Glossary of Symbols: Roman Letters

Symbol	Meaning	Chapter(s)
m_i	Number of elements in cluster i	18
$\bar{m}$	Average cluster size	18
M_2	Average squared deviation	2
M_3	Average cubed deviation	2
M_4	Average of fourth-power deviation	2
n	Sample size	all
n	Number of trials, binomial and hypergeometric distribution	5
N	Population size	all
n_E	Number of occurrences of event E in repeated trials	3
N_E	Number of possible outcomes in event E	3
N_F	Population number of failures	5
N_S	Population number of successes	5
o_i	ith outcome	3
$P_{XY}(x,y)$	Joint probability distribution of discrete random variables X and Y	4, 17
$P_{Y\|x}(y\|x)$	Conditional distribution of discrete random variable Y, given $X=x$	4
$_kP_r$	Number of sequences (permutations) of k things out of r things	5
R^2	Coefficient of determination	13–15
R.R.	Rejection region	9ff
r_s	Rank correlation	13
r_{yx}	Correlation between variables Y and X	13–15
$\binom{r}{k}$	Number of sets (combinations) of k things out of r things	5
$R_{y\cdot x_1\ldots x_k}$	Multiple correlation of variable Y with the best-predicting combination of $X_1,\ldots,X_k$	14, 15
s	Sample standard deviation	all
s^2	Sample variance	all
s_ϵ	Residual standard deviation	13–15
s_p	Pooled standard deviation	10
$s_{\hat{\theta}}$	Estimated standard error of the statistic $\hat{\theta}$	8–15, 18

STATISTICAL THINKING FOR MANAGERS

THE DUXBURY SERIES IN STATISTICS AND DECISION SCIENCES

 ## THE DUXBURY ADVANCED SERIES IN STATISTICS AND DECISION SCIENCES

STATISTICAL THINKING FOR MANAGERS

THIRD EDITION

DAVID K. HILDEBRAND
University of Pennsylvania

LYMAN OTT
Marion Merrell Dow

PWS-KENT Publishing Company
BOSTON

PWS–KENT
Publishing Company

PWS-KENT Publishing Company is a division of Wadsworth, Inc.

Library of Congress Cataloging-in-Publication Data

Hildebrand, David K., 1940–
    Statistical thinking for managers/David K. Hildebrand, Lyman
Ott.—3rd ed.
        p.   cm.
    Includes bibliographical references and index.
    ISBN 0–534–92561–8
    1. Industrial management—Statistical methods.   2. Industrial
management—Statistical methods—Data processing.   3. Economics—
Statistical methods.   4. Statistics—Data processing.   I. Ott,
Lyman.   II. Title.
HD30.215.H54   1991
519.5′024658—dc20   90-19988
                                                                CIP

International Student Edition ISBN: 0-534-98253-0

Printed in the United States of America

1 2 3 4 5 6 7 8 9—95 94 93 92 91

Sponsoring editor: Michael Payne
Assistant editor: Marcia Cole
Editorial assistant: Patricia Schumacher
Production editor: Pamela Rockwell
Manufacturing coordinator: Margaret Sullivan Higgins
Interior design: Chris Crochetière
Cover design: Jean Hammond
Cover illustration: K. Kitagawa/SuperStock, Inc.
Typesetting: Polyglot Pte Ltd
Cover printing: John P. Pow Company, Inc.
Printing and binding: R. R. Donelley & Sons Company

To Pat, Marty, and Jeff
    Sally, Curtis, and Kathy
who all helped

CONTENTS

19   DATA MANAGEMENT AND REPORT PREPARATION   ▪ 890

ABOUT THE AUTHORS

David K. Hildebrand is Professor and former (happily for all concerned) Chair of Statistics at the Wharton School, University of Pennsylvania. Since arriving at Wharton in 1965, he has taught all known varieties of Wharton student (full-time undergraduate, part-time undergraduate, full-time MBA, part-time MBA, and Ph.D.). Besides numerous articles in various statistical journals, he has published two other books, *Prediction Analysis of Cross Classifications* (John Wiley and Sons, 1977) with J. D. Laing and H. Rosenthal, and *Statistical Thinking for Behavioral Scientists* (Duxbury, 1985), and a monograph *Analysis of Ordinal Data* (Sage University Papers, 1977), also with J. D. Laing and H. Rosenthal. He has served the American Statistical Association as an associate editor of its journal and by presenting a short course at its 1979 national meetings. He holds a Ph.D. in statistics from Carnegie-Mellon University and a B.A. in mathematics from Carleton College. In his spare time, he fishes for bass (the bass usually win) and enjoys watching major league baseball (and also the Philadelphia Phillies). He should be blamed for most of the changes in this edition.

Lyman Ott is Managing Director, Systems and Quality Improvement, at Marion Merrell Dow and an Adjunct Professor in the Division of Biostatistics at the University of Cincinnati. At Merrell Dow Research Institute he was responsible for biostatistics, computer services, clinical data processing, laboratory automation, and scientific information services. Prior to his career in the pharmaceutical industry, he was a faculty member in the Department of Statistics at the University of Florida, where he taught service courses and courses for statistics majors at both the undergraduate and graduate levels. He has published many research articles in various statistical journals and several textbooks, including *An Introduction to Statistical Methods and Data Analysis*, 3rd ed.

(Duxbury, 1988), *Understanding Statistics*, 5th ed. (Duxbury, 1990) with W. Mendenhall, and *Elementary Survey Sampling*, 3rd ed. (Duxbury, 1986) with R. Schaeffer and W. Mendenhall. He is a Fellow of the American Statistical Association and has served on the ASA Board of Directors. He holds a Ph.D. in statistics from the Virginia Polytechnic Institute and an undergraduate degree in mathematics and education from Bucknell University. In his spare time, he enjoys tennis and golf and has explored many of the jogging paths of the North American continent. He has served as the voice of reason and moderation for this revision.

PREFACE

In the preface to the second edition of this book, we wrote: "...statistics texts must reflect the wide availability of computers. Now that there are literally dozens of statistical packages available ... the emphasis in managerial statistics courses obviously must shift away from computation and toward thoughtful selection of methods and critical interpretation of results."

We stand by those statements, most emphatically. Now, at almost all colleges and universities, students have easy access to statistical software on a mainframe or personal computer to do the important plotting and computation involved in making sense of data. Endless repetition of routine hand calculations may once have been a justifiable focus for a course; now routine computations are a distraction. The interesting questions—how should one gather the data, what methods of analysis should be used, what assumptions must be made and how can they be checked, what do the results mean—should be the primary focus of a managerial statistics course. We have tried to write a text that emphasizes the interesting questions.

We have made several changes and additions to the text to increase its usefulness as a computer-era text.

- **Quality and Productivity.** The role of statistical thinking in quality control and improvement has been made more explicit. Control charts and Pareto diagrams have been introduced in Chapter 2, accompanied by a brief new section discussing management's role in quality. A non-technical discussion of off-line quality improvement by experimentation, including the ideas of orthogonal array and fractional factorial design, has been included in Chapter 12. These changes should increase the value of the text as a reference.

- **Case Studies.** A case study has been included at the end of each chapter. These cases aren't long (they were called "casettes" and "caselings" at various stages of the project). The presentation of each case asks students to integrate concepts from the chapter and to communicate the results of their analysis in nontechnical language.
- **New Exercises.** We have added numerous new exercises and eliminated some older, less-interesting exercises. A few of the new exercises are conventional pencil-and-paper exercises to fix ideas; the rest are intended to be thought-provoking. Many incorporate computer output of the tedious calculations, allowing students to focus on more important questions and concepts.
- **Computer Exercises.** Many special computer-based exercises have been created. For these exercises, marked by a computer disk icon, the data are stored on a disk available (at no cost to adopters) from the publisher. An instructor can assign these exercises as a means of familiarizing students with whichever computer package is in use. The data sets are formatted as blank-delimited ASCII files without variable-name headers, so they should be readable by almost any package.
- **PC-Based Software.** There is increased emphasis on PC-based computer packages, particularly Minitab, Statgraphics, and Systat. These packages are easier to use than mainframe packages, and their output is usually easier to comprehend.
- **Streamlined Decision Theory.** Formerly separate chapters on basic decision theory and on information in decision theory have been combined, to emphasize the unity of the topics.
- **Influence Concepts in Regression.** High-influence points in regression are explained in Chapters 13 and 14.
- **Earlier Introduction of Bayes' Theorem.** Explicit presentation of Bayes' Theorem has been moved forward to Chapter 4.
- **Solutions Manuals.** A partial solutions manual for students is available, containing extended discussion of the solutions to about 30% of the exercises in the text. The exercises discussed in the solutions manual are numbered with boldface numbers. A complete solutions manual is available to instructors.

Many of the features of the second edition have been retained:

- Review exercises follow sets of several chapters, giving students practice without the artificial clue of exercise placement.
- Several computer simulations of the performance of various statistical methods, under many different conditions, are presented in the text. These simulations provide concrete illustrations of a number of technical concepts. Transparency masters of these and many other simulations are available from the publisher.
- There is heavy emphasis on graphical and exploratory methods, including stem-and-leaf displays, box plots, and normal probability plots. These displays can be produced by any good computer package and

are immensely useful in thoughtful understanding of the data and choice of method.

- There are additional exercises calling for use of calculus methods. These exercises help students to see that calculus methods are natural extensions of algebraic methods. However, calculus isn't a prerequisite to use of the book. Sections and exercises requiring use of differential and integral calculus have been marked by derivative and integral symbols for the convenience of those who wish to skip calculus-based material.
- We have retained a brief chapter describing some of the data management chores necessary before an analysis, as well as guidelines for a statistical analysis and report.

We thank the many individuals who have suggested changes and improvements. We hope that the features we've described are tangible indications that we're listening.

ACKNOWLEDGMENTS

We didn't do this revision all by ourselves. We're most appreciative of the help of several key people. Patricia Hildebrand, our chief computer guru, reprinted clearer tables, suggested improvements in content, helped with word processing, and tolerated one of the authors with perhaps more grace than was warranted. Michael Payne and Marcia Cole were editors, cheerleaders, and taskmasters in most reasonable proportion.

We benefitted greatly from the comments of several thoughtful, and not excessively nasty, reviewers, including

Bruce K. Cooil
Vanderbilt University

C. H. Hesse
University of California, Berkeley

Burt Holland
Temple University

Kevin McCardle
Duke University

John W. Mamer
University of California,
　Los Angeles

Philip J. Mizzi
Arizona State University

Mark Reiser
Arizona State University

Lawrence A. Sherr
University of Kansas

Stanley A. Taylor
California State University,
　Sacramento

Patrick A. Thompson
University of Florida

Nancy Weida
Bucknell University

William B. Widhelm
University of Maryland

John W. Wilkinson
Rensselaer Polytechnic Institute

R. Worthley
University of Hawaii

Of course, we have not always agreed with their suggestions; even those ideas that we didn't buy forced us to rethink and clarify. Our sincere thanks to them all.

1

MAKING SENSE OF DATA

Statistics, as a field of study, is the science and art of making sense of numerical data. The past decade has witnessed an increasing realization that statistical thinking is one of the fundamental keys to good management. When deciding how to formulate a new frozen dinner product, a group of managers can follow its own hunches and tastes or obtain data on which dinners are preferred by a sample of customers. When a foundry's crankshafts for car engines are rejected for inadequate quality, the foundry's design, engineering, purchasing, and production managers can fight over who to blame or they can obtain data on what's causing the problem. When pension managers select an investment advisor, they can choose whoever's currently trendy or they can consider the recorded data on advisors' track records over time. Getting and using data intelligently solves problems.

Virtually every manager—corporate president, cabinet member, hospital director, assistant to the associate vice comptroller—has the need and opportunity to deal with data. The need may be obvious, as it is to loan officers who check the performance of thousands of consumer loans or to hospital managers who track the daily occupancy of beds and operating rooms. The opportunity may be less obvious (and therefore even more valuable); hotel managers, for example, might not realize they could experiment with advance check-in to reduce lines at the registration desk, or the owners of a chain of sound equipment stores might not think to combine sales and inventory data to see that the rush to meet quarterly sales quotas is causing avoidable quarterly inventory problems. Statistical thinking is important for every manager, both in dealing with day-to-day operations and in finding opportunities for improvement.

This book introduces you to the essential ideas of statistical thinking. The ideas in it may be organized around several main topics: How to gather data usefully, how to summarize raw data into understandable form, how to use probability ideas in understanding data, how to infer and predict based on the always-limited available data, and how to use modern computers to aid in the process.

1.1   GATHERING DATA   ■

To be useful, data obviously must be collected and made available. Simply deciding to measure and record relevant data is the necessary beginning for using data to solve problems. But if a manufacturer of microwave ovens records the occurrence of warranty repairs, not the specific malfunction needing repair, then the data are of no help in improving the oven manufacturing process. The first decision, then, concerns what to measure. Often, the variables that are most convenient to measure are not the variables that are most relevant to solving problems. For example, a candy company that must schedule production of its basic chocolate bar would like to know the monthly consumer demand for the bar. It would be relatively easy to record monthly orders from wholesalers and retail chains, but that's not the same as customer demand; some customers may wish to purchase the bar but find it out of stock when shopping. It would be better to obtain not only order data but also stockout data. Giving the problem some thought helps in collecting data on the most relevant variables, not necessarily the easiest variables to measure.

The second decision concerns how to obtain the data. Often data can simply be recorded in the ordinary process of business; with some planning, data on production, warranty, order, and cash flow (for example) can be recorded and made available as a matter of normal procedure. Other times, data must be deliberately sought.

sampling   One important approach to data gathering is **sampling**. A market research group testing consumer reaction to a new design of automobile seats can't possibly talk to every potential car buyer; inevitably, data must be taken from a limited sample of potential buyers. Auditors trying to verify credit card accounts receivable are not about to write to every single cardholder; instead, they will verify a sample of accounts. It's natural, but wrong, to think of statistical sampling only in terms of sampling people; we can equally well sample records or places or times. Generally, statistical sampling is a plausible approach any time potentially valuable data are to be gathered but complete data would be impossible or uneconomical to gather.

experimentation   Another approach to data gathering is **experimentation**. Rather than present only one proposed new automobile seat to (a sample of) potential buyers, a market research group could create several seats combining different features and find out which seat types were most preferred. An operations team seeking to reduce bottlenecks in manufacturing computer boards can experiment with different operating speeds, staffing levels, and flow patterns, measuring the rate of production and the quality of boards. Designed experiments are one of the key components of the recent drive to improve quality of products and processes. Experiments aren't restricted to the lab; virtually any product or process that's part of an organization's business is a potential subject for experimentation.

We'll present some basic ideas about gathering data. Simple random sampling is discussed in Chapter 6, and more complicated sampling ideas are presented in Chapter 18. All of Chapter 12 is devoted to designed experiments. Chapter 19 is a discussion of how data are organized and managed in one industrial setting, the pharmaceutical industry. Other ideas about data gathering are scattered throughout the book.

1.2   SUMMARIZING DATA

Raw data, long lists of numbers, aren't useful as such. They must be summarized in useful, understandable ways. Imagine, just for instance, facing a major national bank's computer printout of the current balances, credit limits, and most recent payments of every Visa cardholder; no one could make sense of that pile of data. Summarization is the first step of data analysis.

The first and most important step in summarizing data is to draw pictures. Relatively simple plots and graphs can make important features of the data obvious. For example, a plot showing what fraction of Visa cardholders had paid about 10% of their outstanding balances, what fraction had paid about 20%, and so on up to 100% would indicate a great deal about potential repayment problems. If there was a sudden shift toward lower payments from one month to the next, the plot would clearly signal that cardholders were changing their habits and possibly having trouble paying their debts. A chart showing how often various parts of a toaster oven were responsible for warranty repairs would indicate quality problems very clearly; if there were 20 problems with a timer for every 1 problem with the heating element, design and production managers would know that timers, not heating elements, needed improvement. The process of making sense of data almost always begins with pictures.

The next obvious step in analyzing data usually is finding some sort of typical, average value. Most people, whether they have formal statistical training or not, have a reasonable idea of what "average" means. Yet some thought is needed even for this simple step. For example, the mean sales price of single-family homes in a suburb will differ from the median sales price. Mean and median are different concepts of "average," and the difference is important to both realtors and tax assessors. Furthermore, an average may not be the most relevant summary statistic for a variable. We would rather not live next to a flood control system that had been designed to handle an *average* year's rainfall; the designers of such systems must consider such extreme values as the every-hundred-years rainfall. Averages are not the only relevant summary figures.

The idea of variability is at least as important in statistical thinking as the idea of average. In fact, understanding variability may be the most important benefit of formal study of statistics. A city's sanitation department will have a budget for overtime pay, but each week's actual overtime will almost surely vary from the budgeted, weekly average amount. Is the variability this week within reasonable limits, or is the variation big enough to deserve special attention? What accounts for the variability? Can it be controlled or predicted? A large part of this book deals with methods for understanding variability—how to summarize it, explain it, reduce it.

A final step in summarizing data is to assess any unusual shapes or patterns in the data. We will want to look for skewness—asymmetry—in data and for outliers—unusual, "freak" values that are far from the bulk of the data. Skewness may make summary figures misleading. For example, a plot of family wealth (monetary value of all assets) will not be symmetric; most families will have small values, some will have moderately large values, and a few will have very large values indeed. If we looked uncritically at only average family wealth, we might be badly fooled. Outliers can also distort averages. Further, outliers can signal unusual cases from which managers can learn; if we saw a supermarket with an outlying low value of cost per dollar of sales, we'd want to know how that market worked.

The basic ideas of summarizing data—data plots, averages, variability, skewness, outliers—are explored in Chapter 2. Normal plots, discussed in Chapter 6, and scatter plots, discussed in Chapter 13, can also provide very useful pictures. The regression methods discussed in Chapters 13–15 are especially relevant to the ideas of accounting for variability.

1.3   THE ROLE OF PROBABILITY   ■

Making sense of data requires some understanding of random variability. There is randomness in sample data. To avoid biasing a sample, we deliberately choose samples at random. Therefore, samples vary randomly from one to another. An element of randomness also occurs in the results of almost any ongoing process. For example, even under seemingly identical conditions, the 6 P.M. check-in lines at a hotel on two different days will differ in size. Therefore, we must allow for some degree of randomness in data from processes as well as in data from samples.

Where there is randomness, there is uncertainty. The results of a sample or process can't be predicted with absolute accuracy. One key to understanding data is understanding the degree of uncertainty that's involved. Probability theory is the mathematical language of randomness and uncertainty. The concepts and theorems of probability theory allow us to specify the likely degree of variation in samples and the probable degree of error in predictions. Probability language gives us a way to think about variability.

In this book, basic probability ideas are developed as they are needed. The basic concepts and language are set forth in Chapters 3 and 4; some basic probability theorems are developed in Chapters 5 and 6. The role of probability in decision making is discussed in Chapter 17. We can indicate only some of the fairly basic ideas of probability; this is not the book for heavy-duty, industrial-strength mathematical probability. Generally, we'll state results without much proof; those who want to know why these results hold should read the appendixes to various chapters.

1.4   MAKING INFERENCES FROM DATA

Data are almost always incomplete. Almost no market research study involves every potential customer. It's also impossible to obtain infinite data on a production process, especially one that has been run under all the different possible combinations of inputs. In using the data, managers must infer characteristics of the larger, underlying population or process based on the limited, actually obtained data. We can never be absolutely sure that the inference is exactly correct. Therefore, users of data must almost always allow for some uncertainty.

Statistical theory makes use of probability results to determine the probable degree of error or uncertainty in an inference. We could run a production process for computer circuit boards in a certain way for 1000 boards and find the proportion of boards that required rework, say 18%. The 1000 boards are only a sample, so the 18% is only an estimate of the long-run proportion of rework boards. But what is the probable degree of error in this estimate? Is it 1%? 10%? Would doubling the run to 2000 boards cut the probable error in half? (No, as it turns out.) We need the statistical theory of inference to answer these questions.

We can also use inference theory to assess whether an apparent change in data is beyond reasonable random variation. If the computer board had been running under one method and yielding 21% rework in the long run, is a reduction to 18% using a new method big enough so we can conclusively say that the new method is better? Again, we need theory to answer the question.

The essential ideas of statistical inference occur in Chapters 7, 8, and 9. Applications of these ideas and specific methods of inference for specific situations are topics for much of the rest of the book.

1.5   THE ROLE OF THE COMPUTER

Making sense of data has become a great deal easier with the advent of modern computers. Computer programs have been written to do even the most tedious calculations described in this book. Some of the methods require so much calculation that they would be utterly impossible without a computer. Perhaps even more important, computers can plot the data easily and clearly. Therefore, managers can explore data rather than rely on cut-and-dried formulas. The results can be communicated effectively and clearly using plots and graphics. Any statistical method involves assumptions; with a decent computer program, it's possible to check the reasonableness of the assumptions. Computers both reduce the tedium of data analysis and make better analyses possible.

The mere fact that data analysis has been done by computer doesn't guarantee that it's any good. The data may be bad, in that the variables aren't really relevant, the data collection was biased, or the assumptions are grossly violated. The choice of the data analysis method may have been a bad one. The results may be correctly calculated but wrongly interpreted. A human being must still decide what data to use, choose the method of analysis, check the assumptions, and interpret the results reasonably. Until artificial intelligence improves greatly, human intelligence will still be required.

Literally hundreds of computer software packages are available to analyze data. Some, such as Minitab, SAS, SPSS, and BMDP, were originally developed for mainframe computers and later adapted for personal computers. Others, such as StatGraphics, Execustat, Systat (for IBM compatibles), and DataDesk (for Apple Macintosh), were originally developed for personal computers. It isn't necessary to know computer programming to use these packages. Most of them can be learned fairly readily, though there are always frustrations from minor errors and misinterpretations. These packages are so useful, both in doing computations and in plotting data, that the investment in learning to use one is most amply repaid.

One needn't learn everything about a package to use it effectively. To begin, you need only learn the steps to obtain the particular results you need. Typically, you'll need to enter the data, assign labels so that the output is readable, select those variables and observations that you want to use in a particular analysis, and call the correct part of the program to carry out the desired step. Depending on the program, the results may be printed or displayed on a monitor.

We will use output from several widely available packages throughout this book. Most of the methods we describe can be carried out with any of these packages. There are so many packages, and they change so quickly, that it's futile to try to describe how to use them all. Instead, we'll concentrate on interpreting the output. *Don't try to interpret every number in the outputs.* The designers of most packages, particularly the older, mainframe-based packages, had to include in the output almost everything that a user could conceivably want to know. As a result, in any particular situation, some of the output is likely to be irrelevant. *Look for the specific results you need; don't worry about the rest.* As you learn more about statistical methods, you'll understand more of the output. In the meantime, select only the specific output you need.

Summary ∎

This chapter sets the agenda for the book. The essential steps in making sense of data are gathering the data, summarizing the data, using pictures and summary numbers, and making inferences and predictions from the limited available data to other data or to the future. The logical structure of the book involves two separate bases—methods for summarizing data (Chapter 2) and concepts of probability (Chapters 3 through 6). These bases are combined to produce the basic theoretical structure of statistical inference (Chapters 7 through 9). Once the basic theory is in place, we will apply it (Chapters 10 through 18) using many methods in many specific situations.

2 SUMMARIZING DATA ABOUT ONE VARIABLE

An unorganized mass of numbers is virtually useless in understanding anything. The first task in making sense out of a data set is to summarize it. In this chapter we focus on three aspects of the data-summarization problem: finding and displaying the frequencies of various data values, calculating a typical value, and indicating the degree of variability around that typical value. Most statistical problems encountered in practice involve several key variables. But an important first step in making sense of such data is to summarize the variables one by one; methods for doing so are described in this chapter.

2.1 THE DISTRIBUTION OF VALUES OF A VARIABLE ■

frequency table

One of the first steps in summarizing data from a single variable is to find the frequencies with which various values occur and to display them in a **frequency table** so that patterns can be seen.

EXAMPLE 2.1

A small firm has a total of 20 salespeople working in four offices. The offices are numbered 1 through 4. The firm's records show that the respective offices of the salespeople (listed in alphabetical order) are

1 4 1 3 3 2 1 1 1 3 4 4 2 2 1 1 2 4 4 1

Summarize the data by displaying the frequencies associated with the values 1, 2, 3, and 4 in a frequency table.

Solution

The easiest way to obtain the frequencies is to list the values and count the frequencies. Then the frequency table is as follows:

Value (office number):	1	2	3	4
Frequency (number of salespeople):	8	4	3	5

■

relative frequency

It's helpful, particularly with large amounts of data, to convert the counts to percentages or proportions. In statistical jargon, the **relative frequency** of a value is the proportion of all observations that have that value. Relative frequency is calculated by dividing the frequency (number of occurrences) of the value by the total number of observations.

EXAMPLE 2.2

Convert the frequencies of Example 2.1 to relative frequencies.

Solution

In Example 2.1, the total number of observations was 20. Therefore,

Value:	1	2	3	4
Relative frequency:	$\frac{8}{20}$ = .40	.20	.15	.25

To convert relative frequencies to percentages, simply multiply them by 100. ■

grouped data

When there are many possible values, it's usually better to combine values into groups. The resulting data are referred to as **grouped data**. Suppose you had a list of the amounts paid by 850 customers at a supermarket's checkout counters in one day. If you listed the amounts to the penny and counted frequencies, you would probably list over 800 values with a frequency of 1 and a few values with frequencies of 2 or 3. That wouldn't be a very useful summary! In such a case you might want to round off the amounts to the nearest dollar or the nearest 5 dollars. This rounding-off process creates groups of similar checkout amounts.

classes

The choice of groups (often called **classes**) for summarizing data from a single variable is somewhat arbitrary, but the selection of classes should conform to the requirement that each measurement falls into one and only one class. In addition, it is desirable to choose the classes so that (1) no gaps appear between the classes, and (2) the classes have a common width. There are many guidelines for determining the number of classes and the class width; here are a few suggestions:

1. **Choose a sufficient number of classes** so that the data are not all lumped into two or three groups but not so many that the frequency table becomes unwieldy. Approximately 5 to 20 classes seems about right for most purposes, with a small number of classes (near 5) for data sets with a small number of observations and more (near 20) in larger data sets. This practice diminishes the possibility of obtaining many classes with a frequency of 0 or 1.
2. **If possible, the classes should have equal width** so that they are comparable. If necessary, an open-ended class such as "over $50" can be used at the high (or low) end of the values. For most purposes, classes such as $0.01 to $10.00, $10.01 to $20.00, $20.01 to $30.00, $30.01 to $40.00, $40.01 and up are preferable to $0.01 to $5.00, $5.01 to $15.00, $15.01 to $40.00, $40.01 and up.
3. **Choose convenient midpoints for the classes.** A frequency chart with midpoints $5, $15, $25 is easier to understand than one with midpoints $7.20, $14.40, $21.60.

4. **Make sure that the class boundaries are not ambiguous.** In suggestion 2 we stated the intervals as $0.01 to $10.00, $10.01 to $20.00,..., rather than as $0 to $10, $10 to $20,..., to avoid the problem that would arise with a purchase of exactly $10.00.

Some statistics textbooks give long, detailed instructions for grouping data and point out some minor, but irritating, pitfalls. The suggestions given here, plus a bit of common sense, should be adequate for simple summaries of data.

EXAMPLE 2.3   Suppose that the 20 salespeople in Example 2.1 had the following commission incomes (excluding salaries) in a certain month:

| $850 | $1265 | $895 | $575 | $2410 | $470 | $660 | $1820 | $1510 | $1100 |
| $620 | $425 | $751 | $965 | $840 | $1505 | $1375 | $695 | $1125 | $1475 |

Use these data to construct a frequency table with suitable class intervals.

Solution   With only 20 observations, we want a small number of classes, such as 5. The incomes range from $425 to $2410; one convenient choice of classes takes incomes to the nearest $500. The results of such a grouping of data are displayed below in a frequency table.

Class:	$250 to $749	$750 to $1249	$1250 to $1749	$1750 to $2249	$2250 to $2749
Frequency:	6	7	5	1	1
Relative frequency:	.30	.35	.25	.05	.05

Note that each measurement (recorded in dollars) falls into exactly one class, that there are no gaps between the intervals, and that the classes have a common interval width of 499.

Some would argue that the common interval width is 500 because theoretically, the class intervals are 250–750, 750–1250,.... Others would argue that the class intervals are really 249.5–749.5, 749.5–1249.5,..., with interval width of 500. We will not quibble with the fine points. Because, for a set of classes, all measurements fall into one and only one class, and because the classes are of equal width and have no gaps, these different groups satisfy the major requirements for the selection of classes.

Many other groupings would be reasonable for the same data. We might redefine the groups as $252 to $751, $752 to $1251,... (which changes the group for the individual who earned exactly $751). We might choose to center the groups at $600, $1000, $1400, $1800, and $2200. While arbitrary choices such as these affect details of the frequency table, they usually do not affect the broad pattern of the data.   ■

Frequency tables are helpful in summarizing data; pictures or graphs derived from these tables are even better, because they allow you to see the basic data pattern easily. There are many kinds of graphical methods for data summarization. We present a few standard ones in this section.

line plot   When there are relatively few observations in the data (no more than 40 or so), one quick and easy method is to mark each observation by a check or X along a line. If 2 or more observations are equal or close to each other, the marks may be piled up. Such a graph might be called a **line plot**.

EXAMPLE 2.4   Draw a line plot for the data of Example 2.3.

Solution   The commission income data of Example 2.3 yield the line plot shown in Figure 2.1. The stacked X's represent the $840 and $850 values, the $1100 and $1125 values, and the $1505 and $1510 values. Note the roughly even spread over most of the range and the two large values.

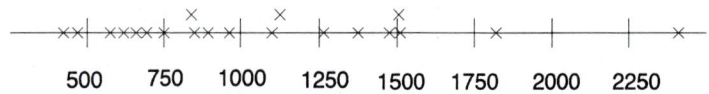

500	750	1000	1250	1500	1750	2000	2250

FIGURE 2.1   Line Plot of Commission Income Data   ■

A line plot is a very easy, rough, "back of an envelope" method that is fine for getting a quick look at the data. For more careful or more formal presentations, bar charts or histograms (among other methods) are preferable.

Bar charts and histograms use rectangles to portray the data. The base of each rectangle indicates a value or a group (class) of values. The height of each rectangle represents the frequency or the relative frequency of each value or class.

bar chart   To create a **bar chart**, label the horizontal axis with values or categories of the variable, label the vertical axis with frequencies, and construct separate rectangles for each value with height corresponding to the frequency or relative frequency of that value. Figure 2.2 shows a bar chart of the data from Example 2.1.

histograms   **Histograms** are constructed in the same way as bar charts. The only difference is that the rectangles in a bar chart are separated by some space, whereas the rectangles in a histogram are directly adjacent. A histogram is often used with grouped data. Figure 2.3 shows a histogram of the commission income data grouped as in Example 2.3.

There are some minor variations in the presentation of histograms. The horizontal axis can be labeled with either class midpoints, as in Figure 2.3, or class endpoints. Thus in Figure 2.3 we could have labeled the edges of the rectangles as $250, $750,... (or equivalently as $249.5, $749.5,...). The vertical axis of a histogram is labeled with frequencies or with relative frequencies. Because relative frequencies are proportional to frequencies, the frequency histogram and the relative frequency histogram have the same shape. The specific choice is mostly a matter of taste.

qualitative   **The distinction between bar charts and histograms is based on the distinction
variable**   **between qualitative and quantitative variables.** The values of **qualitative** variables vary in kind but not degree and hence are not measurements. For example, "office

Frequency

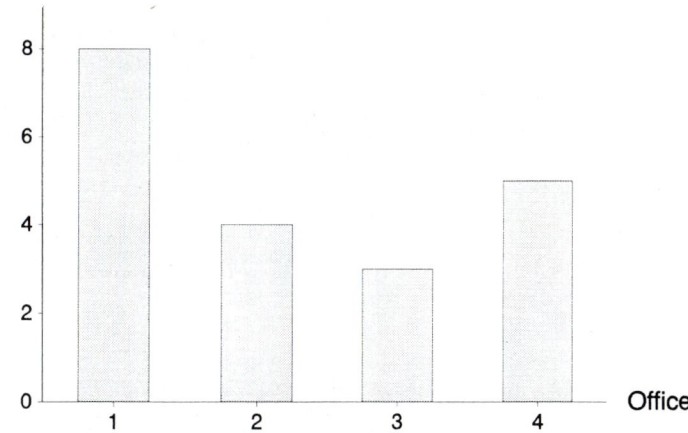

FIGURE 2.2   Bar Chart of Sales Office Data

Frequency

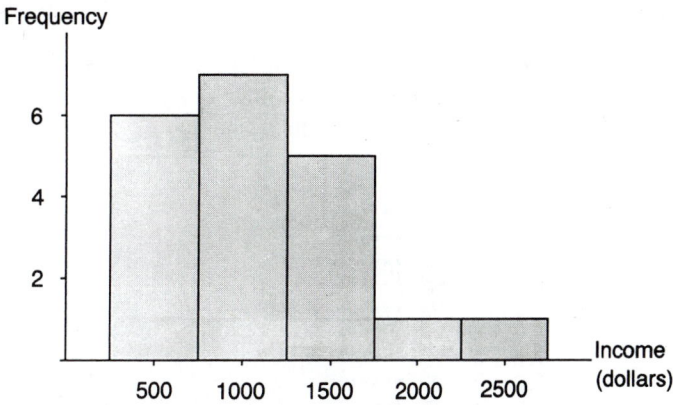

FIGURE 2.3   Histogram of Grouped Commission Income Data

number" in Example 2.1 is a qualitative variable; although the offices were numbered 1, 2, 3, and 4, they could equally well have been labeled New York, Atlanta, Chicago, and San Francisco. Numerical values can be assigned to qualitative variables, as was done in Example 2.1, but these values are only convenient codes. In contrast, values of a **quantitative** variable result from an actual measurement with some sort of yardstick. For example, "commission income" in Example 2.3 is a quantitative variable. A good test for whether a variable should be regarded as qualitative or quantitative is whether a unit of measure can be identified. Commission income is measured in dollars; office

quantitative variable

number has no unit of measurement. Quantitative variables usually have units; qualitative variables don't.*

Bar charts are used with qualitative variables; the separation of rectangles suggests that each value of the variable represents a distinct category. Histograms are used with quantitative variables. The fact that rectangles in a histogram are adjacent (for intervals with nonzero frequencies) suggests that the variable's values are measured along a scale.

EXAMPLE 2.5   Quarterly percentage changes in U.S. gross national product (GNP) from 1965 through the first quarter of 1988 are shown here. Construct a frequency histogram.

1.14	0.75	2.11	1.82	2.99	2.78	1.92	1.55	2.62	1.49	2.09
0.82	1.12	1.41	1.88	0.29	4.37	1.77	1.74	1.26	3.46	2.66
2.17	3.27	3.80	2.36	2.01	3.21	0.92	2.31	2.06	1.81	0.53
2.56	4.09	3.13	3.10	1.79	1.87	2.73	3.04	3.63	3.20	1.53
2.38	5.64	2.65	3.41	2.24	2.23	2.91	1.77	3.16	-0.04	2.32
4.17	4.56	1.31	2.72	0.48	-0.06	1.51	0.63	1.04	1.65	3.12
2.26	2.96	3.64	2.18	1.41	1.16	1.82	1.33	1.74	1.53	1.71
0.89	1.28	0.54	2.08	1.55	1.78	1.83	1.26			

Solution   The data range from −0.06 to 5.64. If we define classes by rounding to the nearest unit (midpoints 0.00, 1.00, etc.), we will have 7 classes, which would be acceptable. We might round to the nearest half unit (midpoints 0.00, 0.50, 1.00, etc.) to see somewhat more detail. A computer-drawn histogram (turned sideways) is based on the latter choice and is shown below.

```
Midpoint   Count
    0.0       2    **
    0.5       5    *****
    1.0       8    ********
    1.5      17    *****************
    2.0      20    ********************
    2.5      11    ***********
    3.0      11    ***********
    3.5       5    *****
    4.0       3    ***
    4.5       2    **
    5.0       0
    5.5       1    *
```

■

Pareto chart   An important use of bar charts in statistical quality control is the **Pareto** (pronounced "pah-RAY-toe") **chart**. Alternative reasons for inadequate quality are specified, the number of occurrences are counted, and the frequencies are displayed in a bar chart. Usually, the reasons are displayed in order of frequency from highest to lowest. A Pareto chart is an effective way to highlight quality

---

* Variables such as sales (in units of dozens) or hotel rooms (simply in units of numbers) can be regarded as quantitative. Sometimes variables such as college grade points ($A = 4$, $B = 3$, and so on) are treated as quantitative, even though there is no obvious unit.

Frequency

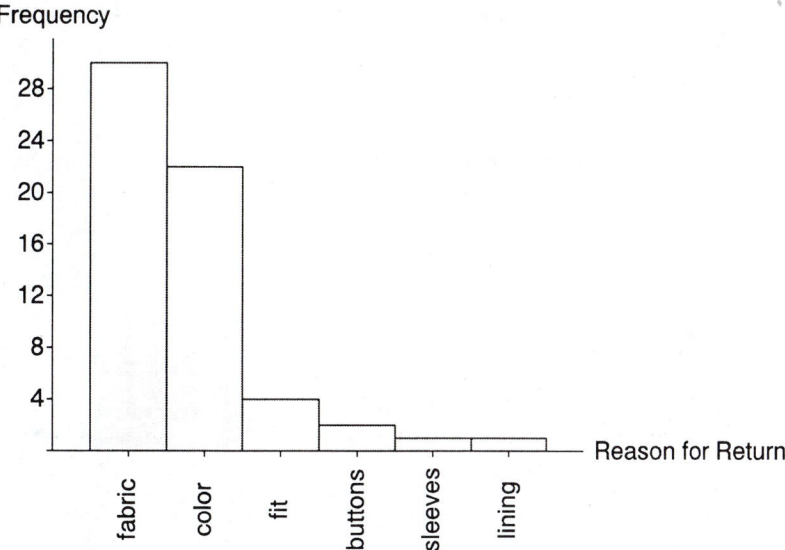

FIGURE 2.4   Pareto Chart of Reasons for Returning Sport Coats

problems. For example, a mail-order firm analyzing reasons for returns of men's sport coats might find that, among the 54 returned coats in the most recent month, there had been 4 returns for poor fit, 22 for disliking the color, 30 for disliking the fabric, 1 for poorly finished sleeves, 2 for improper installation of buttons, and 1 for poor attachment of the lining. Note that there are 60 reasons for 54 returned coats, implying that some coats were returned for multiple reasons; because we're more interested in quality issues than in accounting, we'll count each reason separately. A Pareto chart for these returns is shown in Figure 2.4. (Conventionally, there aren't any spaces between bars in a Pareto chart, but that's not important.) The chart makes clear that color and fabric are major quality concerns *and* that finish (aspects of sewing the sport coats) is *not* a major concern.

stem-and-leaf diagram   A clever device that constructs a histogram-like picture is the **stem-and-leaf diagram**. It is best explained by an example.

EXAMPLE 2.6   Suppose that the grades of 40 job applicants on an aptitude test are as follows. Construct a-stem-and-leaf diagram for these data.

42	21	46	69	87	29	34	59	81	97
64	60	87	81	69	77	75	47	73	82
91	74	70	65	86	87	67	69	49	57
55	68	74	66	81	90	75	82	37	94

Solution   The scores range from 21 to 97. The first digits, 2 through 9, are placed in a column on the left of the diagram. The respective second digits are recorded in the appropriate row. The first three scores, 42, 21, and 46, would be represented as

```
2  |  1
3  |
4  |  2   6
```

The full stem-and-leaf diagram is shown in Figure 2.5.   ■

```
2  |  1 9
3  |  4 7
4  |  2 6 7 9
5  |  9 7 5
6  |  9 4 0 9 5 7 9 8 6
7  |  7 5 3 4 0 4 5
8  |  7 1 7 1 2 6 7 1 2
9  |  7 1 0 4
```

FIGURE 2.5   Stem-and-Leaf Diagram

The diagram can be made a bit neater by ordering the data within a row, from lowest to highest score, but this process is time-consuming if done by hand. The end result of a stem-and-leaf diagram looks much like a histogram turned sideways. The advantage of such a diagram is that it not only reflects frequencies but also contains the actual values. No information is lost.

There are many possible variations. A display of the data from Example 2.6 with more classes is shown in the stem-and-leaf diagram of Figure 2.6. This

```
Stem-and-leaf of Grades     N  = 40
Leaf Unit = 1.0


          LO  21,

     2      2 9
     3      3 4
     4      3 7
     5      4 2
     8      4 679
     8      5
    11      5 579
    13      6 04
    20      6 5678999
    20      7 0344
    16      7 557
    13      8 11122
     8      8 6777
     4      9 014
     1      9 7
```

FIGURE 2.6   Computer Stem-and-Leaf Diagram

Minitab stem-and-leaf diagram divides each interval in half by placing observations from the 90–94 range, for example, in the first 9 row, and observations in the 95–99 range in the second 9 row. Similar subdivisions are made in the other rows. Note also the ordering of observations within a row. The LO 21 entry is a Minitab suggestion that 21 may be an outlier—a wild, extreme value. We would not agree.

The stem-and-leaf diagram, and many other data-summarization ideas, are discussed in Tukey (1977).

SECTION 2.1   EXERCISES

2.1   An automobile manufacturer routinely keeps records on the number of finished (passing all inspections) cars produced per eight-hour shift. The data for the last 28 shifts are

| 366 | 390 | 324 | 385 | 380 | 375 | 384 | 383 | 375 | 339 | 360 | 386 | 387 | 384 |
| 379 | 386 | 374 | 366 | 377 | 385 | 381 | 359 | 363 | 371 | 379 | 385 | 367 | 364 |

a. Construct a histogram using convenient class intervals. Can you think of an explanation for the apparent shape of the histogram?

b. Construct a stem-and-leaf diagram of the data and compare it to the histogram. The left-hand "stem" should have an initial 3 in each value.

2.2   A city manager receives 17 bids for supplying new memory typewriters. The dollar costs per typewriter are

| 847 | 849 | 838 | 841 | 852 | 846 | 812 | 838 | 850 | 836 | 871 | 849 |
| 824 | 846 | 864 | 843 | 839 | | | | | | | |

a. Construct a histogram using an appropriate number of classes.

b. Construct a stem-and-leaf diagram for these data. The left-hand "stem" should start with 81 and end with 87.

2.3   A purchasing agent tests samples of 10 batteries for hand calculators from each of two manufacturers. Each battery is tested in a calculator that is programmed to do a continuous "loop" of typical calculations; the time in hours to failure of each battery is recorded in the table below:

Manufacturer			Time		
E	11.80	11.91	11.95	12.00	12.02
	12.03	12.04	12.07	12.13	12.20
S	12.06	12.14	12.18	12.19	12.20
	12.20	12.21	12.23	12.27	12.33

a. Construct a combined histogram of all 20 times; use 6 or 7 classes.

b. Construct separate histograms with the classes of part (a) for each manufacturer.

c. How do the separate histograms help to explain the appearance of the combined histogram?

2.4   Price–earnings ratios for a sample of 24 publicly owned companies involved in the sale of computer software used in manufacturing operations are given below:

| 7.7 | 8.5 | 9.6 | 10.3 | 13.6 | 14.5 | 19.5 | 10.1 | 9.7 | 11.4 | 17.8 | 15.9 |
| 14.2 | 13.7 | 20.7 | 22.1 | 25.9 | 29.1 | 32.6 | 36.7 | 32.4 | 35.9 | 40.1 | 45.9 |

a. Construct a relative frequency histogram.
b. Use the same, data to construct a stem-and-leaf plot. How can you handle the problem that most of the price–earnings ratios have three digits rather than two? Compare the histogram to the stem-and-leaf plot; which one do you find more informative?

2.5   A hotel kept records over time of the reasons why guests requested room changes. The frequencies were as follows.

Reason	Frequency
Room not cleaned	2
Plumbing not working	1
Wrong type of bed	13
Noisy location	4
Wanted nonsmoking room	18
Didn't like view	1
Room not properly equipped	8
Other, not coded	6

a. Construct a Pareto chart.
b. The hotel management had expected that the primary problems would be connected with maintenance and housekeeping. Does the chart confirm that such reasons were the primary complaints?

2.2   ON THE AVERAGE: TYPICAL VALUES

Frequency tables, bar charts, histograms, and stem-and-leaf displays all give a general sense of the pattern or distribution of values in a data set. They do not indicate a typical, middle, or average value explicitly. In this section we define some standard measures of the typical or average value.

The word *average* has at least three meanings. It can mean the most common value, the mode; it can mean the middle value, the median; or it can mean the arithmetic average, the mean. This section contains more careful definitions of these three basic concepts of typical values.

Mode

The mode of a variable is the value or category with the highest frequency in the data. It is most commonly used with qualitative data but can also be used with quantitative data.

In Example 2.1, the modal category for the qualitative variable "office number" is 1, because that office has the largest number of salespeople.

EXAMPLE 2.7   The data shown below represent the percentage of eligible voters for a sample of 10 voting districts:

63   56   32   48   48   39   45   45   45   41

Determine the modal value.

Solution   It is clear that the modal value is 45%, because the value 45 occurs most frequently in the sample.   ∎

Because we do not usually have the original measurements that have been used to form a frequency table, the mode for grouped data is defined as the midpoint of the class with the highest frequency. This value approximates the mode of the actual (ungrouped) data.

In Example 2.3 the modal commission income is $1000, the midpoint of the class with endpoints of $750 to $1250. Unfortunately, the modal value is very sensitive to small changes in data values or class definitions. Had we defined the classes as $252 to $751, $752 to $1251, and so on in Example 2.3, the frequency table would change slightly, as shown here:

Class	Frequency
252–751	7
752–1251	6
1252–1751	5
1752–2251	1
2252–2751	1

The mode for these grouped data would be 501, the midpoint of the first interval, rather than 1000 as we found previously.

As was illustrated above, a mode calculated from a small amount of data or based on arbitrary class definitions is not too reliable and shouldn't be taken too seriously. One final word about modes: There may be data sets with more than one mode, for example, sets for which there are two or more values (classes) with the highest frequency; these data sets are referred to as bimodal, trimodal, and so on.

Median

The median of a set of data is the middle value when the data are arranged from lowest to highest. If n, the sample size, is odd, the median is the $(n + 1)/2$th value; if n is even, the median is the average of the $n/2$th and $(n + 2)/2$th values.

EXAMPLE 2.8   Suppose that the number of units per day of whole blood used in transfusions at a hospital over the previous 11 days is

25   16   61   12   18   15   20   24   17   19   28

Solution   Arranged in increasing order, the values are

12   15   16   17   18   19   20   24   25   28   61

The median value is the sixth value, 19.   ∎

If n, the number of measurements, is odd, there is no problem in finding the middle value. However, where n is even, there is no value exactly in the middle; for this situation, the median is conventionally defined as the average of the middle two values when the data are ordered from smallest to largest. If in Example 2.8 there had been a twelfth value of 72, the median, would be the average of the sixth and seventh values $(19 + 20)/2 = 19.5$. Whether n is odd or even, there are equal numbers of observations above and below the median.

Mean

The mean of a variable is the sum of the measurements taken on that variable divided by the number of measurements. It is meaningful only for quantitative data.

In Example 2.3 the mean commission income was $(850 + \$1265 + \cdots + \$1475)/20$, or 1066.55. We use two different symbols for the mean, depending on whether we want to regard the data as the entire population of interest or as a sample of measurements from the population of interest.

As we indicated in Chapter 1, a population of measurements is the complete set of measurements of interest to the manager; a sample of measurements is a subset of measurements selected from the population of interest. If we let y_1, $y_2, \ldots, y_n$ represent a sample of n measurements selected from a population, the sample mean is denoted by the symbol $\bar{y}$:

$$\bar{y} = \frac{\sum_i y_i}{n}$$

The corresponding mean of the population from which the sample was drawn is denoted by the Greek letter μ.

In most situations we do not know the population mean; the sample mean is used to make inferences about the corresponding unknown population mean. This is discussed in greater detail beginning in Chapter 7.

The mean is the most useful and convenient measure of the average value; however, any user of statistics should be alert to the possibility of distortions due to skewness or outliers. An extreme value can pull the mean in its direction and cause the mean to appear atypical of the values in the set. For this reason, **trimmed means**   statisticians have developed the idea of **trimmed means**. To find a 40% trimmed mean, for instance, drop the highest 20% and lowest 20% of the values and

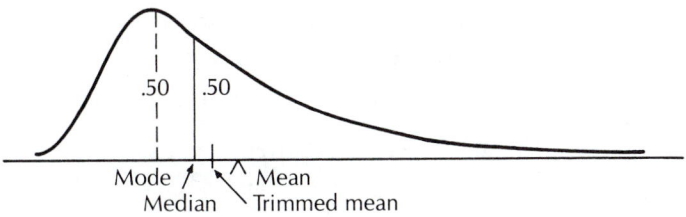

FIGURE 2.7   Measures of Location for Skewed Distribution

outliers

average the remaining values. This trimming process eliminates the effect of **outliers**, data values that lie far above or below the preponderance of the data. Trimmed means are particularly useful in estimation of a population mean based on sample data, because they reduce the impact of possible "freak" values.

measures of location

measures of central tendency

The mode, median, mean, and trimmed means are called **measures of location** or **measures of central tendency**; they indicate the center or general location of data values. The relation among these measures depends on the skewness of the data. If the distribution is mound shaped—symmetric around a single peak—the mode, median, mean, and trimmed means are all equal. For a skewed distribution, one having a long tail in one direction and a single peak, the mean is pulled out toward the long tail; usually the median falls between the mode and the mean, and a trimmed mean between the median and the mean (see Figure 2.7).

The mean is the most widely used measure of central tendency; one reason for this popularity is its utility in statistical inference problems. Another reason is that it is possible to combine subgroup means into an overall mean. This property does not hold for the other measures of central tendency. For example, if the means for three equal-sized subgroups are 23, 25, and 30, the mean for the combined group must be $(23 + 25 + 30)/3 = 26$. However, for the same data, if we know that the subgroup medians are 23, 25, and 30, we know only that the combined group median is somewhere between 23 and 30. Subgroup modes are even less informative. In general, the overall mean is a **weighted average** of the subgroup means, with weights equal to the subgroup sizes; that is, if $\bar{y}_j$ denotes the mean in subgroup j, $j = 1, \ldots, k$, and n_j is the number in subgroup j, then

weighted average

$$\bar{y} = \frac{\sum_j n_j \bar{y}_j}{\sum_j n_j}$$

EXAMPLE 2.9   Find $\bar{y}$ for the following 10 measurements based on the three subgroup means:

Subgroup	Values	Total	$\bar{y}_j$	n_j
1	21, 21, 23, 24, 26	115	23	5
2	23, 26, 26	75	25	3
3	29, 31	60	30	2
	Grand total = 250			$n = 10$

Solution   Substituting into the formula for $\bar{y}$ using subgroup means, we obtain

$$\bar{y} = \frac{5(23) + 3(25) + 2(30)}{5 + 3 + 2} = \frac{250}{10} = 25.0$$

Note that the larger weight given to $\bar{y}_1$ causes the overall mean to fall below the simple average of the three means $(23 + 25 + 30)/3 = 26$.   ■

Statistical thinking focuses very heavily on typical, average values. In many situations, inferences related to average or typical values will suffice, but there is a limit to such thinking. Sometimes the average value isn't important. A single, dramatically effective drug can propel a small pharmaceutical firm's ledger from the red to the black very quickly; a single disaster can propel an insurance firm into bankruptcy court. But it would be foolish to ignore statistical thinking on these grounds. Most products will not be overwhelming successes; most accidents will not be bankruptcy-causing disasters. Managers who assume that their results will always be better than average are in grave danger of becoming ex-managers. Measures of variability provide another dimension to our thinking; they are discussed in Section 2.3.

means chart   In statistical quality control, a remarkably simple, remarkably useful device is a **means chart**, often called an *x*-bar chart. (Because we usually use *y* to denote the variable of interest, we'd call it a *y*-bar chart, but someone else got there first.) A simplified means chart is simply a plot of times (hours, days, weeks, or months) versus means of observations taken at those times. A careful look will show any patterns that indicate trouble—a slow increasing or decreasing trend in the means, a sudden jump or drop, or a cyclic pattern.

A critical aspect of automatic transmissions for cars is the internal fluid pressure of the transmission. The ideal value is 35, in appropriate units. Too low a pressure results in sluggish performance; anything under 32 can be detected and any pressure under 30 results in bad performance. Too high a pressure results in jumpy overperformance; 38 is detectable and 40 is bad. A manufacturer of transmissions randomly samples five units from each day's production and measures the internal pressure on each. A list of the pressures for 40 days and an *x*-bar plot of means versus day is shown here. The initial 3 has been dropped, so 6.01 represents 36.01.

DAY	item1	item2	item3	item4	item5	mean
1	6.01	4.46	4.90	3.83	4.61	4.762
2	6.06	6.26	5.44	3.86	5.88	5.500
3	4.46	6.17	4.07	4.29	4.29	4.656
4	5.08	4.68	4.37	4.50	4.40	4.606
5	4.11	5.84	5.67	4.55	5.62	5.158
6	4.58	5.90	4.35	5.25	4.18	4.852
7	6.04	4.45	4.22	5.09	4.68	4.896
8	4.98	5.19	5.70	4.91	2.97	4.750
9	6.48	5.95	4.53	6.25	6.08	5.858
10	5.30	5.98	5.36	3.83	4.56	5.006
11	3.56	3.95	6.38	4.90	4.86	4.730
12	4.96	6.78	6.56	4.32	5.25	5.574

DAY	item1	item2	item3	item4	item5	mean
13	4.39	3.16	4.31	4.43	6.33	4.524
14	2.88	4.62	5.70	5.77	3.83	4.560
15	2.81	4.27	3.19	6.02	5.94	4.446
16	2.77	3.20	3.60	5.75	4.57	3.978
17	4.88	3.37	4.69	4.02	3.30	4.052
18	6.06	4.49	3.40	5.03	6.63	5.122
19	6.17	2.64	5.90	4.75	5.22	4.936
20	5.85	5.00	3.31	4.58	7.37	5.222
21	5.10	5.39	5.37	4.33	7.28	5.494
22	7.29	2.77	3.54	7.45	5.14	5.238
23	4.44	5.87	5.52	5.03	4.13	4.998
24	4.94	5.97	6.30	8.22	4.72	6.030
25	5.56	5.59	4.63	3.56	6.84	5.236
26	5.48	4.74	6.51	6.76	4.13	5.524
27	5.31	6.87	2.82	3.55	3.47	4.404
28	3.69	4.01	5.16	3.87	4.93	4.332
29	3.32	6.22	2.12	6.01	5.60	4.654
30	5.14	6.57	6.37	6.98	6.66	6.344
31	4.93	6.02	5.10	5.58	6.62	5.650
32	4.93	5.45	2.16	6.25	5.05	4.768
33	6.64	7.00	5.39	4.87	6.76	6.132
34	7.85	4.97	4.68	5.48	4.07	5.410
35	4.02	6.64	7.62	5.91	4.15	5.668
36	4.51	5.42	4.81	5.00	3.74	4.696
37	3.62	5.41	4.78	1.78	3.88	3.894
38	3.06	5.90	6.96	4.96	2.72	4.720
39	2.04	3.22	3.76	3.44	6.76	3.844
40	4.99	6.20	4.73	3.87	3.79	4.716

MTB > plot 'means' vs 'day'

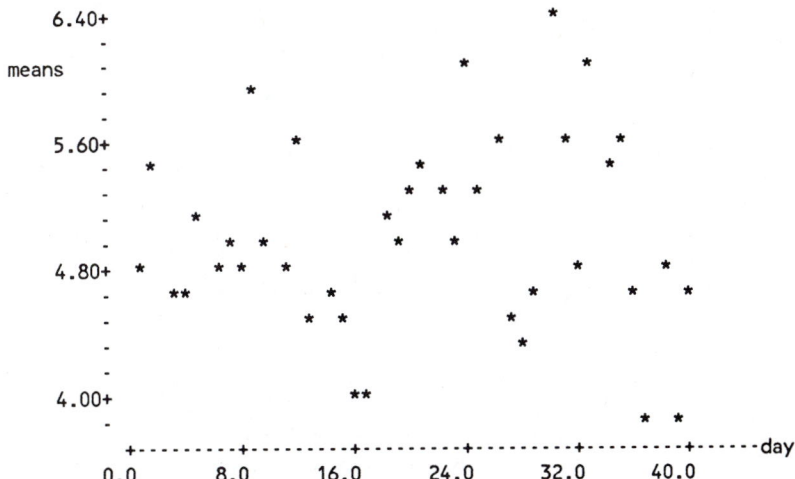

There are no obvious trends up or down, nor are there jumps to new plateaus. The means mostly stay in the 4.00 to 6.00 range, corresponding to mean pressures of 34 to 36 units. Perhaps there are some cycles of a few days' length, but nothing huge. One troubling feature is that the means in days 31–40 seem to "jump around" more. We will need to consider this more when we measure variability in the next section.

EXAMPLE 2.10   A nationwide chain of motels has a national reservation center. Customers phone in reservations to an 800 number. One key measure of the quality of the center's service is the amount of "dead time"—waiting for the phone to be answered, being on hold, waiting for a response once a request has been made—endured by a customer. The chain's four regular inspectors record the dead time (in units of minutes) for their one reservation call each day. The results are averaged over each five-day workweek. A separate analysis is done for weekends and holiday weeks. Means and a simplified x-bar chart are shown below. Is there any clear evidence of a problem?

mean
0.765	0.775	1.025	0.910	0.665	0.815	0.720	0.720	0.795
0.845	0.645	0.905	0.845	0.790	0.950	0.735	0.765	0.710
1.045	1.215	1.085	0.925	1.075	1.100	1.330	1.215	0.995
1.185	1.115	1.110						

```
            -
            -
      1.25+                                      *
            -
mean        -                           *            *   *
            -
            -                              *  * *       * *
      1.00+      *                      *
            -                                *
            -         *            *          *
            -              *    *
            -     *     *    *     *
      0.75+   *                        **
            -                             *
            -        **        *
            -      *         *
            -
            -
            +---------+---------+---------+---------+---------+------week
           0.0       6.0      12.0      18.0      24.0      30.0
```

Solution   For the first 18 weeks, except for week 3, the means are relatively low. Beginning at week 19, the means suddenly increase. The chart clearly signals that we should look for a cause for an increase in deadtime around week 19. ■

In these control charts, means vary from one time period to another. Our next task is to measure and summarize variability. That's the topic of the next section.

SECTION 2.2   EXERCISES

2.6   Compute the mean, median, and mode for the following data:

   11   17   18   10   22   23   15   17   14   13   10   12   18   18   11   14

2.7   The Insurance Institute for Highway Safety published data on the total damage suffered by compact automobiles in a series of controlled, low-speed collisions. The data, in dollars, with brand names removed, are

   361   393   430   543   566   610   763   851   886   887   976   1039
   1124   1267   1328   1415   1425   1444   1476   1542   1544   2048   2197

   a. Draw a histogram of the data, using 6 or 7 categories.
   b. On the basis of the histogram, what would you guess the mean to be?
   c. Calculate the median and mean.
   d. What does the relation between the mean and median indicate about the shape of the data?

2.8   Production records for an automobile manufacturer show the following figures for production per shift (maximum production is 720 cars per shift):

   688   711   625   701   688   667   694   630   547   703   688   697   703
   656   677   700   702   688   691   664   688   679   708   699   667   703

   a. Would the mode be a useful summary statistic for these data?
   b. Find the median.
   c. Find the mean.
   d. What does the relation between the mean and median indicate about the shape of the data?

2.9   Draw a stem-and-leaf plot of the data in Exercise 2.8. The "stem" should include (from highest to lowest) 71, 70, 69, …. Does the shape of the stem-and-leaf display confirm your judgment in part (d) of Exercise 2.8?

2.10   Data are collected on the weekly expenditures of a sample of urban households on food (including restaurant expenditures). The data, obtained from diaries kept by each household, are grouped by number of members of the household. The expenditures were as follows:

1 member:	67	62	168	128	131	118	80	53	99	68	
	76	55	84	77	70	140	84	65	67	183	
2 members	129	116	122	70	141	102	120	75	114	81	106 95
	94	98	85	81	67	69	119	105	94	94	92
3 members:	79	99	171	145	86	100	116	125			
	82	142	82	94	85	191	100	116			
4 members:	139	251	93	155	158	114	108				
	111	106	99	132	62	129	91				
5+ members:	121	128	129	140	206	111	104	109	135	136	

The Statgraphics statistical package calculated summary figures for each group as shown in the table on the next page.

   a. Verify the computation of the mean (average) and median for Level 1 (that is, for the 1-member data).
   b. Within each number of members, the mean is larger than the median. What does this fact suggest about the shape of the data?

c. Construct a stem-and-leaf display of the data for 1 member. Does it confirm your answer to part (b)?

Level	Sample size	Average	Median	Variance	Standard deviation
1	20	93.7500	78.5000	1443.36	37.9915
2	23	98.6522	95.0000	407.510	20.1869
3	16	113.313	100.000	1130.63	33.6248
4	14	124.857	112.500	1993.67	44.6505
5	10	131.900	128.500	829.433	28.7999

2.11 The Statgraphics package was also used to calculate summary statistics for the combined data of Exercise 2.10.

Variable:	foodexp
Sample size	83
Average	108.723
Median	104
Variance	1254.89
Standard deviation	35.4244
Minimum	53
Maximum	251
Skewness	1.21944
Kurtosis	2.56989

a. Can the mean for the combined data be determined by the means and sample sizes for each number of members?

b. Can the median for the combined data be determined by the medians and sample sizes for each number of members?

2.12 The Statgraphics package was used to calculate a three-dimensional histogram for the data of Exercise 2.10, as shown in Figure 2.8 (page 25).

a. Does it appear that number of members of the household is the overwhelming source of variability in food expenditure? That is, is there very little variability left once we take into account the number of household members?

b. Do the histograms seem to overlap? Is your answer confirmed by the original data of Exercise 2.10?

c. Are the expenditures basically symmetrically distributed within each number of household members?

2.3   MEASURING VARIABILITY   ∎

One of the most important unifying ideas in statistics is the notion of variability. Customers vary in time taken to pay bills. Caplets of a particular drug vary in their potency but had better not vary too much. Overtime payments to a city police force vary sharply from week to week. Variability is an absolutely fundamental idea in quality control; in many situations, such as caplets' varying in potency, variability is a major enemy of quality. One of the major themes of

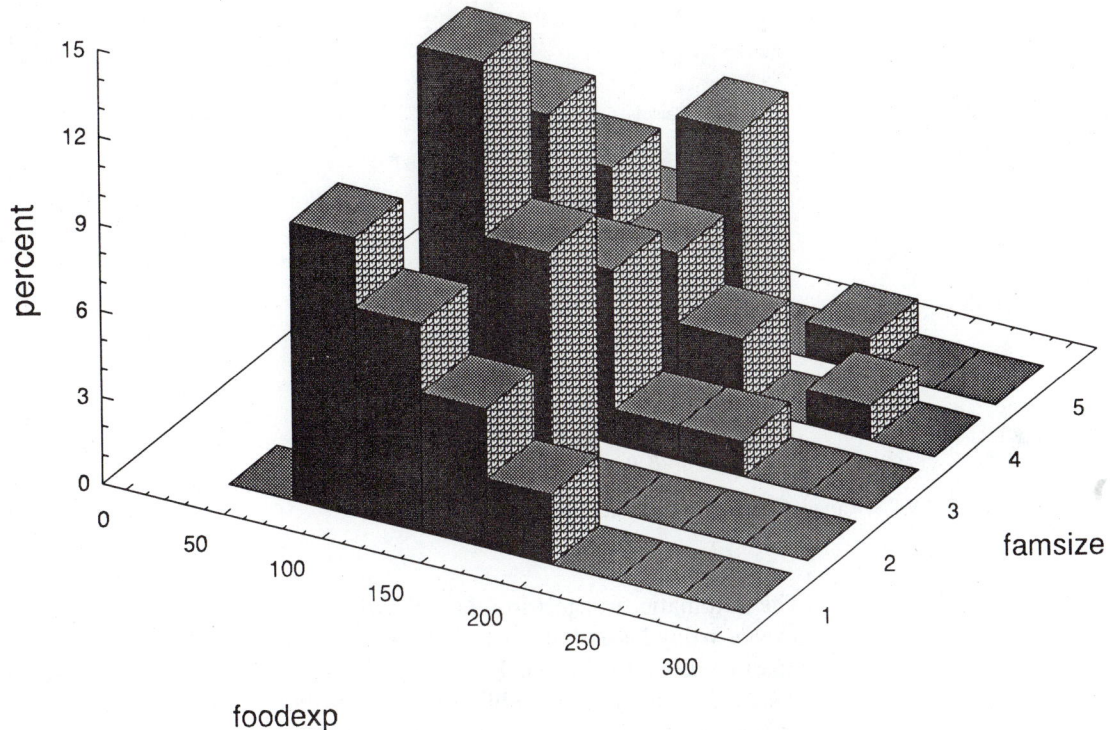

percent

foodexp

famsize

FIGURE 2.8   Three-Dimensional Histogram of Food Expenditures

statistical quality control (and of this book, as well) is accounting for sources of variability.

The first task in dealing with variability is summarizing it. In this section, we'll define several measures of variability and discuss strengths and weaknesses **range** of each. The simplest measure of variability is the **range**—the difference between the largest and smallest values. It's easy to compute, so it is widely used in quality control to measure variability. When data are taken over time and the range **R chart** plotted against time, the result is an **R chart**. For example, in the automatic transmission example from Section 2.2, ranges were also computed as follows:

Day	Range		Day	Range		Day	Range		Day	Range
1	2.18		11	2.82		21	2.95		31	1.69
2	2.40		12	2.46		22	4.68		32	4.09
3	2.10		13	3.17		23	1.74		33	2.13
4	0.71		14	2.89		24	3.50		34	3.78
5	1.73		15	3.21		25	3.28		35	3.60
6	1.72		16	2.98		26	2.63		36	1.68
7	1.82		17	1.58		27	4.05		37	3.63
8	2.73		18	3.23		28	1.47		38	4.24
9	1.95		19	3.53		29	4.10		39	4.72
10	2.15		20	4.06		30	1.84		40	2.41

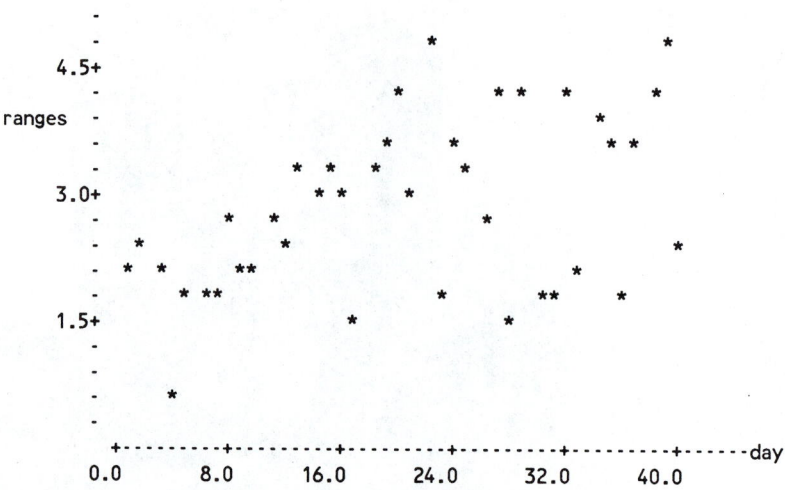

FIGURE 2.9   Range Chart of Automatic Transmission Data

The automatic transmission data shown in Section 2.2 indicate that the largest value in day 1 is 6.01 (item 1) and the smallest value in day 1 is 3.83 (item 4). The range for day 1 is therefore $6.01 - 3.83 = 2.18$, as shown. Note that the actual pressures were 36.01 and 33.83; adding 30 to all the data doesn't change the range, because the 30's cancel. An R chart of range plotted against day is shown in Figure 2.9.

This chart shows that a problem is developing over time. The ranges generally are increasing over time, so there's more and more variability as time goes by. Higher variability means that more transmissions will be either too high or too low in pressure. In seeking the cause, we should notice that there's no sudden jump upward but rather a gradual increase; we should look for a gradual factor such as machine wearout or worker complacency.

EXAMPLE 2.11   Ranges were calculated and an R chart was prepared for the "dead time" data of Example 2.10. They're shown in the figure below. Is there an indication that variability is changing over time?

ranges
1.5	2.5	2.5	2.1	1.5	1.6	2.0	1.6	1.6	3.3	1
1.9	2.1	1.9	1.6	1.5	2.4	2.0	2.8	3.1	3.5	2
2.3	2.0	3.2	3.3	2.3	2.4	3.4	2.9			

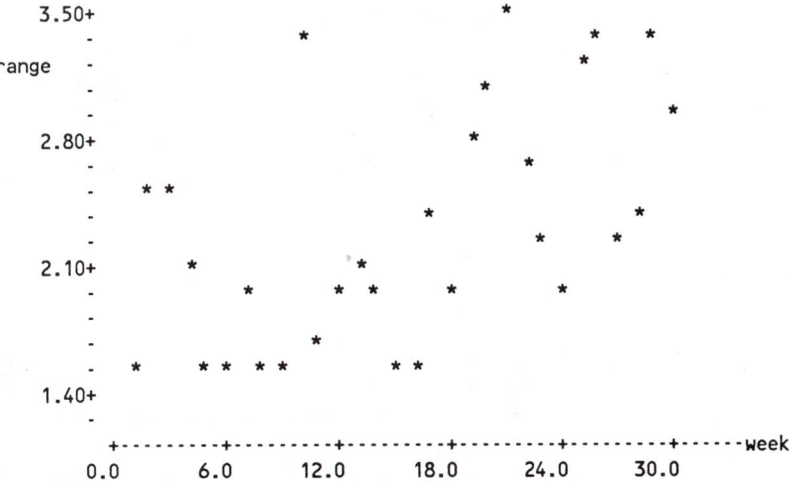

Solution   It appears that the ranges are increasing with week number. In Example 2.10, we found that the means jumped at about week 19. It's not so obvious, but the ranges may have jumped at about that time as well. ■

There are at least two problems with using the range as a measure of variability. First, the range is very sensitive to outliers—"wild" values far from the rest of the data. Second, as the sample size increases, the range tends to increase as well; in the automatic transmission data, adding another 10 measurements to the original 5 per week couldn't decrease the range, and probably would increase it.

deviations from the mean   More useful measures of variability are based on **deviations from the mean**. The deviation of a sample measurement y_i from its mean $\bar{y}$ is defined as $(y_i - \bar{y})$. Some of these deviations are positive, others negative; their algebraic sum is always zero:

$$\sum_i (y_i - \bar{y}) = (y_1 - \bar{y}) + (y_2 - \bar{y}) + \cdots + (y_n - \bar{y})$$

$$= y_1 + y_2 + \cdots + y_n - n\bar{y} = n\bar{y} - n\bar{y} = 0$$

Thus the positive and negative deviations exactly balance. To measure variability, we must look at the magnitudes (ignoring the positive or negative sign) of the deviations; large positive and negative deviations indicate large variability.

average absolute deviation   The simplest measure of the magnitudes of the deviations is the **average absolute deviation** (AD), defined as the average of the absolute values of the deviations:

$$AD = \frac{\sum_i |y_i - \bar{y}|}{n}$$

Regard the data values 11, 12, 13, 14, and 30 as a sample of five measurements selected from a population of interest. Compute the average absolute deviation for the sample data.

It is easy to show that $\bar{y} = 80/5 = 16$, so

$$AD = \frac{|11 - 16| + |12 - 16| + |13 - 16| + |14 - 16| + |30 - 16|}{5}$$

$$= \frac{5 + 4 + 3 + 2 + 14}{5} = 5.6$$

Thus, on the average, an individual measurement deviates 5.6 units from the mean.

The average absolute deviation is easy to compute and to interpret. However, it is difficult to deal mathematically with absolute values. Most statistical methods deal with squared deviations instead.

variance   **The most useful statistical measures of variability are the *variance* and the**
standard deviation   ***standard deviation.*** The variance of a sample of n measurements $y_1, y_2, \ldots, y_n$ is defined as the sum of the squared deviations divided by $(n - 1)$. We denote the sample variance by s^2. The sample standard deviation s of the measurements is the (positive) square root of the variance. The corresponding population variance and standard deviation are denoted by σ^2 and σ, respectively.

$$s^2 = \frac{\sum_i (y_i - \bar{y})^2}{n - 1}$$

$$s = \sqrt{s^2}$$

EXAMPLE 2.12   Compute the sample variance and sample standard deviation for the data in Example 2.11.

Solution   With $\bar{y} = 16$, we can substitute into the formula for s^2 to obtain

$$s^2 = \frac{(11 - 16)^2 + (12 - 16)^2 + (13 - 16)^2 + (14 - 16)^2 + (30 - 16)^2}{5 - 1}$$

$$= \frac{250}{4} = 62.5$$

and thus

$$s = \sqrt{62.5} = 7.906$$ ■

The use of $(n - 1)$ as the denominator of s^2 is not arbitrary. This definition of the sample variance makes it an "unbiased estimator" of the population variance σ^2. This roughly means that if we were to draw a very large number of samples each of size n from the population and if we computed s^2 for each sample, the average sample variance would equal the population variance σ^2. Had we divided by n in the definition of s^2, the average sample variance would be less than the population variance, and hence s^2 would tend to underestimate σ^2.

The definitions of variance and standard deviation depend on whether the data are regarded as a population or as a sample. In practice, the available data are usually only a sample. Unless specifically indicated otherwise, we regard all data sets as samples and consider population means and variances as conceptual quantities to be estimated from the samples.*

Computation of s^2 and s by hand is often simplified by the use of the algebraic identity

$$\sum_i (y_i - \bar{y})^2 = \sum_i y_i^2 - \frac{\left(\sum_i y_i\right)^2}{n}$$

This identity yields a shortcut formula for s^2 and therefore for s.

Shortcut Formula for s^2 and s

$$s^2 = \frac{1}{n-1}\left[\sum_i y_i^2 - \frac{\left(\sum_i y_i\right)^2}{n}\right]$$

$$s = \sqrt{s^2}$$

We have defined the variance and standard deviation but have not yet indicated how to interpret them. What does a standard deviation of $552.51 mean? There are two possible interpretations, one a rough but reasonably accurate approximation, the other a mathematically guaranteed (but not so accurate) inequality. The approximation assumes that the measurements have roughly a mound-shaped histogram—that is, a symmetric, single-peaked histogram that tapers off reasonably smoothly from the peak toward the tails. We call the approximation the **Empirical Rule**.

Empirical Rule

For a set of measurements having a mound-shaped histogram, the interval

$\bar{y} \pm 1s$ contains approximately 68% of the measurements;
$\bar{y} \pm 2s$ contains approximately 95% of the measurements;
$\bar{y} \pm 3s$ contains approximately all of the measurements.

* When a set of data is regarded as a population, the population variance is defined as the sum of squared deviations from the population mean μ, all divided by N, the population size—not by $(N - 1)$.

EXAMPLE 2.13   A sample of 20 days throughout the previous year indicates that the average wholesale price per pound for steers at a particular stockyard was $.61 and that the standard deviation was $.07. If the histogram for the measurements is mound shaped, describe the variability of the data using the Empirical Rule.

Solution   Applying the Empirical Rule, we conclude that

the interval .61 ± .07, or $.54 to $.68, contains approximately 68% of the measurements;

the interval .61 ± .14, or $.47 to $.75, contains approximately 95% of the measurements;

the interval .61 ± .21, or $.40 to $.82, contains approximately all of the measurements. ∎

The mathematically guaranteed bound is known as **Chebyshev's Inequality**.

Chebyshev's Inequality

For any set of measurements and a constant $c > 1$, the interval

$$\bar{y} \pm cs \text{ contains } \textbf{at least } 1 - 1/c^2 \text{ of the measurements.}$$

Thus for $c = 2$ and $c = 3$,

$$\bar{y} \pm 2s \text{ contains } \textbf{at least } 3/4 \text{ of the measurements,}$$

and

$$\bar{y} \pm 3s \text{ contains } \textbf{at least } 8/9 \text{ of the measurements.}$$

Although Chebyshev's Inequality is always mathematically correct, the Empirical Rule is often a better approximation. If the assumption of a mound-shaped histogram is exactly correct (specifically, if the data follow the normal distribution defined in Chapter 5), the Empirical Rule is exactly correct. Even if the data don't follow an exactly mound-shaped distribution, the Empirical Rule is still fairly accurate.

EXAMPLE 2.14   The following data represent the percentages of family income allocated to groceries for a sample of 30 shoppers:

26	28	30	37	33	30
29	39	49	31	38	36
33	24	34	40	29	41
40	29	35	44	32	45
35	26	42	36	37	35

For these data, $\sum_i y_i = 1043$ and $\sum_i y_i^2 = 37{,}331$.

    a. Compute the mean, variance, and standard deviation of the percentage of income spent on food.

    b. Verify that Chebyshev's Inequality holds with $c = 2$. Which is closer to the actual proportion, this inequality or the Empirical Rule?

Solution   The sample mean is

$$\bar{y} = \frac{\sum_i y_i}{30} = \frac{1043}{30} = 34.77$$

The corresponding sample variance and standard deviation are

$$s^2 = \frac{1}{n-1}\left[\sum_i y_i^2 - \frac{\left(\sum_i y_i\right)^2}{n}\right]$$

$$= \frac{1}{29}[37{,}331 - 36{,}261.63] = \frac{1069.37}{29} = 36.87$$

$$s = \sqrt{36.87} = 6.07$$

Chebyshev's Inequality indicates that at least 0.75 of the data should fall in the range $34.77 - 2(6.07)$ to $34.77 + 2(6.07)$, or 22.63 to 46.91. In fact, 29 of the 30 values (a proportion of 0.967) fall within this range; the proportion is much closer to the Empirical Rule value.   ■

squared   Because the standard deviation is based on **squared** deviations from the mean, it is more sensitive to outliers than the mean is, for instance. However, it

S chart   is less outlier-sensitive than the range. Thus an **S chart**, a plot of standard deviations against time, is also a useful quality-control tool in assessing whether there has been a change in variability.

EXAMPLE 2.15   Standard deviations for the automatic transmission data of Section 2.2 were plotted in Figure 2.10 against day number to make an S chart. Is there evidence of a trend?

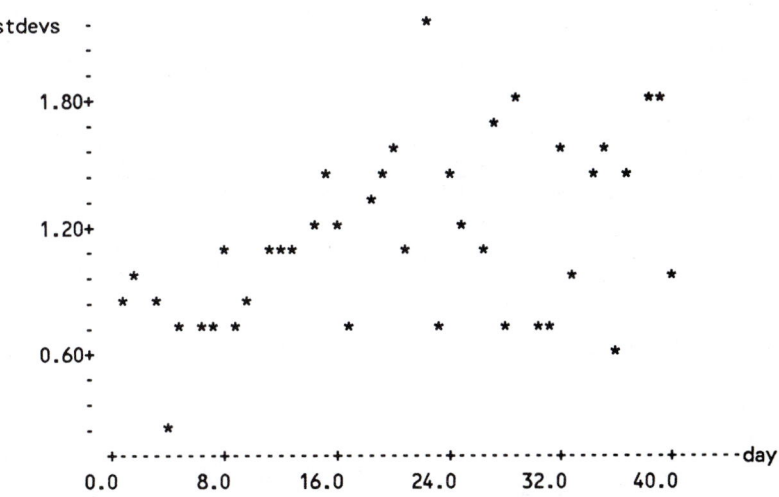

FIGURE 2.10   S Chart of Transmission Pressure Data

Solution   There is a clearly increasing trend in the standard deviations, indicating that variability is increasing with time.   ∎

The standard deviation is also useful in *x*-bar quality-control charts. From data taken when a process is "in control," one can calculate the standard deviation of the means. In a complete *x*-bar chart, upper and lower **control limits** are drawn at the desired mean plus three standard deviations (of the mean) and at the desired mean minus three standard deviations. Any mean that falls outside these limits is taken as evidence that the process is out of control. According to the Empirical Rule, if the process is in control, very few means should fall outside the control limits, so "false alarms" should be rare. If and when the process goes seriously out of control, the means should go outside one control limit or the other. Control limits are very useful in reducing the tendency of managers to go chasing after every minor variation; only deviations that are very likely more than random will fall outside the control limits.

control limits

EXAMPLE 2.16   A control chart for the transmission data of Section 2.2 is shown in Figure 2.11. How does it indicate that there is trouble a-brewing?

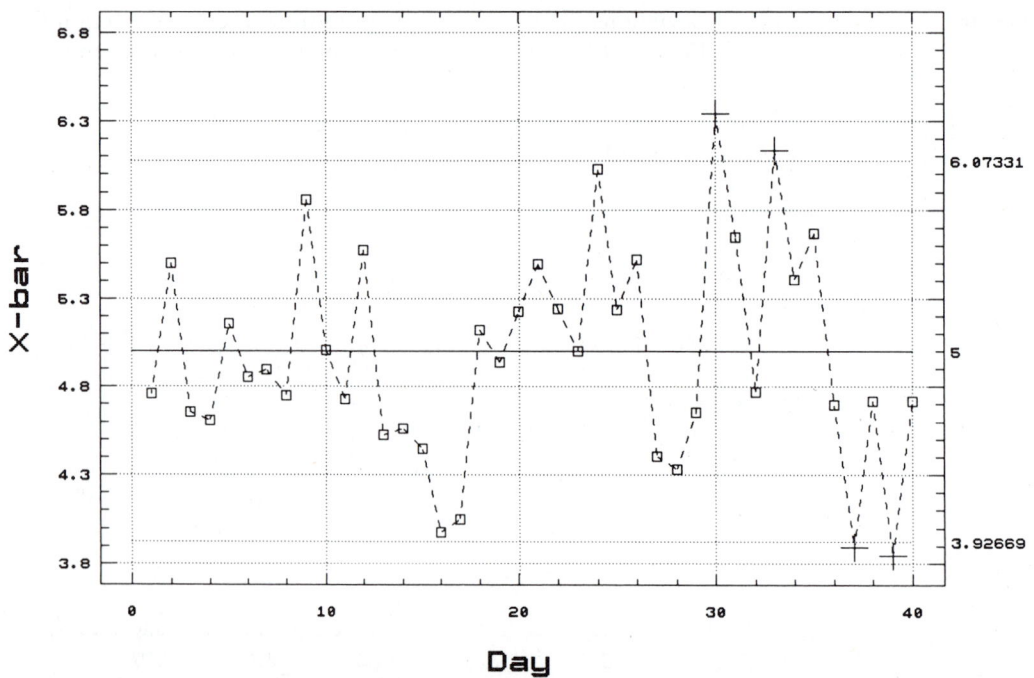

FIGURE 2.11   Control Chart for Automatic Transmission Data

Solution   Near the right-hand side of the chart, the + signs indicate that the mean is outside control limits. Because there is no pattern of consistently high or consistently low readings, it seems reasonable to think that the problem is excessive variability. Results for previous examples confirm this idea. Management's task seems to be to find out why there is such variation in the transmission data.   ■

IQR   An alternative way to approach variability is the **interquartile range** (IQR). The quartiles of a data distribution are the 25th and 75th percentiles—the values that mark the bottom one-fourth and top one-fourth of the data. Tukey (1977) calls these values "hinges" and notes that they can be found by taking medians of each half of the data. The median of the bottom half of the data is the 25th percentile, simply because half of one-half is one-fourth; similarly, the median of the top half of the data is the 75th percentile. The interquartile range is the difference between the two quartiles.

Interquartile Range

To find the quartiles of a set of data on a variable,

1. Sort the data and find the median.
2. Divide the data into top and bottom halves (above and below the median). If the sample size n is odd, arbitrarily include the median in both halves.
3. Find the medians of both halves. These are the 25th and 75th percentiles, or "hinges."
4. IQR = 75th percentile − 25th percentile.   ■

EXAMPLE 2.17   Find the interquartile range for the data of Example 2.14.

Solution   First we sort the data.

24	26	26	28	29	29	29	30	30	31	32	33	33	34	35
35	35	36	36	37	37	38	39	40	40	41	42	44	45	49

Because $n = 30$, the median is the average of the fifteenth and sixteenth values (both of which are 35), namely 35. The bottom half of the data is the lowest 15 values; the top half is the highest 15 values. The median of the bottom half (that is, the 25th percentile) is the eighth value, 30. The 75th percentile is the eighth value from the top, 39. The IQR is $39 - 30 = 9$.   ■

The IQR is most commonly used in checking for outliers. Tukey (1977) defines the inner fences as follows:

lower inner fence = 25th percentile − 1.5 IQR
upper inner fence = 75th percentile + 1.5 IQR

Any value outside the inner fences is an outlier candidate. The choice of the number 1.5 is arbitrary, but it seems to work decently. Similarly, the outer fences are defined as follows:

$$\text{lower outer fence} = \text{25th percentile} - 3.0\ \text{IQR}$$
$$\text{upper outer fence} = \text{75th percentile} + 3.0\ \text{IQR}$$

Any data value outside the outer fences is a serious outlier.   ∎

EXAMPLE 2.18   Calculate the various fences for the data of Example 2.14. Does the fence test identify any outliers? Do there appear to be outliers on visual inspection?

Solution   A plot of the data, or merely a scan by eye, does not indicate that any value should be regarded as an outlier. The closest thing to an outlier is the value 49, but it is close to several other values. The 25th percentile and 75th percentile were found in Example 2.17 to be 30 and 39, so the IQR is 9. The inner fences are $30 - 1.5(9) = 16.5$ and $39 + 1.5(9) = 52.5$. No data value even comes close to the inner fences, so the fence test identifies no outliers.   .   ∎

The interquartile range is the basis for still another Tukey (1977) idea, the box plot, sometimes called the "box-and-whiskers plot."

Box Plot

1. Draw the edges of a box at the 25th and 75th percentiles. Draw a vertical bar through the box at the median.
2. Draw lines ("whiskers") from the edges of the box to the adjacent values—the smallest and largest nonoutliers.
3. Plot each outlier candidate separately, conventionally using a * symbol. Plot each serious outlier, conventionally using a 0 symbol.   ∎

EXAMPLE 2.19   Suppose that the return on investments for 21 companies in a certain industry for a certain year is

−24.6	−2.6	2.4	2.7	3.8	5.6	5.9	6.7	7.0	7.2	7.5
8.0	8.2	8.5	8.6	8.8	9.0	9.2	9.7	10.0	20.5	

Draw a box plot of these data.

Solution   With $n = 21$, the median is the eleventh score, 7.5. The 25th percentile is the median of the bottom 11 scores, namely 5.6. (Note that, because n is an odd number, we include the median in both halves of the data. Thus the bottom half of the data comprises 11 scores, not 10.) The 75th percentile is the median of the top 11 scores, namely 8.8. Thus IQR $= 8.8 - 5.6 = 3.2$. The fences are

$$\text{lower outer fence} = 5.6 - 3.0(3.2) = -4.0$$
$$\text{lower inner fence} = 5.6 - 1.5(3.2) = \ \ \ 0.8$$
$$\text{upper inner fence} = 8.8 + 1.5(3.2) = \ \ 13.6$$
$$\text{upper outer fence} = 8.8 + 3.0(3.2) = \ \ 18.4$$

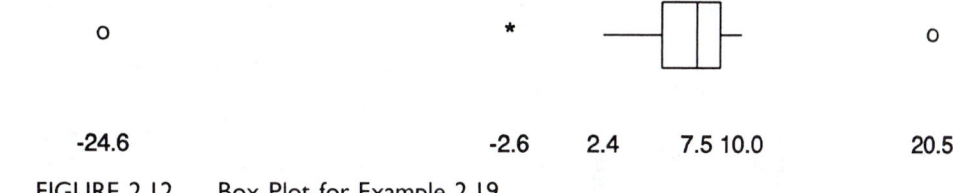

-24.6   -2.6   2.4   7.5 10.0   20.5

FIGURE 2.12   Box Plot for Example 2.19

The fence test identifies two serious outliers, −24.6 and 20.5, and one outlier candidate, −2.6. (A plot of the data indicates that the serious outliers are obviously extreme and that the outlier candidate is debatably out.) The adjacent values are the smallest and largest nonoutliers, 2.4 and 10.0. The resulting box plot is shown in Figure 2.12. ■

SECTION 2.3   EXERCISES

2.13 Suppose that the data from two samples are

Sample 1:   15   19   21   25
Sample 2:   14   17   18   19   19   20   20   20   21   21   22   23   26

  a. Find the range for each sample.
  b. Find the standard deviation for each sample.
  c. Which sample shows more variability? Construct a histogram or line plot to support your opinion.

2.14 Data for car production per shift given in Exercise 2.8 are reproduced here:

688   711   625   701   688   667   694   630   547   703   688   697   703
656   677   700   702   688   691   664   688   679   708   699   667   703

  a. Find the mean and standard deviation.
  b. How well does the Empirical Rule work for the fraction of data falling within one standard deviation of the mean?

2.15 a. Find the median and IQR for the data in Exercise 2.14.
  b. Find the inner and outer fences. Are there outliers?
  c. Draw a box plot of the data.

2.16 Directory assistance (information) operators receive requests for telephone numbers from customers. The procedure for obtaining and reporting numbers is highly computerized so that each operator should be able to handle a large number of calls in a workday. At one office, the minimum standard is regarded as 780 calls cleared per day—roughly, 2 calls cleared per minute. Data were collected for a day on 60 day-shift operators. What sources of variability among operators might be present?

2.17 Data on the 60 operators of Exercise 2.16 were analyzed using Minitab.
  a. Calculate the "mean plus-or-minus one standard deviation" interval used in the Empirical Rule.
  b. Of the 60 scores in 'cleared,' 51 fall within the one standard deviation interval. How does this result compare with the theoretical value of the Empirical Rule? What might explain the discrepancy?

```
MTB > print 'cleared'
cleared
   797    794    817    813    817    793    762    719    804    811    837
   804    790    796    807    801    805    811    835    787    800    771
   794    805    797    724    820    601    817    801    798    797    788
   802    792    779    803    807    789    787    794    792    786    808
   808    844    790    763    784    739    805    817    804    807    800
   785    796    789    842    829

MTB > describe 'cleared'

                N      MEAN    MEDIAN   TRMEAN     STDEV    SEMEAN
cleared        60    794.23    799.00   797.91     34.25      4.42

              MIN       MAX        Q1        Q3
cleared    601.00    844.00    789.00    807.75
```

2.18   A box plot of the data in Exercise 2.17 is shown below. How does the plot explain the failure of the Empirical Rule?

```
MTB > boxplot of 'cleared'
```

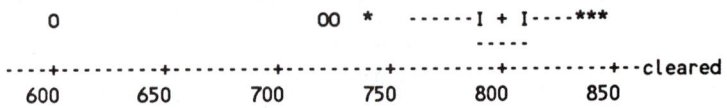

```
                                                        -----
         O                            OO   *   ------I + I----***
                                                        -----
         ----+---------+---------+---------+---------+---------+--cleared
            600       650       700       750       800       850
```

2.19   Operator 28 (the one with the 601 score in the data for Exercise 2.17) was a trainee who wasn't expected to perform to the standard of long-term operators. The data were reanalyzed omitting this operator.
   a. How would you expect omitting the 601 score to affect the mean? the standard deviation?
   b. Minitab output is shown below. How much were the mean and standard deviation affected?

```
MTB > describe 'longterm'

                N      MEAN    MEDIAN   TRMEAN     STDEV    SEMEAN
longterm       59    797.51    800.00   799.02     23.21      3.02

              MIN       MAX        Q1        Q3
longterm   719.00    844.00    789.00    808.00
```

2.20   Scheduling the duration of airplane flights is critical to an airline's service, particularly at "hub" centers. At such centers, flights arrive in groups, passengers transfer to other flights, and these flights depart. If incoming flights require longer-than-scheduled times, passengers may miss connecting flights, or the outgoing flights may have to be delayed. If, however, most flights require less-than-scheduled times, passengers will have to wait a long time for their connecting flights. An operations manager routinely records the actual times taken by 38 flights scheduled to arrive between 4:30 and 5:00 P.M. at a hub. The times are converted to percentage of scheduled time, so a "late percentage" of 100 indicates that a flight is exactly on time. Systat computer output of the 38 percentages is shown below.

a. On average, how well did the flights do in meeting their schedules?

b. What sources of variability can you think of?

c. Find Empirical Rule limits that should include 95% of the flights.

```
TOTAL OBSERVATIONS:   38


                       LATEPERC

N OF CASES               38
MINIMUM              91.000
MAXIMUM             125.000
MEAN                101.579
STANDARD DEV          6.479
```

2.21 A stem-and-leaf display of the data for Exercise 2.20, created by Systat, is shown below.

a. Do the data appear bell shaped, so that the Empirical Rule should work reasonably well?

b. What percentage of the 38 scores fall within the limits calculated in part (c) of Exercise 2.20?

```
        STEM AND LEAF PLOT OF VARIABLE: LATEPERC     , N =    38

MINIMUM IS:        91.000
LOWER HINGE IS:       97.000
MEDIAN IS:        100.000
UPPER HINGE IS:      104.000
MAXIMUM IS:       125.000

             9   1
             9   23
             9   55
             9 H 67777
             9   8999
            10 M 000000
            10   22222333
            10 H 455
            10   67
            10   89
            11   1
       ***OUTSIDE VALUES***
            11   6
            12   5
```

2.22 The late percentage data of Exercise 2.20 were plotted in order of scheduled arrival by Systat. Is there any indication of a trend?

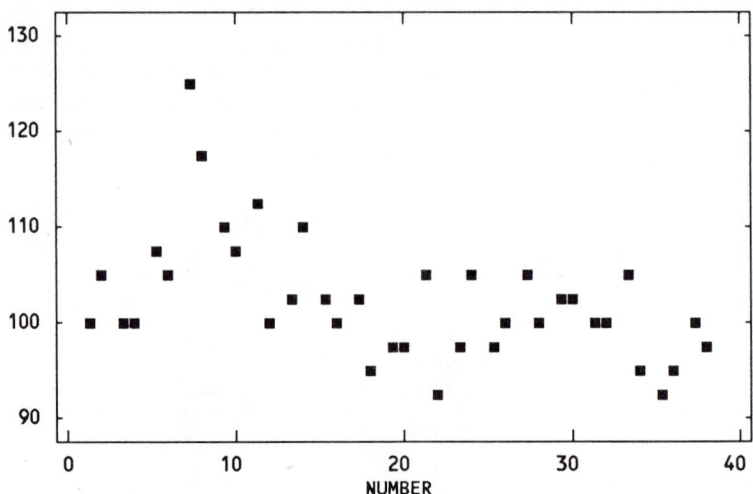

LATEPERC

2.23   The operations manager of Exercise 2.20 also kept track of the lateness percentage of each flight over time. The results for flight 483 for 40 consecutive weekdays were analyzed by Minitab, as shown below.

a. Should one expect essentially the same variability in these numbers as we found for the cross-section data of Exercise 2.20?

b. Which standard deviation turned out smaller?

```
MTB > print 'late%'

late%
    100    107     97    101    103    101     95     92     96     93    104
    109    106    107    112    102    101     99     99     98    104    109
    116    118    104    106     99    105    104    107     97     94    100
    101    102    105    109     99    105     99

MTB > describe 'late%'

                N      MEAN    MEDIAN    TRMEAN    STDEV    SEMEAN
late%          40    102.62    102.00    102.39     5.75      0.91

               MIN       MAX        Q1        Q3
late%        92.00    118.00     99.00    106.00
```

2.24   The lateness percentage data of Exercise 2.23 were plotted against day number, as shown below.

a. Is there any evidence of a time trend?

b. The target percentage is 100. Use the standard deviation from Exercise 2.23 to construct control limits. Were there any days that qualified as out of control?

```
MTB > plot 'late%' vs 'day'
```

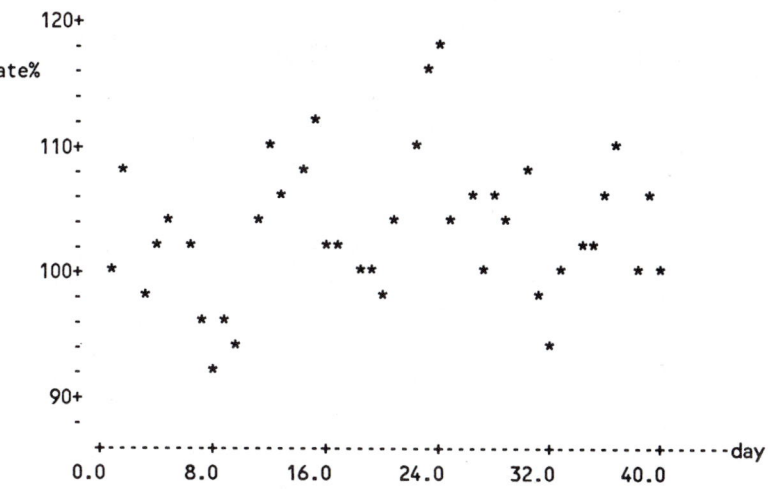

2.25 In Exercise 2.16, we considered calls cleared by directory assistance operators, finding a sample mean equal to 794.23 and a sample standard deviation equal to 34.25. A "sideways histogram" of the data constructed by Minitab is shown below.
   a. Use the histogram (and the indicated midpoints) to find grouped-data approximations to the mean and standard deviation.
   b. How close are these approximations to the correct values?

```
MTB > histogram of 'cleared'

Histogram of cleared    N = 60

Midpoint    Count
    600       1   *
    620       0
    640       0
    660       0
    680       0
    700       0
    720       2   **
    740       1   *
    760       2   **
    780      10   **********
    800      31   *******************************
    820       9   *********
    840       4   ****
```

2.26 The midpoints used in Exercise 2.25 might be considered less than the best. For example, the midpoint shown as 780 should actually be the midpoint of the interval 770–789, namely 779.5. Suppose that we adjust all the midpoints down by 0.5 to satisfy this argument.
   a. Without doing any arithmetic, how should the mean and variability (standard deviation) be changed by this adjustment?
   b. Recompute the grouped-data mean and standard deviation using the adjusted midpoints. Did your results change as predicted in part (a)?

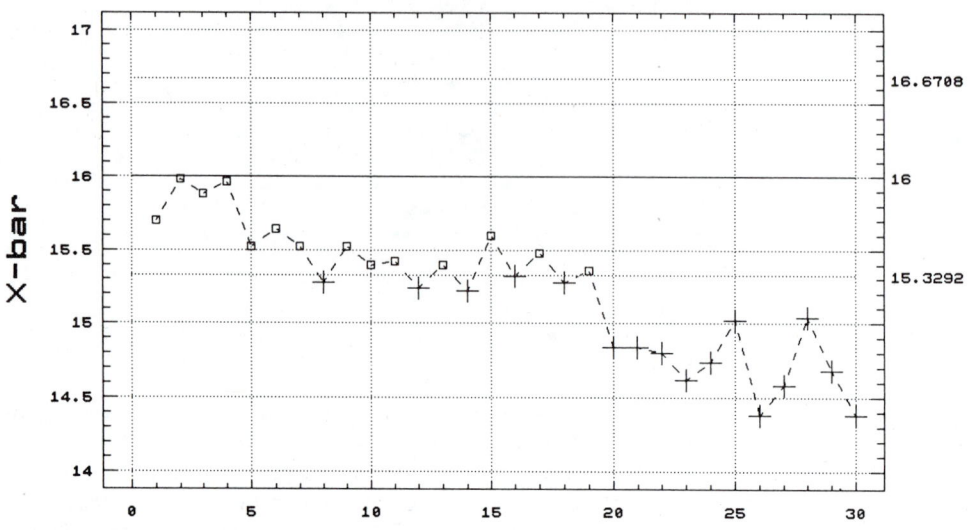

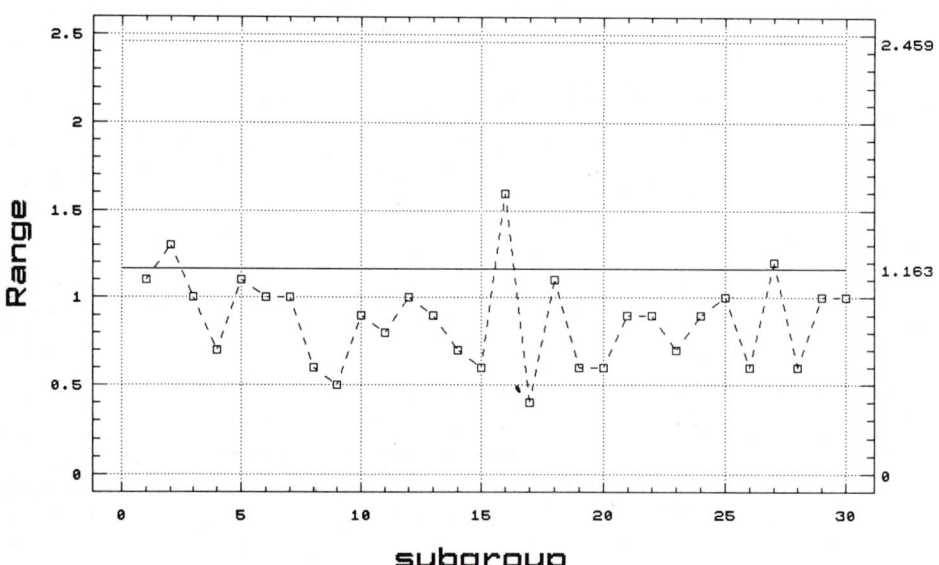

FIGURE 2.13   Control Charts for Bit Hardness Data

2.27   A manufacturer of tools for homeowners and contractors produces a line of masonry bits for drills. One of the critical qualities of these bits is hardness, measured on a standard scale. If the bits are not hard enough, they wear out rapidly. If the bits are too hard, they can be brittle and break; because the bits are used to drill holes in concrete and brick, it can be extremely dangerous to have a bit break. The scale used to measure hardness is quite sensitive; what would seem to an outsider to be small changes in hardness lead to fairly large changes on the scale. The target value on this scale is 16.0. Even when the production process is working well, there is some variability in bit hardness, mostly because of imperfect mixing of metals in the alloy and variation in heating during the tempering process. The target standard deviation is 0.5.

The tool manufacturer instituted a quality-improvement approach involving, among many other actions, use of control charts. Each production day, a sample of five bits was selected randomly from the day's production. The hardness of each bit was measured carefully (by a destructive process, which necessitates using a sample) and recorded. Data for the first 30 days following overhaul of the production process were used in a control chart for the mean and the range, shown in Figure 2.13.

  a. Does the chart indicate that there is a problem with the mean? If so, does it appear that there was a sudden jump, or a gradual trend?
  b. Does the chart indicate that there is a problem of excessive variability? If so, was there a jump or a trend?

2.28   The tool manufacturer in Exercise 2.27 believed that there were two major explanations for unsatisfactory bit hardness. One potential problem would be bad lots of metal. Each lot is used for about six days of production; each lot is completely used up before another lot is begun. A second potential problem is the heating system used to temper the bits. Over time, this system can drift to higher or lower temperatures. Based on the control charts in Figure 2.13, which seems to be the more plausible culprit for any problems you identified in Exercise 2.27?

2.4   OTHER SUMMARY MEASURES OF DATA   ■

The mean and standard deviation are by far the most important and most widely used summary statistics for a set of data. In this section we define some other statistics that are occasionally useful in measuring the skewness and "tail-heaviness" of data.

In Section 2.2 we said that when the data are skewed to the right, the mean is larger than the median; for data that are skewed to the left, the mean is smaller than the median. One simple measure of skewness is

$$\frac{\text{mean} - \text{median}}{\text{standard deviation}}$$

A positive value of this measure indicates that the data are right-skewed; a negative value, left-skewed. This measure is 0 if the data are perfectly symmetric (because the mean and median both equal the point of symmetry). It is also possible that the measure equals 0 for certain patterns of nonsymmetric data.

EXAMPLE 2.20   A random sample of 36 intermediate-level executives from health-related corporations are interviewed to determine their estimated increases in expenditures for research and development over the next 10 years. These data (recorded as percentages of sales) are shown here:

2.10	2.47	1.75	2.94	1.69	2.75	2.82	2.52	2.77	1.98	2.70	2.43
2.17	2.80	2.82	2.38	2.68	2.39	1.99	2.10	2.67	2.65	2.06	2.55
2.22	2.92	3.05	2.77	2.36	1.80	3.09	2.20	2.93	1.85	2.28	1.96

A Minitab output is shown below (some steps are omitted).

```
MTB > histogram of '$R-and-D'

Histogram of $R-and-D    N = 36

Midpoint   Count
     1.6     1   *
     1.8     3   ***
     2.0     4   ****
     2.2     6   ******
     2.4     5   *****
     2.6     5   *****
     2.8     7   *******
     3.0     5   *****

MTB > Describe '$R-and-D'

                N      MEAN    MEDIAN    STDEV
$R-and-D       36    2.4336    2.4500    0.397

MTB > Print k5 = coef of skewness, k6 = kurtosis
K5   -.188922
K6   1.79995
```

a. Use these data to compute $(\bar{y} - \text{median})/s$, a measure of skewness.

b. Do the data suggest a skewness?

Solution   a. The mean is 2.4336, the median is 2.4500, and the standard deviation is 0.397. So $(\bar{y} - \text{median})/s = (2.4336 - 2.45)/0.397 = -0.041$, a very small number.

b. The histogram for the sample data is shown in the output. There is no blatant skewness; if anything, there is a slight left-skewness, because the mean is slightly below the median.   ∎

Another measure of skewness involves raising deviations from the mean to the third power. This measure, called the *coefficient of skewness*, is defined as

$$\frac{M_3}{M_2^{3/2}}$$

where

$$M_3 = \sum(y - \bar{y})^3/n$$
$$M_2 = \sum(y - \bar{y})^2/n$$

This measure also is positive for right-skewed data, negative for left-skewed data, and 0 for symmetric data.

EXAMPLE 2.21   Refer to the data and Minitab output of Example 2.20. Locate the coefficient of skewness.

Solution   The coefficient of skewness $M_3/M_2^{3/2}$ is shown as K5 in the output. The value $K5 = -0.188922$ indicates left-skewness.   ∎

This measure works as a measure of skewness because the cube (third power) of a large number is vastly bigger than the cube of a smaller number. In right-skewed data there are a few relatively large positive deviations, resulting in a positive value for this skewness measure. Unfortunately, this cubing process makes the measure very sensitive to extreme values in the data; for this reason, we prefer to use (mean − median)/s as a measure of skewness.

kurtosis   A measure of the heaviness of the tails of a distribution of data is the **kurtosis**. This involves fourth powers of deviations and can be defined as

$$\frac{M_4}{M_2^2}$$

where

$$M_4 = \sum (y - \bar{y})^4 / n$$
$$M_2 = \sum (y - \bar{y})^2 / n$$

If the data follow a bell-shaped distribution, as shown below, the kurtosis is approximately 3. A symmetric distribution having heavier tails than a bell-shaped distribution has a kurtosis larger than 3. A heavy-tailed distribution is indicated in Figure 2.14. A light-tailed distribution has a kurtosis less than 3.

The difficulty with the kurtosis measure is that, because it uses fourth powers, it is very sensitive to extreme values. Modest changes in extreme values can lead to large changes in the kurtosis measure. However, we know of no other commonly used measure of heavy-tailness that is more satisfactory than the kurtosis. If this measure is to be used, it is important to plot the data to see if one or two very extreme values are present; such values can cause a misleading value of the kurtosis.

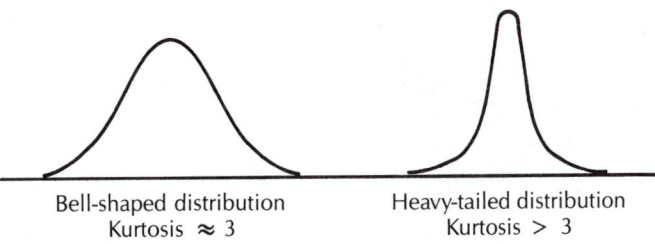

Bell-shaped distribution
Kurtosis ≈ 3

Heavy-tailed distribution
Kurtosis > 3

FIGURE 2.14   **Bell-Shaped and Heavy-Tailed Distributions**

EXAMPLE 2.22   Find the coefficient of kurtosis for the data of Example 2.20.

Solution   The Minitab output from Example 2.20 also displays the coefficient of kurtosis,

1.79995, indicating a light-tailed distribution. The histogram for the sample data indicates no extreme outliers.   ■

SECTION 2.4   EXERCISES

2.29 Use the SAS computer output shown here to answer parts (a)–(c).
   a. Locate the measures of skewness and kurtosis.
   b. Plot the data in convenient form. Does the skewness coefficient indicate the same sign (positive or negative) as does the plot?
   c. Verify the computation of the skewness coefficient.

OBS	1	2	3	4	5	6	7	8	9	10	11	12	13	14	15
CROWD	42.6	12.1	10.6	12.7	14.5	19.2	16.7	20.1	15.5	9.9	14.6	16.1	19.4	23.3	29.7

OBS	16	17	18	19	20	21	22	23	24	25	26	27	28	29	30
CROWD	22.6	15.7	18.9	12.8	19.1	33.5	24.7	18.6	18.2	19.9	15.5	21.2	20.2	16.5	18.6

ATTENDANCE DATA FOR 30 BASEBALL GAMES

VARIABLE	N	MEAN	STANDARD DEVIATION	MINIMUM VALUE	MAXIMUM VALUE	VARIANCE	SKEWNESS	KURTOSIS
CROWD	30	19.10000000	6.76930190	9.90000000	42.60000000	45.82344828	1.76647488	4.37158198

2.30 Refer to the data of Exercise 2.2 (p. 15) and the histogram constructed in part (a) of that exercise.
   a. Calculate the kurtosis coefficient.
   b. Does the coefficient indicate the kind of tailness suggested by the histogram?

2.31 Indicate the skewness pattern you would expect to find in each of the following data situations:
   a. sale prices of existing houses in southern California;
   b. scores on a fairly easy 100-point classroom examination;
   c. lumber yield in a stand of widely spaced, equal-age trees.

2.32 As part of a facilities expansion study, the monthly precipitation (inches) at a major metropolitan airport is obtained for a two-year period. The data are as follows:

Year 1:   0.1   0.7   0.5   4.5   6.7   1.1   0.7   3.2   4.8   1.0   0.9   0.8
Year 2:   7.9   1.8   1.4   0.2   0.7   1.5   2.6   5.5   0.6   0.5   1.7   3.3

   a. Compute $\bar{y}$ and s for each year.
   b. Compute two measures of skewness for each year. Do both measures indicate skewness?

2.33 Combine the data in Exercise 2.32 for both years.
   a. Determine the average monthly precipitation over the two-year period. Can it be found from the yearly averages, or must you go back to the original data?
   b. Use the monthly data to compute the standard deviation of the combined data. Is the combined standard deviation equal to the average of the yearly standard deviations?

2.34 The automobile manufacturer in Exercise 2.8 can produce a maximum of 720 cars per shift. Normally the plant can come close to that maximum, but occasional downtime reduces production.
   a. From this description, what skewness should be observed in the data?
   b. Calculate $(\bar{y} - \text{median})/s$ for the data. Does this measure reflect the expected type of skewness?

2.35 The data in Exercise 2.7 for the amount of damage suffered by automobiles in low-speed crashes are reproduced here:

| 361 | 393 | 430 | 543 | 566 | 610 | 763 | 851 | 886 | 887 | 976 | 1039 |
| 1124 | 1267 | 1328 | 1415 | 1425 | 1444 | 1476 | 1542 | 1544 | 2048 | 2197 | |

a. Does a plot of the data reveal extreme skewness?
b. Does the value $(\bar{y} - \text{median})/s$ indicate extreme skewness?

2.36 Calculate the kurtosis for the data of Exercise 2.35. If a computer package is available to you, this is the spot to use it. What does the value of the kurtosis indicate about the shape of the data?

2.5   CALCULATORS AND COMPUTER SOFTWARE SYSTEMS ■

Inexpensive electronic hand calculators can be quite useful in performing many of the calculations in this chapter, especially for relatively small amounts of data. For example, many calculators have keys for obtaining the mean and standard deviation directly once the data have been entered. Some have special keys or programmable routines that will do more elaborate computations as well. When using a hand calculator, one must be very careful to enter data correctly, because the entries are usually unavailable for later review. It's a good idea to check answers for reasonableness. The mean should be in the middle of the data; if the calculated result is near one end or the other of the data, a data-entry error should be suspected. The Empirical Rule provides a useful check for the size of a standard deviation. If the one standard deviation interval around the mean includes virtually all the data, rather than about 68%, one again suspects a data-entry error.

For larger amounts of data, a computer is extremely useful. There are literally hundreds of programs available for doing statistical analyses by computer. Most of them will carry out virtually all the computations in this book and many more besides. Even more important, the good ones will do data plots very quickly and conveniently.

In general, these packages carry out several steps. First, one must make the data available to the package, either by entry from a keyboard or by importing a data file from a disk or tape. Usually, to make eventual output more readable, a package will have some ability to name variables in a data set. There should be a facility to review the data set and edit it to remove errors. Once the data set is ready for analysis, any package can do plots and computations very quickly and make the results available in a variety of ways.

E notation   Some computer outputs state results in **E notation**. Rather than reporting a mean as 15,326, for example, a particular package may report the mean as 1.5326E04. The E (exponent) part of the expression tells you how many places to the right to move the decimal point. For instance, E04 indicates move the decimal point four places to the right, so that 1.5326E04 = 15,326. Similarly, a negative exponent corresponds to moving the decimal place to the *left*: 1.5326E − 04 = 0.00015326.

We think that the data-plotting ability of computer packages is their most crucial feature. It's so easy to obtain histograms, stem-and-leaf displays, box plots, and other data displays discussed in later chapters that there's little excuse for doing computations before looking at the data. Any good display should alert you to skewness, outliers, or bimodality that distort the meaning of a mean or standard deviation.

It is perfectly possible to use any computer package badly. If you insist on entering "continent" as a numerical variable, with 1 meaning Africa; 2, Asia; 3, Australia; 4, Europe; 5, North America; and 6, South America; and if you ask for the mean continent, any package we know of will calculate it, to lots of decimal places. A good package will have a method for distinguishing qualitative from quantitative variables, but you have to use it. Further, if you ask for a standard deviation from wildly outlier-prone data, any package we know of will give it to you. You must take responsibility for looking at the data and doing sensible things with it.

We will use output from many statistical packages in this book. Remember that not all the output provided by a package will be relevant to a particular problem; rather than trying to interpret every number, find the relevant numbers. Used with thought, these packages can be immensely convenient and useful.

2.6   STATISTICAL METHODS AND QUALITY IMPROVEMENT ■

Statistical tools are a major contributor to quality control and process improvement. We have introduced control charts in this chapter and will describe other statistical quality methods in later chapters. Thinking statistically about averages and especially about variability is crucially important in thinking about quality and its improvement.

Statistical methods alone aren't enough. Control charts have been known in American industry for 60 years. If they cured all quality problems by themselves, American products would universally be the highest quality in the world; however, there are some individuals who assert that American quality is not absolutely the best.

Almost all the people who have studied good-quality and poor-quality operations agree that improving quality requires sustained, long-term, patient commitment by managers and workers at all levels. The best-known quality expert is probably W. Edwards Deming, a professional statistician who introduced statistical quality control and improvement methods in postwar Japan. Deming (1986) has formulated a 14-point program for quality improvement. An interesting outsider's view is given in Walton (1986). Deming insists on the absolute necessity of *sustained* management commitment; he abhors short-term sloganeering ("zero defects") as a substitute for real effort.

Almost all quality experts concentrate on improving processes, as opposed to exhorting people. At bottom, most of the fundamental tasks of organizations are repetitive processes conducted under similar conditions. Most people tend to think of processes and quality control in the context of manufacturing, but the same ideas apply just as well to granting loans, servicing automobiles, handling airline reservations, and many other service-sector activities. One of the key messages to managers from modern quality-improvement experts is to think more about long-run improvements in processes and less about short-run "fire-fighting." Managers should identify the goals of the process, consider what aspects of the process can be varied, and carry out well-considered experiments to find the best possible design for the process.

Rarely does quality leap upward. Instead, quality inches upward in small increments. An improved product design here, a modification of a service process there, improved cooperation with a supplier, a tailoring of a product to better fit customers' needs—all are small steps that must be taken repeatedly to improve quality. The unusual, huge breakthroughs in new products or services get the attention; the common, small gains have a greater cumulative effect. It takes a patient, persevering management to press on for quality improvement without immediate, dramatic payoffs.

One key to improving process quality is intelligent experimentation. Almost any task can be accomplished in many ways, some good, some bad. A remarkably effective method for avoiding quality improvement is to insist on doing a task one way "because we've always done it that way." A not-much-better approach to quality improvement is casual, unplanned experimentation—manipulating one aspect of a process, then another, without pattern or planning. A far more productive approach is planned experimentation, systematically thinking about all the key aspects of a process and deliberately, systematically seeking improvements in all of them. Here's one place where statistical thinking becomes vital. One of the great success stories of recent years in quality improvement has been the effective use of statistically controlled experiments.

Statistical thinking is crucial in considering processes, particularly in dealing with variation within processes. Most accounting systems are designed to deal with averages and totals. Statistical thinking adds the key idea of variability. Any manufacturing or service process will have some degree of natural variability in results. The proverbial widgets will vary from one another because of differences in raw materials, wear on machine parts, changes in temperature and humidity, and many other reasons. Adjustable-rate mortgage loans will sometimes be in default because of a mortgage holder's losing a job, a sharp decline in value of the property, or a change in interest rates. The key question is whether recent variations in process results are within the normal range (and therefore not worth worrying much about) or into the "out of control" range (and therefore a cause for concern). One of the important functions of control charts is to indicate what is *not* worth management attention.

The statistical ideas of variation and experimentation often come together. In many quality-improvement problems, reducing variability is at least as important as improving average quality. A motel chain might institute a change in its reservations process that cuts the average time per reservation by 10%; if that change increased variability in times by 100%, the chain could expect to reduce the demand for its reservations considerably. An airline that reduced the average duration of a Cincinnati–Philadelphia flight by two minutes (98% of the flights arrive three minutes earlier, 2% arrive 47 minutes later) would not make either of the authors happy. A manager who uses statistical experiments and thinks about both averages and variability should be able to make a real difference in quality, given patience and sustained effort.

Summary

■

Chapter 2 presents the basic ideas for summarizing data about a single variable. The methods are data plots, measures of average or location, measures of variability, skewness, and outlier-proneness.

Data plots are the natural first step in summarizing data. Possible plots include histograms for quantitative variables and bar charts for qualitative ones. The Pareto chart of frequencies for various causes of poor quality is a variation of the bar chart. The stem-and-leaf display is a variant of a histogram that shows the actual numerical data. A box plot is a compact plot that also allows for a convenient display of outliers. Each of these plots is helpful in looking for the average value, the extent of variability, the amount and direction of skewness, and the possible presence of outliers.

There are several different concepts of the average value of a variable. The mode, or most frequent value, is used largely for qualitative variables. The median, or middle value, and the mean, or arithmetic average, are for quantitative variables. Skewness typically pulls the mean in the direction of the skew, as compared to the median. An outlier on one side will have the same effect.

Variability may be measured by the range, as it often is in quality-control applications; but the range is heavily influenced by outliers and sample size. The most common measure of variability is the standard deviation, the square root of the average squared deviation around the mean. The Empirical Rule gives a convenient interpretation of the standard deviation that works best for mound-shaped data.

Skewness and kurtosis (outlier-proneness) measures are calculated by some computer packages using third and fourth powers of deviations from the mean. These measures are not as crucial as are the mean and standard deviation measures.

One of the fundamental applications of data-summarization ideas is control charts. By plotting averages, ranges, and standard deviations over time, it is easy to see shifts and patterns in the data that may need management attention. By indicating control limits, control charts also indicate ranges of common variation that do not demand "fire-fighting" attention.

KEY FORMULAS: Summarizing Data from One Variable

1. Sample mean: $\bar{y} = \dfrac{\sum\limits_{i} y_i}{n}$

2. Sample variance: $s^2 = \dfrac{1}{n-1}\left[\sum\limits_{i} y_i^2 - \dfrac{\left(\sum\limits_{i} y_i\right)^2}{n}\right]$

3. Sample standard deviation: $s = \sqrt{s^2}$

CHAPTER 2 EXERCISES

2.37 A study of sick-leave days over one year for a sample of 20 workers in a company yields the following numbers, arranged in increasing order:

0 0 0 0 0 0 1 1 1 1 2 2 2 3 3 4 6 9 14 31

a. Verify that the sample mean is 4.0 and the sample standard deviation is 7.27.
b. What fraction of the observations actually falls within one standard deviation of the mean? What aspect of the data explains the discrepancy between this fraction and the Empirical Rule approximation?
c. Calculate the skewness index $(\bar{y} - \text{median})/s$. Does its sign make sense?

2.38 If a computer package is available to you, use it to find the mean, median, standard deviation, and skewness for the data of Exercise 2.37. What skewness coefficient is calculated? Is the standard deviation calculated with a denominator of $(n-1)$ or n?

2.39 Consider the following artificial data:

8 9 10 10 10 10 10 10 11 12 19 20 20
20 21 28 29 30 30 30 30 30 30 31 32

a. Plot the data using 5 classes. What pattern of skewness and modality do you see?
b. The mean of these values is 20. How can this result be obtained without computation? How about the median?
c. Calculate the standard deviation. What must the skewness coefficient equal?
d. What fraction of the values falls within one standard deviation of the mean? How does this compare with the Empirical Rule fraction? Explain the discrepancy.
e. What fraction of the values falls within two standard deviations of the mean? How does this fraction compare with the Chebyshev Inequality fraction?

2.40 Here is another artificial data set:

−36 −1 −1 −1 −1 0 0 1 1 2 3 4 6 9 14

a. Verify that the mean is 0 and that the standard deviation is 10.84.
b. Calculate the skewness coefficient $(\bar{y} - \text{median})/s$ and $M_3/(M_2)^{3/2}$.
c. Plot the data. Can you identify an obvious skewness?
d. What causes the discrepancy between the two skewness statistics?

2.41 Assembling a circuit board requires several dozen soldering connections. The main soldering operation is automated. However, the process can yield defective connections, usually caused by poor penetration of a flux material used to prepare the connections. Each soldered board must be inspected visually and each defective soldering connection repaired by a relatively expensive hand touchup. The number of defects on each board is recorded. There are 20 boards produced each hour; an average of 2 defects per board is considered in control. The following means were obtained for a 30-hour production week. From the numbers, is there indication of an upward or downward trend?

```
MTB > print 'mean'
```

```
mean
    1.45    1.65    1.50    2.25    1.65    1.60    2.30    2.20    2.70    1.70    2.35
    1.70    1.90    1.45    1.40    2.60    2.05    1.70    1.05    2.35    1.90    1.55
    1.95    1.60    2.05    2.05    1.70    2.30    1.30    2.35
```

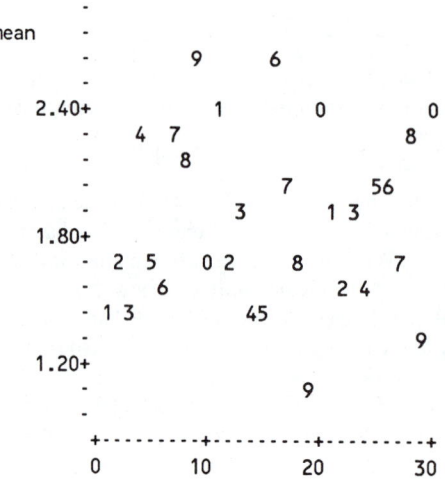

mean

```
mean   -
       -            9      6
       -
2.40+              1         0         0
       -      4   7                 8
       -          8
       -              7        56
       -          3        1 3
1.80+
       -    2 5    0 2    8        7
       -      6            2 4
       - 1 3        45
       -                           9
1.20+
       -                9
       -
       -
       +---------+---------+---------+
       0        10        20        30
```

FIGURE 2.15   Simplified x-bar Chart

2.42   A simplified x-bar chart of the means in Exercise 2.41 is shown in Figure 2.15. Does the chart indicate a trend?

2.43   Experience with the soldering process indicates that the standard deviation applicable to the average number of defectives among 20 boards is 0.38. Recall that the in-control mean is regarded as 2.0.

    a. Calculate upper and lower control limits. Are there any means falling outside these limits?

    b. If a mean fell below the lower control limit, would this indicate a problem?

2.44   The individual board data underlying the mean number of soldering defects was not shown. Obviously, there can't be a negative number of defects; theoretically, there might be dozens of defects on a single board. Assuming that the process is in control (mean number of defects equals 2), what might be expected about the shape of the data? In particular, what kind of skewness might be expected?

2.45   A regional public transit agency runs a fleet of buses from suburban areas to the western terminal of a subway line. One important measure of service quality is how late buses are in arriving at the terminal; typically, riders will not be concerned about a minute or two of lateness, but longer delays indicate deterioration in service. Each weekday morning, a dispatcher records the number of minutes late for a random sample of eight buses scheduled to arrive at the terminal between 7:30 and 8:30 A.M. The means over a 60-day period are shown here:

mean

1.1250	1.3125	1.5000	1.6875	1.6250	1.9375	1.6250	1.6875
1.9375	1.8750	2.0625	1.5000	1.4375	1.3750	1.5000	1.5625
2.2500	1.1875	1.1250	1.8125	2.0000	2.6250	1.5000	1.8125
1.1875	1.7500	2.3750	2.0000	2.0000	2.4375	1.8125	2.4375
1.7500	1.5625	1.7500	2.2500	1.4375	1.6250	2.0625	2.3750
1.7500	1.6875	1.4375	1.6875	2.1250	1.5625	1.8750	1.6875
1.3750	1.6250	1.6875	1.5000	1.3750	4.0000	4.0000	2.0625
4.7500	3.1250						

By looking at the numbers, is it possible to detect where a lateness problem has occurred?

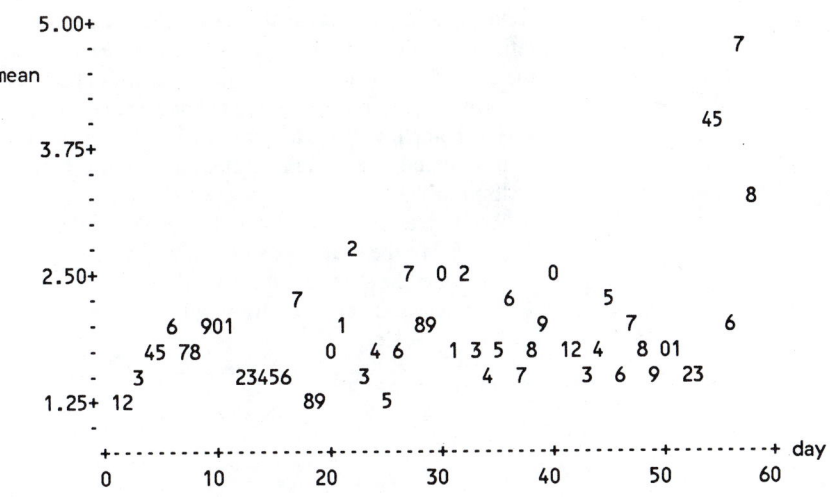

FIGURE 2.16

2.46 A simplified *x*-bar chart for the means in Exercise 2.45 is shown in Figure 2.16. Where were there lateness problems?

2.47 The standard deviation for the mean lateness of eight buses in Exercises 2.45 and 2.46 is about 0.30 minutes.
   a. Construct control limits assuming that the target mean is 1.5 minutes.
   b. On which days did the arrival process appear out of control?

2.48 An S chart for the bus arrival process is shown in Figure 2.17. Do the high variability days essentially coincide with the high mean days?

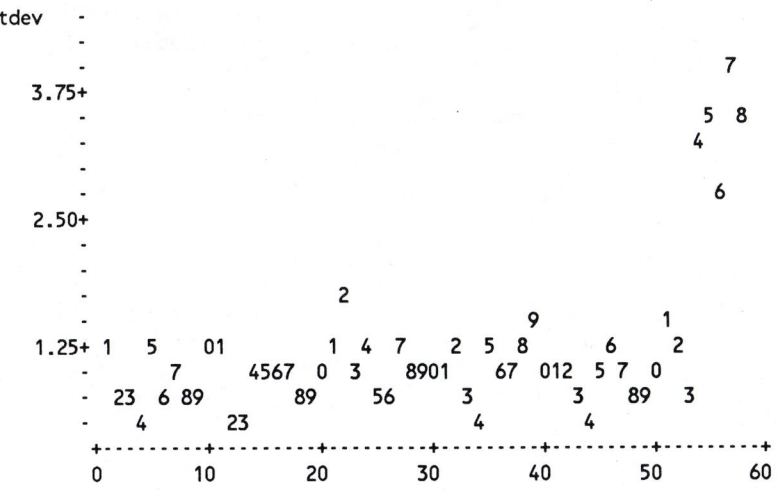

FIGURE 2.17

2.49 A major food products company uses sales representatives to work with wholesalers and supermarket chains. The representatives' chief tasks are to sell new products, secure adequate display space in stores, and coordinate promotions. Each representative is solely responsible for a district. Yearly volume of sales in the district is the primary measure of the representative's effectiveness. The results for the last year (in thousands of dollars) are analyzed in the computer output below.

a. The company had attempted with only partial success to set up the districts to have equal sales volume potential. What other sources of variability can you think of?

b. What does the box plot indicate about the overall shape of the data—in particular, the skewness and outlier-proneness?

c. Calculate the skewness measure based on the mean–median relationship. Does the numerical value confirm your judgment of skewness made in part (b)?

MTB > boxplot of 'volume'

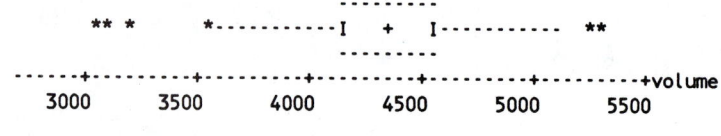

```
                                          ----------
                      ** *       *-----------I   +   I----------   **
                                          ----------
             ------+---------+---------+---------+---------+---------+volume
                 3000      3500      4000      4500      5000      5500
```

MTB > describe 'volume'

	N	MEAN	MEDIAN	TRMEAN	STDEV	SEMEAN
volume	118	4336.2	4334.0	4350.1	401.4	37.0

	MIN	MAX	Q1	Q3
volume	3058.0	5301.0	4154.2	4551.8

2.50   The data underlying Exercise 2.49 were plotted against the identification number of each sales representative. The numbers are in order of seniority, with 1 being the most senior representative. Is there an evident trend in the plot?

MTB > plot 'volume' vs 'idnumber'

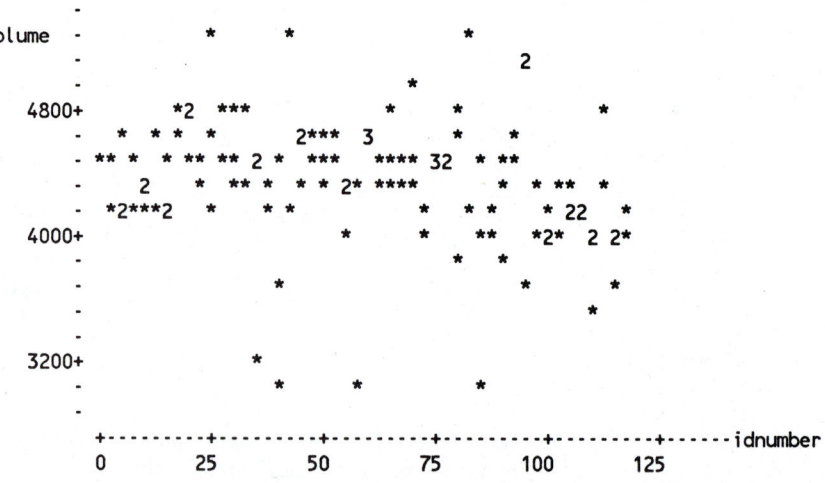

```
volume -         -
       -                   *         *              *
       -                                       2
       -                                *
 4800+         *2   ***          *        *              *
       -    *   *   *    *      2*** 3      *     *
       - ** *   *  ** ** 2 *    ***   **** 32  * **
       -    2     *  ** *  * * 2* ****       *  * ** *
       - *2***2    *     * *        *    * *    * 22    *
 4000+                         *        *    **  *2*  2 2*
       -                                        *   *
       -                  *                     *        *
       -                                              *
       -
 3200+              *
       -          *       *        *
       -
         +---------+---------+---------+---------+---------+------idnumber
         0        25        50        75       100       125
```

2.51 A junior manager, examining the data of Exercise 2.49, noticed that half the sales representatives were performing below average. The manager felt that this fact indicated deficiencies in the company's training or in the representatives' motivation. Is the manager's reasoning valid?

2.52 A publisher of computer science books needs fast action in handling page proofs of forthcoming books. These proofs must be delivered to the authors for a final check of layout, typographical errors, and other features. Because speed is essential in tight publication schedules, the publisher is considering using express delivery services. The last 90 sets of proofs have been randomly allocated to three different services. The number of hours required for delivery of each set has been recorded.

    a. Which would be more desirable to the publisher, a smaller mean or a larger one?

    b. Which would be more desirable to the publisher, a smaller standard deviation or a larger one?

    c. Judging from the box plots, which server has the smallest mean? The smallest standard deviation?

```
MTB > boxplot of 'hoursreq';
SUBC> by 'server'.

server
```

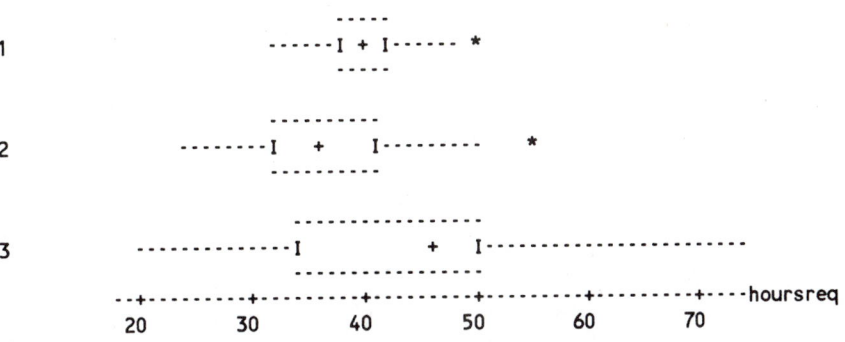

```
                                               -----
    1                                 ------I + I------ *
                                               -----


                                       -----------
    2                       --------I     +    I--------- *
                                       -----------

                                -----------------
    3             --------------I           +    I------------------------
                                -----------------
              --+---------+---------+---------+---------+---------+----hoursreq
                20        30        40        50        60        70
```

2.53 Do the following computed results confirm your opinions from part (c) of Exercise 2.52?

```
MTB > describe 'hoursreq';
SUBC> by 'server'.
```

	server	N	MEAN	MEDIAN	TRMEAN	STDEV	SEMEAN
hoursreq	1	30	40.067	40.000	39.962	4.533	0.828
	2	30	37.17	36.00	36.92	7.25	1.32
	3	30	44.60	45.50	44.04	13.55	2.47

	server	MIN	MAX	Q1	Q3
hoursreq	1	32.000	50.000	37.750	42.500
	2	24.00	55.00	31.75	41.50
	3	20.00	74.00	34.00	50.50

2.54 Most fast-food restaurants have a continuing problem with employee turnover. As a result, they must expend a great deal of time and effort hiring and training new workers. The franchise owner of 13 outlets of a hamburger chain conducted exit interviews with all employees who left any outlet voluntarily, as opposed to being fired. The interviewer judged the primary reason for leaving according to a list of 12 possibilities:

1. don't like the type of work
2. don't like the hours of work
3. don't like the work environment
4. conflict with other employees
5. conflict with managers
6. better pay elsewhere in the food industry
7. better pay elsewhere in a different industry
8. more responsible job elsewhere

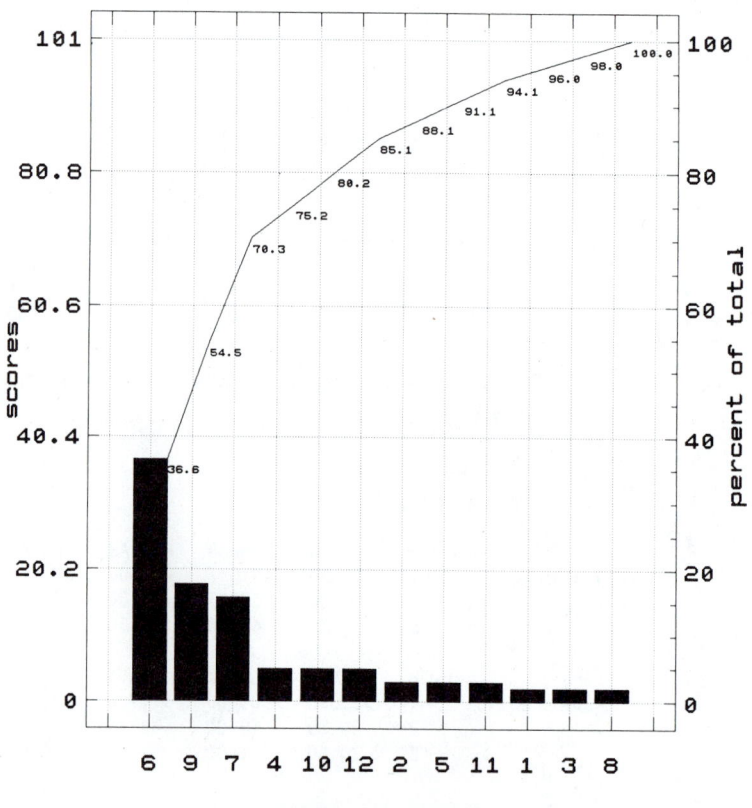

FIGURE 2.18   Reasons for Leaving Employment — Interview Codes

9. pay not enough for loss of free time
10. leaving to enter college
11. moving to different geographical area
12. promotion within the franchise outlets

The interviewer obtained summary statistics from Statgraphics as follows:

```
Variable:              reason
----------------------------------------------------------------
Sample size            101
Average                6.9703
Median                 6
Standard deviation     2.37679
----------------------------------------------------------------
```

The interviewer noted that the mean (average) was quite a bit larger than the median. What does this fact indicate about the data?

2.55 A Pareto chart of the reasons for leaving the hamburger outlet of Exercise 2.54, generated by Statgraphics according to the exit interview codes of that exercise, is shown in Figure 2.18.

a. Which codes account for the great majority of the reasons for leaving? Exactly what constitutes the "great majority" is up to you.

b. Are these codes related in any way?

2.56 Statgraphics combined codes from Exercise 2.54 into four basic categories: Conditions (codes 1, 2, 3, 4, and 5); Improvement (codes 8 and 12); Pay (codes 6, 7, and 9); and Personal (codes 10 and 11). A Pareto chart by categories is shown in Figure 2.19. Does the combining process reveal the essential reason for turnover more clearly in your opinion?

2.57 One of the important factors in a customer's perception of food quality is the age of the product. Even with good, airtight packaging, a food product loses some of its appeal as it gets older. This problem is particularly acute for snack products, various chips and crackers intended for casual munching. A local manufacturer of one such snack visited 63 convenience stores that were outlets for the product. In each store, the age of the frontmost package was determined from the date code stamped on the package. The data were stored as follows using the Statgraphics package:

```
Variable: snackage    (length = 63)
----------------------------------------------------------------
( 1) 29    (19) 25    (37) 20    (55) 20
( 2) 16    (20) 40    (38) 14    (56) 12
( 3) 47    (21) 16    (39) 13    (57) 13
( 4) 49    (22) 12    (40) 20    (58) 27
( 5) 26    (23) 24    (41) 12    (59) 19
( 6) 18    (24) 25    (42) 11    (60) 40
( 7) 17    (25) 25    (43) 21    (61) 15
( 8) 27    (26) 45    (44) 29    (62) 17
( 9) 16    (27) 19    (45) 41    (63) 28
(10) 19    (28) 15    (46) 20
(11) 22    (29) 14    (47) 53
(12) 16    (30) 46    (48) 19
(13) 19    (31) 25    (49) 28
(14) 25    (32) 18    (50) 57
(15) 27    (33) 37    (51) 11
(16) 12    (34) 17    (52) 21
(17) 18    (35) 14    (53) 35
(18) 10    (36) 10    (54) 56
----------------------------------------------------------------
```

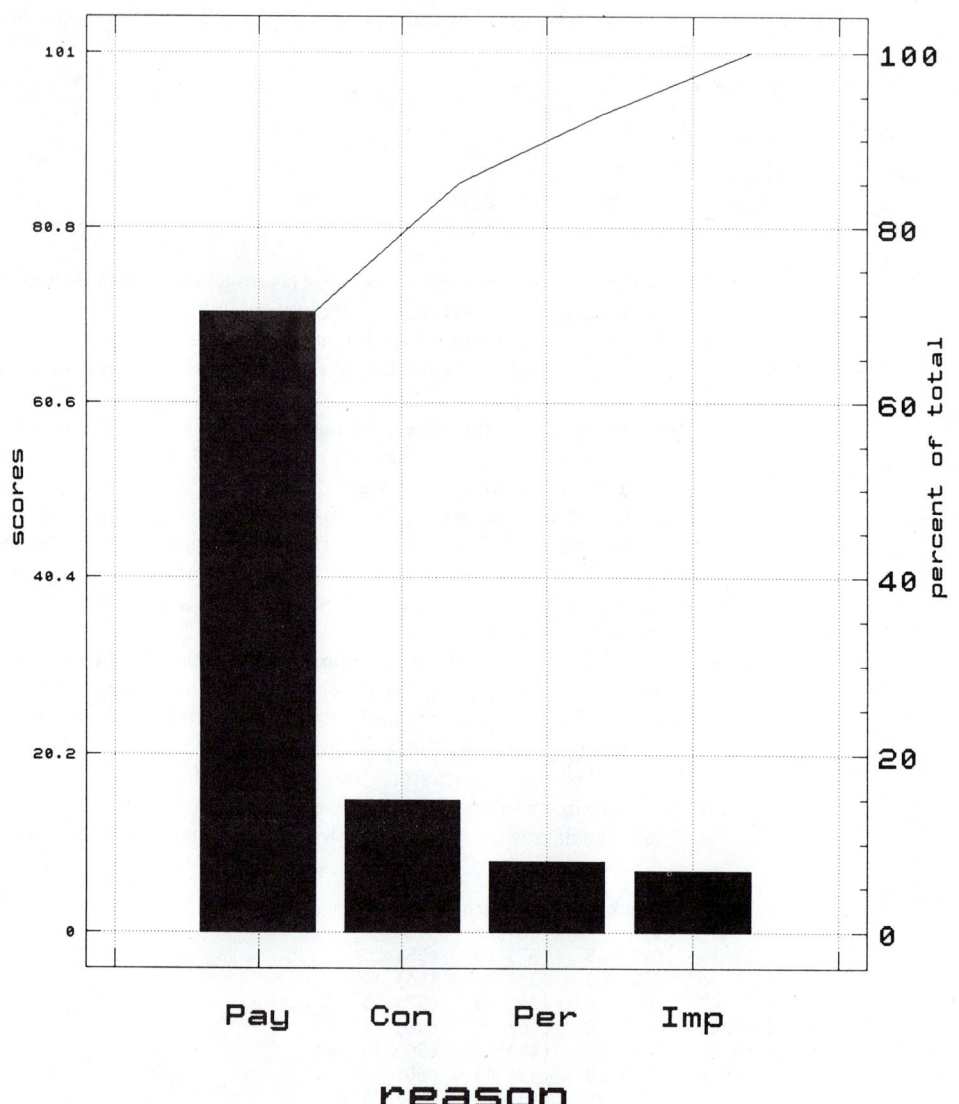

FIGURE 2.19   Reasons for Leaving Employment — Combined Categories

a. Construct a stem-and-leaf display of the data using intervals with a width of 10 days.
b. Redo the stem-and-leaf using intervals with a width of 5 days.
c. Describe the general shape of the data. How much difference does it make which stem-and-leaf you look at?

2.58 A histogram of the snack age data of Exercise 2.57 was constructed using Statgraphics, as shown in Figure 2.20.
a. Does the histogram indicate the same general shape as the stem-and-leaf displays constructed in Exercise 2.57?
b. Why isn't the histogram shape exactly like either stem-and-leaf shape?

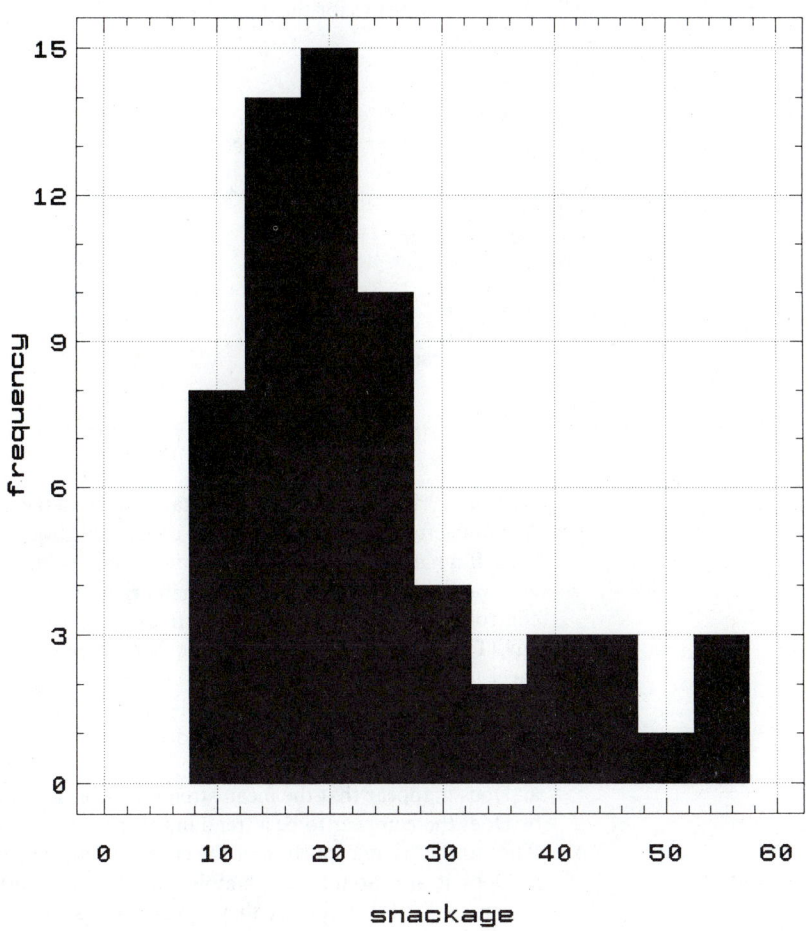

FIGURE 2.20   Histogram of Snack Age Data

Box and Whisker Plot

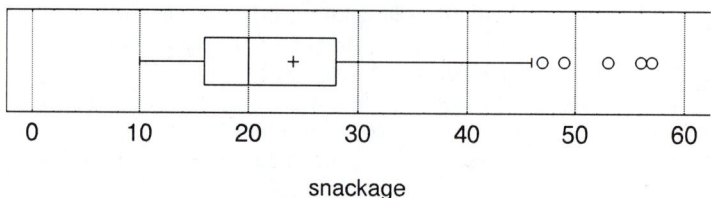

snackage

FIGURE 2.21   Box Plot of Snack Age Data

2.59 The data on age of snack packages from Exercise 2.57 showed clear right-skewness. A box plot of the same data, constructed by the Statgraphics package, is shown in Figure 2.21. How does this plot convey the right-skewness of the data?

2.60 Summary statistics for the data of Exercise 2.57 were obtained using Statgraphics, as follows:

```
Variable:              snackage
-------------------------------------------------------------------
Sample size            63
Average                24
Median                 20
Standard deviation     12.0309
Minimum                10
Maximum                57
Lower quartile         16
Upper quartile         28
Interquartile range    12
Skewness               1.23705
Kurtosis               0.769127
-------------------------------------------------------------------
```

How is the right-skewness of the data reflected in the mean (average) and median?

2.61 A manufacturer of seat belts must be concerned about the breaking strengths of the belts. If a particular belt strength is lower than the design specification, the belt can give way too easily in a crash, causing injury to the wearer. As one part of its quality-control program, the manufacturer finds the breaking strength of five belts each day. (The test involves literally tearing the belt apart, so the manufacturer is less than eager to test all belts.) Design specifications are for a mean strength of 30.0 (in the appropriate units) and a standard deviation of 0.2 units. A Statgraphics control chart for the sample mean and standard deviation for each of the most recent 30 days is shown in Figure 2.22.

a. Does it appear that the mean strength is consistently within the control limits?

b. Does there appear to be a trend in the means, or a sudden jump to a new level?

2.62 Refer to the "sigma" portion of the control chart in Figure 2.22.

a. Does it appear that the sample standard deviations are consistently within control limits? If not, are they too big or too small, generally?

b. What appears to be the primary quality problem for the manufacturer—average level or variability around average?

Control Chart: Belt Strength

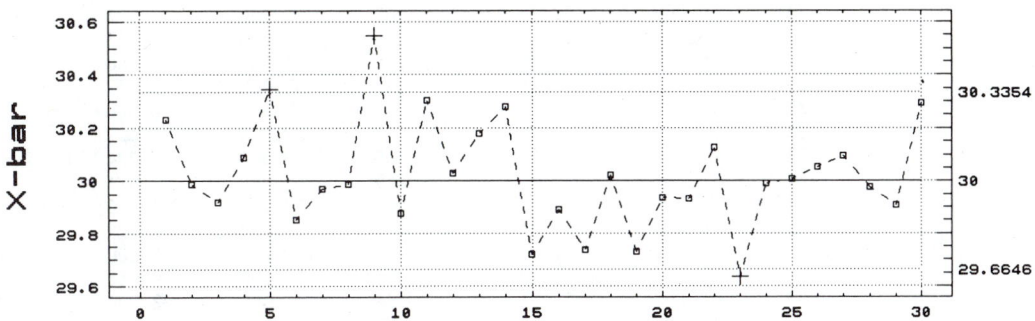

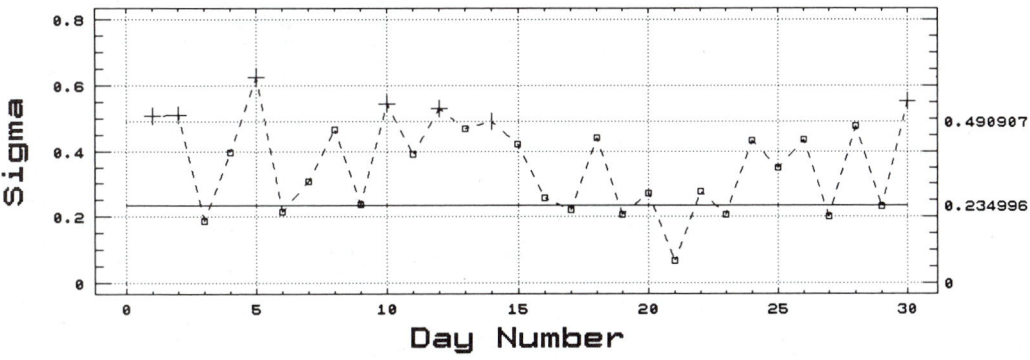

FIGURE 2.22   Control Chart for Seat Belt Strength

2.63   An office supply company does a third of its business supplying local governments and school districts. This business is done by competitive bids. Each potential sale requires a clerk to prepare a bid form. The firm had no real idea of how much effort the bid preparation required, so the bid clerk was asked to record the start and stop times for a sample of 65 bids. The data were recorded two ways: minutes spent per bid (MINPRBID in the Systat output below) and bids per hour BIDPERHR = 60/MINPRBID.

CASE	MINPRBID	BIDPERHR	CASE	MINPRBID	BIDPERHR
1	155.000	0.387	9	54.000	1.111
2	66.000	0.909	10	31.000	1.935
3	134.000	0.448	11	30.000	2.000
4	39.000	1.538	12	149.000	0.403
5	61.000	0.984	13	51.000	1.176
6	46.000	1.304	14	120.000	0.500
7	23.000	2.609	15	23.000	2.609
8	21.000	2.857	16	41.000	1.463

CASE	MINPRBID	BIDPERHR	CASE	MINPRBID	BIDPERHR
17	56.000	1.071	42	24.000	2.500
18	38.000	1.579	43	41.000	1.463
19	25.000	2.400	44	50.000	1.200
20	42.000	1.429	45	82.000	0.732
21	35.000	1.714	46	114.000	0.526
22	28.000	2.143	47	23.000	2.609
23	80.000	0.750	48	49.000	1.224
24	46.000	1.304	49	65.000	0.923
25	24.000	2.500	50	20.000	3.000
26	46.000	1.304	51	22.000	2.727
27	47.000	1.277	52	100.000	0.600
28	73.000	0.822	53	62.000	0.968
29	220.000	0.273	54	24.000	2.500
30	80.000	0.750	55	200.000	0.300
31	25.000	2.400	56	65.000	0.923
32	20.000	3.000	57	50.000	1.200
33	30.000	2.000	58	42.000	1.429
34	76.000	0.789	59	29.000	2.069
35	103.000	0.583	60	145.000	0.414
36	48.000	1.250	61	110.000	0.545
37	29.000	2.069	62	43.000	1.395
38	29.000	2.069	63	40.000	1.500
39	46.000	1.304	64	191.000	0.314
40	26.000	2.308	65	126.000	0.476
41	27.000	2.222			

      a. Scan the MINPRBID columns and give a rough guess as to the mean.

      b. Do the same for the BIDPERHR columns.

2.64 Systat constructed histograms for the data of Exercise 2.63; they're shown here.

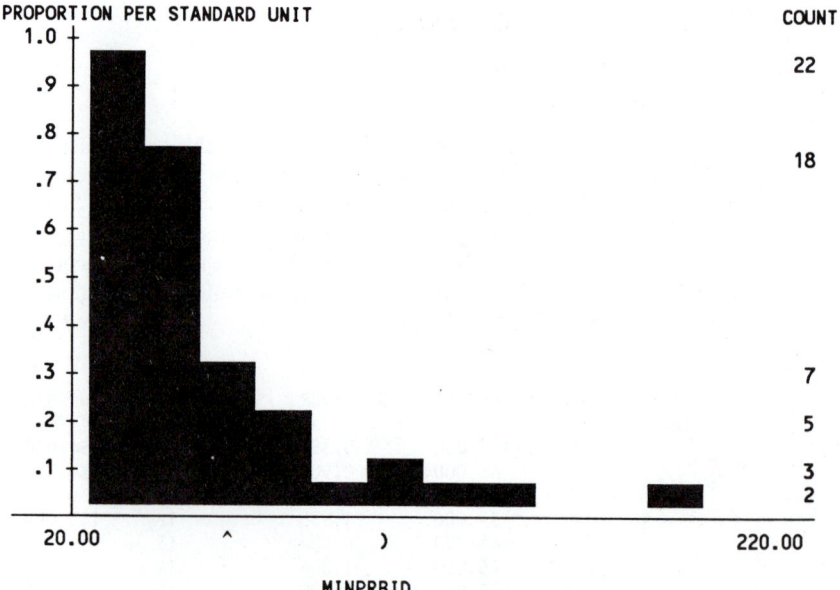

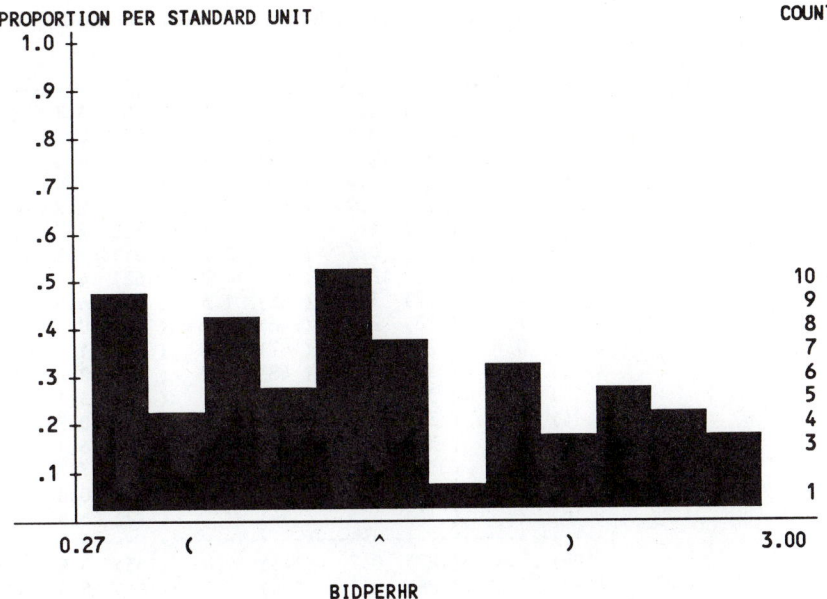

BIDPERHR

a. Use these histograms to check the guesses for the mean that you made in Exercise 2.63.
b. Are the two variables skewed in about the same way?

2.65 Systat actually computed summary figures for the data of Exercise 2.63.

	MINPRBID	BIDPERHR
N OF CASES	65	65
MINIMUM	20.000	0.273
MAXIMUM	220.000	3.000
MEAN	62.462	1.432
VARIANCE	2199.971	0.610
STANDARD DEV	46.904	0.781
SKEWNESS	1.618	0.356

a. Locate the means. Is it true that the mean for BIDPERHR is 60 divided by the mean for MINPRBID?
b. Do the skewness numbers reported by Systat confirm your answer to Exercise 2.64, part (b)?

2.66 An automobile insurance company was considering expanding its sales effort in a middle western city. As one part of its study, the claims department collected data on the size of claims for collision damage over the past year. The data were analyzed by Statgraphics, which printed the data (in thousands of dollars) as follows:

```
-------------------------------------------------------------------------------
(  1) 20.5   ( 19)  4.6   ( 37)  2.6   ( 55)  3.3   ( 73)  4.2   ( 91) 15.2
(  2)  4.8   ( 20)  0.8   ( 38)  4.3   ( 56)  0.7   ( 74)  8.9   ( 92)  5.7
(  3)  5.3   ( 21) 19     ( 39) 10.1   ( 57) 14.4   ( 75)  6.5   ( 93)  1
(  4)  4.6   ( 22)  7.9   ( 40)  6.2   ( 58)  7.4   ( 76)  8.7   ( 94) 13.1
(  5)  0.7   ( 23)  0.9   ( 41)  7.4   ( 59)  2.7   ( 77)  1.1   ( 95) 20.9
(  6)  1.1   ( 24)  4     ( 42)  8.5   ( 60)  2.7   ( 78)  3.5   ( 96) 19.4
(  7)  5.9   ( 25)  0.7   ( 43)  2.7   ( 61)  1.2   ( 79)  3     ( 97)  1.6
(  8)  0.7   ( 26) 12.9   ( 44) 14.2   ( 62)  4.9   ( 80)  1.1   ( 98)  2
(  9)  4.6   ( 27)  3.2   ( 45)  1.3   ( 63) 26.6   ( 81)  4.2   ( 99)  1
( 10)  7.7   ( 28)  2.5   ( 46)  1.2   ( 64) 10.1   ( 82)  4.9   (100)  7.6
( 11)  0.7   ( 29)  1.1   ( 47)  8.3   ( 65) 11     ( 83)  2.5   (101) 16.8
( 12)  5.8   ( 30)  3.7   ( 48)  5.2   ( 66)  2.2   ( 84)  0.9   (102)  1.6
( 13)  4.7   ( 31)  4.2   ( 49)  7.1   ( 67)  3.1   ( 85)  1.1   (103)  0.8
( 14)  0.9   ( 32)  1.3   ( 50)  1.9   ( 68)  0.7   ( 86)  7.7   (104)  3
( 15)  1.2   ( 33)  8.3   ( 51) 11.3   ( 69)  6.1   ( 87)  4.7   (105)  1.9
( 16)  0.7   ( 34)  0.7   ( 52)  1.8   ( 70)  7.7   ( 88)  3.6   (106) 22.6
( 17)  2.3   ( 35)  3.5   ( 53)  8.8   ( 71)  0.8   ( 89)  5.3   (107)  4.2
( 18)  2     ( 36)  1.3   ( 54)  7.3   ( 72)  6.5   ( 90)  5.8   (108)  1.4
-------------------------------------------------------------------------------
(109)  3.6   (127)  0.7   (145)  4.3   (163)  3.5   (181)  0.8
(110)  1.6   (128)  0.9   (146)  7.1   (164)  8.5   (182)  0.7
(111)  6.1   (129)  3.5   (147)  1.3   (165)  1.4   (183) 13.3
(112)  7.2   (130)  0.9   (148)  7.3   (166) 11.4   (184)  1.7
(113)  7.1   (131)  1.1   (149)  5      (167)  1.2   (185)  4.1
(114)  4.4   (132) 33.7   (150)  3      (168)  1.9   (186)  0.8
(115)  2.9   (133)  7.4   (151)  0.9   (169)  6.7   (187) 20.7
(116)  3     (134)  0.9   (152)  2.9   (170)  1.8
(117)  0.7   (135)  2.1   (153)  6      (171)  1.8
(118)  4.4   (136)  1.8   (154)  8.2   (172)  3.6
(119)  1.9   (137)  2.5   (155)  5.7   (173)  3.5
(120)  0.9   (138) 12.9   (156)  3.3   (174)  8.8
(121)  1.3   (139) 11.5   (157)  3.7   (175)  4.6
(122)  9.7   (140)  3.8   (158)  4.6   (176)  2.6
(123)  2     (141) 13.2   (159)  0.7   (177)  1.9
(124)  3.4   (142)  1.6   (160)  2.1   (178) 17.4
(125)  2.3   (143)  0.8   (161)  8.6   (179)  1.2
(126)  0.8   (144)  4.7   (162)  3.3   (180)  4.4
-------------------------------------------------------------------------------
```

a. Construct a histogram using about 8 to 10 classes.

b. Would you say that the data were symmetric around some average value?

2.67 Statgraphics computed a stem-and-leaf display of the data from Exercise 2.66.

```
Stem-and-leaf display for claimsize: unit = 1     1|2  represents 12

  61     0*|00000000000000000000000000000111111111111111111111111111111111
 (39)    0T|222222222222222222233333333333333333333
  87     0F|44444444444444444444444555555555
  56     0S|66666666777777777777777
  35     0o|88888888889
  24     1*|001111
  18     1T|22333
  13     1F|445

         HI|16,17,19,19,20,20,20,22,26,33
```

Note that Statgraphics, like most packages, doesn't round off numbers for a stem-and-leaf display; instead, it simply uses the first two digits of a number.

a. Does the stem-and-leaf display appear roughly symmetric?

b. Can you guess why some of the numbers are displayed in the HI leaf?

2.68 The data on collision insurance claims (in thousands of dollars) from Exercise 2.66 were summarized by Statgraphics as follows:

```
Variable:              claimsize
-----------------------------------------------------------------
Sample size            187
Average                5.17754
Median                 3.5
Standard deviation     5.28388
Minimum                0.7
Maximum                33.7
Skewness               2.23376
Kurtosis               6.40884
-----------------------------------------------------------------
```

a. One standard deviation below the mean is about -0.1, which is an impossible value for an insurance claim. The Empirical Rule doesn't seem to work at all for these data. Why?

b. The mean (average) value is quite a bit larger than the median. Why did that happen?

2.69 A Statgraphics box plot of the claim size data for Exercise 2.66 is shown in Figure 2.23. What does this plot indicate about the shape of the claim size data?

Box and Whisker Plot

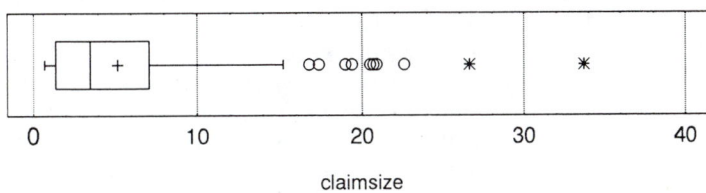

claimsize

FIGURE 2.23   Box Plot of Collision Claims Data

2.70 The customer support service of a word-processing software company must call a customer back if it can't provide a problem-solving suggestion immediately. Call-backs are expensive and less satisfactory for the customer. A set of codes was developed to indicate the reason for each call-back. The frequencies for a period of time were

Code	Explanation	Frequency
01	Problem not covered in manuals	27
02	Operator could not find correct section	56
03	Manuals incorrect	3

Code	Explanation	Frequency
04	Manuals ambiguous	5
11	Customer's problem misstated	42
12	Customer's equipment inadequate	19
13	Task not achievable in customer's version	5
21	Operator's suggestion failed	11
22	Operator answered for wrong version	8
99	All others	17

    a. Construct a Pareto chart.

    b. The company could do little about customer-related errors (codes 11–13). What do the results for other codes suggest about the most important possible improvements to the service?

2.71 The customer service manager for the software company in Exercise 2.70 asked what the average reason for a call-back was. How would you answer this question?

2.72 The editor of a metropolitan newspaper's food section constructed a market basket of 30 items to reflect the "typical" family of four's basic food needs for a week. The editor also put together another list of nonfood items such as cleaning supplies and paper goods typically purchased at supermarkets. Reporters obtained prices for all items on both lists at 53 markets in the metropolitan area. The total cost of the food basket at each market is stored in column 1 of the 'CH2C1.DAT' file on the data disk that accompanies this book. The total cost of the nonfood list is stored in column 2. (Check with your instructor as to how to obtain this disk.)

    a. Use any computer package that is available to you to load the data. Technically, the data are stored as an ASCII (text) file, delimited by blanks, without titles for the columns.

    b. Obtain a histogram of the food cost data. How would you describe the general shape of the data?

    c. From the histogram, make a rough guess what the mean is.

    d. Use the Empirical Rule idea that about 95% of the data should be within two standard deviations of the mean to guess the value of the standard deviation.

    e. Have the computer package calculate the mean and standard deviation.

2.73 a. Obtain a stem-and-leaf display of the nonfood cost data from Exercise 2.72. Describe the general shape.

    b. Obtain the mean, median, and standard deviation of the nonfood cost.

    c. Either using the package or by hand calculate a measure of the skewness of the nonfood cost data.

2.74 a. Have your computer package calculate the ratio of food cost to the sum of food and nonfood costs for the data set of Exercise 2.72. Obtain a box plot of the ratio data.

    b. Does the box plot indicate any outliers?

    c. Is the mean of the ratio data the same as the ratio of the mean food cost to the sum of the means of the two costs?

2.75 A copy center located near a university campus offers self-service copying. The daily number of copies made on self-service machines varies, depending on weather, number of assignments due at the university, number of machines under repair, and many other factors. The copy center recorded the number of copies made each day for 44 days. The data are stored in the 'CH2C2.DAT' file on the data disk; column 1 is number of copies, column 2 is day number. Like all files on this disk, this is an ASCII (text) file, delimited by spaces, without variable labels.

a. Use a computer package to read in the data. Obtain a box plot of the number of copies available.

b. Identify any days that yielded outlier values.

c. Obtain the mean and standard deviation of the number of copies.

d. Delete all outliers from the data and recompute the mean and standard deviation. Which number changes more?

2.76 a. Have a computer package plot the number of copies data of Exercise 2.75 against day number. The package should have a "plot" or "scatterplot" capability; if it has a special capability for plotting time series data, that would be handy here.

b. Can you see an evident upward or downward trend in the plot?

c. Are there evident cycles in the data?

2.77 An office-cleaning service has developed a numerical scale to assess the general cleanliness of an area. The scale ranges from 0 at worst to 100 at best. The target value is 80 or higher. (The service managers believe that shooting for a perfect 100 score would require excessive labor costs.) Supervisors calculated scores for each of four randomly chosen areas on each of 60 days. The data are stored in the 'CH2C3.DAT' file on the data disk, with scores in column 1 and day number in column 2.

a. Read the data into a computer package and obtain a stem-and-leaf display of the cleanliness scores.

b. Identify any evident departures from a normal distribution.

c. The president of the service suspected that supervisors might make a fast guess at the cleanliness score, rather than going through the details. If so, many scores would be likely to end in 0 or 5. Is there evidence of that phenomenon in the stem-and-leaf display?

2.78 a. Obtain the mean and standard deviation of the cleanliness scores from Exercise 2.77.

b. Have the computer package obtain the mean score for each day and compute the standard deviation of those means.

c. If your computer package has the capability, obtain a control chart of the daily means. Use a target mean of 80 and the standard deviation of the means found in part (b) of this exercise.

d. Were there any days when the cleanliness was "out of control"?

C A S E   Summarizing Data

A meat-packer sells portion-controlled sirloin steaks to restaurant chains. The meat is cut, frozen, and packaged on two production lines called (not-too-imaginatively) the Left and Right lines. The target size for each steak is 12 ounces, but there is variability because of differences in meat density, slight differences in cut, slight differences in fat content, and several other factors. Each steak is visually inspected and also weighed by a rough scale along the production line; the scale is supposed to reject any steak that weighs less than 11.5 ounces and set aside any steak that weighs more than 12.6 ounces.

Left Line

Week											Average
1	12.32	12.16	12.34	12.03	11.95	12.05	11.78	12.01	11.95	12.39	12.098
2	12.04	11.98	12.06	11.95	12.12	11.84	12.29	12.10	11.92	12.07	12.037
3	11.78	12.07	12.11	11.71	11.87	11.88	11.61	11.93	12.08	12.01	11.905
4	12.37	11.98	11.94	12.06	11.88	12.24	12.05	12.10	12.32	11.82	12.076
5	12.08	11.95	11.82	11.86	12.51	12.07	12.07	12.25	11.98	12.28	12.087
6	12.12	11.62	12.01	12.04	11.86	12.05	11.80	12.17	12.02	12.20	11.992
7	12.49	12.12	11.92	11.76	11.97	11.78	11.80	11.69	12.04	12.01	11.958
8	11.78	12.29	12.52	12.23	12.32	12.14	11.64	12.12	12.24	12.08	12.136
9	12.00	11.95	12.05	12.15	11.89	12.27	12.23	12.00	12.01	12.22	12.077
10	11.95	11.81	11.99	12.00	11.93	12.01	12.01	11.74	12.50	11.77	11.971
11	11.85	12.13	12.55	12.09	12.28	12.43	11.92	11.96	11.95	12.19	12.135
12	11.81	11.86	11.75	11.86	12.13	12.43	12.14	11.81	12.21	12.19	12.019
13	12.15	11.87	12.36	12.29	12.13	11.82	12.30	11.76	11.88	11.90	12.046
14	12.10	11.82	11.94	12.22	11.61	12.15	11.92	12.06	12.08	12.06	11.996
15	12.19	11.77	11.89	11.96	11.97	11.93	12.18	12.12	12.37	12.27	12.065
16	11.84	12.03	12.07	11.91	11.90	11.86	11.98	12.25	11.96	12.05	11.985
17	12.24	11.80	12.03	12.13	11.88	12.52	12.06	11.90	12.01	11.91	12.048
18	12.08	12.02	11.87	11.89	12.06	12.19	11.91	12.06	11.91	11.85	11.984
19	12.18	12.17	12.03	11.74	11.65	12.01	12.45	11.84	11.88	12.00	11.995
20	12.42	12.00	11.89	11.92	12.06	12.00	11.63	12.12	12.02	12.28	12.034
21	11.60	11.85	12.08	11.68	12.28	12.12	11.96	12.16	11.81	11.93	11.947
22	12.01	11.68	11.96	11.88	11.62	11.82	11.77	12.17	11.78	12.07	11.876
23	12.54	12.35	11.96	12.11	11.94	12.11	11.98	12.16	12.28	11.80	12.123
24	12.25	11.97	12.21	12.03	12.01	11.94	11.76	12.15	11.71	12.07	12.010
25	11.63	12.10	12.14	12.19	11.74	12.19	11.88	12.11	11.76	11.88	11.962

Right Line

Week											Average
1	12.07	11.88	11.89	12.21	11.93	11.94	11.99	12.21	11.90	12.20	12.022
2	11.82	11.83	12.22	12.06	11.96	12.11	11.52	11.96	12.11	11.93	11.952
3	12.34	12.02	12.08	12.33	12.07	12.38	12.06	11.97	11.81	11.97	12.103
4	11.87	12.17	12.01	12.02	12.21	12.33	11.98	12.04	11.80	12.33	12.076
5	12.17	11.60	12.22	11.70	12.12	11.90	12.13	12.08	11.83	11.83	11.981
6	12.00	12.05	11.91	12.24	11.99	12.00	12.21	12.15	11.98	11.73	12.026
7	12.40	11.90	11.72	12.57	11.60	12.20	12.02	12.31	11.82	12.25	12.079
8	11.99	11.95	12.19	12.24	12.19	12.08	12.27	12.15	12.43	12.14	12.163
9	11.83	12.19	11.40	11.69	11.99	11.85	12.14	12.17	12.10	12.04	11.940
10	11.82	12.00	11.89	12.07	11.70	11.67	12.07	11.95	12.06	11.86	11.909
11	11.83	12.04	12.35	12.40	11.82	12.28	11.94	12.21	12.34	12.23	12.144
12	11.81	11.71	11.60	12.03	11.91	11.93	12.10	12.51	12.09	11.86	11.955
13	11.99	12.12	11.67	11.88	12.27	11.50	12.18	12.25	11.71	12.23	11.980
14	12.78	11.34	11.58	12.82	11.40	13.10	11.55	12.70	12.44	12.22	12.193
15	11.59	12.13	11.94	12.45	12.55	11.23	11.52	12.48	12.74	11.07	11.970
16	12.20	12.36	12.00	12.30	11.08	12.21	12.16	12.04	12.50	11.65	12.050
17	12.18	11.70	11.96	12.71	12.07	12.06	11.64	12.78	12.03	11.57	12.070
18	11.96	12.43	11.37	12.54	12.32	12.67	12.21	12.32	12.64	11.90	12.236
19	12.31	12.37	11.74	11.56	11.94	12.24	11.93	12.74	12.06	12.06	12.082
20	11.58	12.06	12.13	12.16	11.94	11.90	11.89	12.33	12.28	12.46	12.073
21	11.90	12.27	11.94	12.37	12.13	11.47	12.26	11.33	11.49	11.63	11.879
22	11.64	11.41	11.90	12.24	11.66	12.23	12.34	12.43	11.57	11.41	11.883
23	11.73	11.34	11.81	12.62	11.43	12.14	12.41	12.46	12.57	11.64	12.015
24	12.15	12.29	12.64	12.40	12.62	12.43	12.47	12.50	11.28	12.08	12.286
25	12.25	12.28	11.94	11.88	12.09	12.24	11.91	11.80	11.62	10.98	11.899

The production managers have noticed an increase in the number of 24-steak packages being rejected by customers for inadequate average weight. The managers traced the source of each rejected package and found that most had come from the Right line. They have written to you for help. "As you know, quality control picks 10 steaks each week from each line for careful testing. Before they're cooked, they're all weighed carefully. We've got weights for each line for the last 25 weeks. During the first 10 weeks, we were running at speeds well below capacity to make sure that our cutting was OK. The last 15 weeks, we've been running at nearly full capacity. What we can't figure out is that the average weights from the two lines are practically identical; if anything, the Right line averages a little heavier. So why are so many more of the Right line packages coming up short?" They enclosed the weights for each week's sample of 10 steaks.

Can you identify any difference between the Left and Right data that might explain the problem? Does the difference show up after the initial 10 weeks or during that period? You may want to use a computer program to do the arithmetic. Write a memorandum to the managers; they don't know any technical terms, so try to use ordinary English as much as possible. ∎

Appendix: Summation Notation

Most readers of this book are familiar with summation notation; however, a brief indication of the way it is used here might be useful. We denote numerical values (observations) by y or x; when there are many observations, we use an indexing subscript such as i or j to differentiate them. For example, if our observations are 11, 30, 12, 14, 13, we let $y_1 = 11, y_2 = 30, \ldots, y_5 = 13$.

The Greek symbol $\sum$ (uppercase sigma) is an instruction to do something—namely, to add up whatever is indicated next. Thus we have $\sum_i y_i = y_1 + \cdots + y_5 = 11 + 30 + 12 + 14 + 13 = 80$. A more elaborate version of the notation indicates which values of the index i are used; in the example, this notation would be $\sum_{i=1}^{5} y_i = y_1 + \cdots + y_5 = 80$. Because we always want to sum over all possible values of the index, we do not use the elaborate form.

EXAMPLE 2.23   Let $y_1 = 2, y_2 = 4, y_3 = 10, y_4 = 1, y_5 = 20, y_6 = 7$, and $y_7 = 3$. Determine $\sum_i y_i$.

Solution
$$\sum_i y_i = y_1 + y_2 + \cdots + y_7$$
$$= 2 + 4 + \cdots + 3$$
$$= 47$$
∎

Most complicated formulas may also be understood by translating $\sum$ as "the sum of." For instance, $\sum_i y_i^2$ means "the sum of the squared observations." In the example, $\sum_i y_i^2 = (11)^2 + \cdots + (13)^2 = 1530$. Note that we square first, then sum. In contrast, the square of the sum of the observations is indicated by $(\sum_i y_i)^2$. In our example, $(\sum_i y_i)^2 = (80)^2 = 6400$. Similarly, translate $\sum_i (y_i - \bar{y})^2$ as "the sum of the squared deviations." For this example, $\sum_i (y_i - \bar{y})^2 = 250$.

EXAMPLE 2.24   Use the data in Example 2.23 to compute $\sum y_i^2$. Also calculate $(\sum_i y_i)^2$.

Solution $\sum_i y_i^2 = 2^2 + 4^2 + \cdots + 3^2 = 579$. From the solution to Example 2.23, we know immediately that $(\sum_i y_i)^2 = (47)^2 = 2209$.   ∎

Basic properties of sums may be demonstrated simply by writing out the sums. We will use the following results in the rest of the book:

$$\sum_i (x_i + y_i) = \sum_i x_i + \sum_i y_i$$

$$\sum_i c y_i = c \sum_i y_i, \text{ where } c \text{ is a constant}$$

$$\sum_i c = nc, \text{ where } c \text{ is a constant and } n \text{ is the number of values of } i$$

EXAMPLE 2.25   Find $\sum_i 3y_i$ and $\sum (y_i + 3)$ using the values for y_i in Example 2.23.

Solution   The values are 2, 4, 10, 1, 20, 7, and 9. Multiplying each value by 3 gives 6, 12, 30, 3, 60, 21, and 27. Therefore, $\sum_i 3y_i = 6 + 12 + \cdots + 27 = 141$. Alternatively, we found in Example 2.23 that $\sum_i y_i = 47$, so $\sum_i 3y_i = 3(47) = 141$.

Adding 3 to each y_i value yields 5, 7, 13, 4, 23, 10, and 12. So $\sum_i (y_i + 3) = 5 + 7 + \cdots + 12 = 68$. Alternatively, $\sum_i (y_i + 3) = \sum_i y_i + \sum_i 3 = 47 + 7(3) = 68$.   ∎

In later chapters we deal with several observations from each of several groups, so we need two indexing subscripts; i, the first subscript, indicates the group, and j, the second subscript, indexes individual observations within the group. Thus $y_{2,5}$ indicates the fifth observation in the second group. The comma is often omitted to save typesetters a second level of subscript, so y_{25} should be read as y-two-five, not y-twenty-five. Then $\sum_{i,j} y_{ij}$ should be read as "the sum of the individual values over all individuals and all groups," while $\sum_j y_{ij}$ should be read as "the sum of the individual values over all individuals in group i." For the latter case, there are as many sums as there are groups.

EXAMPLE 2.26   The following y values have been obtained:

Group 1:   13   8   2   6
Group 2:   5   7   10
Group 3:   6   1   8   7   9

What are y_{12} and y_{21}? Find $\sum_j y_{ij}$ and $\sum_{i,j} y_{ij}$.

Solution y_{12} is the second score in the first group—namely 8; y_{21} is the first score in the second group—namely 5. Adding separately in each group, we get the following:

i	$\sum_j y_{ij}$
1	29
2	22
3	31

Therefore, $\sum_{i,j} = 29 + 22 + 31 = 82$. ∎

Summation notation is merely a device to save words and space. When in doubt, translate the expression into English or write out the sum.

A FIRST LOOK AT PROBABILITY

3

Probability theory is the basis of statistical inference; it is also fundamental in analyzing variability. In this chapter we introduce the basic concepts and principles of probability theory. Before treating the technical aspects of the theory, we sketch some alternative interpretations of probability statements. Then we introduce the concepts of sample space, outcome, and event, the mathematical axioms of probability theory, the basic mathematical principles that underlie the more complex computations, and the important idea of statistical independence. Finally, we describe some techniques that can be used to combine the basic mathematical principles in the solution of more complicated problems.

This is an important foundation chapter for our later discussion of statistical inference. The illustrations and examples that we use are relatively simple—too simple to be completely realistic. They do, however, suggest a wide variety of applications.

3.1   INTERPRETATIONS OF PROBABILITY   ■

The theory of probability forms the basis for statistical inference. If 20% of the work force at a textile company have signed union election cards, and if 8 randomly chosen workers are to be fired, then the probability of choosing 8 workers who have signed the cards is very small. Thus, if it turns out that all 8 workers fired by the company had signed union election cards, then we can make the inference that the firings were related to union activity. The first step in the study of probability is understanding the possible interpretations of probability statements.

The earliest mathematics, and the first interpretation, of probability theory arose from various games of chance. "The probability that a flip of a balanced coin will show heads is 1/2" and "the probability that a card selected at random from a standard deck of 52 cards will be a king is 4/52" are typical examples of this kind of probability statement. The numerical probability values arise from the physical nature of the experiment. A coin flip has only two possible outcomes: heads or tails; the probability that a head occurs should therefore be 1 out of 2. In a standard deck of 52 cards, 4 are kings, so the probability of drawing a king should be 4 out of 52.

classical interpretation   These probability calculations are based on the **classical interpretation** of probability. In this interpretation each distinct possible result of an experiment is called an **outcome**; an **event** is identified with certain of these outcomes. In the card-drawing illustration there are 52 possible outcomes, 4 of which are identified with the event, drawing a king. According to the classical interpretation, the probability of an event E is taken to be the ratio of the number of outcomes favorable to an event N_E to the total number of possible outcomes N, or symbolically,

$$P(\text{event E}) = \frac{N_E}{N}$$

The usefulness of this interpretation depends completely on the assumption that all possible outcomes are **equally likely**. If that assumption is false—if the coin is loaded or the deck marked, for instance—the classical interpretation does not apply.

EXAMPLE 3.1   An ordinary thumbtack is dropped on a hard surface. It can come to rest point up or on its side. Are the two outcomes equally likely?

Solution   There is no reason to assume that the two possible outcomes are equally likely. ∎

random sample   The classical interpretation has some use, even outside the gambling casino. A **random sample**, by definition, is taken in such a way that any possible sample (of a specific size) has the same probability as any other of being selected. Therefore the outcomes (possible samples) are equally likely, and probabilities can be found by counting favorable outcomes. We use this idea extensively throughout this book.

long-run relative frequency   Situations that do not readily allow a classical interpretation sometimes can be given a **long-run relative frequency** interpretation. If an experiment has been repeated over a huge number of trials, and if 24% of these trials have resulted in a particular event E, then the probability of the event E should be .24, at least to a very good approximation. **Symbolically, if an experiment is repeated over n trials and the event E occurs in n_E trials, the probability of event E is approximately n_E divided by n:**

$$P(\text{event E}) \approx \frac{n_E}{n}$$

EXAMPLE 3.2   Suppose that in the thumbtack-tossing experiment of Example 3.1, it is claimed that the probability of the tack landing point up is .70. Give a long-run relative frequency interpretation that would justify the claim.

Solution   The claim could be justified on grounds of long-run relative frequency if a tack had been tossed many times with 70% of the results being point up. ∎

The long-run relative frequency interpretation of probability is based on observations of a large number of trials; just how large must the number of trials be? As we will see in Chapter 8, it is possible to approximate the true probability of an event in a finite number of trials and to assess how good the approximation should be. The relative frequency interpretation is often convenient. We use it whenever it seems sensible to imagine a large number of repeated trials of an experiment.

There are many applications of probability, particularly in management problems, that seem to be "one-shot" situations, those in which it's hard to imagine repeated trials. A product manager who estimates the probability that a new item will receive adequate shelf space is not imagining a long series of trials with this item; it can be introduced as a new product only once. The director of a state welfare agency who estimates the probability that a proposed revision in eligibility rules will pass the state legislature is not imagining a long series of identical proposals; the proposal will be considered only once in the particular legislative session. What then is the meaning of, say, a .6 probability of adequate shelf space or a .3 probability of legislative approval? Such probabilities are **subjective** or **personal** probabilities. One interpretation of such probabilities is that they represent willingness to make certain bets. If someone states that the probability of a certain event is .5, that person regards an even-money bet on the occurrence of that event as a fair bet (and is willing to take either side of the gamble). A subjective probability of .6 for an event means that "lose $6 if the event doesn't occur, win $4 if it does" is regarded as a fair bet. This subjective, betting interpretation of probability is natural in describing the risk-taking questions that confront most managers.

subjective/personal interpretation

Subjective probability estimates are matters of opinion. Two people might well assign very different probabilities to the same event, even if they have the same information. Such diversity of opinion is seen in economic projections for the next calendar year by various economic and investment advisors. Although many of these individuals work from the same data, they formulate diverse opinions about the most probable economic conditions. Such projections are inherently subjective.

The mathematical laws of probability can help one make logically consistent probability estimates, but they cannot guarantee that those estimates are correct. A good manager will take better risks than a bad one and should do better in the long run. But there is no way to guarantee that one assessment of a particular subjective probability is correct and another incorrect. That, as they say, is what makes horse races!

EXAMPLE 3.3   Give a subjective probability interpretation of the statement "the probability that a thumbtack will land point up is .5."

Solution   If you made such a statement, you would be saying that you would take either side of a bet of $1 that the tack would land point up against $1 that it would not.

As we suggested in Example 3.1, we would not agree with you. We believe that the tack is more likely to land point up and would prefer that side of the "even-money" bet.   ■

There are many philosophical arguments about which probability inter-pretation is most appropriate. We do not need to make a hard and fast choice in this book. The mathematics of probability theory is valid regardless of the interpretation chosen. If a particular statistical procedure is most naturally developed under a particular interpretation, we follow it. Otherwise, you're free to impose whichever interpretation seems most sensible.

The classical interpretation of probability gives us a good way to think about basic probability principles. All the basic probability ideas may be de-rived from the random drawing of individuals from a population. For example, suppose that a tasting panel of 200 men, who vary in marital status, test a po-tential new frozen dinner. Table 3.1 shows their opinions, broken down by marital status. For now, we'll regard the panelists as the entire population; in practice, we'd want to regard them as a sample from the much larger pool of potential male customers.

TABLE 3.1   Tasting Panelists' Opinions, by Marital Status

		Opinion				
		Poor	Fair	Good	Excellent	Total
	Never married	5	9	26	10	50
Marital	Divorced	1	4	16	9	30
Status	Married	12	23	37	32	104
	Widowed	2	8	5	1	16
	Total	20	44	84	52	200

Suppose that a panelist is drawn at random. What is the probability that he rates the dinner as poor? Using the classical interpretation, we have 20 poor opinion outcomes and 200 possible outcomes; the probability of poor opinion is $20/200 = .1$. Other probabilities can be found the same way.

The first probability principle is the **addition law**. It has two forms, de-pending on whether or not events are **mutually exclusive**. Events are mutually exclusive if they have no outcomes in common. The events poor opinion and fair opinion are mutually exclusive in drawing a panelist at random; the events poor opinion and widowed are not mutually exclusive. The addition law applies to finding "or" probabilities. What is the probability that a randomly chosen panelist has a poor opinion or fair opinion? There are $20 + 44 = 64$ such pan-elists, so P(poor opinion or fair opinion) $= 64/200 = .32$. P(poor opinion) $= 20/200 = .10$, and P(fair opinion) $= 44/200 = .22$, so P(poor opinion or fair opinion) $= P$(poor opinion) $+ P$(fair opinion).

Addition Law for Mutually Exclusive Events

If events A and B are mutually exclusive, then

$$P(A \text{ or } B) = P(A) + P(B)$$

If events are not mutually exclusive, then adding probabilities double counts the outcomes that belong to both events. If we pick a panelist at random, the events poor opinion and widowed are not mutually exclusive; there are two panelists who are both. To find $P(\text{poor opinion or widowed})$, we must correct for the double counting. $P(\text{poor opinion or widowed}) = P(\text{poor opinion}) + P(\text{widowed}) - P(\text{poor opinion and widowed}) = 20/200 + 16/200 - 2/200 = .10 + .08 - .01 = .17$. Alternatively, we can count the panelists who either have a poor opinion or are widowed, or both; there are $5+1+12+2+8+5+1=34$ such. So $P(\text{poor opinion or widowed}) = 34/200 = .17$, once again.

General Addition Law

For any events A and B, not necessarily mutually exclusive,

$$P(A \text{ or } B) = P(A) + P(B) - P(A \text{ and } B)$$

EXAMPLE 3.4   A direct retailer receives orders from its catalog order forms, from the use of repeat-customer order forms, and by phone. The orders are classified as small (under $25.00), medium ($25.00–$99.99), large ($100.00–$299.99), or major ($300.00 and up). An analysis of the retailer's last 4000 orders yields Table 3.2.

TABLE 3.2   Sources and Sizes of Orders

	Size				
	Small	Medium	Large	Major	Total
Catalog	1021	216	109	14	1360
Repeat	86	371	308	49	814
Phone	1497	230	86	13	1826
Total	2604	817	503	76	4000

a. Catalog and repeat-customer forms must go through an initial entry step. What is the probability that a randomly chosen order went through this step?

b. Major orders and phone orders are held for verification of credit. What is the probability that a randomly chosen order is held?

Solution   a. P(entry step) = P(catalog or repeat)

$$= P(\text{catalog}) + P(\text{repeat}) = \frac{1360}{4000} + \frac{814}{4000}$$

$$= .3400 + .2035 = .5435$$

We needn't worry about double counting, because catalog and repeat are mutually exclusive categories.

b. There are orders that are both major and phone orders. We must use the general addition principle.

$$P(\text{held}) = P(\text{major or phone})$$
$$= P(\text{major}) + P(\text{phone}) - P(\text{major and phone})$$
$$= \frac{76}{4000} + \frac{1826}{4000} - \frac{13}{4000}$$
$$= .01900 + .45650 - .00325 = .47225 \qquad\blacksquare$$

A second probability principle is the **complements law.** It is often easier to find the probability that an event *doesn't* happen than the probability that it does. Because the total probability must equal 1, the complements principle is easy.

Complements Law

If $\bar{A}$ is the event "not A,"

$$P(A) = 1 - P(\bar{A})$$

$\blacksquare$

The tasting panel results in Table 3.1 can be used to illustrate the complements law. To find the probability that a randomly chosen rater gives a poor opinion or fair opinion or good opinion rating, we could note that the complementary event is excellent. So

$$P(\text{poor opinion or fair opinion or good opinion}) = 1 - P(\text{excellent})$$

$$= 1 - \frac{52}{200} = .74$$

Of course, we could have used the addition law and added the probabilities of poor opinion, fair opinion, and good opinion. Very often, there are several ways to solve a probability problem.

EXAMPLE 3.5   As a quality-control measure, the direct retailer in Example 3.4 does an order verification check on all large and major orders, as well as on all catalog and repeat orders. Use the complements law to find the probability that a randomly chosen order will be checked.

Solution   The only orders that are *not* checked are small or medium phone orders.

$$P(\text{checked}) = 1 - P(\text{small or medium phone order})$$
$$= 1 - [P(\text{small and phone}) + P(\text{medium and phone})]$$
$$= 1 - \left(\frac{1497}{4000} + \frac{230}{4000}\right) = .56825$$

Without the complements law, we would have had to add up 10 different probabilities, corresponding to the 10 types of orders that were checked. ∎

The concept of **conditional probability** is important in its own right; and it is also the key to another probability principle, the multiplication law. Many probability questions involve some restriction or condition on randomness. For example, in the tasting panel results of Table 3.1, we might ask for the probability that a randomly chosen married man would rate the product excellent. The condition—that the panelist be married—restricts the random choice to a subgroup, the 104 married men, of the population. Of this group, 32 rated the product excellent, so we should have $P(\text{excellent opinion} \mid \text{married}) = 32/104 = .308$. In the notation $P(B \mid A)$, the condition event is placed after the vertical bar; the bar should be read as "given," so $P(\text{excellent opinion} \mid \text{married})$ should be read as "the probability that a panelist will rate the product excellent given that the panelist is married."

A conditional probability such as $P(\text{excellent opinion} \mid \text{married})$ differs from a joint probability $P(\text{excellent opinion and married}) = 32/200$ in that the conditioning event has already occurred, or is assumed to occur. In the joint probability, the event (such as married) might or might not occur. The following definition of conditional probability indicates that there is a close relationship between conditional and joint probabilities.

 SKiP

Conditional Probability $P(B \mid A)$

$$P(B \mid A) = \frac{P(A \text{ and } B)}{P(A)}$$

According to this definition,

$$P(\text{excellent opinion} \mid \text{married}) = \frac{P(\text{married and excellent opinion})}{P(\text{married})}$$
$$= \frac{32/200}{104/200} = \frac{32}{104}$$

as we found before.

EXAMPLE 3.6   For the direct retailer of Example 3.4, what is the probability that a written (nonphone) order is a repeat order?

Solution   First of all, we're looking for a conditional probability. We're assuming that the order is written. There are $1360 + 814 = 2174$ written orders, of which 814 are repeat. So $P(\text{repeat} \mid \text{written}) = 814/2174 = .374$. Alternatively, we may use the definition of conditional probability. Note that all repeat orders are written orders, so $P(\text{written and repeat}) = P(\text{repeat}) = 814/4000$.

$$P(\text{repeat} \mid \text{written}) = \frac{P(\text{written and repeat})}{P(\text{written})} = \frac{814/4000}{2174/4000}$$

$$= \frac{814}{2174} = .374 \quad \text{once again.} \qquad \blacksquare$$

The **multiplication law** of probability is simply a rewrite of the definition of conditional probability. The multiplication law is used to evaluate "and" probabilities, just as the addition law is used to evaluate "or" probabilities.

Multiplication Law for Joint Probabilities

For any events A and B, $P(A \text{ and } B) = P(A)P(B \mid A)$
$$= P(B)P(A \mid B)$$

In the tasting panelists example of Table 3.1, we could find $P(\text{married and excellent opinion}) = 32/200 = .160$ directly. Alternatively, we could use the multiplication principle. We previously found that $P(\text{excellent opinion} \mid \text{married}) = 32/104 = .308$; also, $P(\text{married}) = 104/200 = .520$. Therefore $P(\text{married and excellent opinion}) = P(\text{married})P(\text{excellent opinion} \mid \text{married}) = (.520)(.308) = .160$, once again.

EXAMPLE 3.7   Table 3.2 in Example 3.4 can be converted to conditional and unconditional probabilities by appropriate division, as shown in Table 3.3.

TABLE 3.3   Conditional Probabilities for Size Given Type of Order, and Unconditional Probabilities for Type of Order

| | *Size* | | | | |
Type of Order	Small	Medium	Large	Major	Total
Catalog	.751	.159	.080	.010	1.000
Repeat	.106	.456	.378	.060	1.000
Phone	.820	.126	.047	.007	1.000

| | *Type of Order* | | | |
	Catalog	Repeat	Phone	Total
Unconditional probability	.3400	.2035	.4565	1.0000

a. How were the .751 and .3400 probabilities obtained?

b. Use the multiplication law to find P(catalog and small).

Solution   a. The .751 probability is P(small|catalog). It was obtained by dividing the number of small catalog orders (1021) by the total number of catalog orders (1360); $1021/1360 = .751$. The .3400 is the unconditional probability of a catalog order. It is the number of catalog orders divided by the total number of all orders (4000); $1360/4000 = .3400$.

b. P(catalog and small) $= P$(catalog)P(small|catalog)

$$= (.3400)(.751) = .255$$

This could also have been obtained by dividing the 1021 small catalog orders by the 4000 total orders: $1021/4000 = .255$. ∎

These basic principles—addition, complements, and multiplication laws, and the definition of conditional probability—form the basis for all probability calculations. In this section, we have considered a special setting for probability: Sampling an individual from a specified population. In the next section, we will consider the same principles in more general settings.

SECTION 3.1   EXERCISES

3.1   For each of the following situations, indicate which interpretation of the probability statement seems most appropriate. (In many situations, it is arguable which is the best interpretation.)

a. A new statistics textbook for managers is about to be published. The editor states that the probability that at least enough copies will sell to break even is .8.

b. A small manufacturing firm produces a certain kind of dial for various electrical devices. A critical component of the dial assembly is a certain gear. The probability that a particular gear fails to satisfy tolerances is .002.

c. A random sample of 100 employees is to be taken from the 13,000 employees of a firm. It is known that 55% of the employees are men. As a check on the sampling process, the number of men in the sample will be counted. The probability that there will be 42 or fewer men in the sample is .0061.

d. The probability that the German inflation rate next year will exceed 6% is .3.

e. The probability that on a given day the demand for coronary-care beds at a local hospital exceeds the normal capacity is .004.

3.2   Give your own subjective probability for each of the following statements. If an entire class does this problem, it might be interesting to tabulate the various probabilities.

a. The Soviet Union will purchase wheat from the United States next year.

b. The next elected president of the United States will be a Democrat.

c. The increase in tuition costs for the major state university in your state will exceed 7% next year.

d. It will rain next week.

3.3   An automobile dealer sells two brands of new cars. One, C, is primarily American in origin; the other, G, is primarily Japanese. The dealer performs repair work under warranty for both brands. Each warranty job is classified according to the primary problem to be fixed. If there is more than one problem in a given job, all problems are listed separately. Records for the past year indicate the following numbers of indicated problems:

		Engine	Transmission	Exhaust	Fit/Finish	Other	Total
				Problem Area			
Brand	C	106	211	67	133	24	541
	G	21	115	16	24	6	182
	Total	127	326	83	137	30	723

a. What is the probability that a randomly chosen problem comes from brand C?
b. Serious problems are those involving the engine or transmission. What is the probability that a randomly chosen problem is serious?
c. The dealer is fully reimbursed for all brand C problems and all brand G engine, transmission, and fit/finish problems. What is the probability that a randomly chosen problem is *not* fully reimbursed?

3.4 a. For the automobile dealer's data in Exercise 3.3, what is the probability that a randomly chosen problem is an engine problem, given that it comes from brand C?
b. Construct a table of conditional probabilities of problem areas, given the brand. Are the probability distributions similar for the two brands?

3.5 The automobile dealer's warranty repair data from Exercise 3.3 were reanalyzed to take into account multiple problems on a particular repair job.

		1	2	3	Total
			Number of Problems		
Brand	C	382	54	17	453
	G	135	16	5	156
	Total	517	70	22	609

a. What is the probability that a randomly chosen job involves more than one problem?
b. What is the probability that a randomly chosen brand C job involves more than one problem?

3.6 Use the data of Exercise 3.5 to construct a table of the conditional probabilities of the number of problems, given the brand. Would you say that the conditional probabilities are similar?

3.7 In both Exercise 3.3 and 3.5, the number of brand C entries is much higher than the number for brand G. Does this fact indicate that brand C is of poorer quality than brand G?

3.8 On a typical day a convenience store recorded 186 sales of gas, 207 sales of dairy products, 188 sales of sodas, 339 sales of packaged foods, and 316 sales of nonfood products: A total of 1236 sales.
a. What is the probability that a randomly chosen sale is gas?

b. What is the probability that a randomly chosen sale is of some food product (including dairy and, by courtesy, soda)?

3.9   In Exercise 3.8, what is the probability that a randomly chosen food sale is a dairy product sale?

3.10 A market research firm regularly assembles panels of consumers to test new television commercials for effectiveness. The consumers are told that they are evaluating a pilot TV program. After viewing the hour-long program, complete with commercials, they are asked many questions about the program and some about the commercial—the actual object of research. A tabulation of results from one panel counted the number of panelists who recalled the product incorrectly, the number who recalled the product correctly and had a favorable opinion, and the number who recalled the product correctly and had an unfavorable opinion.

	Incorrect	Favorable	Unfavorable	Total
Men	42	38	20	100
Women	63	57	30	150
Total	105	95	50	200

a. Use the addition law to find the probability that a randomly chosen consumer recalled the commercial.

b. Use the complements principle to find the same probability.

3.11 In Exercise 3.10, what is the probability that a randomly chosen consumer is either a man or someone who recalled the product favorably?

3.12 a. Use the data of Exercise 3.10 to calculate the conditional probabilities of incorrect, favorable, and unfavorable responses among men. Do the same for women.

b. Are there gender differences in response to the commercial?

3.2   BASIC CONCEPTS AND AXIOMS OF PROBABILITY THEORY

In the previous section we discussed several different interpretations of probability statements. Now we formalize some of the basic definitions and assumptions that enable us to calculate the probability of an event.

experiment   Probabilities are defined for a specified **experiment.** The word *experiment* is used in an extremely broad sense to mean any situation that has more than one possible result; in this usage, experiments are not necessarily conducted under controlled laboratory conditions. An experiment could be

1. recording the total number of hours each of 2200 families spends watching television during a particular week;
2. measuring the sales volume of 194 supermarkets over a one-year period;
3. recording the daily production of an automobile assembly plant for each of 240 working days.

An experiment can be defined by stating all the possible results that might occur. In very small experiments, it is possible to list the possibilities; in most cases, it is necessary to describe but not list the possibilities.

The words *outcomes* and *event* have differing technical meanings in probability theory; they are not synonymous. An outcome is exactly one specific result of an experiment (such as "king of hearts drawn"), whereas an event may include several possibilities (such as "king drawn"). These concepts are formally defined in terms of set theory.

Sample Space *S*

A **sample space** *S* is the set of all distinct possible results of an experiment. An **outcome** is one element of *S*. An **event** is any collection of outcomes, which is a subset of *S*.

An outcome is sometimes called a *simple event* or a *nondecomposable event*, and an event is sometimes called a *compound event*.

EXAMPLE 3.8   A coin is to be flipped three times. Define the sample space by listing all outcomes of the form (result on flip #1, result on flip #2, result on flip #3).

Solution   Because on any toss of the coin we can observe either a head (H) or tail (T), the sample space *S* consists of the 8 possible outcomes

$$S = \{(HHH); (HHT); (HTH); (THH); (HTT); (THT); (TTH); (TTT)\}$$

Note that none of the outcomes can be decomposed. ∎

This same problem can be phrased in more managerial terms as follows. Suppose that intensive audits are performed on the service records of three new car dealers chosen at random from a geographic area of the country. For each company audited, we mark an "H" if there are no unresolved service complaints of more than a two-month duration, and we mark a "T" otherwise. The sample space of Example 3.8 describes the possible outcomes.

EXAMPLE 3.9   In the experiment of Example 3.8, identify these events: A, observe exactly one head; B, observe an odd number of heads; and C, observe no heads.

Solution
A = {(HTT), (THT), (TTH)}
B = {(HTT), (THT), (TTH), (HHH)}
C = {(TTT)} ∎

One way to calculate probabilities of events is to assign probabilities first to each outcome. In many cases, the individual outcomes can be assumed to be equally likely; techniques described later in this chapter can also be used to make the assignment. One of the basic principles of probability is that the probability of any event is the sum of the probabilities of all outcomes in the event.

Addition of Outcome Probabilities

If an event A consists of the outcomes $0_1, \ldots, 0_k$, then

$$P(A) = P(0_1) + \cdots + P(0_k)$$

EXAMPLE 3.10   Assume that each of the outcomes in Example 3.8 has probability 1/8. Find the probabilities of the events A, B, and C defined in Example 3.9.

Solution

$$P(A) = P(\text{exactly one H})$$
$$= P(\text{HTT}) + P(\text{THT}) + P(\text{TTH}) = 1/8 + 1/8 + 1/8 = 3/8$$
$$P(B) = P(\text{odd number of H's}) = P(\text{HTT}) + P(\text{THT})$$
$$+ P(\text{TTH}) + P(\text{HHH})$$
$$= 1/8 + 1/8 + 1/8 + 1/8 = 4/8$$
$$P(C) = P(\text{no heads}) = P(\text{TTT}) = 1/8$$

Note that we could also have taken each probability as

$$\frac{\text{number of outcomes included in the event}}{8}$$

Such classical interpretation probabilities require equally likely outcomes. ■

This approach to calculating probabilities is not always feasible. When there are many possible outcomes with unequal probabilities, it may be excessively difficult to assign probabilities to every outcome. In the rest of this chapter we provide some other methods for calculating probabilities. Regardless of how probabilities are assigned to events, probabilities must satisfy certain mathematical requirements, or axioms.

Probability Axioms

1. For any event A, $0 \leq P(A) \leq 1$.
2. $P(S) = 1$.
3. If the events A and B have no outcomes in common,

$$P(\text{either A or B occurs}) = P(A) + P(B)$$

The first two axioms merely say that probabilities are conventionally taken between 0 and 1, and that a probability of 1 is assigned to the sample space event, which by definition is certain to occur. The third axiom is a generalization of the idea of adding outcome probabilities: As long as events A and B have no outcomes in common, the probability that one or the other occurs is the sum of the separate event probabilities. We build on these ideas in Section 3.3, where we introduce some other ideas for probability calculation.

SECTION 3.2   EXERCISES

3.13 A corporation consists of three divisions, each headed by an executive vice president. Within each division are two groups, each headed by a group vice president. Final decisions about year-end bonuses are made by a committee consisting of one executive vice president and two group vice presidents; membership on the committee each year is determined by a lottery. Define a sample space by listing all possible committees. Designate the executive vice presidents as A, B, and C, and the group vice presidents as 1, 2, 3, 4, 5, and 6.

3.14 In Exercise 3.13, what is the probability that all three committee members belong to the same division? to three different divisions?

3.15 An audit is performed on the receivables of a department store. One hundred accounts are selected at random and verified. Each account is coded 0 (correct) or 1 (erroneous). Describe a typical outcome of the sample space. Should all outcomes be considered equally likely?

3.16 A sample space consists of 6 outcomes with the following probabilities:

Outcome:	1	2	3	4	5	6
Probability:	.25	.20	.20	.15	.15	.05

Event A consists of outcomes 1, 2, 3, and 4; event B consists of outcomes 3, 4, and 5. Find $P(A)$, $P(B)$, $P(A$ and B both occur), and $P(\text{either } A \text{ or } B, \text{ or both, occurs})$.

3.17 In Exercise 3.16, should $P(A \text{ or } B) = P(A) + P(B)$? Why?

3.18 A computer manufacturer sells models 1 through 9. Models 1–6 have standard memory and models 7–9 have expanded memory. Models 1–3 have only a $5\frac{1}{4}''$ disk drive and models 4–9 have both $5\frac{1}{4}''$ and $3\frac{1}{2}''$ drives. Models 1, 4, and 7 have a 20 mB hard disk; models 2, 5, and 8 have a 40 mB hard disk; and models 3, 6, and 9 have an 80 mB hard disk. The manufacturer's sales percentages for the last year were as follows:

Model:	1	2	3	4	5	6	7	8	9
Percent of sales:	27	23	10	13	7	4	5	8	3

One computer sold in the last year is to be chosen at random.

a. Define a sample space so that the outcomes correspond to the models. Should the outcomes be equally likely?

b. What is the probability that the computer has standard memory?

c. What is the probability that the computer has standard memory or both types of disk drives?

3.19 In part (c) of Exercise 3.18, it's not correct to simply add the probabilities of standard memory and of both types of disk drives. Why not?

3.3   PROBABILITY LAWS   ■

Not all probability problems can be solved by the sample-space approach in which we first list all outcomes, assign reasonable probabilities to those outcomes such that $0 \leq P(0_i) \leq 1$ and $P(S) = 1$, and then compute the probability of any event A by summing the probabilities of the outcomes in A. Sometimes merely listing the outcomes becomes a burdensome chore. For example, suppose a judge has ordered the formation of a panel of arbitrators to hear salary demands by the fire and police union of a large metropolitan area. One individual is to be selected from the list of 14 submitted by the fire and police union, one from the list of 29 submitted by the city, and a third arbitrator from another list of 11 neutrals. If we assume that no arbitrator appears on more than one list, there are a total of $14(29)(11) = 4466$ possible outcomes consisting of three arbitrators, one from each list.

In situations such as this, short of listing the entire set of outcomes, we must rely on certain event relationships and probability laws in order to calculate the probability of an event. We stated the basic probability principles in Section 3.1 in the specific context of sampling from a population. Now we want to restate the concepts in a general setting. These concepts are usually stated in the language of set theory, so some preliminary definitions are needed.

Complement, Union, and Intersection

The **complement** of an event A is the set of all outcomes in S that are not included in A; it is denoted as $\bar{A}$ and read as "not A." The **union** of the events A and B is the set of all outcomes that are included in A or in B (or in both); it is denoted as $A \cup B$ and read as "A union B" or "A or B." The **intersection** of the events A and B is the set of all outcomes that are included in both A and B; it is denoted as $A \cap B$ and read as "A intersection B" or "A and B."

These definitions formalize the simplest ideas of logic. The event $\bar{A}$ occurs whenever A does *not* occur, $A \cup B$ occurs whenever A *or* B occurs, and $A \cap B$ occurs whenever A *and* B occur. Often we simply say "not," "or," or "and" in place of the formal complement, union, or intersection.

A handy picture of these concepts is provided by Venn diagrams, as in Figure 3.1. Think of the probability of an event as its area; the whole rectangle, which represents S, has area 1. In Figure 3.1(a), event A is shaded; its complement is the entire white set. In Figure 3.1(b), $A \cup B$ is the entire shaded set, whereas $A \cap B$ is the heavily shaded set.

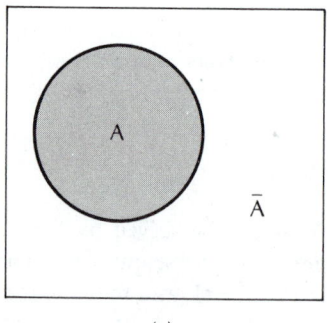
(a)

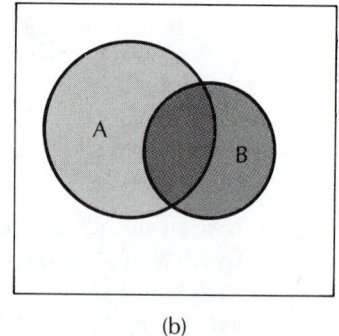
(b)

FIGURE 3.1   Venn Diagrams Illustrating $P(A)$, $P(\bar{A})$, $P(A \cup B)$, and $P(A \cap B)$

We have already used the idea of union in the third probability axiom, which stated that *if* events A and B have no outcomes in common the probability that either A or B occurs—that is, $P(A \cup B)$—is $P(A) + P(B)$. The condition that A and B have no outcomes in common is important enough to warrant a name.

Mutually Exclusive Events

Two events A and B are **mutually exclusive** (or disjoint, or logically incompatible) if they have no outcomes in common. For mutually exclusive events, $A \cap B$ contains no outcomes; the occurrence of one event automatically means that the other cannot occur. Events A, B, C, D, ... are mutually exclusive if all possible pairs of events are mutually exclusive. If one such event occurs, none of the others can occur.

The third axiom of mathematical probability theory can be translated into a basic law for calculating probabilities, using this language of set theory.

Addition Law for Mutually Exclusive Events

If the events A and B are mutually exclusive,

$$P(A \text{ or } B \text{ occurs}) = P(A \cup B) = P(A) + P(B)$$

The logical "or" corresponds to addition of probabilities, provided that the events have been defined to be mutually exclusive. Of course this idea is not restricted to two events; it applies to any finite or infinite number of events.*

In Figure 3.2, no event intersects any other one, so all three events are mutually exclusive. The area of the shaded event, $P(A \cup B \cup C)$, is obviously just the sum of the three separate areas, $P(A) + P(B) + P(C)$.

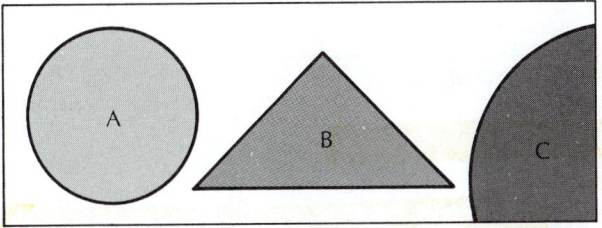

FIGURE 3.2   Three Mutually Exclusive Events

* For mathematical purists: The third axiom can be extended by induction to cover any finite number of events, but it must be restated to cover an infinite number of events.

EXAMPLE 3.11   Events A, B, and C have respective probabilities .2, .5, and .4. Events A and B are mutually exclusive, but A and C are not mutually exclusive, nor are B and C. Which of the probabilities $P(A \cup B)$, $P(A \cup C)$, $P(B \cup C)$, $P(A \cup B \cup C)$ can be calculated with the given information?

Solution   A suitable Venn diagram is shown in Figure 3.3. Because A and B do not have any overlap, $P(A \cup B) = P(A) + P(B) = .2 + .5 = .7$. But because we have no information about the areas of $A \cap C$ and $B \cap C$, we cannot calculate the other probabilities. If we erroneously added probabilities, we would get $P(A \cup B \cup C) = .2 + .5 + 4 = 11$, which is impossible.

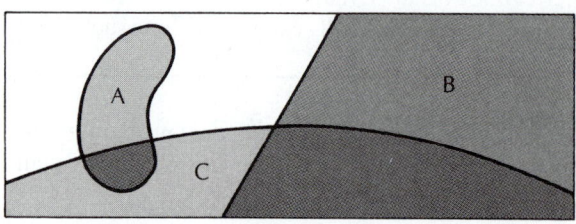

FIGURE 3.3   Venn Diagram for Example 3.11   ■

The addition principle can be extended to handle events that aren't mutually exclusive. The extension can be illustrated by an example.

EXAMPLE 3.12   Assume in Example 3.11 that $P(A \cap C) = .05$ and $P(B \cap C) = .18$. Find $P(A \cup C)$ and $P(B \cup C)$.

Solution   When we add $P(A)$ to $P(C)$ we count the area of the intersection, $P(A \cap C)$, twice. To correct for this, we can subtract the intersection area (once). So $P(A \cup C) = .2 + .4 - .05 = .55$. Similarly, $P(B \cup C) = .5 + .4 - .18 = .72$.   ■

The general addition law follows by the same reasoning.

■

General Addition Law

If A and B are any events,

$$P(A \text{ or } B) = P(A \cup B) = P(A) + P(B) - P(A \cap B)$$

■

When A and B are mutually exclusive, $A \cap B$ contains no outcomes, so $P(A \cap B) = 0$. In this case, the general addition law reduces to simple addition of probabilities. This law can be extended to the case of many events, but accounting for double counts, triple counts, and so on becomes very awkward.

Usually, it's better strategy to break up an event into mutually exclusive components, so that simple addition of probabilities can be used.

EXAMPLE 3.13   In Example 3.12, find $P(A \cup B \cup C)$ and P(exactly one of the events A, B, or C occurs).

Solution   From the information given in Example 3.12, we can deduce the probabilities shown in Figure 3.4. For $P(A \cup B \cup C)$ we add all the probabilities corresponding to the occurrence of one or more of the events:

$$P(A \cup B \cup C) = .15 + .05 + .17 + .18 + .32 = .87$$

For P(exactly one of A, B, or C), we do not add the intersection probabilities .05 and .18, because the intersection represents the occurrence of two events. So P(exactly one of A, B, or C occurs) $= .15 + .17 + .32 = .64$.

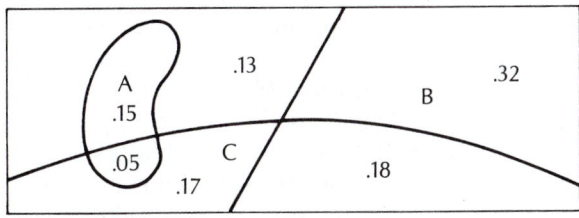

FIGURE 3.4   Venn Diagram for Example 3.13

A useful probability law follows directly from the addition principle. By definition, an event A and its complement $\bar{A}$ are mutually exclusive; $A \cup \bar{A}$ includes the entire sample space and has probability 1. Therefore,

$$P(A \cup \bar{A}) = P(A) + P(\bar{A}) = 1$$

Complements Law

$$P(A) = 1 - P(\bar{A}) = 1 - P(\text{not } A)$$

It is often easier to find the probability that an event does *not* happen. Then, by the complements law, $P(A)$ is simply $1 - P(\bar{A})$.

EXAMPLE 3.14   In putting together a new microcomputer system, it is observed that 16% of the newly assembled systems have exactly one defect, 4% have exactly two defects, and 1% have three or more defects. What is the probability that a randomly chosen system has no defects?

Solution   The event "0 defects" is the complement of the event "1 or more defects": $P(0 \text{ defects}) = 1 - P(1 \text{ or more defects})$. In turn, by the addition principle for mutually exclusive events,

$$P(1 \text{ or more defects}) = P(\text{exactly 1}) + P(\text{exactly 2}) + P(3 \text{ or more})$$
$$= .16 + .04 + .01 = .21$$

Thus $P(0 \text{ defects}) = 1 - .21 = .79$.   ∎

One other concept is crucial in developing basic probability laws: The conditional probability of an event B given that another event A has occurred. For example, it may be that 10% of the purchasers of a luxury automobile order special high-performance audio speakers, so $P(\text{special speakers}) = .1$. But if it is known that the customer has ordered the top-of-the-line stereo receiver for the car, the probability that the customer will also order the high-performance speakers is presumably higher. Thus a condition, in this case that the customer has ordered the special receiver, may change the probability of an event, that the customer will order the high-performance speakers. For another example, suppose that auditors take a random sample from a list of 216 accounts receivable, of which 24 contain errors. The probability that the second account chosen contains an error must be 24/216, if there is no information about the status of the first account. But if it is given that the first account contains an error, then there are only 23 erroneous accounts among the remaining 215; given that the first account contains an error, the probability that the second account also contains an error changes to 23/215. We use the definition of conditional probability in terms of unconditional probabilities heavily in the following chapters.

Definition of Conditional Probability

The conditional probability of event B given that event A occurs denoted by $P(B \mid A)$ and read as "the probability of B given A," is

$$P(B \mid A) = \frac{P(A \cap B)}{P(A)}$$

Similarly,

$$P(A \mid B) = \frac{P(A \cap B)}{P(B)}$$

A conditional probability is formally defined in terms of unconditional probabilities. The definition can be understood in terms of long-run relative frequencies. Imagine a very large number n of trials. We take as given that event A occurs; there will be n_A such trials. The conditional probability is that fraction of the n_A trials in which both A and B occur. There are n_{AB} trials in which A and B both occur, so the conditional probability is

$$\frac{n_{AB}}{n_A}$$

Now divide numerator and denominator of this fraction by n, the total number of trials, to get

$$P(B\,|\,A) = \frac{\dfrac{n_{AB}}{n}}{\dfrac{n_A}{n}}$$

But the numerator is the unconditional probability $P(A \cap B)$ and the denominator is $P(A)$. Therefore, we get back to the definition,

$$P(B\,|\,A) = \frac{P(A \cap B)}{P(A)}$$

EXAMPLE 3.15   Refer to Example 3.8. If event A is "observe 1 or more heads in 3 tosses of a coin" and event B is "observe exactly 1 head," computer $P(B\,|\,A)$ using the definition of conditional probability.

Solution

           A: Composed of all outcomes in S except (TTT); hence $P(A) = 7/8$
           B: Composed of the outcomes (HTT), (THT), and (TTH)
$A \cap B$: Composed of the outcomes (HTT), (THT), and (TTH);
                $P(A \cap B) = 3/8$

The conditional probability of event B given that event A occurs is

$$P(B\,|\,A) = \frac{P(A \cap B)}{P(A)}$$

$$= \frac{3/8}{7/8} = \frac{3}{7}$$

That is, there are 3 chances in 7 of B occurring given that event A has occurred.

∎

EXAMPLE 3.16   Suppose that, in the receivables-auditing illustration discussed on page 88, 16 of the 80 large (over \$10,000) accounts contain errors, and that a single account is chosen at random. What is the probability that the account selected is in error, given that it is large?

Solution   The answer ought to be $16/80 = .2$. According to the definition

$$P(\text{error}\,|\,\text{large}) = \frac{P(\text{error} \cap \text{large})}{P(\text{large})}$$

There are 216 accounts, 80 of which are large and 16 of which are large and in error. Therefore,

$$P(\text{error}\,|\,\text{large}) = \frac{16/216}{80/216} = 16/80$$

as it should be.   ■

The definition of conditional probability leads directly to the multiplication law of probabilities.

Multiplication Law

If A and B are any events,

$$P(\text{A and B}) = P(\text{A} \cap \text{B}) = P(\text{A})P(\text{B}\,|\,\text{A})$$

Note: By reversing the roles of A and B, $P(\text{A} \cap \text{B}) = P(\text{B})P(\text{A}\,|\,\text{B})$.   ■

joint probability
marginal
probability

The only difference between the multiplication law and the definition of conditional probability lies in which probabilities are assumed and which are to be calculated. When the so-called **joint probability** $P(\text{A} \cap \text{B})$ and the **marginal probability** $P(\text{A})$ are assumed to be known, the conditional probability $P(\text{B}\,|\,\text{A})$ can be calculated from the definition. When $P(\text{A})$ and $P(\text{B}\,|\,\text{A})$ are assumed to be known, $P(\text{A} \cap \text{B})$ can be calculated by the multiplication law.

EXAMPLE 3.17   An evaluation team of two people is to be selected from a group of eligible men and women consisting of 10 males and 6 females. If each group of two people has the same chance of being selected, find the probability of selecting an evaluation team composed of two females.

Solution   Let A be the event that the first person selected is female and let B be the event that the second person selected is female. Then we want $P(\text{A} \cap \text{B})$. By the multiplication law,

$$P(\text{A} \cap \text{B}) = P(\text{A})P(\text{B}\,|\,\text{A})$$

It should be clear that $P(\text{A}) = 6/16$ and $P(\text{B}\,|\,\text{A}) = 5/15$. Substituting, we get

$$P(\text{A} \cap \text{B}) = \left(\frac{6}{16}\right)\left(\frac{5}{15}\right) = .125$$ ■

The multiplication law can be extended to deal with the joint probability of three events, or even more:

$$P(\text{A} \cap \text{B} \cap \text{C}) = P(\text{A})P(\text{B}\,|\,\text{A})P(\text{C}\,|\,\text{A} \cap \text{B})$$
$$P(\text{A} \cap \text{B} \cap \text{C} \cap \text{D}) = P(\text{A})P(\text{B}\,|\,\text{A})P(\text{C}\,|\,\text{A} \cap \text{B})P(\text{D}\,|\,\text{A} \cap \text{B} \cap \text{C})$$

and so on.

EXAMPLE 3.18   Suppose that three people are to be selected in Example 3.17. What is the probability that all three are female?

Solution   Define A as the first person selected is female, B as the second person selected is female, and C as the third person selected is female. $P(C|A \cap B)$ must be 4/14, so

$$P(A \cap B \cap C) = P(A)P(B|A)P(C|A \cap B)$$

$$= \left(\frac{6}{16}\right)\left(\frac{5}{15}\right)\left(\frac{4}{14}\right) = .036 \qquad \blacksquare$$

SECTION 3.3   EXERCISES

3.20   A manufacturing firm has two emergency generators, either of which can supply sufficient power for basic operations. Each generator is subject to failure. Let A be the event that generator 1 works properly and B the event that generator 2 works properly. Describe each of the following events verbally: $\bar{A}$; $A \cup B$; $A \cap B$; $\bar{A} \cap \bar{B}$. What is the complement of $A \cup B$?

3.21   Assume in Exercise 3.20 that $P(A) = .96$, $P(B) = .94$, and $P(A \cap B) = .93$. Draw a Venn diagram. Find $P(A \cap \bar{B})$, $P(\bar{A} \cap B)$, and $P(\bar{A} \cap \bar{B})$.

3.22   Use the probabilities in Exercise 3.21 to find $P(B|A)$, $P(\bar{B}|A)$, $P(B|\bar{A})$, and $P(\bar{B}|\bar{A})$. Give a verbal statement of each of these probabilities. Does $P(B|A) + P(\bar{B}|A) = 1$? Does $P(B|A) + P(B|\bar{A}) = 1$?

3.23   Are the events A and B in Exercises 3.20 and 3.21 mutually exclusive? Find $P(A$ or $B)$.

3.24   The director of a federal agency responsible for housing grants to small communities finds that 14.2% of all applications were past deadline, 8.7% were incomplete, and 15.9% were ineligible. Define A as "past deadline," B as "incomplete," and C as "ineligible." Which pairs, if any, of events are logically mutually exclusive? Interpret the event $A \cap B \cap C$.

3.25   For the situation in Exercise 3.24, suppose $P(A \cap B) = .046$, $P(A \cap C) = .092$, $P(B \cap C) = .035$, and $P(A \cap B \cap C) = .016$. Construct a Venn diagram and deduce probabilities for mutually exclusive events. For instance, because $P(A \cap B) = .046$ and $P(A \cap B \cap C) = .016$, it must be true that $P(A \cap B \cap \bar{C}) = .030$.

3.26   Use the Venn diagram constructed in Exercise 3.25 to find $P(\bar{A} \cap \bar{B} \cap \bar{C})$, $P(A \cup B \cup C)$, and $P(\bar{A} \cap \bar{B})$. Give verbal statements of these events.

3.27   In a manufacturing process, a hole must be drilled in a block of metal to rather precise specifications. A defect in drilling can render the block useless, a condition that can be discovered only after assembly. Experience indicates that 90% of the holes are drilled to specification. Each hole is measured by an inspector. If the hole is not drilled to specification, there is a 90% chance that the inspector detects the defect.

    a. What is the probability that a block is defectively drilled and the inspector detects the defect?

    b. What is the probability that a block is defectively drilled and the inspector does not detect the defect?

3.28   Suppose in Exercise 3.27 that, with a reallocation of effort, the rate of drilling to specification can be increased to 99%. With this new strategy, however, less time is available for inspection, so that only 80% of defectively drilled blocks are detected by the inspector.

a. What is the probability that a block is defectively drilled and the inspector does not detect the defect?

b. Compare your answer to part (a) with the answer to part (b) of Exercise 3.27. In which case is the probability of an undetected defect lower? Would it matter to your answer if the rate of defect detection was only 40%, rather than 80%?

3.29   Refer again to Exercise 3.27. Suppose that a defect in a drilled block that is not detected by the inspector is detected during assembly with probability .80. What is the probability that a randomly chosen block is defectively drilled and the defect is not detected either by the inspector or at assembly?

3.4   STATISTICAL INDEPENDENCE

The concept of statistical independence is fundamental in probability theory and particularly in its statistical applications. Suppose that, in the receivables-auditing example of the previous section, 36 of the 216 accounts are "foreign" and 4 of the 36 foreign accounts are in error. Does the probability of error given a foreign account differ from the overall (unconditional) probability of error? Recall that there were 24 erroneous accounts in the group of 216, so $P(\text{error}) = 24/216 = 1/9$. The conditional probability of error given a foreign account is $P(\text{error}|\text{foreign}) = P(\text{foreign and error})/P(\text{foreign}) = (4/216)/(36/216) = 4/36 = 1/9$, also. Because the conditional probability of error is exactly the same as the unconditional probability, the events, observing a foreign account and **statistically** observing an account in error, are said to be **statistically independent**.

independent   The idea of statistical independence is that the occurrence of event A does not change the probability that event B occurs. In other words, the conditional probability $P(B|A)$ is the same as the unconditional probability $P(B)$.

Definition of Independent Events

Events A and B are statistically independent if and only if $P(B|A) = P(B)$. Otherwise they are dependent. Note: If A and B are independent, it also follows that $P(A|B) = P(A)$.

Hereafter, we simply say *independent events* and omit the word *statistically*.

EXAMPLE 3.19   Refer to the receivables-auditing illustration. Determine whether the events "first account erroneous" and "second account erroneous" are independent.

Solution   Because the receivables sampling is done without replacement, the occurrence of an erroneous account on the first draw (slightly) reduces the probability of an erroneous account on the second. Therefore the events are not independent. We know that $P(\text{second is erroneous}|\text{first is erroneous}) = 23/215 = .107$ and that the unconditional probability $P(\text{second is erroneous}) = 24/216 = .111$. The numerical difference in probabilities is very small, so the events are nearly, but not quite, independent.   ■

EXAMPLE 3.20   Suppose that in a university computing center 192 of 960 jobs are high-priority jobs: 128 of these are submitted by students and 64 by faculty. Of all jobs, 640 are from students and 320 from faculty. If one job is selected at random, are the events "high-priority job" and "student job" independent?

Solution   Let A be the event that the job is submitted by a student and B the event that the job is a high-priority job. In order for events A and B to be independent, we must show

$$P(A \mid B) = P(A)$$

or

$$P(B \mid A) = P(B)$$

For this example we can compute $P(B \mid A)$ using the definition of conditional probability:

$$P(B \mid A) = \frac{P(A \cap B)}{P(A)}$$

$$= \frac{128/960}{640/960} = \frac{128}{640} = .200$$

Also, $P(B) = 192/960 = .200$, so the events A and B are independent.   ■

The definition of independent events leads to a special case of the multiplication law that applies to independent events.

Multiplication Law for Independent Events

If events A and B are independent,

$$P(A \cap B) = P(A)P(B)$$

This result is an alternate definition of independence.

EXAMPLE 3.21   Use the multiplication law for independent events to verify that the two events of Example 3.20 are independent.

Solution   We showed previously that $P(A \cap B) = 128/960 = .133$. Similarly, $P(A)P(B) = (640/960) \times (192/960) = .133$. Because $P(A \cap B) = P(A)P(B)$, events A and B are independent.   ■

The definition of independence suggests that we should find $P(A \cap B)$, $P(A)$, and $P(B)$ and then check to determine if the events are independent. Sometimes this is in fact the procedure. More often, independence is a natural assumption. For example, sampling with replacement leads naturally to assumed independence. The multiplication principle is then used to calculate joint probabilities such as $P(A \cap B)$.

EXAMPLE 3.22   Suppose that 70% of the teachers in a school district are rated as satisfactory, that 59% are age 40 or more, and that rating and age are assumed to be independent. What is the probability that a randomly chosen teacher is (a) rated satisfactory and over 40; (b) not rated satisfactory and not over 40; (c) not rated satisfactory, given under 40?

Solution   a. Because the events "rated satisfactory" and "over 40 years of age" are independent, it follows that

$$P(\text{satisfactory} \cap \text{over } 40) = P(\text{satisfactory})P(\text{over } 40)$$
$$= (.70)(.59) = .413$$

b. Because the events "rated satisfactory" and "over 40 years of age" are independent, their complements ("not rated satisfactory" and "not over 40") are also independent. Hence,

$$P(\text{not satisfactory} \cap \text{not over } 40) = (1 - .70)(1 - .59)$$
$$= .123$$

c. $P(\text{not satisfactory} \mid \text{not over } 40) = \dfrac{P(\text{not satisfactory} \cap \text{not over } 40)}{P(\text{not over } 40)}$

$$= \frac{.123}{.41} = .30$$

This is exactly the probability of the event "not rated satisfactory." ∎

The multiplication law can be extended to more than two independent events, but to do so, we need the idea of independent processes. Processes (essentially separate sample spaces) are independent if any event from one process is independent of events from all other processes. If, for instance, there are four independent processes and events A, B, C, and D, then the probability of their intersection is

$$P(A \cap B \cap C \cap D) = P(A)P(B)P(C)P(D)$$

EXAMPLE 3.23   Assume that the probability that a buyer of a new automobile orders factory-installed air conditioning is .6 and that the various buyers' decisions are independent processes. What is the probability that the next five buyers all order factory air conditioning?

Solution   Let A_1, A_2, A_3, A_4, A_5 be the events that buyers 1, 2, 3, 4, 5 order factory air conditioning. Then

$$P(\text{all five order factory air conditioning}) = P(A_1 \cap A_2 \cap A_3 \cap A_4 \cap A_5)$$
$$= P(A_1)P(A_2)P(A_3)P(A_4)P(A_5)$$
$$= (.6)(.6)(.6)(.6)(.6)$$
$$= .07776 \qquad \blacksquare$$

SECTION 3.4   EXERCISES

3.30   A personnel officer for a firm that employs many part-time salespeople tries out a sales-aptitude test on several hundred applicants. Because the test is unproven, results are not used in hiring. Forty percent of applicants show high aptitude on the test and 12% of those hired both show high aptitude and achieve good sales records. The firm's experience shows that 30% of all salespeople achieve good sales. Let A be the event "shows high aptitude" and let B be the event "achieves good sales."
   a. Find $P(A)$, $P(A \cap B)$, and $P(B|A)$.
   b. Are A and B independent?
   c. How useful is the test in predicting good sales achievement?

3.31   Construct a Venn diagram for Exercise 3.30.
   a. Find $P(A \cap \bar{B})$ and $P(\bar{B}|A)$.
   b. Are A and $\bar{B}$ independent?

3.32   A survey of workers in two plants of a manufacturing firm includes the question "How effective is management in responding to legitimate grievances of workers?" In plant 1, 48 of 192 workers respond "poor"; in plant 2, 80 of 248 workers respond "poor." An employee of the manufacturing firm is to be selected randomly. Let A be the event "worker comes from plant 1" and let B be the event "response is poor."
   a. Find $P(A)$, $P(B)$, and $P(A \cap B)$.
   b. Are the events A and B independent?
   c. Find $P(B|A)$ and $P(B|\bar{A})$. Are they equal?

3.33   Show that if A and B are independent, $P(B|A) = P(B|\bar{A})$. (Hint: B and $\bar{A}$ are also independent.)

3.34   A school district must staff two primary schools and one high school. On any particular day, the probability that no substitute for an absent teacher is needed at primary school 1 is .60; the same probability holds for primary school 2. At the high school, the probability that no substitute is needed is .50. Assume that absenteeism at the three schools defines three independent processes. Find the probability that no substitute is needed at any of the schools on a particular day.

3.35   Do you believe that the assumption of independent processes in Exercise 3.34 is realistic?

3.36   In Exercise 3.18, the probability that a randomly chosen computer had standard memory was .84, and the probability that it had both $5\frac{1}{4}''$ and $3\frac{1}{2}''$ disk drives was .40. The probability that it had both types of disk drives and also had standard memory was .24.
   a. Find the probability that a computer has both types of drives, given that it has standard memory.
   b. Find the probability that a computer has standard memory, given that it has both types of drives.
   c. Are the events "standard memory" and "both types of drives" independent?

3.37   In addition to the probabilities given in Exercise 3.36, it follows from the figures in Exercise 3.18 that the probability that a computer has a 20 mB hard disk is .45. The probability that a computer has both types of disk drives and also a 20 mB hard disk is .18. Are the events "both types of disk drives" and "20 mB hard disk" independent?

3.38   An airline keeps track of adjustment problems faced by airport attendants. It finds that 40% of all problems involve a missed connection; 10% of all problems involve mishandled baggage. Is it plausible to assume that 4% of all problems will involve both mishandled baggage and a missed connection?

3.39   A direct-order retailer finds that 40% of all orders arrive by telephone (and the remainder by mail). A partial or complete merchandise return is made in 10% of all orders. Is it reasonable to assume that 4% of all orders will arrive by telephone and involve a merchandise return?

3.5   PROBABILITY TABLES AND PROBABILITY TREES   ∎

Many probability problems require the successive use of several of the basic principles to obtain a solution. These problems can be solved algebraically, but it is helpful to have some devices to keep the logic straight.

EXAMPLE 3.24   A firm has found that 46% of its junior executives have two-career marriages, 37% have single-career marriages, and 17% are unmarried. The firm estimates that 40% of the two-career marriage executives would refuse a transfer to another office, as would 15% of the single-career marriage executives, and 10% of the unmarried executives. If a transfer offer is made to a randomly selected executive, what is the probability that it will be refused?

Solution   First, the event "refused" can be thought of as "(refused ∩ two-career) ∪ (refused ∩ single-career) ∪ (refused ∩ unmarried)." The three possibilities are mutually exclusive, so the addition law yields

$$P(\text{refused}) = P(\text{refused} \cap \text{two-career}) + P(\text{refused} \cap \text{single-career})$$
$$+ P(\text{refused} \cap \text{unmarried})$$

Second, each of the three joint probabilities can be evaluated by the multiplication law. For instance,

$$P(\text{refused} \cap \text{two-career}) = P(\text{two-career})P(\text{refused} \mid \text{two-career})$$
$$= (.46)(.40)$$

Putting the two ideas together, we have

$$P(\text{refused}) = P(\text{two-career})P(\text{refused} \mid \text{two-career})$$
$$+ P(\text{single-career})P(\text{refused} \mid \text{single-career})$$
$$+ P(\text{unmarried})P(\text{refused} \mid \text{unmarried})$$
$$= (.46)(.40) + (.37)(.15) + (.17)(.10) = .2565 \qquad ∎$$

EXAMPLE 3.25   Investments of $100 each are made in two projects. Project A is assumed to yield a net return of $8, $10, or $12, with respective probabilities .2, .6, and .2. Project B is assumed to yield a net return of $8, $10, or $12, with respective probabilities .3, .4, and .3. The returns from the two projects are assumed to be independent. What is the probability that the total of the two returns is exactly $20?

Solution   By the addition law,

$$
\begin{aligned}
P(\text{total} = \$20) = {} & P(\text{A yields } \$8 \cap \text{B yields } \$12) \\
& + P(\text{A yields } \$10 \cap \text{B yields } \$10) \\
& + P(\text{A yields } \$12 \cap \text{B yields } \$8)
\end{aligned}
$$

The multiplication law for independent events may be applied to each joint probability to obtain

$$
\begin{aligned}
P(\text{total} = \$20) = {} & P(\text{A yields } \$8)P(\text{B yields } \$12) \\
& + P(\text{A yields } \$10)P(\text{B yields } \$10) \\
& + P(\text{A yields } \$12)P(\text{B yields } \$8) \\
= {} & (.2)(.3) + (.6)(.4) + (.2)(.3) = .36 \qquad \blacksquare
\end{aligned}
$$

There are no new ideas involved in the solution of such problems, but it is sometimes tricky to find the right order in which to apply the basic principles. With larger, more complicated problems, the difficulty is increased. Several methods have been invented to help clarify the reasoning involved in solving a problem.

One useful approach is to construct a table of joint probabilities. The desired answer can sometimes be found by adding the appropriate table entries.

EXAMPLE 3.26   Construct a joint probability table for marital status versus action on transfer offers for the data of Example 3.24. Use it to find $P(\text{refused})$.

Solution   First, put any known marginal probabilities on the appropriate margins of the table.

	Two-career	Single-career	Unmarried
Refused			
Accepted			
	.46	.37	.17

Now the body of the table can be filled in using the multiplication law. The remaining marginals can be found by addition.

	Two-career	Single-career	Unmarried	
Refused	(.46)(.40) = .1840	(.37)(.15) = .0555	(.17)(.10) = .0170	.2565
Accepted	(.46)(.60) = .2760	(.37)(.85) = .3145	(.17)(.90) = .1530	.7435
	.46	.37	.17	

P(Refused) is shown, in the right margin, to be .2565, as in Example 3.24.   ∎

EXAMPLE 3.27   Construct a joint probability table and find P(total return = $20) for the data of Example 3.25.

Solution   In this case, both sets of marginal probabilities have been specified.

Return from A

		$8	$10	$12	
Return	$8				.3
from	$10				.4
B	$12				.3
		.2	.6	.2	

The multiplication law for independent events can be used to fill in the body of the table.

Return from A

		$8	$10	$12	
Return	$8	.06	.18	.06*	.3
from	$10	.08	.24*	.08	.4
B	$12	.06*	.18	.06	.3
		.2	.6	.2	

The entries that correspond to a total return of $20 are marked with an asterisk. The addition law yields

$$P(\text{total return} = \$20) = .06 + .24 + .06 = .36,$$

as in Example 3.25.   ∎

Probability tables are a convenient, compact way of solving many problems. As a by-product, they often yield the solution to related problems as well. You should have no difficulty, for instance, in finding P(total return = $22) or P(total return = $16) in Example 3.27. For problems involving more than two categories of events, probability tables are at best awkward to use. If there had also been a project C in Example 3.25, some sort of three-dimensional table would have been necessary.

probability tree   Another device that often can be used is a **probability tree**. This method is hard to describe but easy to illustrate.

EXAMPLE 3.28   Use a probability tree to solve Example 3.24.

Solution   First, construct branches for a set of events with known marginal probabilities:

Two-career	.46
Single-career	.37
Unmarried	.17

Then, at the tip of each of these branches, construct branches for another set of events, using conditional probabilities (given the appropriate first branch):

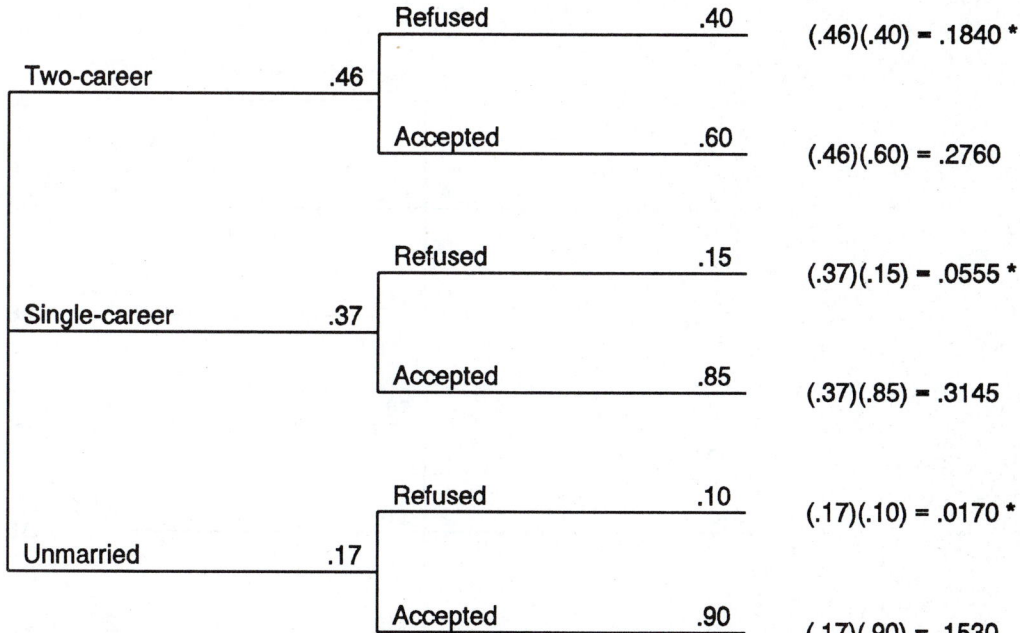

Two-career	.46	Refused .40 → (.46)(.40) = .1840 *
		Accepted .60 → (.46)(.60) = .2760
Single-career	.37	Refused .15 → (.37)(.15) = .0555 *
		Accepted .85 → (.37)(.85) = .3145
Unmarried	.17	Refused .10 → (.17)(.10) = .0170 *
		Accepted .90 → (.17)(.90) = .1530

(Had there been another set of relevant events, we would have added another set of branches.) The probability for each specific path (sequence of branches) is found by multiplying the probabilities along that path, as shown. The probability for an event can be found by adding the probabilities of all paths that satisfy that event. The paths corresponding to "refused" are marked with an asterisk: $P(\text{refused}) = .1840 + .0555 + .0170 = .2565$, once again. ∎

EXAMPLE 3.29   Use a probability tree to solve Example 3.25.

Solution   Marginal probabilities are specified for both project A and project B, so we may use the returns to either project for the first set of branches. Out of sheer perversity, we begin by branching on project B.

B returns   **A returns**

	$8 ____ .2	.06
$8 ____ .3	$10 ____ .6	.18
	$12 ____ .2	.06 *
	$8 ____ .2	.08
$10 ____ .4	$10 ____ .6	.24 *
	$12 ____ .2	.08
	$8 ____ .2	.06 *
$12 ____ .3	$10 ____ .6	.18
	$12 ____ .2	.06

In this case, because of the assumed independence, conditional probabilities of A returns given particular B returns are unnecessary. The path probabilities for a total return of \$20 are marked with an asterisk: $P(\text{total return} = \$20) = .06 + .24 + .06 = .36$. ∎

To give correct answers, a probability tree must be constructed according to the following rules:

Rules for Constructing a Probability Tree

1. Events forming the first set of branches must have known marginal probabilities, must be mutually exclusive, and must exhaust all possibilities (so that the sum of the branch probabilities is 1).
2. Events forming the second set of branches must be entered at the tip of each of the sets of first branches. Conditional probabilities, given the relevant first branch, must be entered, unless assumed independence allows the use of unconditional probabilities. Again, the branches must be mutually exclusive and exhaustive (so that the sum of the probabilities branching from any one tip is 1).
3. If there are further sets of branches, the probabilities must be conditional on all preceding events. As always, the branches must be mutually exclusive and exhaustive.
4. The sum of path probabilities must be taken over all paths included in the relevant event.

With a little practice, most people find probability trees quite easy to use. Trees and tables are both very useful in clarifying the logic of a solution. Both methods in effect construct appropriate sample spaces; a particular outcome corresponds to a path in a probability tree or an entry in a probability table. Trees can be used in a wider variety of problems. The only difficulty with using a tree for a large, complicated problem is that the tree can become impractically large. As long as one is willing to use a lot of paper, it is possible to solve some rather nasty problems surprisingly quickly.

EXAMPLE 3.30   In a certain television game show, a valuable prize is hidden behind one of three doors. You, the contestant, pick one of the three doors. Before opening it, the announcer opens one of the other two doors and you see that the prize isn't behind that door. The announcer offers you the chance to switch to the remaining door. Should you switch, or doesn't it matter?

Solution   Let's make a tree.

Call the door that you select A, the others B and C. Assuming that the prize is distributed randomly among the doors, the probability that it's behind each of the doors is 1/3. If you picked a wrong door in door A, the announcer has no choice: If B contains the prize, the announcer must open C; if C has the prize, he must open B. But if you picked correctly and A has the prize, the announcer does have a choice: Let's assume that the announcer picks B or C randomly, each with probability 1/2 in this situation. We can construct the following tree:

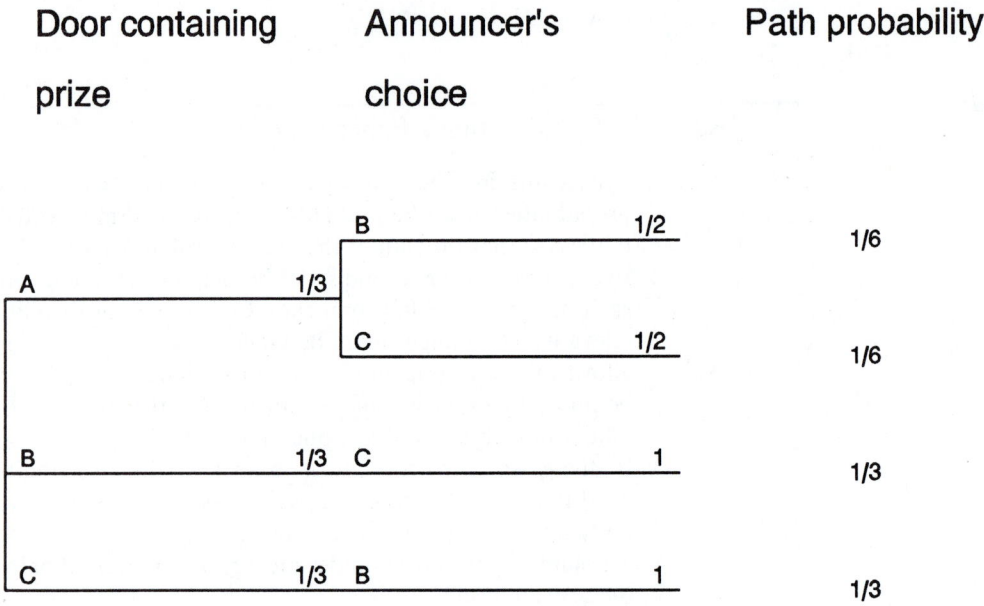

Door containing prize   Announcer's choice   Path probability

Suppose that the announcer has chosen B (and you chose A initially). What is the probability that the prize is behind door C?

$$P(\text{behind C}\,|\,\text{chose B}) = \frac{P(\text{behind C and chose B})}{P(\text{chose B})}$$

$$= \frac{1/3}{1/6 + 1/3} = \frac{1/\ 3}{1/2} = \frac{2}{3}$$

so $P(\text{behind A}\,|\,\text{chose B}) = 1 - 2/3 = 1/3$. You have a better chance of winning if you switch to door C!   ■

EXAMPLE 3.31   Suppose that 40% of all theoretically plausible pharmaceutical drug concepts are biologically active. Of the active drugs, 70% show serious side effects. Of those drugs that prove to be inactive, 20% can be reformulated to be active, and among these reformulated drugs, 80% show serious side effects. All drugs that are to be marketed must be approved by a government agency. The probability that a drug will be approved, given that it is biologically active and shows no side effects, is .90. Of drugs that are biologically active but show side effects, 5% will be approved. If a drug is not biologically active, it will not be approved.

a. What is the probability that a new drug concept will result in an approved drug?

b. What is the probability that a new drug concept will lead to a drug with side effects?

c. If a drug is approved, what is the probability that it will lead to side effects?

Solution A probability tree can be constructed. In this case, as often happens, the natural sequence of branches is chronological. The natural first branch reflects whether or not the drug is active. Whether the drug can be reformulated, whether it shows side effects, and finally whether it is approved are then considered.

Active?	Reformulated?	Side effects?	Approved?	
			Yes .05	.0140
		Yes .70	No .95	.2660
Yes .40			Yes .90	.1080
		No .30	No .10	.0120
			Yes .05	.0048
		Yes .80	No .95	.0912
	Yes .20		Yes .90	.0216
		No .20	No .10	.0024
No .60	No .80		No 1.00	.4800

a. To find the probability that a drug is approved, simply add the probabilities for all paths corresponding to a "yes" branch on the "approved" question:

$$P(\text{approved}) = .0140 + .1080 + .0048 + .0216 = .1484$$

b. Again we must add the appropriate path probabilities. The paths corresponding to existence of side effects are the first, second, fifth, and sixth paths:

$$P(\text{side effects}) = .0140 + .2660 + .0048 + .0912 = .3760$$

Alternatively, we can draw the tree without the "approved" branches and obtain

$$P(\text{side effects}) = .40(.70) + .60(.20)(.80) = .280 + .096 = .376$$

once again.

c. To find a conditional probability like this one, we use the definition of conditional probability:

$$P(\text{side effects} \mid \text{approved}) = \frac{P(\text{side effects} \cap \text{approved})}{P(\text{approved})}$$

In part (a), we found $P(\text{approved}) = .1484$. Note that the first and fifth branches, with respective probabilities .0140 and .0048, are the only ones corresponding to "side effects ∩ approved." Thus

$$P(\text{side effects} \mid \text{approved}) = (.0140 + .0048)/(.1484) \qquad ■$$

SECTION 3.5   EXERCISES

3.40 The experience of a data-processing firm has shown that the first time a new program is tested there is a .6 probability of finding one or more major "bugs"— flaws in the program that cause the program to fail completely. There is a .3 chance of detecting minor bugs—flaws that allow the program to run but produce erroneous results in certain situations—and a .1 chance that no bugs are detected. In each case, an attempt is made to correct all detected programming errors. Then the program is retested on a more extensive basis. The likely results of the retest are summarized in the following table of conditional probabilities:

			Retest	
		Major	Minor	None
First test	Major	.3	.5	.2
	Minor	.1	.3	.6
	None	0	.2	.8

a. Construct a table giving the joint probabilities of all the possible combinations of first test and retest results.
b. Find the probability that major bugs are still found at the retest.
c. Find the probabilities of minor bugs at retest and of no bugs at retest.

3.41 Construct a probability tree to answer Exercise 3.40.

3.42 In the data-processing firm of Exercise 3.40, programs that still show major or minor bugs on retesting are sent through one more round of correction. Programs that had major bugs in retest have a .1 probability of retaining major bugs in the third test (regardless of the result of the initial test) and a .2 probability of showing minor bugs. Those that showed only minor bugs at retesting have essentially no chance of showing major bugs at third test but a .1 chance of showing minor bugs (again regardless of the result of the first test). It is assumed that programs showing no bugs at retesting need not go through a third round.
a. Construct a probability tree for this situation.
b. Find the probability that a program will show major bugs at all three tests.
c. Find the probability that a program will show major bugs at the third test. Why is this answer different from that of part (b)?

d. Find the probability that a program will achieve no-bug status (whether after two or three tests).

3.43 A purchasing unit for a state government has found that 60% of the winning bids for office-cleaning contracts come from regular bidders, 30% from occasional bidders, and 10% from first-time bidders. The services provided by successful bidders are rated satisfactory or unsatisfactory after one year on the job. Experience indicates that 90% of the jobs done by regular bidders are satisfactory, as are 80% of the jobs done by occasional bidders and 60% of the jobs done by first-time bidders.

a. What is the probability that a job will be done by a first-time bidder and will be satisfactory?

b. What is the probability that a job will be satisfactory?

c. Given that a job is satisfactory, what is the probability that it was done by a first-time bidder?

3.44 A manufacturer of snack crackers introduces several new products each year. About 60% of the introductions are failures, 30% are moderate successes, and 10% are major successes. To try to improve the odds, the manufacturer tests new products in a customer tasting panel. Of the failures, 50% receive a poor rating in the panel, 30% a fair rating, and 20% a good rating. For the moderate successes, 20% receive a poor rating, 40% a fair rating, and 40% a good rating. For major successes, the percentages are 10% poor, 30% fair, and 60% good.

a. Find the joint probability of new product being a failure and receiving a poor rating.

b. Construct a probability table of all possible joint probabilities of new product results and panel ratings.

c. If a new product receives a good rating, what is the probability that the product will be a failure?

3.45 Create a probability tree using the probabilities in Exercise 3.44. Use the tree to find the probability that a new product will be a major success, given that it gets a poor rating.

3.46 A trucking company specializing in bulk cargos has contract customers and occasional customers. Company policy dictates that contract customers' calls receive priority; contract calls are 40% of the total. The first four calls each day are assigned immediately to trucks; if at least three of these calls are from contract customers, the dispatcher must decline any further calls that day from occasional customers.

a. Construct a probability tree for the first four calls. The first branch should be for contract or occasional customer on the first call.

b. What is the probability that the dispatcher must decline any further calls from occasional customers?

3.47 In Exercise 3.46, suppose that the dispatcher must decline further calls from occasional customers. What is the probability that all four of the first four calls were from contract customers?

3.6   BAYES' THEOREM, PRIOR AND  POSTERIOR PROBABILITIES

There is one large class of probability problems, readily solved by a probability tree or table, that occurs frequently enough to be given a name. In this section, we introduce Bayes' Theorem, which indicates how to revise probabilities in light of

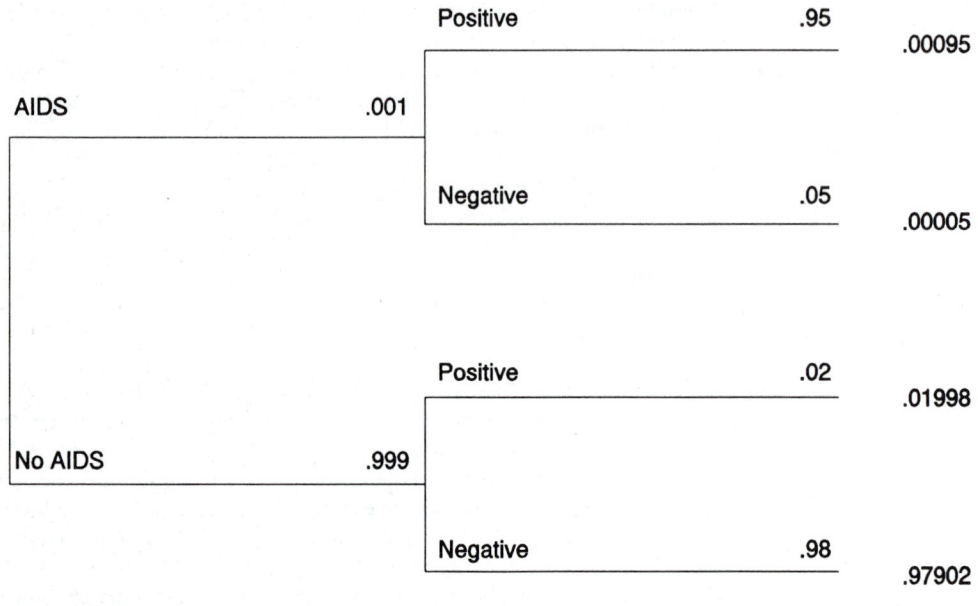

FIGURE 3.5   Probability Tree for AIDS Example

new information. This theorem is not a new concept—it is simply a sometimes-convenient combination of ideas we already know.

Suppose that in a certain population, one-tenth of 1% of all individuals are infected with the HIV virus that causes AIDS. Tests for the presence of the virus are imperfect: Suppose that 95% of those who are infected test positive; 2% of those who really are *not* infected also test positive. If a randomly chosen person tests positive, what is the probability that the person really has AIDS? We could carry out a probability tree calculation as shown in Figure 3.5.

From the tree,

$$P(\text{AIDS}\,|\,\text{positive}) = \frac{P(\text{AIDS and positive})}{P(\text{positive})}$$

$$= \frac{.00095}{.00095 + .01998} = .045$$

prior probabilities   This example has all the elements of Bayes' Theorem. We begin with **prior probabilities** of an event or "state of nature." In this case, the prior probabilities (prior, that is, before we obtain new information) apply to whether or not a randomly chosen person has AIDS. The information—in our case, the test results—is an imperfect indication of the true state; the probabilities of various information outcomes, such as positive or negative diagnoses, are called **likeli-**

likelihoods   **hoods**. These probabilities are combined to yield **posterior probabilities** (that is,
posterior   after obtaining information) of the various states of nature.
probabilities

Bayes' Theorem   skip

If $A_1, \ldots, A_k$ are mutually exclusive states of nature and if $B_1, \ldots, B_m$ are m possible mutually exclusive observable events, then

$$P(A_i \mid B_j) = \frac{P(B_j \mid A_i)P(A_i)}{P(B_j \mid A_1)P(A_1) + P(B_j \mid A_2)P(A_2) + \cdots + P(B_j \mid A_k)P(A_k)}$$

$$= \frac{P(B_j \mid A_i)P(A_i)}{\sum_i P(B_j \mid A_i)P(A_i)}$$

Bayes' Theorem summarizes tree-type calculations. In the AIDS example, the states of nature are A_1 = has AIDS, and A_2 = doesn't have AIDS; the observable events are B_1 = positive, and B_2 = negative. The numerator of Bayes' Theorem is $P(A_i$ and $B_j)$ and is found by multiplying probabilities along one particular path of the tree; for example, $P(\text{AIDS and positive}) = P(A_1$ and $B_1) = .001(.95) = .00095$. The denominator is found by adding probabilities for all paths corresponding to B_j; for example, $P(\text{positive}) = P(B_1) = .00095 + .01998$. When it applies, Bayes' Theorem is a shortcut for a tree calculation.

Sometimes the results are surprising. In the AIDS example, the posterior probability of having AIDS given a positive test result is only .045. Therefore, of all the people who got a positive result (and were terribly frightened as a result), only 4.5% actually have the disease. The positive result did increase the probability of having AIDS, as it should; but the prior probability was so low that even an increased probability is still quite small. Massive screening programs for diseases like AIDS are sometimes proposed; apart from the high cost of such programs, the "false positive" phenomenon illustrated by our example is a strong argument against such programs.

EXAMPLE 3.32   A book club classifies members as heavy, medium, or light purchasers, and separate mailings are prepared for each of these groups. Overall, 20% of the members are heavy purchasers, 30% medium, and 50% light. A member is not classified into a group until 18 months after joining the club, but a test is made of the feasibility of using the first 3 months' purchases to classify members. The following percentages are obtained from existing records of individuals classified as heavy, medium, or light purchasers.

First 3 Months' Purchases	Group		
	Heavy	Medium	Light
0	5%	15%	60%
1	10%	30%	20%
2	30%	40%	15%
3+	55%	15%	5%

a. Identify the states of nature and the observable events.
b. What is the prior probability of a light purchaser?
c. Without calculation, if a member purchases 0 books, what should happen to the probability that the member is a light purchaser?
d. Use Bayes' Theorem to calculate this probability.
e. Use a probability tree to calculate this probability.

Solution   a. There are three possible states of nature, as far as the book club is concerned: A_1 = heavy, A_2 = medium, and A_3 = light. The observable events are the purchases in the first 3 months: $B_1 = 0$, $B_2 = 1$, $B_3 = 2$, and $B_4 = 3+$.

b. Before any information about purchases in the first 3 months is gathered, the probability of being a light purchaser is specified as .50.

c. Purchasing 0 books indicates that the member is more likely to be a light purchaser. Relatively few heavy and medium purchasers buy 0 books in the first 3 months. The posterior probability of light, given 0, should be higher than .50.

d. Bayes' Theorem can be used to compute the posterior probability of light given 0.

$$P(\text{light}\,|\,0) = \frac{P(0\,|\,\text{light})P(\text{light})}{P(0\,|\,\text{light})P(\text{light}) + P(0\,|\,\text{medium})P(\text{medium}) + P(0\,|\,\text{heavy})P(\text{heavy})}$$

$$= \frac{(.60)(.50)}{(.60)(.50) + (.15)(.30) + (.05)(.20)} = .845$$

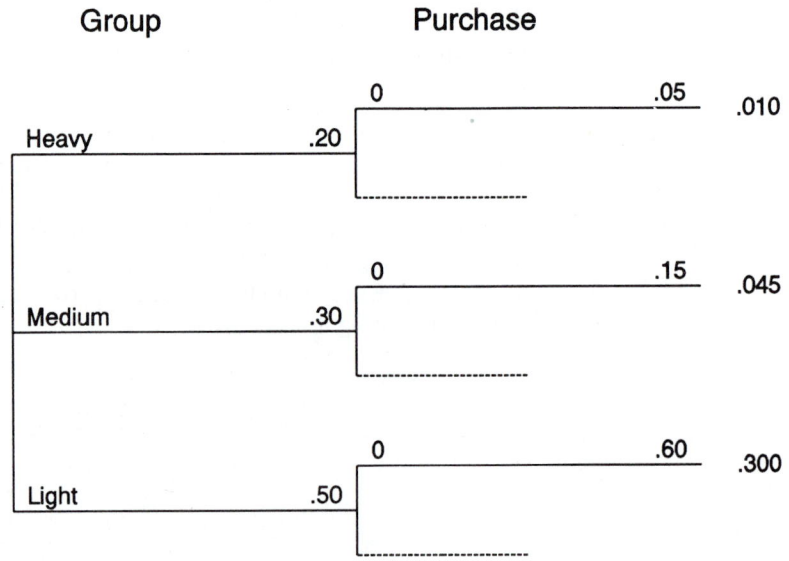

FIGURE 3.6   Probability Tree for Example 3.32

e. Part of a probability tree is shown in Figure 3.6. Only the 0 purchase branches are needed.

$$P(\text{light} \mid 0) = \frac{P(\text{light and } 0)}{P(0)}$$

$$= \frac{.300}{.300 + .045 + .010}$$

$$= .845 \qquad \blacksquare$$

EXAMPLE 3.33   Television commercials vary in their effectiveness. An advertising agency produced a TV commercial for a mature product (radial tires for cars). The brand manager estimates subjectively that the commercial has a 20% chance of being effective (market share increases after its showing), a 70% chance of being adequate (market share unchanged), and a 10% chance of being disastrous (market share decreases). The commercial can be tested by a panel of consumers. Past experience with such panels indicates that they are moderately reliable predictors of effectiveness. The brand manager estimates the likelihoods of positive, neutral, and negative panel reactions (given the eventual result) as follows:

Result of	Panel Reaction		
Commercial	Positive	Neutral	Negative
Effective	.60	.30	.10
Adequate	.40	.30	.30
Disastrous	.10	.30	.60

How should the probability that the commercial will be effective be changed by a neutral panel reaction? Verify your answer using Bayes' Theorem.

Solution   The observable event "neutral reaction" is statistically independent of the states of nature "result of commercial." The (conditional) probability of a neutral reaction is the same for all results. Therefore, the probability of an effective commercial shouldn't be changed at all by a neutral reaction. Using Bayes' Theorem,

$$P(\text{effective} \mid \text{neutral}) = \frac{P(\text{neutral} \mid \text{effective})P(\text{effective})}{P(\text{neutral} \mid \text{effective})P(\text{effective})}$$
$$+ P(\text{neutral} \mid \text{adequate})P(\text{adequate})$$
$$+ P(\text{neutral} \mid \text{disastrous})P(\text{disastrous})$$

$$= \frac{(.20)(.30)}{(.20)(.30) + (.70)(.30) + (.10)(.30)} = .20$$

The posterior probability is the same as the prior probability, as it should be when the observable event is statistically independent of the true state of nature.

■

SECTION 3.6   EXERCISES

3.48   One percent of a finance company's loans are defaulted (not completely repaid). The company routinely runs credit checks on all loan applicants. It finds that 30% of defaulted loans went to poor risks, 40% to fair risks, and 30% to good risks. Of the nondefaulted loans, 10% went to poor risks, 40% to fair risks, and 50% to good risks.
   a. Use a probability tree to calculate the probability that a poor-risk loan is defaulted.
   b. Use Bayes' Theorem to calculate the same probability.

3.49   Refer to Exercise 3.48. Show that the posterior probability of default, given a fair risk, equals the prior probability of default. Explain why this is a reasonable result.

3.50   A manufacturing firm has three machine operators who produce a certain component. Operator A has a 5% defective rate, B has a 3% defective rate, and C has a 2% defective rate. The three operators produce equal numbers of components. Suppose that a randomly selected component is found to be defective. Calculate the posterior probability that the part was produced by A. Compare the result to the prior probability of 1/3.

3.51   An underwriter of home insurance policies studies the problem of home fires resulting from wood-burning stoves. Of all homes having such stoves, 30% own a Type 1 stove, 25% a Type 2 stove, 15% a Type 3, and 30% other types. Five percent of Type 1 stoves, 3% of Type 2, 2% of Type 3, and 4% of other types have resulted in fires over three years of operation. If a fire occurs in a particular home, what is the probability that a Type 1 stove is in the home?

3.52   A reviewer of textbooks has a curious "track record." An editor estimates the following rating percentages for highly successful, moderately successful, and unsuccessful books:

	Reviewer's Rating		
Book	Good	Fair	Poor
Highly successful	5%	20%	75%
Moderately successful	15%	40%	45%
Unsuccessful	50%	30%	20%

About 10% of all books are highly successful, 50% are moderately successful, and 40% are unsuccessful.

If this reviewer rates a book as good, calculate the posterior probability that the book is unsuccessful. Compare the result to the prior probability, .40.

3.53   Conditional probabilities can be useful in diagnosing disease. Suppose that three different, closely related diseases (A_1, A_2, and A_3) occur in 25%, 15%, and 12% of the population. In addition, suppose that any one of three mutually exclusive symptom states B_1, B_2, and B_3 may be associated with each of these diseases. Experience shows that the likelihood $P(B_j|A_i)$ of having a given symptom state when the disease is present is as shown in this table:

Symptom State B_j	Disease State A_i		
	A_1	A_2	A_3
B_1	.08	.17	.10
B_2	.18	.12	.14
B_3	.06	.07	.08
B_4 (no symptoms)	.68	.64	.68

Find the probability of disease A_2 given symptom B_1, B_2, B_3, and B_4, respectively.

3.54 A realtor subjectively estimates that the probability of a weak housing market in the region for the next year is .4, the probability of a normal market is .5, and the probability of a strong market is only .1. Early spring sales are something of an indicator of the year's market. In weak years, the respective probabilities of poor, fair, and good early spring sales are .5, .3, and .2. In normal years, the probabilities are .2, .6, and .2 for poor, fair, and good sales, respectively; in strong years, the probabilities are .1, .3, and .6.
   a. Which probabilities should be regarded as prior probabilities, and which ones should be regarded as likelihoods?
   b. If early sales are good, should the probability of a weak year be increased or decreased? Don't do calculations to answer this question; use your head.
   c. Use Bayes' Theorem to calculate the probability of a weak year, given that early sales are good. Did the probability change as you predicted in part (b)?

3.55 a. Construct a probability tree using the information in Exercise 3.54. Use it to find the probabilities of weak, normal, and strong years, given good early sales.
   b. If early sales are good, is the most probable result for the year a strong market?

3.56 The teachers' contract in a unionized school district is about to expire. The superintendent estimates that there is about a 20% chance of a strike in September. Experience with school negotiations indicates that the initial salary demand is related to eventual strikes. In negotiations that end in strikes, the initial salary demand is for "full catch-up" (to the best salaries in the metropolitan area) in 70% of cases, "partial catch-up" in 20% of cases, and "stay even" in the remaining 10% of cases. In negotiations that do not end in strikes, only 40% of the initial demands are "full catch-up," 50% are "partial catch-up," and 10% are "stay even."
   a. If the initial salary demand in the district is for "full catch-up," should the superintendent increase or decrease the probability of a strike? Why?
   b. Use Bayes' Theorem to calculate the probability of a strike, given a "full catch-up" initial demand.
   c. Construct a probability tree to find this probability.

3.57 In Exercise 3.56, suppose that the initial contract demand is a "stay even" one. Should the probability of a strike increase or decrease from the initial .20? Why?

Summary   ■

The concepts of probability discussed in this chapter will be fundamental to our development of inference and prediction methods later in the book. Probability is the basic language of randomness and uncertainty, which are key concepts in statistical thinking.

Probability statements may be interpreted classically as a ratio of favorable to total outcomes (when the outcomes are assumed equally likely), as long-run relative frequencies, or as subjective expressions of personal opinion. The classical interpretation and the idea of sampling randomly from a population provide a convenient framework for understanding the basic definitions and principles of probability. The same definitions and laws can be stated more generally in terms of set theoretic notions of sample space, outcome, event, union, intersection, and complement.

Key definitions include mutually exclusive events (the occurrence of one such event makes the others impossible); independent events (the occurrence of one such event doesn't change the probability of others at all); and conditional probability. Key laws of probability are addition (for the occurrence of one or another event, most easily done when the events are mutually exclusive); complements (for finding the probability that an event does not happen); and multiplication (for finding the joint probability that several events happen).

There are several useful devices for understanding the reasoning of probability problems. Venn diagrams, probability tables, and probability trees can be tried to see if they help to clarify a probability situation. A particular formula, Bayes' Theorem, is a summary of the calculations involved in using prior probabilities and data likelihoods to find posterior probabilities of states of nature, given data; this formula summarizes work that can also be done using probability trees.

KEY TOPICS AND FORMULAS: A First Look at Probability

1. Interpretations of probability
   a. Classical interpretation: $P(\text{event E}) = \dfrac{N_E}{N}$
   b. Long-run relative frequency: $P(\text{event E}) = \dfrac{n_E}{n}$
   c. Subjective or personal probability
2. Basic concepts
   a. Experiment: Any situation that has more than one possible result
   b. Sample space, S: The set of all possible results for an experiment
   c. Outcome: An element of the sample space
   d. Event: A collection of outcomes
3. Basic axioms of probability for any event A
   a. $0 \leq P(A) \leq 1$
   b. $P(S) = 1$
   c. If two events A and B have no outcomes in common, $P(\text{A or B}) = P(A) + P(B)$.
4. Event relations and probability laws
   a. Complement of an event A: The set of all outcomes in S that are not in A
   b. Union, $A \cup B$: The set of all outcomes either in A or B or in both

c. Intersection, $A \cap B$: The set of outcomes in both A and B
d. Mutually exclusive events: A and B are mutually exclusive if $A \cap B$ contains no outcomes.
e. Addition law: $P(A \cup B) = P(A) + P(B) - P(A \cap B)$
f. Complement law: $P(A) = 1 - P(\bar{A})$
g. Multiplication law: $P(A \cap B) = P(A)P(B|A) = P(B)P(A|B)$
h. Statistical independence: A and B are independent if $P(A|B) = P(A)$, or equivalently, if $P(B|A) = P(B)$, or if $P(A \cap B) = P(A)P(B)$.

5. Bayes' Theorem: $P(A_i|B_j) = \dfrac{P(B_j|A_i)P(A_i)}{\sum P(B_j|A_i)P(A_i)}$

CHAPTER 3 EXERCISES

3.58 Airlines often accept tickets bought for other airlines' flights to the same destination. Suppose that final accounting and settlement of all such tickets is made yearly, and that approximate monthly settlements are made on the basis of random samples of the month's accumulated tickets. Airline A draws a monthly sample of 60 tickets, which may have been bought from airlines B, C, or D. Indicate what a typical outcome of this experiment would be. Should all the outcomes be regarded as equally likely?

3.59 Suppose that in the packaged-cereals industry, 29% of all vice presidents hold MBA degrees, 24% hold undergraduate business degrees, and 8% hold both. A vice president is to be selected at random.
a. Construct a Venn diagram for this situation.
b. What is the probability that the vice president holds either an MBA or an undergraduate business degree (or both)?
c. What is the probability that the vice president holds neither degree?

3.60 In Exercise 3.59, what is the probability that the vice president holds one degree or the other, but not both?

3.61 Suppose that the records of an automobile maker show that, for a certain compact car model, 50% of all customers order air conditioning, 49% order power steering, and 26% order both. An order is selected randomly.
a. Draw a Venn diagram for this situation.
b. What is the probability that air conditioning is ordered but power steering is not?
c. What is the probability that neither option is ordered?

3.62 In Exercise 3.61, suppose that 68% of all customers order automatic transmissions, 19% order automatic transmissions and power steering without air conditioning, 13% order automatic transmissions and air conditioning without power steering, and 21% order all three options.
a. Construct a Venn diagram for this situation.
b. What is the probability that at least one of the options is ordered?
c. What is the probability that exactly one option is ordered?

3.63 Use the data of Exercises 3.61 and 3.62 to find P(automatic transmission $\cap$ air conditioning). Are these events independent?

3.64 Proponents of the random walk theory of stock prices hold that predictions of whether a particular stock will do better or worse than the market in the short run (say, over a one-month period) are no better than what could be obtained by flipping a fair coin. Suppose that a securities analyst selects eight stocks that are predicted to beat the market in the next month.

a. What is the probability that all eight stocks do beat the market, assuming the validity of the random walk theory?

b. State the assumptions you made in answering part (a).

3.65 Refer to Exercise 3.64 and assume that the random walk theory of stock behavior is valid. Suppose that each of 100 different analysts selects eight stocks.

a. What is the probability that no analyst gets eight winners?

b. What is the probability that at least one analyst gets eight winners?

3.66 A paperback book seller estimates the following probabilities for the weekly sales of a particular historical romance:

Sales:	10	20	30	40
Probability:	.40	.30	.20	.10

Assume independence of sales from week to week.

a. Construct a probability table for the joint probabilities of various sales levels in week 1 and week 2.

b. Find the probability that the average sales level per week (over a two-week period) is 25.

3.67 Do you believe that the independence assumption made in Exercise 3.67 is reasonable?

3.68 A purchasing department finds that 75% of its special orders are received on time. Of those orders that are on time, 80% meet specifications completely; of those orders that are late, 60% meet specifications.

a. Find the probability that an order is on time and meets specifications.

b. Construct a probability table or tree for this situation.

c. Find the probability that an order meets specifications.

3.69 For the situation of Exercise 3.68, suppose that four orders are placed.

a. Find the probability that all four orders meet specifications.

b. State what assumptions you made in answering part (a).

3.70 A large credit card company finds that 50% of all cardholders pay a given monthly bill in full.

a. Suppose two cardholders are chosen at random. What is the probability that both pay a monthly bill in full? (The number of cardholders is so large that you need not worry about whether the choice is made with replacement or without.)

b. Suppose a cardholder is chosen at random. What is the probability that the holder pays both of two consecutive monthly bills in full?

c. What did you assume in answering parts (a) and (b)? Does the assumption seem unreasonable in either case?

3.71 A more detailed examination of the records of the credit card company in Exercise 3.70 shows that 90% of the customers who pay one monthly bill in full also pay the next monthly bill in full; only 10% of the customers who pay less than the full amount of one monthly bill pay the next monthly bill in full.

a. Find the probability that a randomly chosen customer pays two consecutive monthly bills in full.

b. Find the probability that a randomly chosen customer pays neither of two consecutive monthly bills in full.

c. Find the probability that a randomly chosen customer pays exactly one of two consecutive monthly bills in full.

3.72 In Exercise 3.71, if a randomly chosen customer pays the second monthly bill in full, what is the probability that that customer also pays the first monthly bill in full?

3.73 Records of a men's clothing shop show that alterations are required for 40% of the suit jackets that are bought and for 30% of the suit trousers. Alterations are required for both jacket and trousers in 22% of the purchases.
   a. Find the probability that no alterations are required in a randomly chosen purchase. You may want to draw a Venn diagram.
   b. Find the probability that alterations are required for either the jacket or the trousers, but not for both.

3.74 Are the events in Exercise 3.73, "alteration to jacket" and "alteration to trousers," independent?

3.75 Suppose that in Exercise 3.73 a customer purchases two suits made by different manufacturers.
   a. What is the probability that both suit jackets require alterations?
   b. What did you assume in answering part (a)? Is the assumption reasonable?

3.76 A computer-supply retailer selected one batch of 10,000 disks and attempted to format them all for a particular machine. There were 8847 perfect disks, 1128 disks that were usable but had bad sectors, and 25 disks that couldn't be used at all.
   a. What is the probability that a randomly chosen disk is not perfect?
   b. If the disk is not perfect, what is the probability that it is not usable at all?

CASE

Probability Principles

The president of a small market research firm faced a problem with the data from a recent survey ordered by a major bank. The bank was considering a shift to consolidated billing of its revolving credit accounts (typically credit cards and equity loans). The change would have the most impact on customers who had multiple accounts with the bank, so the bank was most interested in the opinions of multiple-account customers.

The bank had provided the market research firm with random samples of essentially equal size from three lists of customers. The "pink" list (provided on pink index cards) was sampled from 190,878 customers and supposedly contained customers with no revolving accounts; the "yellow" list, a sample from 48,328 customers supposedly with exactly one such account; and the "blue" list, a sample from 21,539 customers supposedly with two or more accounts. The market researchers conducted phone interviews with all the customers; they asked each customer for an opinion on the proposed billing change and they also asked how many accounts the customer had. Tabulation of the responses showed that the customers disagreed with the bank on how many accounts they had.

		Reported Number of Accounts			
		0	1	2+	Total
	Pink	66	56	28	150
Sample	Yellow	24	90	36	150
	Blue	46	16	89	151
	Total	136	162	153	451

A check with the bank indicated that the lists were several months old, so that many customers had, in the meantime, changed the number of accounts they had with the bank. The market researchers also tabulated opinions on the proposed consolidated billing method.

Pink Sample

		Reported Number of Accounts		
		0	1	2+
	Favor	31	32	16
Opinion	Neutral	20	18	8
	Oppose	15	6	4

Yellow Sample

		Reported Number of Accounts		
		0	1	2+
	Favor	9	41	19
Opinion	Neutral	7	30	9
	Oppose	8	19	8

Blue Sample

		Reported Number of Accounts		
		0	1	2+
	Favor	18	6	44
Opinion	Neutral	21	5	20
	Oppose	7	5	25

The president has asked you for help in estimating the proportions of people in each account group having each opinion. For example, what proportion of those who have two or more accounts favor the change? The president understands that the data are subject to sampling variation, but mostly wants help in obtaining logical estimates of these proportions. In addition, the president is concerned whether these estimates would depend heavily on the numbers of customers from which the lists were drawn; everyone was suspicious of the accuracy of those numbers. Prepare a report: The justification for your answer will be an important part of the firm's report to the bank, so you should explain your logic as clearly as possible.

Review Exercises Chapters 2–3   ■

These exercises are intended to help you check your understanding of the topics in the chapters just completed. The problems are *not* in any particular order, so you can't tell how to do a problem by its location.

R1 Samples of car door locks from four different suppliers are tested to determine the number of times that the locks can be operated before they fail. The data, in thousands, are

Supplier	Operations Before Failure									
A	24.7	19.8	22.0	37.6	21.8	25.4	20.6	48.7	23.9	22.6
B	26.8	25.7	39.7	25.8	28.0	52.4	29.4	31.1	26.0	28.4
C	15.3	35.7	18.2	15.3	21.0	19.9	42.6	21.1	18.9	19.7
D	31.4	21.2	24.5	22.0	26.7	61.0	22.6	23.5	25.0	22.6

 a. Summarize the data separately for each supplier. Be sure to discuss average, variability, and skewness.

 b. Can the Empirical Rule be expected to work well for these data? Why or why not?

R2 Find the mean and variance of the combined data in Exercise R1. Can the mean be found directly from the supplier means in Exercise R1? Can the variance be found directly from the R1 variances?

R3 Prices posted on the shelves of a supermarket do not always match the correct current price of the item, because of errors in posting price changes. Suppose that over time 60% of the price changes are increases and 40% are decreases. Also suppose that 93% of the price increases are posted correctly, as are 98% of the price decreases. If a price change is not posted correctly, what is the probability that the change is a decrease?

R4 A study of small savings and loan associations yielded the following financial information:

Deposits ($000,000)	Capital ($000,000)	Reserves ($000,000)	Bad Debts (Percent of Portfolio)	Type of Bank (1 = Savings, 2 = Joint S & L, 3 = Stock S & L)
3.68	1.14	0.97	1.62	2
11.64	4.03	3.28	0.97	1
31.62	10.63	9.22	2.00	3
2.62	0.85	0.53	3.97	2
1.97	0.61	0.79	0.75	1
15.21	5.21	3.77	1.11	3
3.88	0.65	1.10	1.77	2
5.01	1.00	1.15	0.32	1
7.53	1.16	3.02	4.31	3
3.67	0.89	0.92	1.12	2

a. Calculate means and standard deviations for all relevant variables.

b. Are there any outliers in any of the variables?

R5   A coal-burning electric generator occasionally is improperly stoked and emits unacceptable amounts of various gases. In the long run, this problem occurs in 1% of the generator's operating time. An air sample is taken and analyzed every hour. The analysis is not a perfect indicator of gas emissions. Calibration tests indicate that if the generator is emitting acceptable levels of the gases, the test shows excess emissions 4% of the time, borderline emissions 5% of the time, and acceptable emissions 91% of the time. If the generator is emitting excessive amounts of the gases, the test shows excess emissions 92% of the time, borderline emissions 5% of the time, and acceptable emissions 3% of the time. If the test indicates excess emissions, what is the probability that the generator is in fact emitting unacceptable amounts of the gases?

R6   Show that "borderline emissions in the test" and "unacceptable emissions by the generator" are independent events in Exercise R5.

R7   A supermarket chain does a study of the effectiveness of its own coupons in inducing additional sales in the meat department. The data from the preliminary pilot study were

X_1 Cents Off	X_2 Current Price (Cents)	X_3 Type of Meat	X_4 Normal Sales	X_5 Sales in Coupon Week
29	379	1	37,000	42,000
19	109	2	67,200	79,900
50	399	1	21,200	32,500
25	199	5	11,600	12,900
59	209	4	18,800	22,800
100	379	1	37,000	51,300
20	109	2	67,200	83,100
40	229	3	12,000	13,200
79	399	1	21,200	36,000
50	209	4	18,800	20,100
29	109	2	67,200	83,900
30	379	1	37,000	40,900
50	229	3	12,000	14,100

a. Calculate the mean and standard deviation of X_3.

b. What is the interpretation of the numbers determined in (a)?

R8   Calculate means, medians, and standard deviations of X_4, X_5, and $Y = X_5 - X_4$ in Exercise R7. Is there a simple relation among the means? Does the same relation hold for the medians? for the standard deviations?

R9   Calculate the skewness value of Y as defined in Exercise R8. Does the resulting number confirm your visual impression of the skewness of Y?

R10   Experience indicates that about 10% of new television shows place in the top third of all shows in audience ratings during the first year. About 40% place in the middle third and about 50% place in the bottom third. Of new shows placing in the top third, only 2% are cancelled; 40% of shows placing in the middle third are cancelled, as are 85% of shows placing in the bottom third.

R11 In Exercise R10, are rating and cancellation assumed to be independent? What would independence mean in this context?

R12 Junior managers in a firm are rated by their bosses in terms of current performance and managerial potential. The current performance ratings are 18% excellent, 71% satisfactory, and 11% unsatisfactory. The managerial potential ratings are 24% definite, 40% possible, and 36% unlikely.

a. Find the probability that a randomly selected junior manager will be rated "excellent" on the performance scale and "definite" on the potential scale.

b. What did you assume in answering part (a)? Are the assumptions reasonable? If not, is the probability you calculated likely to be too low or too high?

R13 Records for a sample of employees in a large firm indicate the following distribution of claimed deduction on W-4 tax withholding forms.

Deductions:	0	1	2	3	4	5	6
	7	8	9	10	11	12	
Frequency:	201	287	364	332	151	97	52
	28	11	5	2	0	3	

a. Find the mean number of deductions.

b. Find the standard deviation. Does it make much difference if the data are regarded as a sample rather than a population?

c. How well does the Empirical Rule work for data within one standard deviation of the mean?

R14 A W-4 form is drawn at random from the data of Exercise R13.

a. What is the probability that it claims at least one deduction?

b. If the form claims at least one deduction, what is the probability that it claims at most three?

R15 Data are collected on the total compensation (salary plus bonuses) of samples of men and women junior managers in a firm. The data (in thousands of dollars per year) were

Men:	39.6	28.9	35.4	36.8	33.7	32.8	35.1	36.7	38.4	35.7	33.1
	31.6	34.7	33.8	36.2	34.9	35.7	40.2	36.5	37.4	35.2	36.6
Women:	34.2	31.8	32.7	27.6	33.0	38.1	33.0	31.5	29.8	31.8	44.7
	22.5	30.0	34.3	31.0	32.5	.	.	.	.	.	.

a. From the looks of the data, should the mean and median compensation for men be similar? Calculate them.

b. Show that the smaller group has a larger range than the other. Explain what causes this phenomenon.

R16 Construct box plots for both sets of data in Exercise R15. Include a check for outliers.

R17 Calculate the mean and median compensation for the combined sample of managers in Exercise R15. How do these values relate to the means and medians of the two groups separately?

R18 Data from an automobile manufacturer indicate that, of all cars repaired under warranty, 57% require engine work, 47% require interior work, and 30% require exterior work. Also, 23% require both engine and interior work, 7% both engine and exterior work, and 13% both interior and exterior work; 5% require all three types of work. There are some cars that require other types of work.

a. Find the probability that a car repaired under warranty requires engine work but no interior or exterior work.

b. Find the probability that a car requires exactly one of the three types of work.

c. Are the events "engine work" and "interior work" independent?

R19   A cereal manufacturer collects samples of the time required for workers to clean out the manufacturing line when switching from production of one cereal to production of another. The data, in actual worker-hours expended, were

Previous Flour Base	Time									
Corn	10.0	11.0	11.5	9.5	10.0	12.5	8.5	9.0	10.0	10.5
	11.5	13.0	9.5	16.5	14.5	11.0	10.5	10.0	11.0	15.0
Oats	13.5	11.0	10.0	11.5	12.0	10.5	11.0	16.5	13.0	19.0
	12.5	17.0	11.0	13.5	12.0	11.0	13.5	15.0	.	.
Wheat	28.0	31.0	33.0	35.0	30.0	28.5	27.5	26.5	32.0	24.0
	30.5	32.0	31.5	40.5	31.0	33.0	30.5	33.0	28.5	47.5
	31.0	33.5	35.0	33.5	30.0	36.5	39.5	29.0	30.5	.

a. Draw appropriate plots of the three sets of times. What is the general shape of the data?

b. Calculate the means and medians for the three sets of times. Does the relation between the resulting means and medians confirm your judgment about the shapes?

R20   Calculate the mean and median for the combined samples in Exercise R19. Is this a reasonable summary figure for a typical cleaning time?

4

RANDOM VARIABLES AND PROBABILITY DISTRIBUTIONS

The probability ideas and laws developed in Chapter 3 apply to any kind of experiment, whether it yields qualitative or quantitative results. We will use these probability ideas mostly with numerical quantitative data; we will consider ideas like averaging that apply only to quantitative results. To make connections of probability concepts with ideas like mean and standard deviation from Chapter 2, we need some additional probability ideas. The key ideas are the notions of a random variable (Section 4.1) and probability distribution (Sections 4.2 and 4.3). Once we have these ideas, we can link probability ideas such as independence with ideas of mean and standard deviation in the following sections of this chapter. Finally, in an appendix, we derive some of the relevant mathematics.

4.1   RANDOM VARIABLE: BASIC IDEAS   ∎

Many of the probability issues most relevant to managers involve random, numerical outcomes. For example, the number of no-shows on a particular flight (people holding reservations for the flight who don't actually take the flight) is critically important in establishing an airline's reservation policy. The number of no-shows is random, varying from one flight to another and from day to day on the same flight. Certainly, the number of no-shows is a numerical variable. It makes perfectly good sense to talk about the average number of no-shows. The concept of random variable is the central idea in understanding random, numerical outcomes.

random variable   Informally, a **random variable** is a quantitative (numerical) result from a random experiment. For instance, consider the experiment of selecting a manager randomly from the middle management of an automobile manufacturer. Define the random variable Y to be number of years of formal schooling the manager has had. First of all, Y is numerical; the result will be a number like

12 or 16, not a category like "private college." Secondly, Y is subject to random variation. If the experiment is repeated with a new random selection, the result very likely will change. These two features—numerical result, subject to randomness—are the key aspects of the definition of a random variable.

To specify a random variable, we need to know its possible values and their respective probabilities. For the years of formal schooling example, the possible values could be 0, 1, 2,..., up to some maximum number, perhaps 20. Probabilities could be obtained from company personnel records; for example, if 284 of the 500 managers had completed exactly 4 years of college (after 4 years of high school), the probability that $Y = 16$ would be $284/500 = .568$. Probabilities for other values could be filled in similarly.

Random Variable: Informal Definition

A random variable is any quantitative result from an experiment that is subject to random variability. It is determined by specifying its possible values and the probability associated with each value.

The probability associated with each value of a random variable is found by adding the probabilities for all outcomes that are assigned that value. If Y = number of heads in three flips of a fair coin, we have the following sample space:

Outcome	HHH	HHT	HTH	THH	HTT	THT	TTH	TTT
Probability	1/8	1/8	1/8	1/8	1/8	1/8	1/8	1/8
Value assigned by Y	3	2	2	2	1	1	1	0

Then, for instance,

$$P(Y = 2) = P(\text{HHT}) + P(\text{HTH}) + P(\text{THH}) = \frac{1}{8} + \frac{1}{8} + \frac{1}{8} = \frac{3}{8}$$

To make connections with the probability principles of Chapter 3, we need a more formal definition of a random variable. The definition can be understood by considering what we did in the coin-flipping example in the previous paragraph. We listed all the outcomes in a sample space. Then the nature of the random variable gave us a rule for assigning a *numerical* result to each outcome. Then we could use the sample space to specify possible values and assign probabilities.

Random Variable: Formal Definition

Given a sample space S, a random variable is a rule (function) that assigns a numerical value to each outcome in S.

In practice we don't need to follow the formal definition too rigidly. Stating the values and probabilities for a random variable implicitly defines a sample space; namely, the values themselves. A perfectly valid sample space for the coin-flipping situation is $S = \{0, 1, 2, 3\}$, with the same 1/8, 3/8, 3/8, 1/8 probabilities assumed. There's no logical need to do more than specify possible values and their probabilities unless it is convenient to list all the outcomes first.

The custom is to denote random variables by capital letters at the end of the alphabet; thus we might define X = number of heads observed in three flips of a coin and Y = number of Theater Guild subscribers in a random sample of 200 persons. Possible values of a random variable are usually denoted by the corresponding lowercase letter; we would say that x could be 0, 1, 2, or 3 and y could be 0, 1, 2, ..., 200. The subtle distinction between Y, the random variable itself, and y, one of its possible values, becomes clear with practice.

EXAMPLE 4.1   Suppose that a random sample of two persons is to be selected from a large population consisting of 30% Theater Guild subscribers and 70% nonsubscribers.
  a. List the outcomes that make up the sample space.
  b. Assign probabilities.
  c. Define the quantitative random variable Y as the number of Theater Guild subscribers in the sample. Specify the possible values that the random variable may assume and determine the probability of each.

Solution   a. If we let S designate a subscriber and N a nonsubscriber, then the possible outcomes for the two persons sampled are

$$S = \{(S, S); (S, N); (N, S); \text{ and } (N, N)\}$$

b. From the statement of the problem we know that $P(S) = .3$ and $P(N) = .7$. Under the assumption that the outcomes for the two persons sampled are independent, we have the following probabilities associated with the four outcomes:

$$
\begin{aligned}
P(S, S) &= (.3)^2 = &.09 \\
P(S, N) &= (.3)(.7) = &.21 \\
P(N, S) &= (.7)(.3) = &.21 \\
P(N, N) &= (.7)^2 = &\underline{.49} \\
& &1.00
\end{aligned}
$$

c. If the random variable Y is the number of subscribers in a sample of two from the populations of interest, then the possible values for Y are 0, 1, and 2. The probabilities associated with these values can be determined from probabilities for the outcomes that make up each numerical event.

Outcome	Probability	y	$P(y)$
(N, N)	.49	0	.49
(N, S)	.21	1	.42
(S, N)	.21	1	
(S, S)	.09	2	.09

■

discrete and
continuous
random variables

The random variables we have considered so far have been **discrete**: their possible values have been distinct and separate, like 0 or 1 or 2 or 3. Other random variables are most usefully considered to be **continuous**: Their possible values form a whole interval (or range, or continuum). For instance, the one-year return per dollar invested in a common stock could range from 0 to something quite large. In practice, virtually all random variables assume a discrete set of values; the return per dollar of a million-dollar common-stock investment could be 1.06219423 or 1.06219424 or 1.06219425 or.... But, when there are many, many possible values for a random variable, it is sometimes mathematically useful to treat that random variable as continuous. In fact, one of the most important theoretical probability specifications—the bell-shaped normal distribution—formally applies only to continuous random variables. In Section 4.2 we define some language and notation for discrete random variables. In Section 4.3 we extend these ideas to continuous random variables.

4.2   PROBABILITY DISTRIBUTIONS FOR DISCRETE RANDOM VARIABLES

probability
distribution

The **probability distribution** for a discrete random variable Y is a function $P_Y(y)$ that assigns a probability to each value y of the random variable Y. **The probability distribution for Y can be expressed as a formula, a graph, or a table.**

The properties of the probability distribution for a discrete random variable Y are listed here.

Properties of the Probability Distribution for a Discrete Random Variable Y

1. The probability $P_Y(y)$ associated with each value of Y must lie in the interval

$$0 \le P_Y(y) \le 1$$

2. The sum of the probabilities for all values of Y equals 1.

$$\sum_{\text{all } y} P_Y(y) = 1$$

3. Because different values of Y are mutually exclusive events, their probabilities are additive. Thus

$$P(Y = a \text{ or } Y = b) = P_Y(a) + P_Y(b)$$

For the random variable Y = number of heads in three tosses of a fair coin, we might define $P_Y(y)$ by a table, as follows:

y	0	1	2	3
$P_Y(y)$	1/8	3/8	3/8	1/8

Or we might use the formula

$$P_Y(y) = \frac{3!}{y!(3-y)!}\left(\frac{1}{8}\right)$$

where in general $k! = k(k-1)(k-2)\cdots(1)$ and $0! = 1$ by convention. Substituting $y = 0, 1, 2,$ and 3 into the formula yields the same probabilities as those listed in the previous table:

y	0	1	2	3
$P_Y(y)$	$\dfrac{3\cdot2\cdot1}{(1)(3\cdot2\cdot1)}\dfrac{1}{8}=\dfrac{1}{8}$	$\dfrac{3\cdot2\cdot1}{(1)(2\cdot1)}\dfrac{1}{8}=\dfrac{3}{8}$	$\dfrac{3\cdot2\cdot1}{(2\cdot1)(1)}\dfrac{1}{8}=\dfrac{3}{8}$	$\dfrac{3\cdot2\cdot1}{(3\cdot2\cdot1)(1)}\dfrac{1}{8}=\dfrac{1}{8}$

probability histogram   A graph of this probability distribution, called a **probability histogram**, is shown in Figure 4.1. The discrete random variable Y is the number of heads in three tosses of a fair coin.

cumulative distribution function   The **cumulative distribution function** is another function that is particularly appropriate when calculating probabilities and has applications in the simulation methods to be discussed in Section 6.6. In general, the cumulative distribution function F_Y for a discrete random variable Y is a function that specifies the probability that $Y \leq y$ for all values of y. Thus

$$F_Y(y) = P(Y \leq y) = P_Y(0) + P_Y(1) + \cdots + P_Y(y)$$

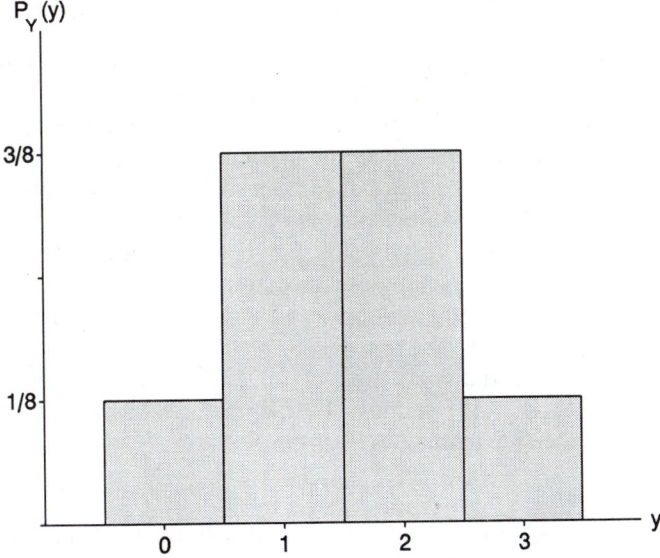

FIGURE 4.1   Graph of $P_Y(y)$ for the Coin-Tossing Experiment

This can be illustrated for the coin-tossing example discussed previously:

y	0	1	2	3
$P_Y(y)$	1/8	3/8	3/8	1/8
$F_Y(y)$	1/8	4/8	7/8	8/8

As the name suggests and these data illustrate, the cumulative distribution function at a particular value y sums all probabilities for $Y \leq y$. For example,

$$F_Y(2) = P(Y \leq 2) = \frac{1}{8} + \frac{3}{8} + \frac{3}{8} = \frac{7}{8}$$

and

$$F_Y(3) = P(Y \leq 3) = 1$$

The cumulative distribution function (abbreviated cdf) is often used in constructing probability tables so that the table user does not have to add up many table entries to find a certain probability. As an illustration, suppose that a large metropolitan teaching hospital has data on the number of acute coronary cases Y arriving at the hospital in a given day. The cdf is tabulated as follows:

y	0	1	2	3	4	5	6	7	8
$F_Y(y)$	.001	.003	.006	.011	.024	.061	.139	.224	.336

y	9	10	11	12	13	14	15	16	17
$F_Y(y)$	.510	.672	.782	.870	.925	.964	.988	.997	1.000

Suppose that the hospital has 14 coronary-care beds available at the beginning of a particular day. The probability that the number of new cases Y is less than or equal to 14 can be read directly from the table as .964. It's almost as easy to find the probability that Y is 15 or more; $P(Y \geq 15) = 1 - P(Y \leq 14) = 1 - .964 = .036$. Had the table been stated in terms of individual probabilities $P(y)$, it would have been necessary to add up many entries to find these probabilities.

General use of cdf tables is easy enough if you draw a probability histogram. A probability histogram for the coronary-care illustration is shown in Figure 4.2; the probability $P_Y(y)$ of each particular value y is indicated by the height of the rectangle erected atop that y value.

For example, suppose we want $P(7 \leq Y \leq 12)$. We want the total area of the rectangles above $y = 7, 8, 9, 10, 11,$ and 12, which are shaded in Figure 4.2. $F_Y(12)$ is the total area of all the rectangles above $y = 0, 1, \ldots, 12$; to find $P(7 \leq Y \leq 12)$ we must subtract the area of the rectangles above $y = 0, 1, 2, 3, 4, 5,$ and 6, namely, $F_Y(6)$, from $F_Y(12)$:

$$P(7 \leq Y \leq 12) = F_Y(12) - F_Y(6) = .870 - .139 = .731$$

Generally, it's useful to draw a probability histogram whenever you want to use tables to calculate probabilities.

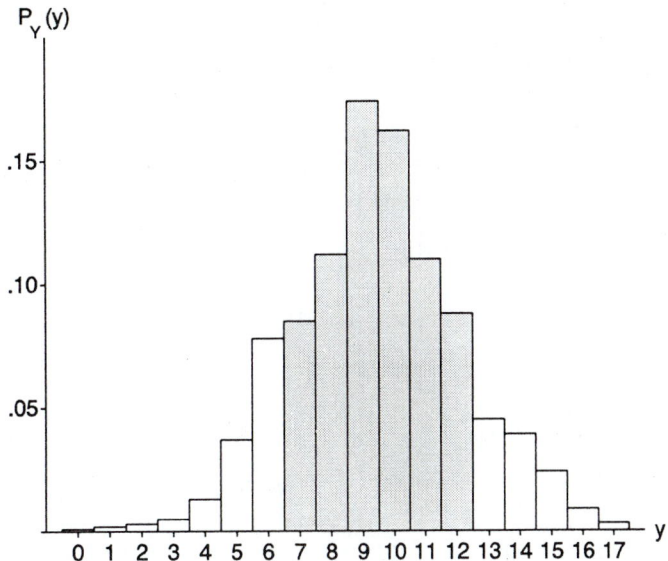

FIGURE 4.2 Probability Histogram for the Coronary-Care Illustration

EXAMPLE 4.2 Suppose that a cosmetic company plans to market a new perfume. The product manager has assessed the following subjective probabilities for the first-year sales (denoted by X) in millions of bottles:

x	0	1	2	3	4	5	6	7	8
$F_X(x)$	.05	.20	.40	.60	.75	.85	.90	.95	1.00

Find the following probabilities, as assessed by the product manager:

a. $P(X \geq 5)$
b. $P(2 \leq X \leq 4)$
c. $P(X \leq 1)$

Solution A probability histogram for this example is shown in Figure 4.3 (page 128). Areas relevant to each problem are indicated by a, b, or c.

a. $P(X \geq 5) = 1 - P(X \leq 4) = 1.00 - .75 = .25$

The area of all the rectangles is 1.00. We must subtract the areas of all rectangles through $x = 4$.

b. Subtract the areas for $x = 0, 1$ from the areas for $x = 0, 1, 2, 3, 4$ to get $P(2 \leq X \leq 4)$;

$$P(2 \leq X \leq 4) = F_X(4) - F_X(1) = .75 - .20 = .55$$

c. By definition, $P(X \leq 1) = F_X(1) = .20$; no subtraction is needed. ∎

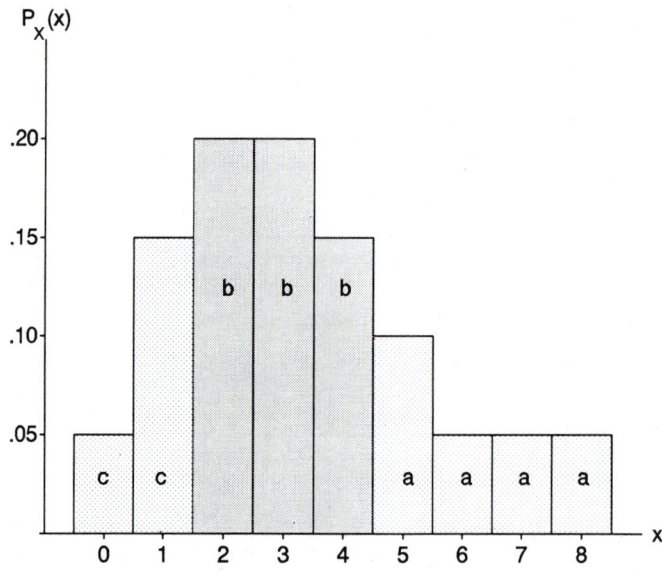

FIGURE 4.3   Probability Histogram for Example 4.2

SECTIONS 4.1 AND 4.2 EXERCISES

4.1   The personnel department of a large firm employs five men and three women as college recruiters. For visits to certain large campuses, a team of two people is sent. Suppose that two of the eight recruiters are chosen at random. Let Y = number of women selected.

a. Construct the sample space; call the recruiters A, B, ..., H.

b. Find the value of Y for each outcome in the sample space.

4.2   In Exercise 4.1, find $P_Y(y)$ by counting. Construct a probability histogram.

4.3   Find the cdf of Y in Exercise 4.1. Plot $F_Y(y)$ against y.

4.4   An appliance store has the following probabilities for Y = number of major appliances sold on a given day:

y:	0	1	2	3	4	5	6	7	8	9	10
$P_Y(y)$:	.100	.150	.250	.140	.090	.080	.060	.050	.040	.025	.015

a. Construct a probability histogram.

b. Find $P(Y \le 2)$.

c. Find $P(Y \ge 7)$.

d. Find $P(1 \le Y \le 5)$.

4.5   Calculate the cdf corresponding to $P_Y(y)$ in Exercise 4.4. Use this cdf to find $P(Y \le 2)$, $P(Y \ge 7)$, and $P(1 \le Y \le 5)$.

4.6   The weekly demand X for copies of a popular word processing program at a computer store has the probability distribution shown here.

x:	0	1	2	3	4	5	6	7	8	9	10
$P_X(x)$:	.06	.14	.16	.14	.12	.10	.08	.07	.06	.04	.03

a. What is the probability that three or more copies of the program will be demanded in a particular week?

b. What is the probability that the demand will be for at least two but no more than six?

c. The store policy is to have eight copies of the program available at the beginning of every week. What is the probability that the demand will exceed the supply in a given week?

4.7 a. Find the cumulative distribution function (cdf) $F_X(x)$ for the probability distribution shown in Exercise 4.6.

b. Use the cdf to recalculate the probabilities requested in Exercise 4.6.

4.3 PROBABILITY DISTRIBUTIONS FOR CONTINUOUS RANDOM VARIABLES (∂, $\int$) ∎

In Section 4.2 we distinguished between discrete random variables, which can assume only distinct, separate values, and continuous random variables, which can assume (for all practical purposes) a complete range of values along some interval. In this section we develop the basic concepts and notation that apply to continuous random variables.

To illustrate, suppose that a U.S. resident is to be chosen at random according to that person's nine-digit Social Security number. Define Y = the Social Security number chosen. Literally speaking, Y is a discrete random variable that can take on any one of the billion possible values 000–00–0000 to 999–99–9999. We are not overly eager to specify one billion different probabilities, so for practical reasons we regard Y as a continuous random variable that can assume all possible values between 0 and 1 billion.

It seems plausible to assume that Y probabilties are **uniform**; no one value is more likely than any other. Suppose we construct a probability histogram. First we consider only the first digit of the Social Security number drawn. Based on the assumption of uniform probability, the histogram should assign equal probabilities to all rectangles, as in Figure 4.4. If we had considered the first two digits, we would have a 100-rectangle histogram, as suggested in Figure 4.5 (page 130).

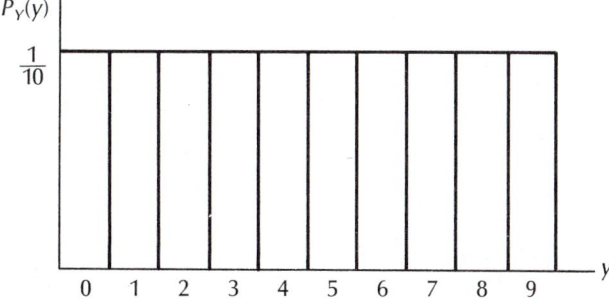

FIGURE 4.4 Uniform Probabilities: First Digit

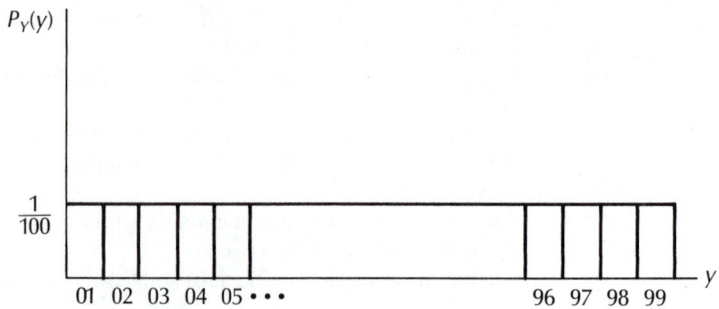

FIGURE 4.5   Uniform Probabilities: First Two Digits

As we refine this process—considering the first three digits, then the first four, and so on, we get more and more, thinner and thinner rectangles. Very soon (and in the limit, mathematically) the rectangles disappear into a continuous blur.

EXAMPLE 4.3   Suppose that a personnel manager measures Y, the actual weekly work time of supermarket employees. Construct histograms that indicate the probability distribution of Y when measurements are made

    a. to the nearest hour;
    b. to the nearest 10 minutes;
    c. to the nearest second.

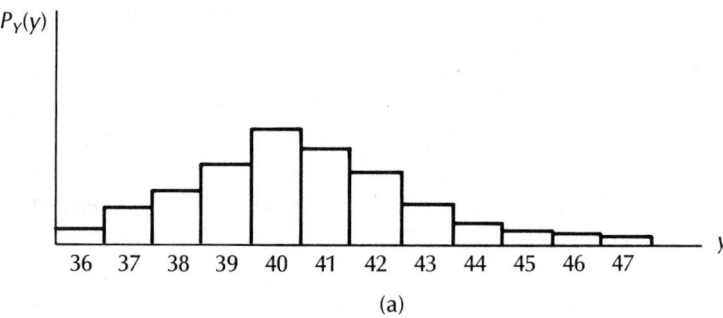

(a)

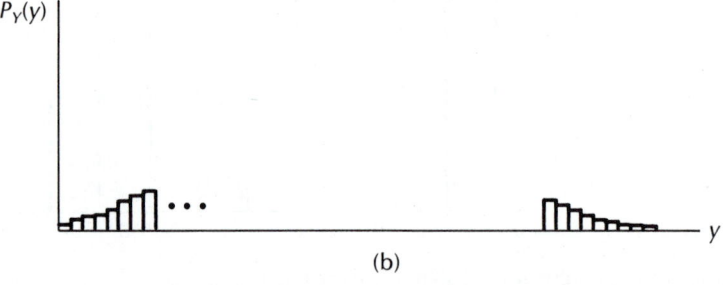

(b)

FIGURE 4.6   Histograms for Weekly Work Time

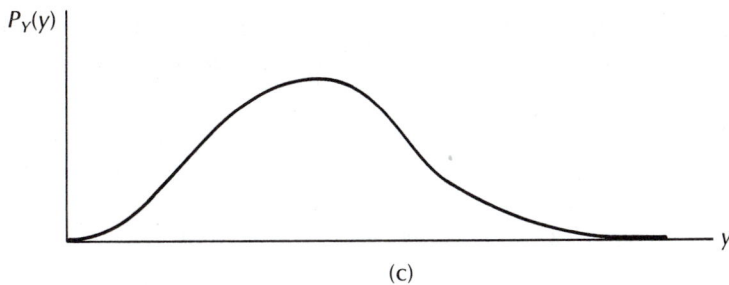

(c)

FIGURE 4.6   (*Continued*)

Solution   a. Assume a nominal 40-hour week with modest overtime. The nearest-hour histogram might look like Figure 4.6a.

b. The nearest 10-minutes histogram might look like Figure 4.6b.

c. For all practical purposes, the nearest-second histogram would look like Figure 4.6c.   ■

Probability histograms were introduced in Section 4.2 when we defined the cumulative distribution function (cdf) F. The cdf idea works just as well with continuous random variables. For a continuous random variable Y, the **cumulative distribution function** is defined as before:

cumulative distribution function

$$F_Y(y) = P(Y \le y)$$

For any particular example of a continuous random variable, the cdf is almost inevitably defined by a formula. For example, suppose that a file-transfer computer program sends lines of a program across a noisy transmission device. One important variable is $X =$ the proportion of lines correctly transmitted. Suppose that, as a model, the cdf is assumed to be

$$F_X(x) = 21x^{20} - 20x^{21}, \qquad \text{for } 0 < x < 1$$

Then the probability that the proportion of correctly transmitted lines is less than .9 is

$$F_X(.9) = 21(.9)^{20} - 20(.9)^{21} = .3647$$

and the probability that the proportion is greater than .9 is

$$1 - F_X(.9) = 1 - .3647 = .6353$$

Furthermore, the probability that the proportion X is between .7 and .9 is

$$F_X(.9) - F_X(.7) = .3647 - .0056 = .3591$$

Recalling the calculations made for discrete random variables, you might expect that in computing $P(.7 \le X \le .9)$ we would subtract $F_X(.6)$ or perhaps $F_X(.69)$ rather than $F_X(.7)$. But the probability that the continuous random variable X equals exactly .7000... is negligibly small; as a mathematical idealization, we may take the probability to be zero. Thus, in the continuous case, we may ignore the probability that the random variable is "right on the boundary."

EXAMPLE 4.4   Suppose that the reservations manager for a large airline assumes that the time T (measured in minutes) between successive phone calls to the reservation center is a continuous random variable with cdf

$$F_T(t) = 1 - e^{-2t}, \qquad \text{for } t \geq 0$$

where

$e \approx 2.7183$, the base of the natural logarithm

Find

    a. $P(T \geq 5)$
    b. $P(2 \leq T \leq 4)$
    c. $P(T \leq 1)$

Solution   The three parts of this example seem to be identical to those of Example 4.2. Because T is continuous, however, the solution procedure differs from that of Example 4.2.

    a. $P(T \geq 5) = 1 - P(T < 5)$

But, because T is a continuous random variable, $P(T = 5.000000 \ldots)$ is assumed to be zero and $P(T < 5) = P(T \leq 5)$.

$$P(T \geq 5) = 1 - P(T \leq 5) = 1 - F_T(5)$$
$$= 1 - (1 - e^{-2(5)}) = .0000454$$

(Values of e^x can be calculated by most calculators or obtained from tables.)

    b. $P(2 \leq T \leq 4) = P(T \leq 4) - P(T < 2)$

The event $T = 2.000 \ldots$ has probability zero, so

$$P(2 \leq T \leq 4) = P(T \leq 4) - P(T \leq 2)$$
$$= F_T(4) - F_T(2)$$
$$= (1 - e^{-2(4)}) - (1 - e^{-2(2)})$$
$$= .0180$$

    c. $P(T \leq 1) = F_T(1)$, by definition
$$= 1 - e^{-2(1)} = .865$$ ∎

The cumulative distribution function F means the same thing for discrete and continuous random variables. For any random variable Y, $F_Y(y) = P(Y \leq y)$. For continuous random variables, another function, the probability density function, is widely used. For a random variable Y, the probability density function is denoted $f_Y(y)$. It is roughly analogous to the probability distribution $P_X(x)$ defined for discrete random variables in that it measures how the probability is spread out—distributed—over the range of possible values of the random variable. But for a continuous random variable Y, the probability that Y exactly equals a particular number is zero. The probability density function does not yield probabilities directly. Instead this function defines a smooth curve; probability is calculated as area under the curve, using integral calculus. If both the cdf $F_Y(y)$ and the probability density function $f_y(y)$ are known, we can compute the probability that Y is between numbers a and b in two ways.

$$P(a \le Y \le b) = F_Y(b) - F_Y(a)$$

or

$$P(a \le Y \le b) = \int_a^b f_Y(y)\, dy$$

In the example in which X = the proportion of lines correctly transmitted, it can be shown that

$$f_X(x) = 21(20)x^{19}(1 - x), \qquad 0 < x < 1$$

The probability that X is larger than .9 can be computed by integrating the probability density over the region $.9 < x < 1$, because X cannot be larger than 1.

$$\begin{aligned}
P(.9 < X) &= \int_{.9}^1 21(20)x^{19}(1 - x)\, dx \\
&= \int_{.9}^1 21(20)(x^{19} - x^{20})\, dx \\
&= (21x^{20} - 20x^{21})\big|_{.9}^1 \\
&= 1 - .3647 = .6353
\end{aligned}$$

as we found previously.

EXAMPLE 4.5   The probability density function for the random variable T of Example 4.4. can be shown to have probability density

$$f_T(t) = 2e^{-2t}, \qquad t \ge 0$$

Calculate the probability that T is between 2 and 4 using this probability density.

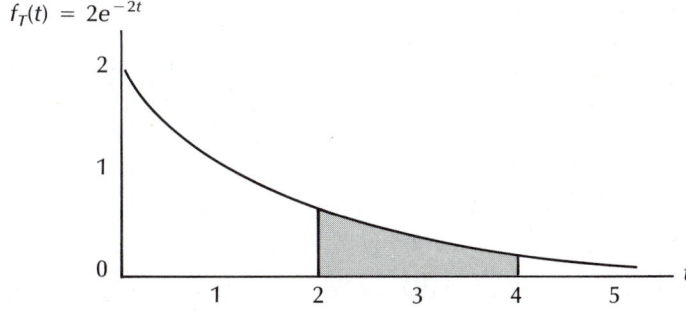

$f_T(t) = 2e^{-2t}$

FIGURE 4.7   Area (Probability) Found in Example 4.5

Solution   To solve this problem, we need the elementary calculus result that the indefinite integral of ce^{-ct} is $-e^{-ct}$. Then

$$P(2 \leq T \leq 4) = \int_2^4 2e^{-2t} \, dt = -e^{-2t} \Big|_2^4$$

$$= -.000335 - (-.018316) = .0180$$

as in Example 4.4. The calculation is shown in Figure 4.7.   ■

The probability density function $f_Y(y)$ of a continuous random variable Y may be either specified directly or derived from the cdf $F_Y(y)$. Because the calculus operation of integration is the opposite of the operation of differentiation, it follows that

$$f_Y(y) = \frac{d}{dy} F_Y(y)$$

For example, we initially specified the cdf of X = the proportion of correctly transmitted lines as

$$F_X(x) = 21x^{20} - 20x^{21}, \quad 0 < x < 1$$

Differentiation yields the expression that we used for the probability density function:

$$f_X(x) = \frac{d}{dx}(21x^{20} - 20x^{21}) = 21(20)x^{19} - 21(20)x^{20}$$

$$= 21(20)x^{19}(1 - x)$$

as previously indicated.

The process of finding the density function from the cdf may be reversed. Just as in the discrete case, where

$$F_X(x) = \sum_{x' \leq x} P_X(x')$$

in the continuous case

$$F_X(x) = \int_{-\infty}^x f_X(x') \, dx'$$

In performing the integration, one must be a bit careful to exclude regions where the random variable cannot occur and thus has a probability density of zero. If a random variable X is by definition nonnegative, the probability that it is less than zero (that is, $\int_{-\infty}^0 f_X(x) \, dx$) is zero.

EXAMPLE 4.6   Show that the probability density specified in Example 4.5 yields the cdf of Example 4.4.

Solution   We note first that T, as an elapsed time measure, cannot be negative. Therefore the probability density function of T must be zero for all values $t < 0$. The probability density of T is stated in Example 4.5 to be $f_T(t) = 2e^{-2t}$, for $t > 0$.

Thus

$$F_T(t) = \int_0^t 2e^{-2t'}\,dt' = -e^{-2t'}\big|_0^t = -e^{-2t} - (-1)$$

$$= 1 - e^{-2t}$$

as stated in Example 4.4. ∎

Generally speaking, every calculation of a discrete random variable involving a summation has an analogous calculation of a continuous random variable involving an integration. The technical difficulties in performing a particular summation or integration should not obscure the fact that the operations of summation and integration are direct analogues.

SECTION 4.3 EXERCISES

4.8 A certain charity is planning a direct mail campaign. The fraction Y of non-respondents is taken to be a continuous random variable with the following cdf:

$$F_Y(y) = 5y^4 - 4y^5, \qquad 0 \le y \le 1$$

a. Calculate $F_Y(y)$ for various values of y between 0 and 1. Sketch the function $F_Y(y)$.
b. Use the graph of $F_Y(y)$ to calculate $P(Y \le .8)$, $P(Y \ge .6)$, and $P(.5 \le Y \le .9)$.

4.9 A data-processing company owns a large computer. Access to the computer is gained via a large number of remote terminals. A reasonable probability model for the time Y (in minutes) between successive job submissions to the computer assumes that

$$F_Y(y) = 1 - e^{-.5y}, \qquad 0 \le y < \infty$$

a. Calculate numerical values of $F_Y(y)$ for $y = 1.0, 2.0, \ldots$, until $F_Y(y)$ exceeds .98 or so. Graph $F_Y(y)$ versus y.
b. Use the graph of $F_Y(y)$ to find $P(Y \le .75)$, $P(Y \ge 4.0)$, and $P(2.0 \le Y \le 3.5)$.

∫, δ 4.10 a. Show that the probability density of Y in Exercise 4.8 is

$$f_Y(y) = 20(y^3 - y^4), \qquad 0 \le y \le 1$$

b. Use this density to calculate $P(.2 \le Y \le .7)$, $P(Y \le .6)$, and $P(Y \ge .5)$.
c. Use the cdf $F_Y(y)$ to find the probabilities indicated in part (b).

∫ 4.11 A securities analyst summarizes some subjective probability estimates for the after-tax profit per share Y of a particular stock in the following continuous probability density:

$$f_Y(y) = \frac{4}{27}(9y - 6y^2 + y^3), \qquad 0 \le y \le 3$$

a. Calculate $f_Y(y)$ for several y values (such as $0, .25, .50, \ldots$) and graph $f_Y(y)$ against y.
b. Find $P(Y \le 1.50)$, $P(Y \ge 2.00)$, and $P(1 \le Y \le 2.50)$.
c. Find $F_Y(y)$ and sketch it.

∫ **4.12** The "back office" of a brokerage house owns a mainframe computer on which it processes all records of transactions. Excess computer time is sold to other companies. To determine how much time to sell, the firm has studied the distribution of Y = the computer time (in minutes) needed daily to process its own transactions. To a good approximation, the density of Y is

$$f_Y(y) = .0009375[40 - .1(y - 100)^2], \quad \text{for } 80 < y < 120$$
$$= 0, \quad \text{outside } 80 < y < 120$$

If the firm reserves 115 minutes of time daily, what is the probability that the actual required time will be longer?

∫ **4.13** Calculate the cdf $F_Y(y)$ for the density in Exercise 4.12. Use the cdf to recalculate the probability in that exercise.

∫ 4.14 The time in worker-hours required to assemble a complex manufactured item is random, with probability density

$$f_Y(y) = 3y^{-4}, \quad \text{for } 1 < y < \infty$$

a. Find the probability that an item will require between two and four worker-hours to assemble. How important is it whether 2.00 and 4.00 hours are included or excluded from the interval?

b. Find the probability that an item will require between 0.5 and 1.5 worker hours. (Think before integrating.)

∫ 4.15 a. Find the cdf $F_Y(y)$ corresponding to the density in Exercise 4.14.

b. Find the 99th percentile of times; that is, solve $F_Y(y) = .99$.

4.4   EXPECTED VALUE, VARIANCE, AND STANDARD DEVIATION: DISCRETE RANDOM VARIABLES ▪

In Sections 4.2 and 4.3 we introduced the language of random variables, distinguishing between discrete and continuous random variables. Now we further characterize the probability distribution for a random variable in terms of its mean (or expected value) and variance. We consider discrete random variables in this section, then extend the concepts to continuous random variables in the next section.

expected value of a discrete random variable   The **expected value of a discrete random variable** Y with probability distribution $P_Y(y)$ is the probability-weighted average of its possible values. The expected value is denoted by $E(Y)$ or μ_Y.

▪

Definition of $E(Y)$

For a discrete random variable Y with probability distribution $P_Y(y)$, the **expected value** of Y is

$$E(Y) = \sum_{\text{all } y} y P_Y(y)$$

▪

To find $E(Y)$, take each possible value y, multiply (weight) it by the associated probability $P_Y(y)$, and add the results.

EXAMPLE 4.7   A firm is considering two possible investments. As a rough approximation, the firm assigns (subjective) probabilities to losing 20% per dollar invested, losing 10%, breaking even, gaining 10%, and gaining 20%. Let Y be the return per dollar invested in the first project and Z the return per dollar invested in the second. The firm's probabilities are

y: $-.20$ $-.10$ 0 $+.10$ $+.20$
$P_Y(y)$:   .1   .2   .4   .2   .1

z: $-.20$ $-.10$ 0 $+.10$ $+.20$
$P_Z(z)$:   .01   .04   .10   .50   .35

Calculate expected returns per dollar invested in each project. Which project appears to be the more attractive investment?

Solution   Project Y, by any reasonable standard, appears less attractive. It is thought to be as likely to lose 20% as to gain 20%, and as likely to lose 10% as to gain 10%. Project Z is thought to be very likely to gain 10% or 20% and relatively unlikely to lose.

Calculations:

y	$P_Y(y)$	$yP_Y(y)$	z	$P_Z(z)$	$zP_Z(z)$
$-.20$	.1	$-.02$	$-.20$	.01	$-.002$
$-.10$	.2	$-.02$	$-.10$	.04	$-.004$
0	.4	0	0	.10	0
$+.10$	.2	$+.02$	$+.10$	.50	$+.050$
$+.20$	.1	$+.02$	$+.20$	.35	$+.070$
		$E(Y) = 0$			$E(Z) = .114$

The expected Y return is (as anticipated) less than the expected Z return.   ∎

interpretations of E(Y)   The expected value (mean) of a random variable Y can be interpreted in several ways. First, it is simply a **probability-weighted average**, a summary figure that takes into account the relative probabilities of different values of Y. Second, it can be thought of as a **long-run average** of Y. For example, imagine that the firm of Example 4.7 could invest in a very large number of projects with the same return probabilities as Project Z. The average return per dollar invested would be .114, or 11.4%. (This fact follows because about 1 of 100 such projects would lose 20%, 4 of 100 would lose 10%, 10 of 100 would break even, 50 of 100 would earn 10%, and 35 of 100 would earn 20%.) Third, the expected value defines, in a certain sense,* the **fair value** of a gamble. Suppose that a casino gambling game pays $3 with probability 12/38 and nothing with probability 26/38. If we let Y = the return on one play of the game, $E(Y) = 3(12/38) + 0(26/38) = 36/38$, or about .947. In a fair game, the casino ought to charge the player 36/38 of a dollar,

---

* This interpretation ignores the risk factor.

or about 94.7¢, to play. (Devotees of the American form of the game of roulette will recognize the nature of the game, the fact that the actual charge is $1, and the long-run effect of the 2/38 increment on casino profitability.) And finally, the expected value of Y represents a **generalization** of the concept of a population mean μ. If Y is a discrete random variable corresponding to a value drawn at random from a discrete population of values, then $E(Y) = \mu$, the mean of the population.

EXAMPLE 4.8

Suppose that a population consists of the following values and associated frequencies:

Value:	1000	2000	3000	4000
Frequency:	80	60	40	20

$(N = 200)$

The population mean is 2000. Let Y denote a single value drawn at random from the population. Find $P_Y(y)$ and $E(Y)$.

Solution

The possible values and their probabilities are

y:	1000	2000	3000	4000
$P_Y(y)$:	$80/200 = .4$	$60/200 = .3$	$40/200 = .2$	$20/200 = .1$

The expected value is

$$E(Y) = 1000(.4) + 2000(.3) + 3000(.2) + 4000(.1)$$
$$= 400 + 600 + 600 + 400 = 2000$$

$E(Y)$ is exactly equal to the population mean. ∎

variance of a discrete random variable

We have discussed the different interpretations associated with the expected value of a discrete random variable. **Equally important characteristics of a discrete random variable are the variance and standard deviation, which measure the probability dispersion or variability of a random variable.** The variance of a random variable Y, Var(Y), is the probability-weighted average of squared deviations from the mean (expected value).

Definition of Var(Y) and σ_Y

If Y is a discrete random variable,

$$\sigma_Y^2 = \text{Var}(Y) = \sum_{\text{all } y} (y - \mu_Y)^2 P_Y(y), \qquad \text{where } \mu_Y = E(Y)$$

The standard deviation of Y, denoted σ_Y, is (as for other standard deviations) the positive square root of the variance

$$\sigma_Y = \sqrt{\text{Var}(Y)}$$

To calculate Var(Y), take each value y, subtract the expected value $\mu_Y = E(Y)$, square the result, multiply by the probability $P_Y(y)$, and sum.

EXAMPLE 4.9 Find the variance and standard deviation for Y and Z in Example 4.7.

Solution In Example 4.7 we found $\mu_Y = E(Y) = 0$ and $\mu_Z = E(Z) = .114$. A worksheet shows the computations required.

y	$P_Y(y)$	$(y - \mu_Y)$	$(y - \mu_Y)^2$	$(y - \mu_Y)^2 P_Y(y)$
$-.20$	.1	$-.20$	.04	.004
$-.10$	.2	$-.10$	.01	.002
0	.4	0	0	0
.10	.2	.10	.01	.002
.20	.1	.20	.04	.004

$$\sigma_Y^2 = .012$$
$$\sigma_Y = \sqrt{.012} = .110$$

z	$P_Z(z)$	$(z - \mu_Z)$	$(z - \mu_Z)^2$	$(z - \mu_Z)^2 P_Z(z)$
$-.20$	.01	$-.314$	.098596	.00098596
$-.10$	.04	$-.214$	.045796	.00183184
0	.10	$-.114$	.012996	.00129960
.10	.50	$-.014$	.000196	.00009800
.20	.35	.086	.007396	.00258860

$$\sigma_Z^2 = .00680400$$
$$\sigma_Z = .082$$

The Y distribution has greater variability. The bulk of the Z distribution is concentrated on the larger values .10 and .20, while the Y probabilities are somewhat more spread out over all possible values. The variance for a return on investment is often taken as a measure of risk, with larger variances indicating greater risk. In this example, the Z investment has both a higher expected return and a lower risk. ■

The computation of a variance can be clumsy, involving lots of many-digit numbers, as in Var(Z) in Example 4.9. There is a shortcut formula for variance computations that can be of help.

Shortcut Method for Var(Y)

If Y is a **discrete random variable**,

$$\text{Var}(Y) = \sum_{\text{all } y} y^2 P_Y(y) - \mu_Y^2, \quad \text{where } \mu_Y = E(Y)$$

We can square the original values, weight by $P_Y(y)$, and add. At the end of that computation we subtract the square of the mean (expected value) to get the variance.

EXAMPLE 4.10   Use the shortcut formula to repeat the variance calculations of Example 4.9.

Solution   For Y it is the same calculation, because $\mu_Y = E(Y) = 0$. It doesn't matter when we subtract 0, or even 0^2. For Z with $\mu_Z = E(Z) = .114$,

z	$P_Z(z)$	z^2	$z^2 P_Z(z)$
$-.20$	.01	.04	.0004
$-.10$	.04	.01	.0004
0	.10	0	0
.10	.50	.01	.0050
.20	.35	.04	.0140
			.0198

So $\mathrm{Var}(Z) = .0198 - (.114)^2 = .006804$, as in Example 4.9.   ∎

Chebyshev's Inequality and the Empirical Rule, introduced for samples and populations in Chapter 2, apply to random variables as well.

Chebyshev's Inequality and the Empirical Rule for Random Variables

If a random variable Y has finite mean and variance,

$P(Y \text{ falls within } c\sigma_Y \text{ of its mean } \mu_Y) \geq 1 - 1/c^2$

If Y has roughly a mound-shaped probability histogram,

$P(Y \text{ falls within one } \sigma_Y \text{ of its mean } \mu_Y) \approx .68,$ and
$P(Y \text{ falls within two } \sigma_Y \text{ of its mean } \mu_Y) \approx .95$

For the random variable Y of Examples 4.7 and 4.9, $E(Y) = 0$ and $\sigma_Y = .110$. The actual probabilities are

$$P(Y \text{ falls within } \sigma_Y \text{ of its mean}) = P(-.110 \leq Y \leq .110)$$
$$= P(Y = -.10) + P(Y = 0) + P(Y = .10)$$
$$= .80$$

and

$$P(Y \text{ falls within two } \sigma_Y \text{ of its mean}) = P(-.220 \leq Y \leq .220) = 1.00$$

Chebyshev's Inequality indicates that these probabilities must be at least $1 - 1/(1)^2 = 0$ and $1 - 1/(2)^2 = .75$, respectively; as usual, the inequalities are true by a large margin. The Empirical Rule approximation is mediocre in this case, in part because Y takes on a small number of values. Had the firm assessed subjective probabilities for returns of, say, $-.25, -.20, -.15, \ldots, +.15, +.20,$

$+.25$, the Empirical Rule would most likely have been a somewhat better approximation, although the distribution might not be mound shaped.

Just as the mean of a random variable is a generalization of the idea of a population mean, so **the variance of a random variable Y is a generalization of a population variance**. If Y is a discrete random variable corresponding to a value drawn randomly from a population, $\sigma_Y^2 = \sigma^2$.

4.5   EXPECTED VALUE, VARIANCE, AND STANDARD DEVIATION: CONTINUOUS RANDOM VARIABLES ($\int$)

We have defined the expected value, variance, and standard deviation for discrete random variables. The mathematical definitions of their counterparts for continuous random variables necessarily involve calculus. The definition of expected value for a continuous random variable Y is as follows.

Expected Value for a Continuous Random Variable

$$E(Y) = \int_{-\infty}^{\infty} y f_Y(y)\, dy$$

Take each value y, multiply (weight) by the probability density $f_Y(y)$, and integrate (instead of adding). The technicalities should not obscure the fact that $E(Y)$ is a probability-weighted average, with the same long-run average and fair-gamble interpretations.

EXAMPLE 4.11   Find $E(T)$, where T is the time between calls of Example 4.4 and $f_T(t) = 2e^{-2t}$, $t \geq 0$. What is the interpretation of this figure?

Solution   Implicitly, $f_T(t) = 0$ for $t < 0$, because $t < 0$ is impossible in this context. It is necessary to know that

$$\int_0^{\infty} t e^{-ct}\, dt = \frac{1}{c^2}$$

Then it follows that

$$E(T) = \int_{-\infty}^{\infty} t f_T(t)\, dt$$

$$= 2 \int_0^{\infty} t e^{-2t}\, dt$$

(because $f_T(t) = 0$ for $t < 0$ and $f_T(t) = 2e^{-2t}$)

$$= 2\left(\frac{1}{2^2}\right) = \frac{1}{2}$$

Because T is the time in minutes between successive calls, $E(T) = 1/2$ means that in the long run, calls come, on the average, half a minute apart. ■

The definition and shortcut formula for $\text{Var}(Y)$ were stated only for discrete random variables. When speaking of continuous random variables we substitute a probability density for a discrete probability distribution, and an integral for a sum.

Definition of Var(Y), Continuous Random Variable

If Y is a **continuous random variable**

$$\text{Var}(Y) = \int_{-\infty}^{\infty} (y - \mu_Y)^2 f_Y(y)\, dy$$

and a shortcut formula is

$$\text{Var}(Y) = \int_{-\infty}^{\infty} y^2 f_Y(y)\, dy - \mu_Y^2$$

EXAMPLE 4.12   Find $\text{Var}(T)$ where T is defined in Examples 4.4 and 4.11. It is known that $\int_0^{\infty} t^2 e^{-ct}\, dt = 2/c^3$.

Solution   Use the shortcut formula and notice that the integral may be taken from 0 to ∞, because $f_T(t) = 0$ for $t < 0$. In Example 4.11 we found $\mu_T = E(T) = 1/2$.

$$\text{Var}(T) = \int_0^{\infty} t^2 f_T(t)\, dt - \mu_T^2$$

$$= \left(\int_0^{\infty} t^2 2e^{-2t}\, dt \right) - \left(\frac{1}{2} \right)^2$$

$$= 2 \int_0^{\infty} t^2 e^{-2t}\, dt - \frac{1}{4}$$

$$= 2 \left(\frac{2}{2^3} \right) - \frac{1}{4} = \frac{1}{2} - \frac{1}{4} = \frac{1}{4}$$ ■

SECTIONS 4.4 AND 4.5   EXERCISES

4.16   The product-development laboratory of a paint manufacturer is asked to develop a modified paint for automobiles. The director of the laboratory estimates the following probabilities for the required development time (in months):

y:	2	3	4	5	6	7	8	9	10	11	12
$P_Y(y)$:	.20	.30	.15	.10	.08	.06	.04	.03	.02	.01	.01

  a. Construct a probability histogram.
  b. Calculate the expected value of Y.
  c. Mark $E(Y)$ on the histogram. How does the shape of the histogram affect $E(Y)$?

4.17 Refer to Exercise 4.16.
  a. Calculate the standard deviation of Y. Use the definition.
  b. Use the shortcut method to calculate σ_Y.

4.18 Refer to Exercise 4.16. What is the actual probability that Y differs from μ_Y by less than one standard deviation? Why does this probability differ from the Empirical Rule estimate?

4.19 An investment syndicate is trying to decide which of two \$200,000 apartment houses to buy. An advisor estimates the following probabilities for the five-year net returns (in thousands of dollars):

Return:	−50	0	50	100	150	200	250
Probability for house 1:	.02	.03	.20	.50	.20	.03	.02
Probability for house 2:	.15	.10	.10	.10	.30	.20	.05

  a. Calculate the expected net return for house 1 and for house 2.
  b. Calculate the respective variances and standard deviations.

4.20 Refer to Exercise 4.19.
  a. Is one investment better than the other in terms of both expected return and risk?
  b. If you had a spare \$200,000 to invest, which investment would you prefer?

4.21 In Exercise 4.6 we considered the probability distribution

x:	0	1	2	3	4	5	6	7	8	9	10
$P_X(x)$:	.06	.14	.16	.14	.12	.10	.08	.07	.06	.04	.03

  a. Find the mean of X.
  b. Use the definition to calculate the variance of X.
  c. Use the shortcut method to recalculate the variance of X.

4.22 Calculate the probability that X in Exercise 4.21 is within two standard deviations of its mean. How does this probability compare to the theoretical values given by the Empirical Rule and by Chebyshev's Inequality?

∫ **4.23** In Exercise 4.14, we defined

$$f_Y(y) = 3y^{-4}, \qquad \text{for } 1 < y < \infty$$

  a. Calculate the mean. What is the interpretation of the resulting number?
  b. Calculate the variance and standard deviation. The shortcut method may be easier.

∫ **4.24** a. Calculate values of the density in Exercise 4.23 for $y = 1.0, 1.5, 2.0, 2.5,$ and 3.0. Sketch the density.
  b. Should the Empirical Rule work well for this density? Find the probability that Y will be within one standard deviation of its mean. Remember that Y can't be less than 1.

∫ **4.25** Specifications call for a metal rod used in an assembly to have a diameter of 10 cm. Rods are inspected, and any rods with diameters less than 9.90 cm or greater than 10.10 cm are discarded. Careful measurements indicate that the density of $Y =$ the diameter of a randomly chosen rod (after inspection) is

$$\begin{aligned} f_Y(y) &= 100(y - 9.9) && \text{if } 9.9 < y < 10 \\ &= 100(10.1 - y) && \text{if } 10 < y < 10.1 \end{aligned}$$

The density is 0 for all other y values.

a. What must the expected value of Y equal?

b. Find the standard deviation of Y.

4.26 A manufacturer of disk controllers subjects each new controller to rigorous testing. Of newly assembled controllers, 84% pass the test with no rework. Controllers that fail the initial test are reworked once; 75% of these machines pass a second test. Those controllers that fail the second test are reworked a second time and retested; 90% of them pass and the rest are scrapped. Define Y to be the number of rework cycles for a randomly chosen controller.

a. Specify the possible values y.

b. Calculate the probability distribution of Y. A small probability tree may be helpful.

4.27 a. Find the expected value of Y in Exercise 4.26. What is the interpretation of this number?

b. Find the variance and standard deviation of Y.

4.28 The manufacturer in Exercise 4.26 could reallocate resources so that 92% of all controllers pass the first test with no rework. However, of those that don't pass, only 60% would pass after one rework cycle. Of those controllers that fail the second cycle, 80% would pass after a second cycle (and the rest would be scrapped).

a. How would these changes alter the probability distribution in Exercise 4.26?

b. How would the probability that a machine is scrapped change?

c. Should these changes increase or decrease the expected value of Y found in Exercise 4.27? Recalculate the expected value to verify your answer.

4.29 An office supply company currently holds 30% of the market for supplying suburban governments. This share has been quite stable and there is no reason to think that it will change. The company has three bids outstanding, prepared by its standard procedure. Let Y be the number of the company's bids that are accepted.

a. Find the probability distribution of Y.

b. What assumptions did you make in answering part (a)? Are any of the assumptions clearly unreasonable?

4.30 Find the expected value and variance of Y in Exercise 4.29.

4.31 It could be argued that if the company in Exercise 4.29 loses on the first bid, that signals that a competitor is cutting prices and the company is more likely to lose the other bids also. Similarly, if the company wins on the first bid, that signals that competitors are trying to improve profit margins and the company is more likely to win the other bids also. If this argument is correct, and the two sides of the argument balance out to a 30% market share for the company, will the expected value and variance of Y be increased or decreased compared to the values found in Exercise 4.30?

4.32 A firm renovates historically certified buildings into upscale apartments. The firm invites individual investors to buy shares in particular buildings; the shareholders may sell back their shares after two years. The price of a share at the end of two years depends on several uncertainties, primarily the level of interest rates and the demand for apartments. The firm estimates that the probability distribution of X, the net return of a share after two years, is

$$f_X(x) = 7.8125(x + 1)^2 e^{-2.5(x + 1)}, \qquad \text{for } -1 < x < \infty$$

a. Find the probability that a shareholder will actually lose money—that is, that the net return will be negative. From calculus, it is known that an antiderivative of $f_X(x)$ is

$$1 - e^{-2.5(x + 1)} - 2.5(x + 1)e^{-2.5(x + 1)} - 6.25(x + 1)^2 e^{-2.5(x + 1)}/2$$

b. Currently, an investor could obtain a no-risk Treasury bill investment that would yield a net return of .176 over two years. If the apartment investment is to be attractive, the probability of a yield larger than .176 must be high. Is it, according to the estimated probability distribution?

∫   4.33   a. Find the expected value of X in Exercise 4.32. What is the economic meaning of this number? The math might be easier if you consider $Y = X + 1$ and remember that the integral from 0 to infinity of $y^k e^{-cy}$ is $k!/c^{k+1}$; the expected value of X can be determined from that of Y.

b. Find the variance of X in Exercise 4.32. Again, you may want to work with $Y = X + 1$.

c. Suppose an investor has an alternative investment, say W, that has an expected value (over the same time period) of 0.24 and a variance of 0.30. Which investment do you think the investor is likely to choose?

4.6   JOINT PROBABILITY DISTRIBUTIONS AND INDEPENDENCE ∎

In Sections 4.2 and 4.3 we developed some basic language for dealing with one random variable. In this section we extend that language to deal with joint probability distributions for two random variables, X and Y. We define everything in terms of two discrete random variables. Those who are tolerably comfortable with calculus should be able to supply the analogues for continuous random variables.

When we deal with two random variables, X and Y, it is convenient to work with joint probabilities. In Chapter 3 the **joint probability** of events A and B was the probability of the intersection, $P(A \cap B)$. Let A be the event $X = x$ and B, the event $Y = y$. Define the **joint probability distribution** $P_{xy}(x, y)$ to be a function that supplies the joint probability for each pair of values, x and y.

joint probability distribution

EXAMPLE 4.13   Suppose that, in the emergency room of a small hospital, the most serious cases involve coronary attack and trauma (injury by violence or severe accident). Define X = number of coronary cases and Y = number of trauma cases arriving on a particular weekday night. It is assumed that

$$P_{xy}(x, y) = \frac{(x + 1)(y + 2)}{84}, \qquad x = 0, 1, 2; y = 0, 1, 2, 3$$

Calculate a numerical table of joint probabilities.

Solution   Simply substitute the desired x and y values to get the joint probabilities: $P_{xy}(0, 3) = P(X = 0 \text{ and } Y = 3) = (0 + 1)(3 + 2)/84 = 5/84$, and so on. A tabular display of the joint probability distribution $P_{xy}(x, y)$ is shown here:

		y		
x	0	1	2	3
0	2/84	3/84	4/84	5/84
1	4/84	6/84	8/84	10/84
2	6/84	9/84	12/84	15/84

marginal probabilities

Once a joint probability distribution has been specified, **marginal probabilities** can be calculated by summation. In Chapter 3, when we dealt with joint probabilities like $P(A \cap B)$, $P(A \cap \bar{B})$, and so on, the term *marginal probability* referred to the probability of one event alone, like $P(A)$. We calculated marginal probabilities by the Additive Law. Because this section is different only notationally from Chapter 3, the same principle can be used here.

EXAMPLE 4.14

Find the marginal probability distribution of X and the marginal probability distribution of Y in Example 4.13.

Solution

Sum across rows to get X probabilities and down columns to get Y probabilities.

			y		
x	0	1	2	3	$P_X(x)$
0	2/84	3/84	4/84	5/84	14/84
1	4/84	6/84	8/84	10/84	28/84
2	6/84	9/84	12/84	15/84	42/84
$P_Y(y)$	12/84	18/84	24/84	30/84	

This idea can be expressed in a formula. To find the probability $P_X(x)$, add up the joint probabilities of that x value and each possible y value:

$$P_X(x) = \sum_{\text{all } y} P_{XY}(x, y)$$

In this example,

$$P(X = 1) = \sum_{\text{all } y} P_{XY}(1, y)$$

$$= P_{XY}(1, 0) + P_{XY}(1, 1) + P_{XY}(1, 2) + P_{XY}(1, 3)$$

$$= \frac{4}{84} + \frac{6}{84} + \frac{8}{84} + \frac{10}{84} = \frac{28}{84}$$

In the same way, the marginal probabilities for Y can be computed as

$$P_Y(y) = \sum_{\text{all } x} P_{XY}(x, y)$$

In this example,

$$P(Y = 1) = \sum_{\text{all } x} P_{XY}(x, 1)$$

$$= P_{XY}(0, 1) + P_{XY}(1, 1) + P_{XY}(2, 1)$$

$$= \frac{3}{84} + \frac{6}{84} + \frac{9}{84} = \frac{18}{84}$$

The idea is simply a translation of the addition principle.*   ■

---

* Now we can explain why we use the apparently redundant notation $P_X(x)$, $P_Y(y)$. If we merely wrote $P(x)$ or $P(y)$, we would not know whether $P(1)$ meant $P(X = 1) = P_X(1)$ or $P(Y = 1) = P_Y(1)$.

We can extend basic probability notation to conditional probabilities. Just as we defined the conditional probability of B given A as

$$P(\mathrm{B} \mid \mathrm{A}) = \frac{P(\mathrm{A} \cap \mathrm{B})}{P(\mathrm{A})}$$

conditional distribution

We can define the **conditional distribution** of Y given $X = x$ as

$$P_{Y|X}(y \mid x)$$

Thus for any value of Y,

$$P(Y = y \mid X = x) = \frac{P(X = x \cap Y = y)}{P(X = x)}$$
$$= \frac{P_{XY}(x, y)}{P_X(x)}$$

The need for this notation arises from the idea of independence. Remember that we had two equivalent definitions of independence for events A and B:

$$P(\mathrm{B} \mid \mathrm{A}) = P(\mathrm{B})$$
$$P(\mathrm{A} \cap \mathrm{B}) = P(\mathrm{A})P(\mathrm{B})$$

equivalent definitions of statistical independence

We also have two **equivalent definitions of statistical independence** for random variables X and Y:

$$P_{Y|X}(y \mid x) = P_Y(y), \qquad \text{for all } x, y$$
$$P_{XY}(x, y) = P_X(x)P_Y(y), \qquad \text{for all } x, y$$

For mathematical ease, we usually use the second form of the independence definition in this text.

EXAMPLE 4.15 Show that X and Y of Examples 4.13 and 4.14 are independent.

Solution In Example 4.14 we found $P_X(x)$ and $P_Y(y)$. When we multiply appropriate $P_X(x)$ and $P_Y(y)$, we get the following table:

x \ y	0	1	2	3	
0	(12/84)(14/84)	(18/84)(14/84)	(24/84)(14/84)	(30/84)(14/84)	14/84
1	(12/84)(28/84)	(18/84)(28/84)	(24/84)(28/84)	(30/84)(28/84)	28/84
2	(12/84)(42/84)	(18/84)(42/84)	(24/84)(42/84)	(30/84)(42/84)	42/84
	12/84	18/84	24/84	30/84	

When we reduce the fractions in this table, we find that every table entry equals the $P_{XY}(x, y)$ entry in Example 4.13. Therefore $P_{XY}(x, y) = P_X(x)P_Y(y)$ for all x and y; that is, X and Y are independent. ■

The assumption of independence was built into the mathematical form of this particular $P_{XY}(x, y)$. In practice, we often assume that X and Y are independent; once we specify $P_X(x)$ and $P_Y(y)$, this assumption lets us calculate $P_{XY}(x, y)$ as the product $P_X(x)P_Y(y)$. Example 4.13 is one situation in which the independence assumption seems reasonable. The number of coronary cases arriving at an emergency room should have no relevance to predictions of the number of trauma cases.

In Section 3.6, we discussed how prior probabilities of various states of nature can be modified by the likelihoods of observable events, using Bayes' Theorem. Sometimes the states of nature and observable events are numerical in nature, so that ideas of average and variability make sense. In such cases, it's useful to write Bayes' Theorem in random variable notation. For example, the agent for an author of best-selling novels wants to estimate the final bid for paperback book publishing rights of a new novel. Based on past results for the author and recent trends in the paperback industry, the agent thinks that the bid could be $100,000, $150,000, $200,000, or $250,000 with respective probabilities of approximately .4, .3, .2, and .1. The agent keeps track of the order of a "bellwether" bookstore chain whose buyer is a fairly good predictor of commercial success. The bookstore chain orders 10,000, 20,000, or 30,000 copies; the agent thinks that the likelihoods of these order sizes, given the eventual bid price, should be roughly as follows:

	Order Amount		
Bid	10,000	20,000	30,000
$100,000	.60	.30	.10
$150,000	.50	.30	.20
$200,000	.30	.40	.30
$250,000	.20	.40	.40

Based on the prior probabilities, the expected value of the paperback bid is $100,000(.4) + $150,000(.3) + $200,000(.2) + $250,000(.1) = $150,000. But now suppose that the bookstore chain orders 30,000 copies; this optimistic note leads the agent to revise the prior probabilities. From Bayes' Theorem (or, equivalently, a probability tree calculation)

$$
P(\$100,000 \mid 30,000) = \frac{P(30,000 \mid \$100,000)P(\$100,000)}{\begin{aligned}&P(30,000 \mid \$100,000)P(\$100,000)\\ &+ P(30,000 \mid \$150,000)P(\$150,000)\\ &+ P(30,000 \mid \$200,000)P(\$200,000)\\ &+ P(30,000 \mid \$250,000)P(\$250,000)\end{aligned}}
$$

$$
= \frac{(.10)(.4)}{(.10)(.4) + (.20)(.3) + (.30)(.2) + (.40)(.1)}
$$

$$
= .20
$$

Similar calculations show that $P(\$150,000\,|\,30,000) = .30$, $P(\$200,000\,|\,30,000) = .30$, and $P(\$250,000\,|\,30,000) = .20$. Using these posterior probabilities, the expected value of the bid is now $\$100,000(.20) + \$150,000(.30) + \$200,000(.30) + \$250,000(.20) = \$175,000$. The expected value of the bid has indeed increased, given the optimistic order.

Bayes' Theorem with Random Variables

For discrete random variables Θ and Y,

$$P_{\Theta|Y}(\theta\,|\,y) = \frac{P_{\Theta}(\theta)P_{Y|\Theta}(y\,|\,\theta)}{\displaystyle\sum_{\theta} P_{\Theta}(\theta)P_{Y|\Theta}(y\,|\,\theta)}$$

For continuous random variables Θ and Y,

$$f_{\Theta|Y}(\theta\,|\,y) = \frac{f_{\Theta}(\theta)f_{Y|\Theta}(y\,|\,\theta)}{\displaystyle\int_{-\infty}^{\infty} f_{\Theta}(\theta)f_{Y|\Theta}(y\,|\,\theta)d\theta}$$

This is merely a notation shift. No new ideas are involved.

SECTION 4.6   EXERCISES

4.34 A manufacturer of television sets sells two principal models. Define X = sales of model A next December (nearest 100,000) and Y = sales of model B next December. The marketing staff estimates that the joint probabilities $P_{XY}(x, y)$ are

		y		
x	1	2	3	4
1	.030	.055	.070	.075
2	.055	.070	.075	.070
3	.070	.075	.070	.055
4	.075	.070	.055	.030

a. Find $P(X = 1, Y = 2)$.
b. Find $P(X \le 2, Y \le 2)$.
c. Find $P_X(x)$ and $P_Y(y)$.
d. Are X and Y independent?

4.35 Show that the formula

$$P_{XY}(x, y) = .005(-10 + 10x + 10y - x^2 - y^2 - 2xy)$$

yields the joint probability table of Exercise 4.34. Can you find a formula for $P_X(x)$?

4.36 The owner of a small sound-system store determines the following probabilities for X = the number of amplifiers sold during a weekday and for Y = the number of speaker systems sold during the same day:

x:	0	1	2	3	4	
$P_X(x)$:	.10	.40	.25	.20	.05	

y:	0	1	2	3	4	5
$P_Y(y)$:	.10	.30	.25	.20	.10	.05

a. Assuming that X and Y are independent, calculate the joint probability distribution $P_{XY}(x, y)$.

b. Check your work by finding the marginal probabilities $P_X(x)$ and $P_Y(y)$.

4.37 Do you believe that independence is a reasonable assumption for Exercise 4.36?

4.38 A small management-consulting firm presents both written and oral proposals in an effort to get new consulting contracts. Records indicate that the probability distribution $P_{XY}(x, y)$ of X = number of oral proposals in a week and Y = number of written proposals in that week is given by the following table:

x	0	1	2	3	4
0	.010	.015	.030	.075	.050
1	.020	.030	.045	.060	.040
2	.030	.045	.100	.045	.030
3	.040	.060	.045	.030	.020
4	.050	.075	.030	.015	.010

a. Find the probability that there are two oral proposals and two written proposals in a particular week.

b. Find the probability that there are exactly two oral proposals and two or fewer written proposals in a particular week.

c. Find the probability that there are two or fewer oral proposals and two or fewer written proposals in a particular week.

4.39 a. Use the probability distribution of Exercise 4.38 to calculate the marginal probability distributions of X and of Y.

b. Assuming these probabilities, are X and Y independent?

4.40 Calculate the conditional distribution of Y given each possible value of X, using the probability distribution of Exercise 4.38. Do these conditional probability distributions indicate that X and Y are independent?

4.7   COVARIANCE AND CORRELATION OF RANDOM VARIABLES

In Section 4.6 we defined the *independence* of two random variables. Now we consider how to measure the degree of *dependence* between two random variables. There are many kinds of dependence that two variables might have and many measures of dependence that one might use. Two measures, covariance and correlation, are particularly important because they are closely related to the concept of variance of a random variable.

Again we begin with an example. A trust officer of a bank assumes the following (subjective) joint probabilities for the percentage returns (interest plus change in market value) of two utility bonds. The returns are labeled X and Y.

			Y			
X	8	9	10	11	12	$P_X(x)$
8	.03	.04	.03	.00	.00	.10
9	.04	.06	.06	.04	.00	.20
10	.02	.08	.20	.08	.02	.40
11	.00	.04	.06	.06	.04	.20
12	.00	.00	.03	.04	.03	.10
$P_Y(y)$	.09	.22	.38	.22	.09	

There is a relation between X and Y. For example, given $x = 8$, the Y probabilities are concentrated on the smaller values $y = 8$, 9, and 10. At the other extreme, given $x = 12$, the Y probabilities are concentrated on the larger values $y = 10$, 11, and 12. In general, there is a tendency for the X and Y outcomes to vary together.

Covariance of Random Variables X and Y

If X and Y are discrete random variables with respective expected values μ_X and μ_Y, and with joint probability distribution $P_{XY}(x, y)$, the **covariance** of X and Y, denoted by $\text{Cov}(X, Y)$ is defined as

$$\text{Cov}(X, Y) = \sum_x \sum_y (x - \mu_X)(y - \mu_Y) P_{XY}(x, y)$$

A shortcut method for computing the covariance is

$$\text{Cov}(X, Y) = \left[\sum_x \sum_y xy P_{XY}(x, y) \right] - \mu_X \mu_Y$$

EXAMPLE 4.16   Compute $\text{Cov}(X, Y)$ for the joint distribution of bond yields given in the preceding discussion. Use the definition first and check to see that the shortcut method gives the same answer.

Solution   From the marginal probabilities $P_X(x)$ and $P_Y(y)$, we get the expected values:

$$\mu_X = 8(.10) + 9(.20) + 10(.40) + 11(.20) + 12(.10) = 10$$
$$\mu_Y = 8(.09) + 9(.22) + 10(.38) + 11(.22) + 12(.09) = 10$$

The covariance can be computed using the definition as follows:

$$\text{Cov}(X, Y) = \sum_x \sum_y (x - \mu_X)(y - \mu_Y) P_{XY}(x, y)$$

$$= (8 - 10)(8 - 10)(.03) + (8 - 10)(9 - 10)(.04)$$
$$+ (8 - 10)(10 - 10)(.03) + \cdots + (12 - 10)(12 - 10)(.03)$$
$$= .60$$

Similarly, using the shortcut method,

$$\text{Cov}(X, Y) = \sum \sum xy P_{XY}(x, y) - \mu_X \mu_Y$$
$$= 8(8)(.03) + 8(9)(.04) + 8(10)(.03) + \cdots + 12(12)(.03) - 10(10)$$
$$= 100.60 - 100 = .60 \qquad \blacksquare$$

The covariance of two random variables is closely related to their correlation.

Correlation of Random Variables X and Y

If X and Y are discrete random variables with respective standard deviations σ_X and σ_Y, their **correlation** ρ_{XY} is defined as

$$\rho_{XY} = \frac{\text{Cov}(X, Y)}{\sigma_X \sigma_Y}$$

It follows that

$$\text{Cov}(X, Y) = \rho_{XY} \sigma_X \sigma_Y$$

EXAMPLE 4.17   Find ρ_{XY} for the bond-yield distribution discussed earlier in this section.

Solution   In Example 4.16 we found $\text{Cov}(X, Y) = .60$. To get ρ_{XY} we need the standard deviations of X and Y, which can be computed from the respective marginal probabilities. The formulas in Sections 4.4 and 4.5 can be used to compute σ_X^2 and σ_Y^2.

$$\sigma_X^2 = \sum_x x^2 P_X(x) - \mu_X^2$$
$$= 8^2(.10) + 9^2(.20) + 10^2(.40) + 11^2(.20) + 12^2(.10) - (10)^2$$
$$= 101.20 - 100 = 1.20$$

and hence $\sigma_X = \sqrt{1.20} = 1.095$.
Similarly, we have

$$\sigma_Y^2 = \sum_y y^2 P_Y(y) - \mu_Y^2 = 1.16$$

and $\sigma_Y = \sqrt{1.16} = 1.077$.
Substituting into the formula for ρ_{XY}, we find

$$\rho_{XY} = \frac{\text{Cov}(X, Y)}{\sigma_X \sigma_Y} = \frac{.60}{1.095(1.077)} = .509 \qquad \blacksquare$$

Covariance and correlation are immensely important ideas in managing portfolios of investments. This application is discussed in Chapter 17.

The correlation between X and Y ranges between -1.00 and $+1.00$. A value of -1.00 or $+1.00$ indicates perfect linear prediction in the population, while a value of zero indicates no linear predictive value.

If the random variables X and Y are independent, there should be no relation (linear or otherwise) between them. Reasonably enough, when X and Y are independent, $\text{Cov}(X, Y) = 0$ and therefore $\rho_{XY} = 0$ also. This fact can be seen easily by using the shortcut method for covariance. Remember that discrete random variables X and Y are independent if $P_{XY}(x, y) = P_X(x)P_Y(y)$ for all possible x and y. In that case,

$$\text{Cov}(X, Y) = \sum_{x,y} xy P_{XY}(x, y) - \mu_X \mu_Y$$

$$= \sum_{x,y} xy P_X(x) P_Y(y) - \mu_X \mu_Y$$

$$= \sum_x x P_X(x) \left[\sum_y y P_Y(y) \right] - \mu_X \mu_Y$$

$$= \mu_X \mu_Y - \mu_X \mu_Y = 0$$

EXAMPLE 4.18   An assembly line can be stopped temporarily to adjust for either bad parts alignment or bad welds. Production records indicate the following joint distribution for X = number of stops in a production shift for bad alignment and Y = number of stops in a production shift for bad welds.

			Y			
X	0	1	2	3	4	
0	.03	.06	.12	.06	.03	.30
1	.04	.08	.16	.08	.04	.40
2	.03	.06	.12	.06	.03	.30
	.10	.20	.40	.20	.10	1.00

    a. What should $\text{Cov}(X, Y)$ equal for these probabilities?
    b. Verify your answer numerically.

Solution   a. In every case $P_{XY}(x, y) = P_X(x)P_Y(y)$. For example, $P_{XY}(2, 4) = .03$ and $P_X(2) \times P_Y(4) = (.30)(.10) = .03$ also. Therefore X and Y are independent, and $\text{Cov}(X, Y)$ should equal zero.

    b. By looking at the marginal probabilities for X and for Y, it is easy to see that $\mu_X = 1$ and $\mu_Y = 2$. So

$$\text{Cov}(X, Y) = [0(0)(.03) + 0(1)(.06) + \cdots + 2(4)(.03)] - 1(2)$$
$$= 2.00 - 2 = 0$$

as it should be.   ■

It is mathematically possible to have $\text{Cov}(X, Y) = 0$ even though X and Y are dependent. The reason is that covariance and correlation measure only the strength of *linear* relation. If there is a relation between X and Y, but that relation cannot be approximated by a linear relation, the covariance can be zero.

EXAMPLE 4.19   Suppose that in Example 4.18 the following probabilities are obtained:

			Y			
X	0	1	2	3	4	
0	.01	.05	.18	.05	.01	.30
1	.03	.10	.14	.10	.03	.40
2	.06	.05	.08	.05	.06	.30
	.10	.20	.40	.20	.10	1.00

Are X and Y independent? What is the covariance between X and Y?

Solution   No, there is dependence. For example, $P_{XY}(0,0) = .01$, but $P_X(0)P_Y(0) = (.10)(.30) = .03$. However,

$$\text{Cov}(X, Y) = [0(0)(.01) + 0(1)(.05) + \cdots + 2(4)(.06)] - 1(2)$$
$$= 2.00 - 2 = 0$$

(Note that $\mu_X = 1$ and $\mu_Y = 2$, as in Example 4.18.) The reason that the covariance is zero is that there is no linear relation. Note that when y is either 0 or 4, the most likely x value is 2; when y is either 1 or 3, the most likely x value is 1; and when y is 2, the most likely x value is 2. Computation of expected X values given each value y also shows a completely nonlinear pattern.   ∎

4.8   JOINT PROBABILITY DENSITIES FOR CONTINUOUS RANDOM VARIABLES ($\int$)   ∎

Our discussion of joint probabilities has, up until now, focused on discrete random variables. Now we turn briefly to continuous random variables. As we shall see once again, every discrete summation has a direct analogue in a continuous integration. The technical details of calculus are needed in this section, but they should not obscure the recurring analogy of continuous integration with discrete summation.

When discussing discrete random variables, we considered joint probabilities $P_{XY}(x, y) = P(X = x \text{ and } Y = y)$. Probabilities for X, Y, or both were obtained by appropriate sums. When we turn to continuous random variables X and Y, we consider joint density functions $f_{XY}(x, y)$. In the continuous case, probabilities are obtained by integration (rather than summation) of the joint probability density. For example, suppose that a study of the time T required to prepare a bid in worker-days and the size of the bid U in millions of dollars indicates that the joint probability density is

$$f_{TU}(t, u) = .02(t + 1)(t + 2)(10 - t)u^t(1 - u), \qquad 0 < t < 10, 0 < u < 1$$

In this case both T and U are continuous random variables, as indicated by the fact that they vary over continuous ranges $0 < t < 10$ and $0 < u < 1$. Thus instead of finding the probability that T and U lie in specified intervals by summing probabilities, we find such probabilities by integrating densities.

Joint Probabilities for Continuous Random Variables

If X and Y are continuous random variables with joint probability density $f_{XY}(x, y)$, then probabilities concerning X and Y are calculated as

$$P(a < X < b, c < Y < d) = \int_{x=a}^{x=b} \int_{y=c}^{y=d} f_{XY}(x, y)\, dy\, dx$$

(Note for those not familiar with double integrals: The integrations are performed "from the inside out." Thus, in the expression above, the first integration is performed with respect to y, with x being regarded as a constant. Once the y variable has been integrated out, the single integration with respect to x is carried out.)

For example suppose that continuous random variables X and Y have joint density

$$f_{XY}(x, y) = (6/17)[4 - (x + y)^2], \qquad 0 < x < 1, 0 < y < 1$$

Find the probability that both X and Y are less than 0.5.

We note first that both X and Y can't be negative, so that we're finding $P(0 < X < .5 \text{ and } 0 < Y < .5)$. Thus

$$P(0 < X < .5 \text{ and } 0 < Y < .5) = (6/17) \int_0^{.5} \int_0^{.5} [4 - (x + y)^2]\, dy\, dx$$

$$= (6/17) \int_0^{.5} \left[4y - \frac{(x + y)^3}{3} \right]\Big|_{y=0}^{y=.5} dx$$

$$= (6/17) \int_0^{.5} \left\{ \left[2 - \frac{(x + .5)^3}{3} \right] + \frac{x^3}{3} \right\} dx$$

$$= (6/17) \left[2x - \frac{(x + .5)^4}{12} + \frac{x^4}{12} \right]\Big|_{x=0}^{x=.5}$$

$$= (6/17) \left[1.0 - \left(\frac{1}{12} - \frac{(.5)^4}{12} \right) + \frac{(.5)^4}{12} \right]$$

$$= .3272$$

EXAMPLE 4.20   Histograms of past data on X = time required to cut bolts of cloth to a pattern and Y = time required to sew the same bolts of cloth for military uniforms (both measured in worker hours) indicate that

$$f_{XY}(x, y) = 72x^2(1 - x)y(1 - y), \qquad \text{for } 0 < x < 1 \text{ and } 0 < y < 1$$

Find the probability that Y will be less than X and X will be between 0 and .5.

Solution   This problem presents some technical difficulties in that the limits for integrating Y depend on the specified x value. We must have $y < x$ and $0 < x < .5$. Thus the region of integration of $f_{XY}(x, y)$ is $0 < x < .5, 0 < y < x$ (because y, by definition, cannot be less than 0). So

$$P(0 < Y < X < .5) = \int_{x=0}^{x=.5} \int_{y=0}^{y=x} 72x^2(1-x)y(1-y)\,dy\,dx$$

$$= \int_{x=0}^{x=.5} 72x^2(1-x) \int_{y=0}^{y=x} y(1-y)\,dy\,dx$$

$$= \int_{x=0}^{x=.5} 72x^2(1-x)\left[\frac{y^2}{2} - \frac{y^3}{3}\right]\Big|_{y=0}^{y=x}\,dx$$

$$= \int_{x=0}^{x=.5} 72x^2(1-x)\left[\left(\frac{x^2}{2} - \frac{x^3}{3}\right) - (0-0)\right]\,dx$$

$$= 36\int_{x=0}^{x=.5} x^4(1-x)\,dx - 24\int_{x=0}^{x=.5} x^5(1-x)\,dx$$

$$= 36\left(\frac{x^5}{5} - \frac{x^6}{6}\right)\Big|_{x=0}^{x=.5} - 24\left(\frac{x^6}{6} - \frac{x^7}{7}\right)\Big|_{x=0}^{x=.5}$$

$$= 36\left[\frac{(.5)^5}{5} - \frac{(.5)^6}{6}\right] - 24\left[\frac{(.5)^6}{6} - \frac{(.5)^7}{7}\right]$$

$$= 0.0955, \text{ after some arithmetic} \qquad\blacksquare$$

In Section 4.6, we showed that we could find the marginal probability distribution of X by summing over y in the joint probability distribution $P_{XY}(x, y)$. You may not be overwhelmingly surprised to hear that, when dealing with continuous random variables, we substitute an integral over y for a sum over y. In the continuous case,

$$f_X(x) = \int_{\text{all } y} f_{XY}(x, y)\,dy$$

For $T =$ time spent in preparing a bid and $U =$ size of the bid, with joint density

$$f_{TU}(t, u) = .02(t + 1)(t + 2)(10 - t)u^t(1 - u), \qquad 0 < t < 10, 0 < u < 1$$

$$f_T(t) = \int_{u=0}^{u=1} .02(t + 1)(t + 2)(10 - t)u^t(1 - u)\,du$$

$$= 0.2(t + 1)(t + 2)(10 - t)\left[\frac{u^{t+1}}{(t+1)} - \frac{u^{t+2}}{(t+2)}\right]\Big|_{u=0}^{u=1}$$

$$= .02(t + 1)(t + 2)(10 - t)\left[\frac{1}{(t+1)} - \frac{1}{(t+2)}\right] = .02(10 - t)$$

EXAMPLE 4.21   Find the marginal density of X in Example 4.20.

Solution
$$f_X(x) = \int_{y=0}^{y=1} 72x^2(1-x)y(1-y)\,dy$$

$$= 72x^2(1-x) \int_{y=0}^{y=1} y(1-y)\,dy$$

$$= 72x^2(1-x)\left[\frac{1}{2} - \frac{1}{3}\right] = 12x^2(1-x) \qquad \blacksquare$$

We may extend the definition of conditional probability distribution to the idea of the conditional density of Y given X. Just as we define the conditional probability distribution in the discrete case as the ratio of the joint probability $P_{XY}(x, y)$ to the marginal probability $P_X(x)$, we can define the conditional density as

$$f_{Y|X}(y\,|\,x) = \frac{f_{XY}(x, y)}{f_X(x)}$$

In particular, we can extend the definition of independence by saying that a continuous random variable Y is independent of another continuous random variable X if

$$f_{Y|X}(y\,|\,x) = f_Y(y)$$

or, equivalently, if $f_{XY}(x, y) = f_X(x)f_Y(y)$ for every x and y. If

$$f_{TU}(t, u) = .02(t+1)(t+2)(10-t)u^t(1-u), \qquad 0 < t < 10, 0 < u < 1$$

we have shown that $f_T(t) = .02(10-t)$, so

$$f_{U|T}(u\,|\,t) = \frac{f_{TU}(t, u)}{f_T(t)} = \frac{.02(t+1)(t+2)(10-t)u^t(1-u)}{.02(10-t)}$$

$$= (t+1)(t+2)u^t(1-u)$$

Because the conditional density of U given $T = t$ is a function of t as well as u, U is not independent of T.

EXAMPLE 4.22   Refer to Example 4.20. Are X and Y independent in this case?

Solution   We defined

$$f_{XY}(x, y) = 72x^2(1-x)y(1-y), \qquad 0 < x < 1, 0 < y < 1$$

In Example 4.21 we showed that

$$f_X(x) = 12x^2(1-x)$$

so

$$f_{YX}(y, x) = \frac{72x^2(1-x)y(1-y)}{12x^2(1-x)} = 6y(1-y)$$

is a function only of y. (We must also be careful to notice that the range of definition of the formula for y is independent of x, as it is here.) Thus X and Y are independent.

Alternatively, we may calculate the marginal probability density of Y as $f_Y(y) = 6y(1 - y)$, for $0 < y < 1$. Thus

$$f_X(x)f_Y(y) = 12x^2(1 - x)6y(1 - y), \qquad 0 < x < 1, 0 < y < 1$$
$$= f_{XY}(x, y)$$

so once again X and Y are independent.   ■

SECTIONS 4.7 AND 4.8   EXERCISES

4.41 In Exercise 4.38 we considered the following joint distribution $P_{XY}(x, y)$ of $X =$ number of oral proposals in a week and $Y =$ number of written proposals in that week as given by the following table:

			y			
x	0	1	2	3	4	Total
0	.010	.015	.030	.075	.050	.180
1	.020	.030	.045	.060	.040	.195
2	.030	.045	.100	.045	.030	.250
3	.040	.060	.045	.030	.020	.195
4	.050	.075	.030	.015	.010	.180
Total	.150	.225	.250	.225	.150	

     a. What are the means of X and Y? (Think, don't calculate.)
     b. Calculate the standard deviations of X and Y.

4.42   a. Find the covariance of X and Y in Exercise 4.41.
     b. Find the correlation of X and Y in Exercise 4.41. What does it indicate about the relation between X and Y? In particular, could X and Y be independent?

4.43 Find the conditional expection of Y, given $X = x$, for the probability distribution of Exercise 4.41. Does the conditional expectation change with X?

4.44 Define $T = X + Y$ to be the total number of proposals made by the firm in Exercises 4.38 and 4.41 in a particular week.
     a. Calculate the probability distribution of T.
     b. Calculate the expected value and variance of T directly from the probability distribution.
     c. Use the results in the appendix to this chapter to recalculate the mean and variance of T.

4.45 In Exercises 3.27 and 3.29 we considered a manufacturing process in which holes are drilled in blocks. The probability that a hole is defectively drilled is .10. Let $X =$ number of defects in a sample of two blocks (there is only one hole per block).
     a. Find the probability distribution of X. You may wish to draw a tree.
     b. Find the expected value and variance of X.
     c. What have you assumed in answering parts (a) and (b)? Under what conditions might the assumption be unreasonable?

4.46   In Exercise 3.29 we assumed that an inspector fails to detect a defect with probability
.10; implicitly we assumed that the inspector does not "detect" defects when in fact
there are none. Let Y = number of detected defects. Use a probability tree to derive
the joint distribution of X (from Exercise 4.45) and Y. Note that Y cannot be larger
than X.

4.47   a. Find the mean and standard deviation of Y in Exercise 4.46.

b. Use the joint distribution of X and Y found in Exercise 4.46 to find the correlation of X and Y.

c. Explain why the correlation should naturally be positive.

4.48   A new-car dealer offers three packages of optional equipment for a particular
model. There is an automatic transmission package, with a profit of \$200 to the
dealer, an air conditioning package, with a profit of \$150, and an interior decor
package, with a profit of \$100. Data indicate that 80% of customers order the
automatic transmission package; 60% of these and 50% of those who don't order
automatic transmissions also order the air conditioning package. Of those who
order both of these packages, 40% order the interior decor package, as do 30% of
those who order exactly one of the transmission and air conditioning packages
and 20% of those who order neither of the other packages. Let Y = the number
of packages ordered on a randomly chosen new car.

a. Find the probability distribution of Y.

b. Find $P(Y \geq 2)$.

c. Find the cumulative distribution function of Y; use it to recalculate $P(Y \geq 2)$.

4.49   Find the mean and standard deviation of Y in Exercise 4.48.

4.50   Let X = the profit from sales of optional packages for the dealer in Exercise 4.48.
Note that X is not directly a function of Y, because the profit depends not only on
how many but also on which packages are sold.

a. Find the probability distribution of X.

b. Find the mean and standard deviation of X.

4.51   Refer to Exercise 4.50. Let T be the total profit from sales of optional packages to 18
randomly chosen customers.

a. Use the results from the appendix to this chapter to find the expected value and
variance of T.

b. What did you assume in answering part (a)? Does any assumption appear clearly
unreasonable?

∫   **4.52**   A daily newspaper in a small city keeps records of the column-inches of classified
ads in a given weekday's paper. Saturday and Sunday editions have different
patterns of ads and are excluded. The probabilities for Y = number of column-
inches (in thousands) on a randomly chosen day are approximated by the density
function

$$f_Y(y) = 30y^4(1 - y), \qquad 0 < y < 1$$

Note that $f_Y(y) = 0$ for y outside the range $0 < y < 1$.

a. Calculate the density for $y = .1, .2, \ldots, .9$ and draw a sketch of the density.

b. Find the probability that between 700 and 900 column-inches are used (that is,
that $.7 < Y < .9$) in a randomly chosen day.

c. Find the probability that $Y > .8$.

∫   **4.53**   Find the mean and standard deviation of the number of column-inches used in
Exercise 4.52 according to the probability density.

∫   **4.54**   The newspaper in Exercise 4.52 also keeps track of X = number of column-inches of commercial ads (in thousands). The distribution of X appears to be

$$f_X(x) = (6/125)x(5 - x), \qquad 0 < x < 5$$

and zero for all other x.
a. Find the cdf of X.
b. Find the probability that X is at least 3.
c. Find the mean and standard deviation of X.

4.55   The random variables X and Y in Exercises 4.54 and 4.52 appear (according to the records of the newspaper) to be independent of each other. If this is assumed, what is the correlation of X and Y?

∫   **4.56**   A company offering overseas telephone service believes that the key variable cost factors for a call are X = number of seconds of computer time used in placing the call and Y = number of minutes of operator time used in placing the call. The probability structure can be represented by the following joint density:

$$f_{XY}(x, y) = (.0625)xe^{-.5y - x/y}, \qquad 0 < x < \infty, 0 < y < \infty$$

a. Find $f_Y(y)$. From calculus, it is known that $\int_0^\infty xe^{-kx} = 1/k^2$.
b. Find the conditional density of X, given $Y = y$.
c. In practice, should X and Y be independent? In this joint density, are they?

∫   **4.57**   Find the conditional expected value of X, given $Y = y$, for the density given in Exercise 4.56.

∫   **4.58**   Find the covariance of X and Y for the density of Exercise 4.56.

Summary ∎

This chapter contains the necessary concepts for extending probability ideas to numerical outcomes. The key idea is that of a random variable, that is, any numerical quantity that is subject to random variation. A random variable is identified by its probability distribution, which is a listing of possible values and the associated probabilities.

Random variables may be either discrete (taking on distinct, separate possible values) or continuous (taking on values through a numerical interval). There are parallel results for discrete and continuous random variables; any computation involving a sum for discrete random variables has an analogous, calculus-based computation involving an integral for continuous random variables.

Because random variables are quantitative (numerical), we can extend the idea of a mean to the idea of expected value (long-run average) of a random variable. The data idea of standard deviation can be extended to random variables as a measure of how much random variation the variable exhibits.

We have also considered joint probability distributions for two or more random variables, and the extension of the independence idea to random variables. Bayes' Theorem can be restated in terms of random variables as well. Covariance and correlation are ways to measure the extent of linear relation between two random variables.

KEY TOPICS AND FORMULAS: Random Variables and
Probability Distributions

1. Properties of the probability distribution $P_Y(y)$ for a discrete random variable Y
   a. $0 \leq P_Y(y) \leq 1$, for all y
   b. $\sum_{\text{all } y} P_Y(y) = 1$
   c Because values of Y are mutually exclusive events, the probabilities are additive.
2. The probability distribution $P_Y(y)$ for a discrete random variable Y can be displayed by a table, a formula, or a graph (called a *probability histogram*).
∫ 3. The probability density function $f_Y(y)$ for a continuous random variable Y allows probabilities to be found by integration:

$$P(a \leq Y \leq b) = \int_a^b f_Y(y)\, dy$$

4. The expected value, variance, and standard deviation for a discrete random variable*

$$\mu_Y = E(Y) = \sum_{\text{all } y} y P_Y(y)$$

$$\sigma_Y^2 = \text{Var}(Y) = \sum_{\text{all } y} (y - \mu_Y)^2 P_Y(y)$$

$$\sigma_Y = \sqrt{\text{Var}(Y)}$$

5. Joint probability distribution, $P_{XY}(x, y)$
   a. Marginal distributions, $P_X(x)$ and $P_Y(y)$
   b. Conditional distribution, $P_{Y|X}(y|x)$
6. The cumulative distribution function (cdf) $F_Y(y) = P(Y \leq y)$ is defined for both discrete and continuous random variables Y.
7. The covariance of random variables X and Y

$$\text{Cov}(X, Y) = \sum_x \sum_y (x - \mu_X)(y - \mu_Y) P_{XY}(x, y)$$

$$= \sum_x \sum_y xy P_{XY}(x, y) - \mu_X \mu_Y$$

   (For continuous random variables, replace summation by integration.)
8. The correlation of X and Y

$$\text{Corr}(X, Y) = \rho_{XY} = \frac{\text{Cov}(X, Y)}{\sigma_X \sigma_Y}$$

9. X and Y are independent if $P_{XY}(x, y) = P_X(x) P_Y(y)$ for all x and y. (For continuous random variables, replace P by f.) If X and Y are independent, $\rho_{XY} = 0$.

---

* For continuous random variables, summation signs are replaced by integration signs and the probability density function replaces $P_Y(y)$.

CHAPTER 4   EXERCISES

4.59   The sales force of a small firm consists of four field engineers (three of whom are over 40 years old) and six sales representatives (two of whom are over 40 years old). One field engineer and two sales representatives are chosen, supposedly at random, to receive special training.

a. Construct the sample space for this experiment. Number the field engineers $1, \ldots, 4$ and the sales representatives $5, \ldots, 10$.

b. Let Y = number of persons selected who are over 40 years old. Find $P_Y(y)$ and $F_Y(y)$ by counting.

4.60   In Exercise 4.59 find $E(Y)$ and σ_Y.

4.61   A state public health agency investigates reported unhealthful practices in restaurants, food stores, and the like. The number of cases varies from week to week. The data indicate the following:

Number of cases/week:	0	1	2	3	4	5	6
Probability:	.02	.13	.20	.30	.19	.15	.01

a. For Y = number of cases in a specified week, find $F_Y(y)$.

b. Find $E(Y)$ and σ_Y.

c. Find $P(\mu_Y - \sigma_Y \leq Y \leq \mu_Y + \sigma_Y)$. Compare to the Empirical Rule approximation.

∫   4.62   Consider the probability density function $f_Y(y) = 20(y^3 - y^4), 0 \leq y \leq 1$:

a. Find $E(Y)$ and σ_Y. Use the shortcut formula

$$\sigma_Y^2 = \int_{all\, y} y^2 f_Y(y)\, dy - \mu_Y^2$$

b. By finding an area under the $f_Y(y)$ curve, find

$$P(\mu_Y - 2\sigma_Y \leq Y \leq \mu_Y + 2\sigma_Y)$$

4.63   The fraction Y of column-inches devoted to display advertising in a certain newspaper on any particular Tuesday can be regarded as a continuous random variable with cdf

$$F_Y(y) = 10y^3 - 15y^4 + 6y^5, \qquad 0 \leq y \leq 1$$

a. Plot $F_Y(y)$.

b. Find $P(Y \leq .5)$, $P(.4 \leq Y \leq .6)$, and $P(Y \geq .7)$.

∂, ∫   **4.64**   a. Show that the probability density in Exercise 4.63 is

$$f_Y(y) = 30y^2 - 60y^3 + 30y^3$$

b. Sketch $f_Y(y)$.

c. Find $E(Y)$ and $Var(Y)$.

d. Find $P(\mu_Y - \sigma_Y \leq Y \leq \mu_Y + \sigma_Y)$. Compare to the Empirical Rule approximation.

4.65   The records of a small auto-body repair shop indicate the following relative frequencies for the number of customers per day:

Number of customers:	0	1	2	3	4	5	6
Relative frequency:	.21	.38	.20	.11	.06	.03	.01

Let Y = number of customers on one particular day.

a. Calculate $F_Y(y)$.

b. Find $E(Y)$ and σ_Y.

4.66 Assume that the numbers of customers on successive days in Exercise 4.65 are independent. Let Y_1 and Y_2 be the respective numbers of customers on two consecutive days.
a. Construct a table for $P_{Y_1 Y_2}(y_1, y_2)$.
b. Define $S = Y_1 + Y_2$, the two-day total number of customers. Find $P_S(s)$.
c. Calculate $E(S)$ and σ_S.

∫ 4.67 Users of a computerized data base have established that X = the number of thousands of lines of instructions and Y = the time in minutes required to run the program have joint density

$$f_{XY}(x, y) = (3/320)(16 - 4x^2 - y^2 + 4xy), \qquad 0 < x < 2, 0 < y < 4$$

a. Find the probability that both X and Y will be less than 0.5.
b. Find the probability that Y will be larger than 1. (X could take any value.)

∫ 4.68 a. Calculate the marginal density of X, for the joint density given in Exercise 4.67.
b. Find $f_{Y|X}(y \mid x)$.

∫ 4.69 Considering their nature, should the random variables X and Y in Exercise 4.67 be independent? According to Exercise 4.68, are they?

∫ **4.70** An insurance firm receives records semiannually from independent agents. From past data, a model for the joint density of X = the proportion of records requiring a coverage update and Y = the proportion of records requiring an address change is

$$f_{XY}(x, y) = 240xy(1 - x)^2(1 - y)^3, \qquad \text{for } 0 < x < 1, 0 < y < 1$$

a. Find the probability that both X and Y are greater than 0.5.
b. Find the probability that Y is between 0.1 and 0.3.

∫ **4.71** a. Find the marginal densities of X and Y in Exercise 4.70.
b. What does the covariance of X and Y equal?

∂, ∫ 4.72 As part of the production process of compact disk (CD) players, the assembled reading unit (a laser-based system that receives digital signals from the disk) is given an initial test. Any unit that fails in reading a test disk, usually because of misalignment, must be reworked at considerable expense. Records are kept of the proportion of units that pass this initial test on each day. If Y is the proportion of passing units on a randomly chosen day, the probability density looks like

$$f_Y(y) = 3990y^{18}(1 - y)^2, \qquad 0 < y < 1$$

a. Calculate values of the density for $y = .70, .75, .80, .85, .90,$ and $.95$. Draw a rough sketch of the density.
b. Find the value y that maximizes the density $f_Y(y)$ (or equivalently, the value y that maximizes the logarithm of the density). In other words, what is the mode of Y?
c. Find the probability that at least 90% of the units pass the initial test on a randomly chosen day. Find the probability that no more than 85% pass.

∫ 4.73 a. Find the expected value of Y for the density of Exercise 4.72.
b. Find the standard deviation.
c. In discussing control charts in Chapter 2, we set one of the control limits at the mean—three standard deviations. What is the probability that Y will fall below this control limit?

∫ **4.74** Stock market analysts watch the "short interest" in the market carefully. An investor sells a stock short by borrowing shares from a broker to sell. The investor hopes that the stock's price will go down, so that the broker can be repaid with lower-priced shares. One analyst said that the distribution of X, the proportion of all sales that are short sales, is

$$f_X(x) = 272x(1 - x)^{15}, \qquad \text{for } 0 < x < 1$$

a. Would you think that X would often be a large proportion like .8? If that happened, what would it mean about the stock market? Calculate a few values of $f_X(x)$. For which x values is the density relatively high?

b. Find the probability that X is less than .10. (In doing the integration, you might find it convenient to substitute $w = 1 - x$, so that $dw = -dx$.)

∫ **4.75** a. Find the expected value of X in Exercise 4.74. It is known from calculus that the integral from 0 to 1 of $x^a(1 - x)^b$ is $a!b!/(a + b + 1)!$

b. Interpret the number you calculated in part (a). In particular, is this the most likely value for the short-sale proportion, X?

c. Find the variance and standard deviation of X. What does the numerical value of the standard deviation tell you about the reasonable range of values for X?

∫ **4.76** The analyst of Exercise 4.74 also considered $Y = $ the daily proportion of sales to individual, noninstitutional investors. The conventional (and rather cynical) wisdom is that individual investors tend to buy at the worst times, right before declines in the stock market, so that high levels of individual purchases are a signal to sell stocks short. The analyst modeled the conditional density of Y given $X = x$ as

$$f_{Y|X}(y|x) = (x + 8)(x + 7)\cdots(x)y^{x-1}(1 - y)^8, \qquad \text{for } 0 < y < 1$$

a. Is the analyst assuming that X and Y are statistically independent? How can you tell?

b. It can be shown that the expected value of Y given $X = x$ is an increasing function of x. Is this fact compatible with statistical independence? Is this fact compatible with the conventional wisdom about individual investors and short sales?

4.77 A food delivery route for a chain of fast food restaurants is scheduled to require 7 hours. Traffic jams and other problems usually extend the actual time to some degree. Records of the required time (in hours), Y, indicate that it may be treated as a continuous random variable with cumulative probability distribution

$$F_Y(y) = 1 - (y - 6)^{-4}, \qquad \text{for } y \geq 7$$

a. The delivery driver must be paid overtime if the route requires more than 8 hours. What is the probability that overtime must be paid?

b. If the route requires more than 9 hours, some of the restaurants run short of product. What is the probability that the route will require overtime, but will not cause restaurants to run short?

∂, ∫ **4.78** a. Find the probability density of the random route time, Y, in Exercise 4.77.

b. Use this density to find the probability that the route will be completed within 7.0 to 7.5 hours.

∫ **4.79** A direct-order retailer keeps track of the fraction of incoming calls each day that are answered within three rings. The quality target is that at least a proportion .80 of calls will be answered promptly. The daily proportion X may be treated as a continuous random variable with density

$$f_X(x) = 30(x^4 - x^5), \qquad \text{for } 0 < x < 1$$

a. What is the probability that the quality target is met?

b. A "disaster day" occurs when less than half of all calls are answered promptly. What is the probability of that disaster?

∫ 4.80 Refer again to X, the proportion of promptly answered calls, in Exercise 4.79. Given that the quality target is met, what is the probability that X will be less than .9?

4.81 The direct-order retailer in Exercise 4.79 also keeps track of the dollar amounts of all telephoned orders. The order size (in hundreds of dollars), Y, of a randomly chosen customer may be regarded as a continuous random variable with cumulative distribution function

$$F_Y(y) = 1 - e^{-2y} - 2ye^{-2y}, \quad \text{for } y > 0$$

a. Find the probability that a randomly chosen customer will place an order of somewhere between $200 and $400.

b. Special expediting is used for all orders larger than $1000. What is the probability that the next call will require some expediting?

∂ 4.82 a. Find the probability density function $f_Y(y)$ of the order size Y in Exercise 4.81.

b. Find the mode of Y, that is, the value y at which the density reaches its maximum.

∫ 4.83 In Exercise 4.77, we considered Y, the time required to complete a restaurant delivery route. Y is a continuous random variable with density

$$f_Y(y) = 4(y - 6)^{-5}, \quad \text{for } y > 7$$

a. Calculate the density for $y = 7, 7.5, 8$, and 8.5. Does the density seem to be symmetric or skewed?

b. Make a rough sketch of the density. Use this density to guess what the mean should be.

c. Calculate the mean (expected value) and standard deviation.

d. Can the Empirical Rule be expected to work well for this density? Calculate the probability that Y falls within one standard deviation of the mean.

∫ 4.84 The proportion X of promptly answered calls in Exercise 4.79 had probability density

$$f_X(x) = 30(x^4 - x^5), \quad \text{for } 0 < x < 1$$

a. Find the expected value. What is the interpretation of this number?

b. Use the shortcut method to find the variance and standard deviation.

4.85 Show that the random variable X of Exercise 4.84 cannot be as much as two standard deviations above its mean. What does this fact suggest about the shape of the distribution?

∫ **4.86** A produce distribution warehouse grades incoming foods. The top grade commands a price premium. The proportions of tomatoes and of lettuce that are rated as top grade varies greatly from day to day. If X = the proportion of top grade tomatoes and Y = the proportion of top grade lettuce, the joint probability density is

$$f_{XY}(x, y) = 3x(1 - xy), \quad \text{for } 0 < x < 1 \text{ and } 0 < y < 1$$

a. Find the probability that less than half the tomatoes, but more than half the lettuce, will receive the top grade.

b. Find the marginal probability densities of X and of Y.

c. Find the probability that X will be less than .5. Find the probability that Y will be greater than .5.

d. Are X and Y independent?

∫ **4.87** The warehouse manager in Exercise 4.86 suspected that the inspectors compensated for low ratings of one food with high ratings of the other. If most of the tomatoes did not receive the top grade, a higher than average proportion of lettuce would receive top grade, and vice versa.

a. If the manager's suspicion is correct, what would be the sign of the covariance (and the correlation) between X and Y?

b. Calculate the covariance of X and Y. Does it have the sign you predicted in part (a)?

c. Find the standard deviations of X and of Y, and the correlation between X and Y. How strong is the correlation?

∫ 4.88 A wholesaler deals with independent hardware stores and has records of the average times of stores between orders and the distribution of interorder times. If X = the average time between orders for a randomly selected hardware store, and Y = the time to the next order for that store, the joint density of X and Y is

$$f_{XY}(x, y) = 12x(1 - x)e^{-y/x}, \qquad \text{for } 0 < x < 1 \text{ and } 0 < y$$

a. Find the density of X alone. What is the probability that X is larger than 0.5?

b. Find the conditional density of Y, given $X = x$. If $X = .5$, what is the probability that Y will be greater than 1?

∫ 4.89 a. Use the conditional density found in part (c) of Exercise 4.88 to find the conditional expected value of Y given $X = x$. In the context of that exercise, does the result make sense?

b. How does the conditional expected value of Y given $X = x$ change as the value x changes? What does this pattern indicate about the sign of the correlation and covariance between X and Y?

∫ 4.90 Calculate the covariance between X and Y for the joint density in Exercise 4.88. It is known that the expected values of X and of Y are both 0.6. Does the sign of the covariance agree with what you expected in part (b) of Exercise 4.89?

C A S E   Probability Distributions

A regional bank was interested in new products and services to expand its customer base. One suggested product was a "debit card." This card works like a credit card in that a cardholder presents it to a merchant as payment. The difference is that the cardholder keeps a balance in an account, from which payments are deducted, rather than effectively borrowing from a bank, which is the case with credit cards. The cardholder does not pay interest on a loan when using a debit card, but the holder must have sufficient funds in the bank to use the card. The bank usually does not charge fees for a debit card; it makes its profit on the difference between interest earned on the cardholder's funds and the costs of servicing the account.

A product manager for the bank carried out a survey of 2150 current bank customers. You are assigned to do a careful analysis of three items from the survey: The reported number of cards in active use by the customer, the reported number that usually have some unpaid balance after a payment, and the reported number of debit cards that the customer would like to have. If we call these items X, Y, and Z, respectively, the survey data yield the following frequencies:

x:	0	0	0	1	1	1	1	1	1	2	2	2	2	2	2
y:	0	0	0	0	0	0	1	1	1	0	0	0	1	1	1
z:	0	1	2	0	1	2	0	1	2	0	1	2	0	1	2
Freq.:	98	45	10	125	110	28	171	203	38	96	87	18	150	228	66

x:	2	2	2	3	3	3	3	3	3	3	3	3	3	3	3
y:	2	2	2	0	0	0	1	1	1	2	2	2	3	3	3
z:	0	1	2	0	1	2	0	1	2	0	1	2	0	1	2
Freq.:	43	160	51	11	15	10	37	78	29	13	51	22	10	23	34

The product manager had a hunch that customers with few cards in active use and customers who had few cards with unpaid balances would like to have more debit cards than those with many cards or with many unpaid balances. Use the survey results as if they perfectly represented the entire population of the bank's current customers (thereby ignoring all variation due to sampling) to investigate these hunches. Write a brief report to the product manager explaining your findings; you should prepare a one-paragraph summary, followed by supporting evidence. The product manager doesn't remember probability theory, so be careful with your use of technical language.

Appendix 4.A Properties of Expected Values and Variances

In this section we present some simple mathematical results about expected values and variances. The results are stated in the language of random variables. Because the notions of expected value and variance of a random variable are generalizations of the corresponding population concepts, the same results apply to populations.

The first results deal with the effect of adding or subtracting a constant. In analyzing the probable return on an investment, there must be a close relation between the gross return (which does not consider the original investment outlay) and net return (which subtracts that outlay).

Effect of Adding a Constant

If a is any constant and Y any random variable,

$$E(Y + a) = E(Y) + a$$
$$\mathrm{Var}(Y + a) = \mathrm{Var}(Y), \qquad \sigma_{Y+a} = \sigma_Y$$

If Y is the gross return and l the investment outlay, then the expected net return $E(Y - l)$ is, reasonably enough, the expected gross return less the investment, $E(Y) - l$. The variances of gross and net return are equal and therefore the standard deviations are also equal. The effect of subtracting l is to shift the whole probability histogram to the left by l units; because that shifting doesn't alter the spread of the histogram, the variance is unchanged. It is fairly easy to prove these two results:

$$E(Y + a) = \sum_{\text{all } y} (y + a)P_Y(y)$$

$$= \sum_{\text{all } y} yP_Y(y) + \sum_{\text{all } y} aP_Y(y)$$

$$= E(Y) + a \sum_{\text{all } y} P_Y(y)$$

$$= E(Y) + a, \qquad \text{because } \sum_{\text{all } y} P_Y(y) = 1$$

$$\text{Var}(Y + a) = \sum_{\text{all } y} [(y + a) - E(Y + a)]^2 P_Y(y)$$

$$= \sum_{\text{all } y} [(y + a) - (E(Y) + a)]^2 P_Y(y)$$

$$= \sum_{\text{all } y} [y - E(Y)]^2 P_Y(y)$$

$$= \text{Var}(Y)$$

Another set of results deals with multiplying or dividing by a constant. This mathematical operation is simply a change in the scale of measurement. For instance, multiplying a dollar amount by 100 changes to units of cents.

Effect of Multiplying by a Constant

If c is any constant and Y any random variable,

$$E(cY) = cE(Y)$$
$$\text{Var}(cY) = c^2 \text{Var}(Y), \qquad \sigma_{cY} = |c|\sigma_Y$$

If $c = 100$ and Y is the cost in dollars, then cY is the cost in cents. The expected cost in cents $E(cY)$ is 100 times the expected cost in dollars, $cE(Y)$. The variance is multiplied by $10{,}000 = (100)^2$ because variance is average squared error; once we take square roots, the standard deviation of the cost in cents σ_{cY} is 100 times the standard deviation of cost in dollars, $c\sigma_Y$.* The proof is a matter of writing down the definitions of expected value and variance, then factoring out c and c^2, respectively.

EXAMPLE 4.23　　A U.S. firm has an investment opportunity in France. The initial outlay is 5,000,000 francs. The firm estimates that the gross return Y has an expected value of 6,200,000 francs and a standard deviation of 500,000 francs. Find the expected value and standard deviation of the net return in dollars, assuming an exchange rate of 5 francs to the dollar.

Solution　　One way to proceed is to work first with net return in francs, then convert to dollars. The net return is $Y - 5{,}000{,}000$, so it has expected value $E(Y) - 5{,}000{,}000$ or 1,200,000 francs, and the standard deviation of 500,000 francs is unchanged. To convert to dollars, divide both the expected value and standard deviation of Y by 5. The expected net return is \$240,000 and the standard deviation is \$100,000. ∎

---

* The absolute value in the standard deviation formula takes care of multiplying by a negative number. Notice that $\sqrt{(-5)^2}$ is $+5$.

The last mathematical results we present involve adding two random variables. This operation arises in a wide variety of situations—the total return on two different investments, the total of cardiac and trauma cases in an emergency room, the total daily output from two automobile assembly lines. Of course there's nothing magical about adding *two* random variables; the results extend immediately to any number of random variables.

Mean and Variance for Sums of Random Variables

For any random variables X and Y,

$$E(X + Y) = E(X) + E(Y)$$

If X and Y are independent, then

$$\text{Var}(X + Y) = \text{Var}(X) + \text{Var}(Y), \qquad \sigma_{X+Y} = \sqrt{\text{Var}(X) + \text{Var}(Y)}$$

The proof of these results is a bit harder than the other proofs.

$$E(X + Y) = \sum_{\text{all } x} \sum_{\text{all } y} (x + y) P_{XY}(x, y)$$

$$= \sum_{\text{all } x} \sum_{\text{all } y} x P_{XY}(x, y) + \sum_{\text{all } x} \sum_{\text{all } y} y P_{XY}(x, y)$$

In the first double sum, think of summing over y first:

$$\sum_{\text{all } y} x P_{XY}(x, y) = x \sum_{\text{all } y} P_{XY}(x, y) = x P_X(x)$$

by definition of the marginal distribution $P_X(x)$. So the first double sum reduces to $\sum_{\text{all } x} x P_X(x) = E(X)$. A similar argument shows that the second double sum is $E(Y)$, which proves the expected value result.

The variance result assumes independence, $P_{XY}(x, y) = P_X(x) P_Y(y)$, and proceeds by expanding the square. Recall that $(a + b)^2 = a^2 + 2ab + b^2$.

$$\text{Var}(X + Y) = \sum_{\text{all } x} \sum_{\text{all } y} (x + y - \mu_{X+Y})^2 P_X(x) P_Y(y)$$

$$= \sum_{\text{all } x} \sum_{\text{all } y} (x - \mu_X + y - \mu_Y)^2 P_X(x) P_Y(y)$$

because we just proved that $\mu_{X+Y} = \mu_X + \mu_Y$. Now expand the square with $a = x - \mu_X$ and $b = y - \mu_Y$:

$$\text{Var}(X + Y) = \sum_{\text{all } x} \sum_{\text{all } y} (x - \mu_X)^2 P_X(x) P_Y(y)$$

$$+ 2 \sum_{\text{all } x} \sum_{\text{all } y} (x - \mu_X)(y - \mu_Y) P_X(x) P_Y(y)$$

$$+ \sum_{\text{all } x} \sum_{\text{all } y} (y - \mu_Y)^2 P_X(x) P_Y(y)$$

The first double sum is

$$\sum_{\text{all } x} (x - \mu_X)^2 P_X(x) \left[\sum_{\text{all } y} P_Y(y) \right] = \sum_{\text{all } x} (x - \mu_X)^2 P_X(x)[1] = \text{Var}(X)$$

The same procedure shows that the third double sum is $\mathrm{Var}(Y)$. The second double sum is $2\,\mathrm{Cov}(X, Y)$, by the definition of covariance given in Section 4.7. Therefore, in general,

$$\mathrm{Var}(X + Y) = \mathrm{Var}(X) + 2\,\mathrm{Cov}(X, Y) + \mathrm{Var}(Y)$$

In Section 4.7 we showed that $\mathrm{Cov}(X, Y) = 0$ when X and Y are independent (as well as in some other cases). Therefore, if X and Y are independent, the covariance term in $\mathrm{Var}(X + Y)$ drops out, and we have $\mathrm{Var}(X + Y) = \mathrm{Var}(X) + \mathrm{Var}(Y)$.

Appendix 4.B Some Reminders about Calculus

Calculus methods are not critical to understanding the essential ideas of this text, but there are a few occasions when it is convenient to use some basic ideas from calculus. This appendix gives a quick refresher in basic calculus methods; it is not intended as an introduction to calculus.

The first key concept is **function**. Informally, a function assigns an "output" number, say, w, to an "input" number, say, x, according to a specified rule. Because we want to reserve the letters f and F for other uses, we use g or G to indicate a function; we write $w = g(x)$.

The **derivative** of a function g at a point $x = a$ is informally defined as the slope of g when $x = a$. We may think of a line tangent to the curve $w = g(x)$ at $x = a$, as in Figure 4.8. The derivative is the slope of the tangent line. The derivative is denoted

$$\frac{d}{dx}g(x)$$

or $g'(x)$. We have no need to emphasize the particular value $x = a$ that is being considered. A very brief table of derivatives is given in Table 4.1.

We sometimes use the **chain rule** for composite functions—functions that are defined in stages; that is, some functions may be thought of as taking an input x, transforming it to an intermediate value $w = g_1(x)$, then transforming w to a final value $v = g_2(w)$. We write such a two-stage function as

$$v = g_2[g_1(x)]$$

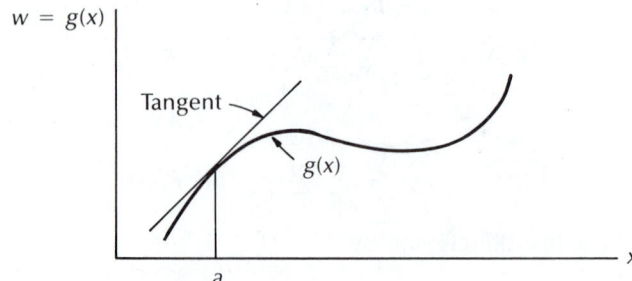

FIGURE 4.8   Tangent Line at $x = a$

TABLE 4.1   Elementary Derivatives

$g(x)$	$\dfrac{d}{dx} g(x)$
c, a constant	0
x^n	nx^{n-1}
e^x	e^x
e^{cx}	ce^{cx}
$\log_e(x)$	$\dfrac{1}{x}$
$ag_1(x) + bg_2(x)$	$a \dfrac{d}{dx} g_1(x) + b \dfrac{d}{dx} g_2(x)$
$g_1(x)g_2(x)$	$g_1(x)\left[\dfrac{d}{dx} g_2(x)\right] + g_2(x)\left[\dfrac{d}{dx} g_1(x)\right]$

For example,

$$v = e^{x^2}$$

can be thought of as a two-stage function. Transform x to $w = x^2$; then transform w to

$$v = e^w = e^{x^2}$$

Alternatively, we write $w = g_1(x) = x^2$ and $v = g_2(w) = e^w$; so $v = g_1[g_2(x)]$. For such "stage-wise" functions, the derivative also goes in stages. First, find the derivative of $g_2(w)$, evaluated at $w = g_1(x)$; next multiply by the derivative of $g_1(x)$. Together, the chain rule asserts that

$$\frac{d}{dx} g_2[g_1(x)] = \left\{\frac{d}{dw} g_2[w = g_1(x)]\right\}\left[\frac{d}{dx} g_1(x)\right]$$

For $g(x) = e^{x^2}$, take $w = g_1(x) = x^2$ and $v = g_2(w) = e^w$. Then

$$\frac{d}{dx} g(x) = \left[\frac{d}{dw} e^w\right]\left[\frac{d}{dx} x^2\right]$$

$$= [e^w[2x] = 2xe^{x^2}$$

from elementary derivatives.

One of the important uses of derivatives is in finding relative maxima and minima. In Figure 4.9 (page 172), notice that at both the peaks and the valleys of the function $g(x)$ the slope (derivative) of $g(x)$ is zero.

Thus to locate a maximum or minimum of $g(x)$, we must solve the equation $(d/dx)g(x) = 0$ for x. In our problems it is usually obvious whether a particular solution is a minimum or a maximum; more sophisticated analyses (such as second-derivative tests) are not needed.

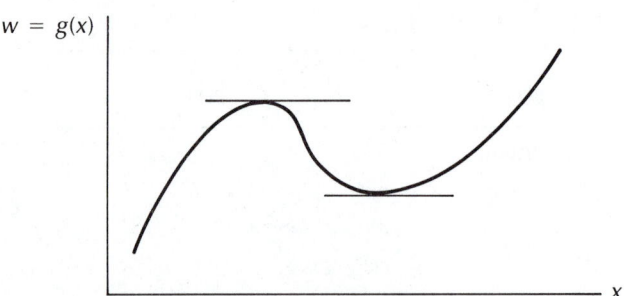

$w = g(x)$

FIGURE 4.9   Derivative Is Zero at Minima and Maxima

The ideas about derivatives discussed so far may be extended to functions of several variables, such as

$$w = g(x_1, x_2, x_3) = x_1^2 e^{3x_2} + \log_e(x_3)$$

We may take **partial derivatives** with respect to each variable by (temporarily) treating the other variables as constants. Partial derivative notation is, for example,

$$\frac{\partial}{\partial x_2}[x_1^2 e^{3x_2} + \log_e(x_3)]$$

In this example, x_1 (and thus x_1^2) and x_3 [and thus $\log_e(x_3)$] should be taken as constants, say, c_1 and c_3. Thus

$$\frac{\partial}{\partial x_2}(c_1 e^{3x_2} + c_3) = c_1 \frac{\partial}{\partial x_2}(e^{3x_2}) + c_3$$

$$= c_1(e^{3x_2})(3) + 0 = 3x_1^2 e^{3x_2}$$

where we have applied the chain rule to get

$$\frac{\partial}{\partial x_2} e^{3x_2} = (e^{3x_2})\frac{\partial}{\partial x_2}(3x_2) = (e^{3x_2})(3)$$

To find a maximum or minimum of a function of several variables, we must equate *all* partial derivatives to zero and solve the resulting set of equations for the values of all the variables. In our problems, it is obvious whether the solution is a minimum or a maximum. To find a minimum or maximum of

$$w = g(x_1, x_2) = (x_1 - 4)^2 + (2x_1 + x_2 - 4)^2$$

we must solve the two equations

$$\frac{\partial}{\partial x_1}[(x_1 - 4)^2 + (2x_1 + x_2 - 4)^2] = 2(x_1 - 4) + 24(2x_1 + x_2 - 4) = 0$$

and

$$\frac{\partial}{\partial x_2}[(x_1 - 4)^2 + (2x_1 + x_2 - 4)^2] = 2(2x_1 + x_2 - 4) = 0$$

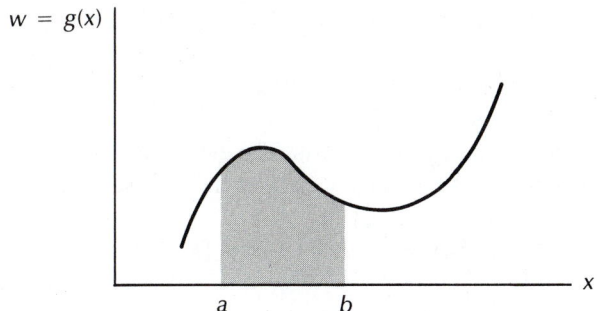

$w = g(x)$

a b x

FIGURE 4.10   Integral as Area

and obtain $x_1 = 4$ and $x_2 = -4$. We note that $g(x_1, x_2)$ is never negative and that $g(4, -4) = (4 - 4)^2 + [2(4) + (-4) - 4]^2 = 0$. Therefore, we have clearly found the only minimum of g; because the given solution is the only one, there is no finite maximum of g.

We have some use for integral calculus as well as the previous differential (derivative) calculus. In general, we need to evaluate **definite integrals** of the form

$$\int_a^b g(x)\,dx$$

Recall that a definite integral is the area under the curve defined by $g(x)$ between the points a and b, as shown in Figure 4.10. The standard way to evaluate definite integrals is to appeal to the Fundamental Theorem of Calculus. According to this theorem we should

1. Find a function $G(x)$ having derivative $g(x)$—called the **antiderivative** of $g(x)$.
2. Evaluate $\int_a^b g(x)\,dx = G(x)\big|_a^b = G(b) - G(a)$

A few of the most useful antiderivatives are shown in Table 4.2.

For example, to evaluate $\int_1^4 2e^{-2x}\,dx$, we find the antiderivative of $g(x) = e^{-2x}$ to be $G(x) = e^{-2x}/(-2)$ and note that the antiderivative of $2e^{-2x}$ is $2e^{-2x}/(-2) = -e^{-2x}$. It follows that

$$\int_1^4 2e^{-2x}\,dx = -e^{-2x}\big|_1^4 = [-e^{-2(4)}] - [-e^{-2(1)}] = e^{-2} - e^{-8}$$

TABLE 4.2   Antiderivatives for Integration

Function, $g(x)$	Antiderivative, $G(x)$
$(x + c)^n,\ n \neq -1$	$(x + c)^{n+1}/(n + 1)$
x^{-1}	$\log_e(x)$
e^{cx}	e^{cx}/c
xe^{cx}	$xe^{cx}/c - e^{cx}/c^2$
$c_1 g_1(x) + c_2 g_2(x)$	$c_1 G_1(x) + c_2 G_2(x)$
$c_n x^n + c_{n-1}x^{n-1} + \cdots + c_0$	$c_n x^{n+1}/(n + 1) + c_{n-1}x^n/n + \cdots + c_0 x$

Occasionally, we need to evaluate integrals with infinite endpoints, such as

$$\int_0^\infty g(x)\,dx = \lim_{M\to\infty} \int_0^M g(x)\,dx$$

assuming that the limit exists. The evaluation of the limit is usually clear, but it can sometimes be tricky. Consider the integral (see Table 4.2)

$$\int_0^\infty xe^{-x}\,dx = \int_0^\infty xe^{(-1)x}\,dx = [xe^{-x}/(-1) - e^{-x}/(-1)^2]|_0^\infty$$

The problem is in evaluating $-xe^{-x}|_0^\infty$. As $x \to \infty$, $e^{-x} \to 0$ and $x \to \infty$, so that the limit of xe^{-x} (as $x \to \infty$) is "$0 \cdot \infty$." An application of a theorem of calculus called L'Hôpital's Rule indicates that $e^{-x} \to 0$ faster than $x \to \infty$, so

$$\lim_{x\to\infty} xe^{-x} = 0$$

Thus,

$$\int_0^\infty xe^{-x}\,dx = (0 - 0) - [0 - (-1)] = 1$$

Finally, we need to evaluate double integrals $\int_a^b \int_c^d g(x_1, x_2) \times dx_1\,dx_2$. Under certain technical conditions (which are always met in our situations), double integrals may be evaluated in two steps. First, regard x_2 as a constant c_2 and perform the integral with respect to x_1. Then integrate the result with respect to x_2. The integral may also be done in the reverse order, with respect to x_2 first, then x_1. For example, we may use the fact that the antiderivative of $(x + c)^n$ is $(x + c)^{n+1}/(n + 1)$ to evaluate

$$\int_0^1 \int_0^2 (x_1 + 2x_2)^2\,dx_1\,dx_2 = \int_0^1 \left[\int_0^2 (x_1 + 2x_2)^2\,dx_1\right] dx_2$$

$$= \int_0^1 \left.\frac{(x_1 + 2x_2)^3}{3}\right|_0^2 dx_2$$

$$= \int_0^1 \left[\frac{(2 + 2x_2)^3}{3} - \frac{(0 + 2x_2)^3}{3}\right] dx_2$$

$$= \left[\frac{8(1 + x_2)^4}{12} - \frac{8(x_2)^4}{12}\right]\Big|_0^1$$

$$= \left[\frac{8(2)^4}{12} - \frac{8(1)^4}{12}\right] - \left[\frac{8(1)^4}{12} - \frac{8(0)^4}{12}\right]$$

$$= 9.3333$$

One may also integrate with respect to x_2 first, then with respect to x_1; the result is once again 9.3333.

SOME SPECIAL PROBABILITY DISTRIBUTIONS

The ideas, notations, and results of the previous chapter apply to any random variables and any probability distributions. Now we identify and present formulas for some particular probability distributions that arise very often in practice. In particular, we describe the kind of situation and the critically important assumptions that justify the use of each distribution.

5.1 COUNTING POSSIBLE OUTCOMES ■

This chapter contains a discussion of the probability distributions that apply to several commonly occurring situations. Among the most common is taking a random sample. The probability distributions that apply to the simplest sampling situations are discussed in Sections 5.2 and 5.3. As we suggested when we discussed the classical interpretation of probability, we have considerable use for the idea that

$$P(\text{event}) = \frac{\text{number of outcomes favoring event}}{\text{total number of outcomes}}$$

To use this idea, we need a method for counting possible outcomes without the labor of actually listing the outcomes. This section contains a brief discussion of counting formulas. These formulas are critical in the development of the probability distributions of the next two sections. They arise as answers to the following two questions:

sequences and subsets

1. How many **sequences** of k symbols can be formed from a set of r distinct symbols, using each symbol no more than once?
2. How many **subsets** of k symbols can be formed from a set of r distinct symbols, using each symbol no more than once?

TABLE 5.1   Subsets and Sequences of the Five Letters A, B, C, D, and E

Subsets	Sequences					
{A, B, C}	ABC	ACB	BAC	CAB	BCA	CBA
{A, B, D}	ABD	ADB	BAD	DAB	BDA	DBA
{A, B, E}	ABE	AEB	BAE	EAB	BEA	EBA
{A, C, D}	ACD	ADC	CAD	DAC	CDA	DCA
{A, C, E}	ACE	AEC	CAE	EAC	CEA	ECA
{A, D, E}	ADE	AED	DAE	EAD	DEA	EDA
{B, C, D}	BCD	BDC	CBD	DBC	CDB	DCB
{B, C, E}	BCE	BEC	CBE	EBC	CEB	ECB
{B, D, E}	BDE	BED	DBE	EBD	DEB	EDB
{C, D, E}	CDE	CED	DCE	ECD	DEC	EDC

The only difference between a sequence and a subset is that order matters for sequences and not for subsets. The sequence ABC is not the same as the sequence CAB, but the subset {A, B, C} is the same as the subset {C, A, B}. As an example, consider sequences and subsets consisting of three of the first five letters. There are 60 sequences but only 10 subsets (Table 5.1).

First we derive a formula for the number of sequences. In the example, we could choose any of five letters to be first, then any of the four remaining letters to form 5×4 or 20 two-letter sequences. We can combine each of these with any of the remaining three letters to form $(5 \times 4)(3) = 60$ three-letter sequences. In general, we have r choices for the first symbol, $r - 1$ for the second symbol, and so on. When we come to choose the kth and last symbol, we have already used up $k - 1$ symbols and have $r - (k - 1) = r - k + 1$ symbols remaining. Therefore,

$$\text{number of sequences} = r(r - 1)\cdots(r - k + 1)$$

permutations

of k symbols from r distinct symbols. This formula looks like a factorial $(r!)$ except that it is truncated at $r - k + 1$ instead of continuing down to 1. The number of sequences is often called the number of **permutations** of r symbols taken k at a time and we denote it as $_kP_r$ or r_k. It can be expressed via factorials as

$$_kP_r = \frac{r!}{(r - k)!} = r(r - 1)\cdots(r - k + 1)$$

The factors $r - k, r - k - 1, \ldots, 3, 2, 1$ in the denominator cancel the corresponding factors in the numerator, leaving only the factors $r, r - 1, \ldots, r - k + 1$.

The number of subsets is called the number of **combinations** of r symbols taken k at a time and is denoted as $_kC_r$ or $\binom{r}{k}$. Table 5.1 suggests an indirect way of finding $\binom{r}{k}$. Each row of the table of sequences corresponds to a particular subset. The six columns correspond to all possible orderings of a given set of three letters. In general, for k symbols, there are $k(k - 1)\cdots 3 \cdot 2 \cdot 1 = k!$ columns, because any of the k symbols may be first, any of the remaining $k - 1$ symbols second, and so on. All k symbols are used, so the factorial is not truncated. Therefore,

$$\text{number of sequences} = (\text{number of rows})(\text{number of columns})$$

$$\frac{r!}{(r-k)!} = (\text{number of subsets})k!$$

Now solve for $\binom{r}{k}$, the number of subsets, and get

$$\binom{r}{k} = \frac{r!}{k!(r-k)!}$$

The symbol $\binom{r}{k}$ is read "r choose k," suggesting a choice of a subset of k things from a set of r things.

The combinations formula is particularly useful in random sampling, because choosing a sample of size k without replacement from a population of size r is exactly the same as choosing a subset of k things from a set of r things. We do not typically care about the ordering of items during sampling, so the permutation formula is somewhat less central.

EXAMPLE 5.1   In auditing the 87 accounts payable of a small firm, a sample of 10 account balances are checked. How many possible samples are there? Assuming that 13 of the accounts contain errors, how many samples contain exactly two erroneous accounts?

Solution   There is no need to consider the sequence (order) in which the 10 accounts are drawn, because all 10 are checked. Therefore we can count the number of combinations. There are $\binom{87}{10} = 87!/10!77! \approx 4{,}000{,}000{,}000{,}000$ possible samples. To obtain all samples with two erroneous accounts, we can combine any of the $\binom{13}{2}$ choices of two from the 13 erroneous accounts with any of the $\binom{74}{8}$ choices of eight from the 74 correct accounts. Because any choice of two erroneous accounts can be matched with any choice of eight correct ones, there are $\binom{13}{2}\binom{74}{8} \approx 1{,}200{,}000{,}000{,}000$ samples with two erroneous and eight correct accounts.   ∎

EXAMPLE 5.2   In a sales contest, the 10 top performers out of 612 salespeople receive prizes, ranging from a free vacation for the overall winner to $50 for the tenth-place finisher. How many different prize lists are possible?

Solution   Here the ordering is certainly relevant, so the permutation formula applies. There are $_{10}P_{612} = 612!/602! \approx 6{,}800{,}000{,}000{,}000{,}000{,}000{,}000{,}000{,}000$ possibilities.   ∎

SECTION 5.1   EXERCISES

5.1   In a certain state, an appeals court consists of seven judges. For a routine case, three judges are chosen at random as a panel to hear a case and render a decision. How many distinct panels can be formed?

5.2   Suppose that five of the seven judges on the appeals court in Exercise 5.1 are considered potentially sympathetic to a particular legal argument. How many panels can be formed having exactly two potentially sympathetic judges? How many panels have at least two such judges?

5.3   A grocery chain wants to taste-test a private-label cola drink. A tester is given eight unmarked glasses, four containing the private-label drink and four containing a nationally advertised cola. The tester is asked to identify the four glasses containing the private-label drink. How many different choices of four glasses can the taster make?

5.4   How many of the choices in Exercise 5.3 include three correct glasses and one incorrect glass?

5.2   BERNOULLI TRIALS AND THE BINOMIAL DISTRIBUTION

The simplest data-gathering process is counting the number of times a certain event occurs. When taking a random sample of registered voters, we can count the number who prefer the incumbent to the challenger. When sampling pistons for an auto engine assembly, we can count the number that fail to meet tolerances. When examining hiring practices, we can count the number of minority workers hired by a firm. When examining credit policies, we can count the number of bad-debt accounts. We can reduce an almost endless variety of situations to this simple counting process.

These examples, and many others, share certain common features. First, the overall process can be thought of as a series of **trials**, each trial yielding exactly one of two possible outcomes. In sampling registered voters, each person constitutes a trial. The incumbent is either preferred or not preferred. In sampling pistons, each trial yields a defective piston or a piston within tolerances. Each person hired is or is not a minority member, and each credit account is or is not a bad debt. The standard language is to call one outcome "success" and the other "failure." Which outcome is called success does not matter; a bad debt account could be called a success.

Second, in each of these situations, it is reasonable to assume that the probability of success π is constant over trials. The probability of finding a registered voter who favors the incumbent does not change in mid-sample (unless the sample is conducted over an extended period of time), nor does the probability of a defective piston, nor does the probability of a bad debt. If relative unemployment rates and the firm's hiring practices do not change, the probability that a given new employee is a minority worker does not change.

And finally, in each situation, the results of the various trials can be assumed to be independent. The preference of one voter for the incumbent should not affect the preference of another voter; at least that shouldn't occur in a carefully designed study. If one account happens to be a bad debt, that fact doesn't change the likelihood that the next account sampled will be good.

These three assumptions—each trial results in either a success or failure, constant probability π of success, and independence of trials—define a series of **Bernoulli trials**. The assumptions are assumptions; not every counting process can reasonably be modeled as Bernoulli trials. Whether these assumptions are reasonable depends on the situation. Success–failure trials are not always independent and identical. But in many cases these assumptions hold to a good approximation, which makes Bernoulli trials a useful model.

EXAMPLE 5.3

Discuss whether or not a series of Bernoulli trials provides a reasonable model for each of the following situations.

a. A telephone researcher involved in a television viewing survey calls different homes (selected at random), one each 15 minutes between 5:30 P.M. and 10:00 P.M. Each person contacted is asked if anyone in the household is watching the ABC network program. A trial consists of contacting a household to determine whether or not someone in the house is watching an ABC network program.

b. A trust officer examines a sample of stock listings from those on the New York Stock Exchange to determine whether or not each stock has risen in price during the past week. Here a trial consists of selecting a stock and determining whether or not the price has risen during the past week.

c. Each of 50 newly hired management trainees is rated outstanding, acceptable, or unsatisfactory at the conclusion of a training program. Determining the rating for a newly hired management trainee constitutes a trial.

Solution

a. The assumption of constant probability from trial to trial is not plausible in this survey, because the level of television watching in general is relatively lower early in the evening. Hence the probability of finding someone watching the ABC network program may vary depending on the time of the call.

b. The independence assumption is very dubious. During any particular time period, there's a moderately strong tendency for stock prices to move up or down together, because of interest rate changes, political news, or the herd instinct of investors. So for the stocks listed in the sample, the outcome on any one trial would depend heavily on price changes for the other stocks.

c. For this problem there are three possible outcomes on each trial, not two. However, if we define a success to be a rating of outstanding and a failure to be the complement (not rated outstanding), Bernoulli trials may be a good model. The key question is whether the trial outcomes are independent. If there is an effective ceiling or quota for the number (or proportion) of outstanding ratings (for instance, a restriction that the supervisor can rate no more than 10% of the group as outstanding), then the independence assumption is violated. But if each trainee is rated according to established, reasonably objective criteria, independence of trials (ratings) should be a reasonable assumption. ∎

There is one additional feature common to all the situations in Example 5.3. We are counting the number of successes that occur in a fixed number n of trials, without regard to the particular order in which successes and failures occur. This would not be true if, for instance, a telephone interviewer called homes at random until 24 television-watching homes had been obtained. In this situation, n is not fixed and the order of successes and failures *is* relevant; the last trial (call) is guaranteed to be a success.

binomial experiment   A collection of a fixed number n of Bernoulli trials in which the researcher is interested in the total number of successes defines a **binomial experiment**. The properties of a binomial experiment are listed here.

Properties of a Binomial Experiment

1. There are n Bernoulli trials; each one results in either a success (S) or a failure (F).
2. The probability of a success, $\pi = P(S)$, remains constant over trials $[P(F) = 1 - \pi]$.
3. The trials are independent. (Assumptions 1–3 define Bernoulli trials.)
4. The random variable of interest is Y, which is the number of successes in n trials. The ordering of successes is not important.

---

binomial random variable
binomial probability distribution   The random variable Y in a binomial experiment is called a **binomial random variable**. It is a discrete random variable that can assume any one of the values $0, 1, 2, \ldots, n$. The **binomial probability distribution** $P_Y(y)$, which assigns probabilities to each value of Y, is best understood by considering a simple example.

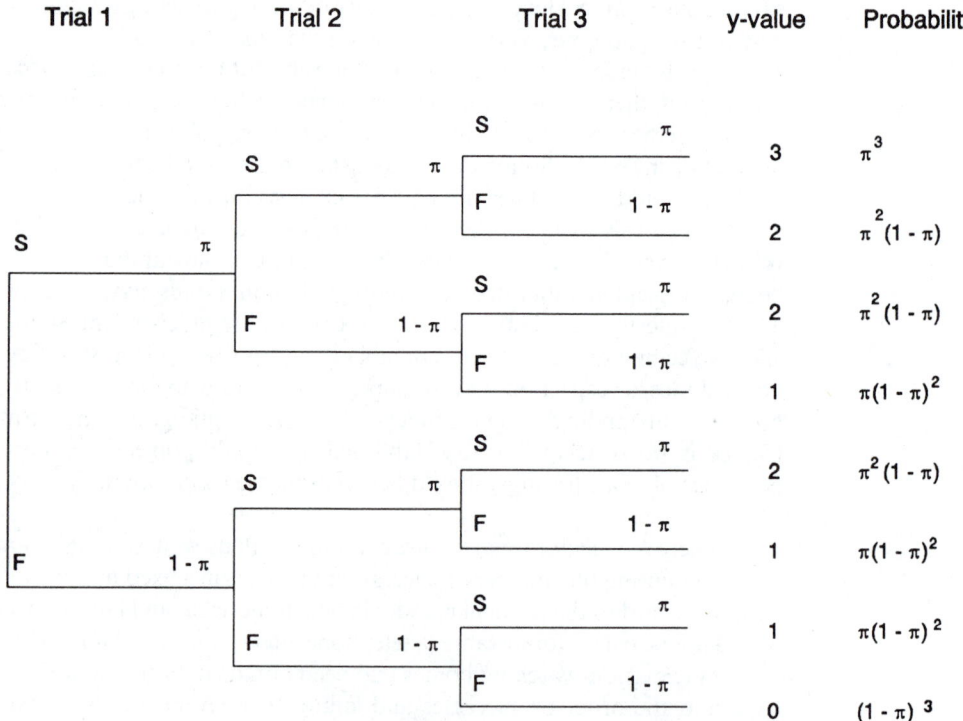

FIGURE 5.1   Probability Tree for Binomial Distribution with $n = 3$

Suppose we take a random sample of three individuals from a population with a proportion π of successes. Figure 5.1 shows a probability tree for calculating the distribution of Y. By adding up the probabilities of appropriate paths, we can find the binomial probability distribution for $n = 3$. For instance, the second, third, and fifth paths (counting from the top) give $y = 2$; each of these paths has probability $\pi^2(1 - \pi)$. We add the path probabilities to get $P(Y = 2)$; $P_Y(2) = \pi^2(1 - \pi) + \pi^2(1 - \pi) + \pi^2(1 - \pi) = 3\pi^2(1 - \pi)$. The complete probability distribution is

y:	0	1	2	3
$P_Y(y)$:	$(1 - \pi)^3$	$3\pi(1 - \pi)^2$	$3\pi^2(1 - \pi)$	π^3

EXAMPLE 5.4   Find the binomial distribution for $n = 4$.

Solution   To save space, we have listed the paths instead of drawing the tree. You may wish to construct the probability tree that gives rise to these paths.

Path Number	Path Sequence	y	Probability
1	SSSS	4	π^4
2	SSSF	3	$\pi^3(1 - \pi)$
3	SSFS	3	$\pi^3(1 - \pi)$
4	SSFF	2	$\pi^2(1 - \pi)^2$
5	SFSS	3	$\pi^3(1 - \pi)$
6	SFSF	2	$\pi^2(1 - \pi)^2$
7	SFFS	2	$\pi^2(1 - \pi)^2$
8	SFFF	1	$\pi(1 - \pi)^3$
9	FSSS	3	$\pi^3(1 - \pi)$
10	FSSF	2	$\pi^2(1 - \pi)^2$
11	FSFS	2	$\pi^2(1 - \pi)^2$
12	FSFF	1	$\pi(1 - \pi)^3$
13	FFSS	2	$\pi^2(1 - \pi)^2$
14	FFSF	1	$\pi(1 - \pi)^3$
15	FFFS	1	$\pi(1 - \pi)^3$
16	FFFF	0	$(1 - \pi)^4$

All the paths corresponding to a particular y value have the same probability; for instance, each of the six paths that yield $y = 2$ has probability $\pi^2(1 - \pi)^2$. So adding up the path probabilities for a particular y value amounts to multiplying the number of paths by the appropriate probability.

y:	0	1	2	3	4
$P_Y(y)$:	$(1 - \pi)^4$	$4\pi(1 - \pi)^3$	$6\pi^2(1 - \pi)^2$	$4\pi^3(1 - \pi)$	π^4

■

We need a formula to save the labor of actually counting paths. We can use the methods of Section 5.1. One way to specify a path in a binomial experiment is to state the trials on which a success occurs. For example, if $n = 5$, the successes occur only at trials 1 and 4—for short, S at $(1, 4)$—specifies the path SFFSF. The ordering of the trial numbers is irrelevant; S at $(4, 1)$ also specifies the path SFFSF. Therefore, in n trials the number of paths containing y successes is the same as the number of subsets of size y out of the first n integers. From Section 5.1, this number is

$$\binom{n}{y} = \frac{(n!)}{y!(n - y)!}$$

Using this expression for the relevant number of paths in a binomial probability tree, we obtain a general expression for the binomial probability distribution.

Binomial Probability Distribution

$$P_Y(y) = \frac{n!}{y!(n - y)!} \pi^y(1 - \pi)^{n-y}, \qquad \text{for } y = 0, 1, \ldots, n$$

Appendix Table 1 (at the end of the book) contains numerical values of binomial probabilities. Each value of n determines a block of probabilities. For values of π below .5, values of π are read at the top of the block and values of y are read on the left. For values of π above .5, values of π are read at the bottom, and values of y on the right.

EXAMPLE 5.5   In Appendix Table 1 of binomial probabilities, find the probability distribution of a binomial random variable for $n = 5$ and (a) $\pi = .2$, (b) $\pi = .5$, and (c) $\pi = .7$.

Solution   We look in the $n = 5$ block of Appendix Table 1. For $\pi = .2$ we read *down* the .20 column; for $\pi = .5$ we use the $\pi = .50$ column; for $\pi = .7$ we read *up* the $\pi = .70$ column. The resulting distribution is

y	0	1	2	3	4	5
$P_Y(y)$ for $\pi = .20$	.3277	.4096	.2048	.0512	.0064	.0003
$P_Y(y)$ for $\pi = .50$	.0313	.1563	.3125	.3125	.1563	.0313
$P_Y(y)$ for $\pi = .70$	.0024	.0284	.1323	.3087	.3602	.1681

EXAMPLE 5.6   In the long run, 20% of all management trainees are rated outstanding, 50% acceptable, and 30% unsatisfactory. In a sample of 20 randomly selected trainees, find the following probabilities:

    a. Exactly 4 trainees are rated outstanding.
    b. At least 4 trainees are rated outstanding.
    c. Exactly 15 trainees are rated outstanding or acceptable.
    d. At least 15 trainees are rated outstanding or acceptable.

Assume that we have a set of Bernoulli trials.

Solution   a. Find the entry for $n = 20$, $\pi = .20$ (on top of the block), and $y = 4$ (to the left). The probability is .2182.

b. Add the entries for $n = 20$, $\pi = .20$, $y = 4, 5, 6, \ldots, 20$, and get .5886.

c. The probability that a rating is outstanding or acceptable is $.20 + .50 = .70$. Find the entry for $n = 20$, $\pi = .70$ (below the block), and $y = 15$ (to the right): .1789. Alternatively, this probability must equal the probability of exactly five unsatisfactory ratings, which has $\pi = .30$ and $y = 5$. This reasoning yields the same table entry: .1789.

d. Add the entries for $n = 20$, $\pi = .70$, $y = 15, 16, \ldots, 20$ to get .4163. Or add the entries for $n = 20$, $\pi = .30$, $y = 5, 4, \ldots, 0$ to get the equivalent probability of 5 or fewer unsatisfactory ratings.   ∎

The expected value and variance of a binomial random variable Y depend, of course, on the values of n and π.

Mean and Variance of a Binomial Random Variable

$$E(Y) = n\pi$$
$$\text{Var}(Y) = n\pi(1 - \pi), \qquad \sigma_Y = \sqrt{n\pi(1 - \pi)}$$

The resulting expected value for a binomial random variable seems intuitively reasonable. If, on average, 30% of all trainees are rated outstanding, then in a sample of 20 trainees we would expect to find $20(.3) = 6$ who are rated outstanding.

SECTION 5.2   EXERCISES

5.5   Let Y be a binomial random variable. Compute $P_Y(y)$ for each of the following situations.
   a. $n = 10$, $\pi = .2$, $y = 3$
   b. $n = 4$, $\pi = .4$, $y = 2$
   c. $n = 16$, $\pi = .7$, $y = 12$

5.6   Let Y have a binomial probability distribution with $n = 6$ and $\pi = .25$.
   a. Calculate $P_Y(y)$ by hand for $y = 1, 2$, and 3. Compare your results to those listed in Appendix Table 1.
   b. Draw a probability histogram of $P_Y(y)$.
   c. Find the mean and standard deviation of Y.

5.7   Let $Y =$ the number of successes in 20 independent trials, where the probability of success on any one trial is .4. Find
   a. $P(Y \geq 4)$
   b. $P(Y > 4)$
   c. $P(Y \leq 10)$
   d. $P(Y > 16)$

5.8   Let Y be a binomial random variable with $n = 20$ and $\pi = .6$. Find $P(Y \leq 16)$ and $P(Y < 16)$. Compare these probabilities to the ones found in parts (a) and (b) of Exercise 5.7.

5.9   A chain of motels has adopted a policy of giving a 3% discount to customers who pay in cash rather than by credit cards. Its experience is that 30% of all customers take the discount. Let Y = the number of discount takers among the next 20 customers.

a. Do you think the binomial assumptions are reasonable in this situation?

b. Assuming that binomial probabilities apply, find the probability that exactly 5 of the next 20 customers take the discount.

c. Find $P(5$ or fewer customers take the discount).

d. What is the most probable number of discount takers in the next 20 customers?

5.10 Find the expected value and standard deviation of the number of discount takers in Exercise 5.9.

5.11 Use the Empirical Rule to approximate the probability that Y in Exercise 5.9 falls within one standard deviation of its expected value. Use binomial tables to find the exact probability. How good is the Empirical Rule approximation?

5.12 A small company uses a parcel service to ship packages of special cheeses ordered as gifts. The company has found that 90% of all orders are delivered on time. A batch of 100 packages is sent out. Let Y = number of packages delivered on time.

a. Do the binomial assumptions seem reasonable in this situation?

b. Assuming that binomial probabilities apply, find $P(Y \geq 85)$.

5.13 Find $E(Y)$ and σ_Y in Exercise 5.12, assuming binomial probabilities.

5.14 A prescription drug manufacturer claims that only 10% of all new drugs that are shown to be effective in animal tests ever pass through all the additional testing required to be marketed. The manufacturer currently has 8 new drugs that have been shown to be effective in animal tests and they await further testing and approval.

a. Find the probability that none of the 8 drugs is marketed.

b. Find the probability that at least 2 are marketed.

c. Find the expected number of marketed drugs among the 8.

5.15 Plot a probability histogram of $P_Y(y)$ in Exercise 5.14.

5.3   HYPERGEOMETRIC DISTRIBUTION   ■

hypergeometric probability distribution

The counting formulas of Section 5.1 can be used to define the **hypergeometric probability distribution**. In this section we state a formula for this distribution and relate it to the binomial distribution.

The situation that leads to the hypergeometric distribution is easily described. There must be a population consisting of some number N_S of successes and some number N_F of failures. The total population size is $N = N_S + N_F$.* A sample of size n is taken from the population without replacement. The relevant random variable is Y = observed number of successes in the sample. Example 5.1 illustrates one such situation: There are 13 successes (erroneous accounts) and 74 failures in the population, and the sample size $n = 10$. That example indicates the basic principle of the hypergeometric distribution, which is straight out of the

---

* These N's are not random variables, though we usually use capital letters to denote random variables. The N's are constants.

classical interpretation of probability:

$$P(\text{event}) = \frac{\text{number of outcomes favoring the event}}{\text{total number of outcomes}}$$

In this context, outcome means sample. There are $\binom{N}{n}$ possible samples of size n that can be drawn from a population of size N. The samples that favor the event are those that have exactly y successes and exactly $n - y$ failures. As indicated in Example 5.1, there are $\binom{N_S}{y}\binom{N_F}{n-y}$ such samples, which leads to the following hypergeometric distribution:

Hypergeometric Probability Distribution

$Y =$ number of S's in a random sample of size n (taken without replacement) from a population consisting of N_S S's and N_F F's.

$$P_Y(y) = \frac{\binom{N_S}{y}\binom{N_F}{n-y}}{\binom{N}{n}}, \qquad y = 0, 1, \ldots, n$$

(If $y > N_S$, take $\binom{N_S}{y}$ and $P_Y(y)$ to be 0; if $n - y > N_F$, take $\binom{N_F}{n-y}$ and $P_Y(y)$ to be 0.)

EXAMPLE 5.7   In Example 5.1, we considered sampling 10 of the 87 accounts of a small firm. Thirteen of the 87 accounts contain errors. Find $P(2$ erroneous accounts in the sample$)$.

Solution   We have $N = 87$, $n = 10$, $N_S = 13$, and therefore $N_F = 74$; we want $P(Y = 2)$.

$$P_Y(2) = \frac{\binom{13}{2}\binom{74}{10-2}}{\binom{87}{10}} \approx \frac{1,175,600,000,000}{4,000,800,000,000} = .294 \qquad \blacksquare$$

Although we could set out many other illustrations of hypergeometric situations, we want to emphasize the close relation of hypergeometric and binomial probabilities. **If the population size N is large (relative to the sample size n), the distinction between the binomial and the hypergeometric is negligible.** If a random sample of 100 is taken from a population of 100,000,000, it does not matter in any serious way whether hypergeometric or binomial probabilities are used.

EXAMPLE 5.8   Find $P(2$ erroneous accounts$)$ in Example 5.7 using a binomial probability distribution.

Solution   We take $n = 10$ and $\pi = 13/87 \approx .149$. Thus $P(2$ erroneous accounts$) = \binom{10}{2}(.149)^2(.851)^8 \approx .275$. We calculated this probability using the binomial probability distribution. It is approximately equal to the probability of two erroneous accounts, .30, which we calculated using the hypergeometric probability distribution. As N gets larger, these probabilities become closer.   ■

The close relation between hypergeometric and binomial probabilities extends to expected values and variances. We don't prove it, but the mean and variance for a hypergeometric probability distribution are as follows:

Expected Value and Variance for a Hypergeometric Random Variable Y

$$E(Y) = n \frac{N_S}{N}$$

$$\text{Var}(Y) = n \frac{N_S}{N}\left(1 - \frac{N_S}{N}\right)\frac{N - n}{N - 1}$$

The ratio N_S/N is exactly π, the probability of success on a single trial. In Example 5.8 we took $\pi = 13/87$. Therefore the expected value of Y for the hypergeometric is $E(Y) = n\pi$, just like the binomial. By substituting $\pi = N_S/N$, the hypergeometric variance reduces to $n\pi(1 - \pi)[(N - n)/(N - 1)]$, as compared to the binomial variance $n\pi(1 - \pi)$. There is an extra factor $(N - n)/(N - 1)$, **finite population** called the **finite population correction**. This factor is exactly equal to 1 when **correction** $n = 1$; otherwise, it is less than 1. For most practical situations in which the sample is a small fraction of the population (n is much smaller than N), the factor $(N - n)/(N - 1)$ is nearly 1. For example, if $n = 100$ and $N = 100,000,000$, then $(N - n)/(N - 1) \approx .999999$. Therefore we do not worry about the distinction between the hypergeometric and the binomial probability distributions in most situations; the distinction makes little numerical difference.

SECTION 5.3   EXERCISES

5.16   Let Y be a hypergeometric random variable with $N_S = 3$, $N_F = 4$, and $n = 3$.
   a. Compute $P_Y(y)$ for $y = 0, 1, 2, 3$.
   b. Graph this probability distribution.

5.17   Find the mean and standard deviation for the random variable Y defined in Exercise 5.16.

5.18   Compute $P_Y(2)$ for a hypergeometric random variable Y in each of the following situations:
   a. $N_S = 2$, $N_F = 3$, $n = 3$

b. $N_S = 4$, $N_F = 4$, $n = 5$
c. $N_S = 5$, $N_F = 1$, $n = 3$

5.19   Compute the probability that $Y = 0$ in both of the following situations:
a. Y is binomial with $n = 5$ and $\pi = .40$.
b. Y is hypergeometric with $N_S = 2$, $N_F = 3$, and $n = 5$.

5.20   Refer to Exercises 5.3 and 5.4 (page 178).
a. Find the probability that the tester selects the 4 correct glasses, assuming random selection.
b. Find $P_Y(y)$, where Y = number of correct choices.

5.21   Assume that in the 2500 business accounts of a bank, 125 have been fraudulently altered. The alterations are sufficiently subtle that only a detailed audit can uncover them. Fifty business accounts are chosen at random for detailed auditing. What is the probability that at least one of the alterations is discovered?

5.22   Find the expected value and variance of the number of altered accounts discovered during audit in Exercise 5.21.

5.23   Use a binomial approximation to answer Exercises 5.21 and 5.22. How close are the numerical answers?

5.4   GEOMETRIC AND NEGATIVE BINOMIAL DISTRIBUTIONS

Bernoulli trials, yielding success or failure on each trial with constant probabilities and independence from trial to trial, were discussed in Section 5.2. There we were concerned with the case in which the number of trials was fixed and the number of successes was random. In a number of cases, the situation is reversed: The number of successes is fixed and the number of trials is random. In this section, we deal with this situation, which leads to the geometric and negative binomial probability distributions.

Many banks supplement their usual teller services with card-operated automatic teller machines. There is some risk of unauthorized use of bank cards at these machines. Suppose that one of every thousand attempted automatic-teller transactions is based on an unauthorized use of a bank card. Regarding each transaction as a trial (and ignoring the possibility of repeated transactions using the same card), we can assume that transactions are a series of Bernoulli trials. The binomial distribution of Section 5.2 would apply to problems such as finding the probability that there are more than 20 unauthorized uses within the next 10,000 transactions. In such a problem, the number of trials (transactions) would be regarded as fixed, and the number of successes (unauthorized uses) as random. Alternatively, we could ask for the number of transactions that occur before the next unauthorized use, or before the tenth unauthorized use. These questions lead to the geometric and negative binomial probability distributions.

The geometric distribution arises when we consider Y = number of trials required to obtain the next success. The probability tree for a geometric random variable is very simple. To require y trials to obtain a success is to require that there be $y - 1$ consecutive failures followed by a success.

Geometric Probability Distribution

In a Bernoulli trials situation, define Y = number of trials required to obtain a success. Then

$$P_Y(y) = \pi(1 - \pi)^{y-1}, \qquad y = 1, 2, 3, \ldots$$

where π is the probability of success on any trial.

These probabilities form a geometric series. If $\pi = .2$, the probabilities are $.2, .2(.8), .2(.8)^2, \ldots$.

EXAMPLE 5.9   The labels on bottles of medication are examined with an optical scanner to see that they are properly affixed to the bottles. Assume that the probability of detecting an improperly affixed label is $\pi = .0001$ and compute the probability that the process will detect an improper label on the very first trial. Also compute the probability that the process will first detect an improper label on exactly the 10,000th bottle.

Solution   The event "improper label at trial 1" is the same as the event "$Y = 1$," where Y = number of trials to find the first improper label. Assuming Bernoulli trials with $P(\text{success}) = \pi = .0001$, the geometric distribution applies. $P(Y = 1) = P_Y(1) = (.0001)(.9999)^{1-1} = .0001$. The event "first improper label at bottle 10,000" is the same as the event "$Y = 10,000$" and has probability $P_Y(10,000) = (.0001)(.9999)^{10,000-1} = .0000368$. Note that, even though we expect one improper label every 10,000 bottles, there is a higher probability that the next bad label will occur at the very next bottle than that it will occur at precisely the next 10,000th bottle.

The mean (expected value) and variance of a geometric random variable may be computed by another convenient shortcut formula:

Mean and Variance for a Geometric Random Variable

$$E(Y) = \frac{1}{\pi}$$

$$\text{Var}(Y) = \frac{1 - \pi}{\pi^2}$$

where π is the probability of success on any given trial.

EXAMPLE 5.10   Find the expected value and variance of the number of labels examined until the next improper label is found, using the assumptions of Exercise 5.9.

Solution   We have $\pi = .0001$, so $E(Y) = 1/(.0001) = 10,000$. It is reasonable that, if one out of every 10,000 labels is improper, we will wait an average of 10,000 bottles to find the next improper label. The variance is $(1 - .0001)/(.0001)^2 = 99,990,000$; therefore, the standard deviation of Y is $\sqrt{99,990,000} = 9999.5$.   ■

The idea of counting the number of trials to the next success may be extended to counting the number of trials to the kth success. For example, a market research firm that needs to obtain $k = 100$ women who have full-time jobs and also watch a certain local television newscast has to interview a random number of potential candidates. Each interview is a trial; the most relevant random variable is $Y =$ number of interviews needed to obtain 100 qualifying women. If the assumptions of Bernoulli trials (success or failure trials, constant probability of success, independent trials) hold, the probability distribution of $Y =$ number of trials required to obtain k successes is a negative binomial.

Negative Binomial Distribution

If $Y =$ number of trials to obtain k successes, then

$$P_Y(y) = \frac{(y - 1)!}{(k - 1)!(y - k)!} \pi^k(1 - \pi)^{y-k}, \qquad y = k, k + 1, \ldots$$

The reason that $y - 1$ and $k - 1$ occur in the expression for the negative binomial distribution is that there must be $k - 1$ successes in the first $y - 1$ trials, followed by one success (at trial y).

EXAMPLE 5.11   In Example 5.9 we assumed that the probability of an improperly affixed label was .0001. Suppose that 50 improperly affixed labels are needed to study the cause of improper label fixing. Write an expression for the probability that 100,000 or more bottles are needed to obtain 50 improper labels.

Solution   We may regard the number of successes (improperly affixed labels) as fixed, and we may find the probability that $Y =$ number of bottles required is at least 100,000:

$$P(Y \geq 100,000) = \sum_{100,000}^{\infty} \frac{(y - 1)!}{(50 - 1)!(y - 50)!}(.0001)^{50}(.9999)^{y-50} \qquad ■$$

Because the negative binomial distribution is simply the extension of the geometric distribution to $k > 1$ successes, it is not surprising that expressions for the mean and variance of the negative binomial distribution are extensions of those for the geometric distribution.

Mean and Variance of the Negative Binomial Distribution

If Y = number of trials required to obtain k successes,

$$E(Y) = \frac{k}{\pi}$$

$$\text{Var}(Y) = \frac{k(1 - \pi)}{\pi^2}$$

EXAMPLE 5.12   Find the expected value and standard deviation of the number of bottles required to find 50 improperly affixed labels, assuming that the probability of an improperly affixed label is .0001.

Solution $E(Y) = 50/.0001 = 500,000$. $\text{Var}(Y) = 50(.9999)/(.0001)^2 = 4,999,500,000$. The standard deviation is $\sqrt{4,999,500,000} = 70,707$.

Not all Bernoulli trials situations can be solved by binomial or negative binomial methods. If Y = number of trials until two consecutive successes occur, then neither the number of trials nor the number of successes is fixed, so neither binomial nor negative binomial probabilities apply. In such cases, one must go back to basic principles to find the relevant probabilities.

5.5   POISSON DISTRIBUTION

A different sort of probability situation occurs when a succession of events seems to happen at random over time. An electrical utility faces occasional thunderstorms that down power lines or damage transformers. Although the long-run probability of occurrence of such storms can be determined quite accurately, the timing of the next storm is rather unpredictable. A company that insures oil tankers cannot predict the time of the next sinking. The manager of a university computer center faces random variation in the timing of job submissions. It's important to be able to protect against probable variation in such situations.

Poisson probability distribution   The **Poisson probability distribution*** is the simplest and most widely used model of events occurring randomly in time. This distribution is the mathematical result of certain assumptions. If the assumptions are not correct, at least approximately, for a particular situation, then the Poisson distribution may be a bad model in that situation. The two crucial assumptions can be translated (without doing much violence to the mathematical niceties) as follows:

1. Events occur one at a time. Two or more events do not occur at precisely the same time.
2. The occurrence of the event of interest in a given period is independent of the occurrence of the event in a nonoverlapping period; that is, the

---

* Named for Simeon Poisson, the mathematician who first derived it.

occurrence (or nonoccurrence) of an event during one period does not change the probability of an event occurring in some later period.

In many discussions on this topic, a third assumption is added: That the expected number of events in a period of specified length stays constant, so that the expected number of events during any one period is the same as during any other period. This third assumption makes the math easier, but it has been proved to be essentially irrelevant. As long as the first two assumptions hold, the Poisson distribution results.

There are two approaches to assessing whether or not a Poisson distribution is a reasonable model in a given situation. One is to see if the assumptions seem reasonable in a given context, the other is to see if the actual data histogram looks like a Poisson probability histogram. Of course the ideal is to have both.

EXAMPLE 5.13   In the three situations described at the beginning of this section, should the Poisson assumptions hold?

Solution   We would expect that the assumption of independence would be shaky for the electrical utility example. It seems to us that if lightning from one storm knocks out some equipment, it is quite likely that lightning from the same storm or another in the vicinity will knock out other equipment. For the oil tanker example, one could argue that, since one large tanker might collide with another, sinking both, the assumption that events happen one at a time doesn't hold. While this is certainly possible, we would guess that such flukes are sufficiently rare that the Poisson distribution is a decent model for the probability of a tanker sinking in a given period. In the computer center, much depends on the situation. If there are only a few terminals, which are tied up during the processing of a job, then the submission of a job now reduces the probability of submission of another job (from the same terminal) a bit later, which violates the assumption of independence. But if there are many terminals or if a terminal is not tied up during processing, the Poisson assumptions look good to us. We would like to see some data! ∎

Poisson Probability Distribution

$$P_Y(y) = \frac{e^{-\mu}\mu^y}{y!}, \qquad y = 0, 1, 2, \ldots$$

where μ is the expected number of events occurring in a given period and $e = 2.71828\ldots$ ∎

A Poisson random variable Y is the number of random events that occur in a fixed period; in principle, there's no upper limit to the values y. In practice, very large values of y are extremely unlikely. Probabilities for the Poisson probability distribution are shown in Appendix Table 2. To find μ, it is often necessary to multiply the expected rate for one time unit (e.g., one hour) times the number of time units per period (e.g., hours per shift).

EXAMPLE 5.14   On Saturday mornings, customers enter a boutique at a suburban shopping mall at an average rate of .50 per minute. Let Y = number of customers arriving in a specified 10-minute interval of time. Find the following probabilities:

   a. $P(Y = 3)$
   b. $P(Y \leq 3)$
   c. $P(Y \geq 4)$
   d. $P(4 \leq Y \leq 10)$

Solution   The Poisson assumptions seem fairly reasonable in this context. We assume that customers don't arrive in groups (or else count the entire group as one arrival) and that the arrival of one customer neither decreases nor increases the probability of other arrivals.

To obtain μ, we note that, at an average rate of .50 per minute over a 10-minute time span, we would expect $\mu = (.50)(10) = 5.0$ arrivals. To find the probabilities, we consult Appendix Table 2.

   a. $P(Y = 3)$ is read directly from Appendix Table 2 with $\mu = 5$ and $y = 3$:
       $P(Y = 3) = .1403$.
   b. $P(Y \leq 3) = P(Y = 0) + P(Y = 1) + P(Y = 2) + P(Y = 3)$
           $= .0067 + .0337 + .0843 + .1403 = .2650$.
   c. $P(Y \geq 4) = 1 - P(Y \leq 3) = 1 - .2650 = .7350$
   d. $P(4 \leq Y \leq 10) = P(Y = 4) + P(Y = 5) + \cdots + P(Y = 10)$
           $= .1755 + .1755 + \cdots + .0181 = .7213$ ∎

As indicated in the definition of the Poisson probability distribution, the expected value is $E(Y) = \mu$. Coincidentally, the variance of a Poisson random variable is also μ.

Mean and Variance for a Poisson Random Variable

If Y has a Poisson distribution, then

$$E(Y) = \mu$$
$$\text{Var}(Y) = \mu$$

EXAMPLE 5.15   Find the standard deviation of Y in Example 5.14.

Solution   We noted in Example 5.14 that $\mu = 5.0$. Thus,

$$\sigma_Y = \sqrt{\text{Var}(Y)} = \sqrt{5.0} = 2.24$$ ∎

Poisson approximation to binomial distributions   The Poisson distribution provides a good approximation to the binomial probability distribution when π is small and n is large but $n\pi$ is less than 5. The Poisson expected value μ is equated to the binomial expected value $n\pi$ for this approximation.

EXAMPLE 5.16   A sample of 1000 patients is treated with a new drug product during a large clinical trial. Compute the probability that none of the patients experiences a particular side effect (such as nausea) if we assume $\pi = .001$.

Solution   The mean of the binomial distribution is $\mu = n\pi = 1000(.001) = 1$. Substituting into the Poisson probability distribution, with $\mu = 1$, we have

$$P_Y(0) = \frac{(1)^0 e^{-1}}{0!} = e^{-1} = .3679$$

The corresponding probability computed using the binomial probability distribution is $\binom{1000}{0}(.001)^0(.999)^{1000} \approx .3677$.   ∎

SECTION 5.5   EXERCISES

5.24   Let Y denote a random variable with a Poisson distribution. Use Appendix Table 2 to calculate
   a. $P_Y(1)$ for $\mu = .4$, $\mu = .7$, and $\mu = 4.8$;
   b. $P(Y \leq 3)$ for $\mu = 1.6$ and $\mu = 7.0$;
   c. $P(Y \leq 10)$ for $\mu = 2.1$ and $\mu = 10.0$.

5.25   Calculate and graph the Poisson probability distribution for $\mu = .5$. Is the distribution roughly symmetric?

5.26   A firm that insures homes against fire assumes that claims arise according to a Poisson distribution at an average rate of 2.25 per week. Let Y be the number of claims arising in a four-week period. Find (a) $P(Y \leq 10)$, (b) $P(Y \geq 7)$, and (c) $P(7 \leq Y \leq 11)$.

5.27   Find the expected value and standard deviation of Y in Exercise 5.26.

5.28   Can you think of insurance situations that would make the Poisson assumption in Exercise 5.26 unreasonable?

5.29   Logging trucks have a particular problem with tire failures due to blowouts, cuts, and large punctures; these trucks are driven fast over very rough, temporary roads. Assume that such failures occur according to a Poisson distribution at a mean rate of 4.0 per 10,000 miles.
   a. If a truck drives 1000 miles in a given week, what is the probability that it does not have any tire failures?
   b. What is the probability that it has at least two failures?

5.30   What is the expected value and standard deviation of the number of tire failures per 1000 miles driven in Exercise 5.29?

5.31   The Poisson distribution also applies to events occurring randomly over an area or in a volume. Chocolate chips spread through well-mixed cookie dough tend to follow a Poisson distribution. A commercial baker produces cookies with an average of 8 chips per cookie.
   a. What is the probability of (horrors!) a chipless cookie?
   b. A cookie is considered acceptable only if it has at least 5 chips. What fraction of the cookies are acceptable?

5.6   THE UNIFORM DISTRIBUTION   ∎

The simplest continuous distribution is the uniform distribution. If Y has a uniform distribution, its probability density is spread out evenly over some range a to b. The uniform density is shown in Figure 5.2 (page 194). The uniform density

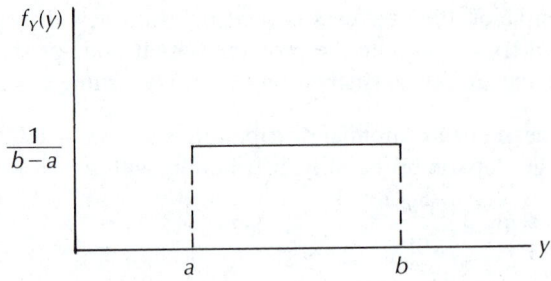

FIGURE 5.2   Uniform Probability Density

arises naturally in random number selection. If $Y = $ a number chosen randomly between 0 and 1, then the probability density of Y is flat over the 0 to 1 range; no one number has higher probability (density) than any other.

The basic formulas—probability density, expected value, and variance—for a uniform random variable are very simple.

Probability Density, Mean, and Variance for a Uniform Random Variable

$$f_Y(y) = \begin{cases} \dfrac{1}{b-a}, & \text{if } a < y < b \\ 0, & \text{otherwise} \end{cases}$$

$$E(Y) = \frac{a+b}{2}$$

$$\text{Var}(Y) = \frac{(b-a)^2}{12}$$

Probabilities for uniform random variables may be found by simple geometry. For example, suppose that Y is uniformly distributed between 0 and 50. What is the probability that Y is between 10 and 40? Figure 5.3 depicts the

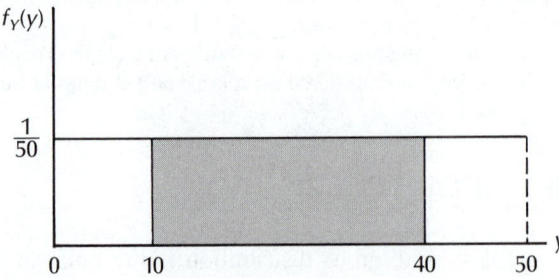

FIGURE 5.3   Probabilities from a Uniform Distribution

situation. The desired probability is the area of a rectangle—the base times the height. Therefore $P(10 < Y < 40) = 30(1/50) = .6$.

Alternatively, we may find uniform probabilities using elementary calculus. If Y is uniformly distributed between 0 and 50,

$$P(10 < Y < 40) = \int_{10}^{40} \left(\frac{1}{50}\right) dy = \frac{y}{50}\Big|_{10}^{40}$$

$$= \frac{(40 - 10)}{50} = .6$$

EXAMPLE 5.17   A mail order company specializing in software programs for microcomputers has found that between 5% and 15% of all orders in a day require special shipping. Suppose that, as a first approximation, we take the distribution of $Y =$ percentage of orders on a randomly chosen day to be uniform over the range 5 to 15. Find the mean and standard deviation of Y and the probability that Y is between 9 and 12.

Solution   We have $a = 5$ and $b = 15$. Therefore,

$$E(Y) = \frac{(5 + 15)}{2} = 10$$

$$\text{Var}(Y) = \frac{(15 - 5)^2}{12} = 8.3333$$

$$\sigma_Y = \sqrt{8.3333} = 2.89$$

The probability that Y is between 9 and 12 is the area of a rectangle with base $12 - 9 = 3$ and height $1/(15 - 5) = .1$. Therefore,

$$P(9 < Y < 12) = 3(.1) = .3 \qquad \blacksquare$$

SECTION 5.6   EXERCISES

5.32   Suppose Y is a uniformly distributed random variable on the interval $10 < y < 120$. Graph the density of Y and find the probability that Y lies in the interval $60 < y < 85$.

5.33   Find the expected value and standard deviation of Y in Exercise 5.32.

5.34   Calculate the following probabilities for a uniform random variable over the interval $0 < y < 200$:
   a. $P(10 < Y < 50)$
   b. $P(Y > 50)$
   c. $P(Y \leq 120)$

5.35   A random telephone-dialing machine picks the last four digits of telephone numbers randomly between 0000 and 9999 (both included). Treat the random variable $Y =$ number selected as continuous (even though there are 10,000 discrete possibilities) and uniformly distributed.
   a. Find $P(0300 < Y \leq 1300)$.
   b. Find the variance of Y.

5.36   On summer days, $Y =$ time that a suburban commuter train is late can be modeled as uniformly distributed between 0 and 20 minutes.
  a. Find the probability that the train is at least 8 minutes late.
  b. Find the standard deviation of the amount of time the train is late.

5.7   EXPONENTIAL DISTRIBUTION ($\int$)   ∎

The Poisson distribution we discussed in Section 5.5 applies to events occurring randomly over time. Specifically, it applies to $Y =$ number of events occurring in a fixed period. If events occur randomly in time, we may also ask about $W =$ waiting time until the next occurrence of an event. Given appropriate assumptions, the probability distribution of W follows an exponential distribution. In contrast to the discrete Poisson random variable, an exponential random variable is continuous.

Recall that the assumptions for a Poisson distribution are that events occur separately and that the occurrence of an event in one period does not change the probability of occurrence in another period. In a waiting-time problem, we must also assume that the expected rate of occurrence is constant over the period. Thus, if there is a rush-hour–off-hour situation in which events occur frequently and then infrequently, exponential probabilities do not apply.

One of the many uses of exponential probabilities is in reliability problems. If a component of a system fails only because of random occurrences (as opposed to wearing out), it's reasonable to assume that nonfailure in previous periods does not change the probability of failure in the next period and also that the rate of failure is constant over time. Of course there can be no clumping of multiple failures of a single component in a single period. Given these assumptions, the probability density $W =$ time to the next event is exponential.

Exponential Density

Assume that events occur randomly over time, with the expected time between events denoted μ. If $W =$ time to the next event, then

$$f_W(w) = \left(\frac{1}{\mu}\right)e^{-w/\mu}, \qquad w > 0$$

$$E(W) = \mu$$
$$\mathrm{Var}(W) = \mu^2$$

The exponential density is often called a "waiting-time" distribution because it is so often used as a model for the length of time one must wait to obtain the next event.

Probabilities involving the exponential density may be found using elementary integral calculus. It is not hard to show that

$$\int_a^b \left(\frac{1}{\mu}\right)e^{-w/\mu}\,dw = e^{-a/\mu} - e^{-b/\mu}$$

Most calculators and many computer programs evaluate e^x automatically.

EXAMPLE 5.18   The average length of time between submissions of jobs to a mainframe computer during the workday is 2.5 minutes. Assume that jobs arrive randomly over time at a constant expected rate.

   a. What is the probability that the waiting time between jobs is between 2 and 5 minutes?
   b. Find the mean and standard deviation of the waiting time between jobs.

Solution   a. It is specified that $\mu = 2.5$ minutes,

$$P(2 < W < 5) = \int_2^5 \left(\frac{1}{2.5}\right) e^{-w/2.5}\, dw$$

$$= e^{-2/2.5} - e^{-5/2.5}$$

$$= .4493 - .1353$$

$$= .3140$$

   b. The mean of W was given as 2.5. The variance is $\mu^2 = (2.5)^2 = 6.25$. The standard deviation is, as always, the square root of the variance, $\sqrt{6.25} = 2.5$. Curiously, the standard deviation equals the mean in this distribution. ■

   The exponential density is only a model. Accurate use of the model requires that the underlying assumptions hold. The assumption of independence over time is particularly critical for the exponential density to apply. The assumption of a constant average rate is also important.

EXAMPLE 5.19   We assumed in Example 5.18 that jobs are submitted to the computer at a rate of 2.5 minutes per job. Suppose that

   a. there is a tendency for one job submission to be followed immediately by another, related submission;
   b. there is a tendency for jobs to be submitted "on the hour," when employees arrive from or leave for meetings.

What assumptions are called into question by each tendency?

Solution   a. Here there is a dependence. If a job is submitted at one period, there is a higher probability that another job will be submitted shortly thereafter.
   b. Here there is a nonconstant average rate of occurrence. The rate is higher "on the hour." ■

SECTION 5.7   EXERCISES

5.37   Use a calculator that finds e^x to compute the value of the exponential density function $f_Y(y)$ for $\mu = 2.5$ and $y = 0, .5, 1.0, 1.5$, and 2.0. Sketch the density function.

5.38   Compute the following probabilities for an exponential random variable with $\mu = 2$.
   a. $P(Y > 2)$
   b. $P(Y > 1)$

c. $P(1 < Y < 2)$

d. $P(1 \leq Y \leq 2)$

(Hint: For part (d), use your head, not your calculator.)

5.39   The time between arrivals at a rural emergency treatment center follows an exponential distribution with an average time between arrivals of 1.25 hours. Find the probability that the time between arrivals is more than 1 hour. Find the probability that the time between arrivals is more than 2 hours.

5.40   Rather than focus on the time between arrivals at the treatment center in Exercise 5.39, focus on the arrivals in a given period. Note that the assumptions for the exponential and Poisson distributions are identical; note also that an average time between arrivals of 1.25 hours indicates an average of $1/1.25 = .80$ arrivals per hour.

   a. Using Poisson probabilities, find the probability that there are no arrivals in 1 hour.

   b. Find the probability that there are no arrivals in 2 hours.

   c. Compare your answers to this exercise with those of Exercise 5.39. What is the explanation?

5.41   The service times for unticketed passengers at an airline ticket counter follow an exponential distribution with a mean of 5 minutes.

   a. Find the probability of a service time less than 2.5 minutes.

   b. Find the probability of a service time longer than 10 minutes.

5.42   Consider the passenger service situation of Exercise 5.41.

   a. What is the expected number of passengers served per minute?

   b. Find the probability that at least one passenger is served within 2.5 minutes.

   c. Find the probability that no passenger is served within 10 minutes.

5.43   "Unusual events"—minor operating problems—occur randomly over time at a nuclear power station. The average time between events is 40 days.

   a. What is the probability that the time to the next "unusual event" is between 20 and 60 days?

   b. Find the standard deviation of the time to the next "unusual event."

5.44   Examination of the records of the power station in Exercise 5.43 shows that "unusual events" occur much more frequently on weekends than on weekdays. What assumption underlying your answers to Exercise 5.43 is called into question?

5.45   A major league baseball team sells individual-game tickets at a downtown ticket office during normal working hours. Ticket buyers arrive at the office at the average rate of 12 per hour. Buyers arrive individually and randomly; the average rate stays essentially constant during the day.

   a. Find the probability that there are more than 5 arrivals in a 10-minute (1/6 hour) period.

   b. Find the probability that the next buyer arrives within 3 minutes. Note that the average time between arrivals is 1/12 hour, or 5 minutes.

5.46   Find a number k such that the probability of k or more arrivals in 1/4 hour in Exercise 5.45 is close to .10.

5.47   The time between "crashes" of a certain mainframe computer appears to have an exponential probability distribution. The average time is 5 days.

   a. What is the probability that the time to the next crash will be at least one (7-day) week?

   b. What is the probability that there will be a two-week period with no crashes?

5.48   What is the probability that there will be 4 or more crashes of the computer in Exercise 5.47 within a specified 7-day week?

5.8   NORMAL DISTRIBUTION ∎

Now we turn to the most fundamental distribution used in statistical theory, the normal distribution. Many standard statistical procedures that we discuss in later chapters are based on the formal mathematical assumption that the underlying population has a normal distribution. Many methods that are widely used in economics, finance, and marketing are based on an assumption of a normal population. This section is therefore important in understanding many later sections of the text.

A normally distributed random variable is continuous. Therefore it has a probability density, as shown below.

Normal Probability Density

$$f_Y(y) = \frac{1}{\sqrt{2\pi}\,\sigma}\,e^{-.5(y-\mu)^2/\sigma^2}$$

---

normal curve

The values μ and σ in the normal density function are in fact the mean and standard deviation of Y (though we don't prove it). A probability histogram, called the **normal curve**, for a normal random variable is bell shaped and symmetric around the mean μ, as shown in Figure 5.4.

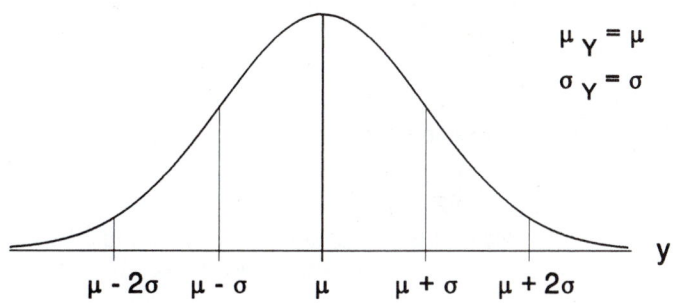

$$\mu_Y = \mu$$
$$\sigma_Y = \sigma$$

$$\mu - 2\sigma \quad \mu - \sigma \quad \mu \quad \mu + \sigma \quad \mu + 2\sigma$$

FIGURE 5.4   Normal Probability Distribution

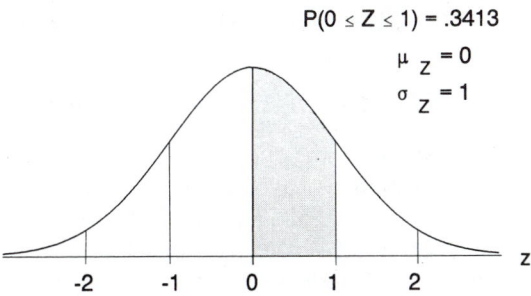

$$P(0 \le Z \le 1) = .3413$$
$$\mu_Z = 0$$
$$\sigma_Z = 1$$

FIGURE 5.5   Standard Normal Probability Distribution

Tables of normal curve areas (probabilities) are always given for the **standard normal distribution**, which has mean 0 and standard deviation 1. Appendix Table 3 gives areas between 0 and a positive number z. For instance, the entry for $z = 1.00$ is .3413; if Z is the standard normal random variable, then $P(0 \leq Z \leq 1.00) = .3413$, as in Figure 5.5 (page 199).

standard normal distribution

EXAMPLE 5.20   Let Z be a standard normal random variable. Find

    a. $P(0 \leq Z \leq 1.96)$
    b. $P(Z > 1.96)$
    c. $P(-1.96 \leq Z \leq 1.96)$
    d. $P(-1.00 \leq Z \leq 1.96)$

Solution   An illustration like Figure 5.5 makes it much easier to use normal tables. The entry for $z = 1.96$ (found by looking in the 1.9 row and .06 column) is .4750. Figure 5.6 is useful.

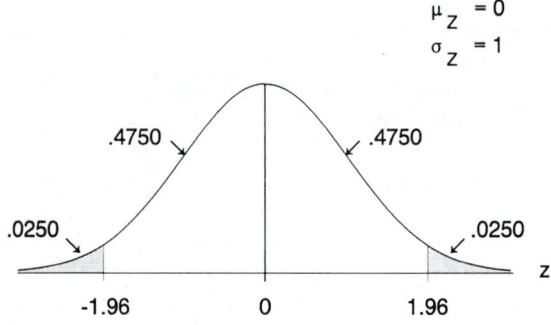

FIGURE 5.6   Solution to Example 5.20

    a. $P(0 \leq Z \leq 1.96) = .4750$.
    b. Because the area to the right of 0 must be .5000 (the normal curve is symmetric and the total area beneath the curve is 1), $P(Z > 1.96) = .5000 - .4750 = .0250$.
    c. By symmetry, the area between -1.96 and 0 must also be .4750. So $P(-1.96 \leq Z \leq 1.96) = .4750 + .4750 = .9500$.
    d. $P(-1.00 \leq Z \leq 1.96) = .3413 + .4750 = .8163$. (Draw a picture.)   ∎

EXAMPLE 5.21   Find k_1 such that $P(0 \leq Z \leq k_1) = .40$ and k_2 such that $P(-k_2 \leq Z \leq k_2) = .60$.

Solution   This problem is in a sense the opposite of Example 5.20. In that problem, values are given and probabilities have to be found. Here probabilities are given and values have to be found. Again, a picture is helpful (see Figure 5.7).
    a. Looking through Appendix Table 3 for an area of .40, we find that the closest z value is 1.28. Therefore $P(0 \leq Z \leq 1.28) = .40$; that is, $k_1 = 1.28$.
    b. An area of .30 (half the desired probability as shown in Figure 5.7) corresponds to $z \approx .84$, so $P(-.84 \leq Z \leq .84) = .60$; that is, $k_2 = .84$.   ∎

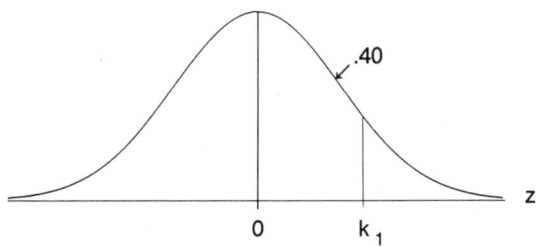 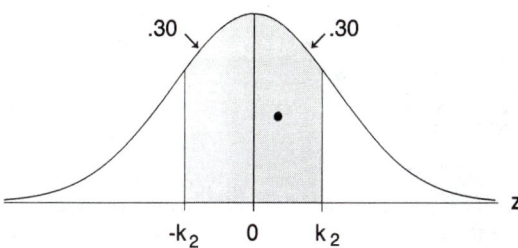

FIGURE 5.7 Solution to Example 5.21

Any normal random variable Y can be transformed to a standard normal random variable Z by subtracting the expected value μ and dividing the result by the standard deviation σ.

$$Z = \frac{Y - \mu}{\sigma}$$

z-score   For a given value of y, the corresponding value of z, sometimes called a **z-score**, is the number of standard deviations that y lies away from μ. If $\mu = 100$ and $\sigma = 20$, a y value of 130 is 1.5 standard deviations above (to the right of) the mean μ and the corresponding z-score is $z = (130 - 100)/20 = 1.50$. A y value of 85 is .75 standard deviations below (to the left of) the mean μ and

$$z = \frac{85 - 100}{20} = -.75$$

The relation between specific values of a normal random variable Y and the corresponding z-scores is shown in Figure 5.8. [Note that $z = (y - \mu)/\sigma$.]

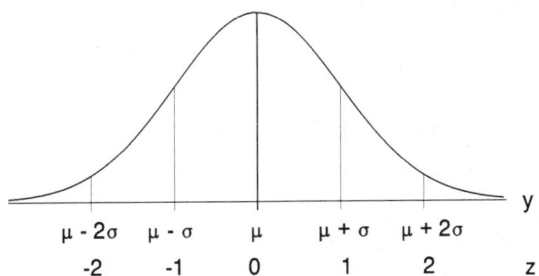

FIGURE 5.8 Relation Between Specific Values of Y and z-Scores

EXAMPLE 5.22   Annual incomes for career service employees at a large university are approximately normally distributed with a mean of $18,600 and a standard deviation of $2700. Find the probability that an employee chosen at random has an annual income less than $15,000; an income greater than $21,000.

Solution   First we draw a figure showing the areas in question (Figure 5.9, page 202). Now we must determine the area between 15,000 and 18,600.

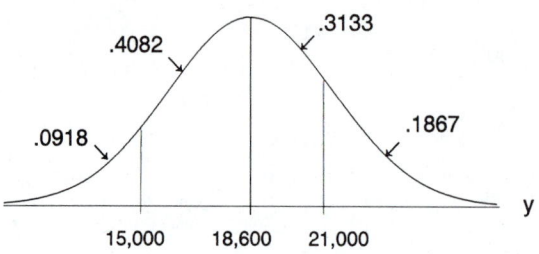

FIGURE 5.9   Areas Greater Than 21,000 and Smaller Than 15,000 for
$\mu = 18,600$ and $\sigma = 2700$; Example 5.22

$$z = \frac{y - \mu}{\sigma} = \frac{15,000 - 18,600}{2700}$$

$$= \frac{-3600}{2700}$$

$$= -1.33$$

The area between the mean of a normal distribution and a value 1.33 standard deviations to the left of the mean, from Appendix Table 3, is .4082. Hence the probability of observing an annual income less than $15,000 is

$$.5 - .4082 = .0918$$

Similarly, to compute the probability of observing a salary over $21,000 we determine the area between 18,600 and 21,000:

$$z = \frac{y - \mu}{\sigma} = \frac{21,000 - 18,600}{2700} = .89$$

The area corresponding to $z = .89$ is .3133. Hence the desired probability is

$$.5 - .3133 = .1867$$ ■

EXAMPLE 5.23   If Y has a normal distribution with mean 500 and standard deviation 100, find

a. $P(500 \leq Y \leq 696)$;
b. $P(Y \geq 696)$;
c. $P(304 \leq Y \leq 696)$;
d. k such that $P(500 - k \leq Y \leq 500 + k) = .60$.

Solution   a. A y value of 696 is 1.96 standard deviations above the mean; $z = (696 - 500)/100 = 1.96$. Of course 500 is zero standard deviations above the mean, so $z = (500 - 500)/100 = 0.00$. Thus $P(500 \leq Y \leq 696) = P(0 \leq Z \leq 1.96) = .4750$.

b. $P(Y \geq 696) = P(Z \geq 1.96) = .0250$.

c. $P(304 \leq Y \leq 696) = P(-1.96 \leq Z \leq 1.96) = .9500$, because 304 corresponds to a z of $(304 - 500)/100 = -1.96$.

d. As in Example 5.21, $P(-.84 \leq Z \leq .84) = .60$, so we want a range for Y from .84 standard deviation below the mean $\mu = 500$ to .84 standard deviation

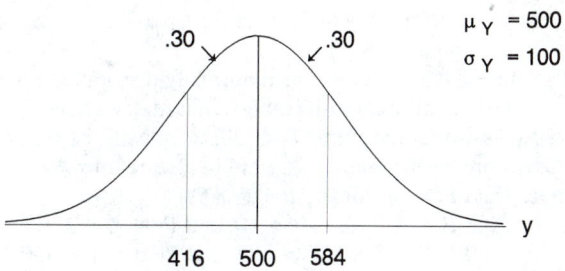

$\mu_Y = 500$

$\sigma_Y = 100$

.30   .30

416   500   584

FIGURE 5.10   Solution to Example 5.23

above the mean: $P[500 - .84(100) \leq Y \leq 500 + .84(100)] = P(416 \leq Y \leq 584)$ $= .60$ (see Figure 5.10). ■

    A little practice with such problems and a habit of drawing pictures makes normal probability calculations fairly easy.

    As we've indicated previously, the concept of a continuous random variable is really an abstraction, because most variables of interest do have a finite number of possible values. But for many situations it is convenient to assume that the random variable of interest has a continuous distribution. In the same way, the normal random variable is an abstraction, because in theory any numerical value, negative as well as positive, is possible and the probability histogram is a smooth, symmetric, bell-shaped curve. In practice, negative values or positive values such as $612.3142769 may be impossible. Such issues often don't really matter. If a random variable Y is assumed normal with mean 500 and standard deviation 100, the probability that $Y < 0$ is by assumption $P(Z < -5)$, which is effectively zero. Whether or not Y can actually assume negative values hardly matters. Similarly, the errors incurred by rounding off $612.3142769 to $612.31 or to $612 are tiny. If a population histogram for a random variable is generally bell shaped, the normal probability distribution usually provides an excellent model for the actual probability distribution.

SECTION 5.8   EXERCISES

5.49   Suppose that Z represents a standard (tabled) normal random variable. Find the following probabilities:

    a. $P(0 \leq Z \leq 1.00)$ f. $P(-1.28 \leq Z \leq 1.28)$

    b. $P(0 \leq Z \leq 1.65)$ g. $P(-1.07 \leq Z \leq 2.33)$

    c. $P(-1.00 \leq Z \leq 0)$ h. $P(Z \geq 2.65)$

    d. $P(-1.28 \leq Z \leq 0)$ i. $P(Z \leq -2.42)$

    e. $P(-1.65 \leq Z \leq 1.65)$ j. $P(Z \geq 1.39 \text{ or } Z \leq -1.39)$

    Draw pictures.

5.50   For the standard normal random variable Z, solve the following equations for k:

    a. $P(Z \geq k) = .01$ d. $P(-k \leq Z \leq k) = .6826$

    b. $P(-k \leq Z \leq k) = .98$ e. $P(-k \leq Z \leq k) = .9544$

    c. $P(Z \leq -k) = .01$ f. $P(Z \geq k) = .95$

    Again, draw pictures.

5.51   Refer to the answers to Exercise 5.50, parts (d) and (e). How do these answers relate to the Empirical Rule?

5.52   Suppose that Y represents a normally distributed random variable with expected value (mean) equal to 100 and standard deviation 15.
   a. Show that the event $(Y \leq 130)$ is equivalent to $(Z \leq 2)$.
   b. Convert the event $(Y \geq 82.5)$ to z-score form.
   c. Find $P(Y \leq 130)$ and $P(Y \geq 82.5)$.
   d. Find $P(Y > 106)$, $P(Y < 94)$, and $P(94 \leq Y \leq 106)$.
   e. Find $P(Y \leq 70)$, $P(Y \geq 130)$, and $P(70 < Y < 130)$.

5.53   Consider the random variable Y of Exercise 5.52. Find the value of k satisfying
   a. $P(100 \leq Y \leq 100 + k) = .45$;   d. $P(Y \leq k) = .30$;
   b. $P(100 - k \leq Y \leq 100 + k) = .90$;   e. $P(Y \leq k) = .80$;
   c. $P(Y \geq k) = .20$;   f. $P(Y \geq k) = .70$.
   Draw appropriate pictures for each part.

5.54   A financial analyst states that the (subjective probability) price Y of a long-term $1000 government bond one year later is normally distributed with expected value $980 and standard deviation $40.
   a. Find $P(Y \geq 1000)$.
   b. Find $P(Y \leq 940)$.
   c. Find $P(960 \leq Y \leq 1060)$.

5.55   Refer to the random variable Y of Exercise 5.54.
   a. Find the value of k satisfying $P(Y \geq k) = .90$.
   b. Find the value k such that the probability that the price of the bond (one year later) exceeds k is .60.

5.56   Assume that the hourly wage rate earned by a worker in a clothing factory (based on a piecework pay system) is normally distributed with expected value $5.10 and standard deviation $0.40.
   a. Find the probability that a worker's hourly rate exceeds $5.40.
   b. Find the probability that a worker's hourly rate is between $4.70 and $5.50.
   c. Find the probability that a worker's hourly rate exceeds a contractual minimum of $3.90.

5.9   NORMAL APPROXIMATIONS TO BINOMIAL AND POISSON PROBABILITIES

One of the many uses of the normal curve is as an approximation to other probability distributions, particularly the binomial and Poisson distributions. This section indicates how such approximations work and when they are reasonably accurate.

Probabilities associated with values of y can be computed for a binomial experiment for any values of n or π, but as you might imagine, the task becomes more difficult when n gets large. For example, suppose a sample of 1000 voters is polled to determine sentiment toward the consolidation of a city and county government. What is the probability of observing 460 or fewer favoring consolidation if we assume that 50% of the entire population favor the change? Here we have a binomial experiment with $n = 1000$; π, the probability of selecting a person favoring consolidation, equals .5. To determine the probability of observing 460 or fewer favoring consolidation in the random sample of

1000 voters, we could compute $P_Y(y)$ using the binomial formula for $y = 460, 459, \ldots, 0$. The desired probability would then be

$$P(Y = 460) + P(Y = 459) + \cdots + P(Y = 0)$$

There would be 461 probabilities to calculate; each one would be somewhat difficult due to the factorials. For example, the probability of observing 460 favoring consolidation is

$$P(Y = 460) = \frac{1000!}{460!540!}(.5)^{460}(.5)^{540}$$

normal
approximation to
binomial

We can approximate the binomial distribution by a normal distribution for certain values of n and π. We can prove this fact by a Central Limit Theorem, which we will discuss in the next chapter. We don't prove the result here; rather, we show how and when to use the approximation. The basic idea is to pretend that a binomial random variable Y has a normal distribution, using the binomial mean $\mu = n\pi$ and standard deviation $\sqrt{n\pi(1 - \pi)}$. For example, we can treat a binomial variable with $n = 400$ and $\pi = .20$ as approximately normally distributed with $\mu = 400(.20) = 80$ and $\sigma = \sqrt{400(.20)(.80)} = 8$. To approximate $P(Y > 96)$, use normal tables to get $P(Y > 96) = P[Z > (96 - 80)/8] = P(Z > 2) = .0228$, or about .02.

EXAMPLE 5.24   A life insurance agency has set as a target that 10% of all prospects contacted buy insurance. Assume that independence holds among prospects, so that binomial probabilities apply. What is the probability that, out of 600 prospects, 30 or fewer buy?

Solution   The exact solution involves binomial probabilities with $n = 600$ and $\pi = .10$, if in fact the target success rate is being achieved. Because we have no tables for $n = 600$, we use a normal approximation with $\mu = n\pi = 600(.10) = 60$ and $\sigma = \sqrt{n\pi(1 - \pi)} = \sqrt{600(.10)(.90)} = 7.348$.

$$P(Y \leq 30) = P\left(Z \leq \frac{30 - 60}{7.348}\right) = P(Z \leq -4.08)$$

which is virtually zero. If an agent sold only 30 policies to the last 600 prospects, we would have to conclude that the agent was not on target; the result (30 successes of 600 trials) can't reasonably be explained as a fluke attributable to chance.   ■

The normal approximation to the binomial distribution can be pretty bad if $n\pi < 5$ or $n(1 - \pi) < 5$. If π, the probability of success, is small, and n, the sample size, is modest, the actual binomial distribution is seriously skewed to the right. In such a case, the symmetric normal curve gives a bad approximation. If π is near 1, so $n(1 - \pi) < 5$, the actual binomial is skewed to the left and again the normal approximation isn't very good. When $n\pi$ and $n(1 - \pi)$ exceed about 10, the normal approximation is quite good. In the middle zone, $n\pi$ or $n(1 - \pi)$ between

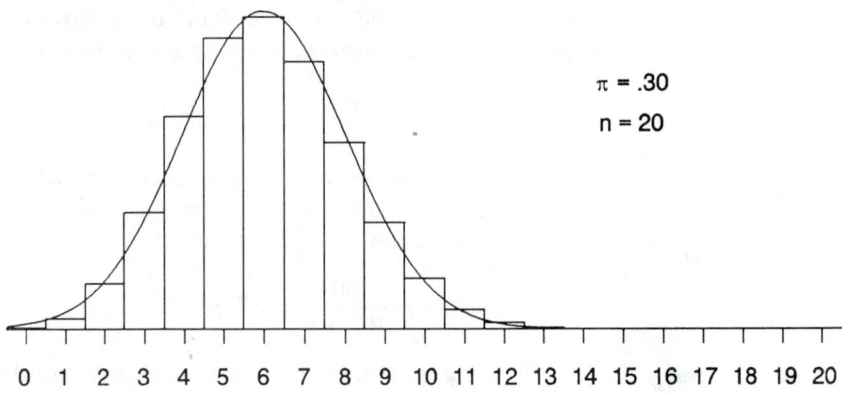

$\pi = .30$

$n = 20$

FIGURE 5.11   Normal Approximation to Binomial Distribution

continuity correction 5 and 10, a modification called a **continuity correction** makes a fairly big difference to the quality of the approximation.

    The reason for the continuity correction is that we are using the continuous normal curve to approximate a discrete binomial distribution. The situation is shown in Figure 5.11. The binomial probability that $Y \le 5$ is the sum of the areas of the rectangles above 5, 4, 3, 2, 1, and 0. We can approximate this probability (area) by the area under the superimposed normal curve to the left of 5. Thus the normal approximation ignores half of the rectangle above 5. The continuity correction simply includes the area between $y = 5$ and $y = 5.5$. For the binomial distribution with $n = 20$ and $\pi = .30$, the correction is to take $P(Y \le 5)$ as $P(Y \le 5.5)$. Instead of $P(Y \le 5) = P\{Z \le [5 - 20(.3)]/\sqrt{20(.3)(.7)}\} = P(Z \le -.49) = .3121$, use $P(Y \le 5.5) = P\{Z \le [5.5 - 20(.3)]/(\sqrt{20(.3)(.7)}\} = P(Z \le -.24) = .4052$. The actual binomial probability, from Appendix Table 1, is .4164. The general idea of the continuity correction is to add or subtract .5 from a binomial value before using normal probabilities. The best way to determine whether to add or subtract is to draw a picture like Figure 5.11.

Normal Approximation to the Binomial Probability Distribution

For large n and π not too near zero or one, a binomial random variable Y may be approximated by a normal distribution with $\mu = n\pi$ and $\sigma = \sqrt{n\pi(1 - \pi)}$. This approximation should be used only if $n\pi \ge 5$ and $n(1 - \pi) \ge 5$. A continuity correction improves the quality of the approximation in cases where n is not overwhelmingly large.

EXAMPLE 5.25   A large drug company has 100 potential new prescription drugs under clinical test. About 20% of all drugs that reach this stage are eventually licensed for sale. What is the probability that at least 15 of the 100 drugs are eventually licensed?

Assume that the binomial assumptions are satisfied, and use a normal approximation with continuity correction.

Solution   The mean (expected value) of Y is $\mu = 100(.2) = 20$; the standard deviation is $\sigma = \sqrt{100(.2)(.8)} = 4.0$. The desired probability is that 15 or more drugs are approved. Because $Y = 15$ is included, the continuity correction is to take the event as $Y \geq 14.5$.

$$P(Y \geq 14.5) = P\left(Z \geq \frac{14.5 - 20}{4.0}\right) = P(Z \geq -1.375)$$

which is about .92.   ■

normal
approximation
to Poisson

The **normal approximation to the Poisson distribution** works the same way. If Y is a Poisson random variable with expected value μ, pretend that Y has a normal distribution; because the variance of a Poisson distribution equals μ, use mean μ and standard deviation $\sqrt{\mu}$.

EXAMPLE 5.26   Assume that Y, the number of jobs arriving at a computer center in a given half-hour period, has a Poisson distribution with mean .2 per minute. Use a normal approximation to find $P(Y \leq 10)$.

Solution $\mu = (.2/\text{minute})(30 \text{ minutes}) = 6$. Then from Appendix Table 3 we have

$$P(Y \leq 10) = P\left(Z \leq \frac{10 - 6}{\sqrt{6}}\right) = P(Z \leq 1.63) = .9484$$

The correct Poisson probability is .9574.   ■

The normal approximation is rather bad for $\mu < 5$ (corresponding to $n\pi < 5$ in the binomial case) and pretty good for $\mu > 10$. In the intermediate case, $5 \leq \mu \leq 10$, the same continuity correction makes the approximation accurate enough for most purposes.

EXAMPLE 5.27   Apply the continuity correction to Example 5.26.

Solution   We still have $\mu = 6$ and $\sigma = \sqrt{6}$. Approximate $P(Y \leq 10)$ by $P(Y \leq 10.5)$. Draw a picture to see why.

$$P(Y \leq 10.5) = P\left(Z \leq \frac{10.5 - 6}{\sqrt{6}}\right) = P(Z \leq 1.84) = .9671$$

The exact Poisson probability, again, is .9574.   ■

SECTION 5.9   EXERCISES

5.57   Suppose that Y has a binomial distribution with $n = 100$ and $\pi = .50$.
   a. Use binomial tables to calculate $P(40 \leq Y \leq 60)$.
   b. Use a normal approximation (without any continuity correction) to calculate the same probability. How good is the approximation?

5.58 Use a continuity-corrected normal approximation to give an answer to Exercise 5.57. Is this approximation much better than the one in Exercise 5.57?

5.59 Input errors to a computerized accounting system occur at a rate of 1.6 per 1000 entries. Under what conditions would you expect the Poisson assumptions to be a reasonable approximation?

5.60 Assume that in Exercise 5.59 Poisson probabilities apply. Let Y = number of errors in a set of 5000 entries.
   a. Find $E(Y)$ and σ_Y.
   b. Find $P(5 \leq Y \leq 11)$.

5.61 Use a normal approximation with continuity correction to answer Exercise 5.60, part (b).

Summary

This chapter presents the most important special probability distributions. Each such distribution arises when certain assumptions are met; those assumptions are an important part of the definition of each distribution. For each distribution, we specified assumptions, the probability distribution, expected value, standard deviation, and (if needed) a table.

The important discrete distributions are: Binomial, for the number of successes in a fixed number of Bernoulli (independent, constant probability) trials; hypergeometric, for sampling without replacement from a population of successes and failures; geometric and negative binomial, for the number of Bernoulli trials until a fixed number of successes; and Poisson, for the number of random (nonclumping, independent) events in a fixed time interval.

The important continuous distributions are: Uniform, for probabilities spread out evenly over an interval; exponential, for the waiting time to the next random event; normal, a widely occurring distribution, the basis for many statistical inference methods, and an approximation (preferably with a continuity correction) to binomial and Poisson probabilities.

KEY TOPICS AND FORMULAS: Some Special Probability Distributions

1. Counting rules
   a. The number of sequences (permutations) of r symbols taken k at a time is

$$_kP_r = \frac{r!}{(r-k)!}$$

   b. The number of subsets (combinations) of r symbols taken k at a time is

$$\binom{r}{k} = \frac{r!}{k!(r-k)!}$$

2. Binomial experiment
   a. There are n trials, each resulting in either success S or failure F.

b. The probability of success $P(S) = \pi$ remains constant for all trials; $P(F) = 1 - \pi$.

c. The trials are independent.

d. The random variable of interest is Y, the number of successes in n trials.

3. Binomial random variable
   a. Binomial probability distribution

   $$P_Y(y) = \frac{n!}{y!(n-y)!}\pi^y(1-\pi)^{n-y}$$

   b. Mean, variance, and standard deviation of Y

   $$E(Y) = n\pi$$
   $$\text{Var}(Y) = n\pi(1-\pi)$$
   $$\sigma_Y = \sqrt{n\pi(1-\pi)}$$

4. Hypergeometric random variable
   a. Hypergeometric probability distribution

   $$P_Y(y) = \frac{\binom{N_S}{y}\binom{N_F}{n-y}}{\binom{N}{n}}$$

   b. Mean, variance, and standard deviation of Y

   $$E(Y) = n\left(\frac{N_S}{N}\right)$$
   $$\text{Var}(Y) = n\left(\frac{N_S}{N}\right)\left(1 - \frac{N_S}{N}\right)\frac{N-n}{N-1}$$
   $$\sigma_Y = \sqrt{n\left(\frac{N_S}{N}\right)\left(1 - \frac{N_S}{N}\right)\frac{N-n}{N-1}}$$

5. Geometric random variable
   a. Probability distribution

   $$P_Y(y) = \pi(1-\pi)^{y-1}, \qquad y = 1,2,\ldots$$

   b. Mean, variance, and standard deviation of Y

   $$E(Y) = \frac{1}{\pi}$$
   $$\text{Var}(Y) = \frac{1-\pi}{\pi^2}$$
   $$\sigma_Y = \frac{\sqrt{1-\pi}}{\pi}$$

6. Negative binomial random variable
   a. Probability distribution

   $$P_Y(y) = \frac{(y-1)!}{(k-1)!(y-k)!} \pi^k (1-\pi)^{y-k}, \qquad y = k, k+1, \ldots$$

   b. Mean, variance, and standard deviation of Y

   $$E(Y) = \frac{k}{\pi}$$

   $$\text{Var}(Y) = \frac{k(1-\pi)}{\pi^2}$$

   $$\sigma_Y = \frac{k\sqrt{(1-\pi)}}{\pi}$$

7. Poisson random variable
   a. Poisson probability distribution

   $$P_Y(y) = \frac{e^{-\mu}\mu^y}{y!}$$

   b. Mean, variance, and standard deviation of Y

   $$E(Y) = \mu$$
   $$\text{Var}(Y) = \mu$$
   $$\sigma_Y = \sqrt{\mu}$$

8. Uniform random variable
   a. Probability density function

   $$f_Y(y) = \frac{1}{b-a}, \qquad a < y < b$$

   b. Mean, variance, and standard deviation of Y

   $$E(Y) = \frac{a+b}{2}$$

   $$\text{Var}(Y) = \frac{b-a}{12}$$

   $$\sigma_Y = \sqrt{\frac{b-a}{12}}$$

9. Exponential random variable
   a. Probability density function

   $$f_Y(y) = \left(\frac{1}{\mu}\right) e^{-y/\mu}, \qquad y > 0$$

   b. Mean, variance, and standard deviation of Y

$$E(Y) = \mu$$
$$\text{Var}(Y) = \mu^2$$
$$\sigma_Y = \mu$$

10. The normal random variable
   a. Probability density function

$$f_Y(y) = \frac{1}{\sqrt{2\pi}\,\sigma}\, e^{-.5\left(\frac{y-\mu}{\sigma}\right)^2}$$

   b. Mean, variance, and standard deviation are μ, σ^2, and σ, respectively.
   c. Standard normal,

$$Z = \frac{Y - \mu}{\sigma}$$

   d. You can obtain areas under a normal curve by first computing a z-score and then referring to Appendix Table 3.

11. Normal approximations to binomial and Poisson probabilities
   a. For a normal approximation to the binomial distribution, use a normal distribution with mean $n\pi$ and standard deviation $\sqrt{n\pi(1-\pi)}$, provided

$$n\pi \geq 5 \qquad \text{and} \qquad n(1-\pi) \geq 5$$

   b. For a normal approximation to the Poisson distribution, use a normal distribution with mean μ and standard deviation $\sqrt{\mu}$, provided $\mu \geq 5$.

CHAPTER 5   EXERCISES

5.62 A telephone-sales firm is considering purchasing a machine that randomly selects and automatically dials telephone numbers. The firm would be using the machine to call residences during the evening; calls to business phones would be wasted. The manufacturer of the machine claims that its programming reduces the business-phone rate to 15%. As a test, 100 phone numbers are to be selected at random from a very large set of possible numbers.
   a. Are the binomial assumptions satisfied in this situation?
   b. Find the probability that at least 24 of the numbers belong to business phones.
   c. If in fact 24 of the 100 numbers turn out to be business phones, does this cast serious doubt on the manufacturer's claim? Explain.

5.63 Refer to Exercise 5.62.
   a. Find the expected value and variance of Y, the number of business phone numbers in the sample.
   b. Use normal approximations (with and without continuity correction) to find $P(Y \geq 24)$. How close are the approximations?

5.64   It is estimated that 5% of all Medicaid claims in a particular city are fraudulent. A random sample of 50 claims is taken.
   a. What is the probability that at most 1 claim in the sample is fraudulent?
   b. What is the probability that at least 4 are faudulent?

5.65   Refer to Exercise 5.64. Use a Poisson approximation to answer parts (a) and (b). How good is the approximation?

5.66   Of 30,000 bank credit cards in circulation in a particular city, 300 are subject to recall (because of theft or nonpayment). A merchant receives 100 different cards in one day.
   a. How many different sets of 100 cards can the merchant receive? Don't work out a numerical answer unless you have an unnatural fondness for very large numbers.
   b. How many sets of 100 cards contain no recallable cards? Again, avoid the arithmetic.
   c. Write an expression for the probability of obtaining no recallable cards in the sample of 100.
   d. Write an expression for the probability of obtaining 2 or fewer recallable cards in the sample.

5.67   Refer to Exercise 5.66, parts (c) and (d).
   a. Write expressions for binomial approximations to these probabilities.
   b. Use a Poisson approximation to get numerical answers to these probabilities.

5.68   Some people claim that female managers tend to be placed in fringe areas, such as public relations or personnel management, as oppposed to the central areas of production, marketing, and finance. Suppose that a firm has 24 male and 6 female managers at the assistant vice president level. Of these positions, 14 are regarded as fringe positions.
   a. In how many distinct ways can the 14 fringe managers be selected?
   b. In how many ways can the fringe managers be selected such that 5 of the 6 women are included?
   c. If the fringe managers had been randomly selected, what is the probability that at least 5 would be women?

5.69   Assume that lost-time industrial accidents occur in a plant according to a Poisson distribution with mean .12 per day. Let Y = number of such accidents in a 10-day period.
   a. Find $P(Y = 1)$ and $P(Y \leq 1)$.
   b. Find $E(Y)$ and σ_Y.

5.70   Would a normal approximation in Exercise 5.69 be very accurate?

5.71   The weekly demand for 5-pound sacks of flour at a particular supermarket is assumed to be approximately normal with mean 72.0 cases and standard deviation 1.6 cases. Let Y = demand in a particular week.
   a. Find $P(Y \leq 72.8)$ and $P(71.2 \leq Y \leq 72.8)$.
   b. Find $P(Y \geq 74.0)$.
   c. The ordering policy of the market is that there be a 1% chance of stockout (demand exceeding supply) in any particular week. How much flour must be stocked to achieve this goal?

5.72   Refer to Exercise 5.71.
   a. What is the probability that demand exceeds 73.0 cases in a particular week?
   b. What is the probability that demand exceeds 73.0 cases in exactly three of four consecutive weeks? Assume independence from week to week.

5.73   A certain amount of material is wasted in cutting patterns for garments. A producer of army uniforms has found that the wastage is normally distributed with mean 4.1% and standard deviation .6%, from lot to lot.

a. In a particular lot, what is the probability that the wastage exceeds 5%?

b. If the actual amount of material required for a lot is 4700 yards, and 5000 yards of material are available, what is the probability that the supply of material is adequate?

5.74 Suppose that in Exercise 5.73 a particular cutter exceeds 5% wastage in 8 of 10 lots.

a. What is the probability of exceeding 5% in at least 8 of 10 lots?

b. Would such a result conclusively indicate that the cutter was inefficient?

5.75 A modem is an electronic device used in communication between computers. The specifications for a particular modem demand that the mean number of errors in transmitting through the device be 1 per 5000 words (or better). A particular modem is to be tested on a 25,000-word transmission. If 8 or more errors occur in transmission, the device will not be accepted. Assume that Poisson probabilities apply and that the modem just meets the 1 per 5000 standard.

a. What is the probability that the device will be accepted?

b. Can you think of a reason why the Poisson assumptions may not hold?

5.76 Assume that the Poisson distribution applies in Exercise 5.75, but also that the modem has a mean error rate of 1 per 2500 words, thus not meeting specifications. What is the probability that the device will be accepted?

5.77 Executives at a soft drink company wish to test a new formulation of their chief product. The new drink is tested in comparison to the current one. Each of 1000 potential customers is given a cup of the current formulation and a cup of the new one. The cups are labeled H and K to avoid bias. Each customer indicates a preference. Assume that, in fact, the customers can't detect a difference and are, in effect, guessing. Define Y to be the number (out of 1000) indicating preference for the new formulation.

a. What probability distribution should apply to Y? Do the assumptions underlying that distribution seem plausible in this context?

b. Find the mean and standard deviation of Y.

5.78 Find the approximate probability that the random variable Y in Exercise 5.77 is no larger than 460. Should the approximation be accurate?

5.79 A firm is considering using telemarketing techniques to supplement traditional marketing methods. It's estimated that 1 of every 100 calls results in a sale. Suppose that 250 calls are made in a single day.

a. Write an expression for the probability that there are 5 or fewer sales. Don't carry out any arithmetic.

b. What did you assume in answering part (a)? Are any of these assumptions grossly unreasonable?

5.80 a. Use a normal approximation to find a numerical value for the probability in Exercise 5.79, part (a).

b. Use a Poisson approximation to find a numerical value for the same probability.

c. Which approximation should be better? Why?

5.81 Refer again to Exercise 5.79. Let Y = number of calls made up to and including the first sale.

a. Find the mean and standard deviation of Y.

b. Find $P(Y = 1)$ and $P(Y = 100)$. Which is larger?

5.82 In the telemarketing situation described in Exercise 5.79, define Y to be the number of calls made up to and including the fourth sale.

a. Write an expression for the probability that Y is at least 400. You need not carry out the arithmetic.

b. Find the variance of Y.

5.83   The chief executive officer (CEO) of a medium-size corporation must select 3 individuals to head the firm's annual drive for community charities. There are three divisions (A, B and C) within the firm and 5, 6, and 4 individuals, respectively, within the divisions who could be chosen.

    a. How many combinations of 3 individuals can be chosen such that 1 individual comes from each of the three divisions?

    b. Suppose that the CEO chooses the individuals at random. What is the probability that at least 2 of them come from division A?

5.84   Refer to Exercise 5.83, part (b). Let Y = number of individuals chosen from division A. Find the expected value and variance of Y.

5.85   The computer that controls a bank's automatic teller machines "crashes" on occasion. The average time between crashes is 5.0 days. Define Y to be the waiting time until the next crash.

    a. Find the probability that the system does not crash in a (7-day) week.

    b. Find the probability that the time until the next crash is at least two weeks.

5.86   Find the expected value and standard deviation of the random variable Y of Exercise 5.85.

5.87   What assumption(s) did you make in Exercise 5.85? If it is known that one crash tends to be followed by another one in a relatively short time, what assumption would be violated?

5.88   An advertising campaign for a new product is targeted to make 20% of the adult population in a metropolitan area aware of the product. After the campaign, a random sample of 400 adults in the metropolitan area is obtained.

    a. Find the approximate probability that 57 or fewer adults in the sample are aware of the product. Use a continuity correction.

    b. Should the approximation be accurate?

    c. The sample shows that 57 adults are aware of the product. The marketing manager argues that the low awareness rate is a random fluke of the particular sample. Based on your answer to part (a), do you agree?

5.89   Brand managers at a consumer-products company regard an introductory advertising campaign for a new product as successful if at least 20% of the target group are made aware of the product. After one such campaign, a market research study finds that 56 of 400 individuals sampled are aware of the product. The target group is all adults who possess driver's licenses in the United States.

    a. Write an expression for the exact probability that 56 or fewer people in the sample are aware of the product, assuming that 20% of the target group are aware of the product. What probability distribution applies? What assumptions have you made?

    b. Use a normal approximation to find a numerical value for this probability.

    c. If you were the brand manager, would you believe that the advertising campaign had beeen successful?

5.90   A certain birth defect occurs with probability .0001; that is, 1 of every 10,000 babies has this defect. If 5000 babies are born at a particular hospital in a given year, what is the approximate probability that there is at least one baby with the defect? What approximation should be used?

5.91   Several states now have a Lotto lottery game. A player chooses 6 distinct integers in the range 1 to 40. If exactly those 6 numbers are selected as the winning numbers, the player receives a very large prize. What is the probability that a particular set of 6 numbers will be drawn? You may wish to think of the 6 numbers drawn as "success" numbers.

5.92   In the Lotto game described in Exercise 5.91, there are smaller prizes for selecting exactly 5 of the 6 winning numbers and even smaller prizes for selecting exactly 4 of the 6 winning numbers.

   a. What is the probability of selecting exactly 4 of the 6 winning numbers?

   b. What is the probability of selecting at least 4 of the 6 winning numbers?

5.93   Suppose that the Lotto game in Exercise 5.91 is changed such that 6 numbers were chosen in the range 1 to 42, rather than 1 to 40.

   a. Without doing any arithmetic, determine if the probability of selecting all 6 winning numbers is larger or smaller than what it was in Exercise 5.91. Will the change be small or large?

   b. Now compute the probability of selecting all 6 winning numbers, chosen from the numbers 1 to 42.

   c. Compare your answer to part (b) with the answer to Exercise 5.91. Did the probability change as you expected in part (a) of this exercise?

5.94   Suppose that, in the Lotto game of Exercise 5.91, 1,000,000 players make independent choices of the 6 numbers.

   a. What probability distribution applies to the random variable Y = number of players selecting all 6 numbers?

   b. Find an expression for $P(Y = 0)$. Don't carry out the arithmetic.

   c. Write an expression for $P(Y \geq 2)$.

5.95   a. Find the expected value and variance of the random variable Y in Exercise 5.94.

   b. Use a Poisson approximation to find $P(Y = 0)$ and $P(Y \geq 2)$. How accurate should the approximation be?

   c. If you have a suitable calculator, calculate a numerical value for the exact probability and compare it to the approximate probability found in part (b).

5.96   Should a normal approximation be used to approximate $P(Y = 0)$ and $P(Y \geq 2)$ in Exercise 5.94? Why?

5.97   If no one selects the correct 6 numbers in the Lotto game described in Exercise 5.94, the largest prize is not awarded; instead, the money is added to the pot for the next drawing. If there are no winners for several consecutive periods, the potential prize can be many millions of dollars. Suppose that, as in Exercise 5.94, 1,000,000 players independently select 6 numbers for each drawing. Define the random variable X = number of drawings required to obtain at least one winner.

   a. What probability distribution applies to X? Defend your statement.

   b. Find the mean and standard deviation of X.

   c. Write an expression for $P(X = 3)$. In terms of what happens in the Lotto game, what does the event $X = 3$ mean?

5.98   There is an objection to the formulation in Exercise 5.97. In fact, if there is no winner in one or two consecutive drawings, the news media report the large potential prize, and many more people play the game. Show that this fact leads to a violation of one of the assumptions made in Exercise 5.97.

5.99   Fires in occupied homes in a particular city occur at the rate of 1 every 2 days.

   a. What is the expected number of fires in homes over a 7-day week?

   b. Find the probability that there are at least 4 fires in a particular week.

   c. What are you assuming about the occurrence of fires in your answer to part (b)? Do any of the assumptions seem grossly unreasonable?

5.100 Refer to Exercise 5.99. Find the probability that at least 3 days elapse without any home fires. What is the expected time between home fires?

5.101 The operator of a mainframe computer system receives unscheduled requests to mount tapes. By policy, these requests must be answered as quickly as possible;

therefore, they interrupt scheduled work flow. Data indicate that the rate of such requests during the 9 A.M.–5 P.M. shift is about 1.5 per hour. Let Y = number of requests received in a particular 9 A.M.–5 P.M. shift.

a. Find the mean and standard deviation of Y.

b. Find $P(Y > 8)$.

5.102 Refer to Exercise 5.101. Find the probability that the time between successive requests is at least two hours.

5.103 The computer system manager in Exercise 5.101 notes that the demand for unscheduled tape mounts varies during the normal workday. Between 9 A.M. and 1 P.M. there is an average of 1 request per hour; between 1 P.M. and 5 P.M. there is an average of 2 requests per hour.

a. Does this fact change your answers to part (a)?

b. Does this fact affect your answer to part (b)?

CASE   Special Probability Distributions

A copy machine provider is about to undergo a major expansion. The company leases and services copiers for businesses and institutions. It is about to absorb another firm in the same business. One major question facing the company is: How many service technicians are required for the combined load of the two firms?

The company distinguishes two categories of copier. Office-use copiers are typically used for small numbers of copies and they are operated by secretaries and casual users. Production-use copiers are typically used for major jobs. They are operated by specialists. The company leases different styles of copiers for the two uses. It maintains separate staffs of service technicians for the two. Because the copiers are standard brands, service is the main area of competition with other providers. The company wants to have an adequate staff of technicians, but it doesn't want to have so many that they are idle a large fraction of the time.

Currently, before absorbing the other firm, the company has 2105 office-use copiers and 386 production-use copiers under lease. Requests for service are treated basically on a first called, first served basis. The service dispatcher logs requests and assigns technicians to them in order of request. Office-use technicians normally can service a maximum of 8 requests per day; production-use technicians typically work on more complex problems and can service a maximum of 4 requests per day. If a sudden burst of requests overloads the supply of technicians, jobs are "bumped" to the next day. The company's president feels that bumped customers are likely to go elsewhere when their contracts expire. The company currently employs 8 technicians for office-use copiers and 7 technicians for production-use copiers. The company uses a guideline that office-use copiers will need service once every 50 workdays (though some think it's once every 40 or once every 60 days) and production-use copiers once every 20 workdays (possibly once every 16 or once every 24 days).

When the company absorbs the other firm, it will have 3185 office-use copiers and 596 production-use copiers under lease. The company president has heard two arguments about the required number of technicians. First, the absorption represents basically a 50% increase in leases, so an increase of 50% in technicians is necessary. The counterargument is that the company maintains an excess of technicians to protect against exceptionally heavy bursts of requests. The law of averages says that the bigger pool of copiers under lease should tend to even out these bursts, so a proportionate increase in technicians isn't necessary.

The president has asked you to examine the question, particularly the risk of "bumping" requests to the next workday. The president is willing to read technical material, but has had no formal training in statistics, so you'll have to explain your ideas clearly.

6

RANDOM SAMPLING AND SAMPLING DISTRIBUTIONS

Now we can combine the ideas of summarizing data from Chapter 2 and the probability concepts from Chapters 3–5 into a central notion of statistics, which is the idea of the sampling distribution of a statistic. Summary statistics—means, medians, standard deviations, anything—vary from one sample to another. Samples from populations are taken randomly, so the means (for example) of two samples from the same population will differ to some degree. Samples from ongoing processes like production or sales are affected by uncontrolled, random influences, so two sample means from the same process will differ randomly. The sampling distribution of a summary statistic is a way to describe the variability of that statistic from one sample to another.

Probability theory can be used to obtain a sampling distribution, given certain assumptions. In fact, probability theory is important to this text for its use in sampling distributions. Such probability concepts as expected value and standard deviation of a random variable will be used repeatedly in this chapter.

One way that randomness and probability relate to summary statistics is by way of random sampling. In Section 6.1, we consider why we want to sample randomly and how to do it. Then we turn to the basic definition of a sampling distribution in Section 6.2, and the use of expected value and standard deviation in that context in Section 6.3. In Section 6.4, we apply the basic ideas to the most important special case, namely the sample mean. In this section, we first encounter a critical mathematical result, the Central Limit Theorem, that we'll use heavily thereafter. In Section 6.5 we consider this theorem, its interpretations and its misinterpretations, more fully. Then in Section 6.6 we consider how the computer can be used to complement the mathematical ideas of this chapter with computer simulation.

This is necessarily a theoretical chapter. The results of this chapter will be used over and over again in the methods of the following chapters. The uses may not be obvious to you at first reading, but we promise that you'll see them later. Bear with us.

6.1   RANDOM SAMPLING   ■

selection bias

Most statistics textbooks, including this one, tell you to use random sampling to collect data. A basic reason for using random sampling is to ensure that the inferences made from the sample data are not distorted by a **selection bias**. A selection bias exists whenever there is a systematic tendency to overrepresent or underrepresent some part of the population. For example, a telephone sample of households in a region, conducted entirely between the hours of 9 A.M. and 5 P.M., would be severely biased toward households with at least one non-working member. Hence any inferences made from the sample data would be biased toward the attitudes or opinions of nonworking members and might not be truly representative of households in the region. Similarly, a sample of charge accounts taken by selecting a set of transactions would be biased toward active, many-transaction accounts, and away from inactive ones. Inferences from these data might not reflect the characteristics of the set of all accounts. A random sampling plan, by definition, avoids this kind of bias.

We indicated earlier that simple random sampling is a process whereby each possible sample of a given size has the same probability of being selected. Obtaining a truly, or even approximately, random sample requires some thought and effort. A random sample is not a casual or haphazard sample. The target population must be identified. In principle, a list of all elements (possible individual values) in the population ought to be constructed with elements to be included in the sample selected randomly from the list, using a table of random numbers.

EXAMPLE 6.1

Suppose that the research staff of a Federal Reserve bank wishes to take a random sample of checks written on individual (nonbusiness) checking accounts to determine average amount, time to clearance, and insufficient-funds rates. How might they do so?

Solution

First, the target population must be defined. Is it all individual checks written in a given period, or is it all checks processed by the Federal Reserve clearing house during that time? There's a difference, because a check that is cashed at the bank on which it was originally drawn never gets to the clearing house. Assume that the clearing-house definition is chosen. The next step is to establish a random sampling method. One could, in principle, put a numerical tag on every one of the 326,274 (or whatever number) checks processed by the center on a particular day. Then a random sample of 1000 could be drawn by selecting six-digit random numbers and the checks with corresponding tags (passing over 000000 and anything larger than 326274).

Obviously, this would be a very impractical and expensive way to obtain a random sample. Such a method only serves as an idealization against which a more practical method can be measured. Another possibility is to sample every 300th check processed. This method is not literally random sampling, because, for instance, two successive checks couldn't be included in the sample. No doubt one could dream up some situations for which sampling every 300th check would introduce some kind of selection bias; however, this process seems to yield a fairly good approximation to random sampling, at a manageable cost.   ■

The applicability of sampling methods is much broader than the familiar political polls and market research studies. Sampling should be considered whenever information is desired and the cost (in dollars, in labor, or in time) of obtaining complete information is excessive. For example, suppose that a processor of potato chips sells the product through 1943 retail outlets. A critical variable for the success of the product is the average amount of shelf space devoted to the product per outlet. It would be absurd for the processor to visit every outlet and measure that shelf space devoted to the product. Assuming that the potato-chip processor had a list of the retail outlets, it would be relatively easy to obtain a random sample of, say, 100 outlets and to measure the average shelf space in that sample.

sampling frame

Ideally, one has a list of the elements of the target population. More often, one has a list that almost, but not quite, equals the target population. The almost-right list is called the **sampling frame**, to indicate that it is not exactly the same as the target population. A good sampling frame is sometimes fairly easy to obtain, as it would be in the case of the potato chip processor, who most likely knows almost all, but not quite all, retail outlets. When sampling human populations, a good sampling frame is harder to develop. People move; a directory or a mailing list can become outdated quickly. Telephone directories are not a completely reliable source for developing a sampling frame; there are unlisted phone numbers and multiple phone numbers. Perhaps the most serious problem is that people without phones tend strongly to be poor people. This problem was a major cause of one of the most notorious failures in sampling, the *Literary Digest* poll before the 1936 U.S. presidential election. The *Literary Digest*, a popular magazine of the time, took a huge survey (2.4 million responses), based in large part on telephone books. In 1936, during the Great Depression, this procedure introduced a substantial bias. The magazine forecast that the Republican candidate would win the election; he won only two states. Much of the effort in conducting a good sampling should go into developing the sampling frame.

Given a decent sampling frame, random sampling can be done with a computer program that generates random numbers, or with a table of random numbers. Appendix Table 9 contains a small random number table. For all practical purposes, such a table can be entered at any point. (One way to enter such a table is to pull a dollar bill from one's wallet and use the first serial number digit to select the row and the second digit to indicate the column.) Suppose that we enter the table at row 3, column 1, go across the row, and use the first three digits. To obtain a random sample of 10 individuals from a population of 916 individuals, we number the individuals in the sampling frame from 000 to 915 and select the first 10 numbers, namely 24130 (using only 241), 483(60), 225(27), 972(75), 763(93), 648(09), 151(79), 248(30), 493(40), and 320(81). If we obtain any random numbers larger than 915, such as 972, we ignore them and draw replacement numbers. We replace the 972 by 306(80), which is the next number in Appendix Table 9. Assuming that we wish to sample without replacement, we also ignore any repetitions of numbers. Of course, there's no need to depend on a table; virtually any decent computer system can generate a series of random numbers that serves equally well.

EXAMPLE 6.2   Suppose that a sample of size 4 is to be taken from a sampling frame of 1943 retail outlets. If we enter Appendix Table 9 of random numbers at row 3, column 1, and read vertically, down columns, the first 10 entries are 24130, 42167, 37570, 77921, 99562, 96301, 89579, 85475, 28918, 63553. Which stores should be sampled?

Solution   One of the many ways that one can use these numbers is to ignore the last digit and select only those values between 0001 and 1943, both inclusive; thus, ignore 2143, 4216, and so on. We continue down the column and pick stores 0942 (row 13), 1036 (row 14), 0711 (row 15), and 0236. We ignore any repetitions, assuming that we are sampling without replacement. (We could also have used a computer to select random samples in the range from 0001 to 1943.)   ■

Careful planning and a certain amount of ingenuity are required to have even a decent approximation to a random sample. This is especially true when the elements in the target population are people. People throw away mail questionnaires, they are not home to answer telephone surveys, and they modify answers to conform to social norms. Too often, surveys of people are done in a haphazard way, using a hastily composed questionnaire mailed (often addressed to "occupant") according to a conveniently chosen mailing list, with no provisions for following up on those who do not respond. The result is bad data, riddled with biases that have unknowable effects. Lots of statistical methods can be applied to such data, but the well-known adage applies: Garbage in, garbage out. Getting reasonable samples of human populations is a considerable art (and a fairly substantial industry); we will not try to capture the essence of that art in a couple of pages.

There are other valid and useful sampling methods, such as stratified sampling. We discuss some of these in Chapter 18. Most uses of probability theory in the remaining chapters are based on simple random sampling. The basic ideas remain the same when other sampling methods are used. The formulas just get a little more complicated.

SECTION 6.1   EXERCISES

6.1   Suppose that we want to select a random sample of $n = 10$ entities from a population of 800 individuals. Use Appendix Table 9 to identify the individuals to be sampled. Start in row 5, column 1, and read down.

6.2   City officials sample the opinions of homeowners in a community about the possibility of raising taxes to improve the quality of local schools. A directory of all homes in the city is used; a computer generates random numbers to identify the addresses to be sampled. An interviewer visits each home between the hours of 3 P.M. and 6 P.M. If no one is home, the address is eliminated from the sample and replaced by another randomly chosen address. Does this process approximate random sampling?

6.3   A university bookstore manager is mildly concerned about the number of textbooks that were underordered and thus unavailable two days after the beginning of classes. The manager instructs an employee to pick a random number, go to the place where that number book is shelved, examine the next 50 titles, and record how many titles are unavailable.

    a. Technically, this process doesn't yield a random sample of the books in the store. Why not?

    b. How could a truly random sample be obtained?

6.4   A professional baseball team has a 20-game ticket plan and a 40-game ticket plan. The sales director wants to assess fan interest in a combination plan by which two separate purchasers of 20-game plans can pool their money and buy a 40-game plan at a modest discount. The target population to be sampled is all current 20-game plan purchasers. An up-to-date list of the 4256 current purchasers is available. Explain how to obtain a random sample of the current purchasers.

6.5   One way to sample the purchasers in Exercise 6.4 is to develop a list of the seat numbers held by purchasers and to take a random sample of seat numbers. Most likely this will not yield a random sample of purchasers. Explain why not.

6.6   A building manager for a 2526-office complex hires a new cleaning contractor. The manager wants to get a rough idea of how satisfactory the contractor's weekend cleaning efforts are. One possible strategy is to select 3 offices on the first three floors and to examine those offices and the 10 offices on either side. Another strategy, which requires roughly the same time, is to select 15 offices completely at random. It is argued that the first strategy is better because it allows for inspection of more offices. Is the argument valid?

6.2   SAMPLE STATISTICS AND SAMPLING DISTRIBUTIONS ■

Once a sample has been selected and numerical data obtained, the first task is to summarize it. In Chapter 2 we defined several summary measures, such as the sample mean and the sample standard deviation. Each of these is an example of a

sample statistic   **sample statistic**.

The numerical value that a sample statistic will have cannot be exactly predicted in advance. Even if we know that a population mean μ is \$216.37 and that the population standard deviation σ is \$32.90—even if we know the complete population distribution—we cannot say that the sample mean $\bar{Y}$ will be exactly \$216.37. A sample statistic is a random variable; it is subject to random variation because it is based on a random sample of measurements selected from the population of interest, and, like any other random variable, a sample statistic has a probability distribution. We call the theoretical probability distribution of

sampling   a sample statistic the **sampling distribution** of that statistic.
distribution   The actual mathematical derivation of sampling distributions is one of the basic problems of mathematical statistics. The techniques we use include the basic probability methods of Chapter 3, Monte Carlo methods (discussed in Section 6.6), and numerous other mathematical manipulations. We first illustrate how the sampling distribution for $\bar{Y}$ can be obtained for a simplified population. Later in the chapter we presented several general results.

EXAMPLE 6.3   The sample mean $\bar{y}$ is to be calculated from a random sample of size 2 taken from a population consisting of the 5 values ($2, $3, $4, $5, $6). Find the sampling distribution of $\bar{Y}$, based on a sample of size 2.

Solution   One way to find $P_{\bar{Y}}(\bar{y})$ is by counting. There are $\binom{5}{2} = 10$ possible samples of 2 items from the 5 items. These are shown here:

Possible samples of size 2:	2, 3	2, 4	2, 5	2, 6	3, 4	3, 5	3, 6	4, 5	4, 6	5, 6
Value of $\bar{y}$:	2.5	3	3.5	4	3.5	4	4.5	4.5	5	5.5

Assuming that each sample of size 2 is equally likely, it follows that the sampling distribution for $\bar{Y}$ based on $n = 2$ observations selected from this population is as indicated here:

y:	2.5	3	3.5	4	4.5	5	5.5
$P_{\bar{Y}}(\bar{y})$:	1/10	1/10	2/10	2/10	2/10	1/10	1/10

This sampling distribution is shown as a graph in Figure 6.1.

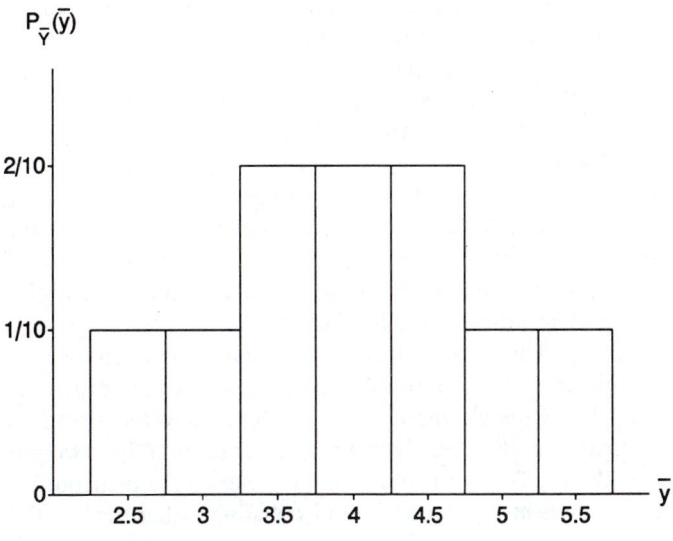

FIGURE 6.1   Sampling Distribution for $\bar{Y}$; Example 6.3   ■

Usually we use a sample statistic as an estimate of a population parameter. For example, we can use a sample mean to estimate the corresponding mean μ of the population from which the sample was drawn. We then use the sampling distribution of a sample statistic to determine how accurate the estimate is likely to be. In Example 6.3 we know that the population mean μ is $4. Obviously, we don't ever know μ in practice. Still, we can use the sampling distribution of $\bar{Y}$ to determine the probability that, for example, the computed value of the sample mean will be more than $.50 away from μ. For Example 6.3, this probability is

$$P_{\bar{Y}}(2.5) + P_{\bar{Y}}(3) + P_{\bar{Y}}(5) + P_{\bar{Y}}(5.5) = \frac{4}{10}$$

In general, a sample statistic is used to make inferences about a population parameter. The sampling distribution of the statistic is crucial in determining how good the inference is likely to be.

interpretations of a sampling distribution   Sampling distributions can be interpreted in at least two ways. One way uses the long-run relative-frequency approach. Imagine taking repeated samples of a fixed size from a given population and calculating the value of the sample statistic for each sample. In the long run, the relative frequencies for the possible values of the sample statistic approach the corresponding sampling distribution probabilities. For example, if you take a large number of samples from the population distribution pr abilities of Example 6.3 and compute the sample mean for each sample, app ximately 20% of the samples will have $\bar{y} = 3.5$.

The other way to interpret a sampling distribution makes use of the classical interpretation of probability. Imagine listing all possible samples that can be drawn from a given population. The probability that a sample statistic has a particular value (say, that $\bar{y} = 3.5$) is then the proportion of all possible samples that yield that value. In Example 6.3, $P_{\bar{y}}(3.5) = 2/10$ corresponds to the fact that 2 of the 10 samples have a sample mean equal to 3.5. Both the repeated-sampling and the classical approach to finding probabilities for a sample statistic are legitimate.

In practice, though, a sample is taken only once, and only one value of the sample statistic is calculated. **A sample distribution is not something you can see in practice; it is not an empirically observed distribution. Rather it is a theoretical concept**, a set of probabilities derived from assumptions about the population and about the sampling method.

There's an unfortunate similarity between the phrase *sampling distribution*, meaning the theoretically derived probability distribution of a statistic, and the phrase *sample distribution*, which refers to the histogram of **individual** values we can actually observe in a particular sample. The two phrases mean very different things. To avoid confusion, we refer to the distribution of sample values as the **sample histogram** or **data distribution** rather than as the sample distribution.

sample histogram or data distribution

EXAMPLE 6.4   Refer to Example 6.3. How could one use a computer to approximate the sampling distribution for $\bar{Y}$ based on $n = 2$ observations?

Solution   Suppose that we decide to simulate 10,000 samples of size 2 from the population of Example 6.3. We can use a computer to generate 10,000 random digits $(0, 1, \ldots, 9)$ from a uniform distribution. As noted in Example 6.3, there are 10 possible samples. The 2, 3 sample $(\bar{y} = 2.5)$ can be assigned to each 0 digit, the 2, 4 sample $(\bar{y} = 3)$ to each 1 digit, $\ldots$, and the 5, 6 sample $(\bar{y} = 5.5)$ to each 9 digit. Thus each possible sample has the same probability. This results in 10,000 $\bar{y}$-values. The values and corresponding relative frequencies are shown below:

Value of $\bar{y}$:	2.5	3.0	3.5	4.0	4.5	5.0	5.5
Frequency:	1024	991	2006	2018	1975	1005	981
Relative frequency:	.1024	.0991	.2006	.2018	.1975	.1005	.0981

Note that these simulated relative frequencies are very close to the theoretical probabilities .1, .1, .2, .2, .2, .1, and .1. This method always yields approximate distributions with the approximation getting better (and more expensive) as the number of repetitions increases. ■

EXAMPLE 6.5   We found that the sampling distribution of $\bar{Y}$ in Example 6.4 assigned probability 2/10 to $\bar{y} = 4.5$. What is the interpretation of this result?

Solution   There are at least two useful interpretations. First, we could suppose that a long series (conceptually, an infinitely long series) of samples of size 2 had been taken from this population. In such a case, the long-run fraction of samples yielding a sample mean of 4.5 would be .2. Alternatively, we could suppose that a list of all possible samples of size 2 was prepared; 2 of every 10 samples would yield a sample mean of 4.5. ■

In this book we derive only some relatively simple theoretical (sampling) distributions. More complicated sampling distributions require sophisticated mathematics, and that's not our priority. Instead, we focus on the assumptions underlying the theory—and the consequences of violating those assumptions. For the derivation of the results we suggest consulting a good mathematical statistics book such as Larsen and Marx (1986).

Of course, sampling distributions can also be calculated for samples taken with replacement. If, in Example 6.3, the sample is taken with replacement, the sampling distribution of $\bar{Y}$ is as follows:

$\bar{y}$:	2.0	2.5	3.0	3.5	4.0	4.5	5.0	5.5	6.0
$P_{\bar{Y}}(\bar{y})$:	.04	.08	.12	.16	.20	.16	.12	.08	.04

A computer-simulation study could be done assuming sampling with replacement. For example, we could draw 10,000 2-digit random numbers, letting each of the numbers 00, 01, 02, and 03 correspond to $\bar{y} = 2$, each of 04 through 11 to $\bar{y} = 2.5$, and so on. The relative frequencies from such a study would be close to the probabilities shown. ■

SECTION 6.2   EXERCISES

6.7   The owner of a chain of laundromats estimates the average between breakdowns of washing machines by determining the time since the previous repair of the 100 most recently repaired machines. What bias may there be in this procedure?

6.8   Can you suggest a better approach to collecting a sample of times to breakdown for 100 machines in Exercise 6.7?

6.9   One way to audit 1% of all transactions passing through a brokerage house is to check all transactions with serial numbers ending in 00. If you were an embezzler working in the back room, what would you think of this approach?

6.10   Suggest an ideal way to sample 1% of all transactions in Exercise 6.9.

6.11   A random sample of size 3 is to be drawn, without replacement, from the population of Example 6.3. The sampling distribution of $\bar{Y}$ can be proved to be

$\bar{y}$:	3.000	3.333	3.667	4.000	4.333	4.667	5.000
$P_{\bar{Y}}(\bar{y})$:	.10	.10	.20	.20	.20	.10	.10

a. Plot histograms of this sampling distribution and the sampling distribution of Example 6.3.

b. Find the probability that $\bar{Y}$ is no more than \$.50 away from the population mean \$4.00, assuming $n = 3$.

6.12   Compute the expected values and variances for the sampling distributions of Example 6.3 and Exercise 6.11. How does the difference in sample size affect the expected values and variances?

6.13   A random sample of size 8 is to be taken with replacement from a population with the following probability distribution:

Value:	4	8	12	16
Probability:	.50	.30	.15	.05

The sampling distributions of $\bar{Y}$, the sample mean, can be shown to be (to 4 decimal places):

$\bar{y}$:	4.0	4.5	5.0	5.5	6.0	6.5	7.0	7.5	8.0
$P_{\bar{Y}}(\bar{y})$:	.0039	.0188	.0488	.0898	.1293	.1535	.1550	.1359	.1048

$\bar{y}$:	8.5	9.0	9.5	10.0	10.5	11.0	11.5	12.0	12.5
$P_{\bar{Y}}(\bar{y})$:	.0718	.0439	.0242	.0119	.0053	.0021	.0008	.0002	.0001

$\bar{y}$:	13.0	13.5	14.0	14.5	15.0	15.5	16.0
$P_{\bar{Y}}(\bar{y})$:	.0000	.0000	.0000	.0000	.0000	.0000	.0000

a. Plot histograms of the population distribution and the sampling distribution of $\bar{Y}$.

b. Verify that the population mean is 7.0.

c. Find the expected value and variance of $\bar{Y}$.

d. Find the probability that $\bar{Y}$ is no more than 1.5 units away from the population mean μ.

6.14   Refer to the histograms plotted in Exercise 6.13, part (a).

a. Which histogram shows a smaller variance? (Determine this without arithmetic.)

b. Which histogram shows less skewness?

6.15   A computer simulation of the sampling process of Exercise 6.13 yields the following:

Mean:	4.0	4.5	5.0	5.5	6.0	6.5	7.0	7.5
Frequency:	3	25	45	91	122	138	165	137

Mean:	8.0	8.5	9.0	9.5	10.0	10.5	11.0	11.5	12.0
Frequency:	115	71	38	23	12	9	3	2	1

a. Plot the simulation frequencies in a histogram.

b. Compare this histogram to the theoretical probabilities shown in Exercise 6.13.

6.3   EXPECTED VALUES AND STANDARD ERRORS OF SAMPLE SUMS AND SAMPLE MEANS

The sampling distribution of a sample statistic is a probability distribution. Its exact form depends on the population distribution being sampled. Fortunately, we can derive the basic properties of the most important sampling distributions, those of sample sums and sample means, from minimal assumptions about the population. In this section we find expected values and variances for these distributions. In the next section we show that the normal distribution is often a good approximation to the exact shapes of these sampling distributions.

The mathematical results shown in Appendix 4A of Chapter 4 extend immediately to give us the desired results for the sampling distribution of a sum. Suppose that we take a random sample of size n from a population of sufficient size N that n is small relative to N. Let Y_i denote the ith observation in the sample and let T denote the sample sum $Y_1 + Y_2 + \cdots + Y_n$. Then it can be shown that the expected value and variance of T are as shown below.

Expected Value and Variance of a Sample Sum

If T is the sum of n values drawn at random from a population with mean μ and variance σ^2, then the expected value, variance, and standard deviation for T are

$$E(T) = \mu + \mu + \cdots + \mu = n\mu$$
$$\text{Var}(T) = \sigma^2 + \sigma^2 + \cdots + \sigma^2 = n\sigma^2$$
$$\sigma_T = \sqrt{\text{Var}(T)} = \sqrt{n}\,\sigma$$

EXAMPLE 6.6   Suppose that the long-run average of the number of Medicare claims submitted per week to a regional office is 62,000, and that the standard deviation is 7000. If we assume that the weekly claims submissions during a 4-week period constitute a random sample of size 4, what are the expected value and standard deviation of the total number of claims in the period?

Solution   We are given that $\mu = 62{,}000$, $\sigma = 7000$, and $n = 4$. It follows that

$$E(T) = (4)(62{,}000) = 248{,}000$$
$$\sigma_T = (\sqrt{4})(7000) = 14{,}000$$

The critical part of the assumption of random sampling is the assumption of independence of the numbers of claims submitted from one week to another. If independence doesn't hold, the expected value of T is still correct but, according to Appendix 4A (Chapter 4), the standard deviation is wrong. ∎

At this point, it is very handy to introduce a new name for an existing concept. We specify many sample statistics and many sampling distributions in the next several chapters; it turns out that there are many different formulas for the standard deviations of the sampling distributions of these statistics. Most of the formulas (like the one for the standard deviation of T) involve the population standard deviation, and it becomes difficult to distinguish between the different standard deviations. From here on, then, we use the term **standard error** to denote the theoretically derived standard deviation of the sampling distribution of a statistic. The standard error of the sample sum T is the standard deviation of its sampling distribution $\sigma_T = \sqrt{n}\sigma$.

standard error

The sampling distribution of a sample mean is even more important than the sampling distribution of a sum; the sample average is the most widely used of all statistics. The expected value, variance, and standard error of this sampling distribution can be found quite easily using the results about a sample sum and the principles introduced in Appendix 4A. If $Y_1, \ldots, Y_n$ represent the n individual values from a random sample, the sample mean is $\bar{Y} = (Y_1 + \cdots + Y_n)/n = T/n$, which is the sample total divided by the sample size. From the Appendix 4A, it follows that we can find the expected value and standard error of the sample mean by dividing the corresponding values for the sample sum T by n.

Expected Value and Standard Error of $\bar{Y}$

If a random sample of size n is drawn from a population, the expected value and standard error of $\bar{Y}$ are

$$E(\bar{Y}) = \frac{n\mu}{n} = \mu$$

$$\sigma_{\bar{Y}} = \frac{\sqrt{n}\sigma}{n} = \frac{\sigma}{\sqrt{n}}$$

EXAMPLE 6.7   In the situation of Example 6.6, find the expected value and standard error of the average weekly number of claims over a 4-week period.

Solution   In Example 6.6, $\mu = 62,000$, $\sigma = 7000$, and $n = 4$. If $\bar{Y}$ is the 4-week average of the weekly number of claims, then

$$E(\bar{Y}) = \mu = 62,000$$

$$\sigma_{\bar{Y}} = \frac{\sigma}{\sqrt{n}} = 7000/\sqrt{4} = 3500 \qquad \blacksquare$$

The fact that $E(\bar{Y}) = \mu$ means that the sample mean estimates the population mean correctly on average. In one particular sample, the sample mean may overestimate the population mean. In another, the sample mean may underestimate. But in the long run there is no **systematic** tendency for a sample mean to overestimate or underestimate the population mean. This is true regardless of the sample size.

The standard deviation of the sampling distribution of the mean (the standard error of the sample mean) is crucial in determining the probable amount of error in an estimate. We just said that there is no systematic tendency to over- or underestimate μ with $\bar{Y}$. This wouldn't be much of a consolation if we knew that half the time we made a huge overestimate, the other half an equally huge underestimate! The standard error of a sample mean $\sigma_{\bar{Y}}$, in conjunction with the Empirical Rule of Chapter 2, can be used to give a good indication of the probable deviation of a particular sample mean from the population mean.

EXAMPLE 6.8   Suppose that a supermarket manager is interested in estimating the mean checkout time for the nonexpress checkout lanes. An assistant manager obtains a random sample of 25 checkout times. If previous data suggest that the population standard deviation is 1.10 minutes, describe the probable deviation of $\bar{Y}$ from the unknown population mean μ.

Solution   The Empirical Rule indicates that approximately 95% of the time $\bar{Y}$ is within two standard errors ($2\sigma_{\bar{Y}}$) of the population mean μ. For $n = 25$,

$$2\sigma_{\bar{Y}} = \frac{2\sigma}{\sqrt{n}} = \frac{2(1.10)}{5} = .44$$

The probable error for $\bar{Y}$ is no more than .44 minute.   ∎

The probable accuracy of a sample mean, as measured by its standard error, is affected by the sample size. Because the standard error of the sample mean is the population standard deviation divided by the square root of the sample size, the standard error decreases as the sample size increases. For example, if the sample size had been either 50 or 100 instead of 25 in Example 6.8, the probable errors ($2\sigma_{\bar{Y}}$) would have been, respectively, .31 or .22.

As the sample size increases to infinity, the standard error of the sample mean decreases toward zero. For a large sample size, the standard error of the mean is very small, and the sample mean based on a huge sample is very close to the true population mean, with very high probability.

In Section 2.3, we defined control limits by adding and subtracting three standard deviations from the desired target value. The standard deviation in question is the standard deviation of the sample mean, based on the sample size used. For example, we discussed an automatic transmission in which the desired internal pressure was 35. The standard deviaton of pressures of individual transmissions was about 1.2, and 5 transmissions were sampled each day. Thus the standard deviation of the sample mean (standard error) should theoretically be 1.2 divided by the square root of 5, or 0.54.

In quality-control practice, there is an additional source of variability that's not found in sampling from fixed populations. Even if a process is in control, it will vary somewhat over time; for example, the true mean pressure for all transmissions may vary somewhat (over time) around 35, even though the process is basically satisfactory. This additional variation often makes the actual standard deviation of sample means slightly higher than the theoretical value. In the transmission example, the actual standard deviation of the means was 0.60.

SECTION 6.3   EXERCISES

6.16   Refer to the sampling distribution of Exercise 6.13. Show that the expected value and variance found in Exercise 6.13 agree with the theoretical results of this section.

6.17   An automobile insurer has found that repair claims have an average of $927 and a standard deviation of $871. Suppose that the next 50 claims can be regarded as a random sample from the long-run claims process.

a. Find the expected value and standard error of the total of the next 50 claims.

b. Find the expected value and standard error of the average of the next 50 claims.

6.18   A computer simulation can itself be regarded as a sampling process. Suppose that a study is done concerning the time required to complete a research and development project. There is considerable variability in the times required to complete the various pieces of the project, so the overall completion time has considerable variability. Assume that the time to completion has a mean of 28.2 months and a standard deviation of 6.9 months.

a. If the simulation involves 1000 independent trials of the project, find the expected value and standard error of the simulation (sample) mean.

b. Find the expected value and standard error if 4000 trials are simulated.

6.4   SAMPLING DISTRIBUTIONS FOR MEANS AND SUMS ∎

In the last section we stated the appropriate expected values and standard errors for two sample statistics: The sample sum T and the sample mean $\bar{Y}$. In this section we show that in most situations a normal distribution provides a good approximation to the sampling distribution for T or $\bar{Y}$.

According to a theorem of mathematical statistics, if a population distribution is (exactly) normal, then the sampling distributions for the sample sum T and the sample mean $\bar{Y}$ are also (exactly) normal. The relevant expected values and standard errors are those given in the previous section.

Suppose that a meat packer provides "12 ounce" steaks that, in fact, have a mean weight of 12.10 ounces and a standard deviation of 0.20 ounces, and they have a normal distribution of weights. Assume that a package of 25 steaks constitutes a random sample from the population (which might also be thought of as a long-run process) of steaks. What is the probability that the mean weight in the package exceeds 12.00 ounces? According to the theorem we just mentioned, if the population distribution is normal, the sampling distribution of sample means is also normal. The expected value for the sample mean will be 12.10, equal to the population mean. The standard deviation for the sample mean will *not* equal the population standard deviation; sample means are less variable than individual scores. The relevant standard deviation for the sample mean is the standard error; $\sigma_{\bar{y}} = \sigma/\sqrt{n} = 0.20/\sqrt{25} = 0.040$. To find the probability that the sample mean will exceed 12.00 ounces, we go through the familiar z calculation, and we make sure that we use the standard error, not the population standard deviation.

$$P(Y > 12.00) = P(z > (12.00 - 12.10)/0.040) = P(z > -2.50)$$
$$= .5000 + .4938 = .9938 \quad \text{(from Appendix Table 3)}$$

EXAMPLE 6.9   A timber company is planning to harvest 400 trees from a very large 50-year-old stand. The yield of lumber from each tree is largely determined by its diameter. Assume that the distribution of diameters in the stand is normal with mean 44 inches and standard deviation 4 inches. Also assume (perhaps unrealistically) that the selection of the 400 trees is effectively random. Find the probability that the average diameter of the harvested trees is between 43.5 and 44.5 inches.

Solution   The population distribution (of the diameters of all trees in the stand) is assumed to be normal. It follows from the previous result that the sampling distribution of $\bar{Y}$ is also normal. The appropriate expected value and standard error are

$$\mu_{\bar{Y}} = \mu = 44$$

$$\sigma_{\bar{Y}} = \frac{\sigma}{\sqrt{n}} = \frac{4}{\sqrt{400}} = .20$$

As usual, we calculate normal probabilities by calculating z-scores (see Figure 6.2):

$$P(43.5 \le \bar{Y} \le 44.5) = P\left(\frac{43.5 - 44}{.20} \le Z \le \frac{44.5 - 44}{.20}\right)$$

$$= P(-2.50 \le Z \le 2.50)$$

$$= 2(.4938) = .9876$$

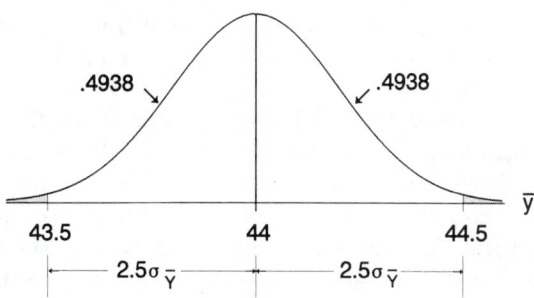

FIGURE 6.2   Probability Calculation for Example 6.9   ■

Use of this theorem, as stated, requires the assumption that the population distribution is exactly normal. In practice, no distribution is exactly normal. **Central Limit** Another theorem, called a **Central Limit Theorem**, implies that the assumption of **Theorem** a normal population is not crucial.

Central Limit Theorem for Sums and Means

For *any* population (with finite mean μ and standard deviation σ), the sampling distributions of the sample sum and of the sample mean are approximately normal if the sample size n is sufficiently large.   ■

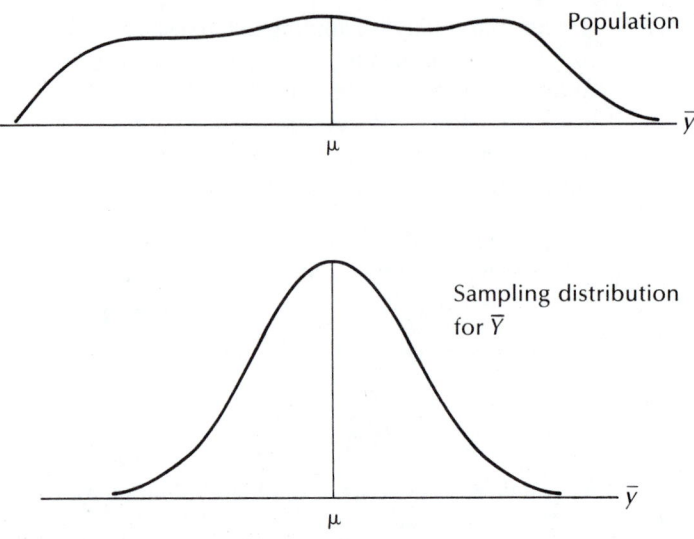

FIGURE 6.3   An Illustration of the Central Limit Theorem

This is a rather remarkable theorem. **Regardless of the nature of the population distribution—discrete or continuous, symmetric or skewed, unimodal or multimodal—the sampling distributions for T and $\bar{Y}$ are always normal as long as the sample size is large enough**. This is illustrated in Figure 6.3 for the sample mean. The condition that the population mean and standard deviation must be finite is almost always satisfied.*

An obvious question is how large a sample is sufficiently large? The Central Limit Theorem is a mathematical theorem—"n sufficiently large" is translated into "as n goes to infinity"—so it does not contain the answer to this question. An enormous number of studies have tried to answer the question, using other mathematical theorems and computer simulations. Many textbooks give a blanket rule: Use the normal approximation anytime n exceeds 30.

This rule is a good basic guide for using the Central Limit Theorem. A better rule would consider the effect of skewness. If the population distribution is very skewed, the actual sampling distribution for $n = 30$ or for $n = 40$ is also somewhat skewed, less so than the population distribution, but enough to make the normal approximation mediocre. If the population distribution is symmetric, the sampling distribution even with $n = 10$ or so is remarkably close to normal. A better rule would be based on a plot of the sample data, and drawing a picture of the data is always a good idea. If a histogram of the sample data shows obvious skewness (and hence suggests skewness for the population distribution), a normal

* The only exception we know of is the case of so-called stable laws, which are sometimes used as models in finance.

approximation should be used skeptically unless n is up around 100. If the histogram has little skewness, the normal approximation may be used confidently, even with an n of 15 or 20.*

EXAMPLE 6.10   A computer program was used to draw 1000 samples each, with sample sizes 4, 10, 30, and 60, from an exponential population having mean and standard deviation both equal to 1. (A discussion of how such computer simulations are done is in Section 6.6.) Histograms of the sample means are shown in Figure 6.4. As the sample size increases, how does the shape of the theoretical (sampling) distribution of means change? How does the variability of sample means change?

Solution   For $n = 4$, the distribution of means is clearly right skewed, although not as skewed as the exponential distribution itself. As the sample size increases, the skewness decreases. For a sample of size 60, the distribution of means appears to be very close to normal. The Central Limit Theorem indicates that the theoretical distribution of sample means should, indeed, approach a normal distribution as the sample size increases.

From the scale at the bottom of each histogram, we can assess the variability of sample means. As n increases, the range of sample means decreases,

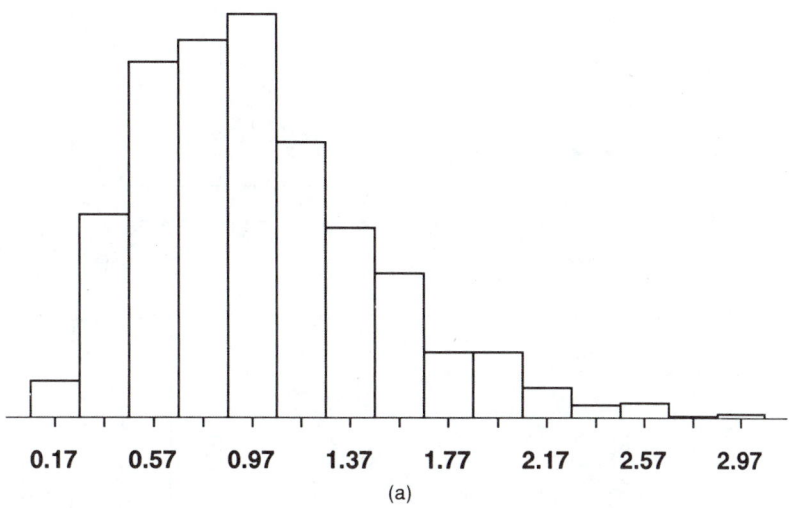

(a)

FIGURE 6.4   Histogram of Sample Means: (a) Sample of Size 4; (b) Sample of Size 10; (c) Sample of Size 30; (d) Sample of Size 60

* The quality of a normal approximation is also slightly affected by how heavy the tails are in the population. Even if a population is nearly symmetric, it may contain many more extremely large and extremely small values than would a near-normal distribution. A heavy-tailed population in a sample is suggested by the presence of outliers—a few individual values that fall very far from the bulk of the data. We discuss the treatment of outliers in later chapters.

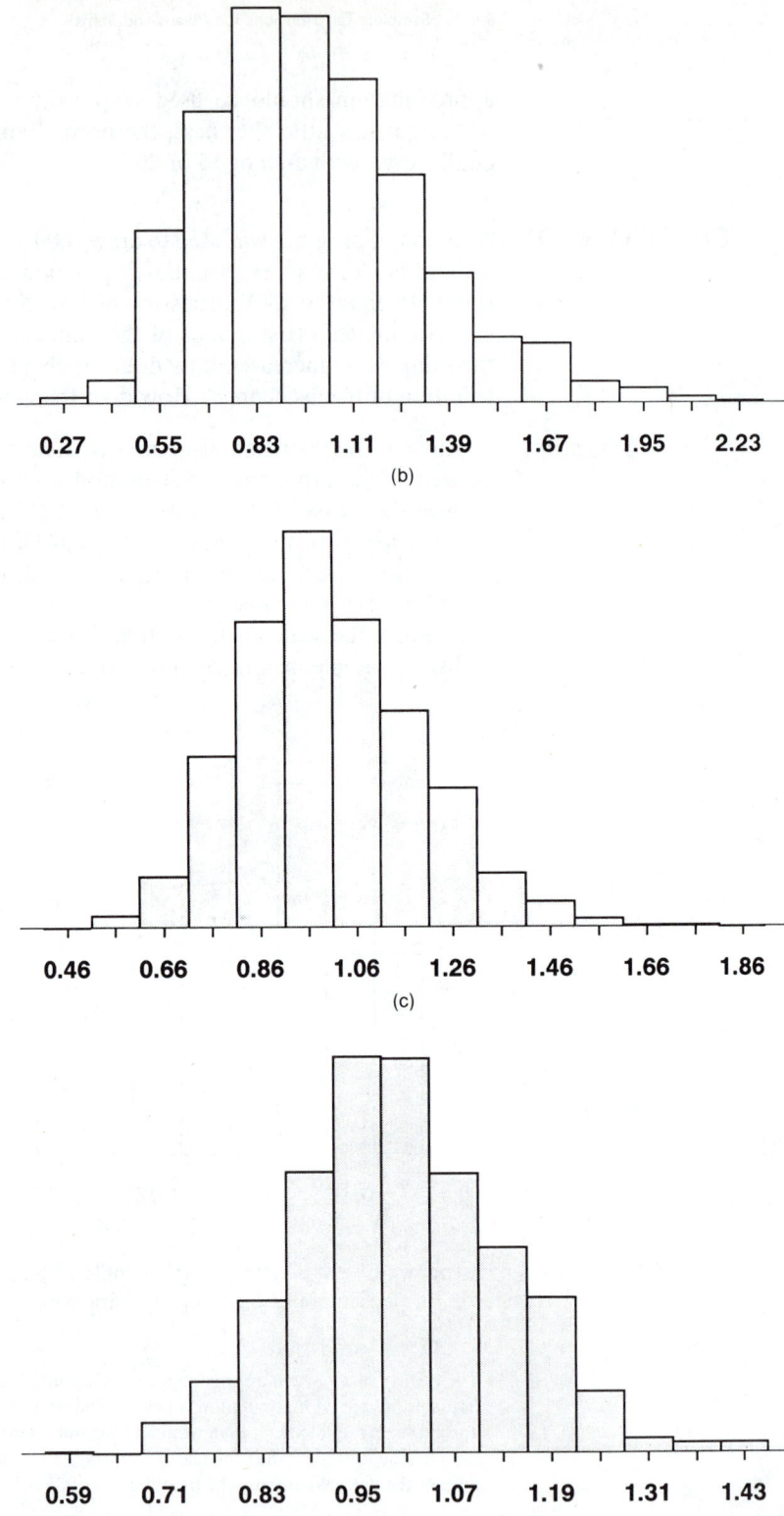

FIGURE 6.4   (Continued)

indicating that variability decreases. The fact that the standard error of the sample mean decreases as n increases indicates that the variability of sample means should decrease as n increases. ∎

Remember that you cannot plot the sampling distribution itself. That is the theoretical, long-run distribution arising from repeated sampling; in practice you take only one sample. The data plot that we refer to is the sample histogram. The sample histogram is useful as a rough indicator of the population shape, which is known to have an effect on the quality of the Central Limit Theorem normal approximation.

EXAMPLE 6.11 In the supermarket checkout time situation of Example 6.8, the following actual times in minutes were observed ($n = 25$): .4, .4, .5, .5, .5, .6, .6, .7, .8, .9, 1.1, 1.2, 1.4, 1.5, 1.8, 2.0, 2.3, 2.6, 2.9, 3.4, 4.2, 5.0, 6.6, 9.2, 16.3 ($\bar{y} = 2.70$). Does it appear that a normal approximation to the sampling distribution of $\bar{Y}$ (for future samples of size $n = 25$, for instance) would be satisfactory?

Solution The sample data suggest that the population distribution of checkout times is likely to be highly skewed. See the histogram in the computer output below. Most times are quite brief, but there are a few people who really slow things up. A sample of 25 is not enough to *deskew* the sampling distribution. Even a sample of 50 isn't really enough in this situation. Therefore the Empirical Rule probabilities (which are based on the normal distribution) in Example 6.8 are most likely inaccurate for $n = 25$ and perhaps for $n = 50$. For $n = 100$, the probabilities should be fairly close.

```
C1
   0.4    0.4    0.5    0.5    0.5    0.6    0.6    0.7    0.8    0.9    1.1
   1.2    1.4    1.5    1.8    2.0    2.3    2.6    2.9    3.4    4.2    5.0
   6.6    9.2   16.3

MTB > describe c1

                N    MEAN   MEDIAN   TRMEAN   STDEV   SEMEAN
C1             25   2.696    1.400    2.204   3.563    0.713

MTB > histogram of c1

Midpoint   Count
    0        10   **********
    2         9   *********
    4         2   **
    6         2   **
    8         0
   10         1   *
   12         0
   14         0
   16         1   *
```
∎

EXAMPLE 6.12 A firm that sells frozen 9-ounce steaks to restaurants is concerned about the fat content of individual steaks. It has claimed that the fat content has mean 8.1%

and standard deviation 1.0%. Use a normal approximation to find the probability that the mean fat content in a random sample of 25 steaks exceeds 8.5%. Would you expect the normal approximation to be accurate?

Solution   The appropriate expected value and standard error are

$$\mu_{\bar{Y}} = \mu = 8.1\%$$

$$\sigma_{\bar{Y}} = \frac{\sigma}{\sqrt{n}} = \frac{1.0}{\sqrt{25}} = 0.2\%$$

The normal approximation yields

$$P(\bar{Y} > 8.5) = P\left(Z > \frac{8.5 - 8.1}{0.2}\right) = P(Z > 2.00) \approx .0228$$

In this situation we would expect the distribution to be fairly symmetric; we would not expect to see fat contents of (say) 15% or more (at least for a firm that stays in business) nor fat contents of practically 0%. (Of course a plot of actual data would be useful in checking our guesses.) If our expectation is correct, the normal approximation should be quite good for $n = 25$.   ■

SECTION 6.4   EXERCISES

6.19 The number of column-inches of classified advertisements appearing on Mondays in a certain daily newspaper is roughly normally distributed with mean 327 inches and standard deviation 34 inches. Assume that the results for 10 consecutive Mondays can be regarded as a random sample.
  a. Find the expected value and standard error of the total number of column-inches of classified advertisements for 10 Mondays.
  b. Find the probability that the total is between 3150 and 3390 inches.
  c. Find the probability that the average number of column-inches per Monday is between 314 and 339.

6.20 Refer to Exercise 6.19. Find a range of the form $327 - k$ to $327 + k$ such that

$$P(327 - k \le \bar{Y} \le 327 + k) \approx .95$$

6.21 Suppose that a certain population has the following distribution:

Value:	200	300	400	500	600
Relative frequency:	.60	.20	.12	.06	.02

The population mean is 270, and the population standard deviation is 102.470. Exact probability computations show the following:

n	$\sigma_{\bar{Y}}$	$P(\bar{Y} < \mu - 2\sigma_{\bar{Y}})$	$P(\bar{Y} < \mu - \sigma_{\bar{Y}})$	$P(\bar{Y} > \mu + \sigma_{\bar{Y}})$	$P(\bar{Y} > \mu + 2\sigma_{\bar{Y}})$
2	72.46	0	0	.2160	.0336
4	51.23	0	.1296	.1965	.0521
8	36.23	0	.1460	.1594	.0319
16	25.62	.0173	.1876	.1486	.0295
32	18.11	.0127	.1543	.1473	.0340

a. Draw a histogram of the population distribution. What is the obvious feature of this histogram?

b. For each sample size, compute the probability that $\bar{Y}$ falls within two standard errors of μ. How good is the normal approximation for various values of n?

c. Repeat part (b) for $\bar{Y}$ within one standard error of μ.

6.22   In Exercise 6.17 we considered an automobile insurer whose repair claims averaged $927 over the past with a standard deviation of $871. A random sample of 50 new claims is taken.

a. Describe the sampling distribution for $\bar{Y}$.

b. Use a normal approximation to calculate $P(\bar{Y} > 1100)$.

6.23   How good would you expect the normal approximation in Exercise 6.22 to be?

6.24   Refer to Exercise 6.22. Suppose $\bar{y} = \$1100$ is observed for the 50 new claims. What do you conclude about repair claims for this year? Would your conclusions change if $\bar{y} = \$1000$?

6.25   The average demand for rental skis on winter Saturdays at a particular area is 148 pairs, which has been quite stable over time. There is variation due to weather conditions and competing areas; the standard deviation is 21 pairs. The demand distribution seems to be roughly normal.

a. The rental shop stocks 170 pairs of skis. What is the probability that demand will exceed this supply on any one winter Saturday?

b. The shop manager will change the stock of skis for the next year if the average demand over the 12 winter Saturdays in a season (considered as a random sample) is over 155 or under 135. These limits aren't equidistant from the long-run process mean of 148 because the costs of oversupply and undersupply are different. If the population mean stays at 148, what is the probability that the manager will change the stock?

6.26   In Exercise 6.25, one could argue that the demand will not be normal. Instead, most Saturdays' demand will be around the mean, but on those few days when skiing conditions are poor, the demand will fall well below the mean.

a. According to this argument, what will be the shape (skewness) of the demand distribution?

b. Will the two answers in Exercise 6.25 be made equally wrong if this argument is correct? Why?

6.27   Computer chips have pins to connect them into sockets on computer boards. The thickness of the pins is important in determining the quality of connection to the board. When the production process is running properly, the mean diameter of pins (relative to the design specification) is 1.000. There is some inevitable variation in diameters; the standard deviation is 0.006 units. The distribution of diameters is normal.

a. A pin will make a highest-quality connection only if its diameter is between 0.997 and 1.003 units. What is the probability that an individual pin will make such a connection?

b. As part of its ongoing quality monitoring, the chip manufacturer takes samples of 20 pins from each lot of 25,000 pins. Assuming that the process is running properly, what is the probability that the mean diameter in the sample will be between 0.997 and 1.003 units?

c. Suppose that the process mean remains at 1.000 units, but the variability increases greatly, so that the standard deviation is 0.020 units. Without doing any arithmetic, what should this change do to the probability that an individual pin will make a highest-quality connection? Verify your answer by computing a revised probability and comparing it to your answer in part (a).

    d. If the standard deviation is 0.020, what is the probability that a mean of a sample of 20 pins will be between 0.997 and 1.003 units?

6.28 In Exercise 6.27, suppose that the mean diameter of the population of pins is 1.000, but that the distribution is not normal. Instead, the standard deviation of 0.006 is the result of most pin diameters being extremely close to 1.000 and a few pin diameters being extremely far from that value. Does this mean that your answer to part (b) of Exercise 6.27 is seriously incorrect? Explain why or why not.

6.29 A downtown hotel runs a special promotion to try to fill rooms that aren't usually occupied on weekends. The long-run average response is 71 rooms per weekend. There is considerable variation due to weather, competing attractions, and other unknown causes. The standard deviation of responses is about 15 rooms. Suppose that the distribution of responses is normal.

    a. The total schedules adequate staff to handle a response of 80 rooms. If more guests arrive, additional staff must be brought in at overtime rates. What is the probability that additional staff will be needed on one particular weekend?

    b. The promotion manager reviews response rates for blocks of 10 weekends, which is regarded as a random sample. If the average demand over the 10-week sample exceeds 80, the manager will increase the scheduled staff. If the long-run mean stays at 71, what is the probability that a 10-week sample mean will exceed 80?

6.30 In Exercise 6.29, we assumed a normal distribution of responses. In fact, the distribution is skewed by a few weekends with extremely heavy demand. Can you assume that your answer to part (b) of that exercise is still correct because of the Central Limit Theorem effect?

6.5   USES AND MISUSES OF THE CENTRAL LIMIT THEOREM

We use the Central Limit Theorem, introduced in Section 6.4, to justify normal approximations to the sampling distributions of sample sums and means. The same mathematical theorem indicates situations in which a **population distribution** can be assumed to be approximately normal. We can use variations on this theorem to show that sampling distributions of other statistics are approximately normal. But the theorem can also be misinterpreted; we now indicate a couple of additional uses for the Central Limit Theorem and a common misconception.

    Here is the formal mathematical statement of the Central Limit Theorem: If $Y_1, Y_2, \ldots, Y_n$ are independent random variables with the same probability density functions $f_Y(y)$, then $T = Y_1 + Y_2 + \cdots + Y_n$ and $\bar{Y} = (Y_1 + Y_2 + \cdots + Y_n)/n$ have approximately normal distributions for sufficiently large values of n. When we are talking about sampling distributions, $Y_1, Y_2, \ldots, Y_n$ represent individual values drawn in a sample of size n, and we interpret T and $\bar{Y}$ as the sample total and mean. There are other practical interpretations of the same mathematical theorem.

    One such situation occurs when each **individual** value in a population can be thought of as a sum of n independent terms. Example 6.9 is such a case; the diameter of an individual tree is the sum of a large number of independent terms, each term being the yearly growth of that tree. It's not unreasonable to assume that the year-by-year increases in diameter are independent, with roughly identical probability distributions.* Therefore, we can expect the individual values of tree diameters, that is, the population, to have a roughly normal distribution. This interpretation of the Central Limit Theorem gives a reason why we can expect some (but by no means all) populations to have roughly normal distributions.

The normal approximation to the binomial probability distribution that was presented in Chapter 5 is another consequence of the Central Limit Theorem. Suppose that we assign the value 1 to all the successes in the population and the value 0 to all the failures. The population mean is the total number of 1s divided by the population size; this is exactly the population proportion of successes π. The population variance turns out to be $\pi(1 - \pi)$. In a sample of size n, the sample mean $\bar{Y}$ is just the sample proportion $\hat{\pi}$. So

$$Z = \frac{\bar{Y} - \mu}{\dfrac{\sigma}{\sqrt{n}}} = \frac{\hat{\pi} - \pi}{\dfrac{\sqrt{\pi(1 - \pi)}}{\sqrt{n}}}$$

has an approximately normal distribution if n is large enough. Furthermore, the sample sum is Y, the number of successes.

$$Z = \frac{Y - n\pi}{\sqrt{n\pi(1 - \pi)}}$$

is an equivalent, approximately normal statistic.

Another important consequence of this Central Limit Theorem is that the Empirical Rule has wide applicability, particularly the 95% portion of the rule. Because the sampling distribution for $\bar{Y}$ is near normal with a single mode and not too much skewness for most reasonable sample sizes, the interval $\mu \pm 2\sigma_{\bar{Y}}$ should contain approximately 95% of the possible values of $\bar{Y}$. This implies that the maximum probable error for estimating μ with $\bar{Y}$ is $2\sigma_{\bar{Y}}$. There is a compensating factor working in our favor. Even though the remaining .05 probability is not evenly split between the two tails, the sum of these tail probabilities is approximately .05, which makes the Empirical Rule work. Thus the Empirical Rule works well even when the sampling distribution for $\bar{Y}$ is somewhat skewed, leaving one tail probability near zero. The other tail probability is near .05.

Versions of a Central Limit Theorem also apply to sample statistics other than sums and means. Mathematical statistics contain many theorems that conclude that such-and-such statistic has an approximately normal distribution when n is sufficiently large. Sample proportions, sample medians, sample variances, and many other statistics all have approximately normal distributions for large samples. Once expected values and standard errors have been found for these statistics, approximate normal probabilities can be calculated.

But the normal distribution does not always apply. The Central Limit Theorem has been misinterpreted to suggest that every distribution—population, observed data, or whatever—must be normal. In particular, some

---

* And fancier versions of the Central Limit Theorem hold even if these assumptions aren't satisfied exactly.

students believe that *any* large population must have a normal distribution. Central Limit Theorems typically refer to sums or averages of many terms, but unless a sum or average is involved, mere largeness does not imply normality. For example, all individuals living in the United States constitute a large population, but the distribution of wealth among these individuals is extremely skewed. In spite of skewness in the distribution of wealth among these individuals, the Central Limit Theorem guarantees that the distribution of the sample mean income ($\bar{Y}$) is approximately normal for sufficiently large values of n. When we deal with individual data, data plots are the best way to examine normality. The normality of theoretical sampling distributions can be tested by simulation methods, which we consider in the next section.

6.6   COMPUTER SIMULATIONS ∎

Thus far in this chapter, the focus has necessarily been theoretical. The concept of a sampling distribution is inevitably a theoretical one. A sampling distribution is best understood as the distribution of a statistic arising from taking many samples under given conditions. In practice, it's unlikely that one would take multiple samples. But one can use a computer to take multiple samples from a specified population, compute any specified statistic for each sample, and calculate the distribution of the results. In this section we discuss the application of such methods to sampling distributions.

procedure for simulating values   The **procedure for simulating values** is based on the assumed cdf $F_Y(y)$. We begin with a random variable that has a uniform distribution (with all values of equal probability). Many methods are known for drawing what look like uniformly distributed variables. One way is to multiply a 15-digit number by another 15-digit number and to take the middle 10 digits as the random number. Another way is to use prepared tables of random numbers. The trick is to convert these uniformly distributed numbers into simulated values from a random variable having the assumed cdf $F_Y(y)$.

Suppose that $F_Y(y)$ is assumed to be

y	9	10	11	12
$F_Y(y)$	.37	.79	.94	1.00
$P_Y(y)$	.37	.42	.15	.06

Also suppose that there is a source of a uniformly distributed 2-decimal random variable U with probabilities $P_U(u) = .01$, for $u = .01, .02, \ldots, 1.00$. Now proceed as follows:

if $.01 \le U \le .37$, assign $Y = 9$
if $.38 \le U \le .79$, assign $Y = 10$
if $.80 \le U \le .94$, assign $Y = 11$
if $.95 \le U \le 1.00$, assign $Y = 12$

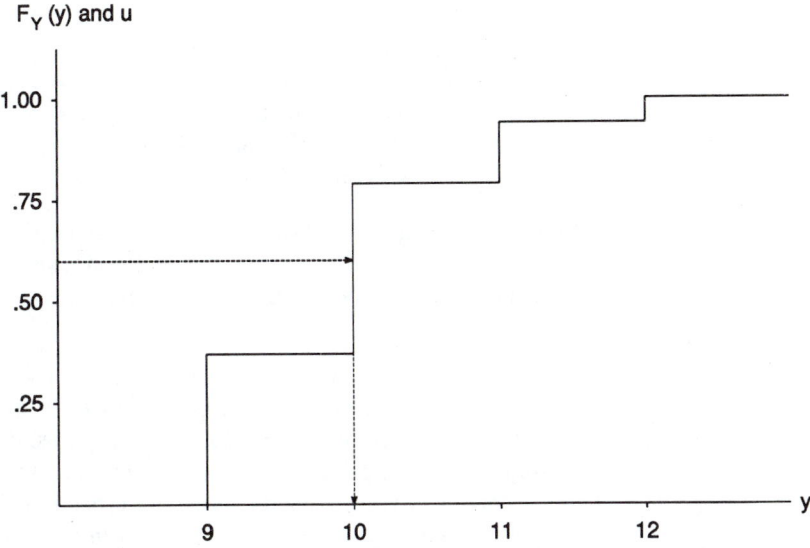

$F_Y(y)$ and u

FIGURE 6.5   Simulating Values from a Random Variable with cdf $F_Y(y)$

Thus, a simulated value, $u = .59$, which falls between .37 and .79, is assigned the value $y = 10$ (see Figure 6.5). All other simulated values are assigned y values in a similar way. The cutoff values for U, namely .37, .79, .94, and 1.00, were obviously taken from the $F_Y(y)$ values shown in Figure 6.5.

This process does yield random Y values; we must still show that these values have the correct probabilities.

$$P(Y = 9) = P(.01 \le U \le .37) = P(U = .01) + \cdots + P(U = .37)$$
$$= .01 + \cdots + .01 = 37(.01) = .37$$
$$P(Y = 10) = P(.38 \le U \le .79) = P(U = .38) + \cdots + P(U = .79)$$
$$= .01 + \cdots + .01 = 42(.01) = .42$$

The probabilities do match the desired ones. The idea can best be seen on a graph such as Figure 6.5. A uniformly distributed random number is drawn, and then we assign the appropriate value of Y from the $F_Y(y)$ table.

EXAMPLE 6.13   Simulate six values of Y in the coronary-care case illustration of Section 4.2 (page 126). Assume that a uniform random-number generator yields the following values: .579, .286, .413, .107, .962, .494. The $F_Y(y)$ table is reproduced below:

y:	0	1	2	3	4	5	6	7	8
$F_Y(y)$:	.001	.003	.006	.011	.024	.061	.139	.224	.336

y:	9	10	11	12	13	14	15	16	17
$F_Y(y)$:	.510	.672	.782	.870	.925	.964	.988	.997	1.000

Solution

$u = .579$ is between .510 and .672; assign $y = 10$
$u = .286$ is between .224 and .336; assign $y = 8$
$u = .413$ is between .336 and .510; assign $y = 9$
$u = .107$ is between .061 and .139; assign $y = 6$
$u = .962$ is between .925 and .964; assign $y = 14$
$u = .494$ is between .336 and .510; assign $y = 9$

If this process had been carried out over a very large number of trials (uniform random numbers), $.672 - .510 = .162$ of the Y assignments should have been $y = 10$, according to the assumed Y probabilities. ∎

Monte Carlo approach

The simulation, or **Monte Carlo approach**—and why that particular gambling casino is so honored, we don't know—is an enormously and widely useful trick. With this technique, it is fairly easy to simulate almost any random situation once appropriate assumptions are made. By varying assumptions, one can test for sensitivity—which aspects are crucial, which are less so. There are many other uses of this technique. We can use the computer to calculate the average value of a statistic, averaged over, say, 1000 samples. This average is a good approximation to the expected value of the statistic, which is the theoretical average value over an infinite number of samples. We can use the computer to calculate the standard deviation of the statistic for 1000 (or whatever number) samples. This standard deviation is a good approximation to the standard error of the statistic; remember that the standard error of a statistic is its theoretical standard deviation over infinitely many samples. To check the shape of the theoretical distribution of a statistic, we may compute the skewness or outlier-proneness of the statistic, or draw histograms. Computer simulation is an extremely flexible way to check the validity of any theoretical results.

Suppose that a computer takes 1000 simple random samples, each of size 25, from a population having a normal distribution with mean 100 and standard deviation 15, and computes the mean for each sample. Further, suppose that after computing all these sample means, the computer calculates the average sample mean to be 99.921, the standard deviations of the sample means to be 3.014, and the median of the sample means to be 100.003. Theoretically, the long-run average should be the expected value of the sample mean, namely, the population mean. The simulation average, 99.921, is very close to the theoretical value, 100. Also, the simulation standard deviation of the sample mean, 3.014, is very close to the theoretical standard error of the sample mean, $15.0/\sqrt{25} = 3.000$. Finally, the theoretical (sampling) distribution should have a normal shape; in particular, the skewness should be zero. The simulation "median of means," 100.003, is very close to the simulation "mean of means," 99.921, suggesting that the distribution of means is at least very close to symmetric. A histogram of the means could be constructed to check on symmetry.

EXAMPLE 6.14   A computer program calculates the sample median for 1000 samples of size 25 taken from a normal population having mean 100 and standard deviation 15. The average median is 100.081, the standard deviation of the medians is 3.763, and a stem-and-leaf display of the medians appears nearly normal. What does each result indicate about the sampling distribution of the sample median in this case?

Solution   The simulation average should approximate the expected value of the sample median. By symmetry, the expected value should be the same as the population mean, 100. The simulation standard deviation should approximate the standard error of the sample median; theoretically the standard error should be 3.760. The histogram suggests that the sampling distribution of a sample median is also normal, at least when sampling from this population. As we mentioned in Section 6.5, for large samples the theoretical sampling distribution of a median is also normal. Apparently, when sampling from a normal distribution, a sample size of 25 is enough to rate as a "large sample."   ■

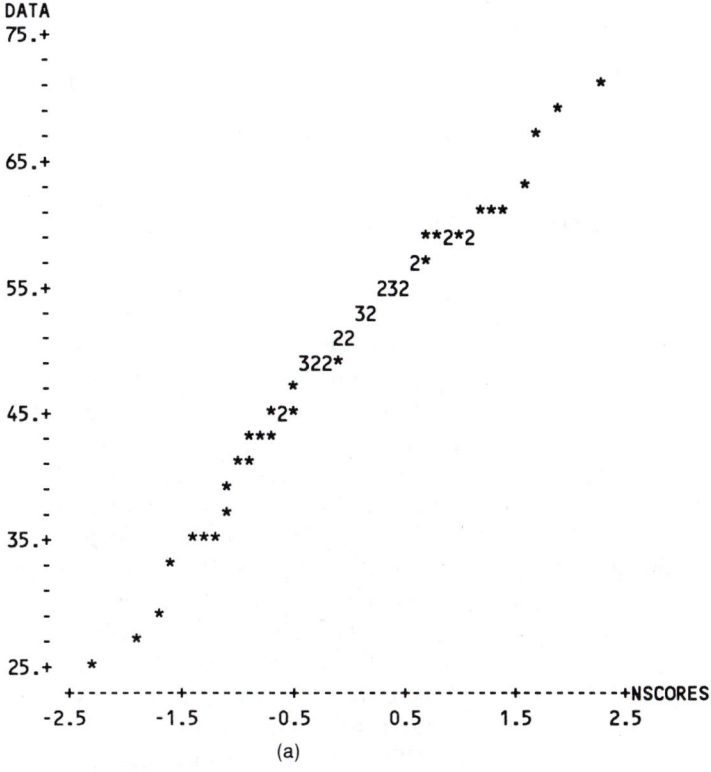

FIGURE 6.6   Normal Plots for (a) Normally Distributed; (b) Right-Skewed; and (c) Outlier-Prone Data (see page 245 for discussion)

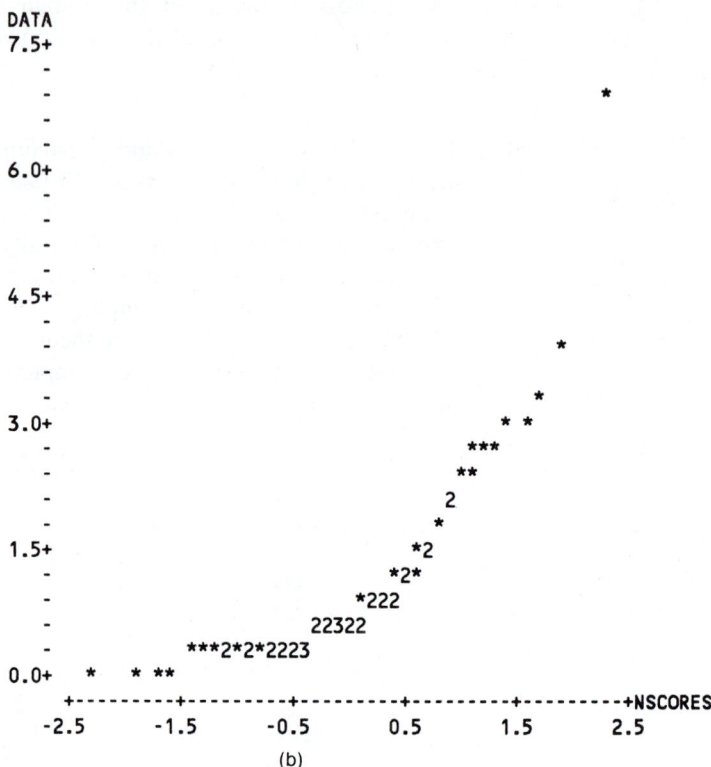

FIGURE 6.6   (*Continued*)

We present the results of many computer simulations in this book. We are concerned not only with the correctness of expected value and standard error formulas, but especially about the correctness of theoretical results about the shape of the sampling distribution. If the sampling distribution of a certain statistic theoretically should be normal, but simulation results indicate that the actual distribution is clearly nonnormal, that indicates that statistical inferences based on the statistic could be seriously wrong.

normal probability plot   A **normal probability plot** is an excellent way to assess whether data (or means in a computer simulation) are close to normally distributed. This plot is based on **normal scores**: The predicted values of data, assuming a normal distribution. The idea is that data will tend to spread out evenly across percentiles. If there are three observations in a sample, we expect the smallest to be at about the 25th percentile, the middle score at the 50th percentile, and the largest at the 75th percentile. If we assume a normal distribution and use Appendix Table 3, we find that these percentiles (in z-score form) are $z = -0.67$, $z = 0.00$, and $z = 0.67$, respectively. Similarly, with nine observations, we expect them

MTB> PLOT 'DATA' VS 'NSCORES'

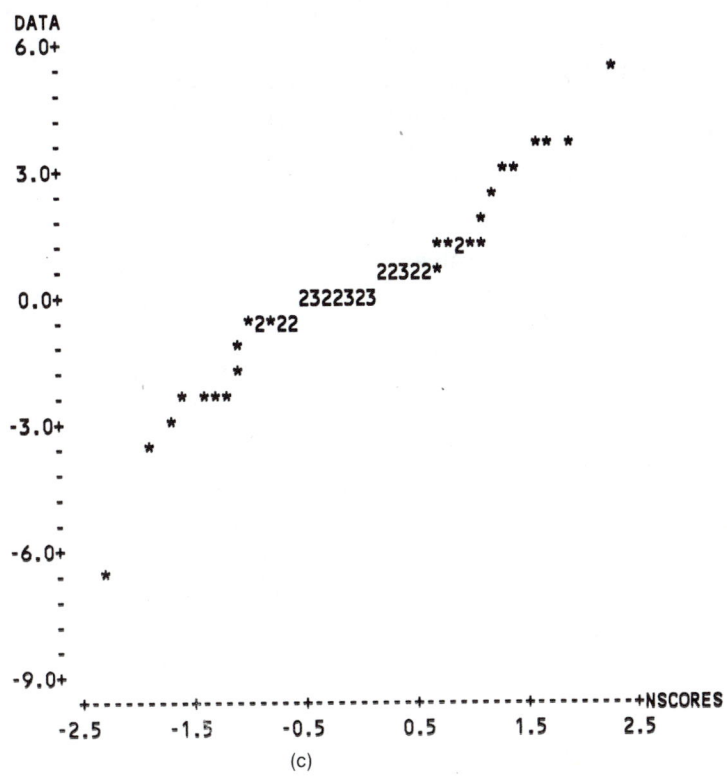

(c)

FIGURE 6.6   (*Continued*)

to be at about the 10th, 20th, ..., 90th percentiles. Assuming normality, these percentiles are $z = -1.28$, $z = -0.84$, ..., $z = 1.28$, respectively. For any sample size, the normal score of the ith smallest score is defined to be the $i/(n + 1)$ percentile of a normal distribution. A computer program that carries out a normal probability plot calculates these normal scores automatically.

A normal plot is a plot of the actual data (or simulation means) against the normal scores. Data that are (essentially) normally distributed yield (essentially) a straight line in a normal plot. It turns out that skewed data plot as (essentially) a single curve. Symmetric, outlier-prone data plot in an S shape. In looking at a computer-generated normal plot, look for the basic, overall pattern rather than the "wiggles and jiggles and bumps." A normal plot is particularly helpful in assessing whether data are outlier-prone; the S shape in a normal plot is often easier to see than the long tails in a histogram. Figure 6.6 shows computer-generated normal plots for, respectively, normally distributed, right-skewed, and outlier-prone data. You should be able to see the basic straight-line, single-curve, and S-shape patterns in the three plots; hold a ruler or other straightedge up to the plot to help you see the patterns.

EXAMPLE 6.15   A normal plot of 1000 means, each based on a sample of size 10 taken from an exponential-shaped population (see Section 5.7) is shown in Figure 6.7. Does the normal plot indicate that the sampling distribution of means is approximately normal in this situation?

values

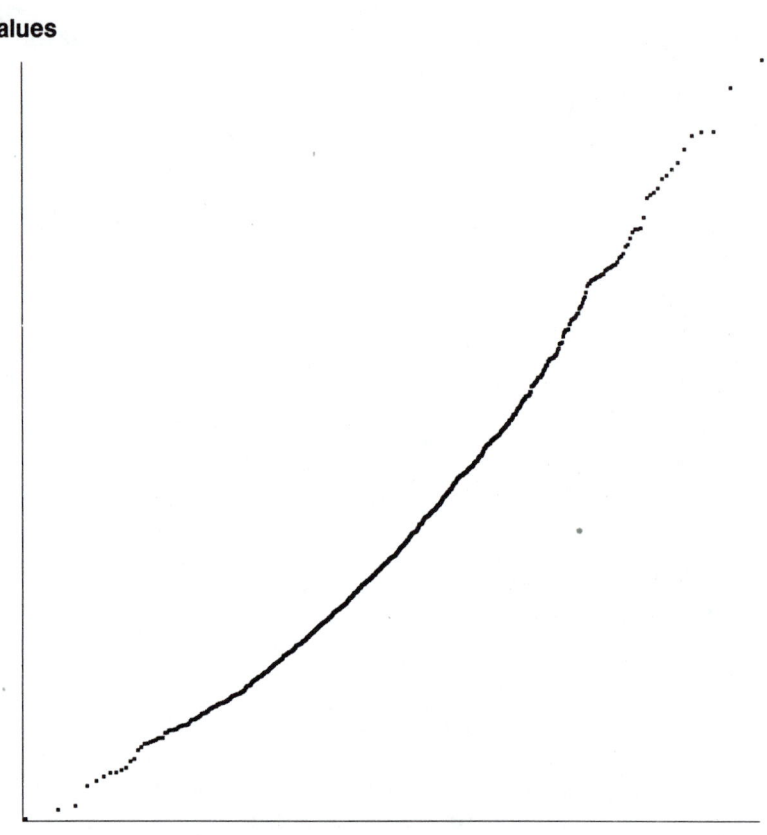

normal scores

FIGURE 6.7   Normal Plot of Means for Example 6.15

Solution   No. There is a clear curve in the plot, indicating that the sampling distribution of the sample means is clearly skewed in this situation.   ■

Computer simulations are a useful supplement to mathematical derivations of sampling distributions, not a substitute for them. A computer simulation necessarily involves very specific assumptions about the statistic and the underlying population, whereas a mathematical theorem often applies much more generally. But as a supplement to, and illustration of mathematical results, computer simulations can be extremely valuable.

EXAMPLE 6.16   Normal plots of 1000 means, based on samples of size 30 and 60 from the exponential distribution, are shown in Figure 6.8 (this page and page 248). What is the effect of increasing sample size?

values

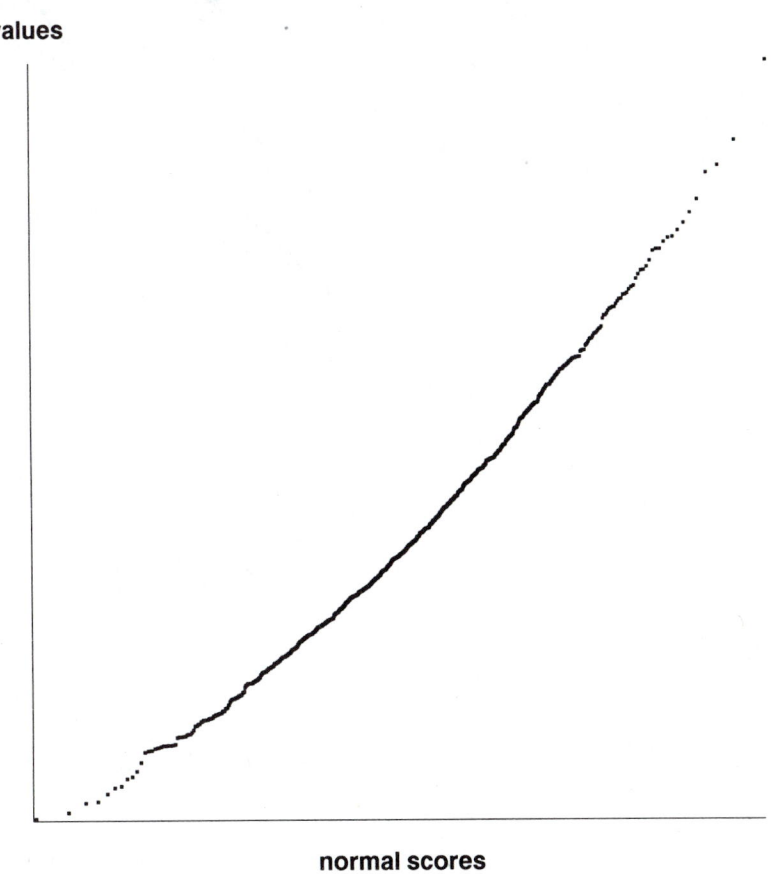

normal scores

(a)

FIGURE 6.8   Normal Plot of Means for Example 6.16: (a) Sample of Size 30; (b) Sample of Size 60

Solution   As the sample size increases, the normal plot comes closer to a straight line, which indicates that the theoretical (sampling) distribution of the sample mean approaches the normal distribution as the same size increases. This is precisely what the Central Limit Theorem states.   ∎

values

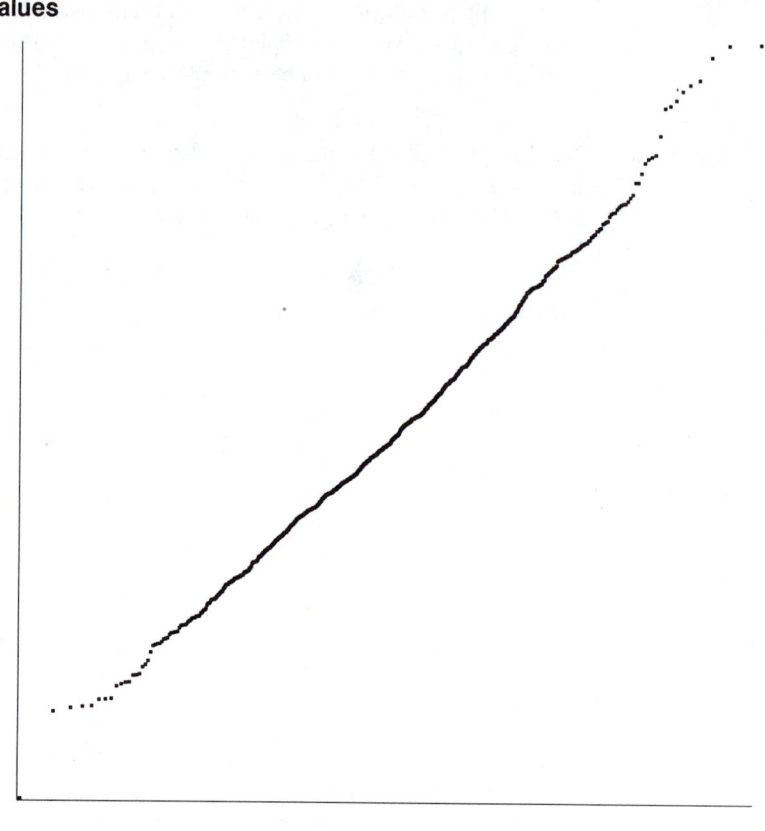

normal scores

(b)

FIGURE 6.8   (*Continued*)

SECTION 6.6   EXERCISES

6.31 Sample means are found for 1000 samples of size 4 taken from a normally distributed population with mean 50 and standard deviation 10. The average of these means is 50.1643 and the standard deviation is 5.0104.

a. What theoretical quantities are being approximated by the average of the means and by the standard deviation of the means?

b. What are the theoretical values of these quantities? Do the simulation results closely approximate these theoretical (infinitely many samples) values?

6.32 Sample medians are found for 1000 samples of size 30 taken from a Laplace population (a symmetric, moderately outlier-prone population). The average of the medians is .0082 and the standard deviation is .2070. What do these results indicate about the theoretical (sampling) distribution of the median?

6.33 A histogram and normal plot of the medians calculated in Exercise 6.32 are shown in Figure 6.9. Do they indicate that the theoretical distribution of the median is approximately normal in this case?

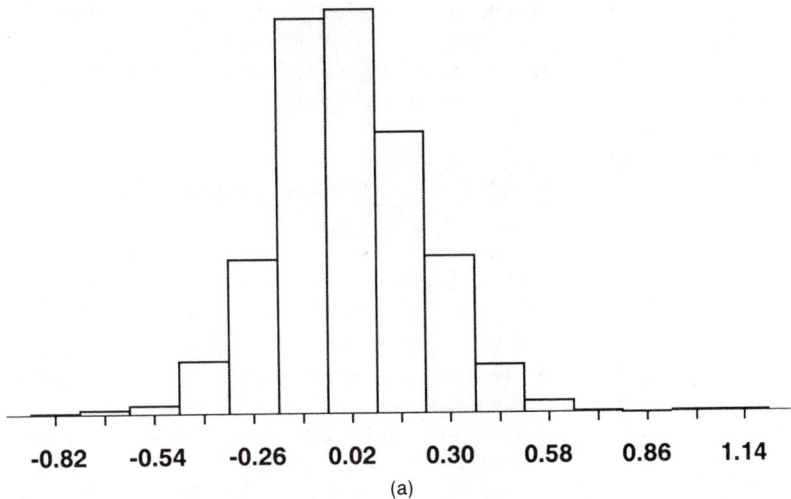

-0.82   -0.54   -0.26   0.02   0.30   0.58   0.86   1.14

(a)

values

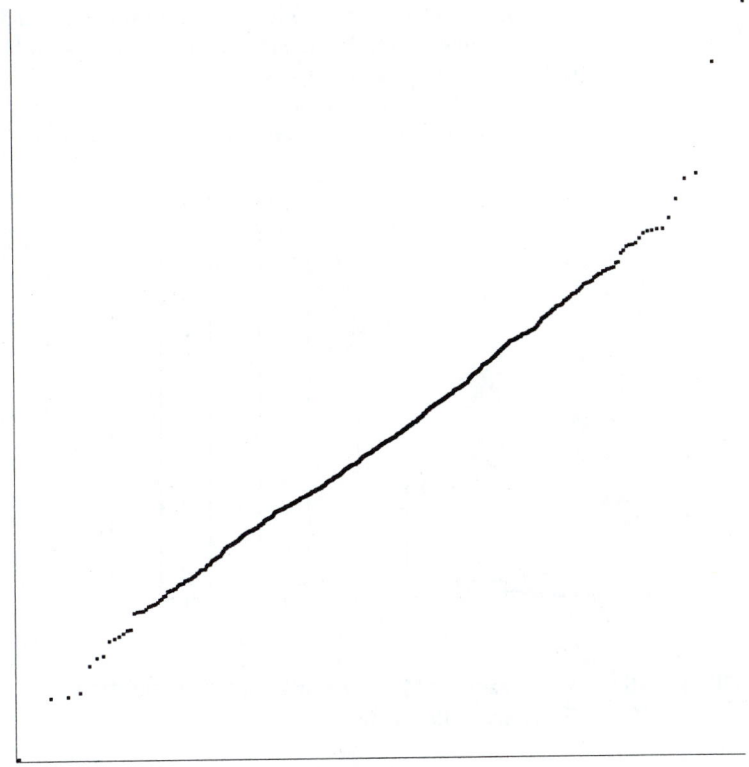

normal scores

(b)

FIGURE 6.9   Histogram (a) and Normal Plot (b) of Medians from a Laplace
                  Population; Exercise 6.33

6.34 Sample means are calculated (for 1000 samples each) from samples of sizes 10 and 30 taken from a discrete population having possible values 1, 2, 3, 4, and 5, with respective probabilities .1, .2, .4, .2, and .1. The averages and standard deviations of these means are as follows:

Sample Size	Mean	Standard Deviation
10	3.0076	.3563
30	2.9986	.2006

a. Calculate the population mean and standard deviation.
b. What are the expected values and standard errors of the sample means for each sample size?
c. How closely do the simulation results agree with the theoretical values calculated in part (b)?

6.35 Sample means are calculated for 1000 samples of size 10 taken from a Laplace population. The population mean is zero and the population variance is 2.00. The average value of the means is .0100 and the standard deviation is .4366.
a. Calculate the theoretical expected value and standard error of the sample mean.
b. How closely do the simulation results agree with the theoretical results?

6.36 A histogram of the means of the data from Exercise 6.35 are shown in Figure 6.10. The Laplace population is somewhat outlier-prone but symmetric. Does it appear that the theoretical distribution of the means is close to normal?

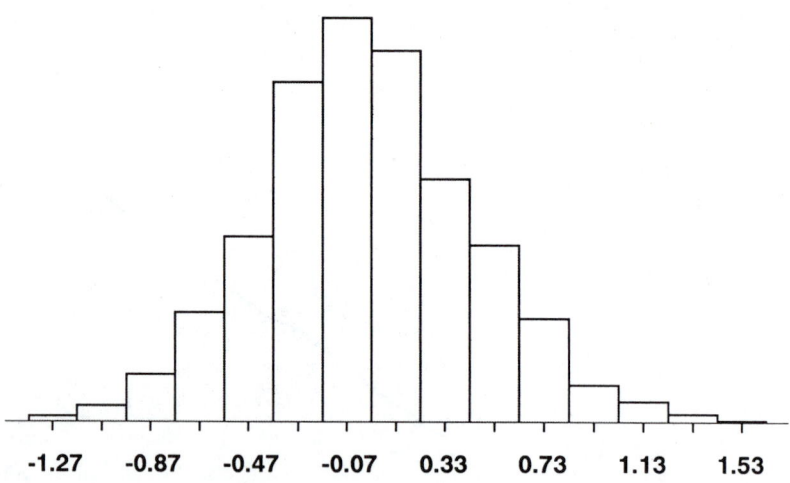

-1.27	-0.87	-0.47	-0.07	0.33	0.73	1.13	1.53

FIGURE 6.10   Histogram for Means from a Laplace Population; Exercises 6.35 – 6.36

Summary

Chapter 6 discusses sampling distributions, the theoretical basis of classical statistical inference. The essential idea is that any summary statistic for a sample is random and will vary from one sample to the next. The randomness may arise from random sampling, which is done to avoid biases (systematic distortions) of the sample, or from the randomness in processes over time. The sampling distribution of any statistic describes its probable variation from one sample to another, which can be derived using either probability theory or computer simulations of repeated samples.

Key features of the sampling distribution of a statistic are its expected value (long-run average over many samples) and its standard error (standard deviation over many samples). These values will vary, depending on the statistic and type of sampling involved. We presented results for the sample mean and sample sum; there will be many other expected value and standard error results later in the book.

An important mathematical result that applies specifically to sums and means is the Central Limit Theorem, which states that virtually any sum or mean of a large number of terms will have an approximately normal distribution. The guidelines for how large a number of terms is needed depend on the skewness (and to a lesser extent, the outlier-proneness and discreteness) of the underlying distribution. A normal plot is a useful device; normality of data appears in a normal plot as a straight line, skewness as a curve, and outlier-proneness as an S shape. The Central Limit Theorem as stated applies only to sums or means, not to any "large" random phenomenon; it must be applied with thought.

KEY TOPICS AND FORMULAS: Random Sampling and Sampling Distributions

1. Statistic: A summary value computed from a random sample
2. Selection bias: Any systematic tendency to overrepresent or underrepresent some part of a population when taking a sample
3. Sampling distribution of a statistic: The theoretical probability distribution of a statistic
4. Standard error of a statistic: The theoretical standard deviation of the statistic's sampling distribution
5. Expected value and standard error of a sample sum T:

$$\mu_T = n\mu$$
$$\sigma_T = \sqrt{n}\,\sigma$$

6. Expected value and standard error of a sample mean $\bar{Y}$:

$$\mu_{\bar{Y}} = \mu$$

$$\sigma_{\bar{Y}} = \frac{\sigma}{\sqrt{n}}$$

7. Central Limit Theorem for sums and means: For any population, the sampling distributions of T and $\bar{Y}$ are approximately normal if n is sufficiently large.

CHAPTER 6   EXERCISES

6.37   While demonstrating the role of variability in statistical quality control, the statistician W. Edwards Deming has seminar participants dip a wooden paddle with 50 holes into a bowl containing 20% red beads and 80% white beads. The beads have been thoroughly mixed.

a. What would you think the expected number of red beads would be in the "paddle sample" of 50 beads?

b. In answering part (a), you made an assumption. What was it, and how might it be wrong?

6.38   In thousands of repetitions of the bead experiment of Exercise 6.37, Deming reports that the average number of red beads is approximately 9.4. What does this fact indicate about the assumption you made in answering Exercise 6.37?

6.39   One important application of sampling ideas in quality control is the inspection of incoming components from suppliers. In the assembly of an automobile door, suppliers must provide window glass, window-lowering mechanisms, door handles, door-lock mechanisms, and trim parts. All of these components can be tested to see if they meet initial fitness and long-term reliability specifications. In particular, suppose that the auto manufacturer specifies that door-lock mechanisms should work smoothly through 50,000 lock-unlock cycles.

a. Why would it be absolutely necessary to use sampling in testing the door-lock mechanisms?

b. One possible sampling method would be to test the first 5 door-lock mechanisms in each 1000-item shipment. Why would this method be unwise?

6.40   One way to specify inspection sampling of the auto door parts in Exercise 6.39 would be to demand that half of one percent of each shipment of each component be randomly sampled and tested. Shipment sizes range from 1000 door handles (from a new supplier of unknown quality) to 50,000 trim parts (from a long-time supplier with an established reputation for high quality). Would the "half a percent" rule yield a reasonable inspection approach?

6.41   Suppose that a random sample of 20 power window mechanisms is taken from each lot of 5000 supplied to the auto manufacturer in Exercise 6.39. Each sampled mechanism is tested by putting it through continuous up-down cycles until it fails. Suppose that in the entire lot, the mean time to failure (under these high-stress conditions) is 4200 cycles and that the standard deviation is 3400. The mean failure time for the sample is recorded.

a. What is the expected value of the sample mean?

b. What is the standard deviation of the sample mean? How much would it matter if the sample of 20 had been taken from a lot of 10,000 rather than a lot of 5000 mechanisms?

c. Would it be reasonable to assume that the distribution of individual failure times should be roughly normal? Should the Empirical Rule apply?

d. Would it be reasonable to assume that the distribution of the sample mean should be roughly normal?

6.42   Assume that the testing method of Exercise 6.41 is modified by testing 40 mechanisms per lot rather than 20. Would this modification result in doubling the accuracy of estimation of the mean failure time?

6.43   Bad sectors on a microcomputer floppy disk cannot be used for data storage. Suppose that in a very large supply of floppy disks the mean bad-sector volume is 2.13 K (kilobytes) per disk, and that the standard deviation is 0.83 K. A retailer assembles packs of 100 floppy disks from the supply.

a. What is the expected total bad-sector volume in a pack?

b. What is the standard deviation of total bad-sector volume in a pack?

6.44 What did you assume about the assembly process of the retailer in Exercise 6.43? If the assumption is wrong, which part of your answer would be affected?

6.45 A purchaser of floppy disks assembles many 100-disk packs, laboriously finds the total bad-sector volume in each pack, and draws a histogram of the data. What would you expect the shape of the histogram to be? Why?

6.46 A newspaper columnist asserts that directors of Fortune 1000 firms paid, on the average, only 19.1% of their gross income in federal income tax the previous year. From the published column, it can be inferred that the claimed standard deviation is 6.8%. Suppose that you, as an Internal Revenue Service officer, are charged with taking a sample of 200 such executives to test this claim.

a. The names of all Fortune 1000 firm directors are publicly available. How can you use such a list to select a random sample? What problems might you encounter?

b. Can you assume that, because $n = 200$ is a fairly large sample, the distribution of percentage of gross income paid in income tax in the sample is approximately normal? Explain.

6.47 In Exercise 5.71 (page 212) we assumed that the weekly demand for 5-pound sacks of flour at a particular supermarket is normally distributed with mean 72.0 cases and standard deviation 1.6 cases.

a. Do you think that a normal distribution might be a decent model?

b. How could you take a reasonable random sample of size 15 from this population?

6.48 Assume that a random sample of size 15 has been taken in Exercise 6.47.

a. What is $P(\bar{Y} > 73.0)$?

b. Find a 95% range for $\bar{Y}$; that is, find a value k such that $P(72.0 - k \le \bar{Y} \le 72.0 + k) = .95$.

6.49 A department store expects the average "inventory shrinkage" (a euphemism for theft by employees and customers) to be 2.2%. The standard deviation from one sale category to another is assumed to be 1.6%. The store has 2571 sales categories, from which a sample of 100 categories is to be selected for detailed inventory checking.

a. How would you select such a random sample?

b. Is a simple random sample desirable here? Granted that you don't know about fancier sampling methods, can you think of other considerations for sampling?

6.50 Suppose that a random sample of 100 categories is chosen in Exercise 6.49.

a. Find the expected value and standard error of the sample average shrinkage.

b. How much difference does it make in part (a) whether you use sampling without replacement or sampling with replacement?

c. Use a normal approximation to calculate $P(\bar{Y} > 2.4\%)$.

6.51 How good do you expect the normal approximation in Exercise 6.50 to be? How would you use the sample data to help indicate how much faith you have in the approximation?

6.52 Suppose that a population has the following distribution:

Values:	10	80	90	100	110	120	190
Relative frequency:	.02	.10	.20	.36	.20	.10	.02

a. Verify that the population mean is 100 and the population standard deviation is 21.07.

b. Draw a histogram of this distribution. What is the obvious feature?

6.53   Refer to Exercise 6.52. The exact sampling distribution of the sample mean (for sample sizes 2, 4, and 8) has the following properties:

Sample Size	Standard Error	$P(\bar{Y} < \mu - 2\sigma_{\bar{Y}})$	$P(\bar{Y} < \mu - \sigma_{\bar{Y}})$	$P(\bar{Y} > \mu + \sigma_{\bar{Y}})$	$P(\bar{Y} > \mu + 2\sigma_{\bar{Y}})$
2	14.90	.0388	.0888	.0888	.0388
4	10.54	.0488	.0899	.0899	.0488
8	7.45	.0333	.1456	.1456	.0333

     a. For each sample size, compute the exact probability that $\bar{Y}$ is within one standard error of μ.

     b. How good is the normal approximation, for each n?

     c. Repeat parts (a) and (b) for $\bar{Y}$ within two standard errors of μ.

6.54   The personnel records of an insurance firm's main office contain data on the number of leave days (for illness or personal reasons) taken in a year by each of 533 employees. The numbers are stored in column 1 of the 'CH6C1.DAT' data set on the data disk for this book.

     a. Obtain a histogram or stem-and-leaf display of the data. Would you say that the population data were roughly normally distributed?

     b. Obtain the mean and standard deviation. A computer program will probably regard the data as a sample, not a population. What difference will that make in the calculations? How important, numerically, will the difference be?

     c. Have the computer program draw 25 random samples from the population, each of size 20, and compute the mean for each sample.

     d. Obtain a histogram or stem-and-leaf display of the 25 sample means. Does this picture have the same shape as the population distribution? What explains the difference?

6.55   Have a computer program calculate the standard deviation of the sample means obtained in Exercise 6.54. What theoretical quantity is being approximated by this standard deviation? Does the numerical value you obtained come close to the theoretical value?

6.56   Many computer programs will choose random numbers that are uniformly distributed between 0 and 1.

     a. Have the program take 100 such samples, each of size 12. Obtain the means of the 100 samples. Have the program draw a histogram of these means. (We will want to repeat this process for an exercise in Chapter 7, so you might want to save the means or remember the method for obtaining them.)

     b. Should the histogram of means be approximately uniformly distributed between 0 and 1? Theoretically, why? Does the histogram you obtained roughly correspond to the theoretical result?

     c. The variance of a uniform distribution (between 0 and 1) is $1/12 = 0.833333$. What is the theoretical standard deviation of the means obtained in part (a)? Have the program compute this standard deviation. How well does it approximate the theoretical value?

     d. What is the mean (expected value) for a uniform distribution between 0 and 1? How does the average of the 100 sample means compare to this theoretical value?

Appendix: Standard Error of a Mean ∎

Some students want to understand *why* the formula for the standard error of $\bar{Y}$ comes out as it does. For their benefit, this appendix contains a sketchy proof. There are two key ideas; each is stated in terms of variance. First, multiplying a random variable by a constant multiplies its variance by the *square* of the constant. Second, the variance of a sum of *independent* random variables is the sum of the component variances. Therefore,

$$\mathrm{Var}(\bar{Y}) = \mathrm{Var}\left(\frac{\sum Y_i}{n}\right)$$

$$= \frac{1}{n^2}\mathrm{Var}\left(\sum Y_i\right) \qquad \text{because dividing by } n \text{ is equivalent to multiplying by } 1/n$$

$$= \frac{1}{n^2}\sum \mathrm{Var}(Y_i) \qquad \text{because the individual variables are, by assumption, independent}$$

$$= \frac{1}{n^2}(\sigma^2 + \sigma^2 + \cdots + \sigma^2) \qquad \text{because the variables are drawn from a population with variance } \sigma^2$$

$$= \frac{n\sigma^2}{n^2} = \frac{\sigma^2}{n}$$

Taking a square root yields the standard error of $\bar{Y}$:

$$\sigma_{\bar{Y}} = \sqrt{\mathrm{Var}(\bar{Y})}$$

$$= \frac{\sigma}{\sqrt{n}}$$

CASE — Sampling and Sampling Distributions

Your employer, a long-distance telephone company, issues charge cards to any customers who request them. Most customers are sales employees and executives of small or medium-sized firms. For such firms, telephone bill payments do not take highest priority and your employer has difficulty collecting payment on about 8% of its charge cards. Therefore, the company is considering a credit-worthiness scoring system (available from a consulting firm) to decide whether or not to issue charge cards to employees of a particular firm.

To try and decide whether to use the system in the future, the company plans to sample its current card users to estimate the average score on the system. Some of the variables in the scoring system are not available on the company's computer, so each firm in the sample requires about an hour of a clerk's time to find and enter the required information. The company can't decide how to take the sample: Some people want to sample individual card users, others want to sample the firms responsible for paying the phone bills. Some people want to sample about 200 accounts; others argue that such a sample would be too small a fraction of the (approximately) 80,000 accounts the company currently has.

No one seems to have thought much about how to take the sample, though the information systems group has available an up-to-date listing of all accounts, classified virtually in any desired way. The consultants aren't willing to specify what the average should be, though they have said that, in other applications of the system, a clear majority of firms tend to score between 75 and 85, and scores between 65 and 75 or between 85 and 95 aren't terribly unusual.

Write a brief position paper on these problems, and focus on how the sample might be taken. Give your recommendations on choosing a sample size of 200 or some other sample size. You can assume that your readers will know what an average is, but don't assume that they know much more about technicial statistical issues. You can also figure that your readers have a one-page attention span.

Review Exercises Chapters 4–6

R21 Scores on an aptitude test for assembly workers are roughly normally distributed with a mean of 200 and a standard deviation of 40.
  a. Find the probability that a randomly chosen individual scores above 210.
  b. Find the probability that the mean of a random sample of 25 individuals is larger than 210.

R22 If the distribution of scores in Exercise R21 is not exactly normal, which answer is a poorer approximation? Why?

R23 Suppose that a random sample of 50 price changes is selected under the conditions of Exercise R3 (page 117). The number of changes made during the period is so large that it doesn't matter whether the sample is taken with or without replacement.
  a. Write an expression for the probability that three or fewer changes are posted incorrectly.
  b. Find a numerical value for the probability in part (a).
  c. What assumptions were made in answering part (a)? Under what conditions might any of these assumptions be in error?

R24 A certain part is kept in inventory at an automobile dealership. The number in stock at a given time follows the probability distribution

$$f_X(x) = \frac{(x+1)}{66}, \qquad x = 0, 1, \ldots, 10$$

  a. Find the mean and standard deviation of the number in stock at a given time.
  b. If the dealer requires 3 of this part on a given day, what is the probability that there is enough in stock?

R25 Suppose that the auto dealer in Exercise R24 has 4 separate parts in stock and that the probability distribution for the number of each in stock is the distribution specified in Exercise R24.
  a. Find the mean and variance of the total stock of the 4 parts.
  b. What additional assumptions, if any, did you make in answering part (a)? For each assumption, is the assumption more critical in determining the mean or in determining the variance?

R26   Now suppose that the dealer in Exercise R24 has 200 separate parts, and that the availability of each part is given by the probability distribution of Exercise R24. Find the approximate probability that the average number in stock (averaged over the 200 parts) is greater than 7. Should the approximation be a good one?

∫   **R27**   The daily demand for propane gas from a particular dealer (in appropriate units of measure) is random, with probability density

$$f_Y(y) = .0012y^2(10 - y), \qquad 0 < y < 10$$

   a. A student attempts to find the probability that the demand is between 5 and 8 units (both included) by calculating $f_Y(5) + f_Y(6) + f_Y(7) + f_Y(8)$. Explain why this procedure doesn't give the right answer.
   b. Calculate the probability sought in part (a).
   c. Find the mean and standard deviation of Y.

∫   **R28**   Of those days when demand exceeds 5 units in Exercise R27, what fraction have a demand less than 8 units?

R29   Suppose that the manufacturing process for glass wire used in fiber-optic transmission introduces impurities at an average rate of .0002 impurities per foot of wire. The wire is cut into 1000-foot sections; if any impurity is found in a section, that section is recycled. What is the probability that a randomly chosen section contains no impurities?

R30   What additional assumptions beyond the stated ones did you make in answering Exercise R29?

R31   A certain radio show has a catalog from which fans of the show may order records or tapes, as well as souvenir items. Suppose that 40% of the orders involve no records or tapes, 30% involve 1 record or tape, 15% involve 2, 10% involve 3, and 5% involve 4. For each possible number of records or tapes ordered, the percentage of orders of 0, 1, 2, 3, 4, or 5 souvenir items is given in the following table:

Records/Tapes Ordered	Souvenirs Ordered (%)					
	0	1	2	3	4	5
0	0	60	30	5	3	2
1	10	40	25	15	5	5
2	5	30	40	10	8	7
3	3	15	22	30	20	10
4	1	4	15	30	40	10

   Calculate the joint probability distribution of X = number of records or tapes ordered and Y = number of souvenirs ordered, in table form. Are the two types of orders independent?

R32   Find the expected number of souvenirs ordered, assuming the probabilities shown in Exercise R31. Also find the standard deviation of the number of souvenirs ordered.

R33   A manufacturing process that is working properly produces 5% defective items because of impurities in materials or other random factors. Suppose that 20 items are selected from the output of the process and inspected. Assume that the process is working properly.
   a. Find the probability that 2 or more of the selected items are defective.
   b. What did you assume in answering part (a)?

R34   An alternative inspection method for the process in Exercise R33 is to inspect every item and stop the process whenever 2 defectives have been found within the most recent 10 inspected. Does this inspection method satisfy the assumptions of a binomial random variable?

R35   In the ratings discussed in Exercise R12 (page 119), suppose that scores of 3, 2, and 1 are assigned to performance ratings of "excellent," "satisfactory," and "unsatisfactory," respectively. Find the mean and variance of the score of a randomly chosen junior executive.

∫ R36   The availability and actual stocking of generic grocery products by supermarkets is surveyed. X is defined as the fraction of all products stocked by a randomly chosen supermarket that are available to that market as generics, and Y is defined as the fraction of available generic products that are actually stocked; the survey results indicate that the joint probability density of X and Y can be approximated by

$$f(x, y) = 6(1 - x - 2y + 2xy + y^2 - xy^2), \qquad 0 < x < 1, 0 < y < 1$$

a. Find the probability that X is less than .3 and Y less than 5.
b. Find the marginal probability density of Y.
c. Are X and Y assumed to be independent in this joint density? Support your answer.

∫ R37   Using the density given in Exercise R36, find the mean and standard deviation of the fraction actually stocked.

∫ R38   Find the expected value and variance of $W = 40X + 20Y$ for the joint density given in Exercise R36.

R39   Suppose that it has been established that the number of program lines per week produced by computer programmers using a commerically available toolbox has a mean of 250 and a standard deviation of 70. Suppose that a random sample of 40 programmers is taken. What is the approximate probability that the average lines produced is greater than 265?

R40   What did you assume in answering Exercise R39? Under what circumstances might the answer to Exercise R39 be a poor approximation?

R41   A realtor believes that, under current conditions, 45% of walk-in customers eventually purchase a home through that realtor. In a random sample of 16 walk-in customers, what is the probability that 3 or fewer eventually purchase a home through the realtor? Provide a numerical answer.

R42   Specify all assumptions you made in answering Exercise R41. Are there any assumptions that appear grossly unreasonable?

R43   A bond broker occasionally calls clients to try to place tax-exempt bonds. Define X = number of calls made to a particular client in a three-month period and Y = number of orders made in that period by the client. Assume that

$$f(x, y) = \frac{(4 - x)(xy + 1)}{30(1 + 2x)}, \qquad x = 1, 2, 3, y = 0, 1, 2, 3, 4$$

a. Find the conditional distribution of Y given X, in either mathematical or tabular form.
b. Are X and Y independent? In context, should they be?

R44   Find the mean and variance of Y in Exercise R43.

R45   A computer software wholesaler occasionally gets special handling orders that must be shipped by air. Such orders are expensive and unprofitable. Records indicate that such orders occur at an average rate of 1.6 per workday. In a week with five workdays, what is the probability that there are 10 or more special handling orders? Provide a numerical answer.

R46 Carefully specify the assumptions you made in answering Exercise R45. Are any of these assumptions obviously wrong?

∫ **R47** When data files are transferred between computers, the files are broken up into packets for transmission. When a packet is received at the destination computer, it goes through a checking program. Define X = time required to transmit a randomly chosen packet and Y = time required to check the packet, both measured in thousandths of a second. Assume that the joint probability density of X and Y is

$$f(x, y) = .00000012y(100 - y)e^{-.02(x - 120)}, \qquad x > 120, 0 < y < 100$$

Find the probability that X is between 200 and 300 and Y is between 30 and 50.

∫ **R48** Find the conditional density of Y given X for the random variables shown in Exercise R47. What does this joint density indicate about the dependence of X and Y?

∫ **R49** Find the expected values and variances of X, Y, and $T = X + Y$ for the random variables of Exercise R47.

∫ **R50** Suppose that we redefine X and Y in Exercise R47 to express them in seconds rather than thousandths of a second. Thus $X' = .001X$ and $Y' = .001Y$. Find the expected values and variances of X', Y', and $T' = X' + Y'$.

R51 Refer again to Exercise R47. A random sample of 250 packets is chosen and the transmission time for each is recorded.

a. Find the approximate probability that the average transmission time in the sample is larger than .180 seconds.

b. Should the approximate probability calculated in part (a) be a good approximation to the unknown exact probability? Explain why.

POINT ESTIMATION

Now we are ready to discuss the basic problems of statistical inference. The objective of statistics is to make inferences about one or more population parameters based on observable sample data. These inferences take several related forms. Conceptually, the simplest inference method is point estimation: The best single guess one can give for the value of the population parameter. Point estimation is the topic of this chapter. Other related inference procedures are interval estimation, in which one uses a point estimate and an allowance for random error to specify a reasonable range for the value of a parameter, and hypothesis testing, in which one isolates a particular possible value for the parameter and asks if this value is plausible given the data. Interval estimation is the topic of Chapter 8 and hypothesis testing is the topic of Chapter 9; the substance of both of these chapters depends greatly on the results established in this chapter. Chapters 10 through 17 extend the basic principles stated in Chapters 7 through 9 to a number of commonly occurring situations.

Within this chapter, we begin in Section 7.1 by discussing some criteria for good procedures for estimating a population parameter. Section 7.2 is a discussion of the relative merits of sampling with and without replacement, and of the relative importance of the absolute sample size compared to the fraction of the population that is being sampled; the results are surprising to many people. Section 7.3 introduces a very general method, called maximum likelihood, which usually yields good point estimates.

7.1   POINT ESTIMATORS

The simplest statistical inference is **point estimation**, where we compute a single value (statistic) from the sample data to estimate a population parameter. How do we decide which sample statistic to compute to give a single, numerical estimate for a population parameter? Suppose that we are trying to estimate a population mean and that we are willing to assume that the population distribution is normal. One natural summary statistic that can be used to estimate the population mean is the sample mean. Because the population mean for a normal distribution is also the population median, the sample median is also a plausible estimating statistic. So is an 80% trimmed mean, the average of the middle 80% of the values. Even if the population is symmetric, the sample is almost sure to be somewhat asymmetric, because of random variation. Thus, for any particular sample, the three methods yield somewhat different estimates. The mean is heavily influenced by outliers. A trimmed mean is less influenced by outliers, but it wastes data by ignoring (for instance) 20% of the data. We can think of the median as an extremely trimmed mean, where one discards all but the middle one or two data points. Which method should we use?

To begin the discussion, we need a technical definition. We use θ as the generic symbol for a population parameter. We use $\hat{\theta}$ to indicate an estimate of θ based on sample data.

Estimator

An **estimator** $\hat{\theta}$ of a parameter θ is a function of random sample values $Y_1, Y_2, \ldots,$ Y_n that yields a point estimate of θ. An estimator is itself a random variable and therefore it has a theoretical (sampling) distribution.

There is a technical distinction between an *estimator* as a function of random variables and an *estimate* as a single number. It is the distinction between a process (the estimator) and the result of that process (the estimate). The important aspect of this definition is that we can only define good processes (estimators), not guarantee good results (estimates). We will show, for example, that when one samples from a normal population, the sample mean is the best estimator. However, we cannot guarantee that the result is always optimal—that is, we cannot guarantee that, in every single sample, the sample mean is always closer to the population mean than, say, the sample median. The best we can do is to find estimators that give good results in the long run.

EXAMPLE 7.1   If Y_1, Y_2, and Y_3 are the (random) results of a sample of three individuals from a population, define a sample mean estimator. If, in a particular sample, the values 106.8, 102.0, and 105.0 are obtained, what is the resulting estimate?

Solution   The estimator

$$\bar{Y} = \frac{Y_1 + Y_2 + Y_3}{3}$$

can be interpreted as the process "take a sample of three values and average them." In the particular sample, $y_1 = 106.8$, $y_2 = 102.0$, and $y_3 = 105.0$ yield $\bar{y} = 104.6$ as an estimate of the population mean from this particular sample.   ■

The first property that we want an estimator (and its sampling distribution) to have is that it estimate the population parameter correctly on the average. For example, it seems wrong to use the sample 90th percentile to estimate the median (50th percentile) of a population as opposed to using the sample median. While it is conceivable that, in a particular sample, the 90th percentile is closer to the population median than is the sample median, generally the sample 90th percentile is too large; that is, the 90th percentile of the sample tends to overestimate the median of the population. We want to use an estimating statistic that does not systematically overestimate or underestimate the desired population parameter.

Unbiased Estimator

An estimator $\hat{\theta}$ that is a function of the sample data Y_1, Y_2, ..., Y_n is called **unbiased** for the population parameter θ if its expected value equals θ; that is, $\hat{\theta}$ is an unbiased estimator of the parameter θ if $E(\hat{\theta}) = \theta$.

An unbiased estimator is correct on the average. We can think of the expected value of $\hat{\theta}$ as the average of $\hat{\theta}$ values for all possible samples, or alternatively as the long-run average of $\hat{\theta}$ values for repeated samples. The condition that the estimator $\hat{\theta}$ be unbiased claims that the **average** $\hat{\theta}$ value is exactly correct. It does not say that a **particular** $\hat{\theta}$ value is exactly correct (see Figure 7.1). If the estimator is biased, the amount of bias is Bias $(\hat{\theta}) = E(\hat{\theta}) - \theta$.

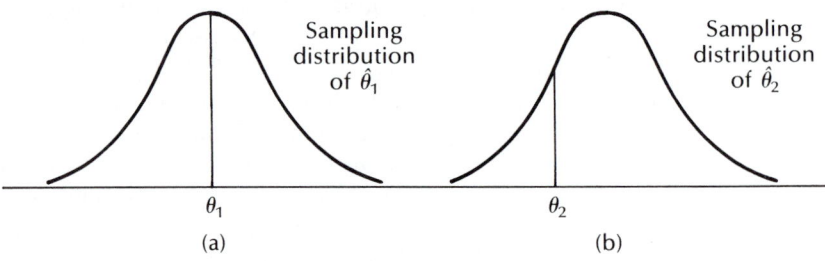

FIGURE 7.1   Illustration of (a) Unbiased and (b) Biased Estimators

EXAMPLE 7.2   Suppose that Y_1, Y_2, ..., Y_n represent the values obtained by a simple random sample from a population having mean μ and variance σ^2. Verify that $\bar{Y}$, the sample mean, is an unbiased estimator of μ.

Solution   In Chapter 4, we showed that $E(\bar{Y}) = \mu$. Thus by definition the sample mean is an unbiased estimator of the population mean. ∎

The requirement that an estimator be unbiased is not very restrictive and it does not rule out many potential estimators. Usually there are many unbiased estimators of any population parameter. For example, when sampling from a

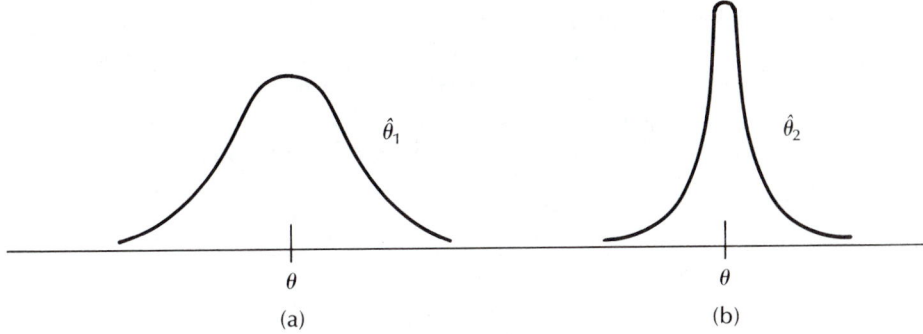

FIGURE 7.2   Sampling Distributions of $\hat{\theta}_1$ and $\hat{\theta}_2$

normal population, the sample mean, median, and trimmed mean are all unbiased estimators of the population mean μ.

Lack of bias is not the only property that we want an estimator to possess.
An estimator that is unbiased but grossly overestimates the parameter of interest
half the time and grossly underestimates it the other half isn't a very good
estimator. A second property that we require of an estimator is that it have a
sampling distribution with most of its probability concentrated near the parameter to be estimated. One measure of this concentration of the sampling distribution of an estimator is given by its standard error: The smaller the standard
error, the more concentration of probability there is near the parameter of interest. Figure 7.2 shows the sampling distributions for two hypothetical unbiased
estimators of a population parameter θ. It is obvious that $\sigma_{\hat{\theta}_1} > \sigma_{\hat{\theta}_2}$ and hence
that $\hat{\theta}_2$ is a more desirable estimator of θ than is $\hat{\theta}_1$.

The standard error of an estimator is also related to the probable degree of
error of an estimator: The smaller the standard error, the smaller the probable
degree of error. Therefore we would like to find an unbiased estimator with the
smallest possible standard error, or equivalently, the smallest probable error.

Efficient Estimator

An estimator is called **most efficient** for a particular problem if it has the smallest
standard error of all possible unbiased estimators.

The word *efficient* is used because the estimator makes the best possible use
of the sample data in a given situation. A most efficient unbiased estimator is
usually preferred to any other, according to standard statistical theory. Given
some very specific assumptions, it is possible to find most efficient estimators. For
example, if the population from which the sample measurements are drawn is
normal, the sample mean has a smaller standard error than the sample median,
any sample trimmed mean, or any other unbiased estimator. Therefore, if there
is good reason to assume a normal population, the sample mean is the best
estimator of the population mean.

EXAMPLE 7.3   A computer program draws 1000 samples, each of size 30, from a normally distributed population having mean 50 and standard deviation 10. For each sample, the mean, median, and trimmed mean (average of the middle 80% of the sample data) are computed. The average value and standard deviation of each set of estimates for the 1000 samples are as follows:

Statistic	Average Value	Standard Deviation
Mean	50.1254	1.8373
Median	50.1696	2.2607
Trimmed mean	50.1196	1.8947

Do the three statistics appear to be unbiased? Which one appears to be most efficient?

Solution   The average value of each estimator is (a simulation approximation to) its expected value. The average value of each estimator is very close to the population mean, 50, so all three estimators appear to be unbiased, at least in this situation. The standard deviation of each estimator is (a simulation approximation to) its standard error. The sample mean has the smallest standard error, so it seems to be most efficient in this situation.   ■

Unfortunately, efficiency claims are heavily dependent on assumptions. The sample mean is not always most efficient when the population distribution is not normal. In particular, when the population distribution has heavy tails, the sample mean is less efficient than a trimmed mean (though it still is unbiased). Heavy-tailed distributions tend to yield lots of extreme, "oddball" values that influence a mean more than a trimmed mean. A great deal of research is being **robust estimator**   conducted to find so-called **robust estimators:** Statistics that are nearly unbiased and nearly efficient for a wide variety of possible population distributions. There is not yet any general agreement on ideal robust estimators, but it's reasonable to assume that such methods will be used increasingly in the near future. We do not spend much space on these methods despite their potential usefulness. The formulas involved in robust estimation are more complicated than those we present, but the basic principles for using the formulas are the same.

EXAMPLE 7.4   A computer is programmed to draw 1000 samples, each of size 30, from an extremely heavy-tailed outlier-prone population having mean zero and standard deviation 9.95. Sample means, medians, and trimmed means are computed for each sample. The average values and standard deviations of the estimates are shown here:

Statistic	Average Value	Standard Deviation
Mean	.0228	1.8757
Median	.0148	.4510
Trimmed mean	.0081	.5667

What do these results indicate about the bias and efficiency of the three estimators when sampling from this population?

Solution   All three averages, approximations to the expected values, are close to zero, so all three estimators seem to be unbiased. In this case the standard error of the median appears to be much smaller than the standard error of the mean and somewhat smaller than that of the trimmed mean. Thus, for this outlier-prone population, the sample median appears to be somewhat more efficient than the trimmed mean and much more efficient than the sample mean. ∎

consistency   One additional criterion of a good estimator is **consistency**. If we're lucky enough to have a very, very large sample, our estimator should be guaranteed to be very close to the population (or process) parameter.

Consistent Estimator

An estimator is consistent if it approaches the parameter with probability one as the sample size goes to infinity. ∎

For example, the sample mean $\bar{Y}$ from a random sample has expected value μ and a standard error that approaches zero as n goes to infinity. Therefore, as the sample size goes to infinity, $\bar{Y}$ will be as close as you want to μ; according to the definition, $\bar{Y}$ is consistent. (All the estimators discussed in this book are consistent, as long as stated assumptions hold.)

An inconsistent estimator is rather clearly a bad one. It is inadvisable to come up with an inaccurate estimate based on infinite data, which could happen if the bias of an estimator didn't approach 0 as n went to infinity. Using the sample 25th percentile to estimate the population median would yield an inconsistent estimator. Inconsistency would also result if the standard error of an estimator didn't go to zero as the sample size increased. Typically, an inconsistent estimator is the result of doing something foolish, or, more likely, the failure of a key assumption.

EXAMPLE 7.5   In Section 4.7, we defined the (population) correlation of two random variables. This parameter can be estimated by sample data if the variables are measured accurately, without measurement error. However, if there is measurement error, the sample correlation approaches a number in between zero and the population correlation (depending on the extent of the measurement error). What does this fact say about the sample correlation as an estimator?

Solution   When there is measurement error the sample correlation is an inconsistent estimator of the true correlation because its bias doesn't disappear as the sample size gets large. ∎

SECTION 7.1   EXERCISES

7.1   A random sample of 20 vice presidents of Fortune 500 firms is taken. The amount each vice president paid in federal income taxes as a percentage of gross income is determined. The data are

| 16.0 | 18.1 | 18.6 | 20.2 | 21.7 | 22.4 | 22.4 | 23.1 | 23.2 | 23.5 |
| 24.1 | 24.3 | 24.7 | 25.2 | 25.9 | 26.3 | 27.9 | 28.0 | 30.4 | 33.7 |

   a. Compute the sample mean and median.
   b. Compute the 20% trimmed mean; that is, delete the lowest 10% and highest 10% of the data and find the mean of the remainder.

7.2   Refer to the data of Exercise 7.1.
   a. Construct a histogram using about 6 classes.
   b. Is there evidence of nonnormality in the data?
   c. Which of the sample statistics computed in Exercise 7.1 would you select to estimate the population mean?

7.3   A Monte Carlo study involves 10,000 random samples of size 16 from a normal population with $\mu = 100$ and $\sigma = 20$. For each sample, the mean, the median, and the 20% trimmed mean are calculated, with the following results:

Estimator	Mean	Median	Trimmed Mean
Average	100.23	99.96	99.98
Variance	26.52	40.61	27.49

   a. What does the study suggest about the bias of the three estimators in this situation?
   b. Which of the three estimators appears most efficient?

7.4   A sample of 30 editions of a weekly newspaper reveals the following numbers of column-inches of classified advertising:

171	185	193	199	204	210	216	218	221	223
225	228	228	230	234	235	237	240	241	243
245	249	251	254	257	262	263	271	280	379

   a. Compute the mean and median.
   b. Compute the 20% trimmed mean, the average of the middle 80% of the values.

7.5   Refer to the data of Exercise 7.4.
   a. Construct a stem-and-leaf display. What is the most conspicuous aspect of the display?
   b. Do the data suggest that the mean is the most efficient estimator for this situation?

7.6   Suppose that Y_1, Y_2, Y_3, and Y_4 represent a random sample of four observations from a population with mean μ and standard deviation σ. Two estimators of the mean might be considered:

$$\hat{\mu}_1 = \bar{Y} = \frac{Y_1 + \cdots + Y_4}{4} \quad \text{and} \quad \hat{\mu}_2 = .2Y_1 + .3Y_2 + .3Y_3 + .2Y_4$$

The results of Chapter 4 indicate that, for independent random variables,

$$E\left(\sum c_i Y_i\right) = \left(\sum c_i\right)\mu$$
$$\text{Var}\left(\sum c_i Y_i\right) = \left(\sum c_i^2\right)\sigma^2$$

a. Are both estimators unbiased?

b. Which estimator has the smaller variance?

7.7 Box plot of means, trimmed means (with the top 10% and bottom 10% of the data deleted), and medians for samples of size 10 from a Laplace (mildly outlier-prone) population are shown in Figure 7.3. The mean of this population is zero.

a. Do the three estimators appear to be unbiased?

b. Which estimator appears to be most efficient?

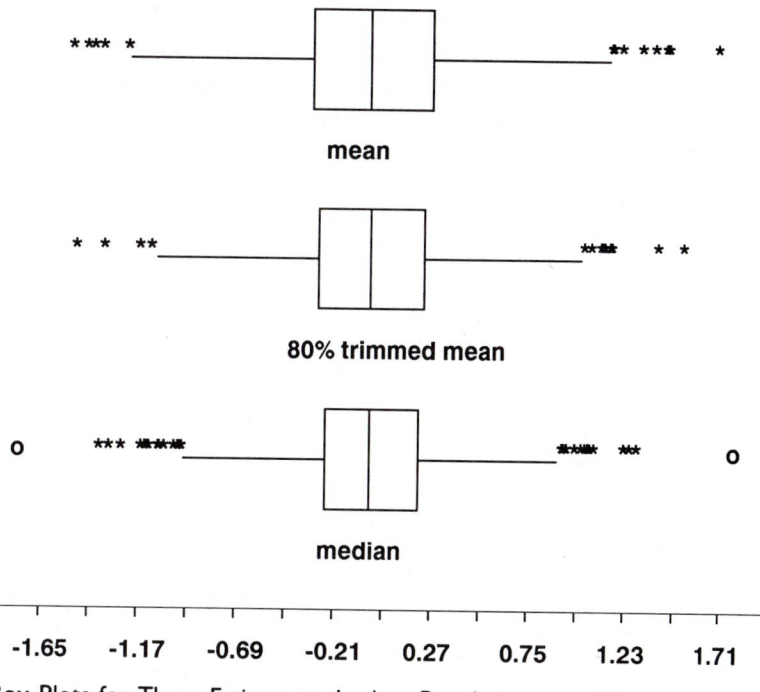

FIGURE 7.3   Box Plots for Three Estimators; Laplace Population, $n = 10$

7.8 The averages and standard deviations for the three estimators in Exercise 7.7 are as follows:

Estimator	Average	Standard Deviation
Mean	.0100	.4366
Trimmed mean	.0040	.3899
Median	.0032	.3704

Are these results consistent with your answers to Exercise 7.7?

7.9   Samples of size 30 are chosen from a uniform population. The population mean is .500 and the population variance is .08333. The population shape is symmetric and absolutely flat; there are no values less than zero or greater than one, so there is no possibility of outliers. The following averages and standard deviations are obtained:

Estimator	Average	Standard Deviation
Mean	.5015	.0504
Trimmed mean	.5017	.0611
Median	.5043	.0644

    a. Should the estimators be unbiased, given the nature of the population? Do they appear to be?

    b. Which of the three estimators appears to be most efficient?

7.10   Box plots for the estimators of Exercise 7.9 are shown in Figure 7.4. Do these plots support your answers to Exercise 7.9?

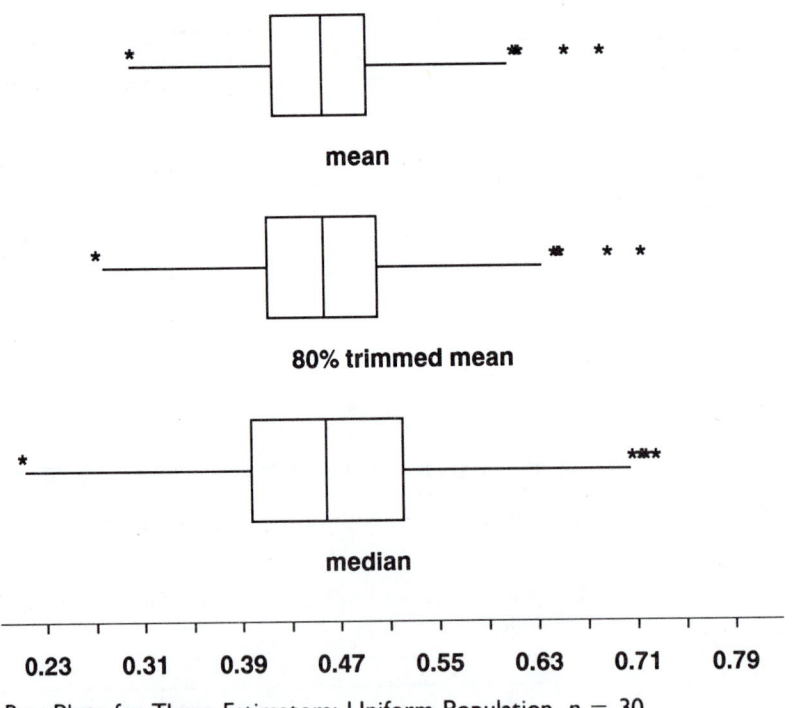

FIGURE 7.4   Box Plots for Three Estimators; Uniform Population, $n = 30$

7.11   The operations manager for the automatic transmission department of an automobile maker obtains data on the operating pressure of a sample of 50 transmissions each week. One of the concerns is the mean for the entire weekly production, which is about 2200 transmissions. (Another concern is the variability around that mean.) Typically, the pressure for most transmissions is very slightly below or above the nominal level of 35 pounds per square inch. A few transmissions can have pressure readings quite far below or above the nominal level. One way to estimate the average for the entire production is to use the midrange of the sample data—the average of the largest and smallest of the 50 data values.

    a. From the (admittedly limited) information that you have, is there reason to believe that this method will systematically underestimate the mean? Systematically overestimate it? What technical statistical concept is in question here?

    b. Even if there is no systematic under- or overestimate, the midrange method may not be an effective use of the data. Explain why not.

7.12 Explain why the operations manager in Exercise 7.11 might not want to use the mean of the 50 sampled pressures as the estimator of the average for the entire weekly production.

7.2   SAMPLING WITH AND WITHOUT REPLACEMENT ∎

In Chapter 6 we derived the formula for the standard error of the sample mean $(\sigma_{\bar{Y}} = \sigma/\sqrt{n})$ under the assumption that successive values of the sampled random variables $Y_1, \ldots, Y_n$ were independent. The assumption is literally correct, in the random-sampling situation, only when sampling with replacement. Yet sampling with replacement seems to be a poor idea in most contexts. In this section we show that the distinction between sampling with and without replacement is not important. As a side benefit, we can clarify the relative importance of the absolute sample size and the fraction of the population that is sampled.

variance of $\bar{Y}$, with and without replacement

    According to the idea of efficiency, unbiased estimators (in our case, sample means taken with and without replacement) may be compared on the basis of variances, or equivalently, of standard errors. It can be proved that the variance of a sample mean (based on a sample size n, a population size N, and a population variance σ^2) is σ^2/n when sampling with replacement, and $(\sigma^2/n)(N-n)/(N-1)$ when sampling without replacement. A standard error can be found, as always, by taking the square root of the associated variance.

EXAMPLE 7.6 Suppose a sample of size 200 is to be taken from a population of size 20,000. Compare the variances and standard errors for the sample mean based on sampling with replacement and sampling without replacement. Which sampling procedure yields the more efficient estimator of μ?

Solution

Sampling Method	With Replacement	Without Replacement
Var($\bar{Y}$)	$\dfrac{\sigma^2}{200} = .005\sigma^2$	$\dfrac{\sigma^2}{200}\left(\dfrac{20{,}000 - 200}{20{,}000 - 1}\right) = .00495\sigma^2$
$\sigma_{\bar{Y}}$	$\dfrac{\sigma}{\sqrt{200}} = .0707\sigma$	$\dfrac{\sigma}{\sqrt{200}}\sqrt{\dfrac{20{,}000 - 200}{20{,}000 - 1}} = .0704\sigma$

Sampling without replacement gives the smaller standard error, but the difference appears in the third significant digit (the fourth decimal place) of the standard error. It's unlikely that this difference would have practical importance. ■

EXAMPLE 7.7 Consider the following two sampling situations where $\bar{Y}$ is used to estimate μ:

    a. sampling 100 items (without replacement) from a population of 1000

    b. sampling 1000 items (without replacement) from a population of 1,000,000

If everything else is assumed equal, which procedure yields the smaller standard error for $\bar{Y}$?

Solution In situation (a) you would sample a larger **fraction of the population**, while in situation (b) you would have a larger **sample size**. To see which effect is more important, we can compute the standard error of $\bar{Y}$ for the two procedures:

$$\text{(a)} \quad \frac{\sigma}{\sqrt{100}} \sqrt{\frac{1000 - 100}{1000 - 1}} = .0949\sigma$$

$$\text{(b)} \quad \frac{\sigma}{\sqrt{1000}} \sqrt{\frac{1,000,000 - 1000}{1,000,000 - 1}} = .0316\sigma$$

Assuming the two populations have equal variances (and therefore equal standard deviations), the standard error of $\bar{Y}$ is much smaller in situation (b). ■

The preceding examples illustrate two general conclusions. First, **the distinction between sampling with and without replacement can safely be ignored except in the rare case that the sample size is at least 10% of the population size.** This is the point of Example 7.6.

The second basic conclusion, which is illustrated in Example 7.7, is surprising to most people. **The absolute sample size is much more important in determining probable accuracy than is the fraction of the population that is sampled.** Of course, for a fixed population size, increasing the sample size also increases the sampling fraction. For virtually any realistic situation, the numerical effect of the change in absolute size is more important. The sample size, not the fraction, determines how much information is in the data.

EXAMPLE 7.8 A computer is programmed to draw 1000 samples of size 20 from a population, sampling both with and without replacement. The population distribution is

Individuals:	00–09	10–29	30–69	70–89	90–99
Value:	1	2	3	4	5

(The population mean is 3.) Sample means are calculated for all the samples, and averages and standard deviations are 2.9996 and .249 with replacement and 3.008 and .216 without replacement.

    a. Does the sample mean appear to be unbiased?

    b. Does sampling with replacement or without appear to be more efficient?

Solution   a. The averages both are very close to 3.0, so the sample mean appears to be unbiased in this case.

b. The standard deviations (simulation approximations to the standard errors) are smaller in the case of sampling without replacement, so sampling without replacement appears to be more efficient.   ∎

EXAMPLE 7.9   The simulation of Example 7.8 is repeated, but with the following changes. The population becomes

Individuals:	0–99	100–299	300–699	700–899	900–999
Value:	1	2	3	4	5

(Again, the population mean is 3.) The sample size in this simulation is 50. Note that the sample size in this example is 2.5 times the sample size in Example 7.8, but that we are sampling only 5% of the population as compared to 20% in Example 7.8. The following results are obtained: With replacement, average = 3.002 and standard deviation = .153; without replacement, average = 2.997 and standard deviation = .150.

What does a comparison of this example to Example 7.8 indicate about the relative importance of sample fraction and sample size?

Solution   In each case, the simulation approximation to the standard error is smaller in this example than in Example 7.8. Thus the effect of increased sample size is shown to be more important than the effect of sampling a smaller fraction of the population.   ∎

SECTION 7.2   EXERCISES

7.13 In Exercise 7.11, we considered a sample of 50 automatic transmissions from a week's production of 2200 transmissions. Certain holiday weeks reduce production by 20%, to 1760 transmissions. Does it follow that the sample size can also be reduced by 20%, to 40, and still have the same accuracy in estimating the weekly average?

7.14 a. Would you expect that the sampling of transmissions in Exercise 7.11 would be done with replacement or without? Why?

b. Assume that the sampling would be done without replacement, that the long-run standard deviation of pressures is 2.40 pounds per square inch, and that the sample size is 50. How much difference does it make to the standard error of the sample mean whether the weekly production is 2200 transmissions or 1760?

7.15. A political candidate running for a state legislature seat noticed that statewide polls sampled 2000 of the state's 8,000,000 registered voters (one of every 4000 voters), and the polls had a probable error of ± 3 percentage points. The candidate planned to sample the same proportion of the 40,000 voters in the legislative district and expected the same probable error. Where's the error in the candidate's reasoning?

7.16 A sample is taken of 90 individuals who are responsible for forecasting within large regional banks. There are 650 individuals who might be sampled. Each forecaster in the sample indicates a predicted percentage growth in real disposable income for the next year. Assume that the population standard deviation of forecasts is .4%.

a. In practice, would the sample be chosen with replacement or without?
b. Assuming sampling with replacement, calculate the standard error of the mean.
c. Assuming sampling without replacement, calculate the standard error of the mean.
d. Which standard error is smaller? by how much?

7.17   Viewers of election-night coverage on television have often heard projections of a statewide winner based on a small percentage of the vote. For states such as New York and California, the projection may be based on 1% of the vote, but for states such as Wyoming and Delaware, the projection is based on a much larger percentage. Why?

7.3   MAXIMUM LIKELIHOOD ESTIMATION (∂)   ■

In Section 7.1 we discussed two desirable properties for estimators of parameters; we want unbiased estimators with small standard errors. How does one go about finding an estimator of a parameter θ in a given sampling situation? One general procedure for selecting an estimator is called the **method of maximum likelihood**.

method of maximum likelihood

There are several reasons why one might use the maximum likelihood estimator for a parameter. Although maximum likelihood estimators are not always unbiased and efficient, they are usually about the best that one can find, because of the following properties: As the sample size increases, the bias of the maximum likelihood estimator tends to zero, its standard error approaches the smallest possible standard error, and its sampling distribution approaches normality. It is because of these properties that many statisticians favor the use of maximum likelihood estimators in many sampling situations.

One of the simplest ways to illustrate the concept of maximum likelihood estimation is by showing how to find a maximum likelihood estimator for a given problem. Suppose that we have a binomial experiment with an unknown probability of success π and that we obtain $y = 2$ successes in $n = 5$ trials. We can use Appendix Table 1 to evaluate the probability of two successes in five trials. For $\pi = .05$, the probability is .0214; for $\pi = .10$, the probability is .0729. As we proceed across the table, the probability of two successes in five trials increases to a maximum (of .3456) at $\pi = .40$ and then decreases. By definition, $\hat{\pi} = .40$ is the maximum likelihood estimate (at least among the values shown in Appendix Table 1) of π when the data are two successes in five trials.

EXAMPLE 7.10   Find the maximum likelihood estimate of π in a binomial experiment with $n = 20$ and $y = 16$.

Solution   If we start using Appendix Table 1 for $n = 20$ and $y = 16$ at $\pi = .05$, we find that the probability of 16 successes in 20 trials increases as we go from $\pi = .05$ to $\pi = .50$. To continue reading the table, we must look at the right-hand edge for the y value and at the bottom for the π value. The probability of 16 successes in 20 trials increases as we go back across the table until it reaches a maximum (of .2182) at $\pi = .80$. Among the values for π shown in Appendix Table 1, $\hat{\pi} = .80$ is the maximum likelihood estimate when $y = 16$ and $n = 20$.   ■

To define maximum likelihood estimation more generally, we need some other definitions.

Likelihood Function

For discrete data $y_1, y_2, \ldots, y_n$, the likelihood function L is the probability of observing the data that are in fact observed:

$$L(y_1, y_2, \ldots, y_n, \theta) = P(y_1, y_2, \ldots, y_n)$$

which we regard as a function of the unknown population parameter θ. If the data are drawn from a continuous distribution $f_Y(y)$, the probability distribution P is replaced by the probability density f:

$$L(y_1, y_2, \ldots, y_n, \theta) = f(y_1, y_2, \ldots, y_n)$$

Assuming that the sample values are drawn independently, we may obtain the probability P or the density f as a product:

$$L(y_1, y_2, \ldots, y_n, \theta) = P(y_1)P(y_2)\ldots P(y_n)$$

or

$$L(y_1, y_2, \ldots, y_n, \theta) = f(y_1)f(y_2)\ldots f(y_n)$$

If, in a binomial experiment with $n = 5$, we obtain $y = 2$, then the likelihood is simply the probability of two successes in five trials taken as a function of the unknown population probability of success π.

EXAMPLE 7.11   Suppose that the number of new orders arriving at a small machine shop on a given day follows a Poisson distribution with unknown mean μ, independently of arrivals on other days. Suppose that one order arrives on the first day of a sample and that four orders arrive on the second (and last) day of the sample. Write down the likelihood function.

Solution   Remember that the Poisson distribution is discrete with

$$P(y) = e^{-\mu}\frac{\mu^y}{y!}$$

The observed values are $y_1 = 1$ and $y_2 = 4$. The likelihood is

$$L(1, 4, \mu) = e^{-\mu}\frac{\mu^1}{1!}e^{-\mu}\frac{\mu^4}{4!}$$

which can be simplified to

$$L(1, 4, \mu) = e^{-2\mu}\frac{\mu^5}{1!4!}$$

Maximum Likelihood Estimate of θ

For observed sample values $y_1, y_2, \ldots, y_n$, the maximum likelihood estimate of a parameter θ is the value $\hat{\theta}$ that maximizes the likelihood function $L(y_1, y_2, \ldots, y_n)$.

In a binomial experiment with $n = 5$ and $y = 2$, the maximum likelihood estimate of π appears from Appendix Table 1 to be .40.

EXAMPLE 7.12   Refer to the likelihood function found in Example 7.11. Indicate how one should use a table of Poisson probabilities to find the maximum likelihood estimate of μ.

Solution   The likelihood found in Example 7.11 was the product of the Poisson probabilities of obtaining $y_1 = 1$ and $y_2 = 4$. Using Appendix Table 2, we can calculate these probabilities and obtain the following:

μ	2.3	2.4	2.5	2.6	2.7
$P_Y(1)$	.2306	.2177	.2052	.1931	.1815
$P_Y(4)$	.1169	.1254	.1336	.1414	.1488
$L(1, 4, \mu)$	.0270	.0273	.0274	.0273	.0270

The value of μ that maximizes the likelihood function appears to be 2.5. Thus the maximum likelihood estimate is $\hat{\mu} = 2.5$.   ■

In principle, one can always find maximum likelihood estimators by numerical computation of the likelihood function. But often it's easier to use elementary calculus to find them. Recall from calculus that to find the maximum of a function one sets the first derivative of the function equal to zero and solves the resulting equation. One should also use a second-derivative check to make sure that one is obtaining a maximum, not a minimum; by and large, the solution of the first-derivative equation gives a maximum likelihood estimator rather than a minimum.

In likelihood problems, it is often convenient to work with the natural logarithm of the likelihood rather than with the likelihood itself. Because the logarithm is an increasing function, as the likelihood increases to its maximum, so does the log-likelihood. For example, consider again a binomial experiment with $n = 5$ and $y = 2$. The likelihood is

$$L(2, \pi) = \frac{5!}{2!3!} \pi^2 (1 - \pi)^3$$

Denoting the log-likelihood by $l(2, \pi)$, we have

$$l(2, \pi) = \log(5!) - \log(2!3!) + 2\log \pi + 3\log(1 - \pi)$$

Set the first derivative equal to zero:

$$\frac{2}{\pi} - \frac{3}{1 - \pi} = 0$$

The solution of this equation is $\hat{\pi} = 2/5 = .40$. Thus calculus yields the same maximum likelihood estimate, $\hat{\pi} = .40$, as is found by numerical methods.

EXAMPLE 7.13   Refer to Example 7.11. Find the maximum likelihood estimate of μ using calculus.

Solution   Again, it is convenient to use the log-likelihood. We found the likelihood in Example 7.11 to be

$$L(1, 4, \mu) = e^{-2\mu} \frac{\mu^5}{1!4!}$$

so the log-likelihood is

$$l(1, 4, \mu) = -2\mu + 5\log(\mu) - \log(1!4!)$$

Setting the first derivative equal to zero gives the equation

$$\frac{\partial l(1, 4, \mu)}{\partial \mu} = -2 + \frac{5}{\mu} = 0$$

so the maximum likelihood estimate of μ is $\hat{\mu} = 5/2 = 2.5$. Once again, the result found by calculus agrees with the result found numerically.   ■

An important problem in statistical theory is estimation of the population mean μ based on a random sample from a normal population. The normal distribution is based on a continuous random variable, with density

$$f(y) = \frac{1}{\sqrt{2\pi}\,\sigma} e^{-.5(y-\mu)^2/\sigma^2}$$

The log-likelihood function for a random sample from a normal population can be found by routine algebra. It is

$$l(y_1, y_2, \ldots, y_n) = \left(\frac{-n}{2}\right)\log(2\pi) - n\log(\sigma) - .5\sum \frac{(y_i - \mu)^2}{\sigma^2}$$

For any specified value of σ, say, 3.72, the derivative of the log-likelihood with respect to μ is

$$\frac{\partial l(\mu)}{\partial \mu} = 0 + 0 + \sum \frac{(y_i - \mu)}{3.72^2}(-1)$$

The maximum likelihood estimator is found by solving this expression set to zero:

$$-\sum \frac{(y_i - \mu)}{3.72^2} = 0$$

One way to see that $\hat{\mu} = \bar{y}$ is the solution to this equation is to note that $\sum(y_i - \bar{y}) = 0$. Obviously the choice of any particular value for σ is irrelevant to the computation of the maximum likelihood estimator of μ; our arbitrary choice of $\sigma = 3.72$ had no effect on the calculation. In general, if the population shape is normal, the sample mean is the most efficient estimator and also the maximum likelihood estimator. Thus we know that the sample mean is a maximum likelihood estimator of the population mean when the population is normal, and also that the sample proportion is the maximum likelihood estimator of the probability of success in a binomial experiment.

SECTION 7.3   EXERCISES

7.18 The times $Y_1, Y_2, \ldots$ between arrivals of customers to a store can often be assumed to have a negative exponential distribution:

$$f_{Y_i}(y) = \theta e^{-\theta y}, \qquad 0 < y < \infty$$

Using a process similar to the one for discrete distributions, we can find the maximum likelihood estimator here for a sample of n measurements $y_1, y_2, \ldots, y_n$ by maximizing the likelihood

$$f_{Y_1}(y_1)f_{Y_2}(y_2)\cdots f_{Y_n}(y_n)$$

Suppose that a sample of size $n = 4$ values yields

$$y_1 = 2.4, \qquad y_2 = .8, \qquad y_3 = .2, \qquad y_4 = 4.6$$

a. Show that the likelihood when $\theta = .5$ is $(.5)^4 e^{-4} = .00114$.

b. Construct a table of likelihoods for the problem, with

$$\theta = .1, .2, .3, .4, .5, .6, .7, .8, .9, 1.0$$

(You will need a calculator that computes exponentials.)

c. What do you think the maximum likelihood estimate of θ is in this situation?

∂ **7.19** a. Use calculus to prove that the maximum likelihood estimate of θ in Exercise 7.18 is $\hat{\theta} = .5$.

b. Show that for a sample of size n from the negative exponential distribution, the maximum likelihood estimator of θ is

$$\hat{\theta} = \frac{n}{\sum\limits_i Y_i} = \frac{1}{\bar{Y}}$$

7.20 One form of the lognormal probability density is given by the following mathematical function:

$$f_Y(y) = \frac{1}{\sqrt{2\pi}\,y} e^{-1/2[(\log y) - \theta]^2}, \qquad 0 < y < \infty$$

where $\pi = 3.14159\ldots$ and $\log y$ is the natural logarithm of y. Suppose that a sample of size 2 yields $y_1 = 4.28$ and $y_2 = 4.69$.

a. Use a calculator that computes natural logarithms to verify the following values.

Hint: The likelihood for $n = 2$ observations is

$$\left(\frac{1}{2\pi y_1 y_2} e^{-1/2(\log y_1 - \theta)^2} e^{-1/2(\log y_2 - \theta)^2} \right)$$

θ:	1.2	1.3	1.4	1.5	1.6
Likelihood:	.00723	.00760	.00783	.00791	.00783

b. What is the maximum likelihood estimate of θ, according to the values?

7.21 a. Use calculus to maximize the likelihood for Exercise 7.20.

b. Show that for general n the maximum likelihood estimator of θ in the lognormal density is

$$\hat{\theta} = \frac{\displaystyle\sum_{i=1}^{n} \log y_i}{n}$$

Hint: To maximize the likelihood, minimize

$$\sum_{i=1}^{n} (\log y_i - \theta)^2$$

7.22 The Laplace density

$$f_Y(y) = .5e^{-|y - \theta|}$$

is symmetric around the value of θ but outlier-prone compared to a normal distribution. Suppose that five observations from a Laplace density yield $y_1 = 2.6$, $y_2 = 5.1$, $y_3 = 4.7$, $y_4 = 9.6$, and $y_5 = 5.0$.

a. Find the mean and median for the sample data.

b. Compute the likelihood function when θ equals each of the values found in part (a).

c. Can the sample mean be the maximum likelihood estimator for a Laplace population? Explain your reasoning.

Summary

This, the first chapter devoted to making inferences from sample data to the underlying population (or process), introduces some principles for choosing a good summary statistic from the sample. There are two fundamental criteria: The statistic should be unbiased (be correct on the average), and should be efficient (have the least possible variability and therefore the smallest possible standard error). The choice of the best estimating statistic depends on assumptions about the underlying population or process; therefore, plots of the data help in selecting reasonably good estimators.

The notion of efficiency can be applied in considering sampling with replacement or without. Our results indicate that sampling without replacement is more efficient, but by a negligibly small amount in most cases. Our results also indicate that the absolute sample size is the important factor in determining estimation accuracy; perhaps surprisingly, the fraction of the population that's being sampled matters very little.

The desire to find efficient, unbiased estimators can usually be achieved by the method of maximum likelihood, given very specific aasumptions about the shape of the underlying population. This method involves finding the value of the population parameter that maximizes the probability of obtaining the data that actually were obtained.

KEY FORMULAS: Point Estimation

1. Unbiased estimator $\hat{\theta}$ of a parameter θ:

$$E(\hat{\theta}) = \theta$$

2. Standard error of $\bar{Y}$

   sampling with replacement: $\sigma_{\bar{y}} = \dfrac{\sigma}{\sqrt{n}}$

   sampling without replacement: $\sigma_{\bar{y}} = \dfrac{\sigma}{\sqrt{n}} \sqrt{\dfrac{N-n}{N-1}}$

3. Likelihood function:

$$L(y_1, y_2, \ldots, y_n, \theta) = P(y_1)P(y_2)\cdots P(y_n)$$

   For continuous random variables, replace the probability $P(y_i)$ by the probability density $f(y_i)$.

CHAPTER 7   EXERCISES

7.23   A Monte Carlo study involves 5000 samples, each of size 30, from a heavy-tailed population having a mean of 300 and a standard deviation of 25. For each sample, the mean, median, and 20% trimmed mean are computed:

Statistic	Mean	Median	Trimmed Mean
Average value	298.91	300.74	299.09
Variance	35.79	41.27	28.47

a. Do the estimators all appear to be unbiased, or nearly so?
b. Which estimator appears to be most efficient?

7.24   Samples of size 30 are taken from an exponential population having mean 1. Recall from Chapter 5 that the exponential distribution is quite severely right-skewed.
   a. Should the sample mean, sample trimmed mean, and median all be unbiased estimators of the population mean?
   b. The average values (over 1000 samples) of these three estimators are 1.0026 for the mean, .8489 for the trimmed mean, and .7149 for the median. Do these results agree with your answer to part (a)?

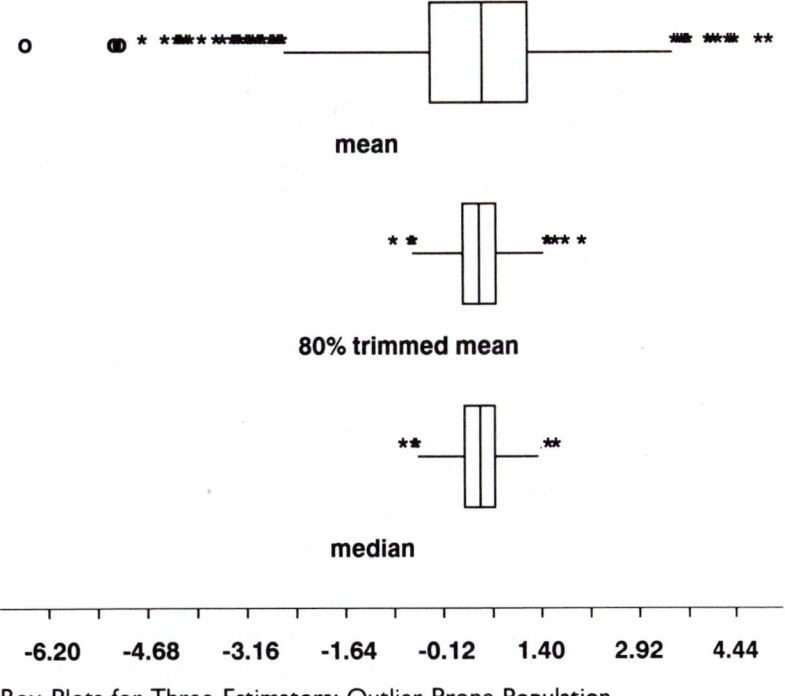

FIGURE 7.5 Box Plots for Three Estimators; Outlier-Prone Population, $n = 60$

7.25 Samples of size 60 are taken from a symmetric but severely outlier-prone population having mean zero and standard deviation 9.95. Box plots of the resulting means, trimmed means, and medians are shown in Figure 7.5.

a. Do the estimators appear to be unbiased?

b. Would the sample mean be the most efficient estimator of the population mean when sampling from this population?

7.26 The averages and standard deviations for the three estimators in Exercise 7.25 are shown below:

Estimator	Average	Standard Deviation
Mean	−.0285	1.3165
Trimmed mean	−.0014	.3699
Median	.0003	.3262

Are these results consistent with your answers to Exercise 7.25?

7.27 A random sample of 50 observations is to be obtained from a population of interest. Under what data shapes might you prefer to use the sample median rather than the sample mean as an estimate of the "center" of the population? For each case, explain why you would prefer to use the median.

7.28 A sample of 400 individuals is taken from a target group of all individuals in the United States that hold driver's licenses. The purpose of the study is to assess the awareness of a new product. There are many, many millions of people in the target group; a sample of 400 is only a microscopic fraction of the population. We can therefore argue that the sample cannot possibly give an accurate estimate of the proportion of individuals who are aware of the product. Is this a valid argument?

7.29 A study yields two random variables, Y_1 and Y_2. Each has expected value μ, the population mean of interest. The variance of Y_1 is 2 and the variance of Y_2 is 8. Three estimators are proposed:

$$\hat{\theta}_1 = .5Y_1 + .5Y_2$$
$$\hat{\theta}_2 = .2Y_1 + .8Y_2$$
$$\hat{\theta}_3 = .8Y_1 + .2Y_2$$

Use the properties of expected values we discussed in Chapter 4 to determine which of these estimators is unbiased.

7.30 Which of the estimators in Exercise 7.29 has the smallest variance? Use the properties of variances we discussed in Chapter 4. Which random variable should be given greater weight, the one with the large variance or the one with the small variance?

7.31 A food service company that operates company dining rooms tries out a new procedure for bidding on contracts. Each of the four offices of the company uses the procedure until three successful bids are made. Office 1 requires 7 bids, office 2 requires 9 bids, office 3 requires 6 bids, and office 4 requires 14 bids. We can assume that the negative binomial distribution (Chapter 5) should apply to $Y =$ required number of bids. Recall that for the negative binomial distribution,

$$P_Y(y) = \frac{(y-1)!}{(k-1)!(y-k)!} \pi^k (1-\pi)^{y-k}$$

where $k =$ number of successes to be obtained and π is the probability of success.
a. What is the value of k in this problem?
b. Calculate the likelihood of the actual results for $\pi = .10, .20, .30, .40, .50$.
c. Which of these values of π appears to be closest to the maximum likelihood estimator?

∂ 7.32 Use calculus to find the maximum likelihood estimator of π in Exercise 7.31.

7.33 An insurance firm uses the Pareto distribution

$$f_Y(y) = \theta(y+1)^{-(\theta+1)}, \qquad y > 0$$

as the assumed probability distribution for $Y =$ dollar amount of settlements for personal liability claims (in thousands). For one class of policies, three claims have $y_1 = .82$, $y_2 = .63$, and $y_3 = 7.55$.
a. Write an expression for the likelihood as a function of θ.
b. Calculate the likelihood for $\theta = 1, 2$, and 3. Which of these values of θ appears closest to the maximum likelihood estimate?

∂ 7.34 Use calculus to find the maximum likelihood estimator of θ in Exercise 7.33. How does the answer generalize to any sample of size n from the Pareto distribution?

7.35 A chain of shoe stores sets a budgeted sales figure for each store. Data are collected on the actual sales of a sample of stores as a fraction of the budgeted sales. The Minitab output shown on page 281 is obtained:
a. Locate the sample mean and median.
b. Which of these values should be the better estimate of the population mean?

7.36 A normal plot for the data of Exercise 7.35 is shown in Figure 7.6.
a. What does the shape of the normal plot indicate about the shape of the sample data?

```
MTB > print 'sales'

sales
  100.8    98.2    99.9    99.5   100.1   100.1   100.7   103.9    80.5
   99.9   100.0    98.3   142.3   101.3    98.2    98.2    98.7    93.2
  101.8    93.6   101.2    99.7    97.7   100.3   119.4    99.3   101.6
   84.0   100.5   100.3    99.1    99.6   100.1   100.2   102.1   100.2
  100.9    99.5   104.8   102.7   109.3    98.0

MTB > describe 'sales'

              N     MEAN   MEDIAN   TRMEAN   STDEV   SEMEAN
sales        42   100.71   100.10   100.09    8.61     1.33

            MIN      MAX      Q1       Q3
sales     80.50   142.30   98.60   101.22

MTB > histogram of 'sales'

Histogram of sales   N = 42

Midpoint   Count
      80       1   *
      85       1   *
      90       0
      95       2   **
     100      32   ********************************
     105       3   ***
     110       1   *
     115       0
     120       1   *
     125       0
     130       0
     135       0
     140       1   *
```

Minitab for Exercise 7.35

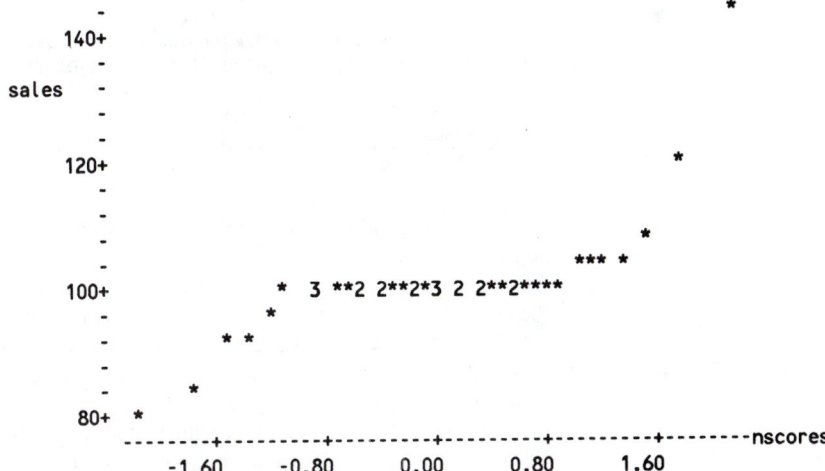

FIGURE 7.6   Normal Plot for Exercises 7.35 – 7.36 Minitab for Exercise 7.37

b. Does the normal plot confirm your answer to part (b) of Exercise 7.35?

7.37 A sales representative for a coffee producer measures the fraction of shelf space for all coffees devoted to the producer's brands. The following results are obtained:

```
MTB > print 'fraction'

fraction
  0.157895    0.160000    0.105263    0.142857    0.250000    0.166667    0.210526
  0.142857    0.200000    0.200000    0.160000    0.210526    0.142857    0.227273
  0.090909    0.125000    0.142857    0.142857    0.210526    0.130435    0.136364
  0.269231    0.136364    0.176471    0.227273    0.120000    0.176471    0.210526
  0.238095    0.210526    0.111111    0.187500    0.142857    0.095238    0.210526
  0.130435    0.192308    0.187500    0.210526    0.117647    0.200000    0.125000
  0.230769    0.190476    0.062500    0.166667    0.083333    0.142857    0.150000
  0.153846

MTB > stem and leaf of 'fraction'

Stem-and-leaf of fraction  N = 50
Leaf Unit = 0.010


     1     0 6
     4     0 899
     7     1 011
    14     1 2223333
    24     1 4444444555
   (6)     1 666677
    20     1 8899
    16     2 0001111111
     6     2 2233
     2     2 5
     1     2 6

MTB > describe 'fraction'

             N     MEAN    MEDIAN   TRMEAN    STDEV    SEMEAN
fraction    50   0.16623   0.16000  0.16631  0.04644   0.00657


            MIN      MAX       Q1       Q3
fraction  0.06250  0.26923  0.13488  0.21053
```

Is there any reason to think that the sample mean is an inefficient estimator of the population mean?

7.38 A normal plot of the data in Exercise 7.37 is shown in Figure 7.7. Does the shape of the normal plot confirm your answer to Exercise 7.37?

7.39 A firm that leases cellular car phones is concerned with the credit-worthiness of its customers. If lease payments aren't made on time (or aren't made at all), the firm experiences serious losses. Typically about 11% of leases are credit problems. The firm has decided to try a credit-scoring system to evaluate future lease customers. The system uses accounting information such as the customer's working capital-to-expense ratio; measures of the customer's stability, such as years in present location; and measures of the customer's industry's stability, such as year-to-year variability in profits. All of this information is combined to give a score: The higher the score,

MTB > plot 'fraction' vs 'nscores'

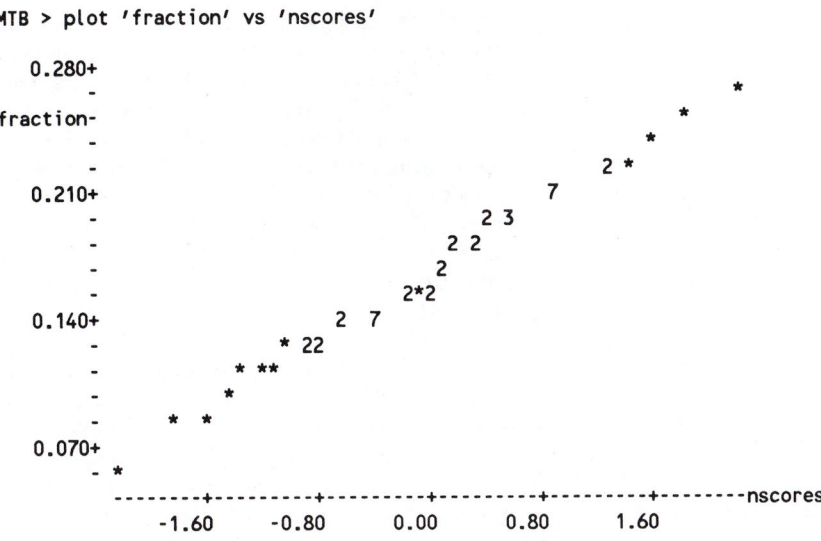

FIGURE 7.7   Normal Plot for Exercises 7.37 – 7.38

the better the customer's credit-worthiness. The car phone firm wants to estimate the 11th percentile of its current customer population on this credit-scoring system, because it plans to use that score as a cutoff for granting credit.

The firm's computer system doesn't contain all the required information, so a clerical worker must spend time gathering some information for each customer. To get results within a reasonable time, the firm plans to rate a random sample of 400 of its current customers. Two different methods for using the sample data to estimate the 11th percentile were proposed. One is simply to use the average of the 44th and 45th scores, arranged in order from lowest to highest; this method will guarantee that 44/400 of the sample scores, which is 11%, will fall below the estimated percentile. The second method uses the fact that the 11th percentile of a z (standard normal) distribution is -1.23; this method uses the sample mean minus 1.23 standard deviations as the estimate of the 11th percentile of scores.

a. If the distribution of credit scores in the firm's entire customer base really is normal, which method would you expect to give the better estimate? Better in what sense? Why do you think so?

b. Which method do you think will be more robust against a violation of the normal-distribution assumption?

c. There is reason to expect that the distribution of credit scores will have many firms in the 80s and 90s (where 100 is the maximum possible score), some scores in the 60s and 70s, and a few scores down as low as the 20s and 30s. If we assume this general pattern, which method seems preferable? Why?

7.40 A computer programmer working for the firm of Exercise 7.39 offers to write a program that will incorporate several different possible assumptions about the distribution of credit scores in the firm's customer base. The program will draw many simulated samples of size 400 and obtain estimates of the 11th percentile based on both methods. How could the output of this program be used to guide the choice of method? What summary figures about the simulation estimates would be helpful in making the choice?

7.41 The car phone leasing firm of Exercise 7.39 will obtain a sample of 400 customer credit scores. The data will be used to estimate not only the 11th percentile, as in Exercise 7.39, but also to estimate the mean. As a "guesstimate," the firm assumes that the standard deviation of scores among its 18,000 customers is about 12.0.

    a. Calculate the standard error of the sample mean assuming sampling with replacement. Do the same calculation, but this time assume sampling without replacement.

    b. In fact, which way would the sampling be done? How much difference does it make?

    c. Should the firm be concerned that less than 3% of its customer base will be sampled?

7.42 An artist made a number of copies of a print from an etched plate, and then destroyed the plate. The total number of prints made was never revealed, but each print had a serial number. A dealer realized that the value of each print depended heavily on how many were made. The dealer discovered that the four copies of the print that were currently for sale had serial numbers $y_1 = 14$, $y_2 = 4$, $y_3 = 21$, and $y_4 = 11$. It seems reasonable to assume that all copies would have the same probability of being for sale, so that the distribution of the serial number Y should be uniform:

$$P_Y(y) = 1/\theta, \quad \text{for } y = 1, 2, \ldots, \theta$$

where θ is the unknown number of prints that were made. (Of course, it's impossible to have a serial number larger than the number of prints made.)

    a. Calculate the likelihood of the observed serial numbers for $\theta = 25, 24, 23, 22, 21$, and (watch it here) 20. Even though the serial numbers aren't really independent—in effect, they are sampled without replacement—you won't lose anything important in this case by assuming independence.

    b. What appears to be the maximum likelihood estimate of theta?

7.43 a. How does the maximum likelihood estimator in the print serial number problem of Exercise 7.42 generalize to have n serial numbers $y_1, y_2, \ldots, y_n$? Again, you may assume independence, even though that isn't a realistic assumption; it turns out not to matter in this case.

    b. Is this estimator unbiased? You shouldn't have to do any math to answer this question.

7.44 In Exercise 6.53, you obtained 100 samples, each of size 12, of random numbers that were uniformly distributed between 0 and 1. Load these samples back into a computer program or obtain a new set of 100 samples.

    a. Have the program obtain means and medians for each sample. Find the average of the means, and the average of the medians. Do both statistics seem to be unbiased?

    b. Have the program obtain the standard deviations of means and medians. Which statistic seems to be more efficient in this situation?

CASE

In the Case of Chapter 6 you played the role of an employee of a long-distance company considering sampling its customers to estimate the average score on a credit-worthiness scoring system. The company has decided to choose a sample of 200 firms (not individual card users) from the current customer list. However, someone finally realized that the key issue wasn't so much the average score as the score that indicated potential problems in getting bills paid.

Specifically, the company needs to get an estimate of the 8th percentile of scores, because about 8 percent of its customer firms have payment problems. Because 8 percent of 200 is 16, one obvious estimate is the 16th-lowest score in the sample (or maybe the average of the 16th and 17th). Your assistant has argued that a sample size of 200 is big enough to assume that the data will be normal, so you should obtain the mean and standard deviation from the sample and estimate the 8th percentile as 1.41 standard deviations below the mean. Also, your assistant still believes that the sample is much too small a fraction of the 80,000-firm customer base.

Write a brief memo to your assistant, responding to the ideas raised. As may already be evident to you, your assistant was not an all-star student of statistics, so you'll have to explain yourself clearly.

INTERVAL ESTIMATION

The discussion in Chapter 7 focused on one type of statistical inference—point estimation. There the task was to find the best single-number guess for the value of a population parameter. The methods developed in Chapter 7 didn't include any explicit indication of the probable degree of error. In this chapter we develop methods that allow for reporting not only the best estimate of a parameter value, but also the probable degree of error of that estimate. The methods of this chapter allow one to state not merely the best single guess for a population parameter, but also an interval of reasonable guesses for that parameter. Because these methods yield a whole numerical interval of reasonable possibilities for a parameter, they are called interval-estimation methods.

In this chapter we build on the point-estimation methods of Chapter 7 to develop interval estimates for parameters. Once we specify general methods, we turn to some specific methods for the most important parameters, such as population means and proportions. Section 8.1 introduces the general concept of a confidence interval; the discussion happens to be stated in terms of means. Section 8.2 extends the concept of a confidence interval to the problem of estimating a proportion. In Section 8.3 we turn to a basic problem in planning statistical studies: How large a sample is needed to achieve a desired accuracy? Section 8.4 contains the basic theory of Student's t distribution, a widely used distribution in establishing confidence intervals and in performing other kinds of statistical inference; the consequences of the use of Student's t distribution in confidence interval problems are discussed in Section 8.5. In Section 8.6 we discuss the assumptions underlying confidence-interval methods, the consequences of violating those assumptions, and methods for detecting possible violations. In Section 8.7 we discuss interval estimation for a population median, as contrasted to methods for a mean, and in Section 8.8 we use confidence intervals for estimation of a standard deviation.

8.1   INTERVAL ESTIMATION OF A POPULATION MEAN WITH KNOWN STANDARD DEVIATION

probable range

The ideas discussed in the previous chapter dealt with point estimation: Finding a best guess for a population parameter. Such point estimates are almost inevitably in error to some degree. Specification of a **probable range** for the parameter—a plus-or-minus range for error—is crucial in indicating the reliability of estimates. A statement like "the estimated response rate is 28%" is less useful than one like "the estimated response rate is 28% ± 2%." And 28% ± 2% indicates a much more reliable estimate than 28% ± 15%. In this section we use the idea of a sampling distribution to construct an **interval estimate** for a population mean. We discuss confidence intervals for proportions later in the chapter.

interval estimate

The idea is best introduced by an example. Suppose that a random sample of size 36 is to be taken, and that the sampling distribution of $\bar{Y}$ is normal.* (If the population can be assumed to be symmetric, the Central Limit Theorem should apply.) Somewhat artificially, we assume that the population standard deviation is known to be 18.0. The expected value of $\bar{Y}$ is the population mean μ, the parameter being estimated, and the standard error of $\bar{Y}$ is $\sigma_{\bar{Y}} = \sigma/\sqrt{n} = 18/\sqrt{36} = 3$. From the properties of a normal distribution, there is a 95% chance that $\bar{Y}$ is within 1.96 standard errors of μ (see Figure 8.1):

$$P[\mu - 1.96(3) \leq \bar{Y} \leq \mu + 1.96(3)] = .95$$

Look at it another way: Any time the observed sample mean $\bar{y}$ lies in the interval $\mu \pm 1.96(3)$, the interval $\bar{y} \pm 1.96(3)$ encloses μ. This is shown in Figure 8.2 (page 288). Because there is a 95% chance that $\bar{Y}$ lies in the interval $\mu \pm 1.96(3)$, there is a 95% chance that the interval $\bar{Y} \pm 1.96(3)$ encloses μ. In practice, we take only a single sample from the population of interest. The interval $\bar{y} \pm 1.96(3)$ that we construct using the observed sample mean is called a **95% confidence interval for μ**.

95% confidence interval for μ

We derive the general formula for a confidence interval for a population mean in the same way. The formula is exactly correct only when the population

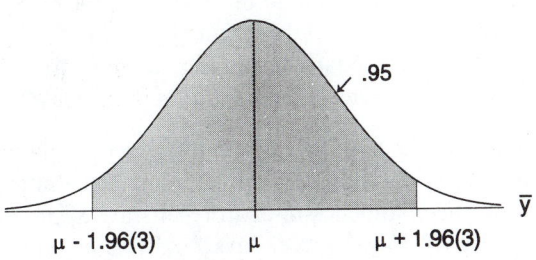

FIGURE 8.1   Sampling Distribution of $\bar{Y}$

---

* Again, we use capital letters for random variables and lowercase letters for the resulting values. Thus, when planning to take a sample, we consider probabilities about $\bar{Y}$. When the sample yields values 90, 96, 100, and 106, $\bar{y} = 98$.

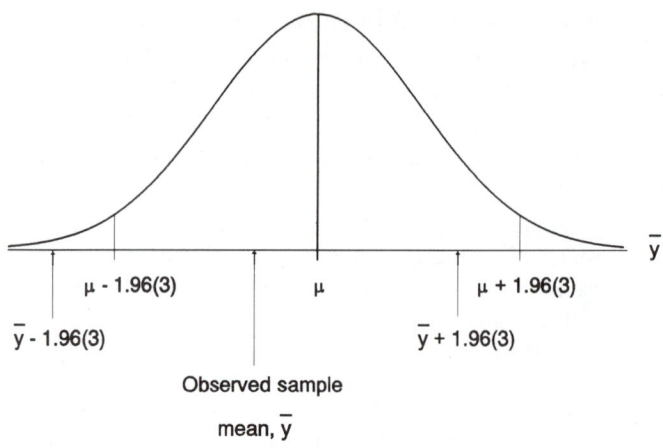

FIGURE 8.2   Sampling Distribution of $\bar{Y}$

distribution is normal and the population standard deviation is known. However, it provides an excellent approximation when the population distribution is symmetric or only modestly skewed, for sample sizes of, say, 30 or more.

$100(1 - \alpha)\%$ Confidence Interval for μ, with σ Known

$$\bar{y} - z_{\alpha/2}\sigma_{\bar{Y}} \leq \mu \leq \bar{y} + z_{\alpha/2}\sigma_{\bar{Y}}$$

where $\sigma_{\bar{Y}} = \sigma/\sqrt{n}$ and $z_{\alpha/2}$ is the tabulated value cutting off a right-tail area of $\alpha/2$ in the standard normal distribution.

EXAMPLE 8.1   An airline needs an estimate of the average number of passengers on a newly scheduled flight. Its experience is that data for the first month of flights are unreliable, but that thereafter the passenger load settles down. Therefore the mean passenger load is calculated for the first 20 weekdays of the second month (regarded as a random sample of 20 days from a hypothetical population of weekdays) after initiation of this particular new flight. If the sample mean is 112.0 and the population standard deviation is assumed to be 25, find a 90% confidence interval for the true, long-run mean number of passengers on this flight.

Solution   We assume that the hypothetical population of daily passenger loads for weekdays is not badly skewed. Then the sampling distribution for $\bar{Y}$ is approximately normal and the confidence-interval results are approximately correct, even for a sample size of only 20 weekdays. For this example $\bar{y} = 112.0$, $\sigma = 25$, and $\sigma_{\bar{Y}} = \sigma/\sqrt{20} = 5.59$. Then for a 90% confidence interval, we use $z_{.05} = 1.645$ in the formula to obtain

$$112 \pm 1.645(5.59), \quad \text{or} \quad 102.80 \text{ to } 121.20$$

We are 90% confident that the long-run mean μ lies in this interval.   ∎

There is a small logical problem in interpreting the "90%" of a 90% confidence interval. In Example 8.1 it is tempting to write

$$P(102.80 \leq \mu \leq 121.20) = .90$$

but, as written, there is no random quantity in the expression: μ is an unknown population constant, while 102.80 and 121.20 are simply numbers. Therefore, in strict logic, we can't apply a probability to one particular interval.

The "90%" refers to the **process** of constructing confidence intervals. Each particular confidence interval either does or does not include the true value of the parameter being estimated. In the long run, 90% of the intervals so constructed

interpretation of a include the population value. So we say that we have 90% confidence that
confidence interval $102.80 \leq \mu \leq 121.20$. This is shorthand for "the interval $102.80 \leq \mu \leq 121.20$ is the result of a process that in the long run has 90% probability of being correct."

EXAMPLE 8.2   A Monte Carlo study considers 5000 samples, each of size 40, from a near-normal population. For each sample, 90% and 95% confidence intervals for the population mean are calculated. A count is made of those samples for which the true mean falls below, within, and above the confidence interval:

	Below	Within	Above
90% interval	236	4513	251
95% interval	129	4753	118

What are the expected frequencies? Compare the theoretical (expected) and the observed frequencies.

Solution   The expected frequencies can be found by multiplying the theoretical probabilities by 5000:

	Below	Within	Above
90% interval	250	4500	250
95% interval	125	4750	125

The simulation frequencies are all quite close to the expected frequencies.   ∎

The discussion in this section has included one rather unrealistic assumption—namely, that the population standard deviation is known. In practice, it's difficult to find situations in which the population mean is unknown but the standard deviation is known. Usually both the mean and the standard deviation must be estimated from the sample. Because σ is estimated by the sample standard deviation s, the actual standard error of the mean $\sigma/\sqrt{n}$ is naturally estimated by $s/\sqrt{n}$. This estimation introduces another source of random error (s varies randomly, from sample to sample, around σ) and, strictly

substituting *s* for σ speaking, invalidates our confidence-interval formula. Fortunately, the formula is still a very good approximation for large sample sizes. As a very rough rule, we can use this formula when n is larger than 30*; a better way to handle this issue is described in Section 8.5.

EXAMPLE 8.3 Suppose that the airline in Example 8.1 takes a sample of 40 days and finds a sample mean of 112.0 and a sample standard deviation of 25. Find a 95% confidence interval for the true mean.

Solution For $\bar{y} = 112$, $s = 25$, and $n = 40$, $\sigma_{\bar{Y}} \approx 25/\sqrt{40} = 3.95$. Then using $z_{.025} = 1.96$, the 95% confidence interval for μ is

$$112 \pm 1.96(3.95) \qquad \text{or} \qquad 104.26 \text{ to } 119.74 \qquad \blacksquare$$

SECTION 8.1   EXERCISES

8.1 The data from Exercise 7.1, what a sample of 20 executives paid in federal income taxes, as a percentage of their gross income, are reproduced below.

16.0	18.1	18.6	20.2	21.7	22.4	22.4	23.1	23.2	23.5
24.1	24.3	24.7	25.2	25.9	26.3	27.9	28.0	30.4	33.7

Assume that the standard deviation for the underlying population is 4.0.
a. Calculate a 95% confidence interval for the population mean.
b. Calculate a 99% confidence interval for the population mean.

8.2 Give a careful verbal interpretation of the confidence interval in part (a) of Exercise 8.1.

8.3 From the appearance of the data in Exercise 8.1, is it reasonable to assume that the sampling distribution of the mean is nearly normal? (This assumption underlies the confidence-interval procedure.)

8.4 A business magazine samples 90 individuals responsible for economic forecasting for regional banks. The population is large enough that the with/without replacement distinction doesn't matter. Suppose that the sample of 90 forecasts yields an average prediction of a 2.7% growth in real disposable income. Assume that the population standard deviation is .4%. Calculate a 90% confidence interval for the population mean forecast.

8.5 In an audit of inventories, an internal auditor takes a sample of 36 items and determines the "shrinkage" (loss due to shoplifting or employee theft) for each item in percentage terms. The sample mean is 5.8% and the standard deviation is 4.2%. Calculate a 95% confidence interval for the true mean shrinkage.

8.6 Do you believe that the sampling distribution of $\bar{Y}$ in Exercise 8.5 would be approximately normal?

8.7 A chain of "quick lube" shops has a standard service for performing oil changes and basic checkups on automobiles. The chain has a standard that says that the average time per car for this service should be 12.5 minutes. There is considerable variability in times, due to differences in layout of engines, degree of time pressure from other

---

* This rule happens to coincide with a standard rule for appealing to the Central Limit Theorem. The latter rule is good only for symmetric or modestly skewed population distributions.

jobs, and many other sources. The standard deviation for the chain has been 2.4 minutes. The manager of one shop picked 48 random times (four per day for 12 days) and timed the next job after each random time. The data were analyzed using Minitab, which gave the following results:

```
MTB > zinterval 95% confidence assuming sigma = 2.4 for 'timeused'

THE ASSUMED SIGMA =2.40
                N      MEAN    STDEV  SE MEAN    95.0 PERCENT C.I.
timeused       48    13.104   2.417   0.346   (  12.424,  13.784)
```

a. Write out the 95% confidence interval for the mean. State what the 95% figure means.
b. Does this interval indicate that the mean for this shop differs from the 12.5 minute standard?

8.8 Minitab also calculated a 90% confidence interval for the mean using the same data as in Exercise 8.7.

```
MTB > zinterval 90% confidence assuming sigma = 2.4 for 'timeused'

THE ASSUMED SIGMA =2.40
                N      MEAN    STDEV  SE MEAN    90.0 PERCENT C.I.
timeused       48    13.104   2.417   0.346   (  12.534,  13.675)
```

Does this interval indicate that the mean for this shop differs from the 12.5 minute standard? Why is the answer here different from the answer in part (b) of Exercise 8.7?

8.9 A box plot of the data in Exercise 8.7 was as follows:

```
MTB > boxplot of 'timeused'
```

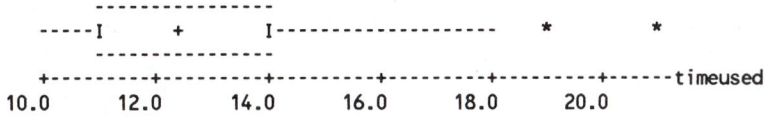

a. What form of nonnormality is indicated by the box plot?
b. Does this nonnormality invalidate the claimed confidence levels in Exercises 8.7 and 8.8?

8.2   CONFIDENCE INTERVALS FOR A PROPORTION ∎

The confidence-interval method in Section 8.1 can be adapted quite directly to give a confidence interval for a population proportion. The method is based on a normal approximation to the sampling distribution of a sample proportion. As such, it is an approximation, and some rules are needed for its use.

The sample proportion of successes, denoted $\hat{\pi}$, is just the number Y of successes divided by the sample size. As the mean and standard deviation for the binomial random variable Y are $n\pi$ and $\sqrt{n\pi(1 - \pi)}$, respectively, it follows (from

**expected value
and standard error
of $\hat{\pi}$**

the properties developed in Chapter 4) that the **expected value and standard error of** $\hat{\pi}$ are, respectively,

$$E(\hat{\pi}) = \pi \quad \text{and} \quad \sigma_{\hat{\pi}} = \sqrt{\pi(1-\pi)/n}$$

For sufficiently large n, $\hat{\pi}$ has an approximately normal distribution; so, for instance

$$P\left(-1.96 \leq \frac{\hat{\pi} - \pi}{\sigma_{\hat{\pi}}} \leq 1.96\right) \approx .95$$

Equivalently,

$$P(\hat{\pi} - 1.96\sigma_{\hat{\pi}} \leq \pi \leq \hat{\pi} + 1.96\sigma_{\hat{\pi}}) \approx .95$$

This looks very much like a confidence-interval formula, but there is the problem that the standard error $\sigma_{\hat{\pi}} = \sqrt{\pi(1-\pi)/n}$ involves the unknown population parameter π. Just as we can replace σ by s in $\sigma_{\bar{y}}$ when n is large, so can we replace $\pi(1-\pi)$ by $\hat{\pi}(1-\hat{\pi})$ in $\sigma_{\hat{\pi}}$. This yields a usable confidence-interval formula for the population proportion:

$100(1 - \alpha)\%$ Confidence Interval for a Proportion

$$\hat{\pi} - z_{\alpha/2}\sqrt{\frac{\hat{\pi}(1-\hat{\pi})}{n}} \leq \pi \leq \hat{\pi} + z_{\alpha/2}\sqrt{\frac{\hat{\pi}(1-\hat{\pi})}{n}}$$

This is the same "sample statistic $\pm$ table value times standard error" that occurs in the confidence interval for a mean. The sample mean $\bar{y}$ is replaced by the sample proportion $\hat{\pi}$. Similarly, $\sigma_{\bar{Y}}$ is replaced by $\sigma_{\hat{\pi}}$.

EXAMPLE 8.4   Suppose that in a sample of 2200 households with one or more television sets, 471 watch a particular network's show at a given time. Find a 95% confidence interval for the population proportion of households watching this show.

Solution   The sample proportion is $\hat{\pi} = 471/2200 = .214$, and $\sqrt{\hat{\pi}(1-\hat{\pi})/n} = .00874$. The z table value that cuts off a right-tail area of .025 is 1.96. The confidence interval is

$$.214 - 1.96(.00874) \leq \pi \leq .214 + 1.96(.00874)$$

or

$$.197 \leq \pi \leq .231$$

You might check the rankings of current television shows to see how much the difference between a 19.7% share and a 23.1% share would make in a show's ranking.   ∎

**normal
approximation
to binomial
distributions**

This confidence-interval method is based on a **normal approximation to a binomial distribution** that is appropriate for sufficiently large n. The rule is that both $n\pi$ and $n(1-\pi)$ should be at least 5, but, because π is the unknown population proportion, the rule has to be based on $n\hat{\pi}$ and $n(1-\hat{\pi})$ instead.

Usually a sample size that violates this rule (or even comes close) yields a confidence interval that is too wide to be informative. For example, if $n = 20$ and $\hat{\pi} = .20$, then $n\hat{\pi} = 4$ and the 95% confidence interval for π is $.025 \leq \pi \leq .375$. This confidence interval is practically useless; we know of few product managers who would consider "your product's market share is between 2.5% and 37.5%" to be very informative. However, even if a sample size satisfies the rule, we are not assured that the interval is informative. The rule judges only the adequacy of the sample size and the accuracy of the confidence interval based on the normal approximation. It is possible to use binomial probabilities to develop exact, if very wide, 90% or 95% confidence intervals.

SECTION 8.2   EXERCISES

8.10   The sales manager for a hardware wholesaler finds that 229 of the previous 500 calls to hardware store owners resulted in new product placements. Assuming that the 500 calls represent a random sample, find a 95% confidence interval for the long-run proportion of new product placements.

8.11   Give a careful verbal interpretation of the confidence interval found in Exercise 8.10.

8.12   As part of a market research study, in a sample of 125, 84 individuals are aware of a certain product. Calculate a 90% confidence interval for the proportion of individuals in the population who are aware of the product.

8.13   Should the normal approximation underlying the confidence interval of Exercise 8.12 be adequate?

8.14   In a sample of 40 middle managers of a large firm, it is found that 8 are actively involved in local civic or charitable organizations. Calculate a 90% confidence interval for the proportion of all middle managers who are so involved.

8.3   HOW LARGE A SAMPLE IS NEEDED?   ■

Information is expensive. Gathering it is costly in terms of salaries, expenses, and time (and profits) lost. Obviously some information is crucial for making management decisions. So the question of how much information (how large a sample) to gather is basic. The confidence interval provides a convenient method for answering this question.

Suppose that an operations officer of a large multibranch bank is concerned about the daily average level of checks left at branches on weeknights. Each day, armored cars take each branch's receipts to a processing center, where checks are recorded and sent to a clearinghouse. The cars must visit some of the branches before the end of banking hours, but a substantial volume of checks can remain uncollected until the next day. The lost interest can be costly. For how many days must the volume of uncollected checks be calculated to get a reasonable idea of the true daily average?

There are two related aspects of the phrase *reasonable idea* to consider in the context of a confidence interval. First, what confidence level should be selected? Second, how wide a confidence interval can be tolerated?

The confidence level is often set at 95% or 90%. In part this is a primitive tribal custom, passed on by generations of statistics textbooks. In part it's a

tolerable width

decent translation of reasonable certainty. It's fairly easy to understand 90 (or 95) chances in 100, but hard to comprehend 999,999 chances in 1,000,000.

The **tolerable width** depends heavily on the context of the problem. Plus or minus $80,000 (or a width of $160,000) is moderately large for the nightly idle-check volume of an entire bank, enormous for the nightly idle volume of one branch, and tiny for the average daily amount cleared by all U.S. banks. The tolerance must be determined by a manager who knows the situation.

When considering a confidence interval for a population mean μ, the plus-or-minus term of a confidence interval is $z_{\alpha/2}\sigma_{\bar{Y}}$, where $\sigma_{\bar{Y}} = \sigma/\sqrt{n}$. Three quantities determine the value of the plus-or-minus term: The desired confidence level (which determines the z table value used), the standard deviation σ, and the sample size (which together with σ determines the standard error $\sigma_{\bar{Y}}$). Usually a guess must be made about the size of the population standard deviation. (Sometimes an initial sample is taken to estimate the standard deviation; this estimate provides a basis for determining the additional sample size that is needed.) For a given tolerable width, once the confidence level is specified and an estimate of σ supplied, the required sample size can be calculated by trial and error or by a formula.

The trial-and-error approach can be illustrated with the idle-check example. Suppose that a 95% confidence interval is desired with a width of no more than $5,000 (a plus-or-minus range no greater than $2,500), and that the long-run standard deviation is assumed to be $10,000. Suppose that we first try $n = 16$. The confidence interval is $\bar{y} \pm 1.96(10,000/\sqrt{16})$ or $\bar{y} \pm 4900$. This interval is about twice as wide as desired; to halve the width of the confidence interval, we must quadruple the sample size because the sample size appears in the standard error formula as $\sqrt{n}$. With $n = 64$, the 95% confidence interval is $\bar{y} \pm 1.96(10,000/\sqrt{64})$ or $\bar{y} \pm 2450$, which is about what we want. Because the assumption that the standard deviation is $10,000 is just a guess, there's not much point in arguing over whether n should be 64 or 63 or 65; a "ballpark" value for n serves the purpose.

We can calculate the required sample size by formula. Set $z_{\alpha/2}\sigma/\sqrt{n}$ equal to the specified plus-or-minus tolerance E and solve for n.

Sample Size Required for a $100(1 - \alpha)$% Confidence Interval of Given Width for μ

The **sample size** required to obtain a $100(1 - \alpha)$% confidence interval for a population mean μ of the form $\bar{y} \pm E$, where $E = z_{\alpha/2}\sigma/\sqrt{n}$, is

$$n = \frac{z_{\alpha/2}^2 \sigma^2}{E^2}$$

The width of the confidence interval is $2E$.

EXAMPLE 8.5   Union officials are concerned about reports of inferior wages being paid to employees of a company under its jurisdiction. How large a sample is needed to obtain a 90% confidence interval for the population mean hourly wage μ with width equal to $1.00? Assume that $\sigma = \$4.00$.

Solution   The desired width is $2E = 1.00$ and $\sigma = 4.00$. Substituting into the sample size formula with $z_{\alpha/2} = 1.645$, we obtain

$$n = \frac{(1.645)^2(4^2)}{(.5)^2} \approx 173$$ ∎

EXAMPLE 8.6   How large a sample is needed to obtain a 95% confidence interval for μ with a width of two-tenths of a (population) standard deviation?

Solution   The desired width $2E = .2\sigma$, so $E = .1\sigma$. Therefore

$$n = \frac{(1.96)^2\sigma^2}{(.1\sigma)^2} = \frac{(1.96)^2}{(.1)^2} \approx 384$$ ∎

Determining sample size for a confidence interval for a proportion is a similar process. The corresponding formula is

$$n = \frac{z_{\alpha/2}^2 \hat{\pi}(1 - \hat{\pi})}{E^2}$$

The only problem is that the sample size depends on $\hat{\pi}$. Until the sample size is determined and the sample taken, we do not know $\hat{\pi}$. There are several possible solutions to our problem. We can substitute $\hat{\pi} = .5$ into the sample size formula, which results in a conservative sample size that is usually larger than is actually required. Another possibility is to substitute a value of $\hat{\pi}$ obtained from either a previous study or a pilot study. The sample-size formula for estimating a binomial proportion is shown here:

Sample Size Required for a $100(1 - \alpha)$% Confidence Interval of Given Width for π

The sample size required to obtain a $100(1 - \alpha)$% confidence interval for π of the form $\hat{\pi} \pm E$, where

$$E = z_{\alpha/2}\sqrt{\frac{\hat{\pi}(1 - \hat{\pi})}{n}}$$

is

$$n = \frac{z_{\alpha/2}^2 \hat{\pi}(1 - \hat{\pi})}{E^2}$$

Note: Use $\hat{\pi} = .5$ for a conservative (large) sample size or use the value of $\hat{\pi}$ from a previous (or pilot) study.

EXAMPLE 8.7   A direct-mail sales company must determine its credit policies quite carefully. Suppose that the firm suspects that advertisements in a certain magazine have led to an excessively high rate of write-offs (accounts regarded as uncollectible). The firm wants to establish a 90% confidence interval for this magazine's write-off proportion that is accurate to $\pm.02$.

      a. How many accounts must be sampled to guarantee this goal?

      b. If this many accounts are sampled and 10% of the sampled accounts are determined to be write-offs, what is the resulting 90% confidence interval?

Solution   a. The sample size formula is

$$n = \frac{z_{\alpha/2}^2 \hat{\pi}(1 - \hat{\pi})}{E^2}$$

Using the conservative estimate $\hat{\pi} = .5$ and substituting $E = .02$ with $z_{\alpha/2} = 1.645$, the required sample size is

$$n = \frac{(1.645)^2(.5)^2}{(.02)^2} \approx 1691$$

      b. If a sample of 1691 accounts shows 169 (essentially 10%) write-offs, the 90% confidence interval for the true write-off proportion is

$$.10 \pm 1.645\sqrt{(.10)(.90)/1691} = .10 \pm .012$$

The conservative nature of the confidence interval that results from a sample size determined by setting $\hat{\pi} = .5$ in the formula is indicated here. The actual confidence interval has $E = .012$, whereas the target was $E = .02$. Had the firm been willing to make an initial guess that $\hat{\pi}$ would be about .10, it could have used a smaller sample size.

$$n = \frac{(1.645)^2(.1)(.9)}{(.02)^2} = 609 \qquad\qquad \blacksquare$$

      As Example 8.7 indicates, **basing a sample-size determination on the assumption that $\hat{\pi}$ is .5 can be excessively conservative.** Whenever there is information to suggest that the sample proportion differs from .5, the substitution $\hat{\pi} = .5$ results in a large (conservative) sample size. The corresponding confidence interval has a smaller width than the target width.

SECTION 8.3   EXERCISES

8.15 a. Refer to Example 8.5. How large a sample is needed to obtain a 90% confidence interval with width $0.50? with width $0.25? with width $0.125?

      b. In general, how much must one increase a sample size to cut the width of a confidence interval in half (using a specified confidence level)?

8.16 Refer to Example 8.6. How large a sample is needed to obtain a width of three-tenths of a standard deviation? four-tenths?

8.17 An automobile insurance firm wants to find the average amount per claim for auto body repairs. Its summary records combine amounts for body repair with all other amounts, so a sample of individual claims must be taken. A 95% confidence interval with a width no greater than $50 is wanted. A "horseback guess" says that the standard deviation is about $400. How large a sample is needed?

8.18   Suppose that the guess of the standard deviation in Exercise 8.17 is somewhere between $300 and $450.

a. Compute the required sample sizes for $\sigma = 300$ and for $\sigma = 450$.

b. What would happen to the width of the confidence interval if the n corresponding to $\sigma = 450$ was used but in fact the standard deviation came out $300?

8.19   Do you think that the sample size used in Exercise 8.17 would be adequate to assume that $\bar{Y}$ had approximately a normal sampling distribution?

8.20   A manufacturer of boxes of candy is concerned about the proportion of imperfect boxes—those containing cracked, broken, or otherwise unappetizing candies.

a. How large a sample is needed to get a 95% confidence interval for this proportion with a width no greater than .02? Use the conservative substitution.

b. How does the answer to part (a) change if we assume that the proportion of imperfect boxes is at least .005 and no more than .08?

8.4   THE t DISTRIBUTION   ■

The estimation procedures for a population mean μ presented in Section 8.1 are based on the assumption that either σ is known or that there is a sufficient number of measurements (e.g., 30 or more) so that the sample standard deviation s can replace σ in the standard error for $\bar{y}$, $\sigma/\sqrt{n}$. Sometimes it is impossible or uneconomical to obtain a large sample when making an inference about a population mean. For example, in a study of rush-hour traffic patterns around a bridge on Friday evenings, it would take more than six months to generate 30 observations on the total Friday evening rush-hour traffic volume. This may be too long before some corrective remedies are proposed.

W. S. Gosset faced a similar problem around the turn of the twentieth century when, as a chemist for Guinness Breweries, he was asked to make judgments on the mean quality of various brews. He was supplied with only small sample sizes to reach his conclusions.

Gosset believed that, for small samples, when he used the z statistic

$$\frac{\bar{Y} - \mu_0}{\sigma/\sqrt{n}}$$

with σ replaced by s, he was underestimating the variability in the statistic. He became intrigued by the problem and set out to derive the sampling distribution of the quantity

$$\frac{\bar{Y} - \mu_0}{s/\sqrt{n}}$$

particularly for $n < 30$.

substituting s for σ   The **substitution of s for σ** in the z statistic

$$z = \frac{\bar{Y} - \mu_0}{\sigma/\sqrt{n}}$$

adds a second source of variability in addition to $\bar{Y}$. We suggested the substitution of s for σ provided $n \geq 30$ in Section 8.1. Now we give confidence intervals for μ for any value of $n > 1$. The procedures are very similar to the large-sample results presented earlier.

Gosset derived the sampling distribution for the statistic

$$\frac{\bar{Y} - \mu}{s/\sqrt{n}}$$

and he published his results in 1908 under the nom de plume "Student" because it was against company policy to publish his results. The statistic

$$t = \frac{\bar{Y} - \mu}{s/\sqrt{n}}$$

Student's t   is frequently referred to as **Student's t** and its distribution as Student's t distribution. We can summarize the properties of a t distribution by comparing it to a standard normal (z) distribution.

Properties of Student's t Distribution

1. The t distribution, like the z distribution, is symmetric about the mean $\mu = 0$.
2. The t distribution is more variable than the z distribution (see Figure 8.3).

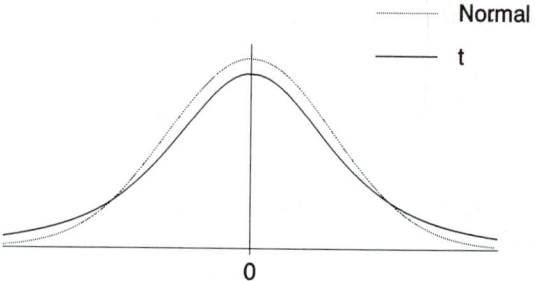

Normal ‑‑‑‑‑‑‑

t ———

0

FIGURE 8.3   A t Distribution with a Normal Distribution Superimposed

3. There are many different t distributions. We specify a particular one by its degrees of freedom, d.f. If a random sample is taken from a normal population, then the statistic

$$t = \frac{\bar{Y} - \mu}{s/\sqrt{n}}$$

has a t distribution with d.f. $= n - 1$.
4. As n increases (or equivalently as the d.f. increase), the distribution of t approaches the distribution of z.

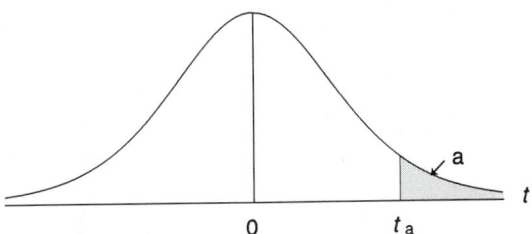

FIGURE 8.4   Illustration of Area Tabulated in Appendix Table 4 for the *t* Distribution

degrees of freedom   A general definition of the term **degrees of freedom** requires n-dimensional geometry and an understanding of linear algebra. We don't go into such detail; rather we try to give an intuitive idea of what the term means. The d.f. refers to the estimated standard deviation and is used to indicate the number of pieces of information available for that estimate. The standard deviation is based on n deviations from the mean; but the deviations must sum to 0, so only $n - 1$ deviations are free to vary. The last (nth) deviation is determined by the other $n - 1$. Therefore, the t statistic is said to have $n - 1$ degrees of freedom.

Although a mathematical formula can be given for the probability density function of the t distribution, it is not important because there are tables to evaluate t probabilities. Because of the symmetry of t, only upper-tail percentage points (probabilities or areas) of the distribution of t have been tabulated. These appear in Appendix Table 4. The degrees of freedom (d.f.) are listed along the left-hand column of the page. An entry in the table specifies a value of t, say, t_a, such that an area a lies to its right (see Figure 8.4). Various values of a appear across the top of the page. Thus, for example, with d.f. = 7, the value of t with an area .05 to its right is 1.895 (found in the $a = .05$ column and d.f. = 7 row).

EXAMPLE 8.8   If a random sample of size $n = 15$ is taken from a normally distributed population, find

$$P\left(\frac{\bar{Y} - \mu}{s/\sqrt{n}} > 2.145\right)$$

and

$$P\left(-2.145 \le \frac{\bar{Y} - \mu}{s/\sqrt{n}} \le 2.145\right)$$

Solution   We must use the t table, Appendix Table 4, with $n - 1 = 14$ d.f. The table indicates values that cut off specific right-tail areas. In particular, $P(t_{14\,\text{d.f.}} > 2.145)$ is shown to be .025, so

$$P\left(\frac{\bar{Y} - \mu}{s/\sqrt{n}} > 2.145\right) = .025$$

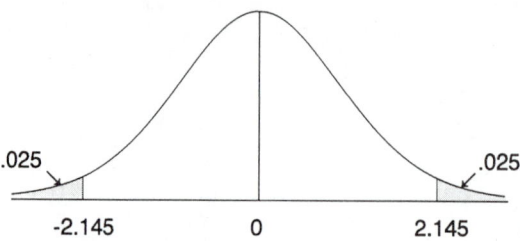

FIGURE 8.5   *t* Distribution with 14 d.f.

(see Figure 8.5). The *t* distribution is symmetric around zero, so the left-tail area $P(t_{14\,\text{d.f.}} < -2.145) = .025$ also. The remaining area after both tails are cut off is .95, so

$$P\left(-2.145 \leq \frac{\bar{Y} - \mu}{s/\sqrt{n}} \leq 2.145\right) = .95$$ ∎

An examination of the *t* table indicates the effect of changing from

$$z = \frac{\bar{Y} - \mu}{\sigma/\sqrt{n}}$$

to

$$t = \frac{\bar{Y} - \mu}{s/\sqrt{n}}$$

For very small *n*, *t* table values are quite large, and for d.f. = 2, the right-tail area of .025 is cut off at 4.303. As the d.f. increases, the *t* table values for a given tail area decrease. At the bottom line, which has infinite degrees of freedom, the *t* table contains the normal distribution (*z*) values.

This phenomenon can be explained by considering how the *t* distribution arises. We get a *t* statistic by replacing the true standard deviation σ by the sample standard deviation *s*, thus introducing an additional source of random variation. When *n* is small, the value of *s* can vary widely from the value of σ, and the *t* distribution must have quite a large variance. As *n* gets larger, there is less random variation of *s* from σ and the *t* distribution's variance gets smaller. As *n* approaches infinity, *s* approaches σ and the only important source of randomness is $\bar{Y}$; the *z* distribution accounts for the variation of $\bar{Y}$ around μ.

When we first discussed replacing σ by *s*, we used a rule that we could use the *z* tables if *n* was greater than or equal to 30. The *t* table values for 30 d.f. are fairly close to normal table values, except for very small tail areas. But there's no need to preserve this rule any longer. We may as well use the *t* tables routinely for all *t* statistics. If the actual d.f. are not shown in the table, rough interpolation is accurate enough for almost all purposes. Alternatively, a conservative approach is to use the next lower d.f. that appears in the table.

EXAMPLE 8.9

For a random sample of size 46 from a normal population, find the cutoff point for a right-tail area of .025; that is, find $t_{.025}$ such that

$$P\left(\frac{\bar{Y} - \mu}{s/\sqrt{n}} > t_{.025}\right) = .025$$

Solution

There are $n - 1 = 45$ d.f. The table entries for 40 and 60 d.f. are 2.021 and 2.000, respectively. As the actual 45 d.f. is closer to 40 than to 60, $t_{.025}$ ought to be closer to 2.021 than to 2.000. We can use a simple diagram, such as that shown here, to find the interpolated value of t.

t value	2.021	$t = ?$		2.000
d.f.	40	45		60

Because 45 is 1/4 the distance from d.f. = 40 to d.f. = 60, we want a t value that is 1/4 the distance from 2.021 to 2.000. With $.021/4 = .005$, the desired t value is $2.021 - .005 = 2.016$. ■

Alternatively, we could go from 45 d.f. to the next lower d.f. in the table, namely 40, and simply use the table value 2.021. This is a conservative choice and close enough for many purposes.

SECTION 8.4 EXERCISES

8.21 A random sample of size 4 is to be taken from a normal population with mean $\mu = 100$. Let

$$t = \frac{\bar{Y} - 100}{s/\sqrt{4}}$$

Evaluate the following probabilities:
a. $P(t > 1.638)$ d. $P(-2.353 < t < 2.353)$
b. $P(t > 5.841)$ e. $P(|t| > 3.182)$
c. $P(t < -2.353)$ f. $P(|t| > 4.541)$
Draw pictures.

8.22 Suppose that the t statistic in Exercise 8.21 is mistakenly assumed to have a normal (z) distribution. Evaluate $P(t > 1.638)$ and $P(|t| > 1.638)$ under this erroneous assumption. Does this assumption cause an overstatement or an understatement of the probabilities?

8.23 A Monte Carlo study is made by taking 1100 samples, each of size 4, from the normal population of Exercise 8.21. The t statistic is defined in that exercise. The results of the study are summarized as follows:

Event	Frequency
$t < -2.353$	44
$-2.353 < t < -1.638$	59
$-1.638 < t < 1.638$	896
$1.638 < t < 2.353$	47
$t > 2.353$	54

a. What are the theoretical relative frequencies?
b. Is there any evidence of a systematic departure from these theoretical relative frequencies?

8.24 For a t statistic with 72 degrees of freedom, use rough interpolation to find 90th, 95th, and 99th percentiles.

8.5 CONFIDENCE INTERVALS WITH THE t DISTRIBUTION

The mathematical development of Section 8.4 can be used to state inference procedures for a mean, which can be used in the typical case that the population standard deviation is not known. This section is devoted to confidence intervals.

The changes in the confidence-interval procedure when σ is unknown are easy enough. Replace the unknown σ by s to get an estimated standard error $s/\sqrt{n}$; use t tables instead of z tables.

EXAMPLE 8.10   Calculate a 95% confidence interval for the population mean if a sample of size $n = 25$ from a nearly normal population yields a sample mean of 96.2; assume that the population standard deviation is 15.0. Recalculate the interval assuming that the population standard deviation is unknown and that the sample standard deviation is 16.2.

Solution   We may use the procedures of Section 8.1 for the first problem:

$$\bar{y} - z_{\alpha/2}\frac{\sigma}{\sqrt{n}} \leq \mu \leq \bar{y} + z_{\alpha/2}\frac{\sigma}{\sqrt{n}}$$

$$96.2 - 1.96\frac{(15.0)}{\sqrt{25}} \leq \mu \leq 96.2 + 1.96\frac{(15.0)}{\sqrt{25}}$$

$$90.32 \leq \mu \leq 102.08$$

In the second problem, we need the t table value for $n - 1 = 24$ d.f. This value must cut off combined left- and right-tail areas of .05 so the desired right-tail area is .025. The t table value is 2.064. Replace $\sigma = 15.0$ by $s = 16.2$ and $z_{.025} = 1.96$ by $t_{.025} = 2.064$.

$$96.2 - 2.064\frac{(16.2)}{\sqrt{25}} \leq \mu \leq 96.2 + 2.064\frac{(16.2)}{\sqrt{25}}$$

$$89.51 \leq \mu \leq 102.89$$

This interval is wider than the previous one because $t_{.025} > z_{.025}$, and also because in this case $s = 16.2$ happens to be greater than the assumed $\sigma = 15.0$.

The general t confidence interval for μ based on a t distribution with d.f. $= n - 1$ is shown here:

$100(1 - \alpha)\%$ Confidence Interval for μ, with σ Unknown

$$\bar{y} - t_{\alpha/2}\frac{s}{\sqrt{n}} \le \mu \le \bar{y} + t_{\alpha/2}\frac{s}{\sqrt{n}}$$

where $t_{\alpha/2}$ is the tabulated t value cutting off a right-tail area of $\alpha/2$, with $n - 1$ d.f.

---

small-sample confidence interval

This formula is often called a **small-sample** confidence interval for the mean, but it is valid for *any* sample size. For a large sample size, the difference between using t tables and z tables is negligible, so the importance of the t versus z distinction is greatest for small sample sizes. The assumption of a normal population is most crucial for small sample sizes, where the Central Limit Theorem has relatively little effect.

EXAMPLE 8.11

An airline has four ticket counter positions at a particular airport. In an attempt to reduce waiting lines for customers, the airline introduces the "snake system." Under this system, all customers enter a single waiting line that winds back and forth in front of the counter. A customer who reaches the front of the line proceeds to the first free position.

Each weekday for three weeks, the airline customer-relations manager charts the waiting time in minutes for the first customer entering after 4 P.M. One observation is excluded because of an unusual condition: The airport was fogged in and many flight plans had to be changed. The data are

| 4.3 | 5.2 | 2.1 | 6.2 | 5.8 | 4.7 | 3.8 | 9.3 | 5.0 | 4.1 | 6.0 | 8.7 | 0.5 | 4.9 |

Find a 95% confidence interval for the long-run mean waiting time on weekdays under normal conditions.

Solution

First calculate $\bar{y} = 5.043$ and $s = 2.266$. The t table value (13 d.f., one-tail area .025) is 2.160. The interval is

$$5.043 - 2.160\frac{(2.266)}{\sqrt{14}} \le \mu \le 5.043 + 2.160\frac{(2.266)}{\sqrt{14}}$$

or

$$3.735 \le \mu \le 6.351$$

It would be better to report this, rounded off to roughly the accuracy of the data, as $3.7 \le \mu \le 6.4$. ∎

sample size required for estimating μ

One of the important uses of confidence intervals is in determining the sample size required to yield a desired degree of statistical accuracy. Accuracy is defined by the level of confidence and the width of the interval. Recall that when we assume σ is known and specify the degree of confidence $100(1 - \alpha)\%$ and the desired confidence interval width $2E$, we find the desired sample size by solving the equation

$$\frac{z_{\alpha/2}\sigma}{\sqrt{n}} = E$$

for n. Now we would like to find n by solving $t_{\alpha/2}s/\sqrt{n} = E$, but there are two difficulties. First, s is not known until the sample is taken, and second, we do not have the d.f. for $t_{\alpha/2}$ until n is specified. The first problem can be handled either by using a rough, ballpark guess for s or by specifying the desired width as some fraction of a standard deviation. (An error in estimating a mean to within .01 standard deviation would be dwarfed by the variation of individual values from the mean, while an error of 1.00 standard deviation would be pretty substantial.) The second problem can be solved by making a preliminary assumption that n is large enough that z can be substituted for t. If the resulting n turns out to be small, trial and error (in the direction of increasing n) usually gets an answer quickly.

EXAMPLE 8.12   Suppose that in Example 8.11 a 95% confidence interval with a plus-or-minus tolerance of half a standard deviation is desired. What sample size is needed?

Solution E is to be $.5s$. For the moment, assume that we can use the z table value 1.96 as an approximation to $t_{.025}$. Solving the equation

$$\frac{1.96s}{\sqrt{n}} = .5s$$

for n, we get

$$n = \frac{(1.96s)^2}{(.5s)^2} = 15.4$$

For $n = 16$ (15 d.f.) we would use $t_{.025} = 2.131$ instead of 1.96 and get an actual value of E equal to

$$\frac{2.131s}{\sqrt{16}} \approx .533(s)$$

which is a bit too large. Try $n = 18$ (17 d.f.); $t_{.025} = 2.110$, and

$$\frac{2.110s}{\sqrt{18}} \approx .497(s)$$

so $n = 18$ will do.   ∎

SECTION 8.5   EXERCISES

8.25   A manufacturer of cookies and crackers does a small survey of the age at sale of one of its brands. A random sample of 23 retail markets in a particular region is chosen. In each store, the number of days since manufacture of the frontmost box of crackers is determined by a date code on the box.

The data (age in days, arranged from lowest to highest) are

27	34	36	36	38	39	39	39	40	40	42	45	47	51	52
57	63	71	75	84	96	110	147							

a. Verify that $\bar{y} = 56.87$ and $s = 28.97$.

b. Calculate a 99% confidence interval for the true mean age.

8.26 Suppose that the manufacturer in Exercise 8.25 wants to obtain a 90% confidence interval with a width of no more than six days. Assuming that the sample standard deviation does not change, how large a sample is needed?

8.27 A consumer group wants to estimate the average delivered price of a certain model of refrigerator in the New York metropolitan area. Prices are determined by comparison shoppers at 14 randomly selected stores in the area. The dollar prices (including taxes) are

| 341 | 347 | 319 | 331 | 326 | 298 | 335 | 351 | 316 | 307 | 335 | 320 | 329 | 346 |

Calculate a 95% confidence interval for the true mean.

8.28 A random sample of 20 taste-testers rate the quality of a proposed new product on a 0–100 scale. The ordered scores are

16	20	31	50	50	50	51	53	53	55	57	59	60	60	61	65
67	67	81	92												

a. Calculate a 95% confidence interval for the population mean score. Should t tables or z tables be used?

b. Plot the data. Is there any reason to think that the use of a mean-based confidence interval is a poor idea?

8.29 A furniture mover calculates the actual weight as a proportion of estimated weight for a sample of 31 recent jobs. The sample mean is 1.13 and the sample standard deviation is .16.

a. Calculate a 95% confidence interval for the population mean using t tables.

b. Assume that the population standard deviation is .16. Calculate a 95% confidence interval for the population mean using z tables.

c. Are the intervals calculated in parts (a) and (b) of roughly similar size?

8.30 When the data underlying Exercise 8.29 are plotted, the plot shows a strong skewness to the right. Does this indicate that the nominal 95% confidence level may be in error?

8.6   ASSUMPTIONS FOR INTERVAL ESTIMATION   ∎

Any statistical method involves assumptions. Some assumptions are general and apply to a wide variety of methods; others are specific to a particular method. We'll have a lot to say about assumptions in future chapters. Because interval estimation of a single parameter (whether it be a mean, a proportion, or a median), is a relatively simple concept, we can deal with the issues of assumptions and assumption violation most clearly in this context.

First, we should emphasize that the methods in this chapter apply only to random samples. The allowance for error inherent in confidence intervals is only an allowance for *random* error; no allowance is made for any biases in data collection. If the data underlying a confidence interval have been collected in a lazy, convenient sample, the confidence interval is very likely to be wrong simply because of the biases in data collection. There are no known methods to compensate for the biases in badly chosen samples.

Within the context of legitimate random samples, there are some specific assumptions that can be problematic. One key assumption is **independence within samples**. All the methods described in this chapter assume that the observations are independent of each other. Not all random-sampling methods yield independent observations. For example, suppose that a real-estate assessor chooses 22 city blocks of homes to evaluate from the tax lists of a city, and then assesses the market value of all homes in each block. Assuming that the assessor does, in fact, choose the blocks randomly, there is no systematic bias in favor of low-value homes or high-value homes. But there is a dependence problem. Given the well-established tendency of high-value homes to cluster together (and low-value homes to occur in bunches), if one home in the sample has higher than average values, so do adjacent homes. The assessment may involve, say, 300 homes; however, the method does not give 300 separate, independent measurements of home values. In fact, the data arising from the assessor's evaluations would be more appropriately evaluated by the cluster-sampling methods we will describe in Chapter 18.

The most common source of problems with the assumption of independence occurs in **time-series** data, data collected in a well-defined chronological order. Suppose, for example, that we measure the dollar volume of back orders for a particular manufacturer on 20 consecutive Friday afternoons. It's reasonable to suppose that a high back-order volume on one Friday is likely to be followed by high back-order volumes on succeeding Fridays, and the same for low volumes. The standard error formulas that we use in confidence intervals depend very heavily on the assumption of independence of observations. When there is dependence, the standard error formulas may underestimate the actual uncertainty in an estimate. Even for modest dependencies, the degree of underestimation may be serious.

In effect, dependence means that we don't have as much information as the value of n indicates. Consider the extreme dependence that would arise in a sample of 25 observations if the first observation was genuinely random, but every succeeding observation had to equal the first one. The confidence interval formula would be based on a sample of 25, but in fact we'd only have a sample of 1.

Whenever the data are taken in time order, it's a good idea to plot the observations against time. If the observations are really independent, there should be no pattern in the plot; the data should look random. Any clear pattern—cycles or trends—in this plot is reason for concern about independence. For example, look for a pattern in the Minitab plot of weekly worker absences in Figure 8.6. There is a clear up-down-up cyclic pattern in the data. We wouldn't be at all happy with an assumption of independence.

Beyond the assumption of independence, methods for means involve an assumption that the underlying population is normally distributed. **In practice, no population is exactly normal**. When we use t-distribution methods for a mean, we are assuming that the underlying population is normal, and this assumption is guaranteed to be more or less wrong.

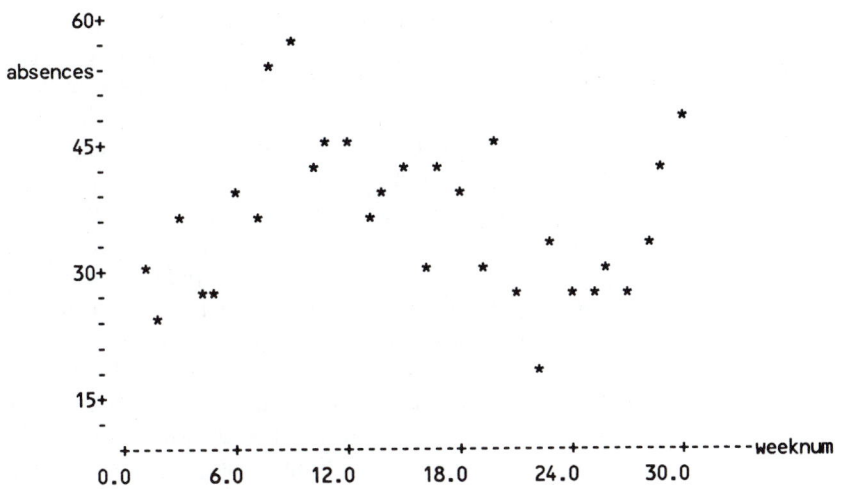

FIGURE 8.6   Plot of Absences by Week

There are two types of issues to consider when populations are assumed to be nonnormal. First, what kind of nonnormality is assumed, and second, what possible effects do these specific forms of nonnormality have on the t-distribution procedures? The most important deviations from normality are skewed distributions and heavy-tailed distributions. (Heavy-tailed distributions show up in otherwise roughly symmetric data by the occurrence of outliers.)

In order to evaluate the effect of nonnormality as exhibited by skewness or heavy tails, we consider whether the t-distribution procedures are still approximately correct for these forms of nonnormality and whether there are other more efficient procedures. Even if a confidence interval for μ based on t gives nearly correct results for, say, a heavy-tailed population distribution, there may be a more efficient procedure (which gives a smaller confidence interval width) based on a trimmed mean.

The question of approximate correctness of t procedures has been studied for quite a long time. The general conclusion of these studies is that the probabilities specified by the t procedures, particularly the confidence level, are fairly accurate even when the population distribution is heavy-tailed (or light-tailed).

sensitivity of one-tailed procedures
In contrast, skewness, particularly with small sample sizes, can have a nasty effect on these probabilities, particularly in one-tailed procedures. A t distribution is symmetric, of course. When the population distribution is skewed, the actual sampling distribution of a t statistic is skewed. The skewness decreases as the sample size increases, but there is no magic sample size that completely deskews the actual sampling distribution.

The second question, that of the efficiency of t procedures, has only recently been studied seriously. There has been a near-unanimous conclusion from these studies. When the population distribution is symmetric but heavy-tailed, various

robust methods
robust procedures are more efficient than the standard t procedures. Virtually all robust procedures eliminate or give low weight to the few largest and smallest observations in the sample. The ordinary sample mean gives equal weight to all

observations and is sensitive to extreme sample values. Therefore when the population distribution is heavy-tailed, robust procedures tend to give more accurate estimates and have smaller standard errors than the ordinary sample mean.

Unfortunately, less work has been done on the effectiveness of these robust procedures when the population distribution is skewed. A 20% trimmed mean, which averages the middle 80% of the data values, is unquestionably a biased estimator of the population mean when the population is skewed. Whether this bias is compensated for by a lower standard error is an open mathematical and conceptual question. However, it would be worrisome to have an estimator with a small standard error that always overestimated the population parameter.

So what is a nonexpert manager to do? First of all, *look at the data.* One of the serious dangers of using available statistical software is that statistical analyses may be done, untouched by human minds. A simple histogram of the data, or some other plotting device, reveals any gross skewness or extreme outliers. We can also calculate the coefficient of skewness for the sample data (see Chapter 2). If there's no blatant nonnormality, the nominal t-distribution probabilities should be reasonably correct and the t procedure should be reasonably efficient. If the data values are obviously skewed or heavy-tailed, the t-distribution probabilities and the efficiency of the t procedure are highly suspect. Whenever possible, you should try something else in these situations. For example, we present a confidence interval for a population median in Section 8.7. Because the median is not as affected by outliers as is the mean, this can be used as an alternative to the interval based on the t statistic.

Other robust procedures are mentioned in this text, but we cannot do complete justice to them. We expect that these procedures will be integrated into some of the statistical software systems in the next few years. If such programs are not available, a manager can at least cultivate an alert skepticism about the accuracy of the stated probabilities.

8.7   CONFIDENCE INTERVALS FOR A MEDIAN   ∎

As early as Chapter 2 we noted that a median is less sensitive than a mean to gross skewness or outliers in data. Therefore we sometimes want to make inferences based on a median rather than a mean. Inferences about a median turn out to be relatively robust methods when the assumption of population normality is shaky. That is, median inferences are generally more believable than mean inferences when the assumptions underlying mean inference are violated. Even when there are large sample sizes, so that mean inferences can be based on the Central Limit Theorem, median inferences may be more precise and efficient. This phenomenon occurs particularly when the data are outlier-prone.

One might expect the confidence interval for a median to follow the conventional "estimate plus or minus table value times standard error" format. It doesn't. Instead, a reformulation of the problem, based on the idea that roughly half the sample data should be above the population median and half below, reduces the problem to a binomial situation.

order statistics   This interval is based on **order statistics**. The kth order statistic in a sample of n measurements is the kth smallest value in the sample. Thus the smallest measurement is the first order statistic, the largest measurement is the nth order statistic, and for an odd number of measurements the sample median is the $(n + 1)/2$th order statistic. A procedure for using order statistics to get a confidence interval for a median is outlined here.

100(1 − α)% Confidence Interval for a Median

1. For a sample of size n, use binomial tables with that n and $\pi = .50$. Add probabilities until just before the total exceeds $\alpha/2$. Call the number of successes at which this occurs k. If the value of n is not in the tables, use the approximate value $k = .5n - .5z_{\alpha/2}/\sqrt{n}$, rounded down.
2. Order the data from lowest to highest, and count $k + 1$ values from each end; that is, find the $k + 1$st and $n - k$th order statistics. These values are the endpoints of the confidence interval.

EXAMPLE 8.13   An insurance adjuster obtains estimates from two garages for repairs on foreign cars that had been damaged in a collision. The adjuster was most interested in the difference of the estimates. A sample of 16 differences was obtained.

Car:	1	2	3	4	5	6	7	8	9	10	11	12	13	14	15	16
Difference:	.3	1.1	1.1	−.2	.3	.5	.4	.9	.2	.6	.3	1.1	.8	.9	.9	.7

Find a 95% confidence interval for the population median of differences.

Solution   For $n = 16$ and $\alpha/2 = .025$, we can see from binomial tables that

$$P(y \leq 3 \,|\, n = 16, \pi = .50) = .0105$$

and

$$P(y \leq 4 \,|\, n = 16, n = .50) = .0383$$

We therefore take $k = 3$. Then the 95% confidence interval for the population median has lower and upper limits of the 4th and 13th order statistics, respectively. For these data, the differences, arranged in order, are

$$-.2 \quad .2 \quad .3 \quad \underset{\uparrow}{.3} \quad .3 \quad .4 \quad .5 \quad .6 \quad .7 \quad .8 \quad .9 \quad .9 \quad \underset{\uparrow}{.9} \quad 1.1 \quad 1.1 \quad 1.1$$

$$\quad\quad\quad\quad\quad\quad \text{4th} \quad\quad\quad\quad\quad\quad\quad\quad\quad\quad\quad\quad\quad \text{13th}$$

The 95% confidence interval for the population median is thus

$$.3 \leq \text{population median} \leq .9$$

EXAMPLE 8.14   Give the order statistics that provide the lower and upper 90% confidence limits for a population median based on $n = 100$ measurements.

Solution   We could use Appendix Table 1. Alternatively, the value of k is the greatest integer less than

$$.5n - .5z_{\alpha/2}\sqrt{n}$$

For $n = 100$ and $\alpha/2 = .05$, we have

$$.5(100) - .5(1.645)10 = 41.775$$

so $k = 41$. The appropriate confidence limits are the 42nd and 59th order statistics.   ∎

There's no reason to use median-based intervals when sampling from a normal population. In that situation, as we know from Chapter 7, the sample mean is the most efficient (smallest standard error) unbiased estimator; when the population is normal, a t (or z) interval has the narrowest, most precise range. But when the data are severely outlier-prone, mean intervals may well have a larger plus-or-minus range than median intervals. Once again, it's useful to plot the data to see which method is most meaningful and appropriate.

EXAMPLE 8.15   A taste test of a proposed new product involved 50 customers rating taste appeal on a 0.0 (best) to 9.9 (worst) scale. The following ratings were obtained.

0.8	1.0	2.9	3.0	3.4	3.5	3.7	3.7	3.8	3.9	4.1	4.1	4.2
4.2	4.2	4.3	4.3	4.3	4.3	4.3	4.3	4.4	4.4	4.4	4.4	4.4
4.4	4.5	4.5	4.5	4.5	4.5	4.5	4.6	4.6	4.6	4.6	4.7	4.7
4.7	4.8	4.8	4.8	4.9	4.9	4.9	5.1	5.1	6.7	6.8		

The mean rating for the 50 tasters is 4.300; the standard deviation is 0.966.

    a. Plot the data. What is the general shape? Are there any outliers?
    b. Calculate a 90% confidence interval for the mean.
    c. Calculate a 90% confidence interval for the median.
    d. According to part (a), which interval should be shorter? Is it?

Solution   a. A stem-and-leaf display or a histogram indicates that the data are close to symmetric. By eye, there seem to be several outliers. The "hinges" (25th and 75th percentiles) are 4.2 and 4.7, giving an IQR of $4.7 - 4.2 = 0.5$. The inner fences are $4.2 - 1.5(0.5) = 3.45$ and $4.7 + 1.5(0.5) = 6.45$. Seven of the 50 scores fall beyond these fences, strongly suggesting that we are sampling from an outlier-prone population.

    b. There is no t table entry for $50 - 1 = 49$ d.f.; conservatively, we use the entry for 40 d.f. and a $(1 - .90)/2 = .05$, 1.684. The interval is

$$4.300 - 1.684\frac{(0.966)}{\sqrt{50}} \le \mu \le 4.300 + 1.684\frac{(0.966)}{\sqrt{50}}$$

or

$$4.07 \le \mu \le 4.53$$

    c. Adding binomial probabilities with $n = 50$ and $\pi = .50$ from the table, we find $P(Y \le 18) = .0313$ and $P(Y \le 19) = .0583$. Thus we take $k = 18$ and the 90% confidence interval ranges from the $k + 1 = 19$th value, 4.3, to the $n - k = 32$nd value, 4.5.

$$4.3 \leq \text{median} \leq 4.5$$

d. We have indicated that using a median is more efficient (gives shorter confidence intervals) when the data are outlier-prone. The confidence interval for the median has width $4.5 - 4.3 = 0.2$; the confidence interval for the mean has width 0.46. ■

EXAMPLE 8.16   A normal plot for the data of Example 8.15, constructed using Minitab, is shown here. Does the plot confirm the judgment of the shape of the data made in Example 8.15?

```
MTB > plot 'rating' vs 'nscores'

           -                                                    *    *
           -
      6.0+
           -
rating     -                                                  2
           -                                          3  3  3
           -                              3    6   6   6   4
      4.0+                          **2
           -                  *  *  2
           -                     *
           -               *
           -
      2.0+
           -
           -          *
           - *
           -
         --------+---------+---------+---------+---------+--------nscores
             -1.60     -0.80      0.00      0.80      1.60
```

Solution   In Example 8.15 we concluded that the data were outlier-prone. The normal plot clearly shows the **S**-shape that is characteristic of outlier-prone data. ■

SECTIONS 8.6 AND 8.7   EXERCISES

8.31   Refer to the data of Exercise 8.27 (page 305).
   a. Plot a histogram or stem-and-leaf display of the data.
   b. Is there any obvious reason to doubt the approximate correctness of the 95% confidence level?

8.32   Using the data of Exercise 8.27, find a 95% confidence interval for the true median price.

8.33   A clothing manufacturer tested a computerized system for cutting bolts of cloth. The main concern was the amount of wasted cloth; a skilled (and expensive) cutter averaged 11.3% waste. A random sample of 18 patterns is chosen and the waste percentage of the computerized system is found. The data are as follows:

10.6   11.3   11.6   11.6   11.8   12.0   12.1   12.2   12.4
12.6   12.8   13.0   13.2   13.3   13.6   13.9   14.3   14.9

(mean 12.622, standard deviation 1.113)
a. Calculate a 95% confidence interval for the mean.
b. Calculate a 95% confidence interval for the median.

8.34   Consider the data of Exercise 8.33.

a. Construct a stem-and-leaf display of the data. Is there clear evidence of nonnormality?

b. What does your answer to part (a) indicate about the relative efficiency of the sample mean versus the sample median? Is your answer confirmed by the relative widths of the two confidence intervals found in Exercise 8.33?

8.35   If a computer program is available to you, construct a normal plot of the data of Exercise 8.33. Does the plot show obvious nonnormality?

8.8   CONFIDENCE INTERVALS FOR A STANDARD DEVIATION

Until now, we've concentrated on confidence intervals for averages (means or medians). In many situations, especially quality control, variability is just as important as average values. Reducing variability is obviously an important goal in mass production of items: A company that produced "3 inch" bolts, half of which were 2.4 inches long and the other half 3.6 inches long, wouldn't be in business for long. Variability is also important in service organizations: If an automatic teller machine made us wait an average of 15 seconds (5 seconds 90% of the time and 105 seconds 10% of the time), we'd be unhappy 10% of the time. One of the most reasonable ways to measure variability is a standard deviation. Therefore, in this section, we turn to confidence interval inference about a standard deviation.

chi-square distribution   The method this section uses a new theoretical (sampling) distribution, the chi-square (χ^2) **distribution**. In the appendix to this chapter, we show that, for independent measurements from a normally distributed population or process, the quantity $(n - 1)(s^2/\sigma^2)$ has a chi-square distribution with $n - 1$ degrees of freedom. Therefore, we need to use χ^2 tables to obtain a confidence interval for a standard deviation. In contrast to the z and t distributions, the χ^2 distribution is not symmetric; therefore, the use of χ^2 tables is a bit more complicated.

Appendix Table 5 gives percentage points—values that cut off a specified right-tail area α. For instance, the value that cuts off a right-tail area of $\alpha = .05$ for a χ^2 distribution with 5 d.f. is 11.07 (see Figure 8.7a). To find a *left*-tail point we must look up the complementary area. For example, the value that cuts off a left-tail area of .05 corresponds to a right-tail area of .95. The tabled value for $\alpha = .95$ and d.f. = 5 is 1.15. A quick sketch like Figure 8.7b clarifies the situation. For large d.f., an approximate value is

$$\chi_a^2 \approx \left(\frac{z_a}{\sqrt{2}} + \sqrt{\text{d.f.} - .5} \right)^2$$

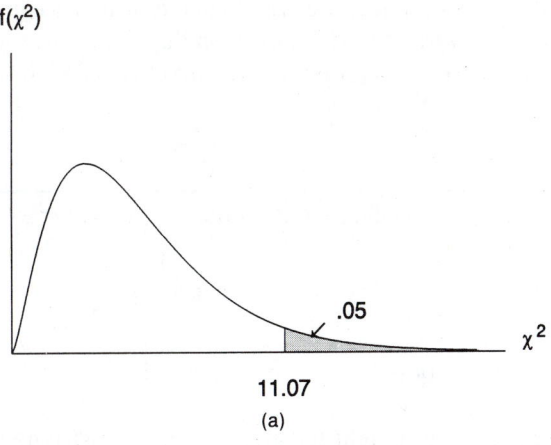

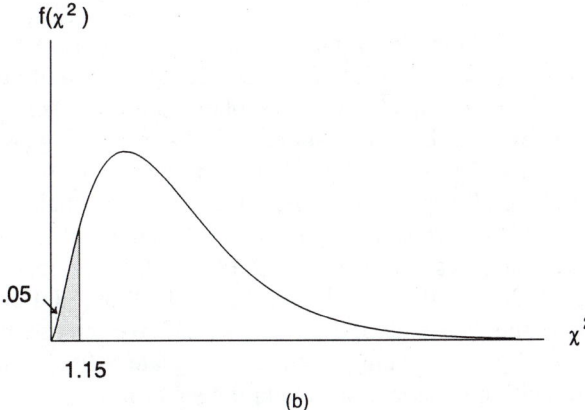

FIGURE 8.7 χ^2 Distribution with d.f. = 5: (a) Upper .05 Value; (b) Lower .05 Value

EXAMPLE 8.17   Use Appendix Table 5 to find values that cut off right-tail and left-tail areas equal to .025, for a χ^2 distribution with 29 d.f. Use the large d.f. approximation to ascertain these same values.

Solution   For the right-tail value, we look in the $a = .025$ column and the 29 d.f. row and find $\chi^2_{.025} = 45.72$. For the left-tail value, we must use the complementary area, $a = .975$; the entry for 29 d.f. is $\chi^2_{.975} = 16.05$. To use the large d.f. approximation, we note that $z_{.025}$ is the now-familiar 1.96. The approximate $\chi^2_{.025}$ value is

$$\chi^2_{.025} \approx (1.96/\sqrt{2} + \sqrt{28.5})^2 = 45.22$$

For the left-tail, the required z-table value must cut off a *left*-tail area of .025 and a right tail area of .975; this value is $z_{.975} = -1.96$. The approximate χ^2 value for the left tail is

$$\chi^2_{.975} \approx (-1.96/\sqrt{2} + \sqrt{28.5})^2 = 15.62$$

Even for 29 d.f., the large d.f. approximation is reasonably accurate.   ∎

The tabled values are used to find a confidence interval for the population (or process) variance. The corresponding confidence interval for the standard deviation may be found by taking square roots of the confidence limits for the variance.

$100(1 - \alpha)\%$ Confidence Intervals for σ^2 and σ

$$\text{For } \sigma^2: (n - 1)\frac{s^2}{\chi^2_{\alpha/2}} \leq \sigma^2 \leq (n - 1)\frac{s^2}{\chi^2_{1-\alpha/2}}$$

$$\text{For } \sigma: \sqrt{(n - 1)\frac{s^2}{\chi^2_{\alpha/2}}} \leq \sigma \leq \sqrt{(n - 1)\frac{s^2}{\chi^2_{1-\alpha/2}}}$$

where χ^2_a cuts off a right-tail area a in the χ^2 distribution with $n - 1$ d.f.

For example, a motel chain operates an 800 number for telephone reservations. One index of service quality is the waiting time, including time on hold, from the first ring of the phone until an agent answers, ready to make reservations. The chain's standard is that the average waiting time should be no more than 30 seconds. The chain has inspectors who travel to the various motels, checking all aspects of service. The inspectors make 30 reservation calls each week and record, among other indicators, the waiting time for each call. For one week, the times in seconds are 12, 13, 13, 14, 14, 14, 15, 15, 16, 17, 17, 18, 18, 19, 19, 25, 25, 26, 27, 30, 33, 34, 35, 40, 40, 51, 51, 58, 59, 83. For this sample, the mean is 28.37 and the standard deviation is 17.37. We can use the table values (16.05 and 45.72) found in Example 8.17 to calculate a 95% confidence interval for the population variance and standard deviation.

$$\frac{(30 - 1)(17.37)^2}{45.72} \leq \sigma^2 \leq \frac{(30 - 1)(17.37)^2}{16.05}$$

or

$$191.38 \leq \sigma^2 \leq 545.16$$

Taking square roots, we get the 95% confidence interval for the waiting time standard deviation.

$$13.83 \leq \sigma \leq 23.35$$

The interval indicates that there is a great deal of variability in waiting times, even though the standard for the mean seems to be met.

EXAMPLE 8.18   A pharmaceutical company manufactures a certain kind of antihistamine tablet. It is important to limit the variability of potency from one tablet to another. The quality control department routinely tests random samples of tablets from each batch. The nominal potency of each tablet is 25 milligrams and the measured potencies of 30 tablets in one sample are

24.1	27.2	26.7	23.6	26.4	25.2
25.8	27.3	23.2	26.9	27.1	26.7
22.7	26.9	24.8	24.0	23.4	25.0
24.5	26.1	25.9	25.4	22.9	24.9
26.4	25.4	23.3	23.0	24.3	23.8

Construct a 95% confidence interval for the standard deviation of tablet potency.

Solution   The usual calculations show that $\bar{y} = 25.097$ and $s^2 = 2.1583$. Because $n = 30$, there are 29 d.f. From Appendix Table 5, the $X^2_{1-\alpha/2}$ and $\chi^2_{\alpha/2}$ values for a 95% confidence interval are $\chi^2_{.975} = 16.05$ and $\chi^2_{.025} = 45.72$. Therefore the 95% confidence interval for σ^2 is

$$(29)\frac{2.1583}{45.72} \leq \sigma^2 \leq (29)\frac{2.1583}{16.05}$$

or

$$1.369 \leq \sigma^2 \leq 3.900$$

Taking square roots, the 95% confidence interval for σ is

$$\sqrt{1.369} \leq \sigma \leq \sqrt{3.900}$$

or

$$1.17 \leq \sigma \leq 1.97 \qquad \blacksquare$$

The justification for this confidence interval is that the event

$$(n-1)\frac{s^2}{\chi^2_{\alpha/2}} \leq \sigma^2 \leq (n-1)\frac{s^2}{\chi^2_{1-\alpha/2}}$$

is algebraically identical to the event

$$\chi^2_{1-\alpha/2} \leq \frac{(n-1)s^2}{\sigma^2} \leq \chi^2_{\alpha/2}$$

We know that $(n-1)s^2/\sigma^2$ has a χ^2 distribution with $n-1$ d.f. and that $\chi^2_{1-\alpha/2}$ and $\chi^2_{\alpha/2}$ cut off left- and right-tail areas of $\alpha/2$, respectively. The probability of the event (the confidence level) is therefore the desired value $1 - \alpha$.

Chi-square inferences about a standard deviation or variance are particularly sensitive to the assumption of a normal population or process. If the population is not normal, claimed probabilities like the confidence level can be seriously wrong. A claimed 95% confidence interval may actually have only an 80% probability (or even less) of including the correct value. The reason is that nothing in the procedure (except the table values, which assume normality) accounts for the uncertainty of the sample variance. The Central Limit Theorem is no help at all; that's a theorem about sample means, not about sample variances. Therefore, it is even more important than usual to plot the data; if the data appear nonnormal, the claimed confidence level is not believable.

Jackknife method

An alternative confidence interval is based on the **jackknife method**, which is a general computer-intensive approach. To perform the jackknife method, leave out one observation at a time from the sample, and recompute the variance. If you've left out a typical value, the variance won't change much; but if you've left out an outlier, the variance will decrease sharply. Thus the jackknife method will warn you if you're dealing with outlier-prone data because the leave-one-out variances will vary greatly. Obviously, you want to jackknife a variance by computer, not by hand; a computer program for that purpose will handle the technical details. (If you must know: The computer calculates "pseudo-values" as n times the logarithm of the variance minus $n-1$ times the logarithm of leave-one-out variances, and then does a t confidence interval using the pseudo-values. You may have to convert back from logarithms, but otherwise you can leave the dirty work to the program.) The jackknife approach does not assume a normal population, and the claimed probability does get more accurate as the sample size gets larger; therefore, it is more believable than the chi-square interval in cases where a data plot suggests nonnormality.

The reservation waiting time data we considered earlier in this section are definitely right skewed, so a jackknife confidence interval ought to be more honest than a χ^2 interval. A Minitab "macro" did the work; we should focus on the results, not the computations.

```
MTB > let k1=1
MTB > execute 'knife1'
MTB > let c50=ck1
MTB > let k2=sum(c50)
MTB > let k3=ssq(c50)
MTB > let k4=count(c50)
MTB > let c49=((k3-c50**2)-((k2-c50)**2)/(k4-1))/(k4-2)
MTB > let c48=2*k4*loge(stdev(c50))-(k4-1)*loge(c49)
MTB > tinterval of c48
             N     MEAN    STDEV   SE MEAN    95.0 PERCENT C.I.
C48         30     5.790    2.333    0.426    (  4.919,   6.661)  MTB > end
MTB > let k5=exponential(4.919)
MTB > let k6=exponential(6.661)
MTB > note k5 and k6 are confidence limits for the variance
MTB > print k5 and k6
K5       136.866
K6       781.332
```

The jackknife interval $136.87 \le \sigma^2 \le 781.33$ is wider then the χ^2 interval $191.38 \le \sigma^2 \le 545.16$ that we found previously. But the claimed 95% confidence for the jackknife interval is far more believable than the claimed 95% confidence of the σ^2 interval, given the nonnormality of the sample data.

EXAMPLE 8.19

A jackknife 95% confidence interval for the standard deviation of tablet potency, based on the data of Example 8.18, is $1.581 \le \sigma^2 \le 3.034$. A stem-and-leaf display of the data is basically flat with nothing close to an outlier. Is there a reason to prefer the jackknife interval to the σ^2 interval $1.369 \le \sigma^2 \le 3.900$ found in Example 8.18?

Solution   There is no indication of skewness or outliers, so the claimed confidence of the χ^2 interval should be reasonably accurate, as should the confidence level for the jackknife. Both are believable, but the jackknife interval is narrower so it is preferable.   ∎

SECTION 8.8   EXERCISES

8.36   Suppose that Y has a χ^2 distribution with 27 d.f.
  a. Find $P(Y > 46.96)$.
  b. Find $P(Y > 18.11)$.
  c. Find $P(Y < 12.88)$.
  d. What is $P(12.8786 < Y < 46.9630)$?

8.37   For a χ^2 distribution with 11 d.f.,
  a. find $\chi^2_{.025}$;
  b. find $\chi^2_{.975}$.

8.38   Suppose that Y has a χ^2 distribution with 277 d.f. Find approximate values for $\chi^2_{.025}$ and $\chi^2_{.975}$.

8.39   A retail seller of modern-design wooden furniture imports many of its items from northern Europe. The furniture is shipped unassembled in flat, compact packages, to economize on shipping costs. The customer assembles the item at home. The customer certainly can't be expected to do high-precision woodworking, so the furniture parts must fit very well. For one popular model, the customer must insert four round legs into predrilled holes. For proper fit, the diameter of the legs must be just slightly less than one centimeter. Inevitably, there is variation in the leg diameters, mostly due to wear on cutting tools and imperfections in the wood; the seller specifies that the mean diameter should be 0.995 centimeters and that the standard deviation should be less than 0.030 centimeters. The seller buys the legs from two suppliers. Random samples of 121 legs from each of the two suppliers were obtained as part of standard quality control procedures. The data for supplier A were analyzed by Minitab, with the following results:

```
MTB > print 'supplA'

SupplA
  0.937   0.947   0.957   0.962   0.963   0.963   0.964   0.967   0.970
  0.970   0.972   0.972   0.973   0.974   0.974   0.975   0.977   0.977
  0.978   0.978   0.978   0.979   0.979   0.980   0.980   0.981   0.981
  0.982   0.982   0.982   0.983   0.983   0.984   0.984   0.985   0.986
  0.986   0.987   0.987   0.987   0.987   0.989   0.989   0.989   0.990
  0.990   0.991   0.991   0.991   0.992   0.992   0.992   0.992   0.993
  0.993   0.993   0.993   0.994   0.995   0.995   0.997   0.997   0.997
  0.998   0.998   0.998   0.999   0.999   1.000   1.000   1.000   1.000
  1.000   1.001   1.001   1.002   1.002   1.002   1.002   1.002   1.002
  1.003   1.003   1.003   1.004   1.004   1.005   1.005   1.005   1.006
  1.006   1.006   1.007   1.008   1.008   1.008   1.009   1.010   1.011
  1.011   1.011   1.012   1.012   1.015   1.015   1.017   1.018   1.019
  1.020   1.021   1.023   1.023   1.024   1.025   1.025   1.025   1.026
  1.028   1.029   1.032   1.038

MTB > describe 'supplA'

               N     MEAN   MEDIAN   TRMEAN    STDEV   SEMEAN
SupplA       121  0.99516  0.99700  0.99548  0.01825  0.00166

              MIN      MAX       Q1       Q3
SupplA    0.93700  1.03800  0.98250  1.00600
```

a. Calculate a 95% confidence interval for the standard deviation of the entire lot of several thousand legs.

b. According to this confidence interval, is it plausible that the true standard deviation is larger than 0.030 centimeters?

8.40 a. The confidence interval in Exercise 8.39 was two-sided. Why might a one-sided, upper-bound confidence interval be more useful?

b. Calculate a 95% upper-bound interval for the standard deviation. What does the interval indicate about the possibility that the true standard deviation is larger than 0.030 centimeters?

8.41 A Minitab macro sequence called "knife1" has been constructed to perform jackknife calculations for a single-sample variance. The results for the data of Exercise 8.39 are shown below.

a. Identify the 95% confidence interval for the population variance.

b. Is this interval much different than the one found in Exercise 8.39?

```
MTB > let k1=1
MTB > execute 'a:knife1'
MTB > let c50=ck1
MTB > let k2=sum(c50)
MTB > let k3=ssq(c50)
MTB > let k4=count(c50)
MTB > let c49=((k3-c50**2)-((k2-c50)**2)/(k4-1))/(k4-2)
MTB > let c48=2*k4*loge(stdev(c50))-(k4-1)*loge(c49)
MTB > tinterval of c48
```

	N	MEAN	STDEV	SE MEAN	95.0 PERCENT C.I.
C48	121	-8.117	1.540	0.140	(-8.394, -7.840)

```
MTB > end
MTB > let k5=expon(-8.394)
MTB > let k6=expon(-7.840)
MTB > note k5 and k6 are the jackknife confidence limits for sigma squared
MTB > print k5 k6
K5        0.000226221
K6        0.000393669
```

8.42 Data and analysis for the second supplier are shown on the next page.

a. Obtain 95% confidence intervals for the standard deviation, using both chi-square and jackknife methods. Are the intervals close to the same?

b. If you had to make a decision, which supplier would you say probably has greater variability? Are the samples informative enough that you can make the choice with near certainty?

Summary

Interval estimation yields a specification of a reasonable range of values for a population parameter. It gives an explicit indication of the degree of uncertainty in an estimate. The form of a confidence interval for a population or process mean is

estimator $\pm$ (table value)(standard error)

where the table value comes from a z table in the (usually unrealistic) case that the population standard deviation is known, and from a t table in the (usually

```
SupplB
 0.907    0.921    0.936    0.945    0.946    0.946    0.948    0.951    0.955
 0.956    0.959    0.959    0.961    0.962    0.963    0.963    0.966    0.967
 0.967    0.968    0.969    0.969    0.970    0.971    0.971    0.973    0.973
 0.973    0.974    0.974    0.975    0.976    0.977    0.978    0.978    0.979
 0.980    0.981    0.981    0.982    0.982    0.984    0.985    0.985    0.985
 0.987    0.987    0.987    0.988    0.989    0.989    0.990    0.990    0.990
 0.991    0.991    0.991    0.993    0.993    0.993    0.996    0.996    0.997
 0.997    0.997    0.997    1.000    1.000    1.000    1.001    1.001    1.001
 1.001    1.002    1.003    1.004    1.004    1.004    1.004    1.004    1.005
 1.005    1.005    1.006    1.006    1.007    1.008    1.009    1.009    1.010
 1.010    1.011    1.012    1.012    1.013    1.013    1.015    1.016    1.017
 1.017    1.018    1.019    1.019    1.023    1.024    1.027    1.027    1.029
 1.031    1.033    1.036    1.036    1.036    1.039    1.039    1.039    1.040
 1.043    1.045    1.050    1.059

MTB > describe 'SupplB'

                N      MEAN    MEDIAN    TRMEAN     STDEV    SEMEAN
SupplB        121    0.99378   0.99600   0.99422   0.02740   0.00249

                MIN       MAX        Q1        Q3
SupplB      0.90700   1.05900   0.97450   1.01050

MTB > let k1=2
MTB > execute 'a:knife1'
MTB > let c50=ck1
MTB > let k2=sum(c50)
MTB > let k3=ssq(c50)
MTB > let k4=count(c50)
MTB > let c49=((k3-c50**2)-((k2-c50)**2)/(k4-1))/(k4-2)
MTB > let c48=2*k4*loge(stdev(c50))-(k4-1)*loge(c49)
MTB > tinterval of c48

               N     MEAN    STDEV   SE MEAN     95.0 PERCENT C.I.
C48          121   -7.273    1.541     0.140   ( -7.550,  -6.995)

MTB > end
MTB > let k7=expon(-7.550)
MTB > let k8=expon(-6.995)
MTB > note k7, k8 are jackknife conf. limits for the SupplB variance
MTB > print k7 k8
K7       0.000526110
K8       0.000916453
```

Minitab for Exercise 8.42

realistic) case that it's not. This same form applies to many, but not all, confidence intervals, with differing standard error formulas for other statistics. Confidence intervals for medians, which require binomial tables, and standard deviations, which require chi-square tables, are intervals that aren't of this form.

Efficient estimators yield precise, narrow confidence intervals. The choice of a confidence interval method depends on the nature of the underlying population or process. Once again, plots of the data can indicate whether skewness or outliers would dictate using something other than a mean.

Deciding on the desired width of a confidence interval and then solving for the required *n* is one useful way of determining how large a sample should be taken. This principle applies by trial and error in many situations; a formula can be given for the specific case of random sampling and a mean.

KEY FORMULAS: Interval Estimation

1. $100(1 - \alpha)\%$ confidence interval for μ, with σ known

$$\bar{y} \pm z_{\alpha/2}\sigma_{\bar{Y}}, \qquad \text{where } \sigma_{\bar{Y}} = \frac{\sigma}{\sqrt{n}}$$

Note that $z_{\alpha/2}$ is the normal table value cutting off a right-tail area equal to $\alpha/2$.

2. $100(1 - \alpha)\%$ confidence interval for π

$$\hat{\pi} \pm z_{\alpha/2}\sqrt{\frac{\hat{\pi}(1 - \hat{\pi})}{n}}$$

3. Sample size required to obtain a $100(1 - \alpha)\%$ confidence interval with width $2E$ for μ

$$n = \frac{z_{\alpha/2}^2\sigma^2}{E^2}$$

4. Sample size required to obtain a $100(1 - \alpha)\%$ confidence interval with width $2E$ for π

$$n = \frac{z_{\alpha/2}^2\hat{\pi}(1 - \hat{\pi})}{E^2}$$

where $\hat{\pi}$ may be estimated from previous information or, conservatively, taken as .50

5. $100(1 - \alpha)\%$ confidence interval for μ

$$\bar{y} \pm t_{\alpha/2}\frac{s}{\sqrt{n}}$$

where $t_{\alpha/2}$ is based on d.f. $= n - 1$

6. $100(1 - \alpha)\%$ confidence interval for median

$$(k + 1)\text{th order statistic } \leq \text{median} \leq (n - k)\text{th order statistic}$$

where

$$P(\text{number of successes} \leq k) \leq \frac{\alpha}{2}$$

and

$$P(\text{number of successes} \leq k + 1) > \frac{\alpha}{2}$$

in Appendix Table 1, $\pi = .50$. For large n, $k \approx .5n - .5z_{\alpha/2}\sqrt{n}$.

7. $100(1 - \alpha)\%$ confidence interval for variance

$$(n - 1)\frac{s^2}{\chi_{\alpha/2}^2} \leq \sigma^2 \leq (n - 1)\frac{s^2}{\chi_{1-\alpha/2}^2}$$

CHAPTER 8   EXERCISES

8.43   A random sample of the year-end statements of 22 small businesses (under $500,000 in yearly sales) in a city shows that the sample mean of gross margin on sales is 5.2% and the standard deviation is 3.3%. Use these results to calculate a 90% confidence interval for the population mean, where the population is (the gross margin of) the several thousand small businesses in the city.

8.44   Refer to Exercise 8.43. Obviously the gross margin of a functioning business can't be negative. The Empirical Rule for two standard deviations would indicate that a substantial fraction of the businesses have negative gross margins.

a. Is it likely that the sample data would appear nearly normal?

b. What does your answer to part (a) indicate about the confidence interval calculated in Exercise 8.43?

8.45   A research project for an insurance company wishes to investigate the mean value of the personal property held by urban apartment renters. A previous study suggested that the population standard deviation should be roughly $10,000. A 95% confidence interval with a width of $1000 (a plus or minus of $500) is desired. How large a sample must be taken to obtain such a confidence interval?

8.46   It could be argued that the data of Exercise 8.45 would be quite skewed, with a few individuals having very large personal-property values. Therefore (the argument goes) the confidence interval would be completely invalid. Is the argument correct?

8.47   Many individuals over the age of 40 develop an intolerance for milk and milk-based products. A dairy has developed a line of lactose-free products that are more tolerable to such individuals. To assess the potential market for these products, the dairy commissions a market research study of individuals over 40 in its sales area. A random sample of 250 individuals shows that 86 of them suffer from milk intolerance. Calculate a 90% confidence interval for the population proportion that suffers milk intolerance based on the sample results.

8.48   A follow-up study to the survey of Exercise 8.47 is planned. A 90% confidence interval is to be constructed. What sample size is needed to estimate the population proportion with an error of no more than .02, under the following conditions?

a. Assume that the sample proportion is approximately the same as that found in Exercise 8.47.

b. Now assume that the population proportion may be anything.

8.49   Shortly before April 15 of a particular year, a team of sociologists conduct a survey to study their theory that tax cheaters tend to allay their guilt by holding certain beliefs. A total of 500 adults are interviewed and asked under what situations they think cheating on an income tax return is justified. The responses include these:

56% agree that "other people don't report all their income."
50% agree that "the government is often careless with tax dollars."
46% agree that "cheating can be overlooked if one is generally law abiding."

Assuming that the data are a simple random sample of the population of taxpayers (or taxnonpayers), calculate 95% confidence intervals for the population proportion that agrees with each statement.

8.50   An editorial writer, commenting on the study of Exercise 8.49, claims that the opinion of 500 individuals out of the total number of taxpayers in the United States is virtually worthless; these might be the "cheatingest" 500 people in the entire country. Criticize this editorial stand.

8.51   The caffeine content (in milligrams) of a random sample of 50 cups of black coffee dispensed by a new machine is measured. The mean and standard deviation are

100 milligrams and 7.1 milligrams, respectively. Construct a 98% confidence interval for the true (population) mean caffeine content per cup dispensed by the machine.

8.52 The machine in Exercise 8.51 is capable of dispensing 3000 cups per day. The caffeine content varies because of variation in caffeine content of the ground coffee beans and because of variation in brewing time.

a. Is the study in Exercise 8.51 questionable because such a small fraction of the machine's output is analyzed?

b. The 50 cups sampled are taken consecutively from the machine. Does this make the study questionable?

8.53 A random sample of the year-end financial statements of a sample of 22 small (under $500,000 in sales) retail businesses in a city show that the average net margin on sales is .0210 and the standard deviation is .0114. Find a 90% confidence interval for the mean net margin for all small retail businesses in the city.

8.54 Tax records indicate that there were 9783 small retail businesses in Exercise 8.53. The sample was taken without replacement. Is it crucial to correct the confidence-interval computations for the without-replacement sampling?

8.55 The data in Exercise 8.53 indicate the the distribution of net margins has a peak at about .015, with some businesses having much larger margins but none having lower margins. What does this fact indicate about the claimed 90% confidence interval?

8.56 A random sample of 100 scores was obtained. The data and Minitab output are shown here.

```
values
40    42    45    47    48    48    49    49    50    51    51    52    53
54    55    55    55    55    56    56    56    56    56    56    57    57
57    57    58    58    58    58    58    59    59    59    59    59    59
60    60    60    60    60    60    60    60    60    61    61    61    61
61    62    62    62    62    63    63    63    64    64    64    65    65
65    65    65    66    66    66    66    66    67    67    67    67    67
67    67    68    68    68    68    69    69    69    69    70    70    72
72    72    73    73    74    76    79    81    81
```

MTB > describe 'values'

	N	MEAN	MEDIAN	TRMEAN	STDEV	SEMEAN
values	100	61.460	61.000	61.478	7.845	0.784

	MIN	MAX	Q1	Q3
values	40.000	81.000	57.000	67.000

MTB > tinterval with 95% confidence for 'values'

	N	MEAN	STDEV	SE MEAN	95.0 PERCENT C.I.
values	100	61.460	7.845	0.784	(59.903, 63.017)

a. Draw a stem-and-leaf display or a histogram. What is the general shape of the data?

b. Should the confidence interval for the mean be wider or narrower than a 95% confidence interval for the median?

c. Calculate a 95% confidence interval for the median. Does the result agree with your answer to part (b)?

8.57 A normal plot of the data in Exercise 8.56, done using Minitab, is shown on the next page. Does the plot confirm your judgment made in part (a) of Exercise 8.56?

MTB > plot 'values' vs 'nscores'

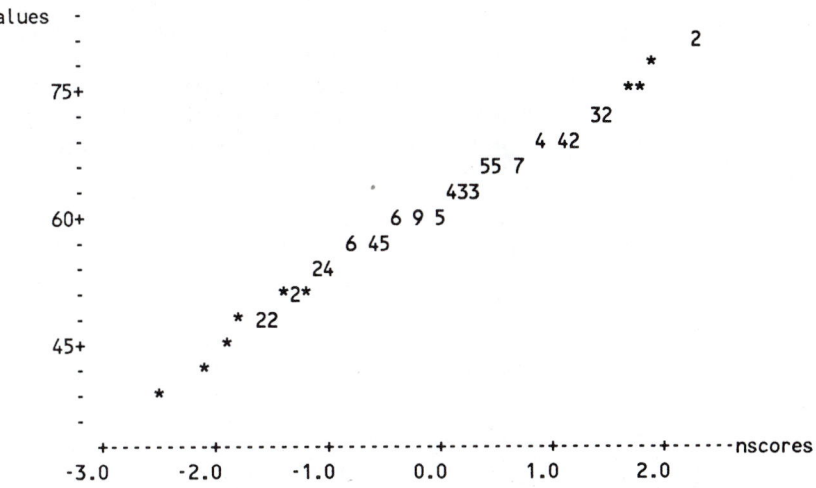

8.58 The police department of a medium-sized city recorded the response time to nonemergency crime calls, usually ones involving burglary or car theft. The times in minutes for 29 calls recorded during one week were thought of as a random sample from the ongoing process. The output from Minitab is shown here.

a. Calculate a 90% confidence interval for the process (long-run) mean time, assuming that the long-run process standard deviation is 6.0 minutes. Locate the result in the output.

b. Recalculate the confidence interval without assuming that the long-run standard deviation is known. Locate this result in the output.

c. Why did the second interval come out wider than the first?

```
MTB > print 'resptime'

resptime
    24    25    18    25    15    11    11    19    36    29    13    21    12
    12    26    16    19    12    21    12    12    18    11    19    16    24
    14    23    17

MTB > describe 'resptime'

                    N      MEAN    MEDIAN    TRMEAN    STDEV    SEMEAN
resptime           29     18.31     18.00     17.93     6.29      1.17

                  MIN       MAX        Q1        Q3
resptime        11.00     36.00     12.00     23.50

MTB > zinterval with 90% confidence sigma = 6.0 data 'resptime'

THE ASSUMED SIGMA =6.00

                    N      MEAN     STDEV    SE MEAN    90.0 PERCENT C.I.
resptime           29     18.31     6.29       1.11    (  16.48,    20.15)

MTB > tinterval with 90% confidence data 'resptime'

                    N      MEAN     STDEV    SE MEAN    90.0 PERCENT C.I.
resptime           29     18.31     6.29       1.17    (  16.32,    20.30)
```

8.59 Plot the data of Exercise 8.58 in a stem-and-leaf display or a histogram. Does it appear that the distribution of response times is approximately normal?

8.60 A state fish hatchery raises trout for stocking streams and lakes. The size of the fish at release time can be controlled to a fair degree by varying the rate of feeding. The target is a mean of 10 ounces; if the fish are too small, those who catch the fish aren't happy, but if the fish are too large, those who buy the feed aren't happy. A sample of 61 fish are weighed at release time. The weights, to the nearest tenth of an ounce, are as follows:

9.3	11.7	11.0	9.8	10.1	8.9	8.7	9.5	10.8	8.7	7.6
10.0	8.8	9.3	9.2	8.1	9.9	9.4	8.3	10.3	9.8	9.5
9.8	9.0	10.7	9.3	9.6	10.4	9.4	9.8	9.8	9.2	11.0
10.2	9.1	11.0	9.4	9.7	12.1	9.8	7.1	8.3	10.3	10.6
10.1	10.2	8.8	9.3	10.3	10.7	10.8	7.5	9.0	10.1	9.2
9.7	10.4	9.1	9.7	10.7	10.6					

mean = 9.6803, standard deviation = 0.95983.

a. Calculate a 95% confidence interval for the mean weight of the entire group of many, many thousands of fish. Should the indicated standard deviation be regarded as a population or a sample standard deviation?

b. Does the confidence interval indicate that the hatchery is clearly not meeting its 10-ounce goal?

8.61 Obtain a stem-and-leaf display of the data of Exercise 8.60. Does the plot indicate that the distribution of weights is roughly normal? If not, would that invalidate the confidence interval that we calculated in Exercise 8.60?

8.62 The data for Exercise 8.60 were obtained by dividing the fish randomly into batches intended for different destinations. Then some fish within each batch were taken out (as randomly as possible). One might suspect that larger fish would be netted first and put into the first few batches. A plot of fish weights against batch numbers is shown below. Is there a clear indication that the weights are decreasing as batch number increases?

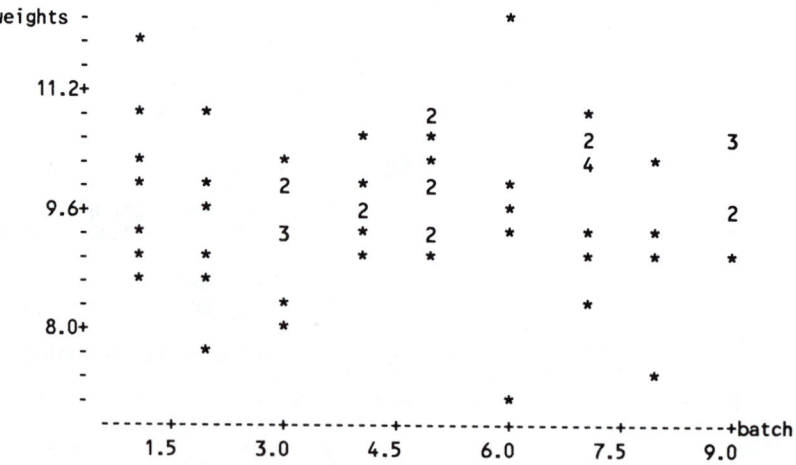

8.63 a. Use the data of Exercise 8.60 to calculate a 95% confidence interval for the population standard deviation.

b. The hatchery hopes for a standard deviation of weights of 0.75 ounces. Does the confidence interval of part (a) indicate that that target is not met in this case?

8.64 A manufacturer of mesh screening tries to limit the number of defects per thousand feet to no more than 5. The defects usually are broken wires in the mesh or "blobs" of paint. Each day, 24 sample sections of wire, each 500 feet long, are inspected for defects. The following data are of defects found in the sampled sections.

```
3   4   3   0   6   1   0   2   1   3   4   4   3   6
4   4   3   4   5   2   1   0   5   2
```

n	mean	median	standard deviation
24	2.917	3.000	1.792

   a. Calculate a 99% confidence interval for the mean number of defects in the entire day's production of many thousands of 500-foot sections.
   b. According to the manufacturer's goal, what should the mean number of defects in 500-foot sections equal? Does the confidence interval indicate that this value is not plausible?

8.65 The data of Exercise 8.64 were collected by visual inspection of the screen for defects. Suppose that the inspection on this particular day was not as thorough as it should have been. What bias should this introduce? Should the confidence interval be too low or too high as a result?

8.66 a. In Exercise 8.64, the mean-minus-two-standard-deviations value is a negative number of defects. What does this fact suggest about the shape of the data?
   b. Plot the data. Does the picture confirm your answer in part (a)?

8.67 a. Calculate a 90% confidence interval for the true population standard deviation of the number of defects.
   b. Assuming that the distribution of number of defects is not normal, what is the effect on the confidence interval for the standard deviation?

8.68 A manufacturer of floppy disks for personal computers is concerned about the reported number of bad sectors when a disk is formatted for a particular computer. A sample of 36 disks is selected from each day's production and it is formatted. The reported size of the bad sectors on each disk, in thousands of bytes, is recorded. Output from one day's data is shown here.

```
MTB > print 'badsects'

badsects
    4.92   10.20   12.88    1.05   12.09    4.54    5.96    7.36   17.21
    6.97    4.69   14.79   15.53   12.43    8.00    7.97    4.85    0.94
    3.91    0.49    7.57    1.03    6.02   26.43    4.19    7.07   48.93
    5.47   26.03    0.63    5.77    1.68    3.68   31.68    3.21    5.43

MTB > stem and leaf of 'badsects'

Stem-and-leaf of badsects   N  = 36
Leaf Unit = 1.0


    14      0  00011133344444
   (11)     0  55556677778
    11      1  02224
     6      1  57
     4      2
     4      2  66
     2      3  1
     1      3
     1      4
     1      4  8
```

(continued)

```
MTB > describe 'badsects'

                 N      MEAN    MEDIAN   TRMEAN    STDEV    SEMEAN
badsects        36      9.49      5.99     8.12    10.02      1.67

               MIN       MAX        Q1       Q3
badsects      0.49     48.93      3.98    12.34

MTB > tinterval 95% confidence of 'badsects'

                 N      MEAN     STDEV   SE MEAN     95.0 PERCENT C.I.
badsects        36      9.49     10.02      1.67   (    6.10,    12.88)

MTB > sinterval 95% confidence of 'badsects'

SIGN CONFIDENCE INTERVAL FOR MEDIAN

                                    ACHIEVED
                 N    MEDIAN      CONFIDENCE      CONFIDENCE INTERVAL     POSITION
badsects        36     5.990         0.9348      (    4.850,    7.970)         13
                                     0.9500      (    4.808,    7.978)        NLI
                                     0.9712      (    4.690,    8.000)         12
```

a. Locate the confidence interval (for the mean) based on t distribution methods.

b. Can this interval be interpreted to mean that 95% of the individual disks have between 6.10 and 12.88 thousand bytes of bad sectors?

8.69 a. Locate a 97.12% confidence interval for the population median in the output for Exercise 8.68.

b. Explain why this interval includes such different values than the confidence interval in Exercise 8.68.

8.70 The bad-sector data in Exercise 8.68 was obtained by taking samples from each of several lots. A plot of the data against the lot number is shown following this exercise. Does it indicate that there is either an evident trend or an evident cycle in the data? Does any other aspect of the data show up clearly in the plot?

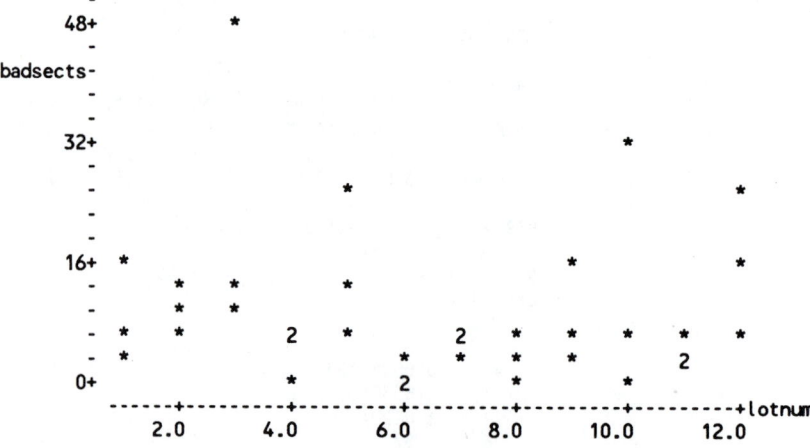

8.71 An automobile rental firm buys new cars and uses them for about six months, then resells them at auction. In effect, the firm is in the used-car futures business. Therefore, the firm wants accurate estimates of the future value of its current fleet of

cars. A consultant proposes a new method of estimating future value. This method
is tried on a sample of cars. The estimates are made initially, the cars are used in the
business, and then the actual auction price for each car is obtained. The data are the
ratio of actual to estimated values for each of 121 cars that had not been damaged
during rental use. The computer output is shown here.

```
MTB > print 'act/est'

act/est
  0.96872    1.02149    1.01100    1.03069    1.01039    1.03266    0.98667
  1.01080    0.96833    1.01814    0.98233    0.98950    1.00423    0.96911
  0.94118    0.97219    1.00409    1.00595    0.98702    0.97397    1.01228
  1.02320    0.97978    0.89570    1.02869    0.99189    1.00378    0.96988
  1.04872    1.01224    0.95713    0.96719    1.07646    1.00463    0.96637
  0.96125    0.95879    0.98965    0.97314    1.02847    1.01319    0.96875
  0.99000    0.99463    1.07783    0.98070    0.95106    1.04667    0.98620
  0.96406    0.96311    1.01996    0.98937    0.99123    1.00000    1.04423
  0.99622    1.06927    0.92623    1.03237    0.99904    1.05807    0.99028
  0.96011    1.03959    0.94857    0.98135    0.93376    1.00000    1.01877
  1.00280    1.02494    0.98779    0.96610    0.94118    0.99445    1.02761
  1.00183    1.04700    0.99011    1.04338    1.06329    0.96900    0.96613
  1.01532    0.99293    1.01865    1.06040    1.03927    0.96418    0.99283
  1.00563    1.05370    0.99537    1.00424    1.00686    1.05361    0.97479
  0.98227    0.97611    1.00074    1.08310    1.01981    1.03604    1.01578
  1.00000    1.00579    0.95124    0.99522    0.96184    0.98585    0.98786
  0.95688    1.02029    0.99295    1.00000    1.00435    1.01088    1.02974
  1.07150    1.01643

MTB > boxplot of 'act/est'


                        ------------
        *     ------------- I    +    I------------------
                        ------------
        ------+---------+---------+---------+---------+---------+act/est
           0.910     0.945     0.980     1.015     1.050     1.085

MTB > tinterval for 'act/est'

               N     MEAN    STDEV  SE MEAN    95.0 PERCENT C.I.
act/est      121   0.99984  0.03404  0.00309  ( 0.99371, 1.00597)

MTB > sinterval for 'act/est'

SIGN CONFIDENCE INTERVAL FOR MEDIAN

                          ACHIEVED
            N    MEDIAN  CONFIDENCE   CONFIDENCE INTERVAL    POSITION
act/est    121   1.000    0.9310     (   0.992,   1.004)        51
                          0.9500     (   0.991,   1.004)       NLI
                          0.9545     (   0.991,   1.004)        50
```

a. Locate the value of the 95% confidence interval for the mean, based on t
   methods.
b. Can the interval be interpreted to mean that the actual price is between 99.371%
   and 100.597% of estimate for 95% of the cars?

8.72 a. Locate the 95.45% confidence interval for the median in the output of Exercise 8.71.

b. Are the confidence intervals for mean and median seriously different for these data? From the boxplot of the data, should the intervals differ much?

8.73 a. Calculate a 95% confidence interval for the population standard deviation, using the data in Exercise 8.71.

b. If the standard deviation is as large as the upper limit of the confidence interval, what can we assume about the accuracy of estimating the price of individual cars?

8.74 The data for Exercise 8.71 were plotted against the actual price of the car to see if there was any trend. Can you see a clear tendency for the ratio of actual to estimate to increase as the actual price increases?

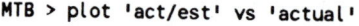

MTB > plot 'act/est' vs 'actual'

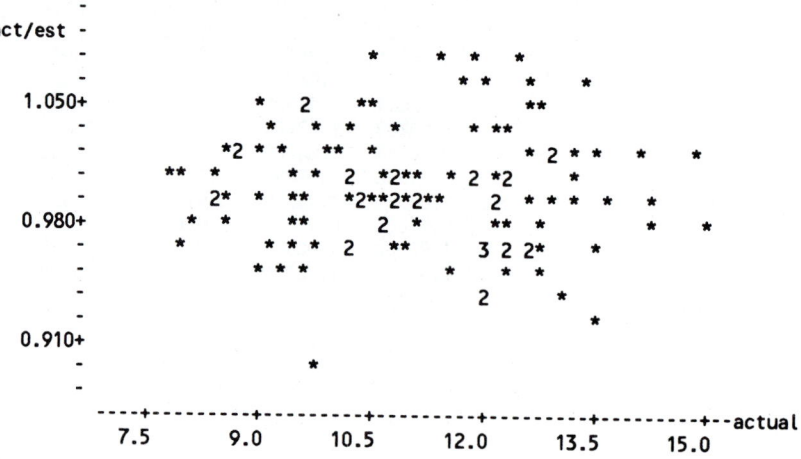

8.75 A restaurant tried to increase business on Monday nights, traditionally the slowest night of the week, by featuring a special $1.00 "Oh, Go Ahead!" dessert menu. The number of diners on each of 12 Mondays was recorded while the special menu was in effect. The data were:

119   139   112   126   121   128   108   63   118   105   131   142
mean 117.67, standard deviation 20.65

a. Calculate a 95% confidence interval for the long-run mean number of diners.

b. Before the special menu, the restaurant averaged 105.2 diners per Monday night. Is it reasonable to interpret the confidence interval from part (a) as indicating that the special menu did not increase the average number of diners?

8.76 a. Use the data of Exercise 8.75 to calculate a confidence interval for the median. Use a confidence level just above 95%, but as close to that figure as possible.

b. How does the width of this interval compare to the width found in Exercise 8.75? Why the difference?

8.77 Use the data of Exercise 8.75 to calculate a 90% confidence interval for the true, long-run standard deviation. Is there any reason to think that the claimed 90% confidence may not be correct?

8.78 A retail lumberyard routinely inspects incoming shipments of lumber from suppliers. For select grade 8-foot 2-by-4 pine shipments, the lumberyard supervisor chooses one gross (144 boards) randomly from a shipment of several tens of thousands of boards. In the sample, 18 boards are not salable as select grade.

    a. Calculate a 95% confidence interval for the proportion of boards in the entire shipment that are not salable as select grade.

    b. If 20% or more of the shipment is not salable as select grade lumber, the shipment is unprofitable. Does the confidence interval indicate that there is reason for concern about possible unprofitability of this shipment?

8.79 a. The lumberyard in Exercise 8.78 must decide how many boards per shipment will be inspected. What sample size is needed to obtain a 95% confidence interval for the proportion of unsalable boards with a width of 0.04? Assume that somewhere between 10% and 20% of a shipment is unsalable.

    b. In this situation, would it be sensible to calculate a sample size based on the worst-case assumption that 50% of the shipment is unsalable?

8.80 a. The sample in Exercise 8.78 is always obtained from the pallet at the right rear of the truckload shipment. A pallet contains 4 gross (576 boards), so the lumberyard selects the 144 gross to sample by rotation—the first shipment, sample upper left; next shipment, sample upper right; and so on. Why isn't this a random sample of the boards? Wouldn't an unethical supplier take advantage of this process?

    b. Do you think it would be feasible to take a simple random sample in this situation? How would you sample to make it more difficult for an unethical supplier to cheat? Of course, there is no single correct answer here.

8.81 An electrical utility offers reduced rates to homeowners who have installed "peak hours" meters. These meters effectively shut off high-consumption electrical appliances (primarily dishwashers and clothes dryers) during the peak electrical usage hours between 3 P.M. and 9 P.M. daily. The utility wants to inspect a sample of these meters to determine the proportion that are not working, either because they were bypassed or because of equipment failure. There are 45,300 meters in use and the utility isn't about to inspect them all.

    a. The utility wants a 90% confidence interval for the proportion with a width of no more than .04. How many meters must be sampled, if one makes no particular assumption about the correct proportion?

    b. How many meters must be sampled if the utility assumes that the true population proportion is between .05 and .15?

    c. Does the assumption in part (b) lead to a substantial reduction in the required sample size?

8.82 The electrical utility in Exercise 8.81 samples 640 meters and finds that 61 are not working, 28 because of bypass and 33 because of equipment failure. Calculate 90% confidence intervals for the population proportions of bypassed meters, equipment-failure meters, and nonworking meters.

8.83 The sample in Exercise 8.82 was obtained by randomly selecting 16 of the 1062 service sectors in the utility's area and inspecting all the meters in each selected sector. Each sector contains 30 to 50 meters. Why isn't this procedure a simple random sample?

8.84 In Exercise 2.66, we considered claims (in thousands of dollars) for automobile collision damage from a particular insurance company. A boxplot of the data is shown in Figure 8.8. Data analysis using the Statgraphics package is shown on the next page.

    a. Interpret the confidence interval for the mean. How critical is it whether the interval is based on t tables or z tables?

    b. Use the confidence interval for the variance to find a 95% confidence interval for the standard deviation.

Box and Whisker Plot

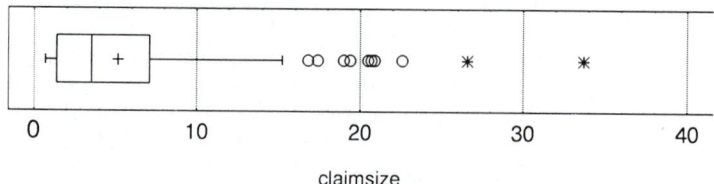

claimsize

FIGURE 8.8   Box Plot of Claim-Size Data

```
                                One-Sample Analysis Results
    ------------------------------------------------------------------------
                                        claimsize
    Sample Statistics: Number of Obs.       187
                       Average           5.17754
                       Variance          27.9194
                       Std. Deviation    5.28388
                       Median            3.5

    Confidence Interval for Mean:         95    Percent
                       Sample 1          4.41509 5.93999      186 D.F.

    Confidence Interval for Variance:     95    Percent
                       Sample 1          23.0123 34.5919      186 D.F.
```

8.85   The box plot in Figure 8.8 indicates that the underlying population distribution is right-skewed. How does this fact affect the credibility of the confidence intervals in Exercise 8.84? Does it affect the credibility of the intervals for the mean and for the variance equally?

8.86   Many newspapers, when reporting results of political polls, say that "with 95% confidence, the results are in error by no more than ± 3 percentage points." The typical sample size is about 1500. The allowance for error is intended to cover both sampling variability and the effect of small biases.
   a. Assume that the poll (sample) indicates that just about 50% of likely voters favor a particular candidate. How large a ± term is required for a 95% confidence interval for the population proportion?
   b. Would the ± term be much different if 40% of likely voters in the sample favored the candidate?
   c. Why is the quoted ± .03 larger than the ± term you calculated in part (a)?

8.87   Consider political polls again, as in Exercise 8.86. When there are many political candidates, as in the early stages of a presidential primary, a particular candidate may be favored by only 2% of poll participants. Given the quoted ± 3 percentage points, the standard joke is that such a candidate may have a negative preference. What ± term should apply, with 95% confidence, if a candidate is favored by 30 of 1500 likely voters in a sample?

8.88   The marketing division of an automobile manufacturer wants to estimate customer satisfaction with a particular new-car dealer, six months after purchase of a car. The marketing managers don't want to use mail surveys because they believe that nonresponse would lead to major biases. Sampling by telephone is feasible because customers' phone numbers are on warranty records. One key question would be "Would you recommend this dealer to your friends and neighbors?" The marketing managers what to estimate the proportion of all customers that would answer "yes," based on a telephone sample.

    a. How large a sample must be taken to obtain a 90% confidence interval for this proportion with a width of .10 (a $\pm$ term of .05)? Use the conservative, worst-case estimate.

    b. Would doubling the sample size cut the width to .05?

8.89 a. By using the worst-case estimate in Exercise 8.88, what are you assuming about customer satisfaction with the dealer? Do you think this would be a sensible assumption in practice?

    b. How would the required sample size in part (a) of Exercise 8.88 change if you assumed that the "yes" proportion would be somewhere between .80 and .95?

8.90 A magazine for attorneys took a sample of 147 law firms to determine the rental cost (in dollars per square foot per year) each law firm is paying for its offices. The data were analyzed using Minitab, with the following results:

```
MTB > describe 'rentals'

             N      MEAN    MEDIAN    TRMEAN     STDEV    SEMEAN
rentals     147    18.366   17.500    18.057     2.949    0.243
            MIN      MAX       Q1        Q3
rentals  15.050   32.550    16.330    19.610

MTB > tinterval 90% confidence based on 'rentals'

             N      MEAN     STDEV    SE MEAN     90.0 PERCENT C.I.
rentals     147    18.366    2.949    0.243    ( 17.963,  18.768)

MTB > sinterval 90% confidence based on 'rentals'

SIGN CONFIDENCE INTERVAL FOR MEDIAN

                             ACHIEVED
             N     MEDIAN   CONFIDENCE    CONFIDENCE INTERVAL    POSITION
rentals     147    17.50     0.9010      ( 17.27,   17.96)         64

MTB > boxplot of 'rentals'
```

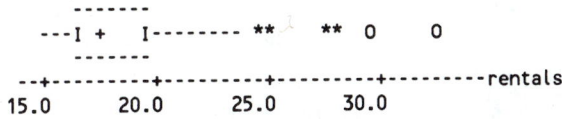

Why are the 'tinterval' and 'sinterval' results so different that they don't overlap at all?

8.91 A sample of 215 urban residents between the ages of 22 and 35 kept diaries for a month recording all expenses on entertainment. The total expenditure for each individual, expressed as a percentage of monthly take-home income, is stored in column 1 of the 'CH8C1.DAT' file on the data disk. (The number of the individual is stored in column 2.) Load the data into a computer program that is available to you.

    a. Obtain the mean and standard deviation of the expenditure sample.

b. Calculate (either by computer or by hand) a 95% confidence interval for the population mean.

c. Interpret the confidence interval carefully.

8.92   a. Obtain a stem-and-leaf display or a boxplot of the expenditure data from Exercise 8.91.

b. On the basis of this plot of the data, is there reason to be concerned that the claimed 95% confidence level in Exercise 8.91 is incorrect?

8.93   An office equipment dealer provides service for leased copiers. All calls for service are logged with the time of request and the time of completion of service. The elapsed times (in minutes) between request and completion for the most recent 61 calls are stored in column 1 of the 'CH8C2.DAT' file on the data disk; column 2 contains the call number, in order from 1 to 61. Load the data into a computer program.

a. Obtain the mean and standard deviation of the elapsed time data.

b. Calculate a 90% confidence interval for the long-run process mean by the program or by hand.

8.94   a. Obtain a normal plot of the elapsed time data for Exercise 8.93. (If the program won't provide that, get a stem-and-leaf display instead.) Does it appear that the data are roughly normally distributed?

b. Have the program plot the elapsed time data against the call number. (The call numbers are the time order of the requests.) Is there an indication of a pattern in this plot? If so, what is indicated about the assumption of independent observations?

8.95   An investment banking firm was considering two spreadsheet programs for possible use in its analysis. A sample of 20 typical analysis problems were carried out using both programs on the firm's standard personal computer. The time in minutes needed to load the data, program the spreadsheet calculations, carry them out, and print the results was recorded for each problem and each program. The data for spreadsheet A is stored in column 1 of the 'CH8C3.DAT' file on the data disk; the corresponding data for spreadsheet B is stored in column 2. Each row of the data corresponds to one of the 20 problems. Load the data into a computer program.

a. Have the program compute the differences of the 20 scores.

b. Obtain a 95% confidence interval for the mean of the differences.

c. Does this confidence interval clearly indicate that either spreadsheet program is better (requires less time on average)?

8.96   a. Obtain a boxplot of the difference data in Exercise 8.95. Are there any outliers?

b. Does it appear that the differences are seriously skewed?

8.97   Calculate (by hand or by computer, at your convenience) a 95% confidence interval for the standard deviation of the differences, using the data in Exercise 8.95.

CASE   Interval Estimation

The benefits manager of a large university was asked to evaluate the costs of a proposed flexible benefits system. Under such a plan, individuals choose a "basket" of benefits best suited to their needs. The most important choices, in terms of cost to the university, are amount of life insurance, amount of medical insurance, and amount of retirement contribution. The benefits manager needed information about the average amounts of each of these choices to assess the university's cost per employee. Each employee would pay part of the cost (above a university-paid minimum), but the university's cost would also increase somewhat with increased benefits.

The manager did not want to survey the entire faculty and staff of the university. First, there were about 17,000 eligible employees, so such a survey would be too large a task. Second, the "flex" plan had not yet been approved, so there was a real danger that a campus-wide survey could be interpreted as a promise that the plan would be available soon. The manager chose to take a sample of eligible employees from the current benefits file. Each employee was interviewed in person, partly to explain the choices and partly to stress the tentative nature of the plan. Data were obtained for 61 employees. The yearly costs, in current dollars, of each employee's choices were calculated. They are the following:

empl	life	medical	retiremt
1	759	1184	915
2	424	239	538
3	157	630	639
4	616	818	862
5	655	867	752
6	559	945	613
7	651	1248	722
8	519	648	750
9	358	361	670
10	456	581	502
11	97	391	590
12	478	837	788
13	129	395	546
14	661	535	633
15	245	472	597
16	602	492	767
17	557	382	706
18	215	672	602
19	331	245	546
20	545	1126	690
21	395	605	748
22	577	435	701
23	345	645	683
24	367	365	540
25	189	181	655
26	716	775	717
27	238	572	507
28	867	776	799
29	475	1123	646
30	369	921	857
31	245	881	724
32	585	740	646
33	472	847	637
34	535	1287	783
35	174	465	481
36	751	1143	794
37	579	751	700
38	666	1098	770
39	596	729	571
40	251	1024	690
41	341	862	409
42	77	398	418
43	225	388	387
44	590	1262	851
45	330	609	742
46	736	1194	667
47	601	713	715
48	555	921	778

empl	life	medical	retiremt
49	775	644	519
50	745	1183	868
51	630	670	715
52	139	790	730
53	521	701	688
54	647	839	683
55	543	529	676
56	699	598	613
57	602	825	759
58	493	1120	882
59	731	481	761
60	267	390	624
61	689	1179	629

The benefits manager wants to know a reasonable range for the average cost to the university of each type of contribution, as well as the average total cost per employee. In addition, the manager's boss wants an idea of how large a survey must be done to estimate that total cost per employee to within plus-or-minus $50. They have asked you to work with the available data and to send them a brief memo answering their questions. Both of them studied statistics some time ago, but they've forgotten most of the concepts, so your report will have to explain any technical terms.

Appendix: The Chi-Square and t Distributions

In this appendix we present a brief sketch of the mathematics underlying the t distribution and the related chi-square (χ^2) distribution. This is the basis for the methods of the preceding chapter and of the next chapters. It should also help to clarify the concept of degrees of freedom.

The formal mathematical assumption is that there are n random variables $Y_1, Y_2, \ldots, Y_n$, each having a normal distribution with mean μ and standard deviation σ; in particular, the assumptions hold for a random sample from a normal population. The corresponding z scores are $Z_1 = (Y_1 - \mu)/\sigma, \ldots,$ $Z_n = (Y_n - \mu)/\sigma$.

First we define the χ^2 distribution with n degrees of freedom (d.f.).

χ^2 Distribution

The χ^2 distribution with n d.f. is the distribution of

$$W = Z_1^2 + \cdots + Z_n^2 = \frac{\sum_i (Y_i - \mu)^2}{\sigma^2}$$

properties of χ^2 distribution

Two properties of the χ^2 distribution follow directly from the definition:

1. If $\bar{Y} = \sum_i Y_i/n$, then $n(\bar{Y} - \mu)^2/\sigma^2$ has a χ^2 distribution with 1 d.f.
2. If W_1 and W_2 are independent random variables having χ^2 distribution with n_1 and n_2 d.f., respectively, then $W_1 + W_2$ has a χ^2 distribution with $n_1 + n_2$ d.f.

The first property follows because $(\bar{Y} - \mu)/(\sigma/\sqrt{n})$ is a z statistic, as shown in Chapter 6. Thus $[(\bar{Y} - \mu)/(\sigma/\sqrt{n})]^2 = n(\bar{Y} - \mu)^2/\sigma^2$ is a Z^2 statistic and can be regarded as a sum with only one term. The definition of a χ^2 distribution implies that $n(\bar{Y} - \mu)^2/\sigma^2$ has a χ^2 distribution with 1 d.f.

The second property follows because both W_1 and W_2 are sums of Z^2 terms, so that $W_1 + W_2$, as a sum of sums, is itself a sum of $(n_1 + n_2)$ Z^2 terms. The assumption of independence of W_1 and W_2 can be shown to allow the assumption that all the Z^2 terms are independent, so that $W_1 + W_2$ has the defining properties of a χ^2 distribution with $n_1 + n_2$ d.f.

These results allow us to relate the χ^2 distribution to the sampling distribution of s^2, the sample variance.

Sampling Distribution of s^2

For a random sample of size n from a normal population, the statistic

$$(n - 1)\frac{s^2}{\sigma^2}$$

has a χ^2 sampling distribution with $n - 1$ d.f.

Recall that $s^2 = \sum(Y_i - \bar{Y})^2/(n-1)$, so that $(n-1)(s^2/\sigma^2) = \sum(Y_i - \bar{Y})^2/\sigma^2$. The proof of the sampling distribution is based on the ideas already developed in this appendix. While we cannot provide a rigorous proof within the scope of this text, we can indicate the basic idea.

The key to the proof is the identity

$$\frac{\sum(Y_i - \mu)^2}{\sigma^2} = \frac{\sum(Y_i - \bar{Y})^2}{\sigma^2} + \frac{n(\bar{Y} - \mu)^2}{\sigma^2}$$

which can be proved by writing $\sum(Y_i - \mu)^2$ as $\sum[(Y_i - \bar{Y}) + (\bar{Y} - \mu)]^2$, expanding the square, and noting that $\sum_{i=1}^{n}(\bar{Y} - \mu)(Y_i - \bar{Y}) = (\bar{Y} - \mu)\sum_{i=1}^{n}(Y_i - \bar{Y}) = 0$.

The quantity $\sum(Y - \mu)^2/\sigma^2$ has, by definition, a χ^2 distribution with n d.f. As we have noted, the $n(\bar{Y} - \mu)^2/\sigma^2$ term has a χ^2 distribution with 1 d.f. Because independent χ^2 statistics add to form χ^2 statistics with more degrees of freedom, it is plausible that the other term $\sum(Y - \bar{Y})^2/\sigma^2$ also has a χ^2 distribution. Further, because degrees of freedom are additive, this term should have $n-1$ d.f. The missing step of the argument is the proof that the two terms on the right side of the equation are independent; this fact is proved only in advanced texts.

These preliminary results on χ^2 distributions are used in developing the t distribution. We first define the t distribution with v d.f.:

t Distribution with v d.f.

The t distribution with v d.f. is the distribution of

$$t = \frac{Z}{\sqrt{W/v}}$$

where Z has a standard normal distribution ($\mu = 0$, $\sigma = 1$) and W a χ^2 distribution with v d.f. Z and W are required to be independent.

We take Z to be $(\bar{Y} - \mu)/(\sigma/\sqrt{n})$ and W to be $(n-1)(s^2/\sigma^2)$, which was just shown to have a χ^2 distribution with $v = n - 1$ d.f. (It can be shown that Z and W are independent.) By definition,

$$t = \frac{\dfrac{(\bar{Y} - \mu)}{\sigma/\sqrt{n}}}{\sqrt{(n-1)\dfrac{s^2}{\sigma^2}\bigg/(n-1)}} = \frac{\bar{Y} - \mu}{s/\sqrt{n}}$$

which is the t statistic used in this chapter.

HYPOTHESIS TESTING

Very often sample data will suggest that something relevant is happening in the underlying population or process. A sample of potential customers may show that a higher proportion prefer a new brand to the existing one. A sampling of telephone response time by reservation clerks may show an increase in mean customer waiting time. A sample of crankshafts produced with a new alloy composition may show a decrease in the standard deviation of metal hardness. In each case, the data are only from a limited sample and therefore they are subject to some degree of random variation.

The question is whether the apparent effect or result in the sample is an indication of something happening in the underlying population (or process) or if the apparent effect is possibly a mere fluke—a result of random variation alone. Statistical hypothesis testing is a means of assessing whether apparent results in a sample conclusively indicate that something is really happening. This chapter is devoted to the basic concepts of hypothesis testing.

We begin in Sections 9.1 and 9.2 with a discussion of a hypothesis test for a proportion, based on binomial probabilities. This test has some practical importance but we discuss it largely as a vehicle to introduce ideas without complicated calculations. Then we turn to a more widely used test for a mean, based on normal probabilities. The mechanics of this z test are set out in Section 9.3 and we consider its theoretical properties in Section 9.4. The p-value of a test, a standard method for indicating the conclusiveness of a test result, is the subject of Section 9.5. With the theory of hypothesis testing established, we can discuss widely used methods: A t test for a mean in Section 9.6, standard checks of assumptions in Section 9.7, a median test in Section 9.8, and an approximate z test for a proportion in Section 9.9. Hypothesis tests and confidence intervals are two ways to deal with the same issue of random variation and uncertainty in samples; the close connection between the two approaches is the topic of Section 9.10. Tests and the related confidence intervals for standard deviations are the subject of Section 9.11. Finally, in Section 9.12, we consider the pros and cons of hypothesis testing as a method for managerial decision making.

Hypothesis testing involves quite a few new concepts and definitions, plus a number of formulas for carrying out computations. While working on these, try not to lose sight of the basic idea. Sample data is subject to random variation, so apparent results from the sample may be misleading. How conclusive is the evidence that sample results indicate a real, more-than-random effect in the underlying population or process?

There are almost always several ways to carry out a hypothesis test. One can carry out a formal test using a five-step procedure described in this chapter, or one can compute a *p*-value to do the test, or one can use a confidence interval as a hypothesis test. These methods are equivalent; they will all lead to the same conclusion. The formal, five-step method is easiest to grasp initially, the *p*-value method is commonly used by computer packages, and the confidence interval approach is easy to interpret (and hard to misinterpret). They are all useful, equivalent ways to solve the problem.

9.1   A TEST FOR A BINOMIAL PROPORTION   ∎

Preliminary market research for a new product often involves a sample of consumers who compare the product to a competitor or to an older version of the product. Suppose that 100 customers indicate a preference either for the new product or for an older version. What results from the sample would conclusively indicate that the new product was superior?

This problem can most easily be handled by using hypothesis testing ideas. There are four key concepts: the null hypothesis, the research hypothesis, the test statistic, and the rejection region.

research hypothesis

The market researchers have a **research hypothesis**—that the new product is superior to the old one. Formally, a research hypothesis, denoted H_a, is a statement about a population parameter. In the example, the relevant parameter is the proportion π of customers in the entire population (not just the sample) who prefer the new product. To say that the new product is superior is to say that more than half of all customers prefer the new product; that is, $H_a: \pi > .50$.

null hypothesis

The **null hypothesis**, denoted H_0, is the denial of the research hypothesis H_a. As the name suggests, the null hypothesis often has a negative quality. In the market research example, if $\pi \leq .50$, the new product is *not* preferred to the older version. We call $H_0: \pi \leq .50$ the null hypothesis because it negates or denies our research hypothesis. Later, we see that the boundary value between H_0 and H_a ($\pi = .50$ in the market research example) is the crucial value of π for the test.

one-sided and two-sided hypotheses

The research hypothesis may be either **one-sided** (directional) or **two-sided** (nondirectional). In the example, we specify a particular direction for H_a relative to H_0. $H_a: \pi > .50$ is a one-sided hypothesis. In contrast, had we specified H_a: $\pi \neq .50$, we would have had a two-sided, nondirectional research hypothesis. The purpose of the study determines the choice of one-sided or two-sided research hypotheses. In comparing a new product to an old one, we want to see if the new product is better, so we use a one-sided research hypothesis. If we are comparing two versions of a new product, we want to test whether either version is clearly superior to the other. If π is the population proportion favoring version 1, we want to know if either $\pi > .50$ or $\pi < .50$; thus, we use the two-sided $H_a: \pi \neq .50$.

EXAMPLE 9.1

A very large supermarket chain supplies freshly baked bread. Inventory theory calculations indicate that, to balance the costs of stale bread and of lost sales and customer goodwill, the chain should run out of bread 20% of all days. A random sample of 50 stores is chosen and the stockout rate determined in these stores on a particular date. Formulate a "no problem" null hypothesis. Should the research hypothesis be taken as one-sided or two-sided?

Solution

The null hypothesis refers to π, the proportion of all stores in the chain (not just the sampled ones) that are out of stock on the date. The desired value for π is .20, so the "no problem" null hypothesis is $H_0: \pi = .20$. In this problem, we should be concerned with stockout rates that are either too low (resulting in too much stale bread) or too high (resulting in lost sales and lost customer goodwill). Therefore, we should take the two-sided $H_a: \pi \neq .20$. ■

The basic strategy in hypothesis testing is to attempt to support the research hypothesis by "contradicting" the null hypothesis. The null hypothesis is "contradicted" if the sample data are highly unlikely given H_0 and more likely given H_a. Thus, to support $H_a: \pi > .50$, we would need to find that the sample results are highly improbable assuming that $H_0: \pi \leq .50$ is true.

test statistic   The data must be summarized in a **test statistic** (T.S.). We calculate this statistic to see if it is reasonably compatible with the null hypothesis. When we are testing a proportion, the test statistic is very simple; we count the number of successes in the sample to find T.S.: $Y =$ number of successes. In our new versus old products example we assume that the old product is at least as good as the new product. Given that assumption, it is very unlikely for Y, the number of customers in the sample who prefer the new product, to be very large. Thus, if Y comes out very large, we reject the null hypothesis and support the research hypothesis that the new product is better. To repeat, the basic logic is as follows:

1. Assume that $H_0: \pi \leq .50$ is true;
2. Calculate the value of T.S.: $Y =$ number of customers in the sample who prefer the new product;
3. If this value is highly unlikely (which, in this case, means very large), reject H_0 and support H_a.

EXAMPLE 9.2

In Example 9.1, π represented the proportion of all stores running out of bread on a particular date. If the null hypothesis is $H_0: \pi = .20$ and the research hypothesis H_a is two-sided, what is an appropriate test statistic? What sort of values of this test statistic would contradict the null hypothesis and therefore support the research hypothesis?

Solution

The natural test statistic is T.S.: $Y =$ number of stores in the sample of 50 that are out of bread on that date. Assuming that $H_0: \pi = .20$ is true, it is likely that Y is close to $50(.20) = 10$. Values of Y far below 10 or far above 10 are unlikely given H_0 and they tend to contradict H_0.   ∎

It's necessary in hypothesis testing to draw the line between values of the test statistic that are relatively likely given the null hypothesis and values that are relatively unlikely. At what value of the test statistic do we start to say that the data support the research hypothesis? Knowledge of the sampling distribution of the test statistic is used to answer this question. Values of the test statistic that are sufficiently unlikely given the null hypothesis (as determined by the sampling distribution) form a **rejection region** (R.R.) for the statistical test.

rejection region

Specification of a rejection region must recognize the possibility of error. Suppose that, for a sample of 100 customers, we set the rejection region at $y = 59$ or more customers who prefer the new product. Even if the null hypothesis H_0: $\pi \le .50$ is true, there is a small probability of observing $y \ge 59$. If such a situation were to occur, the market researchers would erroneously think that the new product was superior to the old one. This error—rejecting a null hypothesis that is, in fact, true—is called a **Type I error**. In establishing a rejection region, an investigator must specify the maximum tolerable probability of a Type I error; this maximum probability is denoted by α.

Type I error

We can compute the α probability in a test of a proportion simply by adding binomial probabilities from Appendix Table 1, because the test statistic Y satisfies all the assumptions for a binomial random variable. For the product-comparison example, if we have $n = 100$, H_0: $\pi \le .50$, and R.R.: $y \ge 59$, then the α risk is*

$$\alpha = \max_{\pi} P(Y \ge 59 \mid \pi \le .50)$$

In principle, to find α we must calculate $P(Y \ge 59)$ for every value of $\pi \le .50$. Looking in Appendix Table 1 with $n = 100$ and $\pi = .50$, we find

$$P(Y \ge 59 \mid \pi = .50) = .0159 + .0108 + \cdots = .0444$$

Looking in the $\pi = .45$ column, we find

$$P(Y \ge 59 \mid \pi = .45) = .0016 + .0009 + \cdots = .0034$$

Similarly,

$$P(Y \ge 59 \mid \pi = .40) = .0001 + .0000 + \cdots = .0001$$

Note that the highest value of $P(Y \ge 59)$ occurs at the boundary value of H_0: $\pi \le .50$, namely, at $\pi = .50$. Thus, if the rejection region is R.R.: reject H_0 if $Y \ge 59$, then $\alpha = .0444$.

Usually we specify α, the maximum allowable value for the probability of Type I error, and then we find a suitable rejection region. For example, in the product-comparison example, suppose that we specify $\alpha = .10$. We know that the

---

* Technically, the conditional probability notation $P(Y \ge 59 \mid \pi \le .50)$ isn't correct, because $\pi \le .50$ is not a random event in a sample space. The notation is very convenient, though, so we continue to use it. To be technically correct, read the "|" symbol as *assuming* rather than as *given*.

important value for π is .50; adding binomial probabilities with $\pi = .50$, we find that

$$P(Y \geq 56 \,|\, \pi = .50) = .1358 \qquad \text{and} \qquad P(Y \geq 57 \,|\, \pi = .50) = .0968.$$

Therefore, a suitable rejection region is $Y \geq 57$.

For most studies, α is specified to be .10, .05, or .01, although the value we chose is somewhat arbitrary. We say more about choosing α in Section 9.11.

EXAMPLE 9.3   Find a rejection region corresponding to $\alpha = .10$ in the bread-inventory problem of Examples 9.1 and 9.2.

Solution   We noted in Example 9.2 that the rejection region should include both very large and very small y values. The most natural way to proceed is to locate the two parts of the rejection region at equal distances from the expected value of Y under H_0, namely $50(.20) = 10$. From Appendix Table 1 with $n = 50$ and $\pi = .20$, we find

$$P(Y \geq 16 \,|\, \pi = .20) = .0308 \qquad \text{and} \qquad P(Y \leq 4 \,|\, \pi = .20) = .0185$$

and

$$P(Y \geq 15 \,|\, \pi = .20) = .0607 \qquad \text{and} \qquad P(Y \leq 5 \,|\, \pi = .20) = .0490$$

We choose the rejection region R.R.: $Y \leq 4$ or $Y \geq 16$, because

$$P(Y \leq 4 \text{ or } Y \geq 16) = .0308 + .0185 = .0493$$

whereas

$$P(Y \leq 5 \text{ or } Y \geq 15) = .0607 + .0490 = .1097$$

which is larger than the allowable α (.10).   ■

The last step in hypothesis testing is to obtain the data and come to a conclusion. For example, suppose that 65 of the 100 customers sampled in the product-comparison example indicate a preference for the new product. We have established a rejection region (for $\alpha = .10$) as R.R.: $Y \geq 59$. The value $y = 65$ falls well within that region. Thus we have contradicted H_0, and the data support the research hypothesis $H_a: \pi > .50$.

EXAMPLE 9.4   Does finding that 14 of the 50 stores were out of stock in the bread-inventory problem of Examples 9.1–9.3 support the research hypothesis?

Solution   We found the R.R.: $Y \leq 4$ or $Y \geq 16$ in Example 9.3. The value $y = 14$ is not in this region. Therefore the data do not support the research hypothesis.   ■

The process of performing a hypothesis test can be summarized conveniently in a five-step list, which we illustrate for the product-comparison example.

■

Five Steps of a Statistical Test

1. Null hypothesis H_0: $\pi \le .50$.
2. Research hypothesis H_a: $\pi > .50$.
3. Test statistic T.S.: Y = number of customers preferring the new product.
4. Rejection region R.R.: for $\alpha = .10$, $Y \ge 57$.
5. Conclusion: Because $y = 66$, reject H_0 and support H_a.   ■

retain H_0

When H_0 is not rejected, we sometimes speak of "accepting" H_0. But when H_0 is not rejected, that only means that we don't have sufficient evidence to support a research hypothesis. Failure to support H_a is *not* conclusive evidence favoring H_0; it may well mean that we don't have enough evidence to say anything in particular! In this situation, we prefer to say that we **retain H_0**, rather than say that we accept it.

This list incorporates the basic strategy of hypothesis testing. We need to formulate a null hypothesis, choose either a one-sided or a two-sided research hypothesis, and select an appropriate test statistic. Then selection of a tolerable α probability allows us to specify a rejection region—those potential values of the test statistic that we will declare to contradict the null hypothesis. Finally, obtaining the actual data allows us to reach a conclusion.

SECTION 9.1 EXERCISES

9.1 Suppose that the prevailing opinion among stock market analysts is that only 35% of all rumored takeover bids actually result in a takeover. One group of analysts believes that even this figure is too high. To test this belief, the group plans to track the next 20 rumored takeover bids to see how many actually result in takeovers.
   a. Define the relevant parameter for a statistical hypothesis test.
   b. Formulate "the prevailing opinion is correct" as a null hypothesis.
   c. Formulate a research hypothesis for the group that believes that the prevailing opinion is wrong.
   d. Suppose that a rejection region is established to reject the null hypothesis if 3 or fewer of the 20 rumored bids actually result in takeovers. What is the corresponding α probability?

9.2 Two of the rumored bids in Exercise 9.1 result in takeovers. Is there sufficient evidence in the data to support the research hypothesis?

9.3 A large chain of realtors offers a guaranteed-purchase plan. Houses that have been listed but not sold for six weeks are bought by the realtor at a predetermined price. Over time, 5% of the houses that the realtor lists are purchased under this plan. Because houses with swimming pools are sometimes hard to sell, it is suspected that a larger fraction of such houses must be bought by the realtor under the plan. The chain has listed 50 houses with pools under the plan, and it can determine how many were bought under the plan.
   a. What is the relevant population parameter for this problem?
   b. Formulate the appropriate research hypothesis. Should it be one-sided or two-sided?

    c. State the null hypothesis.

    d. Use binomial tables to determine a rejection region corresponding to a tolerable $\alpha = .05$.

9.4   Suppose that 7 of 50 houses in Exercise 9.3 are purchased under the plan. Does this evidence support the research hypothesis? Can H_0 be rejected at $\alpha = .05$?

9.5   The long-time city manager of a small city had been awarded grants on 50% of the applications for aid submitted to the federal government. A new city manager is appointed who submits 18 applications to the federal government in the first year. The city council wanted to test whether there is a change in the success rate under the new manager.

    a. Define the appropriate population parameter for a statistical test.

    b. Formulate an appropriate null hypothesis.

    c. Should the research hypothesis be one-sided or two-sided?

    d. Find a rejection region corresponding to $\alpha = .05$, using the test statistic $Y =$ number of successful applications out of the 18 submitted.

9.6   Suppose that 7 of the 18 applications in Exercise 9.5 result in grants. Can H_0 be rejected at $\alpha = .05$?

9.7   Binomial probabilities were used in Exercise 9.5. Under what conditions might binomial distribution be a poor assumption?

9.8   The manager for research and development of a food company finds that historically only 40% of the potential new products brought to consumer testing are ever marketed. The manager institutes a revised selection method to determine which products should be brought to consumer testing.

    a. Formulate the null hypothesis that the revised selection method will have no effect on the proportion of potential new products that are marketed.

    b. What arguments can be made in favor of a two-sided research hypothesis?

    c. If a one-sided research hypothesis is to be used, what should it be?

9.9   A two-sided research hypothesis is used in the situation of Exercise 9.8. A sample of 20 potential new products are brought to consumer testing. Define $Y =$ number of these products that are eventually marketed.

    a. Assuming that the null hypothesis is true, what is the mean (expected value) of Y?

    b. Form a rejection region, symmetric around the mean found in part (a), corresponding to a permissible $\alpha = .05$.

9.10   Binomial tables were used in finding the rejection region for Exercise 9.9. It is noted that several of the products brought to consumer testing are competitive versions of one another, so that if one product is marketed, another is very likely not marketed. Does this fact indicate that binomial probabilities may not be applicable? Explain why.

9.2   TYPE II ERROR, β PROBABILITY, AND POWER OF A TEST ∎

Up to this point, we have been concerned about only one kind of error in hypothesis testing: Type I error, which rejects the null hypothesis when it is true. In the product-comparison example, a Type I error would be a claim that the new product was better than the old one when, in fact, it was not. But there is another possible error; the market researchers might claim that the new product is not

Type II error   superior to the old one, when, in fact, it is superior. This error, a **Type II error**, is the failure to reject the null hypothesis when the research hypothesis is true.

When the null hypothesis is negative, as it often is, a Type I error can be called a *false positive* error; by coming to the erroneous conclusion that a positive hypothesis H_a is true, we commit a false positive, Type I, error. Similarly, a Type II error can be called a *false negative* error—an erroneous conclusion that a negative hypothesis H_0 is true.

EXAMPLE 9.5   In the bread-inventory problem discussed in Examples 9.1–9.4, what are the consequences of Types I and II errors?

Solution $H_0: \pi = .20$ states that the supermarket chain does not have a problem, and $H_a: \pi \neq .20$ states that there is a problem. A Type I error is therefore the incorrect assertion that there is a problem with bread inventory; in effect, a Type I error is a false alarm. A Type II error is the incorrect assertion that the bread inventory is under control; in effect, a Type II error is an erroneous failure to sound an alarm.   ■

The probability that a Type II error will be committed, given that the research hypothesis is true, is denoted by β. The quantity $1 - \beta$ is called the **power** of the test; power is the probability that the test will support the research hypothesis, given that it is in fact true. The possible outcomes of a statistical test and the associated probabilities are summarized in Table 9.1.

TABLE 9.1   Possible Outcomes and Probabilities for a Hypothesis Test

Conclusion	*Condition*	
	H_0 Is True	H_a Is True
Accept H_0	Correct conclusion probability $1 - \alpha$	Type II error probability β
Reject H_0	Type I error probability α	Correct conclusion probability $1 - \beta$ ($=$ power)

EXAMPLE 9.6   Refer to Example 9.5. Under certain conditions, the power of the test is .60. What does this mean?

Solution   Power refers to the probability that a research hypothesis will be correctly supported. The sentence thus means that, if the research hypothesis is true (i.e., the chain has an inventory problem), there is a 60% chance that the test will discover the existence of that problem.   ■

In a binomial test for a proportion, β may be calculated by adding binomial probabilities. The conceptual problem is to specify the value to use for π. The research hypothesis in the product-comparison example asserts only that $\pi > .50$. The probability that we will not reject the null hypothesis depends strongly on whether the research hypothesis is "extremely true," such as $\pi = .90$, or "barely true," such as $\pi = .51$. Thus β should be regarded as a *function* of the true value of the population parameter and it should be computed for several different values. For example, if we hypothesize that $\pi = .55$, we may find β by adding binomial probabilities for the nonrejection region. (Remember that β is the probability that the null hypothesis is not rejected, given that the research hypothesis is true.) The rejection region for the product-comparison example is $Y \geq 57$; to find β, we must add the probabilities of all values of $y \leq 56$. Reading up the $\pi = .55$ column in the $n = 100$ block of Appendix Table 1, we find

$$\beta_{.55} = .0071 + .0108 + .0157 + \cdots = .6172$$

Similar calculations using other columns of Appendix Table 1 determine the values of β shown below:

Value of π in H_a:	.55	.60	.65	.70	.75
β_π:	.6172	.2368	.0389	.0020	.0000

EXAMPLE 9.7   The rejection region corresponding to $\alpha = .10$ in Example 9.3 was found to be $Y \leq 4$ or $Y \geq 16$. Find β and power when $\pi = .30$ and when $\pi = .35$.

Solution   To find β, we must add probabilities for all values of y not in the rejection region, namely $5 \leq y \leq 15$. Power is simply $1 - \beta$. Adding probabilities for $y = 5$, $6, \ldots$, 15 in the $\pi = .30$ and $\pi = .35$ columns of Appendix Table 1 with $n = 50$, we obtain the following values:

π:	.30	.35
β:	.569	.280
Power:	.431	.720

Note that β decreases (and therefore power increases) as the value of π gets farther from the H_0 value, $\pi = .20$.   ∎

The value of β is influenced by a number of factors.

1. All else equal, if α increases, β decreases. Increasing α makes it easier to reject H_0, thus decreasing the probability that we will *not* reject H_0. Note, however, that it is not true that $\alpha + \beta = 1$. Both α and β are conditional probabilities, defined for different conditions; their sum means little, if anything.
2. All else equal, if n increases, β decreases. With more information, we have a lower risk of error.
3. All else equal, if the hypothetical value of the population parameter moves away from H_0, β decreases. It is easier to detect a large deviation from H_0 than a small one.

SECTION 9.2   EXERCISES

9.11   In Exercise 9.1 we had $H_0: \pi = .35$, $H_a: \pi < .35$, $n = 20$, R.R.: $Y \leq 3$, and an actual α of .0445.

    a. Suppose that, in fact, $\pi = .25$. What is the probability that the null hypothesis will not be rejected? What is the technical name for this probability?

    b. If $\pi = .25$, what is the probability that H_0 will be rejected? What is the technical name for this probability?

9.12 How should the probability found in Exercise 9.11, part (a), change if $\pi = .20$ rather than .25? Base your answer on general principles rather than calculations.

9.13 Assume in Exercise 9.3 that 10% of all houses with swimming pools are, in the long run, bought by the realtor. Find the probability that the null hypothesis will not be rejected. Is this an α or a β probability?

9.14 One kind of error we can make in the situation of Exercise 9.3 is a claim that houses with swimming pools are more likely to be bought under the plan than are other houses when in fact houses with pools have the same rate as other houses. According to the formulation of Exercise 9.3, is this error a Type I error or a Type II error?

9.15 Suppose that the sample in Exercise 9.3 is enlarged to 100 houses. The value of α remains .05. Assume, as in Exercise 9.13, that 10% of all houses with swimming pools are, in the long run, bought by the realtor.

    a. Should the probability that the null hypothesis will not be rejected be larger or smaller than the probability found in Exercise 9.13? Base your answer on general principles rather than calculations.

    b. The rejection region with $n = 100$ and $\alpha = .05$ becomes $Y \geq 10$. Calculate the probability that H_0 will not be rejected. Does the result confirm your answer in part (a)?

9.16 Explain what would constitute Type I and Type II errors in Exercise 9.8.

9.17 Find the probability that H_0 in Exercise 9.8 will not be rejected for the following values of π: .45, .50, .55, .65, .75, .80. Sketch a curve of the β probabilities.

9.18 We had $H_0: \pi = .40$, $H_a: \pi \neq .40$, $n = 20$, and R.R.: $Y \leq 3$ or $Y \geq 13$ in Exercise 9.9.

    a. On the hypothesis that the actual value of π is .50, find the power of the test.

    b. If n is increased to 100 but no other changes are made in the specifications, should the power increase or decrease relative to the power found in part (a)? You shouldn't need to make any calculations to answer this question.

9.3 A TEST FOR A POPULATION MEAN WITH KNOWN STANDARD DEVIATION

We introduced hypothesis-testing concepts in the context of testing a binomial proportion. There are many other population parameters and many other statistical tests. In this section we illustrate basic testing concepts in the context of a statistical test for a population mean.

    As usual, we work by example. Suppose that the local bureau of weights and measures is concerned with the actual weight of boxes of a cereal product marked as 16 ounces. There is some variability in weight from one box to another, mostly due to the shape of the cereal pieces. Past experience has shown the standard deviation of box weights to be .1 ounce. Although the bureau doesn't require that every box weigh 16 ounces, it does want to assure the public that the average weight of all such cereal boxes is at least 16 ounces. If the bureau suspects the cereal company of short-weighting (underfilling the boxes), how can it go about testing for such short-weighting?

    Because the boxes must be opened to test the weight of the contents, the bureau cannot test every box coming off the assembly line. Instead, a random sample of boxes must be chosen and tested. Suppose the bureau's sample data consist of the actual weights for the contents of 25 randomly chosen boxes. How should the bureau proceed?

We can formulate this problem in terms of a statistical test about the population mean weight μ for all cereal boxes produced. The bureau is concerned with the basic problem of short-weighting; in particular, the bureau is interested in supporting the research hypothesis $H_a: \mu < 16$ ounces. For this research hypothesis, the corresponding null hypothesis is $H_0: \mu \geq 16$ ounces. The primary concern is with the boundary value, as we indicated in Section 9.1. We denote the boundary value of the hypothesized mean by μ_0; here $\mu_0 = 16$.

The most plausible test statistic is the sample mean weight $\bar{y}$ of the 25 boxes. Sample means much less than μ_0 are unlikely under H_0 and relatively more likely if $H_a: \mu < 16$ is true. Therefore the rejection region is "reject H_0 if $\bar{y}$ is smaller than could reasonably occur by chance."

To determine the exact rejection region, we need to know the sampling distribution of $\bar{Y}$. Recall from Chapter 6 that if the population distribution of weights is normal with mean μ and standard deviation σ, then the sampling distribution of the sample mean is also normal with expected value equal to the population mean weight ($\mu_Y = \mu$) and with standard error equal to $\sigma_{\bar{Y}} = \sigma/\sqrt{n}$. Even if the population distribution is mildly nonnormal, the Central Limit Theorem helps to make this distribution a good approximation. For the bureau's problem, $\sigma = .1$, $n = 25$, and the crucial value for μ is the boundary null hypothesis value $\mu_0 = 16$. Thus if the null hypothesis is true, the sample mean $\bar{Y}$ is normally distributed with $\mu_{\bar{Y}} = 16$ and $\sigma_{\bar{Y}} = .1/\sqrt{25} = .02$. We can use this information about the sampling distribution of the test statistic $\bar{Y}$ to locate a rejection region.

The entire rejection region for $H_0: \mu = 16$, $H_a: \mu < 16$ is in the lower tail of the distribution of $\bar{Y}$. In particular, from our knowledge of the properties of a normal distribution we know that the boundary of the rejection region is located at a distance of 1.645 standard errors ($1.645\sigma_{\bar{Y}}$) below $\mu = 16$ if α is taken to be .05 (see Figure 9.1).

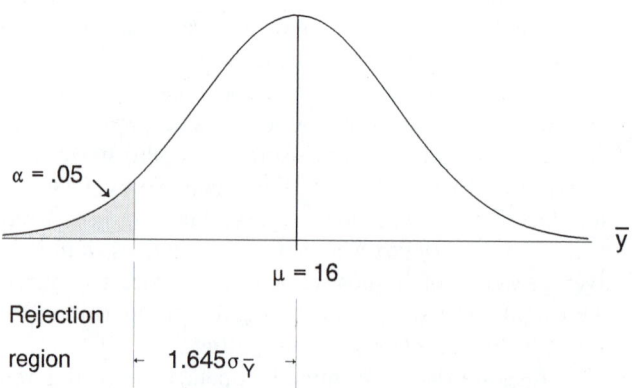

$\alpha = .05$

$\mu = 16$

Rejection region

$1.645\sigma_{\bar{Y}}$

$\bar{y}$

FIGURE 9.1   Rejection Region for the Test Statistic $\bar{y}$ ($\alpha = .05$, one-tailed)

To determine whether or not to reject the null hypothesis, we can also compute the number of standard errors the observed value of $\bar{y}$ lies below $\mu = 16$. **z statistic** This is done by computing a z **statistic** for the observed sample mean $\bar{y}$ using the formula

$$z = \frac{\bar{y} - \mu_0}{\sigma/\sqrt{n}} = \frac{\bar{y} - 16}{.02}$$

This suggests two ways to state the rejection region for a statistical test about μ. First, in terms of the test statistic $\bar{y}$, the rejection region is

rejection region using $\bar{y}$

R.R.: For $\alpha = .05$, reject $H_0: \mu \geq 16$ if the observed value of $\bar{y}$ is more than $1.645\sigma_{\bar{y}}$ below $\mu = 16$ (see Figure 9.1).

An equivalent way to state the rejection region is in terms of the test statistic $z = (\bar{y} - \mu_0)/\sigma_{\bar{y}}$, also called the z statistic:

rejection region using z

R.R.: For $\alpha = .05$, reject $H_0: \mu = 16$ if the computed value of z is less than or equal to -1.645 (see Figure 9.2).

Because the latter approach is shorter and perhaps simpler, we use it throughout this text.

Finally, suppose that the sample mean weight for a sample of $n = 25$ boxes is 15.83 ounces. What can the bureau conclude concerning the population mean fill? The z statistic

$$z = \frac{15.83 - 16}{.1/\sqrt{25}} = -8.5$$

indicates that the sample mean (15.83) lies 8.5 standard errors below the hypothesized mean $\mu = 16$. Because the computed value of the z statistic (-8.5) lies in the rejection region well beyond the critical value -1.645, the bureau can reject the null hypothesis and claim that the company is short-weighting. A summary list displays the bureau's work.

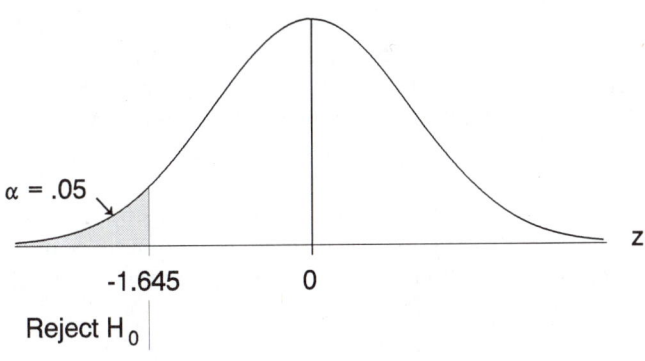

α = .05

-1.645   0   z

Reject H_0

FIGURE 9.2   Rejection Region for the Test Statistic z ($\alpha = .05$, one-tailed)

Summary of One-tailed Test About μ, with σ Known

$$H_0: \mu = \mu_0 \ (\mu_0 = 16 \text{ ounces})$$
$$H_a: \mu < \mu_0$$

$$\text{T.S.: } z = \frac{\bar{y} - \mu_0}{\sigma_{\bar{Y}}}, \qquad \sigma_{\bar{Y}} = \frac{\sigma}{\sqrt{n}}$$

R.R.: For $\alpha = .05$, reject H_0 if $z \leq -1.645$

$$\text{Conclusion: } z = \frac{15.83 - 16}{.1/\sqrt{25}} = -8.5; \text{ reject } H_0$$

Note: For $H_0: \mu = \mu_0$ and $H_a: \mu > \mu_0$, the R.R. for $\alpha = .05$ is $z \geq 1.645$.

For hypothesis tests involving both μ and π, we have noted that the boundary value of the null hypothesis is the important value. In the cereal weight example, suppose that we had taken some other value within H_0 as our mean, such as $\mu = 16.01$. The resulting z statistic would fall even farther into the rejection region:

$$z = \frac{15.83 - 16.01}{.1/\sqrt{25}} = -9.0$$

If the test statistic based on the boundary value leads to rejection of H_0, a test statistic based on any other value in H_0 also leads to rejection of H_0. Up to this point, we have used an inequality sign for H_0 in one-sided tests. Hereafter, we only worry about the crucial boundary value and drop the inequality sign.

EXAMPLE 9.8   A researcher claims that the amount of time urban preschool children age 3–5 watch television per week has a mean of 22.6 hours and a standard deviation of 6.1 hours. A market research firm believes that the claimed mean is too low. The television-watching habits of a random sample of 60 urban preschool children are measured, with the parents of each child keeping a daily log of television watching. If the mean weekly amount of time spent watching television is 25.2 hours and if the population standard deviation σ is assumed to be 6.1 hours, should the researcher's claim be rejected at an α value of .01?

Solution   The marketing firm's research hypothesis is that 22.6 is too small a value for the population mean. Thus the research hypothesis of interest is $H_a: \mu > 22.6$, and the null hypothesis is $H_0: \mu = 22.6$. We summarize the elements of the statistical test for $\alpha = .01$ as follows:

$$H_0: \mu = 22.6$$
$$H_a: \mu > 22.6$$

$$\text{T.S.: } z = \frac{\bar{y} - \mu_0}{\sigma_{\bar{Y}}} = \frac{25.2 - 22.6}{6.1/\sqrt{60}} = 3.30$$

R.R.: For $\alpha = .01$, reject H_0 if $z \geq 2.326$

Conclusion: Because $z = 3.30$ is well within the rejection region, we reject $H_0 : \mu = 22.6$. ■

This test procedure for μ can easily be modified to handle other research hypotheses. For example, if the cereal company wants to establish beyond a reasonable doubt that the true mean weight is more than 16 ounces, it could start with the one-sided research hypothesis $H_a : \mu > 16$. Large values of $\bar{y}$ would then indicate rejection of the null hypothesis $H_0 : \mu = 16$. In particular for $\alpha = .05$, the rejection region would be values of $\bar{y}$ at least $1.645\sigma_Y$ *above* $\mu_0 = 16$, or equivalently, values of $z \geq 1.645$ (see Figure 9.3).

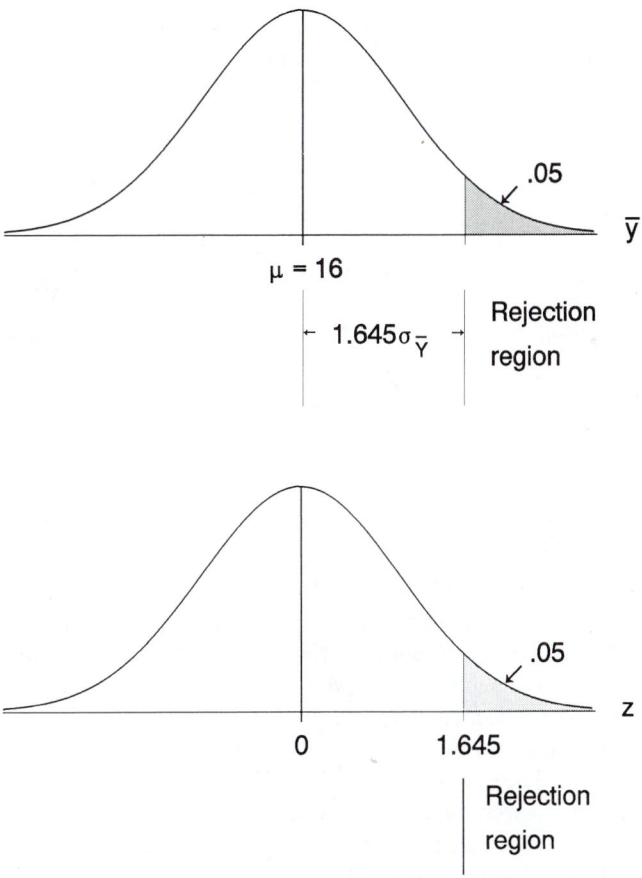

FIGURE 9.3   Rejection Region for $H_a : \mu > 16$, with (a) $\bar{y}$ as Test Statistic; (b) z as Test Statistic

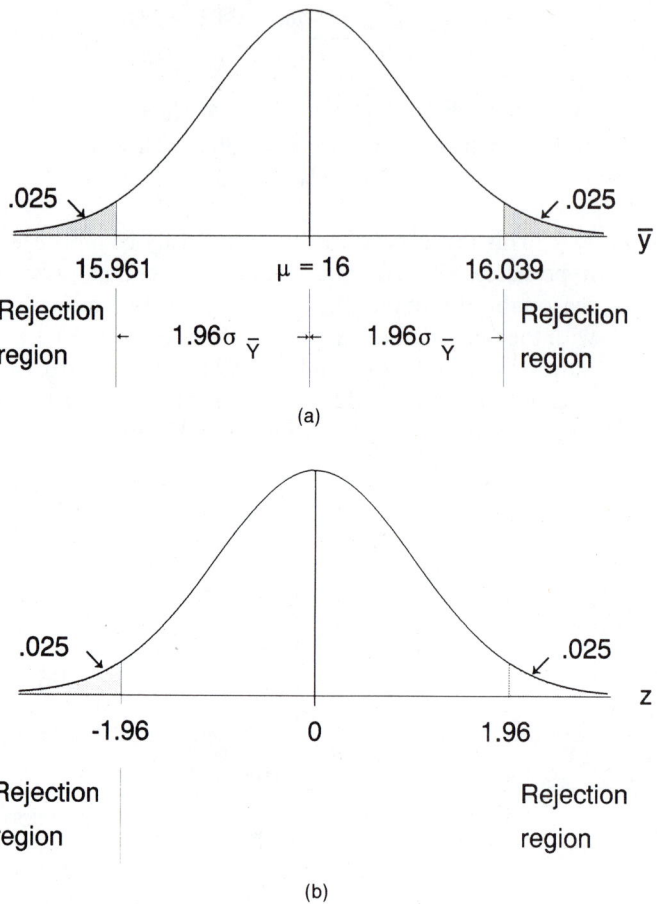

(a)

(b)

FIGURE 9.4   Rejection Region for H_0: $\mu = 16$, with (a) $\bar{y}$ as Test Statistic; (b) z as Test Statistic

A two-tailed test for the research hypothesis H_a: $\mu \neq \mu_0$ follows directly from our discussion of one-tailed tests. For example, the manager of the company who is concerned about possible overfilling or underfilling might well take as a research hypothesis that $\mu \neq 16$. Both large and small values of $\bar{y}$ would indicate rejection of H_0: $\mu = 16$. If we split the rejection region evenly in the tails, the rejection region for $\alpha = .05$ is as shown in Figure 9.4a; the corresponding rejection region based on the z statistic is shown in Figure 9.4b.

The summary chart for the z test can be written to cover all three forms for the research hypothesis. Recall that z_a is the z value that cuts off an area a in the right-hand tail of the z curve; thus $z_{.05} = 1.645$ and $z_{.025} = 1.96$. For a two-tailed test and a given α, the desired cutoff points are $z_{\alpha/2}$ and $-z_{\alpha/2}$. For $\alpha = .05$, we use $z_{.025} = 1.96$ and $-z_{.025} = -1.96$. The first four steps of the statistical test for μ (σ known) are shown here. These steps formulate the problem and establish the rejection region; the last step simply involves drawing a conclusion based on the computed value of the z test statistic. If the computed z value falls within the rejection region, we reject the null hypothesis in favor of the research hypothesis. If the z value does not fall within the rejection region, we reserve judgment until β probabilities can be computed for various values of μ.

Summary for z Test, with σ Known

$H_0: \mu = \mu_0$

$H_a:$ 1. $\mu > \mu_0$

    2. $\mu < \mu_0$

    3. $\mu \neq \mu_0$

T.S.: $z = \dfrac{\bar{y} - \mu_0}{\sigma/\sqrt{n}}$

R.R.: For the probability of a Type I error α, reject H_0 if

    1. $z > z_\alpha$

    2. $z < -z_\alpha$

    3. $z > z_{\alpha/2}$ or $z < -z_{\alpha/2}$

EXAMPLE 9.9

Refer to the television-watching data of Example 9.8. Test the research hypothesis $H_a: \mu \neq 22.6$ using $\alpha = .01$.

Solution

The five steps of the solution are summarized here:

$H_0: \mu = 22.6$

$H_a: \mu \neq 22.6$

T.S.: $z = \dfrac{\bar{y} - \mu_0}{\sigma_{\bar{Y}}} = 3.30$

R.R.: For $\alpha = .01$, reject H_0 if $z \geq 2.576$ or if $z \leq -2.576$

Conclusion: Because the computed value of z (3.30) falls within the rejection region, we reject $H_0: \mu = 22.6$. Practically speaking, because the sample mean is greater than 22.6 and because we reject $H_0: \mu = 22.6$, we can safely conclude that $\mu > 22.6$. ∎

The cereal box example is unrealistic in that we assume a population standard deviation is known. Population parameters such as the standard deviation usually have unknown values. We managed the problem of unknown standard deviations in Chapter 8 by using the t distribution. Hypothesis-testing methods using the t distribution are discussed in Section 9.6. It is convenient to use z tests in our examples for a bit longer, only to avoid minor complications. Recall that for large samples the difference between t and z tables is negligible. Thus, for samples in the hundreds, it doesn't matter whether we use t or z tables.

Suppose that the bureau of weights and measures takes a sample of $n = 100$ cereal boxes and computes the sample mean to be $\bar{y} = 15.83$ ounces and the **sample** standard deviation to be $s = .12$ ounce. Suppose also that the bureau doesn't want to make any unsupported assumptions about the population standard deviation. A reasonable estimate, based on the data, is that the population standard deviation σ is roughly equal to the sample standard deviation s—that is, roughly equal to .12. It seems reasonable to substitute the value of s, the sample standard deviation, as a best guess for σ in the z statistic. According to a theorem of mathematical statistics, if n is large enough, the resulting z statistic does in fact have a z distribution, at least to a good approximation. The bureau can go ahead and do a z test. The summary follows; this time the bureau is using $\alpha = .01$, just for variety.

Summary for Large-Sample Result, with σ Unknown

$$H_0: \mu = 16$$
$$H_a: \mu < 16$$

$$\text{T.S.: } z \approx \frac{\bar{y} - \mu_0}{s/\sqrt{n}} = \frac{15.83 - 16}{.12/\sqrt{100}} = -14.167$$

R.R.: For $\alpha = .01$, reject H_0 if $z \leq -2.326$

Conclusion: Because $z = -14.167$ lies within the rejection region, we reject H_0.

You should be able to verify that -2.326 is the appropriate cutoff point corresponding to $\alpha = .01$.

The large-sample procedure is easy enough: Just substitute the sample standard deviation s for the population standard deviation σ in the z statistic. Further justification for this substitution is given in Section 9.6. For now, assume **sample-size** that this large-sample procedure is a decent approximation if $n \geq 30$ and a good **requirement** approximation if $n \geq 100$. Because the bureau's test statistic fell so far within the rejection tail, the bureau can reject H_0 without any serious concern.

EXAMPLE 9.10   Suppose that the television-watching sample of Example 9.8 yields a standard deviation of 5.8. Use this value to test the research hypothesis $H_a: \mu > 22.6$, at $\alpha = .01$.

Solution   The value of the z statistic with s replacing σ is

$$z = \frac{25.2 - 22.6}{5.8/\sqrt{60}} = 3.47$$

This value falls well within the rejection region $z \geq 2.326$, so H_a is supported.

9.4   THE β PROBABILITY FOR z TESTS   ■

We introduced the β risk—the probability of not rejecting the null hypothesis when the research hypothesis is true—in the test about a binomial proportion in Section 9.2. The same concepts apply to the z test of this section, but the computation of β is a bit trickier than just adding binomial probabilities. We use the original cereal box example for illustration. Recall that, for $H_0: \mu = 16$, $H_a: \mu < 16$, $\sigma = .1$, $n = 25$, and $\alpha = .05$, the rejection region was $z < -1.645$. To calculate the risk of a Type II error (the probability of incorrectly accepting H_0), we must assume some value for μ under H_a. Once again, the value of β depends on the assumed value of μ in H_a. Specifically, let's assume that $\mu = 15.92$; this corresponds to a short-weighting of .5% of the listed weight. What is the probability that the bureau detects this short-weighting?

The calculation is easier to understand if the rejection region is stated in terms of the sample mean $\bar{y}$ rather than the z statistic. If the rejection region is $z < -1.645$; we reject $H_0: \mu = 16$ for values of $\bar{y}$ at least 1.645 standard errors below $\mu = 16$; this is, we reject H_0 if $\bar{y} \leq 16 - 1.645 \, \sigma/\sqrt{n} = 15.9671$. If the true mean is $\mu = 15.92$, the probability β that the sample mean does *not* fall within the rejection region is

$$\beta = P(\bar{Y} > 15.9671 \,|\, \mu = 15.92) = P\left(\frac{\bar{Y} - 15.92}{.1/\sqrt{25}} > \frac{15.9671 - 15.92}{.1/\sqrt{25}}\right)$$

$$= P(z > 2.355) \approx .01$$

The calculation is illustrated in Figure 9.5 (page 354).

Such calculations can be carried out for any test situation, and they can be summarized in a general formula. If μ_0 is the boundary value of μ under H_0 and μ_a is the selected research hypothesis mean, it can be shown that for a one-tailed test

β for a one-tailed test

$$\beta = P\left(z > -z_\alpha + \frac{|\mu_a - \mu_0|}{\sigma/\sqrt{n}}\right)$$

In our cereal example, $-z_\alpha = -z_{.05} = -1.645$, while

$$\frac{|\mu_a - \mu_0|}{\sigma/\sqrt{n}} = \frac{|15.92 - 16|}{.1/\sqrt{25}} = \frac{.08}{.02} = 4$$

(Recall that "| |" indicates absolute value, or magnitude of a number without regard to sign.) Hence

$$\beta = P(z > -1.645 + 4) = P(z > 2.355) \approx .01$$

Therefore the bureau has a small probability ($\beta = .01$) of failing to reject H_0 if the degree of short-weighting is .5% of the claimed weight of 16 ounces. In other words, with this test procedure there is a high probability ($1 - \beta = .99$) of detecting a .5% short-weighting if it exists.

A similar calculation can be made for a two-tailed test. The cereal company's production manager had a rejection region (at $\alpha = .05$) of $z \leq -1.96$

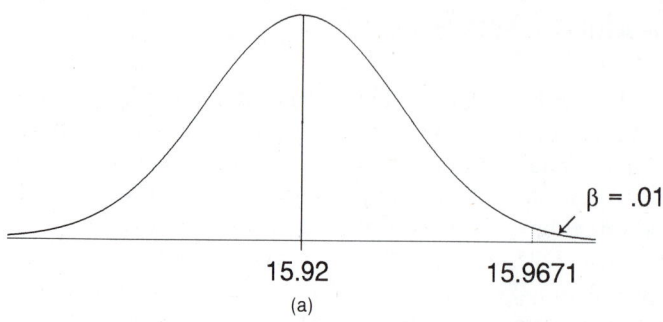

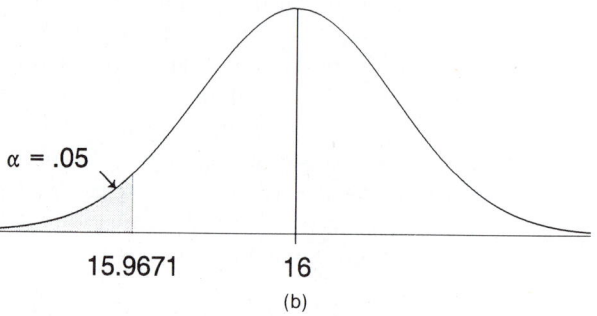

FIGURE 9.5	Calculation of β for One-Tailed z Test: Sampling Distribution for $\bar{Y}$ Under (a) H_a: $\mu = 15.92$; (b) H_0: $\mu = 16.00$

or $z \geq 1.96$, or equivalently,

$$\bar{y} \leq \frac{16 - 1.96(.1)}{\sqrt{25}} = 15.961 \qquad \text{or} \qquad \bar{y} \geq \frac{16 + 1.96(.1)}{\sqrt{25}} = 16.039$$

H_0 is not rejected if $15.961 < \bar{y} < 16.039$. Thus, if the true mean is 15.92, the probability of incorrectly accepting H_0 is

$$\beta = P(15.961 < \bar{Y} < 16.039 \,|\, \mu = 15.92)$$

$$= P\left(\frac{15.961 - 15.92}{.1/\sqrt{25}} < z < \frac{16.039 - 15.92}{.1/\sqrt{25}}\right)$$

$$= P(2.05 < z < 5.95)$$

Note that the upper limit 5.95 (which corresponds to the upper limit of $\bar{y} = 16.039$) has practically no effect, because $P(z \geq 5.95)$ is zero to many decimal places. Hence the value of β is $P(2.05 < z < 5.95) \approx P(z > 2.05) = .02$. This calculation is illustrated in Figure 9.6.

Fortunately, a shortcut version of these calculations can be derived. Recall that μ_0 denotes the boundary value of μ under H_0; similarly, let μ_a denote any selected value of μ within the research hypothesis. The shortcut calculation of β

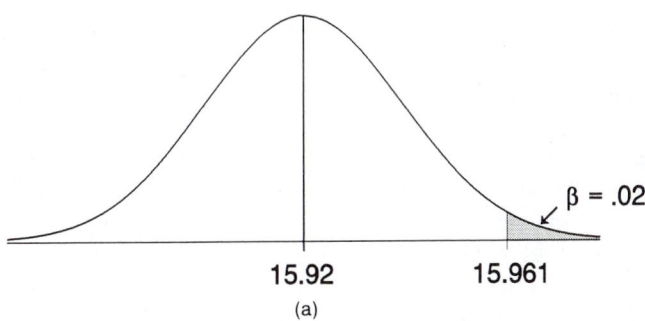

15.92   15.961

(a)

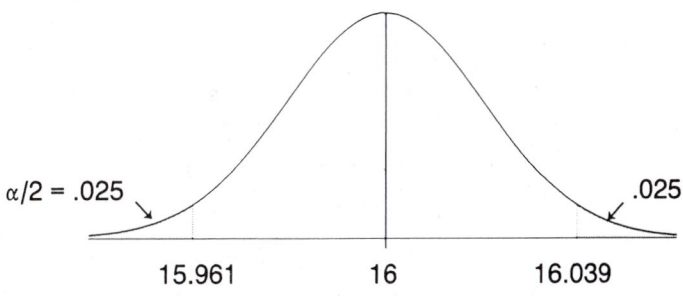

$\alpha/2 = .025$ .025

15.961   16   16.039

FIGURE 9.6   Calculation of β for Two-Tailed z Test: Sampling Distribution for $\bar{Y}$ Under (a) H_a: $\mu = 15.92$; (b) H_0: $\mu = 16.00$

is shown in the following box:

___

Calculation of β for a z Test

One-tailed test: $\beta = P\left(z > -z_\alpha + \dfrac{|\mu_a - \mu_0|}{\sigma/\sqrt{n}}\right)$

Two-tailed test: Replace $-z_\alpha$ in the one-tailed test by $-z_{\alpha/2}$

___

EXAMPLE 9.11   Compute β probabilities for the one-tailed tests of Example 9.8. Assume a true mean of 25.0.

Solution   Because $\alpha = .01$, $\mu_a = 25.0$, $\mu_0 = 22.6$, $\sigma = 6.1$, and $n = 60$,

$$\beta = P\left(z \geq -2.326 + \frac{|25.0 - 22.6|}{6.1/\sqrt{60}}\right)$$

$$= P(z \geq .72) = .2358$$

In Chapter 8 we used confidence intervals to decide how big a sample to take. Alternatively, hypothesis testing can be used to choose a sample size. For example, a chain of inexpensive restaurants that features steaks makes much of its profit from "add-ons"—additional-cost items ordered by diners. Currently, add-ons average $4.24 per check, with a standard deviation of $2.00. An incentive program for waitresses and waiters is being considered, one designed to sell more add-ons (i.e., increase the mean). There is also a concern that the program may backfire and lead to actual reductions. The target is a mean of $4.50. How many checks should be sampled under a trial run of the incentive scheme?

Because of the concern that the program might backfire, a two-sided hypothesis test should be used. To calculate the required sample size, it is necessary to specify both α and β. Suppose we formulate the null hypothesis as $H_0: \mu = \$4.24$ and specify α to be .05 and β to be .10. We take $\mu_a = \$4.50$ as the target and assume that σ continues to be $2.00.

We could proceed by trial and error. Suppose that we try $n = 400$. Then

$$\beta = P\left(z > -1.96 + \frac{|4.50 - 4.24|}{2.00/\sqrt{400}}\right)$$

$$= P(z > .64) = .5000 - .2389 = .2611$$

The β probability is higher than desired; a larger sample is needed. We could keep trying other sample sizes and eventually figure out the required n. Fortunately, it's possible to calculate the required n directly.

Sample Size Required for a Specified α and β

One-tailed test: $n = \dfrac{(z_\alpha + z_\beta)^2 \sigma^2}{(\mu_a - \mu_0)^2}$

Two-tailed test: replace z_α in the one-tailed test by $z_{\alpha/2}$

For the restaurant example, we have a two-tailed test with $\alpha = .05$; therefore we use $z_{\alpha/2} = z_{.05/2} = 1.96$ and $z_\beta = z_{.10} = 1.28$:

$$n = \frac{(1.96 + 1.28)^2(2.00)^2}{(4.50 - 4.24)^2} = 621.16$$

To ensure that the β probability is no greater than .10, we must round n up to 622.

EXAMPLE 9.12   A light-duty parts manufacturing company sometimes uses temporary workers hired through an agency. These workers have a mean production of 2250 items per day and a standard deviation of 260 items per day. Managers at the company propose to get a sample of temporaries from a different agency (one that claims to use more rigorous standards) to see if productivity increases. They propose to use a one-tailed test with $\alpha = .01$. If the long-run (population) mean productivity of temporaries from the new agency is in fact 2380 (half a standard deviation higher), the managers want the test to have power .95. How many temporaries must be tested?

Solution   We assume that the standard deviation for temporaries from the new agency is the same as from the old one, namely $\sigma = 260$. The natural null hypothesis is that the temporaries from the new agency are no better than those from the old agency; H_0: $\mu = \mu_0 = 2250$. We take $\mu_a = 2380$. From Appendix Table 3, $z_{.01} = 2.33$ and $z_{.05} = 1.64$ or 1.65; let's call it 1.645. Thus

$$n = \frac{(2.33 + 1.645)^2(260)^2}{(2380 - 2250)^2} = 63.20$$

Rounding up, we find that the managers need a sample of 64 temporaries. Note that it might be difficult to get a random sample; to get new business, the agency might provide its most productive workers.   ■

SECTIONS 9.3 AND 9.4   EXERCISES

9.19 The manager of a health maintenance organization has set as a target the mean waiting time of nonemergency patients to not exceed 30 minutes. In spot checks, the manager finds the waiting times for 22 patients; the patients are selected randomly on different days. Assume that the population standard deviation of waiting times is 10 minutes.
a. What is the relevant parameter to be tested?
b. Formulate null and research hypotheses.
c. State the test statistic and the rejection region corresponding to $\alpha = .05$.

9.20 Suppose that the mean waiting time for the 22 patients in Exercise 9.19 is 38.1 minutes. Can H_0 be rejected?

9.21 For the test procedure of Exercise 9.19, find the probability that H_0 will not be rejected, assuming a true mean waiting time of 34 minutes. Do the same for other values of μ, and sketch a β curve.

9.22 We stated in Exercise 9.19 that the 22 patients were selected on different days. Why would one not want to select 22 patients on one randomly chosen day?

9.23 A radio station wants to control the time allotted to unpaid public-service commercials. If there are too many such commercials, the station loses revenue; if there are too few, the station loses points with the Federal Communications Commission. The target figure is an average of 1.5 commercial minutes per hour. A sample of 18 hours gives the following times (in minutes) allotted to public-service commercials:

.0	.0	.0	.0	.0	.0	.5	.5	.5	1.0	1.5	1.5
1.5	2.0	2.0	2.5	3.0	6.5	(mean = 1.278)					

Assume that the population standard deviation is 1.60. State all parts of a z test of H_0: $\mu = 1.5$. Should H_a be one- or two-tailed? Use $\alpha = .05$.

9.24 Refer to Exercise 9.23. Calculate β probabilities for $\mu = 1.0, 1.2, 1.4, 1.6, 1.8$, and 2.0. Sketch a β curve.

9.25 The theory underlying the test in Exercise 9.23 assumes that $\bar{Y}$ has an approximately normal distribution. From the appearance of the data, do you believe that the approximation is a good one for this problem?

9.5   THE *p*-VALUE FOR A HYPOTHESIS TEST

In the hypothesis-testing problems we've considered so far, we always come to a reject-don't reject decision, without regard to the conclusiveness of the decision. In practice, this is often an oversimplification. In the product-comparison example of Section 9.1 we specified $H_0: \pi = .50$, $H_a: \pi > .50$, and $n = 100$, and we chose $\alpha = .05$. The corresponding rejection region was $y \geq 59$. Formally, $y = 59$ leads to exactly the same conclusion as $y = 99$. Evidently, the farther the value of the test statistic extends into the rejection region, the more conclusive is the rejection of the null hypothesis. How can we measure the weight of the sample evidence for rejecting a null hypothesis in favor of a research hypothesis?

p-value

The weight of evidence, or conclusiveness index, for rejecting a null hypothesis is called the **p-value** or attained-significance level. The *p*-value is the probability (assuming H_0) of a test statistic value equal to or more extreme than the actually observed value. As the test statistic gets farther into the rejection region, the weight of evidence for rejecting the null hypothesis gets more conclusive and the *p*-value gets smaller. In the product-comparison example, suppose that the observed *y* value is 59. The rejection region is $Y \geq 59$, so formally we would (barely) reject the null hypothesis. We can compute the probability of obtaining the actual *y* value, 59, or a more extreme one (larger, in this case) by using binomial probabilities with $n = 100$ and $\pi = .50$.

$$P(Y \geq 59 \mid \pi = .50) = .0159 + .0108 + \cdots + .0001 = .0444$$

But now suppose that the *y* value is instead 65, much farther into the rejection region. The *p*-value for that result is found by adding binomial probabilities with $n = 100$ and $\pi = .50$.

$$P(Y \geq 65 \mid \pi = .50) = .0009 + .0005 + .0002 + .0001 + .0001$$
$$= .0018$$

which is a much smaller value. The farther within the rejection region the test statistic falls, the smaller the *p*-value is, and the stronger evidence we have to reject the null hypothesis and support the research hypothesis.

Very small *p*-values indicate strong, conclusive evidence for rejecting the null hypothesis. The reason is that a small *p*-value indicates that the actually observed data are very unlikely, assuming that the null hypothesis is true. In the product-comparison example, an observed *y* value of 65 ($p = .0018$) would be much more conclusive than an observed *y* value of 59 ($p = .0444$).

Although no null hypothesis can ever be absolutely disproven, a very small *p*-value leads to its rejection and to support of the research hypothesis beyond a reasonable doubt.

EXAMPLE 9.13   Find the *p*-value if 18 stockouts are observed in a sample of 50 stores in Example 9.1.

Solution   The null and research hypotheses are $H_0: \pi \leq .20$ and $H_a: \pi > .20$. Using binomial tables with $n = 50$ and probability of success (stockout), $\pi = .20$,

$P(Y \geq 18) = .0062$. The p-value is even less than .01, indicating that H_0 can be rejected rather conclusively.   ∎

When the rejection region of the test is two-tailed, the p-value computation must be modified slightly. A more extreme value than the observed test statistic could be in the same tail or in the opposite tail. If the sampling distribution of the test statistic is symmetric (which is the case for most two-tailed tests), the **two-tailed p-value** can be computed by doubling the one-tailed value. In the product-comparison example, the one-tailed p-value corresponding to $y = 59$ is .0444; if H_a had been taken as two-sided, $H_a: \pi \neq .50$, the p-value would be .0888.

two-tailed *p*-value

The computation of p-values is also simple for a z test. In the cereal box example for testing mean fill weight, the bureau of weights and measures used a one-tailed test of $H_0: \mu = 16$ and $H_a: \mu < 16$. The z statistic actually observed was -8.5. Because the last entry in Appendix Table 3, 3.09, corresponds to a tail area of .001, the p-value, $P(z \leq -8.5 \mid \mu = 16)$, is smaller than .001 for this one-tailed test.

For a two-tailed test, such as that for $H_0: \mu = 16$, $H_a: \mu \neq 16$ in the cereal box example, the p-value, $P(z \leq -8.5 \text{ or } z \geq 8.5 \mid \mu = 16)$, is less than .002. More extensive z tables indicate that the one-tailed p-value is less than .0000000001, one chance in 10 billion. Based on the sample data, the bureau can reject H_0 with remarkable confidence. The computation of p-values based on the z statistic proceeds as follows:

p-Values for z Test

1. If $H_a: \mu > \mu_0$, p-value $= P(z > z_{actual})$
2. If $H_a: \mu < \mu_0$, p-value $= P(z < z_{actual})$
3. If $H_a: \mu \neq \mu_0$, p-value $= 2P(z > |z_{actual}|)$

Similarly, p-values for a test about π using the z statistic are computed for one- and two-tailed tests as shown here with π replacing μ.

The computed value of the z statistic is denoted by z_{actual}.   ∎

Most computer programs automatically compute p-values. A very small p-value indicates that the null hypothesis may be rejected at any plausible α value; a large p-value, such as .4 or .6, indicates that the null hypothesis should not be rejected at plausible α values. A very general principle relates p-values to α; the principle is so general that it deserves to be called the Universal Rejection Region.

Universal Rejection Region

If α has been specified, reject the null hypothesis if and only if the p-value is less than the specified α.   ∎

EXAMPLE 9.14   Many computer software programs for statistical analyses routinely compute p-values, usually in two-tailed form.

   a. For the following output, find the appropriate one-tailed p-value.
   b. Verify the p-value computation using z tables.
   c. Can the null hypothesis be rejected at $\alpha = .05$?

```
MTB > ztest of mean = 150 assuming sigma = 20 data in 'Data'

TEST OF MU = 150.000 VS MU N.E. 150.000
THE ASSUMED SIGMA = 20.0
```

	N	MEAN	STDEV	SE MEAN	Z	P VALUE
Data	25	156.480	22.515	4.000	1.62	0.11

Solution   a. The p-value is shown as .11. The one-tailed p-value is half that or about .0515.

   b. The z statistic is shown as 1.62. From the normal tables, the area to the right of 1.62 is $.5000 - .4474 = .0526$.

   c. Because the p-value is not less than .05, we cannot reject H_0 at $\alpha = .05$, although we can come close. Note also that the p-value, .0526, is not less than .05, although it is close. ∎

As we stated previously, the p-value is called the attained-significance level of a statistical test. The results of a statistical test are often summarized by stating that the result is **statistically significant** at the specified p-value. For example, in the product-comparison example, a y value of 59 is statistically significant at $p = .0444$, using a one-tailed test. In the cereal weight example, $z = -8.5$ is statistically significant at $p = .0000000001$. The smaller the p-value, the more conclusive the rejection of the null hypothesis.

statistically significant

The phrase *statistically significant* is unfortunate. The word *significant* suggests "important," "interesting," and "large." Statistical significance does not necessarily imply importance, relevance, or practical significance. Statistical significance only implies that a null hypothesis can be rejected with a specified low risk of error. A better phrase would be *statistically detectable*. To say that a difference is statistically significant or statistically detectable is to say that the observed result cannot reasonably be attributed to random variation alone: The cereal weight problem is a case in point. With a z value of -8.5, the test is statistically significant at the $p \le .0000000001$ level. This allows the bureau to conclude with great confidence that the company is guilty of short-weighting, although the sample mean weight of 15.83 ounces is only about 1% less than the nominal package weight. It's a small but conclusively demonstrated underfilling of the packages.

One should recognize that rarely is any null hypothesis exactly true. For this reason, with a large enough sample size, almost any null hypothesis can be rejected. What does this mean? If the null hypothesis is rejected, it means that a difference has been established fairly conclusively, but no judgment has been made as to the importance or practical significance of the declared difference.

Conversely, a sample result with associated p-value $> .05$ (and considered by some to indicate "not statistically significant") could but may not have been the result of random fluctuation; that is, even though the p-value is greater than .05, there still may be an underlying effect. The problem is that we have not established it beyond a reasonable doubt. All in all, you should be careful not to read too much into statistical significance. The p-value gives the weight of the sample evidence for rejection of the null hypothesis. The experimenter must still judge the practical significance of observed results that are declared statistically significant.

SECTION 9.5   EXERCISES

9.26   Find the p-value for the test of Exercise 9.20.

9.27   A finance company finds that 15% of its customers fall behind in their payments. A revised loan policy is tried on a random sample of 50 customers. If 4 of the sample fall behind in payments, give a p-value for a statistical test of $H_0: \pi = .15$ versus $H_a: \pi < .15$.

9.28   Use normal tables to find the approximate p-value for Exercise 9.27.

9.29   A sales manager believes that a firm's sales representatives should spend about 40% of their working days traveling. If they are on the road for much less, new orders decline and the service and news-gathering functions of the representatives are not adequately met. If they travel much more than 40% of the time, expense accounts eat up any incremental profit. A study of the previous five months (110 working days) shows the following data (number of traveling days by each representative):

32   36   41   45   48   48   51   54   57   64
($\bar{y} = 47.6$, $s = 9.65$, $n = 10$)

A computer output for these data is shown below (based on an assumed population standard deviation of 10.0):

```
MTB > ztest of mean = 44 assuming sigma = 10 data in 'Data'

TEST OF MU = 44.000 VS MU N.E. 44.000
THE ASSUMED SIGMA = 10.0

              N      MEAN     STDEV    SE MEAN      Z     P VALUE
Data         10     47.600    9.652    3.162      1.14     0.26
```

a. Identify the value of the z statistic.

b. Identify the p-value.

c. Is a one-tailed or a two-tailed p-value more appropriate for this problem?

9.30   The sales manager of Exercise 9.29 concludes that the discrepancy between the observed average of 47.6 and the desired average of 44.0 is not statistically significant and therefore the study proves that the travel-days situation is under control.

a. Do you agree that the result is not statistically significant (at the usual α levels)?

b. Do you agree that the study proves that the travel-days situation is under control?

9.31   The battery pack of a hand calculator is supposed to perform 20,000 calculations before needing recharging. A test of 114 battery packs gives an average of 19,695 calculations and a standard deviation of 1103.

a. Formulate null and research hypotheses.

b. Calculate the appropriate test statistic and *p*-value.

9.32   Is the result in Exercise 9.31 statistically significant at the usual α levels? Would you call the result practically significant?

9.6   HYPOTHESIS TESTING WITH THE *t* DISTRIBUTION

The modifications of normal (*z*) procedures to get *t*-distribution confidence intervals also apply to hypothesis tests. Once again, we replace σ by *s* and use *t* tables instead of *z* tables. In this section we summarize the procedure and take care of some other small differences in mechanics.

The basic procedure for any hypothesis-testing method requires formulating null and research hypotheses (H_0 and H_a), choosing a test statistic (T.S.), defining a rejection region (R.R.), calculating the T.S. value, and finally stating a conclusion. Here we are concerned with testing hypotheses about a population mean; we are still making the formal mathematical assumption that the population distribution is exactly normal.

Small-Sample Test of Hypotheses About μ

$H_0: \mu = \mu_0$

$H_a:$ 1. $\mu > \mu_0$

   2. $\mu < \mu_0$

   3. $\mu \neq \mu_0$

T.S.: $t = \dfrac{\bar{y} - \mu_0}{s/\sqrt{n}}$

R.R.: For a given probability α of a Type I error, reject H_0 if

   1. $t > t_\alpha$

   2. $t < -t_\alpha$

   3. $|t| \geq t_{\alpha/2}$

   where t_α cuts off a right-tail area of *a* in a *t* distribution with $n - 1$ d.f.

EXAMPLE 9.15   An airline institutes a "snake system" waiting line at its counters to try to reduce the average waiting time. The mean waiting time under specific conditions with the previous system was 6.1 minutes. A sample of 14 waiting times is taken; the times are measured at widely separated times to eliminate the possibility of dependent observations. The resulting sample mean is 5.043 and the standard deviation is 2.266. Test the null hypothesis of no change against an appropriate research hypothesis, using $\alpha = .10$. Assume that the population of waiting times is approximately normal.

Solution   The population parameter of interest is μ, the long-run mean waiting time under normal conditions using the snake system. The research hypothesis is that the mean is lower than the previous mean, 6.1, so $H_a: \mu < 6.1$. We may take the null hypothesis to be $H_0: \mu = 6.1$ (no change). As usual, we need worry only about the boundary value of the null hypothesis.

$$H_0: \mu = 6.1$$
$$H_a: \mu < 6.1$$

$$\text{T.S.: } t = \frac{5.043 - 6.1}{2.266/\sqrt{14}} = -1.75$$

R.R.: For $\alpha = .10$ and d.f. $= 13$, reject H_0 for $t \leq -1.350$

Because the observed value of t, -1.75, is less than -1.350, we reject H_0 and conclude that the apparent reduction in mean waiting time (from 6.1 to about 5 minutes) is not merely a statistical fluke.   ∎

p-value for a t test

Earlier in this chapter we introduced the p-value as an index of the degree of support for a research hypothesis from a given data set. There we were able to use z tables to compute p-values. Now we must use t tables, which are much less extensive; for given degrees of freedom, a t table gives only a few values. With these tables we can get only approximate p-values (although most statistical software systems give precise p-values). The key to the approximation is the fact that the p-value is the smallest α value that allows rejection of the null hypothesis. If the null hypothesis can be rejected at a particular α level, the p-value must be less than that α. If the null hypothesis cannot be rejected at a particular α level, the p-value must be greater than that α. Therefore we can often bracket the p-value between two numbers. All that is needed is to locate the actually observed t statistic between two t table values. The bounds on the p-value can be read directly.

EXAMPLE 9.16   Find bounds on the p-value in Example 9.15.

Solution   In Example 9.15 we found that we could reject H_0 at $\alpha = .10$ because $t = -1.75$ was below $-t_{.10, 13\text{d.f.}} = -1.350$. Therefore $p < .10$. When we try $\alpha = .05$, we find that we cannot quite reject H_0; the tabulated t value is $-t_{.05, 13\text{d.f.}} = -1.771$. Therefore $p > .05$. We can summarize the approximate p-value as $.05 < p < .10$.   ∎

EXAMPLE 9.17   An insurance adjuster in a small city uses two different garages to handle repairs to foreign cars damaged in collisions. To test whether the garages are competitive in cost, the adjuster obtains estimates from both garages for repair cost on each of 15 such cars. The data are shown in the table below. Test the null hypothesis that the mean difference is zero against an appropriate research hypothesis. What can be said about a p-value?

	Repair Estimates (in Hundreds of Dollars)						
Car	1	2	3	4	5	6	7
Garage 1	7.6	10.2	9.5	1.3	3.0	6.3	5.3
Garage 2	7.3	9.1	8.4	1.5	2.7	5.8	4.9
Difference, d	.3	1.1	1.1	−.2	.3	.5	.4

	Repair Estimates (in Hundreds of Dollars)						
Car	8	9	10	11	12	13	14	15
Garage 1	6.2	2.2	4.8	11.3	12.1	6.9	7.6	8.4
Garage 2	5.3	2.0	4.2	11.0	11.0	6.1	6.7	7.5
Difference, d	.9	.2	.6	.3	1.1	.8	.9	.9

Solution The null hypothesis is that the true mean difference $\mu_d = 0$. As no particular direction has been specified for the research hypothesis, take $H_a: \mu_d \neq 0$. We base the test on the differences (which are designated by d rather than y here). The test statistic is

$$t = \frac{\bar{d} - 0}{s_d/\sqrt{n}}$$

and is based on $n - 1 = 14$ d.f. Routine calculations give $\bar{d} = .613$ and $s_d = .394$, so

$$t = \frac{.613}{.394/\sqrt{15}} = 6.03$$

The largest tabled t value for 14 d.f. is 2.977, corresponding to a one-tail area of .005. Thus even for a (two-tailed) α of .01, H_0 could easily be rejected. The p-value must be less than .01; in fact, we suspect that the p-value is much smaller than .01. Formally, we conclude that the two garages have different average estimates. Practically, it is clear that garage 1 has higher average estimates than garage 2. ■

Evaluation of β and power is more difficult for t tests than for z tests. The method for calculating β stated in Section 9.4 is strictly valid only for z tests, but it can be used as an approximation for t tests. Because a t statistic is more variable than a z statistic, the formula tends to underestimate β and therefore to overestimate power. The easiest way to use the method is to specify a value for

$$\frac{\mu_a - \mu_0}{\sigma}$$

and a value for α. For example, suppose that a t test is run using $n = 25$ and $\alpha = .05$ (two-tailed) and that we hypothesize that the true population mean is .8 standard deviations above the null hypothesis mean;

$$\frac{\mu_a - \mu_0}{\sigma} = .8$$

Then, approximately,

$$\beta = P\left(z > -z_{\alpha/2} + \frac{|\mu_a - \mu_0|}{\sigma/\sqrt{n}}\right)$$

$$= P\left(z > -1.96 + \frac{.8}{1/\sqrt{25}}\right)$$

$$= P(z > 2.04) = .0207$$

It follows that power is approximately $1 - .0207 = .9793$ under these conditions. As we indicated, the calculation underestimates β and overestimates power. Thus the power is not quite as good as the calculation indicates.

EXAMPLE 9.18   In a computer simulation, 1000 samples of size 30 are drawn from a normal population having mean 55 and standard deviation 10. The null hypothesis that the population mean is 50 is tested, based on each sample. The following results are obtained:

Mu	Sigma	n
55.000	10.0000	30

	number of times H0: "mean is 50" is rejected in favor of		
alpha	"mean > 50"	"mean < 50"	total (alpha doubled)
0.100	919	0	919
0.050	856	0	856
0.025	752	0	752
0.010	624	0	624
0.005	541	0	541

The indicated α values are for one-tailed tests. The total shown in the output corresponds to a two-tailed test; as shown, the α value should be doubled. What probability is being approximated by the fraction 919/1000? How close is this approximation to the theoretical probability calculated by formula?

Solution   In this simulation the null hypothesis is false; μ is 55, not 50. The fraction 919/1000 approximates the probability that the test will reject the null hypothesis when it is false; by definition, that probability is $1 - \beta$, the power of the test. We can calculate the theoretical β by formula. For a one-tailed test with $\alpha = .10$, the required table value is $z_{.10} = 1.28$; $\mu_0 = 50$, $\mu_a = 55$, $\alpha = 10$, and $n = 30$. Therefore

$$\beta = P\left(z > -1.28 + \frac{|55 - 50|}{10/\sqrt{30}}\right) = P(z > 1.46)$$

$$= .0721$$

So power $= 1 - .0721 = .9279$. The simulation value, .919, is quite close to the calculated power.   ∎

SECTION 9.6   EXERCISES

9.33 A dealer in recycled paper places empty trailers at various sites; these are gradually filled by individuals who bring in old newspapers and the like. The trailers are picked up (and replaced by empties) on several schedules. One such schedule involves pickup every second week. This schedule is desirable if the average amount of recycled paper is more than 1600 cubic feet per two-week period. The dealer's records for 18 two-week periods show the following volumes (in cubic feet) at a particular site:

1660	1820	1590	1440	1730	1680	1750	1720	1900
1570	1700	1900	1800	1770	2010	1580	1620	1690

$(\bar{y} = 1718.3, \quad s = 137.8)$

Assume that these figures represent the results of a random sample. Do they support the research hypothesis that $\mu > 1600$, using $\alpha = .10$? Write out all parts of the hypothesis-testing procedure.

9.34 Place an upper bound on the p-value of Exercise 9.33. Would you say that $\mu > 1600$ is strongly supported?

9.35 A federal regulatory agency is investigating an advertised claim that a certain device can increase the gasoline mileage of cars. Seven such devices are purchased and installed in seven cars belonging to the agency. Gasoline mileage for each of the cars under standard conditions is recorded both before and after installation.

	Car						
	1	2	3	4	5	6	7
Mpg before	19.1	19.9	17.6	20.2	23.5	26.8	21.7
Mpg after	20.0	23.7	18.7	22.3	23.8	19.2	24.6
Change	.9	3.8	1.1	2.1	.3	−7.6	2.9

The mean change is .50 miles per gallon and the standard deviation is 3.77.

a. Formulate appropriate null and research hypotheses.

b. Is the advertised claim supported at $\alpha = .05$? Carry out the steps of a hypothesis test.

9.36 Use the data of Exercise 9.35 to construct a 90% confidence interval for the mean change. On the basis of this interval, can one reject the hypothesis of no mean change? (Note that the two-sided 90% confidence interval corresponds to a one-tailed $\alpha = .05$ test.)

9.37 Would you say that the agency of Exercises 9.35 and 9.36 has conclusively established that the device has no effect on the average mileage of cars? What does the width of the interval in Exercise 9.36 have to do with your answer?

9.38 A small manufacturer has a choice between shipping via the postal service and shipping via a private shipper. As a test, 10 destinations are chosen and packages shipped to each by both routes. The delivery times, in days, are as follows:

					Destination					
	1	2	3	4	5	6	7	8	9	10
Postal service	3	4	5	4	8	9	7	10	9	9
Private shipper	2	2	3	5	4	6	9	6	7	6
Difference	1	2	2	−1	4	3	−2	4	2	3

a. Calculate the mean and standard deviation of the differences.
b. Test the null hypothesis of no mean difference in delivery times against the research hypothesis that the private shipper has a shorter average delivery time. Use $\alpha = .01$.

9.7   THE EFFECT OF POPULATION NONNORMALITY   ∎

We discussed the effect of population nonnormality on t confidence intervals in Section 8.6. Exactly the same conclusions apply to t tests. The nominal α value and p-value are reasonably accurate if the population is symmetric but heavy- or light-tailed relative to the normal distribution. In this case, a t test may be inefficient. Inefficiency in hypothesis testing terms means that some other test—such as the sign (median) test discussed in the next section—has better power at the same α level. We illustrate these effects of nonnormality with several simulation studies.

EXAMPLE 9.19   A simulation study takes 1000 samples of size 30 from a Laplace population, a symmetric, moderately outlier-prone population. The following results are obtained:

```
                        Checking Alpha

Simulation of One Sample t-test (1000 samples)
Population shape is moderately outlier prone.

        Mu        Sigma        n
      50.000     10.0000      30



one-tail:

        number of times HO:  "mean is  50" is rejected in favor of
alpha    "mean >  50"    "mean <  50"         total (alpha doubled)
0.100       104              95               199
0.050        51              51               102
0.025        28              24                52
0.010         7               6                13
0.005         4               3                 7


average t is 0.0077 with variance of    1.086943
```

Which hypothesis is true in the simulation? Does the outlier-proneness of the Laplace population have a serious effect?

Solution   The output indicates that H_0 is $\mu = 50$, and indeed the population mean is 50. Therefore, fractions such as 104/1000 are approximating α, the probability of Type I error; the fractions are approximations because they are based on 1000 samples, not on an infinite number. Notice that all the fractions are very close to the nominal α values. For example, with a one-tailed α of .025, the observed fractions are .028 and .024. ■

EXAMPLE 9.20   Another simulation study involves samples of size 30 from a Laplace population. In this study, the mean is 55, so $H_0: \mu = 50$ is false. The results of a t test and also of a sign test (a test for the median, which is also 55 by the symmetry of the Laplace population) are shown here:

```
Results for t test
        Mu        Sigma        n
       55.000     10.0000      30

        number of times H0: "mean is  50" is rejected in favor of
alpha   "mean >  50"    "mean <  50"        total (alpha doubled)
0.100      913               0               913
0.050      831               0               831
0.025      745               0               745
0.010      629               0               629
0.005      537               0               537

Simulation of Sign Test (1000 samples)

Simulation results using the normal approximation
        number of times H0: "median is  50" is rejected in favor of
alpha   "median >  50"   "median <  50"     total (alpha doubled)
0.100      956               0               956
0.050      905               0               905
0.025      816               0               816
0.010      686               0               686
0.005      519               0               519
```

Which test appears to have better power, in general?

Solution   Recall that power is the probability that the null hypothesis will be rejected, assuming that it is false. We note that for every α except .005 (one-tailed), the sign test rejects the hypothesis more frequently than does the t test. Therefore the sign test appears generally more powerful for this moderately outlier-prone population. ■

9.8   TESTS ABOUT A POPULATION MEDIAN ■

The median is more robust than the mean. The specific values attained by the few largest and smallest observations affect the mean considerably but the median not at all. In some situations, a population median is a more useful description of the center of a distribution than is the population mean.

As with confidence intervals about a median, hypothesis tests about a median do *not* follow the standard format of inferences about a mean. Instead, a reformulation reduces the problem to a binomial situation. To illustrate, suppose that the null hypothesis is that the median score on a programming aptitude test is 60, with a research (alternative) hypothesis that the median is smaller. The idea is that every observation in a random sample is compared to the hypothesized **median test in** median of 60. Then by letting every observation above 60 denote a success and **terms of a binomial** every observation below 60 denote a failure*, the problem involving a population **distribution** median is translated into one related to a binomial random variable. By definition of a median, the null hypothesis yields a .5 probability of success. If the research hypothesis is true, the probability of a success is something less than .5. Therefore the binomial test described earlier in this chapter applies.

EXAMPLE 9.21   Perform a median test for the data of Example 9.17.

Solution   We take H_0: *Median* difference is zero against a two-sided H_a. Define a success as a difference that is greater than zero. Because no difference equals zero, $n = 15$ and the total number of successes Y in the 15 trials is $y = 14$. From a binomial table, with $n = 15$, $\pi = .5$, $P_Y(y \geq 14) \approx .0005$. For a two-tailed test, we add the two probabilities $P_Y(y \leq 1)$ and $P_Y(y \geq 14)$ to obtain a *p*-value of .0010. Again H_0 can safely be rejected.   ■

EXAMPLE 9.22   Refer to Example 9.20. What does the simulation study indicate about the desirability of using a median test rather than a *t* test for the outlier-prone population?

Solution   As we observed in Example 9.20, the power of the median (sign) test is generally better for outlier-prone data.   ■

SECTION 9.8   EXERCISES

9.39   Refer to the data of Exercise 8.27 (page 305).
   a. Plot a histogram or stem-and-leaf display of the data.
   b. Is there any obvious reason to doubt the approximate correctness of the 95% confidence level?

9.40   Refer again to the data of Exercise 8.27.
   a. Test the null hypothesis that the mean price is $315 against a two-sided H_a. Find bounds on the *p*-value.
   b. Test the null hypothesis that the median price is $315 against a two-sided H_a. Find bounds on the *p*-value.
   c. Is there a serious difference in the conclusions of parts (a) and (b)?

9.41   Find a 95% confidence interval for the true median price, using the data of Exercise 8.27.

---

* If there are values that are exactly equal to the hypothesized median, we can't tell whether to count them as above or below. The easiest solution to this problem, adopted by most computer packages, is to discard such values and reduce *n* by the number discarded.

9.42 Refer to the data of Exercise 8.25 (page 304).
   a. Perform a t test of $H_0: \mu \leq 45$ versus $H_a: \mu > 45$. Use $\alpha = .05$.
   b. Plot the data. Is there reason to be skeptical of your conclusion in part (a)?

9.43 Again refer to Exercise 8.25.
   a. Test the null hypothesis that the true median is less than or equal to 45. Use $\alpha = .05$.
   b. Is there a major difference between your conclusions here and in Exercise 9.42? If there is, what explains the difference?

9.44 Random samples of size 30 are drawn from a normal population having mean 55 and standard deviation 10. Both t and median (sign) tests are performed. The following results are obtained:

```
Simulation of One Sample t-test (1000 samples)

          Mu        Sigma        n
        55.000     10.0000      30

      number of times HO:  "mean is  50" is rejected in favor of
alpha    "mean >  50"    "mean <  50"        total (alpha doubled)
0.100        919              0                    919
0.050        856              0                    856
0.025        752              0                    752
0.010        624              0                    624
0.005        541              0                    541

Simulation of Sign Test (1000 samples)

          Mu        Sigma        n
        55.000     10.0000      30

Simulation results using binomial probabilities

      number of times HO:  "median is  50" is rejected in favor of
alpha    "median >  50"   "median <  50"     total (alpha doubled)
0.100        698              0                    698
0.050        698              0                    698
0.025        564              0                    564
0.010        409              0                    409
0.005        256              0                    256
```

   a. What probabilities are being approximated in this simulation?
   b. What do the results indicate about the relative desirability of the t and sign tests when sampling from a normal population?

9.9   TESTING A POPULATION PROPORTION USING A NORMAL APPROXIMATION

In the first section of this chapter we did a test of a population proportion using binomial tables. The practical problem is that complete binomial tables are not always available, and if available they are cumbersome and necessarily limited. For example, how would you test the null hypothesis that $\pi = .373$ with $n = 277$? Even with a good computer program, binomial probabilities are relatively slow and expensive to compute. The normal-distribution approximation to the binomial allows approximate tests to be run; the method is much like that of Section 9.3 for a statistical test related to μ.

The product-comparison example of Section 9.1 illustrates the method. The null hypothesis is $H_0: \pi = .50$ and the research hypothesis is $H_a: \pi > .50$. Hence we want a one-tailed test. In Chapter 5 we showed that if n is large and π is not too close to 0 or 1, the z statistic for the binomial random variable Y,

$$z = \frac{Y - n\pi}{\sqrt{n\pi(1 - \pi)}}$$

is approximately standard (tabled) normal. This z can be used as the test statistic instead of y; the relevant value for π is the (boundary) null hypothesis value, $\pi_0 = .50$. As with a statistical test for μ, the one-tailed rejection region for $\alpha = .05$ is $z > 1.645$. A little algebra shows that $z > 1.645$ is equivalent to $y > n\pi_0 + 1.645\sqrt{n\pi_0(1 - \pi_0)}$, or, in the product-comparison problem, $y \geq 58.225$. Because y can assume only integer values, this rejection region is equivalent to $y \geq 59$, which is the rejection region we got in Section 9.1 for $\alpha = .05$. Similarly, for $\alpha = .10$, the rejection region is $z \geq 1.282$, or $y \geq 56.41$. Because y can assume only integer values, this is equivalent to $y \geq 57$, which again is the rejection region we got in Section 9.1 for $\alpha = .10$. The observed y value of 68 corresponds to a z score of 3.6:

$$z = \frac{y - n\pi_0}{\sqrt{n\pi_0(1 - \pi_0)}} = \frac{68 - 50}{\sqrt{100(.5)(.5)}} = 3.6$$

Hence we reject $H_0: \pi = .05$ for $\alpha = .05$ (and for $\alpha = .01$). The approximate procedure for testing a population proportion using a z statistic is summarized below.

Summary for Test of a Population Proportion Using the Normal Approximation

$H_0: \pi = \pi_0$

$H_a:$ 1. $\pi > \pi_0$
　　 2. $\pi < \pi_0$
　　 3. $\pi \neq \pi_0$

T.S.: $z = \dfrac{y - n\pi_0}{\sqrt{n\pi_0(1 - \pi_0)}}$

R.R.: For the probability of a Type I error α, reject H_0 if
　　 1. $z > z_\alpha$
　　 2. $z < -z_\alpha$
　　 3. $z > z_{\alpha/2}$ or $z < -z_{\alpha/2}$
Note: π_0 is the (boundary) null-hypothesis value of the population proportion π.

There's another way to write the test statistic z. If $\hat{\pi}$ is the sample proportion (so $\hat{\pi} = y/n$), then z can be written

$$z = \frac{\hat{\pi} - \pi_0}{\sqrt{\pi_0(1 - \pi_0)/n}}$$

For the product-comparison example, $\hat{\pi} = 68/100 = .68$ and again $z = 3.6$. The two forms of z are algebraically equal, so they always give the same answer.

We said that the z test for π is approximate and works best if n is large and π_0 is not too near 0 or 1. A natural next question is, When can we use it? There are several rules to answer the question; none of them should be considered **sample-size** sacred. Our sense of the many studies that have been done is this: If either $n\pi_0$ **requirement** or $n(1 - \pi_0)$ is less than about 2, treat the results of a z test very skeptically. If $n\pi_0$ and $n(1 - \pi_0)$ are at least 5, the z test should be reasonably accurate. For the same sample size, tests based on extreme values of π_0 (e.g., .001) are less accurate than tests for values of π_0 such as .05 or .10. For example, a test of $H_0: \pi = .0001$ with $n\pi_0 = 1.2$ is much more suspect than one for $H_0: \pi = .10$ with $n\pi_0 = 50$. If the issue becomes crucial, it's best to interpret the results skeptically.

9.10   THE RELATION BETWEEN HYPOTHESIS TESTS AND CONFIDENCE INTERVALS

We now have two forms of inference: Confidence intervals and hypothesis tests. Both can be performed on the same data. How are they related? For the cereal box example, a 95% confidence interval for the true mean weight is $\mu \pm 1.96\sigma_{\bar{y}}$. Substituting $\bar{y} = 15.83$, $n = 25$, and $\sigma = .1$, we have

$$15.83 - 1.96\frac{(.1)}{\sqrt{25}} \le \mu \le 15.83 + 1.96\frac{(.1)}{\sqrt{25}} \qquad \text{or} \qquad 15.791 \le \mu \le 15.869$$

In our statistical test of $H_0: \mu \ge 16$, the boundary value $\mu_0 = 16$ does not fall within the 95% confidence interval, so it seems plausible to reject H_0. What is the probability of a Type I error for a statistical test based on a 95% confidence interval? In general, a particular null-hypothesis value, say, θ_0, of any population parameter θ may be rejected with the probability of a Type I error α if and only if θ_0 does not fall in a $(1 - \alpha) \times 100\%$ confidence interval for θ.

For example, because the 95% confidence interval $15.791 \le \mu \le 15.869$ does not include $\mu_0 = 16$, we can reject $H_0: \mu = 16$, based on $\alpha = .05$. In fact, this is a general method for constructing confidence intervals; a 95% confidence interval can be defined as the set of nonrejectable ($\alpha = .05$) null-hypothesis values. For instance, in a two-tailed test a particular μ value is not rejected using $\alpha = .05$ if the z statistic lies in the interval

$$-1.96 \le \frac{\bar{y} - \mu}{\sigma/\sqrt{n}} \le 1.96$$

A little algebra shows that this is equivalent to

$$\bar{y} - 1.96 \frac{\sigma}{\sqrt{n}} \leq \mu \leq \bar{y} + 1.96 \frac{\sigma}{\sqrt{n}}$$

which is the 95% confidence interval for μ. (There's a slight problem with using $<$ or $\leq$. However, the probability that z is exactly equal to 1.96 is so small— theoretically it's zero—that we don't worry about it.) In this sense, confidence intervals and hypothesis tests give equivalent results.

The usual confidence interval is two-sided. As above, such confidence intervals correspond to two-tailed tests. There is such a thing as a one-sided confidence interval. The nonrejection region for a left-tailed test at $\alpha = .05$ is

$$\frac{\bar{y} - \mu}{\sigma/\sqrt{n}} \geq -1.645$$

When solved for μ, this is

$$\mu \leq \bar{y} + 1.645 \frac{\sigma}{\sqrt{n}}$$

one-sided confidence interval

which is a **one-sided confidence interval**. In the cereal box example, this becomes $\mu < 15.863$; because the boundary value $\mu_0 = 16$ does not fall within this interval, $H_0: \mu = 16$ may be rejected using $\alpha = .05$, one-tailed. For the remainder of this text, we use two-sided confidence intervals, which can be used to test two-sided research hypotheses.

EXAMPLE 9.23   For the television-watching data of Example 9.8, use a 99% confidence interval to test $H_0: \mu = 22.6$ versus $H_a: \mu \neq 22.6$.

Solution   The two-sided research hypothesis implies that a two-sided confidence interval may be used to test the null hypothesis. In Example 9.8, $\bar{y} = 25.2$, σ is assumed to be 6.1, and $n = 50$. The 99% confidence interval is

$$25.2 - 2.576 \frac{6.1}{\sqrt{60}} \leq \mu \leq 25.2 + 2.576 \frac{6.1}{\sqrt{60}} \qquad \text{or} \qquad 23.2 \leq \mu \leq 27.2$$

Because the value of μ under H_0, 22.6, does not fall within the interval, we reject H_0 using $\alpha = .01$. Of course, the same conclusion was obtained in Example 9.8.   ∎

confidence interval and β

When the null hypothesis is not rejected, confidence intervals are useful in giving a crude measure of the risk of a Type II error. Roughly speaking, a wide 95% confidence interval indicates a high degree of uncertainty and therefore a high probability β of Type II error. (Of course 95% confidence fixes α at .05.) For example, if a seller of high-intensity lights for portable television cameras claims a mean life of 40 hours and a sample of 10 lights yields a 95% confidence interval of $28.0 \leq \mu \leq 44.0$, the seller's claim cannot be rejected using an $\alpha = .05$ level. Note, too, that the interval is very wide; the lower limit of 28.0 is 30% below the claimed value. If the difference between a mean life of 40 hours and, say, a mean life of 30 hours was crucial in deciding whether to buy, the buyer would not be comfortable in accepting $\mu = 40$. The probability of a Type II error corresponding to $\mu = 30$ would undoubtedly be quite large.

SECTION 9.10   EXERCISES

9.45 In Exercise 2.66, we considered claims (in thousands of dollars) for automobile collision damage from a particular insurance company. A box plot of the data is shown in Figure 9.7. Data analysis using the Statgraphics package is shown below:

```
                       One-Sample Analysis Results
-------------------------------------------------------------------------
                                         claimsize
Sample Statistics: Number of Obs.        187
                   Average               5.17754
                   Variance              27.9194
                   Std. Deviation        5.28388
                   Median                3.5

Confidence Interval for Mean:            95    Percent
                   Sample 1              4.41509 5.93999    186 D.F.

Confidence Interval for Variance:        95    Percent
                   Sample 1              23.0123 34.5919    186 D.F.


Hypothesis Test for HO: Mean = 4.62      Computed t statistic = 1.44293
                   vs Alt: NE            Sig. Level = 0.150723
                   at Alpha = 0.05       so do not reject HO.
```

a. The company's national mean claim size is 4.62 thousand dollars. The data come from a particular midwestern city. Does the confidence interval for the mean indicate that the city's mean claim size might be the same?

b. One claims department staff member said that the deviation from 4.62 was not statistically significant, so that the company could safely assume that the mean for this city was also 4.62. Is this a valid interpretation of the results?

Box and Whisker Plot

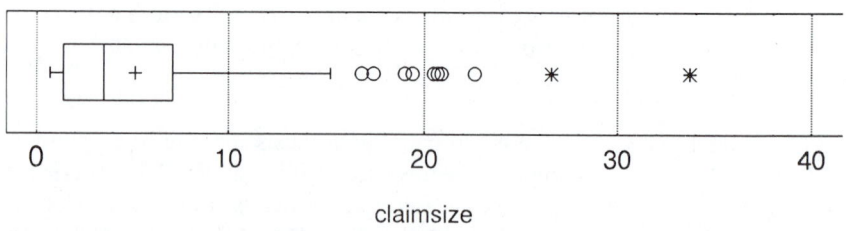

claimsize

FIGURE 9.7   Box Plot of Collision Claims Data

9.46 The box plot of claims data in Figure 9.7 shows some skewness. Does that mean that the claimed probabilities for the test of the mean are wrong?

9.47 In Exercise 9.23 we tested the null hypothesis that the long-run mean number of public service commercials was 1.50. The test was based on a sample of 18 observations with a sample mean of 1.278; the assumed population standard deviation was 1.60. The null hypothesis was retained, using $\alpha = .05$.

  a. Calculate a 95% confidence interval for the population (long-run) mean. Because we're assuming that σ is known, use the z table.

  b. Show that this confidence interval is consistent with the conclusion of Exercise 9.23.

9.48 The null hypothesis in Exercise 9.29, that the mean number of travel days of a population of sales representatives was 44, was barely retained, using $\alpha = .20$. The sample mean was 47.6, the sample size was 10, and the assumed σ was 10.0.

  a. Calculate an 80% confidence interval for the population mean; the required z_{10} value is 1.28.

  b. How does this confidence interval indicate that the null hypothesis must be retained?

  c. How does it indicate that H_0 is barely retained?

9.49 In Exercise 9.31, we tested a claim that the mean life of a battery for a calculator was 20,000 calculations. In a sample of 114 batteries, the mean was 19,695 and the standard deviation was 1103.

  a. Calculate a 99% confidence interval for the population mean lifetime.

  b. Show that the null hypothesis that the mean is 20,000 must be rejected at $\alpha = .01$.

  c. Would it be reasonable to say that, because H_0 is rejected so emphatically, the mean lifetime must be much lower than 20,000?

9.50 The main access road to a suburban shopping mall sometimes becomes severely congested. On weekdays, excluding holidays, the average number of vehicles going toward the mall between 9 A.M. and 7 P.M. that pass a counter is 11,260. The highway department tried to improve traffic flow by changing stoplight cycles and improving turn lanes. For the first five nonholiday weekdays after the changes, the volumes were 10,690, 11,452, 12,316, 12,297, and 12,647. The mean for this sample is 11,880.4 and the standard deviation is 798.68.

  a. Calculate a 95% confidence interval for the long-run (population) mean.

  b. Show that the null hypothesis that the mean is still 11,260 must be retained at $\alpha = .05$.

9.51 A local politician who reviewed the results of Exercise 9.50, said that the data proved that there had been no improvement in traffic volume. Is this a reasonable interpretation of the confidence interval?

9.52 The data for Exercise 9.50 are listed in time order. Is there any suggestion of dependence or a trend over time?

9.53 A clothing manufacturer cuts fabric from bolts. In the process, a certain amount of cloth is wasted. Using standard methods, the wastage is 9.26%. The maker of a computer controlled machine allowed the manufacturer to test the machine on a sample of 762 different cuts. In the sample, the mean wastage was 9.11% and the standard deviation was 1.07%.

  a. Calculate a 99% confidence interval for the mean wastage using the computer controlled machine.

  b. Show that there has been a statistically detectable (significant) change in the mean, using $\alpha = .01$.

9.54 In Exercise 9.53, can the maker of the machine legitimately say that statistics show the machine makes a large improvement in wastage?

9.55 The data underlying Exercise 9.53 were skewed by a few cases with large wastage numbers. Does this fact invalidate the confidence interval and test in Exercise 9.53?

9.11   TESTING A STANDARD DEVIATION   ∎

At the beginning of this chapter we tested a proportion and then turned to hypothesis tests about averages (means or medians). The same basic principles apply to hypothesis tests about a standard deviation. Such tests are particularly relevant in quality control situations. One way to improve quality is to reduce variability. Testing a standard deviation is one way to see if a change in design or process has, in fact, changed variability. Also, we'll show that hypothesis tests and confidence intervals for a standard deviation are related in the same way that they are for means.

A test for a population or process standard deviation is based on the χ^2 distribution, which is also true for the confidence interval for a standard deviation as we discussed in Section 8.8. The test statistic is $\chi^2 = (n-1)s^2/\sigma^2$, with $n-1$ d.f. We state the test procedure in terms of variances; it can be converted to standard deviations as usual by taking appropriate square roots.

Hypothesis Test for σ^2

H_0: $\sigma^2 = \sigma_0^2$

H_a: 1. $\sigma^2 > \sigma_0^2$
    2. $\sigma^2 < \sigma_0^2$
    3. $\sigma^2 \neq \sigma_0^2$

T.S.: $\chi^2 = (n-1)s^2/\sigma^2$

R.R.: 1. Reject H_0 if $\chi^2 > \chi_\alpha^2$
    2. Reject H_0 if $\chi^2 < \chi_{1-\alpha}^2$
    3. Reject H_0 if $\chi^2 > \chi_{\alpha/2}^2$ or $\chi^2 < \chi_{1-\alpha/2}^2$
    where χ_a^2 cuts off right-tail area a in the χ^2 distribution with $n-1$ d.f.

For example, a trucking firm specializing in small lots wants to load trucks with a weight of 20 tons (40,000 pounds). Variability is expensive; loads that are too light aren't economical and loads that are too heavy are illegal and draw fines. The current loading system yields a mean of 36.60 thousand pounds and a standard deviation of 3.010 thousand pounds. A computerized loading system is tried on a sample of 101 truckloads. The mean weight is 36.81 thousand pounds; the standard deviation is 2.064. Is there conclusive evidence that the standard deviation using the computerized system will be different from that of the current system? The null hypothesis is that $\sigma = 3.010$ for the computerized system also; because we are looking for any change, we take a two-sided H_a. The test statistic is $\chi^2 = (101-1)(2.064)^2/(3.010)^2 = 47.02$. The conclusion will depend on the choice of α; for $\alpha = .05$ and a two-tailed test with $101 - 1 = 100$ d.f., the R.R. is $\chi^2 < 74.22$ or $\chi^2 > 129.56$. Because $47.02 < 74.22$ we reject H_0 and we conclude that there is good evidence that the computerized system will yield a different (and, in practice, smaller) standard deviation. Even if we chose $\alpha = .002$ (because $\alpha/2 = .001$ is the smallest area in our χ^2 table), we would reject H_0 because $47.02 < 61.92$, the table value. By the Universal Rejection Region (reject H_0

when and only when the p-value $< \alpha$), the p-value is less than .002, so the evidence is very conclusive.

Another way to carry out the same test is to use a confidence interval. As in Section 9.10, we will reject the null hypothesis value if it is not included in the confidence interval. The χ^2 95% confidence interval for the population variance is

$$\frac{(101 - 1)(2.064)^2}{129.56} \le \sigma^2 \le \frac{(101 - 1)(2.064)^2}{74.22}$$

or $3.288 \le \sigma^2 \le 5.740$. The 95% confidence interval for the standard deviation follows by square roots as $1.81 \le \sigma \le 2.40$. This interval doesn't include the H_0 value, 3.010, so we reject H_0 at $\alpha = .05$ (corresponding to 95% confidence) once again.

EXAMPLE 9.24   Suppose that a pharmaceutical company wants the standard deviation of potencies in any lot of tablets to be no more than 1.40. Can this H_0 be rejected for $\alpha = .10$ if a sample of 30 tablets has a variance of 2.1583?

Solution   The elements of the statistical test for σ^2 are

$$H_0: \sigma^2 = (1.4)^2 = 1.96$$
$$H_a: \sigma^2 > 1.96$$

$$\text{T.S.: } \chi^2 = (n - 1)\frac{s^2}{\sigma_0^2} = \frac{29(2.1583)}{1.96} = 31.934$$

R.R.: The χ_α^2 tabulated value for $\alpha = .10$ and d.f. $= 29$ is 39.09, so there is insufficient evidence to reject H_0.

In this problem, a good case can be made for the argument that $\sigma^2 = (1.40)^2$ is a **maximum** allowable variance and that the research hypothesis should be $H_a: \sigma^2 < 1.96$. A batch of tablets would not be released unless quality control could support $\sigma^2 < 1.96$. This is a tougher standard; for the data $\sigma^2 < 1.96$ is not supported at all. ∎

In Section 8.8, we said that χ^2 methods for a variance were very sensitive to nonnormality. If we sample from a nonnormal population or process, the claimed α probability and p-values will be wrong, possibly very wrong, regardless of sample size. The jackknife method we described in Section 8.8 can be used to perform hypothesis tests that are more believable in the face of nonnormality. An easy jackknife test is to reject H_0 if the H_0 value is not included in the jackknife confidence interval.

SECTION 9.11   EXERCISES

9.56   A sample of 25 observations is drawn from a normal population with unknown mean μ and variance σ^2. Define

$$\chi^2 = \frac{(n - 1)s^2}{\sigma^2}$$

Find the following probabilities:
a. $P(\chi^2 > 12.4)$
b. $P(\chi^2 < 36.4)$
c. $P(9.89 < \chi^2 < 45.56)$

9.57 A packaging line fills nominal 32-ounce tomato juice jars with an actual mean of 32.30 ounces. The process should have a standard deviation smaller than .15 ounce per jar (a larger standard deviation leads to too many underweight and overfilled jars). Samples of 61 jars are regularly taken to test the process. One such sample yields a sample mean of 32.28 ounces and a standard deviation of .132 ounce. Does this indicate (using $\alpha = .05$) that $\sigma < .15$? Carry out a formal hypothesis test.

9.58 Suppose that the research hypothesis in Exercise 9.57 is formulated as $\sigma > .15$. Does this reformulation tend to be more or less generous in terms of what sample results cause the packaging line to be shut down for adjustment?

9.59 A certain part for a small assembly should have a diameter of 4.000 millimeters, and a maximum standard deviation of .011 millimeter is allowed by specifications. A random sample of 26 parts shows the following diameters:

3.952 3.978 3.979 3.984 3.987 3.991 3.995 3.997 3.999 3.999 3.999
4.000 4.000 4.000 4.001 4.001 4.002 4.002 4.003 4.004 4.006 4.009
4.010 4.012 4.023 4.041

a. Calculate the sample mean and standard deviation.
b. Can the research hypothesis that $\sigma > .011$ be supported (at $\alpha = .05$) by these data? State all parts of a statistical hypothesis test.

9.60 Calculate 90% confidence intervals for the true variance and for the true standard deviation for the data of Exercise 9.59.

9.61 Plot the data of Exercise 9.59. Does the plot suggest any violation of the assumptions underlying your answers to Exercises 9.59 and 9.60? Would such a violation have a serious effect on the validity of your answers?

9.62 Baseballs vary somewhat in their rebounding coefficient. A "dead ball" has a relatively low rebound, while a "rabbit ball" has a high rebound. A standard test has been developed. A purchaser of large quantities of baseballs requires that the mean value be 85 and the standard deviation be less than 2 units. A sample of 81 baseballs is tested. The mean value is 84.91 and the standard deviation is 1.80. Can the research hypothesis that $\sigma < 2$ be supported using $\alpha = .05$? Carry out the steps of a formal hypothesis test.

9.63 Place bounds on the p-value in Exercise 9.62.

9.12   HYPOTHESIS TESTING AS A DECISION METHOD ∎

In this chapter, hypothesis testing has been presented as a method for supporting or not supporting research hypotheses. Such hypotheses need not be directly related to a decision. However, there are many situations, such as the television-camera light example in Section 9.10 where a decision such as buy or don't buy is directly involved. In such situations, the research hypotheses is usually called the alternative hypothesis*: The problem is more one of deciding between two hypotheses than of supporting or not supporting a research hypothesis. The two hypotheses usually correspond directly to two possible actions.

* That's why we use the symbol H_a instead of, perhaps, H_r.

The television-camera light problem illuminates how to use a statistical test for decision making. The null hypothesis can be taken as $\mu \geq 40$. Let's assume that the television station would be happy to buy the lights if this null hypothesis is true. The relevant alternative is H_a: $\mu < 40$; if the true mean life is substantially less than 40 hours, the station presumably wouldn't want to buy. Suppose that the buyer plans to observe a sample of 8 lights before reaching a decision. In addition, assume that $\sigma = 10$ hours. (Obviously, in practice we would not know σ and hence we would need a larger n to substitute s for σ in the z statistic.) If the station sets $\alpha = .10$, the rejection region for a statistical test of H_0: $\mu \geq 40$ and H_a: $\mu < 40$ is $z \leq -1.282$. Thus, in terms of a decision procedure, the station will buy the light bulbs if $z > -1.282$ and will not buy if $z \leq -1.282$. In this situation, a Type I error is failing to buy if the claim (H_0: $\mu \geq 40$) is correct.

Suppose that a true mean life of 30 hours would make the lights uneconomical. A Type II error in this situation is buying lights that are uneconomical. The television station would be concerned with the β risk. According to our formula in Section 9.4,

$$\beta_{30} = P\left(z > -1.282 + \frac{|30 - 40|}{10/\sqrt{8}}\right)$$

$$= P(z > 1.55) \approx .06$$

Thus, even a sample of size 8 is enough to yield reasonably low error risks ($\alpha = .10$, $\beta_{30} = .06$), because $\mu_a = 30$ and $\mu_0 = 40$ are rather far apart. The problem of deciding whether or not to buy, based on results from the sample, can be interpreted as a hypothesis-testing problem.

The practical difficulty with this approach is the choice of desirable α and β risks. Of course we'd like to have both risks very low. Usually, though, the only way to do this is to take a very large sample, which can be expensive or impossible. As we've noted previously, for a fixed sample size a decrease in α can be obtained only by an increase in β. It's often hard to see what the right choice is. The choice depends, not only on the relative costs of the two errors, but also on the relative plausibility of the hypotheses. If the cost of bad lights is high and the loss in passing up good lights is low, a Type II error is more costly than a Type I error. So the β risk should be chosen much smaller than the α risk. If the seller is known to be very reliable in its claims, so that the null hypothesis is very plausible, the television station may be relatively more willing to consider a low sample mean as a fluke and reject the null hypothesis only for very extreme z statistic values. A rejection region that rejects the null hypothesis only for very extreme values of a test statistic has a very low α value. The proper choice of α and β depends, not only on the relative costs of the two types of error, but also on the

prior probability   **prior probabilities** of the two hypotheses.

SECTION 9.12   EXERCISES

9.64   A flour miller's contract with a grain seller requires that the average protein content of winter wheat sold to the miller be at least 13.5%. The miller has several samples from each grain shipment analyzed. If the protein content is below 13.5% (to a statistically significant extent), the miller deducts a penalty from the payment to the seller.

  a. Formulate null and alternative hypotheses for this problem.

  b. What actions follow from rejecting and from not rejecting the null hypothesis?

  c. What would be the consequence of setting α at a very small value?

9.65   Assume the following conditions in Exercise 9.64:

  i. Invoking a penalty can lead to legal actions; if the penalty is claimed and the shipment is subsequently found to meet the protein standard, substantial damages must be paid by the miller.

  ii. If the full shipment is deficient in protein, the miller incurs a modest additional cost to supplement the protein content.

  iii. The shipment comes from an established seller and is drawn from grain of an excellent harvest.

  What do these considerations imply about the choice appropriate α and β values?

9.66   A former commissioner of the Food and Drug Administration commented that Congress complains violently whenever the FDA mistakenly allows an unsafe or ineffective drug onto the market but never says a word if a safe, effective drug is not allowed onto the market. If we take the research hypothesis as "drug is safe and effective," what does the ex-commissioner's comment imply about the relative costs of Type I and Type II errors?

Summary

Hypothesis testing is a means for a manager to decide whether an apparent result in a sample is probably an indication that there is a real effect in the underlying population or process, or that the apparent result might plausibly be a fluke of the particular sample. Formally, hypothesis testing was used to "contradict" a negative, null hypothesis that typically says that there is no real effect. The null hypothesis is "contradicted" if the sample data are very unlikely, assuming the null hypothesis is true. Hypothesis tests may be carried out in five steps: Specification of null hypothesis, specification of one-sided or two-sided research hypothesis, choice of test statistic, specification of rejection region, and conclusion from the actual data.

The specification of a rejection region requires consideration of possible false positive (Type I) and false negative (Type II) errors. Typically, α, the probability of a Type I error, is specified and used to determine the R.R.; the β probability of a Type II error (or power, the complement of the β probability) may be calculated given the R.R. and a specification of a particular value in the research hypothesis.

The basic mechanics were introduced in the context of a binomial test for a proportion, mostly because the computations are easy in this test. The same essential steps apply to a z test for a mean with a known population standard deviation and to a t test for a mean with unknown population standard deviation, as well as to a chi-square test for a standard deviation.

The p-value for a statistical test is a conclusiveness index that is widely reported by computer packages and in professional journals. The smaller the p-value (attained significance level), the more conclusively the data support a research hypothesis. Statistical significance, as assessed by the p-value, measures conclusiveness; it does not necessarily imply that there is a large, or practically significant result in the data.

Hypothesis tests and confidence intervals are related forms of inference. A confidence interval immediately allows for a hypothesis test: Reject the null hypothesis at the indicated level when and only when the null hypothesis value is not in the confidence interval. A wide confidence interval indicates a poor (low power) hypothesis test and therefore it indicates that there is little evidence one way or the other.

If hypothesis testing is to be used as a decision method, a manager must consider not only the probabilities of the two kinds of error, but also the relative costs of these two errors and the prior plausibility of the two hypotheses. If the null hypothesis is highly plausible or if falsely rejecting it is highly expensive, then very strong evidence (a very low *p*-value) is needed to reject that hypothesis.

KEY FORMULAS: Statistical Tests

1. Test for μ, σ known
   Null hypothesis: $\mu = \mu_0$

   Test statistic: $\quad z = \dfrac{\bar{y} - \mu_0}{\sigma/\sqrt{n}}$

2. Test for μ, σ unknown, $n \geq 30$: The procedure is the same as for σ known, except that s replaces σ in the formula for the test statistic.

3. Calculation of β for a test on μ
   a. For a two-tailed test:

   $$\beta \approx P\left(z > -z_{\alpha/2} + \frac{|\mu_a - \mu_0|}{\sigma/\sqrt{n}}\right)$$

   b. For a one-tailed test:

   $$\beta = P\left(z > -z_\alpha + \frac{|\mu_a - \mu_0|}{\sigma/\sqrt{n}}\right)$$

4. Sample size required for a specified α and β
   a. One-tailed test:

   $$n = \frac{(z_\alpha + z_\beta)^2 \sigma^2}{(\mu_a - \mu_0)^2}$$

   b. Two-tailed test: Replace z_α by $z_{\alpha/2}$

5. Test for median: Choose as test statistic $Y = $ number of sample values exceeding null hypothesis value of median. Test $H_0: \pi = .50$.

6. Test for π, normal approximation
   Null hypothesis: $\pi = \pi_0$

   Test statistic: $\quad z = \dfrac{y - n\pi_0}{\sqrt{n\pi_0(1 - \pi_0)}}$

7. p-values for z tests:
   a. $H_a: \mu > \mu_0$ (or $\pi > \pi_0$), $p = P(z > z_{\text{actual}})$
   b. $H_a: \mu < \mu_0$ (or $\pi < \pi_0$), $p = P(z < z_{\text{actual}})$
   c. $H_a: \mu \neq \mu_0$ (or $\pi \neq \pi_0$), $p = 2P(z > |z_{\text{actual}}|)$
8. Test for σ^2

$$\text{Test statistic:} \quad \chi^2 = \frac{(n-1)s^2}{\sigma^2} \quad \text{with } n-1 \text{ d.f.}$$

CHAPTER 9   EXERCISES

9.67   A manufacturer of yogurt products stamps a sell date on every container. Yogurt not sold by this date is discarded. As a check on this dating system, 50 containers are kept for 8 days beyond the sell date, the maximum length of time the yogurt should be kept in a home refrigerator. Under such severe conditions, the manufacturer is willing to concede that 10% of the containers will have deteriorated quality. A higher percentage indicates a need for a change in sell-date policy. Assume that 9 of the 50 containers show deteriorated quality. Carry out a statistical test using binomial tables and $\alpha = .05$.

9.68   Find the p-value in Exercise 9.67.

9.69   EPA miles-per-gallon ratings are obtained for all models of cars sold in the United States. One of these figures purports to represent mileage in combined city-country driving. Suppose a consumer group test-drives 8 cars of a model with an EPA rating of 28.2 miles per gallon. If H_0 is $\mu = 28.2$, what argument would lead to a one-sided research hypothesis? What would lead to a two-sided research hypothesis?

9.70   Assume that the population standard deviation is 2.1 and that the mean gas mileage for the 8 cars is 26.7 in Exercise 9.69. Can the two-sided research hypothesis be supported at $\alpha = .01$?

9.71   Find the p-value in Exercise 9.70.

9.72   An official of the consumer group interprets the result of Exercise 9.70 as being not statistically significant. The official concludes that therefore it can reliably be assumed that the true mean is 28.2. Do you agree?

9.73   Compute a 99% confidence interval for the true mean mileage in Exercise 9.70. Use this interval to confirm the result of that exercise. What can we "reliably assume" about the true mean mileage?

9.74   In a nationwide opinion poll based on a random sample of 2417 people, one question is "How do you rate the ethics of business executives of large companies?" A rating of 3 means "no better or worse than most people," a rating of 1 is "much better than most people," and 5 is "much worse than most people." The mean rating is 3.05 and the standard deviation is 0.62.
   a. Calculate a 95% confidence interval for the population mean rating.
   b. Can $H_0: \mu = 3.00$ be rejected (against a two-sided alternative) at $\alpha = .05$?

9.75   A newspaper reporting on the poll of Exercise 9.74 reports that "respondents rated the ethics of big business significantly worse than average."
   a. Is this statement true in the statistical sense?
   b. Do you think it might mislead the general public?

9.76   What can be said about the p-value of Exercise 9.74?

9.77   In Exercise 8.58, a police department obtained data on response times to non-emergency crime calls. The data and Minitab output are reproduced here.

```
MTB > print 'resptime'

resptime
    24   25   18   25   15   11   11   19   36   29   13   21   12
    12   26   16   19   12   21   12   12   18   11   19   16   24
    14   23   17

MTB > describe 'resptime'
```

	N	MEAN	MEDIAN	TRMEAN	STDEV	SEMEAN
resptime	29	18.31	18.00	17.93	6.29	1.17

	MIN	MAX	Q1	Q3
resptime	11.00	36.00	12.00	23.50

a. The department wants to have conclusive evidence that the mean is less than 20 minutes. Formulate this goal as a research hypothesis. What is the corresponding null hypothesis?

b. Assume that the distribution of response times is roughly normal and that the true (population or process) standard deviation is 6.0 minutes. What is the appropriate test statistic?

c. Write out the five parts of a formal hypothesis test, using $\alpha = .05$.

9.78 What is the p-value for the data in Exercise 9.77?

9.79 Plot the data in Exercise 9.77, say as a stem-and-leaf display. Is there a clear indication of a nonnormal distribution? If so, does this completely invalidate your answers in Exercise 9.77?

9.80 In Exercise 9.77, we assumed a population standard deviation of 6.0 minutes. Test the research hypothesis that the population mean is less than 20 minutes, using $\alpha = .05$, without making this assumption.

```
MTB > describe 'resptime'
```

	N	MEAN	MEDIAN	TRMEAN	STDEV	SEMEAN
resptime	29	18.31	18.00	17.93	6.29	1.17

	MIN	MAX	Q1	Q3
resptime	11.00	36.00	12.00	23.50

9.81 In Exercise 8.60, a fish hatchery was concerned that the (population) mean weight of released fish might differ from 10.0 ounces. Differences in either direction were undesirable. The data are reproduced here.

9.3	11.7	11.0	9.8	10.1	8.9	8.7	9.5	10.8	8.7	7.6
10.0	8.8	9.3	9.2	8.1	9.9	9.4	8.3	10.3	9.8	9.5
9.8	9.0	10.7	9.3	9.6	10.4	9.4	9.8	9.8	9.2	11.0
10.2	9.1	11.0	9.4	9.7	12.1	9.8	7.1	8.3	10.3	10.6
10.1	10.2	8.8	9.3	10.3	10.7	10.8	7.5	9.0	10.1	9.2
9.7	10.4	9.1	9.7	10.7	10.6					

mean = 9.6803, standard deviation = 0.95983

a. Formulate a research hypothesis and a null hypothesis.

b. Assume that the population standard deviation is 1.0 ounce. Write down a test statistic.

c. Carry out the five parts of a statistical test with $\alpha = .10$. State the conclusion carefully.

9.82   State a *p*-value for Exercise 9.81. Should it be one-tailed or two-tailed?

9.83   In Exercise 9.82, we obtained a sample mean weight of 9.6803 ounces and a sample standard deviation of 0.95983 ounces, from a sample of 61 fish. Use these results to test the research hypothesis that the population mean weight is not equal to 10.0 ounces. Make no assumption about the population standard deviation.

9.84   Place bounds on a two-tailed *p*-value in Exercise 9.83.

9.85   In Exercise 9.81, a sample of 61 fish yielded a sample standard deviation of 0.95983 ounce. Test the research hypothesis that the population standard deviation is not 1.0 ounce, using $\alpha = .10$.

9.86   In Exercise 8.67, a manufacturer of mesh screening was concerned that the mean number of defects in a two-foot long section of mesh screen might exceed 2.5. A random sample of 24 such sections was inspected and yielded the following data.

```
3   4   3   0   6   1   0   2   1   3   4   4   3   6
4   4   3   4   5   2   1   0   5   2
```

n	mean	median	standard deviation
24	2.917	3.000	1.792

a. Carry out the five steps of a formal hypothesis testing procedure, using $\alpha = .01$. Consider whether the research hypothesis should be one-sided or two-sided, and whether the indicated standard deviation refers to the sample or to the population.

b. Is it a reasonable conclusion to say that the test proves that the mean is not larger than 2.5?

9.87   In Exercise 9.86, what can be said about the size of the *p*-value?

9.88   Show that a 99% confidence interval for the population mean leads to the same conclusion we reached in Exercise 9.86. (We calculated such an interval in Exercise 8.86, if you wish to peek.) How does the width of this interval relate to the answer to part (b) of Exercise 9.86?

9.89   A manufacturer of floppy disks for personal computers tested a sample of 36 disks for bad sectors when formatted in a PC. More extensive testing is to be done if there is clear evidence that the mean size of bad sectors exceeds 7.5 K.

a. Formulate "Do more extensive testing" as a statistical research hypothesis.

b. The sample mean was 9.49 and the sample standard deviation was 10.02. Is there a statistically significant ($\alpha = .05$) increase in the size of bad sectors above 7.5 K?

9.90   What can be said about the size of the *p*-value in Exercise 9.89?

9.91   A stem-and-leaf display of the data of Exercise 9.89 is as follows.

```
0   00011133344444
0   55556677778
1   02224
1   57
2
2   66
3   1
3
4
4   8
```

Does this plot of the data indicate that the probabilities we stated in Exercises 9.89 and 9.90 may be erroneous?

9.92 As cable television availability has increased, broadcast television networks and advertisers have become increasingly concerned with the amount of time that their target audiences spend watching conventional, broadcast television. A sampling of one particular target group recorded the hours of conventional TV watched in one week, to the nearest half hour. A Statgraphics stem-and-leaf display is as follows:

```
Stem-and-leaf display for hrswatched: unit = 0.1    1|2  represents 1.2

          LO|215,225

    4    24o|55
    5    25*|0
    5    25o|
    7    26*|00
    9    26o|55
   15    27*|000000
   21    27o|555555
   (5)   28*|00000
   18    28o|555
   15    29*|0000
   11    29o|55
    9    30*|0

       HI|330,335,335,335,335,390,415,435
```

a. What do the LO and HI entries indicate about the shape of the data?
b. Is it fair to say that the data appear close to normally distributed?

9.93 A normal probability plot of the data of Exercise 9.92 is shown in Figure 9.8 (page 386). (Note that the data are on the horizontal axis and the theoretical, normal-distribution scores are on the vertical axis, which is the reverse of other normal plots shown in this text.) Would you judge that the data fell close to the indicated straight line? If not, what sort of nonnormality seems to be present?

9.94 For the target population of Exercise 9.92, the mean (and median) hours watched was 30.4, according to a very extensive survey made two years previously. The data of Exercise 9.92 were analyzed by the Statgraphics package, with the following results:

```
                      One-Sample Analysis Results
-------------------------------------------------------------------------

                                    hrswatched
Sample Statistics: Number of Obs.   44
                   Average          28.8977
                   Variance         18.4486
                   Std. Deviation   4.29518
                   Median           28

Confidence Interval for Mean:       90    Percent
                   Sample 1         27.809 29.9865    43 D.F.

Confidence Interval for Variance:   90    Percent
                   Sample 1         13.3768 27.3881   43 D.F.
```

a. According to the confidence interval for the mean, is there conclusive evidence that the mean hours watched has changed since the previous survey?
b. The plots of Exercises 9.92 and 9.93 indicated that the data are not normally

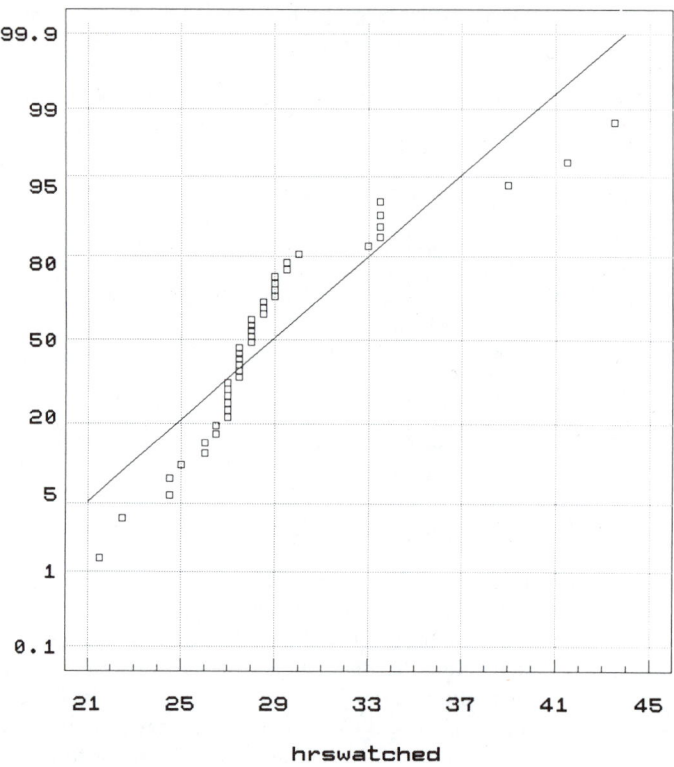

Normal Probability Plot

FIGURE 9.8   Normal Probability Plot — Television-Watching Hours

distributed. Does that fact indicate that the claimed confidence of the interval for the mean is seriously incorrect?

9.95   Does the apparent nonnormality of the data of Exercise 9.92 have any effect on the correctness of the confidence interval for the variance shown in Exercise 9.94? If so, is it more or less serious than the effect on the confidence interval for the mean?

9.96   The Statgraphics output from Exercise 9.94 also included the result of a formal hypothesis test, as follows:

```
Hypothesis Test for H0: Mean = 30.4      Computed t statistic = -2.32003
                  vs Alt: LT             Sig. Level = 0.0125765
              at Alpha = 0.1             so reject H0.
```

a. According to the computed t statistic, can the null hypothesis be rejected using $\alpha = .10$ and a two-tailed test? The output indicated 43 d.f.

b. Is your answer consistent with the answer to part (a) of Exercise 9.94?

c. How is the p-value shown in the output? Does this p-value indicate that the null hypothesis should be rejected using $\alpha = .10$?

9.97   A communications firm has an "intrapeneur" program, by which managers and employees with business ideas are awarded yearly bonuses based on the profitability of the ideas. The bonuses are not enormous; last year, the average was \$3550. In the current year, 144 bonuses were awarded. The director of the program was concerned that the average size of the bonuses would decrease as the most evident and profitable ideas were used up. The data (expressed in thousands of dollars per award) were analyzed using Statgraphics, yielding the following output:

```
                         One-Sample Analysis Results
--------------------------------------------------------------------------

                                          award
Sample Statistics: Number of Obs.         144
                   Average                3.21875
                   Variance               6.12042
                   Std. Deviation         2.47395
                   Median                 2.5

Confidence Interval for Mean:             95    Percent
                   Sample 1               2.81114 3.62636     143 D.F.

Confidence Interval for Variance:         95    Percent
                   Sample 1               4.91695 7.82968     143 D.F.


Hypothesis Test for HO: Mean = 3.55       Computed t statistic = -1.60674
                  vs Alt: LT              Sig. Level = 0.0551582
               at Alpha = 0.05            so do not reject HO.
```

a. Show that the output indicates that there has not been a statistically significant decrease in the mean award amount, using $\alpha = .05$.
b. The manager interpreted the output as proof that there had been no decrease in the mean award amount. Is this a valid interpretation?

9.98 A box plot, produced by Statgraphics, of the data of Exercise 9.97 is shown in Figure 9.9.

Box-and-Whisker Plot

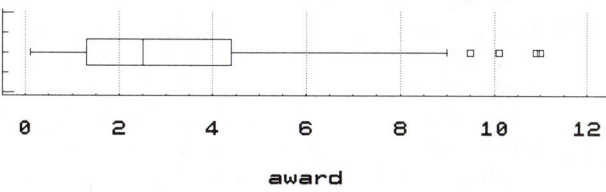

award

FIGURE 9.9   Box Plot of Intrapeneurship Awards

a. What form of nonnormality is indicated by the box plot?
b. Does this nonnormality indicate that the probabilities shown in the output (which assume a normal population) are seriously wrong?

9.99 a. Use the output of Exercise 9.97 to calculate a 95% confidence interval for the standard deviation.

b. Is it correct to say that any nonnormality in the underlying award process doesn't affect the correctness of the confidence interval because the sample size is so large?

9.100 The data of Exercise 9.97 are all the awards that the firm made in the current year. In what sense, if any, can the data be regarded as a sample?

9.101 A package delivery service adopted a new dispatching system to try to reduce the total mileage required by its truck fleet to make deliveries. The new system would be worth the cost if it reduced the fleet mileage by more than 5% from its current level of 2420 miles per day (i.e., decrease it to less than 2299 miles per day). The miles required for each of 49 days under a trial of the new system are recorded in column 1 of the 'CH9C1.DAT' file on the data disk; day number is recorded in column 2. Load the data into a computer package.

a. Obtain the mean and standard deviation of the miles data.

b. Using the computer package, if possible, test the research hypothesis that the long-run mean will be less than 2299. Obtain a p-value. (Note: Many packages will test a null hypothesis that a mean is 0. To convert the problem to that form, subtract 2299 from each observation.)

c. Is there conclusive evidence that the new system is worthwhile?

9.102 a. Obtain a stem-and-leaf display of the miles data from Exercise 9.101. Is there reason to think that there is a problem of nonnormality?

b. The data are a time series. Obtain a plot of miles against day number. Is there evidence of a trend? Of cycles, indicating day-to-day dependence in the data?

9.103 An inexpensive restaurant featuring steak dinners makes most of its profits from side orders suggested to diners by the staff. As an experiment, the restaurant owner rewarded each server with 10% of the price of all side orders made through that server. After 10 days, the owner computed the side order volume per customer for each of 41 servers. The data are stored in column 1 of the 'CH9C2.DAT' file on the data disk; server number is stored in column 2. Load the data into a computer package.

a. Obtain the mean and standard deviation of the volume data.

b. The reward policy will be profitable if the mean volume is more than $2.40 per customer. Is there strong evidence in the data that the policy will, in fact, be profitable?

9.104 a. Obtain a boxplot of the volume data of Exercise 9.103. Are there any outliers?

b. Obtain a normal plot of the data. What nonnormality, if any, appears to be present?

9.105 The human resources director for a large corporation tested an incentive policy to try to reduce the number of personal leave days taken by employees. A sample of 50 employees (out of several hundred in the company) were offered bonuses if the average number of leave days taken could be reduced from the current level of 5.7 per employee per year. After a year, the number of leave days was computed for each employee. The data are stored in column 1 of the 'CH9C3.DAT' file on the data disk. Employee ID number is in column 2. Load the data into whatever statistical computer package you can use.

a. Obtain the mean, median, and standard deviation of the leave-days data. What does this information suggest about the skewness of the data?

b. Get a stem-and-leaf display or histogram of the data. Does the plot confirm your impression about the skewness in the data?

9.106 a. Have the computer package test the null hypothesis that the mean leave days is still 5.7. You may have to subtract 5.7 from all the data to be able to test the hypothesis that the mean is 0.

b. Obtain a *p*-value for the test. Is it one-sided or two-sided in the computer output? Do you think a one-sided test or a two-sided test is more appropriate in this situation?

CASE   Hypothesis Testing

A manufacturer of heavy-duty leaf springs for trucks begins by making basic castings. The most important factor in the quality of a casting is its length. Ideally, the casting should be 8.05 inches. (The basic casting is finished to a specification length of 8.00 inches.) There is substantial variation of casting lengths, even if the process is working properly, because of variations in outside temperature and humidity and variations in the quality of the steel raw material. Experience has indicated that the standard deviation of lengths of basic castings is about 0.180 inches, when the casting process is working well.

Systematic problems with the process tend to show up mostly in incorrect mean lengths, rather than in increased variability. Therefore, the length of each casting is measured. After each set of 16 castings, the average length is found. If the mean for any sample of 16 castings is too far away from the desired mean, 8.05 inches, the casting process is halted and a lengthy (and moderately expensive) reset procedure is carried out to bring the process back to standard. One major problem is the definition of "too far away" from 8.05 inches. The casting-process manager wants to establish limits of 7.915 inches and 8.185 inches, but the finishing-process manager favors limits of 8.000 inches and 8.100 inches. Both of them agree with an official target that says that the long-run mean (over many thousands of castings) must be kept within the range of 7.95 to 8.15 inches; they disagree over the implications of this target for the samples of 16 castings.

Write a report to both managers and explain the implications of the choice of limits. Indicate what seem to be the important issues, and what other facts may need to be found to come to a reasonable conclusion. Neither manager knows much statistical theory, so try to explain any technical ideas carefully. ∎

Review Exercises Chapters 7–9 ∎

R52 A large computer software firm installs a new editor for use by a random sample of its programmers. After the programmers have learned to use the editor comfortably, the firm measures the number of lines of debugged code produced by each programmer. (The programming tasks are of comparable difficulty.) The data are

178	183	199	201	204	210	218	218	219	220	225	227	231
232	232	233	233	235	238	239	241	243	244	246	247	249
250	251	264	266	270	271	271	273	275	276	277	279	283
284	285	286	289	289	298	303	306	315	315	345

For these data, the sample size is 50, the sample mean is 253.32, and the sample standard deviation is 36.1.

a. The population standard deviation using the previous editor was 35.4. Assume that this population standard deviation applies to the new editor as well. Calculate a 99% confidence interval for the population mean using the new editor.

b. Is there clear evidence in the data that the sample mean is likely to be an inefficient estimator of the population mean?

R53   Refer to the confidence interval calculated in part (a) of Exercise R52. The population mean using the old editor was 230.2. Can we reject the null hypothesis that the mean for the new editor is 230.2, using $\alpha = .01$, based on the confidence interval?

R54   Carry out a formal hypothesis test of the null hypothesis that the population mean remains 230.2 against the research hypothesis that it is not equal to 230.2 for the data of Exercise R52. Use $\alpha = .01$ and assume that the population standard deviation is 35.4.

R55   For the hypothesis test performed in Exercise R54, state a p-value. Should it be one-sided or two-sided?

R56   Redo Exercises R52–R55 without making the assumption that the population standard deviation is 35.4. Do any of your conclusions change substantially?

R57   Using the data of Exercise R52, calculate a 99% confidence interval for the population median. On the basis of this interval, can one reject the null hypothesis that the population median is 230, using $\alpha = .01$?

R58   Which 99% confidence interval is wider, the interval calculated in Exercise R56 or the one in R57? What does your answer suggest about the efficiency of the sample mean as compared to the sample median in this particular case?

R59   It is claimed that 45% of all walk-in customers at a particular real estate office eventually buy a home through that office. To test the claim, they plan to regard the next 100 customers as a random sample. Set up a formal test of the research hypothesis that the population proportion is less than .45, using $\alpha = .05$.

R60   How does the rejection region in Exercise R59 change if the maximum allowable α is set at .01?

R61   Suppose that the head of the real estate office in Exercise R59 determines that 32 of the 100 walk-in customers eventually buy homes through the office. Does this fact support H_a if α is set at .05?

R62   Does the result indicated in Exercise R61 lead to rejection of H_0 if α is set at .01? What does your answer indicate about the p-value for the data?

R63   A forester needs to test a new method for growing pine trees for lumber, one designed to minimize the loss to browsing deer. A five-year trial is needed. A sample of 25 stands is to be planted and tended using the new method. The current yield has a mean of 272.6 and a standard deviation of 67.3, in appropriate units of measurement.

a. Formulate reasonable null and research hypotheses. In particular, should the research hypothesis be one-sided or two-sided?

b. Set up the first four parts of a formal test of the null hypothesis. Assume that the population standard deviation remains unchanged. The desired α value is .05.

R64   Suppose that the population mean yield under the new growing method in Exercise R63 is 305. Calculate the probability that the test in Exercise R63 will not reject the null hypothesis. What is the technical name for this probability?

R65   Assume that the population mean yield is 295 rather than the 305 assumed in Exercise R64. Should the probability that the null hypothesis will not be rejected using the test in Exercise R63 be larger or smaller than the probability calculated in Exercise R64?

R66 Assume that the experiment of Exercise R64 results in the following yield data:

135 185 231 247 262 285 300 304 310 312 313 319 322
322 324 328 335 362 366 368 370 384 384 385 401
$(\bar{y} = 314.16, \quad s = 64.0)$

What is the conclusion of the test specified in Exercise R64?

R67 Refer to Exercises R64 and R66. Find the probability that a sample mean is equal to or larger than 314.16, given a population mean of 272.6. What is the technical name for this probability?

R68 Plot the data of Example R66. Is there any reason to believe that the sample mean is not the best estimator of the population mean?

R69 A market research firm is trying to estimate the proportion of shoppers at a suburban mall that are regular readers of two particular newspapers in order to judge the relative merits of the two papers as advertising vehicles. Employees of the firm are instructed to sample shoppers randomly until they find a shopper who is a regular reader of both newspapers; once a regular reader is found, a value of $X =$ number of other shoppers interviewed is recorded. Under reasonable assumptions, the probability distribution of X is geometric:

$$f(x) = \pi(1 - \pi)^x \qquad \text{for } x = 0, 1, 2, \ldots,$$

Suppose that six values of X are recorded: $x_1 = 5$, $x_2 = 8$, $x_3 = 2$, $x_4 = 9$, $x_5 = 0$, $x_6 = 6$. Calculate the likelihood of these values for values of π ranging from .2 through .5. From the numerical results, what seems to be the best estimate of π?

∂ R70 a. For the data of Exercise R69, use calculus to find the maximum likelihood estimate.

b. Generalize the derivation in part (a) to arbitrary values of $x_1, \ldots, x_n$.

R71 It can be proved that the long-run average (over many samples) of the estimator found in Exercise R70 is larger than π, although the long-run average decreases rapidly toward π as the sample size increases. What desirable property of an estimator is (slightly) violated by this particular estimator?

R72 A computer center that serves, among other clients, small savings and loan associations needs to know the proportion of jobs from these businesses that require intervention by the computer operator. In a random sample of 133 such jobs, 22 require operator intervention. Calculate a 95% confidence interval for the population proportion of jobs requiring intervention.

R73 Suppose that the confidence interval found in Exercise R72 is felt to be too wide. Calculate the sample size required to obtain a 95% confidence interval with a width of .06 (a plus or minus of .03) under each of two assumptions:

a. Assume that the sample proportion continues to equal 22/133.

b. Assume that the sample proportion may take any value.

R74 A normal approximation was used in answering Exercises R72 and R73. Can we be confident that the approximation is a good one?

R75 An auditor wishes to verify transaction records of a firm. The transactions are placed in random order. An auditor trainee keeps a cumulative total of the dollar amounts of the transactions; every time the total moves over a $100,000 increment (that is, when the total passes $100,000, $200,000, $300,000, etc.), the transaction is set aside for verification. Show that this process does not yield a random sample of the transactions.

R76 The process of Exercise R75 yields 241 transactions. The mean size of the transactions is $5381 and the standard deviation is $2271. The amounts, when plotted, show substantial right skewness.

    a. Calculate a supposed 95% confidence interval for the population mean transaction size.

    b. This interval is in fact quite likely not to include the actual mean transaction size of the population. Explain why.

R77   A chemical manufacturer doing a pilot study of yields obtains a sample of 26 small batches. The yields, expressed as percentages of the theoretical maximum, are

67.6 68.5 74.7 77.6 78.4 79.3 79.5 80.3 80.3 80.7 80.8 80.8 80.9
81.2 81.4 81.4 81.5 82.5 82.5 82.9 82.9 83.8 84.4 84.4 85.4 86.0
$(\bar{y} = 80.37, \quad s = 4.37)$

Calculate a 90% confidence interval for the population mean yield.

R78   Use the data in Exercise R77 to calculate a 90% confidence interval for the population median.

R79   Compare the widths of the intervals in Exercises R77 and R78. What do the widths indicate about the relative efficiency of using the sample mean versus the sample median in this situation? Does a plot of the data indicate the same thing?

R80   Use the data in Exercise R77 to test the null hypothesis that the population mean is 82.0 against a two-sided research hypothesis. State bounds on the p-value.

R81   The complete pilot study for Exercise R77 eventually involves a sample of 150 batches. Assuming that the population standard deviation is about 4.4, and that the population mean is 80.4, find the probability that H_0: population mean = 82.0 will be rejected. Assume an α of .05.

R82   The probability calculated in Exercise R81 is *not* a p-value. Explain why not.

∂ **R83**   The Pareto density is sometimes used as a model in insurance situations that can result in many small claims and a few enormous ones. One form of Pareto density is

$$f(y) = \frac{1}{\theta}(y + 1)^{-1-1/\theta} \qquad \text{for } y > 0$$

Given a sample with $y_1 = 2.730$, $y_2 = 5.124$, $y_3 = .798$, and $y_4 = 36.215$, find a good estimate of θ.

∂ **R84**   Find a good estimator of the parameter θ in Exercise R83 for arbitrary values $y_1, \ldots, y_n$.

R85   The estimator of Exercise R84 has the following properties: Its long-run average value is θ, and among all estimators with average value θ it has the smallest standard error. What do these properties indicate about this estimator?

10

COMPARING TWO SAMPLES

Until now we have discussed basic principles of statistical inference in the context of a single sample. The basic ideas of estimation, confidence intervals, and hypothesis tests have much wider applications. In this chapter, we extend them to deal with comparisons of two samples.

Comparison is a fundamental issue. If we want to ask how much a market research panel likes a new product, we need to compare that product to another one. If we want to assess the effect of production speed on variability of the resulting products, we should compare two (or more) speeds. If we want to look at the effect of tax-auditing procedures for state income taxes, we can compare the results for states with two different auditing methods.

In this chapter we develop methods for comparison. Section 10.1 contains theoretical results that are used in Section 10.2 to find confidence intervals and hypothesis tests for comparing two means. Section 10.3 describes an alternative approach to inference based on ranking data from lowest to highest. Sections 10.4 and 10.5 describe methods for comparison when two samples are based on paired or matched individuals. Section 10.6 deals with methods for comparing proportions, and Section 10.7 with methods for comparing standard deviations. An appendix contains some of the relevant mathematics.

This chapter is an extension of the basic principles we discussed in the last three chapters. The formulas get a little longer, but the basic principles are those we've already learned.

10.1 COMPARING THE MEANS OF TWO POPULATIONS WITH KNOWN STANDARD DEVIATIONS ∎

The basic principles underlying the statistical methods for two-sample inferences are the same as those developed in the preceding chapters for single-sample inferences. To make the transition to two-sample problems easier, we initially make the artificial assumption that both population standard deviations are known. As in the one-sample problem, this assumption is not crucial for large sample sizes. As you might expect, when we drop this assumption we use sample variances and t tables; the more realistic situation of unknown standard deviations is the topic of the next section.

The procedures of this section are based on the following formal mathematical assumptions:

Formal Assumptions for Two-Sample Inferences Concerning Means

1. A random sample is selected from each of the two populations. The samples are independent. The notation is

Group 1		Group 2
μ_1	population mean	μ_2
σ_1^2	population variance	σ_2^2
n_1	sample size	n_2
$\bar{y}_1$	sample mean	$\bar{y}_2$
s_1^2	sample variance	s_2^2

2. Each population distribution is normal.
3. We are interested in inferences concerning $\mu_1 - \mu_2$, the difference of the two population means.

(We discuss the effect of violations of these assumptions at the end of Section 10.2.)

The obvious way to form a point estimator of the difference in population means $\mu_1 - \mu_2$ is to use the difference in sample means $\bar{Y}_1 - \bar{Y}_2$. Because each sample mean is an unbiased estimator of the corresponding population mean, $\bar{Y}_1 - \bar{Y}_2$ is an **unbiased estimator of $\mu_1 - \mu_2$**.

unbiased estimator of $\mu_1 - \mu_2$

$$E(\bar{Y}_1 - \bar{Y}_2) = E(\bar{Y}_1) - E(\bar{Y}_2) = \mu_1 - \mu_2$$

The key to inference problems related to $\mu_1 - \mu_2$ is that the variances of $\bar{Y}_1$ and $\bar{Y}_2$ can be added, because the random variables $\bar{Y}_1$ and $\bar{Y}_2$ are independent.

Variance of $\bar{Y}_1 - \bar{Y}_2$; Independent Samples

$$\text{Var}(\bar{Y}_1 - \bar{Y}_2) = \text{Var}(\bar{Y}_1) + \text{Var}(\bar{Y}_2) = \frac{\sigma_1^2}{n_1} + \frac{\sigma_2^2}{n_2}$$

---

standard error of $\bar{Y}_1 - \bar{Y}_2$

The **standard error of** $\bar{Y}_1 - \bar{Y}_2$ is

$$\sigma_{\bar{Y}_1 - \bar{Y}_2} = \sqrt{\frac{\sigma_1^2}{n_1} + \frac{\sigma_2^2}{n_2}}$$

EXAMPLE 10.1

Suppose that samples of respective sizes 50 and 32 are drawn from populations with the following characteristics:

	Group 1	Group 2
Population mean	85	75
Population standard deviation	10	16

Find the expected value and standard error of the difference in sample means, $\bar{Y}_1 - \bar{Y}_2$.

Solution

$$E(\bar{Y}_1 - \bar{Y}_2) = 85 - 75 = 10$$

$$\sigma_{\bar{Y}_1 - \bar{Y}_2} = \sqrt{\frac{\sigma_1^2}{n_1} + \frac{\sigma_2^2}{n_2}}$$

$$= \sqrt{\frac{(10)^2}{50} + \frac{(16)^2}{32}}$$

$$= \sqrt{10.00} = 3.16$$

Note that the standard error of the difference in means is not the sum of the standard errors (and certainly not the difference of them). ∎

The crucial condition for the use of this formula for the standard error is that the two samples are independent. The formula is not appropriate when there is any matching up or pairing of entities in the two samples, as in "before" and **paired samples** "after" measurements on the same individuals. Methods for **paired samples** are discussed in Section 10.4.

Given this standard error formula, confidence-interval and hypothesis-testing procedures are direct extensions of the one-sample methods. We first state these two-sample procedures under the artificial assumption that both population variances are known. As in the one-sample case, these procedures can be used with sample variances replacing population variances, provided that both sample sizes are large, say, 30 or more. Procedures for smaller sample sizes are discussed in the next section.

We presented one-sample estimation procedures in Chapters 7 and 8. These results can be summarized as follows: If θ represents the unknown parameter, $\hat{\theta}$ is an unbiased estimator of θ, and $\sigma_{\hat{\theta}}$ is the standard error of the estimator $\hat{\theta}$, then the large sample $100(1 - \alpha)\%$ confidence interval for θ is $\hat{\theta} \pm z_{\alpha/2}\sigma_{\hat{\theta}}$. This same format holds for two-sample problems with $\theta = \mu_1 - \mu_2$, $\hat{\theta} = \bar{Y}_1 - \bar{Y}_2$, and $\sigma_{\hat{\theta}} = \sigma_{\bar{Y}_1 - \bar{Y}_2}$.

■

**100($1 - \alpha$)% Confidence Interval for $\mu_1 - \mu_2$;
Large, Independent Samples**

$$\bar{y}_1 - \bar{y}_2 - z_{\alpha/2}\sigma_{\bar{Y}_1 - \bar{Y}_2} \leq \mu_1 - \mu_2 \leq \bar{y}_1 - \bar{y}_2 + z_{\alpha/2}\sigma_{\bar{Y}_1 - \bar{Y}_2}$$

where

$$\sigma_{\bar{Y}_1 - \bar{Y}_2} = \sqrt{\frac{\sigma_1^2}{n_1} + \frac{\sigma_2^2}{n_2}}$$

If both n_1 and n_2 exceed 30, unknown population variances (σ_1^2 and σ_2^2) may be replaced by the respective sample variances s_1^2 and s_2^2.

■

EXAMPLE 10.2   A health insurer gathers data on the length of hospitalization (in days) of patients operated on for appendicitis. Random samples from two different hospitals yielded the following results:

	Hospital 1	Hospital 2
Sample mean	8.2	9.4
Sample standard deviation	3.6	2.9
Sample size	56	38

Find a 90% confidence interval for $\mu_1 - \mu_2$, the difference in long-run average lengths of hospitalization.

Solution   The difference in sample means is $\bar{y}_1 - \bar{y}_2 = 8.2 - 9.4 = -1.2$ and the appropriate z value for a 90% confidence interval is $z_{.05} = 1.645$. Because both sample sizes exceed 30, we can replace the unknown variances (σ_1^2 and σ_2^2) by the corresponding sample variances to obtain

$$\sigma_{\bar{Y}_1 - \bar{Y}_2} \approx \sqrt{\frac{(3.6)^2}{56} + \frac{(2.9)^2}{38}} = .673$$

Substituting into the formula, we obtain the 90% confidence interval for $\mu_1 - \mu_2$:

$$-1.2 - 1.645(.673) \leq \mu_1 - \mu_2 \leq -1.2 + 1.645(.673)$$

or

$$-2.3 \leq \mu_1 - \mu_2 \leq -.1$$

We are 90% confident that the long-run length of hospitalization is from .1 to 2.3 days shorter for hospital 1.   ■

Hypothesis testing for two samples is also a direct extension of the one-sample procedure. If $\hat{\theta}$ is an unbiased estimator of the unknown parameter of interest, and $\sigma_{\hat{\theta}}$ represents the standard error of $\hat{\theta}$, then the large-sample statistical test for θ takes this form:

$$H_0: \theta = \theta_0 (\theta_0 \text{ is specified})$$
$$H_a: 1. \ \theta > \theta_0$$
$$2. \ \theta < \theta_0$$
$$3. \ \theta \neq \theta_0$$

$$\text{T.S.: } z = \frac{\hat{\theta} - \theta_0}{\sigma_{\hat{\theta}}}$$

R.R.: For Type I error rate α
1. Reject H_0 if $z > z_\alpha$
2. Reject H_0 if $z < -z_\alpha$
3. Reject H_0 if $|z| > z_{\alpha/2}$

This same format applies to a two-sample test with $\theta = \mu_1 - \mu_2$, $\hat{\theta} = \bar{y}_1 - \bar{y}_2$, and $\sigma_{\hat{\theta}} = \sigma_{\bar{Y}_1 - \bar{Y}_2}$.

Hypothesis Test for $\mu_1 - \mu_2$; Large, Independent Samples

$$H_0: \mu_1 - \mu_2 = D_0 \ (D_0 \text{ is specified; often } D_0 = 0)$$
$$H_a: 1. \ \mu_1 - \mu_2 > D_0$$
$$2. \ \mu_1 - \mu_2 < D_0$$
$$3. \ \mu_1 - \mu_2 \neq D_0$$

$$\text{T.S.: } z = \frac{(\bar{y}_1 - \bar{y}_2) - D_0}{\sqrt{\dfrac{\sigma_1^2}{n_1} + \dfrac{\sigma_2^2}{n_2}}}$$

R.R.: For a Type I error rate α
1. Reject H_0 if $z > z_\alpha$
2. Reject H_0 if $z < -z_\alpha$
3. Reject H_0 if $|z| > z_{\alpha/2}$

If n_1 and n_2 both exceed 30, σ_1^2 and σ_2^2 may be replaced by s_1^2 and s_2^2, respectively.

EXAMPLE 10.3   Refer to Example 10.2. Test the null hypothesis of equal long-run average stay against a general (two-sided) alternative; use $\alpha = .10$.

Solution

$$H_0: \mu_1 - \mu_2 = 0$$
$$H_a: \mu_1 - \mu_2 \neq 0$$

$$\text{T.S.: } z = \frac{(\bar{y}_1 - \bar{y}_2) - 0}{\sqrt{\dfrac{s_1^2}{n_1} + \dfrac{s_2^2}{n_2}}} = \frac{(8.2 - 9.4)}{\sqrt{\dfrac{(3.6)^2}{56} + \dfrac{(2.9)^2}{38}}} = -1.78$$

R.R.: Reject H_0 if $|z| > z_{.05} = 1.645$

Conclusion: $|z| = 1.78 > 1.645$; reject H_0.

We conclude that the mean lengths of stay differ. (Practically, it is clear that the mean stay for hospital 1 is shorter.)

This conclusion also follows from the fact that the 90% confidence interval for $\mu_1 - \mu_2$ in Example 10.2 does not include the value zero.   ■

SECTION 10.1   EXERCISES

10.1 A manufacturer of puffed cereal tries two different preventive-maintenance approaches on two of the "guns" used in processing. The number of hours of operation between required shutdowns is recorded:

	Machine 1	Machine 2
Mean	62.4	55.8
Standard deviation	37.1	42.2
n	126	155

a. Calculate a 95% confidence interval for the difference in true means.

b. Can the hypothesis of equal mean operation times be rejected at $\alpha = .05$?

10.2 Calculate the p-value in Exercise 10.1.

10.3 A wholesaler specializing in drugstore items incurs considerable labor costs in "picking" every order. In an effort to reduce the time per order, a minicomputer is programmed to list the items in an efficient order. Two programs, based on different efficiency principles, are tested. One hundred orders are run through each program, and the total labor time per order is recorded. The data yield the following:

	Program 1	Program 2
Mean (hours)	1.64	1.89
Standard deviation	1.02	0.94

a. Calculate a 90% confidence interval for the difference in long-run mean times.

b. Test the null hypothesis of equal means against a two-sided alternative. Use $\alpha = .10$.

10.4 Find the p-value of the test in Exercise 10.3, part (b).

10.5 What would you guess the skewness of the data underlying Exercise 10.3 might be? If you feel that there may be substantial skewness, does this invalidate your conclusions in Exercises 10.3 and 10.4?

10.6 Two agencies supply temporary workers for light manufacturing. Both agencies give their workers a test of dexterity. The two populations at a particular time have the following means and standard deviations.

	Agency K	Agency R
Mean	78.28	75.79
Standard deviation	9.63	11.25

Samples of 8 workers from agency K and 12 from agency R are sent to a manufacturer on one particular day. Each worker's dexterity score is recorded.
a. What is the expected value of the difference of mean dexterity scores (agency K − agency R)?
b. Find the standard error of this difference.

10.7   Suppose that the sample in Exercise 10.6 had been 12 from agency K and 8 from agency R. How, if at all, would your answers to Exercise 10.6 change?

10.8   A trucking firm specializes in LTL (less-than-truckload) shipments for mail order firms. The firm uses two priority classes and charges fees accordingly. The mean delivery time for class 1 is 7.20 working days and the standard deviation is 4.21 working days. For class 2, the mean is 11.41 and the standard deviation is 6.33. In checking to see whether these times have changed, the firm routinely takes separate random samples of 25 shipments from each of the two priority classes and finds the sample mean delivery times.
a. What is the expected difference in the sample means?
b. What is the variance of the difference of the means?

10.9   Suppose that the samples in Exercise 10.8 are not taken completely randomly. Instead, all shipments are placed into 25 distance categories (with category 1 being nearest and category 25 being farthest). Then one class 1 shipment and one class 2 shipment are chosen randomly from each category. Do your answers to Exercise 10.8 remain valid?

COMPARING THE MEANS OF TWO POPULATIONS

10.2   WITH UNKNOWN STANDARD DEVIATIONS ■

The confidence interval for a population mean μ is of the form $\bar{y} \pm z_{\alpha/2}\sigma/\sqrt{n}$. In Chapter 8 we learned that when the unknown σ is replaced by s, $t_{\alpha/2}$ values (with $n - 1$ d.f.) are used instead of $z_{\alpha/2}$ values in confidence intervals and the statistical test. It would perhaps seem natural that, in the two-sample case with small sample sizes when σ_1 and σ_2 are replaced by the sample standard deviations s_1 and s_2, we would use $t_{\alpha/2}$ values rather than $z_{\alpha/2}$ values for the corresponding confidence intervals and test. However, this is *not* the case.

assumption of equal variances   When the standard deviations are unknown, inferences about $\mu_1 - \mu_2$ based on independent random samples require an additional assumption besides independence and population normality. We also assume that the two unknown population variances are equal: $\sigma_1^2 = \sigma_2^2$. The common unknown variance is designated σ^2.

To help motivate the results, note that if $\sigma_1^2 = \sigma_2^2 = \sigma^2$, the large-sample confidence interval for $\mu_1 - \mu_2$ can be written

$$\bar{y}_1 - \bar{y}_2 - z_{\alpha/2}\sigma\sqrt{\frac{1}{n_1} + \frac{1}{n_2}} \leq \mu_1 - \mu_2 \leq \bar{y}_1 - \bar{y}_2 + z_{\alpha/2}\sigma\sqrt{\frac{1}{n_1} + \frac{1}{n_2}}$$

The corresponding confidence interval for $\mu_1 - \mu_2$ is shown here.

■

100(1 − α)% Confidence Interval for $\mu_1 - \mu_2$, with σ's Unknown and Independent Samples

$$\bar{y}_1 - \bar{y}_2 - t_{\alpha/2} s_p \sqrt{\frac{1}{n_1} + \frac{1}{n_2}} \le \mu_1 - \mu_2 \le \bar{y}_1 - \bar{y}_2 + t_{\alpha/2} s_p \sqrt{\frac{1}{n_1} + \frac{1}{n_2}}$$

where

$$s_p = \sqrt{\frac{(n_1 - 1)s_1^2 + (n_2 - 1)s_2^2}{n_1 + n_2 - 2}}$$

and

$$\text{d.f.} = n_1 + n_2 - 2$$

Note: This procedure can be used for all samples sizes.   ■

The quantity s_p in the confidence interval for $\mu_1 - \mu_2$ is an estimate of the common population standard deviation σ and is formed by combining information from the two independent samples. The two estimates s_1^2 and s_2^2 are weighted by their respective degrees of freedom to form the **pooled variance** s_p^2. For the special case in which the sample sizes are the same ($n_1 = n_2$), the formula for s_p^2 reduces to $s_p^2 = (s_1^2 + s_2^2)/2$, the average of the two sample variances. The degrees of freedom for s_p^2 combine the degrees of freedom for s_1^2 and s_2^2; d.f. $= (n_1 - 1) + (n_2 - 1) = n_1 + n_2 - 2$.

pooled variance

EXAMPLE 10.4   A taxicab company wants to test two programs for improving the gasoline mileage of its drivers. Under program A, drivers are assigned a target mileage and receive modest bonuses for better performance. Under program B, drivers are allowed a maximum monthly quota of gasoline; if it runs out, a driver has to pay for extra gasoline out of pocket. All taxis used are standard models and they are given standard maintenance. After three months, each driver's mileage per gallon is calculated. The data are as follows:

A: 15.9   17.5   19.1   16.9   18.3   17.3   17.0   16.2   16.8   17.1
B: 16.1   15.8   15.3   16.5   14.9   15.5   16.4   16.0   16.7   17.2

Find a 95% confidence interval for the difference in mean gasoline mileage.

Solution

Program	Mean	Variance	Standard Deviation	Sample Size
A	17.21	.8788	.9374	10
B	16.04	.4804	.6931	10

The required table value for a 95% confidence interval with $10 + 10 - 2 = 18$ d.f. is $t_{.025}$; from Appendix Table 4, $t_{.025} = 2.101$. The pooled sample variance is

$$s_p^2 = \frac{9(.8788) + 9(.4804)}{18} = .6796$$

so

$$s_p = \sqrt{.6796} = .8244$$

The confidence interval is

$$(17.21 - 16.04) - 2.101(.8244)\sqrt{\frac{1}{10} + \frac{1}{10}}$$

$$\leq \mu_A - \mu_B \leq (17.21 - 16.04) + 2.101(.8244)\sqrt{\frac{1}{10} + \frac{1}{10}}$$

or

$$.40 \leq \mu_A - \mu_B \leq 1.94 \qquad \blacksquare$$

The corresponding t test for comparing μ_1 and μ_2 based on independent samples with the standard deviations unknown is summarized here:

Hypothesis Test for $\mu_1 - \mu_2$; Independent Samples and σ's Unknown

$H_0: \mu_1 - \mu_2 = D_0(D_0$ is specified; often $D_0 = 0)$

$H_a:$ 1. $\mu_1 - \mu_2 > D_0$
     2. $\mu_1 - \mu_2 < D_0$
     3. $\mu_1 - \mu_2 \neq D_0$

T.S.: $t = \dfrac{(\bar{y}_1 - \bar{y}_2) - D_0}{s_p\sqrt{\dfrac{1}{n_1} + \dfrac{1}{n_2}}}$

R.R.: 1. $t > t_\alpha$
     2. $t < -t_\alpha$
     3. $|t| > t_{\alpha/2}$

where t_a cuts off a right-tail area a for the t distribution with $n_1 + n_2 - 2$ d.f. Note: This method can be used for all sample sizes.

EXAMPLE 10.5   Refer to Example 10.4. Test the research hypothesis that program A yields a higher mean mileage than program B. Use $\alpha = .10$.

Solution $H_0: \mu_A - \mu_B = 0$

$H_a: \mu_A - \mu_B > 0$

T.S.: $t = \dfrac{(\bar{y}_A - \bar{y}_B) - 0}{s_p\sqrt{\dfrac{1}{n_1} + \dfrac{1}{n_2}}} = \dfrac{(17.21 - 16.04)}{.8244\sqrt{\dfrac{1}{10} + \dfrac{1}{10}}} = 3.17$

R.R.: Reject H_0 if $t > t_{.10,18\text{ d.f.}} = 1.330$

Conclusion: Because $t = 3.17 > 1.33$, the mean mileage under A is significantly greater than under B based on $\alpha = .10$. In fact, because H_0 can be rejected at $\alpha = .01$ ($t_{.01, 18} = 2.552$), the p-value is less than .01.   ∎

The two-sample t test and confidence interval are based on several mathematical assumptions. Once again, these assumptions are not exactly satisfied in practice. The most crucial assumption is the independence of the two samples. If this assumption is not valid, the procedures can be grossly erroneous. If the samples are taken from different populations, and if there is no connection between the elements of one sample and those of the other, the **independence assumption** should be valid. But if the two measurements are taken on the same elements at different times or if there is any connection between elements of the samples, the two-sample t test is not appropriate and other methods of analysis must be used. For example, if one sample represents measurements on product awareness for individuals before an advertising campaign and the second sample represents measurements of product awareness on these same individuals after advertising exposure, the two-sample t test is not appropriate. The paired-sample procedures of Sections 10.4 and 10.5 should be used to compare the difference in mean awareness before and after.

independence assumption

The assumption that both populations are normally distributed is less crucial because of the Central Limit Theorem. Even if the populations are not normal, the sampling distributions of $\bar{Y}_1$ and $\bar{Y}_2$ are approximately normal for modestly large sample sizes. In fact, we believe that the quality of the Central Limit Theorem normal approximation is determined largely by the total sample size $n_1 + n_2$. Even moderate population skewness is not a serious problem. If both populations are skewed in the same direction, the fact that we are dealing with a difference in means tends to make the sampling distribution of $\bar{Y}_1 - \bar{Y}_2$ more symmetric. Generally, if $n_1 + n_2$ is at least 30 or so, we are confident of the t probabilities; if the data are reasonably symmetric within each sample, even a total sample of 15 or so should serve. Of course, with small samples, confidence intervals are wide and β probabilities high. The point is that the t probabilities are reasonably accurate. A nonparametric alternative to the two-sample t test (called Wilcoxon's rank sum test) that does not require normality of the two populations is presented in Section 10.3.

normality assumption

The new assumption is that of equal population variances; even though two **population** variances are equal, the **sample** variances differ because of random variation. Many studies have been made about the effect of unequal population variances. The universal conclusion is that for *equal* sample sizes, even substantial differences in variances (such as $\sigma_1^2 = 3\sigma_2^2$) have remarkably little effect. The most dangerous situation is one in which the larger population variance is associated with the smaller sample size. If n_1 is only half the size of n_2 but σ_1^2 is, say, twice σ_2^2, the nominal t probabilities may be seriously in error. The best cure for this problem is to take equal sample sizes.

assumption of equal variances

When the sample variances (s_1^2 and s_2^2) suggest that there may be a problem in assuming that the two population variances are equal, we can modify the usual t statistic to obtain an approximate t test. Welch (1938) showed that the distribution of the statistic

$$t' = \frac{\bar{y}_1 - \bar{y}_2}{\sqrt{\dfrac{s_1^2}{n_1} + \dfrac{s_2^2}{n_2}}}$$

can be approximated by a t distribution using Welch's approximation:

Welch's Approximation for the t' Statistic; Independent Samples

1. $H_0: \mu_1 - \mu_2 = 0$
2. The test statistic is

$$t' = \frac{\bar{y}_1 - \bar{y}_2}{\sqrt{(s_1^2/n_1) + (s_2^2/n_2)}}$$

3. The rejection region for t' can be obtained from Appendix Table 4 for

$$\text{d.f.} = \frac{(n_1 - 1)(n_2 - 1)}{(n_2 - 1)c^2 + (1 - c)^2(n_1 - 1)}$$

where

$$c = \frac{s_1^2/n_1}{s_1^2/n_1 + s_2^2/n_2}$$

Note: If d.f. is not an integer, round *down* to the nearest integer.

---

separate variance
t test

The test based on the t' statistic is sometimes referred to as the **separate variance t test** because the test statistic is identical to that (presented in Section 10.1) for large samples. The statistic replaces each population variance (σ_1^2 and σ_2^2) with the separate sample variances s_1^2 and s_2^2.

EXAMPLE 10.6   A firm has a generous but rather complicated policy concerning end-of-year bonuses for its lower-level managerial personnel. The policy's key factor is a subjective judgment of "contribution to corporate goals." A personnel officer takes samples of 24 female and 36 male managers to see if there are any differences in bonuses, expressed as a percentage of yearly salary. The data are listed here:

Gender	Bonus Percentage								
F	9.2	7.7	11.9	6.2	9.0	8.4	6.9	7.6	7.4
	8.0	9.9	6.7	8.4	9.3	9.1	8.7	9.2	9.1
	8.4	9.6	7.7	9.0	9.0	8.4			
M	10.4	8.9	11.7	12.0	8.7	9.4	9.8	9.0	9.2
	9.7	9.1	8.8	7.9	9.9	10.0	10.1	9.0	11.4
	8.7	9.6	9.2	9.7	8.9	9.2	9.4	9.7	8.9
	9.3	10.4	11.9	9.0	12.0	9.6	9.2	9.9	9.0

A computer program yields the following output:

TTEST PROCEDURE

VARIABLE: PERCENT

SEX	N	MEAN	STD DEV	STD ERROR	MINIMUM	MAXIMUM	VARIANCES	T
F	24	8.53333333	1.18895887	0.24269521	6.20000000	11.90000000	UNEQUAL	-3.9013
M	36	9.68333333	1.00384973	0.16730829	7.90000000	12.00000000	EQUAL	-4.0367

FOR H0: VARIANCES ARE EQUAL, F'=   1.40 WITH 23 AND 35 DF   PROB > F'= 0.3584

WILCOXON SCORES (RANK SUMS)

LEVEL	N	SUM OF SCORES	EXPECTED UNDER H0	STD DEV UNDER H0	MEAN SCORE
F	24	481.00	732.00	66.15	20.04
M	36	1349.00	1098.00	66.15	37.47

a. Identify the value of the pooled-variance t statistic.
b. Identify the value of the t' statistic.
c. Use both statistics to test the research hypothesis of unequal means at $\alpha = .05$ and at $\alpha = .01$. Does the conclusion depend on which statistic is used?

Solution

a. The pooled-variance statistic is $t = -4.0367$.
b. $t' = -3.9013$.
c. The t statistic based on the pooled variance has d.f. $= 24 + 36 - 2 = 58$. For a two-sided H_a, we reject H_0 at $\alpha = .05$ if $|t| > t_{.025} \approx 2.00$; with $\alpha = .01$, reject if $|t| > t_{.005} \approx 2.66$. Because $|t| = 4.037$, we can easily reject H_0 even at $\alpha = .01$. For the t' statistic based on separate variances the degrees of freedom can be computed using the formula

$$\text{d.f.} = \frac{(n_1 - 1)(n_2 - 1)}{(n_2 - 1)c^2 + (1 - c)^2(n_1 - 1)}, \qquad \text{with } c = \frac{s_1^2/n_1}{s_1^2/n_1 + s_2^2/n_2}$$

For these data,

$$c = \frac{1.4137/24}{1.4137/24 + 1.0076/36} = \frac{.0589}{.0589 + .0280} = .6778$$

and

$$c^2 = .4594, \qquad (1 - c)^2 = .1038$$

Then

$$\text{d.f.} = \frac{23(35)}{35(.4594) + .1038(23)}$$

$$= \frac{805}{16.0790 + 2.3876}$$

$$= \frac{805}{18.4671} = 43.59$$

Rounding down to the nearest integer, d.f. = 43. For a two-sided research hypothesis and $\alpha = .05$, we reject H_0 if $|t'| > t_{.025, 43} \approx 2.02$. For $\alpha = .01$, we reject H_0 if $|t'| > t_{.005, 43} = 2.70$. Because $|t'| = 3.90$, we can easily reject H_0 even at $\alpha = .01$. The conclusions from the t and t' tests are essentially the same and the research hypothesis is quite conclusively supported. ∎

We have presented several different approaches in the last two sections. In this section we developed pooled-variance t methods based on an assumption of equal population variances. In addition, we introduced the t' statistic for an approximate t when the variances are not equal. In Section 10.1 we used separate variances in a z statistic and appealed to large-sample theory. Confidence intervals and hypothesis tests based on these different procedures (t, t', or z) need not give identical results. Standard computer packages often report the results of both the pooled-variance and separate-variance t tests. Which should a manager believe?

The choice depends on the evidence about underlying assumptions. If plots of each sample appear roughly normal, and if the sample variances are roughly equal, the pooled-variance t test should be valid and most efficient. If plots of each sample are normal but the sample variances are clearly different (especially if the sample sizes differ), the separate-variance t' test is more believable. If the sample sizes are equal, the pooled-variance and separate-variance t tests will usually give the same results; in fact, the test statistics are algebraically equal for equal sample sizes. But if the data in one or both samples are obviously nonnormal, the rank sum approach discussed in the next section is preferred. As usual, a little thought and some careful looks at the data will let a manager make a reasonable choice.

EXAMPLE 10.7   A simulation study involves samples from independent, normal populations. The following results are obtained:

```
            Checking Alpha (different sample sizes and sigmas)

Simulation of Two Sample t-test (1000 samples)

Popn      Mu        Sigma        n
  1     50.000     14.1421      10
  2     50.000     10.0000      20

using the pooled variance t test

one-tail:

          number of times H0:   "mu1-mu2 is   0" is rejected in favor of
  alpha    "mu1-mu2 >   0"      "mu1-mu2 <   0"    total (alpha doubled)
  0.100         137                 127                  264
  0.050          70                  71                  141
  0.025          36                  34                   70
  0.010          14                  16                   30
  0.005          11                  10                   21
```

```
using separate variances (t')

one-tail:

        number of times H0:  "mu1-mu2 is   0" is rejected in favor of
alpha   "mu1-mu2 >  0"   "mu1-mu2 <  0"   total (alpha doubled)
0.100        104              99                203
0.050         44              41                 85
0.025         20              21                 41
0.010         10              10                 20
0.005          4               4                  8


average pooled t is 0.0047 with variance of   1.354355
average t' is 0.0071 with variance of   1.122882
```

What do these results indicate about the choice of pooled-variance t versus t?

Solution   One of the assumptions underlying the pooled-variance t test has been violated; the population variances aren't equal. The null hypothesis is true because the population means are equal. The pooled-variance t test rejects the null hypothesis more frequently than the nominal α value would indicate. For example, for a nominal α of .05 (one-tailed test), we would expect 50 and 50 rejections, but we get 70 and 71 rejections. The t' test rejects the null hypothesis just about as often as α indicates. ∎

EXAMPLE 10.8

Another simulation study is done with samples from independent normal populations, with the following results.

```
              Checking Alpha (different sample sizes and sigmas)

Simulation of Two Sample t-test (1000 samples)

Popn      Mu      Sigma        n
  1     50.000   10.0000      10
  2     50.000   14.1421      20

using the pooled variance t test

one-tail:

        number of times H0:  "mu1-mu2 is   0" is rejected in favor of
alpha   "mu1-mu2 >  0"   "mu1-mu2 <  0"   total (alpha doubled)
0.100         71              84                155
0.050         32              36                 68
0.025         13              16                 29
0.010          4               7                 11
0.005          1               3                  4
```

```
using separate variances (t')

one-tail:

        number of times HO:   "mu1-mu2 is   0" is rejected in favor of
alpha    "mu1-mu2 >   0"    "mu1-mu2 <   0"    total (alpha doubled)
0.100          103                104                  207
0.050           43                 48                   91
0.025           21                 20                   41
0.010            7                  9                   16
0.005            1                  5                    6


average pooled t is -0.0196 with variance of   0.873156
average t' is -0.0226 with variance of   1.088475
```

What do these results indicate about t versus t'?

Solution   Again, the assumption of equal variances is violated. This time, however, the smaller variance is associated with the smaller sample size; in Example 10.7 the smaller variance was associated with the larger sample size. In this example, we find that the number of false rejections of the null hypothesis is consistently *smaller* than would be indicated by the nominal α. Again, the t' test rejects the null hypothesis just about as often as α indicates. ∎

SECTION 10.2   EXERCISES

10.10 A processor of recycled aluminum cans is concerned about the levels of impurities (principally other metals) contained in lots from two sources. Laboratory analysis of sample lots yields the following data (kilograms of impurities per hundred kilograms of product):

Source I: 3.8   3.5   4.1   2.5   3.6   4.3   2.1   2.9   3.2   3.7   2.8   2.7
             mean = 3.267, standard deviation = .676

Source II: 1.8   2.2   1.3   5.1   4.0   4.7   3.3   4.3   4.2   2.5   5.4   4.6
             mean = 3.617, standard deviation = 1.365

a. Calculate the pooled variance and standard deviation.
b. Calculate a 95% confidence interval for the difference in mean impurity levels.
c. Can the processor conclude, using $\alpha = .05$, that there is a nonzero difference in means?

10.11 Calculate the p-value in Exercise 10.10, part (c).

10.12 In a computer simulation study, 1000 samples were taken from each of two populations. Both populations were normal, and both populations had means equal to 50. The first population had a standard deviation of 20, the second had a standard deviation of 10. The first sample size was 5, the second sample size was 20. The null hypothesis of equal means was rejected at $\alpha = .05$ in 203 of the samples, using the pooled-variance t test; this hypothesis was rejected, again at $\alpha = .05$, in 48 samples using the t' test.

a. Should the pooled-variance t test or the t' test be better in this situation? What does "better" mean?
b. Does the computer simulation result confirm your judgment in part (a)?

10.13 Construct separate plots of the impurities data from each source in Exercise 10.10. Which of the assumptions (if any) of the t test seem suspect? Do you think that there is serious reason to doubt the conclusion of Exercise 10.10, part (c)?

10.14 Company officials are concerned about the length of time a particular drug retains its potency. A random sample (sample 1) of 10 bottles of the product is drawn from current production and analyzed for potency. A second sample (sample 2) is obtained, stored for one year, and then analyzed. The readings obtained are

Sample 1:	10.2	0.5	10.3	10.8	9.8	10.6	10.7	10.2	10.0	10.6
Sample 2:	9.8	9.6	10.1	10.2	10.1	9.7	9.5	9.6	9.8	9.9

The data are analyzed by a standard program package (SAS). The relevant output is shown on the top of the next page.

TTEST PROCEDURE

VARIABLE: POTENCY

SAMPLE	N	MEAN	STD DEV	STD ERROR	MINIMUM	MAXIMUM	VARIANCES	T	DF	PROB > |T|
1	10	10.37000000	0.32335052	0.10225241	9.80000000	10.80000000	UNEQUAL	4.2368	16.6	0.0006
2	10	9.83000000	0.24060110	0.07608475	9.50000000	10.20000000	EQUAL	4.2368	18.0	0.0005

FOR HO: VARIANCES ARE EQUAL, F'=   1.81 WITH 9 AND 9 DF   PROB > F'= 0.3917

   a. Identify the sample means and standard deviations.
   b. Locate the value of the t statistic. Is the pooled-variance t statistic identified as "equal variance" or "unequal variance"?
   c. Locate the value of the t' statistic.
   d. Why are these two statistics equal in this case?

10.15 a. Plot the data of Exercise 10.14. Use separate plots for the two samples.
   b. Does it seem that there are serious violations of the assumptions underlying the pooled-variance test?

10.16 a. Locate the p-value for the pooled-variance t test in the output of Exercise 10.14. Is it one-tailed or two-tailed?
   b. What conclusion would you reach concerning the possibility of a decrease in mean potency over one year?

10.17 To compare the performance of microcomputer spreadsheet programs, teams of three students each choose whatever spreadsheet program they wish. Each team is given the same set of standard accounting and finance problems to solve. The time (minutes) required for each team to solve the set of problems is recorded. The following data are obtained for the two most widely used programs.

Program	Time										$\bar{y}$	s	n
A	39	57	42	53	41	44	71	56	49	63	51.50	10.46	10
B	43	38	35	45	40	28	50	54	37	29			
	36	27	52	33	31	30					38.00	8.67	16

   a. Calculate the pooled variance.
   b. Use this variance to find a 99% confidence interval for the difference of population means.
   c. According to this interval, can the null hypothesis of equal means be rejected at $\alpha = .01$?

10.18 Redo parts (b) and (c) of Exercise 10.17 using a separate-variance (t') method. Which method is more appropriate in this case? How critical is it which method is used?

10.19 A manufacturer of modems uses microcomputer chips from two different sources. As part of quality-control testing, the manufacturer obtains data on the rate of defective chips per thousand for each lot of chips. The following results are obtained; note that the rate is not necessarily an integer number because the lot sizes are not exactly 1000 chips per lot.

Source	Number of Defectives/1000									
I	9.8	9.9	10.2	10.5	10.7	10.8	11.7	13.9	19.2	27.6
II	10.6	11.0	11.5	11.8	11.9	12.7	14.2	16.8	21.7	29.9

    a. Calculate means and standard deviations for both sources.
    b. Calculate the pooled-variance t statistic for testing the null hypothesis of equal means.
    c. Calculate the t' statistic for testing the same hypothesis.
    d. Explain why t and t' are equal for these data.

10.20 a. Can the null hypothesis in Exercise 10.19 be rejected at $\alpha = .05$ in favor of a two-sided research hypothesis? Use the pooled-variance t statistic.
    b. State bounds on the p-value.
    c. Calculate the approximate d.f. for the t' statistic.
    d. Redo parts (a) and (b) using the t' statistic.

10.3 A NONPARAMETRIC ALTERNATIVE: THE WILCOXON RANK SUM TEST

The two-sample t test we described in the previous section is based on several mathematical assumptions. In particular, we assume that both populations have normal distributions with equal variances. When the assumptions are not satisfied, the t test may still be valid, in the sense that the nominal probabilities are approximately correct, particularly if the sample sizes are large and equal. Even so, there is another hypothesis-testing method that requires weaker mathematical assumptions, is almost as powerful when the t assumptions are satisfied, and is more powerful in other situations. We describe this test, called the *Wilcoxon rank sum test*, in this section.

The mathematical assumption for this test is that independent random samples are taken from two populations; the null hypothesis is that the two population distributions are identical (but not necessarily normal). The Wilcoxon rank sum test probabilities are exactly correct for any two populations with identical continuous distributions and are generally conservative for two populations with identical discrete distributions.

ranking sample data   The test is based on the ranks of the sample data values. The rank of an individual observation is its position in the combined sample: Rank 1 indicates the smallest value, rank 2 indicates the next smallest value, and so on. As the phrase *rank sum test* indicates, the Wilcoxon rank sum test is based on the sum of the ranks in either sample. Under the null hypothesis of identical population distributions, the sum of the ranks in one sample is proportional to the sample size. If one population is shifted to the right of another, that is, if the first population tends to yield larger observations, the rank sum for the first sample tends to be large. Of course a small rank sum for the first sample indicates that the first population is shifted to the left of the second. Define T to be the sum of the ranks in the first sample. Under the null hypothesis, the expected value and variance of T have been determined:

$$\mu_T = \frac{n_1(n_1 + n_2 + 1)}{2} \qquad \sigma_T^2 = \frac{n_1 n_2}{12}(n_1 + n_2 + 1)$$

If both n_1 and n_2 are 10 or larger, the sampling distribution of T is approximately normal. This allows use of a z statistic in testing the hypothesis of equal distributions.

Wilcoxon Rank Sum Test

H_0: The two populations are identical

H_a: 1. Population 1 is shifted to the right of population 2
2. Population 1 is shifted to the left of population 2
3. Population 1 is shifted to the right or left of population 2

T.S.: $z = \dfrac{T - \mu_T}{\sigma_T}$

where T denotes the rank sum for sample 1

R.R.: 1. $z > z_\alpha$
2. $z < -z_\alpha$
3. $|z| > z_{\alpha/2}$

Note: The normal approximation is reasonably accurate if $n_1 \geq 10$ and $n_2 \geq 10$. Special tables are available for smaller values of n_1 and n_2 (e.g., Hollander and Wolfe, 1973).

EXAMPLE 10.9   Perform a rank sum test for Example 10.5.

Solution   The first step is to rank the observations. It helps in doing the ranking to order the values in each sample from lowest to highest.

					Program A					
Value:	15.9	16.2	16.8	16.9	17.0	17.1	17.3	17.5	18.3	19.1
Rank:	5	8	12	13	14	15	17	18	19	20

					Program B					
Value:	14.9	15.3	15.5	15.8	16.0	16.1	16.4	16.5	16.7	17.2
Rank:	1	2	3	4	6	7	9	10	11	16

The sum of the ranks in the A sample is

$$T = 5 + 8 + \cdots + 20 = 141$$

Under the null hypothesis

$$\mu_T = \frac{10(10 + 10 + 1)}{2} = 105$$

$$\sigma_T^2 = \frac{(10)(10)}{12}(10 + 10 + 1) = 175$$

$$\sigma_T = \sqrt{175} = 13.23$$

So

$$z = \frac{T - \mu_T}{\sigma_T}$$

$$= \frac{141 - 105}{13.23}$$

$$= 2.72 \qquad \blacksquare$$

In Example 10.5, the research hypothesis H_a was that the mean for program A was larger than the mean for program B. The corresponding research hypothesis for the rank sum test is that the program A distribution is shifted to the right of the program B distribution. This research hypothesis is supported and the null hypothesis is rejected if T (and therefore z) is too large to be attributed to chance. The one-tailed p-value for $z = 2.72$ is .0033, so the null hypothesis is rejected for $\alpha = .10, .05, .01$, or even .005. As $n_1 = n_2 = 10$, we are barely within the adequacy range of the normal approximation. It is conceivable that the real p-value is a bit larger than .0033, but still the null hypothesis should be rejected at any conventional α level.

EXAMPLE 10.10   Refer to the computer output of Example 10.6.
a. Identify the value of the rank sum statistic.
b. Find the test statistic for the null hypothesis of equal distribution of bonuses by gender.
c. State an approximate two-tailed p-value for the test in part (b).
d. How does the conclusion of this test compare with that found in Example 10.6?

Solution   a. The sum of the ranks in sample 1 is shown as 481.0.
b. Because $n_1 = 24$ and $n_2 = 36$, a normal approximation should be quite good.

$$\mu_T = \frac{24(24 + 36 + 1)}{2} = 732.0$$

$$\sigma_T^2 = \frac{(24)(36)(24 + 36 + 1)}{12} = 4392.0$$

$$z = \frac{481.0 - 732.0}{\sqrt{4392.0}} = -3.79$$

c. The z value is beyond the range of our z tables. The largest table entry, 3.09, corresponds to a one-tailed area of .001. Therefore a z value of -3.79 must correspond to a two-tailed area less than $2(.001) = .002$.

d. As in Example 10.6, we have conclusive support for the research hypothesis. ∎

treatment of ties

The theory behind the rank sum test assumes that the population distributions are continuous, so there is zero probability that two observations are exactly equal. In practice there are often ties—two or more equal observations. Each observation in a set of tied values is assigned the average of the ranks for the set. If two observations are tied for ranks 2 and 3, each is given rank 2.5; the next larger value gets rank 4, and so on. There is a correction to the variance formula for the case of tied ranks (see Ott, 1984). The variance formula given above is generally conservative and usually very close, unless there are many, many ties.

The Wilcoxon rank sum test is a direct competitor of the two-sample t test. Both tests are sensitive to differences in location (mean or median) as opposed to dispersion or spread. The rank sum test requires fewer assumptions than the t test (in particular it does not assume population normality), but it uses less information from the data; only ordering information is relevant to the rank sum test.* When the assumptions underlying the t test are close to correct, the t test is better. Both theoretical results and simulations clearly indicate that a t test (using the pooled variance if the sample variances are equal or if the sample sizes are equal, but separate variances if both variances and sample sizes aren't equal) will have correct α values and optimal power for normal populations. For obvious nonnormal data, the rank sum test has a more believable α value (especially for small samples) and it usually has better power.

EXAMPLE 10.11

To investigate the effect of skewness on the pooled-variance t test as well as the rank sum test, 1000 samples are drawn from a squared-exponential population; this population is extremely right-skewed. The following results are obtained.

```
          Checking Alpha (different sample sizes; same sigmas)

Simulation of Two Sample t-test (1000 samples)

Popn      Mu        Sigma       n
  1     50.000    10.0000       5
  2     50.000    10.0000      25
```

---

* Therefore the rank sum test can be used when the observations are qualitative and ordinal, as when 1 = strongly opposed, 2 = opposed, 3 = neutral, and so on.

```
using the pooled variance t test
one-tail:
        number of times HO:  "mu1-mu2 is   0" is rejected in favor of
alpha   "mu1-mu2 >   0"    "mu1-mu2 <   0"    total (alpha doubled)
0.100         146              35                  181
0.050          95               3                   98
0.025          51               0                   51
0.010          25               0                   25
0.005          15               0                   15
```

```
Results of Wilcoxon Rank Sum Test using Z as test statistic

        number of times HO:  "two populations are identical" rejected in favor of
alpha   Popn1 rt of Popn2   Popn1 left of Popn2    total (alpha doubled)
0.100         102                   93                   195
0.050          37                   51                    88
0.025          15                   30                    45
0.010           5                   14                    19
0.005           4                    3                     7
```

What do the results indicate about the effect of skewness on the two tests?

Solution   The null hypothesis is true in this simulation; both means are 50. The actual number of rejections of the null hypothesis by the t test is far from what is indicated by the nominal α value for one-tailed probabilities. The rank sum test, which doesn't assume normal populations, appears to be rejecting the null hypothesis the correct number of times. ∎

EXAMPLE 10.12   A simulation study investigating the effect of outliers on the t and rank sum tests involves independent samples from Laplace (mildly outlier-prone) populations. One part of the study has both population means equal; a second part involves different means. The following results are obtained:

```
              Checking Alpha (same sample sizes and sigmas)

Simulation of Two Sample t-test (1000 samples)

Popn      Mu       Sigma        n
 1      50.000    10.0000       30
 2      50.000    10.0000       30

using the pooled variance t test

one-tail:

        number of times HO:  "mu1-mu2 is   0" is rejected in favor of
alpha   "mu1-mu2 >   0"    "mu1-mu2 <   0"    total (alpha doubled)
0.100         106              98                  204
0.050          50              47                   97
0.025          22              22                   44
0.010           7              10                   17
0.005           3               5                    8
```

```
Results of Wilcoxon Rank Sum Test using Z as test statistic

        number of times HO:  "two populations are identical" rejected in favor of
alpha   Popn1 rt of Popn2   Popn1 left of Popn2    total (alpha doubled)
0.100         111                   98                   209
0.050          53                   47                   100
0.025          21                   21                    42
0.010           7                   12                    19
0.005           5                    4                     9
```

Checking Power (same sample sizes and sigmas)

Simulation of Two Sample t-test (1000 samples)

Popn	Mu	Sigma	n
1	50.000	10.0000	30
2	60.000	10.0000	30

using the pooled variance t test

one-tail:

number of times HO: "mu1-mu2 is 0" is rejected in favor of

alpha	"mu1-mu2 > 0"	"mu1-mu2 < 0"	total (alpha doubled)
0.100	0	996	996
0.050	0	986	986
0.025	0	962	962
0.010	0	912	912
0.005	0	864	864

Results of Wilcoxon Rank Sum Test using Z as test statistic

number of times HO: "two populations are identical" rejected in favor of

alpha	Popn1 rt of Popn2	Popn1 left of Popn2	total (alpha doubled)
0.100	0	999	999
0.050	0	998	998
0.025	0	993	993
0.010	0	966	966
0.005	0	937	937

What do these results indicate about the choice of the *t* or rank sum test when the populations are outlier-prone?

Solution The results for both tests when the null hypothesis is true indicate that the nominal α is (very close to) correct. The simulation obtained just about the expected number of false rejections. When the research hypothesis is true, as in the second part of the study, we want to reject the null hypothesis. The rank sum test consistently yields more rejections than does the *t* test. The rank sum test is more powerful in this situation. ■

SECTION 10.3 EXERCISES

10.21 The computer package used in Exercise 10.14 also calculated rank sums. The relevant output is shown at the top of page 415.
  a. Identify the rank sums.
  b. Locate the value of the *z* statistic.
  c. Formulate appropriate null and research hypothesis.
  d. Is H_a supported at $\alpha = .01$?

10.22 a. Locate the *p*-value in the output of Exercise 10.21. Is it one-tailed or two-tailed? What *p*-value should be reported in Exercise 10.21?
  b. What conclusion would be reached in using the rank sum test? How does it compare to the conclusion of the *t* test? Does it matter much which test is used?

```
                 DRUG POTENCY DATA                14:25 THURSDAY, SEPTEMBER 11, 1986


    ANALYSIS FOR VARIABLE POTENCY CLASSIFIED BY VARIABLE  SAMPLE

            AVERAGE SCORES WERE USED FOR TIES



                WILCOXON SCORES (RANK SUMS)


                       SUM OF   EXPECTED    STD DEV      MEAN
       LEVEL        N   SCORES   UNDER HO    UNDER HO    SCORE

       1           10   146.00    105.00      13.17     14.60
       2           10    64.00    105.00      13.17      6.40

        WILCOXON 2-SAMPLE TEST (NORMAL APPROXIMATION)
        (WITH CONTINUITY CORRECTION OF .5)
        S=  146.00     Z= 3.0743      PROB >|Z|=0.0021

        T-TEST APPROX. SIGNIFICANCE=0.0062
```

Output for Exercise 10.21

10.23 The data for Exercise 10.17 are reproduced here:

Program	Time										$\bar{y}$	s	n
A	39	57	42	53	41	44	71	56	49	63	51.50	10.46	10
B	43	38	35	45	40	28	50	54	37	29			
	36	27	52	33	31	30					38.00	8.67	16

    a. Find the ranks of the combined data. It's much easier if you sort the data in each sample first.

    b. Find the rank sums.

    c. Is there a statistically significant difference ($\alpha = .01$) between programs according to the rank sum test?

10.24 Do the data of Exercise 10.17 (and 10.23) indicate that the rank sum test is preferable to a t test? Explain, preferably with pictures.

10.25 The data of Exercise 10.19 are as follows:

Source	Number of Defectives/1000									
I	9.8	9.9	10.2	10.5	10.7	10.8	11.7	13.9	19.2	27.6
II	10.6	11.0	11.5	11.8	11.9	12.7	14.2	16.8	21.7	29.9

    a. Use a rank test to test the null hypothesis that both sources have the same distribution of defectives per 1000. Use $\alpha = .05$ and a two-sided research hypothesis.

    b. Find the two-tailed p-value.

10.26 Is there reason to think that a rank test is more appropriate than a *t* test for the data of Exercise 10.19 (and 10.25)?

10.27 Another simulation study compares the pooled-variance *t*, *t'*, and rank sum tests when the research hypothesis of unequal means is true. The populations are both the severely skewed squared-exponential shape. The results are as follows:

```
            Checking Power (same sample sizes and sigmas)

Popn        Mu        Sigma        n
  1       50.000     10.0000      10
  2       60.000     10.0000      10

using the pooled variance t test

one-tail:

         number of times HO:  "mu1-mu2 is   0" is rejected in favor of
alpha    "mu1-mu2 >   0"   "mu1-mu2 <   0"     total (alpha doubled)
0.100           0               858                   858
0.050           0               789                   789
0.025           0               728                   728
0.010           0               655                   655
0.005           0               586                   586


using separate variances (t')

one-tail:

         number of times HO:  "mu1-mu2 is   0" is rejected in favor of
alpha    "mu1-mu2 >   0"   "mu1-mu2 <   0"     total (alpha doubled)
0.100           0               850                   850
0.050           0               779                   779
0.025           0               716                   716
0.010           0               625                   625
0.005           0               550                   550


Results of Wilcoxon Rank Sum Test using Z as test statistic

         number of times HO:  "two populations are identical" rejected in favor
alpha    Popn1 rt of Popn2   Popn1 left of Popn2    total (alpha doubled)
0.100           0               984                   984
0.050           0               971                   971
0.025           0               940                   940
0.010           0               879                   879
0.005           0               760                   760
```

a. Why is the "Checking Power" title justified?

b. Which of the three tests appears to have the best power in this situation?

10.4   PAIRED-SAMPLE METHODS

The methods of the preceding two sections are appropriate for the analysis of two independent samples. We have emphasized that those methods are not appropriate for situations in which each measurement in one sample is matched or paired with a corresponding measurement in the other. In this section we discuss methods for paired-sample data.

control of variability   The advantage of pairing observations is the **control of variability** that would otherwise obscure a real difference in means. For example, suppose that an office manager wants to test two new word processors to find which one yields greater average speed. One test procedure would be to assign 10 secretaries randomly to one model and another 10 secretaries to the other. This procedure would yield two independent samples. Another procedure would be to have 10 randomly chosen secretaries type on both models; the 10 typing speeds on each model would constitute paired or matched samples. Of course, there are large differences in speed among secretaries. These differences would cause large variability in the independent-samples experiment and would tend to conceal any real differences between the two models. In the paired-sample experiment, the manager can calculate the difference in the two models' speeds for the same secretaries; individual variability in speed cancels out of the difference. The individual-variability factor does not cause random variability in the paired-sample experiment.

As indicated in the secretary example, statistical methods for working with paired samples are all based on the same idea. Calculate all differences of matched scores and apply single-sample methods to the resulting sample of differences. In particular, the t-distribution methods for confidence intervals and hypothesis tests described in Chapters 8 and 9 may be used.

EXAMPLE 10.13   Insurance adjusters investigate the relative automobile repair costs at two garages. Each of 15 cars recently involved in accidents is taken to both garages 1 and 2 for separate estimates of repair costs. The resulting data are analyzed incorrectly as coming from two independent samples, and correctly as coming from paired samples. Use the following computer printouts to compare the resulting t statistics. What accounts for the difference in these statistics? (Costs are entered in hundreds of dollars.)

	1	2	
Sample size	15	15	
Mean	6.84667	6.23333	diff. = 0.613333
Variance	10.2655	8.65095	ratio = 1.18664
Std. deviation	3.20399	2.94125	

Hypothesis Test - Difference of Means

```
Null hypothesis: difference of means = 0
Alternative: not equal
Equal variances assumed: yes

Computed t statistic = 0.546163
            P value = 0.5893

Equal variances assumed: no

Computed t statistic = 0.546163
            P value = 0.5893
```

(continued)

```
                              Sample1          Sample2         differences

Sample size                   15               15              15
Mean                          6.84667          6.23333         0.613333
Variance                      10.2655          8.65095         0.155524
Std. deviation                3.20399          2.94125         0.394365


                         Hypothesis Test - Mean Difference


Null hypothesis: mean = 0
Alternative: not equal

Computed t statistic = 6.02343
            P value = 0.0000
```

Solution   The pooled-sample and separate-sample (t') statistics are equal because $n_1 = n_2$; the value is only .546. For 28 (or 27) d.f., this value does not approach statistical significance at any reasonable α level. The difference t statistic equals 6.02, which is "off the tables"—significant at all reasonable α levels. The reason is that there is huge variability in the severity of damage to the 15 cars. This source of variability makes the standard error very large and therefore the t' quite small. Because the difference t is based on differences between the two garages' estimates on the same cars, it is not affected by the variability among cars.   ∎

EXAMPLE 10.14   A tasting panel of 15 people is asked to rate two new kinds of tea on a scale ranging from 0 to 100; 25 means "I would try to finish it only to be polite," 50 means "I would drink it but not buy it," 75 means "it's about as good as any tea I know," and 100 means "it's superb; I would drink nothing else." (What 0 means is left to your imagination.) The ratings are as follows:

	Person							
	1	2	3	4	5	6	7	8
Tea S	85	40	75	81	42	50	60	15
Tea J	65	50	43	65	20	65	35	38
Difference	+20	−10	+32	+16	+22	−15	+25	−23

	Person						
	9	10	11	12	13	14	15
Tea S	65	40	60	40	65	75	80
Tea J	60	47	60	43	53	61	63
Difference	+5	−7	0	−3	+12	+14	+17

a. Calculate a 95% confidence interval for the population difference in mean ratings.

b. Test the null hypothesis of no difference against a two-sided alternative using $\alpha = .05$.

c. What advantage does matching have in this situation?

Solution   a. If we call the differences d_i, then $\bar{d} = 7.00$ and $s_d = 16.08$. Of course

$$\bar{d} = \frac{\sum d_i}{15} \quad \text{and} \quad s_d^2 = \frac{\sum (d_i - \bar{d})^2}{14}$$

The population mean of the differences is the same as the difference in means, so $\mu_d = \mu_S - \mu_J$. Because our calculations are based on 15 differences, there are 14 d.f., and the required t table value is 2.145. The confidence interval is

$$7.00 - 2.145 \frac{16.08}{\sqrt{15}} \le \mu_S - \mu_J \le 7.00 + 2.145 \frac{16.08}{\sqrt{15}}$$

or

$$-1.9 \le \mu_S - \mu_J \le 15.9$$

b. Because the value 0 is included in this 95% confidence interval, it follows that $H_0: \mu_S - \mu_J = 0$ cannot be rejected at $\alpha = .05$ using a two-tailed test. The t statistic is

$$t = \frac{7.00 - 0}{16.08/\sqrt{15}} = 1.69$$

which has a two-tailed p-value a little larger than .10.

c. The matching is somewhat useful in accounting for individual differences in taste. There is some tendency for those who give high scores to S to also give high scores to J, and for those who give low S scores to also give low J scores. Had we erroneously used the two-sample formula, we would have had a standard error

$$s_p \sqrt{\frac{1}{15} + \frac{1}{15}} = 6.21$$

rather than the correct standard error

$$s_d/\sqrt{15} = 4.15 \qquad \blacksquare$$

The formal statement of these matched-pairs procedures merely requires replacing y's by d's in the one sample t-distribution procedures. These are summarized here:

100$(1 - \alpha)$% Confidence Interval for μ_d Based on Matched Samples

$$\bar{d} - t_{\alpha/2} s_d/\sqrt{n} \le \mu_d \le \bar{d} + t_{\alpha/2} s_d/\sqrt{n}$$

where n is the number of pairs of observations (and therefore the number of differences) and $t_{\alpha/2}$ cuts off a right-tail area of $\alpha/2$ for the t distribution with $n - 1$ d.f.

Hypothesis Test for Matched Samples

H_0: $\mu_d = D_0$ (D_0 is specified; often $D_0 = 0$)

H_a: 1. $\mu_d > D_0$

    2. $\mu_d < D_0$

    3. $\mu_d \neq D_0$

T.S.: $t = \dfrac{\bar{d} - D_0}{s_d/\sqrt{n}}$

R.R.: 1. $t > t_\alpha$

    2. $t < -t_\alpha$

    3. $|t| > t_{\alpha/2}$

In fact, Example 10.14 was an illustration of the paired-sample t test.

10.5   THE SIGNED-RANK METHOD

In the previous section, we considered a t test for paired samples. Like any t test, it is based on an assumption that the underlying population (or process) has something reasonably close to a normal distribution. But what if a histogram, stem-and-leaf display, or box plot clearly indicates a nonnormal distribution? There are alternatives to the t test that are more effective in clear nonnormal cases. One could test the null hypothesis that the *median* difference is zero, using the test described in Section 9.8. In this context, a median test is usually called a

sign test

sign test, because counting the number of successes (values above the hypothesized median, zero) is counting the number of plus signs in the data. The sign test, or equivalently a median confidence interval, is often a good choice in the case of a highly skewed distribution, especially if the sample size is too small to place much reliance on the Central Limit Theorem.

    An alternative test, designed for data that are basically symmetric but outlier-prone, is the **Wilcoxon signed-rank** test. The formal null hypothesis for this test is that the true distribution of differences is symmetric around a specified number D_0; almost always D_0 is taken to be zero. The test is primarily sensitive to the distribution being shifted to the right or left of D_0; one- or two-sided research hypotheses may be tested. Again the test works with differences (if D_0 is not zero, D_0 is subtracted from each difference). Discard all differences that are exactly zero and reduce n accordingly. Then the differences are ranked in order of absolute value, smallest to largest. The appropriate sign is attached to each rank. Define

T_+ and T_-

$T_+ =$ the sum of the positive ranks; if there are no positive ranks, $T_+ = 0$

$T_- =$ the sum of the negative ranks; if there are no negative ranks, $T_- = 0$

and $n =$ the number of nonzero differences

The Wilcoxon signed-rank test is presented next.

Wilcoxon Signed-Rank Test

H_0: The distribution of differences is symmetric around D_0 (D_0 is specified; usually D_0 is zero)

H_a: 1. the differences tend to be larger than D_0
2. the differences tend to be smaller than D_0
3. the differences tend to be shifted away from D_0

T.S.: 1. $T = |T_-|$
2. $T = T_+$
3. $T =$ smaller of $|T_-|$, T_+

R.R.: ($n \leq 50$): For a specified value of α (one-tailed .05, .025, .01, or .005; two-tailed .10, .05, .02, .01) and fixed number of nonzero differences n, reject H_0 if the value of T is less than or equal to the appropriate entry in Appendix Table 7. ($n > 50$): Compute the test statistic

$$z = \frac{T - \dfrac{n(n + 1)}{4}}{\sqrt{\dfrac{n(n + 1)(2n + 1)}{24}}}$$

For cases 1 and 2, reject H_0 if $z < -z_\alpha$; for case 3 reject H_0 if $z < -z_{\alpha/2}$.

EXAMPLE 10.15

Refer to the data of Example 10.14. Use the signed-rank test to test the null hypothesis of symmetry around $D_0 = 0$ against a two-sided alternative. Use $\alpha = .05$.

Solution

The differences and their signed ranks are presented below:

					Person					
	1	2	3	4	5	6	7	8	9	10
Difference	+20	−10	+32	+16	+22	−15	+25	−23	+5	−7
Signed rank	+10	−4	+14	+8	+11	−7	+13	−12	+2	−3

			Person		
	11	12	13	14	15
Difference	0	−3	+12	+14	+17
Signed rank	X	−1	+5	+6	+9

The 0 difference (person 11) is discarded, so $n = 14$.

$$T_+ = 10 + 14 + 8 + 11 + 13 + 2 + 5 + 6 + 9 = 78$$
$$T_- = -4 - 7 - 12 - 3 - 1 = -27$$

(A good check is that $T_+ - T_-$ must always equal $n(n + 1)/2$, which equals 105 here.) For a two-sided research hypothesis, $T = \{$smaller of $|-27|$ and $78\} = 27$. As $n = 14 < 50$, we find the $\alpha = .05$ (two-sided) entry in Appendix Table 7; it is 21. Because $T = 27 > 21$, we cannot reject H_0 at $\alpha = .05$. We cannot reject at $\alpha = .10$ either; the table value is 26. Although we do not need the large-sample $(n > 50)$ approximation in this problem, it can be computed:

$$z = \frac{27 - (14)(15)/4}{\sqrt{\dfrac{(14)(15)(29)}{24}}} = -1.60$$

For $\alpha = .10$ (two-tailed), we reject if $z < -z_{.05} = -1.645$; if we had used the z approximation we would not have rejected H_0 at $\alpha = .10$. ∎

EXAMPLE 10.16   Use the signed-rank information in the computer printout of Example 10.13 to test the research hypothesis that garage 1's estimates tend to be higher than garage 2's. How does the result of the signed-rank test compare with the result of the t test of Example 10.13?

Solution   For this one-sided research hypothesis, the test statistic $T = |T_-|$; from the printout, $T_- = -1.5$, so $T = 1.5$. According to Appendix Table 7 of critical values for the signed rank test, H_0 is rejected (at $\alpha = .005$ with $n = 15$) if $T \leq 16$. Because 1.5 is much less than 16, we can reject H_0 conclusively. Although $n = 15$ is too small to give us much faith in a normal approximation,

$$z = \frac{1.5 - (15)(16)/4}{\sqrt{\dfrac{(15)(16)(31)}{24}}} = -3.32$$

This z value is "off the table." Even if the normal approximation is poor, this strongly indicates that the null hypothesis can be rejected even at extremely low α values. The same conclusion applies to the t value of 6.023 found in Example 10.13. ∎

choice of method   The choice of the appropriate paired-sample test from this section follows the guidelines of Chapter 9. If the assumptions of the t test are satisfied—in particular, if the distribution of differences is roughly normal—the t test is more powerful. If the distribution of differences is grossly skewed, the nominal t and signed-rank probabilities may be misleading. If the distribution is roughly symmetric but has heavy tails (as indicated by the presence of outliers), the signed-rank test may be more powerful. Often, as in Examples 10.14 and 10.15, the tests yield essentially the same conclusion.

Unless there are very obvious features (such as severe skewness or major outliers) in the data, these three methods will often give very similar conclusions. With a computer package, it's not difficult to obtain tests or confidence intervals using all three methods. If the results are similar, you can report them with comfort. If the results are clearly different, you should be able to find the "data gremlin" that is causing the difference; in such a case, use the analysis that is least sensitive to the particular problem you found.

SECTIONS 10.4 AND 10.5 EXERCISES

10.28 A manufacturer of an air compressor and tire pump wants to test two possible point-of-purchase displays. The product is sold through independent auto parts stores, which vary greatly in sales volume. A total of 30 stores agree to feature the display for one month. The stores are matched on the basis of annual sales volume. One of the two largest stores is randomly chosen to receive display A, while the other receives B. The same thing is done for the third and fourth largest stores, and so on down to the two smallest. Sales for the one-month period are recorded:

															Pairing
Display	1	2	3	4	5	6	7	8	9	10	11	12	13	14	15
A	46	39	40	37	32	26	21	23	20	17	13	15	11	8	9
B	37	42	37	38	27	19	20	17	20	12	12	9	7	2	6
Difference	+9	−3	+3	−1	+5	+7	+1	+6	0	+5	+1	+6	+4	+6	+3

The mean of the differences is 3.47 and the standard deviation is 3.31.
   a. Use a paired-sample t test to test the research hypothesis of unequal means. Use $\alpha = .10$.
   b. Calculate a 90% confidence interval for the true mean difference.

10.29 a. Carry out the signed-rank test for the data of Exercise 10.28. Use a two-tailed test with $\alpha = .10$.
   b. How does the conclusion of this test compare with that of the t test in Exercise 10.28?

10.30 Place bounds on the p-values for the tests in Exercises 10.28 and 10.29.

10.31 Consider the situation of Exercise 10.28. An alternative approach would be to assign display A to 15 randomly chosen stores and display B to the rest.
   a. Suppose that the data of Exercise 10.28 were obtained in this way. Carry out the appropriate t test.
   b. Does there seem to be any advantage to the pairing process actually used in Exercise 10.28?

10.32 Again refer to Exercise 10.28. Carry out a binomial (sign) test of the null hypothesis that the proportion of positive differences equals the proportion of negative differences. What should you do about a zero difference?

10.33 A simulation study compares the power of t and signed-rank tests. In the simulation, the population of differences is the symmetric, mildly outlier-prone Laplace population, with a population mean of 5 and a population standard deviation of

10. The (incorrect) null hypothesis is that the mean was 0. The sample size is 30. The null hypothesis is rejected (as it should be) 745 times at $\alpha = .05$ by the t test and 839 times by the signed-rank test. What do these results indicate about the relative desirability of the two tests for this mildly outlier-prone population?

10.34 A manufacturer can use either the postal service or a private shipper to deliver its small shipments. To help in making a choice, the manufacturer selects 10 destinations and ships parcels to each destination by each carrier. The delivery times (in days) are

	Destination									
	1	2	3	4	5	6	7	8	9	10
Postal	3	4	5	4	8	9	7	10	9	9
Private	2	2	3	5	4	6	9	6	7	6

Computer output (Statgraphics) for this study is shown below:

	Postal	Private	differences
Sample size	10	10	10
Mean	6.8	5	1.8
Variance	6.62222	5.11111	3.95556
Std. deviation	2.57337	2.26078	1.98886

Hypothesis Test - Mean

```
Null hypothesis: mean = 0
Alternative: not equal

Computed t statistic = 2.86199
            P value = 0.0187
```

Hypothesis Test - Median (Ranks Method)

```
Sample median = 0
Null hypothesis: median = 0
Alternative: not equal
Average rank of 8 values above 0 = 6.125
Average rank of 2 values below 0 = 3
0 values equal to 0 ignored.

Computed z statistic = 2.1574 (continuity correction applied)
            P value = 0.0310
```

a. Locate the value of the t statistic.

b. Locate the value of the signed-rank statistic.

c. Use each statistic separately to test the hypothesis of equal mean delivery times. Use a two-sided H_a and $\alpha = .05$.

10.35 Find p-values for both test statistics in Exercise 10.34. How conclusive would you say the apparent difference in means is?

10.36 Why is the experiment in Exercise 10.34 more effective than randomly assigning 10 packages to the postal service and another 10 to the private shipper? How would you select the 10 destinations?

10.37 A direct mail company tests two different versions of a special-offer catalog. A sample of ZIP codes is chosen. Each version of the catalog is sent to half the people on the firm's mailing list within each of the selected ZIP codes. The response per thousand catalogs is recorded for each ZIP code. The data are as follows:

ZIP code :	1	2	3	4	5	6	7	8	9	10	11	12
Version A:	10.8	13.4	8.9	10.6	17.0	14.1	11.2	13.4	9.9	10.7	11.3	14.2
Version B:	11.3	15.0	9.9	10.0	17.7	12.6	11.8	13.7	10.4	9.9	12.8	14.9

   a. Why should this experiment be regarded as a paired-sample study?
   b. Calculate the mean and standard deviation of the differences.
   c. Can the research hypothesis that version B yields a higher average response rate be supported using a t test at $\alpha = .05$?
   d. State bounds on the p-value for testing the research hypothesis in part (c).

10.38 a. Perform a signed-rank test for the data of Exercise 10.37. Use $\alpha = .05$ and a one-sided H_a.
   b. Put bounds on the p-value.
   c. Do the signed-rank and t tests come to the same conclusion?

10.39 An analyst of the data in Exercise 10.37 interprets the results as proving that version B is no better than version A. Do you agree?

10.40 An organization keeps an extensive file of volunteers coded according to skills and desired activities. Two data-base management programs are tested. A sample of 10 combinations of skills and activities is specified; then both programs are used to find all volunteers with the specified combination. The time required (seconds) is recorded for every search. The data are as follows:

Combination:	1	2	3	4	5	6	7	8	9	10	Mean	s
Program 1:	136	298	187	192	100	170	240	200	102	155	178.0	60.756
Program 2:	158	391	206	128	120	194	272	221	119	184	199.3	83.225

   a. Explain why this is a paired-sample experiment.
   b. Calculate a 95% confidence interval for the population mean of differences.
   c. According to this interval, can the null hypothesis that the means for programs 1 and 2 are equal be rejected in favor of a two-sided research hypothesis? What is the effective α?

10.41 Perform a signed-rank test, using the data of Exercise 10.40, of the null hypothesis that the differences are symmetric around zero. Can we reject the hypothesis at $\alpha = .05$ using a two-tailed test?

10.42 What plot(s) of the data should we draw to decide whether a t test or a signed-rank test will be more effective for the data of Exercise 10.40? Which test would you choose? Does the choice of test affect the conclusion?

10.43 a. Using the data of Exercise 10.40 and a pooled-variance t method, calculate a 95% confidence interval for the difference of population means.
   b. Compare the width of this interval to the width of the interval found in Exercise 10.40. What does the comparison indicate about the desirability of pairing in this study?

10.44 A maker of over-the-counter pain relief products feels ethically bound to put its products in child-resistant packages. However, many of its sales were to older people who might also have problems opening the packages. Two package designs were proposed. A sample of 40 older customers opened both packages; the time required (in seconds) was recorded. The data were input to the Systat computer package, as follows:

		PACKAGE1	PACKAGE2	DIFF21
CASE	1	100.000	138.000	38.000
CASE	2	52.000	56.000	4.000
CASE	3	72.000	55.000	-17.000
CASE	4	37.000	30.000	-7.000
CASE	5	21.000	38.000	17.000
CASE	6	31.000	37.000	6.000
CASE	7	46.000	49.000	3.000
CASE	8	18.000	21.000	3.000
CASE	9	127.000	75.000	-52.000
CASE	10	56.000	50.000	-6.000
CASE	11	14.000	17.000	3.000
CASE	12	34.000	37.000	3.000
CASE	13	28.000	53.000	25.000
CASE	14	11.000	20.000	9.000
CASE	15	58.000	53.000	-5.000
CASE	16	79.000	71.000	-8.000
CASE	17	23.000	33.000	10.000
CASE	18	14.000	21.000	7.000
CASE	19	16.000	18.000	2.000
CASE	20	19.000	28.000	9.000
CASE	21	13.000	19.000	6.000
CASE	22	29.000	35.000	6.000
CASE	23	43.000	44.000	1.000
CASE	24	28.000	44.000	16.000
CASE	25	25.000	39.000	14.000
CASE	26	59.000	62.000	3.000
CASE	27	31.000	51.000	20.000
CASE	28	19.000	23.000	4.000
CASE	29	42.000	46.000	4.000
CASE	30	19.000	26.000	7.000
CASE	31	31.000	44.000	13.000
CASE	32	34.000	36.000	2.000
CASE	33	11.000	18.000	7.000
CASE	34	32.000	28.000	-4.000
CASE	35	45.000	57.000	12.000
CASE	36	18.000	21.000	3.000
CASE	37	39.000	52.000	13.000
CASE	38	27.000	25.000	-2.000
CASE	39	30.000	28.000	-2.000
CASE	40	47.000	34.000	-13.000

Construct a stem-and-leaf display of the difference data. Do these scores seem to be roughly normally distributed?

10.45 A normal probability plot of the data from Exercise 10.44 was created using Systat. The actual data are plotted on the horizontal axis and the normal scores on the vertical axis as shown at the top of page 427. Does this plot show that the data aren't normally distributed?

10.46 Use the output summary information from Systat to calculate a t statistic for the null hypothesis that the mean difference is 0. Find bounds on the two-sided p-value.

10.47 Systat also performed sign and signed-rank tests of the null hypothesis that the median difference is 0, using the data of Exercise 10.44. The tests were based on the differences, although the output may be unclear on that point.

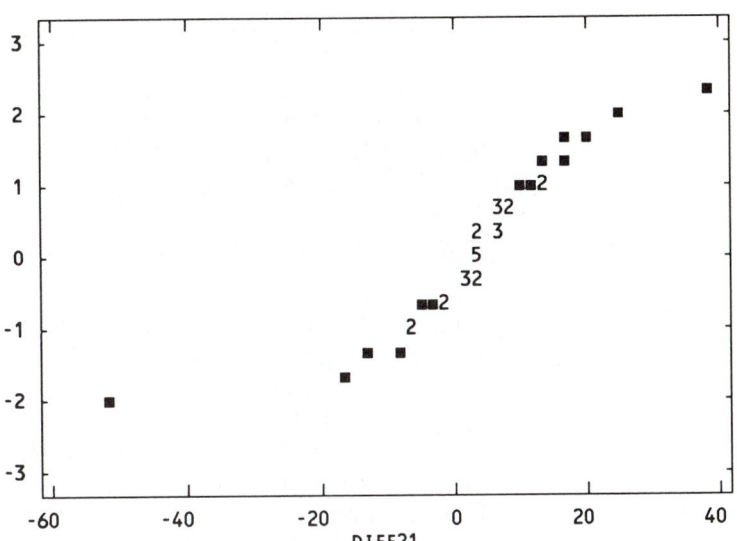

Figure for Exercise 10.45

	PACKAGE1	PACKAGE2	DIFF21
N OF CASES	40	40	40
MINIMUM	11.000	17.000	-52.000
MAXIMUM	127.000	138.000	38.000
MEAN	36.950	40.800	3.850
VARIANCE	592.869	479.446	181.721
STANDARD DEV	24.349	21.896	13.480

Output for Exercise 10.46

SIGN TEST RESULTS
  COUNTS OF DIFFERENCES (ROW VARIABLE GREATER THAN COLUMN)

	PACKAGE1	PACKAGE2
PACKAGE1	0	10
PACKAGE2	30	0

  TWO-SIDED PROBABILITIES FOR EACH PAIR OF VARIABLES

	PACKAGE1	PACKAGE2
PACKAGE1	1.000	
PACKAGE2	.003	1.000

WILCOXON SIGNED RANKS TEST RESULTS

  TWO-SIDED PROBABILITIES USING NORMAL APPROXIMATION

	PACKAGE1	PACKAGE2
PACKAGE1	1.000	
PACKAGE2	.007	1.000

Output for Exercise 10.47

a. Does the sign test indicate that the null hypothesis should be rejected at $\alpha = .01$?

b. Does the signed-rank test indicate that the null hypothesis should be rejected at $\alpha = .01$?

c. How do the results of these tests compare to the results of the t test in Exercise 10.46? If there is a difference in the conclusion of the tests, what accounts for it?

10.6   TWO-SAMPLE PROCEDURES FOR PROPORTIONS

So far in this chapter we have concentrated entirely on tests and confidence intervals for means. In this section we consider procedures for proportions. The methods are based on the normal approximation to the binomial distribution, so some consideration of required sample size is necessary.

We assume that two **independent** random samples of sizes n_1 and n_2 are taken. The respective sample proportions are denoted as $\hat{\pi}_1$ and $\hat{\pi}_2$, and the (unknown) population proportions are called π_1 and π_2. Our goal is to make inferences about the difference, if any, in the population proportions. The natural estimator is the difference in sample proportions $\hat{\pi}_1 - \hat{\pi}_2$. It is unbiased: $E(\hat{\pi}_1 - \hat{\pi}_2) = \pi_1 - \pi_2$. To calculate confidence intervals and perform hypothesis tests, we need a standard error formula. Recall from Chapter 6 that the variance of a sample proportion $\hat{\pi}$ is $\pi(1 - \pi)/n$. By the assumed independence of the two samples, we may add the variances of $\hat{\pi}_1$ and $\hat{\pi}_2$ to obtain

$$\text{Var}(\hat{\pi}_1 - \hat{\pi}_2) = \frac{\pi_1(1 - \pi_1)}{n_1} + \frac{\pi_2(1 - \pi_2)}{n_2}$$

$$\sigma_{\hat{\pi}_1 - \hat{\pi}_2} = \sqrt{\frac{\pi_1(1 - \pi_1)}{n_1} + \frac{\pi_2(1 - \pi_2)}{n_2}}$$

standard error of
$\hat{\pi}_1 - \hat{\pi}_2$

The confidence interval for $\hat{\pi}_1 - \hat{\pi}_2$ follows the familiar form $\hat{\theta} \pm z_{\alpha/2}\sigma_{\hat{\theta}}$, where $\hat{\theta}$ is now $\hat{\pi}_1 - \hat{\pi}_2$ and $\sigma_{\hat{\theta}}$ is $\sigma_{\hat{\pi}_1 - \hat{\pi}_2}$. Because the standard error $(\sigma_{\hat{\pi}_1 - \hat{\pi}_2})$ depends on the unknown population proportions π_1 and π_2, in practice we must substitute the sample proportions $\hat{\pi}_1$ and $\hat{\pi}_2$ into the standard-error formula. If both sample sizes are sufficiently large (say, at least 30), this substitution can be made without affecting the normal approximation.

$100(1 - \alpha)\%$ Confidence Interval for $\pi_1 - \pi_2$

$$(\hat{\pi}_1 - \hat{\pi}_2) - z_{\alpha/2}\sigma_{\hat{\pi}_1 - \hat{\pi}_2} \leq \pi_1 - \pi_2 \leq (\hat{\pi}_1 - \hat{\pi}_2) + z_{\alpha/2}\sigma_{\hat{\pi}_1 - \hat{\pi}_2}$$

where

$$\sigma_{\hat{\pi}_1 - \hat{\pi}_2} \approx \sqrt{\frac{\hat{\pi}_1(1 - \hat{\pi}_1)}{n_1} + \frac{\hat{\pi}_2(1 - \hat{\pi}_2)}{n_2}}$$

EXAMPLE 10.17   A new product is test-marketed in the Grand Rapids, Michigan, and Wichita, Kansas, metropolitan areas. Adertising in the Grand Rapids area is based almost entirely on television commercials. In Wichita, a roughly equal dollar amount is spent on a balanced mix of television, radio, newspaper, and magazine ads. Two months after the ad campaign begins, surveys are taken to determine consumer awareness of the product.

	Grand Rapids	Wichita
Number interviewed	608	527
Number aware	392	413

Calculate a 95% confidence interval for the regional difference in the proportion of all consumers who are aware of the product.

Solution   The sample awareness proportion is higher in Wichita, so let's make Wichita region 1.

$$\hat{\pi}_1 = 413/527 = .784; \qquad \hat{\pi}_2 = 392/608 = .645$$

The estimated standard error is

$$\sqrt{\frac{(.784)(.216)}{527} + \frac{(.645)(.355)}{608}} = .0264$$

Therefore the 95% confidence interval is

$$(.784 - .645) - 1.96(.0264) \le \pi_1 - \pi_2 \le (.784 - .645) + 1.96(.0264)$$

or

$$.087 \le \pi_1 - \pi_2 \le .191$$

which indicates that somewhere between 8.7% and 19.1% more Wichita consumers than Grand Rapids consumers are aware of the product.   ∎

rule for sample sizes   This confidence-interval method is based on the normal approximation to the binomial distribution. In Chapter 6 we indicated as a general rule that $n\hat{\pi}$ and $n(1 - \hat{\pi})$ should both be at least 5 to use this normal approximation. For this confidence interval to be used, the rule should hold for each sample. In practice, sample sizes that come even close to violating this rule aren't very useful, because they lead to excessively wide confidence intervals. For instance, even though $n\hat{\pi}$ and $n(1 - \hat{\pi})$ are greater than 5 for both samples when $n_1 = 30$, $\hat{\pi}_1 = .20$ and $n_2 = 60$, $\hat{\pi}_2 = .10$, the 95% confidence interval is $-.06 \le \pi_1 - \pi_2 < .26$; π_1 could be anything from 6 percentage points lower than π_2 to 26 percentage points higher.

Hypothesis testing about the difference between two population proportions is based on the z statistic from a normal approximation. The typical null hypothesis is that there is no difference between the population proportions, though any specified value for $\pi_1 - \pi_2$ may be hypothesized. The procedure is summarized at the top of page 430.

Hypothesis Test for $\pi_1 - \pi_2$

$H_0: \pi_1 - \pi_2 = D_0$ (D_0 is specified; often $D_0 = 0$)
$H_a:$ 1. $\pi_1 - \pi_2 > D_0$
    2. $\pi_1 - \pi_2 < D_0$
    3. $\pi_1 - \pi_2 \neq D_0$

$$\text{T.S.: } z = \frac{(\hat{\pi}_1 - \hat{\pi}_2) - D_0}{\sqrt{\dfrac{\hat{\pi}_1(1 - \hat{\pi}_1)}{n_1} + \dfrac{\hat{\pi}_2(1 - \hat{\pi}_2)}{n_2}}}$$

R.R.: 1. $z > z_\alpha$
    2. $z < -z_\alpha$
    3. $|z| > z_{\alpha/2}$

Note: This test should be used only if $n_1\hat{\pi}_1$, $n_1(1 - \hat{\pi}_1)$, $n_2\hat{\pi}_2$, and $n_2(1 - \hat{\pi}_2)$ are all at least 5.

EXAMPLE 10.18   Refer to Example 10.17. Test the hypothesis of equal population-awareness proportions against a two-sided alternative. State a p-value.

Solution $\hat{\pi}_1 = .784, n_1 = 527, \hat{\pi}_2 = .645,$ and $n_2 = 608$. The general rule for using a z test is amply met; the smallest of the four indicators is $n_1(1 - \hat{\pi}_1) = 114$.

$$z = \frac{(.784 - .645) - 0}{\sqrt{\dfrac{(.784)(.216)}{527} + \dfrac{(.645)(.355)}{608}}}$$

$$= \frac{.139}{.0264} = 5.26$$

A z value of 5.26 is far beyond the range of our z table. The p-value is some very small number.

There is a slight variation on this test. Under the null hypothesis $H_0: \pi_1 - \pi_2 = 0$, the two populations have an equal proportion, call it π, of successes. The natural estimator of this common proportion is $\bar{\pi}$, the total number of successes divided by the total sample size. This estimator is, by easy algebra, a weighted average of the two sample proportions $\hat{\pi}_1$ and $\hat{\pi}_2$:

$$\bar{\pi} = \frac{n_1\hat{\pi}_1 + n_2\hat{\pi}_2}{n_1 + n_2}$$

The modification to the z test uses a standard error:

$$\sqrt{\frac{\bar{\pi}(1 - \bar{\pi})}{n_1} + \frac{\bar{\pi}(1 - \bar{\pi})}{n_2}}$$

that is, the unknown population proportions π_1 and π_2 are replaced by $\bar{\pi}$, rather than by $\hat{\pi}_1$ and $\hat{\pi}_2$, in the standard-error formula. In practice, the numerical effect of this modification is usually negligible.

EXAMPLE 10.19   Perform the modified z test for Example 10.17. How does the modification affect your conclusion?

Solution   The total sample size is $608 + 527 = 1135$; the total number of successes is $392 + 413 = 805$. Note that $413 = n_1\hat{\pi}_1 = 527(.784)$ and $392 = n_2\hat{\pi}_2 = 608(.645)$. Therefore,

$$\bar{\pi} = \frac{805}{1135} = \frac{527(.784) + 608(.645)}{527 + 608}$$

$$= .709$$

The modified standard error is

$$\sqrt{\frac{\bar{\pi}(1-\bar{\pi})}{n_1} + \frac{\bar{\pi}(1-\bar{\pi})}{n_2}} = \sqrt{\frac{(.709)(.291)}{527} + \frac{(.709)(.291)}{608}}$$

$$= .0270$$

compared to the previous standard error of .0264. The modified z statistic is

$$z = \frac{(.784 - .645)}{.0270} = 5.15$$

compared to the previous z value of 5.26. The conclusion remains the same: The null hypothesis is emphatically rejected. The p-value is so small as to go beyond our normal table. ■

SECTION 10.6   EXERCISES

10.48 A consumer finance company considers its bad-debt experience for married and unmarried couples. A sample of 3200 loans yields the following data:

Status	Number of Loans	Bad Debts
Married	2128	102
Unmarried	1072	31

Calculate a 90% confidence interval for the true difference in proportions of bad debts.

10.49 Refer to Exercise 10.48.
   a. Test the null hypothesis of equal proportions. Let H_a be two-sided. Use $\alpha = .10$.
   b. In performing this test, how important is the modification of the standard error (using the pooled proportion $\bar{\pi}$)? Does this modification affect the conclusion?

10.50 Find p-values for the unmodified and modified z statistics in Exercise 10.49.

10.51 In a survey, it is found that 1697 of 2961 urban-area residents regularly watch a network television news program, whereas 674 of 983 rural or small-town residents are regular watchers.
   a. Calculate a 95% confidence interval for the difference in proportions.
   b. Test the research hypothesis that a higher percentage of rural (small-town) residents are regular watchers. Use $\alpha = .05$.

10.52 Find the *p*-value in Exercise 10.51. How conclusive is the evidence favoring the research hypothesis?

10.53 Recalculate the test statistic and *p*-value for the data of Exercise 10.51 using the modified ($\bar{\pi}$) standard error. How important is the modification?

10.54 A retail computer dealer is trying to decide between two methods for servicing customers' equipment. The first method emphasizes preventive maintenance; the second emphasizes quick response to problems. Samples of customers are each served by one of the two methods. After six months, it is found that 171 of 200 customers served by the first method are very satisfied with the service, as compared to 153 of 200 customers served by the second method.

   a. Test the research hypothesis that the population proportions are different. Use $\alpha = .10$. State your conclusion carefully.

   b. State a *p*-value for the test in part (a).

10.55 Redo Exercise 10.54 using $\bar{\pi}$, the pooled proportion, in the standard error. How much difference does it make which method is used?

10.56 The media-selection manager for an advertising agency inserts the same advertisement for a client bank in two magazines. The ads are similarly placed in each magazine. One month later, a market research study finds that 226 of 473 readers of the first magazine are aware of the banking services offered in the ad, as are 165 of 439 readers of the second magazine (readers of both magazines are excluded).

   a. Calculate a 95% confidence interval for the difference of proportions of readers who are aware of the advertised services.

   b. Are the sample sizes adequate to use the normal approximation?

   c. Does the confidence interval indicate that there is a statistically significant difference using $\alpha = .05$?

10.57 Using the data of Exercise 10.56, perform a formal test of the null hypothesis of equal populations. Use $\alpha = .05$. How important is it whether or not the pooled proportion is used in the standard error?

10.58 Samples of 30 electric motors for dot matrix printers are subjected to severe testing for reliability. Of the motors from supplier 1, 22 pass the test; of the motors from supplier 2, only 16 pass.

   a. Show that the difference is not statistically significant at $\alpha = .05$ (two-tailed).

   b. Can we claim to have shown that the two suppliers provide equally reliable motors?

10.59 Use the data of Exercise 10.58 to calculate a 95% confidence interval for the difference of proportions. Interpret the result carefully in terms of the relative reliability of the two suppliers.

10.7 TWO-SAMPLE PROCEDURES FOR STANDARD DEVIATIONS

Another important two-sample problem has to do with variability. In quality control and process improvement, one goal is to reduce variability. For example, if we test two dispatching methods for bulk-material trucks on different samples of days, which method yields lower variability in delivery times? Or, if we try two methods for mixing raisins into bran flakes for a breakfast cereal, which method yields lower variability of raisin weight per box?

In this section we describe comparisons of variances and standard deviations for data from two independent samples. These methods are based on

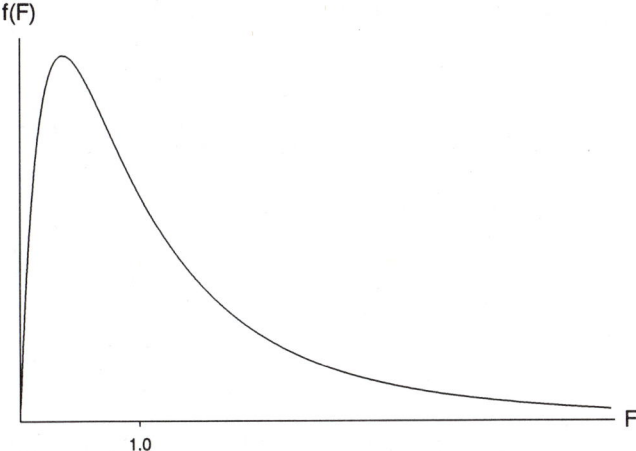

f(F)

1.0

F

FIGURE 10.1   Typical *F* Distribution

another theoretical probability distribution, the *F* distribution. Formally, an *F* statistic is defined as a ratio:

$$F = \frac{\chi_1^2/\text{d.f.}_1}{\chi_2^2/\text{d.f.}_2}$$

where χ_1^2 and χ_2^2 are independent statistics having χ^2 distributions with respective degrees of freedom d.f.$_1$ and d.f.$_2$. The *F* distribution has degrees of freedom for both numerator and denominator. An *F* statistic cannot take on negative values; the *F* distribution is typically skewed to the right, as in Figure 10.1. The mean of this distribution is close to 1; the mode and median are somewhat less.

F distribution   Because the **F distribution** depends on two d.f. numbers, tables are either bulky or sparse. Appendix Table 6 gives upper-tail areas. The numerator degrees of freedom (d.f.$_1$) indexes columns, and the denominator degrees of freedom (d.f.$_2$) indexes rows. For example, for d.f.$_1 = 3$ and d.f.$_2 = 9$, $P(F > 3.86) = .05$ and $P(F > 6.99) = .01$.

A test of the null hypothesis of equal variances for two populations follows from the definition of an *F* statistic and the fact that (under certain assumptions) the statistic $(n - 1)s^2/\sigma^2$ has a χ^2 distribution with $n - 1$ d.f. Suppose that we have two independent samples of respective sizes n_1 and n_2. The population variances are σ_1^2 and σ_2^2, and the sample variances are s_1^2 and s_2^2. Then

$$F = \frac{\chi_1^2/\text{d.f.}_1}{\chi_2^2/\text{d.f.}_2} = \frac{(n_1 - 1)\dfrac{s_1^2}{\sigma_1^2}\bigg/(n_1 - 1)}{(n_2 - 1)\dfrac{s_2^2}{\sigma_2^2}\bigg/(n_2 - 1)}$$

$$= \frac{s_1^2/\sigma_1^2}{s_2^2/\sigma_2^2}$$

Under the null hypothesis $H_0: \sigma_1^2 = \sigma_2^2$, the test statistic becomes $F = s_1^2 / s_2^2$. The test procedure is outlined next:

F Test for Equality of Variances

$H_0: \sigma_1^2 = \sigma_2^2$

$H_a:$ 1. $\sigma_1^2 > \sigma_2^2$
     2. $\sigma_1^2 < \sigma_2^2$
     3. $\sigma_1^2 \neq \sigma_2^2$

T.S.: $F = \dfrac{s_1^2}{s_2^2}$

R.R.: 1. Reject H_0 if $F > F_{\alpha, n_1 - 1, n_2 - 1}$, the tabled value cutting off a right-tail area of the F distribution with d.f.$_1 = n_1 - 1$ and d.f.$_2 = n_2 - 1$.
     2. Reject H_0 if $F < 1/F_{\alpha, n_2 - 1, n_1 - 1}$. Note that $F_{\alpha, n_2 - 1, n_1 - 1}$ is the tabled F value with **numerator** d.f. $= n_2 - 1$ and **denominator** d.f. $= n_1 - 1$.
     3. Reject H_0 if $F > F_{\alpha/2, n_1 - 1, n_2 - 1}$ or if $F < 1/F_{\alpha/2, n_2 - 1, n_1 - 1}$.

The reason for the transposition of degrees of freedom is that the choice of which sample variance to put in the numerator is arbitrary.

EXAMPLE 10.20 A study compares the variabilities in strengths of 1-inch-square sections of a synthetic fiber produced under two different procedures. Samples of 9 squares from each procedure are obtained, yielding the following strengths (in pounds per square inch):

Procedure 1: 74   90   103   86   75   102   97   85   69
Procedure 2: 59   66   73   68   70   71   82   69   74

Test the research hypothesis of unequal variability using $\alpha = .10$.

Solution Standard computations yield

	$\bar{y}$	s^2	n
Procedure 1	86.778	153.944	9
Procedure 2	70.222	38.944	9

The test can be summarized as follows:

$H_0: \sigma_1^2 = \sigma_2^2$
$H_a: \sigma_1^2 \neq \sigma_2^2$

$$\text{T.S.: } F = \frac{s_1^2}{s_2^2} = \frac{153.944}{38.944} = 3.95$$

R.R.: Because d.f.$_1$ = d.f.$_2$ = 8 and $F_{.05, 8, 8} = 3.44$, we reject H_0 if
$$s_1^2/s_2^2 > 3.44 \text{ or if } s_1^2/s_2^2 < 1/3.44 = .291$$

Conclusion: Because $F = 3.95 > 3.44$, we reject H_0 and conclude that the variability for procedure 1 is greater than that for procedure 2. ∎

It is convenient to use the ratio of two sample variances, rather than their difference, to construct a confidence interval for comparing two population variances.

$100(1 - \alpha)\%$ Confidence Interval for σ_1^2/σ_2^2 or σ_1/σ_2

$$\frac{s_1^2}{s_2^2} \frac{1}{F_{\alpha/2, n_1 - 1, n_2 - 1}} \leq \frac{\sigma_1^2}{\sigma_2^2} \leq \frac{s_1^2}{s_2^2} F_{\alpha/2, n_2 - 1, n_1 - 1}$$

For comparing standard deviations, take square roots throughout. ∎

EXAMPLE 10.21   Calculate a 90% confidence interval for the ratio of procedure standard deviations based on the data of Example 10.20.

Solution   In Example 10.20 we found that the ratio of sample variances was $s_1^2/s_2^2 = 3.95$ and $F_{.05, 8, 8} = 3.44$. The 90% confidence interval for the ratio of the population variances is

$$3.95\left(\frac{1}{3.44}\right) \leq \frac{\sigma_1^2}{\sigma_2^2} \leq 3.95(3.44)$$

or

$$1.148 \leq \frac{\sigma_1^2}{\sigma_2^2} \leq 13.588$$

Taking square roots,

$$1.072 \leq \frac{\sigma_1}{\sigma_2} \leq 3.686$$

Note that a ratio of 1.00 is not included in the 90% confidence interval. This corresponds to the rejection of $H_0: \sigma_1^2 = \sigma_2^2$ at $\alpha = .10$ in Example 10.20. ∎

One critical assumption for these procedures is the assumption of normal population or process distributions. If either or both of the underlying distri-
normality   butions is moderately skewed or heavy-tailed (outlier-prone), the claimed F prob-
assumption   abilities (alpha, confidence level, p-value) can be seriously wrong, regardless of sample sizes. The jackknife procedure we introduced in Section 8.8 can be

extended to two independent samples. Recall that the basic jackknife idea is to delete one observation at a time from the data and recompute the sample variance. If these leave-one-out variances vary greatly, the overall variance estimates are quite uncertain and a very wide confidence interval is called for. Obviously, a great deal of arithmetic is needed for jackknife methods; a computer program should be used for the heavy lifting. The technical details can be left to the program; you need only know that the final result is a two-sample t' test or confidence interval, usually in terms of the logarithms of the variances.

EXAMPLE 10.22   The data for Example 10.20 were put into a Minitab macro that performed a two-sample jackknife test of the null hypothesis of equal variances.

```
MTB > let k1=1
MTB > let k2=2
MTB > execute 'knife2'
MTB > let c49=ck1
MTB > let c50=ck2
MTB > let k3=sum(c49)
MTB > let k4=sum(c50)
MTB > let k5=ssq(c49)
MTB > let k6=ssq(c50)
MTB > let k7=count(c49)
MTB > let k8=count(c50)
MTB > let c47=((k5-c49**2)-((k3-c49)**2)/(k7-1))/(k7-2)
MTB > let c48=((k6-c50**2)-((k4-c50)**2)/(k8-1))/(k8-2)
MTB > let c45=2*k7*loge(stdev(c49))-(k7-1)*loge(c47)
MTB > let c46=2*k8*loge(stdev(c50))-(k8-1)*loge(c48)
MTB > twosample t for 90% confidence, c45 vs. c46

TWOSAMPLE T FOR C45 VS C46
         N      MEAN     STDEV    SE MEAN
C45  9         5.09      1.00       0.33
C46  9         3.90      2.22       0.74

90 PCT CI FOR MU C45 - MU C46: (-0.27, 2.65)

TTEST MU C45 = MU C46 (VS NE): T= 1.46  P=0.17  DF=  11
MTB > end
MTB > let k9=exponential(-0.27)
MTB > let k10=exponential(2.98)
MTB > note k9, k10 conf. lim. for jackknife interval (var.ratio)  MTB > print k9 k10
K9       0.763380
K10      19.6878
```

Does the jackknife procedure give the same result as the F procedure for testing the research hypothesis of unequal variability? Which method is preferable in this case?

Solution   The p-value in the output is shown as $P = 0.17$. Because this is larger than $\alpha = .10$, we can't support the research hypothesis as we could using the F test in Exercise 10.20. The 90% confidence interval in $K9$ and $K10$ is wider than the F interval of Example 10.21; because the jackknife interval includes a possible ratio of 1.00, we again can't support the research hypothesis.

If we could believe the claimed F probabilities, the F method would be more conclusive and therefore preferable. We would like to check the data for nonnormality; with samples of only 9 each, pictures aren't very helpful. We suspect that the underlying distribution of fiber strengths would be skewed to the left by a few very weak squares. Therefore, we would be skeptical of the claimed F probabilities and we would tend to believe the jackknife procedure.   ■

SECTION 10.7   EXERCISES

10.60 The total sales for antidepressants throughout the United States during a given year represents a sizable amount of money, and competition among drug companies is keen. Suppose that one company markets drug A and a second company markets drug B. Both of these prescription drugs are for the relief of depression. One factor in the treatment of depressed patients is the patient's perceived benefit from the therapy; the time to first perception of relief (onset of relief) can therefore be an important variable to examine. The table below summarizes the perceived time to onset of relief (in numbers of days) for a random sample of 20 patients treated with drug A, and for a second random sample of 20 patients treated with drug B.

	n	$\bar{y}$	s
Drug A	20	8.3	3.1
Drug B	20	10.2	2.5

  a. Would you expect the data to be normal?
  b. Assuming that the data are approximately normal, run a two-sided test of H_0: $\sigma_1^2 = \sigma_2^2$ using $\alpha = .05$.

10.61 Refer to the data of Exercise 10.60. Construct a 95% confidence interval for the ratio σ_1^2/σ_2^2.

10.62 A simulation study involves 1000 independent samples of size 20 from each of two populations. Both populations have the same variance. Both are moderately outlier-prone. The following results are obtained for the variance ratio (F) test.

```
one-tail:

        number of times H0:  "variances equal" is rejected in favor of
 alpha    "var1 > var2"    "var1 < var2"    total (alpha doubled)
 .100         194              196                 390
 .050         139              134                 273
 .025          97               93                 190
 .010          63               65                 128
 .005          41               43                  84
```

Does the presence of outliers have a serious effect on the accuracy of the claimed α for the variance ratio test?

10.63 Refer to suppliers A and B data from Exercises 8.39 and 8.42 (pages 317–319).
  a. Calculate a 95% confidence interval for the ratio of the two variances.
  b. Does this interval clearly indicate that one supplier has a lower standard deviation than the other?

10.64 A Minitab macro called 'knife2' calculates a jackknife confidence interval for the ratio of variances. Results of 'knife2' for the data of Exercises 8.39 and 8.42 are shown below.

a. Identify the confidence interval for the ratio of variances.
b. Does this interval indicate that one supplier's variation is clearly less than the other's?
c. Compare the confidence interval found in this exercise to the interval found in Exercise 10.63. Are they similar, or would you call them quite different?

```
MTB > twosample t for c45 vs. c46

TWOSAMPLE T FOR C45 VS C46
          N      MEAN     STDEV    SE MEAN
C45   121       8.12      1.54       0.14
C46   121      -7.27      1.54       0.14


95 PCT CI FOR MU C45 - MU C46: (-1.23, -0.45)

TTEST MU C45 = MU C46 (VS NE): T= -4.26  P=0.0000  DF=  239
MTB > end
MTB > let k9=expon(-1.23)
MTB > let k10=expon(-0.45)
MTB > note k9, k10 are jacknife conf. limits for ratio of variances
MTB > print k9 k10
K9        0.292293
K10       0.637628
MTB > note ratio is 'SupplA' divided by 'SupplB'
```

Summary

∎

Methods for comparing samples are extensions of the basic inference procedures we developed in Chapters 7–9. These methods are widely used in their own right and they can also be extended to the methods in the next two chapters.

There are three methods for comparing means in independent (nonpaired) samples. The pooled-variance t method is most effective when both samples appear nearly normal and when we can assume the underlying population (process) standard deviations are equal. The pooled-variance t method is most safely used in the case of balanced design (equal sample sizes). The separate variance t' method assumes normality but not equal variability; it is safer than the pooled-variance t for unbalanced data. (The t' method becomes a large-sample z method for very large n's.) The rank sum method uses rankings rather than actual values and it is therefore more effective in the case of skewed or outlier-prone data.

For inferences about averages in paired samples, a t analysis based on differences works best if the difference data appears nearly normal. A median approach works best if the differences appear skewed; a signed-rank approach is defined for symmetric but nonnormal cases.

Not all comparisons involve means. A large-sample method for comparing proportions, and an F method for comparing standard deviations were also presented. The F method is sensitive to nonnormality for any sample size; a jackknife approach is safer if the data appear nonnormal.

KEY FORMULAS: Comparing Two Samples

1. Confidence interval for $\mu_1 - \mu_2$ (large, independent samples)

$$(\bar{y}_1 - \bar{y}_2) \pm z_{\alpha/2}\sqrt{\frac{\sigma_1^2}{n_1} + \frac{\sigma_2^2}{b_2}}$$

If $n_1 \geq 30$ and $n_2 \geq 30$, s_1^2 and s_2^2 can replace σ_1^2 and σ_2^2, respectively.

2. Statistical test for $\mu_1 - \mu_2$ (large, independent samples)

Null hypothesis: $\mu_1 - \mu_2 = D_0$ (D_0 is specified)

Test statistic: $z = \dfrac{(\bar{y}_1 - \bar{y}_2) - D_0}{\sqrt{\dfrac{\sigma_1^2}{n_1} + \dfrac{\sigma_2^2}{n_2}}}$

3. Confidence interval for $\mu_1 - \mu_2$ (independent samples, standard deviations unknown)

$$(\bar{y}_1 - \bar{y}_2) \pm t_{\alpha,2} s_p \sqrt{\frac{1}{n_n} + \frac{1}{n_2}}$$

where

$$s_p = \sqrt{\frac{(n_1 - 1)s_1^2 + (n_2 - 1)s_2^2}{n_1 + n_2 - 2}}$$

and

$$\text{d.f.} = n_1 + n_2 - 2$$

4. Statistical test for $\mu_1 - \mu_2$ (independent samples, standard deviations unknown)

Null hypothesis: $\mu_1 - \mu_2 = D_0$

Test statistic: $t = \dfrac{(\bar{y}_1 - \bar{y}_2) - D_0}{s_p\sqrt{\dfrac{1}{n_1} + \dfrac{1}{n_2}}}$

5. Wilcoxon rank sum test (independent samples, $n_1, n_2 \geq 10$)

Null hypothesis: The two populations are identical

Test statistic: $z = \dfrac{T - \mu_T}{\sigma_T}$

where T = rank sum for sample 1

$$\mu_T = \frac{n_1(n_1 + n_2 + 1)}{2}$$

$$\sigma_T = \sqrt{\frac{n_1 n_2}{12}(n_1 + n_2 + 1)}$$

6. Confidence interval for μ_d (paired samples)

$$\bar{d} \pm t_{\alpha/2} \frac{S_d}{\sqrt{n}}$$

7. Statistical test for μ_d (paired data)

Null hypothesis: $\mu_d = D_0$

Test statistic: $t = \dfrac{\bar{d} - D_0}{s_d/\sqrt{n}}$

8. Wilcoxon signed-rank test (paired data)

Null hypothesis: The distribution of d values is symmetric about D_0

Test statistic: a. For $n \leq 50$, T (see Appendix Table 7 for critical values)

b. For $n > 50$, $z = \dfrac{T - \mu_T}{\sigma_T}$

where

$$\mu_T = \frac{n(n + 1)}{4}$$

$$\sigma_T = \sqrt{\frac{n(n + 1)(2n + 1)}{24}}$$

9. Confidence interval for $\pi_1 - \pi_2$

$$(\hat{\pi}_1 - \hat{\pi}_2) \pm z_{\alpha/2}\sigma_{\hat{\pi}_1 - \hat{\pi}_2}$$

where

$$\sigma_{\hat{\pi}_1 - \hat{\pi}_2} \approx \sqrt{\frac{\hat{\pi}_1(1 - \hat{\pi}_1)}{n_1} + \frac{\hat{\pi}_2(1 - \hat{\pi}_2)}{n_2}}$$

10. Statistical test for $\pi_1 - \pi_2$

Null hypothesis: $\pi_1 - \pi_2 = D_0$

Test statistic: $z = \dfrac{(\hat{\pi}_1 - \hat{\pi}_2) - D_0}{\sigma_{\hat{\pi}_1 - \hat{\pi}_2}}$

11. Confidence interval for $\dfrac{\sigma_1^2}{\sigma_2^2}$

$$\frac{s_1^2}{s_2^2} \frac{1}{F_{\alpha/2, n_1 - 1, n_2 - 1}} \leq \frac{\sigma_1^2}{\sigma_2^2} \leq \frac{s_1^2}{s_2^2} F_{\alpha/2, n_2 - 1, n_1 - 1}$$

> 12. Statistical test for $\sigma_1^2 = \sigma_2^2$
>
> $$\text{T.S.: } F = \frac{s_1^2}{s_2^2}$$
>
> $$\text{R.R} > \text{(two-tailed test): } F > F_{\alpha/2,\, n_1 - 1,\, n_2 - 1} \text{ or } F < \frac{1}{F_{\alpha/2,\, n_2 - 1,\, n_1 - 1}}$$

CHAPTER 10 EXERCISES

10.65 An auditor for a national bank credit card samples the accounts of two local banks that process cardholders' accounts. The results are

Bank	Accounts Audited	Accounts in Error	Mean Error	Standard Deviation
A	475	41	$41.27	$19.42
B	384	39	$60.38	$31.68

The mean and standard deviations are based on only those accounts that are in error.
a. Calculate a 95% confidence interval for the difference in true error proportions.
b. Can the research hypothesis of unequal proportions be supported using $\alpha = .05$?

10.66 Find the p-value for the test in Exercise 10.65.

10.67 Refer to the data of Exercise 10.65.
a. Calculate a 90% confidence interval for the difference in means.
b. Give a careful interpretation of this confidence interval. To what population(s) does it apply?
c. Test the research hypothesis of unequal means, using the large-sample test of Section 10.1. Use $\alpha = .05$.

10.68 Find the p-value for the test of Exercise 10.67.

10.69 a. Use the pooled-variance t test of the hypothesis of Exercise 10.67.
b. Use the t' statistic for this hypothesis. How does t' relate to the large-sample z test of Section 10.1?

10.70 A fruit grower plants 12 stands of each of two varieties of apple tree. At maturity, the following yields are observed (in bushels per 100 trees):

Variety R: 64.2 71.1 59.8 74.6 37.1 58.7 61.6 54.0 47.3 53.2 68.0 61.1
Variety K: 59.9 72.0 62.1 66.7 32.4 49.0 57.4 50.8 49.0 48.6 61.9 60.0

Assume that the 24 stands are randomly selected from the grower's available acreage and that the yields are listed in an arbitrary order.
a. Use the t test to test the research hypothesis that the mean yield of variety R exceeds that of variety K. Use $\alpha = .10$.
b. Use an appropriate rank test for the same hypothesis. Again use $\alpha = .10$.

10.71 Plot the data of Exercise 10.70. Which of the tests in that exercise seems more appropriate? Does it matter (to the conclusion) which test is used?

10.72   Find p-values for the tests of Exercise 10.70.

10.73   Refer to the data of Exercise 10.70. Now assume that the grower plants the two varieties side by side on 12 plots, and that the data are presented by plot number.

   a. Use a t test for the research hypothesis that the mean yield of variety R exceeds that of variety K. Use $\alpha = .10$.

   b. Use a rank test for this hypothesis, again using $\alpha = .10$.

10.74   Plot the relevant data for Exercise 10.73. Which of the tests in that exercise seems more appropriate? Does it matter (to the conclusion) which test is used?

10.75   Find p-values for the tests of Exercise 10.73.

10.76   Exercises 10.70 and 10.73 indicate two alternative experimental designs. What is the advantage of the design in Exercise 10.73? If this design is adopted, how would you select the plots to ensure that the yield ratings were reasonably valid for the grower's entire farm?

10.77   Two possible methods for retrofitting jet engines to reduce noise are being considered. Identical planes are fitted with two systems. Noise recording devices are installed directly under the flight path of a major airport. Each time one of the planes lands at the airport, a noise level is recorded. The data are analyzed by a computer package (SAS). The relevant output is:

VARIABLE: DBREAD

SYSTEM	N	MEAN	STD DEV	STD ERROR	MINIMUM	MAXIMUM	VARIANCES	T	DF	PROB > |T|
H	42	100.90476190	2.99438111	0.46204304	95.00000000	110.00000000	UNEQUAL	4.4491	21.5	0.0002
R	20	92.50000000	8.19178022	1.83173774	79.00000000	111.00000000	EQUAL	5.9126	60.0	0.0001

   a. Locate the t statistic.

   b. Locate the t' statistic.

   c. Can the research hypothesis of unequal means be supported using $\alpha = .01$? Does it matter which statistic is used?

10.78   Based on the output of Exercise 10.77, which of the test statistics in that exercise seems more reliable? How crucial is the choice?

10.79   The data of Exercise 10.77 are also used in a rank sum test. The relevant output is shown below:

WILCOXON SCORES (RANK SUMS)

LEVEL	N	SUM OF SCORES	EXPECTED UNDER HO	STD DEV UNDER HO	MEAN SCORE
H	42	1608.00	1323.00	66.22	38.29
R	20	345.00	630.00	66.22	17.25

WILCOXON 2-SAMPLE TEST (NORMAL APPROXIMATION)
(WITH CONTINUITY CORRECTION OF .5)
S= 345.00   Z=-4.2963   PROB > |Z|=0.0000

T-TEST APPROX. SIGNIFICANCE=0.0001

   a. Locate the rank sum statistic.

   b. Locate the z statistic and p-value.

   c. How does the conclusion of the rank sum test compare to the conclusion reached in Exercise 10.77?

10.80 A coffee company wished to test its current method for grinding premium coffee against an experimental "coarse grind." The market research staff assembled 80 coffee drinkers as a test panel. Each panelist was present when pots of both grinds were brewed (because aroma during brewing was thought to be a cause of customer preference) and each tasted cups of coffee made from both grinds. The panelists evaluated taste and aroma on a 10-point scale where 1 was worst, 10 best.

    a. Why might the research staff want to make the study "blind," so that the panelists didn't know which coffee was which? How could blinding be arranged?

    b. Why might the staff want to present the coffees in random order? How could that be done?

10.81 The panelists' ratings in Exercise 10.80 were entered into Minitab and analyzed.

    a. Why should we regard the study as a paired-sample experiment?

    b. One part of the Minitab output is the following:

```
MTB > tinterval 95% confidence for differences in c3
```

	N	MEAN	STDEV	SE MEAN	95.0 PERCENT C.I.
diff	80	0.350	1.476	0.165	(0.021, 0.679)

    The differences were taken as "coarse"—"original". What does the interval indicate about the null hypothesis that $\mu_d = 0.00$?

    c. Calculate a 99% confidence interval for the mean difference. What does this interval indicate about the null hypothesis that $\mu_d = 0.00$?

10.82 Further Minitab output for Exercise 10.81 is the following:

```
MTB > ttest of mu = 0 for data in c3

TEST OF MU = 0.000 VS MU N.E. 0.000
```

	N	MEAN	STDEV	SE MEAN	T	P VALUE
diff	80	0.350	1.476	0.165	2.12	0.037

    Explain why the p-value shown in the output is compatible with your answers in parts (b) and (c) of Exercise 10.81.

10.83 The data from Exercise 10.81 are also analyzed using a pooled-variance t method.

    a. Explain why this method should *not* be used in this situation.

    b. The Minitab results are as follows:

```
MTB > twosample t for c2 vs c1;
SUBC> pooled.

TWOSAMPLE T FOR coarse VS original
```

	N	MEAN	STDEV	SE MEAN
coarse	80	6.18	1.97	0.22
original	80	5.82	1.88	0.21

```
95 PCT CI FOR MU coarse - MU original: (-0.25, 0.95)

TTEST MU coarse = MU original (VS NE): T= 1.15  P=0.25  DF= 158

POOLED STDEV =     1.93
```

    What do the confidence interval and p-value in the output indicate about the null hypothesis of equal means?

c. How does the width of this confidence interval compare to the width of the interval based on differences? What does the comparison indicate about the effectiveness of the pairing of observations?

10.84   A confidence interval and test based on the signed rank method was also obtained for the data of Exercise 10.81.

```
MTB > winterval for data in c3

                    ESTIMATED   ACHIEVED
                N     MEDIAN   CONFIDENCE  CONFIDENCE INTERVAL
    diff       80     0.5000        95.0  (0.000,     0.500)

MTB > wtest of center = 0 data in c3

TEST OF MEDIAN = 0.000000000 VERSUS MEDIAN N.E. 0.000000000

                N FOR    WILCOXON               ESTIMATED
                N   TEST  STATISTIC  P-VALUE     MEDIAN
    diff       80    58    1107.5     0.052      0.5000
```

Would you call these results substantially different from those we obtained in Exercises 10.81 and 10.82?

10.85   A stem-and-leaf display of the differences in Example 10.81 was obtained from Minitab.

```
MTB > stem and leaf of 'diff' data

Stem-and-leaf of diff        N  = 80
Leaf Unit = 0.10
    2    -3 00
   10    -2 00000000
   21    -1 00000000000
   32    -0 00000000000
  (11)    0 00000000000
   37     1 0000000000000000000
   18     2 000000000000
    6     3 000000
```

Are the data so nonnormal that a t method should not be used?

10.86   A large corporation is considering using its computer network for electronic mail to cut down the flow of paper. The MIS department has a choice of two access methods, and it decides to run a small experiment to see which is preferable. The department has a list of all current managers who could use the network. Two random samples of 32 managers each (out of several hundred total) were chosen. Access method A was given to the first sample, B to the second. The first week was used for training and learning; the department counted the number of network communications by each manager in the second week.

The data were analyzed by Systat, and a two-sample t test was performed.

```
INDEPENDENT SAMPLES T-TEST ON   NUMCOMM     GROUPED BY    METHOD
    GROUP         N     MEAN          SD
    1.000        32    27.594        27.793
    2.000        32    43.625        38.333
  POOLED VARIANCES T =     1.915 DF =     62 PROB = .060
```

a. Is there a statistically detectable (significant) difference in means at $\alpha = .05$?
b. Is it fair to say that the result shows that there is no difference in mean number of communications for the two access methods?

10.87 In Exercise 10.86, note that the standard deviations are about as large as the means. Of course, number of communications can't be negative. What do these facts suggest about the normality of the data?

10.88 Systat gives stem-and-leaf displays of the data for Exercise 10.86.

```
THE FOLLOWING RESULTS ARE FOR:
      METHOD      =        1.000

      STEM AND LEAF PLOT OF VARIABLE:  NUMCOMM   , N =   32
         0    0113
         0    579
         1 H  2344
         1    577
         2 M  0000123
         2    99
         3 H  01
         3    7
         4
         4    9
         5    3
      ***OUTSIDE VALUES***
         6    48
         9    0
        12    9


THE FOLLOWING RESULTS ARE FOR:
      METHOD      =        2.000

      STEM AND LEAF PLOT OF VARIABLE:  NUMCOMM   , N =   32
         0    067
         1 H  1255679
         2    069
         3 M  1668
         4    0135
         5 H  13359
         6    5
         7    77
         8    2
      ***OUTSIDE VALUES***
        13    2
        18    9
```

a. Do these plots indicate that the underlying populations are normal?

b. What does the "OUTSIDE VALUES" warning indicate about the data?

10.89 Systat also performed a rank sum test on the data for Exercise 10.86.

a. Would you expect a rank sum method to be more effective than a t test? Why?

b. The results are as follows.

```
DEPENDENT VARIABLE IS  NUMCOMM
GROUPING VARIABLE IS   METHOD

   GROUP      COUNT    RANK SUM

   1.000      32        880.0
   2.000      32       1200.0


MANN-WHITNEY U TEST STATISTIC =     352.
PROBABILITY IS  .032 ASSUMING CHI-SQUARE DISTRIBUTION WITH  1 DF
```

In fact, is the rank sum test more conclusive than the t test of Exercise 10.86?

10.90   Recently a number of opticians established on-site laboratories for preparing prescription eyeglasses. These labs provide much more rapid service than conventional off-premises labs. Conventional opticians have questioned the accuracy of on-site labs. As a test, eyeglasses prescribed for nearsightedness were prepared by both types of labs. The glasses were evaluated by very accurate devices that determine the percentage deviation from the prescribed correction. A minus sign indicates that the actual correction was less than prescribed; a plus sign, more than prescribed. The data were analyzed by Systat; source 1 is conventional labs, source 2 is on-site labs.

```
THE FOLLOWING RESULTS ARE FOR:
          SOURCE      =       1.000

             DISCREP
  N OF CASES              43
  MEAN                 -0.245
  VARIANCE             12.757
  STANDARD DEV          3.572

THE FOLLOWING RESULTS ARE FOR:
          SOURCE      =       2.000

             DISCREP
  N OF CASES              26
  MEAN                 -0.365
  VARIANCE             50.218
  STANDARD DEV          7.086

OVERALL MEAN =       -0.290 STANDARD DEVIATION =       5.133
POOLED WITHIN GROUPS STANDARD DEVIATION =       5.171
T STATISTIC =         .094 PROBABILITY =  .926
```

a. Is there a statistically detectable (significant) difference of means, according to the output?

b. Can the result be interpreted that there is no evidence of a difference between conventional and on-site labs?

10.91   a. Use the computer output of Exercise 10.90 to test the null hypothesis of equal standard deviations, using a two-sided research hypothesis. Find bounds on the p-value.

b. What does the result of this test indicate about the relative quality of the two sources?

10.92   Boxplots of the data for Exercise 10.90 were obtained using Systat and are shown in Figure 10.2.

a. What do the plots indicate about the relative values of the medians for the two sources?

b. What do the plots indicate about relative amounts of variability?

c. Is there evidence of major deviations from normal distributions (as far as can be detected by box plots)? If so, are the deviations so serious that they invalidate your conclusions from Exercises 10.90 and 10.91?

10.93   One component of housing expenses for a family is heating. Heating costs will vary, not only because of differences in the basic cost of fuel (gas, oil, electricity) but also because of differences in climate, age of housing, and construction. A survey of heating costs compared samples of single-family homes in two northern

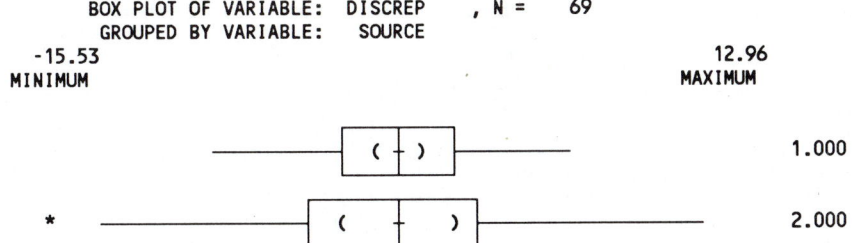

```
          BOX PLOT OF VARIABLE:  DISCREP    , N =    69
             GROUPED BY VARIABLE:   SOURCE
          -15.53                                                        12.96
          MINIMUM                                                       MAXIMUM
```

FIGURE 10.2   Box Plots for Exercise 10.92

cities and recorded the yearly heating cost (in hundreds of dollars). The following Statgraphics output was obtained:

```
                        Two-Sample Analysis Results
------------------------------------------------------------------------------
                                     city1exp    city2exp    Pooled
Sample Statistics: Number of Obs.    37          53          90
                   Average           20.9135     30.5811     26.6067
                   Variance          77.0729     234.883     170.324
                   Std. Deviation    8.77912     15.3259     13.0508
                   Median            21.4        28          23.65

Difference between Means = -9.66762
Conf. Interval For Diff. in Means:      99    Percent
 (Equal Vars.)    Sample 1 - Sample 2   -17.03 -2.30522     88 D.F.
 (Unequal Vars.)  Sample 1 - Sample 2   -16.3938 -2.94147   85.2 D.F.

Ratio of Variances = 0.328133
Conf. Interval for Ratio of Variances:  95    Percent
                Sample 1 ÷ Sample 2   0.181479 0.613857    36   52 D.F.

Hypothesis Test for H0: Diff = 0      Computed t statistic = -3.45779
                vs Alt: NE            Sig. Level = 8.41203E-4
              at Alpha = 0.05         so reject H0.
```

a. Which confidence interval shown in the output used the pooled-variance method?

b. According to this interval, is there conclusive evidence that the mean heating costs for all single-family homes are unequal in the two cities?

c. Is your answer to part (b) confirmed by the formal hypothesis test shown in the output?

d. Does your answer to part (b) change if the t' method is used instead of the pooled-variance method?

10.94 According to the output of Exercise 10.93, is there a statistically detectable (significant) difference in variability between the two cities? What value of alpha is being used?

10.95 Statgraphics boxplots of the heating cost data of Exercise 10.93 are shown in Figure 10.3 (page 448).

a. Is there evidence that the underlying population distributions are nonnormal? If so, what seems to be the type of nonnormality?

b. Is there reason to think that nonnormality will affect your conclusions of Exercises 10.93 and 10.94? If so, which conclusion will be most seriously affected?

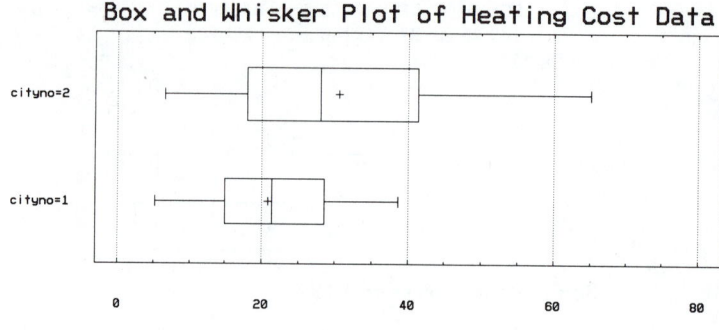

FIGURE 10.3   Box Plots of Heating Cost Data

10.96   Statgraphics also carried out a rank sum test for the data of Exercise 10.93, yielding the following output:

```
                              Comparison of Two Samples
- - - - - - - - - - - - - - - - - - - - - - - - - - - - - - - - - - - - - - - - - - -
Sample 1: city1exp

Sample 2: city2exp

Test based on: Ranks

Average rank of first group = 36.2297 based on 37 values.
Average rank of second group = 51.9717 based on 53 values.
Large sample test statistic Z = 2.80866
Two-tailed probability of equaling or exceeding Z = 4.97496E-3

NOTE:  90 total observations.
```

a. Does this test indicate conclusively that there is a difference in typical heating costs between the two cities?

b. Does this test yield a substantially different conclusion than the test of Exercise 10.93?

10.97   An accountant decided to test whether submitting federal income tax forms electronically would speed the delivery of refunds. The accountant submitted one sample of forms electronically, and sent another sample by mail. The number of business days until a refund was received was recorded in column 1 of the 'CH10C1.DAT' file on the data disk. Column 2 contains a code for the type of submission; a 1 indicates electronic submission, a 2 indicates mail submission. Load the data into the statistical computer package you use.

a. Obtain means, standard deviations, and sample sizes for the two samples.

b. Obtain separate plots of the two samples (histograms, stem-and-leaf displays, or normal plots, as you prefer).

c. Based on this information, which of the several possible methods for comparing the average values in the samples seems most appropriate to you? Why?

d. Carry out a formal test of the null hypothesis of equal means, using the method you selected in part (c). Locate the p-value.

10.98 a. Obtain a 99% confidence interval for the difference of means in Exercise 10.97. Use the method you selected in that exercise.

b. How does the interval confirm the result of the test in part (d) of Exercise 10.97?

10.99 Test the null hypothesis of equal standard deviations, using the data of Exercise 10.97. You should be able to use a computer package to get the sample standard deviations (depending on the package you have, you may need to do some computations by hand). Is there conclusive evidence that the long-term, population standard deviations will differ?

10.100 A magazine conducted an experiment concerning investment advisers. The editors prepared 50 descriptions of the financial positions of hypothetical families with the husband earning a larger share of the income; they prepared an additional 50 descriptions that were identical, except that the wife earned the larger share of the income. Each description was sent to one of 100 advisers, who recommended a portfolio of investments. The editors calculated the previous year's yield on each investment. The yields are stored in the 'CH10C2.DAT' file on the data disk, with the husband-larger-income descriptions in column 1 and the matching wife-larger-income descriptions in column 2. Load the data into a statistical computer package that you can use.

a. Explain why the data should *not* be analyzed using pooled-variance t methods.

b. Have the package compute differences. Obtain a normal plot of the differences. Is there a clear indication of nonnormality?

c. Obtain a t statistic for the null hypothesis that the mean of the differences is 0. Obtain a p-value.

d. Should a one-sided or two-sided test be used here? (This question might just possibly provoke some gender-based disagreement.)

10.101 a. Have the computer package perform a signed-rank test of the null hypothesis that the differences are symmetric around 0, using the difference data from Exercise 10.100. Which result is more conclusive, the signed-rank or the t test of Exercise 10.100?

b. Test the null hypothesis that the *median* difference is 0 using the same data. Is this test more or less conclusive than the other two, or do they all give about the same conclusion?

10.102 a. Ignore the fact that the pooled-variance t test isn't appropriate for the data of Exercise 10.100 and have the computer package use that method to test the null hypothesis of equal means. Locate the p-value.

b. Is the pooled-variance t result more conclusive (that there is a detectable difference) than the t test on differences, or less so? What does the comparison of results indicate about the usefulness of matching descriptions.

10.103 A supermarket mailed coupons good for 25 cents off the price of cleaning products. At random, either product 1 or product 2 received the cents-off promotion. The supermarket wanted to find out which product would attract better-spending shoppers. The amount spent by each shopper who redeemed a coupon is recorded in column 1 of the 'CH10C3.DAT' file on the data disk; the product receiving the cents off for that coupon is shown in column 2. Load the data into your computer package.

a. Obtain histograms or stem-and-leaf displays of the purchase amounts separately for the two products. Do the plots appear roughly normal?

b. Obtain a 95% confidence interval for the difference of means, using the pooled-variance t method. Also, obtain a similar interval using the separate variance

(t') method. For each interval, can we reject the null hypothesis of equal means using $\alpha = .05$?

c. Are the two intervals we obtain in part (b) essentially identical? If not, which one should be believed?

10.104 a. Carry out formal t tests (both pooled variance and t') of the null hypothesis of equal means for the spending data of Exercise 10.103. Obtain two-tailed p-values for both tests.

b. Carry out a test of the null hypothesis of equal distributions, using a rank sum test. Again, obtain a two-tailed p-value.

c. Which of the three test results appears to be most conclusive? Can the p-value for this test be believed?

CASE   Comparing Two Samples

A maker of crackers and other snack food was market-testing two versions of a microwaved snack. A total of 200 adult volunteers was recruited to appear at a suburban shopping mall one evening. Each person filled out a brief questionnaire concerning age, education, income, and similar facts. From these facts, each person received a Target Customer Score (TCS) based on how desirable the person would be as a customer. Then the questionnaires were sorted from lowest to highest TCS score. Customers with TCS scores 1, 4, 5, 8, 9, 12, and so on were assigned to Group K; TCS scores 2, 3, 6, 7, 10, 11, and so on went to Group S. (The letters meant nothing, deliberately.) Customers in both groups evaluated several other products and a number of possible television commercials. The important

```
Group K
 33   67   39   48   69   55   66   52   58   43   57   77   58
 58   71   40   54   52   60   69   70   76   62   73   69   72
 56   54   68   55   45   82   82   66   63   67   59   69   65
 73   65   66   62   83   59   77   62   68   67   71   75   74
 59   65   59   73   71   75   59   76   72   61   79   63   58
 64   68   77   85   68   58   88   65   74   60   62   59   58
 66   77   65   60   68   73   74   78   68   60   71   67   75
 71   84   65   63   57   83   75   72   67

Group S
 27   64   48   43   66   45   64   52   45   35   62   69   70
 55   66   52   48   45   61   72   64   57   61   60   63   85
 55   51   76   68   48   81   80   67   70   68   68   63   63
 76   67   66   62   76   67   73   59   66   61   66   85   65
 60   78   56   78   74   76   72   78   62   72   76   64   66
 70   72   73   86   84   60   87   78   82   73   61   59   68
 73   81   69   66   84   82   75   78   69   67   80   72   86
 74   78   67   62   71   86   79   82   70
MTB > describe 'Group K', 'Group S'
```

	N	MEAN	MEDIAN	TRMEAN	STDEV	SEMEAN
Group K	100	65.76	66.50	66.14	10.15	1.01
Group S	100	67.42	68.00	67.97	11.65	1.16

	MIN	MAX	Q1	Q3
Group K	33.00	88.00	59.00	73.00
Group S	27.00	87.00	61.25	76.00

data were approval ratings of two versions (also labeled K and S) of the microwaved snack product. The ratings were based on a bidding system that the company believed gave accurate readings of actual preferences. The company thought that each additional bidding point, on average, would result in about three-tenths of a point of additional market share for the selected version of the product.

The data, in order from lowest to highest TCS score, and some very preliminary analyses have been supplied to you. You have been selected as a consultant to decide whether the study has provided adequate information to decide which microwaved snack is better, and by how much. Perform whatever additional analyses you feel are necessary and prepare a consultant's report to the company. In your report, try to minimize the use of technical jargon. ∎

Appendix: The Mathematics of Pooled-Variance t Methods ∎

In developing the pooled-variance t statistic, we made the seemingly arbitrary assumption that the population variances were equal. The χ^2 and t distribution results of the appendix to Chapter 8 can be used to indicate why this assumption was made.

The definition of a t statistic is

$$t = \frac{z}{\sqrt{W/v}}$$

where W has a χ^2 distribution with v d.f. As the true standard error of $\bar{Y}_1 - \bar{Y}_2$ is $\sqrt{\sigma_1^2/n_1 + \sigma_2^2/n_2}$, the desired Z statistic is

$$Z = \frac{(\bar{Y}_1 - \bar{Y}_2) - (\mu_1 - \mu_2)}{\sqrt{\dfrac{\sigma_1^2}{n_1} + \dfrac{\sigma_2^2}{n_2}}}$$

Because $(n_1 - 1)s_1^2/\sigma_1^2$ and $(n_2 - 1)s_2^2/\sigma_2^2$ are (independently) χ^2 distributed, as argued in the appendix to Chapter 8, the appropriate χ^2 statistic is the sum

$$W = (n_1 - 1)\frac{s_1^2}{\sigma_1^2} + (n_2 - 1)\frac{s_2^2}{\sigma_2^2}$$

with $(n_1 - 1) + (n_2 - 1) = n_1 + n_2 - 2$ d.f.

Substituting these expressions for Z and W into the definition of a t statistic yields the following result:

$$t = \frac{\dfrac{(\bar{Y}_1 - \bar{Y}_2) - (\mu_1 - \mu_2)}{\sqrt{\dfrac{\sigma_1^2}{n_1} + \dfrac{\sigma_2^2}{n_2}}}}{\sqrt{\left((n_1 - 1)\dfrac{s_1^2}{\sigma_1^2} + (n_2 - 1)\dfrac{s_2^2}{\sigma_2^2}\right) \Big/ (n_1 + n_2 - 2)}}$$

Without further assumptions, this can't be simplified, and the t statistic depends on the unknown population variances. To solve this problem, we assumed $\sigma_1^2 = \sigma_2^2$. Then the common variance can be factored out of the square roots. With a little algebra, the t definition becomes

$$t = \frac{(\bar{Y}_1 - \bar{Y}_2) - (\mu_1 - \mu_2)}{\sqrt{\dfrac{(n_1 - 1)s_1^2 + (n_2 - 1)s_2^2}{n_1 + n_2 - 2}}\sqrt{\dfrac{1}{n_1} + \dfrac{1}{n_2}}}$$

$$= \frac{(\bar{Y}_1 - \bar{Y}_2) - (\mu_1 - \mu_2)}{s_p\sqrt{\dfrac{1}{n_1} + \dfrac{1}{n_2}}}$$

which is the form used in this chapter. In summary, the assumption that $\sigma_1^2 = \sigma_2^2$ is made so that the defining condition for t yields a t statistic that does not depend on unknown population variances.

11

METHODS FOR PROPORTIONS AND QUALITATIVE VARIABLES

Most of the methods we've considered so far are intended for quantitative, numerical variables where ideas like averaging or ranking are meaningful. Sometimes it's impossible to obtain quantitative measurements of a variable. The variable "automobile model" is not completely captured by numerical measurements of length, weight, or engine displacement. The variable "college major field" is inherently qualitative, not numerical. In a telephone survey of opinions about a new billing system for credit cards, we could get ordinal information as to whether a customer liked or disliked the change, but it would be very hard to get a numerical measure of how strong the opinion was.

In this chapter, we turn briefly to some basic methods for dealing with qualitative, categorical variables. Section 11.1 describes a test of how well the frequencies of various categories fit to a theoretical set of probabilities. Section 11.2 describes a hypothesis test for the relation of two qualitative variables. Section 11.3 looks at the strength of the relation of variables, as opposed to the statistical detectability (significance) of the relation.

11.1   TESTS FOR SEVERAL PROPORTIONS   ∎

In Chapter 9 we discussed hypothesis testing about a single proportion, often using an approximate z statistic. In this section, we'll extend the test to a single statistic for testing whether several deviations of sample data from theoretical proportions could plausibly have occurred by chance. The test uses the χ^2 distribution and table we introduced in Chapter 8, in the context of estimating a variance or standard deviation. The χ^2 table (Table 5) gives critical values that cut off a specified right-tail area a, for given degrees of freedom (d.f.). In this respect, the χ^2 table is similar to the t table we used in the past few chapters. The χ^2 distribution is not symmetric; in this section we need only be concerned about values in the upper tail of the distribution, so the asymmetry won't be crucial.

goodness-of-fit test

The χ^2 **goodness-of-fit test** is used to test the hypothesis that several proportions have specified numerical values. For instance, suppose that a life insurance company has a mix of 40% whole life policies, 25% level term policies, 15% decreasing term policies, and 20% other types. A change in this mix could signal a need to change commission, reserve, or investment practices, but the company does not want to react to random short-term fluctuations. If the company does a study of the last 1200 policies issued (regarded as a random sample), the χ^2 goodness-of-fit test can be used to test the statistical significance of deviations from the historical percentages.

In Chapter 9 we developed a test for a single binomial proportion; we often used a z approximation. We could run a separate test on the proportion for each policy type. The trouble with such a procedure is that although the Type I error is controlled at some level α for each test, the overall probability of error (incorrectly rejecting the null hypothesis in at least one test) may be much larger than α. If four separate tests are run at $\alpha = .05$, what is the probability of at least one Type I error? The tests are not independent. If one sample proportion is too high, the others tend to be too low, because the sample proportions must add to 1. But there is no way to get an accurate assessment of the overall probability of error from combining several z tests. The goodness-of-fit method yields a combined test of all proportions with a specified overall α level.

multinomial sampling

The χ^2 procedure assumes **multinomial sampling**. This is the extension of binomial sampling to more than two categories. Now we have k categories, and in each of n independent trials, the probability of observing a member of category i is π_i. This probability is assumed to be constant over trials.

expected number

The procedure works by comparing the observed number in each category to the **expected number** in that category. If there are n items in a sample and the probability of any items falling in category i is π_i, then, by the binomial distribution, the expected number in category i is

$$E_i = n\pi_i$$

The test procedure is summarized next:

Goodness-of-fit Test for Several Proportions

H_0: $\pi_i = \pi_{i,0}$ for categories $i = 1, \ldots, k$; $\pi_{i,0}$ are specified probabilities or proportions

H_a: H_0 is not true

T.S.: $\chi^2 = \sum_i \dfrac{(n_i - E_i)^2}{E_i}$ where n_i is the observed number in category i and $E_i = n\pi_{i,0}$ is the expected number under H_0.

R.R.: Reject H_0 if $\chi^2 > \chi_\alpha^2$, the right-tail α percentage point of a χ^2 distribution with d.f. $= k - 1$. Note that the d.f. depends on k, the number of categories, not on n, the number of observations.

EXAMPLE 11.1   Suppose that, in the insurance company illustration at the beginning of this section, the previous 1200 policies issued consist of 439 whole life policies, 323 level term policies, 197 decreasing term policies, and 241 others. Assess the statistical significance (at $\alpha = .10$) of any shift from the historical policy mix.

Solution   The following table summarizes the calculations:

Category, i	Whole Life	Level Term	Decreasing Term	Other	Total
Historical proportion, $\pi_{i,0}$	.40	.25	.15	.20	1.00
Observed number, n_i	439	323	197	241	1200
Expected number, $E_i = 1200\pi_{i,0}$	480	300	180	240	1200
$n_i - E_i$	−41	+23	+17	+1	0
$\dfrac{(n_i - E_i)^2}{E_i}$	3.502	1.763	1.606	.004	6.875

The number of categories is $k = 4$, so there are $k - 1 = 3$ d.f.; $\chi^2_{.10} = 6.25$ for 3 d.f. Because $\chi^2 = 6.875 > 6.25$, H_0 is rejected, and the shift from the historical mix is statistically significant at $\alpha = .10$. It appears that term policies are becoming more popular and whole life policies less so. (Note: The $\alpha = .05$ percentage point is 7.81. H_0 could not be rejected at $\alpha = .05$, therefore the p-value is somewhere between .05 and .10.)   ∎

multinomial assumptions   As with the binomial distribution, the key **multinomial assumptions** are independence of trials and constant probabilities over trials. Independence would be violated if several of the policies were sold to the same person or within the same family. Constant probability would be violated if the 1200 policies were sold over a long enough period that a time trend could matter. The most serious possible violation would occur if the policies were sold by relatively few agents and if there were major differences in product mix among agents.

The statistic for the χ^2 goodness-of-fit test is the sum of k terms, which is why d.f. depends on k, not n. There are $k - 1$ d.f. instead of k because the sum of the $n_i - E_i$ terms must always equal $n - n = 0$; $k - 1$ of these terms are free to vary but the kth is determined by this requirement.

The mathematics underlying this test is based on an approximation that is a lineal descendant of the normal approximation to the binomial distribution. The quality of this approximation has been extensively studied. A fairly conservative general rule is that the approximation is adequate if all E_i are at least 5.0.

The goodness-of-fit test is used extensively to test the adequacy of various scientific theories. One problem of such applications is that the hypothesis of interest is formulated as the null hypothesis, not the research hypothesis. If a scientist has a pet theory and wants to show that it gives a good fit to the data, the scientist wants to accept the null hypothesis. But the potential error in accepting it is Type II, and β probabilities of Type II errors are hard to calculate. In general,

good fit conclusion

the null hypothesis tends to be accepted (the β probability is high) if n is small, or if there are many categories. Even if the general rule that all E_i are at least 5.0 is satisfied, the β risk can be large. **A "good fit" conclusion is always suspect.** Perhaps the best procedure for a manager is to look at deviations of sample proportions from theoretical proportions and to use the χ^2 test results as an indicator of the degree of potential random variation.

EXAMPLE 11.2

Suppose that in a test of a random walk theory of stock price changes, 125 security analysts are each asked to select four stocks listed on the New York Stock Exchange that are expected to outperform the Standard and Poor's Index over a 90-day period. According to one random walk theory of stock price changes, the analysts should do no better than coin flipping; the number of correct guesses by any particular analyst should follow a binomial distribution with $n = 4$ and probability of success .50. The data are

Number correct: 0   1   2   3   4
Frequency: 3   23 51 39 9

Test the random walk hypothesis at $\alpha = .05$ and at $\alpha = .10$.

Solution

Number correct	0	1	2	3	4
Theoretical proportion (based on binomial probability)	.0625	.2500	.3750	.2500	.0625
Observed proportion	.0240	.1840	.4080	.3120	.0720
n_i	3	23	51	39	9
E_i	7.8125	31.250	46.875	31.250	7.8125
$\dfrac{(n_i - E_i)^2}{E_i}$	2.9645	2.1780	0.3630	1.922	0.1805

$$\chi^2 = \sum \frac{(n_i - E_i)^2}{E_i} = 7.608$$

The tabled .05 and .10 points for χ^2 with $5 - 1 = 4$ d.f. are 9.49 and 7.78, respectively. Thus H_0 cannot be rejected at $\alpha = .05$ or even at $\alpha = .10$, and the data might be declared "a good fit" to the random walk theory. But the actual proportions of analysts who are correct for two, three, or four stocks are larger than those predicted by the theory. The result of the χ^2 test indicates that this fact could conceivably have been a collective lucky break for the analysts. We would say that such data would suggest, though by no means conclusively prove, that analysts can do somewhat better than the random walk theory would indicate. ∎

SECTION 11.1   EXERCISES

11.1   The director of a data-processing center wants to test the Poisson distribution model for arrivals of jobs to a central computer. The mean arrival rate during the relevant period is 3.8 jobs per minute. Records are kept on the number of arrivals in each of 2000 1-minute periods. The results are

Arrivals:	0	1	2	3	4	5	6	7	8	9+
Frequency:	38	155	328	392	415	399	170	61	27	15

   a. Use Poisson tables ($\mu = 3.8$) to calculate probabilities for each category of number of arrivals.
   b. Calculate expected frequencies.
   c. Is the Poisson model a good fit to the data? Use $\alpha = .01$.

11.2   Can you detect any systematic discrepancy between the observed frequencies and the expected (Poisson model) frequencies in the data of Exercise 11.1?

11.3   A gift shop owner believes that 30% of the customers who enter the shop buy no items, 45% buy 1 item, and 25% buy 2 or more items. Observation of 25 customers yields the following data:

Number of purchases:	0	1	2+
Frequency:	10	6	9

   a. Calculate the expected frequencies, assuming that the owner's hypothesis is valid.
   b. Test the owner's hypothesis using $\alpha = .05$. Can the owner claim a good fit based on these data?

11.4   Suppose that the data in Exercise 11.3 are based on 250 customers, with respective frequencies 100, 60, and 90.
   a. Test the owner's hypothesis at $\alpha = .05$.
   b. Explain the discrepancy in the conclusion between this exercise and Exercise 11.3.

11.2   CHI-SQUARE TESTS OF INDEPENDENCE ▪

When we first introduced probability ideas in Chapter 3, we started by using tables of frequencies (counts). At the time, we treated these counts as if they represented the whole population. In practice, we'll hardly ever know the complete population data; we'll usually have only a sample. When we have

cross tabulations or contingency tables
counts from a sample, they're usually arranged in **cross tabulations** or **contingency tables** such as those in Chapter 3. In this section, we'll describe one particular test that is often used for such tables, a chi-squared test of independence.

In Chapter 3 we introduced the idea of independence. In particular we
dependence
discussed the idea that **dependence** of variables means that one variable has some value for predicting the other. With sample data there usually appears to be some degree of dependence. In this section we develop a χ^2 test that assesses whether the perceived dependence in sample data may be a fluke—the result of random variability rather than real dependence.

First, the frequency data are to be arranged in a cross-tabulation with r rows and c columns. The possible values of one variable determine the rows of the table and the possible values of the other determine the columns. We denote the population proportion (or probability) falling in row i, column j as π_{ij}. The total proportion for row i is $\pi_{i.}$, and the total proportion for column j is $\pi_{.j}$. If the row and column proportions (probabilities) are independent, then $\pi_{ij} = \pi_{i.}\pi_{.j}$. For instance, suppose that a personnel manager for a large firm wants to assess the popularity of three alternative flexible time-scheduling (flextime) plans among clerical workers in four different offices. The following indicates a set of proportions (π_{ij}) that exhibit independence. The proportion of all clerical workers who favor plan 2 and work in office 1 is $\pi_{21} = .03$; the proportion of all workers favoring plan 2 is $\pi_{2.} = .30$ and the proportion working in office 1 is $\pi_{.1} = .10$. Independence holds for that cell because $\pi_{21} = .03 = (\pi_{2.})(\pi_{.1}) = (.30)(.10)$. Independence also holds for all other cells.

			Office		
Favored Plan	1	2	3	4	Total
1	.05	.20	.15	.10	.50
2	.03	.12	.09	.06	.30
3	.02	.08	.06	.04	.20
Total	.10	.40	.30	.20	

The null hypothesis for this χ^2 test is independence. The research hypothesis specifies only that there is some form of dependence, that is, that it is not true that $\pi_{ij} = \pi_{i.}\pi_{.j}$ in every cell of the table. The test statistic is once again the sum over all cells of

(Observed value − expected values)²/expected value

The computation of expected values E_{ij} under the null hypothesis is different for the independence test than for the goodness-of-fit test. The null hypothesis of independence does not specify numerical values for the row probabilities $\pi_{i.}$ and column probabilities $\pi_{.j}$, so these probabilities must be estimated by the row and column relative frequencies. If $n_{i.}$ is the actual frequency in row i, estimate $\pi_{i.}$ by $\hat{\pi}_{i.} = n_{i.}/n$; similarly $\hat{\pi}_{.j} = n_{.j}/n$. Assuming the null hypothesis of independence is true, it follows that $\hat{\pi}_{ij} = \hat{\pi}_{i.}\hat{\pi}_{.j} = (n_{i.}/n)(n_{.j}/n)$.

Estimated Expected Values $\hat{E}_{ij}$

Under the hypothesis of independence the estimated expected value in row i, column j is

$$\hat{E}_{ij} = n\hat{\pi}_{ij} = n\frac{(n_{i.})}{n}\frac{(n_{.j})}{n} = \frac{(n_{i.})(n_{.j})}{n}$$

the row total multiplied by the column total divided by the grand total.

EXAMPLE 11.3   Suppose that in the flexible time-scheduling illustration a random sample of 216 workers yields the following frequencies:

Favored Plan	Office				Total
	1	2	3	4	
1	15	32	18	5	70
2	8	29	23	18	78
3	1	20	25	22	68
Total	24	81	66	45	216

Calculate a table of $\hat{E}_{ij}$ values.

Solution   For row 1, column 1 the estimated expected number is

$$\hat{E}_{11} = \frac{(\text{row 1 total})(\text{column 1 total})}{\text{grand total}} = \frac{(70)(24)}{216} = 7.78$$

Similar calculations for all cells yield the table below:

Plan	Office				Total
	1	2	3	4	
1	7.78	26.25	21.39	14.58	70.00
2	8.67	29.25	23.83	16.25	78.00
3	7.56	25.50	20.78	14.17	68.01
Total	24.01	81.00	66.00	45.00	216.01

Note that the row and column totals in the $\hat{E}_{ij}$ table equal (except for round-off error) the corresponding totals in the observed (n_{ij}) table. ∎

The χ^2 test of independence is summarized in the following:

χ^2 Test of Independence

H_0: The row and column variables are independent

H_a: The row and column variables are dependent (associated)

T.S.: $\chi^2 = \sum_{i,j}(n_{ij} - \hat{E}_{ij})^2/\hat{E}_{ij}$

R.R.: Reject H_0 if $\chi^2 > \chi_\alpha^2$, where χ_α^2 cuts off area α in a χ^2 distribution with $(r-1)(c-1)$ d.f.; $r = $ number of rows, $c = $ number of columns.

EXAMPLE 11.4   Carry out the χ^2 test of independence for the data of Example 11.3. First use $\alpha = .05$, then obtain a bound for the p-value.

Solution   The term for cell $(1,1)$ is $(n_{11} - \hat{E}_{11})^2/\hat{E}_{11} = (15 - 7.78)^2/7.78 = 6.70$. Similar calculations are made for each cell. Substituting into the test statistic, we find $\chi^2 = 6.70 + \cdots + 4.33 = 27.12$. For $(3 - 1)(4 - 1) = 6$ d.f., the tabled χ^2 value (6 d.f., $\alpha = .05$) is 12.59. The observed χ^2 value of 27.12 far exceeds 12.59, so H_0 is rejected at $\alpha = .05$. In fact, 27.12 exceeds the tabled value even for $\alpha = .001$ (the smallest α in the table), namely 21.46. Therefore H_0 is rejected even for $\alpha = .001$ and p-value $< .001$. ∎

d.f. for table   The degrees of freedom for the χ^2 test of independence relate to the number of cells in the two-way table that are free to vary while the marginal totals remain fixed. For example, in a 2×2 table (2 rows, 2 columns) only one cell entry is free to vary. Once that entry is fixed, we can determine the remaining cell entries by subtracting from the corresponding row or column total (see Figure 11.1a). Similarly, with a 2×3 table (2 rows, 3 columns), two of the cell entries are free to vary. Once these entries are set, the remaining cell entries are determined by subtracting from the appropriate row or column total (see Figure 11.1b). In general, for a table with r rows and c columns, $(r - 1)(c - 1)$ of the cell entries are free to vary. This number represents the degrees of freedom for the χ^2 test of independence.

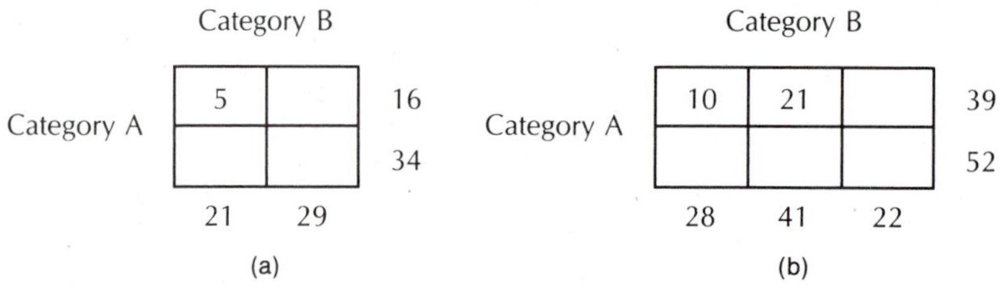

FIGURE 11.1   (a) One Degree of Freedom for a 2 × 2 Table; (b) Two Degrees of Freedom for a 2 × 3 Table

This χ^2 test of independence is also based on an approximation. A conservative rule is that each $\hat{E}_{ij}$ must be at least 5 to use the approximation comfortably. Standard practice if some $\hat{E}_{ij}$'s are too small is to lump together those rows (or columns) with small totals until the rule is satisfied.

The only function of this χ^2 test is to determine whether apparent dependence in sample data may be a fluke, plausibly a result of random variation. Rejection of the null hypothesis indicates only that the apparent association is not reasonably attributable to chance. It does not indicate anything about the **strength of association**   **strength** or type **of association**. The percentage analysis and the λ measure defined in Section 11.3 are used to indicate how strong the dependence is.

The same χ^2 test statistic applies to a slightly different sampling procedure. An implicit assumption of our discussion surrounding the χ^2 test of independence is that the data result from a single random sample from the whole population. Often, separate random samples are taken from the subpopulations defined by the column (or row) variable. In the flextime example (11.3) the data might well have resulted from separate samples (of respective sizes 24, 81, 66, and 45) from the four offices rather than from a single random sample of 216 workers. The null hypothesis of independence is then stated (in an equivalent form) as H_0: The conditional probability of row i given column j is the same for all columns j. **test of homogeneity**   The test is called a **test of homogeneity** of distributions (that is, that the probabilities or proportions by column are equal). The mechanics and conclusions sions of the test are identical, so the distinction is minor.

EXAMPLE 11.5   A poll of attitudes toward five possible energy policies is taken. Random samples of 200 individuals from major oil- and natural-gas-producing states, 200 from coal states, and 400 from other states are drawn. Each respondent indicates the most preferred alternative from among the following:

1. primarily emphasize conservation
2. primarily emphasize domestic oil and gas exploration
3. primarily emphasize investment in solar-related energy
4. primarily emphasize nuclear-energy development and safety
5. primarily reduce environmental restrictions and emphasize coal-burning activities

The results are as follows:

Policy Choice	Oil/Gas States	Coal States	Other States	Total
1	50	59	161	270
2	88	20	40	148
3	56	52	188	296
4	4	3	5	12
5	2	66	6	74
Total	200	200	400	800

Conduct a χ^2 test of homogeneity of distributions for the three groups of states. Give the p-value for this test.

Solution   A test that the corresponding population distributions are different makes use of the following table of expected values:

Policy Choice	Oil/Gas States	Coal States	Other States
1	67.5	67.5	135
2	37	37	74
3	74	74	148
4	3	3	6
5	18.5	18.5	37

The table violates our general rule that all $\hat{E}_{ij}$'s be at least 5. There is no obvious choice for combining policy 4 with some other. Therefore we leave the table as is, but we realize that the nominal χ^2 probabilities are slightly suspect. The test procedure is outlined here:

H_0: The column distributions are homogeneous

H_a: The column distributions are not homogeneous

$$\text{T.S.: } \chi^2 = \sum (n_{ij} - \hat{E}_{ij})^2 / \hat{E}_{ij}$$
$$= (50 - 67.5)^2 / 67.5 + (88 - 37)^2 / 37 + \cdots + (6 - 37)^2 / 37$$
$$= 289.22$$

R.R. and Conclusion: Because the tabled value of χ^2 for d.f. $= 8$ and $\alpha = .001$ is 26.12, the p-value is $<.001$.

Even recognizing the limited accuracy of the χ^2 approximation, we can reject the hypothesis of homogeneity at some very small p-value. Percentage analysis, particularly of state type for a given policy choice, shows dramatic differences; for instance, 1% of those living in oil/gas states favor policy 5, compared to 33% of those living in coal states who favor policy 5.   ■

The χ^2 test described in this section has a limited, but important, purpose. This test only assesses whether the data indicate a statistically detectable (significant) relation among various categories. It doesn't measure how strong the apparent relation might be. A weak relation in a large data set may be detectable (significant); a strong relation in a small data set may be nonsignificant. Methods for assessing the apparent strength of relation in a data set are discussed in Section 11.3.

SECTION 11.2   EXERCISES

11.5   A personnel director for a large, research-oriented firm categorizes colleges and universities as most desirable, good, adequate, and undesirable for purposes of hiring their graduates. Data are collected on 156 recent graduates, and each is rated by a supervisor.

| | Rating | | |
School	Outstanding	Average	Poor
Most desirable	21	25	2
Good	20	36	10
Adequate	4	14	7
Undesirable	3	8	6

Output from a standard computer package (SPSS) is shown below:

```
                 RATING
        COUNT |
              |OUTSTAND AVERAGE  POOR      ROW
              |ING                        TOTAL
              |    1.00|    2.00|    3.00|
SCHOOL  -------+--------+--------+--------+
         1.00 |   21   |   25   |   2   |    48
MOST DESIRABLE|        |        |       |   30.8
              +--------+--------+--------+
         2.00 |   20   |   36   |  10   |    66
GOOD          |        |        |       |   42.3
              +--------+--------+--------+
         3.00 |    4   |   14   |   7   |    25
ADEQUATE      |        |        |       |   16.0
              +--------+--------+--------+
         4.00 |    3   |    8   |   6   |    17
UNDESIRABLE   |        |        |       |   10.9
              +--------+--------+--------+
       COLUMN     48       83      25       156
       TOTAL     30.8     53.2    16.0     100.0
```

CHI-SQUARE	D.F.	SIGNIFICANCE	MIN E.F.	CELLS WITH E.F.< 5
15.96704	6	0.0139	2.724	2 OF 12 (16.7%)

STATISTIC	SYMMETRIC	WITH SCHOOL DEPENDENT	WITH RATING DEPENDENT
LAMBDA	0.00613	0.01111	0.00000
UNCERTAINTY COEFFICIENT	0.04716	0.04211	0.05357
SOMERS' D	0.26573	0.28627	0.24794
ETA		0.31150	0.30639

a. Locate the value of the χ^2 statistic.

b. Locate the p-value.

c. Can the director safely conclude that there is a relation between school type and rating?

d. Is there any problem in using the χ^2 approximation?

11.6 Calculate rating percentages for each school. Do the percentages reflect the existence of the relation we found in Exercise 11.5?

11.7 A study of potential age discrimination considers promotions among middle managers in a large company. The data are

	Age				
	Under 30	30–39	40–49	50 or Over	Total
Promoted	9	29	32	10	80
Not promoted	41	41	48	40	170
Total	50	70	80	50	

a. Find the expected numbers under the hypothesis of independence.
b. Calculate the degrees of freedom.
c. Is there a statistically significant relation between age and promotions, using $\alpha = .05$?

11.8 Place bounds on the p-value in Exercise 11.7.

11.9 The data of Exercise 11.7 are combined as follows:

	Age		
	Up to 39	40 or Over	Total
Promoted	38	42	80
Not promoted	82	88	170
Total	120	130	

a. Can the hypothesis of independence be rejected using a reasonable α?
b. What is the effect of combining age categories? Compare the answers to Exercises 11.7 and 11.9.

11.3   MEASURING STRENGTH OF RELATION

The χ^2 test we discussed in Section 11.2 has a built-in limitation. By design, the test only answers the question, Is there a statistically detectable (significant) relation among the categories? It cannot answer the question of whether the relation is strong, interesting, or relevant. This is not a criticism of the test; no hypothesis test can answer these questions. In this section we discuss methods for assessing the strength of relation shown in cross-tabulated data.

The simplest (and often the best) method for assessing the strength of a relation is simple percentage analysis. If there is no relation (that is, if complete independence holds), then percentages by row or by column show no relation. For example, suppose that a direct mail company tests two different offers to see if the response rates differ. Their results are as shown here:

	Response		
Offer	Yes	No	Total
A	40	160	200
B	80	320	400
Total	120	480	600

To check the relation, if any, we calculate percentages of response for each offer. We see that $(40/200) = .20$ (that is, 20%) respond to offer A and $(80/400) = .20$ respond to offer B. Because the percentages are exactly the same, there is no indication of a relation. Alternatively, we note that one-third of the "yes" respondents and one-third of the "no" respondents were given offer A. Because these fractions are exactly the same, there is no indication of a statistical relation.

Of course it is rare to have data that show absolutely no relation in the sample. More commonly the percentages by row or by column differ, which suggests some relation. For example, a firm planning to market a cleaning product commissions a market research study of the leading current product. The variables of interest are the frequency of use and the rating of the leading product. The data are shown below:

		Rating		
Use	Fair	Good	Excellent	Total
Rare	64	123	137	324
Occasional	131	256	129	516
Frequent	209	171	45	425
Total	404	550	311	1265

One natural analysis of the data takes the frequencies of use as givens and looks at the ratings as functions of use. The analysis essentially looks at conditional probabilities of the rating factor, given the use factor, but it recognizes that the data are only a sample, not the population. When use is rare, the best estimate is that $64/324 = .1975$ (or 19.75%) will rate the product as fair, that $123/324 = .3796$ will rate it good, and that $137/324 = .4228$ will rate it excellent. The corresponding proportions for occasional users are $131/516 = .2539$, $256/516 = .4961$, and $129/516 = .2500$. For frequent users the proportions are .4918, .4024, and .1059. The proportions (or percentages, if one multiplies by 100) are quite different for the three use categories, which indicates that rating is related to use. Alternatively, we may calculate the use categories as percentages of the rating categories. In either case, there appears to be a relation. Because the proportions of ratings differ quite a bit as one varies use (or the proportions of use differ quite a bit as one varies rating), there is a suggestion that there is a fairly strong relation between use and rating.

Another way to analyze relations in data is to consider predictability. The stronger the relation exhibited in data, the better one can predict the value of one variable from the value of the other. We could imagine a situation where every rare user rated the product as excellent, every occasional user rated the product as good, and every frequent user rated the product as fair. In such a case, there would be a perfect statistical relation; in terms of predictability, given the use, one could predict the rating exactly. Of course in practice prediction and relation are not perfect; we need a measure of the strength of relation defined as degree of predictability.

dependent and independent variables   We need to distinguish between a **dependent variable**—the variable one is trying to predict—and an **independent variable**—the variable one is using to make the prediction. If one is trying to predict rating given use, use serves as the independent variable and rating as the dependent variable. No cause-and-effect connotations are intended; the choice of independent and dependent variables is entirely up to the person who is analyzing the data.

The simplest prediction rule is to predict the most common value (the mode) of the dependent variable; this rule is the basis of the λ (lambda) predictability measure. In our use-rating example, when use is rare, the most common rating is excellent, with 137 responses; if one predicts excellent for every rare case, one makes $187 = 64 + 123 = 324 - 137$ prediction errors. Similarly for occasional use, a prediction of rating as good gives $260 = 131 + 129 = 516 - 25$ errors; given frequent use, a prediction of rating as fair gives $216 = 171 + 45 = 425 - 209$ errors. The total number of errors is $187 + 260 + 216 = 663$. By comparison, if use is not known, we would have to predict the most common rating, namely good; we would make $715 = 404 + 311 = 1265 - 550$ errors. Reasonably enough, given information about use, we do better in predicting rating than when we have no information. The λ measure indicates how much better we predict. When use is the independent variable and rating is the dependent variable, the difference in prediction errors is $715 - 663 = 52$; we take this difference as a fraction of the errors made not knowing the independent variable, namely 715. If use is the independent variable,

$$\lambda = \frac{\begin{array}{c}\text{errors with unknown independent variable} \\ - \text{ errors with known independent variable}\end{array}}{\text{errors with unknown independent variable}}$$

$$= \frac{715 - 663}{715} = .115$$

The value of λ ranges between 0 and 1; $\lambda = 1$ indicates that, at least in the sample, the dependent variable is predicted perfectly given the independent variable. A value of $\lambda = 0$ occurs if there is independence in the data, or if the same value of the dependent variable is always predicted. To interpret other values of λ, note that it is a proportionate reduction in error (PRE) measure. The value $\lambda = .115$ that we found means that we make 11.5% fewer errors predicting rating given use than we would predicting rating without information about use. Values of λ above about .30 are rare in real data; thus $\lambda = .115$ indicates a modest relation between rating and use. Note that the value of λ depends on which variable is taken as the dependent variable. For rating predicting use, $\lambda = .073$.

Calculation of λ

For every level of the independent variable (every row or every column), find the modal value of the dependent variable. If there are two or more modal values with equal frequency, choose one arbitrarily. Add the frequencies in all nonmodal cells to find K = number of prediction errors with known independent variable value.

Refer to the marginal (total) frequencies of the dependent variable. Add the frequencies in all nonmodal categories to find U = number of prediction errors with unknown independent variable values.

$$\lambda = (U - K)/U$$

∎

EXAMPLE 11.6   An internal survey of samples of clerical workers, supervisory personnel, and junior managers is taken to obtain opinions on a proposed flextime schedule. The following output (SAS) is obtained:

TABLE OF OPINION BY LEVEL

OPINION   LEVEL

FREQUENCY EXPECTED COL PCT	clerical	superv	junior manager	TOTAL
strongly oppose	5 9.8 12.50	8 7.3 26.67	9 4.9 45.00	22
oppose	8 10.2 20.00	10 7.7 33.33	5 5.1 25.00	23
favor	14 11.1 35.00	7 8.3 23.33	4 5.6 20.00	25
strongly favor	13 8.9 32.50	5 6.7 16.67	2 4.4 10.00	20
TOTAL	40	30	20	90

STATISTICS FOR TABLE OF OPINION BY LEVEL

STATISTIC	DF	VALUE	PROB
CHI-SQUARE	6	12.110	0.060

STATISTIC	VALUE	ASE
GAMMA	-0.428	0.114
LAMBDA ASYMMETRIC C|R	0.120	0.106
LAMBDA ASYMMETRIC R|C	0.123	0.079
LAMBDA SYMMETRIC	0.122	0.083

SAMPLE SIZE = 90
ASE IS THE ASYMPTOTIC STANDARD ERROR.
R|C MEANS ROW VARIABLE DEPENDENT ON COLUMN VARIABLE.

a. What does the χ^2 test indicate about the relation shown in the data?

b. What can you see by examining the column percentages?

c. Locate the value for λ with opinion taken as the dependent variable. Interpret the number.

d. Verify the calculation of λ.

Solution
a. The χ^2 statistic is shown as CHI-SQUARE = 12.110 with 6 d.f. The *p*-value is shown as PROB = .060. We cannot reject the null hypothesis of independence at $\alpha = .05$, but we can reject it at $\alpha = .10$. There is only limited evidence that the apparent relation is nonrandom; therefore we should not place too much reliance on any apparent dependence.

b. The clerical staff seems to be largely in favor (35%) or strongly in favor (32.5%). The junior managers are largely strongly opposed (45%) or opposed (25%) and the supervisors are more or less evenly spread out over various opinions. Again, the result of the χ^2 test indicates that we can't rely too heavily on this apparent relation; it could conceivably have arisen by sheer random variation.

c. Here the row variable is the dependent variable. The statement that R|C MEANS ROW VARIABLE DEPENDENT ON COLUMN VARIABLE indicates that we want LAMBDA ASYMMETRIC R|C, which is .123.

d. The predicted cells, with the column listed first, are (CLERICAL, FAVOR), (SUPERV, OPPOSE), (JUNIOR MANAGER, STRONGLY OPPOSE). Adding the frequencies in all other cells, we find $K = 5 + 8 + 13 + 8 + 7 + 5 + 5 + 4 + 2 = 57$. In the TOTAL column for OPINION, we find that the most frequent opinion is FAVOR. Adding the frequencies for the other categories, we find $U = 22 + 23 + 20 = 65$. Therefore

$$\lambda = \frac{65 - 57}{65} = .123 \qquad \blacksquare$$

Percentage analyses and values of λ play a fundamentally different role than does the χ^2 test. The point of a χ^2 test is to see how much evidence there is that there *is* a relation, whatever the size may be. The point of percentage analyses and λ is to see *how strong* the relation appears to be, taking the data at face value. The two types of analyses are complementary.

KEY FORMULAS: Chi-Square and *F* Methods

1. χ^2 goodness-of-fit test

$$H_0: \pi_i = \pi_{i0}, \qquad i = 1, \ldots, k$$

$$\text{T.S.: } \chi^2 = \sum_i \frac{(n_i - E_i)^2}{E_i}$$

where $E_i = n\pi_{i0}$ and d.f. $= k - 1$

2. χ^2 test of independence or homogeneity

$$H_0: \text{The row and column variables are independent}$$

$$\text{T.S.: } \chi^2 = \sum_{i,j} \frac{(n_{ij} - \hat{E}_{ij})^2}{\hat{E}_{ij}}$$

where

$$\hat{E}_{ij} = \frac{(n_{i.})(n_{.j})}{n}$$

and

$$\text{d.f.} = (r-1)(c-1)$$

Summary

This is a tangential chapter devoted to methods for judging qualitative data and proportions, rather than quantitative, measured data. There are two chi-square tests: A goodness-of-fit test to see whether the observed frequencies are reasonably compatible with a specified set of probabilities, and a test of independence (also called homogeneity) to see whether there is evidence of a more-than-random degree of relation between two qualitative variables. These two tests each compare observed frequencies to expected frequencies, but the computation of expected frequencies differs with the two tests. We also discussed ways of assessing the strength of relation between two qualitative variables, based on the measure of how well one variable predicts the other, and the proportionate reduction of prediction error.

CHAPTER 11   EXERCISES

11.10 A speaker who advises managers on how to avoid being unionized claims that only 25% of industrial workers favor union membership, 40% are indifferent, and 35% are opposed. In addition, the advisor claims that these opinions are independent of actual union membership. A random sample of 600 industrial workers yields the following data:

	Favor	Indifferent	Opposed	Total
Members	140	42	18	200
Nonmembers	70	198	132	400
Total	210	240	150	600

  a. What part of the data is relevant to the 25%, 40%, 35% claim?
  b. Test this hypothesis using $\alpha = .01$.

11.11 What can be said about the p-value in Exercise 11.10?

11.12 Test the hypothesis of independence in the data of Exercise 11.10. How conclusively is it rejected?

11.13 Calculate (for the data of Exercise 11.10) percentages of workers in favor of unionization, indifferent, and opposed; separately for members and for nonmembers. Do the percentages suggest that there is a strong relation between membership and opinion?

11.14 Calculate the λ value for predicting opinion given membership, using the data of Exercise 11.10. Does the value of λ indicate that there is a strong relation between membership and opinion?

11.15 Three different television commercials are advertising an established product. The commercials are shown separately to theater panels of consumers; each consumer views only one of the possible commercials and then states an opinion of the product. Opinions range from 1 (very favorable) to 5 (very unfavorable). The data are

		Opinion				
Commercial	1	2	3	4	5	Total
A	32	87	91	46	44	300
B	53	141	76	20	10	300
C	41	93	67	36	63	300
Total	126	321	234	102	117	900

a. Calculate expected frequencies under the null hypothesis of independence.
b. How many degrees of freedom are available for testing this hypothesis?
c. Is there evidence that the opinion distributions are different for the various commercials? Use $\alpha = .01$.

11.16 State bounds on the p-value for Exercise 11.15.

11.17 In your judgment, is there a strong relation between type of commercial and opinion in the data of Exercise 11.15? Support your judgment with computation of percentages and a λ value.

11.18 A direct-mail retailer experimented with three different ways of incorporating order forms into its catalog. In Type 1 catalogs, the form was at the end of the catalog, in Type 2, it was in the middle, and in Type 3, there were forms both in the middle and at the end. Each form was sent to a sample of 1000 potential customers, none of whom had previously bought from the retailer. A code on each form allowed the retailer to determine which type it was; the number of orders received on each type of form was recorded. The following Systat results were obtained from the data; a 0 value for RECEIVED indicates no order received, 1 indicates that an order was received.

```
TABLE OF TYPEFORM     (ROWS) BY RECEIVED     (COLUMNS)

ROW PERCENTS

                  0        1      TOTAL

         1     94.40     5.60     100.00

         2     96.10     3.90     100.00

         3     91.50     8.50     100.00

TOTAL          94.00     6.00     100.00
```

TEST STATISTIC	VALUE	DF	PROB
PEARSON CHI-SQUARE	19.184	2	.000
LIKELIHOOD RATIO CHI-SQUARE	19.037	2	.000

COEFFICIENT	VALUE	ASYMPTOTIC STD ERROR
PHI	.0800	
CRAMER V	.0800	
CONTINGENCY	.0797	
GOODMAN-KRUSKAL GAMMA	.1708	.06631
KENDALL TAU-B	.0470	.01836
STUART TAU-C	.0258	.01018
SPEARMAN RHO	.0499	.01945
SOMERS D (COLUMN DEPENDENT)	.0193	.00764
LAMBDA (COLUMN DEPENDENT)	.0000	.00000
UNCERTAINTY (COLUMN DEPENDENT)	.0140	.00632

    a. What does the null hypothesis of statistical independence indicate about the three types of order form?

    b. Can this null hypothesis be retained at normal α levels?

11.19 Locate the value of λ for predicting RECEIVED knowing TYPEFORM. Does it capture the relation between the two variables?

11.20 A programming firm had developed a more elaborate, more complex version of its spreadsheet program. A "beta test" copy of the program was sent to a sample of users of the current program. From information supplied by the users, the firm rated the sophistication of each user, where 1 indicated standard, basic applications of the program and 3 indicated the most complex applications. Each user indicated a preference between the current version and the test version, where 1 indicated a strong preference for the current version, 3 indicated no particular preference between the two versions, and 5 indicated a strong preference for the new version. The data were analyzed using Systat. Partial output is shown here.

TABLE OF SOPHIST   (ROWS) BY   PREFER   (COLUMNS)

FREQUENCIES

	1	2	3	4	5	TOTAL
1	38	24	16	8	9	95
2	11	16	29	13	8	77
3	2	3	5	8	15	33
TOTAL	51	43	50	29	32	205

ROW PERCENTS

	1	2	3	4	5	TOTAL
1	40.00	25.26	16.84	8.42	9.47	100.00
2	14.29	20.78	37.66	16.88	10.39	100.00
3	6.06	9.09	15.15	24.24	45.45	100.00
TOTAL	24.88	20.98	24.39	14.15	15.61	100.00

TEST STATISTIC	VALUE	DF	PROB
PEARSON CHI-SQUARE	56.346	8	.000
LIKELIHOOD RATIO CHI-SQUARE	51.918	8	.000

COEFFICIENT	VALUE	ASYMPTOTIC STD ERROR
GOODMAN-KRUSKAL GAMMA	.5159	.07201
LAMBDA (COLUMN DEPENDENT)	.2013	.04381

    a. Do the ROW PERCENT entries suggest that there is a relation between SOPHIST and PREFER? If the data showed no relation, what would be true of the ROW PERCENTS?

    b. Does the (PEARSON) CHI-SQUARE computation indicate that there is a statistically detectable (significant) relation, at usual values of α?

11.21 Interpret the value of λ shown in the output of Exercise 11.20. What does it indicate about the predictability of PREFER knowing SOPHIST?

11.22 The Systat output of Exercise 11.20 also included 95% confidence intervals for the overall proportion of users in each PREFER category. The Systat manual did not spell out the details of how the intervals were computed, but indicated that the method should be quite accurate. Output is shown below.

TABLE OF VALUES FOR   PREFER

95 PERCENT APPROXIMATE CONFIDENCE INTERVALS SCALED AS CELL PERCENTS

1	2	.3	4	5
33.22	28.98	32.70	21.29	22.97
17.32	13.97	16.90	8.36	9.53

    a. Use the method of Section 8.2 to calculate a confidence interval for the proportion in category 3. (You will need to refer to the output of Exercise 11.20.) Multiply the results by 100 for comparability to the CELL PERCENTS shown by Systat.

    b. Are your results the same as those shown by Systat? Which intervals (yours or Systat's) are more conservative?

11.23 A chain of video rental stores did a survey (a more-or-less random sample) of its customers. The two responses of most interest to the store were customers' frequency of renting and customers' rating of the adequacy of the stores' selection. The responses are stored in the 'CH11C1.DAT' file of the data disk, which you should load into the computer package you use. Column 1 contains codes for the frequency of renting, with code 1 indicating the lowest frequency and 4 the highest. Similarly, column 2 contains codes for rating the adequacy of selection, with code 1 being the poorest rating and code 4 the best.

    a. Obtain the frequencies for each category of adequacy of selection rating.

    b. Test the null hypothesis that the categories are equally likely. (Many computer packages won't do a goodness-of-fit test easily, so you may have to do some hand computation.) Can the hypothesis be rejected at $\alpha = 10$? What about $\alpha = .01$?

11.24 a. Use the data of Exercise 11.23 and test the null hypothesis that frequency and selection adequacy are statistically independent. What does the p-value indicate about this null hypothesis?

    b. Is there any reason to think that the expected frequencies are so low that the claimed p-value in part (a) is a poor approximation?

11.25 Use the data of Exercise 11.24 and obtain percentages of customers in each adequacy rating, separately for each frequency code. Can you find any trend in the percentages as the frequency of renting increases?

11.26 The benefits manager for a major bank surveyed a sample of 353 employees (out of several thousand) to obtain their opinions of two alternative medical benefits plans. The variables of interest were: age (five categories, with 1 being a code for the youngest employees, 5 for the oldest); opinion (five categories, with 1 being most in favor of a health maintenance organization option, 5 being most in favor of a traditional fee-for-service option, and 3 being neutral); and a code for whether the employee has dependents covered by the plan (0 if not, 1 if so). The responses are listed (in the order stated for columns 1–3) in the 'CH11C2.DAT' file of the data disk. Load that file into your computer package.

a. Obtain a table of frequencies for each combination of age and opinion codes. If the computer package will do so, obtain percentages in each opinion code for each age category. Are the opinion percentages similar for the various age codes?

b. Have the computer package carry out a formal test of the null hypothesis that age and opinion are independent. Can the null hypothesis be rejected at $\alpha = .05$?

11.27 The benefits manager in Exercise 11.26 suspected that there might be an indirect relation between age and opinion: Age might be related to whether dependents are covered, and whether dependents are covered might be related to opinion.

a. Have the computer package test for dependence between age and dependents. Is the relation conclusively established?

b. Do the same analysis for dependents and opinion.

c. Have the computer package test for dependence between age and opinion. Have the computer package test separately for those employees with dependents covered and for those employees without dependents covered. In these tests, is there any evidence of a relation?

CASE

Testing a Relation

In the case for Chapter 4, a bank was considering three variables from a sample survey of 2150 customers as part of a plan to offer a "debit card". The relevant variables were X = number of active credit cards held by a customer, Y = number of credit cards carrying unpaid balances, and Z = number of debit cards desired. The following frequencies were reported in the case for Chapter 4:

x:	0	0	0	1	1	1	1	1	1	2	2	2	2	2	2
y:	0	0	0	0	0	0	1	1	1	0	0	0	1	1	1
z:	0	1	2	0	1	2	0	1	2	0	1	2	0	1	2
Freq.:	98	45	10	125	110	28	171	203	38	96	87	18	150	228	66

x:	2	2	2	3	3	3	3	3	3	3	3	3	3	3	3
y:	2	2	2	0	0	0	1	1	1	2	2	2	3	3	3
z:	0	1	2	0	1	2	0	1	2	0	1	2	0	1	2
Freq.:	43	160	51	11	15	10	37	78	29	13	51	22	10	23	34

Recall that the product manager thought that customers with low values of X (or of Y) would tend to have high values of Z. Construct cross-tabulations of X and Z and also of Y and Z. Supplement your analysis of the Chapter 4 case with appropriate tests of the hypothesis of no relation. What do the results of these tests indicate? In particular, do they generally support the product manager's belief?

12

ANALYSIS OF VARIANCE AND DESIGNED EXPERIMENTS

One of the most notable trends in management during the past decade has been the use of scientifically controlled, carefully designed experiments. Controlled experiments are especially useful to managers in the assessment of the likely effect of changes. To assess the probable results of a change in product, process, or policy, one can perform an experiment on carefully chosen samples, make the change, and measure the results. Well-designed experiments convert a discussion from speculative opinion to the assessment of actual data. That's an improvement.

This chapter is devoted to Analysis of Variance (ANOVA) methods that were specifically developed to analyze experimental data. (These methods are also useful in certain nonexperimental situations.) Typically, the data resulting from an experiment consist of multiple samples, so we must extend the two-sample methods from Chapter 10 to apply to many samples. In Section 12.1, we discuss ANOVA methods for **one-factor** experiments in which the multiple samples are obtained by changing the values of a single experimental variable. We explore a rank-based alternative method in Section 12.2. We list some more detailed methods for exploring specific parts of the data when we discuss the topic of multiple comparisons in Section 12.3. The recent realization of the value of experiments has led to much more interest in complex multifactor experiments, which we discuss in Sections 12.4–12.7. In particular, in Section 12.7, we have all the ideas we need to consider the crucial applications of statistical experiments to quality improvement.

12.1   TESTING THE EQUALITY OF SEVERAL POPULATION MEANS

The simplest experiments vary only one variable, and measure the results on another, response variable. The experimental variable, which often is qualitative, **factor** is called a **factor**. The response variable, which is quantitative, is called a **depen-**

dependent variable

dent variable, or simply the response. For example, suppose that a manufacturing firm is considering possible policies for selecting supervisors for work areas. Three possible policies are A, to promote from within the work force using in-house training; B, to promote from within, using a local community college for supervisory training; and C, to hire only experienced supervisors from outside. The firm has supervisors hired under each of the three conditions. Ideally, these supervisors would be assigned completely at random to work areas to avoid any biases caused by the assignment process. This is an idealization; without randomization, we may have to make an unverified assumption that there are no biases. Suppose that no evident source of bias can be identified, so that we're willing to use the data, which are effectiveness ratings on the firm's standard 100-point scale. The data are

								Mean	Variance	n
Policy A	39	51	58	61	65	72	86	61.71	225.24	7
Policy B	22	38	43	47	49	54	72	46.43	232.95	7
Policy C	18	31	41	43	44	54	65	42.29	229.24	7

It appears that the policy A supervisors have substantially higher average ratings, but there is a great deal of variability within each group and the sample sizes are very small. Is it plausible that the apparent differences in average ratings are merely the result of random variation?

We might be tempted to run two-sample t tests on all pairs of means, using the methods of Chapter 10. Resist the temptation. If we ran many t tests, each at a

overall risk

given alpha level, we wouldn't know what the **overall risk** of Type I (false positive) error is. Certainly, the more tests one runs, the greater the risk of a false positive conclusion somewhere among the tests. The analysis of variance (ANOVA) method leads to a single test statistic for comparing all the means, so the overall risk of Type I error can be controlled. Therefore, ANOVA is preferable to multiple t tests.

The analysis of variance is based on "taking apart" the variability in the data into (1) a part attributable to variation between groups, and (2) another remaining part attributable to variation within groups. Variation is assessed by

sums of squares

sums of squares (SS). To begin with, we calculate the total sum of squares as the sum of squared deviations of individual values around the grand mean of all scores. For the example, we can calculate the grand mean by averaging all 21 values or by averaging the 3 group means:

$$\bar{y} = \frac{(39 + 51 + 58 + \cdots + 44 + 54 + 65)}{21}$$
$$= (61.71 + 46.43 + 42.29)/3 = 50.14$$

Then SS(Total) is by definition the sum of all squared deviations around this mean.

$$SS(\text{Total}) = (39 - 50.14)^2 + (51 - 50.14)^2 + (58 - 50.14)^2 + \cdots$$
$$+ (44 - 50.14)^2 + (54 - 50.14)^2 + (65 - 50.14)^2$$
$$= 5590.57$$

variability between groups   Variability between groups is denoted SS(Between) or SS(Factor). It is the sum of squared deviations of each group mean from the grand mean, multiplied by the sample size for the group.

$$SS(\text{Between}) = 7(61.71 - 50.14)^2 + 7(46.43 - 50.14)^2 + 7(42.29 - 50.14)^2$$
$$= 1466.00$$

If the means for the various groups (the various levels of the experimental factor) are nearly the same, there is little variability attributed to the factor, and SS(Between) will be small. But if the means differ greatly, there will be large variability attributed to the factor and a large SS(Between) value.

variability within groups   To evaluate variability within groups, we look at deviations within each group from the mean *for that group*. The calculation can be done either from the raw data or from the group variances multiplied by the respective degrees of freedom.

$$SS(\text{Within}) = (39 - 61.71)^2 + (51 - 61.71)^2 + \cdots + (22 - 46.43)^2$$
$$+ (38 - 46.43)^2 + \cdots + (18 - 42.29)^2 + \cdots + (65 - 42.29)^2$$
$$= (7 - 1)225.24 + (7 - 1)232.95 + (7 - 1)229.24$$
$$= 4124.57$$

If all the data in each group are close together and therefore close to the group mean, the variances and SS(Within) will be small.

ANOVA calculations are based on the following notation; they can be done by most statistical packages. See Table 12.1.

$y_{ij} = j$th sample measurement in group i

$$i = 1, 2, \ldots, I; \qquad j = 1, 2, \ldots, n_i$$

n_i = sample size for group i
$\bar{y}_i$ = sample mean for group i
$\bar{y}$ = average of all the sample measurements
n = the total sample size. For the above data $n = n_1 + n_2 + \cdots + n_I$

With this notation it is possible to express the variability of the n sample measurements about $\bar{y}$ as

SS(Total) $$SS(\text{Total}) = \sum_{i,j} (y_{ij} - \bar{y})^2$$

and to partition this quantity into two components, SS(Between) and SS(Within).

$$\sum_{i,j} (y_{ij} - \bar{y})^2 = \sum_i n_i (\bar{y}_i - \bar{y})^2 + \sum_{i,j} (y_{ij} - \bar{y}_i)^2$$

$$SS(\text{Total}) = SS(\text{Between}) + SS(\text{Within})$$

SS(Within)   Because **SS(Within)** is based on deviations from specific group means, it is not affected by possible deviations of these sample means from each other; SS(Within) reflects only random variation within the samples. In contrast,

| TABLE 12.1 | Notation for Sample Data in an ANOVA |

Group	Sample Data	Sample Mean	Unknown Group Mean
1	$y_{11} y_{12} \cdots y_{1n_1}$	$\bar{y}_1$	μ_1
2	$y_{21} y_{22} \cdots y_{2n_2}$	$\bar{y}_2$	μ_2
$\vdots$	$\vdots \quad \vdots \qquad \vdots$	$\vdots$	$\vdots$
I	$y_{I1} y_{I2} \quad y_{In_i}$	$\bar{y}_I$	μ_I

SS(Between)

SS(Between) is strongly affected by discrepancies among group means. If the true groups means μ_i are equal, the sample means $\bar{y}_i$ are close to each other and therefore close to the grand mean $\bar{y}$, and SS(Between) tends to be small. But if the true group means are different, the sample means tend to be far apart and **SS(Between)** tends to be large. If SS(Between) is large relative to SS(Within), the null hypothesis that the true group means are equal should be rejected.

To make a precise statement of the analysis of variance (ANOVA) test, we need to do a little mathematics. We make the following formal mathematical assumptions:

Assumptions for an ANOVA

1. The sample measurements $y_{i1}, y_{i2}, \ldots, y_{in_i}$ are selected from a normal population ($i = 1, 2, \ldots, I$).
2. The samples are independent.
3. The unknown population mean and variance for the measurements from sample i are μ_i and σ^2, respectively.

The null hypothesis for analysis of variance is $H_0: \mu_1 = \mu_2 = \cdots = \mu_I$. By assumption, the true variances are also equal. Therefore, under the null hypothesis, all the sample measurements y_{ij} may be regarded as a large sample from a normal population. It follows that

$$\frac{\sum_{i,j} (y_{ij} - \bar{y})^2}{\sigma^2} = \frac{\text{SS(Total)}}{\sigma^2}$$

has a χ^2 distribution with $n - 1$ degrees of freedom, just as in Chapters 8 and 11. In the Appendix to this chapter we show that

$$\frac{\text{SS(Total)}}{\sigma^2} = \frac{\text{SS(Between)}}{\sigma^2} + \frac{\text{SS(Within)}}{\sigma^2}$$

According to a very useful mathematical fact, Cochran's Theorem, these components are independent and have χ^2 distributions.

d.f. for SS(Within) and SS(Between)

The degrees of freedom for SS(Within) can be found by realizing that there are $n_i - 1$ d.f. for squared deviations within group i and that d.f.'s can be added across the groups. Therefore, there are $(n_1 - 1) + (n_2 - 1) + \cdots + (n_I - 1) = n - I$ d.f. for SS(Within). The quantity SS(Between) $= \sum_i n_i (\bar{y}_i - \bar{y})^2$ has I terms, but because the constraint $\sum_i n_i(\bar{y}_i - \bar{y}) = 0$ determines one term (once the remaining $I - 1$ have been found), there are $I - 1$ d.f. for SS(Between).

We can use these results to develop a test statistic for the null hypothesis $H_0: \mu_1 = \mu_2 = \cdots = \mu_I$. In Chapter 11 the F statistic was defined to be the ratio of two independent χ^2 variables each divided by its degrees of freedom:

$$F = \frac{\chi_1^2/\text{d.f.}_1}{\chi_2^2/\text{d.f.}_2}$$

Therefore

$$F = \frac{\dfrac{\text{SS(Between)}}{\sigma^2}\bigg/(I-1)}{\dfrac{\text{SS(Within)}}{\sigma^2}\bigg/(n-I)} = \frac{\text{SS(Between)}/(I-1)}{\text{SS(Within)}/(n-I)}$$

mean square (MS) is an F statistic under $H_0: \mu_1 = \mu_2 = \cdots = \mu_I$. The term **mean square (MS)** is given to any sum of squares divided by its degrees of freedom. With this terminology, the F statistic for our analysis of variance is

$$F = \frac{\text{MS(Between)}}{\text{MS(Within)}}$$

Large values of MS(Between) relative to MS(Within) indicate differences among the population means and lead to the rejection of the null hypothesis.

The ANOVA test of the null hypothesis is summarized next:

ANOVA for Testing the Equality of I Group Means

$H_0: \mu_1 = \mu_2 = \cdots = \mu_I$
$H_a:$ Not all μ_i are equal

$$\text{T.S.: } = F = \frac{\text{MS(Between)}}{\text{MS(Within)}} = \frac{\sum_i n_i(\bar{y}_i - \bar{y})^2/(I-1)}{\sum_{ij}(y_{ij} - \bar{y}_i)^2/(n-I)}$$

R.R.: For specified α, reject H_0 if $F > F_\alpha$, where F_α cuts off a right-tail area of α in the F distribution with $I - 1$ numerator and $n - I$ denominator d.f.

We calculated the necessary sums of squares for the supervisor-effectiveness data given near the beginning of this section. The results are usually organized in a so-called ANOVA table, as shown here:

Source	SS	d.f.	MS	F
Between	1466.00	2	733.00	3.20
Within	4124.57	18	229.14	
Total	5590.57	20		

For a test at $\alpha = .05$, we compare the F value of 3.20 to the tabled .05 point (2 and 18 d.f.), namely 3.55. Because $3.20 < 3.55$, we would retain the null hypothesis.

The ANOVA arithmetic is often done by a computer program, but without such help, the pain of hand computation can be eased by shortcut formulas.

Shortcut Formulas for ANOVA Sums of Squares

$$SS(\text{Within}) = \sum_{i,j} y_{ij}^2 - \frac{\sum_i \left(\sum_j y_{ij} \right)^2}{n_i}$$

$$SS(\text{Between}) = \frac{\sum_i \left(\sum_j y_{ij} \right)^2}{n_i} - \frac{\left(\sum_{i,j} y_{ij} \right)^2}{n}$$

$$SS(\text{Total}) = \sum_{i,j} y_{ij}^2 - \frac{\left(\sum_{i,j} y_{ij} \right)^2}{n}$$

$$= SS(\text{Within}) + SS(\text{Between})$$

Alternatively, we can compute the mean $\bar{y}_i$ and variance s_i^2 for each group, indexed by i.

Alternative Method for Computation of Sums of Squares

$$SS(\text{Within}) = \sum_i (n_i - 1)s_i^2$$

$$SS(\text{Between}) = \sum_i n_i (\bar{y}_i - \bar{y})^2$$

$$= \sum_i (n_i \bar{y}_i^2) - n\bar{y}^2$$

where

$$\bar{y} = \frac{\sum_i n_i \bar{y}_i}{n}, \qquad \text{and} \qquad n = \sum n_i$$

EXAMPLE 12.1   A panel of potential cereal-product consumers is asked to rate one of four potential new products. Each member of the panel rates only one of the products and compares it to a standard, existing cereal on a 100-point scale. The scores are

Product I:	16	31	57	62	67	71	73	75				
Product II:	30	35	52	60	64	65	65	67	70	71	75	82
Product III:	43	51	53	54	56	58	61	64	64	67	68	70	71	75	79
Product IV:	29	39	46	50	59	61	62					

Test the hypothesis of equal mean product scores by an ANOVA. First use $\alpha = .05$, then find a p-value.

Solution   A worksheet is shown below:

Product	$\sum_j y_{ij}$	$\left(\sum_j y_{ij}\right)^2$	n_i	$\left(\sum_j y_{ij}\right)^2 \Big/ n_i$	$\sum_j y_{ij}^2$
I	452	204,304	8	25,538.000	28,794
II	736	541,696	12	45,141.333	47,754
III	934	872,356	15	58,157.067	59,508
IV	346	119,716	7	17,102.286	18,024
Total	2468		42	145,938.686	154,080

$$SS(\text{Within}) = 154{,}080 - 145{,}938.686 = 8141.314$$
$$SS(\text{Between}) = 145{,}938.686 - (2468)^2/42 = 914.305$$

We can also use a calculator to find the following results:

Product	$\bar{y}_i$	s_i^2	n_i
I	56.50000	465.1429	8
II	61.33333	237.5152	12
III	62.26667	96.4952	15
IV	49.42857	153.6190	7

The grand mean is

$$\bar{y} = [8(56.50000) + 12(61.33333) + 15(62.26667) + 7(49.42857)]/42$$
$$= 58.76191$$
$$SS(\text{Within}) = 7(465.1429) + 11(237.5152) + 14(96.4952) + 6(153.6190)$$
$$= 8141.314$$
$$SS(\text{Between}) = 8(56.50000)^2 + 12(61.33333)^3 + 15(62.26667)^2$$
$$+ 7(49.42857)^2 - 42(58.76191)^2 = 914.305$$

The ANOVA table is

Source	SS	d.f.	MS	F
Between	914.305	3	304.768	1.422
Within	8141.314	38	214.245	
Total	9055.619	41		

Because $F = 1.422$ is less than 2.84, the $F_{.05}$ value based on 3 and 38 d.f., H_0 is retained. The p-value is larger than .05, most likely quite a bit larger. The observed deviations of sample means are well within the range of random variation. ∎

EXAMPLE 12.2   Suppose that a drug company testing two new products against a currently used drug is concerned about the possible side effect of increased blood pressure. In a clinical trial of the drugs, 12 patients are tested under each drug, at standard dosages. Blood pressures are recorded initially and again one hour after a single dose of the assigned drug product. Blood pressure changes are as follows:

Drug	Blood Pressure Changes											
A	−10	−10	−8	−5	0	3	5	7	8	10	12	15
B	0	5	8	10	12	15	16	17	20	22	25	25
C	−5	−1	0	2	5	8	8	10	14	16	20	20

An ANOVA is performed on the data, using the SAS software, and the output is shown below. Identify the following: The sample means, the mean squares MS(Between) and MS(Within), the value of the F statistic, and the p-value for $H_0: \mu_A = \mu_B = \mu_C$.

ONE FACTOR ANOVA OF BLOOD PRESSURE INCREASES

ANALYSIS OF VARIANCE PROCEDURE

DEPENDENT VARIABLE: CHGBLPR

SOURCE	DF	SUM OF SQUARES	MEAN SQUARE	F VALUE	PR > F	R-SQUARE	C.V.
MODEL	2	913.55555556	456.77777778	6.61	0.0039	0.286055	100.0806
ERROR	33	2280.08333333	69.09343434		ROOT MSE		CHGBLPR MEAN
CORRECTED TOTAL	35	3193.63888889			8.31224605		8.3055555

MEANS

DRUG	N	CHGBLPR
A	12	2.2500000
B	12	14.5833333
C	12	8.0833333

Solution   The sample means are shown as MEANS and they are, respectively, 2.2500000, 14.5833333, and 8.0833333. The mean square for MODEL in this case is MS(Between), namely 456.77777778. MS(Within) is the ERROR mean square, 69.09343434. F is 6.61, and the p-value is PR > F, 0.0039. Thus the evidence for differences in mean blood-pressure change with different drugs is quite conclusive.   ■

normality assumption   Like all statistical inference procedures, this F test is based on certain assumptions. The three basic assumptions are population normality, equal group variances, and independence of observations. The **normality assumption** is perhaps the least crucial. The ANOVA test is a test on means (despite its name); the Central Limit Theorem has its effect. If the populations are badly skewed and if the sample sizes are small (such as 10 each), the Central Limit Theorem effect doesn't take over and the nominal F probabilities may be in error. If the population distributions are roughly symmetric but have heavy tails, as indicated by outliers in the sample data, the F probabilities are reasonably accurate, but alternative procedures may be more efficient (make better use of the data).

assumption of equal variance balanced design

The assumption of equal true variances for each group is important if the sample sizes are substantially different. Many studies have indicated that when all n_i's are equal, in a so-called **balanced design**, the effect of even grossly unequal variances is minimal. However, if the n_i's are substantially different—say, if the largest n_i is at least twice the smallest—then unequal variances can cause major distortions in the nominal F probabilities. The worst case is when large variances occur in groups with small sample sizes. The best way to avoid problems is to strive for equal n_i's.

independence assumption

Violation of the **assumption of independence** can cause a great deal of trouble. When the data arise from a cross-sectional random sample taken at a specific time, independence holds virtually by definition. If the data arise by measurements taken repeatedly over time, there is a possibility of dependence from one measurement to the next. In such situations, nominal F probabilities are very suspect.

EXAMPLE 12.3

Refer to the data of Example 12.1. Is there any indication of trouble because of violation of assumptions?

Solution

The data are cross-sectional, so independence is not a problem. But the data appear to be left-skewed, particularly in groups I and IV, where the sample sizes are small. The variances appear substantially different, and the big variances go with the small n's. The conclusions of the F test in Example 12.1 are very shaky. ∎

12.2   COMPARING SEVERAL DISTRIBUTIONS BY A RANK TEST

In Section 12.1, we noted that one assumption underlying the ANOVA F test was that all populations were normal. If that assumption is incorrect, as evidenced by substantial skewness or outliers in the samples, the nominal probabilities given by the F table may be in error. In addition, the F test may not be efficient. In this section, we introduce the Kruskal-Wallis rank sum test, which doesn't require the normal-population assumption.

The Kruskal-Wallis test is an extension of the Wilcoxon rank sum test we described in Section 10.3. The formal null hypothesis is that all the populations have the same distribution, not necessarily a normal distribution. The formal research hypothesis is that the populations differ in any way; the test is largely sensitive to differences of location (means or medians), rather than differences of variances.

To carry out the test, all the data values are combined and ranked from lowest to highest. In case of ties, average ranks are assigned, as in the Wilcoxon rank sum test. The Kruskal-Wallis statistic may be thought of as

$$H = \frac{12}{n(n+1)} \text{SS(Between, ranks)}$$

where SS(Between, ranks) is the SS(Between) obtained for the rankings rather than the original data, and n is the combined sample size. Thus if the average rank in every sample is equal, H will be 0, but if the average ranks differ greatly among samples (indicating a clear difference in locations), H will be large. Conventionally, the Kruskal-Wallis statistic is stated in terms of T_i, the sum of the ranks in group i, rather than in terms of the average rank. Of course, the average is simply the sum divided by the relevant sample size, so the test could be stated either way.

Kruskal-Wallis Test

H_0: The distributions are identical (effectively, the populations have equal means)

H_a: The distributions differ in location

$$\text{T.S.: } H = \left\{ \frac{12}{n(n+1)} \sum_i \frac{T_i^2}{n_i} \right\} - 3(n+1)$$

where n_i = sample size in sample i, $(i = 1, 2, \ldots, I)$, n = total sample size, and T_i = sum of combined-sample ranks for measurements in sample i

R.R.: For specified α, reject H_0 if $H > \chi_\alpha^2$ where χ_α^2 cuts off a right-tail area α for the χ^2 distribution with $I - 1$ d.f.

EXAMPLE 12.4   Perform a Kruskal-Wallis test for the data of Example 12.1. First use $\alpha = .05$, then find a p-value.

Solution   The data, ranks, and T_i values are shown below:

I		II		III		IV	
Score	Rank	Score	Rank	Score	Rank	Score	Rank
16	1	30	3	43	7	29	2
31	4	35	5	51	10	39	6
57	15	52	11	53	12	46	8
62	21.5	60	18	54	13	50	9
67	29	64	24	56	14	59	17
71	35	65	26.5	58	16	61	19.5
73	37	65	26.5	61	19.5	62	21.5
75	39	67	29	64	24	$T_1 = 83.0$	
	$T_1 = 181.5$	70	32.5	64	24		
		71	35	67	29		
		75	39	68	31		
		82	42	70	32.5		
			$T_1 = 291.5$	71	35		
				75	39		
				79	41		
					$T_1 = 347.0$		

Ties are handled by averaging ranks. For instance, the three 64 scores are tied for ranks 23, 24, and 25 and are all assigned rank 24. Here $n = 42$ (and, as a check, the highest rank is 42).

$$H = \frac{12}{(42)(43)}\left\{\frac{(181.5)^2}{8} + \frac{(291.5)^2}{12} + \frac{(347)^2}{15} + \frac{(83)^2}{7}\right\} - 3(43)$$

$$= \frac{12}{(42)(43)}(20,210.212) - 3(43) = 5.287$$

The right-tail .05 point for χ^2 with $4 - 1 = 3$ d.f. is 7.81; because $H = 5.287 < 7.81$, H_0 is retained. At $\alpha = .10$, the table value is 6.25, so the p-value $> .10$. The result agrees with the F test result of Example 12.1. Had there been a conflict, we would have believed the Kruskal-Wallis result because of the major violations of F test assumptions we discussed in Example 12.3. ∎

SECTIONS 12.1 AND 12.2 EXERCISES

12.1 A test is made of five different incentive-pay schemes for piecerate workers. Eight workers are assigned randomly to each plan. The total number of items produced by each worker over a 20-day period is recorded.

	Plan				
	A	B	C	D	E
Production	1106	1214	1010	1054	1210
	1203	1186	1069	1101	1193
	1064	1165	1047	1029	1169
	1119	1177	1120	1066	1223
	1087	1146	1084	1082	1161
	1106	1099	1062	1067	1200
	1101	1161	1051	1109	1189
	1049	1153	1029	1083	1197
Mean	1104.38	1162.62	1059.00	1073.88	1192.75
Variance	2136.55	1116.84	1137.71	662.41	409.93
$\sum y_{ij}$	8835	9301	8472	8591	9542
$\sum y_{ij}^2$	9,772,109	10,821,393	8,979,812	9,230,297	11,384,090

a. Calculate the grand mean.
b. Calculate SS(Between) from the definition (page 476).
c. Use the fact that SS(Within) $= \sum_i (n_i - 1)s_i^2$ to calculate SS(Within).
d. What are the appropriate degrees of freedom for these sums of squares?

12.2 Refer to the data of Exercise 12.1. Use the shortcut formula (page 479) to calculate SS(Between) and SS(Within).

12.3 Perform the ANOVA F test for the data of Exercise 12.1. State bounds on the p-value. What would you conclude?

12.4   Plot the data of Exercise 12.1 by plan. Do there appear to be any blatant violations of assumptions?

12.5   Perform a Kruskal-Wallis test on the data of Exercise 12.1. Place bounds on the *p*-value.

12.6   How do the results of the *F* test and Kruskal-Wallis test on the data of Exercise 12.1 compare? Does it matter much which test is used?

12.7   A data-processing firm administers an aptitude test to all applicants for programming jobs. The results of these tests are analyzed by the source (general advertising, trade journal advertising, employment agency, personal recommendation, or off the street).

Source						Score								
Genadv	36	47	38	51	62	78	60	47	49	53	26	38	61	39	43
Tradej	58	64	62	47	71	90	65	82	61	59				
Agency	47	59	48	81	66	50	42	53						
Recomm	67	61	82	97	65	72	54	69	58					
Street	38	47	80	41	38	66	50							

An SAS analysis of this data is given below:

```
                              ANALYSIS OF VARIANCE PROCEDURE

DEPENDENT VARIABLE: SCORE

SOURCE            DF    SUM OF SQUARES    MEAN SQUARE    F VALUE    PR > F    R-SQUARE       C.V.

MODEL              4    3478.17505669    869.54376417      4.92    0.0023    0.308890    23.1247

ERROR             44    7782.06984127    176.86522367                ROOT MSE          SCORE MEAN

CORRECTED TOTAL   48   11260.24489796                              13.29906853        57.51020408

                                          MEANS

                          SOURCE      N        SCORE

                          AGENCY      8     55.7500000
                          GENADV     15     48.5333333
                          RECOMM      9     69.4444444
                          STREET      7     51.4285714
                          TRADEJ     10     65.9000000

                                                        PROGRAMMER APTITUDE SCORE

        ANALYSIS FOR VARIABLE SCORE CLASSIFIED BY VARIABLE  SOURCE

               AVERAGE SCORES WERE USED FOR TIES

            WILCOXON SCORES (RANK SUMS)

                          SUM OF    EXPECTED    STD DEV      MEAN
        LEVEL        N    SCORES    UNDER HO    UNDER HO     SCORE

        GENADV      15    247.00    375.00       46.05       16.47
        TRADEJ      10    331.50    250.00       40.27       33.15
        AGENCY       8    187.00    200.00       36.93       23.37
        RECOMM       9    329.50    225.00       38.69       36.61
        STREET       7    130.00    175.00       34.96       18.57

        KRUSKAL-WALLIS TEST (CHI-SQUARE APPROXIMATION)
        CHISQ= 16.10    DF= 4    PROB > CHISQ=0.0029
```

a. Find the sums of squares.

b. Locate the value of the F statistic.

c. Test the null hypothesis of equal mean aptitude, using $\alpha = .01$.

12.8 Plot the data of Exercise 12.7 by source. Are there any obvious violations of the ANOVA assumptions?

12.9 a. Locate the value of the Kruskal-Wallis statistic for the output of Exercise 12.7.

b. Can the hypothesis of equal locations be rejected at $\alpha = .05$?

c. Compare the conclusions of the F test and the Kruskal-Wallis test. Does it matter much which test is used?

12.10 A supermarket experimented with three different staffing policies to try to determine when to open new cash registers or add more staff in service areas (such as the deli section). The time of most concern is weekdays between 5 and 6 P.M. when the store is.crowded with impatient shoppers. The manager of the store was told to vary the three different staffing policies in a random way. A hired shopper came in each weekday shortly after 5 P.M. and measured the waiting time (in minutes) needed to obtained a standard set of items. The data were as follows:

day	wait	policy	day	wait	policy
1	6.5	1	19	8.3	1
2	5.4	1	20	2.4	2
3	6.5	2	21	1.0	2
4	4.4	1	22	3.4	2
5	3.4	3	23	5.1	1
6	3.2	3	24	4.3	3
7	1.6	2	25	1.3	2
8	7.4	3	26	11.6	1
9	9.6	3	27	7.5	1
10	2.8	3	28	6.6	1
11	15.5	3	29	4.8	3
12	4.7	1	30	6.3	2
13	3.7	2	31	8.2	1
14	7.3	1	32	12.2	1
15	6.6	3	33	0.5	2
16	8.5	1	34	17.9	3
17	4.4	1	35	17.7	1
18	0.9	2	36	8.7	1

a. Find mean and standard deviation of times for each policy. Find the grand mean.

b. Verify that SS(Between) $= 183.9$ and SS(Within) $= 477.8$.

c. Calculate df and MS values, between and within groups.

12.11 a. Calculate the F statistic for testing the null hypothesis of equal means, using the results of Exercise 12.10.

b. Can this null hypothesis be rejected at $\alpha = .01$?

c. Place bounds on the p-value.

12.12 a. Construct stem-and-leaf displays of the waiting time data in Exercise 12.10.

b. Based on the data plots and on your own experience waiting in supermarkets, would it seem reasonable to you to assume normal populations?

c. If the populations are, in fact, moderately nonnormal, does that mean that the conclusions of Exercise 12.11 are completely invalid?

12.13 a. Plot the data of Exercise 12.10 against day number. Is there clear evidence of an upward or downward trend, or of a cyclic pattern?

b. Suppose a cyclic pattern had been found, with high values usually followed by other high values, and lows usually followed by lows. Which assumption underlying analysis of variance would be called into question?

12.14 a. A Kruskal-Wallis test was performed on the waiting time data of Exercise 12.10. The following results were obtained.

$$H = 14.34$$
$$H(\text{ADJ. FOR TIES}) = 14.34$$

Recall that we were comparing times among three groups. According to the Kruskal-Wallis results, is there a statistically detectable (significant) difference in times among the groups?

b. Apparently, there is an adjustment made to the test when there is tied data (equal values). In this case, how important is the adjustment?

c. Is the result we found here greatly different from the result we found by an F test in Exercise 12.11?

12.15 A nationwide chain of automobile repair shops had a standard procedure for dealing with complaints of improper work. As part of a systematic practice of checking customer satisfaction, regional managers reviewed records of all complaints; one particular concern was the number of business days required before each complaint was resolved. A regional manager obtained samples of records from each of the districts in the region. Computer output of the results is shown here.

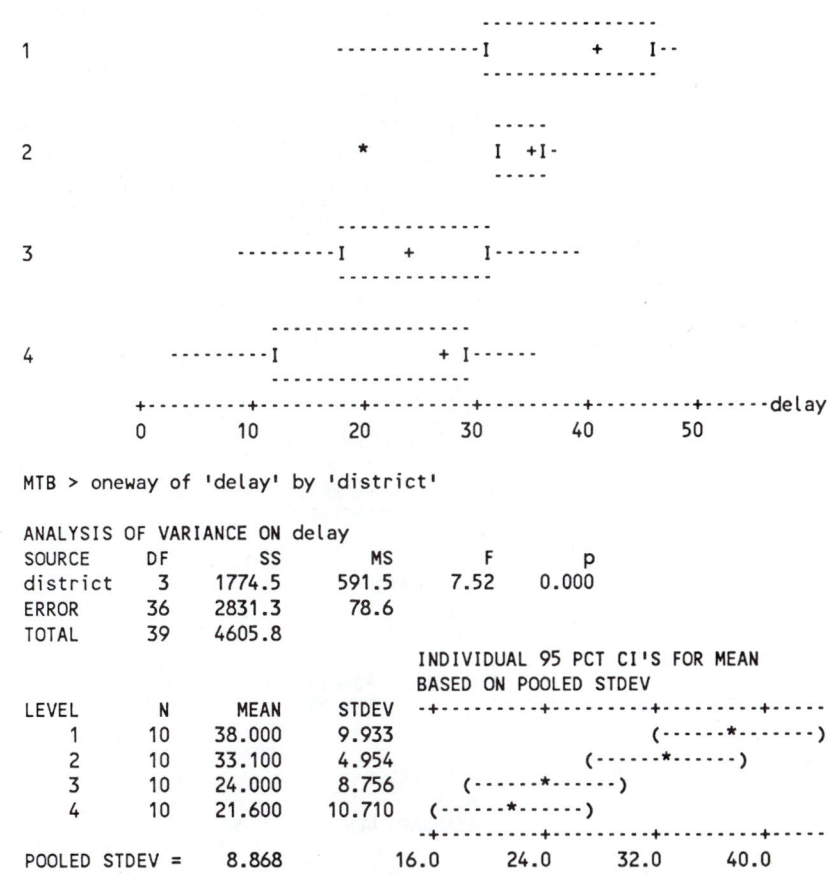

```
district

1                                      -------------I     +    I--
                                       ----------------

                                           -----
2                       *              I  +I-
                                           -----

                            ---------------
3                       --------I     +     I--------
                            ---------------

                        -------------------
4              --------I              + I------
                        -------------------
       +---------+---------+---------+---------+---------+------delay
       0        10        20        30        40        50

MTB > oneway of 'delay' by 'district'

ANALYSIS OF VARIANCE ON delay
SOURCE      DF      SS        MS       F        p
district     3    1774.5    591.5    7.52    0.000
ERROR       36    2831.3     78.6
TOTAL       39    4605.8
                                    INDIVIDUAL 95 PCT CI'S FOR MEAN
                                    BASED ON POOLED STDEV
LEVEL        N    MEAN      STDEV    -+---------+---------+---------+-----
    1       10    38.000    9.933                          (------*-------)
    2       10    33.100    4.954                    (------*------)
    3       10    24.000    8.756         (------*------)
    4       10    21.600   10.710    (------*------)
                                    -+---------+---------+---------+-----
POOLED STDEV =     8.868              16.0      24.0      32.0      40.0
```

a. Is the value of F statistically significant at $\alpha = .05$?

b. What is the meaning of the indicated p-value?

12.16 According to the boxplots shown in Exercise 12.15, is there strong evidence that the data are not coming from normal populations? If so, does that mean that the conclusions drawn in Exercise 12.15 are likely to be wrong?

12.17 A Kruskal-Wallis test of the delay time data for the repair chain was performed and yielded the following computer output:

```
MTB > kruskal wallis of 'delay' by 'district'

LEVEL    NOBS    MEDIAN  AVE. RANK    Z VALUE
  1        10     41.00     29.8        2.90
  2        10     34.50     25.6        1.61
  3        10     24.00     14.1       -2.00
  4        10     26.50     12.4       -2.51
OVERALL    40               20.5

H = 16.01
H(ADJ. FOR TIES) = 16.05
```

Is there a statistically significant difference among the four levels (which were the four districts in a particular region), say using $\alpha = .01$?

12.18 For the Kruskal-Wallis analysis in Exercise 12.17, state bounds on the p-value. Is there a radical difference between this p-value and the one from the F test of Exercise 12.15?

12.19 In Exercise 11.18, we considered the rate of response to a direct-mail catalog. The retailer used three different ways of incorporating an order form into the catalog. In the exercise, we found that there was a distinct difference in the probability of receiving an order, given the different types of order form. Another relevant question for the retailer is the dollar amount of each order. The total sale for each order received was recorded; the data were analyzed by Systat. Here are some of the results.

```
THE FOLLOWING RESULTS ARE FOR:
          FORMTYPE      =      1.000

                  SALETOT
N OF CASES            56
MEAN              63.610
STANDARD DEV      57.695

THE FOLLOWING RESULTS ARE FOR:
          FORMTYPE      =      2.000

                  SALETOT
N OF CASES            39
MEAN              53.026
STANDARD DEV      68.825

THE FOLLOWING RESULTS ARE FOR:
          FORMTYPE      =      3.000

                  SALETOT
N OF CASES            85
MEAN              65.534
STANDARD DEV      58.942
```

ANALYSIS OF VARIANCE

SOURCE	SUM OF SQUARES	DF	MEAN SQUARE	F	PROBABILITY
BETWEEN GROUPS	4338.442	2	2169.221	.586	.557
WITHIN GROUPS	654908.800	177	3700.050		

    a. Are there statistically detectable differences among the means, using any reasonable alpha value?

    b. How much evidence is there that the type of order form influences the amount of sale?

12.20 In the output of Exercise 12.19, the standard deviations are about as big as the means, so a value that is one standard deviation below the mean would be essentially $0. The Empirical Rule indicates that a substantial proportion of individual scores should be even less than one standard deviation below the mean, but a negative order amount is impossible (the retailer fervently hopes).

    a. What do these facts suggest about the shape of the data?

    b. What assumption of analysis of variance seems likely to be violated in this situation?

12.21 Further Systat output for the data of Exercise 12.19 was obtained and is shown here.

```
KRUSKAL-WALLIS ONE-WAY ANALYSIS OF VARIANCE FOR 180 CASES
    DEPENDENT VARIABLE IS  SALETOT
    GROUPING VARIABLE IS FORMTYPE

    GROUP     COUNT   RANK SUM
        1.000   56      5245.0
        2.000   39      3021.0
        3.000   85      8024.0

KRUSKAL-WALLIS TEST STATISTIC =    3.12
PROBABILITY IS  .210 ASSUMING CHI-SQUARE DISTRIBUTION WITH  2 DF
```

    Does the Kruskal-Wallis result conclusively indicate that there is a difference in the average SALETOT for the three FORMTYPE groups?

12.3   SPECIFIC COMPARISONS AMONG MEANS   ■

The ANOVA F test and the Kruskal-Wallis test developed in Section 12.1 test for an overall pattern of discrepancies among the group means. Rejection of the hypothesis that all population (group) means are equal does not indicate specifically which means are not equal. In this section we outline one of many possible methods for assessing differences among specified means. Several other methods are discussed in Ott (1984), and there are other minor variations available. We state this method in terms of confidence intervals. As usual, we can use the resulting intervals to perform hypothesis tests.

    One approach would be to use the t methods of Chapter 10 to construct t-type confidence intervals for all possible pairs of means. The objection to this is essentially the same as our objection to multiple t tests in the previous section. While the confidence level for each interval separately may be 95%, there is no way to measure the overall confidence that all the intervals are correct. We use the Tukey method in this section to yield a desired overall confidence level.

Formally, we again assume that the data constitute independent random samples from I groups or subpopulations. The groups are labeled by the index i, where $i = 1, 2, \ldots I$, and the sample size for group i is n_i. We assume that the population distribution in group i is normal with mean μ_i and variance σ^2. There is no subscript on σ^2 because we assume that the population variances for all groups are identical. The estimate $\hat{\sigma}^2$ is MS (Within), which is a generalization of the pooled variance we defined in Chapter 10.

Tukey method   The **Tukey method** is designed specifically to compare any two means, say, $\bar{y}_i$ and $\bar{y}_{i*}$. The underlying mathematical theory assumes that all sample sizes are equal: $n_1 = n_2 = \cdots = n_I$. The common sample size is usually denoted n. Note that here n means the individual sample size, *not* the overall sample size.

100(1 − α)% Confidence Intervals for All Pairs of Means, Using Tukey's Method

$$(\bar{y}_i - \bar{y}_{i*}) - q_\alpha(I, \text{d.f.}_2)\sqrt{\text{MS(Within)}/n} < \mu_i - \mu_{i*}$$
$$< (\bar{y}_i - \bar{y}_{i*}) + q_\alpha(I, \text{d.f.}_2)\sqrt{\text{MS(Within)}/n}$$

where n is the sample size for each sample, I is the number of samples, d.f._2 is the degrees of freedom for MS(Within) and $q_\alpha(I, \text{d.f.}_2)$ is found in Appendix Table 8. There is 100(1 − α)% confidence that **all possible** intervals comparing two means are correct.

EXAMPLE 12.5   Construct (overall) 95% confidence intervals for the differences in mean blood-pressure increase for the data of Example 12.2.

Solution   The relevant summary statistics are

Drug i	A	B	C
$\bar{y}_i$	2.25	14.58	8.08
n_i	12	12	12
MS(Within) = 69.09			

The desired $q_\alpha(I, \text{d.f.}_2)$ value has $\alpha = .05$, $I = 3$, and $\text{d.f.}_2 = 33$. There is no $\text{d.f.}_2 = 33$ entry in Appendix Table 8, so we use $\text{d.f.}_2 = 30$, $q_{.05}(3, 30) = 3.49$. It's clear from the table that $q_{.05}(3, 30)$ is just a little larger than the desired $q_{.05}(3, 33)$, so we err slightly on the conservative (wider interval) side. The desired 95% confidence intervals are

$$(14.58 - 2.25) - 3.49\sqrt{69.09/12} \leq \mu_B - \mu_A$$
$$\leq (14.58 - 2.25) + 3.49\sqrt{69.09/12}$$

$$(8.08 - 14.58) - 3.49\sqrt{69.09/12} \leq \mu_C - \mu_B$$
$$\leq (8.08 - 14.58) + 3.49\sqrt{69.09/12}$$

$$(8.08 - 2.25) - 3.49\sqrt{69.09/12} \leq \mu_C - \mu_A$$
$$\leq (8.08 - 2.25) + 3.49\sqrt{69.09/12}$$

or

$$3.96 \leq \mu_B - \mu_A \leq 20.70$$
$$-14.87 \leq \mu_C - \mu_B \leq 1.87$$
$$-2.54 \leq \mu_C - \mu_A \leq 14.20$$

Recall that confidence intervals may be used to conduct (two-sided) hypothesis tests. The natural null hypothesis, $H_0: \mu_i - \mu_{i*} = 0$, is rejected if zero does not fall in the interval. In Example 12.5, the 95% confidence intervals indicate that at $\alpha = 0.05$ we can reject $\mu_B - \mu_A = 0$ but must retain $\mu_C - \mu_B = 0$ and $\mu_C - \mu_A = 0$. We conclude that the mean blood-pressure increase under drug B is higher than under drug A. Drug C is in the middle, and the difference of $\bar{y}_C$ from either $\bar{y}_A$ or $\bar{y}_B$ could be the result of random variation. ■

The formal assumption in the Tukey method that $n_1 = n_2 = \cdots = n_I$ may be relaxed somewhat. As long as the n_i's are not drastically indifferent, say, if the largest n_i is no more than twice the smallest, the Tukey method may be used with

$$n = \frac{1}{\dfrac{1}{n_1} + \dfrac{1}{n_2} + \cdots + \dfrac{1}{n_I}}$$

harmonic mean   the so-called **harmonic mean** of the n_i's.

SECTION 12.3   EXERCISES

12.22 Refer to the data of Exercise 12.1.
   a. Calculate overall 95% confidence intervals for all possible differences of means.
   b. Which differences can be declared significant at $\alpha = .05$?

12.23 a. Instead of the Tukey method of Exercise 12.22, calculate 10 separate 99.5% confidence intervals for all 10 possible differences in means. The required t-table value is 2.977.
   b. If each interval has probability .005 of being wrong, do you think that the overall probability of error exceeds .05? Justify your answer.

12.24 Compare the widths of the intervals in Exercises 12.22 and 12.23.

12.25 Refer to the data of Exercise 12.7. Which pairs of means can be declared significantly different using $\alpha = .01$? Note the unbalanced design.

12.26 a. The means, standard deviations, sample sizes, and MS(Within) for the supermarket waiting times in Exercise 12.10 are shown here.

MS(Within) = 14.5, 33 degrees of freedom

Policy	n	mean	st. dev.
1	16	7.944	3.487
2	10	2.760	2.188
3	10	7.550	5.294

Calculate overall 95% confidence intervals for the differences of all pairs of means. You will need to use the modification for unequal sample sizes.

b. Based on these confidence intervals, which means, if any, are detectably (significantly) different?

12.27 The data in Exercise 12.10 were collected by asking the store manager to specify a policy for the day haphazardly. What would be a better way to obtain the data?

12.28 The relevant computer output for the delay time data for Exercise 12.15 is reproduced here.

```
MTB > oneway of 'delay' by 'district'

ANALYSIS OF VARIANCE ON delay
SOURCE      DF       SS       MS       F       p
district     3    1774.5    591.5    7.52    0.000
ERROR       36    2831.3     78.6
TOTAL       39    4605.8
                                      INDIVIDUAL 95 PCT CI'S FOR MEAN
                                      BASED ON POOLED STDEV
LEVEL       N      MEAN    STDEV   -+---------+---------+---------+-----
    1      10    38.000    9.933                     (------*------)
    2      10    33.100    4.954                (------*------)
    3      10    24.000    8.756        (------*------)
    4      10    21.600   10.710    (------*------)
                                    -+---------+---------+---------+-----
POOLED STDEV =    8.868           16.0      24.0      32.0      40.0
```

Calculate 99% Tukey confidence intervals for the differences of all pairs of means. Do the results indicate that any of the pairs are significantly different?

12.4   TWO-FACTOR EXPERIMENTS

Until now, we have considered only single-factor experiments in which one variable is manipulated. Often managers can learn more with more complex experiments. It is perfectly possible to vary several experimental factors in the same experiment. In this section, we describe the basic ideas and computations that arise when there are two factors being varied. In this context, we will describe a fundamental statistical idea, interaction.

For example, a clothing contractor who supplies military uniforms must cut fabric for coats, shirts, and pants (in many different sizes) from layers of fabric. The fabric is expensive, so wastage has a big effect on profitability. The contractor has a choice among three computer-aided cutting machines, A, B, and C. Rather than guessing which machine would give the least wastage, the contractor can experiment by having each machine cut several lots for coats, several more for shirts, and several more for pants. This experiment has two factors—the machine and the type of garment. One possible set of mean wastage percentages is shown in the next table.

| | Factor 2 (Type of Garment) | | | |
Factor 1 (Machine)	Coats	Shirts	Pants	Avg.
A	7.6	9.1	7.3	8.0
B	6.5	8.0	6.2	6.9
C	5.1	6.6	4.8	5.5
Avg.	6.4	7.9	6.1	6.8

In this table, there's a consistent pattern. Machine A is consistently 1.1 percentage points higher (poorer) in wastage than machine B, whether we consider coats, shirts, or pants. In turn, machine B is consistently 1.4 percentage points higher than machine C. The consistency goes the other direction, too; shirts have a 1.5 percentage point higher wastage than coats and a 1.8 percentage point higher wastage than pants, which is consistent in all three machines.

Alternatively, the means might look like the following table.

| | Factor 2 (Type of Garment) | | | |
Factor 1 (Machine)	Coats	Shirts	Pants	Avg.
A	5.1	11.1	7.8	8.0
B	8.1	8.5	4.1	6.9
C	6.0	4.1	6.4	5.5
Avg.	6.4	7.9	6.1	6.8

interaction

In this second table, the averages across rows or down columns are exactly the same as in the first table, but the pattern is *not* consistent. For example, machine A is 3.0 percentage points lower than B for coats, but 2.6 points *higher* for shirts, and 3.7 points higher for pants. The second table shows an **interaction** between machine and garment type factors; there is no such interaction in the first table.

Interaction can be described in several equivalent ways. **Two experimental factors interact in their effect on a response variable if the effect of changing one factor depends on the level of the other factor.** In the second table, changing from machine A to machine B increases the wastage by 3.0 points for coats, decreases it 2.6 points for shirts, and decreases it 3.7 points for pants. Which machine is better? It depends on what type of garment we're cutting. This "it depends" answer is characteristic of interaction. What type of garment has the lowest wastage in the second table? It depends on which machine we're using.

Another way to say the same thing is that, when interaction is present, differences for one factor themselves differ as we change the other factor. The difference between A and B changes as we change type of garment in the second table.

effect

A more mathematical description of interaction depends on the idea of effect of a factor. The (main) **effect** of one level of a factor is the difference between its mean response and the grand mean. In either of the preceding tables, the effect of machine A is $8.0 - 6.8 = 1.2$, the effect of B is $6.9 - 6.8 = 0.1$, and the effect of C is $5.5 - 6.8 = -1.3$. (In passing, note that the effects must sum to 0, because they are deviations from a mean. With three levels of a factor, only two of the effects are free to vary, so there are two degrees of freedom, as we said in Section 12.1.) Similarly, the garment type effects are -0.4 for coats, 1.1 for shirts, and -0.7 for pants.

Effects are used to define models for cell means, where a cell is a particular combination of a row and a column (just like spreadsheet computer programs). The **additive model** is

additive model

cell mean = grand mean + row effect + column effect

For example, for machine A working on coats the additive model would predict a mean of $6.8 + (1.2) + (-0.4) = 7.6$; for machine C working on pants, the model predicts a mean of $6.8 + (-1.3) + (-0.7) = 4.8$. These predictions for the additive model are exactly correct for the first table. **When there is no interaction, the additive model is exactly correct. When there is interaction, effects are not additive, and the additive model is incorrect.** Another way to define interaction is that there is a "combination effect" for the levels of the two factors that cannot be predicted by adding the separate effects of the levels. For example, in the second table, adding the effects of machine A and of coats to the grand mean yields a predicted mean of 7.6; but this particular combination actually yields a mean of 5.1, substantially lower than we would predict from the separate effects of machine A and of coats.

EXAMPLE 12.6   A drug company tests the average decrease in blood pressure for both female and male patients. A table of means, based on sufficiently large samples that we can ignore sampling error, is shown here.

Drug	Gender		Average
	Female	Male	
A	10.8	12.8	11.8
B	9.8	10.4	10.1
C	8.2	9.2	8.7
Average	9.6	10.8	10.2

a. Is there some degree of interaction between the drug and gender factors?

b. Construct a table of predicted means, using the additive model. Does a comparison of actual means with additive model values indicate the presence of interaction here?

Solution   a. There are several ways to check for interaction. We could compare drug A to drug B; the difference is $10.8 - 9.8 = 1.0$ for females and $12.8 - 10.4 = 2.4$ for males. The difference between mean blood pressure decreases for drugs A and B depends on the gender of the patient, so there is interaction. Also, the B − C difference is 1.6 for females and 1.2 for males, so again interaction is shown. In this case, the interaction is not extremely large. Drug A shows the highest decrease in blood pressure for both females and males, drug C the lowest for both.

b. It's convenient to put the effects (mean−grand mean) in the rows and columns of the table. For example, the effect for drug A is $11.8 − 10.2 = 1.6$; the effect for females is $9.6 − 10.2 = −0.6$. Then we can fill in the cells for an additive model. We show the computations for females; the ones for males are similar.

Drug	Gender		
	Female	Male	Effect
A	$10.2 + 1.6 − 0.6 = 11.2$	12.4	$(+1.6)$
B	$10.2 − 0.1 − 0.6 = 9.5$	10.7	$(−0.1)$
C	$10.2 − 1.5 − 0.6 = 8.1$	9.2	$(−1.5)$
Effect	$(−0.6)$	$(+0.6)$	Gr. mean 10.2

The results for the additive model do not equal the actual means, so again we see interaction. The actual mean for (A, Female) is 10.8; the additive model for this cell is 11.2, a slightly different number. Note that the additive model values are close to the actual means, though not identical; again, the interaction seems to be small.   ■

profile plot   A very convenient check for interaction is a **profile plot**. Label the horizontal axis with levels of one factor—it doesn't matter which one—and the vertical axis for means. Plot each mean as a point, and connect the points corresponding to a level of the other factor. For example, Figure 12.1 (page 496) shows profile plots for the two tables of wastage means for the military clothing contractor example at the beginning of this section. The first table shows no interaction at all. Notice that the profile lines are exactly parallel. When there's no interaction, the differences between means for levels of one factor are equal over all levels of the other factor; that's why the no-interaction profiles are parallel. The second table has large interaction and the profile plot shows the interaction by definite nonparallel profiles.

EXAMPLE 12.7   In Example 12.6, we noted that the means exhibited interaction, but the interaction didn't seem large. Construct a profile plot. How does it display the small interaction.

Solution   Several computer packages can produce plots with labels on each point. The following plot (Figure 12.2, page 497) is from Minitab, with the drugs identified as A, B, and C. Gender = 1 was (arbitrarily) taken as Female, 2 as Male. If you draw lines connecting the two A's, the two B's, and the two C's, you will see that they aren't parallel. Therefore, the profile plot shows interaction. They are not far from parallel though, which indicates that the interaction is small.   ■

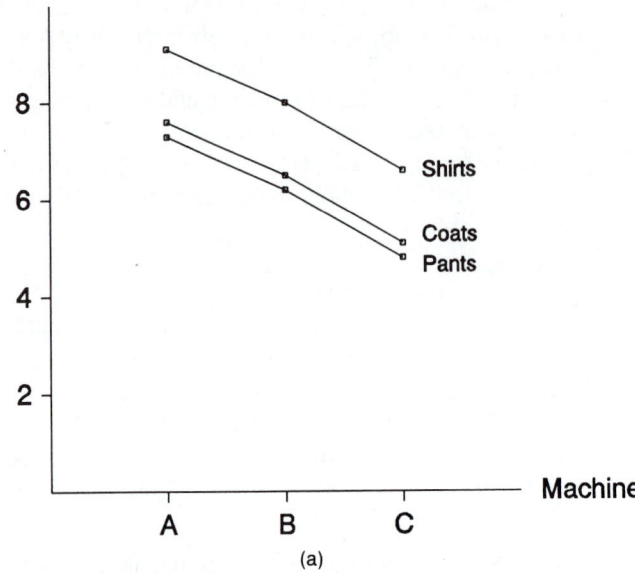

(a)

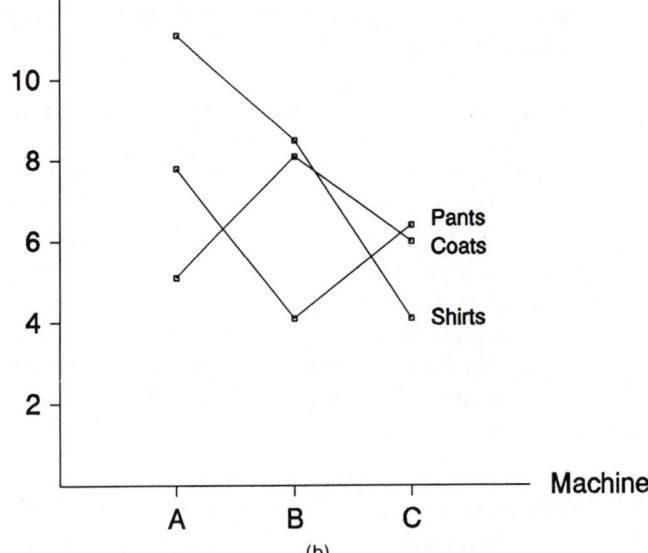

(b)

FIGURE 12.1   Profile Plots for Wastage Means: (a) No Interaction; (b) Interaction

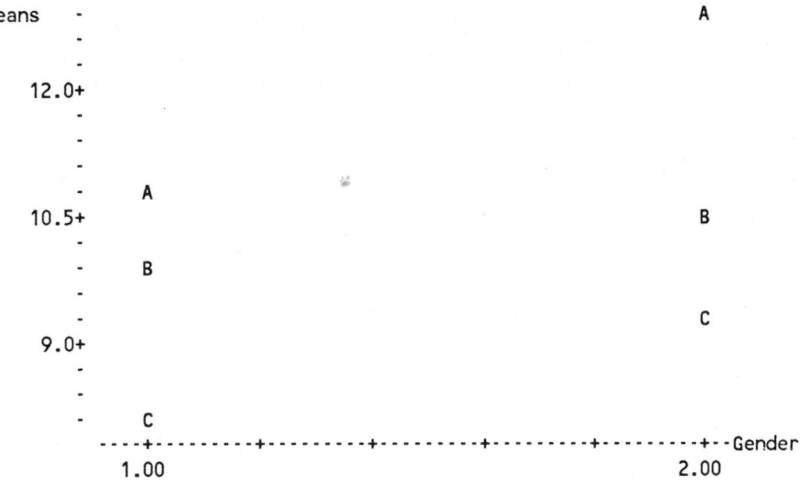

FIGURE 12.2   Profile Plot for Blood Pressure Means

A full model for a two-factor experiment allows for possible interaction of the factors. The **general model** is

general model

Individual score = grand mean + row factor effect
$$+ \text{ column factor effect } + \text{ interaction } + \text{ random error}$$

or

$$Y_{ijk} = \mu + \alpha_i + \beta_j + \delta_{ij} + \varepsilon_{ijk}$$

The additive model assumes that the δ_{ij} (interaction) term is 0. An analysis of variance (ANOVA) for a two-factor experiment will take apart SS(Total), which is the total squared variation (of individual scores around the grand mean) into components that correspond to terms in the model:

$$\text{SS(row effect} + \text{SS(column effect)} + \text{SS(interaction)} + \text{SS(error)}.$$

There's enough arithmetic involved to make a computer package very useful. We will discuss how to use computer output for two-factor experiments first, before we consider how the arithmetic is done.

balanced design

One key to computer analysis is that most packages assume **balanced design**—equal numbers of observations in all cells. The analysis for unbalanced designs is possible but more subtle. Whenever possible, multiple-factor experiments should have balanced designs; we will assume balance throughout the rest of this section.

Virtually every computer package will produce an ANOVA table for a two-factor experiment. The table consists of sums of squares for rows, columns, interaction, and error—in that order unless otherwise specified—the associated degrees of freedom (d.f.), and mean squares, defined as sums of squares divided by d.f. For example, consider an experiment to measure the heat loss through four different types of commercial thermal window glass. Five different levels of exterior temperature setting are used. Three panes of each type are tested at each temperature setting, and the heat loss is recorded for each pane. The data are shown here.

Exterior Temperature i	Pane Type j			
	A	B	C	D
60	3.2	7.5	10.3	12.4
	3.9	8.3	11.5	13.6
	4.3	8.0	10.9	12.9
50	5.7	10.6	12.9	15.0
	6.6	10.1	13.4	14.8
	6.1	9.7	13.0	15.5
40	7.5	11.0	13.4	15.5
	7.0	11.6	14.6	16.1
	6.5	10.7	14.0	16.2
30	8.0	12.0	14.6	17.5
	7.7	12.4	15.0	17.1
	8.2	11.7	15.3	16.4
20	10.1	13.6	17.1	18.8
	9.9	14.0	17.0	19.2
	10.0	14.5	16.8	18.8

The Minitab package produced the following ANOVA table:

```
SOURCE        DF       SS        MS
Temp           4   243.288    60.822
Panetype       3   689.244   229.748
INTERACTION   12     0.074     0.006
ERROR         40     7.353     0.184
TOTAL         59   939.960
```

A similar table could be obtained from most packages. The names for the sums of squares may vary; in particular, the error SS is sometimes called the within-cell SS or the residual SS. Interaction is often indicated by "multiplication" of factor names; for example, some packages might indicate the interaction of Temp and Panetype by Temp*Panetype or T*P. Don't treat this "multiplication" notation as literal multiplication; for our purposes, it's just conventional notation.

The first task in any two-factor experiment is to check for interaction. A profile plot is always a good idea; the profiles for the heat-loss data are very close to parallel, which indicates little or no interaction. The ANOVA tables allow for a formal F test of the null hypothesis of no interaction.

Test for Interaction

1. H_0: No interaction, $\delta_{ij} = 0$ for all i, j
2. H_a: Interaction, $\delta_{ij} \neq 0$ for at least some i, j
3. T.S.: $F = MS(\text{Interaction})/MS(\text{Error})$
4. R.R.: $F > F$; the numerator d.f. are the indicated d.f. for interaction, the denominator d.f. are the error d.f.

For the heat-loss data, the computer output yields $F = 0.006/0.184 = 0.03$, with 12 numerator d.f. and 40 denominator d.f. There's no need to even look this value up in the table; the expected value of an F statistic when H_0 is true is about 1.0, so $F = 0.03$ isn't even close to the expected value, let alone to the right-tail rejection region. (Note that all entries in the F table are greater than 1.0.) Thus we have no indication of interaction, either by the formal F test or by the profile plot.

EXAMPLE 12.8   A consultant tested three different sets of materials for teaching basic statistical concepts. Three groups were the target audiences: College students, production workers, and staff managers. Randomly, 20 individuals from each group were taught with each set of materials. A score that measures ability to use statistical ideas in context was obtained for each individual. The data were analyzed using Systat and the following ANOVA table was obtained:

SOURCE	SUM-OF-SQUARES	DF	MEAN-SQUARE	F-RATIO	P
GROUP	195.300	2	97.650	0.992	0.373
MATERIAL	1435.633	2	717.817	7.291	0.001
GROUP* MATERIAL	6633.667	4	1658.417	16.845	0.000
ERROR	16835.200	171	98.451		

The means were condensed from (rather long) Systat output:

	Material		
Group	A	B	C
Students	72.10	74.00	75.65
Workers	82.50	69.00	63.05
Managers	66.50	84.90	68.85

Is there evidence of interaction?

Solution   The F test for interaction is shown, using the "multiplication" notation GROUP*MATERIAL, as $F = 16.845$, with a p-value 0.000. Interaction is significant (detectable) at any reasonable alpha value. Just by looking at the means, we can see the interaction. As we go from A to B to C, the mean increases slightly for students, decreases sharply for workers, and first increases then decreases for managers. A profile plot would be thoroughly nonparallel. There is substantial, significant interaction. ∎

Further analysis of two-factor experiments usually depends on the result of the interaction check. If interaction is not close to significant (perhaps with a p-value around .25 or higher), or if the profile plots are close enough to parallel that we consider interaction to be negligible, we can assume the additive model

$$Y_{ijk} = \mu + \alpha_i + \beta_j + \varepsilon_{ijk}$$

main effects   with $\gamma_{ij} = 0$. In this case the **main effects** α_i and β_j become relevant. These are differences between row (or column) averages and the grand mean. Thus, if the means for all levels of the row factor are equal—and therefore are equal to the grand mean—the row effects are 0. To say that the row factor means differ is to say that there are nonzero row effects. The ANOVA table also yields an F test for row effects and for column effects. Technically, these tests are valid only for **fixed factors**, those for which the levels constitute the entire set of relevant levels. Most management experiments meet this condition; the exceptional **random factors**, in which the levels are only a sample of the relevant levels (like a sample of teachers leading classes, or a sample of possible orderings of a report) must be handled by more advanced methods.

Test for Row and Column Effects

1. H_0: No row effects; $\alpha_i = 0$ for all i
2. H_a: There are row effects
3. T.S.: $F = $ MS(Row factor)/MS(Error)
4. R.R.: Reject H_0 if $F > F_\alpha$, the tabled F value with numerator d.f. = d.f. for row factor and denominator d.f. = error d.f.

Note: To test column effects, replace "row" by "column"

In the example of four types of window panes, the relevant effect to test is Panetype; we don't need a statistical test to know that outside temperature has an effect on heat loss through windows. For Panetype, the output yields $F = 229.748/0.184$ with 3 and 40 d.f.; this is a huge number, far beyond all table values. Therefore we have conclusive evidence that there are real, more than random, differences in mean heat loss among types. Recall that in this example we found that there was no temperature-panetype interaction. Therefore we may also conclude that the panetype differences are consistent across different temperatures.

When there is significant interaction, or when the profile plots are substantially nonparallel (whether significant or not), then the tests for row and column effects often don't mean much. Interaction means that the effect of varying levels of the row factor depends on which column we're talking about;

the overall average obscures this fact. Occasionally, the test makes sense. For example, suppose that we had found interaction between outside temperature and type of pane in our heat loss example, and suppose that the temperatures used were representative of the range of temperatures that the windows will actually be exposed to. We can't change window panes every time the outside temperature changes, so the pane that is best on average is the one to use, even if its relative effectiveness depends on the temperature. Usually, though, when there is interaction, the main effects (averages) aren't very relevant.

EXAMPLE 12.9   In Example 12.8, what do the *F* tests for main GROUP and MATERIAL effects tell us?

Solution   Not much. There is a large interaction. The materials that are most effective for one group are relatively ineffective for other groups. There is no need to use the same materials for all groups, so there's no reason to consider the overall average scores for each set of materials. Similarly, the performance of each group depends so heavily on the materials used that the average scores don't indicate much.

■

Even if interaction is present, Tukey comparisons of cell means are still possible and useful. In effect, we simply consider the *IJ* cell means as if they were means from a single factor.

100%(1 − α)% Confidence Intervals for $\mu_{ij} - \mu_{i*j*}$ in a Two-Factor ANOVA Using the Tukey Method

$$(\bar{y}_{ij} - \bar{y}_{i*j*}) - q_\alpha(IJ, \text{d.f.}_2)\sqrt{\text{MS(Within)}/n} \le \mu_{ij} - \mu_{i*j*}$$
$$\le (\bar{y}_{ij} - \bar{y}_{i*j*}) + q_\alpha(IJ, \text{d.f.}_2)\sqrt{\text{MS(Within)}/n}$$

where *IJ* is the number of cells, d.f.$_2$ = $IJ(n-1)$ is the d.f. for MS(Within), $q_\alpha(IJ, \text{d.f.}_2)$ is given by Appendix Table 8, and n = sample size per cell.   ■

EXAMPLE 12.10   A state environmental agency tests two different methods of burning bituminous coal to generate electricity, in connection with four different "scrubbers" to reduce the resulting air pollution. The primary concern is the emission of particulate matter. Four trials are run with each scrubber combined with each burning method. Particulate emission is measured for each trial. The data are:

		Scrubber		
Method	1	2	3	4
A	18.9	8.8	23.7	23.6
	16.1	16.5	15.9	22.1
	14.7	11.7	16.2	16.7
	16.9	13.0	18.0	18.9

		Scrubber		
Method	1	2	3	4
B	24.3	24.0	9.3	18.4
	21.1	27.1	12.1	8.6
	18.0	22.6	15.6	15.1
	16.2	23.1	12.4	9.9

Computer output from an ANOVA program is shown below:

```
DEPENDENT VARIABLE: EMISSION

SOURCE                DF          ANOVA SS       F VALUE      PR > F

METHOD                1           1.16281250       0.12       0.7366
SCRUBBER              3          48.03093750       1.59       0.2168
METHOD*SCRUBBER       3         475.47343750      15.78       0.0001
```

```
                                         MEANS

                             METHOD       N        EMISSION

                               A          16      16.9812500
                               B          16      17.3625000

                             SCRUBBER     N        EMISSION

                               1          8       18.2750000
                               2          8       18.3500000
                               3          8       15.4000000
                               4          8       16.6625000

                    METHOD    SCRUBBER    N        EMISSION

                       A         1        4       16.6500000
                       A         2        4       12.5000000
                       A         3        4       18.4500000
                       A         4        4       20.3250000
                       B         1        4       19.9000000
                       B         2        4       24.2000000
                       B         3        4       12.3500000
                       B         4        4       13.0000000
```

Construct a profile plot. Does it indicate that interaction is present? Does the ANOVA table confirm your answer?

Solution   A profile plot is shown in Figure 12.3. The profiles aren't close to parallel, indicating that interaction is present. The ANOVA table in the output shows the interaction SS, using the METHOD*SCRUBBER multiplication notation. The output shows a large F value and a very small p-value, confirming that interaction is present.   ■

EXAMPLE 12.11   Because there is considerable interaction in the situation of Example 12.10 (page 501), we would like to compare the performance of each method when

Sample mean

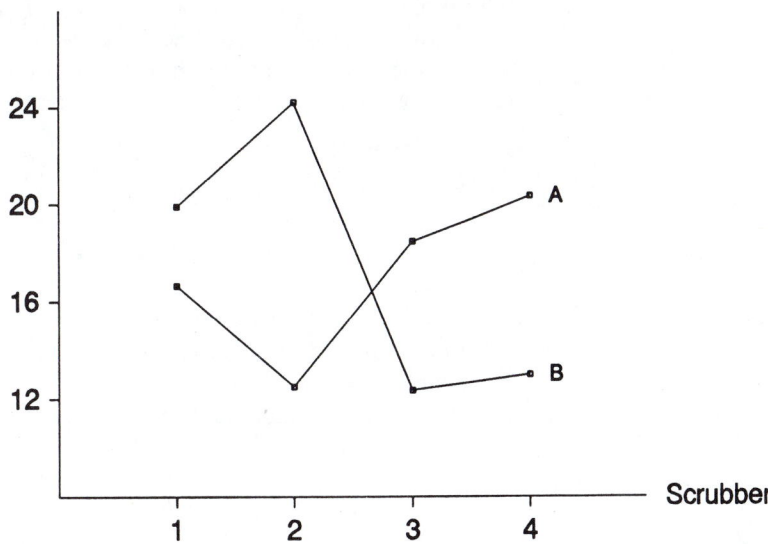

FIGURE 12.3   Profile Plots for Emission Means

mated with the best scrubber. Construct a 95% Tukey confidence interval for the difference in best-scrubber performance for each method.

Solution   The best scrubber for Method A is scrubber 2, with $\bar{y}_{A2} = 12.500$. The best scrubber for Method B is scrubber 3, with $\bar{y}_{B3} = 12.350$. For a 95% confidence interval with $IJ = 8$, $\text{d.f.}_2 = 24$, the value of $q_{.05}(8, 24)$ is 4.68. Substituting into the formula with $n = 4$ and $\text{MS(Within)} = 10.0407$, we have

$$(12.500 - 12.350) - 4.68\sqrt{10.0407/4} \le \mu_{A2} - \mu_{B3} \le (12.500) - 12.350)$$
$$+ 4.68\sqrt{10.0407/4}$$

or

$$-7.265 \le \mu_{A2} - \mu_{B3} \le 7.565 \qquad \blacksquare$$

When interaction is not substantial or significant or when a manager is willing to ignore it and compare equally weighted means, the Tukey method still applies.

100(1 − α)% Confidence Intervals for Comparisons of Row Means

Tukey method for pairwise comparison

$$(\bar{y}_{i..} - \bar{y}_{i*.}) - q_\alpha(I, \text{d.f.}_2)\sqrt{\text{MS(Within)}/nJ} \le \mu_{i..} - \mu_{i*.} \le (\bar{y}_{i..} - \bar{y}_{i*.})$$
$$+ q_\alpha(I, \text{df}_2)\sqrt{\text{MS(Within)}/nJ}$$

In this section, we have relied on computer output for ANOVA tables and the resulting inferences. This is the way we usually analyze two-factor experiments; occasionally, the work must be done by hand. Therefore, for the record, we present methods for computing the ANOVA table by hand.

The formulas for these sums of squares use the following notation:

y_{ijk}: kth observation at the ith level (row) of factor 1 and the jth level (column) of factor 2

$$i = 1, 2, \ldots, I$$
$$j = 1, 2, \ldots, J$$
$$k = 1, 2, \ldots, n$$

Note that n is the number of observations per cell, not the overall sample size.

$\bar{y}_{ij.}$: sample mean response for the ith level of factor 1 and the jth level of factor 2

$$\bar{y}_{ij.} = \sum_k \frac{y_{ijk}}{n}$$

$\bar{y}_{i..}$: sample mean response for the ith level of factor 1

$$\bar{y}_{i..} = \sum_{j,k} \frac{y_{ijk}}{nJ}$$

$\bar{y}_{.j.}$: sample mean response for the jth level of factor 2

$$\bar{y}_{.j.} = \sum_{i,k} \frac{y_{ijk}}{nI}$$

$\bar{y}_{...}$: grand mean for all sample observations

$$\bar{y}_{...} = \sum_{i,j,k} \frac{y_{ijk}}{nIJ}$$

two-factor sums of squares   With this notation, the sums of squares for a two-factor ANOVA are defined as follows:

Factor 1: $\text{SS(Rows)} = nJ \sum_i (\bar{y}_{i..} - \bar{y}_{...})^2$

Factor 2: $\text{SS(Columns)} = nI \sum_j (\bar{y}_{.j.} - \bar{y}_{...})^2$

Interaction: $\text{SS(Interaction)} = n \sum_{i,j} (\bar{y}_{ij.} - \bar{y}_{i..} - \bar{y}_{.j.} + \bar{y}_{...})^2$

$$\text{SS(Within)} = \sum_{i,j,k} (y_{i,j,k} - \bar{y}_{ij.})^2$$

EXAMPLE 12.12   Compute the sums of squares for an ANOVA of the heat-loss data (page 498).

Solution   The following table of means can be used to compute these sums of squares. Entries in the body of the table are the $\bar{y}_{ij.}$'s. Note that $n = 3$, $I = 5$, and $J = 4$.

Exterior	Pane Type j				
Temperature i	A	B	C	D	$\bar{y}_{i\cdot\cdot}$
60	3.800	7.933	10.900	12.967	8.900
50	6.133	10.133	13.100	15.100	11.117
40	7.000	11.100	14.000	15.933	12.008
30	7.967	12.033	14.967	17.000	12.992
20	10.000	14.033	16.967	18.933	14.983
$\bar{y}_{\cdot j\cdot}$	6.980	11.047	13.987	15.987	$\bar{y}_{\cdots} = 12.000$

Substituting (unrounded) means from this table we find

$$SS(\text{Rows}) = (3)(4)[(-3.100)^2 + (-.883)^2 + (.008)^2 + (.992)^2 + (2.983)^2]$$
$$= 243.288$$
$$SS(\text{Columns}) = (3)(5)[(-5.020)^2 + (-.953)^2 + (1.987)^2 + (3.987)^2]$$
$$= 689.244$$
$$SS(\text{Interaction}) = 3[(-.080)^2 + (-.014)^2 + \cdots + (-.037)^2] = .074$$

The within-cell sum of squares must be calculated from the original data. For this example,

$$SS(\text{Within}) = (3.2 - 3.800)^2 + (7.5 - 7.933)^2 + \cdots + (3.9 - 3.800)^2$$
$$+ (8.3 - 7.933)^2 + (4.3 - 3.800)^2 + (8.0 - 7.933)^2$$
$$+ \cdots + (18.8 - 18.933)^2$$
$$= 7.353 \qquad\blacksquare$$

SECTION 12.4   EXERCISES

12.29 Three products are tested in each of five geographic regions. A mean approval rating is found in each case. The sample sizes are large enough that the means can be regarded essentially as population means.

Region	Product		
	A	B	C
1	68	80	77
2	55	64	58
3	62	72	67
4	67	76	70
5	58	68	63

a. Calculate the grand mean. Interpret this value.
b. Calculate region effects and product effects.
c. What does the difference in effects of products A and B represent?

12.30 Refer to the means of Exercise 12.29. Calculate a table of interaction effects.

12.31 Construct a profile plot for the means of Exercise 12.29. (Arbitrarily, put products along the horizontal axis.)

12.32 a. Is there interaction in the means? Refer to Exercise 12.29.

b. Is there a consistent superiority of any one product over all regions?

12.33 An experiment on workfare programs is undertaken by a state welfare agency. Three plans are tested. Plan A requires that all physically able welfare recipients work at assigned jobs for minimum wages. Plan B allows recipients to select or reject jobs, and welfare benefits are reduced by \$1 for every \$2 earned. Plan C is a "control": Welfare officials visit plan C recipients as often as subjects in plans A and B and encourage job searching, but they offer no special job-taking incentives. Each plan is used with 20 families in each of four geographic areas of the state. For each family, the one-year increase in income is found. The following means (in thousands of dollars) are observed:

	Area			
Plan	1	2	3	4
A	2.1	1.7	1.3	1.7
B	1.9	1.8	1.7	1.8
C	.8	.7	.6	.7

An ANOVA table follows:

Source	SS	d.f.	MS
Plan	59.20	2	29.60
Area	4.80	3	1.60
Interaction	2.40	6	.40
Error	273.60	228	1.20
	340.00	239	

a. Find the grand mean.

b. Find the row and column effects.

c. Verify the computation of SS(Plan).

12.34 Refer to Exercise 12.33. Calculate F tests for the effects of (a) plan, (b) area, and (c) interaction. Use $\alpha = .05$ in each case. State a conclusion for each test..

12.35 a. Construct a profile plot for the data of Exercise 12.33. Arrange plans along the horizontal axis.

b. Does this plot suggest the possibility that interaction is present?

c. Does the F test of Exercise 12.34 indicate that interaction is present? Is there a conflict between the plot and the test? If so, what is a possible explanation?

12.36 Refer to the data of Exercise 12.33. Use a Tukey test with $\alpha = .05$ to see if any of the plan mean differences can be declared statistically significant.

12.37 An experiment tests four types of tanks for the commercial growing of shrimp. One of each type of tank is placed at each of eight locations. The shrimp yields (in pounds) are recorded:

Tank	Location							
Type	1	2	3	4	5	6	7	8
1	150	138	159	180	97	180	84	103
2	130	135	171	170	89	160	85	89
3	125	116	149	129	78	129	77	94
4	116	128	139	151	73	147	75	84

An SPSS output is shown below.

SOURCE OF VARIATION	SUM OF SQUARES	DF	MEAN SQUARE	F	SIGNIF OF F
MAIN EFFECTS	33236.250	10	3323.625	40.19067	0.000
TANKTYPE	3259.375	3	1086.458	13.13791	0.000
LOCATION	29976.875	7	4282.411	51.78471	0.000
EXPLAINED	33236.250	10	3323.625	40.19067	0.000
RESIDUAL	1736.625	21	82.696		
TOTAL	34972.875	31	1128.157		

a. Locate the sums of squares for location and tank type.
b. Locate the values of F statistics for location and tank type.
c. Can you conclude that there are significant ($\alpha = .01$) differences among the tank types?

12.38 Refer to the computer output of Exercise 12.37. Locate the p-value for the test of tank-type effect.

12.39 Refer again to the data of Exercise 12.37. Suppose that the data had been incorrectly analyzed as a one-factor ANOVA, ignoring the location effect. Would the conclusion have been different? Carry out the analysis.

12.40 a. Calculate the mean yields by tank type for the data of Exercise 12.37.
b. Which pairs of means can be declared significantly different ($\alpha = .01$) using the Tukey method?

12.41 A maker of packaged cake mixes wants consistently good results from its mixes, and therefore minimal variation in quality from one box to another. Standard procedure in testing any new mix is to prepare four versions of the mix. Six batches of each version are tested at each of three geographical altitudes. Typically, there is greater variability at higher altitudes. Most customers are at altitude 1, the lowest altitude, and most of the rest are at the middling altitude, 2. A standard measure of variability is computed for the cakes baked from each batch. The variability measure reflects differences in the height and texture among cakes, which is ideally very small. The data were analyzed by Statgraphics to obtain the following averages of the variation measure:

Table of means for variation				altitude by mixture			
Level	Count	Average		1	1	6	64.666667
				1	2	6	59.233333
altitude				1	3	6	54.083333
1	24	61.075000		1	4	6	66.316667
2	24	72.341667		2	1	6	69.900000
3	24	77.587500		2	2	6	53.200000
mixture				2	3	6	73.633333
1	18	57.177778		2	4	6	92.633333
2	18	67.627778		3	1	6	36.966667
3	18	71.983333		3	2	6	90.450000
4	18	84.550000		3	3	6	88.233333
				3	4	6	94.700000
				Total		72	70.334722

a. Would it be sensible to say that mixture 1, which has the lowest average score, appears to be the most desirable mixture?

b. Construct a profile plot of the means, with mixture number on the horizontal axis and one profile for each altitude. What does this plot say about your answer to part (a)?

12.42 The data for Exercise 12.41 also were analyzed to yield an ANOVA table. The Statgraphics output is as follows.

Analysis of Variance for variation					
Source of variation	Sum of Squares	d.f.	Mean square	F-ratio	Sig. level
MAIN EFFECTS	10351.000	5	2070.1999	6.199	.0001
altitude	3416.954	2	1708.4768	5.116	.0089
mixture	6934.046	3	2311.3487	6.922	.0004
2-FACTOR INTERACTIONS	11666.572	6	1944.4287	5.823	.0001
altitude mixture	11666.572	6	1944.4287	5.823	.0001
RESIDUAL	20035.972	60	333.93286		
TOTAL (CORR.)	42053.543	71			

a. Show that there is a statistically detectable (significant) interaction at any reasonable alpha value.

b. Explain what interaction means in this context. In particular, how does interaction relate to your answers to Exercise 12.41?

c. How meaningful are the tests for the main effects in this case?

12.43 A supermarket chain wanted to select a new "house brand" of instant coffee. A taste test was arranged. Three different methods for preparing the coffee were used. Also, three different ages of coffee were tested. Age 1 was as fresh as the distribution system would allow, age 2 was the maximum age allowed for selling the coffee, and age 3 was basically "What's this stuff in the back of the cupboard?" The chain manager obtained six jars of each method of coffee at each age and prepared coffee from every jar. A consensus rating was obtained for each jar from a tasting panel; the ideal rating was 100. Mean ratings were obtained from Systat output as follows:

		Method		
		1	2	3
	1	63.000	55.000	57.167
Age	2	50.667	43.667	40.167
	3	46.333	37.000	27.667

a. Which method seems to obtain the best ratings?

   b. Is there an evident effect of age? Does the pattern of changes in means make sense in this context?

   c. Are differences between methods reasonably consistent across different ages? What effect is being considered here?

12.44 The data underlying Exercise 12.43 were given to the Systat package, which yields the following ANOVA output:

```
DEP VAR: RATING      N:  54    MULTIPLE R:  .731    SQUARED MULTIPLE R:  .535
                            ANALYSIS OF VARIANCE
     SOURCE    SUM-OF-SQUARES    DF   MEAN-SQUARE    F-RATIO      P

      AGE         4215.593        2     2107.796     18.749     0.000
    METHOD        1287.259        2      643.630      5.725     0.006
     AGE*
    METHOD         306.519        4       76.630      0.682     0.608

     ERROR        5059.000       45      112.422
```

   a. Is there clear evidence that the effect of METHOD depends on which AGE is considered? That is, is there clear evidence of an interaction effect?

   b. What does the p-value for AGE indicate about the main effect of AGE?

   c. Is there conclusive evidence of a more-than-random difference of METHOD averages?

12.45 Use the means from Exercise 12.43 and the output from Exercise 12.44 to test for significant differences of all pairs of METHOD means. You'll need to compute METHOD means by hand from the cell means. Do the results indicate a clear choice of the method to adopt?

12.5   RANDOMIZED BLOCK DESIGNS   ∎

The ANOVA methods we discussed in this chapter extend the basic methods of comparing two means to the more general problem of comparing several means. We applied the procedure in two experimental settings—one-factor ANOVA, which we described in Section 12.1, and two-factor ANOVA, which we described in Section 12.4. In this section we describe an experimental design that is a hybrid of these settings, the **randomized block design**.

randomized block design

A chain of personal-computer stores wants to test three possible point-of-purchase displays of a new type of holder for computer disks. The chain managers propose to test-market the displays in three stores in each of three sales districts. One approach is to assign displays completely randomly to stores. The only factor is the type of display; the one-factor ANOVA methods of Section 12.1 can be used to analyze the resulting sales-volume data. One problem with this approach is that there is a chance of obtaining an assignment such as the following:

	Products Displayed		
District 1:	A	A	A
District 2:	B	B	B
District 3:	C	C	C

confounded effects

This would be a disastrous assignment. Because all the displays of a given type are in one district, there is no way to tell whether differences in sales volume are due to differences in displays or to differences in districts; that is, with this assignment, effect of display and effect of district are **confounded**. But even if the assignment of displays to stores does not turn out to be confounded, there is another objection to a one-factor experiment. By not controlling for district, this design implies that any district-to-district differences are part of random error. If there are, in fact, large district-to-district differences, MS(Error) is large; by failing to control for district, this design leads to very wide confidence intervals and to tests with very poor power.

The one-factor experimental design can be modified to control for differences among districts. The chain's managers can restrict the random assignment of displays to stores by requiring that each display be used once in each district. One such randomization is shown below. Note that each display is placed in one (randomly chosen) store in each district.

	Products Displayed		
District 1:	A	C	B
District 2:	B	A	C
District 3:	A	B	C

treatment factor

block factor

This experimental setting is referred to as a randomized block design. Characteristically, there is one factor, called the **treatment factor**, that is of primary interest; in this example, the treatment factor is type of display. In addition, there is another factor, called a **block factor**, that is of less interest in itself but should be controlled to avoid confounding and to reduce random error. In this example, districts would be considered block factors. Randomized block methods can be thought of as extensions of the paired-sample methods of Chapter 10; had the chain been considering only displays A and B, the sales-volume data could be regarded as paired by district. One reason for blocking is the same as the reason for pairing—to reduce the amount of random variation.

A randomized block is a two-factor (treatments and blocks) experiment with a one-factor focus; that is, the primary aim of the design is to compare means for the treatment factor. The block factor tends to be regarded as a "nuisance" factor; it is controlled, not so much to find out what its effects are as to avoid having those effects contaminate the analysis of the treatment factor.

There is another difference between a randomized block design and the two-factor designs we discussed in Section 12.4. There is typically only $n = 1$ observation per cell in a randomized block design. In the ANOVA table for a two-factor design, the d.f. for error is $IJ(n - 1)$; if we used two-factor methods for a randomized block design, we would have no d.f. for error, no MS(Error) number, and no way to do tests or confidence intervals. To avoid this problem, we assume that there is no interaction between treatments and blocks; the degrees of freedom that would have been used up in estimating interaction become available, given the assumption of no interaction, for estimating error.

The model for a randomized block design is

$$Y_{ij} = \mu + \alpha_i + \beta_j + \epsilon_{ij}$$

where Y_{ij} is the response for treatment i in block j, μ is the population grand mean, α_i is the true (population) effect of treatment i, β_j is the true effect of block j, and ϵ_{ij} is random error. Note that, by assumption, there is no interaction term in the model.

The ANOVA computations for a randomized block design are similar to those of a two-factor ANOVA, with the exception that there is, by assumption, no SS(Interaction).

Computation of Sums of Squares for a Randomized Block Design

$$\text{SS(Treatment)} = J \sum (\bar{y}_{i.} - \bar{y}_{..})^2, \quad \text{with d.f.} = I - 1$$
$$\text{SS(Block)} = I \sum (\bar{y}_{.j} - \bar{y}_{..})^2, \quad \text{with d.f.} = J - 1$$
$$\text{SS(Error)} = \sum (y_{ij} - \bar{y}_{i.} - \bar{y}_{.j} + \bar{y}_{..})^2, \quad \text{with d.f.} = (J - 1)(J - 1)$$
$$\text{SS(Total)} = \sum (y_{ij} - \bar{y}_{..})^2$$
$$= \text{SS(Treatment)} + \text{SS(Block)} + \text{SS(Error)},$$
$$\text{with d.f.} = IJ - 1$$

In these formulas, $\bar{y}_{i.}$ is the mean for treatment i, $\bar{y}_{.j}$ is the mean for block j, and $\bar{y}_{..}$ is the grand mean; I is the number of treatments and J is the number of blocks. Usually, the easy way is to compute SS(Treatment), SS(Block), and SS(Total), and then find SS(Error) by subtraction.

Suppose that the sales-volume data for the three different displays in three different districts is as follows:

Display	District 1	District 2	District 3	Average
A	86	97	96	93.0
B	55	82	79	72.0
C	60	88	77	75.0
Average	67.0	89.0	84.0	80.0

Then

$$\text{SS(Treatment)} = \text{SS(Display)}$$
$$= 3[(93.0 - 80.0)^2 + (72.0 - 80.0)^2 + (75.0 - 80.0)^2]$$
$$= 774.0$$

$$SS(Block) = SS(District)$$
$$= 3[(67.0 - 80.0)^2 + (89.0 - 80.0)^2 + (84.0 - 80.0)^2]$$
$$= 798.0$$
$$SS(Total) = (86 - 80.0)^2 + (97 - 80.0)^2 + \cdots + (77 - 80.0)^2$$
$$= 1684.0$$
$$SS(Error) = SS(Total) - SS(Treatment) - SS(Block)$$
$$= 1684.0 - 774.0 - 798.0$$
$$= 112.0$$

The ANOVA table and F tests are completed just as in previous sections. The results for the sales-volume data are as follows:

Source	SS	d.f.	MS	F
Treatment (display)	774.0	2	387.0	13.82
Block (district)	798.0	2	399.0	14.25
Error	112.0	4	28.0	
Total	1684.0	8		

The F statistics are obtained, as usual, by dividing the indicated MS by MS(Error); the degrees of freedom for the F statistic are those indicated by the ANOVA table. For the sales-volume data, both F statistics have $d.f._1 = 2$ and $d.f._2 = 4$; for these d.f., $F_{.025} = 10.65$ and $F_{.01} = 18.00$. For the display factor, the F statistic falls between 10.65 and 18.00; the p-value is therefore between .025 and .01. Thus the chain's managers have fairly conclusive evidence that there are real, more than random, differences in mean sales volume by type of display. The F test for the district factor also shows that there are differences in mean volume by district; the managers knew that very well already. Note that the block factor does indeed account for a large fraction of SS(Total); had the managers not adopted a randomized block design, the SS(Error) would have been much larger, possibly concealing the effect of the display factor.

The Tukey method for comparing pairs of means works the same way as for other designs. The role of MS(Within) is taken by MS(Error) and the d.f. are those for error. In a randomized block design, the sample size per mean, n, is equal to the number of blocks; however, it can also be calculated as the total number of observations divided by the number of treatments. For example, suppose that there had been 4 levels of a treatment factor applied within each of 11 blocks; there would be a total of 44 observations (and 43 total d.f.). If an ANOVA table showed MS(Error) $= 16.0$ with 30 d.f., the Tukey plus-or-minus for $\alpha = .05$ (95% confidence) would be $q_{.05}(I = 4, d.f. = 30)\sqrt{MS(Error)/n} = 3.85\sqrt{16.0/11} = 4.64$. The Tukey procedure is the same for randomized block designs as for other designs, given the proper interpretation of the various entries.

Most computer packages can compute the ANOVA table for a randomized block design. Alternatively, the definitions or the following shortcut formulas may be used:

Shortcut Formulas for a Randomized Block Design

$$SS(\text{Treatment}) = \frac{\sum A_i^2}{J} - \frac{T^2}{IJ}$$

$$SS(\text{Block}) = \frac{\sum B_j^2}{I} - \frac{T^2}{IJ}$$

$$SS(\text{Total}) = \sum y_{ij}^2 - \frac{T^2}{IJ}$$

$$SS(\text{Error}) = SS(\text{Total}) - SS(\text{Treatment}) - SS(\text{Block})$$

---

where

$$A_i = \sum_j y_{ij}$$

$$B_j = \sum_i y_{ij}$$

$$T = \sum_{i,j}$$

SECTION 12.5   EXERCISES

12.46 An information-systems manager tests four data-base management systems for possible use. A key variable is speed of execution of programs. The manager chooses six representative tasks and writes programs within each management system. The following times are recorded:

			Task			
System	1	2	3	4	5	6
I	58	324	206	94	39	418
II	47	331	163	75	30	397
III	73	355	224	106	59	449
IV	38	297	188	72	25	366

a. Compute means for each system and each task. Find the grand mean.
b. Use the definitions to find SS(System), SS(Task), and SS(Total). Find SS(Error).
c. Is there a statistically detectable (significant) difference among system means? State bounds on the p-value.

12.47 Recompute the sums of squares in Exercise 12.46 using the shortcut formulas.

12.48 Test all pairs of means for significant differences in Exercise 12.46 using $\alpha = .05$.

12.49 An experiment compares four different mixtures of the components of a rocket propellant; the mixtures contain differing proportions of oxidizer, fuel, and binder.

To compare the mixtures, five different samples of propellant are prepared for each mixture. Each of five investigators is randomly assigned one sample of each of the four mixtures and is asked to measure the propellant thrust. The data are shown here:

Mixture	Investigator				
	1	2	3	4	5
1	2340	2355	2362	2350	2348
2	2658	2650	2665	2640	2653
3	2449	2458	2432	2437	2445
4	2403	2410	2418	2397	2405

a. Identify the blocks and treatments for this design.
b. Why would one want to use this design, as opposed to assigning mixtures completely randomly to investigators?

12.50 a. Refer to Exercise 12.49. Use the computer output shown below to conduct an ANOVA. Use $\alpha = .05$.
b. Which mixture appears to have the best (highest) mean? Is its mean significantly ($\alpha = .05$) higher than each of the other three means?

ANOVA FOR ROCKET PROPELLANT DATA

ANALYSIS OF VARIANCE PROCEDURE

DEPENDENT VARIABLE: THRUST

SOURCE	DF	SUM OF SQUARES	MEAN SQUARE	F VALUE	PR > F	R-SQUARE	C.V
MODEL	7	261713.45000000	37387.63571429	542.96	0.0001	0.996853	0.336
ERROR	12	826.30000000	68.85833333		ROOT MSE		THRUST MEA
CORRECTED TOTAL	19	262539.75000000			8.29809215		2463.7500000

SOURCE	DF	ANOVA SS	F VALUE	PR > F
MIXT	3	261260.95000000	1264.73	0.0001
INVEST	4	452.50000000	1.64	0.2273

MEANS

MIXT	N	THRUST
1	5	2351.00000
2	5	2653.20000
3	5	2444.20000
4	5	2406.60000

12.51 Is there evidence of a significant investigator effect in the computer output of Exercise 12.50? What would such an effect indicate about the accuracy of the investigators?

12.52 As one part of a taste-testing experiment, three different formulations of a new frozen dinner product are tested. Samples of each formulation are given, in random order, to each of 12 testers. Each tester gives a score to each formulation. A Minitab analysis of the data is shown here:

```
MTB > twoway ANOVA of 'rating' by 'form' and 'person'

ANALYSIS OF VARIANCE   rating

SOURCE      DF       SS        MS
form        2       767.4     383.7
person     11      5301.2     481.9
ERROR      22      1532.6      69.7

MTB > table by 'form';
SUBC> means of 'rating'.

 ROWS: form

        rating MEAN
   1    57.667
   2    46.917
   3    49.250
 ALL    51.278
```

a. Perform an F test of the null hypothesis of equal score (RATING) means by formulation (FORM). State bounds on the p-value.

b. Are there statistically significant ($\alpha = .01$) differences among taste-tester (PERSON) means? What does the result of the test indicate about the people in the experiment?

12.53 a. Calculate 95% confidence intervals for all pairwise differences of score means for the three formulations, using the results in Exercise 12.52. Note that each mean is an average of 12 scores.

b. According to these intervals, which pairwise differences, if any, are statistically significant at $\alpha = .05$?

12.54 Use the means shown in Exercise 12.52 to verify SS(FORM). Note that, because of rounding off, your answer may differ from that shown in the output.

12.6   MORE COMPLEX EXPERIMENTS   ∎

Carefully designed experiments have become an important tool for managers in the past few years. Experiments have always been relevant in the context of the research and development laboratory; recently, they have also become important in market research and in quality control. The most important concepts of experimental design have already been introduced in this chapter. In this section, we sketch some elaborations of the basic ideas.

Perhaps the most widely known role of designed experiments is in quality control. The quality of a manufactured product is the result of a number of different factors, including the quality of the parts supplied, the design of the product, and the skill of the workers who assemble the product. One of the key ideas from the modern quality-control literature is that finding a quality problem by varying one factor at a time is not an effective approach. Instead, there should be carefully planned experiments that control all critical factors. For example, suppose that the quality of a video monitor is measured by an index that reflects the brightness of display, the size of flaws on the screen, and the appearance of the case. After some consideration, three key factors are isolated: Which of three suppliers of the internal electronic "gun" is used, which of two types of glass is used for the screen, and which of four assembly teams puts together the product?

It would not be wise to have teams A and B always use glass 1 and teams C and D always use glass 2, with team A using guns from supplier 1, team B guns from supplier 2, and teams C and D guns from supplier 3. In this situation, one can't separate the effect of the supplier from the effect of the gun, and neither can be separated from the effect of the assembly team. Or suppose that only the source of the gun varies across assembly teams. If teams A and B consistently put out inferior products in such a situation, it can't be determined whether their work is poor or whether glass 1 is inferior. Instead, all teams should use all gun suppliers and all glass types. The most convenient and effective way to vary team, supplier, and glass type is in a balanced design.

factorial experiment

Measuring the quality index as a function of team, gun supplier, and glass type in a balanced design is a **factorial experiment** with three factors. The data can be analyzed in terms of main effects, two-way interactions (team by supplier, team by glass type, and supplier by glass type), and a three-way interaction. If a quality problem arises, the analysis will suggest the appropriate remedy. For example, if the mean for supplier 1 is consistently low, that supplier should bring up quality standards, but if there is a strong supplier-by-glass-type interaction, the technical compatibility of the guns and glass type should be investigated. The computations required for a multifactor experiment are similar to those for a two-factor experiment, but they are tedious enough to be left to a computer. Analyses by F tests and Tukey methods are obvious extensions of these methods for two-factor studies. In particular, one should check for interactions before considering overall averages (main effects).

For example, suppose that samples of eight monitors each are taken from the production of each combination of team, supplier, and glass type, and that the computer output on page 517 is obtained.

First, we look for interactions. SAS uses an asterisk to denote interactions; we see that TEAM*SUPPLIER, TEAM*TYPE, SUPPLIER*TYPE, and TEAM*SUPPLIER*TYPE all have p-values (shown as $PR > F$) that are relatively large. The only interaction that is even close to statistically significant is SUPPLIER*TYPE (p-value 0.0979).

Then, we look for main effects. There is a huge SUPPLIER effect; the SS for SUPPLIER is extremely large, the F value is enormous at 105.06, and the p-value ($PR > F$) is tiny at 0.0001. The computed MEANS clearly show that SUPPLIER 2 has a very low quality average. There also is a clear evidence of a significant effect of TEAM ($PR > F = 0.0003$); the TEAM 1 mean is high and the TEAM 2 mean is low. There is a marginally significant ($PR > F = 0.0362$) TYPE effect; TYPE 2 has a slightly higher mean than TYPE 1. Tukey method tests could be performed for each main effect to verify that the apparent differences of means are statistically detectable.

Careful experimentation isn't easy. Everyone who is involved in the study must understand the importance of balanced design and of randomization. The effort required has a real payoff. A well-designed, well-executed experiment can

THREE-WAY ANOVA FOR QUALITY CONTROL DATA

ANALYSIS OF VARIANCE PROCEDURE

DEPENDENT VARIABLE: QUALITY

SOURCE	DF	SUM OF SQUARES	MEAN SQUARE	F VALUE	PR > F	R-SQUARE	C.V.
MODEL	23	24557.95312500	1067.73709239	10.94	0.0001	0.599609	4.3901
ERROR	168	16398.62500000	97.61086310		ROOT MSE		QUALITY MEAN
CORRECTED TOTAL	191	40956.57812500			9.87982101		225.04687500

SOURCE	DF	ANOVA SS	F VALUE	PR > F
TEAM	3	1957.89062500	6.69	0.0003
SUPPLIER	2	20509.96875000	105.06	0.0001
TEAM*SUPPLIER	6	203.15625000	0.35	0.9109
TYPE	1	435.00520833	4.46	0.0362
TEAM*TYPE	3	303.05729167	1.03	0.3786
SUPPLIER*TYPE	2	460.01041667	2.36	0.0979
TEAM*SUPPLIER*TYPE	6	688.86458333	1.18	0.3213

MEANS

TEAM	N	QUALITY
1	48	229.645833
2	48	220.625000
3	48	225.145833
4	48	224.770833

SUPPLIER	N	QUALITY
1	64	231.953125
2	64	210.437500
3	64	232.750000

TYPE	N	QUALITY
1	96	223.541667
2	96	226.552083

reveal the important variables much more clearly than any other data-gathering method.

off-line quality control

Designed experiments are crucial for "off-line" quality control—the design of products and processes to achieve high effectiveness and, equally important, low variability. This approach was popularized in Japan by Taguchi [see Taguchi (1980)]. Experts in the product or process of interest are asked to specify what factors would influence the quality of the result. These factors may be categorized as *control* factors (those that can be set as desired) and *noise* factors (those that are impossible or very expensive to control).

In a typical off-line quality-control experiment, there will be many, many factors. For example, Lin and Kacker (1986) discuss a study of how to solder circuit pack assemblies; there were 17 distinct factors, 7 having two levels and 10 having three levels. Practically, it is often impossible to study every possible combination of levels. In the soldering study, there would be $2^7 3^{10} = 7,558,272$ possible combinations of levels of the factors; at one hour per combination, 24 hours per day, 365.25 days per year, evaluating all possible combinations would take about 860 years! Therefore, most off-line quality experiments need a

TABLE 12.2   Orthogonal Array OA_8

			Column				
Row	1	2	3	4	5	6	7
1	1	1	1	1	1	1	1
2	1	1	1	2	2	2	2
3	1	2	2	1	1	2	2
4	1	2	2	2	2	1	1
5	2	1	2	1	2	1	2
6	2	1	2	2	1	2	1
7	2	2	1	1	2	2	1
8	2	2	1	2	1	1	2

method to reduce the number of experimental runs, while still preserving the essential balanced-design property.

orthogonal array
Taguchi suggested **orthogonal array** designs. An example, OA_8 (which stands for orthogonal array with 8 rows), is shown in Table 12.2. These designs are "pairwise balanced"; that is, within any two columns, all pairs of numbers occur exactly the same number of times. In OA_8, the pairs $(1, 1)$, $(1, 2)$, $(2, 1)$, and $(2, 2)$ appear exactly twice in any pair of columns. Each factor is assigned to a column; thus, a seven-factor experiment (each factor having two levels) could be handled using OA_8. It isn't necessary to use every column. If an experiment had six two-level factors, the OA_8 design could be used by omitting any one column. Notice that instead of $2^7 = 128$ runs, an OA_8 experiment requires only 8 runs. Shoemaker and Kacker (1988) discuss these designs and show several orthogonal arrays.

EXAMPLE 12.13
Another orthogonal array design, OA_9, is shown in Table 12.3. How many factors and levels does it accomodate? How many runs (rows) would be required to obtain all possible combinations of the levels? How does the pairwise-balanced property show in this design?

TABLE 12.3   Orthogonal Array OA_9

		Column		
Row	1	2	3	4
1	1	1	1	1
2	1	2	2	2
3	1	3	3	3
4	2	1	2	3
5	2	2	3	1
6	2	3	1	2
7	3	1	3	2
8	3	2	1	3
9	3	3	2	1

Solution   There are four columns, so a four-factor study could be handled by this design. Because the numbers 1, 2, and 3 appear in each column, all four factors could have three levels. Therefore, there are $3^4 = 81$ combinations of the levels of the four factors. The pairwise-balanced property is reflected by the fact that in any two columns, the pairs $(1, 1), (1, 2), (1, 3), (2, 1), \ldots, (3, 3)$ all appear exactly once.   ∎

These orthogonal array designs make it possible to perform experiments even when there are enormous numbers of factors. The cost is that it is difficult or impossible to discover interactions among factors. The whole point of orthogonal array designs is to avoid using all combinations of factor levels, but interaction is by definition the effect of specific combinations. Alternatively, we may see the problem by considering degrees of freedom (d.f.). In OA_8, only 8 measurements are taken on the response variable, which corresponds to the 8 rows; thus, there are $8 - 1 = 7$ total d.f. If all 7 columns are used for 7 two-level factors, one degree of freedom will be used to assess the effect of each factor. With all 7 d.f. used up, there is no available information about interaction.

EXAMPLE 12.14   In the OA_9 design, if all four columns are used for factors, will there be any information about interactions?

Solution   There are $9 - 1 = 8$ total d.f. Because each factor has three levels, the main effect of each factor accounts for two d.f. The main effects account for $4(2) = 8$ d.f., which leaves none for interaction.   ∎

fractional factorial design   The most useful variety of orthogonal array designs is **fractional factorial designs**. Rather than having a full factorial experiment with all combinations of factor levels represented, these designs pick only a fraction of the combinations. The selected combinations are chosen so that some balance is preserved. The simplest example involves factors A, B, and C, each having levels 1 and 2. Table 12.4 shows the $2^3 = 8$ possible combinations of levels. The * denotes those combinations selected in a "1/2 replication" fractional factorial. This design can be displayed as an orthogonal array, OA_4, shown in Table 12.5.

These fractional factorial designs often allow for at least some interactions to be estimated. A good description of fractional factorial designs is given in Box, Hunter, and Hunter (1978). Shoemaker and Kacker (1988) suggest that a good strategy is to have a fractional factorial design for the control factors and to have each row of this design tested with each combination of the noise factors. Thus, if there were 5 two-level control factors and 2 two-level noise factors, we could use

TABLE 12.4   Fractional Factorial for Three Two-Level Factors

	Factor A = 1		Factor A = 2	
	B		B	
	1	2	1	2
C 1	*		1	*
C 2		*	2	*

TABLE 12.5 OA_4

Row	Column 1	2	3
1	1	1	1
2	1	2	2
3	2	1	2
4	2	2	1

an OA_8 design for the control factors (omitting two columns) with level 1 of both noise factors; then another OA_8 design with level 1 of noise factor A and level 2 of noise factor B; still another OA_8 with A = 2 and B = 1; and finally another OA_8 with A = 2 and B = 2. If there were many noise factors, we could have another orthogonal array design (preferably a fractional factorial) for the noise factors and we could combine every row of the control OA with every row of the noise OA.

In off-line quality-control experiments, several dependent variables are usually measured for each run (row) of the experiment. For example, suppose that we were experimenting with a process that deposits a coating on silicon wafers. We could measure the coating thickness of each of several wafers during each run (row) of the experiment. One obvious measure of interest would be the deviation of the average thickness from the target value. Another important measure would be the variability in thickness from one wafer to another. Rather than using the variance to measure variability, it's usually better to measure the

control of variance

logarithm of the variance to minimize the effect of occasional very large, outlying variances. Shoemaker and Kacker (1988) indicate that in their experience, a variability measure is usually more important because it's harder to control. They suggest finding combinations of some of the factors that minimize variability and using other factors to make the mean close to the target.

Once the experiment is designed and the data collected, it's possible to use many computer programs to perform an analysis of variance (ANOVA). One difficulty is deciding which effects can be estimated from the data. One good approach is to count degrees of freedom (d.f.), as we did earlier in this section. The maximum d.f. available for estimating effects is the number of runs (rows) in the orthogonal array, less one. (If many observations of a response variable are made within each run, this information is useful for measuring random error and reducing standard errors, but the information does not add d.f. for measuring the effects of factors.) If, as we saw previously, these d.f. may be completely used up in estimating main effects, then no interactions can be estimated. If an interaction can't be estimated, the computer program should return an error message. Shoemaker and Kacker (1988) and the references cited therein discuss more sophisticated approaches.

EXAMPLE 12.15

Certain packaged cereals will settle in the box before reaching the customer. Although the box contains the advertised weight, it appears only partially filled; customers aren't happy when this happens. Engineers at the cereal plant identify four control factors: Cut, the size of the bits of dough to be baked into the cereal; moisture, the wetness of the dough; temperature, the heat in the baking ovens; and speed, the rate at which a package-filling machine fills boxes. An experiment used columns 1, 2, 4, and 7 of OA_8 for these factors. Cartons from morning and afternoon runs for each row of the OA were selected, labelled to indicate the experimental conditions under which they were produced, and shipped by the usual process to a distant store. Each box in each carton was opened and the degree of settling, in inches, was carefully measured. The mean and variance of settling degree was calculated for each carton. The experimenters attempted to use Systat to perform an analysis of variance involving the main effects of all four factors and four interactions that they thought might be relevant. They obtained a message "***ERROR*** A DESIGN MATRIX WAS SINGULAR." Why did they get that message?

Solution   In trying to evaluate four main effects of two-level factors and four interactions, they needed eight d.f. But OA_8 has eight rows, therefore only seven available d.f.

∎

Shoemaker and Kacker also suggest that it's important to have a small follow-up experiment that uses the levels of the various factors that seem to be best. The reason for the follow-up experiment is that the factors may interact in ways that can't be analyzed by the experimental design, so the chosen levels of the factors may not give the predicted results.

EXAMPLE 12.16   The cereal engineers in Example 12.15 reanalyzed their data using Systat and omitted one of the interaction terms. They obtained the following output. What factors and/or interactions have a detectable influence on the logarithm of the variance (LOGVAR)? What has detectable influence on the mean (MEANSET)? How should the engineers proceed to design a follow-up study?

DEP VAR: MEANSET   N: 16   MULTIPLE R: .980   SQUARED MULTIPLE R: .961

ANALYSIS OF VARIANCE

SOURCE	SUM-OF-SQUARES	DF	MEAN-SQUARE	F-RATIO	P
C	0.449	1	0.449	161.766	0.000
M	0.001	1	0.001	0.225	0.648
T	0.000	1	0.000	0.081	0.783
S	0.001	1	0.001	0.324	0.585
C*M	0.006	1	0.006	2.306	0.167
M*T	0.087	1	0.087	31.360	0.001
C*T	0.005	1	0.005	1.766	0.221
ERROR	0.022	8	0.003		

DEP VAR: LOGVAR   N: 16   MULTIPLE R: .784 SQUARED MULTIPLE R: .614
ANALYSIS OF VARIANCE

SOURCE	SUM-OF-SQUARES	DF	MEAN-SQUARE	F-RATIO	P
C	0.897	1	0.897	1.120	0.321
M	1.673	1	1.673	2.089	0.186
T	0.103	1	0.103	0.128	0.730
S	6.143	1	6.143	7.670	0.024
C*M	0.418	1	0.418	0.522	0.491
M*T	0.947	1	0.947	1.183	0.309
C*T	0.011	1	0.011	0.014	0.910
ERROR	6.408	8	0.801		

Solution   The rightmost column of the output is presumably the *p*-value corresponding to each *F* statistic. Only the *S* (speed) factor has detectable effect on LOGVAR, with a *p*-value of 0.024. In the output for MEANSET, the *p*-values for C and M∗T are very small, which indicates that cut and the moisture-temperature interaction have detectable effect on mean settling. The engineers should select the speed setting that consistently gave lower variance, and the setting for cut and combination of settings for moisture and temperature that gave the most desirable (in this case, least) mean settling. These settings and perhaps other similar ones should be used in a follow-up study to verify that no neglected interactions cause trouble.   ■

SECTION 12.6   EXERCISES

12.55 An experiment is designed to determine factors that affect electricity usage in single-family homes. In a new suburban development, there are two basic home layouts: Equal numbers of houses were built with two levels of insulation (*M* being the suggested minimum and *H* a larger amount). Another factor is the size of family living in the home (0, 1, 2, or more children). The electricity usage for each house is determined. An SAS analysis of the data is shown below:

a. Locate the *F* statistics.
b. Which factors and interactions are significant at $\alpha = .01$?

ELECTRICITY USAGE STUDY

ANALYSIS OF VARIANCE PROCEDURE

DEPENDENT VARIABLE: ELECUSE

SOURCE	DF	SUM OF SQUARES	MEAN SQUARE	F VALUE	PR > F	R-SQUARE	C.V
MODEL	11	2529.16666667	229.92424242	17.74	0.0001	0.844275	6.615
ERROR	36	466.50000000	12.95833333		ROOT MSE		ELECUSE MEAN
CORRECTED TOTAL	47	2995.66666667			3.59976851		54.4166666

SOURCE	DF	ANOVA SS	F VALUE	PR > F
INSUQUAL	1	432.00000000	33.34	0.0001
LAYOUT	1	320.33333333	24.72	0.0001
INSUQUAL*LAYOUT	1	0.33333333	0.03	0.8735
FAMTYPE	2	1147.79166667	44.29	0.0001
INSUQUAL*FAMTYPE	2	0.37500000	0.01	0.9856
LAYOUT*FAMTYPE	2	627.54166667	24.21	0.0001
INSUQ*LAYOU*FAMTY	2	0.79166667	0.03	0.9699

MEANS

INSUQUAL	N	ELECUSE
H	24	51.4166667
M	24	57.4166667

LAYOUT	N	ELECUSE
A	24	51.8333333
B	24	57.0000000

(continued)

INSUQUAL	LAYOUT	N	ELECUSE
H	A	12	48.9166667
H	B	12	53.9166667
M	A	12	54.7500000
M	B	12	60.0833333

FAMTYPE	N	ELECUSE
0	16	49.4375000
1	16	52.7500000
2	16	61.0625000

LAYOUT	FAMTYPE	N	ELECUSE
A	0	8	42.8750000
A	1	8	49.3750000
A	2	8	63.2500000
B	0	8	56.0000000
B	1	8	56.1250000
B	2	8	58.8750000

12.56 Refer to the output of Exercise 12.55.
   a. Draw the interaction profiles for insulation quality by layout.
   b. Draw the interaction profiles for layout by family type.

12.57 Refer to the output of Exercise 12.55.
   a. Use the Tukey method to calculate a 95% confidence interval for the difference in mean electricity usage for the two insulation levels.
   b. Do you think it makes sense to compare the layout means ignoring family type?
   c. Treat the means by layout and family type as a set of six means. Which pairs differ significantly ($\alpha = .05$)?

12.58 Pignatiello and Ramberg (1985) report on an experiment to determine factors that affect the quality of leaf springs for trucks. They indicate four controllable factors, each at two levels.

Code	Factor	Level 1	Level 2
B	High heat temperature ($^\circ$F)	1840	1880
C	Heating time (seconds)	25	23
D	Transfer time (seconds)	12	10
E	Hold down time (seconds)	2	3

They also have a noise factor 0, which is quench oil temperature. Level 1 of the quench oil temperature is about 140°, level 2 is about 160°. The dependent variable is the height of the resulting spring. The target value is 8.00 inches and variability around that value in either direction is costly. Three springs were manufactured at each of 16 combinations of factors, as shown at the top of page 524.
   a. Show that the assignment of levels to B, C, D, and E are pairwise balanced.
   b. Show that the experimental design involves eight rows for the B, C, D, and E combinations at each level of a noise factor.
   c. In fact, the levels for the B, C, D, and E factors came from the orthogonal array OA_8. Which columns were used?

B	C	D	E	O	Spring heights		
1	1	1	1	1	7.78	7.78	7.81
1	1	1	1	2	7.50	7.25	7.12
2	1	1	2	1	8.15	8.18	7.88
2	1	1	2	2	7.88	7.88	7.44
1	2	1	2	1	7.50	7.56	7.50
1	2	1	2	2	7.50	7.56	7.50
2	2	1	1	1	7.59	7.56	7.75
2	2	1	1	2	7.63	7.75	7.56
1	1	2	2	1	7.94	8.00	7.88
1	1	2	2	2	7.32	7.44	7.44
2	1	2	1	1	7.69	8.09	8.06
2	1	2	1	2	7.56	7.69	7.62
1	2	2	1	1	7.56	7.62	7.44
1	2	2	1	2	7.18	7.18	7.25
2	2	2	2	1	7.56	7.81	7.69
2	2	2	2	2	7.81	7.50	7.59

12.59 The data in Exercise 12.58 were analyzed to find the factors that influenced mean height. SAS output follows:

ANALYSIS OF VARIANCE PROCEDURE

DEPENDENT VARIABLE: LEAFHGT

SOURCE	DF	SUM OF SQUARES	MEAN SQUARE	F VALUE	PR > F	R-SQUARE	C.V.
MODEL	15	2.43621458	0.16241431	9.81	0.0001	0.821395	1.6849
ERROR	32	0.52973333	0.01655417		ROOT MSE		LEAFHGT MEAN
CORRECTED TOTAL	47	2.96594792			0.12866300		7.63604167

SOURCE	DF	ANOVA SS	F VALUE	PR > F
B	1	0.58741875	35.48	0.0001
C	1	0.37276875	22.52	0.0001
D	1	0.00991875	0.60	0.4446
E	1	0.12916875	7.80	0.0087
B*C	1	0.00350208	0.21	0.6487
B*D	1	0.00460208	0.28	0.6017
C*D	1	0.01505208	0.91	0.3475
O	1	0.80860208	48.85	0.0001
B*O	1	0.08585208	5.19	0.0296
C*O	1	0.32835208	19.84	0.0001
D*O	1	0.03466875	2.09	0.1576
E*O	1	0.00880208	0.53	0.4712
B*C*O	1	0.00130208	0.08	0.7809
B*D*O	1	0.01960208	1.18	0.2846
C*D*O	1	0.02660208	1.61	0.2141

a. Which factors are conclusively (say at $\alpha = .01$) shown to affect mean height?

b. Are there any interactions that appear to be statistically significant at $\alpha = .05$?

12.60 The SAS output from Exercise 12.59 also contains means for various factors.

a. Which value of each factor that was found to be significant in Exercise 12.59 appears to increase the mean height?

b. What combination of C and O values appears to increase the mean height?

MEANS

B	N	LEAFHGT
1	24	7.52541667
2	24	7.74666667

C	N	LEAFHGT
1	24	7.72416667
2	24	7.54791667

D	N	LEAFHGT
1	24	7.65041667
2	24	7.62166667

E	N	LEAFHGT
1	24	7.58416667
2	24	7.68791667

O	N	LEAFHGT
1	24	7.76583333
2	24	7.50625000

C	O	N	LEAFHGT
1	1	12	7.93666667
1	2	12	7.51166667
2	1	12	7.59500000
2	2	12	7.50083333

12.61 Variances were calculated for each set of three heights from the data of Exercise 12.58. The natural logarithms of these variances were analyzed by SAS, with the following results:

DEPENDENT VARIABLE: LOGS2

SOURCE	DF	SUM OF SQUARES	MEAN SQUARE	F VALUE	PR > F	R-SQUARE	C.V.
MODEL	15	35.08418527	2.33894568	.		1.000000	0.0000
ERROR	0	0.00000000	0.00000000		ROOT MSE		LOGS2 MEAN
CORRECTED TOTAL	15	35.08418527			0.00000000		-4.93131272

SOURCE	DF	ANOVA SS	F VALUE	PR > F
B	1	14.30152886	.	.
C	1	1.29362276	.	.
D	1	0.24501624	.	.
E	1	0.18584162	.	.
B*C	1	0.00000999	.	.
B*D	1	0.72144506	.	.
C*D	1	1.79810574	.	.
O	1	0.31251768	.	.
B*O	1	1.38647540	.	.
C*O	1	1.42946513	.	.
D*O	1	4.93508450	.	.
E*O	1	0.06671034	.	.
B*C*O	1	4.74597590	.	.
B*D*O	1	0.74812365	.	.
C*D*O	1	2.91426240	.	.

a. Why doesn't the output perform F tests?

b. Which factors and interactions individually account for more than 10% of SS(Total)?

12.62 Means for the log-variance were obtained by SAS for factor B. Which setting of B appears to give the better log-variance, and therefore the better variance?

MEANS

B	N	LOGS2
1	8	-5.87674678
2	8	-3.98587866

12.63 What settings for the factors B, C, D, E, and O would you recommend for a follow-up experiment?

12.64 Phadke (1986) reported a study on improving the life of router bits. These bits are used to cut the edges of panels to be made into wiring boards. As these bits wear, they leave increasing amounts of dust on the edges, which must then be cleaned. Changing the router bits requires stopping the process, which is expensive. Engineers familiar with the process identified nine factors as follows:

Factor	Level 1	Level 2	Level 3	Level 4
A. Suction (inches of mercury)	1	2		
B. x-y feed (inches/minute)	60	80		
C. In-feed (inches/minute)	10	50		
D. Type of bit	1	2	3	4
E. Spindle position	1	2	3	4
F. Suction foot	Ring	Brush		
G. Stacking height (inches)	3/16	4/16		
H. Depth of slot (mils)		60	100	
I. Speed (thousands of rpm)	30	60		

Factors A, F, and H relate to the process of removing dust from the edges. Factors B, I, and G determine how many boards are cut per operating hour. Factor C indicates how fast the bit was lowered onto the board; it was thought that lowering it too fast might tend to break or damage the point. Factor D reflects bits available from different suppliers. Factor E is included to find levels of others factors that worked with all four positions.

The factor settings and bit lifetimes (in hundreds of inches, cut before the bit broke or wore out) were reported by Phadke to be:

Factor A	B	C	D	E	F	G	H	I	Lifetime
1	1	1	1	1	1	1	1	1	3.5
1	1	1	2	2	2	2	1	1	0.5
1	1	1	3	4	1	2	2	1	0.5
1	1	1	4	3	2	1	2	1	17.5
1	2	2	3	1	2	2	1	1	0.5
1	2	2	4	2	1	1	1	1	2.5
1	2	2	1	4	2	1	2	1	0.5
1	2	2	2	3	1	2	2	1	0.5
2	1	2	4	1	1	2	2	1	17.5
2	1	2	3	2	2	1	2	1	2.5
2	1	2	2	4	1	1	1	1	0.5
2	1	2	1	3	2	2	1	1	3.5
2	2	1	2	1	2	1	2	1	0.5

(continued)

Factor A	B	C	D	E	F	G	H	I	Lifetime
2	2	1	1	2	1	2	2	1	2.5
2	2	1	4	4	2	2	1	1	0.5
2	2	1	3	3	1	1	1	1	3.5
1	1	1	1	1	1	1	1	2	17.5
1	1	1	2	2	2	2	1	2	0.5
1	1	1	3	4	1	2	2	2	0.5
1	1	1	4	3	2	1	2	2	17.5
1	2	2	3	1	2	2	1	2	0.5
1	2	2	4	2	1	1	1	2	17.5
1	2	2	1	4	2	1	2	2	14.5
1	2	2	2	3	1	2	2	2	0.5
2	1	2	4	1	1	2	2	2	17.5
2	1	2	3	2	2	1	2	2	3.5
2	1	2	2	4	1	1	1	2	17.5
2	1	2	1	3	2	2	1	2	3.5
2	2	1	2	1	2	1	2	2	0.5
2	2	1	1	2	1	2	2	2	3.5
2	2	1	4	4	2	2	1	2	0.5
2	2	1	3	3	1	1	1	2	17.5

Notice that the 16 runs (rows) associated with factor I = 1 are exactly the same as the 16 runs associated with I = 2.

a. Show that the runs for factors A, B, and C were obtained from columns 1, 2, and 3 of OA_{16}, shown below.

b. Show that the runs for factor D may be obtained by combining columns 7 and 9 of OA_{16}. (Hint: We could make 1, 1, correspond to D = 1, and 1, 2 correspond to D = 2, etc.)

```
            Column
                  1 1 1 1 1 1
Row | 1 2 3 4 5 6 7 8 9 0 1 2 3 4 5
--- | -----------------------------
 1  | 1 1 1 1 1 1 1 1 1 1 1 1 1 1 1
 2  | 1 1 1 1 1 1 1 2 2 2 2 2 2 2 2
 3  | 1 1 1 2 2 2 2 1 1 1 1 2 2 2 2
 4  | 1 1 1 2 2 2 2 2 2 2 2 1 1 1 1
 5  | 1 2 2 1 1 2 2 1 1 2 2 1 1 2 2
 6  | 1 2 2 1 1 2 2 2 2 1 1 2 2 1 1
 7  | 1 2 2 2 2 1 1 1 1 2 2 2 2 1 1
 8  | 1 2 2 2 2 1 1 2 2 1 1 1 1 2 2
 9  | 2 1 2 1 2 1 2 1 2 1 2 1 2 1 2
10  | 2 1 2 1 2 1 2 2 1 2 1 2 1 2 1
11  | 2 1 2 2 1 2 1 1 2 1 2 2 1 2 1
12  | 2 1 2 2 1 2 1 2 1 2 1 1 2 1 2
13  | 2 2 1 1 2 2 1 1 2 2 1 1 2 2 1
14  | 2 2 1 1 2 2 1 2 1 1 2 2 1 1 2
15  | 2 2 1 2 1 1 2 1 2 2 1 2 1 1 2
16  | 2 2 1 2 1 1 2 2 1 1 2 1 2 2 1
```

12.65 The data in Exercise 12.64 were analyzed using Systat. The following ANOVA table was obtained:

```
DEP VAR:LIFETIME    N: 32    MULTIPLE R:   .882    SQUARED MULTIPLE R:   .778

                          ANALYSIS OF VARIANCE
```

SOURCE	SUM-OF-SQUARES	DF	MEAN-SQUARE	F-RATIO	P
A	0.000	1	0.000	0.000	1.000
B	105.125	1	105.125	4.073	0.063
C	8.000	1	8.000	0.310	0.587
D	367.375	3	122.458	4.744	0.017
E	93.625	3	31.208	1.209	0.343
F	98.000	1	98.000	3.797	0.072
G	220.500	1	220.500	8.542	0.011
H	3.125	1	3.125	0.121	0.733
I	180.500	1	180.500	6.993	0.019
I*B	4.500	1	4.500	0.174	0.683
I*G	171.125	1	171.125	6.630	0.022
I*C	10.125	1	10.125	0.392	0.541
G*B	4.500	1	4.500	0.174	0.683
ERROR	361.375	14	25.812		

a. Which factors and interactions clearly appear statistically significant, say using $\alpha = .05$?

b. Are there other factors that are close to significant?

c. For which factors and interactions is there little or no evidence of an effect?

12.66 The data of Exercise 12.64 were analyzed by Minitab to obtain mean bit lifetimes for different levels of various factors.

a. According to the output of Exercise 12.65, what must be true of the means for levels of factor A?

b. The means for factor D were obtained by Minitab as:

```
ROWS: D

      Lifetime
        MEAN

  1     6.125
  2     2.625
  3     3.625
  4    11.375
ALL     5.937
```

Which level of D (type of bit) appears to be best?

12.67 Which pairs of means are significantly ($\alpha = .05$) different according to a Tukey approach? Note that there were 32 observations in all, so each mean is an average of 8 values.

12.68 Mean bit lifetimes for all combinations of factors I and G were also obtained by Minitab for the data of Exercise 12.64.

```
ROWS: I     COLUMNS: G

            1        2      ALL

    1     3.875    3.250   3.563
    2    13.250    3.375   8.312
  ALL     8.562    3.312   5.937
```

a. The output in Exercise 12.64 indicates that there was an I*G interaction. How does it appear in the output?
b. Which levels of the two factors appear to give the best results? Does the combination of these levels appear to give the best cell mean?

Summary

This is the key chapter for constructing and analyzing planned experiments, which is an increasingly important managerial tool. The chapter proceeds from relatively simple experiments to quite complex ones; the same basic principles· apply throughout.

The simplest experiment involves varying a single experimental factor. The significance of differences among means may be tested by an F test, which we describe in Section 12.1. For seriously nonnormal data, the Kruskal-Wallis test of Section 12.2 will be more effective. If the aim is to compare all pairs of means, the Tukey procedure of Section 12.3 is useful.

When two factors are varied in an experiment, the key concept of interaction applies. Two factors interact in their effect on a response if the effect of changing one factor depends on the level of the other. Interaction implies a nonadditive, combination effect. The analysis of a two-factor study depends on whether substantial interaction is judged to be present. If not, F and Tukey methods apply to the main effects from row and column averages. When there is major interaction, main effects often aren't very relevant; Tukey inferences on cell means often reveal more.

Blocking, an extension of the pairing idea of Chapter 10, is a control for a nuisance source of variability, which thereby reduces random variability and yields more precise conclusions. Randomized block studies involve a treatment factor of interest and a nuisance block factor. Once again, F and Tukey methods apply.

Experiments that involve many factors are important in quality improvement and in market research studies. Often it is uneconomical or impossible to use all combinations of factor levels. In this case, orthogonal array (OA) designs, especially fractional factorial experiments, obtain information on main effects and some interactions. The drawback of OA designs is that they ignore most interactions.

KEY FORMULAS: Introduction to the Analysis of Variance

1. Testing the equality of I group means

$$H_0: \mu_1 = \mu_2 = \cdots = \mu_I$$

$$\text{T.S.: } F = \frac{\text{MS(Between)}}{\text{MS(Within)}}$$

where

$$\text{MS(Between)} = \sum_i n_i(\bar{y}_i - \bar{y})^2/(I - 1)$$

$$\text{MS(Within)} = \sum_{i,j}(y_{ij} - \bar{y}_i)^2/(n - I)$$

2. Shortcut formulas for ANOVA sums of squares

$$\text{SS(Total)} = \sum_{i,j} y_{ij}^2 - \frac{\left(\sum_{i,j} y_{ij}\right)^2}{n}$$

$$\text{SS(Between)} = \sum_i \left(\sum_j y_{ij}\right)^2 \bigg/ n_i - \frac{\left(\sum_{i,j} y_{ij}\right)^2}{n}$$

$$\text{SS(Within)} = \text{SS(Total)} - \text{SS(Between)}$$

3. $\text{SS(Between)} = \sum n_i(\bar{y}_i - \bar{y})^2$

$$\text{SS(Within)} = \sum (n_i - 1)s_i^2$$
$$\text{SS(Total)} = \text{SS(Between)} + \text{SS(Within)}$$

where

n_i is the number of observations in level i
$\bar{y}_i$ is the sample mean for level i
s_i^2 is the sample variance for level i

4. Kruskal-Wallis test (a nonparametric alternative to the ANOVA for testing I group means)

H_0: The distributions are identical (effectively, the populations have equal means)

$$\text{T.S.: } H = \frac{12}{n(n + 1)} \sum_i \frac{T_i^2}{n_i} - 3(n + 1)$$

where T_i is the sum of the ranks for the n_i measurements in sample i and
d.f. $= I - 1$

5. Tukey's $100(1 - \alpha)\%$ confidence interval for $\mu_i - \mu_{i*}$

$$(\bar{y}_i - \bar{y}_{i*}) \pm q_\alpha(I, \text{d.f.}_2)\sqrt{\text{MS(Within)}/n}$$

6. Shortcut formulas for sums of squares in two-factor ANOVA

$$SS(\text{Rows}) = \sum_i \frac{A_i^2}{nJ} - \frac{T^2}{nIJ}$$

$$SS(\text{Columns}) = \sum_j \frac{B_j^2}{nI} - \frac{T^2}{nIJ}$$

$$SS(\text{Within}) = \sum_{i,j,k} y_{ijk}^2 - \sum_{i,j} \frac{C_{ij}^2}{n}$$

$$SS(\text{Total}) = \sum_{i,j,k} y_{ijk}^2 - \frac{T^2}{nIJ}$$

$$SS(\text{Interaction}) = SS(\text{Total}) - SS(\text{Rows}) - SS(\text{Columns}) - SS(\text{Within})$$

7. Two-factor ANOVA

H_0: 1. all $\delta_{ij} = 0$ (no interaction effect)
    2. all $\alpha_i = 0$ (no row effect)
    3. all $\beta_j = 0$ (no column effect)
T.S.: 1. $F = MS(\text{Interaction})/MS(\text{Within})$
    2. $F = MS(\text{Rows})/MS(\text{Within})$
    3. $F = MS(\text{Columns})/MS(\text{Within})$

8. Tukey $100(1 - \alpha)\%$ confidence interval for $\mu_{ij} - \mu_{i*j*}$

$$(\bar{y}_{ij} - \bar{y}_{i*j*}) \pm q_\alpha(IJ, \text{d.f.}_2)\sqrt{MS(\text{Within})/n}$$

9. Randomized block design

$$SS(\text{Treatment}) = J \sum (\bar{y}_{i.} - \bar{y}_{..})^2 = \frac{(\sum A_i^2)}{J} - \frac{T^2}{IJ}$$

where

$$A_i = \sum_j y_{ij}, \; T = \sum_i \sum_j y_{ij}$$

$$SS(\text{Block}) = I \sum (\bar{y}_{.j} - \bar{y}_{..})^2 = \frac{(\sum B_j^2)}{I} - \frac{T^2}{IJ}$$

where

$$B_j = \sum_i y_{ij}, \; T = \sum_i \sum_j y_{ij}$$

$$SS(\text{Total}) = \sum (y_{ij} - \bar{y}_{..})^2 = \sum (y_{ij}^2) - \frac{T^2}{IJ}$$

$$SS(\text{Error}) = \sum (y_{ij} - \bar{y}_{.j} - \bar{y}_{i.} + \bar{y}_{..})^2$$
$$= SS(\text{Total}) - SS(\text{Treatment}) - SS(\text{Block})$$

10. *F* tests for randomized block design

For H_0: No treatment effect,

$$F = \frac{SS(Treatment)/(I - 1)}{SS(Error)/(I - 1)(J - 1)}$$

For H_0: No block effect

$$F = \frac{SS(Block)/(J - 1)}{SS(Error)/(I - 1)(J - 1)}$$

CHAPTER 12   EXERCISES

12.69   Three different designs of video recording equipment are subjected to accelerated use testing, and the times to failure (in hours) of each unit are recorded:

					Time					
Design A:	226	400	462	489	510	541	547	563	581	603
Design B:	329	366	409	451	465	490	517	546	577	615
Design C:	421	484	506	566	589	605	619	634	651	600

a. Calculate means and variances for each design.
b. Use these results to calculate SS(Between) and SS(Within).
c. Use the shortcut formulas to calculate the sums of squares.

12.70   Refer to Exercise 12.69. Is the research hypothesis of unequal means supported? First use $\alpha = .05$, then place bounds on the *p*-value.

12.71   Perform the Kruskal-Wallis test for the hypothesis of Exercise 12.70. Is the conclusion substantially different from that of Exercise 12.70?

12.72   Plot the data of Exercise 12.69. Do there appear to be any major violations of ANOVA assumptions?

12.73   Use the Tukey procedure to calculate overall 95% confidence intervals for the pairwise differences among the means of Exercise 12.69.

12.74   In a study of the effects of television commercials on 7-year-old children, the attention span of children watching commercials for clothing, food products, and toys is measured. To reduce the effects of outliers, only the median attention span for each commercial is used.

Commercial					Median Attention Span (Seconds)							
Clothes	21	30	23	37	21	18	30	42	36			
Food	32	51	46	30	25	41	38	50	45	53	57	41
Toys	48	59	51	47	58	56	49	55	52	49	60	

SAS output is shown on the next page.

DEPENDENT VARIABLE: ATTSPAN   ATTENTION SPAN

SOURCE	DF	SUM OF SQUARES	MEAN SQUARE	F VALUE	PR > F	R-SQUARE	C.V.
MODEL	2	2953.64299242	1476.82149621	23.10	0.0001	0.614386	18.9378
ERROR	29	1853.82575758	63.92502612		ROOT MSE		ATTSPAN MEAN
CORRECTED TOTAL	31	4807.46875000			7.99531276		42.21875000

MEANS

COMMTYPE	N	ATTSPAN
DUDS	9	28.6666667
FOODS	12	42.4166667
TOYS	11	53.0909091

WILCOXON SCORES (RANK SUMS)

LEVEL	N	SUM OF SCORES	EXPECTED UNDER HO	STD DEV UNDER HO	MEAN SCORE
TOYS	11	274.50	181.50	25.19	24.95
FOODS	12	193.50	198.00	25.67	16.12
DUDS	9	60.00	148.50	23.84	6.67

KRUSKAL-WALLIS TEST (CHI-SQUARE APPROXIMATION)
CHISQ= 18.87   DF= 2   PROB > CHISQ=0.0001

    a. Locate the value of the F statistic for the null hypothesis of equal means.

    b. Can this hypothesis be rejected using $\alpha = .01$?

    c. Locate the p-value for this test.

12.75 a. Calculate the value of the Kruskal-Wallis statistic in Exercise 12.74.

    b. Can the hypothesis of equal means (or more properly "locations") be rejected using $\alpha = .01$?

12.76 a. Plot the data of Exercise 12.74.

    b. Do there appear to be serious violations of ANOVA assumptions?

    c. Does it matter much whether an F test or a Kruskal-Wallis test is used?

12.77 Calculate 99% Tukey confidence intervals for differences in means for the data of Exercise 12.74. Which differences, if any, are significant at $\alpha = .01$?

12.78 A township manager had four appraisers estimate the fair market value of 12 houses. The estimates, in thousands of dollars, are

					Home							
Appraiser	1	2	3	4	5	6	7	8	9	10	11	12
A	86	76	93	110	73	55	96	74	96	140	88	72
B	81	75	95	105	70	53	91	75	95	120	75	68
C	89	80	97	110	80	61	89	80	100	130	90	75
D	90	76	96	108	78	63	99	77	99	135	94	75

Computer output from the SAS package is shown at the top of page 534.

    a. How relevant is the null hypothesis of equality of house prices? Is this hypothesis rejected?

    b. Locate the value of the F statistic for testing the null hypothesis of the equality of appraiser effects.

    c. Can the null hypothesis be rejected at typical α levels? What is the indicated p-value?

HOME VALUATIONS BY APPRAISERS

ANALYSIS OF VARIANCE PROCEDURE

DEPENDENT VARIABLE: VALUE   FAIR MARKET VALUE OF HOUSE

SOURCE	DF	SUM OF SQUARES	MEAN SQUARE	F VALUE	PR > F	R-SQUARE	C.V.
MODEL	14	16467.62500000	1176.25892857	98.60	0.0001	0.976651	3.9166
ERROR	33	393.68750000	11.92992424		ROOT MSE		VALUE MEAN
CORRECTED TOTAL	47	16861.31250000			3.45397224		88.18750000

SOURCE	DF	ANOVA SS	F VALUE	PR > F
APPRAISR	3	381.56250000	10.66	0.0001
HOME	11	16086.06250000	122.58	0.0001

MEANS

APPRAISR	N	VALUE
1	12	88.2500000
2	12	83.5833333
3	12	90.0833333
4	12	90.8333333

12.79 Use the Tukey method to test ($\alpha = .05$) the significance of pairwise differences in appraiser effects for the data of Exercise 12.78.

12.80 The data of Exercise 12.78 were also analyzed incorrectly as a one-way ANOVA experiment, with the following output:

HOME VALUATION IGNORING HOME FACTOR

ANALYSIS OF VARIANCE PROCEDURE

DEPENDENT VARIABLE: VALUE   FAIR MARKET VALUE OF HOUSE

SOURCE	DF	SUM OF SQUARES	MEAN SQUARE	F VALUE	PR > F	R-SQUARE	C.V.
MODEL	3	381.56250000	127.18750000	0.34	0.7968	0.022629	21.9453
ERROR	44	16479.75000000	374.53977273				
CORRECTED TOTAL	47	16861.31250000	ROOT MSE		VALUE MEAN		
			19.35303007		88.18750000		

a. Would the null hypothesis of equal appraiser means be rejected at $\alpha = .05$?

b. How important is it to control for the effect of house differences in Exercise 12.78?

12.81 As part of an environmental impact study, an offshore oil driller tests three different drilling-rig designs at two different depths. The dependent variable of interest is the fish catch in a small net alongside the rig. The data are

	Design		
Depth	A	B	C
1	1025	896	925
	988	914	984
	1104	953	963

Depth	Design		
	A	B	C
2	721	630	665
	785	687	741
	655	652	706

SAS output is given below:

FISH CATCH AROUND OIL RIGS

ANALYSIS OF VARIANCE PROCEDURE

DEPENDENT VARIABLE: CATCH

SOURCE	DF	SUM OF SQUARES	MEAN SQUARE	F VALUE	PR > F	R-SQUARE	C.V.
MODEL	5	378554.00000000	75710.80000000	38.65	0.0001	0.941536	5.313
ERROR	12	23506.00000000	1958.83333333		ROOT MSE		CATCH MEA
CORRECTED TOTAL	17	402060.00000000			44.25870912		833.0000000

SOURCE	DF	ANOVA SS	F VALUE	PR > F
DEPTH	1	350005.55555556	178.68	0.0001
DESIGN	2	24892.00000000	6.35	0.0131
DEPTH*DESIGN	2	3656.44444444	0.93	0.4200

MEANS

DEPTH	DESIGN	N	CATCH
1	A	3	1039.00000
1	B	3	921.00000
1	C	3	957.33333
2	A	3	720.33333
2	B	3	656.33333
2	C	3	704.00000

    a. Plot an interaction profile.

    b. Test the null hypothesis of no interaction at $\alpha = .05$.

    c. Does it appear that there is substantial interaction?

12.82 Refer to the output of Exercise 12.81.

    a. Are there significant effects of design? State the p-value.

    b. Are there significant depth effects at $\alpha = .05$?

12.83 Refer to the output of Exercise 12.81. Calculate overall 95% confidence intervals for differences among design effects.

12.84 A food manufacturer tests several formulations of an orange juice product. Three different sweetness levels are tested, in combination with two acidity levels and two color levels. Six panels rate each combination on a 1–99 scale. The ratings are shown below:

Sweetness	Acidity	Color	Rating					
1	1	1	40	35	45	42	48	45
1	1	0	62	56	60	54	60	65
1	2	1	38	32	50	40	46	35

Sweetness	Acidity	Color	Rating					
1	2	0	60	50	48	61	55	53
2	1	1	45	56	50	45	55	48
2	1	0	72	56	63	75	67	68
2	2	1	47	53	46	52	56	47
2	2	0	60	66	56	64	72	70
3	1	1	35	50	35	40	43	35
3	1	0	56	48	52	45	59	52
3	2	1	25	35	30	24	34	34
3	2	0	40	36	32	31	34	38

The SAS analysis is shown below:

Analysis of Juice Experiment

ANALYSIS OF VARIANCE PROCEDURE

DEPENDENT VARIABLE: RATING

SOURCE	DF	SUM OF SQUARES	MEAN SQUARE	F VALUE	PR > F	R-SQUARE	C.V.
MODEL	11	8769.77777778	797.25252525	29.01	0.0001	0.841755	10.7465
ERROR	60	1648.66666667	27.47777778		ROOT MSE		RATING MEAN
CORRECTED TOTAL	71	10418.44444444			5.24192501		48.77777778

SOURCE	DF	ANOVA SS	F VALUE	PR > F
SWEET	2	4149.52777778	75.51	0.0001
ACIDITY	1	624.22222222	22.72	0.0001
SWEET*ACIDITY	2	488.52777778	8.89	0.0004
COLOR	1	3200.00000000	116.46	0.0001
SWEET*COLOR	2	203.08333333	3.70	0.0307
ACIDITY*COLOR	1	80.22222222	2.92	0.0927
SWEET*ACIDITY*COLOR	2	24.19444444	0.44	0.6459

MEANS

SWEET	ACIDITY	COLOR	N	RATING
High	1	Enhanced	6	39.6666667
High	1	Natural	6	52.0000000
High	2	Enhanced	6	30.3333333
High	2	Natural	6	35.1666667
Low	1	Enhanced	6	42.5000000
Low	1	Natural	6	59.5000000
Low	2	Enhanced	6	40.1666667
Low	2	Natural	6	54.5000000
Medium	1	Enhanced	6	49.8333333
Medium	1	Natural	6	66.8333333
Medium	2	Enhanced	6	50.1666667
Medium	2	Natural	6	64.6666667

a. Does there appear to be a significant three-factor interaction?

b. Plot the acidity–color interaction profile. Does it appear that this interaction is substantial?

12.85 Summarize the results of the F tests shown in the output of Exercise 12.84.

12.86 Refer to Exercise 12.84.

a. Calculate a 95% confidence interval for the mean difference in rating by the two acidity levels. Is the difference statistically significant at $\alpha = .05$?

b. Which differences among the 12 cell means are statistically significant ($\alpha = .05$) according to the Tukey method?

12.87 A paint manufacturer experimented with six possible formulations for a new economy-grade paint. Six samples of each formulation were tested in a high-stress laboratory environment. The time to paint failure was recorded for each sample. High scores are preferable and the company regarded 40 as a minimum acceptable score. The following results were obtained:

LEVEL	N	MEAN	STDEV
1	6	42.000	6.542
2	6	51.833	7.139
3	6	48.833	4.956
4	6	45.000	4.733
5	6	55.333	3.615
6	6	49.500	5.167

POOLED STDEV =   5.485

a. Verify that the sum of squares between formulations is 678.2 and that the sum of squares within formulations is 902.5.

b. Find d.f. and MS values and construct an ANOVA table.

c. Is there a statistically detectable difference among means, using $\alpha = .05$? What can be said about the p-value?

12.88 According to the Tukey method of paired comparisons, which pairs of means in Exercise 12.87 are detectably different, using $\alpha = .05$?

12.89 The 36 samples in Exercise 12.87 were collected and then tested in the lab in completely random order. Why is this method preferable to (for example) testing all of formulation 1 first, all of formulation 2 next, and so on?

12.90 The six paint formulations in Exercise 12.87 were in fact put together as all combinations of three bases and two coloring agents. It we wanted to separate the effect of different bases from the effect of different coloring agents, how should we reanalyze the data?

12.91 The data of Exercise 12.87 were treated as a two-factor ANOVA. The following computer output was obtained:

```
MTB > twoway of c1 by c3 c4

ANALYSIS OF VARIANCE  failtime

SOURCE        DF       SS       MS
base           2     613.2    306.6
coloring       1      51.4     51.4
INTERACTION    2      13.7      6.9
ERROR         30     902.5     30.1
TOTAL         35    1580.7

MTB > table by c3 c4;
SUBC> means of c1.
```

(continued)

```
ROWS: base      COLUMNS: coloring

           1        2       ALL

   1    42.000   45.000   43.500
   2    51.833   55.333   53.583
   3    48.833   49.500   49.167
  ALL   47.556   49.944   48.750

CELL CONTENTS --
          failtime:MEAN
```

    a. Is there evidence of statistically significant interaction between the factors?

    b. Show that the effect of coloring is not statistically significant at usual α levels, but the effect of base is statistically significant.

12.92 Use the Tukey method to construct 95% confidence intervals for all differences of "base" means, using the computer output in Exercise 12.91. Are any of the differences of means significant at $\alpha = .05$?

12.93 A manufacturer of laser printers is trying to improve the design of the toner cartridge, which determines much of the perceived quality of the printer output. In particular, the manufacturer wants to increase the life of the cartridge as measured by the number of thousands of pages printed satisfactorily. Four cartridge designs are tested. Sixteen cartridges of each design are tested and the number of thousands of pages produced is obtained for each cartridge. A computer analysis of the data yields the following output:

```
MTB > oneway of c1 by c2

ANALYSIS OF VARIANCE ON copies
SOURCE      DF        SS        MS         F         p
design       3      7022      2341     17.08     0.000
ERROR       60      8222       137
TOTAL       63     15244
                                    INDIVIDUAL 95 PCT CI'S FOR MEAN
                                    BASED ON POOLED STDEV
LEVEL        N      MEAN     STDEV   ----+---------+---------+---------+--
    1       16    123.31     12.40                  (----*----)
    2       16    109.44     12.59   (----*----)
    3       16    137.25     10.75                            (----*----)
    4       16    115.00     10.97        (----*----)
                                    ----+---------+---------+---------+--
POOLED STDEV =    11.71           108       120       132       144

MTB > kruskal wallis of c1 by c2

LEVEL      NOBS    MEDIAN   AVE. RANK    Z VALUE
    1       16     122.0       35.5        0.75
    2       16     107.0       18.4       -3.50
    3       16     138.5       51.2        4.63
    4       16     116.5       24.9       -1.88
OVERALL     64                 32.5

H = 28.32
H(ADJ. FOR TIES) = 28.35
```

According to the ANOVA table, is there a statistically significant difference some-where among the means, using $\alpha = .05$?

12.94 According to the Kruskal-Wallis output shown in Exercise 12.93, is there a sig-nificant difference among the cartridges in their average life? Again, use $\alpha = .05$. Does the result differ greatly from the result for the F test?

12.95 In the output for Exercise 12.93, which design seems to be best? (The first question is whether high or low scores are best.) Use the Tukey approach with $\alpha = .05$ to see if this design has a significantly better mean than each of the other designs.

12.96 Most people believe that televised sports events last considerably longer than nontelevised ones. Suppose that records are kept of the length (in minutes) of college football games in three categories: typetv $= 1$ for nationally televised games, typetv $= 2$ for regionally televised games, and typetv $= 3$ for nontelevised games. Statgraphics output from the data included the following:

Table of means for gamelength by typetv

Level	Count	Average	Stnd. Error (internal)	Stnd. Error (pooled s)	95 Percent Tukey HSD intervals for mean	
1	8	196.87500	5.1040513	4.4217775	189.33087	204.41913
2	13	192.92308	3.0497195	3.4687277	187.00498	198.84118
3	34	176.94118	2.1577457	2.1448771	173.28174	180.60062
Total	55	183.61818	1.6863998	1.6863998	180.74096	186.49540

a. Do the averages appear to be consistent with the opinion about television effect?

b. The confidence interval for the mean in level 3 doesn't overlap the other inter-vals at all. What does this fact suggest about the statistical significance of the difference in means?

12.97 A more formal statistical test of the data in Exercise 12.96 was provided by the following Statgraphics output:

One-Way Analysis of Variance

Data: gamelength
Level codes: typetv

Analysis of variance

Source of variation	Sum of Squares	d.f.	Mean square	F-ratio	Sig. level
Between groups	4047.3014	2	2023.6507	12.938	.0000
Within groups	8133.6804	52	156.4169		
Total (corrected)	12180.982	54			

a. Show that the null hypothesis of equal mean game lengths may be rejected at any plausible α value.

b. Can we interpret this result as showing that television makes a very large difference in the length of games?

12.98   Pairs of means from Exercise 12.96 were tested using the Tukey approach, with compensation for the unequal sample sizes. Statgraphics reported the results using a standard code. The means are divided into "homogeneous groups" using Tukey's test. Means that are *not* significantly different each have an asterisk (*) in the same column. If two means do not have an asterisk in the same column, they are significantly different according to the Tukey procedure, as shown.

```
          Multiple range analysis for gamelength by typetv
-----------------------------------------------------------------------------
Method: 95 Percent Tukey HSD Intervals
Level    Count      Average    Homogeneous Groups
-----------------------------------------------------------------------------
  3         34      176.94118    *
  2         13      192.92308         *
  1          8      196.87500         *
-----------------------------------------------------------------------------
```

Do these results indicate that televised games are detectably longer than nontelevised ones?

12.99   Box plots of the data for Exercise 12.96 are shown in Figure 12.4.
   a. Does there appear to be a problem of nonnormality?
   b. Does there appear to be a problem of nonconstant variance?

12.100 Statgraphics also produced a Kruskal-Wallis test for the football game–length data of Exercise 12.96:

```
-----------------------------------------------------------------------------
Kruskal-Wallis analysis of gamelength by typetv
-----------------------------------------------------------------------------
Level             Sample Size      Average Rank
-----------------------------------------------------------------------------
  1                    8             41.3125
  2                   13             38.3077
  3                   34             20.9265
-----------------------------------------------------------------------------
Test statistic = 17.5554  Significance level  = 1.54132E-4
```

Does this test yield a substantially different conclusion than the F test of Exercise 12.97?

12.101 A hotel is renovating rooms and needs to select the type of curtains to use for windows. One consideration is how much light the curtains let in. The designer has three choices of fabric, two choices of liner, and two choices for how the curtains close. All 18 combinations are put together in 18 different rooms. The light entering each room at 7:00 A.M. is measured on each of 5 successive days. The first analysis of the data was done using Statgraphics, which yields the ANOVA table on page 542. (The IND entry in the Source column may be ignored, and read the CROSS entry as indicating interaction.)

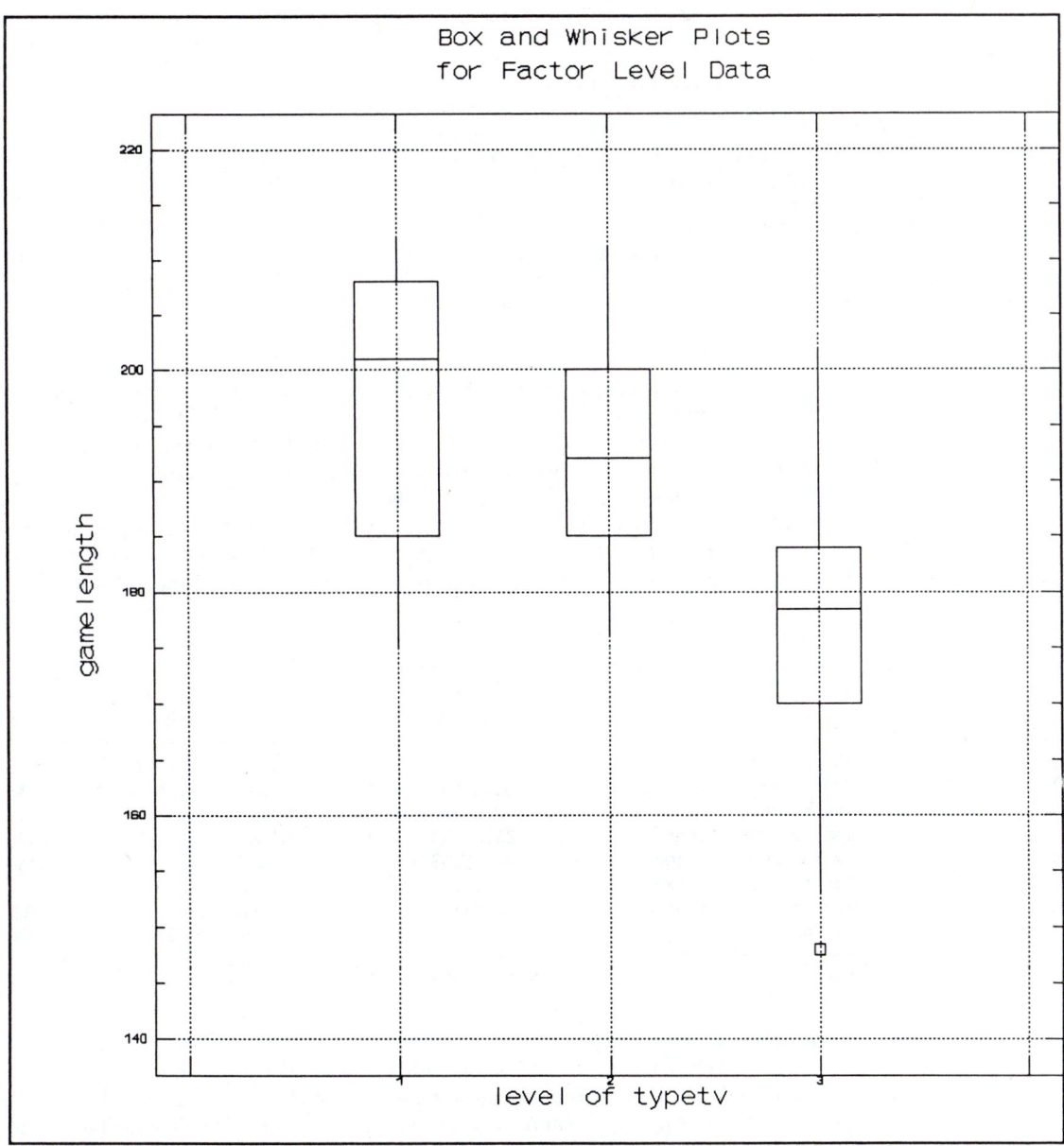

FIGURE 12.4   Box Plots: Lengths of Football Games

Further ANOVA for Variables in the Order Fitted

Source	Sum of Squares	DF	Mean Sq.	F-Ratio	P-value
IND fabric	1689.10000	2	844.55000	18.19	.0000
IND liner	88.81667	1	88.81667	1.91	.1730
IND closure	2.81667	1	2.81667	.06	.8091
fabric CROSS liner	21.23333	2	10.61667	.23	.7964
fabric CROSS closure	24.03333	2	12.01667	.26	.7730
liner CROSS closure	.01667	1	.01667	.00	.9852
fabric CROSS liner CROSS cl	10.83333	2	5.41667	.12	.8901
Model	1836.85000	11			

a. Are there any statistically detectable (significant) interactions for the data as analyzed? How crucial is it which α value is used?

b. Which main effects, if any, are significant for the data as analyzed?

12.102 In Exercise 12.101, there is at least one important source of variability that wasn't included in the analysis. What is it?

12.103 The data from Exercise 12.101 were reanalyzed, with day number included as another factor (in effect, a blocking factor). The Statgraphics output follows. (Again, ignore the IND notation and read CROSS as indicating interaction).

Further ANOVA for Variables in the Order Fitted

Source	Sum of Squares	DF	Mean Sq.	F-Ratio	P-value
IND fabric	1689.10000	2	844.55000	62.89	.0000
IND liner	88.81667	1	88.81667	6.61	.0136
IND closure	2.81667	1	2.81667	.21	.6541
fabric CROSS liner	21.23333	2	10.61667	.79	.4599
fabric CROSS closure	24.03333	2	12.01667	.89	.4160
liner CROSS closure	.01667	1	.01667	.00	.9724
fabric CROSS liner CROSS cl	10.83333	2	5.41667	.40	.6705
IND daynumber	1637.10000	4	409.27500	30.48	.0000
Model	3473.95000	15			

a. Which interactions are statistically significant at reasonable α levels?

b. Which main effects are detectable (significant)?

c. Does it appear that the type of linear is important in determining how much light is in the room?

12.104 Compare the results of Exercises 12.101 and 12.103. What do the differences indicate about the relevance of the "daynumber" factor?

12.105 As part of a market test of a new package design, a cereal manufacturer prepared boxes in each of two colors with each of two new type styles. Each color–type-style combination was tested in 12 randomly assigned supermarkets in the test area. Sales of the cereal over a three-day period were recorded. The data are recorded in the "CH12Cl.DAT' file on the data disk. Load the data into your computer program. Sales are shown in column 1, color code (1 or 2) in column 2, and type-style code (1 or 2) in column 3.

a. Obtain mean sales for each combination of color code and type-style code.

b. Does there appear to be a large interaction between color and type style, based on these means?

12.106 a. Obtain an analysis of variance (ANOVA) table for the data of Exercise 12.105, with sales as the dependent variable. Is there a relatively large interaction sum of squares?

b. Are there statistically detectable (significant) effects of color and of type style? Obtain p-values if the program will do so; otherwise, try $\alpha = .05$ and $\alpha = .01$.

12.07 If the computer program will do so conveniently, obtain "residuals" (actual sales minus mean for the color–type-style combination) for the data of Exercise 12.105. Obtain a histogram, stem-and-leaf display, or normal plot of the residuals. Is there any evidence of serious nonnormality in the data?

12.108 A furniture store targeted eight ZIP codes for promotional activity. The store's records for the past two months indicated all purchases by residents of each ZIP code. The data are stored in the 'CH12C2.DAT' file on the data disk, which should be read into your computer package. Sales amounts are stored in column 1 of the file, and numbers 1–8 for the eight ZIP codes are stored in column 2.

a. Obtain boxplots of the sales data separately for each ZIP code. Do these boxplots indicate that the data are roughly normally distributed within each ZIP code?

b. Obtain an ANOVA table for testing the null hypothesis of equal means. Can this hypothesis be rejected at conventional α values?

12.109 a. Use the computer program to perform a Kruskal-Wallis test of the null hypothesis of equal distributions for the data of Exercise 12.108. Can the null hypothesis be rejected at conventional α values?

b. Do the F and Kruskal-Wallis tests give similar conclusions? If not, what explains the difference in results?

12.110 A company wanted to select a long-distance telephone service on the basis of lowest cost. A clerk took 50 calls at random from the list of those made by the company in the last three months, and determined what each call would cost using each service. The results are in the 'CH12C3.DAT' file on the data disk. Cost of the call is in column 1, call number is in column 2, and service company number is in column 3. Load the data into your statistical computer program.

a. Obtain an analysis of variance (ANOVA) table using call number and service number as factors.

b. Is there a statistically detectable (significant) effect of service number? If possible, obtain a p-value.

c. Explain why there shouldn't be an interaction term between the two factors in the ANOVA model.

12.111 If your computer program will do so conveniently, perform Tukey tests of significance for all pairwise differences among service company means in Exercise 12.110, using $\alpha = .05$. If the computer isn't programmed to do so, obtain the means for each service and do the tests by hand. Is there a clear-cut lowest-cost service among the four?

12.112 a. Reanalyze the data of Exercise 12.110, ignore the call number factor, and treat the service company number as the only factor. Obtain an ANOVA table.

b. Does the error mean square for this analysis differ much from the error mean square in the two-factor analysis? If so, what does that fact say about the wisdom of blocking, using call numbers (as opposed to allocating 200 calls completely at random, 50 to each of the four service companies)?

12.113 a. If possible, have the computer program find predicted values and residuals (actual − predicted) for the data of Exercise 12.110. Obtain a plot of residuals against predicted values. Does the variability around predicted values appear to be constant?

   b. Have the computer program calculate the logarithms, either natural (base e) or common (base 10), of the costs. Obtain a new ANOVA table and use the logarithm of cost as the dependent variable, with call number and service company number as factors. Is there a statistically detectable (significant) service company effect?

   c. Obtain a plot of residuals against predicted values for the logarithm model. Does the variability around predicted values appear constant?

CASE   Designed Experiments

A large insurance company employs many clerical workers for routine computer-based tasks. The flow of tasks is enormous and never-ending, so worker efficiency is crucial to the company's smooth operation. The director of human resources feels that new working conditions could improve productivity by a few percentage points, more than enough to cover the cost of the changes. What isn't clear is *which* new conditions would have the best effect on productivity. An experiment was carried out to test the effects.

The director of human resources has written you a memo asking you to analyze the results. The relevant part of the memo says:

> We took three divisions: Claims (1), data processing (2), and investments (3). The way it turned out, we could get 33 clerical people in each division to participate. We picked the people randomly from personnel lists and—even though there were a few refusals so we had to pick other people—we think that the groups are reasonably representative. Then we had everybody draw numbers from a hat. Number 1 meant that the person went to a flextime schedule, 2 meant a four-day work week, and 3 meant a regular week in an enhanced work environment. We ignored the data for the first two weeks while people were getting used to the new setup. Then we measured percentage efficiency gains for everybody over the next four weeks. The efficiency measures are good enough that we think they'll be accurate for our purposes. We think we did the study pretty well.
>
> We can't figure out the results. The averages for the three conditions are practically the same, so it seems like it didn't make much difference. But I've got some supervisors who think that one or another of the new conditions is doing great things for efficiency, and other supervisors who think some condition is actually hurting efficiency. Are they nuts, or is there something in the results that we haven't noticed?

The data and means are reproduced here for you. Reanalyze the data—you might want to use a computer program—and see what you can find about average efficiency gains. Write a memo to the director and explain your findings. The director doesn't remember any statistical theory, so try to use ordinary language.

ROW	%improve	dept	conditn	ROW	%improve	dept	conditn	ROW	%improve	dept	conditn
1	5.5	1	1	41	12.7	2	1	81	10.0	3	2
2	5.5	1	1	42	21.2	2	1	82	14.7	3	2
3	7.1	1	1	43	10.6	2	1	83	17.5	3	2
4	-2.1	1	1	44	16.6	2	1	84	17.2	3	2
5	4.2	1	1	45	-1.1	2	2	85	13.4	3	2
6	-0.9	1	1	46	-7.2	2	2	86	16.0	3	2
7	8.9	1	1	47	-5.9	2	2	87	17.5	3	2
8	3.5	1	1	48	-4.3	2	2	88	22.4	3	2
9	6.9	1	1	49	-2.1	2	2	89	6.7	3	3
10	3.3	1	1	50	-2.0	2	2	90	7.0	3	3
11	5.7	1	1	51	-4.0	2	2	91	8.4	3	3
12	-3.7	1	2	52	-5.1	2	2	92	11.1	3	3
13	8.1	1	2	53	-9.0	2	2	93	9.5	3	3
14	6.6	1	2	54	-6.2	2	2	94	10.7	3	3
15	5.3	1	2	55	-5.3	2	2	95	13.3	3	3
16	-0.1	1	2	56	-0.3	2	3	96	7.3	3	3
17	-0.6	1	2	57	4.1	2	3	97	10.0	3	3
18	6.3	1	2	58	1.4	2	3	98	8.4	3	3
19	0.9	1	2	59	4.0	2	3	99	10.8	3	3
20	5.7	1	2	60	4.5	2	3				
21	2.9	1	2	61	-2.3	2	3				
22	3.0	1	2	62	6.7	2	3				
23	5.3	1	3	63	4.4	2	3				
24	11.5	1	3	64	-1.6	2	3				
25	5.9	1	3	65	1.5	2	3				
26	5.2	1	3	66	2.0	2	3				
27	4.0	1	3	67	0.4	3	1				
28	-1.7	1	3	68	-3.0	3	1				
29	6.4	1	3	69	-7.2	3	1				
30	1.8	1	3	70	-6.8	3	1				
31	2.9	1	3	71	-4.2	3	1				
32	0.6	1	3	72	-8.2	3	1				
33	4.3	1	3	73	-5.0	3	1				
34	19.5	2	1	74	-11.4	3	1				
35	17.9	2	1	75	-6.6	3	1				
36	19.7	2	1	76	-5.9	3	1				
37	17.5	2	1	77	-4.3	3	1				
38	16.4	2	1	78	21.5	3	2				
39	14.4	2	1	79	19.3	3	2				
40	19.3	2	1	80	16.1	3	2				

ROWS: dept

	%improve MEAN
1	3.885
2	4.788
3	6.867
ALL	5.180

ROWS: conditn

	%improve MEAN
1	5.188
2	5.085
3	5.267
ALL	5.180

Appendix: Sums of Squares ■

In this appendix we sketch a proof that SS(Total) = SS(Between) + SS(Within) for a one-factor design. Similar proofs apply to more complicated ANOVA problems, as long as the design is balanced. The quantity SS(Total) can be written as follows

$$SS(Total) = \sum_{i,j}(y_{ij} - \bar{y})^2$$

$$= \sum_{i,j}(y_{ij} - \bar{y}_i + \bar{y}_i - \bar{y})^2$$

$$= \sum_{i,j}(y_{ij} - \bar{y}_j)^2 + 2\sum_i\left[\sum_j(y_{ij} - \bar{y}_i)\right](\bar{y}_i - \bar{y}) + \sum_{i,j}(\bar{y}_i - \bar{y})^2$$

by expanding $(a + b)^2$ as $a^2 + 2ab + b^2$. For a fixed group i, the quantity in square brackets of the second term is a sum of deviations from a mean, which is always zero. Therefore the middle term is zero. The first term is SS(Within) by definition. The last term involves $\sum_j (\bar{y}_i - \bar{y})^2$; the quantity being summed is a constant (with respect to j) summed n_i times. Therefore the last term is SS(Between), and the desired result holds.

Review Exercises Chapters 10–12

   ■

R86 A sample of 40 testers rates the thirst-quenching property of an old formulation of a soft drink and a new formulation. The drinks are scored on a 0–100 scale. The results are

Formulation	Mean	Standard Deviation
Old	41.15	14.7
New	45.55	17.8

  a. Calculate a 95% confidence interval for the difference of the true (population) means using a pooled-variance procedure.

  b. Based on this interval, can the null hypothesis of equal means be rejected, using $\alpha = .05$?

  c. In fact, it's a very bad idea to use a pooled-variance procedure for these data. Why?

R87 The differences between ratings of the new formulation and the old one in Exercise R86 are shown here:

4	3	−1	9	−4	7	−6	4	−2	7	2	4	14	1
2	12	−7	11	12	9	4	10	−5	−7	−2	−3	10	
−1	23	2	7	5	15	4	0	1	5	−4	16	15	

The mean of the differences is 4.40 and the standard deviation is 7.05.

  a. Calculate a 95% confidence interval for the population mean difference.

  b. Based on this interval, can the null hypothesis that the mean difference is zero be rejected using $\alpha = .05$?

  c. Is there any evidence of a serious violation of assumptions for this procedure?

R88 Perform an appropriate rank test for the difference data of Exercise R87, using $\alpha = .05$ (two-sided). Does this test lead to the same conclusion as the t test of that exercise?

R89 Place bounds on the p-values in Exercises R87 and R88. Are the p-values similar in the two exercises?

R90 Compare the widths of the confidence intervals found in Exercises R86 and R87. What do the relative sizes of the intervals indicate about the effect of having the same tasters rate both formulations (as opposed to having different tasters rating each formulation)?

R91 A large corporation has a pool of individuals responsible for most word-processing jobs. As a means of providing a pleasant and productive atmosphere, the company plays taped music during the workday. Some individuals complain that the music occasionally becomes distracting. As an experiment, the company provides varying degrees of control over the music's volume (ranging from 1 = no control to

4 = complete control) to samples of size 16 each of word-processing operators. An efficiency score is obtained for each person.

	Degree of Control			
Efficiency	1	2	3	4
	42	55	63	66
	57	50	57	63
	37	65	24	64
	52	22	55	57
	58	65	64	64
	58	56	56	60
	56	63	61	62
	57	58	60	62
	41	65	63	58
	49	57	64	54
	53	52	67	65
	55	61	66	60
	53	64	66	63
	42	57	52	64
	48	65	47	49
	48	66	65	61
$\bar{y}$	50.38	57.56	58.13	60.75
s	6.80	10.76	10.71	4.45

a. Test the null hypothesis that the four population means are equal, using $\alpha = .01$. State the conclusion carefully.
b. Place bounds on the p-value.
c. Is there any indication that any of the formal mathematical assumptions have been violated? If so, do the violations make your answers to parts (a) and (b) seriously wrong?

R92 a. Using the data of Exercise R91, calculate simultaneous 99% confidence intervals for the differences of all pairs of means.
b. Which pairs of means, if any, are significantly different at $\alpha = .05$?

R93 For the data of Exercise R91, the value of the Kruskal-Wallis statistic is 17.18.
a. Can the null hypothesis that the four groups' distributions are equal be rejected at $\alpha = .01$?
b. Place bounds on the p-value of the statistic.
c. Does this test yield essentially the same conclusion as the test in Exercise R91?

R94 In the study of Exercise R91, the participants who have some degree of control also rate that control as not useful, somewhat useful, or very useful. The frequencies are

	Degree of Control			
Rating	1	2	3	Total
Not useful	7	3	2	12
Somewhat useful	4	7	5	16
Very useful	5	6	9	20
Total	16	16	16	48

a. Is there a statistically significant relation between rating and degree of control, using $\alpha = .05$?

b. Place bounds on the p-value for the test statistic used in part (a).

c. Is there any reason to be skeptical of the (approximate) p-value bounds?

R95   Do the frequencies in Exercise R94 indicate a moderately strong relation, whether or not the relation is statistically significant?

R96   One person interprets the results of Exercise R94 as proving that there is no relation between rating and degree of control. Is this interpretation appropriate?

R97   A real-estate firm in the headquarter city of a large corporation is contracted by the corporation to find housing and mortgages for the corporation's newly arriving managers. One concern is the length of mortgage contracts. Samples are taken of managers arriving by transfer from other corporation offices and of newly hired managers. The data are taken over a time when mortgage availability and terms are stable. The following lengths (in months) of mortgage contracts are obtained:

Transfer: 180 240 300 360 240 180 144 300 240 240 360 180 180
           300 240   ($n = 15$, $\bar{y} = 245.6$, $s = 66.9$)

New hires: 360 360 360 240 270 300 360 360 300 360 360 300 300
           240 300 360 360 360 360 360 300 300 360 240 360 360
           360 360 300 360 360 300   ($n = 32$, $\bar{y} = 329.1$, $s = 41.4$)

Use pooled-variance methods to calculate a 95% confidence interval for the difference of population means. Based on this interval, can you conclude that there is a statistically significant difference? What α are you using?

R98   The use of pooled-variance methods in Exercise R97 is a poor idea for (at least) two reasons. Discuss the reasons.

R99   Recalculate the confidence interval of Exercise R97 using a more appropriate method. Does the new interval lead to the same conclusion about the significance of the difference?

R100   When the data of Exercise R97 are ranked, the sum of the ranks in the transfers sample is 198.0. Test the null hypothesis that the distribution of mortgage lengths is the same in the transfers and new-hires populations against a general research hypothesis. State a bound on the p-value.

R101   Test the null hypothesis of equal variances, using the data of Exercise R97. Use a two-sided research hypothesis.

a. Can the null hypothesis be rejected at $\alpha = .01$?

b. Is there any reason to suspect that the nominal α of .01 might be in error? Why?

R102 An income-tax preparation service tests three microcomputer programs designed to help its staff prepare state and federal tax returns. Random samples of 10 experienced and 10 inexperienced preparers are assigned to each of three programs. The time required to prepare a standard return is obtained for each of the 60 preparers. The following means and (standard deviations) are calculated:

Program	Experienced	Inexperienced
A	36.60 (5.190)	40.50 (3.342)
B	28.30 (6.201)	41.70 (3.164)
C	34.00 (6.600)	40.60 (4.971)

a. Verify that SS(Program) = 129.7 and that SS(Error) = 1393.5.

b. Is there a statistically significant difference among the program means, using $\alpha = .05$?

R103 Which pairs of program means in Exercise R102, if any, are significantly different, using $\alpha = .05$?

R104 Refer to the means of Exercise R102. Construct a profile plot. Is there any reason to think that the overall program means might not be a good indication of the relative merits of the programs? It might be relevant to know that the service has relatively low turnover among its preparers; only about 15% of the preparers are inexperienced.

R105 Is there evidence of a nonconstant variance problem in Exercise R102?

R106 An analyst of microcomputer software firms keeps track of the number of test cycles of new programs before release for public sale. The following frequencies are obtained:

Number of cycles: 1   2   3   4   5+
Frequency: 39   16   5   3   12   (total = 75)

One theory indicates that the probability that there are exactly x cycles is $.4(.6)^{x-1}$, for $x = 1, 2, \ldots$. Are the actual frequencies consistent with this theory if one allows a .05 risk of Type 1 error?

R107 One possible objection to the test used in Exercise R106 is that there are fewer than five observations in the $x = 4$ category. Is this a valid objection?

R108 Data are collected on the price-to-earnings ratio (P/E) of common stocks of companies in two industries, electric utilities and computer services. The data are

Utilities:	5.8	6.6	6.1	5.7	5.4	6.0	6.0	5.5	5.9	5.6	6.0	6.0	5.8
	5.8	5.9	6.2	6.2	6.0	6.0	6.1	($n = 20, \bar{y} = 5.92, s = .291$)
Computer services:	6.2	6.7	5.9	6.8	6.7	6.2	6.5	6.5	6.8	6.6	7.5	6.2	7.9
	6.4	6.9	4.7	6.9	6.5	6.5	6.4	($n = 20, \bar{y} = 6.54, s = .624$)

Basic financial concepts suggest that the mean P/E should be higher for the computer service industry than for utilities. Do the data support this hypothesis? Use the appropriate t method. State a bound on the p-value.

R109 Test the hypothesis in Exercise R108 using rank methods. Again, state a bound on the p-value.

R110 From the appearance of the data in Exercise R108, is a t test or a rank test more appropriate? How much difference does the choice of test make in the conclusion?

R111 The P/E ratios should be more variable in the computer services stocks than in the utilities in Exercise R108. Is this hypothesis supported by the data, using $\alpha = .01$?

R112 What are the critical assumptions underlying your method in Exercise R111? Do these assumptions appear reasonable?

R113 A package-delivery company tests its current dispatching rule against a computerized rule. One of the methods is selected randomly for use on a given day; a key customer records the service as excellent, good, fair, or poor for each day. The following frequencies are obtained:

	Excellent	Good	Fair	Poor	Total
Current rule	36	39	15	10	100
Computerized rule	48	42	8	2	100

a. Calculate a 95% confidence interval for the difference of proportions of ratings of excellent between the current and computerized rules.

b. Use this interval to test the null hypothesis of equal proportions. What conclusion can be reached?

R114 Perform a formal hypothesis test for the null hypothesis of equal proportions of ratings of excellent using the data of Exercise R113. Assume that $\alpha = .05$.

R115 In gathering the data of Exercise R113, it is noted that there may be carryover effects from one day to the next such that one poor day may tend to be followed by another poor day. If in fact there are carryover effects, does this violate any of the assumptions underlying the method of Exercises R113 and R114?

R116 Using the data of Exercise R113, test the null hypothesis that the distribution of opinion is the same for the current rule as for the computerized rule. State bounds on the p-value.

R117 Other than the potential problem cited in Exercise R115, are there any violations of assumptions for the test in Exercise R116?

R118 A law firm tests two models of printers for use in its office. A random sample of 20 documents is chosen; each document is printed out by each printer. The time required (in seconds) is recorded. The data are as follows:

	Document													
	1	2	3	4	5	6	7	8	9	10	11	12	13	14
Printer A	24	40	16	28	28	43	18	25	19	17	17	21	37	25
Printer B	22	36	29	21	20	36	16	27	15	13	11	13	30	20
A − B	2	4	−13	7	8	7	2	−2	4	4	6	8	7	5

	15	16	17	18	19	20	$\bar{y}$	s
Printer A	43	22	38	30	32	41	28.20	9.32
Printer B	36	23	29	24	25	30	23.80	7.83
A − B	7	−1	9	6	7	11	4.40	5.21

a. Perform an appropriate t test for the null hypothesis of equal means against a two-sided research hypothesis. Use $\alpha = .05$.

b. State a bound on the p-value for the test in part (a). Can one safely come to a conclusion about the relative speed of the two printers?

R119 Use a rank test for the data of Exercise R118 to test the null hypothesis that the mean difference is zero. Does this test give the same conclusion as the t test of Exercise R118?

R120 Compare the standard deviation of the differences to the A and B standard deviations in Exercise R118. What does this comparison indicate about the desirability of printing out the same 20 documents on both printers rather than using one set of 20 documents for one printer and a different set for the other printer?

R121 As part of a performance review, junior managers are rated on a 50-point scale of managerial potential. The following results are obtained:

Undergraduate Major	n	$\bar{y}$	S
Business	12	21.17	8.26
Engineering	9	15.44	7.32
Liberal arts	18	27.39	8.15

Source	SS	d.f.	MS
Between	897.7	2	448.9
Within	2306.2	36	64.1
Total	3203.9	38	

a. Verify the computation of the sums of squares.

b. Is there a statistically significant difference among the means, using $\alpha = .05$?

R122 The rank sums for the data of Exercise R121 are business, 217.0; engineering, 101.0; and liberal arts, 462.0. Perform the appropriate rank test of the null hypothesis that the distribution of managerial potential is the same in the three groups.

R123 Examination of the data in Exercise R121 shows a definite right-skewness in all three samples. What does this fact indicate about the relative appropriateness of the tests in Exercises R121 and R122?

R124 The scale underlying the data of Exercise R121 is interpreted such that a score under 20 indicates little potential, a score between 20 and 29 indicates some potential, and a score above 30 indicates high potential. Examination of the data gives the following frequencies:

	Potential			
	Little	Some	High	Total
Business	7	3	2	12
Engineering	8	0	1	9
Liberal arts	2	9	7	18
Total	17	12	10	39

Test the null hypothesis that rated managerial potential is unrelated to type of education. Use $\alpha = .05$.

R125 Is there evidence that the nominal α probability in Exercise R124 is a poor approximation? How critical is the quality of the approximation to the general conclusion?

LINEAR REGRESSION AND CORRELATION METHODS

One of the most important uses of statistics for managers is prediction. A manager may want to forecast the cost of a particular contracting job given the size of that job; to forecast the sales of a particular product given the current rate of growth of gross national product; or to forecast the number of parts that will be produced given a certain size work force. The statistical method most **regression analysis**   widely used in making predictions is **regression analysis**.

In the regression approach, past data on the relevant variables are used to develop and evaluate a prediction equation. The variable that is being predicted **dependent and**   by this equation is the **dependent variable**. A variable that is used to make the pre-**independent**   diction is an **independent variable**. In this chapter we discuss regression methods **variables**   involving a single independent variable. In Chapter 14 we extend these methods to multiple regression, which is the case of more than one independent variable.

There are a number of tasks that can be accomplished in a regression study.

1. The data can be used to obtain a prediction equation.
2. The data can be used to estimate the amount of variability or uncertainty around the equation.
3. Because the data are only a sample, inferences can be made about the true population values for the regression quantities.
4. The prediction equation can be used to predict a reasonable range of values for future values of the dependent variable.
5. The data can be used to estimate the degree of correlation between dependent and independent variables, which indicates how strong the relation is.

In this chapter these tasks are carried out for the case of one independent variable.

Like any statistical method, regression analysis is based on a model that incorporates some assumptions. We begin in Section 13.1 by describing the simplest regression model and its assumptions. Methods for estimating the prediction equation and estimating the variability around it are given in Section 13.2. We discuss basic inference methods for regression in Section 13.3. In Section 13.4 we deal with prediction of future values of the dependent variable. Section 13.5 contains methods for assessing correlation. Finally in Section 13.6 we examine correlation based on ranks, an approach that is sometimes useful when assumptions underlying the ordinary correlation coefficient aren't met.

13.1 THE LINEAR REGRESSION MODEL ∎

Predicting future values of a variable is a crucial management activity. Financial officers must predict future cash flows, production managers must predict needs for raw materials, and human resources managers must predict future personnel needs. Explanation of past variation is also important. Explaining the past variation in number of clients of a social service agency can help to understand the demand for the agency's services. Finding the variables that explain deviations from an automobile component's specifications can help to improve the quality of that component. The basic idea of regression analysis is to use data on a quantitative independent variable to predict or explain variation in a quantitative dependent variable. We can distinguish between prediction (reference to future values) and explanation (reference to current or past values).

prediction vs explanation

(The virtues of hindsight indicate that explanation is easier than prediction.) However, it is often clearer to use "prediction" to include both cases. Therefore, in this book, we will sometimes blur the distinction between prediction and explanation.

For prediction (or explanation) to make much sense, there must be some connection between the variable we're predicting (the dependent variable) and the variable we're using to make the prediction (the independent variable). No doubt, if you tried long enough, you could find 26 common stocks whose price changes over a year have been accurately predicted by the won-loss percentage of the 26 major league baseball teams on the Fourth of July. But such a prediction seems absurd, because there is no connection between the two variables.

unit of association

Prediction requires a **unit of association**. There should be an entity that relates the two variables. With time series data, the unit of association may be simply time. The variables may be measured at the same time period or, for genuine prediction, the independent variable may be measured one time period before the dependent variable. For cross-sectional data, there should be an economic or physical entity that connects the variables. If we're trying to predict the change in market share of various soft drinks, we should consider the promotional activity for those drinks, not the advertising for various brands of potato chips. The need for a unit of association seems obvious, but there are many, many attempts made at prediction in which no such unit is evident.

simple regression

In this chapter, we consider simple linear regression analysis, in which there is a single independent variable and the equation for predicting a dependent variable y is a linear function of a given independent variable x. Suppose, for example, that the director of a county highway department wants to predict the cost of a resurfacing contract that is up for bids. We could reasonably predict the costs to be a function of the road miles to be resurfaced. A reasonable first attempt is to use a linear prediction function. Let y = total cost of a project in thousands of dollars, x = number of miles to be resurfaced, and $\hat{y}$ = the predicted cost, also in thousands of dollars. A prediction equation $\hat{y} = 2.0 + 3.0x$ (for example) is a linear equation. The constant term, such as the 2.0, is the **intercept** term and it is interpreted as the predicted value of y when $x = 0$. In the road resurfacing example, we may interpret the intercept as the fixed cost of beginning the project. The coefficient of x, such as the 3.0, is the **slope** of the line, the predicted change in y when there is a one-unit change in x. In the road resurfacing example, if two projects differed by one mile in length, we would predict that the longer project cost three thousand dollars more than the shorter one. In general, we write the prediction equation as

$$\hat{y} = \hat{\beta}_0 + \hat{\beta}_1 x$$

where $\hat{\beta}_0$ is the intercept and $\hat{\beta}_1$ is the slope. See Figure 13.1.

  The basic idea of simple linear regression is to use data to fit a prediction line that relates a dependent variable Y and a single independent variable X. The first assumption in simple regression is that the relation is, in fact, linear.

linearity assumption   According to the assumption of linearity, the slope of the equation does not change as X changes.* In the road resurfacing example, we would assume that there were no (substantial) economies or diseconomies from projects of longer mileage. There is little point in using simple linear regression unless the linearity assumption makes sense (at least roughly).

  Linearity is not always a reasonable assumption. For example, if we tried to predict Y = number of drivers that are aware of a car dealer's midsummer sale using X = number of repetitions of the dealer's radio commercial, the assumption of linearity means that the first broadcast of the commercial leads to no greater an increase in aware drivers than the thousand-and-first. (You've heard commercials like that.) We strongly doubt that such an assumption is valid. It

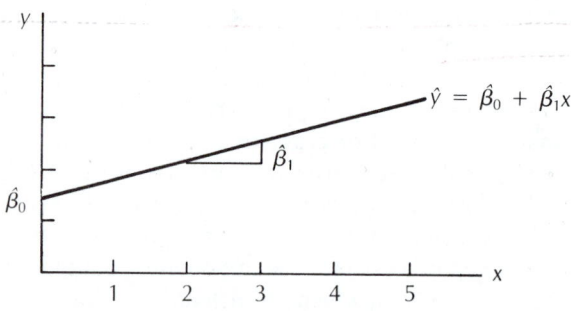

FIGURE 13.1   Linear Prediction Function

* In terms of calculus, we assume the first derivative of the equation (of total cost with respect to mileage) to be constant.

makes far more sense to us that the effect of repetition would diminish as the number of repetitions got larger, so a straight-line prediction wouldn't work well.

Assuming linearity, we would like to write $y = \beta_0 + \beta_1 x$. However, according to such an equation y is an exact linear function of x; no room is left for the inevitable errors (deviations of actual y values from their predicted values). Therefore, corresponding to each y we introduce a **random error term** ϵ_i and assume the model

random error term

$$Y_i = \beta_0 + \beta_1 x_i + \epsilon_i$$

We assume the random variable Y to be made up of a predictable part (a linear function of x) and an unpredictable part (the random error ϵ_i). The coefficients β_0 and β_1 are interpreted as the true underlying intercept and slope. The error term ϵ_i includes the effects of all other factors, known or unknown. In the road resurfacing project, unpredictable factors such as strikes, weather conditions, and equipment breakdowns would contribute to ϵ_i; so would factors such as hilliness or pre-repair condition of the road, that might have been used in prediction but were not. The combined effects of unpredictable and ignored factors yield the random error terms ϵ_i.

For example, one way to measure the gas mileage of various new cars would be to assign each car to a different driver, say, for a one-month period. What unpredictable and ignored factors might contribute to prediction error? Unpredictable (random) factors in this study would include the driving habits and skills of the drivers, the type of driving done (city vs. highway), and the number of stoplights encountered. Factors that would be ignored in a regression analysis of mileage and weight would include engine size and type of transmission (manual vs. automatic).

In regression studies, the values of the independent variable (the x_i values) are usually taken as predetermined constants, so the only source of randomness is the ϵ_i terms. While most economic and business applications have fixed x_i values, this is not always the case. For example, suppose that x_i is the score of an applicant on an aptitude test and Y_i is the productivity of the applicant. If the data are based on a random sample of applicants, X_i (as well as Y_i) is a random variable. The question of fixed versus random in regard to X is not crucial for regression studies. If the X_i's are random, we can simply regard all probability statements as conditional on the observed x_i's.

the assumption of fixed independent variables

When we assume that the x_i's are constants, the only random portion of the model for Y_i is the random error term ϵ_i. We make the following formal assumptions:

Formal Assumptions of Regression Analysis

1. The errors all have expected value zero; $E(\epsilon_i) = 0$ for all i.
2. The errors all have the same variance; $\text{Var}(\epsilon_i) = \sigma_\epsilon^2$ for all i.
3. The errors are independent of each other.
4. The errors are all normally distributed; ϵ_i is normally distributed for all i.

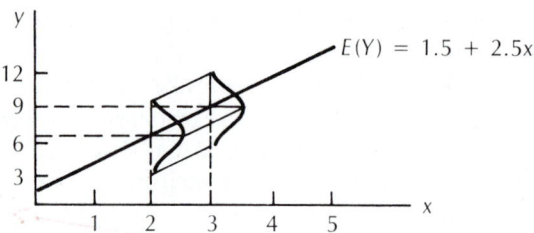

FIGURE 13.2 Theoretical Distribution of Y in Regression

These are formal assumptions, made in order to derive the significance tests and prediction methods that follow. In practice, any or all of them may not hold exactly. We discuss detection and the effects of deviations from these assumptions in Chapter 15.

The assumptions on ϵ_i may be translated into probability statements about the dependent variable $Y_i = \beta_0 + \beta_1 x_i + \epsilon_i$. Because x_i is a constant, so is $\beta_0 + \beta_1 x_i$. Adding a constant $(\beta_0 + \beta_1 x_i)$ to a normally distributed random variable (ϵ_i) yields another normally distributed random variable (Y_i). From properties of expectations, it follows that $E(Y_i) = E(\beta_0 + \beta_1 x_i + \epsilon_i) = \beta_0 + \beta_1 x_i$ and $V(Y_i) = V(\beta_0 + \beta_1 x_i + \epsilon_i) = \sigma_\epsilon^2$. By assumption then, **$Y_i$ is normally distributed with expected value $\beta_0 + \beta_1 x_i$ and variance σ_ϵ^2 and is independent of other Y values.** For example, suppose $\beta_0 = 1.5$, $\beta_1 = 2.5$, and $\sigma_\epsilon^2 = 6.1$. Then for $x_i = 2.0$, Y_i is normal with mean $1.5 + 2.5(2.0) = 6.5$ and variance 6.1. For $x_i = 3.0$, Y_i is normal with mean $1.5 + 2.5(3.0) = 9.0$ and the same variance, 6.1. Figure 13.2 shows that there is a theoretical normal distribution of Y's at each x value. We assume the expected values for these theoretical distributions to be along the true regression line $y = \beta_0 + \beta_1 x$; the variances are all the same.

In practice, only sample data are available. The population parameters β_0, β_1, and σ_ϵ^2 all have to be estimated from limited sample data. The formal assumptions we made in this section allow us to make inferences about the true parameter values from the sample data.

13.2 ESTIMATING MODEL PARAMETERS ∎

The quantities β_0 and β_1 in the regression model

$$Y = \beta_0 + \beta_1 x + \epsilon$$

are population quantities. We must estimate these values from sample data. The error variance σ_ϵ^2 is another population parameter that must be estimated. The first regression problem is to obtain estimates of the slope, intercept, and variance; we discuss how to do so in this section.

The road resurfacing example of Section 13.1 is a convenient illustration. Suppose the following data for similar resurfacing projects in the recent past are available:

Cost y_i (in thousands of dollars):	6.0	14.0	10.0	14.0	26.0
Mileage x_i (in miles):		1.0	3.0	4.0	5.0	7.0

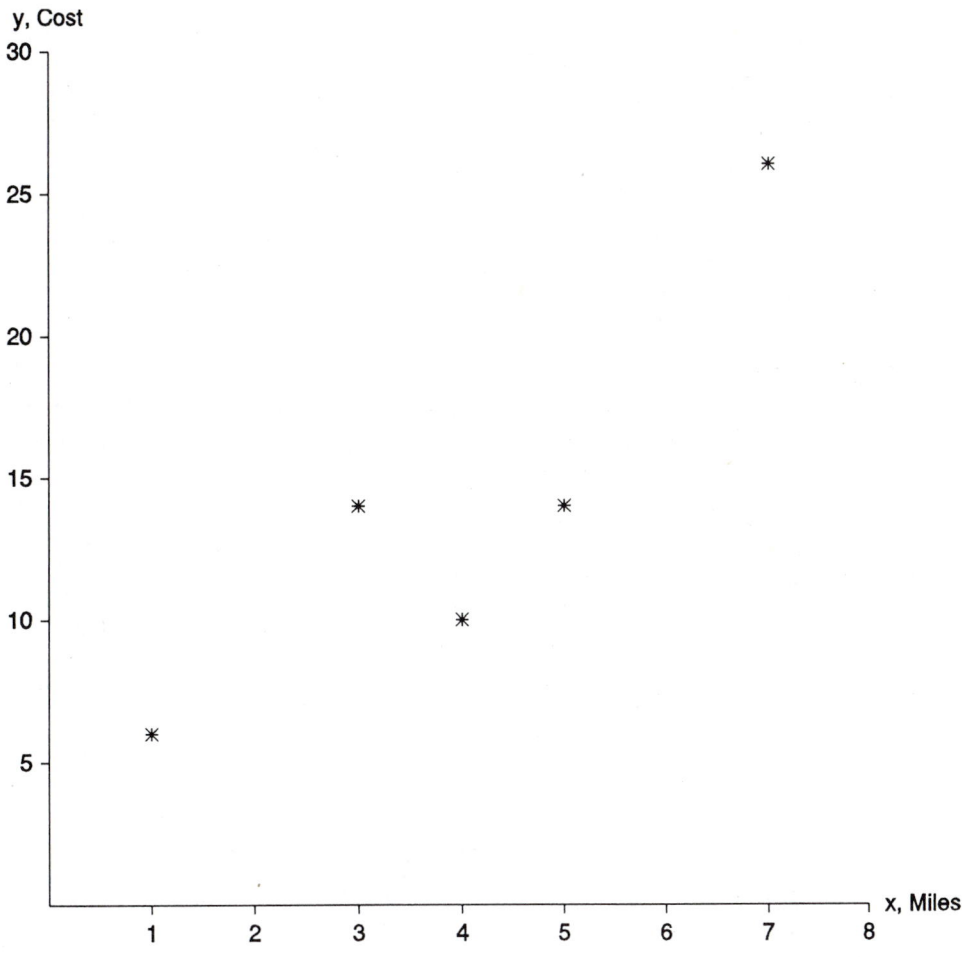

FIGURE 13.3   Scatter Plot of Cost Versus Mileage

A first step in examining the relation between y and x is to plot the data as a
scatter plot   **scatter plot**, where each point represents the (x, y) coordinates of one data entry,
as in Figure 13.3. The plot makes it clear that there is an imperfect but generally
increasing relation between x and y. A straight-line relation appears plausible.
The regression analysis problem is to find the best straight-line prediction.
The criterion for "best" is based on squared prediction error. We find the equa-
tion of the prediction line, that is, the slope $\hat{\beta}_1$ and intercept $\hat{\beta}_0$ that minimize the
total squared prediction error. The method that accomplishes this goal is called
least-squares   the **least-squares** method, because it chooses $\hat{\beta}_0$ and $\hat{\beta}_1$ to minimize the quantity

$$\sum_i (y_i - \hat{y}_i)^2 = \sum_i [y_i - (\hat{\beta}_0 + \hat{\beta}_1 x_i)]^2$$

The prediction errors are shown on the plot of Figure 13.4 (page 558) as
vertical deviations from the line. The deviations are taken as vertical distances
because we're trying to predict y values and errors should be taken in the y

direction. For these data the least-squares line can be shown to be $\hat{y} = 2.0 + 3.0x$; one of the deviations from it is indicated by the smaller brace. For comparison, the mean $\bar{y} = 14.0$ is also shown; deviation from the mean is indicated by the larger brace. The least-squares estimates are obtained as follows:

$$\hat{\beta}_1 = \frac{S_{xy}}{S_{xx}} \qquad \text{and} \qquad \hat{\beta}_0 = \bar{y} - \hat{\beta}_1 \bar{x}$$

where

$$S_{xy} = \sum_i x_i y_i - \frac{\sum_i x_i \sum_i y_i}{n} \qquad \text{and} \qquad SS_{xx} = \sum_i x_i^2 - \frac{\left(\sum_i x_i\right)^2}{n}$$

(When calculating by hand, be careful of the order of operation. In S_{xy}, divide the product of the sums by n first, then subtract the result from the sum of the xy

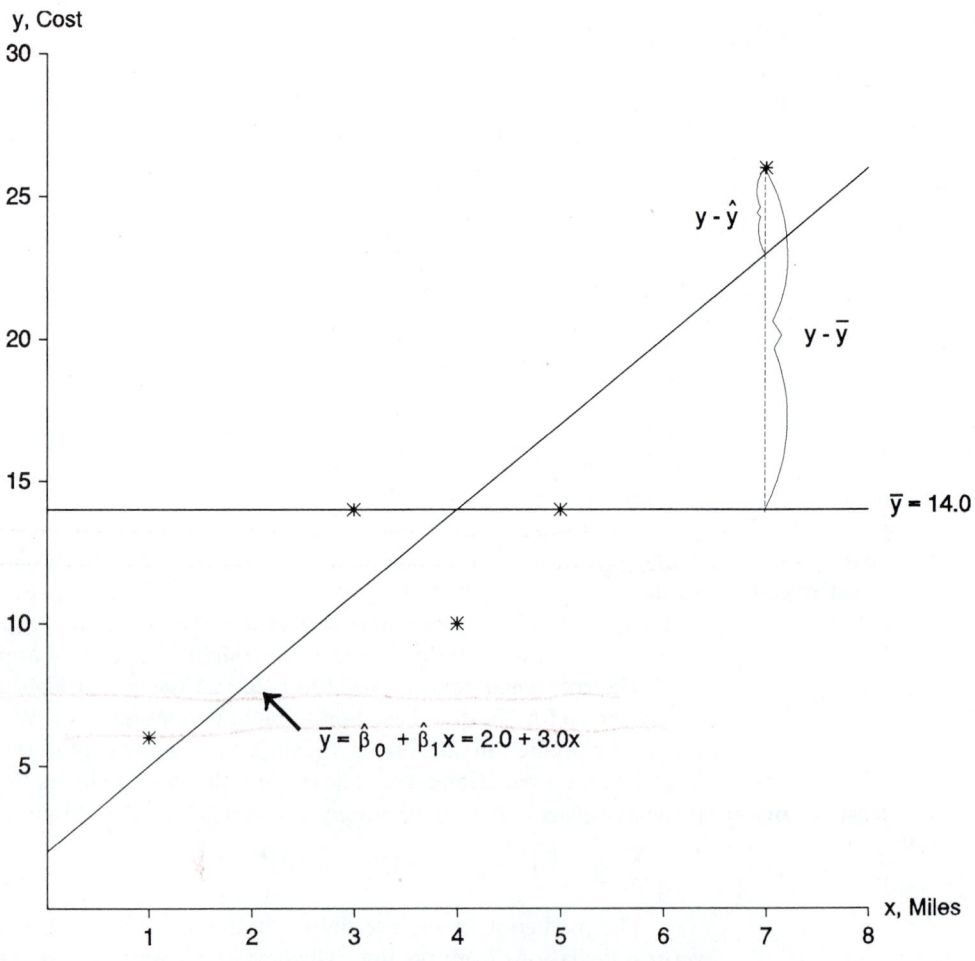

FIGURE 13.4   Deviations from the Least-Squares Line and from the Mean

products. Similarly, in S_{xx}, divide the square of the sum by n and subtract the result from the sum of x^2 values.)

For the road resurfacing data, $n = 5$ and

$$\sum x_i = 1.0 + \cdots + 7.0 = 20.0$$

Similarly,

$$\sum y_i = 70.0$$

Also

$$\sum x_i^2 = (1.0)^2 + \cdots + (7.0)^2 = 100.00$$

and

$$\sum x_i y_i = (1.0)(6.0) + \cdots + (7.0)(26.0) = 340.0$$

Therefore,

$$S_{xy} = 340.0 - \frac{(20.0)(70.0)}{5} = 60.0$$

and

$$S_{xx} = 100.0 - \frac{(20.0)^2}{5} = 20.0$$

So

$$\hat{\beta}_1 = \frac{60.0}{20.0} = 3.0$$

and

$$\hat{\beta}_0 = \frac{70.0}{5} - (3.0)\frac{20.0}{5} = 2.0$$

The equation $\hat{y} = 2.0 + 3.0x$ is also shown in Figure 13.4.

EXAMPLE 13.1   Data from a sample of 10 pharmacies are used to examine the relation between prescription sales volume and the percentage of prescription ingredients purchased directly from the supplier. The sample data are shown here:

Pharmacy	Sales Volume, y (in $1000)	% of Ingredients Purchased Directly, x
1	25	10
2	55	18
3	50	25
4	75	40
5	110	50
6	138	63
7	90	42
8	60	30
9	10	5
10	100	55

a. Find the least-squares estimates for the regression line $\hat{y} = \hat{\beta}_0 + \hat{\beta}_1 x$.
b. Predict sales volume for a pharmacy that purchases 15% of its prescription ingredients directly from the supplier.
c. Plot the x, y data and the prediction equation, $\hat{y} = \hat{\beta}_0 + \hat{\beta}_1 x$.

Solution   a. The least squares estimates can be obtained from the calculations performed in the following table:

y	x	xy	x^2
25	10	250	100
55	18	990	324
50	25	1250	625

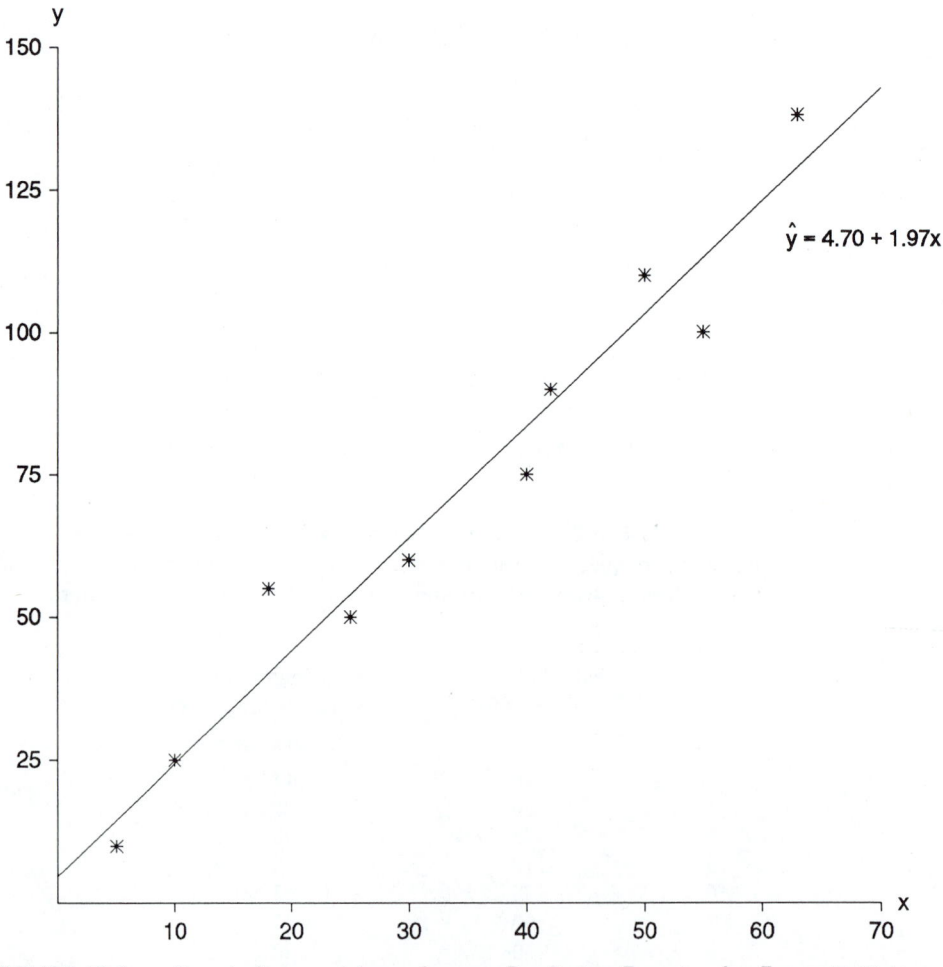

FIGURE 13.5   Sample Data and Least-Squares Prediction Equation for Example 13.1

	y	x	xy	x^2
	75	40	3000	1600
	110	50	5500	2500
	138	63	8694	3969
	90	42	3780	1764
	60	30	1800	900
	10	5	50	25
	100	55	5500	3025
Totals	713	338	30,814	14,832

$$S_{xx} = \sum x^2 - \frac{(\sum x)^2}{n} = 14{,}382 - \frac{(338)^2}{10} = 3407.6$$

$$S_{xy} = \sum xy = \sum xy - \frac{(\sum x)(\sum y)}{n} = 30{,}814 - \frac{(338)(713)}{10} = 6714.6$$

Substituting into the formulas for $\hat{\beta}_0$ and $\hat{\beta}_1$,

$$\hat{\beta}_1 = \frac{S_{xy}}{S_{xx}} = \frac{6714.6}{3407.6} = 1.9704778, \text{ rounded to } 1.97$$

$$\hat{\beta}_0 = \bar{y} - \hat{\beta}_1 \bar{x} = 71.3 - 1.9704778(33.8) = 4.6978519, \text{ rounded to } 4.70$$

b. When $x = 15\%$, the predicted sales volume is $\hat{y} = 4.70 + 1.97(15) = 34.25$ (i.e., \$34,250). The prediction equation is shown in Figure 13.5. ∎

EXAMPLE 13.2   Use the SAS output shown below to identify the least-squares estimates for the road resurfacing data.

DEPENDENT VARIABLE: TOTCOST

SOURCE	DF	SUM OF SQUARES	MEAN SQUARE	F VALUE	PR > F	R-SQUARE	C.V.
MODEL	1	180.00000000	180.00000000	12.27	0.0394	0.803571	27.3551
ERROR	3	44.00000000	14.66666667		ROOT MSE		TOTCOST MEAN
CORRECTED TOTAL	4	224.00000000			3.82970843		14.00000000

SOURCE	DF	TYPE I SS	F VALUE	PR > F	DF	TYPE III SS	F VALUE	PR > F
MILES	1	180.00000000	12.27	0.0394	1	180.00000000	12.27	0.0394

PARAMETER	ESTIMATE	T FOR H0: PARAMETER=0	PR > |T|	STD ERROR OF ESTIMATE
INTERCEPT	2.00000000	0.52	0.6376	3.82970843
MILES	3.00000000	3.50	0.0394	0.85634884

Solution   The intercept is shown as $\hat{\beta}_0 = 2.000$. The slope (coefficient of $x =$ miles) is $\hat{\beta}_1 = 3.000$. ∎

high influence
point

The estimate of the regression slope can be greatly affected by **high influence points**, sometimes called high leverage points. These are points that have very high or very low values of the independent variable—outliers in the X direction. They carry great weight in the estimate of the slope. A high influence point that happens to correspond to a Y outlier can alter the slope and twist the line badly. Consider the two scatter plots in Figure 13.6. In plot (a) the point in the upper left corner is far to the left of the other points; it has a much lower x value and therefore it has high influence. If we drew a line through the other points, it would fall far below this point, so the point is an outlier in the Y direction as well. Including this point would change the slope of the line greatly. In contrast, in plot (b) the Y-outlier point corresponds to an x value very near the mean, having low influence. Including this point would pull the line upward, increasing the intercept, but it wouldn't increase or decrease the slope much at all.

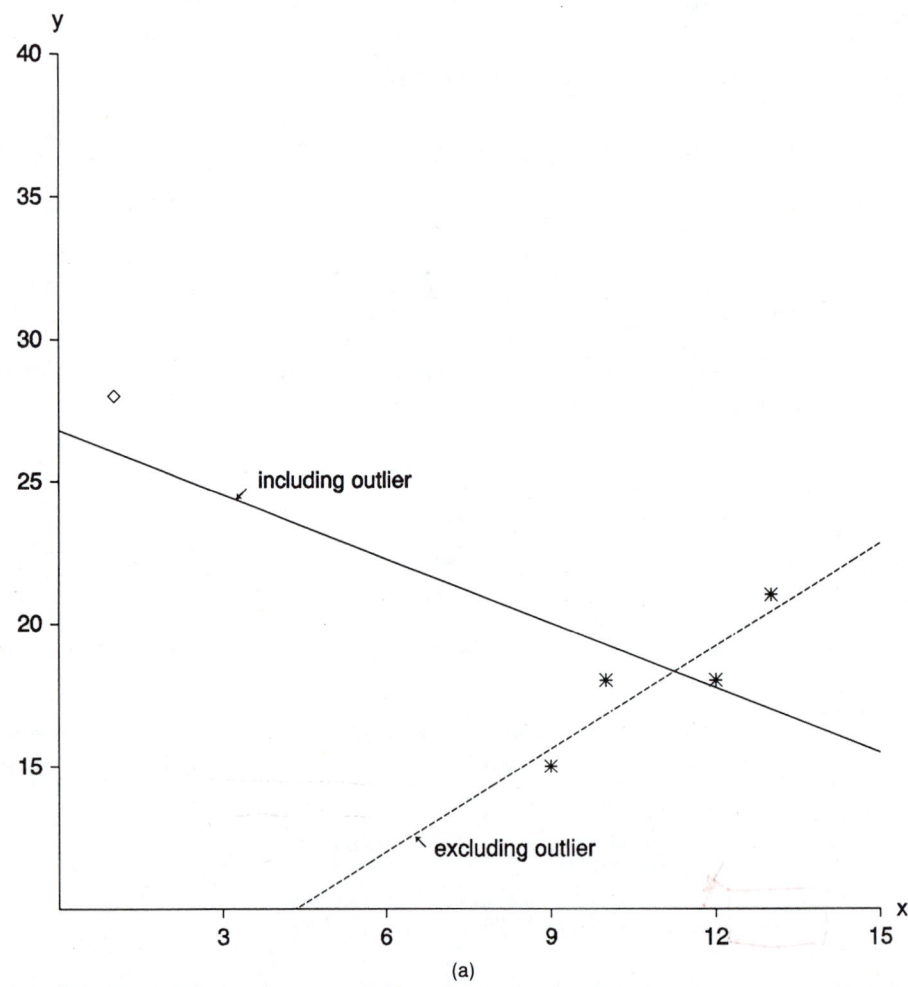

FIGURE 13.6   (a) High Influence and (b) Low Influence Points

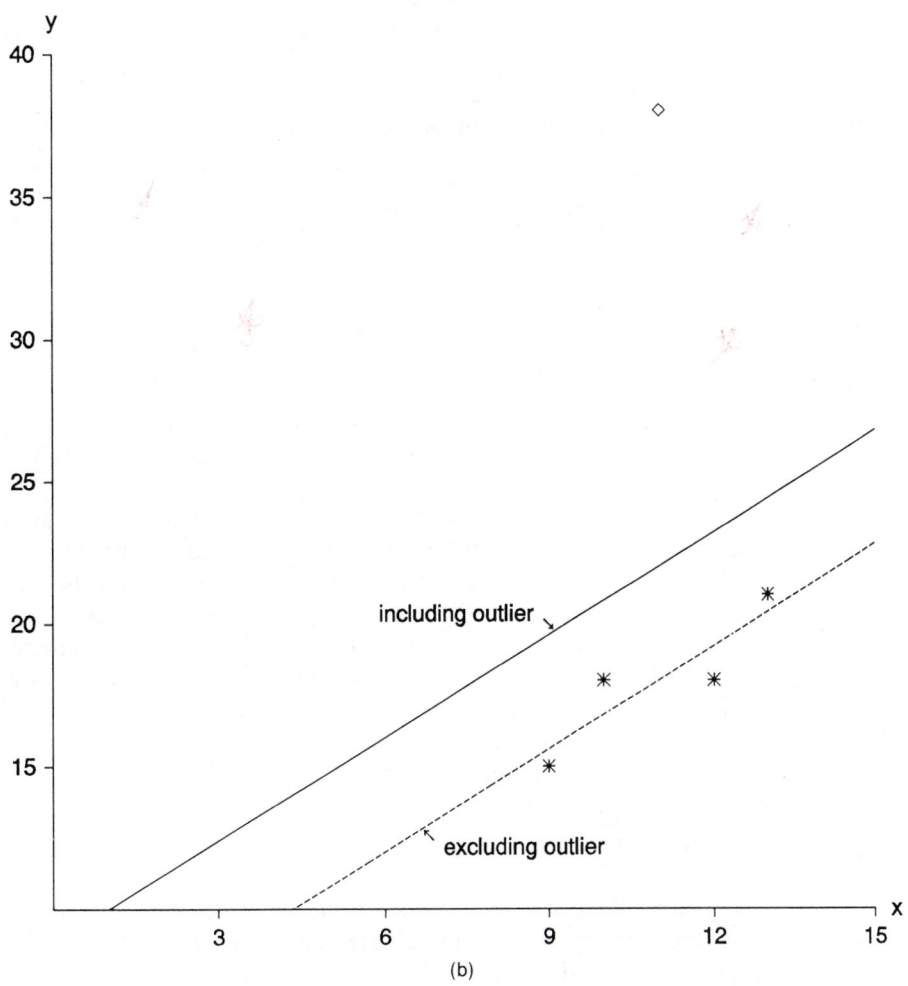

FIGURE 13.6   (*Continued*)

Mathematically, the effect of a point's influence can be seen in the S_{xy} term that enters into the slope calculation. One of the many ways this term can be written is

$$S_{xy} = \sum (x_i - \bar{x}) y_i$$

We can think of this equation as a weighted sum of y values. The weights are large positive or negative numbers when the x value is far from its mean and has high influence. The weight is almost 0 when x is very close to its mean and has low influence.

Most computer programs that perform regression analyses will calculate **diagnostic measures** one or another of several **diagnostic measures** of influence. We won't try to summarize all of these measures. We only note that very large values of any of these measures correspond to very high influence points, those that are X-outliers.

It is possible to prove that both estimators $\hat{\beta}_0$ and $\hat{\beta}_1$ are unbiased,

$$E(\hat{\beta}_0) = \beta_0, \qquad E(\hat{\beta}_1) = \beta_1$$

standard errors of and that in linear regression, the variances and standard errors for $\hat{\beta}_0$ and $\hat{\beta}_1$ are,
$\hat{\beta}_0, \hat{\beta}_1$ respectively,

$$\text{Var}(\hat{\beta}_0) = \sigma_\epsilon^2 \left[\frac{1}{n} + \frac{\bar{x}^2}{S_{xx}} \right], \qquad \sigma_{\hat{\beta}_0} = \sigma_\epsilon \sqrt{\frac{1}{n} + \frac{\bar{x}^2}{S_{xx}}}$$

and

$$\text{Var}(\hat{\beta}_1) = \sigma_\epsilon^2 \left[\frac{1}{S_{xx}} \right], \qquad \sigma_{\hat{\beta}_1} = \sigma_\epsilon \sqrt{\frac{1}{S_{xx}}}$$

Finally, we can prove that the sampling distributions of $\hat{\beta}_0$ and $\hat{\beta}_1$ are both normal. These facts are most readily proved using matrix concepts (see Johnston, 1977).

The variances for $\hat{\beta}_0$ and $\hat{\beta}_1$ indicate their probable accuracy as estimates of the true parameter values. Both of these variances depend on the theoretical error variance σ_ϵ^2. The smaller the error variance, the more accurate the estimates. For the extreme case where all the errors ϵ_i are zero, all values of Y_i lie on the population regression line $Y_i = \beta_0 + \beta_1 x_i$ and $\sigma_\epsilon^2 = 0$. Obviously there is no error in estimating the values β_0 and β_1 from sample data, and the error variances for $\hat{\beta}_0$ and $\hat{\beta}_1$ are zero.

The formula for the standard error of $\hat{\beta}_1$ indicates that the variability of $\hat{\beta}_1$ is influenced by two quantities, σ_ϵ^2 and S_{xx}.

$$\sigma_{\hat{\beta}_1} = \frac{\sigma_\epsilon}{\sqrt{S_{xx}}}$$

The greater the variability σ_ϵ of the y value for a given value of x, the larger $\sigma_{\hat{\beta}_1}$ is. The greater the spread in the x value (as measured by S_{xx}), the smaller $\sigma_{\hat{\beta}_1}$ is. This result is illustrated in Figure 13.7.

In each part of Figure 13.7, the solid line represents the regression line through the data including the points marked with asterisks (*) and the circled point. The dashed line represents the modified regression line if the circled point is moved by random error up to the point marked by a plus sign. In Figure 13.7(a), the points are close together on the x axis, so S_{xx} is small; the random error causes the slope to increase considerably. In Figure 13.7(b), the points are far apart on the x axis, so S_{xx} is large; the random error causes the slope to increase very little. A wide spread of x values dampens the effect of random error, permitting more accurate estimation of the slope.

The variance of the estimated intercept $\hat{\beta}_0$ is influenced by n, naturally, and also by the size of $\bar{x}^2$ relative to S_{xx}. The predicted y value when $x = 0$ is represented by $\hat{\beta}_0$; if all the x_i, are, for instance, large positive numbers, predicting Y at $x = 0$ is a huge extrapolation from the actual data. Such extrapolation magnifies small errors, and $\text{Var}(\hat{\beta}_0)$ is large. The ideal situation for estimating $\hat{\beta}_0$ is when $\bar{x} = 0$.

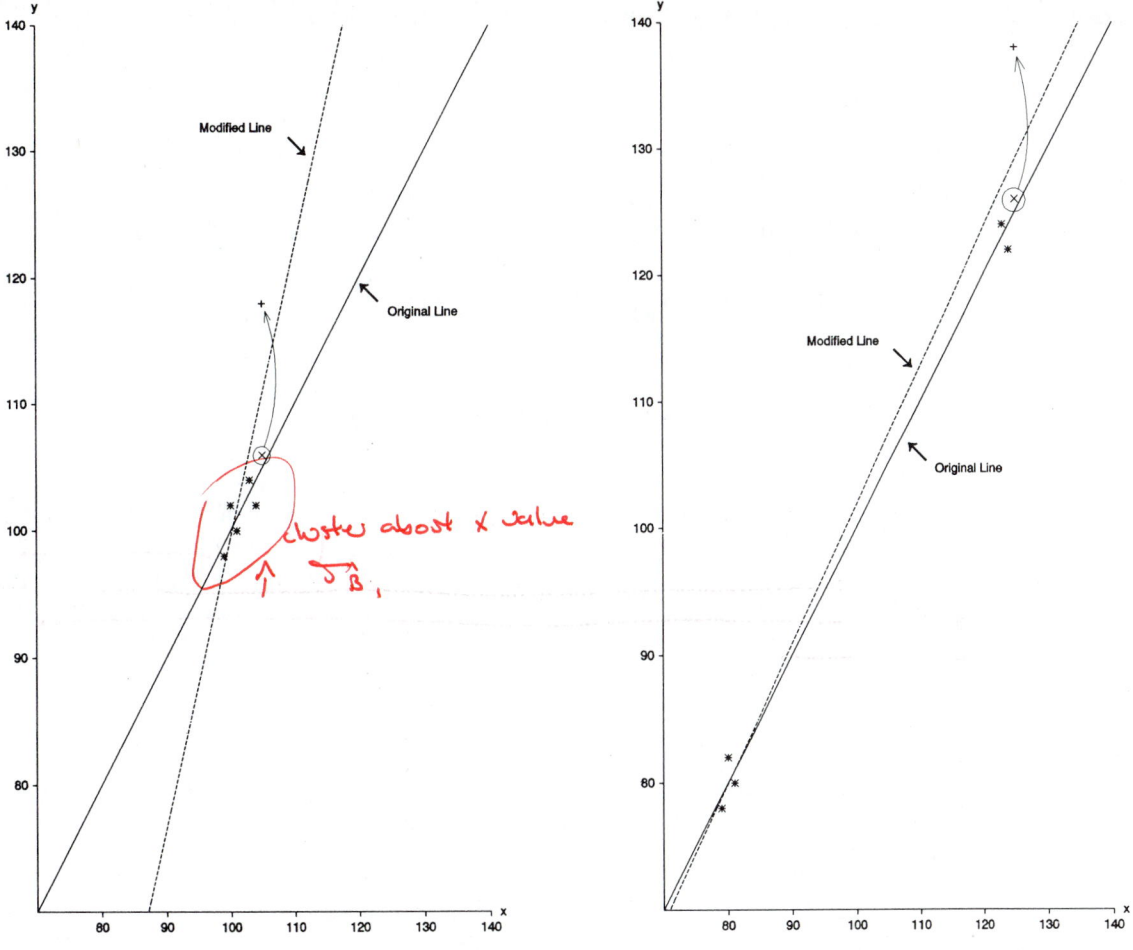

Handwritten annotations on figure (a): "cluster about x value", "$\sigma_{\hat{\beta}_1}$"

FIGURE 13.7 The Effect of S_{xx} on σ_{β_1}: (a) Small S_{xx}; (b) Large S_{xx}

EXAMPLE 13.3 Suppose that in a particular regression study $\sigma_\epsilon^2 = 6.1$. (In practice, the true error variance would not be known, so this is a hypothetical exercise.) The x values for the regression study are

18.1 20.0 20.8 21.5 22.0 22.4 22.9 24.0 25.4 27.3

Find the variances and standard errors for $\hat{\beta}_0$ and $\hat{\beta}_1$.

Solution For these data, $\sum x_i = 224.4$ and $\sum x_i^2 = 5099.12$. It follows that

$$\bar{x} = \frac{224.4}{10} = 22.44$$

and

$$S_{xx} = 5099.12 - \frac{(224.4)^2}{10} = 63.584$$

Substituting $\sigma_\epsilon^2 = 6.1$, $\bar{x} = 22.44$, and $S_{xx} = 63.584$, we have

$$\text{Var}(\hat{\beta}_0) = 6.1\left[\frac{1}{10} + \frac{(22.44)^2}{63.584}\right] = 48.92$$

and

$$\text{Var}(\hat{\beta}_1) = \frac{6.1}{63.584} = .0959, \qquad \sigma_{\hat{\beta}_1} = \sqrt{.0959} = .31 \qquad \blacksquare$$

To this point, we have considered only the estimates of intercept and slope. We also have to estimate the true error variance σ_ϵ^2. We can think of this quantity as "variance around the line," or as the mean squared prediction error. The estimate of σ_ϵ^2 is based on the **residuals** $y_i - \hat{y}_i$, which are the prediction errors in the sample. The estimate of σ_ϵ^2 based on the sample data is

residuals

$$s_\epsilon^2 = \frac{\sum_i (y_i - \hat{y}_i)^2}{n - 2} = \frac{\text{SS(Residual)}}{n - 2}$$

where SS again stands for sum of squares. The quantity SS(Residual) is sometimes called SS(Error). In the computer output for Example 13.2, SS(Error) is shown to be 44.0.

Just as we divide by $n - 1$ rather than n in the ordinary sample variance s^2 (in Chapter 2), we divide by $n - 2$ in s_ϵ^2, the estimated variance around the line. To see why, suppose our sample size is $n = 2$. No matter how large or small σ_ϵ^2 may be, the estimated regression line goes exactly through the two points and the residuals are automatically zero. Thus for $n = 2$ we simply don't have enough information to estimate σ_ϵ^2 at all. In our definition, s_ϵ^2 is undefined for $n = 2$, as it should be. Another argument for dividing by $n - 2$ is that

$$E(s_\epsilon^2) = \sigma_\epsilon^2$$

Dividing by $n - 2$ makes s_ϵ^2 an unbiased estimator of σ_ϵ^2. In the computer output of Example 13.2, $n - 2$ is shown as DF (degrees of freedom) for ERROR, and s_ϵ^2 is shown as MEAN SQUARE for ERROR. The formula for hand calculation of s_ϵ^2 is

$$s_\epsilon^2 = \frac{\text{SS(Residual)}}{n - 2} = \frac{\sum y_i^2 - \hat{\beta}_0 \sum y_i - \hat{\beta}_1 \sum x_i y_i}{n - 2}$$

As we indicated previously, s_ϵ^2 is an unbiased estimator of σ_ϵ^2. The square root s_ϵ of the sample variance is called the **sample standard deviation around the regression line** or the **residual standard deviation**. Because s_ϵ estimates σ_ϵ, the standard deviation of Y_i, s_ϵ estimates the standard deviation of the population of y values associated with a given value of the independent variable x. The SAS output labels s_ϵ as STD. DEV.; for our Example 13.2, s_ϵ is 3.830.

The estimates $\hat{\beta}_0, \hat{\beta}_1$, and s_ϵ are basic in regression analysis. They specify the regression line and the probable degree of error associated with y values for a given value of x. The next step is to use these sample estimates to make inferences about the true parameters.

EXAMPLE 13.4   For the following data,

  a. construct a scatter plot;
  b. compute the least-squares estimates for β_0 and β_1 in the model $Y = \beta_0 + \beta_1 x + \epsilon$;
  c. predict y for $x = 19.5$;
  d. compute s_ϵ, the sample standard deviation about the regression line.

y:	31.5	33.1	27.4	24.5	27.0	27.8	23.3	24.7	16.9	18.1
x:	18.1	20.0	20.8	21.5	22.0	22.4	22.9	24.0	25.4	27.3

Solution   a. A scatter plot is shown in Figure 13.8 (page 568); the indicated line will be shown to be the least-squares line in part (b).
  b. First we must calculate $\hat{\beta}_0$ and $\hat{\beta}_1$. Direct calculations yield $\sum x_i = 224.4$, $\sum x_i^2 = 5099.12$, $\sum y_i = 254.3$, $\sum y_i^2 = 6706.91$, and $\sum x_i y_i = 5595.30$. Substituting these values,

$$\hat{\beta}_1 = \frac{S_{xy}}{S_{xx}} = \frac{\sum x_i y_i - (\sum x_i)(\sum y_i)/n}{\sum x_i^2 - (\sum x_i)^2/n}$$

$$= \frac{5595.30 - (224.4)(254.3)/10}{5099.12 - (224.4)^2/10} = -1.7487$$

and

$$\hat{\beta}_0 = \bar{y} - \hat{\beta}_1 \bar{x}$$
$$= 25.43 - (-1.7487)(22.44) = 64.672$$

c. The least-squares prediction equation is

$$\hat{y} = 64.672 - 1.7487x$$

Substituting $x = 19.5$, the predicted value of y is $\hat{y} = 30.57$.
  d. The hand-calculation formula for s_ϵ^2 yields

$$s_\epsilon^2 = \frac{\sum y_i^2 - \hat{\beta}_0 \sum y_i - \hat{\beta}_1 \sum x_i y_i}{n-2}$$

$$= \frac{6706.91 - (64.672)(254.3) - (-1.7487)(5595.30)}{10-2}$$

$$= 5.6652$$

Therefore, $s_\epsilon = \sqrt{s_\epsilon^2} = \sqrt{5.6652} = 2.380$.
  Note that the prediction equation is shown in Figure 13.8.   ■

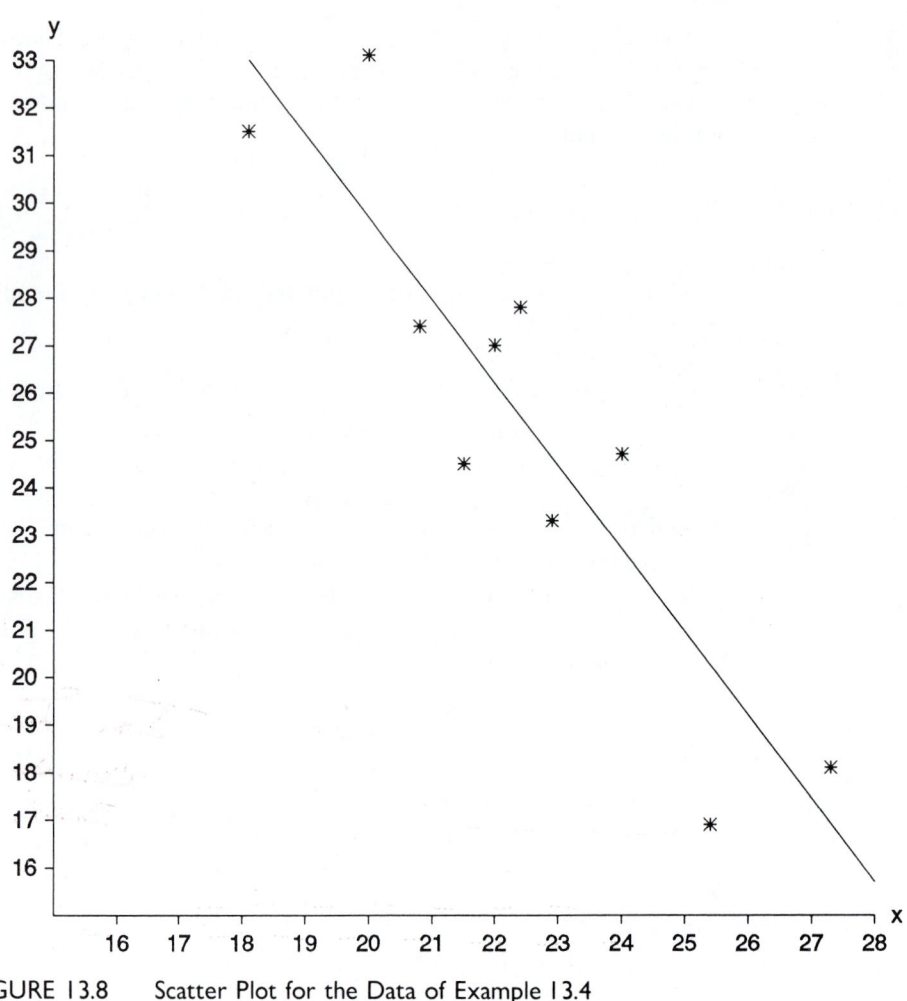

FIGURE 13.8   Scatter Plot for the Data of Example 13.4

SECTIONS 13.1 AND 13.2   EXERCISES

13.1   The following data are obtained:

x:	1	1	1	3	3	3
$x' = \log_{10} x$:	.000	.000	.000	.477	.477	.477
y:	13.5	15.4	16.1	18.3	19.9	20.9

x:	5	5	5	7	7	7
$x' = \log_{10} x$:	.699	.699	.699	.845	.845	.845
y:	20.8	23.1	22.1	22.8	24.9	24.5

a. Plot y versus x. Draw an approximate regression line through the plot.
b. Separately, plot y versus x'. Draw an approximate regression line through the plot.
c. Which plot appears more nearly linear to you?

13.2   Refer to the data of Exercise 13.1.
   a. Calculate the least-squares equation $\hat{y} = \hat{\beta}_0 + \hat{\beta}_1 x$.
   b. Calculate the residual standard deviation.

13.3   Refer to the data of Exercise 13.1.
   a. Calculate the least-squares equation $\hat{y} = \hat{\beta}_0 + \hat{\beta}_1 x'$.
   b. Calculate the residual standard deviation.

13.4   Compare the residual standard deviations s_ϵ in Exercises 13.2 and 13.3. Which is smaller? Does this confirm your opinion about the choice of model based on the plots of Exercise 13.1?

13.5   As one part of a study of commercial bank branches, data are obtained on the number of independent businesses (x) located in sample ZIP code areas and the number of bank branches (y) located in these areas. The commercial centers of cities are excluded.

x:	92	116	124	210	216	267	306	378	415	502	615	703
y:	3	2	3	5	4	5	5	6	7	7	9	9

$\sum x_i = 3944$ $\sum y_i = 65,$ $\sum x_i y_i = 26,208$
$\sum x_i^2 = 1,732,524,$ $\sum y_i^2 = 409,$ $n = 12$

   a. Plot the data. Does a linear equation relating y to x appear plausible?
   b. Calculate the regression equation (with y as the dependent variable).
   c. Calculate the sample residual standard deviation s_ϵ.

13.6   Does it appear that variability of y increases with x in the data plot of Exercise 13.5? (This would violate the assumption of constant variance.)

13.7   Manufacture of cases for sound equipment requires drilling holes for metal screws. The drill bits wear out and must be replaced. There is expense not only for the cost of the bits but also for lost production. Engineers varied the rotation speed of the drills and measured the lifetime Y (thousands of holes drilled) of four bits at each of five speeds X. The data were:

X:	60	60	60	60	80	80	80	80	100	100
Y:	4.6	3.8	4.9	4.5	4.7	5.8	5.5	5.4	5.0	4.5

X:	100	100	120	120	120	120	140	140	140	140
Y:	3.2	4.8	4.1	4.5	4.0	3.8	3.6	3.0	3.5	3.4

   a. Create a scatter plot of the data. Does there appear to be a relation? Does it appear to be linear?
   b. Is there any evident outlier? If so, does it have high influence?

13.8   a. Calculate the intercept and slope of the least squares regression line, using the data of Exercise 13.7. The following sums can be obtained:

$$\sum x = 2000, \quad \sum x^2 = 216,000, \quad \sum y = 286.6,$$
$$\sum y^2 = 386.80, \quad \sum xy = 8388.00.$$

The sample size was 20.
   b. What does the sign of the slope indicate about the relation between speed and bit lifetime?
   c. Calculate the residual standard deviation. Interpret the resulting number.

13.9   a. Use the regression line of Exercise 13.8 to calculate predicted values for $x = 60$, 80, 100, 120, and 140.
   b. For which x values are most of the actual Y values larger than the predicted values? For which x values are most Y values lower than predicted? What does this pattern indicate about whether there is a linear relation?

13.10 A realtor studied the relation between X = yearly income (in thousands of dollars per year) of home purchasers and Y = sale price of the house (in thousands of dollars). Data were obtained from mortgage applications for 24 sales in the realtor's basic sales area in one season.

x:	25.0	28.5	29.2	30.0	31.0	31.5	31.9	32.0	33.0
y:	84.9	94.0	96.5	93.5	102.9	99.5	101.0	105.0	99.9

x:	33.5	34.0	35.9	36.0	39.0	39.0	40.5	40.9	42.5
y:	110.0	100.0	116.0	110.0	125.0	119.9	130.6	120.8	129.9

x:	44.0	45.0	50.5	54.6	65.0	70.0
y:	135.5	140.0	150.7	170.0	110.0	185.0

a. Create a scatter plot. Does the relation appear to be basically linear?

b. Are there any apparent outliers? If so, which ones seem to have high influence?

13.11 a. Calculate the least-squares regression equation for the data of Exercise 13.10. The following summary numbers were obtained:

$$n = 24, \quad \sum x = 942.50, \quad \sum x^2 = 39{,}915.53, \quad \sum y = 2830.60,$$
$$\sum y^2 = 347{,}868.94, \quad \sum xy = 116{,}392.67$$

b. Interpret the slope coefficient. Is the intercept meaningful?

c. Find the residual standard deviation.

13.12 Recalculate the regression line for the data of Exercise 13.10 and omit the point with $X = 65.0$ and $Y = 110.0$. Does the slope change substantially? Why?

13.3   INFERENCES ABOUT PARAMETERS

The t distribution can be used to make significance tests and confidence intervals for the true slope and intercept. One natural null hypothesis is that the true slope $\beta_1 = 0$. If this H_0 is true, a change in x yields no predicted change in y, and it follows that x has no value in predicting y. We know from the previous section that the sample slope $\hat{\beta}_1$ has expected value β_1 and standard error

ie. no rela. exists

$$\sigma_{\hat{\beta}_1} = \sigma_\epsilon \sqrt{\frac{1}{S_{xx}}}$$

t test for β_1   In practice, σ_ϵ is not known and must be estimated by s_ϵ in this formula. Combining these facts, we get the t statistic

$$t = \frac{\hat{\beta}_1 - \beta_1}{\text{estimated standard error } (\hat{\beta}_1)} = \frac{\hat{\beta}_1 - \beta_1}{s_\epsilon \sqrt{\dfrac{1}{S_{xx}}}}$$

We indicate the use of this statistic in testing $H_0: \beta_1 = 0$ in the following summary.

Summary for t Test of H_0: $\hat{\beta}_j = 0$

H_0: $\beta_1 = 0$

H_a: 1. $\beta_1 > 0$
   2. $\beta_1 < 0$
   3. $\beta_1 \neq 0$

T.S.: $t = \dfrac{\hat{\beta}_1 - 0}{s_\epsilon \sqrt{\dfrac{1}{S_{xx}}}}$

R.R.: For d.f. $= n - 2$ and Type I error α,
   1. reject H_0 if $t > t_\alpha$
   2. reject H_0 if $t < -t_\alpha$
   3. reject H_0 if $|t| > t_{\alpha/2}$

EXAMPLE 13.5   Use the computer output of Example 13.2 to locate the value of the t statistic for testing H_0: $\beta_1 = 0$ in the road resurfacing example. Give the observed level of significance for the test.

Solution   It is clear from the output that the value of the test statistic in the column labeled T FOR H0: PARAMETER $= 0$ is $t = 3.50$. The p-value for the two-tailed alternative H_a: $\beta_1 \neq 0$, labeled as PR $> |T|$, is .0394. Because this value is small, we can reject the hypothesis that mileage has no effect in predicting cost. ∎

EXAMPLE 13.6   The following data show mean ages of executives of 15 firms in the food industry and the previous year's percentage increase in earnings per share of the firms. Test the hypothesis that executive age has no predictive value. Should a one-sided or two-sided alternative be used?

Mean age, x:	38.2	40.0	42.5	43.4	44.6	44.9	45.0	45.4
Change, earnings per share, y:	8.9	13.0	4.7	−2.4	12.5	18.4	6.6	13.5
x:	46.0	47.3	47.3	48.0	49.1	50.5	51.6	
y:	8.5	15.3	18.9	6.0	10.4	15.9	17.1	

Solution   In the model $Y = \beta_0 + \beta_1 x + \epsilon$, the null hypothesis is H_0: $\beta_1 = 0$. The myth in American business is that younger managers tend to be more aggressive and harder driving, but it is also possible that the greater experience of the older executives leads to better decisions. Therefore there is good reason to choose a two-sided research hypothesis, H_a: $\beta_1 \neq 0$.

For the t test, we need $\hat{\beta}_1$, s_ϵ, and S_{xx}. The necessary summary figures are

$$\sum x_i = 683.8, \qquad \sum y_i = 167.3, \qquad \sum x_i y_i = 7741.74$$
$$\sum x_i^2 = 31{,}358.58, \qquad \sum y_i^2 = 2349.61, \qquad n = 15$$

$$\hat{\beta}_1 = \frac{\sum x_i y_i - (\sum x_i)(\sum y_i)/n}{\sum x_i^2 - (\sum x_i)^2/n}$$

$$= \frac{115.09067}{186.41733} = .6173818$$

Note that

$$S_{xx} = \sum x_i^2 - (\sum x_i)^2/n = 186.41733$$

and that

$$\hat{\beta}_0 = \bar{y} - \hat{\beta}_1 \bar{x} = -16.991045$$

The interpretation of $\hat{\beta}_0$ is rather interesting in this example; (much) younger is not necessarily better.

Now

$$s_\epsilon^2 = \frac{\sum y_i^2 - \hat{\beta}_0 \sum y_i - \hat{\beta}_1 \sum x_i y_i}{n - 2}$$

$$= \frac{412.60245}{13} = 31.73865$$

and $s_\epsilon = \sqrt{31.73865} = 5.6337066$. Therefore

$$t = \frac{\hat{\beta}_1}{s_\epsilon \sqrt{\dfrac{1}{S_{xx}}}} = \frac{.6173818}{5.6337066 \sqrt{\dfrac{1}{186.41733}}} = 1.4962451$$

threshold

or about 1.50. The tabulated t value (13 d.f., two-sided $\alpha = .10$) is 1.771. Therefore we cannot reject H_0 even at $\alpha = .10$.   ∎

It is also possible to calculate a confidence interval for the true slope:

$100(1 - \alpha)\%$ Confidence Interval for Slope $\hat{\beta}_j$

$$\hat{\beta}_1 - t_{\alpha/2} s_\epsilon \sqrt{\frac{1}{S_{xx}}} \leq \beta_1 \leq \hat{\beta}_1 + t_{\alpha/2} s_\epsilon \sqrt{\frac{1}{S_{xx}}}$$

EXAMPLE 13.7   Compute a 95% confidence interval for the slope β_1 using the output from Example 13.2.

Solution   In the SAS output the estimated standard error of $\hat{\beta}_1$ is $s_\epsilon \sqrt{1/S_{xx}} = .856$, rounded off. The corresponding confidence interval β_1 is then

$$3.00 \pm 3.182(.856), \quad \text{or} \quad .276 \text{ to } 5.724$$

The predicted cost per additional mile of resurfacing could be anywhere from $276 to $5724. The large width of this interval results largely from the small sample size.   ∎

There is an alternative test, an F test, for the null hypothesis of no predictive value. This test gives the same result as a two-sided t test of $H_0: \beta_1 = 0$ in simple linear regression. The F test is summarized next.

F Test for H_0: $\beta_1 = 0$

$H_0: \beta_1 = 0$
$H_a: \beta_1 \neq 0$

T.S.: $F = \dfrac{\text{SS(Regression)}/1}{\text{SS(Residual)}/(n-2)} = \dfrac{\text{MS(Regression)}}{\text{MS(Residual)}}$

R.R.: with d.f.$_1 = 1$ and d.f.$_2 = n - 2$, reject H_0 if $F > F_\alpha$

Note: SS(Regression) $= \hat{\beta}_0 \sum y_i + \hat{\beta}_1 \sum x_i y_i - (\sum y_i)^2/n$ and
SS(Residual) $= \sum y_i^2 - \hat{\beta}_0 \sum y_i - \hat{\beta}_1 \sum x_i y_i$

Virtually all computer packages calculate this F statistic. In the road resurfacing example, the SAS output shows $F = 12.27$ with a p-value of .0394. Again the hypothesis of no predictive value can be rejected. It is always true for simple linear regression problems that $F = t^2$; in the example, $12.27 \approx (3.50)^2$. Therefore the F and two-sided t tests are equivalent here.

EXAMPLE 13.8   For the data of Example 13.4, use the F test for $H_0: \beta_1 = 0$. Show that $t^2 = F$.

Solution   The required sums of squares are

$$\begin{aligned}
\text{SS(Regression)} &= \hat{\beta}_0 \sum y_i + \hat{\beta}_1 \sum x_i y_i - (\sum y_i)^2/n \\
&= (64.672)(254.3) + (-1.7487)(5595.30) - (254.3)^2/10 \\
&= 194.74 \\
\text{SS(Residual)} &= \sum y_i^2 - \hat{\beta}_0 \sum y_i - \hat{\beta}_1 \sum x_i y_i \\
&= 6706.91 - (64.672)(254.3) - (-1.7487)(5595.30) \\
&= 45.32.
\end{aligned}$$

Therefore,

$$F = \frac{\text{SS(Regression)}/1}{\text{SS(Residual)}/(n-2)} = \frac{194.74/1}{45.32/8}$$

$$= 34.37$$

This value of the F statistic lies beyond all tabled values with d.f.$_1 = 1$ and d.f.$_2 = 8$. Hence we may reject H_0. For the t statistic, we have

$$t = \frac{\hat{\beta}_1}{s_\epsilon \sqrt{1/S_{xx}}} = \frac{-1.7487}{2.380\sqrt{1/63.58}} = -5.86$$

Note that $F = 34.37 = t^2 = (-5.86)^2$.

You should be able to work out comparable hypothesis-testing and confidence-interval formulas for the intercept β_0 using the estimated standard error of $\hat{\beta}_0$ as $s_\epsilon\sqrt{1/n + \bar{x}^2/S_{xx}}$. In practice this parameter is of less interest than the slope. In particular, there is often no reason to hypothesize that the true intercept is zero (or any other particular value). Computer packages almost always test $H_0: \beta_1 = 0$, but some don't bother with a test on the intercept term.

It is also possible to calculate a confidence interval for the true error variance σ_ϵ^2. The only change from the χ^2 variance-inference methods of Chapter 8 is in degrees of freedom. Now s_ϵ^2 has $n - 2$ d.f.

$100(1 - \alpha)\%$ Confidence Interval for σ_ϵ^2

$$s_\epsilon^2 \frac{n-2}{\chi_{\alpha/2}^2} \leq \sigma_\epsilon^2 \leq s_\epsilon^2 \frac{n-2}{\chi_{1-\alpha/2}^2}$$

where χ_a^2 cuts off area a in the right tail of the χ^2 distribution with $n - 2$ d.f.
Note: $(n - 2)s_\epsilon^2 = $ SS(Residual).

EXAMPLE 13.9   For the data of Example 13.6, calculate 95% confidence intervals for σ_ϵ^2 and for σ_ϵ.

Solution   The tabled $\chi_{.025}^2$ and $\chi_{.975}^2$ values for $n - 2 = 13$ d.f. are, respectively, 24.74 and 5.01. Because s_ϵ^2 is 31.73865 in Example 13.6, the 95% confidence interval for σ_ϵ^2 is

$$(31.73865)\left(\frac{13}{24.74}\right) \leq \sigma_\epsilon^2 \leq (31.73865)\left(\frac{13}{5.01}\right)$$

or

$$16.677544 \leq \sigma_\epsilon^2 \leq 82.355778$$

The confidence interval for σ_ϵ may be found by taking square roots:

$$4.0838149 \leq \sigma_\epsilon \leq 9.0750085$$

SECTION 13.3   EXERCISES

13.13 Refer to the data of Exercise 13.5.
  a. Calculate a 90% confidence interval for β_1.
  b. What is the interpretation of $H_0: \beta_1 = 0$ in Exercise 13.5?
  c. What is the natural research hypothesis H_a for that problem?
  d. Do the data support H_a at $\alpha = .05$?

13.14 Find the p-value of the test of $H_0: \beta_1 = 0$ for Exercise 13.13.

13.15 Calculate a 95% confidence interval for σ_ϵ using the data of Exercise 13.5.

13.16 A firm that prints automobile bumper stickers investigates the relation between the total direct cost of a lot of stickers and the number produced in the printing run. The data are analyzed by a standard computer package. The relevant output is shown below:

```
MULTIPLE R              0.9982        STD. ERROR OF EST.       12.2068
MULTIPLE R-SQUARE       0.9964
```

ANALYSIS OF VARIANCE

	SUM OF SQUARES	DF	MEAN SQUARE	F RATIO	P(TAIL)
REGRESSION	1167746.5000	1	1167746.5000	7836.946	0.0000
RESIDUAL	4172.1484	28	149.0053		

VARIABLE		COEFFICIENT	STD. ERROR	STD. REG COEFF	T	P(2 TAIL)	TOLERANCE
INTERCEPT		99.77704					
RUNSIZE	1	51.91785	0.58647	0.998	88.527	0.0000	1.00000

a. Plot the data. Do you detect any difficulties with using a linear regression model? Can you see any blatant violations of assumptions? The raw data are

Runsize:	2.6	5.0	10.0	2.0	.8	4.0	2.5	.6	.8	1.0	2.0	
Total cost:	230	341	629	187	159	327	206	124	155	147	209	

Runsize:	3.0	.4	.5	5.0	20.0	5.0	2.0	1.0	1.5	.5	1.0	1.0
Total cost:	247	135	125	366	1146	339	208	150	179	128	155	143

Runsize:	.6	2.0	1.5	3.0	6.5	2.2	1.0
Total cost:	131	219	171	258	415	226	159

b. Write the estimated regression equation indicated in the output. Find the residual standard deviation.

c. Calculate a 95% confidence interval for the true slope. What are the interpretations of the intercept and slope in this problem?

13.17 Refer to the computer output of Exercise 13.16.

a. Locate the value of the *t* statistic for testing $H_0: \beta_1 = 0$.

b. Locate the *p*-value for this test. Is the *p*-value one-tailed or two-tailed? If necessary, calculate the *p*-value for the appropriate number of tails.

13.18 Refer to the computer output of Exercise 13.16.

a. Locate the value of the *F* statistic and the associated *p*-value.

b. How do the *p*-values for this *F* test and the *t* test of Exercise 13.17 compare? Why should this relation hold?

13.19 Calculate a 90% confidence interval for σ_ϵ using the information in Exercise 13.16.

13.4   PREDICTING NEW *Y* VALUES USING REGRESSION ∎

In all the regression analyses we've done so far, we have been summarizing and making inferences about relations in data that have already been observed. Thus we've been predicting the past. One of the most important uses of regression is in trying to forecast the future. In the road resurfacing example, the county highway director wants to predict the cost of a new contract that is up for bids. In this section we discuss how to make such regression forecasts and how to determine the plus-or-minus probable error factor.

There are two possible interpretations of a Y prediction based on a given x. Suppose that the highway director substitutes $x = 6$ miles in the regression equation $\hat{y} = 2.0 + 3.0x$ and gets $\hat{y} = 20$. This can be interpreted as either

"the average cost $E(Y)$ of *all* resurfacing contracts for 6 miles of road will be $20,000,"

or

"the cost Y of *this specific* resurfacing contract for 6 miles of road will be $20,000."

The best-guess prediction in either case is 20, but the plus-or-minus factor differs. It's easier to predict an average value $E(Y)$ than an individual Y value. We discuss the plus-or-minus range for predicting an average first, with the understanding that this is an intermediate step toward solving the specific-value problem.

In the mean-value forecasting problem, suppose that the value of the predictor x is known. Because the previous values of x have been designated $x_1, \ldots, x_n$, call the new value x_{n+1}. Then $\hat{y}_{n+1} = \beta_0 + \beta_1 x_{n+1}$ is used to predict $E(Y_{n+1})$. As $\hat{\beta}_0$ and $\hat{\beta}_1$ are unbiased, $E(\hat{y}_{n+1}) = \beta_0 + \beta_1 x_{n+1} = E(Y_{n+1})$; thus $\hat{y}_{n+1}$ is an unbiased predictor of $E(Y_{n+1})$. The standard error of $\hat{y}_{n+1}$ can be shown to be

$$\sigma_\epsilon \sqrt{\frac{1}{n} + \frac{(x_{n+1} - \bar{x})^2}{S_{xx}}}$$

where S_{xx} is the sum of squared deviations of the original n values of x_i. Again σ_ϵ must be estimated by s_ϵ, and t tables must be used. The usual approach to forming a confidence interval, namely, estimate $\pm t$ (standard error of estimate), yields a confidence inverval for $E(Y_{n+1})$ as shown here:

$100(1 - \alpha)\%$ Confidence Interval for $E(Y_{n+1})$

$$\hat{y}_{n+1} - t_{\alpha/2} s_\epsilon \sqrt{\frac{1}{n} + \frac{(x_{n+1} - \bar{x})^2}{S_{xx}}} \leq E(Y_{n+1})$$

$$\leq \hat{y}_{n+1} + t_{\alpha/2} s_\epsilon \sqrt{\frac{1}{n} + \frac{(x_{n+1} - \bar{x})^2}{S_{xx}}}$$

where t_a cuts off area a in the right tail of the t distribution with $n - 2$ d.f.

For the resurfacing example, the computer output at the top of page 577 shows the estimated value of $E(Y)$ to be 20 when $x = 6$. The corresponding 95% confidence interval on $E(Y)$ is 12.29 to 27.21.

The forecasting plus-or-minus term in the confidence interval for $E(Y_{n+1})$ depends on the sample size n and the standard deviation around the regression line, as one might expect. It also depends on the squared distance of x_{n+1} from $\bar{x}$ (the mean of the previous x_i values) relative to S_{xx}. As x_{n+1} gets farther from $\bar{x}$,

PARAMETER	ESTIMATE	T FOR H0: PARAMETER=0	PR > |T|	STD ERROR OF ESTIMATE
INTERCEPT	2.00000000	0.52	0.6376	3.82970843
MILES	3.00000000	3.50	0.0394	0.85634884

OBSERVATION	OBSERVED VALUE	PREDICTED VALUE	RESIDUAL	LOWER 95% CL FOR MEAN	UPPER 95% CL FOR MEAN
1	6.00000000	5.00000000	1.00000000	-4.82631770	14.82631770
2	14.00000000	11.00000000	3.00000000	4.90597646	17.09402354
3	10.00000000	14.00000000	-4.00000000	8.54933964	19.45066036
4	14.00000000	17.00000000	-3.00000000	10.90597646	23.09402354
5	26.00000000	23.00000000	3.00000000	13.17368230	32.82631770
6 *	.	20.00000000	.	12.29160220	27.70839780

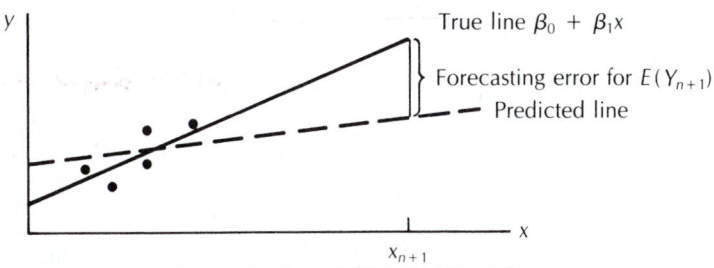

FIGURE 13.9   Effects of Extrapolation on Forecast Error

the term $(x_{n+1} - \bar{x})^2/S_{xx}$ gets larger. When x_{n+1} is far away from the other x values, so that this term is large, the prediction is a considerable extrapolation from the data. Small errors in estimating the regression line are magnified by the extrapolation, as in Figure 13.9. The term $(x_{n+1} - \bar{x})^2/S_{xx}$ could be called an **extrapolation penalty** because it increases with the degree of extrapolation. This penalty term actually understates the risk of extrapolation. It is based on the assumption of a linear relation, and that assumption gets very shaky for large extrapolations.

extrapolation penalty

EXAMPLE 13.10   For the data of Example 13.4, calculate a 95% confidence interval for $E(Y_{n+1})$ based on an assumed x_{n+1} of 22.4. Compare the width of this interval to one based on an assumed x_{n+1} of 30.4.

Solution   For $x_{n+1} = 22.4$,

$$\hat{y}_{n+1} = 64.672 + (-1.7487)(22.4) = 25.5$$

The estimated standard error for estimating $E(Y_{n+1})$ is

$$s_\epsilon \sqrt{\frac{1}{n} + \frac{(x_{n+1} - \bar{x})^2}{S_{xx}}} = 2.380 \sqrt{\frac{1}{10} + \frac{(22.4 - 22.44)^2}{5099.12 - (224.4)^2/10}} = .753$$

* Observation 6 designates the predicted value $\hat{y}_{n+1} = 20$ and the 95% confidence limits for $E(Y_{n+1})$.

The tabled t value ($n - 2 = 8$ d.f., $\alpha = .025$) is 2.306. The 95% confidence interval is

$$25.5 - (2.306)(.753) \le E(Y_{n+1}) \le 25.5 + (2.306)(.753) \qquad \text{or}$$

$$23.764 \le E(Y_{n+1}) \le 27.236$$

For $x_{n+1} = 30.4$,

$$\hat{y}_{n+1} = 64.672 + (-1.7487)(30.4) = 11.5$$

with standard error

$$2.380\sqrt{1/10 + (30.4 - 22.44)^2/[5099.12 - (224.4)^2/10]} = 2.492$$

The 95% confidence interval is

$$11.5 - (2.306)(2.492) \le E(Y_{n+1}) \le 11.5 + (2.306)(2.492), \qquad \text{or}$$

$$5.753 \le E(Y_{n+1}) \le 17.247 \qquad \textit{Much bigger cuz further down } \bar{x}$$

The interval for $E(Y_{n+1})$ when $x_{n+1} = 22.4$ is much shorter than that for $E(Y_{n+1})$ when $x_{n+1} = 30.4$. An x value of 30.4 is well outside the range of x values in the data, so the extrapolation penalty is severe. ∎

Usually, the more relevant forecasting problem is that of predicting an individual Y_{n+1} value rather than $E(Y_{n+1})$. The same best-guess $\hat{y}_{n+1}$ is used but the forecasting plus-or-minus term is larger when predicting Y_{n+1} rather than $E(Y_{n+1})$. In fact, it can be shown that the plus-or-minus forecasting error using $\hat{y}_{n+1}$ to predict Y_{n+1} is

$$\sigma_\epsilon \sqrt{1 + \frac{1}{n} + \frac{(x_{n+1} - \bar{x})^2}{S_{xx}}}$$

If the population standard deviation σ_ϵ is estimated by s_ϵ, the prediction interval for Y_{n+1} is as follows:

$100(1 - \alpha)$% Prediction Interval for Y_{n+1}

$$\hat{y}_{n+1} - t_{\alpha/2} s_\epsilon \sqrt{1 + \frac{1}{n} + \frac{(x_{n+1} - \bar{x})^2}{S_{xx}}} \le Y_{n+1}$$

$$\le \hat{y}_{n+1} + t_{\alpha/2} s_\epsilon \sqrt{1 + \frac{1}{n} + \frac{(x_{n+1} - \bar{x})^2}{S_{xx}}}$$

where t_a cuts off area a in the right tail of the t distribution with $n - 2$ d.f. ∎

In the road resurfacing example, the corresponding 95% prediction limits for Y_{n+1} when $x = 6$ are 5.58 to 34.42, as shown in the output below. The 95%

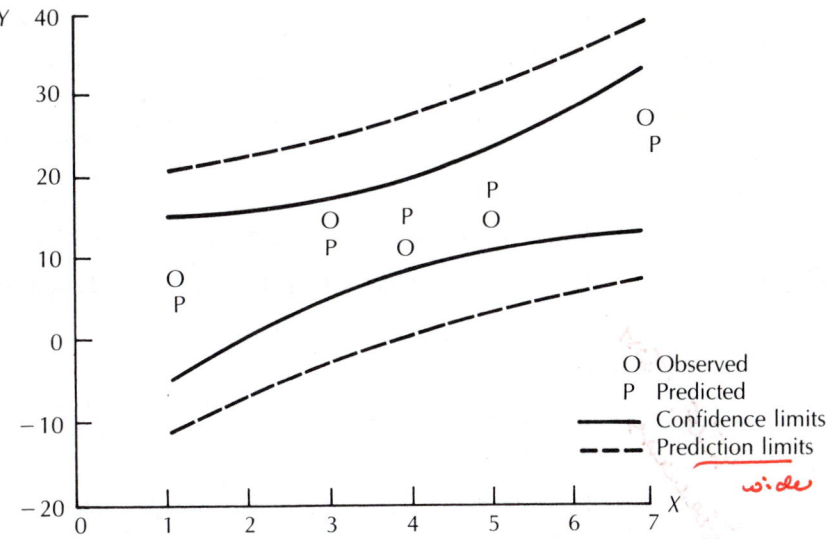

FIGURE 13.10   Predicted Versus Observed Values with 95% Limits; Example 13.2

OBSERVATION	OBSERVED VALUE	PREDICTED VALUE	RESIDUAL	LOWER 95% CL INDIVIDUAL	UPPER 95% CL INDIVIDUAL
1	6.00000000	5.00000000	1.00000000	-10.65582994	20.65582994
2	14.00000000	11.00000000	3.00000000	-2.62665089	24.62665089
3	10.00000000	14.00000000	-4.00000000	0.64866336	27.35133664
4	14.00000000	17.00000000	-3.00000000	3.37334911	30.62665089
5	26.00000000	23.00000000	3.00000000	7.34417006	38.65582994
6 *	.	20.00000000	.	5.57890821	34.42109179

intervals for $E(Y_{n+1})$ and for Y_{n+1} are shown in Figure 13.10; the inner curves are for $E(Y_{n+1})$ the outer ones for Y_{n+1}.

The only difference between prediction of a mean $E(Y_{n+1})$ and prediction of an individual value Y_{n+1} is the term $+1$ in the standard error formula. The presence of this extra term indicates that predictions of individual values are less accurate than predictions of means. The extrapolation penalty term still applies, as does the warning that it understates the risk of extrapolation. If n is large and the extrapolation term is small, the $+1$ term dominates the square root factor in the prediction interval. In such cases the interval becomes, approximately, $\hat{y}_{n+1} - t_{\alpha/2}s_\epsilon \le Y_{n+1} \le \hat{y}_{n+1} + t_{\alpha/2}s_\epsilon$. Thus, for large n, roughly 68% of the residuals (forecast errors) are less than $\pm 1s_\epsilon$ and 95% less than $\pm 2s_\epsilon$. There isn't much point in devising rules for when to ignore the other terms in the square root factor. They are easy to calculate and it does no harm to include them.

EXAMPLE 13.11   For the data of Example 13.4, find a 95% prediction interval for Y_{n+1} with $x_{n+1} = 22.4$, and find the interval with $x_{n+1} = 30.4$. Compare these to widths estimated by the $\pm 2s_\epsilon$ rules above.

Solution   As in Example 13.10, $\hat{y}_{n+1} = 25.5$ if $x_{n+1} = 22.4$. The estimated standard error for predicting Y_{n+1} is

$$s_\epsilon \sqrt{1 + \frac{1}{n} + \frac{(x_{n+1} - \bar{x})^2}{S_{xx}}} = 2.380 \sqrt{1 + \frac{1}{10} + \frac{(22.4 - 22.44)^2}{5099.12 - (224.4)^2/10}}$$

$$= 2.496$$

The tabled t value ($n - 2 = 8$ d.f., $\alpha = .025$) is 2.306. The prediction interval is

$$25.5 - (2.306)(2.496) \le Y_{n+1} \le 25.5 + (2.306)(2.496), \qquad \text{or}$$

$$19.744 \le Y_{n+1} \le 31.256$$

The $\pm 2s_\epsilon$ range is

$$25.5 - (2)(2.380) \le Y_{n+1} \le 25.5 + (2)(2.380), \qquad \text{or}$$
$$20.74 \le Y_{n+1} \le 30.26$$

The latter is too narrow, mostly because the tabled t value with only 8 d.f. is larger than 2.

For $x_{n+1} = 30.4$, $\hat{y}_{n+1} = 11.5$ as in Example 13.10. The estimated standard error for predicting Y_{n+1} is

$$2.380 \sqrt{1 + \frac{1}{10} + \frac{(30.4 - 22.44)^2}{5099.12 - (224.4)^2/10}} = 3.446$$

The 95% prediction interval is

$$11.5 - (2.306)(3.446) \le Y_{n+1} \le 11.5 + (2.306)(3.446), \qquad \text{or}$$

$$3.554 \le Y_{n+1} \le 19.446$$

The $\pm 2s_\epsilon$ range is

$$11.5 - (2)(2.380) \le Y_{n+1} \le 11.5 + (2)(2.380), \qquad \text{or}$$

$$6.74 \le Y_{n+1} \le 16.26$$

The latter is much too narrow. Not only is the tabled t value larger than 2, but also the large extrapolation penalty is not reflected. ∎

SECTION 13.4   EXERCISES

13.20 Refer to the data of Exercise 13.16.
   a. Predict the mean total direct cost for all bumper sticker orders with a print run of 2000 stickers (that is, with RUNSIZE = 2.0).
   b. Calculate a 95% confidence interval for this mean.

13.21 Does the prediction in Exercise 13.20 represent a major extrapolation?

13.22 Refer to Exercise 13.20.
   a. Predict the total direct cost for a particular bumper sticker order with a print run of 2000 stickers. Calculate a 95% prediction interval.
   b. Would an actual total direct cost of $250 be surprising for this order?

13.23 Refer to the data of Exercise 13.5.

a. Predict the number of bank branches located in a ZIP code area that has 1267 independent businesses. Give a 90% prediction interval.

b. Do you think that this is a reasonable prediction, given the data?

13.24 Refer to the data of Exercise 13.1.

a. If the model with Y a linear function of x is adopted (as in Exercise 13.2), what is the predicted Y when $x = 20$?

b. If the model with Y a linear function of $x' = \log_{10} x$ is adopted (as in Exercise 13.3), what is the predicted value of Y when $x = 20$?

c. Which of the two predictions seems more reasonable (or perhaps less unreasonable)?

13.25 Give a 95% prediction interval for the prediction you selected in Exercise 13.24.

13.5   CORRELATION   ∎

Once we've found the prediction line, we need to measure how well it predicts actual values. In the road resurfacing example, if we were given the mileage values x_i, we could use the prediction equation $\hat{y}_i = 2.0 + 3.0x_i$ to predict costs. The

residuals   deviations of actual values from predicted values, called **residuals**, measure prediction errors. These errors are summarized by the sum of squared residuals $SS(\text{Residual}) = \sum (y_i - \hat{y}_i)^2$, which is 44 for these data. For comparison, if we were not given the x_i values, the best squared error predictor of y would be the mean value $\bar{y} = 14$, and the sum of squared prediction errors would, in this case, be $\sum_i (y_i - \bar{y})^2 = SS(\text{Total}) = 224$. The proportionate reduction in error would be

$$\frac{SS(\text{Total}) - SS(\text{Residual})}{SS(\text{Total})} = \frac{224 - 44}{224} = .804$$

which indicates a fairly strong relation between the mileage to be resurfaced and the cost of resurfacing.

correlation   This proportionate reduction in error is closely related to the **correlation**
coefficient   **coefficient** of x and y. **The general idea of a correlation is that it measures the strength of the linear relation between x and y.** The stronger the correlation, the better x predicts y. The mathematical definition of the correlation coefficient, denoted r_{yx}, is

$$r_{yx} = \frac{S_{xy}}{\sqrt{S_{xx}S_{yy}}}$$

where S_{xy} and S_{xx} are defined as before and

$$S_{yy} = \sum_i y_i^2 - \frac{\left(\sum_i y_i\right)^2}{n}$$

In the example, $r_{yx} = 60/\sqrt{(20)(224)} = .896$.

Generally, the correlation r_{yx} is a positive number if y tends to increase as x increases; r_{yx} is negative if y tends to decrease as x increases; and r_{yx} is zero if either there is no relation between changes in x and changes in y, or there is a nonlinear relation such that patterns of increase and decrease in y (as x increases) cancel each other.

EXAMPLE 13.12

Consider the following data:

y:	25	41.	47	59	54	56	49	43	30
x:	10	20	20	30	30	30	40	40	50

a. Should the correlation be positive or negative?

b. Calculate the correlation.

Solution

a. Notice that as x increases from 10 to 50, y first increases, then decreases. Therefore the correlation should be small. The y values don't decrease quite back to where they started, so the correlation should be positive.

b. Calculations show $\sum x = 270, \sum x^2 = 9300, \sum y = 404, \sum y^2 = 19{,}198, \sum xy = 12{,}260$, and $n = 9$. Therefore

$$S_{xx} = 9300 - \frac{(270)^2}{9} = 1200$$

$$S_{yy} = 19{,}198 - \frac{(404)^2}{9} = 1062.8889$$

$$S_{xy} = 12{,}260 - \frac{(270)(404)}{9} = 140$$

$$r_{yx} = \frac{140}{\sqrt{(1200)(1062.8889)}} = .1240$$

The correlation is indeed a small positive number.   ∎

Correlation and regression predictability are closely related. The proportionate reduction in error for regression we defined earlier is called the **coefficient of determination**. The coefficient of determination is simply the square of the correlation coefficient,

$$r_{yx}^2 = \frac{SS(Total) - SS(Residual)}{SS(Total)}$$

coefficient of determination

which is the proportionate reduction in error. In the resurfacing example, $r_{yx} = .896$ and $r_{yx}^2 = .804$.

A correlation of zero indicates no predictive value using the equation $y = \hat{\beta}_0 + \hat{\beta}_1 x$; that is, one can predict y as well without knowing x as one can knowing x. A correlation of 1 or -1 indicates perfect predictability—a 100% reduction in error attributable to knowledge of x. A correlation coefficient should routinely be interpreted in terms of its squared value, the coefficient of determination. Thus, correlation of $-.3$, say, indicates only a 9% reduction in squared prediction error. Many books and most computer programs use the equation

$$SS(Total) = SS(Residual) + SS(Regression)$$

where

$$SS(Regression) = \sum_i (\hat{y}_i - \bar{y})^2$$

Because the equation can be expressed as $SS(Residual) = (1 - r_{yx}^2) SS(Total)$, it follows that $SS(Regression) = r_{yx}^2 SS(Total)$, which again says that regression on x explains a proportion r^2 of the total squared error of y.

EXAMPLE 13.13   Find SS(Total), SS(Regression), and SS(Residual) for the data of Example 13.12.

Solution $SS(Total) = S_{yy}$, which we computed to be 1062.8889 in Example 13.12. We also found that $r_{yx} = .1240$, so $r_{yx}^2 = (.1240)^2 = .0154$. Using the fact that $SS(Regression) = r_{yx}^2 SS(Total)$, we have $SS(Regression) = (.0154)(1062.8889) = 16.3685$. Because $SS(Residual) = SS(Total) - SS(Regression)$, $SS(Residual) = 1062.8889 - 16.3685 = 1046.5204$.

Note that SS(Regression) and r_{yx}^2 are very small. This suggests that x is not a good predictor of y. The reality, though, is that the relation between x and y is extremely nonlinear. A *linear* equation in x does not predict y very well, but a nonlinear equation would do far better. ∎

The sample correlation r_{yx} is the basis for estimation and significance testing of the population correlation ρ_{yx}. Statistical inferences are always based on formal mathematical assumptions. The formal assumptions of regression analysis—linear relation between x and y, and constant variance around the **assumptions for** regression line, in particular—are also assumed in correlation inference. In **correlation** regression analysis, we regard the x values as predetermined constants. In **inference** correlation analysis, we regard the x values as randomly selected (and the regression inferences are conditional on the sampled x values). If the x's are not drawn randomly, it is possible that the correlation estimates are biased. In some texts, the additional assumption is made that the x values are drawn from a normal population. (This assumption, together with the regression assumptions, implies that the x, y, values are drawn from a bivariate normal population.) The inferences we make do not depend crucially on this normality assumption.

bias in estimating ρ   The most basic inference problem is potential bias in estimation of ρ_{yx}. Under the assumptions we've given, the sample correlation is not quite an unbiased estimator. However, the degree of bias is small, and not worth correcting. A more serious problem arises when the x values are predetermined, as often happens in regression analysis. The choice of x values can systematically increase or decrease the sample correlation. In general, a wide range of x values tends to increase the magnitude of the correlation coefficient and a small range to decrease it. This effect is shown in Figure 13.11 (page 584). If all the points in this scatter plot are included, there is an obvious, strong correlation between x and y. But suppose we consider only x values in the range between the dashed vertical lines. By eliminating the outside parts of the scatter diagram, the sample correlation coefficient is still positive, but much weaker. It's clear then that the correlation coefficient (and the coefficient of determination) can be affected by systematic choices of x values. Thus it's a good idea to consider the residual

FIGURE 13.11   Effect of Limited x Range on Sample Correlation Coefficient

standard deviation s_ϵ and the magnitude of the slope when you decide how well a linear regression line predicts y.

EXAMPLE 13.14   Suppose that a company has the following data on productivity y and aptitude test score x for 12 data entry operators:

y:	41	39	47	51	43	40	57	46	50	59	61	52
x:	24	30	33	35	36	36	37	37	38	40	43	49

Find the correlation coefficient and the residual standard deviation based on all 12 observations. Compare these to the correlation and residual standard deviation based on the 6 observations with the highest x scores.

Solution   For all 12 observations,

$$\sum x_i = 438, \qquad \sum x_i^2 = 16{,}414, \qquad \sum y_i = 586$$
$$\sum y_i^2 = 29{,}232, \qquad \sum x_i y_i = 21{,}720$$

Therefore

$$r_{yx} = \frac{\sum x_i y_i - (\sum x_i)(\sum y_i)/n}{\sqrt{\sum x_i^2 - (\sum x_i)^2/n}\sqrt{\sum y_i^2 - (\sum y_i)^2/n}}$$

$$= \frac{21{,}720 - (438)(586)/12}{\sqrt{16{,}414 - (438)^2/12}\sqrt{29{,}232 - (586)^2/12}}$$

$$= .646$$

Also, $\hat{\beta}_1 = .775$, $\hat{\beta}_0 = 20.54$, and $s_\epsilon = 6.021$. For the six highest x scores

$$\sum x_i = 244, \qquad \sum x_i^2 = 10{,}032, \qquad \sum y_i = 325$$
$$\sum y_i^2 = 17{,}771, \qquad \sum x_i y_i = 13{,}242$$

Therefore

$$r_{yx} = \frac{13{,}242 - (244)(325)/6}{\sqrt{10{,}032 - (244)^2/6}\sqrt{17{,}771 - (325)^2/6}} = .188$$

Also, $\hat{\beta}_1 = .232$, $\hat{\beta}_0 = 44.74$, and $s_\epsilon = 6.292$.

In going from all 12 observations to the 6 observations with the highest x values, the correlation has decreased drastically but the residual standard deviation has hardly changed at all.   ∎

Just as it is possible to test the null hypothesis that a true slope is zero, we can also test $H_0: \rho_{yx} = 0$. The procedure is summarized in the following:

Summary for a Test of $H_0: \rho_{yx} = 0$

$H_0: \rho_{yx} = 0$
H_a: 1. $\rho_{yx} > 0$
    2. $\rho_{yx} < 0$
    3. $\rho_{yx} \neq 0$
T.S.: $t = r_{yx}\sqrt{n-2}/\sqrt{1-r_{yx}^2}$
R.R.: With $n-2$ d.f. and Type I error probability α,
    1. $t > t_\alpha$
    2. $t < -t_\alpha$
    3. $|t| > t_{\alpha/2}$

We tested the hypothesis that the true slope is zero (in predicting resurfacing cost from mileage) in Example 13.5; the resulting t statistic was 3.50. For that data, we can calculate r_{yx} as .896421 and r_{yx}^2 as .803571. Hence the correlation t statistic is $.896\sqrt{3}/\sqrt{1 - .803571} = 3.50$. In general, the t tests for a slope and for a correlation give identical results; it doesn't matter which form is used. It follows that the t test is valid for any choice of x values. The bias we mentioned previously does not affect the sign of the correlation.

EXAMPLE 13.15   Perform t tests for the null hypotheses of zero correlation and zero slope for the data of Example 13.14 (all observations). Use an appropriate one-sided alternative.

Solution   First, the appropriate H_a ought to be $\rho_{yx} > 0$ (and therefore $\beta_1 > 0$). It would be nice if an aptitude test had a positive correlation with the productivity score it was predicting! In Example 13.15, $n = 12$, $r_{yx} = .646$, and

$$t = \frac{.646\sqrt{12-2}}{\sqrt{1-(.646)^2}} = 2.68$$

Because this value falls between the tabled t values for d.f. $= 10$, $\alpha = .025$ (2.228) and for d.f. $= 10$, $\alpha = .01 (2.764)$, the p-value lies between .010 and .025. Hence H_0 may be rejected.

The t statistic for testing the slope β_1 is

$$t = \frac{\hat{\beta}_1}{s_\epsilon \sqrt{\dfrac{1}{S_{xx}}}} = \frac{.775}{6.021 \sqrt{\dfrac{1}{16,414 - (438)^2/12}}}$$

$$= 2.66$$

which equals (to within round-off error) the correlation t statistic, 2.68.

The test for a correlation provides a neat illustration of the difference between statistical significance and statistical importance. Suppose that a psychologist has devised a skills test for production line workers and tests it on a huge sample of 40,000. If the sample correlation between test score and actual productivity is .02, then

$$t = \frac{0.2\sqrt{39{,}998}}{\sqrt{1 - (.02)^2}} = 4.0$$

We would reject the null hypothesis at any reasonable α level, so the correlation is "statistically significant." However, the test accounts for only $(.02)^2 = .0004$ of the squared error in skill scores, so it is almost worthless as a predictor. Remember, the rejection of the null hypothesis in a statistical test is the conclusion that the sample results cannot plausibly have occurred by chance if the null hypothesis is true. The test itself does not address the practical significance of the result. Clearly, for a sample size of 40,000, even a trivial sample correlation like .02 is not likely to occur by mere luck of the draw. There is no practically meaningful relationship between these test scores and productivity scores.

EXAMPLE 13.16   Suppose that a study is made of forecast profits and actual realized profits for 40 new products introduced by chemical industry firms within the previous four years. Forecast five-year profit (per $1000 invested) is the independent variable x and actual first-year profit (per $1000 invested) is the dependent variable y. Summary results are

$$\sum x_i = 2480, \quad \sum y_i = 1860, \quad \sum x_i y_i = 128{,}860$$
$$\sum x_i^2 = 187{,}660, \quad \sum y_i^2 = 124{,}530, \quad n = 40$$

a. Find the regression equation and residual standard deviation.
b. Find the sample correlation coefficient and coefficient of determination. What does this indicate about the apparent success of current forecasting methods?
c. Test (at $\alpha = .05$) the hypothesis that x has no value in a (linear) prediction of y.
d. Give a 95% prediction interval for the actual first-year profit per thousand dollars invested for a project with a forecast profit of $50.00.

Solution   a. $\hat{\beta}_1 = \dfrac{S_{xy}}{S_{xx}} = \dfrac{\sum x_i y_i - (\sum x_i)(\sum y_i)/n}{\sum x_i^2 - (\sum x_i)^2/n} = \dfrac{13{,}540}{33{,}900} = .39941003$

$\hat{\beta}_0 = \bar{y} - \hat{\beta}_1 \bar{x} = 21.736578$

So $\hat{y} = 21.74 + .40x$, rounding off to reasonable numbers,

$$s_\varepsilon^2 = \frac{\sum y_i^2 - \hat{\beta}_0 \sum y_i - \hat{\beta}_1 \sum x_i y_i}{n - 2} = \frac{32{,}631.988}{38}$$

$$= 858.73654$$

So $s_\varepsilon = \sqrt{858.73654} = 29.304207$, or about 29.30.

b. $r_{yx} = \dfrac{S_{xy}}{\sqrt{S_{xx}}\sqrt{S_{yy}}} = \dfrac{13{,}540}{\sqrt{33{,}900}\sqrt{38{,}040}} = .37704967$

$r_{yx}^2 = (.37704967)^2 = .14216645$

This indicates that knowledge of the forecast profits reduces squared error in predicting actual profits by only about 14.2%.

c. Because we just calculated the sample correlation, it's convenient to use the correlation t statistic. We take H_0: $\rho_{yx} = 0$. If there is any correlation between forecast and actual, we would hope it is positive, so we take H_a: $\rho_{yx} > 0$.

The test statistic $t = \dfrac{r_{yx}\sqrt{n-2}}{\sqrt{1-r_{yx}^2}} = \dfrac{.37704967\sqrt{38}}{\sqrt{1 - .14216645}}$

$$= 2.5095095, \text{ or about } 2.51$$

The tabled t value for 38 d.f., $\alpha = .05$ (one-tailed) lies somewhere between the values for 30 d.f. and 40 d.f., namely, 1.697 and 1.684; let's assume it is 1.69. The observed t statistic falls beyond either value, so we may reject H_0 at $\alpha = .05$ and conclude that the modest observed correlation is not merely the result of chance. (In fact, the t tables indicate that we could also reject H_0 at $\alpha = .01$ but not at $\alpha = .005$. Therefore the one-tailed p-value would be somewhere between .005 and .01).

d. For $x_{n+1} = 50.00$, the predicted profit is

$$\hat{y}_{n+1} = 21.736578 + .39941003(50) = 41.70708$$

or about 41.71. By rough approximation, take the two-tailed tabled t value to be 2.02. The 95% prediction interval is

$$41.71 - 2.02(29.30)\sqrt{1 + \frac{1}{40} + \frac{\left(50.00 - \frac{2480}{40}\right)^2}{33{,}900}} \le Y_{n+1}$$

$$\le 41.71 + 2.02(29.30)\sqrt{1 + \frac{1}{40} + \frac{\left(50.00 - \frac{2480}{40}\right)^2}{33{,}900}}$$

or

$$-18.34 \le Y_{n+1} \le 101.76$$

This very wide interval confirms the finding in part (b) that current forecasting methods are quite poor. ∎

13.6   RANK CORRELATION

The ordinary correlation coefficient r_{yx} assesses the degree to which x and y are linearly related. It can happen that y generally increases as x increases, but not necessarily in a linear fashion. In such a case, the ordinary correlation does not

rank correlation

completely reflect the extent of the relation between y and x. There are two reasonable approaches for measuring the association between x and y in such a situation: Use a nonlinear prediction rule, or find a general measure of the tendency for y to increase (linearly or not) with x. Nonlinear prediction can be handled by methods we will discuss in the next two chapters. The **rank correlation coefficient** is another way to measure the extent to which y increases with x.

The calculation of a rank correlation is quite simple. Rank all the x scores from lowest to highest; rank the y scores likewise. Calculate the correlation based on the ranks; this is the rank correlation r_s that we sometimes refer to as Spearman's rank order correlation coefficient.

EXAMPLE 13.17   Calculate the rank correlation coefficient r_s for the data of Example 13.4.

Solution   First, rank the y scores and the x scores separately, from lowest to highest.

y_i:	31.5	33.1	27.4	24.5	27.0	27.8	23.3	24.7	16.9	18.1
rank y_i:	9	10	7	4	6	8	3	5	1	2

x_i:	18.1	20.0	20.8	21.5	22.0	22.4	22.9	24.0	25.4	27.3
rank x_i:	1	2	3	4	5	6	7	8	9	10

Then $\sum \text{rank } x_i = 55$, $\sum (\text{rank } x_i)^2 = 385$, $\sum \text{rank } y_i = 55$, $\sum (\text{rank } y_i)^2 = 385$, and $\sum (\text{rank } x_i)(\text{rank } y_i) = 234$. The rank correlation is

$$\frac{\sum (\text{rank } x_i)(\text{rank } y_i) - (\sum \text{rank } x_i)(\sum \text{rank } y_i)/n}{\sqrt{\sum (\text{rank } x_i)^2 - (\sum \text{rank } x_i)^2/n} \sqrt{\sum (\text{rank } y_i)^2 - (\sum \text{rank } y_i)^2/n}}$$

$$= \frac{234 - (55)(55)/10}{\sqrt{385 - (55)^2/10} \sqrt{385 - (55)^2/10}}$$

$$= -.830$$ ■

When there are no ties in rankings, the calculation is even simpler. In this case, it can be proved that

$$r_s = 1 - \frac{6 \sum d_i^2}{n(n^2 - 1)}$$

where d_i is the difference between the y rank and the x rank of observation i.

EXAMPLE 13.18   Use the simplified formula above to recalculate the rank correlation coefficient for the data of Example 13.4.

Solution   The ranks and the differences in ranks are

rank y_i:	9	10	7	4	6	8	3	5	1	2
rank x_i:	1	2	3	4	5	6	7	8	9	10
d_i:	8	8	4	0	1	2	−4	−3	−8	−8

$\sum d_i^2 = 302$, so

$$r_s = 1 - \frac{(6)(302)}{10(100 - 1)} = -.830$$ ■

The rank correlation may be tested for statistical significance. The null hypothesis is that there is no general tendency for y to either increase or decrease with x. This is true if x and y are independent. The same t statistic and degrees of freedom are used for rank correlation as for ordinary correlation. In the case of rank correlation, the test is approximate because the formal normality assumptions underlying the t test don't hold for ranks. However, the approximation is accurate enough for $n \geq 10$ or so.

EXAMPLE 13.19   Test the significance of the rank correlation for the data of Example 13.4.

Solution

$$t = \frac{r_s \sqrt{n-2}}{\sqrt{1-r_s^2}}$$

$$= \frac{-.830\sqrt{10-2}}{\sqrt{1-(-.830)^2}} = -4.21$$

This value falls beyond tabulated t values with $10 - 2 = 8$ d.f., so the null hypothesis may be rejected conclusively. ∎

SECTIONS 13.5 AND 13.6   EXERCISES

13.26 Refer to the data of Exercise 13.5. Calculate the correlation coefficient r_{yx}.

13.27 Refer to the data of Exercise 13.5.
  a. Test the hypothesis of no true correlation between x and y. Use a one-sided H_a and $\alpha = .05$.
  b. Compare the result of this test to that of Exercise 13.13, part (d).

13.28 Refer to the computer output of Exercise 13.16.
  a. Locate r_{yx}^2.
  b. The estimated slope $\hat{\beta}_1$ is positive; what must be the sign of the sample correlation coefficient?

13.29 Suppose that the study in Exercise 13.16 had been restricted to RUNSIZE values less than 1.8. Would you anticipate a larger or a smaller r_{yx} value?

13.30 Suppose that an advertising campaign for a new product is conducted in 10 test cities. The intensity of advertising X is varied across cities; the awareness percentage Y is found by survey after the ad campaign.

x:	4.0	4.5	5.0	5.5	6.0	6.5	7.0	7.5	8.0	8.5
y:	10.1	10.3	10.4	21.7	36.7	51.5	67.0	68.5	68.2	69.3

$\sum x_i = 62.5,$ $\sum y_i = 413.7,$ $\sum x_i y_i = 2930.45$
$\sum x_i^2 = 411.25,$ $\sum y_i^2 = 23{,}421.27,$ $n = 10$

  a. Calculate the correlation coefficient r_{yx}.
  b. Calculate the rank correlation coefficient r_s.
  c. Plot the data. Does the relation appear linear to you? Does it appear to be generally increasing?

13.31 A survey of recent M.B.A. graduates of a company obtained data on first-year salary and years of prior work experience. The data are shown at the top of page 590 as printed out by Systat.
  a. By scanning the numbers, can you sense that there is a relation? In particular, does it appear that those with less experience have smaller salaries?
  b. Can you notice any cases that seem to fall outside the pattern?

CASE	SALARY	EXPER	CASE	SALARY	EXPER
1	53.900	8.000	27	51.700	7.000
2	52.500	5.000	28	56.200	9.000
3	49.000	5.000	29	48.900	6.000
4	65.100	11.000	30	51.900	6.000
5	51.600	4.000	31	36.100	4.000
6	52.700	3.000	32	53.500	6.000
7	44.500	3.000	33	50.400	5.000
8	40.100	3.000	34	38.700	1.000
9	41.100	0.000	35	60.100	13.000
10	66.900	13.000	36	38.900	1.000
11	37.900	14.000	37	48.400	6.000
12	53.500	10.000	38	50.600	2.000
13	38.300	2.000	39	41.800	4.000
14	37.200	2.000	40	44.400	1.000
15	51.300	5.000	41	46.600	5.000
16	64.700	13.000	42	43.900	1.000
17	45.300	1.000	43	45.000	4.000
18	47.000	5.000	44	37.900	1.000
19	43.800	1.000	45	44.600	2.000
20	47.400	5.000	46	46.900	7.000
21	40.200	5.000	47	47.600	5.000
22	52.800	7.000	48	43.200	1.000
23	40.700	4.000	49	41.600	1.000
24	47.300	3.000	50	39.200	0.000
25	43.700	3.000	51	41.700	1.000
26	61.800	7.000			

13.32 The data in Exercise 13.31 were plotted by Systat's "influence plot." This plot is a scatter plot with each point identified as to how much its removal would change the correlation. A point with low influence is marked with a 0, which indicates that removing the point would change the correlation by .0something (less than .1). Removing a point marked with à 1 would change the correlation by .1something, which indicates higher influence. (In principle, points could be marked 2, 3, up to 9.) The plot is shown here.

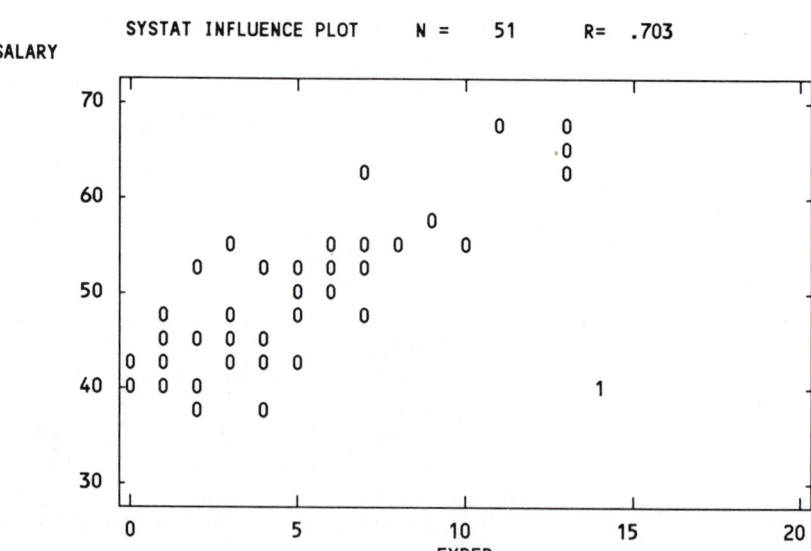

Does there appear to be an increasing pattern in the plot? Are there any points that clearly fall outside the basic pattern?

13.33 Systat computed a regression equation with SALARY as the dependent variable. The output is shown here.

```
DEP VAR: SALARY     N:  51    MULTIPLE R: .703   SQUARED MULTIPLE R: .494
ADJUSTED SQUARED. MULTIPLE R: .484     STANDARD ERROR OF ESTIMATE:    5.402

   VARIABLE     COEFFICIENT    STD ERROR     STD COEF TOLERANCE     T    P(2 TAIL)

  CONSTANT        40.507        1.257      0.000 1.0000000    32.219    0.000
    EXPER          1.470        0.213      0.703 1.0000000     6.916    0.000


                       ANALYSIS OF VARIANCE

  SOURCE     SUM-OF-SQUARES   DF  MEAN-SQUARE    F-RATIO       P

REGRESSION      1395.959       1    1395.959     47.838     0.000
  RESIDUAL      1429.868      49      29.181
```

a. Write out the prediction equation. Interpret the coefficients. Is the constant term (intercept) meaningful in this context?
b. Locate the residual standard deviation. What does the number mean?
c. Is the apparent relation statistically detectable (significant)?
d. How much of the variability in salaries is accounted for by variation in years of prior work experience?

13.34 The 11th person in the data of Exercise 13.31 went to work for a family business in return for a low salary but a large equity in the firm. This case (the high-influence point in Exercise 13.32) was removed from the data and the results reanalyzed by Systat, as follows:

```
DEP VAR: SALARY     N:  50    MULTIPLE R: .842   SQUARED MULTIPLE R: .709
ADJUSTED SQUARED MULTIPLE R: .703     STANDARD ERROR OF ESTIMATE:    4.071

   VARIABLE     COEFFICIENT    STD ERROR     STD COEF TOLERANCE     T    P(2 TAIL)

  CONSTANT        39.188        0.971      0.000 1.0000000    40.353    0.000
    EXPER          1.863        0.172      0.842 1.0000000    10.812    0.000


                       ANALYSIS OF VARIANCE

  SOURCE     SUM-OF-SQUARES   DF  MEAN-SQUARE    F-RATIO       P

REGRESSION      1937.311       1    1937.311    116.906     0.000
  RESIDUAL       795.433      48      16.572
```

a. Should removing the high-influence point in Exercise 13.32 increase or decrease the slope? Did it?
b. How should removal of this point change the residual standard deviation? How large was the change?
c. How could removal of this point change the correlation? How large was this change?

Summary ▪

In preceding sections, we considered various statistical inferences (estimation and testing problems) related to linear regression and correlation. The underlying assumptions for a linear regression model $Y = \beta_0 + \beta_1 x + \epsilon$ (namely, fixed x values, random error, normal with mean zero and variance σ_ϵ^2, independence) allow us to state the sampling distributions for the least-squares estimators $\hat{\beta}_0$ and $\hat{\beta}_1$. Based on these results, we are able to specify the form of a statistical test of $H_0: \beta_1 = 0$ and a corresponding confidence interval for the unknown slope.

The prediction of future values of the dependent variable based on specific values of the independent variable x is a problem of particular interest in regression. We discussed prediction of future values using the linear regression prediction equation and developed an appropriate prediction interval. Finally, we considered inferences related to the population correlation coefficient ρ_{yx}. The rank correlation coefficient provides an alternative to r_{yx} when two variables appear related but are not necessarily linearly related.

KEY FORMULAS: Linear Regression and Correlation Methods

1. Linear regression model

$$Y_i = \beta_0 + \beta_1 x_i + \epsilon_i$$

2. Least-squares estimates of β_0 and β_1

$$\hat{\beta}_1 = \frac{S_{xy}}{S_{xx}},$$

where

$$S_{xy} = \sum xy - \frac{(\sum x)(\sum y)}{n} \text{ and } S_{xx} = \sum x^2 - \frac{(\sum x)^2}{n}$$

$$\hat{\beta}_0 = \bar{y} - \hat{\beta}_1 \bar{x}$$

3. $\text{SS(Residual)} = \sum y^2 - \hat{\beta}_0 \sum y - \hat{\beta}_1 \sum xy$
   $\text{SS(Regression)} = \hat{\beta}_0 \sum y + \hat{\beta}_1 \sum xy - (\sum y)^2/n$

4. Estimated standard errors for $\hat{\beta}_0$ and $\hat{\beta}_1$

$$s_{\hat{\beta}_0} = s_\epsilon \sqrt{\frac{1}{n} + \frac{\bar{x}^2}{S_{xx}}}$$

$$s_{\hat{\beta}_1} = s_\epsilon \sqrt{\frac{1}{S_{xx}}}$$

where

$$s_\epsilon^2 = \frac{\text{SS(Residual)}}{n - 2}$$

5. Inferences about β_1

   a. t test

   $H_0: \beta_1 = 0$

   T.S.: $t = \dfrac{\hat{\beta}_1}{s_\epsilon \sqrt{\dfrac{1}{S_{xx}}}}$, where d.f. $= n - 2$

   b. F test

   $H_0: \beta_1 = 0$

   T.S.: $F = \dfrac{\text{MS(Regression)}}{\text{MS(Residual)}}$, where d.f.$_1 = 1$ and d.f.$_2 = n - 2$

   c. $100(1 - \alpha)\%$ confidence interval

   $\hat{\beta}_1 \pm t_{\alpha/2} s_\epsilon \sqrt{1/S_{xx}}$

6. $100(1 - \alpha)\%$ confidence interval for σ_ϵ^2

   $s_\epsilon^2 \dfrac{(n - 2)}{\chi_{\alpha/2}^2} \leq \sigma_\epsilon^2 \leq s_\epsilon^2 \dfrac{(n - 2)}{\chi_{1 - \alpha/2}^2}$, where d.f. $= n - 2$

7. $100(1 - \alpha)\%$ confidence interval for $E(Y_{n+1})$

   $\hat{y}_{n+1} \pm t_{\alpha/2} s_\epsilon \sqrt{\dfrac{1}{n} + \dfrac{(x_{n+1} - \bar{x})^2}{S_{xx}}}$

8. $100(1 - \alpha)\%$ prediction interval for Y_{n+1}

   $\hat{y}_{n+1} \pm t_{\alpha/2} s_\epsilon \sqrt{1 + \dfrac{1}{n} + \dfrac{(x_{n+1} - \bar{x})^2}{S_{xx}}}$

9. Sample correlation coefficient

   $r_{yx} = \dfrac{S_{xy}}{\sqrt{S_{xx}} \sqrt{S_{yy}}}$

10. SS(Total) $= \sum (y_i - \bar{y})^2$
    $= \sum y_i^2 - (\sum y_i)^2/n$

    Proportionate reduction in error $= \dfrac{\text{SS(Total)} - \text{SS(Residual)}}{\text{SS(Total)}}$

    $= r_{yx}^2$

11. t test concerning ρ_{xy}

    $H_0: \rho_{yx} = 0$

    T.S.: $t = \dfrac{r_{yx} \sqrt{n - 2}}{\sqrt{1 - r_{yx}^2}}$

12. $r_s = 1 - 6 \sum d_i^2/n(n^2 - 1)$, where d_i is the difference between the y rank and the x rank of observation i (valid only if there are no ties)

CHAPTER 13   EXERCISES

13.35 Consider the data shown here:

x: 10   12   14   15   18   19   23
y: 25   30   36   37   42   50   55

a. Plot the data.
b. Using the data, find the least-squares estimates for the model $Y_i = \beta_0 + \beta_1 x_i + \epsilon_i$.
c. Predict Y when $x = 21$.

13.36 Refer to Exercise 13.35.

a. Calculate s_ϵ, the residual standard deviation.
b. Compute the residuals for these data. Do most lie within $\pm 2s_\epsilon$ of zero?

13.37 A government agency responsible for awarding contracts for much of its research work is under careful scrutiny by a number of private companies. One company examines the relationship between the amount of the contract ($\times \$10,000$) and the length of time between submission of the contract proposal and contract approval:

Length (in months), y: 3   4   6   8   11   14   20
Size ($\times \$10,000$), x: 1   5   10   50   100   500   1000

a. Plot y versus x.
b. Fit the line $Y = \beta_0 + \beta_1 x + \epsilon$.
c. Conduct a test of the null hypothesis $H_0: \beta_1 = 0$. Give the p-value for your test for $H_a: \beta_1 > 0$.

13.38 Refer to the data of Exercise 13.37.

a. Plot y versus $\log x$.
b. Fit a linear regression line using $\log x$ as the independent variable.
c. Conduct a test of $H_0: \beta_1 = 0$ and give the level of significance for a one-sided alternative, $H_a: \beta_1 > 0$.

13.39 Use the results of Exercises 13.37 and 13.38 to determine which linear regression line provides the better fit. Give reasons for your choice.

13.40 Refer to the data of Exercise 13.35.

a. Give a 90% confidence interval for β_1, the slope of the linear regression line.
b. Construct a 95% confidence interval for σ_ϵ^2.

13.41 A pharmaceutical company is interested in testing a drug that was developed to treat hypertension (high blood pressure). Six rats selected from a colony of rats bred to be hypertensive are randomly assigned to each of four groups. Group 1 is designated as the control group. These rats are injected with a solution that contains no drug. Groups 2–4 are designated as drug groups. Group 2 rats are all injected with a dose of .1 mg/kg, those in group 3 received .2 mg/kg, and those in group 4 received .4 mg/kg. The response of interest is y, the decrease in blood pressure at two hours post-dose compared to the corresponding pre-dose blood pressure. The data are

Blood Pressure Decreases (mm)					
Group 1 (control)	2	5	6	4	3	1
Group 2 (.1 mg/kg)	10	12	15	16	13	11
Group 3 (.2 mg/kg)	25	22	26	19	18	24
Group 4 (.4 mg/kg)	30	32	35	27	26	29

a. Use a computer software program to fit the model

$$Y = \beta_0 + \beta_1 \sqrt{x} + \epsilon$$

b. Conduct a two-sided test of $H_0: \beta_1 = 0$.

13.42 Use the data of Exercise 13.37 to predict the length of time in months before approval of a $750,000 contract. Give a 95% prediction interval.

13.43 An airline studying fuel usage by a certain type of aircraft obtains data on 100 flights. The air mileage x in hundreds of miles and the actual fuel use y in gallons are recorded. Summary values are

$$\bar{x} = 8.00, \quad \bar{y} = 550.0$$
$$S_{xx} = 1621.0, \quad S_{yy} = 4{,}947{,}000, \quad S_{xy} = 81{,}242$$

a. Calculate the regression equation.
b. Calculate the sample correlation coefficient and coefficient of determination.

13.44 a. Use the fact that $\sum(y_i - \hat{y}_i)^2 = (1 - r_{xy}^2)\sum(y_i - \bar{y})^2$ to calculate SS(Residual) and the residual standard deviation in Exercise 13.43.
b. Calculate the estimated standard error of $\hat{\beta}_1$. Calculate a 95% confidence interval for β_1.
c. Is there any point in testing $H_0: \beta_1 = 0$?

13.45 Refer to the data and calculations of Exercises 13.43 and 13.44.
a. Predict the mean fuel usage of all 1000-mile flights. Give a 95% confidence interval.
b. Predict the fuel usage of a particular 1000-mile flight. Would a usage of 570 gallons considered exceptionally low? (A 95% prediction interval might help in answering the question.)

13.46 What is the interpretation of $\hat{\beta}_1$ in the situation of Exercise 13.43? Is there a sensible interpretation of $\hat{\beta}_0$?

13.47 A group of investors interested in the acquisition of a corporation examine the quarterly sales volumes and the corresponding advertising volumes for the preceding 10 quarters.
a. Use the data shown here to compute the sample correlation coefficient.
b. Conduct a one-sided test of $H_0: \rho_{yx} = 0$. Give the p-value for your test.

Quarter	Sales ($10,000) y	Advertising Expense ($1000) x
1	50	10
2	70	12
3	80	14
4	90	15
5	62	12
6	68	13
7	92	14
8	106	16
9	65	14
10	76	15
11	85	17
12	110	19

13.48 Refer to Exercise 13.47.
   a. What conclusion can be drawn from the sample data?
   b. What other (uncontrolled) factors might affect sales in addition to the amount of advertising? How are these factors represented in the regression model?
   c. In what sense, if any, do these data represent a random sample from the population of interest?

13.49 Refer to Exercise 13.47. Construct a 99% prediction interval for quarterly sales, given a quarterly advertising expense of $18,000.

13.50 The high interest rates being charged for mortgage money in previous years had an impact on the number of housing starts throughout the United States. The data below summarize the prevailing interest rates by quarter and the corresponding number of housing starts for that quarter in a given locale.

Month	Interest Rate (%) x	Number of Housing Starts y
1	11.5	260
2	11.4	250
3	11.6	241
4	12.4	256
5	12.8	270
6	13.2	220
7	13.5	190
8	13.0	195
9	12.7	200
10	12.9	210
11	12.5	230
12	12.0	245

   a. Plot the data.
   b. Fit a linear regression line to these data. Is $\hat{\beta}_1$ significantly different from zero?
   c. Predict the number of housing starts for an interest rate of 11.0%. Use a 95% prediction interval.

13.51 Refer to Exercise 13.50.
   a. Calculate the rank correlation coefficient.
   b. Run a test of the hypothesis that the number of housing starts y decreases with the interest rate x.
   c. Draw conclusions from parts (a) and (b).

13.52 Refer to Exercise 13.41.
   a. Use a computer software package to run a one-way analysis of variance.
   b. What percentage of the total variability in the y values, SS(Total), do the four groups account for?

13.53 Refer to Exercise 13.47. Additional factors such as interest rates and inflation rate (as measured by the CPI) could help to explain the sales data. One factor that reflects some of these rate changes is the variable "year." For convenience, let the coded variable year x_2 take on the following values.

x_2:	1	1	1	1	2	2	2	2	3	3	3	3
Quarter:	1	2	3	4	5	6	7	8	9	10	11	12

a. Fit the model $Y = \beta_0 + \beta_2 x_2 + \varepsilon$.

b. Conduct a test of $H_0: \beta_2 = 0$. Give the level of significance for a two-sided test.

13.54 One use for regression analysis is to find a trend line. The sales y in thousands of units of a certain model of microwave oven are tabulated by month x. A regression line is calculated by a standard computer package (SAS) and is shown below:

VARIABLE	MEAN	VARIANCE	STANDARD DEVIATION
MONTH	10.50000000	35.00000000	5.91607978
SALES	80.00000000	205.68421053	14.34169483

DEP VARIABLE: SALES

ANALYSIS OF VARIANCE

SOURCE	DF	SUM OF SQUARES	MEAN SQUARE	F VALUE	PROB>F
MODEL	1	3552.435	3552.435	179.837	0.0001
ERROR	18	355.5654	19.75363		
C TOTAL	19	3908			

ROOT MSE	4.444506	R-SQUARE	0.9090	
DEP MEAN	80	ADJ R-SQ	0.9040	
C.V.	5.555633			

PARAMETER ESTIMATES

VARIABLE	DF	PARAMETER ESTIMATE	STANDARD ERROR	T FOR H0: PARAMETER=0	PROB > |T|
INTERCEP	1	55.73158	2.064613	26.994	0.0001
MONTH	1	2.311278	0.1723506	13.410	0.0001

DURBIN-WATSON D   0.348

a. Write the trend equation (regression line).

b. Calculate the residual standard deviation.

13.55 Use the data of Exercise 13.54 to calculate sales forecasts for months 21 and 40. How does the plus-or-minus term increase as one forecasts farther into the future? Note: $S_{xx} = (n-1)s_x^2$.

13.56 Calculate a 95% confidence interval for β_1 in Exercise 13.54. What does β_1 mean in this problem?

13.57 The management science staff of a grocery products manufacturer is developing a linear programming model for the production and distribution of its cereal products. The model requires transportation costs for a monstrous number of origins and destinations. It is impractical to do the detailed tariff analysis for every possible combination, so a sample of 50 routes is selected. For each route, the mileage x and shipping rate y (in dollars per 100 pounds) are found. A regression analysis is performed, with the following output:

```
Multiple R              .99291      Analysis of Variance
R Square                .98587                    DF      Sum of Squares      Mean Square
Adjusted R Square       .98556      Regression     1        15558.63206       15558.63206
Standard Error         2.20210      Residual      46          223.06460           4.84923

                                    F =    3208.47441      Signif F =  .0000

------------------ Variables in the Equation ------------------

Variable            B        SE B       Beta        T   Sig T

MILEAGE          .050115  8.8475E-04   .992908    56.643  .0000
(Constant)      9.770917   .474035                20.612  .0000
```

The data are as follows:

Mileage:	50	60	80	80	90	90	100	100	100	110	110	110
Rate:	12.7	13.0	13.7	14.1	14.6	14.1	15.6	14.9	14.5	15.3	15.5	15.9

Mileage:	120	120	120	120	130	130	140	150	170	190	200	230
Rate:	16.4	11.1	16.0	15.8	16.0	16.7	17.2	17.5	18.6	19.3	20.4	21.8

Mileage:	260	300	330	340	370	400	440	440	480	510	540	600
Rate:	24.7	24.7	18.0	27.1	28.2	30.6	31.8	32.4	34.5	35.0	36.3	41.4

Mileage:	650	700	720	760	800	810	850	920	960	1050	1200	1650
Rate:	46.4	45.8	46.6	48.0	51.7	50.2	53.6	57.9	56.1	58.7	75.8	89.0

    a. Write the regression equation and the residual standard deviation.

    b. Calculate a 90% confidence interval for β_1.

13.58 Plot the data of Exercise 13.57. Do you see any problems with the data?

13.59 Predict the shipping rate for a 340-mile route. Calculate a 95% prediction interval. How serious is the extrapolation problem in this exercise?

13.60 Suburban towns often spend a large fraction of their municipal budgets on public safety (i.e., police, fire, and ambulance) services. A taxpayers' group felt that very small towns were likely to spend large amounts per person, just because they have such small financial bases. The group obtained data on the per capita expenditure for public safety of 29 suburban towns in a metropolitan area, as well as the population of each town. The data were analyzed using the Statgraphics package. A regression model with dependent variable "expendit" and independent variable "townpopn" yields the following output:

```
Linear model: expendit = 118.957 + 0.0005324*townpopn
```

Table of Estimates

	Estimate	Standard Error	t Value	P Value
Intercept	118.957	23.2626	5.11	0.0000
Slope	0.0005324	0.00061809	0.86	0.3966

```
R-squared =  2.67%
Correlation coeff. =  0.164
Standard error of estimation = 43.3126
Durbin-Watson statistic = 1.66182
Mean absolute error = 24.861
```

Fitted model plot

(Linear model)

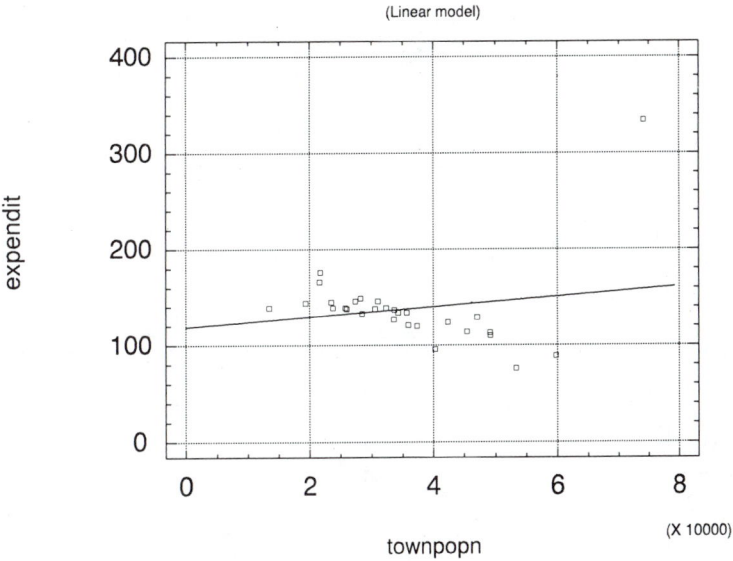

FIGURE 13.12   Scatter Plot (Statgraphics) for Expenditure Data

a. If the taxpayers' group is correct, what sign should the slope of the regression model have?

b. Does the slope in the output confirm the opinion of the group?

13.61 Statgraphics produced a scatterplot of the data of Exercise 13.60, shown as Figure 13.12. Does this plot indicate that the regression line (which is also shown in the figure) is misleading? Why?

13.62 One town in the data base of Exercise 13.60 is the home of an enormous regional shopping mall. A very large fraction of that town's expenditure on public safety is related to the mall; the mall management pays a yearly fee to the township that covers these expenditures. That town's data were removed from the data base and the remaining data were reanalyzed by Statgraphics. A scatter plot including the revised regression line is shown in Figure 13.13.

a. Explain why removing this one point from the data changed the regression line.

b. Does the revised regression line appear to confirm the opinion of the taxpayers' group in Exercise 13.60?

13.63 Regression output for the data of Exercise 13.62, excluding the one unusual town, is shown on page 600. How has the slope changed from the one obtained in Exercise 13.60?

13.64 In Exercise 13.60, data on population and per capita expenditures for public safety were collected for 28 suburban towns. The regression line had a positive slope. However, when one unusual observation, a town that contains a huge regional shopping mall, was removed from the data, the slope of the regression line became negative. How should the removal of one town from the data base affect the sign of the correlation coefficient?

13.65 Statgraphics output for the regression models of Exercises 13.60 (with the unusual town) and 13.63 (without it) yields the information shown at the top of page 601 about the correlation between "expendit" and "townpopn."

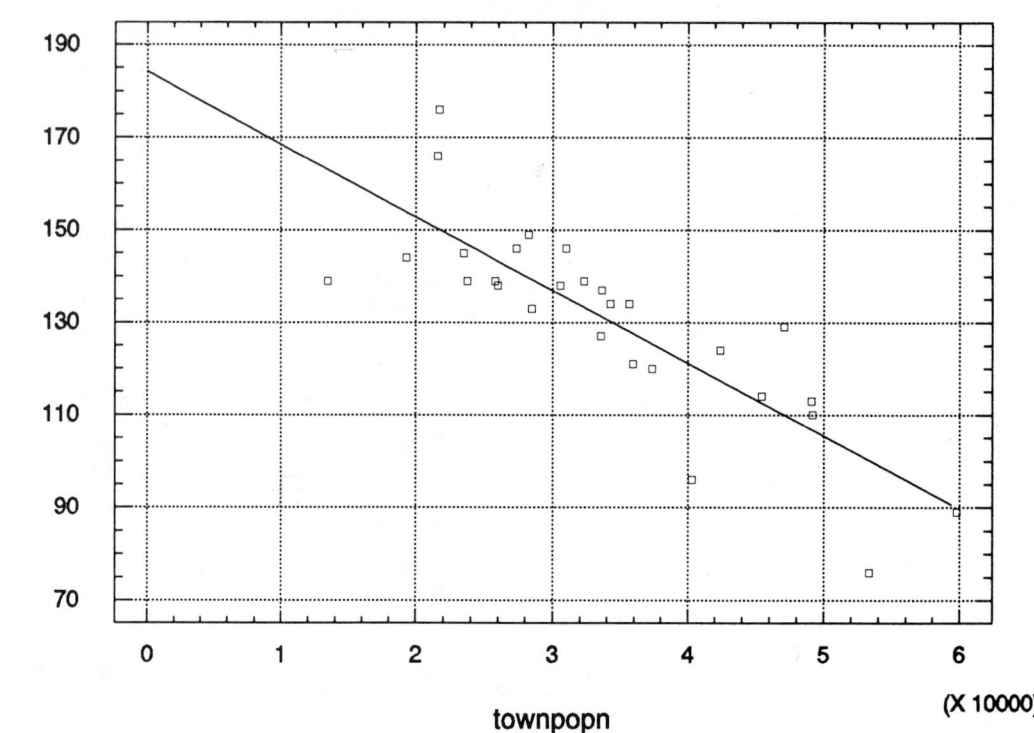

FIGURE 13.13   Scatter Plot with Unusual Town Data Removed

Linear model: expendit = 184.24 - 0.00157657*townpopn

Table of Estimates

	Estimate	Standard Error	t Value	P Value
Intercept	184.24	7.48122	24.63	0.0000
Slope	-0.00157657	0.000209869	-7.51	0.0000

R-squared = 68.46%
Correlation coeff. = -0.827
Standard error of estimation = 12.1442
Durbin-Watson statistic = 2.04747
Mean absolute error = 9.01159

Output for Exercise 13.63

	expendit	townpopn
expendit		0.1635
townpopn	0.1635	

The table shows estimated product-moment correlation

(a)

	expendit	townpopn
expendit		-0.8274
townpopn	-0.8274	

The table shows estimated product-moment correlation

(b)

Output for Exercise 13.65

    a. Did the sign of the correlation change as you predicted in Exercise 13.64?

    b. Why was the magnitude of the change in correlation so large?

13.66 A realtor in a suburban area attempted to predict house prices solely on the basis of size. From a multiple listing service, the realtor obtained size in thousands of square feet and asking price in thousands of dollars. The information is stored in the 'CH13C1.DAT' file on the data disk, with price in column 1 and size in column 2. Have your statistical computer program read this file.

    a. Obtain a plot of price against size. Does it appear that there is an increasing relation?

    b. Locate an apparent outlier in the data. Is it a high-leverage outlier?

    c. Obtain a regression equation and include the outlier in the data.

    d. Delete the outlier and obtain a new regression equation. How much does the slope change without the outlier? Why?

    e. Locate the residual standard deviations for the outlier-included and outlier-excluded models. Do they differ much? Why?

13.67 Obtain the outlier-excluded regression model for the data of Exercise 13.66.

    a. Interpret the intercept (constant) term. How much meaning does this number have in this context?

    b. What would it mean in this context if the slope were 0? Can the null hypothesis of zero slope be emphatically rejected?

    c. Calculate a 95% confidence interval for the true population value of the slope. The computer output should give you the estimated slope and its standard error, but you'll probably have to do the rest of the calculations by hand.

13.68 a. If possible, use your computer program to obtain a 95% prediction interval for the asking price for a home of five thousand square feet, based on the outlier-excluded data of Exercise 13.66. If you must do the computations by hand, obtain the mean and standard deviation of the size data from the computer, and find $S_{xx} = (n - 1)s^2$ by hand. Would this be a wise prediction to make, based on the data?

    b. Obtain a plot of the price against size. Does the constant-variance assumption seem reasonable, or does variability increase as size increases?

    c. What does your answer to part (b) say about the prediction interval obtained in part (a)?

13.69 A lawn-care company tried to predict the demand for its service by ZIP code, using the housing density in the ZIP code area as a predictor. The owners obtained the number of houses and the geographic size of each ZIP code, and calculated their sales per thousand homes and the number of homes per acre. The data are stored in the 'CH13C2.DAT' file on the data disk. Sales data are in column 1 and density (homes/acre) are in column 2. Read the data into your computer package.

a. Obtain the correlation between the two variables. What does its sign mean?

b. Obtain a prediction equation with sales as the dependent variable and density as the independent variable. Interpret the intercept (yes, we know the interpretation will be a bit strange) and the slope numbers.

c. Obtain a value for the residual standard deviation. What does this number indicate about the accuracy of prediction?

13.70 a. Obtain a value of the t statistic for the regression model of Exercise 13.69. Is there conclusive evidence that density is a predictor of sales?

b. Calculate a 95% confidence interval for the true value of the slope. The package should have calculated the standard error for you.

13.71 Obtain a plot of the data of Exercise 13.69, with sales plotted against density. Does it appear that straight-line prediction makes sense?

13.72 a. Have your computer program calculate a new variable as 1/density. What is the interpretation of the new variable? In particular, if the new variable equals 0.50, what does that mean about the particular ZIP code area?

b. Plot sales against the new variable. Does a straight-line prediction look reasonable here?

c. Obtain the correlation of sales and the new variable. Compare its magnitude to the correlation obtained in Exercise 13.69 between sales and density. What explains the difference?

13.73 A manufacturer of paint used for marking road surfaces developed a new formulation that needs to be tested for durability. One question concerns the concentration of pigment in the paint. If the concentration is too low, the paint will fade quickly; if the concentration is too high, the paint will not adhere well to the road surface. The manufacturer applies paint at various concentrations to sample road surfaces and obtains a durability measure for each sample. The data are stored in the 'CH13C3.DAT' file of the data disk, with durability in column 1 and concentration in column 2.

a. Have your computer program calculate a regression equation with durability predicted by concentration. Interpret the slope coefficient.

b. Find the coefficient of determination. What does it indicate about the predictive value of concentration?

13.74 In the regression model of Exercise 13.73, is the slope coefficient significantly different from 0 at $\alpha = .01$?

13.75 Obtain a plot of the data of Exercise 13.73, with durability on the vertical axis and concentration on the horizontal axis.

a. What does this plot indicate about the wisdom of using straight-line prediction?

b. What does this plot indicate about the correlation found in Exercise 13.73?

CASE   Regression and Correlation

In the case for Chapter 8, the benefits manager of a large university obtained data from a sample of 61 employees on their intended use of a possible flexible benefits plan. Now the manager wants to analyze the data in more detail. In particular, the manager is interested in the relation between monthly life insurance cost and age of the employee. This relation is a matter of increasing concern because the age of the employee group has been rising and it will continue to rise. A work-study student took age and life insurance cost data from the sample and performed some basic Minitab analysis, as shown.

employee	age	life		employee	age	life
1	52	759		32	47	585
2	28	424		33	32	472
3	42	157		34	65	535
4	51	616		35	22	174
5	42	655		36	52	751
6	44	559		37	39	579
7	46	651		38	43	666
8	49	519		39	35	596
9	51	358		40	61	251
10	25	456		41	51	341
11	33	97		42	27	77
12	59	478		43	28	225
13	35	129		44	51	590
14	44	661		45	53	330
15	30	245		46	47	736
16	37	602		47	50	601
17	32	557		48	40	555
18	41	215		49	40	775
19	29	331		50	52	745
20	48	545		51	46	630
21	61	395		52	58	139
22	38	577		53	44	521
23	32	345		54	55	647
24	33	367		55	29	543
25	24	189		56	44	699
26	43	716		57	53	602
27	43	238		58	54	493
28	50	867		59	45	731
29	55	475		60	38	267
30	56	369		61	49	689
31	68	245				

```
MTB > correlation of 'age' and 'life'

Correlation of age and life = 0.271

MTB > regress 'life' on 1 var 'age'

The regression equation is
life = 259 + 5.07 age

Predictor      Coef      Stdev     t-ratio       p
Constant      258.9      105.7        2.45     0.017
age           5.073      2.344        2.16     0.035

s = 195.3      R-sq = 7.4%      R-sq(adj) = 5.8%

Analysis of Variance

SOURCE       DF          SS          MS        F        p
Regression    1       178624      178624     4.68    0.035
Error        59      2250734       38148
Total        60      2429357
```

(continued)

```
Unusual Observations
Obs.      age      life      Fit Stdev.Fit  Residual    St.Resid
 31      68.0     245.0    603.9     62.0    -358.9      -1.94 X
 52      58.0     139.0    553.1     41.7    -414.1      -2.17R
```

R denotes an obs. with a large st. resid.
X denotes an obs. whose X value gives it large influence.

MTB > plot c6 vs c2

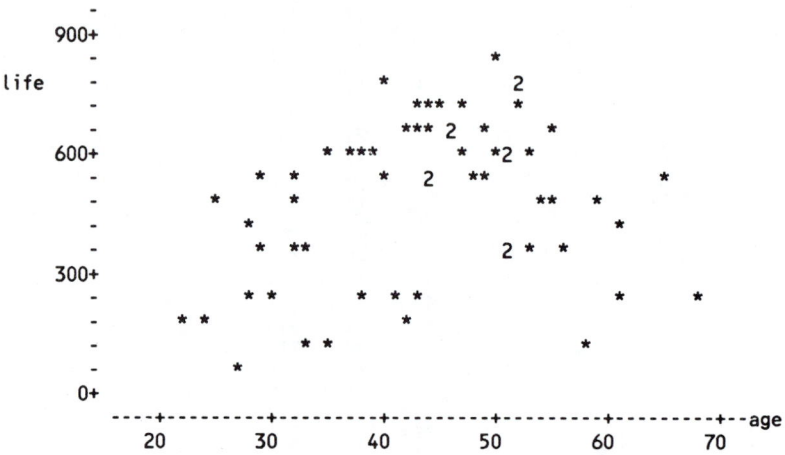

In a cover note to you accompanying the output, the benefits manager said "I don't understand this very well. There doesn't seem to be a very good correlation, but the work-study student says that it's significant. Can you explain what's going on in the output for me?" Explain what you think are the most important conclusions to be obtained from the output, in language the manager can understand. You're welcome to suggest and carry out any further analysis that might help interpret the data.

Appendix: The Mathematics of Least Squares (∂)

In this appendix we use calculus to show that the formulas given in Chapter 13 do in fact give the least-squares intercept $\hat{\beta}_0$ and slope $\hat{\beta}_1$. Then we give an algebraic justification for the interpretation of r_{yx}^2.

First, the least-squares estimate of

$$E(Y_i) = \beta_0 + \beta_1 x_i$$

requires that we choose $\hat{\beta}_0$ and $\hat{\beta}_1$ to minimize

$$\sum_i (y_i - \hat{y}_i)^2 = \sum_i (y_i - \hat{\beta}_0 - \hat{\beta}_1 x_i)^2$$

Standard calculus methods indicate that we should take partial derivatives with respect to $\hat{\beta}_0$ and to $\hat{\beta}_1$ and equate them to zero. (While it is logically possible that this procedure yield a maximum or a saddle point, the solution is a minimum; a second derivative test verifies this.) The resulting equations are

$$\sum 2(y_i - \hat{\beta}_0 - \hat{\beta}_1 x_i)(-1) = 0$$

and

$$\sum 2(y_i - \hat{\beta}_0 - \hat{\beta}_1 x_i)(-x_i) = 0$$

Dividing by 2 and collecting terms yields

$$\sum y_i = n\hat{\beta}_0 + \left(\sum x_i\right)\hat{\beta}_1$$

and

$$\sum x_i y_i = \left(\sum x_i\right)\hat{\beta}_0 + \left(\sum x_i^2\right)\hat{\beta}_1$$

To solve for $\hat{\beta}_1$, multiply the first equation by $\left(\sum x_i\right)/n$ and subtract the result from the second to get

$$\frac{\sum x_i y_i - \left(\sum x_i\right)\left(\sum y_i\right)}{n} = \left[\frac{\sum x_i^2 - \left(\sum x_i\right)^2}{n}\right]\hat{\beta}_1$$

or

$$\hat{\beta}_1 = \frac{\sum x_i y_i - \left(\sum x_i\right)\left(\sum y_i\right)/n}{\sum x_i^2 - \left(\sum x_i\right)^2/n}$$

Then $n\hat{\beta}_0 = \sum y_i - \hat{\beta}_1 \sum x_i$ from the first equation, so

$$\hat{\beta}_0 = \bar{y} - \hat{\beta}_1 \bar{x}$$

Thus we have shown that the least-squares principle yields the indicated slope and intercept estimates.

Our next task is to establish that the proportion of the squared error of y values explained by regression is r_{yx}^2. To do so we need to establish a relation between the correlation r_{yx} and the slope $\hat{\beta}_1$. The defining equations are

$$r_{yx} = \frac{S_{xy}}{\sqrt{S_{xx}}\sqrt{S_{yy}}}$$

and

$$\hat{\beta}_1 = \frac{S_{xy}}{S_{xx}}$$

Therefore

$$\hat{\beta}_1 = r_{yx}\frac{\sqrt{S_{yy}}}{\sqrt{S_{xx}}}$$

SS(Regression) is defined as $\sum(\hat{y} - \bar{y})^2$. Substituting for $\bar{y}$, we have

$$
\begin{aligned}
\text{SS(Regression)} &= \sum(\hat{\beta}_0 + \hat{\beta}_1 x_i - \bar{y})^2 \\
&= \sum[(\bar{y} - \hat{\beta}_1 \bar{x}) + \hat{\beta}_1 x_i - \bar{y}]^2 \\
&= (\hat{\beta}_1)^2 \sum(x_i - \bar{x})^2 \\
&= r_{yx}^2 \frac{S_{yy}}{S_{xx}} \sum(x_i - \bar{x})^2
\end{aligned}
$$

Because $S_{xx} = \sum x^2 - (\sum x^2)^2/n$ is the shortcut formula for $\sum(x - \bar{x})^2$ and because S_{yy} is the shortcut formula for $\sum(y - \bar{y})^2 = \text{SS(Total)}$, it follows that

$$
\begin{aligned}
\text{SS(Regression)} &= r_{yx}^2 \frac{S_{yy}}{S_{xx}} \sum(x - \bar{x})^2 \\
&= r_{yx}^2 \text{SS(Total)}
\end{aligned}
$$

14 MULTIPLE REGRESSION METHODS

Multiple regression uses many independent variables to predict or explain variation in a quantitative dependent variable. It's an extremely useful way to assess the explanatory value of many different, plausible predictors. In many management situations, there are several possible predictors of a result. We use multiple regression to try to sort out which of these plausible predictors really do explain variation in the dependent variable, and which others add little or no predictive value. It is probably the statistical technique most widely used by managers.

We'll devote two chapters to multiple regression. In this chapter, we'll develop the basic theoretical concepts, the assumptions, and the methods. We'll consider what the multiple regression model is and how it's interpreted (Section 14.1); how the coefficients can be estimated from data (Section 14.2); how inferences can be made from the limited data base of the model (Sections 14.3 and 14.4); and how to use the model in forecasting new cases (Section 14.5). In Section 14.6 we'll show the underlying mathematics for those who wish to see those results. Then, in Chapter 15, we'll describe how all the concepts fit together in developing a multiple regression study.

14.1 THE MULTIPLE REGRESSION MODEL ■

Every manager faces situations in which changes or variations in something need to be understood and predicted, and in which there are many plausible indicators pointing (in possibly conflicting ways) to predicted changes. In every publicly held company, changes in the price of the company's common stock are of more than mild interest. There are both internal predictors of the price (such as earnings, growth rate, market share of primary products, and debt/equity ratio) and external predictors (such as interest rates, consumer confidence levels, and current unemployment). Variation in the cost of a print job depends on the number of pages, the number of graphic displays, the hours needed to set up, and the number of copies. Variation in the sales of a new product can be predicted by the size of the market, the rate of growth of that market, consumer satisfaction in tests of the product, and type of sales outlet for the product. Multiple regression is a method for using data to sort out the predictive value of the competing predictors.

Given the data, the first task in multiple regression is to specify a model, the mathematical form of the prediction equation. The simplest model takes each predictor, multiplies it by a numerical weight (coefficient), and adds the resulting quantities to an intercept term. For example, a multiple regression model for variation in price of a common stock over time might be

$$\text{Price} = -12.72 + 5.21\ \text{Earnings} + 3.34\ \text{Growth} - 0.68\ \text{D/E}$$

where Price = closing price of the stock at the end of each quarter; Earnings = reported earnings per share in the quarter; Growth = change in earnings from the same quarter of the previous year; and D/E = ratio of corporate debt to corporate equity. The intercept term, -12.72 in the example, is the predicted dependent variable value when all the independent variables equal 0. In many cases, the intercept has little meaning because the condition that all predictors are 0 is economically absurd. There can't be a stock with a price of -12.72 (even the ones we own), but the conditions of 0 earnings, 0 growth, and 0 debt-to-equity are so far outside of reasonable economic values that we needn't worry about the impossible value.

The coefficients of the predictor variables are usually the interesting ones.

partial slopes   They are the **partial slopes** and they measure the predicted change in the dependent variable for a one-unit change in the independent variable, *holding other independent variables constant*. In the stock price example, if we compare two quarters when the company had the same growth and debt/equity ratio, we'd predict that the price would be $5.21 higher for the quarter in which the earnings per share were $1 higher. Similarly, if we had two quarters when earnings and growth were the same, but D/E was 1.0 higher in quarter A than in quarter B, we would predict that the price would be $0.68 *lower* (because of the minus sign) in quarter A.

EXAMPLE 14.1   The manager of a copy center must estimate costs for jobs that differ in number of pages, number of copies, setup hours, and number of graphics. Data from past jobs were put into a computer multiple regression program and yielded a model:

```
The regression equation is
cost = - 160 + 7.43 pages + 1.84 copies + 4.44 setup + 2.67 graphics
```

Interpret each numerical value in the model.

Solution   The intercept, -160, refers to a job with no pages, no copies, no setup, and no graphics—in other words, to a nonjob! It is not interpretable. The partial slope for "pages" is the predicted difference in cost between two jobs with the same number of copies, setup hours, and graphics, differing by one page. The partial slope for "copies" is the predicted difference in cost between two jobs of equal number of pages, setup hours, and graphics, differing by one copy. Similar interpretations hold for the other slopes. Note that the total number of copied pages can be obtained by multiplying "pages" by "copies"; we'd expect that product term to be a useful predictor. ∎

Symbolically, we write the multiple regression model as

$$Y = \beta_0 + \beta_1 x_1 + B_2 x_2 + \cdots + \beta_k x_k + \epsilon$$

where Y is the dependent variable to be predicted, the x's are independent predictor values, and ϵ is the error term (in recognition of the fact that every prediction is in error to some degree). The intercept term is β_0; β_1 though β_k are the partial slopes. (For those who know some calculus, the partial slope β_j is exactly the partial derivative of predicted Y with respect to x_j. $\beta_j = (\partial/\partial_{x_j})\hat{Y}$.) If we want to emphasize an individual case, we'll add a subscript i for the individual:

$$Y_i = \beta_0 + \beta_1 x_{i1} + \beta_2 x_{i2} + \cdots + \beta_k x_{ik} + \epsilon_i$$

Whether or not we use the i subscript isn't terribly critical; both forms for the regression model are commonly used and mean the same thing.

first-order model   This simplest regression model is called a **first-order model**. It contains each predictor by itself without mathematical transformations such as squared terms or logarithms. It doesn't combine predictors in such forms as product terms. Using a first-order model implicitly makes assumptions about the nature of the relation between Y and the predictors. First, it assumes that Y changes at a consistent rate as x_j changes, over the entire range of x_j—as opposed to, say, increasing at a decreasing rate or increasing to a maximum and then decreasing. In our first-order stock price model, we're implicitly assuming that, holding growth and D/E constant, an increase of \$1 in earnings leads to a \$5.21 increase in price per share, whether the earnings dollar is the first or the 379th. That may not be a good assumption; in the stock-price case, it might well be that the price is very sensitive to changes in earnings on the low end of the scale, but less sensitive when earnings start out very high. A first-order model also implicitly assumes **interaction**   that there is no **interaction** among predictors. We encountered the idea of interaction in Chapter 12: The effect of changing one experimental factor depends on the level of another factor. Interaction in regression means the same thing. Two independent variables interact in their effect on the dependent variable if the predicted effect of a change in one predictor, holding the other constant, depends on *where* that other variable is held constant. In our stock-price example, it wouldn't be surprising to have earnings and debt/equity ratio interact. At low D/E levels, higher earnings might have little effect; at high D/E levels, the leveraging effect might make stock prices very sensitive to changes in earnings.

EXAMPLE 14.2   A brand manager for a new food product took data on Y = brand recognition (percent of potential consumers who can describe what the product is), x_1 = length in seconds of an introductory TV commercial, and x_2 = number of repetitions of the commercial over a two-week period. What does the brand manager assume if a first-order model

$$Y = 0.31 + 0.042x_1 + 1.41x_2$$

is used to predict Y?

Solution   First, there is an assumption of a straight-line, consistent rate of change. The manager assumes that a one-second increase in length of the commercial will lead to a 0.042 percentage point increase in recognition, whether the increase is from, say, 10 to 11 seconds or from 59 to 60 seconds. Also, every additional repetition of the commercial is assumed to give a 1.41 percentage point increase in recognition, whether it is the second repetition or the twenty-second.

Second, there is a no-interaction assumption. The first-order model assumes that the effect of an additional repetition (that is, an increase in x_2) of a given length commercial (that is, holding x_1 constant) doesn't depend on *where* that length is held constant (at 10 seconds, 27 seconds, 60 seconds, whatever). ∎

A first-order model is often a good starting point. In many managerial situations, there is no obvious reason to expect curvature or interaction. In such situations, a first-order model is a natural first try. In Section 15.3, we'll have more to say about other, mathematically more complicated models. Until then, we simply note that a first-order multiple regression model is a useful possibility, but not the only one.

The error term ϵ_i plays exactly the same role in multiple regression as in simple linear regression. It includes all the effects of unpredictable and ignored factors. (The basic hope of multiple regression is to make the ϵ_i values small by including all or most of the relevant predictive factors.) The formal assumptions on the ϵ_i's, which are identical to those stated in Chapter 13, are listed here:

Formal Assumptions for ϵ_i in Multiple Regression

1. $E(\epsilon_i) = 0$ for all i.
2. $V(\epsilon_i) = \sigma_\epsilon^2$ for all i.
3. The ϵ_i's are independent.
4. ϵ_i is normally distributed

$$i = 1, 2, \ldots, n$$

The effect of violations of these formal assumptions is discussed in Chapter 15.

EXAMPLE 14.3   Find the error terms ϵ_i for the data below under each of the following models:

    a. $Y_i = 30 + 4x_{i1} - .6x_{i2} + \epsilon_i$
    b. $Y_i = 78 - 36x_{i1} + .4x_{i2} + 6x_{i1}^2 + \epsilon_i$

Y_i	x_{i1}	x_{i2}
35.2	2	10
31.8	3	20
27.7	3	10
36.7	4	20

Solution   a.   For the first model we have

Y_i	$30 + 4x_{i1} - .6x_{i2}$	ϵ_i
35.2	32.0	3.2
31.8	30.0	1.8
27.7	36.0	-8.3
36.7	34.0	2.7

b. For the second model,

Y_i	$78 - 36x_{i1} + .4x_{i2} + 6x_{i1}^2$	ϵ_i
35.2	34.0	1.2
31.8	32.0	$-.2$
27.7	28.0	$-.3$
36.7	38.0	-1.3

Note that the ϵ terms for the second model are much smaller (in absolute value) than those for the first model.   ∎

general linear model   The equation, $Y_i = \beta_0 + \beta_1 x_{i1} + \beta_2 x_{i2} + \cdots + \beta_k x_{ik} + \epsilon_i$, together with the indicated assumptions on the x_{ij} and ϵ_i terms, is often called the **general linear model**. The word *linear* is used in a slightly peculiar way. Because some X predictors may be nonlinear functions of other ones, the expression does not necessarily mean that $E(Y)$ is a linear function of the independent variables. For example, the general linear model $Y_i = \beta_0 + \beta_1 x_{i1} + \beta_2 x_{i1}^2 + \beta_3 x_{i2} + \beta_4 x_{i1} x_{i2} + \epsilon_i$ is certainly not linear in the independent variables x_{i1}, x_{i2}. But if we view the general linear model as a function of the β parameters, with the x's regarded as given numbers, it is linear. Any predictive equation that is linear in the β parameters satisfies the general linear model. Thus

$$Y_i = 20 + 5x_i + 2v_i + \epsilon_i$$

and

$$Y_i = 20 + 5x_i + 2x_i^2 + \epsilon_i$$

are both linear models in this sense.

We turn our attention now to the important problem of determining estimates for the coefficients (the intercept β_0 and the partial slopes $\beta_1, \ldots, \beta_k$) in the multiple regression model in order to obtain the multiple regression forecasting equation.

14.2   ESTIMATING MULTIPLE REGRESSION COEFFICIENTS   ■

The first task of a multiple regression analysis is to estimate the intercept β_0, the partial slopes $\beta_1, \beta_2, \ldots, \beta_k$, and the error variance σ_ϵ^2. The basic principle is least-squares estimation, just as in linear regression. The arithmetic involved in multiple regression gets heavy very quickly, so the work is usually done by a computer. The only examples we work out by hand here involve a small number of independent variables and unrealistically few observations.

In simple linear regression, the least-squares principle leads to two equations, the normal equations. These must be solved to obtain the estimated slope and intercept (see the Appendix to Chapter 13). In multiple regression using k independent variables, there are $k + 1$ equations to solve for the intercept and the k partial slopes. If you recall the time and effort required to solve, say, four equations in four unknowns, you can appreciate why multiple regression is virtually always done by a computer package. There is a pattern to the normal equations for any number of independent variables that can be programmed. Therefore, a single program can handle any number of independent variables, up to the limits of computer storage.

Literally thousands of computer programs have been written to perform the calculations needed in multiple regression. The output of such programs typically has a list of variable names, together with the estimated partial slopes, labeled COEFFICIENTS (or ESTIMATES or PARAMETERS). The intercept term $\hat{\beta}_0$ is usually called INTERCEPT (or CONSTANT); sometimes it is shown along with the slopes, but with no variable name.

EXAMPLE 14.4   The data for three variables (shown next) are analyzed with the Minitab software package. Identify the estimates of the partial slopes and the intercept.

y:	25	34	28	40	36	42	44	53	49
x_1:	-10	-10	-10	0	0	0	10	10	10
x_2:	-5	0	5	-5	0	5	-5	0	5

```
MTB > regress c1 on 2 variables in c2 and c3

The regression equation is
Y = 39.0 + 0.983 X1 + 0.333 X2

Predictor        Coef        Stdev      t-ratio
Constant       39.000       1.256        31.05
X1             0.9833       0.1538         6.39
X2             0.3333       0.3076         1.08

s = 3.768      R-sq = 87.5%      R-sq(adj) = 83.3%
```

Analysis of Variance

SOURCE	DF	SS	MS
Regression	2	596.83	298.42
Error	6	85.17	14.19
Total	8	682.00	

SOURCE	DF	SEQ SS
X1	1	580.17
X2	1	16.67

Solution   This output gives the values twice, once by printing THE REGRESSION EQUATION IS $Y = 39.0 + 0.983x_1 + 0.333x_2$ and once in the column headed COEF. Note that the intercept value 39.0000 does not have a variable name; the estimated partial slopes .9833 and .3333 are associated with x_1 and x_2, respectively.   ∎

The coefficient of an independent variable x_j in a multiple regression equation does not, in general, equal the coefficient that would apply to that variable in a simple linear regression. In multiple regression, the coefficient refers to the effect of changing that x_j variable while other independent variables stay constant. In simple linear regression, all other potential independent variables are ignored. If other independent variables are correlated with x_j (and therefore don't tend to stay constant while x_j changes), simple linear regression with only x_j as an independent variable captures not only the direct effect of changing x_j but also the indirect effect of the associated changes in other x's. Multiple regression is a method for isolating only the direct effect of changing x_j alone.

EXAMPLE 14.5   a. Fit the simple linear regression model $\hat{Y}_i = \hat{\beta}_0 + \hat{\beta}_1 x_{i1}$ using the data shown.
b. Compare the coefficient of x_1 for this model and the one obtained for the multiple regression model, which is $\hat{Y} = 10 + 1x_1 + 3x_2$

y	x_1	x_2
3	−2	−1
10	−1	0
12	0	0
12	1	0
13	2	1

Solution   a. Using the formulas $\hat{\beta}_1 = S_{x_1 y}/S_{x_1 x_1}$ and $\hat{\beta}_0 = \bar{y} - \hat{\beta}_1 \bar{x}_1$ from Chapter 13, it can be shown that the simple linear regression equation is $\hat{y} = 10 + 2.2x_1$.
b. The coefficients for the simple linear regression model are different (1 and 2.2) because the coefficient of x_1 in the simple linear regression represents the expected change in y for a unit change in x_1 (allowing x_2 to vary), while in

the multiple regression equation the coefficient of x_1 is the expected change in y when x_2 is held constant.   ∎

In addition to estimating the intercept and partial slopes, it is important to estimate the residual standard deviation s_ϵ. The residuals are defined as before, the difference between the observed value and the predicted value of Y:

$$y_i - \hat{y}_i = y_i - (\hat{\beta}_0 + \hat{\beta}_1 x_{i1} + \hat{\beta}_2 x_{i2} + \cdots + \hat{\beta}_k x_{ik})$$

The sum of squared residuals SS(Residual), also called SS(Error), is defined exactly as it sounds:

$$SS(\text{Residual}) = \sum (y_i - \hat{y}_i)^2$$
$$= \sum [y_i - (\hat{\beta}_0 + \hat{\beta}_1 x_{i1} + \hat{\beta}_2 x_{i2} + \cdots + \hat{\beta}_k x_{ik})]^2$$

A shortcut computing formula is

$$SS(\text{Residual}) = \sum y_i^2 - \hat{\beta}_0 \sum y_i - \hat{\beta}_1 \sum x_{i1} y_i - \hat{\beta}_2 \sum x_{i2} y_i$$
$$- \cdots - \hat{\beta}_k \sum x_{ik} y_i$$

The d.f. for this sum of squares is $n - (k + 1)$. One d.f. is subtracted for the intercept and one d.f. is subtracted for each of the k partial slopes. The mean square residual MS(Residual), also called MS(Error), is the residual sum of squares divided by $n - (k + 1)$. Finally, the residual standard deviation s_ϵ is the square root of MS(Residual).

$$s_\epsilon = \sqrt{MS(\text{Residual})}$$
$$= \sqrt{\frac{SS(\text{Residual})}{n - (k + 1)}}$$

EXAMPLE 14.6   a. Calculate the SS(Residual) both from the definition and by the shortcut formula for the multiple regression model of Example 14.5. The required sums are $\sum y_i^2 = 566$, $\sum y_i = 50$, $\sum x_{i1} y_i = 22$, and $\sum x_{i2} y_i = 10$.
b. Calculate the residual standard deviation.

Solution   a. To get the residuals, we need the predicted values $\hat{y}_i$. These values can be found by plugging the appropriate x_{i1} and x_{i2} values into the equation $\hat{y}_i = 10 + 1x_1 + 3x_2$.

y_i	$\hat{y}_i$	$y_1 - \hat{y}_i$	$(y_i - \hat{y}_i)^2$
3	5	-2	4
10	9	1	1
12	10	2	4
12	11	1	1
13	15	-2	4
		0	14

As shown, SS(Residual) = 14. Also

$$SS(\text{Residual}) = \sum y_i^2 - \hat{\beta}_0 \sum y_i - \hat{\beta}_1 \sum x_{i1} y_i - \hat{\beta}_2 \sum x_{i2} y_i$$
$$= 566 - 10(50) - 1(22) - 3(10)$$
$$= 14$$

b. The d.f. is $5 - (2 + 1) = 2$, so the residual standard deviation is

$$s_\epsilon = \sqrt{\frac{14}{2}} = 2.646$$ ■

EXAMPLE 14.7   Identify SS(Residual) and s_ϵ in the output of Example 14.4.

Solution   In the section of the output labeled ANALYSIS OF VARIANCE, SS(Residual) is shown as 85.17, with 6 d.f. The residual standard deviation is indicated by $s = 3.768$.   ■

The residual standard deviation is crucial in determining the probable error of a prediction using the regression equation. The precise standard error to be used in forecasting an individual Y value is stated in Section 14.6. As in simple linear regression, this standard error depends on the sample size and the degree of extrapolation involved in the forecast. The standard error must be multiplied by an appropriate t table value to give the probable error. A rough approximation, ignoring extrapolation and d.f. effects, is that the probable error is $\pm 2s_\epsilon$. This approximation can be used as a rough indicator of the forecasting quality of a regression model.

EXAMPLE 14.8   The admissions office of a business school develops a regression model that uses aptitude test scores and class rank to predict the grade average (4.00 = straight A; 2.00 = C average, the minimum graduation average; 0.00 = straight F). The residual standard deviation is $s_\epsilon = .46$. Does this value suggest highly accurate prediction?

Solution   A measure of the probable error of prediction is $2s_\epsilon = .92$. For example, if a predicted average is 2.80, then an individual's grade is roughly between $2.80 - .92 = 1.88$ (not good enough to graduate) and $2.80 + .92 = 3.72$ (good enough to graduate magna cum laude). This is not an accurate forecast.   ■

coefficient of determination   The final topic we will discuss in this section is the **coefficient of determination**, R^2. This quantity is defined and interpreted very much like the r^2 value in Chapter 13. (The customary notation is R^2 for multiple regression and r^2 for linear regression.) As in Chapter 13, we define the coefficient of determination as the proportional reduction in the squared error of Y, which we obtain by knowing the values of $x_1, \ldots, x_k$. For example, if we have the multiple regression model $Y = \beta_0 + \beta_1 x_1 + \beta_2 x_2 + \beta_3 x_3 + \epsilon$ and $R^2_{Y \cdot x_1 x_2 x_3} = .736$, then we can account for 73.6% of the variability of the Y values by variability in $x_1, x_2,$

and x_3. Formally

$$R^2_{Y \cdot x_1 \cdots x_k} = \frac{\text{SS(Total)} - \text{SS(Residual)}}{\text{SS(Total)}}$$

where

$$\text{SS(Total)} = \sum y_i^2 - \frac{(\sum y_i)^2}{n}$$

EXAMPLE 14.9   Calculate $R^2_{y \cdot x_1 x_2}$ for the data of Example 14.5.

Solution   In Example 14.7, SS(Residual) was calculated to be 14. SS(Total) can be calculated as

$$\sum y_i^2 - \frac{(\sum y_i)^2}{n} = 566 - \frac{(50)^2}{5} = 66$$

Therefore

$$R^2_{y \cdot x_1 x_2} = \frac{66 - 14}{66} = .788 \qquad \blacksquare$$

EXAMPLE 14.10   Locate the value of $R^2_{y \cdot x_1 x_2}$ in the computer output of Example 14.4.

Solution   We want R-SQ = 87.5%, not the one that is ADJ. Alternatively, SS(Total) = 682.00 and SS(Residual) = 85.17 are shown on the output and we can compute $R^2_{y \cdot x_1 x_2} = (682.00 - 85.17)/682.00 = .875$. $\qquad \blacksquare$

There is no general relation between the multiple R^2 from a multiple regression equation and the individual coefficients of determination $r^2_{yx_1}, r^2_{yx_2}, \ldots, r^2_{yx_k}$ other than $R^2 \geq \max_j(r^2_{yx_j})$. If all the independent variables are themselves uncorrelated, then coefficients of determination can be added. If the x's are correlated, it is difficult to take apart the overall predictive value of $x_1, x_2, \ldots, x_k$ as measured by $R^2_{y \cdot x_1 \cdots x_k}$, into separate pieces that can be attributable to x_1 alone, to x_2 alone, ..., to x_k alone. When the independent variables are themselves correlated, **collinearity** (sometimes called **multicollinearity**) is present. Collinearity is usually present to some degree in a multiple regression study, which is a slight problem for slightly correlated x's but a more severe one for highly correlated x's. Thus, if collinearity occurs in a regression study, and it usually does to some degree, it is almost impossible to take apart the overall $R^2_{y \cdot x_1 x_2 \cdots x_k}$ into separate components associated with each x variable. The correlated x's account for overlapping pieces of the variability in y, so that often, but not inevitably,

collinearity

$$R^2_{y \cdot x_1 x_2 \cdots x_k} < r^2_{yx_1} + r^2_{yx_2} + \cdots + r^2_{yx_k}$$

EXAMPLE 14.11   a. Calculate r_{yx_1}, r_{yx_2}, and $r_{x_1 x_2}$ for the data of Example 14.5.
b. Is collinearity present?
c. Does $R^2_{y \cdot x_1 x_2} = r^2_{yx_1} + r^2_{yx_2}$?

Solution   a. The formula for r_{yx} in Chapter 13 becomes

$$r_{yx_1} = \frac{S_{x_1y}}{\sqrt{S_{x_1x_1}}\sqrt{S_{yy}}}$$

$$= \frac{22 - 0(50)/5}{\sqrt{10 - (0)^2/5}\sqrt{566 - (50)^2/5}}$$

$$= .8563$$

Similarly,

$$r_{yx_2} = \frac{S_{x_2y}}{\sqrt{S_{x_2x_2}}\sqrt{S_{yy}}}$$

$$= \frac{10 - (0)(50)/5}{\sqrt{2 - (0)^2/5}\sqrt{566 - (50)^2/5}}$$

$$= .8704$$

and

$$r_{x_1x_2} = \frac{S_{x_1x_2}}{\sqrt{S_{x_1x_1}}\sqrt{S_{x_2x_2}}}$$

$$= \frac{4 - (0)(0)/5}{\sqrt{10 - (0)^2/5}\sqrt{2 - (0)^2/5}}$$

$$= .8944$$

b. Because $r_{x_1x_2} \neq 0$, collinearity is present, and indeed it is serious.

c. Because

$$r_{yx_1}^2 = (.8563)^2 = .733$$
$$r_{yx_2}^2 = (.8704)^2 = .758$$

and

$$R_{y \cdot x_1x_2}^2 = .788$$

$R_{y \cdot x_1x_2}^2$ is less than the sum of $r_{yx_1}^2$ and $r_{yx_2}^2$.   ∎

sequential sums of squares   Many statistical computer programs will report **sequential sums of squares**. These SS are *incremental* contributions to SS(Regression), when the independent variables enter the regression model in the order you specify to the program. The data for Example 14.5 have SS(Regression) = 52.0 and SS(Total) = 66.0. We found that $r_{yx_1}^2 = .733$, in Example 14.11. If we had asked a computer program for sequential SS, specifying $X1$ as the first predictor and $X2$ as the second, the program would report the sequential SS for $X1$ as $(.733)(66.0) = 48.4$ and the sequential SS for $X2$ *given* $X1$ as the remainder of SS(Regression), namely $52.0 - 48.4 = 3.6$. Therefore, $X1$ accounts for most of the explainable variation in Y and $X2$ adds little to the explanation.

Sequential sums of squares depend heavily on the particular order in which the independent variables enter the model. If we had specified $X2$ as the first predictor and $X1$ as the second, the program would report the sequential SS for $X2$ as 50.0 and the sequential SS for $X1$ given $X2$ as 2.0. Now it seems that $X2$ accounts for most of the explainable variation in Y and $X1$ adds little to the explanation!

Again, the trouble is collinearity. When all variables in a regression study are strongly and positively correlated (as often happens in economic data), whichever independent variable happens to be entered first typically accounts for most of the explainable variation in Y and the remaining variables add little to the sequential SS. The explanatory power of any X given all the other X's (which is sometimes called the *unique predictive value* of that X) is small. When the data exhibit severe collinearity, separating out the predictive value of the various independent variables is very difficult indeed.

SECTIONS 14.1 AND 14.2   EXERCISES

14.1   A manufacturer of industrial chemicals investigates the effect on its sales of promotion activities (primarily direct contact and trade show), direct development expenditures, and short-range research effort. Data are assembled for 24 quarters (6 years) and analyzed by a standard multiple regression program (SAS) as shown below (in \$100,000 per quarter).

DEPENDENT VARIABLE: SALES

SOURCE	DF	SUM OF SQUARES	MEAN SQUARE	F VALUE	PR > F	R-SQUARE	C.V.
MODEL	3	43901.76502960	14633.92167653	22.28	0.0001	0.769693	8.1489
ERROR	20	13136.23497040	656.81174852		ROOT MSE		SALES MEAN
CORRECTED TOTAL	23	57038.00000000			25.62833878		314.50000000

PARAMETER	ESTIMATE	T FOR H0: PARAMETER=0	PR > |T|	STD ERROR OF ESTIMATE
INTERCEPT	326.38940741	1.35	0.1918	241.61283337
PROMO	136.09828861	4.84	0.0001	28.10758630
DEVEL	-61.17527129	-1.20	0.2438	50.94101324
RESEARCH	-43.69507838	-0.90	0.3766	48.32295140

a. Write the estimated regression equation.
b. Calculate the residual standard deviation.
c. Locate SS(Residual).

14.2   State the interpretation of $\hat{\beta}_1$, the estimated coefficient of promotion expenses, of Exercise 14.1.

14.3   The following artificial data are designed to illustrate the effect of correlated and uncorrelated independent variables:

y:	17	21	26	22	27	25	28	34	29	37	38	38
x:	1	1	1	1	2	2	2	2	3	3	3	3
w:	1	2	3	4	1	2	3	4	1	2	3	4
v:	1	1	2	2	3	3	4	4	5	5	6	6

a. Plot x versus w, x versus v, and w versus v.

b. Which of these plots indicate zero correlations?

c. Show that the simple linear regression equation for predicting y from x is

$$\hat{y} = 14.5 + 7.0x$$

The following sums are needed:

$$\sum x_i = 24, \quad \sum y_i = 342, \quad \sum x_i y_i = 740$$
$$\sum x_i^2 = 56, \quad \sum y_i^2 = 10{,}282, \quad n = 12$$

d. Calculate the residual standard deviation.

e. Calculate r_{yx}^2.

14.4 The Minitab computer package yields the following output for the data of Exercise 14.3.

```
MTB > correlations of c1-c4

            Y         X         W
X         0.856
W         0.402     0.000
V         0.928     0.956     0.262

MTB > regress c1 on 3 variables in c2 c3 c4

The regression equation is
Y = 10.0 + 5.00 X + 2.00 W + 1.00 V

Predictor     Coef      Stdev      t-ratio
Constant     10.000     5.766       1.73
X             5.000     6.895       0.73
W             2.000     1.528       1.31
V             1.000     3.416       0.29

s = 2.646      R-sq = 89.5%    R-sq(adj) = 85.6%

Analysis of Variance

SOURCE        DF         SS          MS
Regression     3       479.00      159.67
Error          8        56.00        7.00
Total         11       535.00
```

a. Write the least-squares prediction equation. Locate the residual standard deviation s_ϵ.

b. Show that the multiple R^2 is larger than the r^2 of Exercise 14.3. Is the residual standard deviation smaller?

14.5 A chemical firm tests the yield that results from the presence of varying amounts of two catalysts. Yields are measured for five different amounts of catalyst 1 paired with four different amounts of catalyst 2. A second-order model is fit to approximate the anticipated nonlinear relation. The variables are $y =$ yield, $x_1 =$ amount of catalyst 1, $x_2 =$ amount of catalyst 2, $x_3 = x_1^2$, $x_4 = x_1 x_2$, and $x_5 = x_2^2$. The data are analyzed by a standard computer package (SAS). Selected output is shown below:

```
DEPENDENT VARIABLE: YIELD

SOURCE              DF      SUM OF SQUARES      MEAN SQUARE     F VALUE      PR > F      R-SQUARE         C.V.

MODEL               5         448.19324829      89.63864966      17.55       0.0001      0.862437      3.7611

ERROR              14          71.48900671       5.10635762                  ROOT MSE                 YIELD MEAN

CORRECTED TOTAL    19         519.68225500                                  2.25972512               60.08150000


                                    T FOR H0:     PR > |T|      STD ERROR OF
PARAMETER           ESTIMATE      PARAMETER=0                    ESTIMATE

INTERCEPT          50.01950000         11.39       0.0001         4.39050111
CAT1                6.64357143          3.30       0.0052         2.01211633
CAT2                7.31450000          2.67       0.0183         2.73977110
CAT1SQ             -1.23142857         -4.08       0.0011         0.30196847
CAT1CAT2           -0.77240000         -2.42       0.0299         0.31957339
CAT2SQ             -1.17550000         -2.33       0.0355         0.50528990
```

    a. Write the estimated regression equation.

    b. Locate SS(Residual) and the residual standard deviation.

14.6 Refer to Exercise 14.5. Calculate $R^2_{y \cdot x_1 x_2 x_3 x_4 x_5}$.

14.3   INFERENCES IN MULTIPLE REGRESSION

The ideas of the preceding section involve point (best-guess) estimation of the regression coefficients, the standard deviation s_ϵ, and the coefficient of determination R^2. In this section we discuss inferences about the partial slope parameters in the multiple regression model.

First we present a test of an overall null hypothesis about the partial slopes $(\beta_1, \beta_2, \ldots, \beta_k)$ in the multiple regression model. According to this hypothesis, $H_0: \beta_1 = \beta_2 = \cdots = \beta_k = 0$, none of the variables included in the multiple regression has any predictive value at all. The research hypothesis is a very general one, namely, H_a: At least one $\beta_j \neq 0$. The test statistic is an F statistic very similar to the F statistics of Chapter 12. To state the test, we must first define the sum of squares attributable to the regression of Y on the variables $x_1, x_2, \ldots, x_k$. We designate this sum of squares SS(Regression).

SS(Regression)

$$\text{SS(Regression)} = \sum (\hat{y}_i - \bar{y})^2$$
$$\text{SS(Total)} = \sum (y_i - \bar{y})^2$$
$$= \text{SS(Regression)} + \text{SS(Residual)}$$

Unlike SS(Total) and SS(Residual), we don't interpret SS(Regression) in terms of prediction error. Rather, it measures the extent to which the predictions

$\hat{y}_i$ vary as the x's vary. If SS(Regression) = 0, the predicted y values ($\hat{y}$) are all the same. In such a case, information about the x's is useless in predicting y. If SS(Regression) is large relative to SS(Residual), the indication is that there is real predictive value in the independent variables $x_1, x_2, \ldots, x_k$. We state the test statistic in terms of mean squares rather than sums of squares. As always, a mean square is a sum of squares divided by the appropriate d.f.

F Test of H_0: $\beta_1 = \beta_2 = \cdots = \beta_k = 0$

H_0: $\beta_1 = \beta_2 = \cdots = \beta_k = 0$

H_a: At least one $\beta_j \neq 0$

T.S.: $F = \dfrac{\text{SS(Regression)}/k}{\text{SS(Residual)}/[n - (k + 1)]} = \dfrac{\text{MS(Regression)}}{\text{MS(Residual)}}$

R.R.: With d.f.$_1 = k$ and d.f.$_2 = n - (k + 1)$, reject H_0 if $F > F_\alpha$

EXAMPLE 14.12   Carry out the F test of H_0: $\beta_1 = \beta_2 = 0$ for the data of Example 14.5. Use $\alpha = .05$.

Solution   From previous work in Example 14.9 we found that SS(Total) = 66, and in Example 14.6 we computed SS(Residual) = 14. It follows that

$$\text{SS(Regression)} = \text{SS(Total)} - \text{SS(Residual)}$$
$$= 66 - 14 = 52$$

The test procedure is then

H_0: $\beta_1 = \beta_2 = 0$

H_a: At least one of the β's $\neq 0$

T.S.: $F = \dfrac{\text{MS(Regression)}}{\text{MS(Residual)}} = \dfrac{52/2}{14/2} = 3.714$

with $n = 5$ and $k = 2$

R.R.: For d.f.$_1 = $ d.f.$_2 = 2$ and $\alpha = .05$, the rejection region is $F > 19.00$.

Conclusion: Because the computed value of F is less than 19.00, we cannot reject H_0. Of course, because n is so small, the risk of a Type II error in accepting H_0 could be quite high. ∎

EXAMPLE 14.13   a. Locate SS(Regression) in the computer output of Example 14.4.
b. Calculate the F statistic.
c. Can we safely conclude that the independent variables x_1 and x_2 together have predictive power?

Solution   a. SS(Regression) is shown in the ANALYSIS OF VARIANCE section of the output as 596.83.

b. The MS(Regression) and MS(Residual) values are also shown there:

$$F = \frac{MS(Regression)}{MS(Residual)} = \frac{298.42}{14.19} = 21.0$$

c. For $d.f._1 = 2$, $d.f._2 = 6$, and $\alpha = .01$, the tabled F value is 10.92. Therefore we have strong evidence (p-value well below .01) to reject the null hypothesis and to conclude that the x's collectively have at least some predictive value. ∎

Rejection of the null hypothesis of this F test is not an overwhelmingly impressive conclusion. **This rejection merely indicates that there is some degree of predictive value somewhere among the independent variables.** It does not give any indication of which individual independent variables are useful. The next task, therefore, is to make inferences about the individual partial slopes.

To make these inferences, we need the estimated standard error of each partial slope. These standard errors are computed and shown by most regression computer programs. The formula that we present for the standard error is useful in considering the effect of collinearity (correlated independent variables), but it is not a good way to do the computation.

Estimated Standard Error of $\hat{\beta}_j$ in a Multiple Regression

$$s_{\hat{\beta}_j} = s_\epsilon \sqrt{\frac{1}{\sum (x_{ij} - \bar{x}_j)^2 (1 - R^2_{x_j \cdot x_1 \cdots x_{j-1} x_{j+1} \cdots x_k})}}$$

where $R^2_{x_j \cdot x_1 \cdots x_{j-1} x_{j+1} \cdots x_k}$ is the R^2 value obtained by letting x_j be the **dependent** variable in a multiple regression with all other x's independent variables. Note that s_ϵ is the residual standard deviation for the multiple regression of y on $x_1, x_2, \ldots, x_k$.

EXAMPLE 14.14   Compute the estimated standard error of $\hat{\beta}_1$ for the data of Example 14.5.

Solution   The standard deviation, from Example 14.6, is $s_\epsilon = 2.646$, and

$$\sum (x_{i1} - \bar{x}_1)^2 = \sum x_{i1}^2 - (\sum x_{i1})^2/n = 10.$$

The R^2 value obtained by treating x_1 as a dependent variable and x_2 (the only other x variable) as independent is simply $r^2_{x_1 x_2}$. From Example 14.11, this is $(.8944)^2 = .800$. Therefore the estimated standard error of $\hat{\beta}_1$ is

$$s_{\beta_1} = 2.646 \sqrt{\frac{1}{10(1 - .800)}} = 1.871$$ ∎

effect of collinearity   The most important use of the formula for estimated standard error is to illustrate the **effect of collinearity**. If the independent variable x_j is highly collinear with one or more other independent variables, $R^2_{x_j \cdot x_1 \cdots x_{j-1} x_{j+1} \cdots x_k}$ is by definition very large and $1 - R^2_{x_j \cdot x_1 \cdots x_{j-1} x_{j+1} \cdots x_k}$ is near zero. Division by a near-zero number yields a very large standard error. Thus the most important effect of severe collinearity is that it results in very large standard errors of partial slopes.

A large standard error for any estimated partial slope indicates a large probable error for the estimate. The partial slope $\hat{\beta}_j$ of x_j estimates the effect of increasing x_j by one unit while all other x's remain constant. If x_j is highly collinear with other x's, when x_j increases the other x's also vary rather than staying constant. Therefore, it is difficult to estimate β_j and its probable error is large when x_j is severely collinear with other independent variables.

The standard error of each estimated partial slope $\hat{\beta}_j$ is used in a confidence interval and statistical test for β_j. The confidence interval follows the familiar format of estimate $\pm$ (table values)(estimated standard error).

$100(1 - \alpha)\%$ Confidence Interval for $\hat{\beta}_j$

$$\hat{\beta}_j - t_{\alpha/2}s_{\hat{\beta}_j} \leq \beta_j \leq \hat{\beta}_j + t_{\alpha/2}s_{\hat{\beta}j}$$

where $t_{\alpha/2}$ cuts off area $\alpha/2$ in the tail of a t distribution with d.f. $= n - (k + 1)$.

EXAMPLE 14.15   Calculate a 95% confidence interval for β_1 for the data of Example 14.5.

Solution $\hat{\beta}$ was found to be 1.00 in Example 14.5 and $s_{\hat{\beta}_1}$ was 1.871. The t value that cuts off an area of .025 in a t distribution with d.f. $= n - (k + 1) = 5 - (2 + 1) = 2$ is 4.303. The confidence interval is $1.00 - 4.303(1.871) \leq \beta_1 \leq 1.00 + 4.303(1.871)$, or $-7.051 \leq \beta_1 \leq 9.051$. ∎

EXAMPLE 14.16   Locate the estimated partial slope for x_2 and its standard error in the output of Example 14.4. Calculate a 90% confidence interval for β_2.

Solution $\hat{\beta}_2$ is .3333 with standard error (labeled STDEV) .3076. The tabled t value is 1.943 [tail area .05, $9 - (2 + 1) = 6$ d.f.]. The desired interval is $.3333 - 1.943(.3076) \leq \beta_2 \leq .3333 + 1.943(.3076)$, or $-.2644 \leq \beta_2 \leq .9310$. ∎

interpretation of   The usual null hypothesis for inference about β_j is $H_0: \beta_j = 0$. This hy-
$H_0: \beta_j = 0$ pothesis does not assert that x_j has no predictive value by itself. It asserts that it has no *additional* predictive value over and above that contributed by the other independent variables; that is, if all other x's had already been used in a regression model and then x_j was added last, no improvement in prediction would result. We interpret $H_0: \beta_j = 0$ to mean that x_j has no additional predictive value as the "**last**
last predictor in   **predictor in**." The t test of this H_0 is summarized below.

Summary for Testing H_0: $\beta_j = 0$

$H_0: \beta_j = 0$

$H_a:$ 1. $\beta_j > 0$

2. $\beta_j < 0$

3. $\beta_j \neq 0$

$$\text{T.S.: } t = \hat{\beta}_j / s_{\hat{\beta}_j}$$
$$\text{R.R.: 1. } t > t_\alpha$$
$$\text{2. } t < -t_\alpha$$
$$\text{3. } |t| > t_{\alpha/2}$$

where t_a cuts off a right-tail area a in the t distribution with d.f. $= n - (k + 1)$

EXAMPLE 14.17

a. Use the information given in Example 14.15 to test $H_0: \beta_1 = 0$ at $\alpha = .05$. Use a two-sided alternative.

b. Is the conclusion of the test compatible with the confidence interval?

Solution

a. The test statistic for $H_0: \beta_1 = 0$ versus $H_a: \beta_1 \neq 0$ is $t = \hat{\beta}_1 / s_{\hat{\beta}_1} = 1.00/1.871 = .534$. Because the .025 point for the t distribution with $5 - (2 + 1) = 2$ d.f. is 4.303, H_0 must be retained; x_1 does not appear to have any additional predictive power in the presence of the other independent variable x_2.

b. The 95% confidence interval includes zero, which also indicates that $H_0: \beta_1 = 0$ must be retained at $\alpha = .05$, two-tailed.   ∎

EXAMPLE 14.18

Locate the t statistic for testing $H_0: \beta_2 = 0$ in the output of Example 14.4. Can $H_a: \beta_2 > 0$ be supported at any of the usual α levels?

Solution

The t statistics are shown under the heading T–RATIO. For x_2 the t statistic is 1.08. The t table value for 6 d.f. and $\alpha = .10$ is 1.440, so H_0 cannot be rejected even at $\alpha = .10$.   ∎

The multiple regression F and t tests that we discuss in this chapter test different null hypotheses. It sometimes happens that the F test results in the rejection of $H_0: \beta_1 = \beta_2 = \cdots = \beta_k = 0$, while no t test of $H_0: \beta_j = 0$ is significant. In such a case, we can conclude that there is predictive value in the equation as a whole, but we cannot identify the specific variables that have predictive value. Remember that each t test is testing "last predictor in" value. When the predictor variables are highly correlated among themselves, it often happens that no x_j can be shown to have significant "last in" predictive value, even though the x's together have been shown to be useful.

SECTION 14.3   EXERCISES

14.7 Refer to the computer output of Exercise 14.1.
   a. Locate the F statistic.
   b. Can the hypothesis of no overall predictive value be rejected at $\alpha = .01$?
   c. Locate the t statistic for the coefficient of promotion $\hat{\beta}_1$.
   d. Test the research hypothesis that $\beta_1 \neq 0$. Use $\alpha = .05$.
   e. State the conclusion of the test in part (d).

14.8 Locate the p-value for the test of Exercise 14.7, part (d). It is one-tailed or two-tailed?

14.9 Summarize the results of the t tests in Exercise 14.7. What null hypotheses are being tested?

14.10 Refer to the computer output of Exercise 14.4.
    a. Locate MS(Regression) and MS(Residual).
    b. What is the value of the F statistic?
    c. Determine the p-value for the F test.
    d. What conclusion can be established from the F test?

14.11 A metalworking firm conducts an energy study using multiple regression methods. The dependent variable is Y = energy consumption cost per day (in thousands of dollars), and the independent variables are x_1 = tons of metal processed in the day, x_2 = average external temperature $- 60°F$ (a union contract requires cooling of the plant whenever outside temperatures reach $60°$, x_3 = rated wattage for machinery in use, and $x_4 = x_1x_2$. The data are analyzed by a standard program (SAS). Selected output is shown here.

DEPENDENT VARIABLE: ENERGY

SOURCE	DF	SUM OF SQUARES	MEAN SQUARE	F VALUE	PR > F	R-SQUARE	C.V.
MODEL	4	257.04891106	64.26222777	9.86	0.0001	0.663592	4.9894
ERROR	20	130.31108894	6.51555445		ROOT MSE		ENERGY MEAN
CORRECTED TOTAL	24	387.36000000			2.55255841		51.16000000

PARAMETER	ESTIMATE	T FOR H0: PARAMETER=0	PR > |T|	STD ERROR OF ESTIMATE
INTERCEPT	7.20439073	0.41	0.6855	17.53227919
METAL	1.36291836	1.47	0.1559	0.92438439
TEMP	0.30588336	0.19	0.8522	1.62104565
WATTS	0.01024173	2.16	0.0427	0.00473218
METXTEMP	-0.00277728	-0.04	0.9717	0.07722576

    a. Write the estimated model.
    b. Summarize the results of the various t tests.

INFERENCES BASED ON THE COEFFICIENT

14.4   OF DETERMINATION ■

The methods of the previous section yield tests for the null hypothesis of no overall predictive value of all variables (F test) and of no incremental predictive value of one variable (t test). Other null hypotheses, such as that of no incremental predictive value of a set of variables, may be tested by way of the coefficient of determination R^2.

    Recall that $R^2_{y \cdot x_1 \cdots x_k}$ measures the reduction in squared error for y attributed to knowledge of all the x predictors. The F test of Section 14.3 can be stated in terms of $R^2_{y \cdot x_1 \cdots x_k}$. Because the regression of y on the x's accounts for a proportion $R^2_{y \cdot x_1 \cdots x_k}$ of the total squared error in y,

$$SS(\text{Regression}) = R^2_{y \cdot x_1 \cdots x_k} SS(\text{Total})$$

The remaining fraction, $1 - R^2$, is incorporated in the residual squared error

$$SS(\text{Residual}) = (1 - R^2_{y \cdot x_1 \cdots x_k}) SS(\text{Total})$$

F and R²   The F test statistic of Section 14.3 can be rewritten as

$$F = \frac{\text{MS(Regression)}}{\text{MS(Residual)}} = \frac{R^2_{y \cdot x_1 \cdots x_k}/k}{(1 - R^2_{y \cdot x_1 \cdots x_k})/[n - (k + 1)]}$$

This statistic is to be compared with tabulated F values for d.f.$_1$ = k and d.f.$_2$ = $n - (k + 1)$.

EXAMPLE 14.19   A large city bank studies the relation of average account size in each of its branches to per capita income in the corresponding ZIP code area, number of business accounts, and number of competitive bank branches. The data are analyzed by a multiple regression program, shown below:

```
DEPENDENT VARIABLE. . . . . . . . . . . . . . .        1 ACCTSIZE

MULTIPLE R            0.8699        STD. ERROR OF EST.        2.9108
MULTIPLE R-SQUARE     0.7567

ANALYSIS OF VARIANCE
                 SUM OF SQUARES    DF    MEAN SQUARE    F RATIO    P(TAIL)
   REGRESSION        447.9653       3     149.3218      17.624     0.0000
   RESIDUAL          144.0339      17       8.4726
```

VARIABLE		COEFFICIENT	STD. ERROR	STD. REG COEFF	T	P(2 TAIL)	TOLERANCE
INTERCEPT		1.15862					
INCOME	2	2.66675	1.35716	1.017	1.965	0.0660	0.05343
BUSIN	3	-0.13453	0.22016	-0.193	-0.611	0.5493	0.14313
COMPET	4	0.03470	1.56340	0.007	0.022	0.9825	0.13187

a. Identify the multiple regression prediction equation.
b. Use the R^2 value shown to test $H_0: \beta_1 = \beta_2 = \beta_3 = 0$. (Note: $n = 21$.)

Solution   a. From the output, the multiple regression forecasting equation is

$$\hat{y} = 1.15862 + 2.66675x_1 - 0.13453x_2 + 0.0347x_3$$

b. The test procedure based on R^2 is

$H_0: \beta_1 = \beta_2 = \beta_3 = 0$
H_a: At least one β_j differs from zero

$$\text{T.S.: } F = \frac{R^2_{y \cdot x_1 x_2 x_3}/3}{(1 - R^2_{y \cdot x_1 x_2 x_3})/(21 - 4)}$$

$$= \frac{.7567/3}{.2433/17} = 17.624$$

R.R.: For d.f.$_1$ = 3 and d.f.$_2$ = 17, the critical .05 value of F is 3.20.

Because the computed F statistic, 17.624, is greater than 3.20, we reject H_0 and conclude that one or more of the x values has some predictive power. Note that the F value we compute is the same as that shown in the output.   ∎

F test for several β_j's

There is another F test for the hypothesis that several $(<k)\beta_j$'s are zero. For example, if we have the multiple regression model.

$$y = \beta_0 + \beta_1 x_1 + \beta_2 x_2 + \beta_3 x_3 + \beta_4 x_4 + \beta_5 x_5 + \epsilon$$

with $k = 5$ independent variables, we can test the null hypothesis

$$H_0: \beta_4 = \beta_5 = 0$$

According to this null hypothesis, the independent variables x_4 and x_5 together have no predictive value once x_1, x_2, and x_3 are included as predictors. The t test of Section 14.3 tests a single coefficient on a "last predictor in" basis. Now we are testing x_4 and x_5 on a "last two predictors in" basis.

The idea is to compare the R^2 values when x_4 and x_5 are excluded and when they are included in the prediction equation. When they are included, the R^2 is automatically at least as large as the R^2 when they are excluded, because we can predict at least as well with more information as with less. The F test for this null hypothesis tests whether the gain in R^2 is more than could be expected by chance alone. In general, let k be the total number of predictors, and let g be the number of predictors with coefficients not hypothesized to be zero $(g < k)$. Then $k - g$ represents the number of predictors with coefficients that are hypothesized to be zero. The idea is to find R^2 values using all predictors (the **complete model**) and using only the g predictors that do not appear in the null hypothesis (the **reduced model**). Once these have been computed, the test proceeds as outlined below. The notation is easier if we assume that the reduced model contains $\beta_1, \beta_2, \ldots, \beta_g$.

complete and reduced models

An F Test of $H_0: \beta_{g+1} = \beta_{g+2} = \cdots = \beta_k = 0$

$H_0: \beta_{g+1} = \beta_{g+2} = \cdots = \beta_k = 0$

$H_a: H_0$ is not true

T.S.: $F = \dfrac{(R^2_{\text{complete}} - R^2_{\text{reduced}})/(k - g)}{(1 - R^2_{\text{complete}})/[n - (k + 1)]}$

R.R.: $F > F_\alpha$, where F cuts off a right-tail of area α of the F distribution with d.f.$_1 = (k - g)$ and d.f.$_2 = [n - (k + 1)]$ ∎

EXAMPLE 14.20   A state fisheries commission wants to estimate the number of bass caught in a given lake during a season in order to restock the lake with the appropriate number of young fish. The commission could get a fairly accurate assessment of the seasonal catch by extensive "netting sweeps" of the lake before and after a season, but this technique is much too expensive to be done routinely. Therefore the commission samples a number of lakes and records y, the seasonal catch (thousands of bass per square mile of lake area); x_1, the number of lakeshore residences per square mile of lake area; x_2, the size of the lake in square miles; $x_3 = 1$ if the lake has public access, 0 if not; and x_4, a structure index. (*Structures* are weed beds, sunken trees, dropoffs, and other living places for bass.) The data are

y	x_1	x_2	x_3	x_4
3.6	92.2	.21	0	81
.8	86.7	.30	0	26
2.5	80.2	.31	0	52
2.9	87.2	.40	0	64
1.4	64.9	.44	0	40
.9	90.1	.56	0	22
3.2	60.7	.78	0	80
2.7	50.9	1.21	0	60
2.2	86.1	.34	1	30
5.9	90.0	.40	1	90
3.3	80.4	.52	1	74
2.9	75.0	.66	1	50
3.6	70.0	.78	1	61
2.4	64.6	.91	1	40
1.9	50.0	1.10	1	22
2.0	50.0	1.24	1	50
1.9	51.2	1.47	1	37
3.1	40.1	2.21	1	61
2.6	45.0	2.46	1	39
3.4	50.0	2.80	1	53

The commission is convinced that x_1 and x_2 are important variables in predicting y because they both reflect how intensively the lake has been fished. There is some question as to whether x_3 and x_4 are useful as additional predictor variables. Therefore regression models (with all x's entering linearly) are run with and without x_3 and x_4. Relevant portions of the Minitab output follow.

```
MTB > regress c1 on 4 variables in c2-c5

The regression equation is
Y = - 1.94 + 0.0193 X1 + 0.332 X2 + 0.836 X3 + 0.0477 X4

Predictor        Coef           Stdev        t-ratio
Constant       -1.9378         0.9081         -2.13
X1              0.01929        0.01018         1.90
X2              0.3323         0.2458          1.35
X3              0.8355         0.2250          3.71
X4              0.047714       0.005056        9.44

s = 0.4336      R-sq = 88.2%     R-sq(adj) = 85.0%
```

Analysis of Variance

```
SOURCE         DF            SS            MS
Regression     4         21.0474        5.2619
Error          15         2.8206        0.1880
Total          19        23.8680
```

MTB > regress c1 on 2 variables in c2 and c3

The regression equation is
Y = - 0.11 + 0.0310 X1 + 0.679 X2

```
Predictor       Coef        Stdev       t-ratio
Constant       -0.107       2.336        -0.05
X1             0.03102      0.02650       1.17
X2             0.6794       0.6178        1.10
```

s = 1.138   R-sq = 7.7%   R-sq(adj) = 0.0%

Analysis of Variance

```
SOURCE         DF            SS            MS
Regression     2         1.845         0.922
Error          17        22.023        1.295
Total          19        23.868
```

a. Write the complete and reduced models.
b. Write the null hypothesis for testing that the omitted variables have no (incremental) predictive value.
c. Perform an F test for this null hypothesis.

Solution   a. The complete and reduced models are, respectively,

$$Y_i = \beta_0 + \beta_1 x_{i1} + \beta_2 x_{i2} + \beta_3 x_{i3} + \beta_4 x_{i4} + \epsilon_i$$

and

$$Y_i = \beta_0 + \beta_1 x_{i1} + \beta_2 x_{i2} + \epsilon_i$$

The corresponding multiple regression forecasting equations based on the sample data are

Complete: $\hat{y} = -1.94 + .0193x_1 + .332x_2 + .836x_3 + .0477x_4$
Reduced: $\hat{y} = -.11 + .0310x_1 + .679x_2$

b. The appropriate null hypothesis of no predictive power for x_3 and x_4 is

$$H_0: \beta_3 = \beta_4 = 0$$

c. The test statistic for the H_0 of part (b) makes use of $R^2_{\text{complete}} = .882$, $R^2_{\text{reduced}} = .077$, $k = 4$, $g = 2$, and $n = 20$:

$$\text{T.S.: } F = \frac{(R^2_{\text{complete}} - R^2_{\text{reduced}})/(4-2)}{(1 - R^2_{\text{complete}})/(20-5)} = \frac{(.882 - .077)/2}{(1 - .882)/15} = 51.165$$

R.R.: The .01 F value for d.f.$_1 = 2$ and d.f.$_2 = 15$ is 6.36, so we can reject H_0 convincingly. The variables x_3 and x_4 are useful predictors in the multiple regression equation. ∎

SECTION 14.4 EXERCISES

14.12 Refer to the output shown in Exercise 14.1.
  a. Locate the R^2 value.
  b. Calculate the F statistic (based on R^2) for the null hypothesis that none of the independent variables has predictive value.
  c. Compare the value of this F statistic to that shown in the output.

14.13 Another regression analysis of the data of Exercise 14.1 is done using only developmental expenditures as an independent variable. The SAS output is shown below:

SOURCE	DF	SUM OF SQUARES	MEAN SQUARE	F VALUE	PR > F	R-SQUARE	C.V.
MODEL	1	20094.34500769	20094.34500769	11.97	0.0022	0.352298	13.0298
ERROR	22	36943.65499231	1679.25704511		ROOT MSE		SALES MEAN
CORRECTED TOTAL	23	57038.00000000			40.97873894		314.50000000

  a. Locate R^2 for the reduced model.
  b. Use this R^2 and that given in Exercises 14.1 to calculate an F statistic.
  c. What is the mathematical null hypothesis of this test? Give a careful interpretation of this hypothesis in terms of predictive value.
  d. What is the conclusion of this F test using $\alpha = .01$?

14.14 Another regression equation is calculated based on the data of Example 14.19 (page 626). The only independent variable used is INCOME. The output is shown below:

DEPENDENT VARIABLE. . . . . 1 ACCTSIZE

MULTIPLE R	0.8628	STD. ERROR OF EST.	2.8219
MULTIPLE R-SQUARE	0.7444		

ANALYSIS OF VARIANCE

	SUM OF SQUARES	DF	MEAN SQUARE	F RATIO	P(TAIL)
REGRESSION	440.7036	1	440.7036	55.344	0.0000
RESIDUAL	151.2956	19	7.9629		

  a. Locate R^2 for the reduced model.
  b. Locate R^2 for the complete model in the output of Example 14.19.
  c. Calculate the F statistic based on the incremental R^2. What null hypothesis is being tested?

14.15 For the chemical data of Exercise 14.5, a regression model is fit using only the first-order variables x_1 and x_2. Selected output is shown at the top of page 631.
  a. Write the estimated complete model from Exercise 14.5.
  b. Write the estimated reduced model.

DEPENDENT VARIABLE: YIELD

SOURCE	DF	SUM OF SQUARES	MEAN SQUARE	F VALUE	PR > F	R-SQUARE	C.V.
MODEL	2	305.80784100	152.90392050	12.15	0.0005	0.588452	5.9036
ERROR	17	213.87441400	12.58084788		ROOT MSE		YIELD MEAN
CORRECTED TOTAL	19	519.68225500			3.54694909		60.08150000

PARAMETER	ESTIMATE	T FOR H0: PARAMETER=0	PR > |T|	STD ERROR OF ESTIMATE
INTERCEPT	70.31000000	27.36	0.0001	2.57000878
CAT1	-2.67600000	-4.77	0.0002	0.56082189
CAT2	-0.88020000	-1.24	0.2315	0.70938982

c. Locate R^2 for the complete model in Exercise 14.6 and R^2 for the reduced model here.

d. Is there convincing evidence that the addition of the second-order terms x_3, x_4, and x_5 has improved the predictive value of the model?

14.5   FORECASTING USING MULTIPLE REGRESSION   ∎

One of the major uses of multiple regression models is in forecasting a y value given certain values of the independent x variables. The best-guess forecast is easy; just substitute the assumed x values into the estimated regression equation. In this section we discuss the relevant standard errors for such forecasts.

As in Chapter 13, the problem of forecasting y given values of the x's can be interpreted in two ways. We can think of the resulting $\hat{y}$ value as a best guess of $E(Y)$, the long-run average y value that results from averaging infinitely many observations of y when the x's have the designated values. Alternatively, and usually more interesting, we can think of $\hat{y}$ as a forecast of the actual y value that occurs given the x's. Of course it's harder to forecast an individual value than a mean, so the standard error for individual y forecasts is larger than the one for $E(Y)$. Because the relevant formulas for standard error require an understanding of matrix algebra that is not required for this text, we present crude approximations to these standard errors that ignore the major problem of extrapolation.

Extrapolation is not a problem if each x_j value is equal to the mean of the sample x_j values used in fitting the multiple regression model. In this case (and only in this case) the standard errors are quite simple. The estimated standard errors in forecasting $E(Y)$ and individual y values when there is no extrapolation are, respectively,

$$s_\epsilon \sqrt{\frac{1}{n}} \quad \text{and} \quad s_\epsilon \sqrt{1 + \frac{1}{n}}$$

In fact, these no-extrapolation standard errors would be obtained by setting the extrapolation penalty term to zero in the Chapter 13 formulas.

However, the relevant values for $x_1, x_2, \ldots, x_k$ used in a forecast are hardly ever precisely equal to the respective sample means, so some degree of extrapolation is required. Although it would be helpful to use matrices to compute approximate standard errors, we rely on computer output to get numerical values for these standard errors. Computer programs typically give a standard error for an individual y forecast. While this information can also be used to find a standard error for estimating $E(Y)$, the individual y forecast is usually more relevant. The appropriate plus-or-minus term for forecasting can be found by multiplying the standard error by a tabled t value with d.f. $= n - (k + 1)$. In fact, many computer programs give the plus-or-minus term directly.

EXAMPLE 14.21   An advertising manager for a manufacturer of prepared cereals wants to develop an equation to predict sales (s) based on advertising expenditures for children's television (c), daytime television (d), and newspapers (n). Data were collected monthly for the previous 30 months (and divided by a price index to control for inflation). A multiple linear regression is fit, yielding the following computer output (SAS):

PARAMETER	ESTIMATE	T FOR H0: PARAMETER=0	PR > |T|	STD ERROR OF ESTIMATE
INTERCEPT	0.34954867	0.65	0.5214	0.53776104
C	0.06488372	3.80	0.0008	0.01706376
D	0.00628634	0.26	0.7949	0.02393904
N	0.05785077	2.74	0.0110	0.02113293

OBSERVATION	OBSERVED VALUE	PREDICTED VALUE	RESIDUAL	LOWER 95% CL INDIVIDUAL	UPPER 95% CL INDIVIDUAL
27	2.34000000	2.42060156	-0.08060156	2.02320918	2.81799394
28	1.99000000	1.93924981	0.05075019	1.53145179	2.34704784
29	2.15000000	2.07381038	0.07618962	1.67063254	2.47698822
30	2.35000000	2.49656474	-0.14656474	2.11575518	2.87737430
31 *	.	3.08658507	.	2.61561332	3.55755682

OBSERVATION	OBSERVED VALUE	PREDICTED VALUE	RESIDUAL	LOWER 95% CL FOR MEAN	UPPER 95% CL FOR MEAN
27	2.34000000	2.42060156	-0.08060156	2.28427805	2.55692507
28	1.99000000	1.93924981	0.05075019	1.77504681	2.10345282
29	2.15000000	2.07381038	0.07618962	1.92144316	2.22617759
30	2.35000000	2.49656474	-0.14656474	2.42120349	2.57192599
31 *	.	3.08658507	.	2.79939561	3.37377453

a. Write the regression equation.
b. Locate the predicted y value $(\hat{y})$ when $c = 31$, $d = 5$, and $n = 12$. Locate the lower and upper limits for a 95% confidence interval for $E(Y)$ and the upper and lower 95% prediction limits for an individual Y value.

Solution   a. The column labeled ESTIMATE yields the equation

$$\hat{y} = .34955 + .06488c + .00629d + 0.5755n$$

b. The predicted y value is shown as OBSERVATION 31. Note that no OBSERVED VALUE is shown for this observation. As can be verified by substituting $c = 31, d = 5$, and $n = 12$ into the equation, the predicted y is 3.0866. The 95% confidence limits for the mean $E(Y)$ are shown as 2.7994 to 3.3738, while the wider prediction limits for an individual y value are 2.6156 to 3.5576.   ∎

extrapolation in multiple regression

The notion of extrapolation is more subtle in multiple regression than in simple linear regression. Briefly, the extrapolation error depends not only on the range of each separate x_j predictor used to develop the regression equation but also on the correlations among the x_j values. In Figure 14.1, the circled point has an x_1 value well within the range of previous x_1 values, as it does for the x_2 value. Yet the point itself lies far outside the range of previous points, because of the very strong (negative, in this case) correlation of previous x_1 and x_2 values. To avoid gross extrapolation, a manager must select x values that are within (or at least close to) the range of previous values not only variable by variable, but also in combination. Those who try to forecast without regard to the data base on which the regression equation is built display a touching, childlike, and possibly expensive faith in statistical magic.

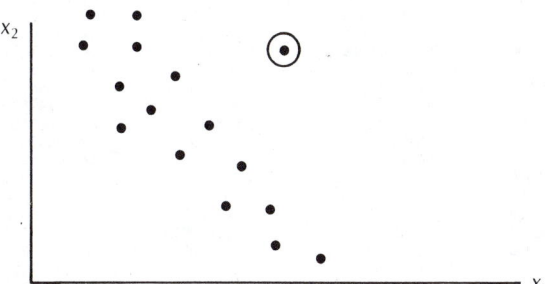

FIGURE 14.1   Extrapolation in Multiple Regression

SECTION 14.5 EXERCISES

14.16 Refer to the chemical firm data of Exercise 14.5. Predicted yields for $x_1 = 3.5$ and $x_2 = 3.5$ (observation 21) and also for $x_1 = 3.5$ and $x_2 = 2.5$ (observation 22) are calculated based on the model $\hat{y} = 50.0195 + 6.6436x_1 + 7.3145x_2 - 1.2314x_1^2 - .7724x_1x_2 - 1.1755x_2^2$ of Exercise 14.5 and on the model $\hat{y} = 70.3100 - 2.6760x_1 - .8802x_2$ of Exercise 14.15. Selected output is shown on page 634.
  a. Locate the 95% confidence limits for individual prediction in the model $\hat{y} = 50.0195 + 6.6436x_1 + 7.3145x_2 - 1.2314x_1^2 - .7724x_1x_2 - 1.1755x_2^2$.
  b. Locate the 95% confidence limits for individual prediction in the model $\hat{y} = 70.3100 - 2.6760x_1 - .8802x_2$.
  c. Are the confidence limits for the model of part (a) much tighter than those for the model of part (b)?

OBSERVATION	OBSERVED VALUE	PREDICTED VALUE	RESIDUAL	LOWER 95% CL INDIVIDUAL	UPPER 95% CL INDIVIDUAL
1	58.01000000	60.79824286	-2.78824286	54.78096039	66.81552532
2	65.89000000	62.97512857	2.91487143	57.49639919	68.45385795
3	62.70000000	62.68915714	0.01084286	57.24575991	68.13255438
4	58.22000000	59.94032857	-1.72032857	54.46159919	65.41905795
5	55.83000000	54.72864286	1.10135714	48.71136039	60.74592532
6	66.69000000	63.81384286	2.87615714	58.28481389	69.34287182
7	63.93000000	65.21832857	-1.28832857	60.00318599	70.43347115
8	62.83000000	64.15995714	-1.32995714	58.89199760	69.42791669
9	63.52000000	60.63872857	2.88127143	55.42358599	65.85387115
10	52.96000000	54.65464286	-1.69464286	49.12561389	60.18367182
11	62.53000000	64.47844286	-1.94844286	58.94941389	70.00747182
12	65.27000000	65.11052857	0.15947143	59.89538599	70.32567115
13	65.71000000	63.27975714	2.43024286	58.01179760	68.54771669
14	58.04000000	58.98612857	-0.94612857	53.77098599	64.20127115
15	51.09000000	52.22964286	-1.13964286	46.70061389	57.75867182
16	63.74000000	62.79204286	0.94795714	56.77476039	68.80932532
17	63.43000000	62.65172857	0.77827143	57.17299919	68.13045795
18	56.72000000	60.04855714	-3.32855714	54.60515991	65.49195438
19	55.16000000	54.98252857	0.17747143	49.50379919	60.46125795
20	49.36000000	47.45364286	1.90635714	41.43636039	53.47092532
21 *	.	59.92597500	.	54.70811858	65.14383142
22 *	.	62.36787500	.	57.08293311	67.65282689

OBSERVATION	OBSERVED VALUE	PREDICTED VALUE	RESIDUAL	LOWER 95% CL INDIVIDUAL	UPPER 95% CL INDIVIDUAL
1	58.01000000	66.75380000	-8.74380000	58.42067813	75.08692187
2	65.89000000	64.07780000	1.81220000	56.00061828	72.15498172
3	62.70000000	61.40180000	1.29820000	53.41175332	69.39184668
4	58.22000000	58.72580000	-0.50580000	50.64861828	66.80298172
5	55.83000000	56.04980000	-0.21980000	47.71667813	64.38292187
6	66.69000000	65.87360000	0.81640000	57.81376993	73.93343007
7	63.93000000	63.19760000	0.73240000	55.40267825	70.99252175
8	62.83000000	60.52160000	2.30840000	52.81700484	68.22619516
9	63.52000000	57.84560000	5.67440000	50.05067825	65.64052175
10	52.96000000	55.16960000	-2.20960000	47.10976993	63.22943007
11	62.53000000	64.99340000	-2.46340000	56.93356993	73.05323007
12	65.27000000	62.31740000	2.95260000	54.52247825	70.11232175
13	65.71000000	59.64140000	6.06860000	51.93680484	67.34599516
14	58.04000000	56.96540000	1.07460000	49.17047825	64.76032175
15	51.09000000	54.28940000	-3.19940000	46.22956993	62.34923007
16	63.74000000	64.11320000	-0.37320000	55.78007813	72.44632187
17	63.43000000	61.43720000	1.99280000	53.36001828	69.51438172
18	56.72000000	58.76120000	-2.04120000	50.77115332	66.75124668
19	55.16000000	56.08520000	-0.92520000	48.00801828	64.16238172
20	49.36000000	53.40920000	-4.04920000	45.07607813	61.74232187
21 *	.	57.86330000	.	50.02807100	65.69852900
22 *	.	58.74350000	.	51.05254533	66.43445467

Output for Exercise 14.6

14.6   SOME MULTIPLE REGRESSION THEORY ∎

In this section matrix notation is used to sketch some of the mathematics underlying multiple regression. The ideas in this section indicate how multiple regression calculations are actually done, whether by hand or by computer. We do not prove most of the results; proofs are available in many specialized texts, such as Draper and Smith (1981).

The starting point for the use of matrix notation is the multiple regression model itself. Recall that a model relating a response Y to a set of independent variables of the form

$$Y = \beta_0 + \beta_1 x_1 + \beta_2 x_2 + \cdots + \beta_k x_k + \epsilon$$

is called the general linear model. The least-squares estimates $\hat{\beta}_0, \hat{\beta}_1, \ldots, \hat{\beta}_k$ of the intercept and partial slopes in the general linear model can be obtained using matrices.

Let the $n \times 1$ matrix **Y**

$$\mathbf{Y} = \begin{bmatrix} y_1 \\ y_2 \\ \vdots \\ y_n \end{bmatrix}$$

be the matrix of observations, and let the $n \times (k + 1)$ matrix **X**

$$\mathbf{X} = \begin{bmatrix} 1 & x_{11} & \cdots & x_{1k} \\ 1 & x_{21} & \cdots & x_{2k} \\ \vdots & \vdots & & \vdots \\ 1 & x_{n1} & \cdots & x_{nk} \end{bmatrix}$$

be a matrix of settings for the independent variables augmented with a column of 1's. The first row of **X** contains a 1 and the settings for the k independent variables for the first observation. Row 2 contains a 1 and corresponding settings on the independent variables for y_2. Similarly, the other rows contain settings for the remaining observations.

Next we turn to the least-squares estimates $\hat{\beta}_0, \hat{\beta}_1, \ldots, \hat{\beta}_k$ of the intercept and partial slopes in the multiple regression model. Recall that the least-squares principle involves choosing the estimates to minimize the sum of squared residuals. Those familiar with the calculus will see that the solution can be found by differentiating SS(Residual) with respect to $\hat{\beta}_j$ ($j = 0, \ldots, k$) and setting the result to zero. The resulting normal equations, in matrix notation, are

$$(\mathbf{X}'\mathbf{X})\,\hat{\boldsymbol{\beta}} = \mathbf{X}'\mathbf{Y}$$

where

$$\hat{\boldsymbol{\beta}} = \begin{bmatrix} \hat{\beta}_0 \\ \hat{\beta}_1 \\ \vdots \\ \hat{\beta}_k \end{bmatrix}$$

is the desired vector of estimated coefficients. Provided that the matrix $\mathbf{X}'\mathbf{X}$ has an inverse (it does as long as no x_j is perfectly collinear with other x's), the solution is

$$\hat{\boldsymbol{\beta}} = (\mathbf{X}'\mathbf{X})^{-1}\mathbf{X}'\mathbf{Y}$$

EXAMPLE 14.22   Suppose that in a given experimental situation,

$$\mathbf{Y} = \begin{bmatrix} 25 \\ 19 \\ 33 \\ 23 \end{bmatrix} \quad \text{and} \quad \mathbf{X} = \begin{bmatrix} 1 & -2 & 5 \\ 1 & -2 & -5 \\ 1 & 2 & 5 \\ 1 & 2 & -5 \end{bmatrix}$$

Obtain the least-squares estimates for the prediction equation

$$\hat{y} = \hat{\beta}_0 + \hat{\beta}_1 x_1 + \hat{\beta}_2 x_2$$

Solution For these data,

$$\mathbf{X'X} = \begin{bmatrix} 4 & 0 & 0 \\ 0 & 16 & 0 \\ 0 & 0 & 100 \end{bmatrix}$$

$$\mathbf{X'Y} = \begin{bmatrix} 100 \\ 24 \\ 80 \end{bmatrix}$$

The $\mathbf{X'X}$ matrix is a diagonal one, so inverting the matrix is easy. The solution is

$$\hat{\beta} = (\mathbf{X'X})^{-1}\mathbf{X'Y}$$

$$= \begin{bmatrix} .25 & 0 & 0 \\ 0 & .0625 & 0 \\ 0 & 0 & .01 \end{bmatrix} \begin{bmatrix} 100 \\ 24 \\ 80 \end{bmatrix} = \begin{bmatrix} 25 \\ 1.5 \\ 0.8 \end{bmatrix}$$

and the prediction equation is

$$\hat{y} = 25 + 1.5x_1 + .8x_2. \qquad \blacksquare$$

The hard part of the arithmetic in multiple regression is computing the inverse of $\mathbf{X'X}$. For most realistic multiple regression problems, this task takes hours by hand and fractions of a second by computer. This is the major reason that most multiple regression problems are done with computer software.

Once the inverse of the $\mathbf{X'X}$ matrix is found and the $\hat{\beta}$ vector is calculated, the next task is to compute the residual standard deviation. The hard work is to compute SS(Residual) $= \sum(y_i - \hat{y}_i)^2$. The shortcut formula given in Section 14.2 can be written as SS(Residual) $= \mathbf{Y'Y} - \hat{\beta}'(\mathbf{X'Y})$.

EXAMPLE 14.23 Compute SS(Residual) for the data of Example 14.22.

Solution $\hat{\beta}$ and $\mathbf{X'Y}$ were calculated to be

$$\begin{bmatrix} 25 \\ 1.5 \\ 0.8 \end{bmatrix} \quad \text{and} \quad \begin{bmatrix} 100 \\ 24 \\ 80 \end{bmatrix}$$

respectively, and

$$\mathbf{Y'Y} = \begin{bmatrix} 25 & 19 & 33 & 23 \end{bmatrix} \begin{bmatrix} 25 \\ 19 \\ 33 \\ 23 \end{bmatrix} = 2604$$

The shortcut formula yields

$$SS(Residual) = 2604 - [25 \quad 1.5 \quad 0.8] \begin{bmatrix} 100 \\ 24 \\ 80 \end{bmatrix} = 4$$ ■

Similar calculations yield SS(Total) and SS(Regression). While the formulas for these sums can be expressed artificially in pure matrix notation, the easy way is to mix matrix and algebraic notation:

$$SS(Regression) = \hat{\beta}'(X'Y) - \frac{(\sum y_i)^2}{n}$$

$$SS(Total) = Y'Y - \frac{(\sum y_i)^2}{n}$$

EXAMPLE 14.24   Calculate SS(Regression) and SS(Total) for the data of Example 14.22.

Solution $\sum y_i = 100$ and $n = 4$. The relevant matrix calculations were performed in the previous example.

$$SS(Regression) = 2600 - \frac{(100)^2}{4} = 100$$

$$SS(Total) = 2604 - \frac{(100)^2}{4} = 104$$

Note that SS(Total) = 104 = 100 + 4 = SS(Regression) + SS(Residual).   ■

These sum-of-squares calculations are necessary to make inferences based on R^2 using F tests. For inferences about individual coefficients using t tests, the estimated standard errors of the coefficients are necessary. In Section 14.3 we presented a conceptually useful but computationally cumbersome formula for these estimated standard errors. There is a much easier way to compute them that involves only the standard deviation s_ϵ and the main diagonal elements of the $(X'X)^{-1}$ matrix.

Estimated Standard Error of $\hat{\beta}_j$

$$s_{\hat{\beta}_j} = s_\epsilon \sqrt{v_{jj}}$$

where s_ϵ is the standard deviation from the regression equation and v_{jj} is the entry in row $j + 1$, column $j + 1$ of $(X'X)^{-1}$

$$(X'X)^{-1} = \begin{bmatrix} v_{00} & & & \\ & v_{11} & & \\ & & \ddots & \\ & & & v_{kk} \end{bmatrix}$$

Because the $(X'X)^{-1}$ matrix must be computed to obtain the $\hat{\beta}_j$'s, it is easy to get the estimated standard errors.

EXAMPLE 14.25   Calculate the residual standard deviation s_ϵ and the estimated standard errors of $\hat{\beta}_0$, $\hat{\beta}_1$, and $\hat{\beta}_2$ for the data of Example 14.22.

Solution   From Example 14.23, we know that SS(Residual) = 4 with d.f. $= n - (k + 1) = 4 - (2 + 1) = 1$, so MS(Residual) $= 4/[4 - (2 + 1)] = 4$ and $s_\epsilon = \sqrt{\text{MS(Residual)}} = 2.0$. The $(\mathbf{X'X})^{-1}$ matrix is

$$\begin{bmatrix} .25 & 0 & 0 \\ 0 & .0625 & 0 \\ 0 & 0 & .01 \end{bmatrix}$$

so the standard errors for $\hat{\beta}_0$, $\hat{\beta}_1$, and $\hat{\beta}_2$ are, respectively,

$$s_{\hat{\beta}_0} = 2.0\sqrt{.25} = 1.0$$
$$s_{\hat{\beta}_1} = 2.0\sqrt{.0625} = .50$$
$$s_{\hat{\beta}_2} = 2.0\sqrt{.01} = 0.20$$ ∎

One other use of matrix notation occurs when a multiple regression model is used to estimate the expected value of Y at new settings of the x's or to predict an individual value of Y at new settings of the x's. In Chapter 13, standard errors were shown for the linear regression case. These standard errors involve the residual standard deviation, the sample size, and an extrapolation penalty. The matrix notation formulas for these standard errors once again involve the $(\mathbf{X'X})^{-1}$ matrix. We designate the future value of Y and $E(Y)$ as Y_{n+1} and $E(Y_{n+1})$, respectively.

Standard Error for Estimating $E(Y_{n+1})$

$$s_{\hat{Y}_{n+1}} = s_\epsilon\sqrt{\mathbf{X}_{n+1}(\mathbf{X'X})^{-1}\mathbf{X}_{n+1}}$$

where

$$\mathbf{X}_{n+1} = \begin{bmatrix} 1 \\ x_{n+1,\,1} \\ x_{n+1,\,2} \\ \vdots \\ x_{n+1,\,k} \end{bmatrix}$$

is the vector of settings of the independent variables at which $E(Y_{n+1})$ is to be predicted.

Standard Error for Predicting Y_{n+1}

$$s_{\hat{Y}_{n+1}} = s_\epsilon\sqrt{1 + \mathbf{X}'_{n+1}(\mathbf{X'X})^{-1}\mathbf{X}_{n+1}}$$

When each x_j is equal to its sample mean $\bar{x}_j$, the term $\mathbf{X}'_{n+1}(\mathbf{X}'\mathbf{X})^{-1}\mathbf{X}_{n+1}$ reduces to $1/n$. Otherwise there is an extrapolation penalty.

EXAMPLE 14.26   Find standard errors for $E(Y_{n+1})$ and Y_{n+1} for the data of Example 14.22.

a. Assume that x_1 and x_2 are both zero (that is, when $x_{n+1,1} = \bar{x}_1$ and $x_{n+1,2} = \bar{x}_2$).
b. Examine the extrapolation penalty when $x_{n+1,1} = 1$ and $x_{n+1,2} = 6$.

Solution   The residual standard deviation was found to be $s_\epsilon = 2.0$. The desired $\mathbf{X}_{n+1}$ vector is

$$\mathbf{X}_{n+1} = \begin{bmatrix} 1 \\ x_{n+1,1} \\ x_{n+1,2} \end{bmatrix} = \begin{bmatrix} 1 \\ 0 \\ 0 \end{bmatrix}$$

Thus

$$\mathbf{X}'_{n+1}(\mathbf{X}'\mathbf{X})^{-1}\mathbf{X}_{n+1} = \begin{bmatrix} 1 & 0 & 0 \end{bmatrix} \begin{bmatrix} .25 & 0 & 0 \\ 0 & .0625 & 0 \\ 0 & 0 & .01 \end{bmatrix} \begin{bmatrix} 1 \\ 0 \\ 0 \end{bmatrix} = .25 = \frac{1}{n}$$

The standard errors for estimating $E(Y_{n+1})$ and predicting Y_{n+1} are, respectively,

$$2.0\sqrt{.25} = 1.0$$

and

$$2.0\sqrt{1 + .25} = 2.236$$

b. For $x_{n+1,1} = 1$ and $x_{n+1,2} = 6$,

$$\mathbf{X}_{n+1} = \begin{bmatrix} 1 \\ 1 \\ 6 \end{bmatrix}$$

and

$$\mathbf{X}'_{n+1}(\mathbf{X}'\mathbf{X})^{-1}\mathbf{X}_{n+1} = \begin{bmatrix} 1 & 1 & 6 \end{bmatrix} \begin{bmatrix} .25 & 0 & 0 \\ 0 & .0625 & 0 \\ 0 & 0 & .01 \end{bmatrix} \begin{bmatrix} 1 \\ 1 \\ 6 \end{bmatrix} = .6725$$

Thus the estimated standard errors for estimating $E(Y_{n+1})$ and predicting Y_{n+1} when $x_{n+1,1}$ 1 and $x_{n+1,2} = 6$ are, respectively,

$$2.0\sqrt{.6725} = 1.6401$$

and

$$2.0\sqrt{1 + .6725} = 2.5865$$

Note that these errors are larger than their counterparts when there is no extrapolation. ∎

SECTION 14.6   EXERCISES

14.17 The effects of temperature settings and lighting levels on office productivity are studied. The variables are y, a measure of work production; x_1, office temperature $-68°$; and x_2, lighting level -60. The data are

y:	43	42	49	39	47	57	46	48	53
x_1:	-4	-4	-4	-2	-2	-2	0	0	0
x_2:	-5	0	5	-5	0	5	-5	0	5

y:	49	51	63	56	54	64
x_1:	2	2	2	4	4	4
x_2:	-5	0	5	-5	0	5

a. Write the **X** matrix and **Y** vector for these data.
b. Verify that

$$\mathbf{X'X} = \begin{bmatrix} 15 & 0 & 0 \\ 0 & 120 & 0 \\ 0 & 0 & 250 \end{bmatrix} \quad \text{and} \quad \mathbf{X'Y} = \begin{bmatrix} 761 \\ 200 \\ 265 \end{bmatrix}$$

c. Calculate the $\hat{\boldsymbol{\beta}}$ vector.

14.18 Refer to the data of Exercise 14.17.
a. Calculate $\mathbf{Y'Y}$
b. Calculate SS(Residual) $= \mathbf{Y'Y} - \hat{\boldsymbol{\beta}}'(\mathbf{X'Y})$.
c. Calculate s_ϵ. The d.f. for SS(Residual) is $n - 3 = 12$.

14.19 Refer to the data of Exercise 14.17.
a. Calculate the value of the F statistic.
b. Can we reject the null hypothesis that neither x_1 nor x_2 has predictive value? Use $\alpha = .01$.

14.20 Perform t tests for the partial slope coefficients $\hat{\beta}_1$ and $\hat{\beta}_2$ in Exercise 14.17. What conclusion follows from each test?

14.21 In a small regression study, the following data are observed:

y:	15	18	12	13	19	17	16	25	20	21	26	21	22	20	29	26
x_1:	-3	-2	-2	-1	-1	-1	0	0	0	0	1	1	1	2	2	3
x_2:	-5	-3	-3	-2	-2	-1	-1	0	0	1	1	2	2	3	3	5

a. Verify that

$$\mathbf{X'X} = \begin{bmatrix} 16 & 0 & 0 \\ 0 & 40 & 64 \\ 0 & 64 & 106 \end{bmatrix} \quad \text{and} \quad \mathbf{X'Y} = \begin{bmatrix} 320 \\ 91 \\ 148 \end{bmatrix}$$

b. Calculate the least-squares coefficient vector $\hat{\boldsymbol{\beta}}$.
c. Calculate the residual standard deviation.

14.22 Refer to the data of Exercise 14.21.
a. Calculate the estimated standard errors of $\hat{\beta}_1$ and $\hat{\beta}_2$.
b. Calculate 90% confidence intervals for β_1 and β_2.
c. Test the hypothesis that $\beta_1 > 0$. Use $\alpha = .05$.

14.23 Refer to Exercise 14.21.
a. Calculate SS(Regression), SS(Residual), and SS(Total).
b. Calculate $R^2_{y \cdot x_1 x_2}$.
c. Test $H_0: \beta_1 = \beta_2 = 0$ at $\alpha = .01$.

14.24 Refer to Exercise 14.21.
  a. Predict Y when $x_{n+1,1} = 2$ and $x_{n+1,2} = 3$.
  b. Give a 90% prediction interval for the prediction in part (a).
  c. Predict Y when $x_{n+1,1} = 2$ and $x_{n+1,2} = -3$.
  d. Give a 90% prediction interval for the prediction in part (c).

Summary

In this chapter we introduced the multiple regression model

$$Y = \beta_0 + \beta_1 x_1 + \beta_2 x_2 + \cdots + \beta_k x_k + \epsilon$$

where β_0 is the intercept and $\beta_1, \ldots, \beta_k$ are the partial slopes.

Many inferences are possible using sample data and a multiple regression equation. We can make an overall F test of the null hypothesis

$$H_0: \beta_1 = \beta_2 = \cdots = \beta_k = 0$$

Or, in other words, we can test the null hypothesis that none of the independent variables contributes to the prediction of y. We can also be more specific. The sample data can be used to test $H_0: \beta_j = 0$ or to place a confidence interval about the parameter β_j. These last two inferences relate to a single β and focus on the contribution of an individual predictor variable when entered last.

Not all inferences related to a multiple regression equation can be phrased in terms of all the x's or a single x. Sometimes we much consider the contribution of a subset of predictor variables. We discussed an F test of the null hypothesis that a subset of $(k - g)$ β's are identically zero $(g < k)$.

Finally, in this chapter we expanded on the interpretation of the coefficient of determination and we presented the important concepts of forecasting (with a corresponding prediction error) using a multiple regression. We discussed briefly the underlying mathematics of multiple regression using matrix notation.

KEY FORMULAS: Multiple Regression

1. Multiple regression model

$$Y_i = \beta_0 + \beta_1 x_{i1} + \beta_2 x_{i2} + \cdots + \beta_k x_{ik} + \epsilon_i$$

2. $SS(\text{Residual}) = \sum y_i^2 - \hat{\beta}_0 \sum y_i - \hat{\beta}_1 \sum x_{i1} y_i - \hat{\beta}_2 \sum x_{i2} y_i$
$$- \cdots - \hat{\beta}_k \sum x_{ik} y_i$$

3. $s_\epsilon = \sqrt{MS(\text{Residual})} = \sqrt{SS(\text{Residual})/[n - (k + 1)]}$

4. Coefficient of determination

$$R^2_{Y \cdot x_1 x_2 \cdots x_k} = \frac{SS(\text{Total}) - SS(\text{Residual})}{SS(\text{Total})}$$

5. F test for $\beta_1, \ldots, \beta_k$

$$H_0: \beta_1 = \beta_2 = \cdots = \beta_k = 0$$

T.S.: $F = \dfrac{\text{MS(Regression)}}{\text{MS(Residual)}}$

where $\text{d.f.}_1 = k$ and $\text{d.f.}_2 = n - (k + 1)$

6. Estimated standard error of $\hat{\beta}_j$

$$s_{\hat{\beta}_j} = s_\epsilon \sqrt{\dfrac{1}{\sum (x_{ij} - \bar{x}_j)^2 (1 - R^2_{x_j \cdot x_1 \cdots x_{j-1} x_{j+1} \cdots x_k})}}$$

7. $100(1 - \alpha)\%$ confidence interval for β_j

$$\hat{\beta}_j \pm t_{\alpha/2} s_{\hat{\beta}_j}$$

8. Statistical test for β_j

$$H_0: \beta_j = 0$$

T.S.: $t = \dfrac{\hat{\beta}_j}{s_{\hat{\beta}_j}}$, where $\text{d.f.} = n - (k + 1)$

9. F test for $\beta_1, \ldots, \beta_k$ based on R^2

$$H_0: \beta_1 = \beta_2 = \cdots = \beta_k = 0$$

T.S.: $F = \dfrac{\text{MS(Regression)}}{\text{MS(Residual)}} = \dfrac{R^2_{y \cdot x_1 \cdots x_k}/k}{(1 - R^2_{y \cdot x_1 \cdots x_k})/[n - (k + 1)]}$

10. F test for a set of β's

$$H_0: \beta_{g+1} = \beta_{g+2} = \cdots = \beta_k = 0$$

T.S.: $F = \dfrac{(R^2_{\text{complete}} - R^2_{\text{reduced}})/(k - g)}{(1 - R^2_{\text{complete}})/[n - (k + 1)]}$

11. Formulas using matrices

$$\hat{\boldsymbol{\beta}} = (\mathbf{X'X})^{-1}\mathbf{X'Y}$$

$$\text{SS(Residual)} = \mathbf{Y'Y} - \hat{\boldsymbol{\beta}}'\mathbf{X'Y}$$

$$s_{\hat{\beta}_j} = s_\epsilon \sqrt{v_{jj}}$$

$s_{\hat{Y}_{n+1}} = s_\epsilon \sqrt{\mathbf{X}'_{n+1}(\mathbf{X'X})^{-1}\mathbf{X}_{n+1}}$ for estimating $E(Y_{n+1})$

$s_{\hat{Y}_{n+1}} = s_\epsilon \sqrt{1 + \mathbf{X}'_{n+1}(\mathbf{X'X})^{-1}\mathbf{X}_{n+1}}$ for predicting Y_{n+1}

CHAPTER 14   EXERCISES

14.25 A study of demand for imported subcompact cars consists of data from 12 metropolitan areas. The variables are

DEMAND: Imported subcompact car sales as a percentage of total sales
EDUC: Average number of years of schooling completed by adults
INCOME: Per capita income

POPN: Area population
FAMSIZE: Average size of intact families

BMDP output is shown below:

| MULTIPLE R | 0.9811 | STD. ERROR OF EST. | 2.6863 |
| MULTIPLE R-SQUARE | 0.9625 | | |

ANALYSIS OF VARIANCE

	SUM OF SQUARES	DF	MEAN SQUARE	F RATIO	P(TAIL)
REGRESSION	1295.7041	4	323.9260	44.890	0.0000
RESIDUAL	50.5125	7	7.2161		

VARIABLE		COEFFICIENT	STD. ERROR	STD. REG COEFF	T	P(2 TAIL)	TOLERANCE
INTERCEPT		-1.31949					
EDUC	2	5.54983	2.70228	0.446	2.054	0.0791	0.11363
INCOME	3	0.88514	1.30846	0.099	0.676	0.5205	0.25194
POPN	4	1.92483	1.37081	0.131	1.404	0.2031	0.61124
FAMSIZE	5	-11.38928	6.66931	-0.438	-1.708	0.1314	0.08156

   a. Write the regression equation. Place the standard error of each coefficient below the coefficient, perhaps in parentheses.
   b. Locate R^2 and the residual standard deviation.

14.26 Summarize the conclusions of the F test and the various t tests in the output of Exercise 14.25.

14.27 Another analysis of the data of Exercise 14.25 uses only EDUC and FAMSIZE to predict DEMAND. The output is shown below:

| MULTIPLE R | 0.9707 | STD. ERROR OF EST. | 2.9389 |
| MULTIPLE R-SQUARE | 0.9423 | | |

ANALYSIS OF VARIANCE

	SUM OF SQUARES	DF	MEAN SQUARE	F RATIO	P(TAIL)
REGRESSION	1268.4828	2	634.2414	73.432	0.0000
RESIDUAL	77.7338	9	8.6371		

VARIABLE		COEFFICIENT	STD. ERROR	STD. REG COEFF	T	P(2 TAIL)	TOLERANCE
INTERCEPT		-19.16498					
EDUC	2	7.79256	2.49031	0.626	3.129	0.0121	0.16014
FAMSIZE	5	-9.46411	5.20709	-0.364	-1.818	0.1025	0.16014

   a. Locate the R^2 value for this reduced model.
   b. Test the null hypothesis that the true coefficients of INCOME and POPN are zero. Use $\alpha = .05$. What is the conclusion?

14.28 The manager of documentation for a computer software firm wants to forecast the time required to document moderate-size computer programs. Records are available for 26 programs. The variables are y = number of writer-days needed, x_1 = number of subprograms, x_2 = average number of lines per subprogram, $x_3 = x_1 x_2$, $x_4 = x_2^2$, and $x_5 = x_1 x_2^2$. A portion of the output from a regression analysis (SAS) of the data is shown below:

MODELS PROCEDURE

DEPENDENT VARIABLE: Y

SOURCE	DF	SUM OF SQUARES	MEAN SQUARE	F VALUE	PR > F	R-SQUARE	C.V.
MODEL	5	2546.02735209	509.20547042	44.31	0.0001	0.917195	11.9597
ERROR	20	229.85726330	11.49286316		ROOT MSE		Y MEAN
CORRECTED TOTAL	25	2775.88461538			3.39011256		28.34615385

PARAMETER	ESTIMATE	T FOR H0: PARAMETER=0	PR > |T|	STD ERROR OF ESTIMATE
INTERCEPT	-16.81979712	-1.45	0.1636	11.63104920
X1	1.47018752	4.02	0.0007	0.36594367
X2	0.99477822	1.63	0.1194	0.61144114
X1X2	-0.02400705	-1.01	0.3243	0.02375645
X2SQ	-0.01031004	-1.40	0.1774	0.00737400
X1X2SQ	0.00024957	0.71	0.4862	0.00035178

a. Write the multiple regression model and locate the residual standard deviation.

b. What does the variable x_3 represent in terms of the problem?

c. Does x_3 have a statistically significant predictive value as "last predictor in"?

14.29 The model $Y = \beta_0 + \beta_1 x_1 + \beta_2 x_2 + \epsilon$ is fit to the data of Exercise 14.28. Selected output is shown here:

DEPENDENT VARIABLE: Y

SOURCE	DF	SUM OF SQUARES	MEAN SQUARE	F VALUE	PR > F	R-SQUARE	C.V.
MODEL	2	2516.12160091	1258.06080045	111.39	0.0001	0.906422	11.8558
ERROR	23	259.76301448	11.29404411		ROOT MSE		Y MEAN
CORRECTED TOTAL	25	2775.88461538			3.36066126		28.34615385

PARAMETER	ESTIMATE	T FOR H0: PARAMETER=0	PR > |T|	STD ERROR OF ESTIMATE
INTERCEPT	0.84008527	0.24	0.8089	3.43374955
X1	1.01583472	12.81	0.0001	0.07929252
X2	0.05582624	1.08	0.2897	0.05150660

a. Write the complete and reduced-form estimated models.

b. Is the improvement in R^2 obtained by adding x_3, x_4, and x_5 statistically significant at $\alpha = .05$? What is the p-value for this test?

14.30 A chain of small convenience food stores performs a regression analysis to explain variation in sales volume among 16 stores. The variables in the study are

SALES: Average daily sales volume of a store, in thousands of dollars

SIZE: Floor space in thousands of square feet

PARKING: Number of free parking spaces adjacent to the store

INCOME: Estimated per household income of the ZIP code area of the store

Output from a regression program is shown at the top of page 645.

a. Write down the regression equation. Indicate the standard errors of the coefficients.

b. Carefully interpret each coefficient.

c. Locate R^2 and the residual standard deviation.

MULTIPLE R		0.8895	STD. ERROR OF EST.		0.7724		
MULTIPLE R-SQUARE		0.7912					

ANALYSIS OF VARIANCE

		SUM OF SQUARES	DF	MEAN SQUARE	F RATIO	P(TAIL)
	REGRESSION	27.1296	3	9.0432	15.158	0.0002
	RESIDUAL	7.1592	12	0.5966		

VARIABLE		COEFFICIENT	STD. ERROR	STD. REG COEFF	T	P(2 TAIL)	TOLERANCE
INTERCEPT		0.87272					
SIZE	2	2.54794	1.20083	0.385	2.122	0.0554	0.52842
PARKING	3	0.22028	0.15539	0.249	1.418	0.1817	0.56477
INCOME	4	0.58932	0.17806	0.479	3.310	0.0062	0.83117

14.31 Summarize the results of the F and t tests for the output of Exercise 14.30.

14.32 A producer of various feed additives for cattle conducts a study of the number of days of feedlot time required to bring beef cattle to market weight. Eighteen steers of essentially identical age and weight are purchased and brought to a feedlot. Each steer is fed a diet with a specific combination of protein content, antibiotic concentration, and percentage of feed supplement. The data are

STEER:	1	2	3	4	5	6	7	8	9
PROTEIN:	10	10	10	10	10	10	15	15	15
ANTIBIO:	1	1	1	2	2	2	1	1	1
SUPPLEM:	3	5	7	3	5	7	3	5	7
TIME:	88	82	81	82	83	75	80	80	75

STEER:	10	11	12	13	14	15	16	17	18
PROTEIN:	15	15	15	20	20	20	20	20	20
ANTIBIO:	2	2	2	1	1	1	2	2	2
SUPPLEM:	3	5	7	3	5	7	3	5	7
TIME:	77	76	72	79	74	75	74	70	69

Computer output from a regression analysis follows:

MULTIPLE R		0.9490	STD. ERROR OF EST.		1.7096	
MULTIPLE R-SQUARE		0.9007				

ANALYSIS OF VARIANCE

		SUM OF SQUARES	DF	MEAN SQUARE	F RATIO	P(TAIL)
	REGRESSION	371.0832	3	123.6944	42.323	0.0000
	RESIDUAL	40.9166	14	2.9226		

VARIABLE		COEFFICIENT	STD. ERROR	STD. REG COEFF	T	P(2 TAIL)	TOLERANCE
INTERCEPT		102.70834					
PROTEIN	2	-0.83333	0.09870	-0.711	-8.443	0.0000	1.00000
ANTIBIO	3	-4.00000	0.80590	-0.418	-4.963	0.0002	1.00000
SUPPLEM	4	-1.37500	0.24675	-0.469	-5.572	0.0001	1.00000

    a. Write down the regression equation.
    b. Find the standard deviation.
    c. Find the R^2 value.

14.33 Refer to Exercise 14.32.
   a. Predict the feedlot time required for a steer fed 15% protein, 1.5% antibiotic concentration, and 5% supplement.
   b. Do these values of the independent variables represent a major extrapolation from the data?
   c. Give a 95% confidence interval for the mean time predicted in part (a).

14.34 The data of Exercise 14.32 are also analyzed by a regression model using only protein content as an independent variable, with the following output:

MULTIPLE R	0.7111	STD. ERROR OF EST.	3.5678
MULTIPLE R-SQUARE	0.5057		

ANALYSIS OF VARIANCE

	SUM OF SQUARES	DF	MEAN SQUARE	F RATIO	P(TAIL)
REGRESSION	208.3332	1	208.3332	16.367	0.0009
RESIDUAL	203.6667	16	12.7292		

VARIABLE	COEFFICIENT	STD. ERROR	STD. REG COEFF	T	P(2 TAIL)	TOLERANCE
INTERCEPT	89.83334					
PROTEIN 2	-0.83333	0.20599	-0.711	-4.046	0.0009	1.00000

   a. Write the regression equation.
   b. Find the R^2 value.
   c. Test the null hypothesis that the coefficients of ANTIBIO and SUPPLEM are zero at $\alpha = .05$.

14.35 A sex discrimination suit alleges that a small college discriminated in salaries against women. A regression study considers the following variables:

SALARY: Base salary per year (thousands of dollars)
SENIOR: Seniority at the college (years)
SEX: 1 for men, 0 for women
RANKD1:   1 for full professors, 0 for others
RANKD2:   1 for associate professors, 0 for others
RANKD3:   1 for assistant professors, 0 for others
DOCT: 1 for holders of doctorate, 0 for others

Note that lecturers and instructors have value 0 for all 3 RANKD variables. Computer output from the study is shown below:

ANALYSIS OF VARIANCE

SOURCE	DF	SUM OF SQUARES	MEAN SQUARE	F VALUE	PROB>F
MODEL	6	2119.347	353.2245	64.646	0.0001
ERROR	23	125.6717	5.463985		
C TOTAL	29	2245.019			

ROOT MSE	2.337517	R-SQUARE	0.9440	
DEP MEAN	31.92667	ADJ R-SQ	0.9294	
C.V.	7.321519			

PARAMETER ESTIMATES

VARIABLE	DF	PARAMETER ESTIMATE	STANDARD ERROR	T FOR H0: PARAMETER=0	PROB > |T|
INTERCEP	1	18.67841	1.378787	13.547	0.0001
SENIOR	1	0.5420351	0.07615423	7.118	0.0001
SEX	1	1.207423	1.064854	1.134	0.2685
RANKD1	1	8.777947	1.93803	4.529	0.0001
RANKD2	1	4.421096	1.779685	2.484	0.0207
RANKD3	1	2.716527	1.423856	1.908	0.0690
DOCT	1	0.9224809	1.258893	0.733	0.4711

    a. Write down the regression equation.

    b. What is the interpretation of the coefficient of SEX?

    c. What is the interpretation of the coefficient of RANKD1?

14.36 Refer to Exercise 14.35.

    a. Test the hypothesis that the coefficient of SEX is positive. Use $\alpha = .05$.

    b. What does the conclusion of this test indicate about allegations of discrimination?

14.37 a. Locate the value of the F statistic in Exercise 14.35.

    b. What null hypothesis is being tested by this statistic?

    c. Is this null hypothesis rejected at $\alpha = .01$? How plausible is this null hypothesis?

14.38 Another regression model of the data of Exercise 14.35 omits SEX and DOCT from the list of independent variables. The output is shown below:

SOURCE	DF	SUM OF SQUARES	MEAN SQUARE	F VALUE	PROB>F
MODEL	4	2110.925	527.7313	98.389	0.0001
ERROR	25	134.0934	5.363737		
C TOTAL	29	2245.019			

ROOT MSE	2.315974	R-SQUARE	0.9403	
DEP MEAN	31.92667	ADJ R-SQ	0.9307	
C.V.	7.254044			

PARAMETER ESTIMATES

VARIABLE	DF	PARAMETER ESTIMATE	STANDARD ERROR	T FOR H0: PARAMETER=0	PROB > |T|
INTERCEP	1	19.71134	1.077636	18.291	0.0001
SENIOR	1	0.5571643	0.07439458	7.489	0.0001
RANKD1	1	9.241436	1.821404	5.074	0.0001
RANKD2	1	5.105024	1.587501	3.216	0.0036
RANKD3	1	3.224291	1.32044	2.442	0.0220

    a. Locate R^2 for this reduced model.

    b. Test the null hypothesis that the true coefficients of SEX and DOCT are zero. Use $\alpha = .01$.

14.39 A survey of information systems managers was used to predict the yearly salary of beginning programmer/analysts in a metropolitan area. Managers specified their standard salary for a beginning programmer/analyst, the number of employees in the firm's information processing staff, the firm's gross profit margin in cents per dollar of sales, and the firm's information processing cost as a percentage of total administrative costs. The data are stored in the 'CH14C1.DAT' file on the data disk, with salary in column 1, number of employees in column 2, profit margin in column 3, and information processing cost in column 4.

   a. Obtain a multiple regression equation with salary as the dependent variable and the other three variables as predictors. Interpret each of the (partial) slope coefficients.

   b. Is there conclusive evidence that the three predictors together have at least some value in predicting salary? Locate a p-value for the appropriate test.

   c. Which of the independent variables, if any, have statistically detectable ($\alpha = .05$) predictive value as the "last predictor in" the equation?

14.40 a. Locate the coefficient of determination (R^2) for the regression model in Exercise 14.39.

   b. Obtain another regression model with number of employees as the only independent variable. Find the coefficient of determination for this model.

   c. By hand, test the null hypothesis that adding profit margin and information processing cost does not yield any additional predictive value, given the information about number of employees. Use $\alpha = .10$. What can you conclude from this test?

14.41 Obtain correlations for all pairs of predictor variables in Exercise 14.39. Does there seem to be a major collinearity problem in the data?

14.42 A government agency pays research contractors a fee to cover overhead costs, over and above the direct costs of a research project. Although the overhead cost varies considerably among contracts, it is usually a substantial share of the total contract cost. An agency task force obtained data on overhead cost as a fraction of direct costs, number of employees of the contractor, size of contract as a percentage of the contractor's yearly income, and personnel costs as a percentage of direct cost. These four variables are stored (in the order given) in the 'CH14C2.DAT' file on the data disk.

   a. Obtain correlations of all pairs of variables. Is there a severe collinearity problem with the data?

   b. Plot overhead cost against each of the other variables. Locate a possible high-influence outlier.

   c. Obtain a regression equation (overhead cost as dependent variable) using all the data including any potential outlier.

   d. Delete the potential outlier and get a revised regression equation. How much did the slopes change?

14.43 Consider the outlier-deleted regression model of Exercise 14.42.

   a. Locate the F statistic. What null hypothesis is being tested? What can we conclude based on the F statistic?

   b. Locate the t statistic for each independent variable. What conclusions can we reach based on the t tests?

14.44 Use the outlier-deleted data of Exercise 14.42 to predict overhead cost of a contract when the contractor has 500 employees, the contract is 2.50% of the contractor's income, and personnel cost is 55% of the direct cost. Obtain a 95% prediction interval. Would an overhead cost equal to 88.9% of direct cost be unreasonable in this situation?

14.45 The owner of a rapidly growing computer store tried to explain the increase in biweekly sales of computer software, using four explanatory variables: Number of titles displayed, display footage, current customer base of IBM compatible computers, and current customer base of Apple compatible computers. The data are stored in time series order in the 'CH14C3.DAT' file of the data disk, with sales in column 1, titles in 2, footage in 3, IBM base in 4, and Apple base in 5.

    a. Before doing the calculations, consider the economics of the situation and state what sign you would expect for each of the partial slopes.

    b. Obtain a multiple regression equation with sales as the dependent variable and all other variables as independent. Does each partial slope have the sign you expected in part (a)?

    c. Calculate a 95% confidence interval for the coefficient of the titles variable. The computer output should contain the calculated standard error for this coefficient. Does the interval include 0 as a plausible value?

14.46 a. In the regression model of Exercise 14.45, can the null hypothesis that none of the variables have predictive value be rejected at normal α levels?

    b. According to t tests, which predictors, if any, add statistically detectable predictive value ($\alpha = .05$) given all the others?

14.47 Obtain correlation coefficients for all pairs of variables from the data of Exercise 14.45. How severe is the collinearity problem in the data?

14.48 Compare the coefficient of determination (R^2) for the regression model of Exercise 14.45 to the square of the correlation between sales and titles in Exercise 14.47. Compute the incremental F statistic for testing the null hypothesis that footage, IBM base, and Apple base add no predictive value, given titles. Can this hypothesis be rejected at $\alpha = .01$?

CASE   Multiple Regression

Engineers for a manufacturer of power tools for home use were trying to design an electric drill that didn't heat up under strenuous use. The three key design factors are insulation thickness, quality of the wire used in the motor, and size of the vents in the body of the drill. The engineers had learned a little about off-line quality control, so they designed an experiment that varied these design factors. They created 10 drills using each combination of the three design factors, split them into two lots, and tested the lots under two (supposedly equivalent) "torture tests." The temperature of each drill was measured at the end of each test; for each lot, the mean temperature and the logarithm of the variance of temperatures were computed. The engineers wanted to minimize both the mean and (the logarithm of) the variance.

    The engineers have asked you to analyze the resulting data. They present you with the following data and explain that they included squared terms to try to capture any curves in the relation. Average temperature is "avtem," logarithm of variance is "logv," insulation thickness is IT, quality of wire is QW, vent size is VS, and the "2" variables are the respective squared terms. The squared terms are of the form

$$(\text{predictor} - \text{mean of predictor})^2$$

They have asked you to try to figure out which of the predictors seem to affect the mean (and by how much), which affect the variance, which squared terms seem to matter, and finally whether the lot number (corresponding to the type of test) is relevant. They don't know any statistical jargon, so please write your report without it.

avtem	logv	IT	QW	VS	I2	Q2	V2	lot
185	3.6	2	6	10	4	1	1	1
176	3.7	2	6	10	4	1	1	2
177	3.6	2	6	11	4	1	0	1
184	3.7	2	6	11	4	1	0	2
178	3.6	2	6	12	4	1	1	1
169	3.4	2	6	12	4	1	1	2
185	3.2	2	7	10	4	0	1	1
184	3.2	2	7	10	4	0	1	2
180	3.2	2	7	11	4	0	0	1
184	3.5	2	7	11	4	0	0	2
179	3.0	2	7	12	4	0	1	1
173	3.2	2	7	12	4	0	1	2
179	2.9	2	8	10	4	1	1	1
185	2.7	2	8	10	4	1	1	2
180	2.8	2	8	11	4	1	0	1
180	2.7	2	8	11	4	1	0	2
169	2.9	2	8	12	4	1	1	1
177	2.8	2	8	12	4	1	1	2
172	3.6	3	6	10	1	1	1	1
171	3.9	3	6	10	1	1	1	2
172	3.8	3	6	11	1	1	0	1
167	3.6	3	6	11	1	1	0	2
165	3.3	3	6	12	1	1	1	1
159	3.4	3	6	12	1	1	1	2
169	3.0	3	7	10	1	0	1	1
174	3.3	3	7	10	1	0	1	2
163	3.3	3	7	11	1	0	0	1
170	3.3	3	7	11	1	0	0	2
169	3.2	3	7	12	1	0	1	1
163	3.2	3	7	12	1	0	1	2
178	2.7	3	8	10	1	1	1	1
165	2.7	3	8	10	1	1	1	2
167	2.8	3	8	11	1	1	0	1
171	2.8	3	8	11	1	1	0	2
166	2.9	3	8	12	1	1	1	1
166	2.7	3	8	12	1	1	1	2
161	3.7	4	6	10	0	1	1	1
162	3.7	4	6	10	0	1	1	2
169	3.4	4	6	11	0	1	0	1
162	3.7	4	6	11	0	1	0	2
159	3.5	4	6	12	0	1	1	1
168	3.4	4	6	12	0	1	1	2
169	3.1	4	7	10	0	0	1	1
165	3.2	4	7	10	0	0	1	2
163	3.2	4	7	11	0	0	0	1
168	3.4	4	7	11	0	0	0	2
160	2.9	4	7	12	0	0	1	1
154	3.1	4	7	12	0	0	1	2
169	2.8	4	8	10	0	1	1	1
156	2.9	4	8	10	0	1	1	2
168	2.7	4	8	11	0	1	0	1
161	2.7	4	8	11	0	1	0	2
156	2.6	4	8	12	0	1	1	1
158	2.7	4	8	12	0	1	1	2
164	3.7	5	6	10	1	1	1	1
163	3.7	5	6	10	1	1	1	2
161	3.7	5	6	11	1	1	0	1
158	3.4	5	6	11	1	1	0	2
154	3.4	5	6	12	1	1	1	1
162	3.7	5	6	12	1	1	1	2
163	2.8	5	7	10	1	0	1	1
166	3.0	5	7	10	1	0	1	2
159	3.3	5	7	11	1	0	0	1
156	3.3	5	7	11	1	0	0	2
152	3.3	5	7	12	1	0	1	1
150	3.3	5	7	12	1	0	1	2
165	2.9	5	8	10	1	1	1	1
156	2.7	5	8	10	1	1	1	2
155	2.8	5	8	11	1	1	0	1
155	3.2	5	8	11	1	1	0	2
149	2.6	5	8	12	1	1	1	1
152	2.9	5	8	12	1	1	1	2
165	3.4	6	6	10	4	1	1	1
160	3.7	6	6	10	4	1	1	2
157	3.7	6	6	11	4	1	0	1
149	3.7	6	6	11	4	1	0	2
149	3.8	6	6	12	4	1	1	1
145	3.7	6	6	12	4	1	1	2
154	3.4	6	7	10	4	0	1	1
153	3.2	6	7	10	4	0	1	2
150	3.0	6	7	11	4	0	0	1
156	3.1	6	7	11	4	0	0	2
146	3.2	6	7	12	4	0	1	1
153	3.3	6	7	12	4	0	1	2
161	2.8	6	8	10	4	1	1	1
160	2.9	6	8	10	4	1	1	2
156	2.9	6	8	11	4	1	0	1
150	2.7	6	8	11	4	1	0	2
149	2.9	6	8	12	4	1	1	1
151	2.8	6	8	12	4	1	1	2

CONSTRUCTING A MULTIPLE REGRESSION MODEL

This chapter presents some suggestions for actually creating a useful multiple regression model. It is, we hope, a practical chapter that builds on and extends the material of Chapter 14.

four steps in a multiple regression study

A typical multiple regression study passes through at least four steps. First, we select potentially useful predictor (independent) variables. Qualitative variables can be incorporated by the "dummy variable" device that we discuss in Section 15.2. Additional variables may be created (in time-series data) by lagging independent variables; we discuss this process in Section 15.3. The second step is tentative selection of plausible forms for the multiple regression model. This may require transformation or combination of either the dependent variable or the independent variables, as we discuss in Section 15.4. The third step, which usually requires fitting several candidate models, is the selection of a particular model that is appropriate and useful for the given situation. This step may be done simply by comparing the results of several models or, more elaborately, by the process of stepwise regression, which we discuss in Section 15.5. The fourth step is checking the selected model for potential violations of assumptions. At this step, the residuals (actual y values minus predicted y values) are examined for evidence of severe nonnormality or nonconstant variance, as we discuss in Section 15.6. If, in addition, the multiple regression model involves time-series data, it is also necessary to check the residuals for nonindependence (autocorrelation), as we discuss in Section 15.7. With luck, a satisfactory multiple regression model can be found by one pass through this four-step process. Usually, several passes are necessary.

We should ideally make a fifth step before the model is put into use. This step is checking the results of the model on new data, which we discuss in Section 15.8. This check is to confirm that the selected model has the indicated predictive value and that it is not merely an artifact of too much "data massaging."

Obviously, a great deal of calculating is required in the process of selecting a model, and access to statistical software programs is a practical necessity.

15.1   SELECTING CANDIDATE INDEPENDENT VARIABLES
(Step 1)

Perhaps the most critical decision in constructing a multiple regression model is the initial selection of independent variables. In later sections of this chapter we consider many methods for refining a multiple regression analysis but first we must make a decision about which independent (x) variables to consider for inclusion and hence which data to gather. While initially it may appear that an optimum strategy might be to construct a monstrous multiple regression model with very many variables, these models are difficult to interpret and are much more costly from a data-gathering and computer-usage standpoint. How can a manager make a reasonable selection of initial variables to include in a regression analysis?

selection of the independent variables

Knowledge of the problem area is critically important in the initial selection of data. First, identify the dependent variable to be studied. Individuals who have had experience with this variable by observing it, trying to predict it, and trying to explain changes in it often have remarkably good insight as to what factors (independent variables) affect the variable. As a consequence, the first step involves consulting those who have the most experience with the dependent variable of interest. For example, suppose that the problem is to forecast the next quarter's sales volume of an inexpensive brand of computer printer for each of 40 districts. The dependent variable Y is then district sales volume. Certain independent variables, such as the advertising budget in each district and the number of sales outlets, are obvious candidates. A good district sales manager undoubtedly could suggest others.

collinearity

A major consideration in selecting predictor variables is the problem of **collinearity**, severely correlated independent variables (we discussed them in Sections 14.2 and 14.3). A partial slope in multiple regression estimates the predictive effect of changing one independent variable while holding all others constant. But when some or all of the predictors vary together, it can be almost impossible to separate out the predictive effects of each one. A common result when predictors are highly correlated is that the overall F test is highly significant but none of the individual t tests comes close to significance. The significant F result indicates only that there is detectable predictive value somewhere among the independent variables; the nonsignificant t values indicate that we can't detect **additional** predictive value for any variable, given all the others. The reason is that highly correlated predictors are surrogates for each other; any of them individually may be useful, but adding others will not be. When seriously collinear independent variables are all used in a multiple regression model, it can be virtually impossible to decide which predictors are in fact related to the dependent variable.

correlation matrix

There are several ways to assess the amount of collinearity in a set of independent variables. The simplest method is to look at a matrix of correlation coefficients, which can be produced by almost all computer packages. The higher these correlations, the more severe the collinearity problem is. In most situations, any correlation over .9 or so definitely indicates a serious problem. The correlation matrix may not reveal the full extent of the problem. Sometimes two predictors together predict a third all too well, even though either of the two by itself shows a more modest correlation with the third one. (Direct labor hours and indirect labor hours together predict total labor hours remarkably well, even if either one predicts the total imperfectly.) There are a number of more sophisticated ways of diagnosing collinearity built into various computer packages. The books by Cook and Weisberg (1982) and by Belsley, Kuh, and Welsch (1980) define several of them. The manuals for most statistical computer programs will indicate which of these can be computed and what the results indicate.

One of the best ways to avoid collinearity problems is to choose predictor variables intelligently, right at the beginning of a regression study. Try to find independent variables that should correlate decently with the dependent variable but do not have obvious correlations with each other. If possible, try to find independent variables that reflect various components of the dependent variable. For example, suppose that we want to predict the sales of inexpensive printers for personal computers in each of 40 sales districts. Total sales are made up of several sectors of buyers. We might identify the important sectors as college students, home users, small businesses, and computer network workstations. Therefore, we might well try number of college freshmen, household income, small business starts, and new network installations as independent variables. Each one makes sense as a predictor of printer sales, and there is no screamingly obvious correlation among the predictors. People who are knowledgable about the variable you want to predict can often identify separate components and suggest reasonable predictors for the different components.

EXAMPLE 15.1   A firm that sells and services minicomputers is concerned about the volume of service calls. The firm maintains several district service branches within each sales region, and computer owners requiring service call the nearest branch. The branches are staffed by technicians trained at the main office. The key problem is whether technicians should be assigned to main-office duty or to service branches; assignment decisions have to be made monthly. The required number of service-branch technicians grows in almost exact proportion to the number of service calls. Discussion with the service manager indicates that the key variables in determining the volume of service calls seem to be the number of computers in use, the number of new installations, whether or not a model change has been introduced recently, and the average temperature. (High temperatures, or possibly the associated high humidity, lead to more frequent computer troubles, especially in imperfectly air-conditioned offices.) Which of these variables can be expected to be correlated with each other?

Solution   It is hard to imagine why temperature should be correlated with any of the other variables. There should be some correlation between number of computers in use and number of new installations, if only because every new installation is a computer in use. Unless the firm has been growing at an increasing rate, we wouldn't expect a severe correlation (we would, however, like to see the data). The correlation of model change to number in use and new installations isn't at all obvious; surely data should be collected and correlations analyzed.   ∎

15.2 USING QUALITATIVE PREDICTORS: DUMMY VARIABLES (Step 1)

dummy variable

One special type of independent variable that could be included in the multiple regression model is the **dummy** or **indicator variable**. Such variables are used to represent qualitative (categorical) variables such as geographic region, type of incentive plan, or "protected-class" membership in a discrimination suit. The simplest dummy-variable situation occurs when the qualitative variable has only two categories, such as female-male or protected-not protected; then the dummy variable is defined by assigning one category of the qualitative variable the value 1, and the other the value 0. For example, suppose that y is the total production cost (in dollars) of a print run, x_1 is the number of items printed (in thousands of items), and x_2 is a dummy variable that equals 1 when the run is on a rush basis and 0 when it is on a regular basis. Assume that the multiple regression prediction equation is

$$\hat{y} = 86.2 + 5.1x_1 + 20.5x_2$$

The coefficient $\hat{\beta}_2 = 20.5$ of x_2 may be interpreted as the estimated difference in cost between a rush job ($x_2 = 1$) and a regular job ($x_2 = 0$) for any specified run size (x_1).

By substituting $x_2 = 1$ into the multiple regression prediction equation, we get an equation relating y to x_1 for rush jobs. The corresponding equation relating y to x_1 for regular jobs is obtained by substituting $x_2 = 0$.

Rush jobs: $\hat{y} = 86.2 + 5.1x_1 + 20.5(1) = 106.7 + 5.1x_1$
Regular jobs: $\hat{y} = 86.2 + 5.1x_1 + 20.5(0) = 86.2 + 5.1x_1$

Note that the two prediction equations (corresponding to $x_2 = 0$ or $x_2 = 1$) are parallel lines with different intercepts. These equations are shown in Figure 15.1.

If a qualitative variable can take on more than two levels, definition of the dummy variable is a bit more complicated. We do not want to code residence as $0 =$ urban, $1 =$ suburban, and $2 =$ rural and then use the resulting x in a regression. A one-unit increase in this x could mean either a change from urban to suburban or a change from suburban to rural. There is no reason to assume that the two possible changes would predict the same change in any y; the coefficient of such a variable wouldn't mean much. Instead, we could use two dummy variables to define residence: Define $x_1 = 1$ if residence $=$ suburban and $x_1 = 0$ otherwise, and define $x_2 = 1$ if residence $=$ rural and $x_2 = 0$ otherwise. If both

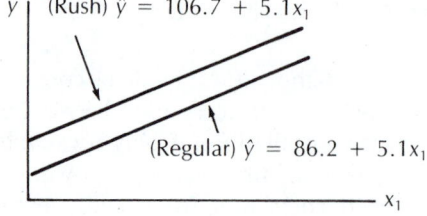

y | (Rush) $\hat{y} = 106.7 + 5.1x_1$

(Regular) $\hat{y} = 86.2 + 5.1x_1$

x_1

FIGURE 15.1   Effect of a Two-Value Dummy Variable

x_1 and x_2 are zero, it follows by elimination that residence = urban. In general, with this scheme, a qualitative variable with k categories can be coded using $k - 1$ dummy variables. If all $k - 1$ dummies are zero for an observation, the observation must fall in the kth category.

interpreting coefficients   The interpretation of regression coefficients in the prediction equation requires some thought. Suppose that x_1 and x_2 are the dummy variables for the qualitative variable residence, x_3 is education in years, and y is income in thousands of dollars. An appropriate multiple regression model is

$$Y = \beta_0 + \beta_1 x_1 + \beta_2 x_2 + \beta_3 x_3 + \epsilon$$

where

$$x_1 = \begin{cases} 1 \text{ if suburban} \\ 0 \text{ otherwise} \end{cases} \qquad x_2 = \begin{cases} 1 \text{ if rural} \\ 0 \text{ otherwise} \end{cases}$$

The interpretations assigned to the β's for the dummy variables x_1 and x_2 can be seen by examining the corresponding expectations $E(Y)$.

For urban residence ($x_1 = x_2 = 0$): $E(Y) = \beta_0 + \beta_3 x_3$
For suburban residence ($x_1 = 1, x_2 = 0$): $E(Y) = \beta_0 + \beta_1 + \beta_3 x_3$
For rural residence ($x_1 = 0, x_2 = 1$): $E(Y) = \beta_0 + \beta_2 + \beta_3 x_3$

It follows that β_1 is the difference in expected income between suburban and urban residents for a fixed number of years of education x_3. Similarly, β_2 is the difference in expected income for rural and urban residents for a fixed number of years of education x_3. It follows, too, that $\beta_2 - \beta_1$ is the difference in expected income for rural and suburban residents at a fixed education level.

Knowing the interpretations of the β's, one can make sense of a least-squares prediction equation. Suppose that the least-squares prediction equation based on sample data is

$$\hat{y} = 3.05 + 5.91 x_1 - 1.84 x_2 + .12 x_3$$

The coefficient of x_1 is the estimated difference in incomes (in thousands of dollars) for suburban residents when compared to urban residents with the same years of education. Similarly, the coefficient of x_2 is the predicted difference in average income for rural and urban residents with the same education. With years of education x_3 fixed, the regression equation tells us that suburban residents average $5910 higher income than urban residents, while rural residents average $1840 lower than urban residents. The "undummied" category (urban residents in the example) serves as the comparison standard. A comparison of rural and suburban residents can be made by comparing each to an urban resident. For education held constant, a suburban resident is predicted to earn $5.91 - (-1.84) = 7.75$ thousand dollars more than a rural resident.

EXAMPLE 15.2   A regression model relates Y = a person's percentage salary increase to seniority in years, gender, and location of the workplace (urban, suburban, or rural). The prediction equation is

$$\hat{y} = 1.31 + 0.09 x_1 - 0.43 x_2 + 1.02 x_3 - 0.66 x_4$$

where $x_1 =$ seniority in years,

$$x_2 = \begin{cases} 1 \text{ if female} \\ 0 \text{ otherwise} \end{cases} \qquad x_3 = \begin{cases} 1 \text{ if suburban} \\ 0 \text{ otherwise} \end{cases} \qquad x_4 = \begin{cases} 1 \text{ if rural} \\ 0 \text{ otherwise} \end{cases}$$

Interpret the coefficients ($\hat{\beta}$'s) in the general linear model.

Solution   Because there are several dummy variables and one quantitative independent variable, the easiest way to interpret the coefficients is to obtain expected values $E(Y)$ for each combination of settings of the dummy variables. These expected values are listed below.

	Urban $(x_3 = 0, x_4 = 0)$	Suburban $(x_3 = 1, x_4 = 0)$	Rural $(x_3 = 0), x_4 = 1)$
Male $\hat{y} = 1.31 + 0.09x_1$ $(x_2 = 0)$		$\hat{y} = 1.31 + 0.09x_1 + 1.02$	$\hat{y} = 1.31 + 0.09x_1 - 0.66$
Female $\hat{y} = 1.31 + 0.09x_1 - 0.43$ $(x_2 = 1)$		$\hat{y} = 1.31 + 0.09x_1 - 0.43 + 1.02$	$\hat{y} = 1.31 + 0.09x_1 - 0.43 - 0.66$

From this table, it is clear that β_2 is the difference in mean salary increase $E(Y)$ for females and males, for a given level of seniority (x_1) and location of residence. For example, at a given level of x_1 in an urban district, the difference in mean salary increases for females and males is

$$(\beta_0 + \beta_1 x_1 + \beta_2) - (\beta_0 + \beta_1 x_1) = \beta_2$$

This result also applies for any other fixed geographic location. Similarly, β_3 is the difference in mean salary increase between suburban and urban residences for females (or males) at a given seniority level, and β_4 is the difference in mean salary increase in the rural and urban districts for females (or males) at a given seniority level. ∎

EXAMPLE 15.3   The minicomputer firm of Example 15.1 is concerned with recent model changes as a source of service calls. The firm feels that most of the effects of model changes occur in the first two months. After that time, minor manufacturing changes eliminate any blatant problems. Discuss how dummy variables could be used in a regression model (based on monthly data) to treat the issue of model change.

Solution   There are three possibilities in any given month: Model has changed that month, model has changed the previous month, or neither of these. Two dummies are needed, and one way to define them is

$$x_1 = \begin{cases} 1 \text{ if model has changed this month} \\ 0 \text{ if not} \end{cases}$$

$$x_2 = \begin{cases} 1 \text{ if model has changed the previous month} \\ 0 \text{ if not} \end{cases}$$

A problem with this approach is that it does not reflect the *number* of new installations in the model-change months.   ■

15.3   LAGGED PREDICTOR VARIABLES (Step I)   ◾

lagged variables   In many time-series regression problems, the independent variables in the equation should be **lagged**. A regional sales manager may try to forecast monthly sales (s) given the number of initial calls (c) and the number of sales presentations (p) by salespeople. For many types of products, the calls and presentations will result in sales some months later, rather than immediately. The sales manager does not want an equation of the form

$$\hat{s}_t = \hat{\beta}_0 + \hat{\beta}_1 c_t + \hat{\beta}_2 p_t$$

but rather an equation something like

$$\hat{s}_t = \hat{\beta}_0 + \hat{\beta}_1 c_{t-2} + \hat{\beta}_2 p_{t-1}$$

In this example, initial calls are lagged two months behind sales, and presentations one month behind. The implicit idea is that initial calls in one month tend to generate presentations the next month, which in turn tend to generate sales a month later.

Lagging variables is often necessary when regression is to be used for forecasting. A sales forecasting equation like

$$\hat{s}_t = \hat{\beta}_0 + \hat{\beta}_1 c_t + \hat{\beta}_2 p_t$$

is most likely useless, because the values of c_t and p_t are not known when the forecast has to be made. To make regression useful in forecasting, the predictor variables must be lagged at least far enough so that their values can be known at forecast time.

The major problem with lagging variables is deciding the number of periods to lag. Should the sales manager lag the presentation variable by one month, two months, or what? It's tempting to include many lags in a single regression equation, such as

$$\hat{s}_t = \hat{\beta}_0 + \hat{\beta}_1 c_{t-1} + \hat{\beta}_2 c_{t-2} + \hat{\beta}_3 c_{t-3} + \hat{\beta}_4 c_{t-4} + \hat{\beta}_5 c_{t-5}$$
$$+ \hat{\beta}_6 p_{t-1} + \hat{\beta}_7 p_{t-2} + \hat{\beta}_8 p_{t-3} + \hat{\beta}_9 p_{t-4} + \hat{\beta}_{10} p_{t-5}$$

There are two problems with this strategy. First, the number of independent variables is large. Because one must have more observations than variables in a regression (the d.f. for error is number of observations − number of predictors − 1), this strategy requires a lot of data. Second, the lagged variables are likely to be severely correlated (for further discussions of problems related to correlated predictor variables, see Section 14.2).

Econometricians have proposed several other strategies for deciding on lags (see Johnston, 1977). These strategies typically involve rather severe assumptions that are difficult to verify. If one has no inkling of plausible lag structures, these methods are worth a try.

Often it's possible to find reasonable lags by thoughtful trial and error. The sales manager may well try lagging presentations by one month in one regression equation, and by both one and two in a second. If the second equation doesn't forecast much better than the first, and if most sales result within a month or so of presentations, there is no reason to try further lags. Knowledge of the basic process involved is almost always useful in choosing lags.

EXAMPLE 15.4   An automobile dealer offers a 12-month or 12,000-mile warranty on new cars and a 3-month or 3000-mile warranty on used cars. As a consequence, the dealer's repair department handles a certain number of warranty-covered repair jobs each month. Data are collected on y_t, the number of warranty repair jobs in month t; x_{t1}, the number of new car sales in month t; and x_{t2}, the number of used car sales in month t. The data are analyzed by two regression models:

$$Y_t = \beta_0 + \beta_1 x_{t1} + \beta_2 x_{t2} + \epsilon_t$$
$$Y_t = \beta_0 + \beta_1 x_{t1} + \beta_2 x_{t-1,1} + \beta_3 x_{t-2,1} + \beta_4 x_{t2} + \beta_5 x_{t-1,2}$$
$$+ \beta_6 x_{t-2,2} + \epsilon_t$$

Computer output is shown below: variable 7 is y_t, variable 1 is x_{t1}, variable 4 is x_{t2}; variables 2 and 3 are $x_{t-1,1}$ and $x_{t-2,1}$; variables 5 and 6 are $x_{t-1,2}$ and $x_{t-2,2}$.

a. Write the regression equation for the nonlagged model, together with the residual standard deviation and R^2 values.
b. Do the same for the lagged model.
c. Is there reason to believe that the lagged variables are useful in prediction?

```
MTB > regress c7 on 2 variables in c1 and c4

The regression equation is
Y = 0.33 + 0.312 X1 + 0.171 X2

Predictor        Coef         Stdev       t-ratio
Constant        0.326         6.535         0.05
X1              0.3115        0.1412        2.21
X2              0.1715        0.1857        0.92

s = 5.174      R-sq = 38.3%     R-sq(adj) = 34.3%

Analysis of Variance

SOURCE        DF          SS            MS
Regression     2        514.50        257.25
Error         31        829.74         26.77
Total         33       1344.24

MTB > regress c7 on 6 variables in c1-c6

The regression equation is
Y = - 25.1 + 0.176 X1 + 0.141 X1lag1 + 0.123 X1lag2 + 0.264 X2 - 0.003 X2lag1
          + 0.259 X2lag2
```

(continued)

```
Predictor        Coef         Stdev      t-ratio
Constant       -25.052        5.776       -4.34
X1              0.17643       0.08728      2.02
X1lag1          0.14055       0.09187      1.53
X1lag2          0.12297       0.08970      1.37
X2              0.2644        0.1082       2.44
X2lag1         -0.0030        0.1060      -0.03
X2lag2          0.2590        0.1241       2.09

s = 2.903        R-sq = 83.1%        R-sq(adj) = 79.3%

Analysis of Variance

SOURCE        DF          SS            MS
Regression     6        1116.72       186.12
Error         27         227.51         8.43
Total         33        1344.24
```

Solution   a. For this model, the regression equation is

$$\hat{y}_t = .33 + .312x_{i1} + .171x_{i2}$$

The corresponding values of s_ϵ and R^2 are

$$s_\epsilon = 5.174 \quad \text{and} \quad R^2 = .383$$

b. The regression equation for the second model is

$$\hat{y}_t = -25.1 + .176x_{t1} + .141x_{t-1,1} + .123x_{t-2,1} + .264x_{t2}$$
$$- .003x_{t-1,2} + .259x_{t-2,2}$$

The values of s_ϵ and R^2 are

$$s_\epsilon = 2.903 \quad \text{and} \quad R^2 = .831$$

c. The inclusion of lagged variables has helped in the prediction of y. The value of R^2 has been increased considerably, and s_ϵ is much smaller.   ∎

EXAMPLE 15.5   In Example 15.3 new-model introduction affected service calls for two months. What lags should be used in a (monthly) data base?

Solution   New installations reflect only the current month. To capture the two-month effect, the new-installations variable should also be lagged by a month. As a check on the belief that the new-model effect lasts only two months, it woundn't be totally inappropriate to lag new installations by another month as well.   ∎

SECTIONS 15.1–15.3   EXERCISES

15.1   A city probation office tries to use various reported crime rates to forecast the volume of new cases. The total number of nonviolent crimes reported in the city is determined for 12 quarters, as is the volume of new cases. The data are

Quarter, t:	1	2	3	4
Crimes (thousands), x_t:	6.4	5.6	5.8	6.6
New cases (hundreds), y_t:	13.1	13.5	12.7	12.9

5	6	7	8	9	10	11	12
7.0	6.7	6.5	7.1	7.2	6.9	6.8	6.7
14.3	14.8	14.4	13.9	15.0	15.5	15.1	14.6

a. Calculate the correlation between x_t and y_t.
b. Calculate the "lag 1" correlation—the correlation between x_{t-1} and y_t. Note that the effective sample size is 11, not 12.
c. Which of the correlations is stronger? Does this result seem sensible?

15.2 Refer to the data of Exercise 15.1.
a. Calculate the regression equation $\hat{y}_t = \hat{\beta}_0 + \hat{\beta}_1 x_{t-1}$.
b. Calculate the residual standard deviation.
c. Give a 95% prediction interval for the volume of new cases in quarter 13.

15.3 Refer to the data of Exercise 15.1 What would happen if you tried to calculate lag 10 and lag 11 correlations?

15.4 A textbook polisher begins a sales forecasting system. The chief editors for each of three divisions forecast first-year sales for all new books published in a certain year. These forecasts are later compared to actual sales. Computer output from a regression study (SAS) follows:

DEPENDENT VARIABLE: ACTUAL

SOURCE	DF	SUM OF SQUARES	MEAN SQUARE	F VALUE	PR > F	R-SQUARE	C.V.
MODEL	3	894.74508876	298.24836292	109.47	0.0001	0.924030	13.9768
ERROR	27	73.56200801	2.72451882		ROOT MSE		ACTUAL MEAN
CORRECTED TOTAL	30	968.30709677			1.65061165		11.80967742

PARAMETER	ESTIMATE	T FOR H0: PARAMETER=0	PR > |T|	STD ERROR OF ESTIMATE
INTERCEPT	-1.86308649	-1.86	0.0738	1.00171014
FORECAST	1.35417285	16.33	0.0001	0.08292934
DIV2	-4.00656296	-5.67	0.0001	0.70677705
DIV3	0.91579423	1.25	0.2205	0.73021786

a. Identify the dummy variables.
b. What is the interpretation of the coefficients of these dummy variables?
c. Do the t statistics suggest that the dummy variables separately have some predictive value?

15.5 For the data of Exercise 15.4, what additional computer output would you need to test the null hypothesis that the dummy variables collectively have no predictive value once the forecast value has been included in the regression equation?

15.6 Refer to Exercise 15.4.

    a. What null hypothesis is being tested by the F statistic? What does this hypothesis say about the forecasting system?

    b. Can this null hypothesis be rejected at $\alpha = .01$? Locate the p-value.

15.7 Refer to Exercise 15.4.

    a. If the forecast sales had been exactly correct on the average within each division, what would the regression equation be? In particular, what would the coefficient of forecast equal?

    b. Calculate a 95% confidence interval for the forecast coefficient. Does it include the value you specified in part (a)?

15.4   NONLINEAR REGRESSION MODELS (Step 2)   ■

In Section 14.1, we pointed out that use of a first-order regression model (one containing only linear terms in the x's) assumes linearity in each variable separately and also assumes that there are no interactions among the independent variables. In this section we discuss how to modify a first-order model to handle some kinds of nonlinearities.

In some situations it is evident that a model that is linear in all the independent variables is inadequate. A regression model that predicts y, a taste-test preference score for a lime drink, as a linear function of x_1, lime concentration, and x_2, sweetness, is very dubious. In other cases, scatter plots of the data reveal nonlinearities. In linear regression, the ordinary plot of y versus x is adequate. In multiple regression, the effect of variables in other x's can obscure the nonlinearity. For this reason, a standard strategy is to fit a first-order model and then plot the residuals from this model against each independent variable. If a more appropriate model contains, for instance, a term in x_1^2, then the plot of residuals against x_1 shows a nonlinear pattern. Because the use of a first-order model removes the linear effect of the other independent variables, nonlinearities often show up more clearly in these residual plots.

residual plots

Interactions among variables are harder to detect in scatter plots. If x_1 and x_2 interact in determining y, three variables are involved; unfortunately, three-dimensional plots are hard to draw. Common sense may be the best approach to determine whether interactions are present. For the special case in which one of the independent variables is a qualitative variable represented by one or more dummy variables, interaction may be detected by plotting residuals (from a first-order model) against the other independent variables. Separate plots should be made for observations in each category of the qualitative variable. The first-order, no-interaction model implies that these plots should be parallel. If the separate residual plots are not close to parallel, the possibility of interaction should be considered.

EXAMPLE 15.6

In Example 15.3 we noted that the new-model dummy variables did not reflect the number of new installations in new-model months. Data for 29 months are collected on the following variables.

Variable	Description
7	Total number of service calls in the month
1	Number of minicomputers in use, beginning of month
2	Number of new installations this month
3	Number of new installations, previous month
4	1 if model change in this month, 0 if not
5	1 if model change in previous month, 0 if not
6	Average temperature this month

A first-order model is fit to the data. Plots of residuals against varibles 2 and 3 are shown in Figure 15.2. Is there evidence that interaction terms should be used?

To see if the effect of this month's installations depends on whether or not there was a model change this month, we plot residuals against variable 2 and circle the cases for variable 4 = 1. Similarly, to see if the effect of installations in the previous month depends on whether or not there was a model change last month, we plot residuals against variable 3 and circle the cases corresponding to variable 5 = 1.

Solution   Certainly a strong pattern doesn't exactly leap off the page at you. There is no obvious positive or negative slope in either plot. There is no visually obvious reason to include the interaction terms, but the theoretical reasoning behind the idea is strong enough that we may want to test it anyway.   ∎

Once potential nonlinearity has been discovered, we can deal with it either by transforming existing variables or by adding additional, higher-order terms in the x's. Often we use both of these strategies. Transformations may be suggested either by the nature of the problem or by the look of the data.

With economic variables and time-series data, growth often occurs at a roughly constant percentage rather than at an absolute rate. For instance, total sales of a large company may grow at the rate of 8% per year, as opposed to $8 million per year. Of course, if initial sales are $100 million, 8% growth in the first year is the same as $8 million growth. But in later years, constant percentage growth and constant additive growth differ. The table below shows the total sales for a company over a five-year period, based on each of the two types of growth.

	Year					
	0	1	2	3	4	5
8% growth	100.0	108.0	116.6	126.0	136.0	146.9
$8 million growth	100.0	108.0	116.0	124.0	132.0	140.0

```
MTB > lplot c19 c2 id by c4
```

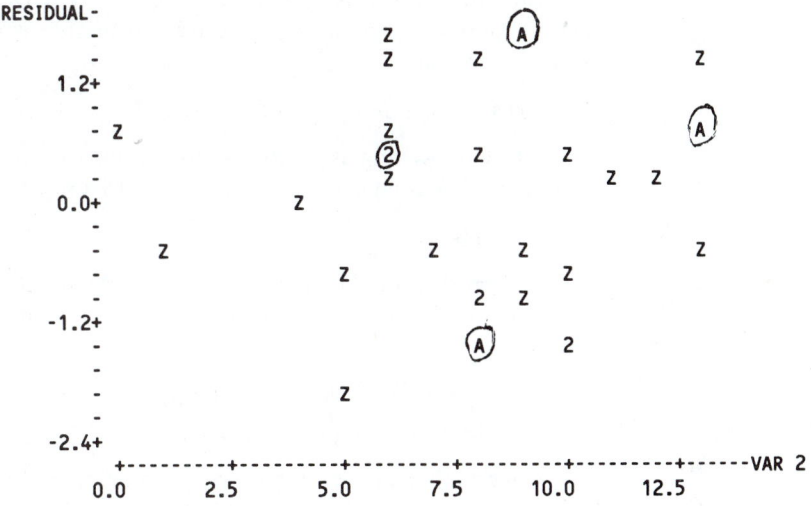

```
MTB > lplot c19 c3 id by c5
```

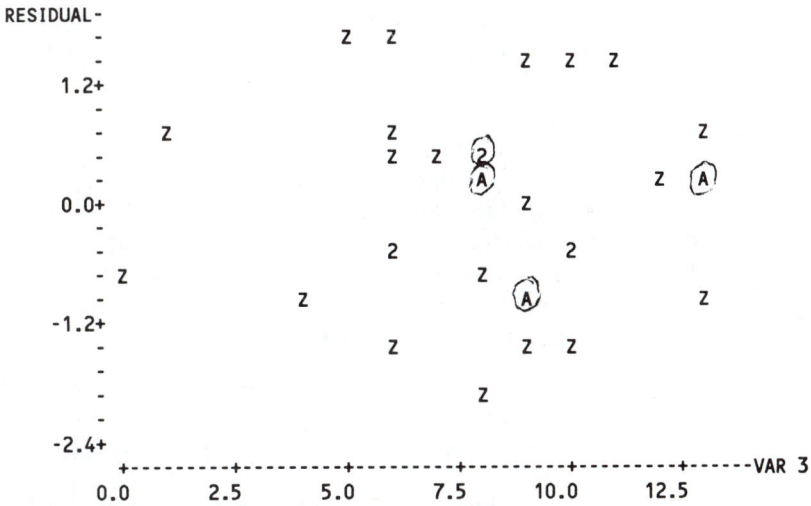

FIGURE 15.2   Residual Plot for Example 15.6

Most basic finance books show that if a quantity y grows at a rate r per unit time (continuously compounded), the value of y at time t is

$$y_t = y_0 e^{rt}$$

where y_0 is the initial value. This relation may be converted into a linear relation between Y_t and t by a **logarithmic transformation**

$$\log y_t = (\log y_0) + rt$$

logarithmic transformation

The linear regression method of Chapter 13 can be used to fit data for this regression model with $\beta_0 = \log y_0$ and $\beta_1 = r$. When y is an economic variable such as total sales, the logarithmic transformation is often used in a multiple regression model:

$$\log Y_i = \beta_0 + \beta_1 x_{i1} + \beta_2 x_{i2} + \cdots + \beta_k x_{ik} + \epsilon_i$$

The Cobb-Douglas production function is another standard example of a nonlinear model that can be transformed into a regression equation:

$$y = cI^\alpha k^\beta$$

where y is production, I is labor input, k is capital input, and α and β are unknown constants. Again, to transform the dependent variable we take logarithms to obtain

$$\log y = (\log c) + \alpha(\log I) + \beta(\log k)$$
$$= \beta_0 + \beta_1(\log I) + \beta_2(\log k)$$

This suggests that a regression of log production on log labor and log capital is linear.

EXAMPLE 15.7   An important economic concept is the *price elasticity of demand*, defined as the negative of the percentage change in quantity demanded per percentage change in price. It can be shown that a price elasticity of 1 means that a (small) price change yields no change in total revenue. An inelastic demand (elasticity less than 1) means that a small price increase yields an increase in revenue; elastic demand is the opposite.

Data are obtained on y, daily demand for lettuce (in heads sold per hundred customers) for varying levels of price (dollars per head). As much as possible, other conditions that might affect demand are held constant; all participating stores are located in middle class suburbs, no competitors are running sales on lettuce, and so on. The data are

x:	.79	.79	.84	.84	.89	.89	.94	.94	.99	.99
y:	40.2	37.1	37.4	34.9	32.8	35.5	30.6	34.2	31.2	29.8
xy:	31.758	29.309	31.416	29.316	29.192	31.595	28.764	32.148	30.888	29.502

 a. What economic quantity does xy represent?
 b. Does there appear to be any trend in xy values as x increases?
 c. If xy is constant, what is true of $\log x + \log y$?
 d. If a product has price elasticity equal to 1, what does the regression equation of $\log y$ versus $\log x$ look like?

Solution   a. The term xy is price per head times heads per hundred customers. Therefore it represents revenue per hundred customers.

 b. No trend is apparent in a plot of the data. Revenue, xy, appears constant.

 c. Because $\log xy = \log$ constant $= \log x + \log y$, $\log x + \log y$ should be constant.

d. A price elasticity of 1 means that $\log y = \text{constant} - \log x$. The regression equation with $\log y$ as dependent variable and $\log x$ independent should have a slope nearly equal to -1 (plus-or-minus random error). Thus a regression model in $\log y$ and $\log x$ is useful in elasticity studies.   ■

A fairly extensive discussion of possible transformations is found in Tukey (1977).

Sometimes nonlinearity can be handled by adding extra terms in the independent variables. Quadratic terms, such as x_1^2, are particularly useful when we think that y increases to a maximum and then decreases (or decreases to a minimum and then increases) as x_1 increases. If a plot of residuals (from a first-order model) versus an independent variable shows a parabolic pattern, a quadratic term should be added.

EXAMPLE 15.8   For the service-call situation of Example 15.6, the effect of temperature may not be linear. A regression model is calculated using the independent variables and interaction terms indicated in Example 15.6. Residuals are plotted against average temperature, as shown in Figure 15.3. Does this plot suggest that a quadratic term would be a useful predictor?

Solution   Again, there is certainly nothing blatant here. If not for the point at the lower right, there would not be any pattern at all. We would not base any decision on a couple of odd points.   ■

Interaction terms may also be added to the multiple regression model to cure some forms of nonlinearity. Unfortunately, multiple regression was not designed to capture interaction effects. The experimental design, ANOVA

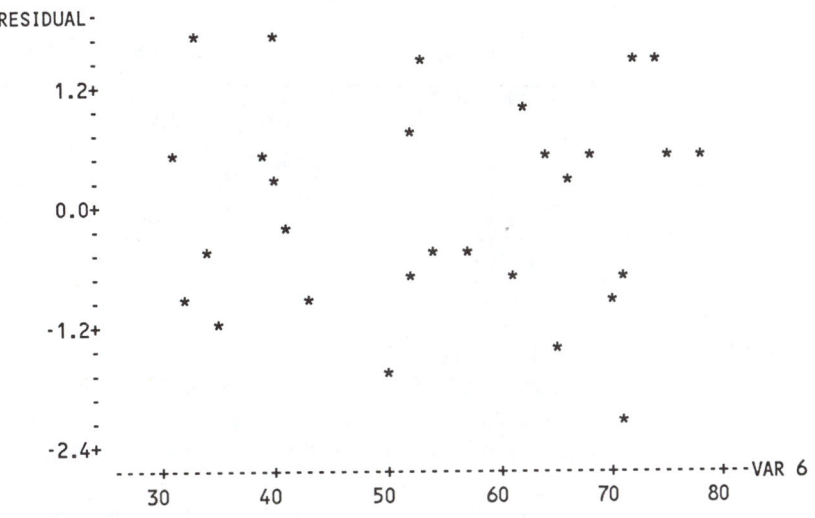

FIGURE 15.3   Residual Plot for Example 15.8

approach (where every possible value of one predictor is combined with each possible value of every other predictor) yields a much more clearly intelligible treatment of this form of nonlinearity. In practice, however, it may not be possible to plan the neatly balanced data-gathering schemes of the ANOVA approach. In such situations, the regression approach may be modified to yield some information (however imperfect) about interaction effects.

cross-product terms   One basic but mechanical device is to include **cross-product terms**, as we indicated in Chapter 14. A sales forecasting equation such as

$$\hat{y} = .40 + .04c + .01d + .005cd$$

allows for a certain type of interaction between d and c. If $c = 200$, the predicted change in y per unit change in d is $.01 + .005(200)$. If $c = 500$, the predicted change in sales y per unit change in d is $.01 + .005(500)$. In general, if

$$\hat{y} = \hat{\beta}_0 + \hat{\beta}_1 c + \hat{\beta}_2 d + \hat{\beta}_3 cd$$

the predicted change in y per unit change in d is $\hat{\beta}_2 + \hat{\beta}_3 c$ for a given value of c. Thus the effect of a change in d depends in a certain way on the level of c. This is one form of interaction, though by no means the only one. A cross-product term such as cd may be treated as just another predictor variable. Its coefficient may be tested for statistical significance by a t test, and its predictive value may be assessed by the increase in squared correlation. Therefore this approach to the problem of interaction can be done routinely within the ordinary regression structure.

EXAMPLE 15.9   Salary data for 427 teachers are examined for a seniority and unionization study. Product terms are created: $x_6 = x_1 x_2$ and $x_7 = x_1 x_3$. A summary computer output is shown for the model $Y = \beta_0 + \beta_1 x_1 + \beta_2 x_2 + \cdots + \beta_7 x_7 + \epsilon$. Test the hypotheses that x_6 and x_7 individually have no incremental predictive value.

VARIABLE	COEFF	ST.ERROR	T-STATISTIC
INTERCEPT	10.243	------	------
X1	2.070	7.912	0.262
X2	2.963	0.031	16.065
X3	1.475	0.203	7.249
X4	1.932	0.396	5.590
X5	0.808	0.301	2.686
X6	0.177	0.032	5.554
X7	0.093	0.011	8.183

Solution   For these data, $n = 427$. The d.f. for the t test is $427 - (7 + 1) = 419$, so the relevant t table is effectively the normal table. The t statistics for x_6 and x_7 fall far beyond normal table values. Therefore we may conclude that some degree of interaction between x_1 and x_2 and between x_1 and x_3 has been shown.   ∎

Insertion of cross-product terms into the regression equation is sometimes thought to be the only way to handle interaction in regression. Certainly this approach does not handle all possible kinds of interaction, but it does provide a useful approximation to solving the problem of interaction within regression. A manager who believes that interaction effects are crucial in predicting a dependent variable may well spend the extra money to gather data in the neatly balanced form of ANOVA methods.

Finally, thoughtful consideration of underlying economic relations may suggest other combinations of variables to address questions of nonlinearity. For example, suppose that a regression study is made of the total yearly expenditures of cities (y) on water supply systems. Natural independent variables are x_1, the population size; x_2, the total water consumption; and x_3, the number of miles of water lines (of course, there are other possibilities). A regression analysis based on these variables would be bedeviled by collinearity; every other variable would be strongly correlated with city size. A better analysis would take the dependent variable as y/x_1, the per capita expenditure. Natural independent variables would be x_2/x_1, x_3/x_1, and perhaps x_1 itself.

EXAMPLE 15.10

The data of Example 15.6 indicated (to no one's surprise) that variable 7, the number of service calls, increases as variable 1, the number of minicomputers in use, increases. What would be the interpretation of a new variable, defined as variable 7 divided by variable 1? Why might the new variable be an appropriate dependent variable?

Solution

The new variable represents the number of service calls per computer. For a growing business such as the minicomputer firm, defining the variables as fractions of the number of computers in use might well reduce collinearity. ■

EXAMPLE 15.11

A manufacturer of feed for chickens faces a great deal of month-to-month variability in sales. A regression study attempts to forecast monthly sales volumes. The feed is used largely for chickens age 20–50 days, so the number of chicken starts in the previous month is expected to be a critical predictor variable. Monthly data on starts are available. In addition, feed sales are expected to be quite sensitive to price. The prices of the manufacturer's feed and the primary competitor's feed, as well as the wholesale price of chickens, are very plausible predictor variables.

The working group charged with performing the regression study argues over the form of the regression equation. The following suggestions are made:

1. A linear (first-order) model in starts, price, competitor's price, and chicken price;
2. A first-order model in starts, difference in price (between manufacturer and competitor), and chicken price;
3. A first-order model in starts and the price difference as a fraction of chicken price.

Write the three suggested models. Is there a simple relation between one model and any other?

Solution   Let

$$y = \text{monthly sales of the manufacturer's feed}$$
$$x_1 = \text{starts in the previous month}$$
$$x_2 = \text{current price of manufacturer's feed}$$
$$x_3 = \text{current price of competitor's feed}$$
$$x_4 = \text{current price of chickens}$$

Model 1 is a first-order model in these variables:

$$Y = \beta_0 + \beta_1 x_1 + \beta_2 x_2 + \beta_3 x_3 + \beta_4 x_4 + \epsilon$$

Model 2 involves x_2 and x_3 only through their difference:

$$Y = \beta_0^* + \beta_1^* x_1 + \beta_2^*(x_2 - x_3) + \beta_3^* x_4 + \epsilon$$

Model 3 involves the difference as a fraction of chicken price x_4:

$$Y = \beta_0^{**} + \beta_1^{**} x_1 + \beta_2^{**}(x_2 - x_3)/x_4$$

Model 2 is equal to model 1 if $\beta_2^* = \beta_2$ and $-\beta_2^* = \beta_3$.
Model 3 is not a first-order model in $x_1, \ldots, x_4$, so there is no simple relation between it and the others.   ■

SECTION 15.4   EXERCISES   ■

15.8   A consultant who specializes in corporate gifts to charities, schools, cultural institutions, and the like is often asked to suggest an appropriate dollar amount. The consultant undertakes a regression study to try to predict the amount contributed by corporations to colleges and universities and is able to obtain information on the contributions of 38 companies. Financial information about these companies is available from their annual reports. Other information is obtained from such sources as business magazines. From experience, the consultant believes that the level of contributions is affected by the profitability of a firm, the size of the firm, whether the firm is in a high-education industry (such as data processing, electronics, or chemicals), the educational level of the firm's executives, and whether the firm matches the contributions of employees. Profitability can be measured by pre-tax or post-tax income, size by number of employees or gross sales, and educational level by average number of years of education or by percentage of executives holding advanced degrees.

   a. Would you expect pre-tax and post-tax income to be highly correlated? How about number of employees and gross sales?

   b. Discuss how to define profitability, size, and educational level so that the correlations among these variables are not automatically huge.

15.9   The consultant of Exercise 15.8 proposes to define an industry-type variable as follows:

$$\text{INDUSTRY} = \begin{cases} 3 \text{ if firm is primarily in the electronics industry} \\ 2 \text{ if firm is primarily in the data-processing industry} \\ 1 \text{ if firm is primarily in the chemical industry} \\ 0 \text{ otherwise} \end{cases}$$

  a. Explain why this is not a good idea.
  b. Suggest an alternative approach for indicating these industries.
  c. How could the factor of whether or not the firm matches employee contributions be incorporated into a regression model?

15.10 The consultant of Exercise 15.8 collects data on the following variables:

CONTRIB:	Millions of dollars contributed
INCOME:	Pre-tax income, in millions of dollars
SIZE:	Number of employees, in thousands
DPDUMMY:	1 if firm is primarily in the data-processing industry
	0 if not
ELDUMMY:	1 if firm is primarily in the electronics industry
	0 if not
CHDUMMY:	1 if firm is primarily in the chemical industry
	0 if not
EDLEVEL:	Proportion of executives holding advanced degrees
MATCHING:	1 if firm matches employee contributions
	0 if not

  a. Does it seem like a good idea to take CONTRIB as the dependent variable, with all other variables as independent variables?
  b. What does the variable CONTRIB/INCOME represent?

15.11 Refer to Exercise 15.10. The consultant suspects that the effect of SIZE on CONTRIB/INCOME differs greatly among firms in the data-processing, electronics, chemical, and other industries. How can the regression model be modified to test this suspicion?

15.12 Refer to Exercise 15.10. The consultant suspects that the effect of increasing EDLEVEL is itself increasing; that is, all else being equal, there is little difference in CONTRIB/INCOME for firms with EDLEVEL = .2 versus .3, more for firms with EDLEVEL = .4 versus .5, and still more for firms with EDLEVEL = .6 versus .7.
  a. How can a regression model be formulated to test this suspicion?
  b. If the consultant's suspicion is correct, and if the residuals from a first-order regression model are scatter-plotted against EDLEVEL, what pattern of residuals would you expect to see?

15.13 A company that has developed a plastic film for use in wrapping food (such as crackers and cookies) has a problem with film stiffness. To be useful with modern packaging machines, stiffness (as given by an accepted measure) must be high. Stiffness is thought to be the result of certain variables of the production process. A regression study attempts to predict film stiffness for various combinations of these variables. A total of 32 pilot plant runs are made. Data are recorded on the following variables:

STIFF:	Stiffness	REPEL:	Percentage of recycled
MELT:	Melt temperature (°F)		pelletized material used
CHILL:	Chill temperature (°F)	SPEED:	Line production speed
			(feet per minute)
		KNIFE:	Setting of vacuum knife

There is considerable uncertainty among the firm's chemical engineers as to the mathematical form of the relation among these variables. The following output is obtained for a first-order model:

```
PEARSON CORRELATION COEFFICIENTS / PROB > |R| UNDER HO:RHO=0 / N = 32

                STIFF      MELT     CHILL     REPEL     SPEED     KNIFE


      STIFF   1.00000   0.05933   0.13753  -0.88640   0.02966  -0.30752
              0.0000    0.7470    0.4529    0.0001    0.8720    0.0869


      MELT    0.05933   1.00000   0.00000   0.00000   0.00000   0.00000
              0.7470    0.0000    1.0000    1.0000    1.0000    1.0000


      CHILL   0.13753   0.00000   1.00000   0.00000   0.00000   0.00000
              0.4529    1.0000    0.0000    1.0000    1.0000    1.0000


      REPEL  -0.88640   0.00000   0.00000   1.00000   0.00000   0.00000
              0.0001    1.0000    1.0000    0.0000    1.0000    1.0000


      SPEED   0.02966   0.00000   0.00000   0.00000   1.00000   0.00000
              0.8720    1.0000    1.0000    1.0000    0.0000    1.0000


      KNIFE  -0.30752   0.00000   0.00000   0.00000   0.00000   1.00000
              0.0869    1.0000    1.0000    1.0000    1.0000    0.0000
```

a. How much collinearity is present in these data?

b. The 32 observations involved one measurement of each combination of MELT = 510, 530, 550, 570 with CHILL = 70, 80, 90, 100, and REPEL = 20, 30. How much correlation should there be between MELT and CHILL and between MELT and REPEL?

15.14 A first-order model is fit to the data of Exercise 15.13. The following (SAS) output is obtained and plotted in Figure 15.4 (pages 671–672). Is there any evidence, by eye, of nonlinearity? RESSTIFF is the name of the residuals.

DEPENDENT VARIABLE: STIFF

SOURCE	DF	SUM OF SQUARES	MEAN SQUARE	F VALUE	PR > F	R-SQUARE	C.V.
MODEL	5	3106.40000000	621.28000000	48.73	0.0001	0.903581	2.8780
ERROR	26	331.47500000	12.74903846		ROOT MSE		STIFF MEAN
CORRECTED TOTAL	31	3437.87500000			3.57057957		124.06250000

PARAMETER	ESTIMATE	T FOR H0: PARAMETER=0	PR > |T|	STD ERROR OF ESTIMATE
INTERCEPT	170.96250000	8.34	0.0001	20.50947556
MELT	0.02750000	0.97	0.3389	0.02822791
CHILL	0.12750000	2.26	0.0325	0.05645582
REPEL	-1.83750000	-14.56	0.0001	0.12623905
SPEED	0.00687500	0.49	0.6303	0.01411396
KNIFE	-0.31875000	-5.05	0.0001	0.06311953

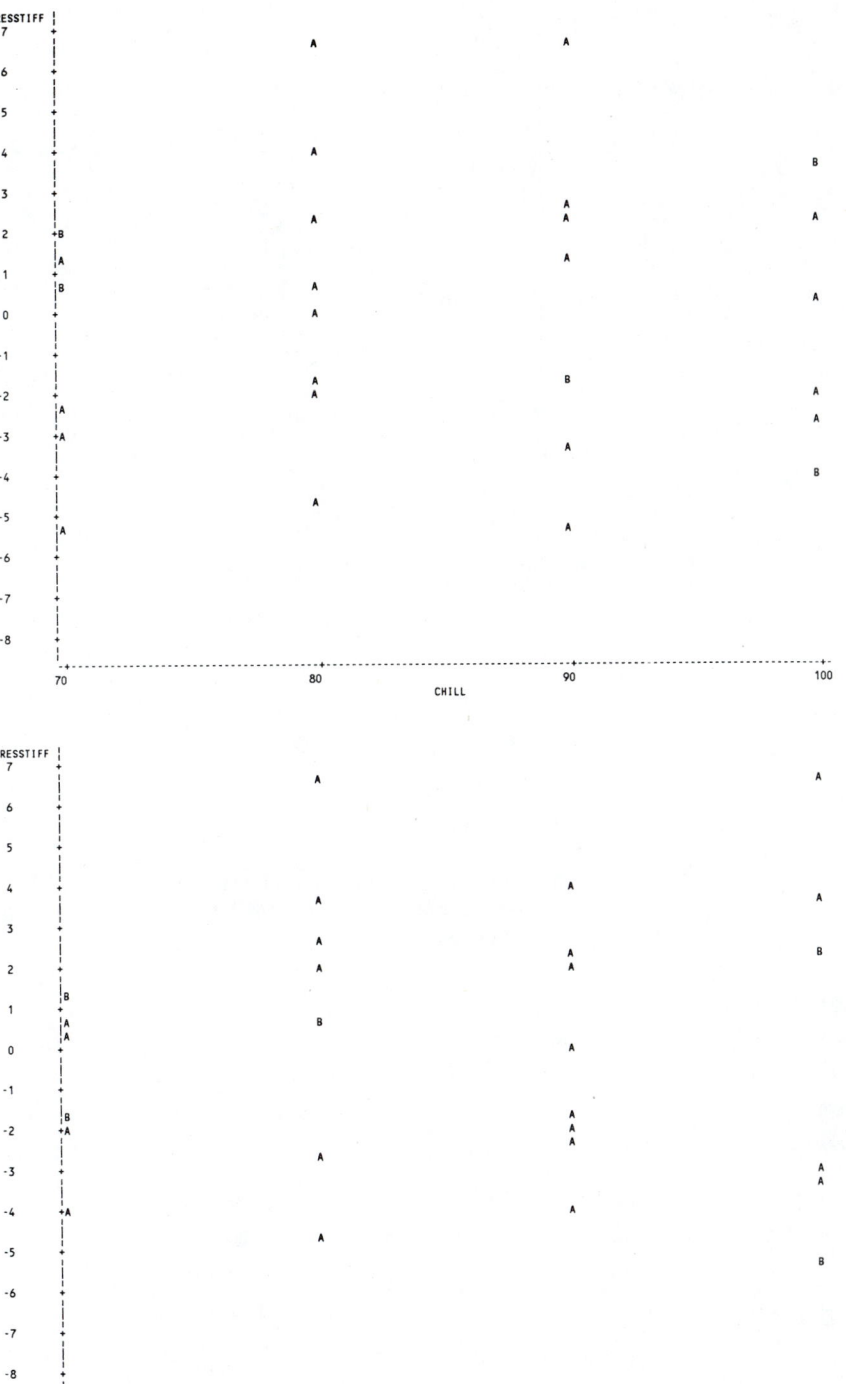

FIGURE 15.4   Residual Plots for Exercise 15.14

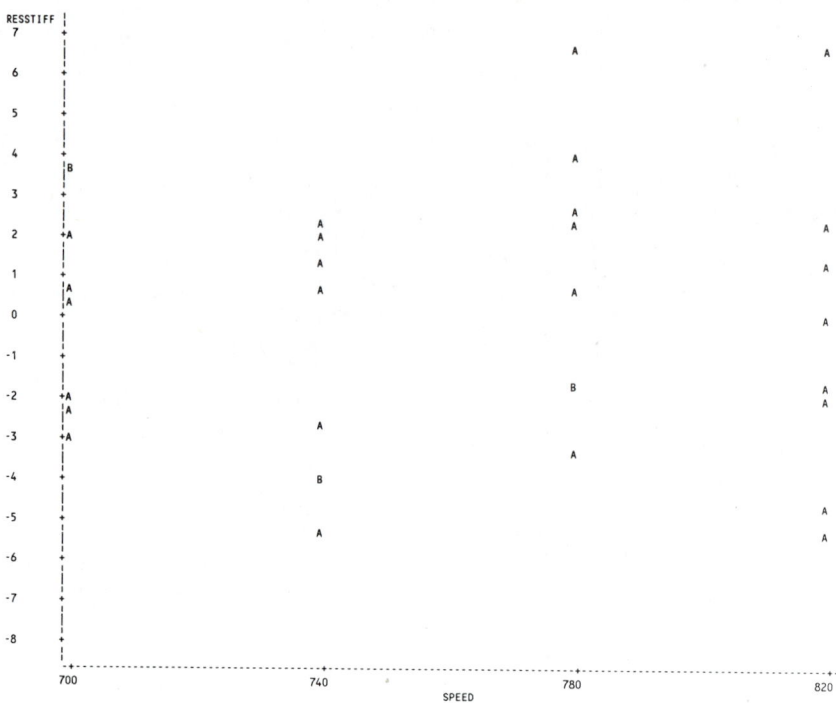

FIGURE 15.4 (*Continued*)

15.15 In an attempt to detect nonlinearity in the data of Exercise 15.13, a second-order model (containing squared MELT and CHILL terms) is run, and the output below is obtained.

DEPENDENT VARIABLE: STIFF

SOURCE	DF	SUM OF SQUARES	MEAN SQUARE	F VALUE	PR > F	R-SQUARE	C.V.
MODEL	7	3141.62500000	448.80357143	36.36	0.0001	0.913828	2.8319
ERROR	24	296.25000000	12.34375000		ROOT MSE		STIFF MEAN
CORRECTED TOTAL	31	3437.87500000			3.51336733		124.06250000

PARAMETER	ESTIMATE	T FOR H0: PARAMETER=0	PR > |T|	STD ERROR OF ESTIMATE
INTERCEPT	-308.00000000	-0.67	0.5086	459.03091353
MELT	1.37750000	0.82	0.4195	1.67714997
CHILL	3.63375000	1.54	0.1370	2.36158010
REPEL	-1.83750000	-14.79	0.0001	0.12421629
SPEED	-0.03437500	-1.11	0.2793	0.03105407
KNIFE	-0.31875000	-5.13	0.0001	0.06210815
MELTSQ	-0.00125000	-0.81	0.4287	0.00155270
CHILLSQ	-0.02062500	-1.49	0.1505	0.01388780

a. How much larger is the R^2 for this model than the R^2 for the first-order model of Exercise 15.14?

b. Use the F test for complete and reduced models to test the null hypothesis that the addition of the squared terms yields no additional predictive value. Use $\alpha = .05$.

c. Do the t statistics indicate that either squared term is a statistically significant ($\alpha = .05$) predictor as "last predictor in"?

15.5   CHOOSING AMONG REGRESSION MODELS (Step 3) ∎

In the previous sections of this chapter we have suggested many reasons to include variables in a regression study. The variables may be defined directly or they may be defined by using dummy variables, lagged variables, transformed variables, interaction cross-product variables, or some other combination. Most of these suggestions involve adding more independent variables to the study. A manager who begins a regression study may well suffer from the "kitchen-sink syndrome" and try to throw every possible variable into a regression model. Some sensible guidelines are needed for selecting the independent variables, from all candidates, to be used in the final regression model.

Stepwise regression is a device for computerized selection of the "best" independent variables. There are several types of stepwise regression procedure; **forward selection** we concentrate on the simplest one, **forward selection**.

Forward-selection stepwise regression selects independent variables for inclusion in a regression model one at a time. The first variable included is the one that has the highest r^2 value for predicting y; assume that this variable is called x_1. The second variable included is the one that, when combined with x_1, yields the highest R^2 value; call the second variable x_2. If there is any degree of collinearity among the x's, x_2 may not have the second-largest r^2_{yx} value. In fact $R^2_{y \cdot x_1 x_2}$ may not even have the highest R^2 value of any two-x regression model.

The third variable included by forward selection yields the highest R^2 value when combined with x_1 and x_2. The process continues in this same manner. Obviously, a considerable amount of computation is necessary. That is why we would never attempt stepwise regression without access to a computer.

When should the selection process stop? There are several criteria, depending in part on which stepwise computer program is used. A common one uses the t test for statistical significance of a single regression coefficient. When a variable is selected for possible inclusion, a t test is performed on the coefficient. If the null hypothesis, $H_0: \beta_j = 0$, can be rejected at an α level specified by the user, the variable x_j is included and stepwise selection continues. If the null hypothesis is retained, the variable is not included and selection stops. To avoid stopping too early, a relatively large α such as .10 or .20 is typically used. Of course it is also possible to force the procedure to include all variables, one at a time, if the α value is too large.

EXAMPLE 15.12   A forward-selection stepwise regression analysis is performed for the data of Example 15.6 (first-order model). The variables are as indicated in that example, and the row labeled R-SQ gives the value at each step of R^2. Thus variable 1 explains .6419 of the variation in variable 7, variable 2 an additional .2513 (for a total of .8932), and so on.

STEP	1	2	3	4	5	6
CONSTANT	72.39	-83.73	-101.94	-98.54	-97.08	-97.47
var1	1.137	1.527	1.484	1.467	1.450	1.451
T-RATIO	6.96	14.72	16.51	16.37	16.19	15.39
var2		9.0	8.3	8.0	7.5	7.5
T-RATIO		7.82	8.25	7.82	7.06	5.91
var6			0.61	0.63	0.70	0.70
T-RATIO			3.23	3.39	3.65	3.25
var5				10.5	13.2	13.1
T-RATIO				1.31	1.60	1.54
var4					10.7	10.8
T-RATIO					1.26	1.22
var3						0.1
T-RATIO						0.07
S	30.8	17.1	14.7	14.5	14.3	14.6
R-SQ	64.19	89.32	92.46	92.97	93.42	93.42

a. Which variables are not statistically significant at $\alpha = .10$ as "last predictor in"?

b. How much higher an R^2 value does the six-variable model have than the model with only variables 1, 2, and 6?

Solution   a. The table t value with $29 - (6 + 1) = 22$ d.f. and one-tailed area .05 (presumably a two-tailed test should be used) is 1.717. Only variables 1, 2, and 6 have t statistics larger than that in the STEP 6 column.

b. The six-variable R^2 is .9342 as compared to the R^2 of .9246 given by variables 1, 2, and 6 alone. The difference is .0094. This modest gain in R^2 is not close to being statistically significant. The F statistic for incremental R^2 (discussed in Section 14.4) is 1.05, with a p-value greater than .25.   ∎

backward elimination

There are many variations in stepwise procedures. Variables may be successively removed from the model in **backward elimination**. This process begins with all variables included in the model. Then, one at a time, variables that offer very little predictive value are deleted. Additionally, forward or backward selection can be modified to use various check-up procedures for retesting variables already included in, or excluded from, the model. For example, in forward selection a variable included at one step can be found at a later step to be of little use; a check-up procedure allows later elimination of the variable. There are sophisticated stepwise procedures that incorporate these and other checks.

Stepwise regression can be of great value in suggesting reasonable models. Like any other statistical method, it requires thinking and judgment for proper use.

stepwise bias   One technical problem is that some biases are introduced by stepwise regression. Because stepwise regression selects variables to yield a large R^2 value, it is quite likely that the resulting R^2 is an overestimation of the actual predictive value of the variables in the model. The magnitudes of the resulting coefficients also tend to be too large.

Additionally, stepwise regression involves decisions that are based on differences of R^2 values. These differences contain an element of random error, which can be quite large for small differences in R^2 values. For example, suppose that in a forward selection based on 28 y values, the correlation between y and the first selected variable x_1 is $r_{yx_1} = .6$ (hence $r^2_{yx_1} = .36$). A 95% confidence interval on $r^2_{yx_1}$, calculated by a method not shown in this text, ranges from .09 to .64. Because of this large sampling variation, one variable could be selected over another for inclusion in the regression model, even though the selected variable has less actual predictive value than others not selected.

Stepwise methods usually involve some form of hypothesis test to select among models. An alternative approach to model selection is based on Mallows' (1973) C_p statistic. If a model contains p coefficients—typically one intercept and $p - 1$ slopes corresponding to $p - 1$ independent variables—then

$$C_p = \frac{SS(\text{Residual, } p \text{ coefficients})}{MS(\text{Residual, all coefficients})} - (n - 2p)$$

$$= \frac{(n - p)\, MS(\text{Residual, } p \text{ coefficients})}{MS(\text{Residual, all coefficients})} - (n - 2p)$$

where the last step follows because the d.f. for MS(Residual, p coefficients) is $n - (k + 1) = n - (p - 1 + 1) = n - p$. If the p-coefficient model contains all the useful predictors, MS(Residual, p coefficients) is essentially the same as MS(Residual, all coefficients). In this case, C_p roughly equals $(n - p) - (n - 2p) = p$. But if the p-coefficient model is inadequate, C_p is substantially larger than p. One plausible model-selection strategy is to select the regression model with the fewest independent variables having C_p approximately equal to p.

EXAMPLE 15.13   Assume that data are collected for 20 independent pharmacies in an attempt to predict prescription volume (sales per month). The independent variables are total floor space, percentage of floor space allocated to the prescription department, number of available parking spaces, whether or not the pharmacy is in a shopping center, and per capita income for the surrounding community. The data and SAS output are shown below. What does the C_p statistic suggest as the most reasonable model?

OBS	VOLUME	FLOOR_SP	PRESC_RX	PARKING	SHOPCNTR	INCOME
1	22	4900	9	40	1	18
2	19	5800	10	50	1	20
3	24	5000	11	55	1	17
4	28	4400	12	30	0	19
5	18	3850	13	42	0	10
6	21	5300	15	20	1	22
7	29	4100	20	25	0	8
8	15	4700	22	60	1	15
9	12	5600	24	45	1	16
10	14	4900	27	82	1	14
11	18	3700	28	56	0	12
12	19	3800	31	38	0	8
13	15	2400	36	35	0	6
14	22	1800	37	28	0	4
15	13	3100	40	43	0	6
16	16	2300	41	20	0	5
17	8	4400	42	46	1	7
18	6	3300	42	15	0	4
19	7	2900	45	30	1	9
20	17	2400	46	16	0	3

ALL SUBSETS PREDICTION OF DRUGSTORE VOLUME

N=20   REGRESSION MODELS FOR DEPENDENT VARIABLE: VOLUME   MODEL: MODEL1

NUMBER IN MODEL	R-SQUARE	C(P)	VARIABLES IN MODEL
1	0.00480421	30.4539	PARKING
1	0.03353172	29.1129	FLOOR_SP
1	0.04105340	28.7618	SHOPCNTR
1	0.14798995	23.7702	INCOME
1	0.43933184	10.1709	PRESC_RX

NUMBER IN MODEL	R-SQUARE	C(P)	VARIABLES IN MODEL
2	0.04210776	30.7126	PARKING SHOPCNTR
2	0.06855667	29.478	FLOOR_SP PARKING
2	0.20543099	23.089	PARKING INCOME
2	0.23487329	21.7147	FLOOR_SP INCOME
2	0.25653635	20.7035	FLOOR_SP SHOPCNTR
2	0.49576794	9.53661	SHOPCNTR INCOME
2	0.53142435	7.87224	PRESC_RX PARKING
2	0.54748785	7.12242	PRESC_RX INCOME
2	0.64706473	2.47436	PRESC_RX SHOPCNTR
2	0.66566267	1.60624	FLOOR_SP PRESC_RX

3	0.25569607	22.7427	FLOOR_SP PARKING INCOME
3	0.26507110	22.3051	FLOOR_SP PARKING SHOPCNTR
3	0.49828073	11.4193	PARKING SHOPCNTR INCOME
3	0.50012580	11.3332	FLOOR_SP SHOPCNTR INCOME
3	0.60243233	6.55772	PRESC_RX PARKING INCOME
3	0.64711563	4.47198	PRESC_RX SHOPCNTR INCOME
3	0.66259120	3.74961	PRESC_RX PARKING SHOPCNTR
3	0.66641145	3.57129	FLOOR_SP PRESC_RX INCOME
3	0.67943313	2.96346	FLOOR_SP PRESC_RX PARKING
3	0.69072432	2.43641	FLOOR_SP PRESC_RX SHOPCNTR

4	0.50128901	13.2789	FLOOR_SP	PARKING	SHOPCNTR	INCOME	
4	0.66300855	5.73013	PRESC_RX	PARKING	SHOPCNTR	INCOME	
4	0.68058567	4.90966	FLOOR_SP	PRESC_RX	PARKING	INCOME	
4	0.69326657	4.31774	FLOOR_SP	PRESC_RX	SHOPCNTR	INCOME	
4	0.69873952	4.06228	FLOOR_SP	PRESC_RX	PARKING	SHOPCNTR	
5	0.70007369	6	FLOOR_SP	PRESC_RX	PARKING	SHOPCNTR	INCOME

Solution   Note that for k variables in the model, $p = k + 1$; there are k slopes and one intercept. For the one-variable models, no C_p is close to $p = 2$. The two-variable model using FLOOR SP and PRESC RX has $C_p = 1.606$, actually below $p = 3$. On the C_p criterion, this model appears to be a good one. Note also that the R^2 value for this model is almost as large as the R^2 value for the "kitchen-sink" model involving all variables.   ∎

Mallows (1973) points out the C_p statistic is as susceptible to random variation as any other statistic; it is not an infallible guide. Neither is any other statistical method. In selecting a regression model, a manager should use experience and judgment as well as statistical results. If one model involves highly reasonable relations and variables, yet does somewhat less well than another, less plausible model on a purely statistical basis, a manager might well choose the first model anyway.

SECTION 15.5   EXERCISES

15.16 A forward-selection stepwise regression is run using a first-order model for the data of Exercise 15.13. The following SAS output is obtained:

STEPWISE REGRESSION OF FILM STIFFNESS DATA

FORWARD SELECTION PROCEDURE FOR DEPENDENT VARIABLE STIFF

STEP 1	VARIABLE REPEL ENTERED		R SQUARE = 0.78569611	C(P) =	29.78867185		
			B VALUE	STD ERROR	TYPE II SS	F	PROB>F
	INTERCEPT		170.00000000				
	REPEL		-1.83750000	0.17520821	2701.12500000	109.99	0.0001

STEP 2	VARIABLE KNIFE ENTERED		R SQUARE = 0.88026761	C(P) =	6.28674862		
			B VALUE	STD ERROR	TYPE II SS	F	PROB>F
	INTERCEPT		201.87500000				
	REPEL		-1.83750000	0.13320081	2701.12500000	190.30	0.0001
	KNIFE		-0.31875000	0.06660041	325.12500000	22.91	0.0001

(continued)

```
STEP 3    VARIABLE CHILL ENTERED      R SQUARE = 0.89918191      C(P) =    3.18636398

                              B VALUE          STD ERROR        TYPE II SS            F        PROB>F

              INTERCEPT    191.03750000
              CHILL          0.12750000       0.05562951       65.02500000         5.25       0.0296
              REPEL         -1.83750000       0.12439138     2701.12500000       218.21       0.0001
              KNIFE         -0.31875000       0.06219569      325.12500000        26.27       0.0001

----------------------------------------------------------------------------------------------------------

STEP 4    VARIABLE MELT ENTERED       R SQUARE = 0.90270152      C(P) =    4.23727280

                              B VALUE          STD ERROR        TYPE II SS            F        PROB>F

              INTERCEPT    176.18750000
              MELT           0.02750000       0.02782635       12.10000000         0.98       0.3318
              CHILL          0.12750000       0.05565269       65.02500000         5.25       0.0300
              REPEL         -1.83750000       0.12444320     2701.12500000       218.03       0.0001
              KNIFE         -0.31875000       0.06222160      325.12500000        26.24       0.0001

----------------------------------------------------------------------------------------------------------
```

NO OTHER VARIABLES MET THE 0.5000 SIGNIFICANCE LEVEL FOR ENTRY INTO THE MODEL.

a. List the order in which the independent variables enter the regression model.

b. List the independent variables from largest (in absolute value) to smallest correlation with STIFF. Correlations are shown in Exercise 15.13.

c. Compare the ordering of the variables given by the two lists.

15.17 Refer to Exercise 15.16. Use the F test for complete and reduced models described in Section 14.4 to test the hypothesis that the last two variables entered in the stepwise regression have no predictive value.

15.18 The consultant of Exercise 15.10 runs a regression model with CONTRIB/INCOME as the dependent variable. The key to the variables in the following output is as follows:

$$1 = \text{INCOME}$$
$$2 = \text{SIZE}$$
$$3 = \text{DPDUMMY}$$
$$4 = \text{ELDUMMY}$$
$$5 = \text{CHDUMMY}$$
$$6 = \text{EDLEVEL}$$
$$7 = \text{MATCHING}$$
$$8 = \text{CONTRIB}$$
$$9 = \text{CONTRIB/INCOME}$$

```
Predictor       Coef        Stdev      t-ratio
Constant      0.024569    0.004707       5.22
INCOME       -0.0000711   0.0001946     -0.37
SIZE          0.001146    0.002087       0.55
DPDUMMY       0.006555    0.006736       0.97
ELDUMMY       0.01557     0.01126        1.38
CHDUMMY       0.007371    0.005187       1.42
EDLEVEL      -0.03033     0.02558       -1.19
MATCHING      0.000284    0.002013       0.14

s = 0.005533    R-sq = 19.2%    R-sq(adj) = 0.4%
```

Analysis of Variance

SOURCE	DF	SS	MS
Regression	7	0.00021843	0.00003120
Error	30	0.00091855	0.00003062
Total	37	0.00113698	

a. Can the hypothesis that none of the independent variables has predictive value be rejected (using reasonable α values)?

b. Which variables have been shown to have statistically significant (say, $\alpha = .10$) predictive value as "last predictor in"?

15.19 A simpler regression model than that of Exercise 15.18 is obtained by regressing the dependent variable (variable 9) on the independent variables 3, 4, 6, and 7. The following output is obtained:

Predictor	Coef	Stdev	t-ratio
Constant	0.022158	0.002713	8.17
DPDUMMY	-0.004729	0.004531	-1.04
ELDUMMY	-0.002143	0.007182	-0.30
EDLEVEL	0.01237	0.01678	0.74
MATCHING	-0.000254	0.001948	-0.13

s = 0.005692   R-sq = 6.0%   R-sq(adj) = 0.0%

Analysis of Variance

SOURCE	DF	SS	MS
Regression	4	0.00006774	0.00001693
Error	33	0.00106924	0.00003240
Total	37	0.00113698	

a. What is the increment to R^2 for the model of Exercise 15.18, as opposed to the model considered here?

b. Is this increment statistically significant at $\alpha = .05$?

c. Which model do you think is more sensible, given the information you have?

15.6   RESIDUALS ANALYSIS: NONNORMALITY AND NONCONSTANT VARIANCE (Step 4) ∎

Once independent variables, including any polynomial or cross-product terms, have been defined and a tentative model selected, the next step in a careful regression analysis is to check for any gross violations of assumptions. The basic method for this check is analysis of the residuals from the model.

We have already discussed residuals analysis in Section 15.3. There we suggested plotting the residuals from a first-order (linear terms only) model against each independent variable, and looking for evidence of nonlinearity. In this section we discuss the use of residuals analysis for detecting nonnormality (including outliers) and nonconstant variance.

skewness   A simple histogram of the residuals reveals severe **skewness** or wild outliers. Skewness is not a terribly serious problem for sample sizes of 30 or more. The Central Limit Theorem allows us to use normal-distribution methods to make inferences about means, even if the population distribution is not normal. A more complicated version of the theorem allows us to make inferences about the coefficients and correlations if the distribution of errors isn't normal. In particular, the t and F tests of Chapter 14 are valid to a good approximation for even modestly large sample sizes ($n \geq 30$). The guidelines given in discussing inferences about means also apply in regression.

Nonnormality arising from skewness may have some effect when predicting individual y values. Because the prediction is about one particular y value, there is no averaging involved, and the Central Limit Theorem doesn't apply. If serious skewness is detected in a histogram of residuals, the "95%" of a 95% prediction interval must be taken with a grain of salt.

outlier   An **outlier** is a data point that falls far away from the rest of the data. Sometimes it is possible to isolate the reason for the outlier, other times it is not. For example, such a point may arise because of an error in recording the data, or in entering it into a computer, or because the observation is obtained under different conditions than the other observations. No matter what the source or reason for outliers, if they go undetected they can cause serious distortions in a regression equation.

EXAMPLE 15.14   Suppose the data for a regression study are as shown below.

x: 10   13   16   18   20   22   24   27   30
y: 31   35   42   45   51   53   59   31   70

Draw a scatter plot of the data, identify the outlier, and fit the model $Y = \beta_0 + \beta_1 x + \epsilon$ with and without the outlier point.

Solution   A scatter plot of the data (Figure 15.5) shows that any line with slope about 2 and intercept about 10 fits all the data points fairly well, except for the $x = 27$, $y = 31$ point. If that point is included, the least-squares equation is

$$\hat{y} = 19.94 + 1.32x$$

If it is excluded, the equation is

$$\hat{y} = 9.93 + 2.00x$$

The scatter plot shows clearly that the observation $(27, 31)$ is a high-influence outlier and that the regression equation is distorted by inclusion of this point. ■

Outliers cause particularly serious distortions because regression is based on minimizing total squared error. Rather than fitting a line with many small errors and one or two large ones (which yield huge squared errors), the least-squares method accepts numerous moderate errors to avoid large ones. The effect is to twist the line in the direction of the outlier.

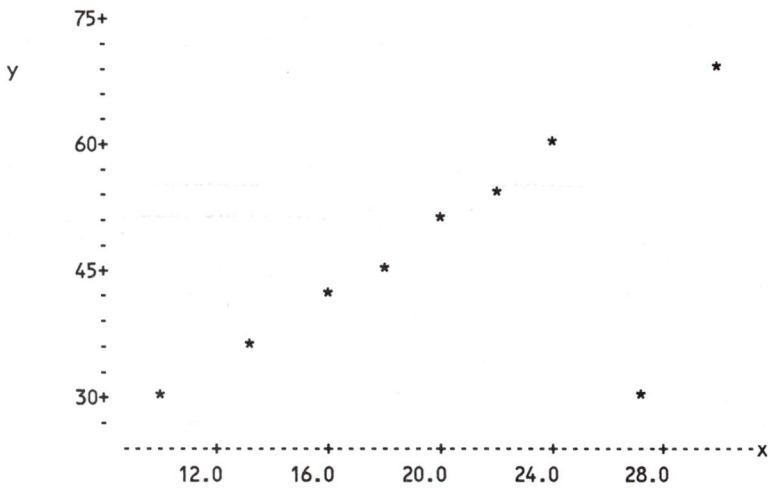

FIGURE 15.5   Effect of an Outlier; Example 15.14

The first problem with outliers is detection. In simple linear regression, a scatter plot of y versus x reveals outliers very clearly. In multiple regression, because it is not possible to plot all variables at once, scatter plots of y against each x separately are sometimes helpful. However, examination of the residuals (prediction errors) often provides more information regarding outliers than the separate scatter plots. A large residual suggests that the data point may be an outlier, but the fact that the regression line is twisted toward outliers (as indicated in the sample linear regression situation) sometimes causes an outlier to have a modest residual while residuals for perfectly legitimate data points are larger.

EXAMPLE 15.15   Use the computer output shown below and the residual $(y - \hat{y})$ for each observation to identify potential outliers for the data of Example 15.14.

Solution   From the output the residual for the data point $x = 27$, $y = 31$ is $31 - 55.57 = 24.57$. The next largest residual is 10.47 for the data point $x = 30$, $y = 70$. Most other residuals are quite a bit smaller. Note that the outlier data point $x = 27$, $y = 31$ twists the least-squares line down, making larger residuals for the data points near $x = 27$.

PARAMETER ESTIMATES

VARIABLE	DF	PARAMETER ESTIMATE	STANDARD ERROR	T FOR H0: PARAMETER=0	PROB > |T|
INTERCEP	1	19.9428	12.29563	1.622	0.1488
X	1	1.319527	0.5878062	2.245	0.0597

(*continued*)

OBS	ACTUAL	PREDICT VALUE	RESIDUAL
1	31	33.1381	-2.1381
2	35	37.0966	-2.0966
3	42	41.0552	0.944773
4	45	43.6943	1.30572
5	51	46.3333	4.66667
6	53	48.9724	4.02761
7	59	51.6114	7.38856
8	31	55.57	-24.57
9	70	59.5286	10.4714

■

jackknife method   Another approach to detecting outliers is the **"jackknife" method**. This involves calculating a series of regression equations, each time excluding one data point. When an outlier is excluded, coefficients in the regression equation change substantially. In principle, one could try excluding two or three points at a time, but the number of equations to calculate and examine would become prohibitive. The one-at-a-time jackknife method may not always catch multiple outliers, but often it does.

In practice, it may be necessary to consider a combination of techniques for examining the sample data for outliers. First, simple x, y scatter plots may suggest that certain observations are outliers. An examination of the residuals may (or may not) confirm this suspicion. If neither the scatter plots nor residuals suggest the existence of one or more outliers, one can probably end the search. However, identification of possible outliers could require additional work with jackknife techniques to isolate specific outliers.

If you detect outliers, what should you do with them? Of course recording or transcribing errors should simply be corrected. Sometimes an outlier obviously comes from a different population than the other data points. For example, a Fortune 500 conglomerate firm doesn't belong in a study of small manufacturers. In such situations, the outliers can reasonably be omitted from the data. Unless a compelling reason can be found, throwing out a data point **robust regression**   seems like cheating. There are **"robust regression"** methods that retain possible outliers and try to minimize distortions caused by them. One such method minimizes the sum of absolute (rather than squared) deviations. These methods should be used if there appear to be outliers that cannot be justifiably excluded from the data.

EXAMPLE 15.16   Apply a jackknife procedure, eliminating one data point at a time, to the data of Example 15.15. Examine the estimated slopes and intercepts to locate possible outliers.

Solution   The estimated slopes and intercepts are listed below. Note that the last two data points appear to be outliers.

Data Point Excluded	Slope	Intercept
10,31	1.21286	22.47672
13,35	1.26116	21.42333
16,42	1.33281	19.55234
18,45	1.32834	19.60120
20,51	1.31953	19.35947
22,53	1.29235	19.97601
24,59	1.21563	21.04531
27,31	2.00354	9.93239
30,70	.79712	28.42905

Thus, while the scatter plot of Figure 15.5 identified one potential outlier (the point 27, 31), an examination of the residuals as well as the jackknife procedure detects a second potential outlier (the point 30, 70). An examination of residuals from the regression omitting the point 27, 31 indicates that the point 30, 70 is not in fact an outlier. ∎

constant variance

Another formal assumption of regression analysis is that the (true, population) error variance σ_ϵ^2 is constant, regardless of the values of the x predictors. This assumption may also be violated in practice. In particular, it often occurs that combinations of x values leading to large predicted values of y also lead to relatively large variance around the predicted value. We here consider the consequences, detection, and possible cure of the problem of nonconstant error variance.

When the variance around the prediction equation is not constant, there are two basic consequences. Ordinary least-squares regression does not give the most accurate possible estimate of the regression equation, and the plus-or-minus error of prediction given in Chapters 13 and 14 may be seriously in error.

The estimation problem is less serious. If the error variance is not constant, the usual least-squares estimates are still valid in the sense of being unbiased. Furthermore, various studies have indicated that the F and t statistics still give about the same conclusions. The issue here is one of "opportunity cost"; if

heteroscedasticity

weighted least squares

heteroscedasticity (nonconstant variance) is recognized, it is possible to improve the estimation of the regression equation and the various related statistics. The technique of **weighted least squares**, as described in Johnston (1977), for example, yields somewhat more accurate estimates of the regression coefficients than does ordinary least-squares regression (more accurate estimates have smaller standard errors). The same technique makes the F and t statistics more powerful for testing the appropriate null hypotheses. Weighted least squares, in the presence of heteroscedasticity around the equation, makes more efficient use of the data.

The more serious problem arises in making forecasts. The best-guess forecast based on ordinary least-squares regression is still unbiased, but (given nonconstant error variance) the usual plus-or-minus formulas can be badly wrong. If the forecast y value falls in a high-variance zone, the theoretical plus-or-minus term may be much too small.

Probably the best way to detect heteroscedasticity is by eye and by data plot. The most useful plot is predicted y versus actual y, or predicted y versus residual $y - \hat{y}$. Most standard statistical computer programs can calculate predicted, actual, and residual values. Some have commands that produce the desired plots. In such plots, look for evidence that the variability of actual y values (or of residuals) increases as predicted y increases. There are several statistical significance tests for the research hypothesis of nonconstant variance. They generally tend to confirm the evidence of the "eyeball test," and the theory behind these tests leans heavily (uncomfortably so) on the normal-distribution assumption. We tend to prefer the eyeball method for detecting heteroscedasticity.

EXAMPLE 15.17   A very crude model for predicting the price of common stocks might take price per share (y) as a linear function of previous year's earnings per share (x_1), change in earnings per share (x_2), and asset value per share (x_3). A scatter plot of residuals versus predicted y values for a regression study of 26 stocks is shown in Figure 15.6. Is there evidence of a problem of heteroscedasticity?

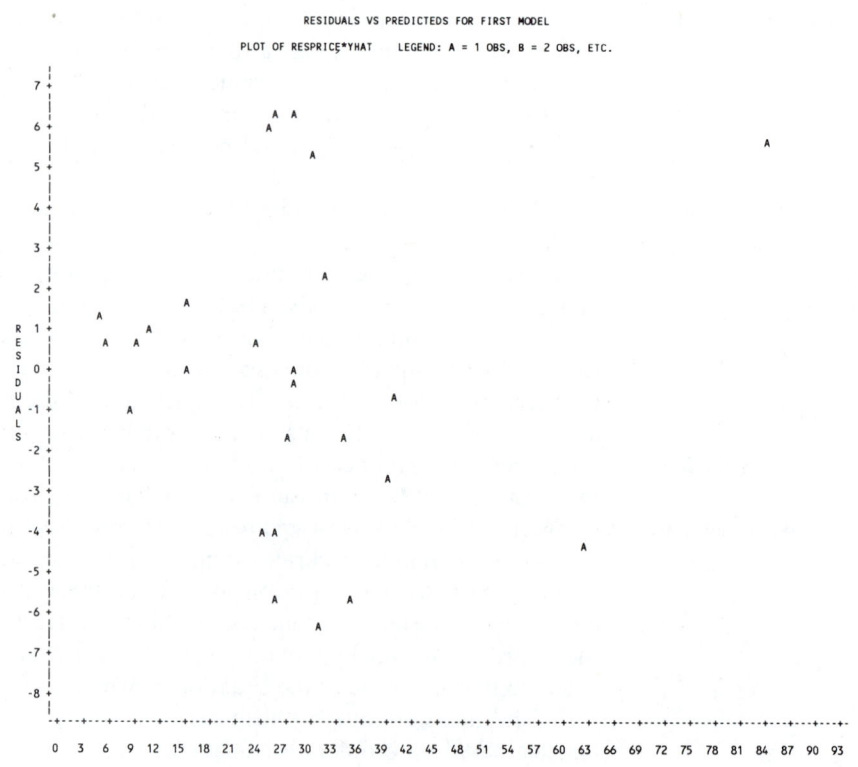

FIGURE 15.6   Residuals Versus Predicted Values; Example 15.17

Solution   In the plot of residuals versus predicted values, there is a general tendency for the magnitude of the residuals to increase as $\hat{y}$ increases. All residuals on the left are small. Therefore there seems to be a problem of nonconstant variance.   ■

Once we detect the problem of nonconstant variance, there are two basic cures. One is weighted least squares. The other, which often turns out to be equivalent to weighted least squares, is appropriate reexpression of the dependent variable. For example, one may try to predict the number of airline tickets sold for a particular airport from the population of the relevant metropolitan area, the average disposable income in the area, the number of Fortune 500 companies in the area, and so on. Almost certainly, there will be larger variance in number of tickets sold at larger airports. If the dependent variable is redefined as number of tickets sold per capita, the problem of heteroscedasticity may well disappear. A little thought in defining the regression equation often goes a long way.

EXAMPLE 15.18   The dependent variable in Example 15.17 is redefined to be price per share divided by earnings per share (the P/E ratio). The SAS output is shown on the next page, and the revised model is plotted in Figure 15.7.

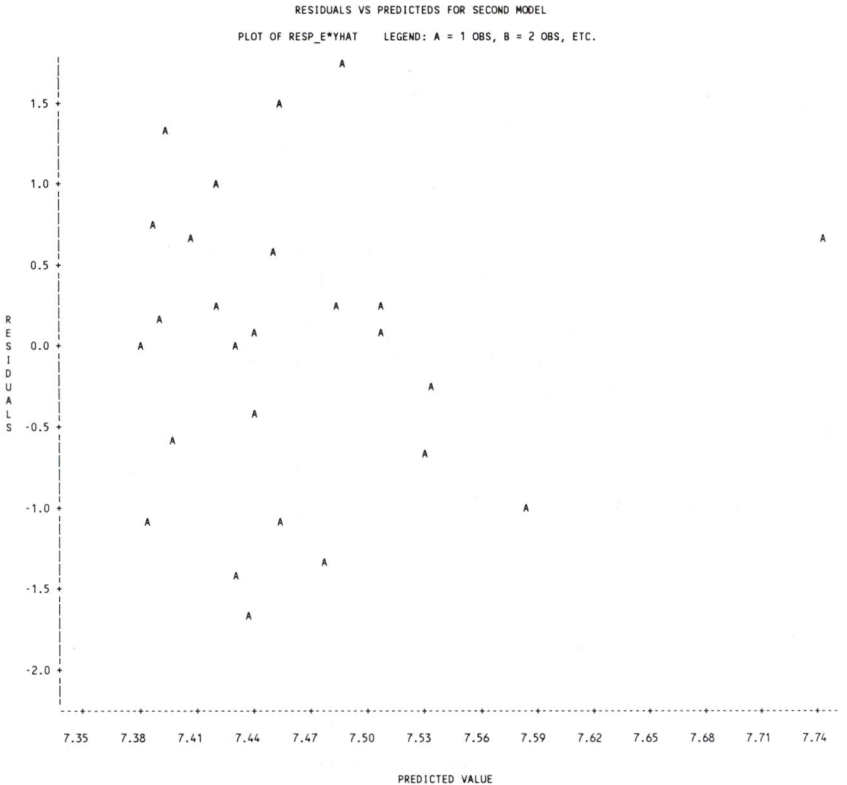

FIGURE 15.7   Residuals Versus Predicted Values; Example 15.18

SECOND MODEL

ANALYSIS OF VARIANCE

SOURCE	DF	SUM OF SQUARES	MEAN SQUARE	F VALUE	PROB>F
MODEL	2	0.1520641	0.07603204	0.083	0.9209
ERROR	23	21.15736	0.9198854		
C TOTAL	25	21.30943			

ROOT MSE	0.9591066	R-SQUARE	0.0071	
DEP MEAN	7.46351	ADJ R-SQ	-0.0792	
C.V.	12.85061			

PARAMETER ESTIMATES

VARIABLE	DF	PARAMETER ESTIMATE	STANDARD ERROR	T FOR H0: PARAMETER=0	PROB > |T|
INTERCEP	1	7.372642	0.3967074	18.585	0.0001
DEARN	1	-0.459169	1.85963	-0.247	0.8072
ASSET	1	0.00891629	0.02395633	0.372	0.7132

a. Write the model for Example 15.17.
b. Divide this model equation by the earnings variable to obtain the revised model.
c. Identify the estimated coefficients in the revised model.
d. Does there appear to be a problem of nonconstant variance with the revised model (see Figure 15.7)?
e. Use the revised model to predict the price of a stock with earnings 3.00, growth .27, and assets 14.25.

Solution   a. $Y = \beta_0 + \beta_1 x_1 + \beta_2 x_2 + \beta_3 x_3 + \epsilon$.
b. $Y/x_1 = \beta_1 + \beta_2(x_2/x_1) + \beta_3(x_3/x_1) + \epsilon$, where we omit the term β_0/x_1.
c. $\hat{\beta}_1 = 7.373$, $\hat{\beta}_2 = -.459$, and $\hat{\beta}_3 = .0089$.
d. The residual plot is much better for the revised model.
e. Substituting $x_1 = 3.00$, $x_2 = .27$, and $x_3 = 14.25$ into the ratio model, we have $\hat{y} = 7.373 - .459(.27/3) + .0089(14.25/3) = 7.374$.   ∎

EXAMPLE 15.19   A first-order model is developed for predicting feed sales using the independent variables defined in Example 15.11. A plot of residuals versus starts is shown in Figure 15.8. Is there evidence of nonconstant variance?

Solution   There appears to be a definite increase in variability as starts increase. This seems reasonable, and we would not be surprised to see more variability in high-activity months.   ∎

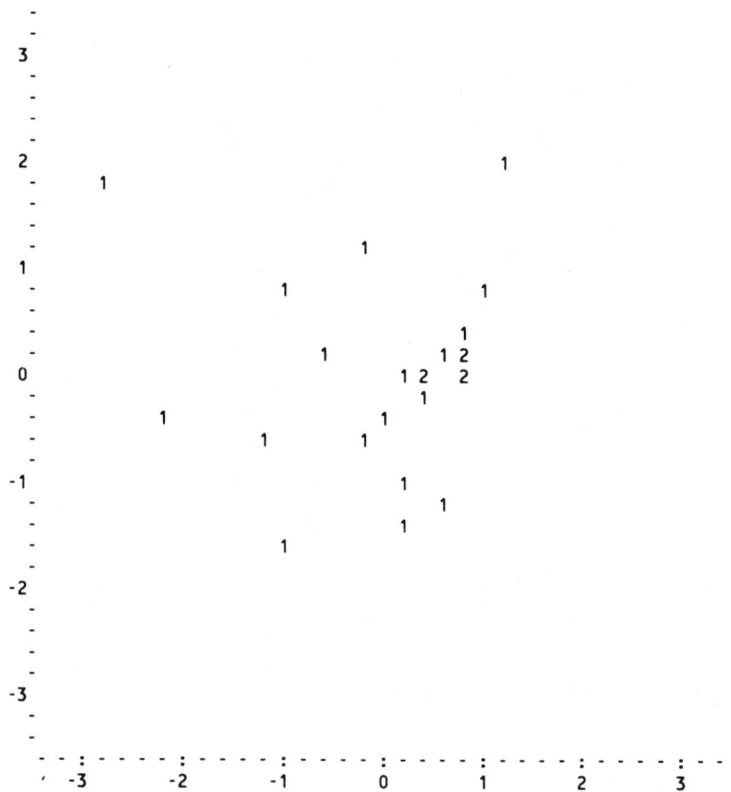

FIGURE 15.8   Standardized Residuals Versus Starts; Example 15.19

15.7   RESIDUALS ANALYSIS: AUTOCORRELATION (Step 4) ■

One of the crucial assumptions of regression analysis is that the error terms ϵ_i, which might be called the "true residuals," are independent. Much of the statistical theory of regression depends heavily on this assumption. In practice the assumption may be wrong. Time-series data, where the data points are measured at successive times, often shown more-or-less cyclic behavior. If such behavior is shown by a dependent variable y, and if no x variable matches the apparent cycles, the sample residuals show evidence of dependence. This problem, which is largely restricted to time-series data, is called **autocorrelation**.

autocorrelation

To see why autocorrelation (dependence of the error terms) is a problem, assume that we have the linear regression model

$$Y_i = \beta_0 + \beta_1 x_i + \epsilon_i$$

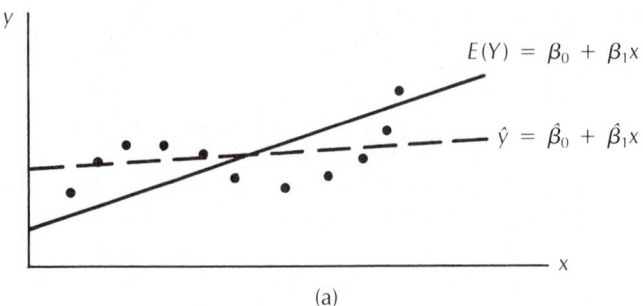

(a)

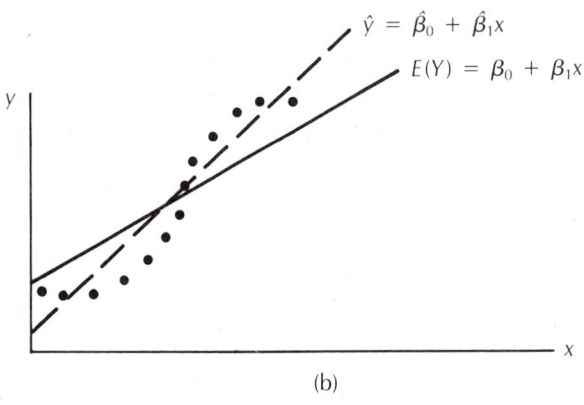

(b)

FIGURE 15.9   Two Possible Results of Autocorrelation

where x_i represents the time when observation y_i is obtained and the least-squares prediction equation is

$$\hat{y}_i = \hat{\beta}_0 + \hat{\beta}_1 x_i$$

Now, for illustration purposes, suppose that the values of the parameters β_0 and β_1 are known, so that we can draw the line $E(Y_i) = \beta_0 + \beta_1 x_i$. Two such regression lines are shown by solid lines, one in Figure 15.9a and a second in Figure 15.9b. The observations in these figures are designated by data points, and the least-squares prediction equations are shown by dashed lines.

In each figure the y values (and hence the error terms ϵ) show a definite nonrandom pattern about the true regression line $E(Y) = \beta_0 + \beta_1 x$. In Figure 15.9a, a series of several y values above the true regression line (positive errors) is followed by a series of y values below the true regression line (negative errors). In Figure 15.9b the negative errors occur first, followed by the positive errors. If the errors (ϵ) are independent, the pattern of positive and negative errors should be random. The cyclic pattern of the y values (and hence the errors) clearly indicates that autocorrelation is present.

effect of autocorrelation   What are the **effects of autocorrelation** on the usual types of inferences that we make in regression? Figure 15.9 illustrates some of the difficulties. In both situations (where autocorrelation exists), the least-squares prediction equation provides too good a fit to the sample data; that is, the least-squares line is closer to the y values than is the true regression line. Because of this, the residuals (the observed errors, $y - \hat{y}$) are smaller than the true errors (the ϵ's) and the residual standard deviation s_ϵ provides an underestimate of the population standard deviation σ_ϵ. The net effect is that all formulas for standard error involving s_ϵ underestimate the actual standard errors. Further, if the residual standard deviation is too small in the presence of autocorrelation, the coefficient of determination is too large.

In practice, the detection of autocorrelation is based on the residuals, because the true errors (the ϵ's) are unknown. If a plot of the residuals versus time shows a cyclic, nonrandom pattern, it is likely that the true errors are dependent, and hence that autocorrelation is present.

EXAMPLE 15.20   Suppose that the data for a simple regression study are as follows:

y:	6.1	6.0	6.1	6.3	6.8	6.8	7.0	7.1	7.0	6.7	6.8	7.0	7.2	7.4	7.5
x:	1	2	3	4	5	6	7	8	9	10	11	12	13	14	15

Calculate and graph the least-squares regression line on a scatter plot of the data. Does there seem to be an autocorrelation problem?

Solution   The regression line $\hat{y} = 5.98 + .10x$. It is shown on a scatter plot of the data in Figure 15.10. The cyclic pattern (several negative residuals followed by several positive residuals, etc.) clearly indicates that autocorrelation is present.   ■

Durbin-Watson statistic   A formal test for autocorrelation uses the **Durbin-Watson statistic**. This statistic is based on the idea that, given (positive) autocorrelation, any one residual tends to be close to the following residual; a large positive residual tends

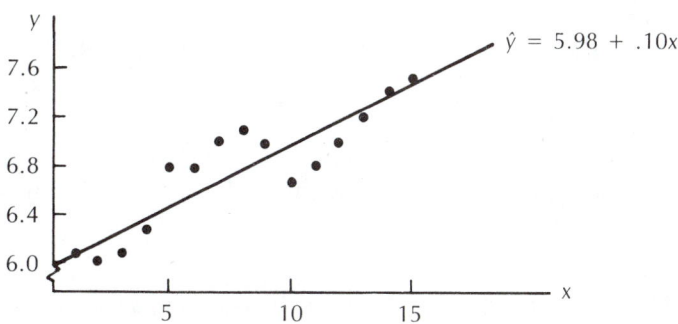

FIGURE 15.10   Correlated Residuals; Example 15.20

to be followed by another large positive one, and so on. Therefore the squared differences of successive residuals tend to be smaller under positive autocorrelation than they are when independent. The Durbin-Watson statistic is

$$d = \frac{\sum_{t=1}^{n-1} (\hat{\epsilon}_{t+1} - \hat{\epsilon}_t)^2}{\sum_{t=1}^{n} \hat{\epsilon}_t^2}$$

where $\hat{\epsilon}_t$ is the residual at time t. If the true errors are in fact independent, the expected value of d is about 2.0. Positive autocorrelation tends to make $\hat{\epsilon}_{t+1}$ close to $\hat{\epsilon}_t$ and therefore to make d less than 2.0. Tables for a formal hypothesis test based on d are available (see Johnston, 1977). In practice, though, we would hope to accept the null hypothesis of zero autocorrelation. Because accepting any null hypothesis leads to the nasty question of Type II errors, we prefer to use the Durbin-Watson statistic as an index rather than as a formal test. Any value of d less than 1.5 or 1.6 leads us to suspect autocorrelation.

EXAMPLE 15.21   Calculate the Durbin-Watson statistic for the data of Example 15.20. Does it indicate an autocorrelation problem?

Solution

x_t	y_t	$\hat{y}_t = 5.98 + .10x_t$	$\hat{\epsilon}_t = y_t - \hat{y}_t$	$\hat{\epsilon}_{t+1} - \hat{\epsilon}_t$	$(\hat{\epsilon}_{t+1} - \hat{\epsilon}_t)^2$	$\hat{\epsilon}^2$
1	6.1	6.08	+.02	−.20	.04	.0004
2	6.0	6.18	−.18	.00	.00	.0324
3	6.1	6.28	−.18	+.10	.01	.0324
4	6.3	6.38	−.08	+.40	.16	.0064
5	6.8	6.48	+.32	−.10	.01	.1024
6	6.8	6.58	+.22	+.10	.01	.0484
7	7.0	6.68	+.32	.00	.00	.1024
8	7.1	6.78	+.32	−.20	.04	.1024
9	7.0	6.88	+.12	−.40	.16	.0144
10	6.7	6.98	−.28	.00	.00	.0784
11	6.8	7.08	−.28	+.10	.01	.0784
12	7.0	7.18	−.18	+.10	.01	.0324
13	7.2	7.28	−.08	+.10	.01	.0064
14	7.4	7.38	+.02	.00	.00	.0004
15	7.5	7.48	+.02	—	—	.0004
					.46	.638

The Durbin-Watson statistic $d = .46/.638 = .721$. This value is far below the ideal value of 2.0 and the cutoff of 1.5. Autocorrelation is clearly a problem.   ∎

EXAMPLE 15.22   Data for 24 months for the feed manufacturer of Example 15.11 are shown below. STARTS is the number of starts in the previous month, RELPRI is the manufacturer's feed price in the month (relative to an index), CHICKP is the monthly average price of chickens, COMPPR is the chief competitor's price (also relative to an index), and SALES is monthly feed sales by the manufacturer.

ROW	STARTS	RELPRI	CHICKP	COMPPR	SALES
* 1 *	6.46000	16.21000	0.49300	15.99000	241.00000
* 2 *	7.20000	16.19000	0.51700	16.31000	264.00000
* 3 *	6.68000	16.06000	0.46200	16.26000	259.00000
* 4 *	7.01000	15.97000	0.49000	16.12000	258.00000
* 5 *	7.47000	16.31000	0.53600	16.41000	265.00000
* 6 *	7.68000	16.58000	0.59400	16.49000	255.00000
* 7 *	7.65000	16.97000	0.57000	17.00000	267.00000
* 8 *	7.49000	17.21000	0.53800	17.01000	243.00000
* 9 *	7.38000	17.08000	0.49900	16.96000	251.00000
* 10 *	7.46000	17.00000	0.48600	17.21000	268.00000
* 11 *	7.58000	17.15000	0.52500	17.47000	277.00000
* 12 *	7.56000	17.31000	0.49000	17.22000	260.00000
* 13 *	7.60000	17.08000	0.47300	17.11000	269.00000
* 14 *	7.31000	17.11000	0.43100	17.01000	252.00000
* 15 *	7.04000	16.97000	0.45600	16.99000	248.00000
* 16 *	7.03000	16.90000	0.46400	17.16000	278.00000
* 17 *	7.36000	16.84000	0.47700	17.24000	295.00000
* 18 *	7.53000	17.17000	0.50900	17.38000	277.00000
* 19 *	7.68000	17.52000	0.49200	17.46000	264.00000
* 20 *	7.73000	17.67000	0.47400	17.81000	284.00000
* 21 *	7.51000	17.65000	0.51000	17.70000	267.00000
* 22 *	7.84000	17.34000	0.49500	17.47000	291.00000
* 23 *	7.67000	17.59000	0.50100	17.50000	263.00000
* 24 *	7.70000	17.52000	0.42300	17.63000	279.00000

A first-order model is run with independent variables STARTS, RELPRI, CHICKP, and COMPPR (using the IDA package). The following selected output is obtained. The plot of residuals is shown in Figure 15.11 (page 692). Is there evidence of autocorrelation?

```
> coef

VARIABLE  B(STD.V)      B       STD.ERROR(B)    T

STARTS     0.6048   2.9846E+01  5.5488E+00    5.379
RELPRI    -2.2814  -7.5555E+01  6.5053E+00  -11.614
CHICKP    -0.1547  -6.7000E+01  3.4754E+01   -1.928
COMPPR     2.3187   7.5660E+01  6.8608E+00   11.028
CONSTANT   0        7.0308E+01  4.5134E+01    1.558

> summ

            MULTIPLE R   R-SQUARE
UNADJUSTED    0.9651      0.9315
 ADJUSTED     0.9576      0.9171

STD. DEV. OF RESIDUALS = 4.8684E+00
N =   24

> durb
DURBIN-WATSON STAT. =        1.5574
```

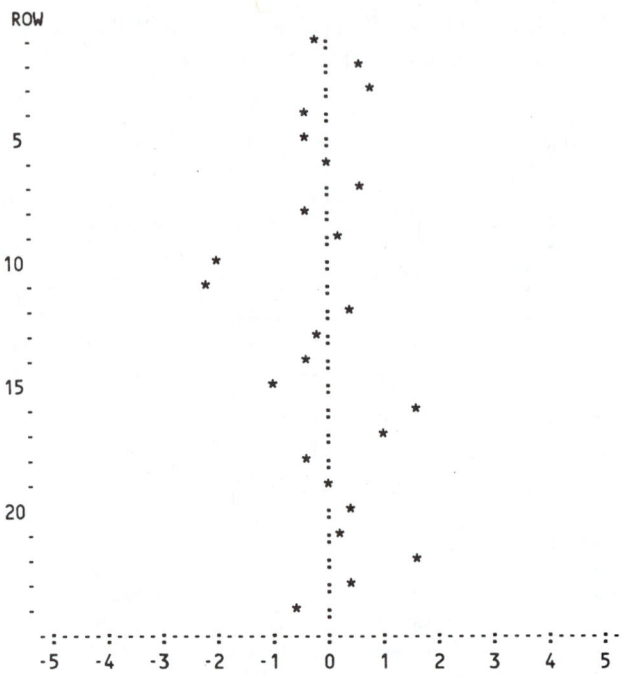

FIGURE 15.11   Sequence Plot of Standardized Residuals; Example 15.22

Solution   There is some suggestion of autocorrelation. The Durbin-Watson statistic is 1.5574 and there is perhaps a hint of a pattern in the sequence plot of residuals; that is, there seems to be some roughly cyclic behavior in the sequence of residuals.   ∎

EXAMPLE 15.23   In an attempt to solve the problem of nonconstant variance detected in Example 15.19, a revised model is run. The dependent variable is SHARE = SALES/STARTS. The independent variables are RELPRI and RELDIF = (RELPRI − COMPPR)/CHICKP. Selected output is shown below, and the residuals are plotted in Figure 15.12. Is there evidence of an autocorrelation problem?

```
> coef

VARIABLE  B(STD.V)      B       STD.ERROR(B)    T

RELPRI    -0.0672 -2.5317E-01  3.2385E-01   -0.782
RELDIF    -0.9103 -5.3179E+00  5.0192E-01  -10.595
CONSTANT    0      3.9351E+01  5.5075E+00    7.145

> durb

DURBIN-WATSON STAT. =        1.4008
```

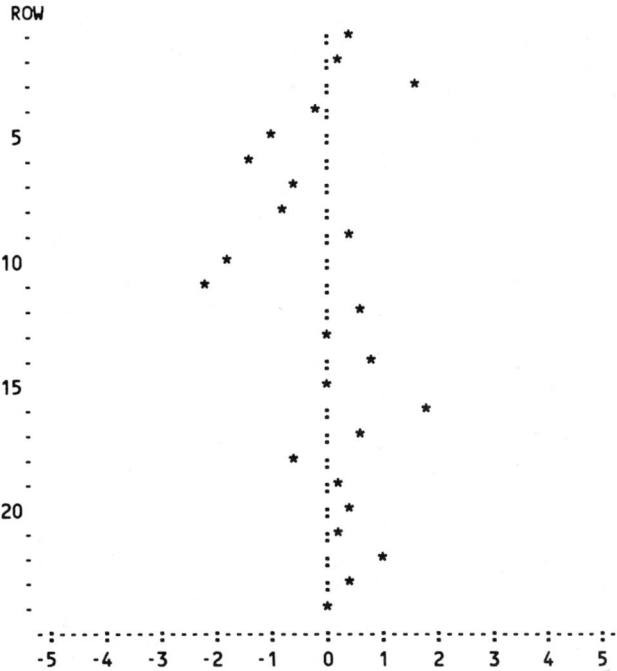

FIGURE 15.12   Sequence Plot of Standardized Residuals; Example 15.23

Solution   The Durbin-Watson statistic is 1.4 and the sequence plot of residuals clearly suggests autocorrelation. ■

If autocorrelation is suspected, either because of a plot of residuals versus time or because of a Durbin-Watson statistic less than about 1.5 or 1.6, what should be done about the regression model? Ideally, we should adopt an auto-correlation model for the error terms. One simple error model is the **first-order autoregressive model**

first-order autoregressive model

$$\epsilon_t = u_t + \rho u_{t-1}$$

where the u_t values are independent and ρ is a model parameter; $\rho > 0$ yields positive autocorrelation.* If this model is correct and if (miraculously) ρ is known, then it can be proven that

$$Y_t - \rho Y_{t-1} = \beta_0(1 - \rho) + \beta_1(x_{t1} - \rho x_{t-1,1})$$
$$+ \cdots + \beta_k(x_{tk} - \rho x_{t-1,k}) + (\epsilon_t - \rho \epsilon_{t-1})$$

---

* This is the simplest of the Box-Jenkins models we will discuss in Chapter 16.

is a model satisfying the assumption of independent error. In practice, the problem is to estimate the unknown error parameter ρ.

use of differences

A quick approach to the problem is to assume $\rho = 1$. This leads to a regression of the differences $y_t - y_{t-1}$ on the differences $x_{t1} - x_{t-1,1}, \ldots, x_{tk} - x_{t-1,k}$. Often, using differences eliminates any autocorrelation problems. This method also tends to reduce collinearity, which is often a major problem with time-series data.

Cochran-Orcutt method

Regression of differences is a crude approach because it assumes that the autocorrelation parameter $\rho = 1$. A more sophisticated approach is the Cochran-Orcutt method. In this method, we begin with a raw-data regression, estimate ρ, re-regress on $y_t - \rho y_{t-1}$, reestimate ρ, and so on to convergence. Alternatively, it is possible to search for the least-squares value of ρ. For details, consult a time-series specialist.

Alternatively, the presence of cyclic residuals (autocorrelation) sometimes suggests new independent variables that should be included in the regression model. It may well be that inclusion of another variable, whose "highs" match the positive residuals and whose "lows" match the negative ones, will improve the model. There should be an explanation, that is, a theoretical reason, why the newly included variable relates to the dependent variable. Of course it's always risky to throw new variables into a model blindly.

EXAMPLE 15.24

First differences of the variables of Example 15.23 are calculated and a regression run. Selected IDA output is shown on the top of the next page. Note that although there were 24 observations initially, we now have 23 first differences.

```
> coef

VARIABLE  B(STD.V)      B       STD.ERROR(B)    T

DRELPR    -0.0811 -8.7320E-01   1.1592E+00   -0.753
DRELDF    -0.8684 -4.7008E+00   5.8276E-01   -8.066
CONSTANT   0       4.0462E-02   2.0865E-01    0.194

> durb

DURBIN-WATSON STAT. =       2.6979
```

The variables are DSHARE, DRELPR, and DRELDF, where the initial D in the variable names indicates that the quantities are differences. Is there evidence of an autocorrelation problem of a problem of nonconstant variance (see Figure 15.13)?

Solution

The Durbin-Watson statistic is just about 2.7, and the sequence plot of residuals (Figure 15.13a) shows a pattern of alternating positive and negative signs. If anything, the differencing method has produced overkill; positive autocorrelation

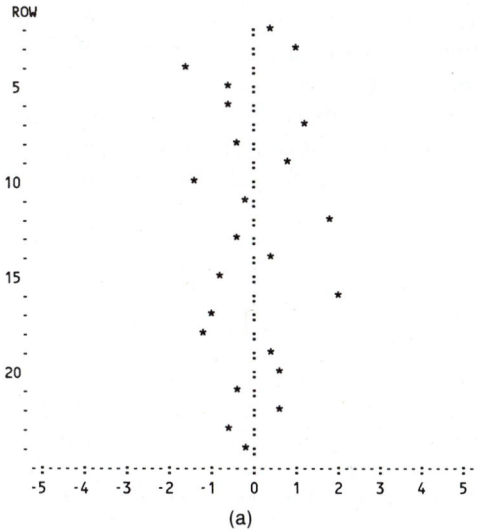

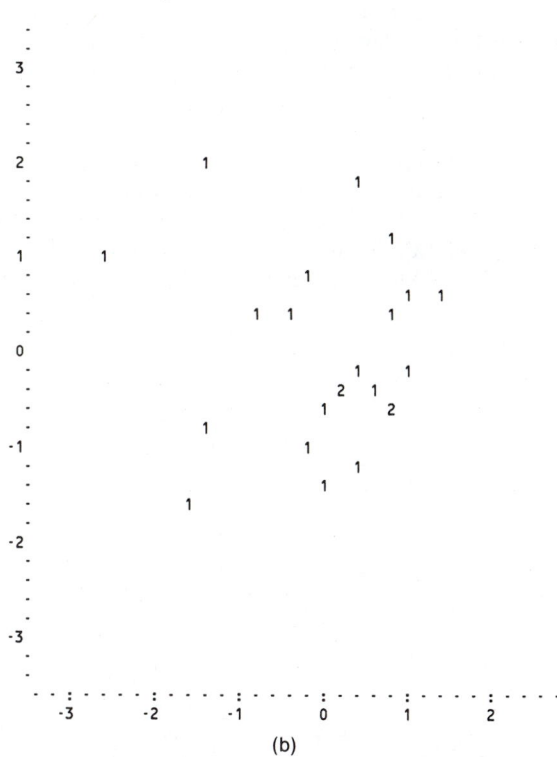

FIGURE 15.13   Example 15.24: (a) Sequence Plot of Standardized Residuals;
(b) Plot of Standardized Residuals Versus Starts

has been converted to apparent negative autocorrelation. Negative autocorrelation at least yields conservative results. A Cochran-Orcutt or search method might make more efficient use of the data.

The plot of residuals versus starts (Figure 15.13b) shows no problem of nonconstant variance. A plot of residual versus predicted values might be worthwhile to see if variability increases with increasing values of $\hat{y}$.   ■

SECTIONS 15.6 AND 15.7   EXERCISES

15.20   Residual plots for the regression model of Exercise 15.19 are shown in Figure 15.14 (a few of the marks on the plot represent two observations rather than one).
a. Is there any strong suggestion of nonlinearity?
b. Is there any strong suggestion of nonconstant variance?

15.21   The district sales office for a particular automobile is interested in predicting the sales of the "top of the line" luxury car in the district. It is obvious that sales are affected by the rated gasoline mileage of the car and by the car loan interest rate charged by the company's financing agency. It also seems plausible that sales are affected by gasoline prices and by the price of the car. Data are collected for 48 months; the last 6 months are reserved for model validation (to be discussed in Section 15.8). The variables are

MILAGE: Rated gas mileage of the car
GASPRI: Average price per gallon (in cents) in the district
PREGAS: Average gas price in the previous month
INTRAT: Interest rate (percent per year)
CARPRI: Sticker price divided by the consumer price index

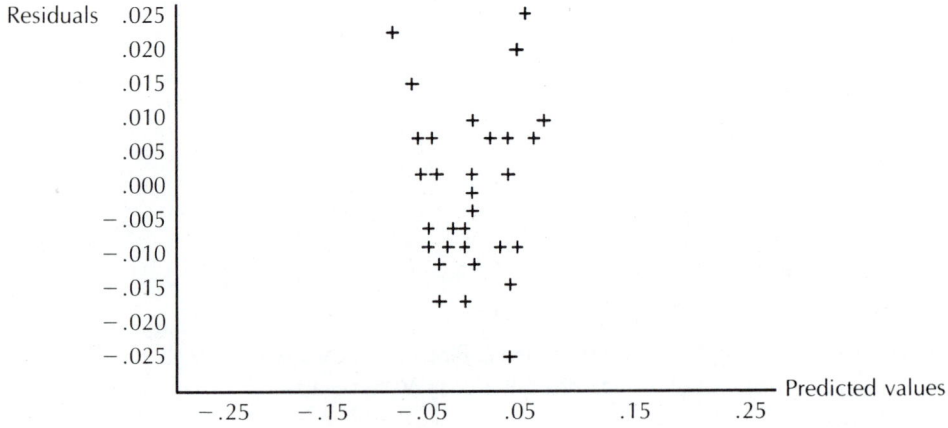

FIGURE 15.14   Residual Plot; Exercise 15.20

A first-order model is fit, using the IDA package. Selected output is shown below. Figure 15.15 (page 698) shows the sequence plot of residuals.

a. Write the estimated regression model.

b. Locate the standard deviation.

```
VARIABLE  B(STD.V)      B        STD.ERROR(B)     T

MILAGE     0.5277   2.3079E+02   5.3907E+01     4.281
GASPRI    -0.4004  -8.4934E+00   1.7006E+00    -4.994
PREGAS    -0.6884  -1.4538E+01   1.6374E+00    -8.878
INTRAT    -0.5310  -2.5170E+02   9.4153E+01    -2.673
CARPRI    -0.3382  -5.6437E+01   4.2268E+01    -1.335
CONSTANT   0         5.7597E+03   2.0978E+03    2.746

MEAN      =  0.0000E+00
STD. DEV. =  4.7543E+01
SAMPLE SIZE =   42
DURBIN-WATSON STAT. =        0.7999
```

15.22 Refer to the output for the model for Exercise 15.21 and to Figure 15.15.

    a. Does the Durbin-Watson statistic indicate that there is a problem of (positive) autocorrelation?

    b. Does the sequence plot of residuals indicate that autocorrelation is a problem?

15.23 The auto-sales forecasting model of Exercise 15.21 is modified in two ways. First, the gas price variables are divided by the mileage figure to yield rated gas price per mile driven. The current month's price per mile is called PRIMIL, and the previous month's is LAGPRM. Second, differences of the variables SALES, PRIMIL, LAGPRM, INTRAT, and CARPRI are calculated; the names are prefaced by a C. A regression model based on these differences is fit, with the following results (IDA). The sequence plot of residuals is shown in Figure 15.16 (page 699).

```
VARIABLE  B(STD.V)      B        STD.ERROR(B)     T

CPRIMI    -0.3537  -8.9662E+01   1.6951E+01    -5.289
CLAGPR    -0.8760  -2.2195E+02   1.5782E+01   -14.064
CINTRA    -0.0865  -1.0950E+02   8.5126E+01    -1.286
CCARPR     0.0095   5.8950E+00   3.9183E+01     0.150
CONSTANT   0       -6.6169E-01   6.6030E+00    -0.100

             MULTIPLE R   R-SQUARE
UNADJUSTED     0.9276      0.8605
ADJUSTED       0.9192      0.8450

STD. DEV. OF RESIDUALS = 3.7339E+01
N =   41

DURBIN-WATSON STAT. =        1.8867
```

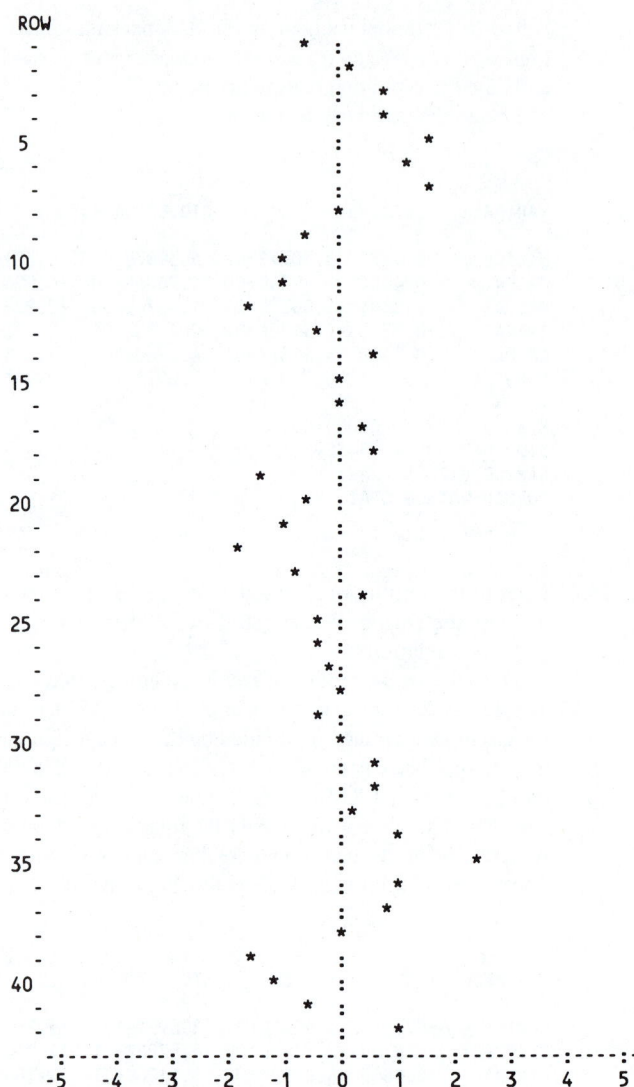

FIGURE 15.15   Sequence Plot of Residuals; Exercise 15.21

a. Write the regression equation.
b. Locate the residual standard deviation.
c. Is the residual standard deviation larger for the difference model than for the original? Why would this be a common result?

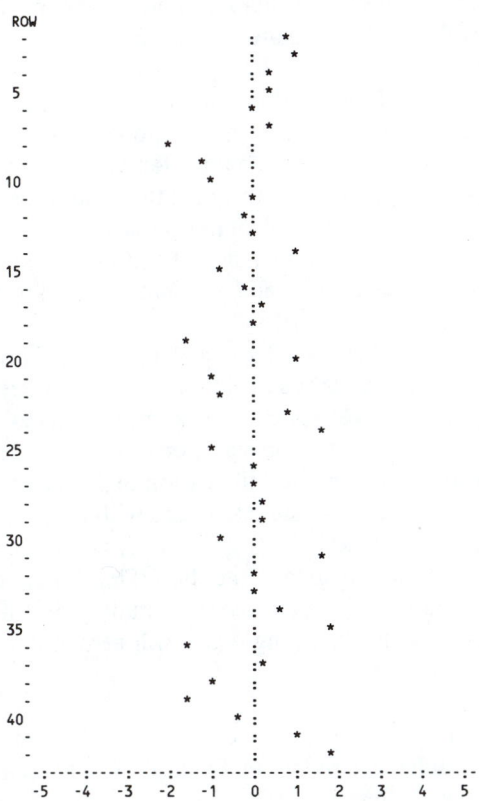

FIGURE 15.16   Sequence Plot of Residuals; Exercise 15.23

15.8   MODEL VALIDATION

In this computer era, data can be "massaged" repeatedly at little cost. Regressions can be run with every conceivable combination of variables, transformations, and lags. It isn't unusual to have a hundred different regression equations run to try to predict a variable y. The statistical theory of regression analysis implicitly assumes that the choice of predictors x and dependent variable y has been made, once and for all, and that a single regression equation is found. The gap between theory and practice is wide.

The practice of calculating many regression equations and selecting the best one often leads to overoptimism. The apparent predictability decreases when the equation is used with new data—for two reasons. First, any regression equation is based on predicting the past; the equation is chosen to yield the best fit to available data. Second, when one selects the best of many equations, one runs a risk of "capitalizing on chance." Even purely random phenomena can be explained after the fact by some combination of variables, if you search long enough.

A good practical approach to selecting an appropriate prediction equation is to validate the chosen regression equation with new data. In a time-series study, we can withhold the most recent data from the original regression study. Then we can use the chosen regression equation to predict recent values. The resulting standard deviation gives a good indication of the future predictive value of the equation. We can use the same procedure with cross-section data. Select some subset of observations (perhaps 10% or 20%) at random, withhold them from the original study, and use them for validation. The chosen regression typically does not perform quite as well in the validation study. If it still works reasonably well, that's good grounds for believing that it will be useful in practice.

EXAMPLE 15.25   An additional 12 months' data are collected for the feed manufacturer of Example 15.11. The difference model of Example 15.24 is used with these data. The results are shown below.

Actual DSHARE	Predicatd DSHARE	Error
.6243	1.4735	−.8492
2.7931	1.7694	1.0237
−1.4616	−1.6785	.2169
−2.1039	−.4668	−1.6371
1.0487	.2520	.7967
3.4225	1.3979	2.0246
.8994	1.9018	−1.0024
−1.1583	−.7206	−.4377

(continued)

	Actual DSHARE	Predicatd DSHARE	Error
	1.2767	.4526	.8241
	4.0023	4.2146	−.2123
	−2.9046	−3.9520	1.0474
	−.8726	−.5465	−.3261
Mean	.4638	.3414	.1224
Standard deviation	2.2153	2.0665	1.0520

a. Is there any flagrant bias in the predictions?

b. The residual standard deviation for the model of Example 15.24 is .9293. Is the error standard deviation grossly different?

Solution   a. There's no obvious systematic error. The mean error is small (.1224) relative to the size of the actual values and to the error standard deviation. Exactly half of the errors are positive.

   b. The error standard deviation (1.0520) is only slightly larger than .9293. ∎

SECTION 15.8   EXERCISES

15.24 The auto-sales difference model of Exercise 15.23 is tested against data for months 43–48, which have been reserved for validation purposes. Selected output is shown here.

ROW	Y (OBSERVED)	YPRED (PREDICTED)	ERROR (Y-PRED)	SE (STD.ERROR)	ERROR/SE SQUARED
43	1.1000E+02	1.4230E+02	-3.2302E+01	3.9539E+01	6.6743E-01
44	-5.0000E+00	6.0607E+01	-6.5607E+01	3.8738E+01	2.8683E+00
45	2.7000E+01	2.8318E+01	-1.3177E+00	3.8475E+01	1.1729E-03
46	-4.5000E+01	-1.2990E+01	-3.2010E+01	4.3213E+01	5.4873E-01
47	8.1000E+01	-2.0403E+01	1.0140E+02	3.7939E+01	7.1439E+00
48	1.1000E+01	-6.8245E+00	1.7825E+01	3.8408E+01	2.1537E-01
MEAN	2.9833E+01		-2.0016E+00		1.9075E+00
S.D.	5.6958E+01		5.8224E+01		2.7649E+00

a. Is there strong evidence that the model systematically over- or underestimates the new y values?

b. Is the residual standard deviation about the same size as that of Exercise 15.23?

15.25 The consultant of Exercise 15.8 obtains data on eight more firms for purposes of model validation. These firms have the same general characteristics as the firms in the original study; no outrageous extrapolation is needed. The output results are obtained for the full model of Exercise 15.18 and the simpler model of Exercise 15.19.

ROW	Y (OBSERVED)	YPRED (PREDICTED)	ERROR (Y-PRED)	SE (STD.ERROR)	ERROR/SE SQUARED
39	2.1689E-02	2.2258E-02	-5.6888E-04	7.6159E-03	5.5796E-03
40	1.7102E-02	3.4139E-02	-1.7037E-02	9.9448E-03	2.9350E+00
41	1.4938E-02	2.1126E-02	-6.1886E-03	6.1308E-03	1.0190E+00
42	3.3333E-02	3.3550E-02	-2.1669E-04	1.5649E-02	1.9172E-04
43	1.5500E-02	1.7715E-02	-2.2154E-03	7.0702E-03	9.8182E-02
44	2.4333E-02	2.4698E-02	-3.6496E-04	1.7031E-02	4.5922E-04
45	6.4453E-03	2.5253E-02	-1.8808E-02	7.9858E-03	5.5467E+00
46	1.4333E-02	1.9342E-02	-5.0086E-03	6.6630E-03	5.6506E-01
MEAN	1.8459E-02		-6.3010E-03		1.2713E+00
S.D.	8.0226E-03		7.5135E-03		1.9935E+00

ROW	Y (OBSERVED)	YPRED (PREDICTED)	ERROR (Y-PRED)	SE (STD.ERROR)	ERROR/SE SQUARED
39	2.1689E-02	2.2246E-02	-5.5692E-04	6.3994E-03	7.5735E-03
40	1.7102E-02	2.2736E-02	-5.6335E-03	8.1305E-03	4.8010E-01
41	1.4938E-02	2.1881E-02	-6.9436E-03	6.2911E-03	1.2182E+00
42	3.3333E-02	2.5490E-02	7.8428E-03	6.3051E-03	1.5472E+00
43	1.5500E-02	2.5243E-02	-9.7431E-03	6.1848E-03	2.4817E+00
44	2.4333E-02	2.3854E-02	4.7956E-04	7.0329E-03	4.6495E-03
45	6.4453E-03	2.4755E-02	-1.8309E-02	6.0808E-03	9.0664E+00
46	1.4333E-02	2.4260E-02	-9.9268E-03	5.9659E-03	2.7687E+00
MEAN	1.8459E-02		-5.3489E-03		2.1968E+00
S.D.	8.0226E-03		7.9447E-03		2.9647E+00

a. Is there any systematic bias that is obvious from either prediction?
b. The standard deviation is estimated to be .006 in both models. Is there any evidence that the standard deviation has increased in the validation?
c. Is there any strong reason to abandon the simpler model?

Summary

In this chapter we have discussed some of the "tricks of the trade" for constructing satisfactory multiple regression models. To summarize, we present a series of steps for attempting a regression analysis.

Step 1 a. Try to identify and collect data on the most relevant independent variables. Ask those who are familiar with the problem what they think might be important predictors. Make sure the variables are well defined, but don't worry much about delicate distinctions. If two variables differ only in fine detail, either one should be about as satisfactory as the other.

    b. Consider what dummy variables or lagged variables should be added to the model.

    c. Think about whether a first-order model makes sense. Are additional nonlinear terms required? What transformations of the dependent variable might be sensible?

Step 2   Calculate a first-order model that involves all the variables and plot the residuals against each variable. Look for nonlinear patterns of the residuals. (This is a good spot to look for outliers as well.) Based on an interpretation of these plots, add appropriate quadratic terms, cross products, or other transformed variables to the model.

Step 3   Either by trial and error or by formal stepwise regression methods, add or delete variables. Consider both the technical issues (values of t statistics, C_p, and changes in R^2, in particular) and also whether the model is reasonable in context.

Step 4 a. Once a tentative model has been selected, fit the model and look at the residuals from that model. Look again for outliers or gross skewness. Plot residuals against predicted values to look for non-constant variance. If this problem appears serious, consider possible transformations of the dependent variable and redo the analysis using the transformed Y.

    b. With time-series data, plot the data against time and look for auto-correlation. If this plot and the Durbin-Watson statistic indicate that autocorrelation is a problem, reanalyze the data using differences or the Cochran-Orcutt method (if an appropriate computer program is available).

Step 5   Once a model has been chosen, validate it using new data. Expect to find some modest increase in the residual standard deviation. If the model consistently underpredicts or overpredicts or if the errors become much larger in magnitude, try whatever model you identified as second best.

    This agenda may seem impossibly long and time-consuming. In fact, most of the time and effort are required at the first step—deciding which variables to use, collecting the sample data, entering the data, and constructing the necessary data files prior to analysis. The actual machine-run time may only be a small portion of this time. The extra effort involved in developing a thoughtful, non-mechanical regression analysis is not that great, and the payoff can be large.

CHAPTER 15 EXERCISES

15.26 The residuals from the regression study of Example 14.19 (page 626) are plotted against the predicted values, as shown in Figure 15.17 (page 704).

    a. Is there evidence of any problem with this regression study? If so, what?

    b. Recall that the dependent variable in Example 14.19 is average account size per branch. Suppose that the dependent variable is redefined as average account size as a fraction of per capita income. What effect would you expect this redefinition to have on the problem of part (a)?

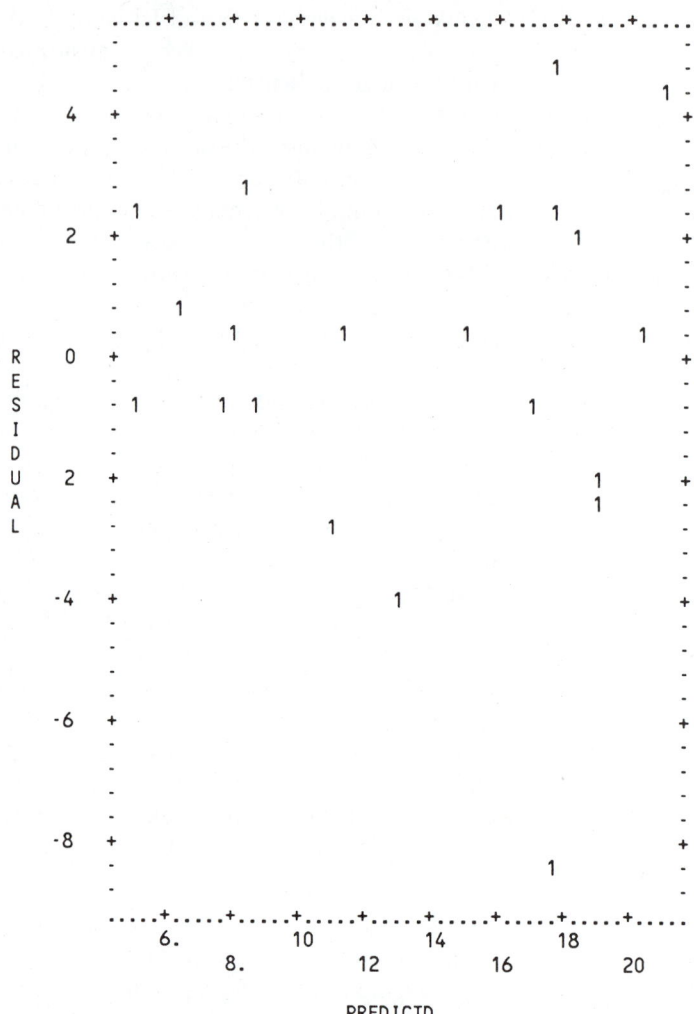

FIGURE 15.17   Scatter Plot for Exercise 15.26

15.27 Refer to the feedlot study of Exercise 14.32 (page 645).
   a. Is there a problem of collinearity?
   b. Would you expect to find a problem of autocorrelation?
   c. What additional information would you need to assess possible hetero-scedasticity? Might this be a problem?

15.28 Residuals from the regression of Exercise 14.27 are plotted in Figure 15.18 on the next page.
   a. What potential problems could you detect in such a plot?
   b. Do you find any evidence of such problems?

15.29 A firm that manufactures and sells moderately sophisticated word-processing equipment budgets a certain dollar amount for post-sale support activities. This

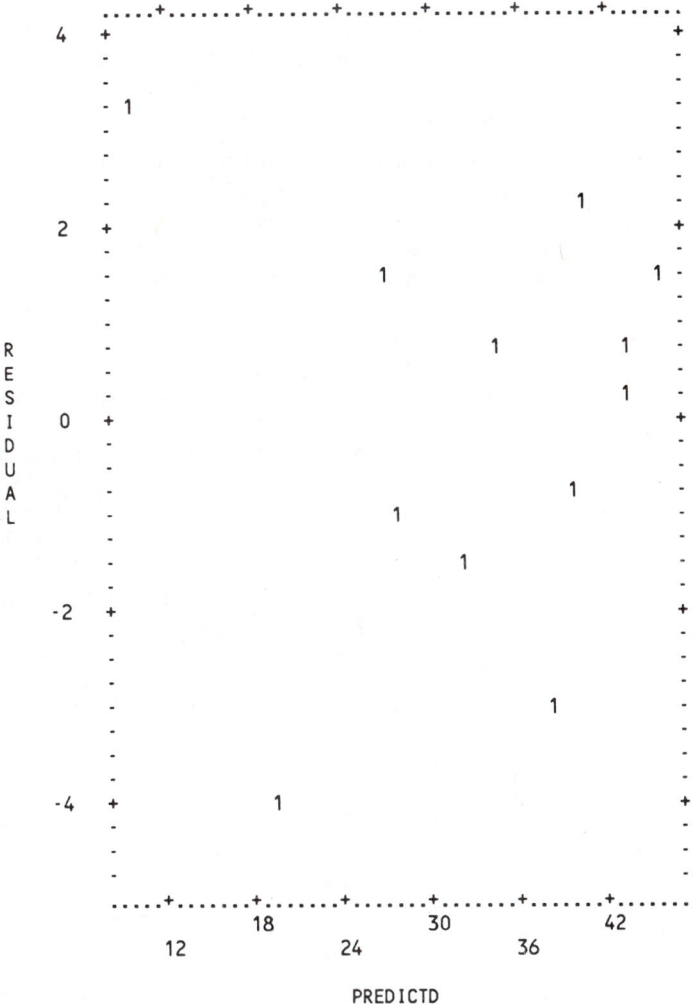

FIGURE 15.18   Scatter Plot for Exercise 15.28

support is provided by field representatives who train users initially and by home-office representatives who answer questions by telephone. Individuals shuttle between home and field-representative positions frequently, so it is not very meaningful to separate the positions in the budget. A regression study is made in an attempt to forecast the required support budget.

Analysis of the support requirements suggests that the training aspect of post-sales support typically involves users who have installed the equipment in the current and preceding months. For the next four months, there is substantial call-back support as users forget aspects of training or add new equipment operators. After that period, support activity is mostly trouble-shooting and new application work. Therefore the installation data to be used as independent variables are broken down as

1. number of installations in budget month (known in previous month)
2. number of installations in previous month
3. number of installations in preceding four months

These data are collected separately for the two levels of sophistication (A and B) of equipment (the A class requires more sophisticated training). Thus six independent variables are entered.

There is some question as to whether support costs increase in proportion to the number of installations. One opinion holds that the cost per installation decreases as installations increase because of improved user's manuals and more efficient training methods.

a. Identify any lagged variables.
b. Does the description of the situation indicate that any severe interaction can be expected?
c. Is there any indication of possible need for nonlinear terms in a regression model?

15.30 The firm of Exercise 15.29 collects data on the budgeted number of representatives (y) and the six independent variables described in that exercise. Data are available for 36 months, and the most recent 6 months' data are reserved for validation. A first-order regression model is fit to the remaining 30 months' data. A plot of the residuals against time is shown in Figure 15.19.

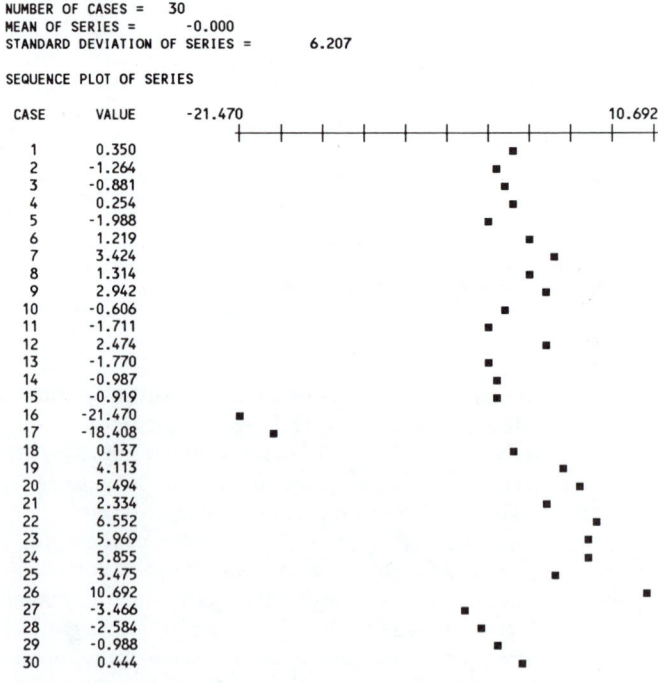

```
PLOT OF RESIDUAL
NUMBER OF CASES =    30
MEAN OF SERIES =        -0.000
STANDARD DEVIATION OF SERIES =        6.207

SEQUENCE PLOT OF SERIES

   CASE     VALUE      -21.470                                        10.692

     1       0.350
     2      -1.264
     3      -0.881
     4       0.254
     5      -1.988
     6       1.219
     7       3.424
     8       1.314
     9       2.942
    10      -0.606
    11      -1.711
    12       2.474
    13      -1.770
    14      -0.987
    15      -0.919
    16     -21.470
    17     -18.408
    18       0.137
    19       4.113
    20       5.494
    21       2.334
    22       6.552
    23       5.969
    24       5.855
    25       3.475
    26      10.692
    27      -3.466
    28      -2.584
    29      -0.988
    30       0.444
```

FIGURE 15.19   Residuals Versus Time; Exercise 15.30

      a. Is there any indication of possible outliers?

      b. Is there any indication of autocorrelation?

15.31 Investigation of the data of Exercise 15.30 shows that the support budget in months 16 and 17 had been cut back drastically in a spasm of cost cutting. This action led to many user complaints, so the attempt was abandoned. The budget numbers of those months are changed in the data base to the figures that had been planned before the cost-cutting attempt. A first-order model yields the plots of residuals versus predicted values shown in Figure 15.20. Is there any indication of possible heteroscedasticity (nonconstant variance)?

15.32 The square of the current month's installations (both A and B types) are added as independent variables. A stepwise (forward selection) regression analysis yields the Systat output on the top of page 708.

      a. List the sequence in which the variables are added.

      b. How much of an increment to R^2 is obtained by inclusion of the last four variables?

15.33 Additional output from the regression analysis of Exercise 15.32, for the model with all variables included, yields the scatter plots shown in Figure 15.21 (page 708).

      a. Is there evidence of serious autocorrelation?

      b. Is there evidence of nonconstant variance?

15.34 Differences for all variables in the data of Exercise 15.33 are calculated, and a stepwise (forward selection) regression is run. The output is on page 709. Is the sequence in which the variables are added similar to that found in Exercise 15.32?

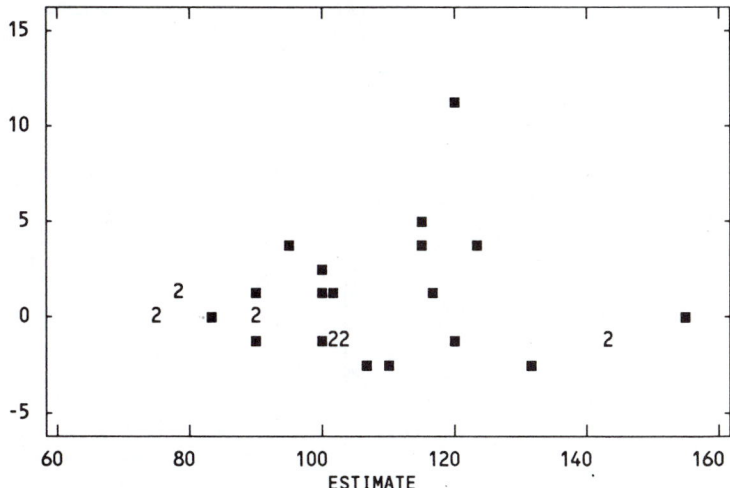

FIGURE 15.20   Residuals Versus Predicted Values; Exercise 15.31

```
DEP VAR:    SUPP      N:  30    MULTIPLE R:  .992    SQUARED MULTIPLE R:  .984
ADJUSTED SQUARED MULTIPLE R:  .978      STANDARD ERROR OF ESTIMATE:      3.088
```

VARIABLE	COEFFICIENT	STD ERROR	STD COEF	TOLERANCE	T	P(2 TAIL)
CONSTANT	-12.629	12.609	0.000	1.0000000	-1.002	0.328
ACURR	1.372	0.661	0.324	.0317871	2.075	0.050
APREV	0.986	0.153	0.227	.6247882	6.434	0.000
APREC4	0.148	0.075	0.087	.3976707	1.973	0.062
BCURR	2.264	0.913	0.597	.0133587	2.481	0.022
BPREV	0.573	0.150	0.156	.4652845	3.825	0.001
BPREC4	0.206	0.062	0.168	.3022238	3.310	0.003
ACURRSQ	0.006	0.025	0.039	.0285971	0.234	0.817
BCURRSQ	-0.021	0.018	-0.291	.0128034	-1.183	0.250

ANALYSIS OF VARIANCE

SOURCE	SUM-OF-SQUARES	DF	MEAN-SQUARE	F-RATIO	P
REGRESSION	12117.087	8	1514.636	158.815	0.000
RESIDUAL	200.279	21	9.537		

STEPWISE REGRESSION WITH ALPHA-TO-ENTER= .990 AND ALPHA-TO-REMOVE= .990

```
STEP=  1    ENTER  BCURRSQ    R=  .838    RSQUARE=  .701
STEP=  2    ENTER  ACURRSQ    R=  .912    RSQUARE=  .831
STEP=  3    ENTER   BPREV     R=  .958    RSQUARE=  .918
STEP=  4    ENTER   APREV     R=  .972    RSQUARE=  .945
STEP=  5    ENTER  BPREC4     R=  .984    RSQUARE=  .968
STEP=  6    ENTER   BCURR     R=  .989    RSQUARE=  .978
STEP=  7    ENTER   ACURR     R=  .990    RSQUARE=  .981
STEP=  8    ENTER  APREC4     R=  .992    RSQUARE=  .984
```

Systat for Exercise 15.32

RESIDUAL

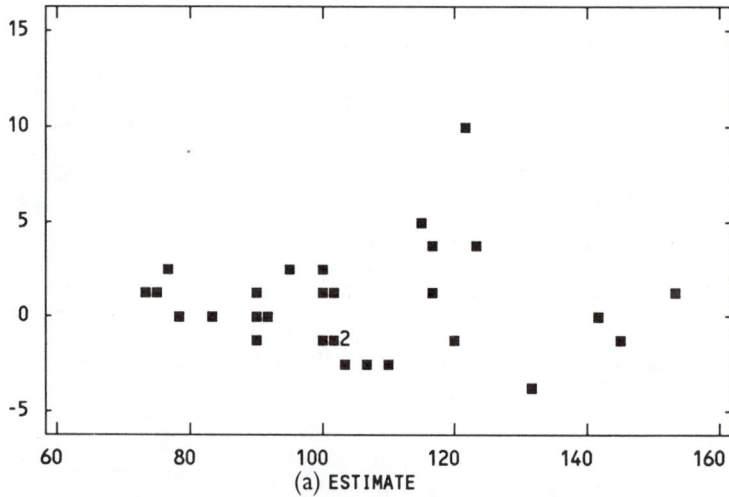

(a) ESTIMATE

FIGURE 15.21   Residual Plots for Exercise 15.33: (a) Residuals and Predicted Values;
(b) Residuals and Time

```
PLOT OF RESIDUAL
NUMBER OF CASES =    30
MEAN OF SERIES =        -0.000
STANDARD DEVIATION OF SERIES =        2.584

SEQUENCE PLOT OF SERIES

   CASE      VALUE      -4.141                                        9.006
                        +--+--+--+--+--+--+--+--+--+--+
     1        0.820
     2       -0.204
     3        1.414
     4       -0.360
     5       -1.764
     6       -0.824
     7        0.314
     8       -0.006
     9        2.131
    10       -2.012
    11       -2.298
    12        0.153
    13       -2.826
    14       -1.405
    15       -2.986
    16       -2.576
    17       -2.498
    18       -1.685
    19        1.947
    20        2.985
    21        2.680
    22        4.326
    23        0.896
    24        0.823
    25        0.529
    26        9.006
    27       -0.435
    28       -4.141
    29       -2.462
    30        0.458
```

FIGURE 15.21   (*Continued*)   (b)

```
STEPWISE REGRESSION WITH ALPHA-TO-ENTER= .999 AND ALPHA-TO-REMOVE= .999


    STEP=  1      ENTER   DACURR      R=  .681      RSQUARE=  .464
    STEP=  2      ENTER   DAPREV      R=  .864      RSQUARE=  .747
    STEP=  3      ENTER   DBCURR      R=  .954      RSQUARE=  .911
    STEP=  4      ENTER   DBPREV      R=  .964      RSQUARE=  .930
    STEP=  5      ENTER DBCURRSQ      R=  .968      RSQUARE=  .936
    STEP=  6      ENTER   DAPREC4     R=  .970      RSQUARE=  .940
    STEP=  7      ENTER DACURRSQ      R=  .970      RSQUARE=  .941
    STEP=  8      ENTER   DBPREC4     R=  .970      RSQUARE=  .941


    DEP VAR:  DSUPP      N:  29    MULTIPLE R:  .970   SQUARED MULTIPLE R:  .941
    ADJUSTED SQUARED MULTIPLE R:  .918      STANDARD ERROR OF ESTIMATE:      3.356
```

Systat for Exercise 15.34

(*continued*)

VARIABLE	COEFFICIENT	STD ERROR	STD COEF	TOLERANCE	T	P(2 TAIL)
CONSTANT	0.521	0.763	0.000	1.0000000	0.683	0.503
DACURR	1.335	0.540	0.624	.0460098	2.470	0.023
DAPREV	1.063	0.152	0.497	.5771369	6.974	0.000
DAPREC4	0.119	0.111	0.066	.7834705	1.073	0.296
DBCURR	2.025	0.686	1.004	.0253851	2.953	0.008
DBPREV	0.396	0.173	0.174	.5106955	2.292	0.033
DBPREC4	0.058	0.141	0.028	.6455454	0.414	0.683
DACURRSQ	0.010	0.020	0.121	.0467664	0.484	0.633
DBCURRSQ	-0.020	0.012	-0.542	.0257820	-1.608	0.124

ANALYSIS OF VARIANCE

SOURCE	SUM-OF-SQUARES	DF	MEAN-SQUARE	F-RATIO	P
REGRESSION	3610.604	8	451.326	40.084	0.000
RESIDUAL	225.189	20	11.259		

DURBIN-WATSON D STATISTIC   2.462
FIRST ORDER AUTOCORRELATION -.267

Systat for Exercise 15.34

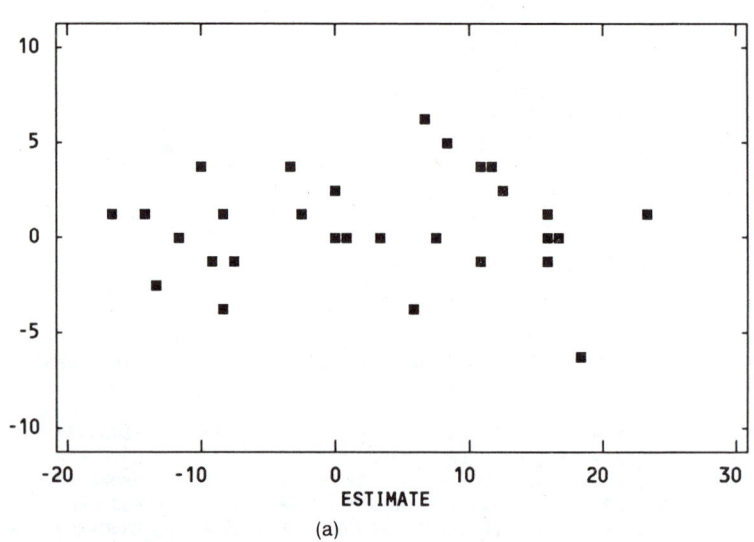

(a)

FIGURE 15.22   Residual Plots for Exercise 15.35: (a) Residuals and Predicted Values;
(b) Residuals and Time (on p. 711)

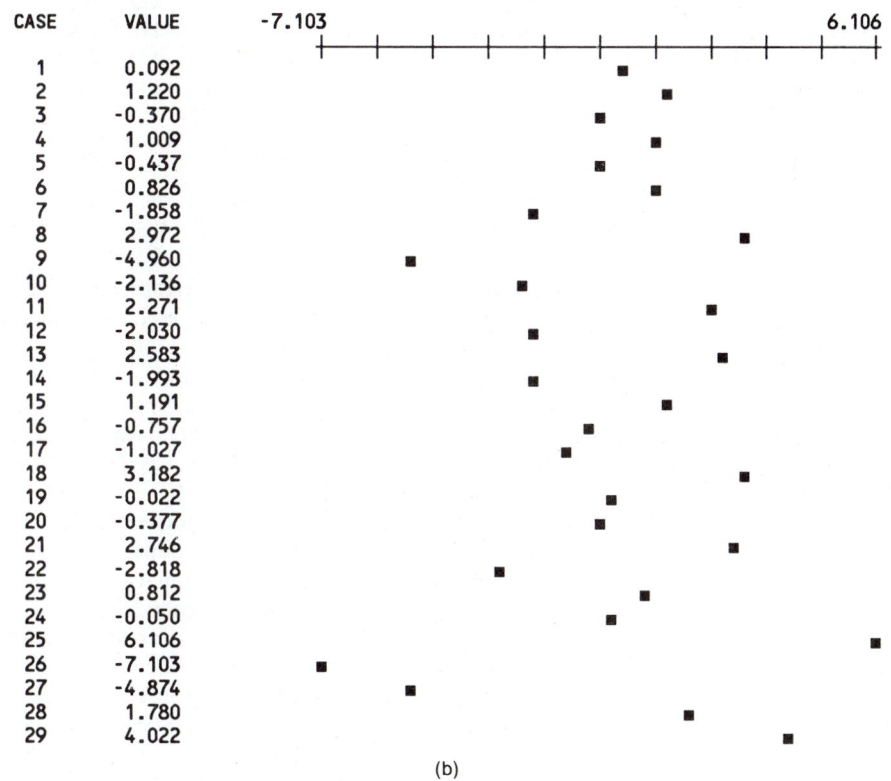

```
PLOT OF RESIDUAL
NUMBER OF CASES =    29
MEAN OF SERIES =        -0.000
STANDARD DEVIATION OF SERIES =        2.787

SEQUENCE PLOT OF SERIES

    CASE      VALUE      -7.103                                        6.106
      1       0.092
      2       1.220
      3      -0.370
      4       1.009
      5      -0.437
      6       0.826
      7      -1.858
      8       2.972
      9      -4.960
     10      -2.136
     11       2.271
     12      -2.030
     13       2.583
     14      -1.993
     15       1.191
     16      -0.757
     17      -1.027
     18       3.182
     19      -0.022
     20      -0.377
     21       2.746
     22      -2.818
     23       0.812
     24      -0.050
     25       6.106
     26      -7.103
     27      -4.874
     28       1.780
     29       4.022
```

(b)

FIGURE 15.22   (*Continued*)

15.35 Additional output from the all-variables model of Exercise 15.34 is shown in Figure 15.22.
   a. Is there an autocorrelation problem with the differenced data?
   b. Is there evidence of heteroscedasticity?

15.36 Consider the output from the regression study of Exercise 15.34.
   a. Write the regression model.
   b. Can the null hypothesis that all partial slopes are zero be rejected at reasonable α levels?
   c. Which variables have coefficients that differ significantly (at $\alpha = .05$) from zero as "last predictor in"?
   d. Identify and interpret the R^2 value.
   e. Identify the residual standard deviation.

15.37 In Exercise 15.30 the most recent six months' data were reserved for validation. These values, in difference form, are shown on the next page, along with the predicted values given by the model of Exercise 15.34.

ACURR	APREV	APREC4	BCURR	BPREV	BPREC4	ACURRSQ	BCURRSQ	Actual Support	Predicted Support
−2	−3	9	5	3	1	−80	−135	2	5.78
5	−2	3	−6	5	1	215	−80	−3	−.97
−4	5	−1	4	−6	3	−176	215	5	2.99
−4	−4	−7	−6	4	8	−144	−176	−5	−9.94
14	−4	−4	7	−6	6	644	−144	17	15.29
−2	14	−5	4	7	−3	−116	644	11	12.78

a. Calculate the residuals and their standard deviation.

b. Is this residual standard deviation much larger than the one found in Exercise 15.34?

c. Previous forecasts of the budget were often in error by as much as ±20 units. Does it appear that the regression model will be useful in predicting the budget figure?

15.38 A wholesale hardware company fills orders at a large warehouse. The volume of orders fluctuates substantially from day to day, and the company has a policy of filling each order on the day of receipt. Orders are phoned or mailed, and they are received by 10 A.M. The warehouse supervisor estimates the total time required for each order and assigns the required number of workers to order filling. Excess workers, if any, are assigned to other tasks and cannot be recalled until the next day. The supervisor's estimates of time per order are often quite erroneous, so that sometimes workers are idle and other times substantial overtime must be paid. A regression study is attempted to improve the prediction of required time per order. The minicomputer used for order processing and inventory control can easily calculate predicted times once a model is determined.

Items in the order are classified as frequently, moderately, or rarely ordered. The rarely ordered items are stored in the most distant parts of the warehouse and therefore require more time to obtain. Both the number of items ordered in each category and the average size per item are thought to influence the order-filling time. Most items ordered are in carton units, and less-than-carton items (which are mostly rarely ordered) are filled as "loose-box" items. Certain orders require special packing to protect fragile items. The supervisor assigns each such order to either packing station A or B. All items are assembled at a central station and placed on skids. A forklift is used to move the skids from the assembly station to delivery trucks.

A sample of 50 orders is selected; care is taken to include relatively extreme types of order (small and large, mostly loose-box and mostly carton, mostly frequent and mostly rare). Values for each of the following variables are recorded:

TIME:	Time (in worker-minutes) needed to fill order
NUMFREQ:	Number of frequently ordered items in the order
NUMMOD:	Number of moderately ordered items in the order
NUMRARE:	Number of rarely ordered items in the order
NUMLOOSE:	Number of loose-box items
AVSZCAR:	Average size of carton items (cartons/item)
AVSZLB:	Average size of loose-box items (pieces/item)

SPECIALS: 0 if no special packing need
             1 if special packing done at station A
             2 if special packing done at station B
SKIDS: Number of skids needed

The supervisor thinks that the most important predictor variables are the NUM ones, because much of the order-filling time is taken up by workers moving to the appropriate locations. However, this travel time is not likely to be directly proportional to the number of items, because a worker can combine items found in the same general area of the warehouse. The order size of each item is also relevant, because some time is used in taking each item from the shelf. This time is expected to be in proportion to AVSZ. The time spent moving skids is expected to be in proportion to SKIDS. The only other major time factor is assembly-station time, which is expected to depend on a combination of NUM and AVSZ variables.

a. Explain why the SPECIALS variable should be recoded as two variables:

SPECIALA = 1 if special packing done at station A, 0 if not

SPECIALB = 1 if special packing done at station B, 0 if not

b. Explain the interpretation of the coefficients of these two variables.
c. According to the information given by the supervisor, which independent variables might be transformed?
d. Is there any indication that interaction terms might be useful?

```
              Model fitting results for: TIME
-----------------------------------------------------------------
Independent variable      coefficient  std. error  t-value  sig.level
-----------------------------------------------------------------
CONSTANT                    12.58383    2.695224    4.6689   0.0000
NUMFREQ                      0.139473    0.053193    2.6220   0.0123
NUMMOD                       0.234382    0.108601    2.1582   0.0370
NUMRARE                      0.542355    0.155061    3.4977   0.0012
NUMLOOSE                     1.171283    0.253927    4.6127   0.0000
AVSZCAR                     -0.216187    0.621999   -0.3476   0.7300
AVSZLB                       0.497549    0.318769    1.5608   0.1264
SPECIALA                     0.701185    1.783779    0.3931   0.6963
SPECIALB                     1.819549    2.300707    0.7909   0.4337
SKIDS                        1.351252    0.23116     5.8455   0.0000
-----------------------------------------------------------------
R-SQ. (ADJ.) = 0.9163  SE=   4.340919  MAE=      2.399476  DurbWat=  2.100
```

15.39 The data for the study of Exercise 15.38 are shown on the next page. A first-order model is fit, and the Statgraphics output and scatter plot shown in Figure 15.23 (page 715) are obtained.
   a. Is there any indication of outliers?
   b. Is there any indication of nonconstant variance?
   c. Is there any indication of autocorrelation? Would autocorrelation be expected in this study?

15.40 It was discovered that observation 27 of the data in Exercise 15.39 was taken during a brief strike. The order was filled by the president and vice president of the firm, who couldn't find most of the items. This observation is deleted from the data set. Regression runs are made using logarithms of the NUM variables and using the

TIME	NUMFREQ	NUMMOD	NUMRARE	NUMLOOSE	AVSZCAR	AVSZLB	SPECIALA	SPECIALB	SKIDS
27	16	6	3	4	1.6	3.5	1	0	2
57	70	25	2	2	3.2	2.7	0	0	18
39	25	6	8	4	2.4	3.3	0	0	8
20	10	2	1	1	6.2	4	0	0	4
55	50	30	6	7	2.6	3	0	0	12
95	85	43	16	10	4.7	6.2	0	1	25
19	12	3	1	1	2.4	3	0	0	3
35	10	12	13	3	5	6	0	0	5
61	87	12	4	6	3	4	1	0	16
44	50	22	8	2	4	1.5	0	0	9
23	12	8	8	2	1.4	3.5	0	0	2
47	27	6	12	14	1.6	7.2	0	0	4
53	64	8	1	2	3	2.5	0	0	14
70	71	34	7	10	2.1	4.6	0	0	16
32	25	1	2	2	2.8	5	0	0	10
39	16	10	3	8	2	4.7	1	0	6
32	25	12	4	2	1.8	6	0	0	4
30	40	6	1	1	2.6	3	0	0	7
38	72	21	8	3	2	2.7	0	0	6
78	64	37	21	6	3	4.3	0	1	20
30	23	6	2	1	4.2	2	0	0	6
38	35	13	7	1	1.4	8	0	0	5
25	16	4	2	4	1.6	9.3	0	0	3
47	19	17	10	6	3.2	2.7	1	0	8
42	31	12	16	3	1.4	2.3	0	1	4
46	46	8	11	2	4	2.5	0	0	13
48	12	6	1	5	2	6.2	0	0	3
28	16	4	4	2	6.1	1.5	0	0	5
28	37	8	2	1	2.2	2	1	0	3
32	21	9	6	4	1.8	6.5	0	0	3
51	58	4	3	6	4	8.3	0	0	11
48	24	15	1	8	3	9.1	0	1	10
49	36	12	9	2	4	6	0	0	15
42	51	18	3	5	1.8	2.8	0	0	8
58	77	30	15	12	1.2	1.2	1	0	6
37	24	6	2	2	4	6	0	0	10
37	16	8	5	1	6	10	0	0	9
46	36	12	4	6	2.6	5.1	0	1	8
58	74	15	16	4	1.8	1.5	0	0	13
49	51	10	3	8	3.7	4.5	0	0	16
41	24	6	8	3	4.1	3.3	1	0	9
31	36	8	1	1	2.7	5	0	0	6
31	21	4	5	6	1.6	1.3	0	0	3
49	42	10	2	2	4	8.5	0	1	18
29	16	3	4	2	2.7	3.5	0	0	7
29	28	15	2	1	3	6	0	0	5
66	73	18	15	5	1.9	4.2	0	0	12
31	15	8	8	6	1.2	2.3	0	0	4
36	23	4	10	4	1.5	2.8	0	0	6
36	44	9	2	1	4	5	1	0	10

Data for Exercise 15.39

square roots of these variables. The resulting residual standard deviations and R^2 values are

	Logarithms	Square Roots
s_ϵ	3.4804	3.0561
R^2	.9570	.9669

Which transformation appears more effective?

15.41 A forward-selection stepwise regression is run on the data resulting from Exercise 15.40. The square-root transformation is used. The output on pages 715–718 is obtained.

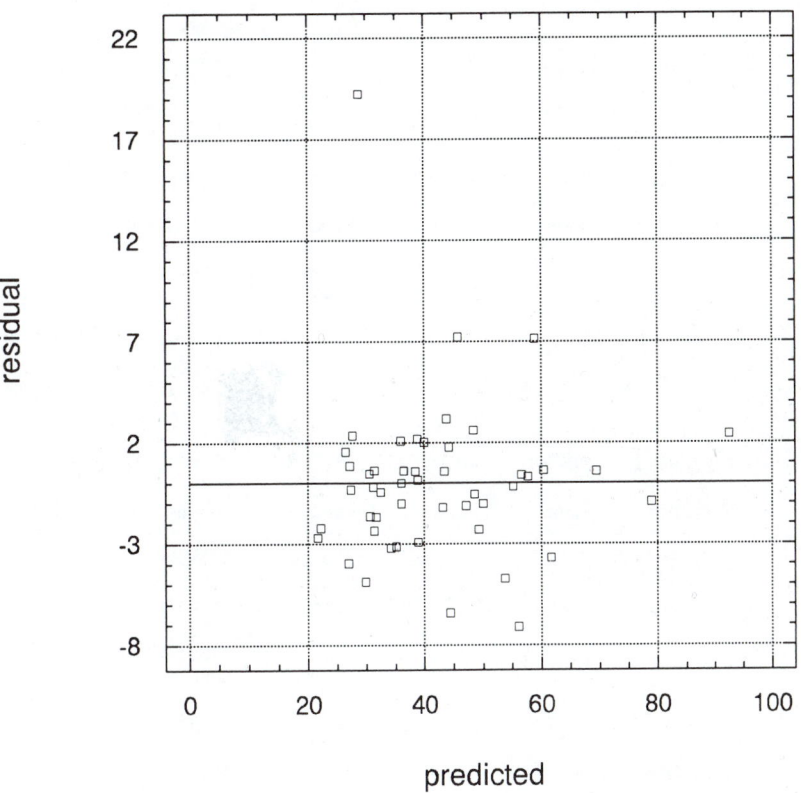

FIGURE 15.23   Scatter Plot for Exercise 15.39

a. How much does inclusion of the last variable increase R^2?
b. Test the null hypothesis that the last two variables have no incremental predictive value.

```
                    Stepwise Selection for TIME
-------------------------------------------------------------------
Selection: Forward        Maximum steps: 500        F-to-enter: 4.00
Control: Manual              Step: 1                F-to-remove: 4.00

R-squared:  .71880     Adjusted: .71281      MSE: 65.7734      d.f.: 47

Variables in Model      Coeff.  F-Remove  Variables Not in Model P.Corr. F-Enter
-------------------------------------------------------------------
```

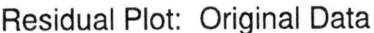

(continued)

```
9. SKIDS                2.43382  120.1384   1. SQTNUMF    .5197   17.0231
                                            2. SQTNUMM    .6902   41.8533
                                            3. SQTNUMR    .6884   41.4352
                                            4. NUMLOOSE   .7285   52.0295
                                            5. AVSZCAR    .4720   13.1822
                                            6. AVSZLB     .0978    .4443
                                            7. SPECIALA   .1654   1.2934
                                            8. SPECIALB   .2183   2.3024
```

R-squared: .86805   Adjusted: .86231   MSE: 31.5349   d.f.: 46

Variables in Model	Coeff.	F-Remove	Variables Not in Model	P.Corr.	F-Enter
4. NUMLOOSE	1.93220	52.0295	1. SQTNUMF	.5387	18.3993
9. SKIDS	2.16751	187.9069	2. SQTNUMM	.6534	33.5319
			3. SQTNUMR	.6473	32.4471
			5. AVSZCAR	.2812	3.8652
			6. AVSZLB	.1826	1.5513
			7. SPECIALA	.0481	.1042
			8. SPECIALB	.1733	1.3938

R-squared: .92439   Adjusted: .91935   MSE: 18.4716   d.f.: 45

Variables in Model	Coeff.	F-Remove	Variables Not in Model	P.Corr.	F-Enter
2. SQTNUMM	3.76762	33.5319	1. SQTNUMF	.3738	7.1448
4. NUMLOOSE	1.44632	42.6284	3. SQTNUMR	.5678	20.9399
9. SKIDS	1.74510	152.5233	5. AVSZCAR	.1654	1.2371
			6. AVSZLB	.0788	.2748
			7. SPECIALA	.0263	.0304
			8. SPECIALB	.1116	.5550

R-squared: .94877   Adjusted: .94411   MSE: 12.7998   d.f.: 44

Variables in Model	Coeff.	F-Remove	Variables Not in Model	P.Corr.	F-Enter
2. SQTNUMM	2.74049	21.8495	1. SQTNUMF	.4927	13.7820
3. SQTNUMR	2.88554	20.9399	5. AVSZCAR	.1691	1.2654
4. NUMLOOSE	1.22869	41.6281	6. AVSZLB	.0408	.0717
9. SKIDS	1.79848	231.5026	7. SPECIALA	.0990	.4253
			8. SPECIALB	.1071	.4989

R-squared: .96120   Adjusted: .95669   MSE: 9.91851   d.f.: 43

Variables in Model	Coeff.	F-Remove	Variables Not in Model	P.Corr.	F-Enter
1. SQTNUMF	1.52926	13.7820	5. AVSZCAR	.0392	.0645
2. SQTNUMM	1.84518	10.4917	6. AVSZLB	.2469	2.7267
3. SQTNUMR	2.99877	29.0976	7. SPECIALA	.0563	.1335
4. NUMLOOSE	1.19112	50.3026	8. SPECIALB	.2943	3.9815
9. SKIDS	1.55219	158.2161			

Output for Exercise 15.41

(continued)

```
                    Stepwise Selection for TIME
-----------------------------------------------------------------------
Selection: Forward        Maximum steps: 500        F-to-enter: 4.00
Control: Manual                Step: 1              F-to-remove: 4.00

R-squared:  .71880     Adjusted: .71281        MSE: 65.7734     d.f.: 47

Variables in Model    Coeff.  F-Remove  Variables Not in Model P.Corr. F-Enter
-----------------------------------------------------------------------
  9. SKIDS            2.43382 120.1384  1. SQTNUMF            .5197   17.0231
                                        2. SQTNUMM            .6902   41.8533
                                        3. SQTNUMR            .6884   41.4352
                                        4. NUMLOOSE           .7285   52.0295
                                        5. AVSZCAR            .4720   13.1822
                                        6. AVSZLB             .0978    .4443
                                        7. SPECIALA           .1654   1.2934
                                        8. SPECIALB           .2183   2.3024


R-squared:  .86805     Adjusted: .86231        MSE: 31.5349     d.f.: 46

Variables in Model    Coeff.  F-Remove  Variables Not in Model P.Corr. F-Enter
-----------------------------------------------------------------------
  4. NUMLOOSE         1.93220  52.0295  1. SQTNUMF            .5387   18.3993
  9. SKIDS            2.16751 187.9069  2. SQTNUMM            .6534   33.5319
                                        3. SQTNUMR            .6473   32.4471
                                        5. AVSZCAR            .2812   3.8652
                                        6. AVSZLB             .1826   1.5513
                                        7. SPECIALA           .0481    .1042
                                        8. SPECIALB           .1733   1.3938


R-squared:  .92439     Adjusted: .91935        MSE: 18.4716     d.f.: 45

Variables in Model    Coeff.  F-Remove  Variables Not in Model P.Corr. F-Enter
-----------------------------------------------------------------------
  2. SQTNUMM          3.76762  33.5319  1. SQTNUMF            .3738    7.1448
  4. NUMLOOSE         1.44632  42.6284  3. SQTNUMR            .5678   20.9399
  9. SKIDS            1.74510 152.5233  5. AVSZCAR            .1654   1.2371
                                        6. AVSZLB             .0788    .2748
                                        7. SPECIALA           .0263    .0304
                                        8. SPECIALB           .1116    .5550


R-squared:  .94877     Adjusted: .94411        MSE: 12.7998     d.f.: 44

Variables in Model    Coeff.  F-Remove  Variables Not in Model P.Corr. F-Enter
-----------------------------------------------------------------------
  2. SQTNUMM          2.74049  21.8495  1. SQTNUMF            .4927   13.7820
  3. SQTNUMR          2.88554  20.9399  5. AVSZCAR            .1691   1.2654
  4. NUMLOOSE         1.22869  41.6281  6. AVSZLB             .0408    .0717
  9. SKIDS            1.79848 231.5026  7. SPECIALA           .0990    .4253
                                        8. SPECIALB           .1071    .4989


R-squared:  .96120     Adjusted: .95669        MSE: 9.91851     d.f.: 43

Variables in Model    Coeff.  F-Remove  Variables Not in Model P.Corr. F-Enter
-----------------------------------------------------------------------
  1. SQTNUMF          1.52926  13.7820  5. AVSZCAR            .0392    .0645
  2. SQTNUMM          1.84518  10.4917  6. AVSZLB             .2469   2.7267
  3. SQTNUMR          2.99877  29.0976  7. SPECIALA           .0563    .1335
  4. NUMLOOSE         1.19112  50.3026  8. SPECIALB           .2943   3.9815
  9. SKIDS            1.55219 158.2161
```

Output for Exercise 15.41

(continued)

```
                    Model fitting results for: TIME
-----------------------------------------------------------------------
Independent variable        coefficient  std. error   t-value   sig.level
-----------------------------------------------------------------------
CONSTANT                       1.802562    1.773467    1.0164    0.3151
SQTNUMF                        1.529262    0.411933    3.7124    0.0006
SQTNUMM                        1.84518     0.56966     3.2391    0.0023
SQTNUMR                        2.99877     0.555923    5.3942    0.0000
NUMLOOSE                       1.191118    0.167942    7.0924    0.0000
SKIDS                          1.552191    0.123401   12.5784    0.0000
-----------------------------------------------------------------------
```

Output for Exercise 15.41

15.42 The independent variable in Exercise 15.41 is redefined to be the time *per item*, that is

$$\frac{\text{TIME}}{\text{NUMFREQ} + \text{NUMMOD} + \text{NUMRARE}}$$

All independent variables (including the dummy variables) are divided by (NUMFREQ + NUMMOD + NUMRARE). The output below results from a regression run on the transformed data.

a. Write the regression model and the residual standard deviation.
b. Is any violation of assumptions shown by the residual plots on pages 719–722?

```
                Analysis of Variance for the Full Regression
-----------------------------------------------------------------------
Source           Sum of Squares    DF    Mean Square    F-Ratio   P-value
-----------------------------------------------------------------------
Model               3.16378         9     0.351532      145.132    .0000
Error               0.0944638      39     0.00242215
-----------------------------------------------------------------------
Total (Corr.)       3.25825        48
```

R-squared = 0.971008   Stnd. error of est. = 0.0492153
R-squared (Adj. for d.f.) = 0.964317 Durbin-Watson statistic = 2.09397

```
                    Model fitting results for: TIMEPER
-----------------------------------------------------------------------
Independent variable        coefficient  std. error   t-value   sig.level
-----------------------------------------------------------------------
CONSTANT                       0.024358    0.040596    0.6000    0.5520
SQTNFPER                       1.801329    0.322713    5.5818    0.0000
SQTNMPER                       1.631093    0.550287    2.9641    0.0052
SQTNRPER                       2.734805    0.401163    6.8172    0.0000
NUMLPER                        1.149122    0.134476    8.5452    0.0000
ASZCRPER                       0.360024    0.163308    2.2046    0.0335
ASZLBPER                       0.210388    0.127899    1.6450    0.1080
SPECAPER                       1.875247    0.854948    2.1934    0.0343
SPECBPER                       2.924934    1.411255    2.0726    0.0449
SKIDSPER                       1.288203    0.123421   10.4374    0.0000
-----------------------------------------------------------------------
```

15.43 A validation study of the model obtained in Exercise 15.42 is based on an additional 10 orders. The results are shown below.

Actual Time	Time per Item	Regression Forecast	Superintendent's Forecast
36	.6316	.6691	.7895
24	1.0000	.9057	.8333
26	.7647	.8482	.7692
42	.7925	.6558	.9434
34	.5667	.5608	.8333
31	.9688	.9021	.7813
27	.8182	.9247	.9091
32	.6531	.7567	.8163
34	.8293	.9272	.7317
38	.7451	.7479	.7843

a. Compute the standard deviation of the regression prediction errors and the standard deviation of the superintendent's prediction errors.
b. Has the regression standard deviation increased from the standard deviation shown in Exercise 15.42?
c. Does the result of this study suggest that the regression model will yield better forecasts than the superintendent's forecasts?

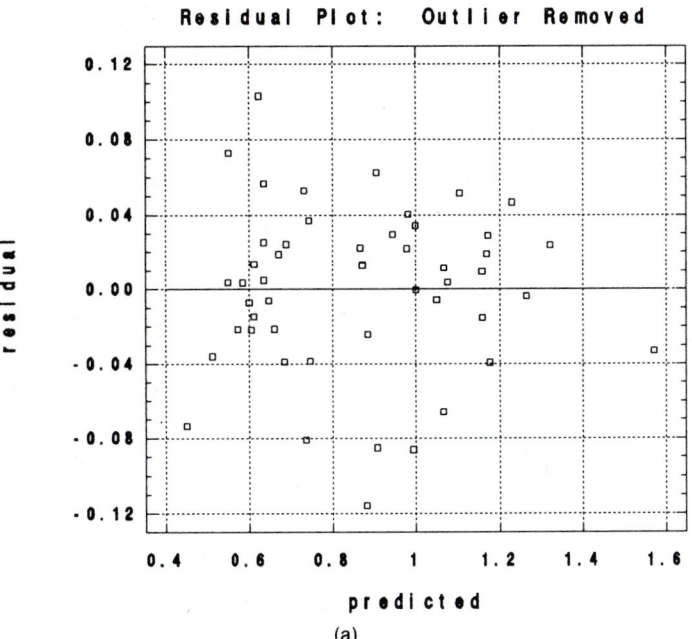

(a)

Residuals for Exercise 15.42

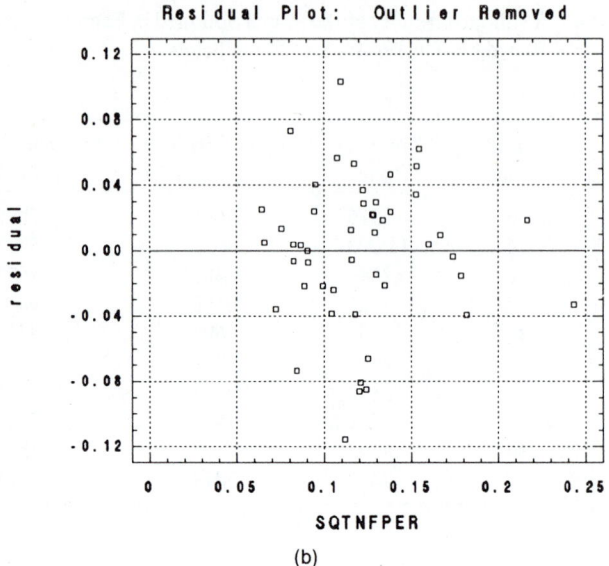

(b)

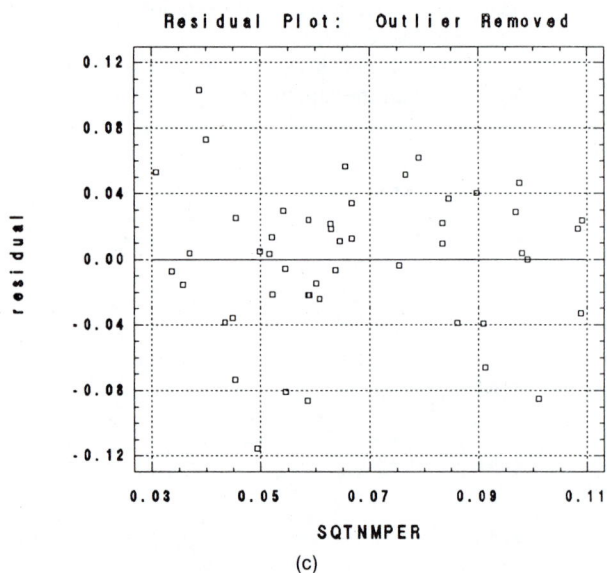

(c)

Residuals for Exercise 15.42 (*continued*)

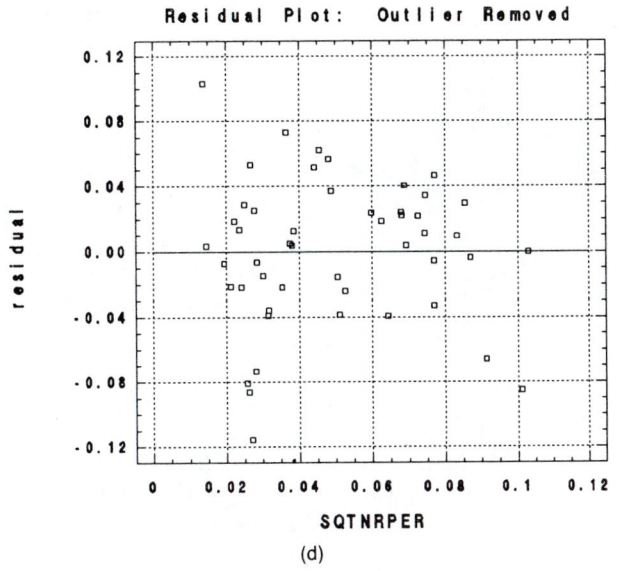

(d)

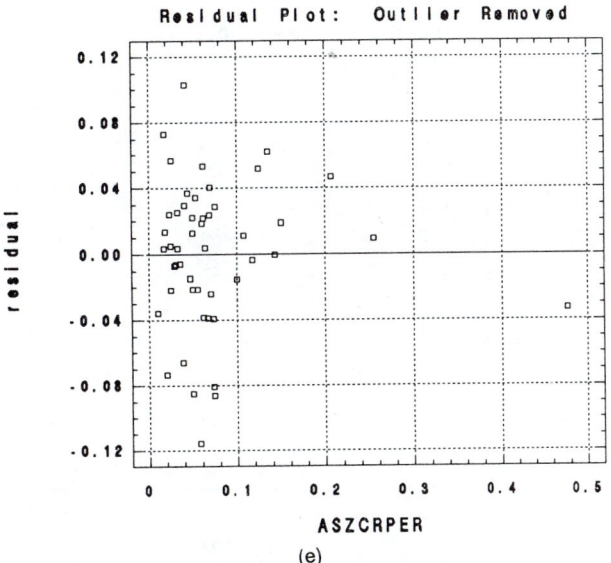

(e)

Residuals for Exercise 15.42 *(continued)*

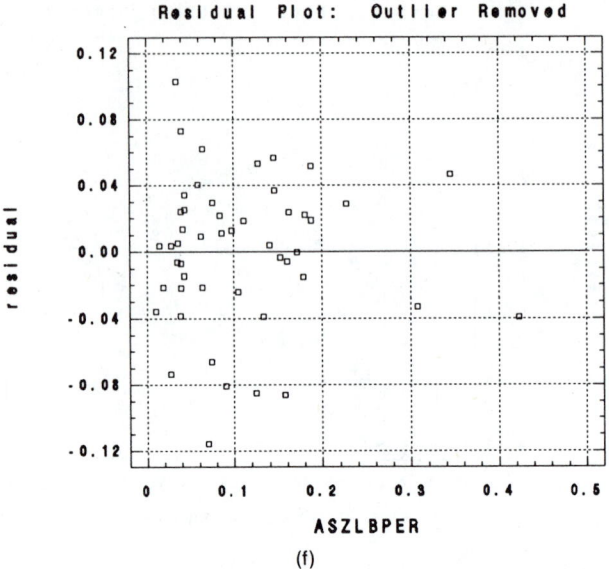

(f)

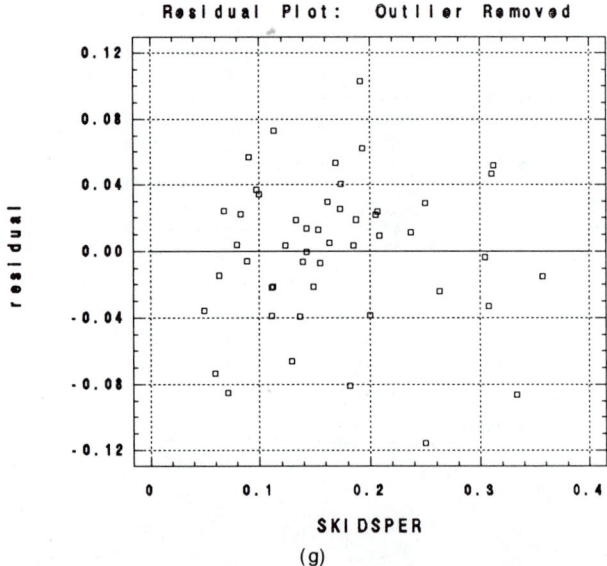

(g)

Residuals for Exercise 15.42 (*continued*)

15.44 An airline that is the major carrier at its airport hub analyzed its sales of full-fare seats on flights to various other cities. These sales are most profitable for the airline, so it would like to reserve adequate space; full-fare passengers almost always reserve seats in the last few days before the flight. In addition, any exceptionally low sales figures may indicate a problem in scheduling or in operations at the destination city. For each of the airline's 315 weekly flights, the full-fare demand, averaged over 10 weeks, was determined; this demand included any requests for seats that couldn't be accommodated. In addition, the day of the flight (Sunday = 1 through Saturday = 7), the scheduled departure time (in military time, so 1700 = 5:00 P.M., for example), the airline's share of the gates at the destination airport, and the per capita income of the destination metropolitan area were recorded. The data are in the 'CH15C1.DAT' file of the data disk. Column 1 contains demand, column 2 has the day code, column 3 lists the departure time, column 4 is a dummy variable indicating the peak travel times (portions of Sunday afternoon, Monday morning, and Friday afternoon), column 5 contains the gate share, and column 6 has income.

a. Explain why it would not make sense to include day and departure time as independent variables in a first-order model for predicting demand.

b. Obtain a first-order regression equation using the peak-time dummy variable, gate share, and income as independent variables.

c. Have the computer program create two new variables by multiplying the dummy variable by gate share and by income. Obtain a regression equation including the previous three independent variables plus the two new ones.

d. Test the null hypothesis that the new product variables add no predictive value, given the previous three variables. Can this hypothesis be rejected at $\alpha = .05$? What does this test indicate about interaction in the data?

15.45 Obtain residuals from the regression equation without product terms found in Exercise 15.44.

a. Plot the residuals against predicted values. Is there a clear indication that variability increases as the predicted value increases?

b. Plot the residuals against gate share and against income. Is there a clear reason to incorporate nonlinear terms in these variables?

c. Plot the residuals against the dummy variable. Does this plot reveal anything?

15.46 The data in Exercise 15.44 are time series data, in the sense that they are entered in the time order of the flights.

a. Plot the residuals calculated in Exercise 15.45 against observation number (time). Is there any evidence of a roughly cyclic pattern, which indicates autocorrelation?

b. Obtain the Durbin-Watson statistic for the model without product terms. Does this statistic indicate that there is a serious autocorrelation problem?

15.47 An auto-supply store had 60 months of data on variables that were thought to be relevant to sales. The data, stored in the 'CH15C2.DAT' file of the data disk, include monthly sales in thousands of dollars (column 1), average daily low temperature in degrees Fahrenheit (column 2), advertising expenditure for the month in thousands of dollars (column 3), used-car sales in the previous month (column 4), and month number (column 5).

a. Identify any variables that are already in lagged form.

b. Obtain a regression equation using temperature, current month's advertising, previous month's used-car sales, and month number as the independent variables.

c. Have your computer program create a one-month lagged variable for advertising expense. Use this lagged variable in place of the current month's advertising, and obtain a new regression equation. Does this new model have a smaller residual standard deviation (and therefore a smaller mean square error) than the model in part (b)?

15.48 Consider the regression model using temperature, previous month's advertising, previous month's used-car sales, and month number, as in part (b) of Exercise 15.47.

a. Obtain correlations; is there a major collinearity problem?

b. Test to see if the four predictors together have at least some predictive value. Locate a *p*-value.

c. Test to see if each predictor adds statistically detectable predictive value, given the others. Locate *p*-values.

15.49 Obtain residuals for the model of Exercise 15.48.

a. Plot to see if there is evidence of nonconstant variance.

b. Plot to see if there is evidence of nonlinearity.

c. Plot to see if there is evidence of autocorrelation.

d. Obtain the Durbin-Watson statistic. What does it tell you?

15.50 Based on the results you obtained in the last three exercises, determine what changes, if any, you want to make in the regression model. Carry out these changes and see if the resulting regression model is more satisfactory.

15.51 A construction firm wanted to use regression methods to estimate the amount of concrete-block foundation that could be constructed in a day, using various combinations of workers and delivery vehicles. Data on a sample of recent projects are included in the 'CH15C3.DAT' file on the data disk. The variables are: Completion rate, the number of square feet of foundation wall constructed in a day (column 1); number of skilled workers (column 2); number of helpers (column 3); and number of delivery vehicles (column 4).

a. Obtain correlations. Is there an obvious collinearity problem?

b. Are there any variables that should be replaced by dummy variables? Would it make sense to have lagged variables?

c. Obtain a first-order regression model to predict completion rate and use the other variables as they are. Locate the coefficient of determination.

15.52 Obtain residuals from the regression model of Exercise 15.51.

a. Plot the residuals against the predicted values. Is there a "fan" shape characteristic of increasing variability? Is there any other evident problem?

b. Plot the residuals against each of the predictors. Is there any evidence of a high-influence outlier? Is there any other evident problem?

c. Why wouldn't the Durbin-Watson statistic be of much relevance in this problem?

15.53 Have your computer program calculate logarithms (say to base *e*, if that's convenient) of all the variables from Exercise 15.51.

a. Obtain a regression equation using the logarithm of completion as the dependent variable, and the other logarithm variables as independent.

b. Obtain residuals for this model and plot them against each (logarithm form) independent variable. Is there an evident curve in any of the plots?

c. Convert (by hand) the logarithmic model back to a model in the original variables. Remember that the logarithm of a product is the sum of the logarithms of each component, and that the logarithm of a variable raised to a power is the power times the logarithm of the variable.

CASE

Building a Regression Model

The marketing managers of an office products company have some difficulty in evaluating the field sales representatives' performance. The representatives travel among the outlets for the company's products, create displays, try to increase volume, introduce new products, and discover any problems that the outlets are having with the company's products. The job involves a great deal of travel time. The marketing managers believe that one important factor in the representatives' performance is the motivation to spend a great deal of time on the road. Other variables also have an effect. Some sales districts have more potential than others, either because of differences in population or differences in the number of retail outlets. Large districts are difficult because of the extra travel time.

One important variable is compensation. Some of the representatives are paid a salary plus a commission on sales; others work entirely for a larger commission on sales. The marketing managers suspect that there is a difference between the two groups in their effectiveness, although some of them argue that the important factor is the combination of commission status and number of outlets. In particular, they suspect that commission-only representatives with many outlets to cover are highly productive.

Data are collected on 51 representatives. The data include DISTRICT number, PROFIT (net profit margin for all orders placed through the representative—the dependent variable of interest), AREA (of the district in thousands of square miles), POPN (millions of people in the district), OUTLETS (number of outlets in the district), and COMMIS, which is 1 for full-commission representatives and 0 for partially salaried representatives.

Use the tabulated data to perform a multiple regression analysis. Find out if the variables suspected by the managers as having an effect on PROFIT actually do have an effect; in particular, try to discover if there is a combination effect of COMMIS and OUTLETS. Omit variables that show little predictive value. Locate and, if possible, correct any serious violations of assumptions. Write a brief report to the marketing managers and explain your findings; the managers are not familiar with the technical language of statistics, although they do have an idea what a standard deviation is.

DIST	PROFIT	AREA	POPN	OUTLETS	COMMIS
1	1011	16.96	3.881	213	1
2	1318	7.31	3.141	158	1
3	1556	7.81	3.766	203	1
4	1521	7.31	4.587	170	1
5	979	19.84	3.648	142	1
6	1290	12.37	3.456	159	1
7	1596	6.15	3.695	178	1

(continued)

DIST	PROFIT	AREA	POPN	OUTLETS	COMMIS
8	1155	14.21	3.609	182	1
9	1412	7.45	3.801	181	1
10	1194	14.43	3.322	148	1
11	1054	6.12	5.124	227	0
12	1157	11.71	4.158	139	1
13	1001	9.36	3.887	179	0
14	831	19.14	2.230	124	1
15	857	11.75	4.468	205	0
16	188	40.34	.297	85	1
17	1030	7.16	4.224	211	0
18	1331	9.37	3.427	145	1
19	643	7.62	4.031	205	1
20	992	27.54	2.370	166	1
21	795	15.97	3.903	149	1
22	1340	12.97	3.423	186	1
23	689	17.36	2.390	141	0
24	1726	6.24	4.947	223	1
25	1056	11.20	4.166	176	0
26	989	18.09	4.063	187	1
27	895	13.32	3.105	131	1
28	1028	14.97	4.116	170	0
29	771	21.92	1.510	144	1
30	484	34.91	.741	126	1
31	917	8.46	5.260	234	0
32	1786	7.52	5.744	210	0
33	1063	14.43	2.703	141	1
34	1001	15.37	3.583	158	0
35	1052	11.20	4.469	167	1
36	1610	7.20	4.951	174	1
37	1486	13.49	3.474	211	1
38	1576	6.56	4.637	172	1
39	1665	9.35	3.900	185	1
40	878	11.12	3.766	166	0
41	849	10.58	3.876	189	0
42	775	17.82	2.753	164	0
43	1012	10.03	4.449	193	0
44	1436	10.01	4.680	157	1
45	798	10.70	4.806	200	0
46	519	24.38	2.367	142	0
47	1701	6.57	5.563	199	0
48	1387	6.64	4.357	166	1
49	1717	9.24	4.670	221	1
50	1032	11.62	3.993	180	0
51	973	12.85	3.923	193	0

Review Exercises Chapters 13–15   ■

R126 A contractor bids on many small jobs. The current process of preparing bids is expensive and time consuming. An attempt is made to predict y, the total direct cost of a job, based on x, the direct labor hours required. Data are collected on 26 jobs:

x:	214	228	235	239	247	248	278	289	291
y:	7444	7223	10,509	8931	9674	8084	11,784	10,067	11,344

x:	298	306	314	319	333	353	364	464	495
y:	7355	14,946	15,088	7409	15,475	11,524	13,209	16,012	22,570

x:	505	607	625	651	738	771	796	840
y:	26,285	18,427	22,892	20,689	33,636	28,465	22,018	29,744

The following sums are obtained:

$$\sum x = 11,048 \qquad \sum y = 410,804$$
$$\sum x^2 = 5,705,438 \qquad \sum y^2 = 7,991,850,900$$
$$\sum xy = 209,738,350$$

a. Calculate the least-squares regression equation.
b. What is the economic interpretation of the slope coefficient?
c. What is the economic interpretation of the intercept coefficient?
d. Calculate the residual standard deviation. Interpret its numerical value.

R127 Find the correlation between x and y for the data of Exercise R126. Interpret the resulting number.

R128 Refer again to Exercise R126.
a. Calculate the estimated standard error of the slope.
b. Find a 95% confidence interval for the true value of the slope.

R129 In Exercise R126, is the null hypothesis that the slope is zero economically plausible? Can this hypothesis be rejected conclusively by the data?

R130 a. The contractor in Exercise R126 has a new job with $x = 890$ hours. Calculate the predicted y value and a 90% prediction interval for the actual Y value.
b. The contractor has another new job with $x = 436$ hours. Calculate a 90% prediction interval for the actual Y value.
c. Which of the intervals calculated in parts (a) and (b) is wider? Why?

R131 A plot of the residuals from the regression analysis of the data in Exercise R126 against the x values shows that residuals corresponding to small x values are small positive or negative numbers, but that several of the residuals corresponding to large x values are relatively large in magnitude.
a. What regression assumption is called into question by this finding?
b. Which of your answers to Exercises R126–R130 is most questionable because of this finding?

R132 A bank that offers charge cards to customers studies the yearly purchase amount on the card as related to the age, income, and years of education of the cardholder, and whether or not the cardholder owns or rents a home. The following Minitab output is obtained; the variables are self-explanatory, except for OWNER, which equals 1 if the cardholder owns a home and 0 if the cardholder rents a home.
a. Locate the least-squares regression equation.
b. Explain what each slope coefficient means.
c. How meaningful is the intercept term?

```
MTB > correlations of C1-C5

          purch      age    income    owner
age       0.932
income    0.928    0.837
owner     0.462    0.212    0.686
educn     0.222    0.057    0.310    0.476

MTB > regress c1 on 4 variables c2-c5 put residuals in c19, preds in c20

The regression equation is
purch = - 0.744 + 0.0329 age + 0.00900 income + 0.115 owner + 0.00818 educn

Predictor        Coef       Stdev     t-ratio
Constant      -0.74439     0.06978     -10.67
age           0.032896    0.003809       8.64
income        0.008999    0.005075       1.77
owner         0.11502     0.04982        2.31
educn         0.008176    0.003611       2.26

s = 0.09263      R-sq = 94.6%     R-sq(adj) = 94.4%

Analysis of Variance

SOURCE        DF        SS         MS
Regression     4     23.1295     5.7824
Error        155      1.3301     0.0086
Total        159     24.4596
```

R133 Refer to the output of Exercise R132.
    a. What would the hypothesis that all slopes are zero mean about predictability in this context?
    b. Show that this null hypothesis may be rejected emphatically.
    c. What do the various t statistics indicate about the incremental predictive value of the variables?

R134 Is there evidence of collinearity in the data of Exercise R132?

R135 Additional predictor variables for the problem of Exercise R132 are created by multiplying OWNER by each of the other independent variables. Minitab output is shown below.

```
MTB > regress c1 on 7 variables in c2-c8 put residuals in c19, preds in c20

The regression equation is
purch = - 0.916 + 0.0272 age + 0.0204 income + 0.247 owner + 0.00536 educn
        + 0.00043 X1X3 - 0.0066 X2X3 + 0.00510 X3X4

Predictor        Coef       Stdev     t-ratio
Constant      -0.9156      0.1332      -6.87
age           0.027249    0.005535      4.92
income        0.020373    0.008714      2.34
owner         0.2468      0.2083        1.18
educn         0.005361    0.005250      1.02
X1X3          0.000432    0.009902      0.04
X2X3          -0.00656    0.01312      -0.50
X3X4          0.005105    0.007254      0.70

s = 0.09217      R-sq = 94.7%     R-sq(adj) = 94.5%
```

Analysis of Variance

SOURCE	DF	SS	MS
Regression	7	23.1682	3.3097
Error	152	1.2914	0.0085
Total	159	24.4596	

SOURCE	DF	SEQ SS
age	1	21.2586
income	1	1.7745
owner	1	0.0524
educn	1	0.0440
X1X3	1	0.0327
X2X3	1	0.0018
X3X4	1	0.0042

a. What is the reason for introducing the product terms X1X3, X2X3, and X3X4?

b. Test the null hypothesis that the coefficients of all the product terms are zero.

R136 Residuals for the model in Exercise R135 are plotted against predicted values, as shown in Figure R.1. Are there any obvious violations of regression assumptions?

R137 A revised regression model for Exercise R135 is attempted. The original variables in the study are each divided by INCOME, then a regression model is calculated for the transformed variables. A plot of the residuals against the predicted values is shown in Figure R.2 (page 730). What problem is evident in the plot?

R138 Another regression model for the data of Exercise R135 is attempted using the natural logarithm of INCOME, rather than INCOME, as an independent variable. The output from Minitab is shown on page 730.

MTB > plot residuals in c19 vs. predicted values in c20

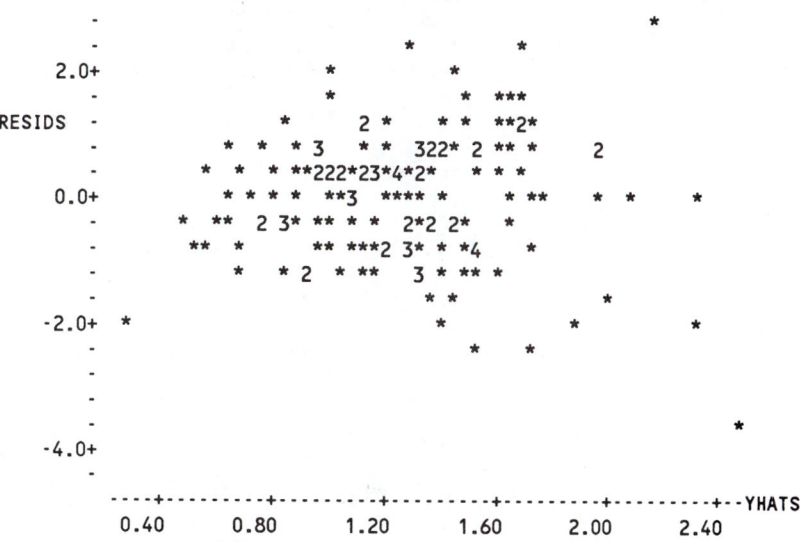

FIGURE R.1   Residuals Versus Predicted Values; Exercises R135–R136

MTB > plot residuals in c19 vs. predicted values in c20

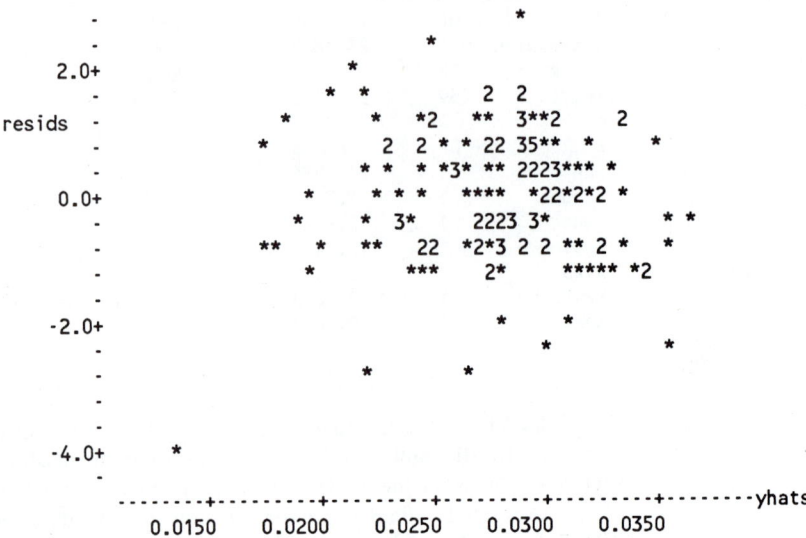

FIGURE R.2   Residuals Versus Predicted Values; Exercise R137

MTB > regress c1 on 4 vars c2 c6 c4 c5 put residuals in c19 yhats in c20

The regression equation is
purch = - 3.38 + 0.0247 age + 0.913 loginc + 0.0118 owner + 0.00784 educn

Predictor	Coef	Stdev	t-ratio
Constant	-3.3834	0.6754	-5.01
age	0.024719	0.003765	6.57
loginc	0.9134	0.2273	4.02
owner	0.01183	0.04916	0.24
educn	0.007844	0.003462	2.27

s = 0.08904   R-sq = 95.0%   R-sq(adj) = 94.8%

Analysis of Variance

SOURCE	DF	SS	MS
Regression	4	23.2306	5.8076
Error	155	1.2290	0.0079
Total	159	24.4596	

SOURCE	DF	SEQ SS
age	1	21.2586
loginc	1	1.9296
owner	1	0.0016
educn	1	0.0407

Minitab for Exercise R138

a. As compared to the original model, has predictive value improved?

b. As compared to the original model, is the incremental predictive value of the LOGINC variable greater?

c. Is the LOGINC variable more statistically significant than the INCOME variable in the original model?

R139 A regression model is constructed to predict the spread between interest rates of government bonds (risk-free) and corporate bonds rated BAA (somewhat risky). The independent variables are a privately constructed leading economic indicator (LEADING), a measure of the relative supply of corporate and governmental bonds in a given month (SUPPLY), the actual rate of government bonds in that month (RATE), and the month number (MONTH). SAS output is shown below. Is there evidence of collinearity in the data?

```
                   CORRELATIONS OF ORIGINAL VARIABLES

PEARSON CORRELATION COEFFICIENTS / PROB > |R| UNDER HO:RHO=0 / N = 24

                 SPREAD   LEADING   SUPPLY    RATE    MONTH


     SPREAD     1.00000 -0.85042  0.67591  0.87240 -0.86171
                0.0000   0.0001   0.0003   0.0001   0.0001


     LEADING   -0.85042  1.00000 -0.22698 -0.98189  0.99688
                0.0001   0.0000   0.2862   0.0001   0.0001


     SUPPLY     0.67591 -0.22698  1.00000  0.25868 -0.24415
                0.0003   0.2862   0.0000   0.2223   0.2502


     RATE       0.87240 -0.98189  0.25868  1.00000 -0.98638
                0.0001   0.0001   0.2223   0.0000   0.0001


     MONTH     -0.86171  0.99688 -0.24415 -0.98638  1.00000
                0.0001   0.0001   0.2502   0.0001   0.0000
```

R140 A regression model is constructed using the data of Exercise R139, omitting MONTH. SAS output is shown below.

```
                   REGRESSION FOR ORIGINAL VARIABLES
```

DEP VARIABLE: SPREAD

```
                          ANALYSIS OF VARIANCE

                        SUM OF        MEAN
          SOURCE    DF   SQUARES      SQUARE      F VALUE    PROB>F

          MODEL      3  1.245096    0.4150321     321.310    0.0001
          ERROR     20  0.02583373  0.001291686
          C TOTAL   23  1.27093


          ROOT MSE  0.03594004    R-SQUARE     0.9797
          DEP MEAN  3.181728      ADJ R-SQ     0.9766
          C.V.      1.129576
```

PARAMETER ESTIMATES

VARIABLE	DF	PARAMETER ESTIMATE	STANDARD ERROR	T FOR H0: PARAMETER=0	PROB > |T|
INTERCEP	1	-0.0141918	2.156388	-0.007	0.9948
LEADING	1	-0.00826552	0.007199793	-1.148	0.2645
SUPPLY	1	3.75408	0.2566032	14.630	0.0001
RATE	1	0.2269971	0.07023813	3.232	0.0042

DURBIN-WATSON D   0.807
(FOR NUMBER OF OBS.)   24
1ST ORDER AUTOCORRELATION   0.518

a. Show that the null hypothesis that all slopes are zero can be rejected at any reasonable level of significance.

b. Do all the t tests of individual slopes lead to rejection of the null hypothesis?

R141 Locate the residual standard deviation in Exercise R140. What does it indicate about the predictive value of the equation? (The SPREAD variable has a standard deviation of about .2.)

R142 The residuals for the model in Exercise R140 are plotted against time in Figure R.3.

a. Does there appear to be a violation of regression assumptions?

b. Show that the output of Exercise R140 indicates a violation.

c. What are the consequences of this violation?

R143 The data of Exercise R140 are converted to differences and the model is recalculated. SAS output is shown below.

REGRESSION FOR DIFFERENCED VARIABLES

DEP VARIABLE: DSPREAD

ANALYSIS OF VARIANCE

SOURCE	DF	SUM OF SQUARES	MEAN SQUARE	F VALUE	PROB>F
MODEL	3	0.5252236	0.1750745	260.674	0.0001
ERROR	19	0.01276081	0.0006716217		
C TOTAL	22	0.5379844			

ROOT MSE	0.02591566	R-SQUARE	0.9763
DEP MEAN	-0.0260657	ADJ R-SQ	0.9725
C.V.	-99.4246		

PARAMETER ESTIMATES

VARIABLE	DF	PARAMETER ESTIMATE	STANDARD ERROR	T FOR H0: PARAMETER=0	PROB > |T|
INTERCEP	1	0.004044871	0.009158125	0.442	0.6637
DLEADING	1	-0.0106223	0.008161656	-1.301	0.2087
DSUPPLY	1	3.351632	0.1313994	25.507	0.0001
DRATE	1	0.2139063	0.03623192	5.904	0.0001

DURBIN-WATSON D   2.003
(FOR NUMBER OF OBS.)   23
1ST ORDER AUTOCORRELATION -0.072

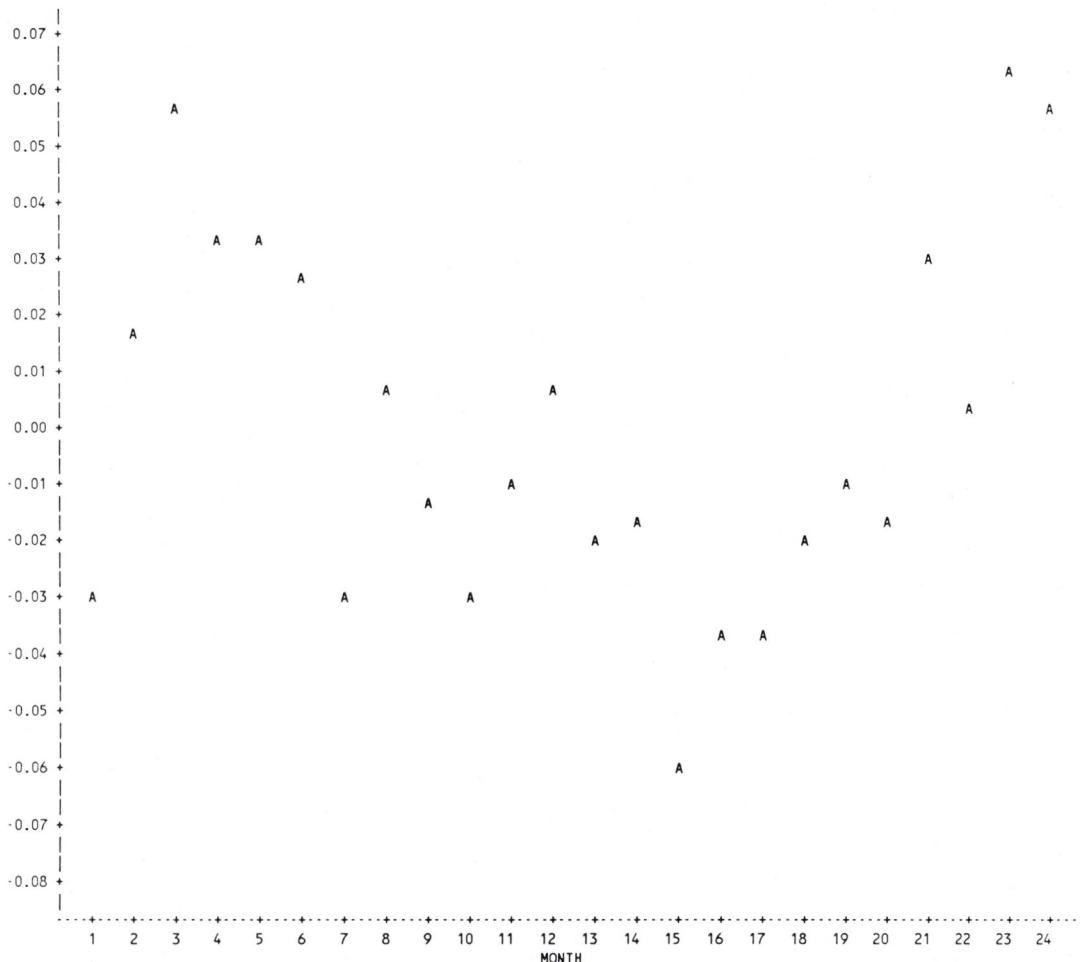

RESIDUAL PLOT FOR ORIGINAL VARIABLES

PLOT OF RESIDS*MONTH   LEGEND: A = 1 OBS, B = 2 OBS, ETC.

FIGURE R.3   Residuals Versus Time; Exercises R140–R142

a. How much have the coefficients changed as compared to those in Exercise R140?

b. Have the results of F and t tests changed, as compared to the results in Exercise R140? If so, which set of tests are more believable?

c. Does it appear that working with differences has cured the violation of assumptions found in Exercise R142?

R144 The residuals from the model of Exercise R143 are plotted against month number in Figure R.4 (page 734). Is there a clear pattern in this plot? Should there be, given the results in Exercise R143?

R145 Correlations for the difference data are shown on page 735. Has differencing decreased collinearity?

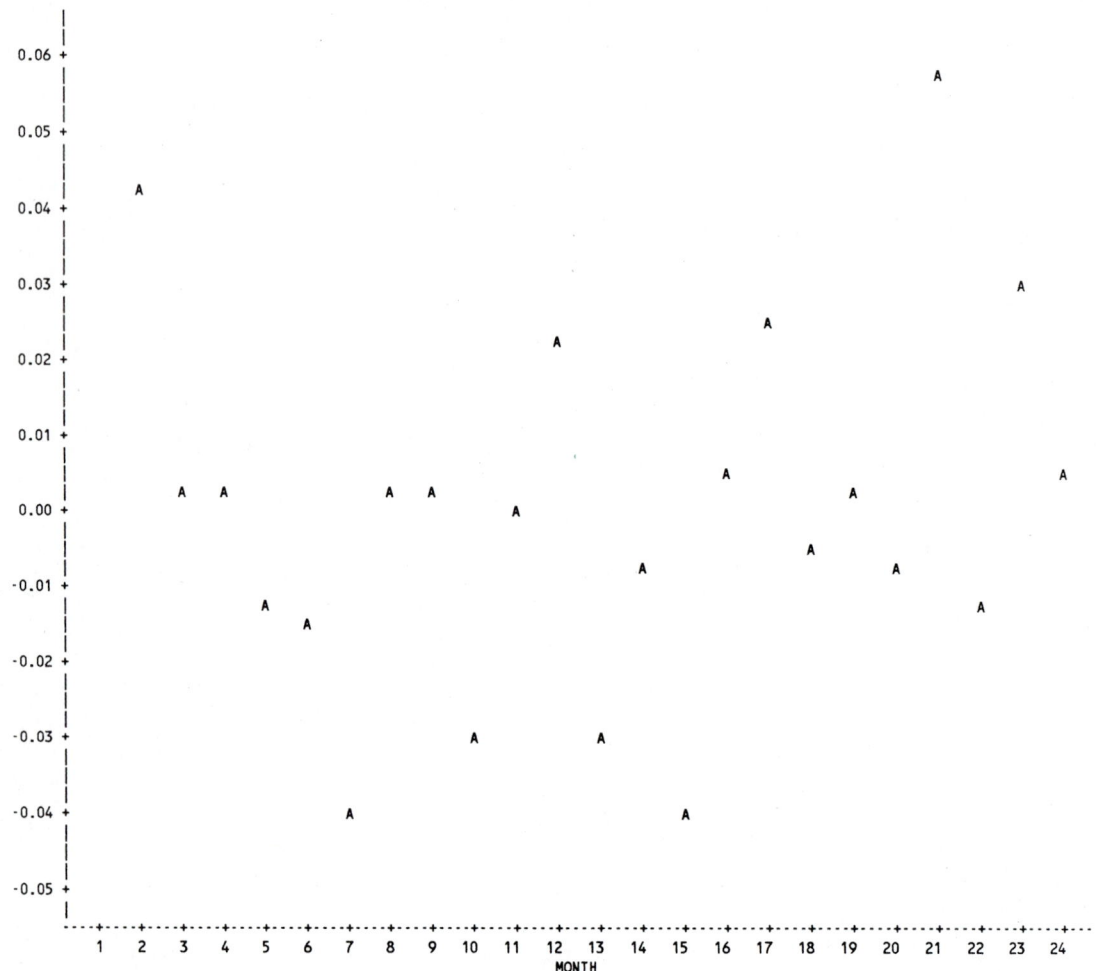

FIGURE R.4   Residuals Versus Time; Exercises R143–R144

R146 An oil company does a small study of the sale of kerosene at its service stations. The dependent variable is the monthly sales (thousands of gallons) of kerosene. The independent variables are monthly sales of gasoline (thousands of gallons), average income in the census tract where the station is located, and a rough index of the amount of traffic past the station. The sample is of 21 company stations in a particular month. Statgraphics output is shown on pages 735–736.
  a. Locate the least-squares regression equation. Interpret each of the slopes.
  b. Negative sales are impossible; should we be concerned about a negative intercept?

CORRELATIONS OF DIFFERENCED VARIABLES

PEARSON CORRELATION COEFFICIENTS / PROB > |R| UNDER H0:RHO=0 / NUMBER OF OBSERVATIONS

	DSPREAD	DLEADING	DSUPPLY	DRATE
DSPREAD	1.00000	0.25674	0.96542	0.34370
	0.0000	0.2370	0.0001	0.1083
	23	23	23	23
DLEADING	0.25674	1.00000	0.29280	0.12873
	0.2370	0.0000	0.1752	0.5583
	23	23	23	23
DSUPPLY	0.96542	0.29280	1.00000	0.14566
	0.0001	0.1752	0.0000	0.5072
	23	23	23	23
DRATE	0.34370	0.12873	0.14566	1.00000
	0.1083	0.5583	0.5072	0.0000
	23	23	23	23

SAS for Exercise R145

	Kero	Gas	Avginc	Traffic
Kero		0.7559	0.3736	0.5601
Gas	0.7559		0.5321	0.5659
Avginc	0.3736	0.5321		0.3768
Traffic	0.5601	0.5659	0.3768	

The table shows estimated product-moment correlation

Dependent variable: Kero

Table of Estimates

	Estimate	Standard Error	t Value	P Value
Constant	-3.33279	8.68157	-0.38	0.7058
Gas	0.0793746	0.0240985	3.29	0.0043
Avginc	-0.131951	0.392495	-0.34	0.7408
Traffic	7.86137	7.3042	1.08	0.2968

R-squared = 59.99%
Adjusted R-squared = 52.93%
Standard error of estimation = 4.34061
Durbin-Watson statistic = 1.90866
Mean absolute error = 3.00421

Statgraphics for Exercise R146

(continued)

Analysis of Variance

Source	Sum of Squares	D.F.	Mean Square	F-Ratio	P Value
Model	480.172	3	160.057	8.50	0.0011
Error	320.295	17	18.8409		
Total (corr.)	800.467	20			

Conditional Sums of Squares

Source	Sum of Squares	D.F.	Mean Square	F-Ratio	P Value
Gas	457.428	1	457.428	24.28	0.0001
Avginc	0.918619	1	0.918619	0.05	0.8302
Traffic	21.8248	1	21.8248	1.16	0.2968
Model	480.172	3			

Statgraphics for Exercise R146 (*Continued*)

R147 Refer to the output of Exercise R146.
   a. Locate SS(Regression).
   b. Find the sequential contribution of each independent variable to SS(Regression).
   c. What do these results suggest about deleting one or more independent variables from the model?
   d. Do the results of t tests also suggest deleting one or more independent variables from the model?

R148 a. Does the output in Exercise R146 indicate a serious collinearity problem?
   b. Does the output indicate a serious autocorrelation problem? Would one expect autocorrelation in this study?

R149 A plot of residuals versus predicted values is shown in Figure R.5 (page 738). Is there evidence of nonconstant variance? Are there any potentially serious outliers?

R150 It is discovered that station number 9 in the sample of Exercise R146 has a rather large contract to supply kerosene to a group of stores. No other station known to the company has a similar contract. Therefore station 9 is deleted from the sample and the regression is recalculated. The variables are given an N- (no contracts) prefix. Output is shown below.
   a. Have the regression slopes changed because of the omission of station 9?
   b. How has the residual standard deviation changed?
   c. How has the coefficient of determination changed?

	NKero	NGas	NAvginc	NTraffic
NKero		0.6931	0.1631	0.3829
NGas	0.6931		0.4396	0.4522
NAvginc	0.1631	0.4396		0.2579
NTraffic	0.3829	0.4522	0.2579	

The table shows estimated product-moment correlation

Dependent variable: NKero

Table of Estimates

	Estimate	Standard Error	t Value	P Value
Constant	7.81713	7.15908	1.09	0.2910
NGas	0.0640065	0.0185461	3.45	0.0033
NAvginc	-0.27926	0.297238	-0.94	0.3614
NTraffic	2.90331	5.63937	0.51	0.6137

R-squared = 51.34%
Adjusted R-squared = 42.21%
Standard error of estimation = 3.25854
Durbin-Watson statistic = 1.64667
Mean absolute error = 2.32787

Analysis of Variance

Source	Sum of Squares	D.F.	Mean Square	F-Ratio	P Value
Model	179.213	3	59.7376	5.63	0.0079
Error	169.889	16	10.6181		
Total (corr.)	349.102	19			

Conditional Sums of Squares

Source	Sum of Squares	D.F.	Mean Square	F-Ratio	P Value
NGas	167.721	1	167.721	15.80	0.0011
NAvginc	8.67761	1	8.67761	0.82	0.3889
NTraffic	2.81432	1	2.81432	0.27	0.6191
Model	179.213	3			

R151 Refer to the output in Exercise R150. Test the null hypothesis that the coefficients of NAVGINC and NTRAFF are both zero. Can this hypothesis be rejected at the usual α values?

R152 Data are collected on the yield of a chemical under various combinations of temperature and pressure. The data were as follows:

TEMP	PRES	YIELD	TEMP	PRES	YIELD	TEMP	PRES	YIELD
2200	3.8	75.50	2250	3.8	76.80	2300	3.8	78.50
2200	4.2	77.90	2250	4.2	79.20	2300	4.2	80.20
2200	3.8	75.90	2250	3.8	76.00	2300	3.8	78.80
2200	4.2	77.90	2250	4.2	78.90	2300	4.2	80.20

a. Plot TEMP versus PRES.
b. What must the value of $r_{TEMP, PRES}$ be?
c. How severe is the collinearity problem for these data?

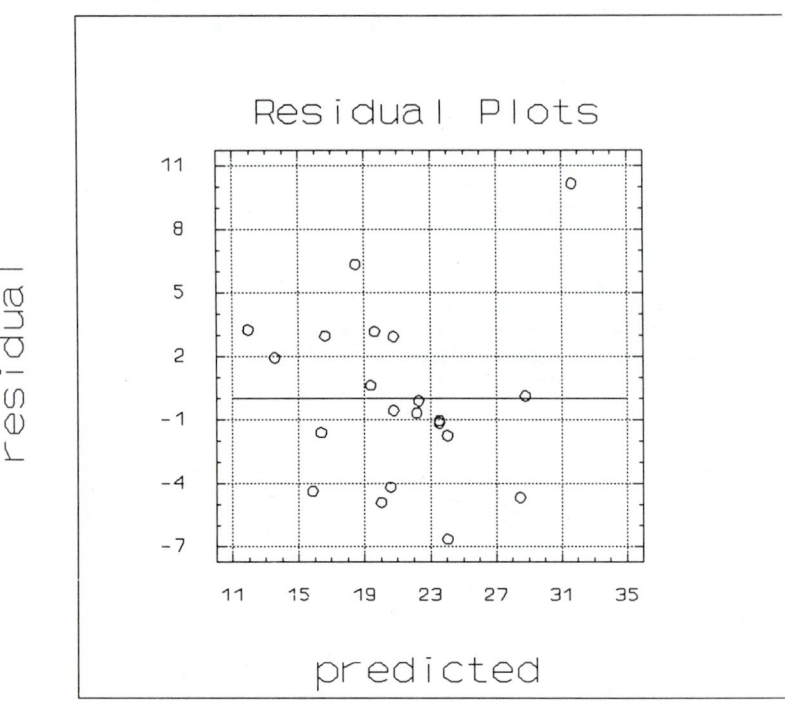

FIGURE R.5   Residuals Versus Predicted Values; Exercises R146–R149

R153 A regression model is fit to the data of Exercise R152. The output is shown on page 739.
   a. Locate the prediction equation.
   b. Roughly, what is the width of a 95% prediction interval for a value of YIELD? Assume that any extrapolation penalty can be neglected.

R154 Perform F and t tests for Exercise R153. What do the results indicate about the predictive value of TEMP and PRES?

R155 A residual plot against values of TEMP for the model of Exercise R153 is shown in Figure R.6 (page 740). Is there any evidence of a problem shown by this plot?

R156 Based on the plot of Exercise R155, a new variable, TEMPSQ = $(TEMP - 2250)^2$, is created. A new regression analysis is performed. The output is shown on page 740.
   a. Have the coefficients of TEMP and PRESS changed much?
   b. Does adding TEMPSQ greatly improve the prediction of YIELD? Indicate the parts of the output that support your judgment.

R157 A store manager for a supermarket chain does a regression study of the weekly sales of the store and the volume of promotional activity (advertising and coupons) the previous week. Systat output is shown on page 741.
   a. Is there evidence of a statistically significant predictive value of PROMO for predicting SALES?
   b. How much of the variability (squared error) of SALES is accounted for by PROMO?

```
MTB > regress c3 on 2 variables in c1 c2 put residuals in c19 yhats in c20
```

The regression equation is
yield = - 2.41 + 0.0262 temp + 5.33 pres

Predictor	Coef	Stdev	t-ratio
Constant	-2.412	6.915	-0.35
temp	0.026250	0.002889	9.09
pres	5.3333	0.5897	9.04

s = 0.4085   R-sq = 94.8%   R-sq(adj) = 93.7%

Analysis of Variance

SOURCE	DF	SS	MS
Regression	2	27.435	13.717
Error	9	1.502	0.167
Total	11	28.937	

SOURCE	DF	SEQ SS
temp	1	13.781
pres	1	13.653

Minitab for Exercise R153

R158 The output of Exercise R157 indicates that there is a serious violation of at least one assumption. What is it, how do you know that this violation has occurred, and what are the consequences of the violation on your answers in Exercise R157?

R159 Differences are calculated for the data of Exercise R157 and a new regression equation is found. The output is shown on page 741.
   a. Is there statistically significant predictive value of DPROMO for predicting DSALES?
   b. How much of the variability of DSALES is accounted for by variation in DPROMO?
   c. How do your answers here compare to the answers of Exercise R157?

R160 Did the use of differences eliminate the violation of assumptions in Exercise R158?

R161 In a paper mill, a liquid slurry of wood fibers is forced through a screen. The yield of fibers is known to increase as the difference in pressure between the two sides of the screen increases. Data are collected and a regression equation found. The output is shown on page 742.
   a. What would the null hypothesis that the true slope is zero mean in this situation?
   b. Show that this hypothesis can be conclusively rejected.

R162 Locate and interpret the residual standard deviation in the output of Exercise R161.

R163 A plot of the residuals from Exercise R161 versus values of CHGPRES is shown in Figure R.7 (page 743).
   a. Is there an indication that a nonlinear equation may give a better fit to the data?
   b. Are there any severe outliers?

R164 The square root of the pressure change is calculated for the data of Exercise R161 and a new regression is calculated. The output is shown on page 742. Has the square-root transformation improved the fit of the model?

```
MTB > plot 'resids' vs. 'temp'
```

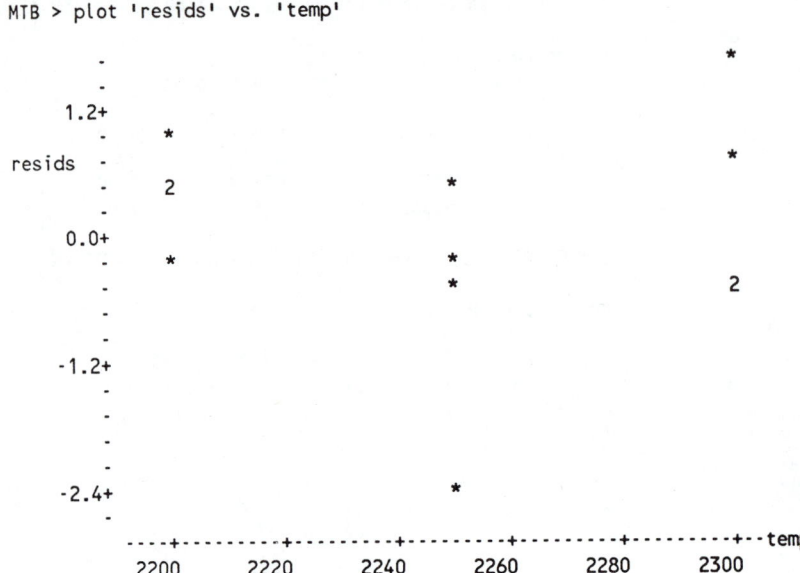

FIGURE R.6   Residuals Versus Temperature; Exercises R152–R155

```
MTB > regress c3 on 3 vars in c1 c2 c4 put residuals in c19 yhats in c20

The regression equation is
yield = - 2.67 + 0.0262 temp + 5.33 pres +0.000155 tempsq
```

Predictor	Coef	Stdev	t-ratio
Constant	-2.671	6.283	-0.43
temp	0.026250	0.002624	10.00
pres	5.3333	0.5356	9.96
tempsq	0.00015500	0.00009090	1.71

s = 0.3711   R-sq = 96.2%   R-sq(adj) = 94.8%

Analysis of Variance

SOURCE	DF	SS	MS
Regression	3	27.8350	9.2783
Error	8	1.1017	0.1377
Total	11	28.9366	

SOURCE	DF	SEQ SS
temp	1	13.7812
pres	1	13.6533
tempsq	1	0.4004

Minitab for Exercise R156

```
DEP VAR:  SALES      N:  24    MULTIPLE R:  .871    SQUARED MULTIPLE R:  .759
ADJUSTED SQUARED MULTIPLE R:  .748      STANDARD ERROR OF ESTIMATE:      12.964

    VARIABLE      COEFFICIENT    STD ERROR    STD COEF TOLERANCE     T    P(2 TAIL)

CONSTANT            -7.790        24.950       0.000 1.0000000   -0.312    0.758
PROMO                5.313         0.638       0.871 1.0000000    8.325    0.000


                        ANALYSIS OF VARIANCE

    SOURCE     SUM-OF-SQUARES   DF   MEAN-SQUARE      F-RATIO      P

REGRESSION        11647.283      1    11647.283       69.306     0.000
  RESIDUAL         3697.217     22      168.055


DURBIN-WATSON D STATISTIC      .433
FIRST ORDER AUTOCORRELATION    .668
```

Systat for Exercise R157

```
DEP VAR:  DSALES     N:  23    MULTIPLE R:  .970    SQUARED MULTIPLE R:  .940
ADJUSTED SQUARED MULTIPLE R:  .937      STANDARD ERROR OF ESTIMATE:       8.328

    VARIABLE      COEFFICIENT    STD ERROR    STD COEF TOLERANCE     T    P(2 TAIL)

CONSTANT            -1.696         1.737       0.000 1.0000000   -0.976    0.340
DPROMO               5.019         0.276       0.970 1.0000000   18.159    0.000


                        ANALYSIS OF VARIANCE

    SOURCE     SUM-OF-SQUARES   DF   MEAN-SQUARE      F-RATIO      P

REGRESSION        22870.318      1    22870.318      329.736     0.000
  RESIDUAL         1456.551     21       69.360


DURBIN-WATSON D STATISTIC     1.431
FIRST ORDER AUTOCORRELATION    .197
```

Systat for Exercise R159

REGRESSION WITH ORIGINAL DATA

DEP VARIABLE: YIELD

ANALYSIS OF VARIANCE

SOURCE	DF	SUM OF SQUARES	MEAN SQUARE	F VALUE	PROB>F
MODEL	1	2455.976	2455.976	414.234	0.0001
ERROR	28	166.0107	5.928955		
C TOTAL	29	2621.987			

ROOT MSE	2.434945	R-SQUARE	0.9367
DEP MEAN	78.11	ADJ R-SQ	0.9344
C.V.	3.117328		

PARAMETER ESTIMATES

VARIABLE	DF	PARAMETER ESTIMATE	STANDARD ERROR	T FOR H0: PARAMETER=0	PROB > |T|
INTERCEP	1	60.78444	0.9603551	63.294	0.0001
CHGPRES	1	0.6300202	0.03095505	20.353	0.0001

SAS for Exercise R161

REGRESSION WITH TRANSFORMED DATA

DEP VARIABLE: YIELD

ANALYSIS OF VARIANCE

SOURCE	DF	SUM OF SQUARES	MEAN SQUARE	F VALUE	PROB>F
MODEL	1	2474.3	2474.3	469.102	0.0001
ERROR	28	147.6871	5.274541		
C TOTAL	29	2621.987			

ROOT MSE	2.296637	R-SQUARE	0.9437
DEP MEAN	78.11	ADJ R-SQ	0.9417
C.V.	2.94026		

PARAMETER ESTIMATES

VARIABLE	DF	PARAMETER ESTIMATE	STANDARD ERROR	T FOR H0: PARAMETER=0	PROB > |T|
INTERCEP	1	47.75158	1.463042	32.639	0.0001
SQRTPRES	1	6.042607	0.2789912	21.659	0.0001

SAS for Exercise R164

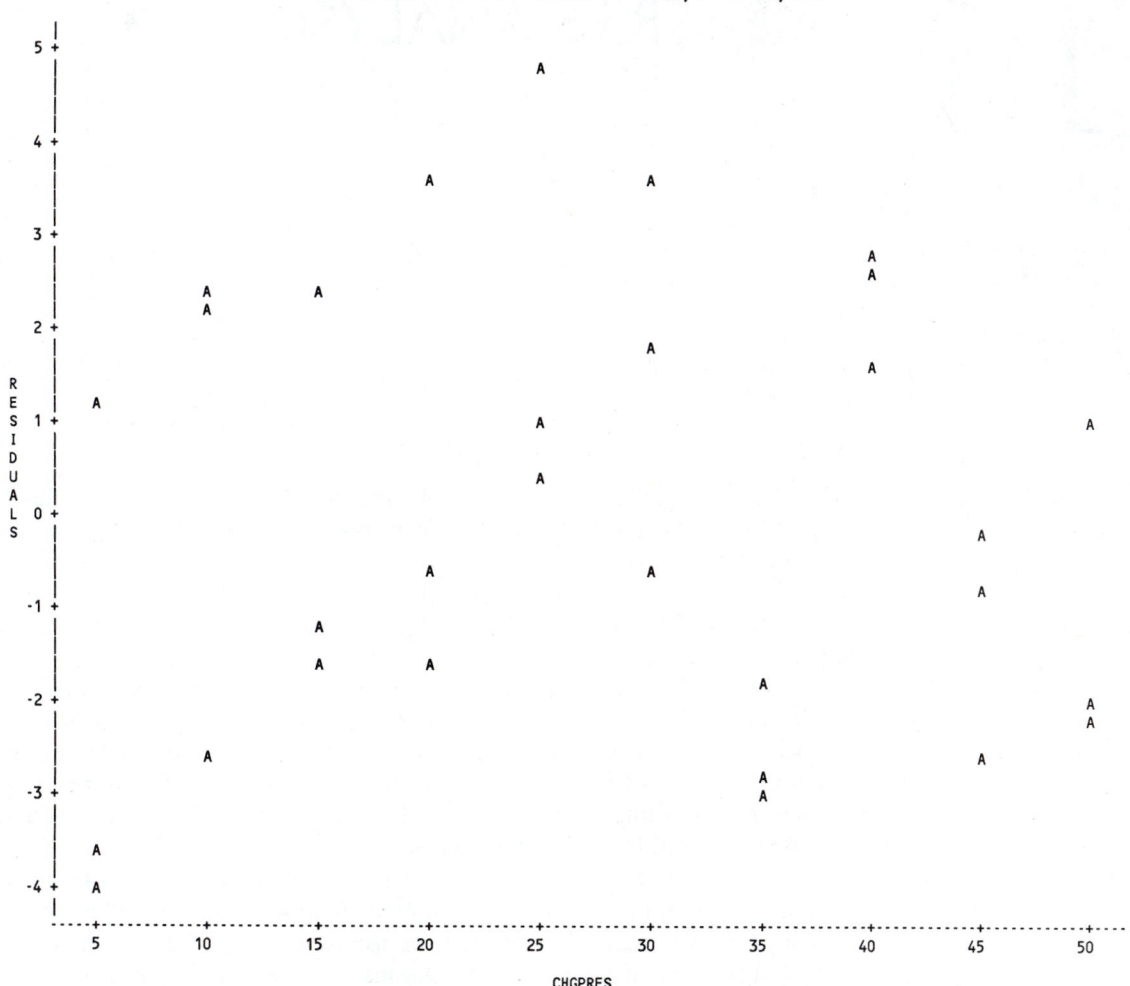

FIGURE R.7   Residuals Versus Change in Pressure; Exercises R161–R163

TIME-SERIES ANALYSIS

One part of statistical analysis of great relevance to managers is analysis of **time-series** data collected on the same variable for many time periods. From macro-economic data such as disposable income to microeconomic data such as weekly sales of one particular product at one particular store, time series are basic data for managers. In Chapter 15 we discussed how we can apply multiple regression methods to time-series data. The emphasis there was on the special problems that such data presented, particularly the problem of autocorrelated errors.

If time-series data present problems, they also present opportunities. One of the very best predictors of the future behavior of a variable is its past behavior. Intelligent analysis of time-series data can often yield insights that help in under-standing and predicting the future values of the series. In this chapter we discuss some useful ways of looking at time-series data.

The key aspect of this chapter is that the behavior of a time series is considered in isolation. We don't look at prediction of one time series by other series, as we did in regression. Instead, we use past values of a time series to predict future values of the same series. One major virtue of this approach is that the data requirements are minimal. As long as the series have been defined consistently over time (as, unfortunately, some series aren't), there's no need to bring together many different sets of data. Therefore the methods in this chapter are very useful in situations such as inventory control, where very many forecasts must be made and the value of a little extra accuracy is not huge.

One part of time-series analysis is the construction of index numbers to reflect changes in prices over time. We discuss methods for constructing and using such indices in Section 16.1. In Section 16.2 we turn to the classical breakdown of time series into trend, seasonal, cyclic, and irregular components. In Section 16.3 we discuss some smoothing methods that can be used as simple forecasting methods and also as methods for clearing up the effect of irregular, random movements of the series. The Box-Jenkins methods of Section 16.4 are poten-tially very valuable, both in the context of a single series and as a way to com-bine concepts of regression and time series.

16.1   INDEX NUMBERS   ∎

Index numbers are probably the best-known results of statistical reasoning. The value of the Dow-Jones Industrial Index is reported daily by newspapers and broadcasts. Many news radio stations interrupt their regular broadcasts to give the monthly Consumer Price Index as soon as it is released. Many cost-of-living adjustments are based on such indices, as are Social Security payments. In this section we discuss some basic ideas of index-number construction, with primary emphasis on price indices.

There are essentially two types of indices—price indices and quantity indices. A price index measures the change in the prices of a group of items over time; a quantity index measures the change in the amount of a group of goods or services produced over time. Stock market indices such as the Dow Jones Industrial Average or the Standard and Poor's 500 are price indices; production indices for automobiles, steel, and the like are quantity indices.

A price index is useful in its own right as an indicator of the general level of prices. Also, measurements of general economic activity such as the gross national product are divided by a price index to separate the effect of price changes from actual changes in activity. If all prices change by a constant percentage, any price index serves these functions; the interpretation of a price index gets more delicate when prices vary differently.

Once again we work by example. Suppose that we want to construct an index for the price of entertainment. The following price data are available:

		Price	
Item	1988	1989	1990
Color television set 19″ console	$500	$550	$525
Movie ticket suburban theater	$5.00	$5.50	$5.50
Baseball ticket reserved seat	$5.00	$5.50	$6.00
Theater admission season subscription	$70.00	$77.00	$105.00

There is no problem when comparing 1988 and 1989 entertainment prices. Every price shown increased by 10% from 1988 to 1989. No matter how the entertainment index is calculated, if 1988 is taken as the base year with an index value of 100, the 1989 index value must be 110, a 10% increase.

There is a problem with comparing 1990 to 1988 prices, because the price changes are not consistent. Color televisions are up 5% (1990 over 1988), movie tickets 10%, baseball tickets 20%, and theater admissions 50%. One solution, not a very good one, is to take the ratio of total prices in 1990 to total prices in 1988. Conventionally, this ratio is multiplied by 100 so that we state the index in percentage terms. This index value is

$$\frac{525 + 5.50 + 6.00 + 105.00}{500 + 5.00 + 5.00 + 50.00} \times 100 = 110.6$$

which indicates a 10.6% rise in prices from 1988 to 1990. This is an example of a simple aggregate index. A formal definition follows:

Simple Aggregate Price Index

A simple aggregate price index for year k, denoted I_k, is the ratio of a sum of prices in year k to the sum of prices in the base year (year 0), expressed as a percentage:

$$I_k = \frac{\sum p_{ki}}{\sum p_{0i}} \times 100$$

where p_{ki} and p_{0i} are the prices of item i in year k and year 0, respectively.

The Dow-Jones Industrial Index began as a simple aggregate index of the prices of 30 blue chip stocks. So many modifications have been made over the years that it is no longer recognizable as such an index.

EXAMPLE 16.1

Closing 1988 and 1989 stock prices for a group of nonprescription drug wholesalers are shown here. Construct a simple aggregate price index for 1989 using 1988 as the base year.

	Closing Stock Price	
Wholesaler	1988	1989
Begley	$15\frac{1}{2}$	$16\frac{1}{4}$
Bindley	$9\frac{7}{8}$	19
Durr-Fillauer	$10\frac{1}{4}$	$15\frac{1}{4}$
Ketchum	$15\frac{1}{4}$	$20\frac{1}{4}$
Med. Shoppe	19	24

Solution

$$I_{1989} = \frac{16\frac{1}{4} + 19 + 15\frac{1}{4} + 20\frac{1}{4} + 24}{15\frac{1}{2} + 9\frac{7}{8} + 10\frac{1}{4} + 15\frac{1}{4} + 19} = 1.356$$

A stockholder owning one share of each wholesaler would have seen a 35.6% increase in the price of the portfolio.

The obvious objection to a simple aggregate index is that it does not reflect the amounts of various goods that are typically purchased. Our entertainment price index implicitly assumes that the relevant consumer buys as many color televisions as movie tickets. For most purposes, it is more reasonable to weight each price by an appropriate quantity to form a weighted aggregate index.

Weighted Aggregate Price Index

A weighted aggregate price index for year k is the ratio of a weighted sum of prices in year k to a weighted sum of prices in the base year 0 expressed as a percentage. The weights q_i are appropriately chosen quantities of each item:

$$I_k = \frac{\sum p_{ki} q_i}{\sum p_{0i} q_i} \times 100$$

EXAMPLE 16.2

In constructing an entertainment index using the data in this section, assume that a representative family buys a new color television set every eight years, ten movie tickets and two baseball tickets per year, and a subscription theater admission once every five years. Calculate the weighted aggregate price index values for 1989 and 1990.

Solution

The appropriate quantities can all be translated into amounts per year; for television sets the quantity is $1/8 = .125$ per year, for movie and baseball tickets ten and two per year, and for theater admissions $1/5 = .2$ per year. The price index value for 1990 is

$$I_{1989} = \frac{550(.125) + 5.50(10) + 5.50(2) + 57.00(.2)}{500(.125) + 5.00(10) + 5.00(2) + 70.00(.2)} \times 100 = 110.0$$

The price index value for 1990 is

$$I_{1990} = \frac{525(.125) + 5.50(10) + 6.00(2) + 105(.2)}{500(.125) + 5.00(10) + 5.00(2) + 70(.2)} = 112.5$$

The 1989 index value reflects the uniform 10% price increase. The 1990 index value (112.5) is substantially higher than the simple aggregate value (110.6) found previously. The basic reason is that the price of television sets increased relatively little. This price receives much less weight in the weighted aggregate index than it does in the simple aggregate index, while the larger increases receive more weight.

The major difficulty in defining a weighted aggregate index is, of course, the specification of appropriate items and the weights attached to the items. The Bureau of Labor Statistics, in preparing the Consumer Price Index, selected **choice of weights** about 300 carefully defined items. The quantities q_i are obtained by a sample of wage earners and their families. The selection of items and quantities inevitably becomes less appropriate as time goes by. Thus almost any index must be revised periodically.

In a sense, the whole exercise of fixed-quantity weighted price indices is a denial of elementary economics. When a particular commodity becomes more expensive, we buy less of it. When a new product of superior quality appears on the market, we change our purchasing behavior. On the other hand, if product quality declines, we may receive less utility for a given expenditure. Ideally, a price index would not be so closely tied to specific products but rather would reflect the cost of obtaining certain goals. Instead of basing a food price index on the price of so much steak, so much beans, and so many apples, we would prefer a food price index based on the total cost of a diet meeting specified nutrition and taste standards. The difficulties involved in pinning down such elusive goals, however, are formidable. At least the current fixed-quantity approach to price indices provides an objective, if somewhat arbitrary, standard. As we noted earlier in this section, the choice of weights matters only to the extent that price changes differ among products. All in all, we suggest that price indices should be treated like any other statistical quantities—as estimates that are subject to error.

SECTION 16.1   EXERCISES

16.1 Data for a price index based on eight commodities are collected over a three-year period, yielding the following results:

	Commodity							
	1	2	3	4	5	6	7	8
Price								
year 1	6.00	7.25	6.60	10.50	4.60	12.50	25.00	300.00
year 2	6.58	7.80	7.25	11.58	5.05	13.75	27.48	329.50
year 3	7.25	8.59	7.99	12.75	5.50	15.10	30.21	362.45
Quantity								
per year	6.25	4.00	2.50	1.00	.80	.25	.10	.01

a. Compute simple aggregate price indices for years 2 and 3, using year 1 as the base period.

b. Compute weighted aggregate price indices for years 2 and 3, using year 1 as the base period.

16.2 An analyst of the computer-calculator industry gathers data on the cost and quantity sold of calculating and computing devices for a four-year period. The data are collected in six major categories, as follows:

	Category					
	A	B	C	D	E	F
Year 1						
price	20.00	50.68	989	35,416	195,626	651,928
quantity	2,060,000	121,200	86,104	82,147	21,047	1306
Year 2						
price	18.64	48.21	1021	37,215	206,114	721,200
quantity	2,547,000	142,900	89,216	81,021	21,926	1339

	Category					
	A	B	C	D	E	F
Year 3						
price	16.93	47.03	1096	40,462	215,963	790,087
quantity	2,997,000	163,800	95,114	76,050	20,875	1575
Year 4						
price	16.61	46.89	1129	41,943	229,120	864,326
quantity	3,451,000	177,500	94,397	71,194	19,975	1498

a. Compute simple aggregate price indices for years 2, 3, and 4, using year 1 as the base period.
b. Compute weighted aggregate price indices for these years, using year 1 quantities as weights. (Base-year weights are used in Laspeyres indices.)
c. Compute weighted aggregate price indices for these years, using the quantities for each year as weights for that year. (Current-year weights are used in Paasche indices.)

16.3 Refer to the price indices you computed in Exercise 16.2.
   a. Is there a serious difference between the unweighted, simple aggregate index and the index that is weighted by yearly quantities? Why?
   b. Is there a serious difference between the year 1 weighted index and the year 4 weighted index? Why?

16.4 A manufacturer of small electric appliances uses mostly stainless steel sheets, copper wire, a plastic substance, and glass. As a part of its pricing policy, the company routinely calculates a raw-material cost index. Price data (P) for the previous five years and utilization data (Q) are as follows. The quantities are measured in special units used only by the manufacturer.

	Steel		Copper		Plastic		Glass	
Year	P	Q	P	Q	P	Q	P	Q
1	280	220	450	30	24	40	48	21
2	306	244	430	34	38	43	51	24
3	327	256	492	36	36	45	53	25
4	360	280	582	38	39	49	54	30
5	396	308	573	44	44	52	56	35

a. Compute simple aggregate price index values for years 2–5, using year 1 as the base period.
b. Compute weighted aggregate price indices (using year 1 quantity weights) for these years.
c. Explain any major discrepancies you find between the two sets of values.

16.2 THE CLASSICAL TREND, CYCLIC, AND SEASONAL APPROACH   ∎

One way to examine a time series is to break it into components. A standard approach is to find components corresponding to a long-term trend, any cyclic behavior, seasonal behavior, and a residual, irregular part. For example, data have been collected on the ridership of the PATCO public transit line running between southern New Jersey and Philadelphia. The data (supplied by Bruce Allen of the Wharton School) are recorded in 13 four-week blocks per year:

Period	1983	1984	1985	1986	1987	1988	1989
1	882712	820304	761622	777819	763648	792936	844229
2	854016	806592	784017	794289	815377	845591	842124
3	861124	807453	802528	824552	825763	866940	850269
4	832343	804755	795945	817406	834137	839738	868484
5	824050	800477	793017	806742	831219	853809	858221
6	800650	754132	761957	775087	824524	826061	825535
7	763825	750522	782769	772918	826191	814283	813425
8	778466	749987	783530	789186	823712	830701	842028
9	747695	726420	740151	751060	817463	811976	
10	844658	805096	802746	839767	877116	834676	
11	870317	823609	840390	835142	883962	878721	
12	814071	779037	785039	786395	839698	840804	
13	797018	783205	797048	797011	859494	1066242	

What can we see from the plot of these data in Figure 16.1? First, there's an obvious outlier in period 78 (the last period of 1988). We couldn't find any reason to exclude that value. It's correct and not attributable to any special situation we know of. Therefore, we left it in the data and will have to be careful that it doesn't distort our analysis too badly. Second, there appears to be a slight upward **trend**. Third, there is a **seasonal** pattern. Ridership in periods 6 through 9 of each year tends to be somewhat below the trend; these periods fall during the summer, when potential riders are on vacation. There may be a **cyclic** effect. Ridership may be somewhat below the trend in 1984 and 1985 and somewhat above it earlier and later. Finally, there is a **random**, irregular aspect; even if we knew the trend, seasonal, and cyclic behavior exactly, we still couldn't predict ridership exactly.

EXAMPLE 16.3   Monthly data on the number of paid admissions (in thousands) to an indoor sports and entertainment arena for 72 months are given below and plotted in Figure 16.2 (page 752). Identify any apparent trend, seasonal, and cyclic effects.

J	F	M	A	M	J	J	A	S	O	N	D
89	101	116	111	94	59	44	44	73	78	99	93
96	110	118	116	107	69	52	54	85	92	113	109
120	136	155	155	129	98	69	78	116	143	154	166
183	199	227	219	198	148	94	108	160	201	215	246
242	264	359	308	265	193	150	146	243	260	332	293
323	377	470	422	345	239	176	182	288	342	380	379

Solution   The upward trend in admissions is obvious in the figure. The trend may not be linear, however. Rather, it may be **S**-shaped, involving initial slow growth, a period of more rapid growth, and then a tapering-off. (One consideration sug-

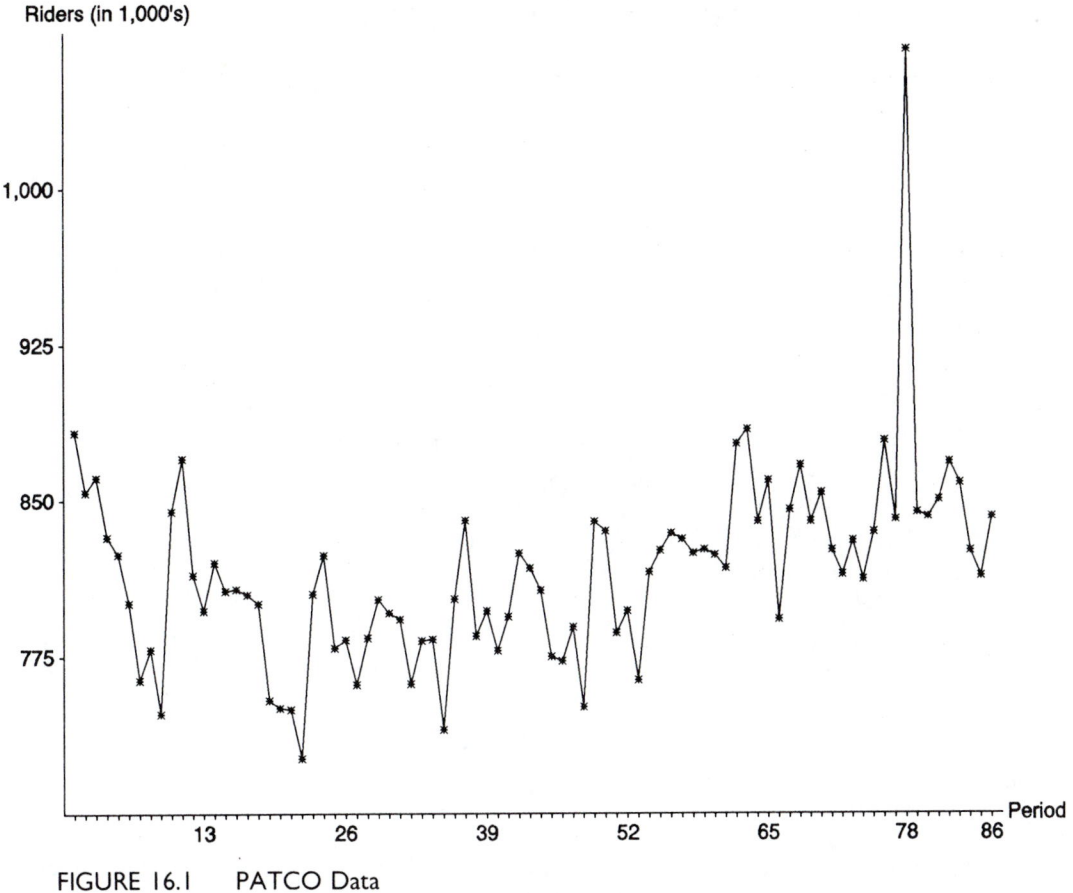

FIGURE 16.1   PATCO Data

gests that the trend cannot increase forever. Paid admissions to the arena are limited by the available number of dates and seats.) There is a strong seasonal effect; admissions drop dramatically in the summer months. If there's any cyclic component, it's not apparent in the figure.   ■

One natural approach to the analysis of a time series is to remove the trend first, then the seasonal effects. The hope is that this procedure will bring out any longer-term cycles more clearly. The key decision that must be made in removing a trend is the specification of the mathematical form of a trend equation. Denote the values of the time series variable as y_t, where t runs from time 1 to some time T. Several mathematical forms for trends are widely used:

Linear: $Y_t = \beta_0 + \beta_1 t + \epsilon_t$

Exponential: $Y_t = \beta_0 e^{\beta_1 t} \epsilon_t$

Logistic: $Y_t = \dfrac{\beta_0}{1 + \beta_1 e^{\beta_2 t}} \epsilon_t$

Gompertz: $Y_t = \beta_0 e^{\beta_1 e^{\beta_2 t}} \epsilon_t$

Admissions to Arena

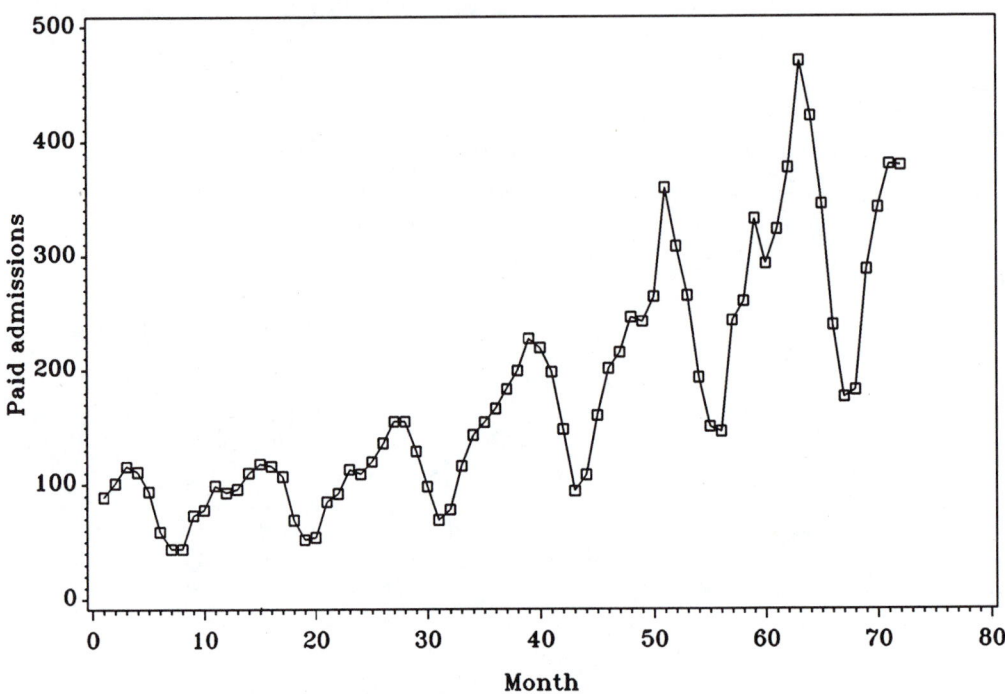

FIGURE 16.2   Admissions to Arena; Example 16.3

linear trend

The **linear trend** equation is the simplest. The coefficient β_1 represents the average increase in y per unit time. This increase is measured in absolute terms (e.g., dollars) rather than in percentage terms. A linear trend equation should be used when there is no evident curvature in the plot of y_t against t. A good way to estimate β_0 and β_1 is by least squares, as in simple linear regression, with t as the independent variable.

EXAMPLE 16.4

The PATCO ridership data shown previously in this section are used in a linear regression, with period number as the independent variable. The output shown here indicates the equation and the trend values.

```
The regression equation is
riders = 784639 + 714 C4
```

785353	786067	786781	787495	788208	788922	789636	790350	791064	791778	792492	793206	793920
794634	795348	796062	796776	797490	798204	798918	799631	800345	801059	801773	802487	803201
803915	804629	805343	806057	806771	807485	808199	808913	809627	810340	811054	811768	812482
813196	813910	814624	815338	816052	816766	817480	818194	818908	819622	820335	821049	821763
822477	823191	823905	824619	825333	826047	826761	827475	828189	828903	829617	830331	831044
831758	832472	833186	833900	834614	835328	836042	836756	837470	838184	838898	839612	840326
841040	841754	842467	843181	843895	844609	845323	846037					

Write the estimated trend equation. Interpret the slope.

Solution   The trend equation is ridership $= 784{,}639 + 714t$ where t is the time period. The slope indicates that, over time, the transit line is gaining about 714 riders per four-week period.   ∎

exponential trend   We use the **exponential trend** equation when the trend reflects a roughly constant percentage growth; e^{β_1} is the percentage growth rate per time, while β_0 is the value of the trend at time $t = 0$. For instance, if at time 0 the trend value is 250, and the trend reflects an 8% growth rate per year, the trend equation is

$$\hat{y}_t = 250(1.08)^t$$

Because $e^{.077} = 1.08$, or equivalently $\log_e 1.08 = .077$, the trend equation can be rewritten as

$$\hat{y}_t = 250\,e^{.077t}$$

The exponential trend equation should be used if a plot of the natural logarithm of y_t against t appears roughly linear. If

$$Y_t = \beta_0 e^{\beta_1 t}\epsilon_t$$

then

$$\log Y_t = (\log \beta_0) + \beta_1 t + \log \epsilon_t$$

We can estimate the coefficients $(\log \beta_0)$ and β_1 by regressing $\log y_t$ against $x_t = t$.

EXAMPLE 16.5

An exponential trend is fit to the PATCO ridership data. The output shown below results from a least-squares fit of $\log Y_t$ to $t(t = 1,\ldots,85)$. Trend values are shown by period.

```
The regression equation is
C5 = 13.6 +0.000859 C4
```

785334	786009	786684	787360	788037	788714	789391	790070	790749	791428	792109	792790	793470
794152	794835	795518	796201	796886	797571	798256	798942	799629	800315	801003	801692	802380
803070	803760	804451	805142	805834	806527	807219	807913	808608	809302	809998	810694	811391
812088	812786	813485	814183	814883	815584	816284	816985	817688	818390	819093	819798	820502
821207	821913	822619	823326	824033	824742	825450	826160	826870	827581	828291	829003	829716
830428	831142	831857	832571	833287	834003	834719	835437	836155	836874	837592	838312	839033
839753	840475	841198	841920	842644	843368	844093	844818					

a. Identify the least-squares estimates of $(\log \beta_0)$ and β_1.
b. Write the estimated trend equation and identify the monthly percentage increase in sales.
c. Does a linear trend or an exponential trend appear more appropriate?

Solution   a. The intercept term is 13.6, while the slope is $+0.000859$.

b. The prediction equation is obtained by taking $e^{13.6} = 806{,}000$ for the initial constant. The equation is

$$\hat{y}_t = 806{,}000 e^{0.000859t}$$

The estimated change in ridership is $e^{0.000859}$, or 1.00886, a .086% per period increase.

c. The choice is not blatantly obvious. The plot of the data and the trend equations suggest that a linear trend fits the data as well as anything.   ■

It is risky to assume that exponential growth will continue indefinitely. The sales history of a product may reveal a consistent 15% growth rate in unit sales per year, but sooner or later the sales must approach some saturation level and the percentage growth must slow down. The **logistic** and **Gompertz trend** equations yield very similar **S**-shaped trends. Figure 16.3 shows typical logistic and Gompertz curves.

logistic and Gompertz trends

Fitting either logistic or Gompertz trend equations is a bit harder than fitting linear or exponential trends. It is not possible to transform either **S**-shaped curve into a regression model. There are more complicated numerical methods for fitting such equations.

The trend, cyclic, seasonal, and irregular aspects of a time series can be combined in either of two ways. The **multiplicative model** is

multiplicative model

$$y_t = T_t C_t S_t I_t$$

where T_t, C_t, S_t, and I_t are the trend, cyclic, seasonal, and irregular components at time t. This model can be understood in terms of percentage changes. For instance, a seasonal index for a particular month equal to 1.08 means that the series tends to be 8% above the value predicted by trend and cycle alone. (By

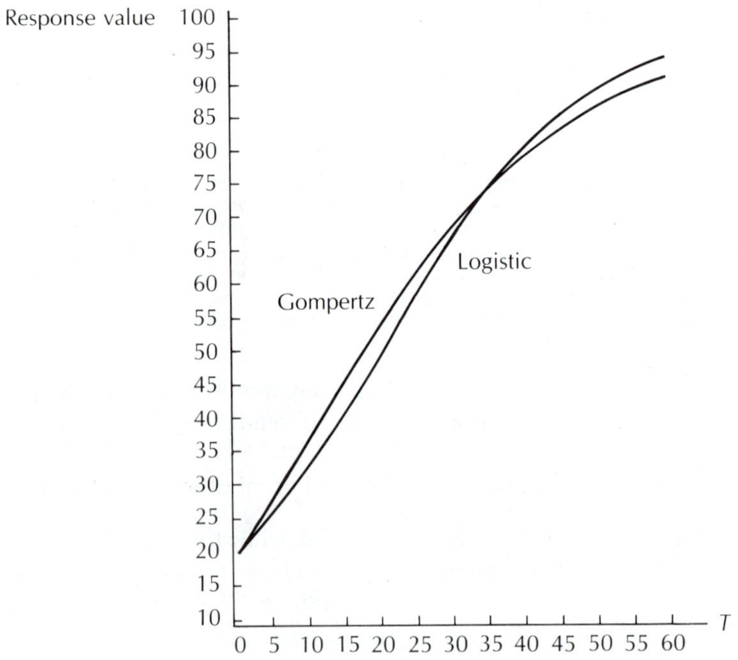

FIGURE 16.3   Typical Logistic and Gompertz Curves

additive model   definition, the irregular component is unpredictable.) The **additive model** is

$$y_t = T_t + C_t + S_t + I_t$$

This model can be understood in absolute units as opposed to percentages. For instance, a seasonal index for daily water consumption in a city might have a value of 8 million gallons per day for August. That means that the water-consumption series for August would tend to be 8 million gallons above what was predicted by trend and cycle. A multiplicative model may be converted to an additive one by taking logarithms (to any base):

$$\log y_t = \log T_t + \log C_t + \log S_t + \log I_t$$

An additive model is very convenient when the trend equation is linear; a multiplicative model is convenient for an exponential trend. (Recall that we estimated an exponential trend by regressing the logarithm of y_t on t.) For most economic series, percentage changes tend to be more stable, and the multiplicative model is more commonly used. Therefore most or our examples use the multiplicative model.

Once a trend equation has been estimated, the influence of trend can be
detrended series   removed from the data, yielding a "**detrended**" time series. For the multiplicative model, divide the actual y_t by the trend value:

$$\frac{y_t}{T_t} = \frac{T_t C_t S_t I_t}{T_t} = C_t S_t I_t$$

contains no trend. If $y_t/T_t = 1.052$, for example, then the actual y_t is 5.2% above trend. For the additive model, subtract the trend value from y_t:

$$y_t - T_t = T_t + C_t + S_t + I_t - T_t = C_t + S_t + I_t$$

If $y_t - T_t = 620$, then y_t is 620 units above trend.
seasonal index   Next, the detrended values can be used to construct a **seasonal index**. There are several methods that can be used. The simplest method applies to an additive model. To construct a seasonal index value for, say, October, simply average all the available detrended October values. For instance, if 60 months of data are available and the five October detrended values are .982, .965, .961, .976, and .966, the seasonal index is the mean, .970. The same method could perhaps be used in a multiplicative model. Alternatively, because the multiplicative model is additive in logarithms, we can average the logarithms of detrended values, then take the antilogarithm to obtain the index. The logarithms (base 10) of the five October detrended values are $-.0078885$, $-.0154727$, $-.0172766$, $-.0105502$, and $-.0150229$, which have a mean of $-.0132422$. Take the antilogarithm by calculating $10^{-.0132422} = .970$. The two methods do not yield identical answers (in this case the difference is in the fifth decimal place), but if the detrended values are not too variable, as is the case here, the difference is small. The interpretations of the additive and multiplicative seasonal indices are very different. The additive index of .970 means that October values tend to be .970 units above the trend; the multiplicative index of .970 means that October values tend to be 97.0% of the trend.

For the PATCO ridership data shown at the beginning of this section, the detrended values are

97359	67949	74343	44848	35841	11728	-25811	-11884	-43369	52880	77825	20865	3098
25670	11244	11391	7979	2987	-44072	-48395	-49644	-73925	4037	21836	-23450	-19996
-42293	-20612	-2815	-10112	-13754	-45528	-25430	-25383	-69475	-7594	29336	-26729	-15434
-35377	-19621	9928	2068	-9310	-41679	-44562	-29008	-67848	20145	14806	-34654	-24752
-58829	-7814	1858	9518	5886	-1523	-570	-3763	-10726	48213	54345	9367	28449
-38822	13119	33754	5838	19195	-9267	-21759	-6055	-25494	-3508	39823	1192	225916
3189	370	7802	25303	14326	-19074	-31898	-4009					

To compute a seasonal index, we simply average the values for each period, obtaining

Period:	1	2	3	4	5	6	7
Index:	-7015	6376	19466	12206	7882	-21345	-28346

Period:	8	9	10	11	12	13
Index:	-18535	-48473	19029	39662	-8902	32880

Thus ridership in period 1 tends to be 7015 passengers below the trend. Notice that in periods 6 through 9, the summer periods, ridership is substantially lower.

deseasonalized data

Once seasonal indices have been calculated, detrended data can be **deseasonalized**. Simply divide by the index value (in the multiplicative model) or subtract the index value (in the additive model).

cyclic patterns

Detrended, seasonally adjusted values are useful in attempting to identify **cyclic patterns**. Only cyclic and irregular (random) components remain in such values. Even so, identification of cyclic patterns is a tricky business. The basic problem is identifying the peak-to-peak or trough-to-trough length (called the *period*) of a supposed cycle. Seasonal patterns don't present any such problem. By definition, seasonal cycles have a one-year period. But identifying longer-term cyclic behavior is difficult. What do you do with data that appear to encompass $3\frac{1}{2}$ cycles, with peak-to-peak distances of $2\frac{1}{12}$ years, $3\frac{7}{12}$ years, and $4\frac{10}{12}$ years? One simpleminded idea is to take the mean distance ($3\frac{1}{2}$ years) as the apparent period of the cycle. But there is no guarantee that this is a very accurate estimate.

spectral analysis

There is a much more sophisticated version of time-series analysis, **spectral analysis**, which is related to the idea of cyclic behavior. The sophisticated mathematics of spectral analysis, called *Fourier analysis*, is borrowed from physics and electrical engineering. The idea can be stated, without too much distortion, in terms of regression. A sine curve is a cyclic pattern, as shown in Figure 16.4; any period may be specified for a sine curve.

If several sine curves with different periods are specified and weights are assigned to each curve, very complicated cyclic patterns can be reconstructed as weighted sums of sine curves. Spectral analysis can be regarded as the result of regressing a (detrended or seasonally adjusted) time series on all possible sine

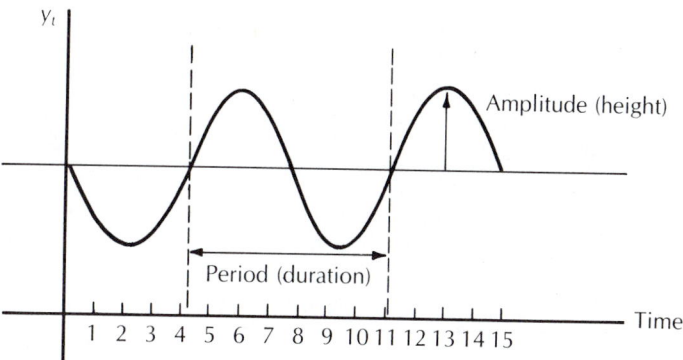

FIGURE 16.4   Sine Wave

curves. The **spectrum** of the time series indicates how much of the variation in y_t is explained by the sine curve having each possible period. If y_t shows a very strong cyclic pattern with a given period, spectral analysis shows that a sine curve with that period explains much of the variation in y_t, and the spectrum has a sharp "peak" corresponding to that period. Estimating the spectrum of a time series is not a job for amateurs. For our purposes, it is enough to say that spectral analysis is an available method for analyzing cyclic data.

SECTION 16.2   EXERCISES

16.5 A supplier of high-quality audio equipment for automobiles accumulates monthly sales data on speakers and receiver-amplifier units for five years. The data (in thousands of units per month) are shown here:

Year	J	F	M	A	M	J	J	A	S	O	N	D
1	101.9	93.0	93.5	93.9	104.9	94.6	105.9	116.7	128.4	118.2	107.3	108.6
2	109.0	98.4	99.1	110.7	100.2	112.1	123.8	135.8	124.8	114.1	114.9	112.9
3	115.5	104.5	105.1	105.4	117.5	106.4	118.6	130.9	143.7	132.2	120.8	121.3
4	122.0	110.4	110.8	111.2	124.4	112.4	124.9	138.0	151.5	139.5	127.7	128.0
5	128.1	115.8	116.0	117.2	130.7	117.5	131.8	145.5	159.3	146.5	134.0	134.2

Plot the sales data. Do you see any overall trend in the data? Do there seem to be any cyclic or seasonal effects?

16.6 Fit a linear trend equation to the data of Exercise 16.5. The following summary figures will be useful; y_t represents sales in month t, $t = 1, \ldots, 60$.

$$\sum y_t = 7122.0, \qquad \sum t = 1830, \qquad \sum y_t^2 = 858{,}693.02$$
$$\sum t^2 = 73{,}810, \qquad \sum t y_t = 227{,}951.30$$

16.7 The data of Exercise 16.5 are detrended by dividing by the trend equation values of Exercise 16.6, with the following results:

Year	J	F	M	A	M	J	J	A	S	O	N	D
1	1.014	.920	.919	.918	1.019	.913	1.017	1.114	1.218	1.115	1.007	1.013
2	1.011	.908	.909	.909	1.004	.904	1.006	1.104	1.205	1.101	1.002	1.003
3	1.003	.903	.903	.901	.999	.900	.998	1.096	1.198	1.096	.997	.996
4	.996	.897	.896	.895	.996	.896	.991	1.089	1.199	1.091	.994	.991
5	.987	.888	.886	.891	.989	.885	.988	1.086	1.183	1.083	.986	.984

Plot the detrended values against time. Do they show a seasonal effect?

16.8 A simple seasonal index is constructed by averaging the detrended values of Exercise 16.7. The index values are

J	F	M	A	M	J	J	A	S	O	N	D
1.002	.903	.903	.903	1.001	.900	1.000	1.098	1.199	1.097	.997	.997

a. Construct detrended, deseasonalized data for year 5.
b. Construct forecast values for year 6 by calculating the trend values and then multiplying by the seasonal factor.

16.9 Plot the detrended, seasonally adjusted data from Exercise 16.5. Is there any visual evidence of a cyclic pattern?

16.10 A machine-tool firm that produces a variety of products for manufacturers has quarterly records of total activity for the previous eight years. The data reflect activity rather than price, so inflation is irrelevant. The data are

	Quarter			
Year	1	2	3	4
1	97.2	100.2	102.8	102.6
2	106.1	107.8	110.5	110.6
3	116.5	117.3	119.9	119.3
4	126.1	125.7	128.3	132.1
5	133.2	133.8	141.1	142.1
6	144.2	146.1	151.6	154.0
7	155.8	158.6	165.8	167.0
8	171.1	172.6	176.5	179.7

a. Plot the data against time (quarters 1–32).
b. Does there appear to be a clear trend? If so, what form of trend equation would you suggest?
c. Can you detect cyclic or seasonal features?

16.11 Fit an exponential trend to the data of Exercise 16.10. The following summary figures are relevant:

$$\sum \log y_t = 156.41, \qquad \sum t = 528, \qquad \sum (\log y_t)^2 = 765.59$$
$$\sum t^2 = 11{,}440, \qquad \sum t \log y_t = 2634.48$$

16.12 Detrended values for the data of Exercise 16.10 are calculated by dividing by trend values, using the trend equation of Exercise 16.11. The detrended values are

Year	Quarter			
	1	2	3	4
1	.9939	1.0046	1.0106	.9890
2	1.0028	.9990	1.0041	.9854
3	1.0177	1.0048	1.0070	.9825
4	1.0182	.9952	.9960	1.0055
5	.9941	.9792	1.0125	.9998
6	.9948	.9882	1.0055	1.0015
7	.9935	.9916	1.0165	1.0038
8	1.0084	.9974	1.0001	.9984

a. Plot the detrended values against time (quarters 1–32).
b. Can you detect possible seasonal or cyclic effects?

16.13 Use the trend equation of Exercise 16.11 to forecast activity for quarters 33–36.

16.3   SMOOTHING METHODS   ■

The classical approach described in the previous section does not lead directly to forecasts, though forecasts can be derived as a by-product. An alternative approach to time-series analysis is **smoothing**, which attempts to get rid of the irregular, random component of the series but does not concern itself with details of trends, seasons, and cycles.

Most smoothing methods yield forecasts that are, in one sense or another, averages of past values. If the data show a pronounced trend, these forecasts therefore tend to lag behind the trend. In addition, these methods usually ignore seasonal factors. We discuss smoothing methods for no-trend, no-seasonal data.

moving averages   One of the most widely used smoothing methods is **moving averages**: Averaging the M most recent values to forecast the next value.

EXAMPLE 16.6   One of the key elements of the budget of a small-town television station is the monthly advertising-time sales. In the previous 36 months, the monthly sales (measured in minutes per day) of paid, local advertising have been the following:

Month:	1	2	3	4	5	6	7	8	9	10	11	12
Sales:	86	80	85	93	96	102	97	89	96	87	82	81

Month:	13	14	15	16	17	18	19	20	21	22	23	24
Sales:	87	89	97	88	95	87	81	79	82	85	96	93

Month:	25	26	27	28	29	30	31	32	33	34	35	36
Sales:	99	103	96	85	78	83	90	96	85	82	89	96

Construct 3-month and 5-month moving-average forecasts. Plot forecast values against actual values by month.

Solution The first 3-month moving average is $(86 + 80 + 85)/3 = 83.6667$, shown as 83.7 in the output. The first 5-month moving avarage is $(86 + 80 + 85 + 93 + 96)/5 = 88.0$, as shown.

3-month moving average:

—	—	83.7	86.0	91.3	97.0	98.3	96.0	94.0	90.7	88.3	93.3
83.3	85.7	91.0	91.3	93.3	90.0	87.7	82.3	80.7	82.0	87.7	91.3
96.0	98.3	99.3	94.7	86.3	82.0	83.7	89.7	90.3	87.7	85.3	89.0

5-month moving average:

—	—	—	—	88.0	91.2	94.6	95.4	96.0	94.2	90.2	87.0
86.6	85.2	87.2	88.4	91.2	91.2	89.6	86.0	84.8	82.8	84.6	87.0
91.0	95.2	97.4	95.2	92.2	89.0	86.4	86.4	86.4	87.2	88.4	89.6

The 3-month and 5-month moving averages are plotted, with the original time series, in Figure 16.5. ∎

running medians A variation on the idea of moving-average smoothing is the method of moving (or running) medians. The **running-median** smoothing method involves calculating the median instead of the mean of the M most recent values of the time series. Because a median is not affected by extreme values as a mean is, running-median forecasts are unaffected by the occasional fluke value, whether that value is extremely large or extremely small.

EXAMPLE 16.7 Calculate 3-month and 5-month running medians for the data of Example 16.6. How do these forecasts compare with the moving-average forecasts of that example?

Solution The first 3-month running median is median $(86, 80, 85) = 85$. The first 5-month running median is median $(86, 80, 85, 93, 96) = 86$. The series of running medians is shown here.

3-month running median:

—	—	85	85	93	96	97	97	96	89	87	82	82
87	89	89	95	88	87	81	81	81	81	82	85	93
96	99	99	96	85	83	83	90	90	85	85	89

5-month running median:

—	—	—	—	86	93	96	96	96	96	89	87
87	87	87	88	89	89	88	87	82	82	82	85
93	96	96	96	96	85	85	85	85	85	89	89

The 3-month and 5-month running medians are plotted, with the original time series, in Figure 16.6 (page 762). ∎

Monthly Sales

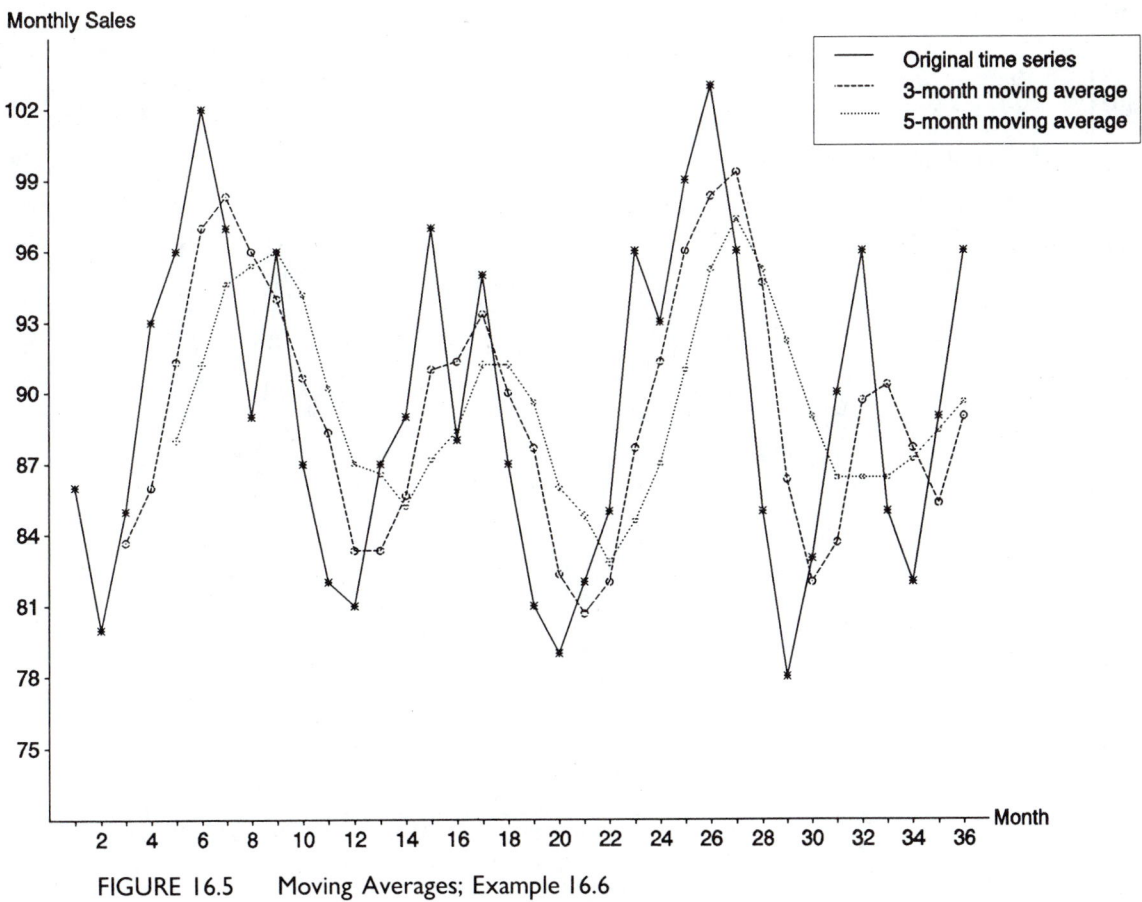

FIGURE 16.5   Moving Averages; Example 16.6

choice of time periods   How many time periods should be used in a moving average or running median? An extremely large value of M (the number of periods) causes the forecast to change very slowly, and such forecasts are not effective in picking up short-term variations. An extremely small value for M causes the forecasts to be very "jittery." In the extreme case of $M = 1$, the forecast for the next period is simply the current value. This forecast incorporates all the random, irregular features of the time series. If the series moves in fairly smooth waves with modest randomness, a small number of periods (such as 3) is desirable. If the series exhibits a great deal of randomness around a vaguely cyclic pattern, greater averaging (such as 5 or 7 periods) is preferred. Comparison of the past forecasting performance of several possible values of M often clarifies the choice.

exponential smoothing   The moving-average and running-median smoothing methods are open to critcism on the grounds that they give the same weight to relatively old values as to the most recent values. The forecasts tend to be somewhat slow in responding to short-run trends or cycles. An alternative method, **exponential smoothing**, gives higher weight to the most recent values and often can be more effective in reacting to shifts or cycles in the series.

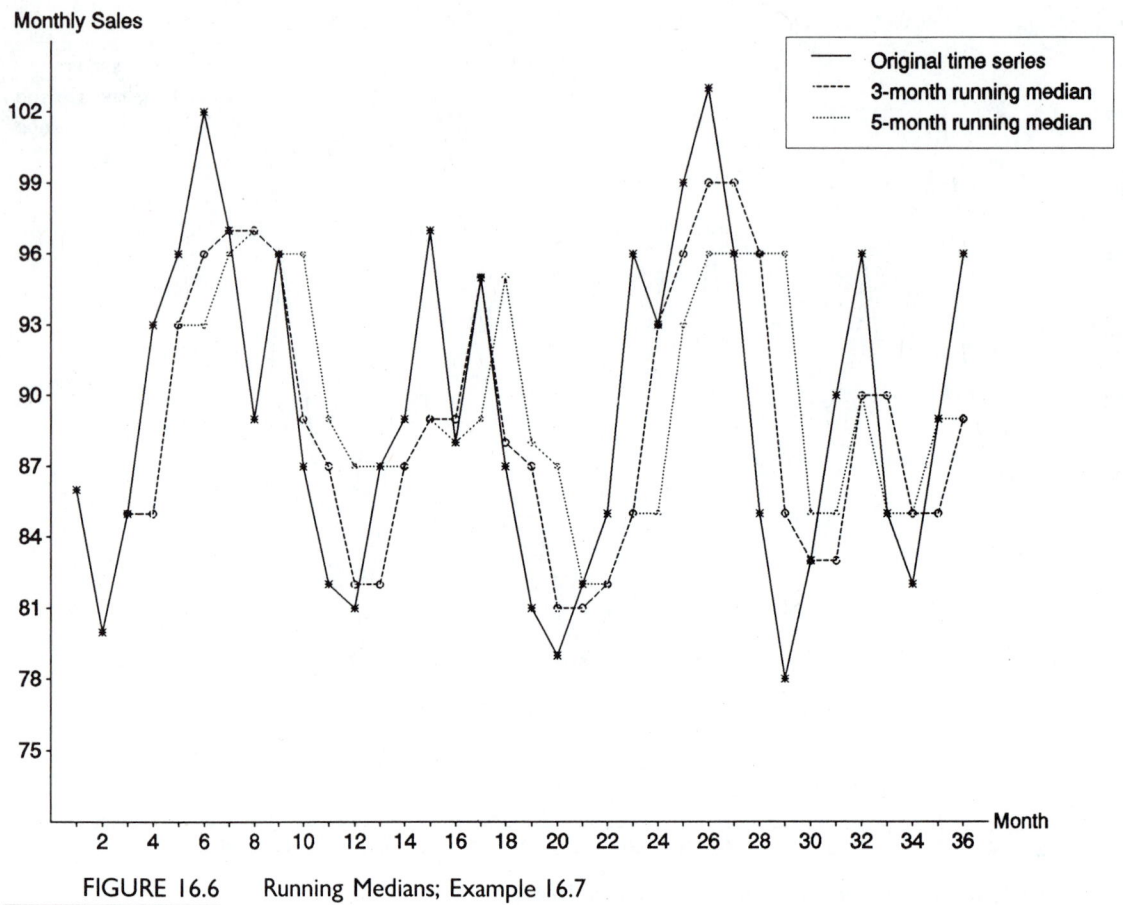

FIGURE 16.6   Running Medians; Example 16.7

The exponential-smoothing forecast $\hat{y}_{t+1}$ of the actual value y_{t+1} is defined as

$$\hat{y}_{t+1} = \alpha y_t + \alpha(1 - \alpha)y_{t-1} + \alpha(1 - \alpha)^2 y_{t-2} + \cdots$$

The number α (no relation to α, the probability of Type I error) lies between 0 and 1 and is called the **smoothing constant**; an appropriate choice of α will be discussed shortly. For example, suppose that α is chosen to be .6. Then

smoothing constant

$$\hat{y}_{t+1} = .6y_t + .24y_{t-1} + .096y_{t-2} + .0384y_{t-3} + \cdots$$

The most recent value of the time series is given the heaviest weight, and the weights given to previous values drop off rapidly. In fact, the weights α, $\alpha(1 - \alpha)$, $\alpha(1 - \alpha)^2$, $\alpha(1 - \alpha)^3, \ldots$ decrease exponentially to zero. Hence the name *exponential smoothing*.

There is an alternative way of finding exponentially smoothed forecasts that is easier computationally and also helps to indicate the effect of various choices of the smoothing constant α:

$$\hat{y}_{t+1} = \alpha y_t + (1 - \alpha)\hat{y}_t$$

The next forecast value is the weighted average of the current actual value and the current forecast value. To use this formula in computation, an initial (time 1) forecast must be chosen; the effect of the initial forecast dies out quite rapidly. One good choice is $\hat{y}_1 = y_1$. Then

$$\hat{y}_2 = \alpha y_1 + (1 - \alpha)\hat{y}_1 = y_1$$
$$\hat{y}_3 = \alpha y_2 + (1 - \alpha)\hat{y}_2 = \alpha y_2 + (1 - \alpha)y_1$$
$$\hat{y}_4 = \alpha y_3 + (1 - \alpha)\hat{y}_3 = \alpha y_3 + \alpha(1 - \alpha)y_2 + (1 - \alpha)^2 y_1$$
$$\hat{y}_5 = \alpha y_4 + (1 - \alpha)\hat{y}_4 = \alpha y_4 + \alpha(1 - \alpha)y_3 + \alpha(1 - \alpha)^2 y_2 + (1 - \alpha)^3 y_1$$

and so on.

With this choice of $\hat{y}_1$, the forecasts rapidly approach the infinite series value

$$\hat{y}_{t+1} = \alpha y_t + \alpha(1 - \alpha)y_{t-1} + \alpha(1 - \alpha)^2 y_{t-2} + \cdots$$

EXAMPLE 16.8 Compute the exponentially smoothed forecast values for the data of Example 16.6, using $\alpha = .4$. Plot the observed time series and the smoothed time series.

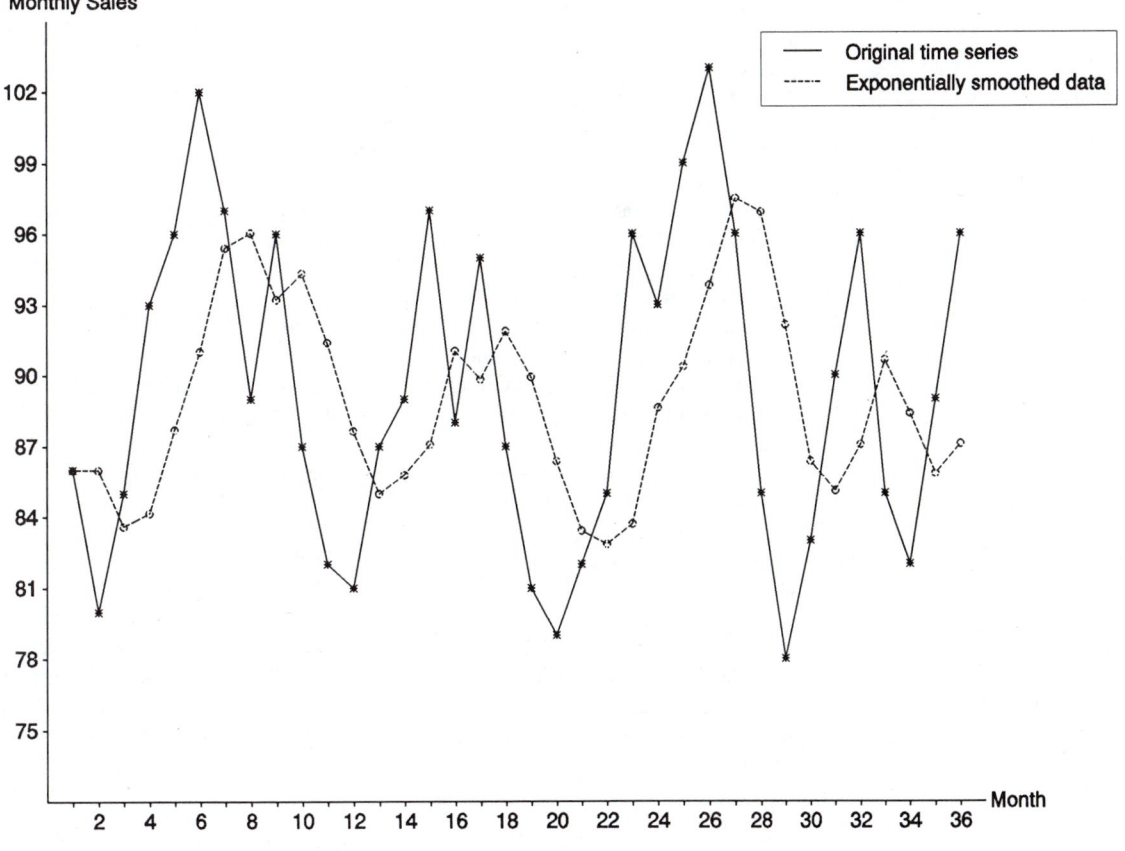

FIGURE 16.7   Exponential Smoothing; Example 16.8

Solution   The exponentially smoothed values, calculated by a computer, are plotted with the original time series in Figure 16.7.   ■

choice of α   The **choice of α** is important in exponential smoothing. A large value of α, such as .7, makes the next forecast value very sensitive to the current value. Therefore the forecast picks up shifts or short-run trends in the series quite quickly, at the cost of being very sensitive to random fluctuations in the series. A small value of α, such as .2, makes the forecast less affected by random fluctuations, but also less effective in picking up shifts or trends. One fairly simple way to select α is to try various α's on historical data; that is, select the α that minimizes average absolute or average squared error in the data.

SECTION 16.3   EXERCISES

16.14 As part of an inventory-management method, the monthly demands for various products are recorded and used for future forecasting. The demands for the previous 24 months of one particular product are

Month:	1	2	3	4	5	6	7	8	9	10	11	12
Demand:	89	97	101	168	120	107	100	96	89	97	143	105

Month:	13	14	15	16	17	18	19	20	21	22	23	24
Demand:	96	84	93	110	125	110	93	95	89	93	105	110

    a. Calculate 3-month and 5-month moving averages.
    b. Plot the original time series, together with the 3-month and 5-month moving averages.
    c. Calculate the average squared error for the 3-month moving average used as a forecast of the next month's demand. Do the same for the 5-month moving average.

16.15 Refer to Exercise 16.14.
    a. Calculate 3-month and 5-month running medians.
    b. Plot the original, 3-month, and 5-month smoothed data.
    c. Calculate the average squared error for the 3-month running median used as a forecast of the next month's demand. Do the same for the 5-month moving average.

16.16 a. Calculate exponentially smoothed forecasts of the demands in Exercise 16.14. Use a smoothing constant of .8.
    b. Compute the average squared error for this forecast.

16.17 Compare the average squared error for the forecasts generated in Exercises 16.14–16.16. On the basis of this criterion, which forecast appears to be preferred?

16.18 A large supermarket tries to forecast volume (total number of transactions) to assist in its short-term staffing decisions. Of particular interest are the weekday evening (Monday–Thursday, 5 P.M.–11 P.M.) volumes, which fluctuate because of competitors' actions, weather, and many unknown factors. The average weekday evening volume is collected for 40 weeks. These volumes and 3- and 5-week moving averages are shown below:

Data:

40.2	43.1	44.2	43.6	45.1	47.3	45.9	46.3	45.7	43.9
44.1	43.8	43.1	41.5	42.1	41.6	40.8	42.4	44.5	46.9

Data:

49.4	50.0	51.6	52.3	51.8	53.1	51.9	48.7	49.2	47.1
45.2	41.1	43.8	46.0	41.7	39.4	41.2	43.1	42.5	44.9

3-week moving average:

—	—	42.5	43.6	44.3	45.3	46.1	46.5	46.0	45.3
44.6	43.9	43.7	42.8	42.2	41.7	41.5	41.6	42.6	44.6
46.9	48.8	50.3	51.3	51.9	52.4	52.3	51.2	49.9	48.3
47.2	44.5	43.4	43.6	43.8	42.4	40.8	41.2	42.3	43.5

5-week moving average:

—	—	—	—	43.2	44.7	45.2	45.6	46.1	45.8
45.2	44.8	44.1	43.3	42.9	42.4	41.8	41.7	42.3	43.2
44.8	46.6	48.5	50.0	51.0	51.8	52.1	51.6	50.9	50.0
48.4	46.3	45.3	44.6	43.6	42.4	42.4	42.3	41.6	42.2

a. Plot the actual data and the moving averages on the same graph.

b. Which moving average appears to track the actual values better?

16.19 The data of Exercise 16.18 leads to the following 3- and 5-week running medians:

3-week running median:

—	—	43.1	43.6	44.2	45.1	45.9	46.3	45.9	45.7
44.1	43.9	43.8	43.1	42.1	41.6	41.6	41.6	42.4	44.5
46.9	49.4	50.0	51.6	51.8	52.3	51.9	51.9	49.2	48.7
47.1	45.2	43.8	43.8	43.8	41.7	41.2	41.2	42.5	43.1

5-week running median:

—	—	—	—	43.6	44.2	45.1	45.9	45.9	45.9
45.7	44.1	43.9	43.8	43.1	42.1	41.6	41.6	41.6	42.1
42.4	44.5	46.9	49.4	50.0	51.6	51.8	51.9	51.9	51.8
44.2	48.7	47.1	45.2	45.2	43.8	41.7	41.7	41.7	42.5

a. Plot the actual data and running medians on the same graph.

b. Which running median seems to give better forecasts?

16.20 The average squared error and average absolute error for the forecasts of Exercises 16.18 and 16.19 are shown below.

	Mean Squared Error	Mean Absolute Error
3-week moving average	.626	.604
5-week moving average	2.183	1.166
3-week running median	.608	.438
5-week running median	2.420	1.154

Does the same forecast method appear to be best on each criterion?

16.21 An evening newspaper records the number of pages of display (unclassified) advertisements over a 70-month period. Monthly averages are computed. The data, plus exponentially smoothed forecasts, are shown below:

Sales:

69.2	67.6	68.0	70.5	73.4	65.2	68.7	72.5	74.1	76.9
70.0	73.2	78.0	75.6	74.9	72.2	70.9	74.3	69.1	63.5
66.7	68.0	64.7	68.9	69.0	69.7	71.3	74.5	70.8	75.6
74.8	73.5	72.8	69.9	71.5	70.4	68.5	67.1	63.5	66.8
67.9	69.0	68.3	71.1	73.2	72.9	74.6	76.1	75.3	77.9
78.3	75.4	72.9	73.6	71.5	69.9	67.3	69.3	67.2	67.4
63.8	64.7	65.8	68.0	67.2	68.7	70.2	72.5	73.6	71.7

Exponential smoothing, $\alpha = .2$:

—	69.20	68.88	68.70	69.06	69.93	68.98	68.93	69.64	70.53
71.81	71.45	71.80	73.04	73.55	73.82	73.50	72.98	73.24	72.41
70.63	69.84	69.48	68.52	68.60	68.68	68.88	69.37	70.39	70.47
71.50	72.16	72.43	72.50	71.98	71.89	71.59	70.97	70.20	68.86
68.45	68.34	68.47	68.44	68.97	69.81	70.43	71.27	72.23	72.85
73.86	74.75	74.88	74.48	74.30	73.74	72.98	71.84	71.33	70.51
69.88	68.67	67.87	67.46	67.57	67.49	67.74	68.23	69.08	69.99

Exponential smoothing, $\alpha = .8$:

—	69.20	67.92	67.98	70.00	72.72	66.70	68.30	71.66	73.61
76.24	71.25	72.81	76.96	75.87	75.09	72.78	71.28	73.70	70.02
64.80	66.32	67.66	65.29	68.18	68.84	69.53	70.95	73.79	71.40
74.76	74.79	73.76	72.99	70.52	71.30	70.58	68.92	67.46	64.29
66.30	67.58	68.72	68.38	70.56	72.67	72.85	74.25	75.73	75.39
77.40	78.12	75.94	73.51	73.58	71.92	70.30	67.90	69.02	67.56
67.43	64.53	64.67	65.57	67.51	67.26	68.41	69.84	71.97	73.27

a. Plot the actual data. Is there a pronounced trend?
b. Plot the exponentially smoothed forecasts for $\alpha = .2$ and $\alpha = .8$.
c. Which forecast method seems to overrespond to random variation?

16.22 The mean squared error and mean absolute error for the most recent two years of data in Exercise 16.21 are calculated for each exponentially smoothed forecast.

	Mean Squared Error	Mean Absolute Error
$\alpha = .2$	11.735	2.852
$\alpha = .8$	7.224	2.221

Which α value seems better?

16.4 THE BOX-JENKINS APPROACH

Both the classical analysis (which takes into account the trend, seasonal, and cyclic components of time-series data) and the smoothing methods of the previous section have the problem that they don't reflect any theoretical structure. Instead, they are rough-and-ready methods for cleaning up time-series data without much regard to the process that generated the data in the first place. In this section we sketch some of the basic ideas of what is known as the Box-Jenkins approach to the analysis of time-series data.

autoregressive model
The simplest Box-Jenkins model is the **autoregressive model**. The idea of an autoregressive model is to use the past values of a time series as independent variables in predicting future values. The simplest autoregressive model is a first-order model, designated AR(1):

$$Y_t = \phi_0 + \phi_1 Y_{t-1} + \epsilon_t$$

The *order* of a Box-Jenkins model refers to the maximum time lag used, not to the maximum power of a variable as in regression analysis. In this model we assume only the most recent y value to be a useful predictor. The ϵ_t term, which reflects only pure random error, is assumed to have mean zero, constant variance, no autocorrelation, and a normal distribution, just as in regression. The ϵ_t pro-

white noise
cess is sometimes called **white noise**.

stationary series
As stated, the autoregressive model does not contain a trend. Box-Jenkins models were designed for **stationary** time series—ones with no trend, constant variability, and stable correlations over time. In particular, the series should be detrended. If the time series shows only a linear trend, taking (first) differences $y_t - y_{t-1}$ often yields an approximately stationary series. For an exponential trend, differences in logarithms of y values will serve.

Autoregressive models often yield data with a distinct cyclic pattern, despite the lack of any cyclic function (such as a sine curve) in the model.

EXAMPLE 16.9   The following 25 values of a time series are available:

129.60	139.79	147.89	152.69	157.22	163.91	173.49	182.40	189.16
195.74	202.14	207.51	212.02	215.44	221.54	229.93	237.05	244.31
250.46	257.50	260.77	265.78	268.97	272.17	278.49		

a. Is there evidence of a trend?
b. Convert the data to approximately stationary form.

Solution
a. A plot (not shown) of the data indicates a roughly linear trend.
   b. The first differences of the series are

10.19	8.10	4.80	4.53	6.69	9.58	8.92	6.76	6.58	6.39	5.37	4.51
3.42	6.10	8.40	7.11	7.26	6.15	7.03	3.27	5.01	3.19	3.20	6.32

■

EXAMPLE 16.10   Plot the difference data of Example 16.9 against time. Does it appear cyclic?

Solution
A plot of the differences is shown in Figure 16.8 (page 768). The dashed line indicates the mean value. There appears to be a definite cyclic pattern.   ■

Earlier in this chapter we noted that trying to determine the period of a particular type of cycle might not be fruitful, and that an alternative strategy is to seek models that tend to produce roughly cyclic behavior. Box-Jenkins models provide one very rich class of possible models.

correlogram
autocorrelation
coefficients
An important part of the Box-Jenkins method is the **correlogram**. This is a plot (against time) of the **autocorrelation coefficients** of a time series y_t. Autocorrelation coefficients are almost, but not quite, the same as ordinary

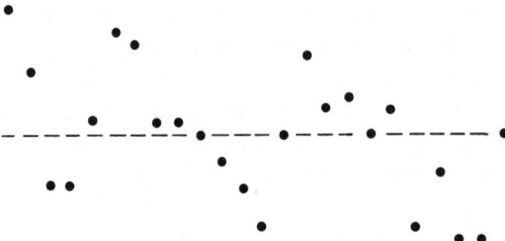

FIGURE 16.8   First Differences; Example 16.10

correlations of the time series with the same series lagged by a number (j) of periods. For example, we might take the series shown below and lag it one period, as indicated:

Time, t:	1	2	3	4	5	6	7	8	9
Series, y_t:	86	81	82	85	90	93	89	86	—
Lagged series, y_{t-1}:	—	86	81	82	85	90	93	89	86

Omitting times 1 and 9 (because one series or the other does not have a value there), we can compute the correlation of y_t and y_{t-j} using the sample-correlation formula of Chapter 13. The autocorrelation coefficient r_j of y_t and a variable y_{t-j} is only slightly different than the sample correlation between y_t and y_{t-j}. The formula is

$$r_j = \frac{\sum\limits_{t=j+1}^{T} (y_t - \bar{y})(y_{t-j} - \bar{y})}{\sum\limits_{t=1}^{T} (y_t - \bar{y})^2}$$

where T is the number of periods of data available and

$$\bar{y} = \frac{\sum\limits_{t=1}^{T} y_t}{T}$$

You should be able to verify that $\bar{y} = 86.5$ for the data shown in this paragraph and that the lag 1 autocorrelation is

$$r_1 = \frac{(81 - 86.5)(86 - 86.5) + \cdots + (86 - 86.5)(89 - 86.5)}{(86 - 86.5)^2 + \cdots + (86 - 86.5)^2} = .5855$$

(The ordinary correlation is .5867.) While shortcut formulas can be used, the calculation of autocorrelations is almost always done by computer.

The correlogram is simply a scatter plot of lags versus autocorrelations r_j.

EXAMPLE 16.11   The autocorrelations [up to a maximum lag of 10 for the (difference)] data of Example 16.9 are

Lag j:	1	2	3	4	5	6	7	8	9	10
r_j:	.455	−.008	−.189	−.121	−.047	−.144	−.077	.137	.333	.206

Construct the correlogram.

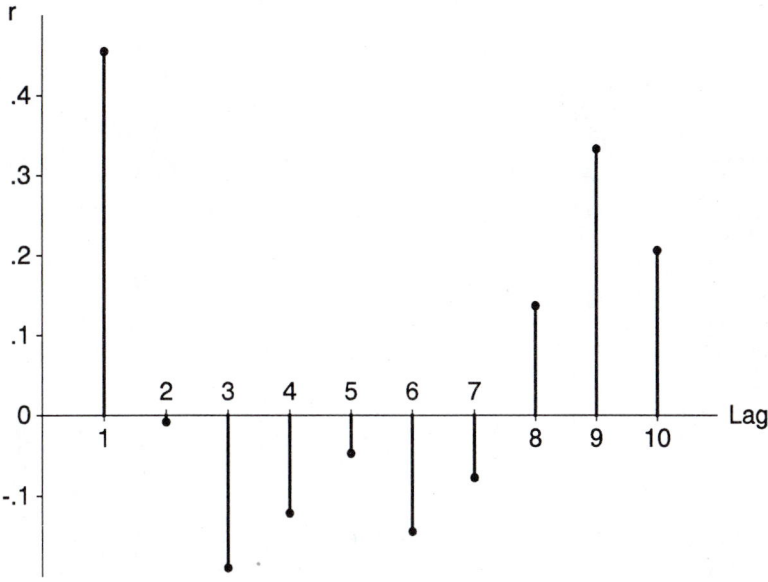

FIGURE 16.9   Sample Autocorrelations; Example 16.11

Solution   The correlogram is shown in Figure 16.9.   ■

The sample correlogram in Figure 16.9 should be compared to a theoretical correlogram. For any particular Box-Jenkins model, theoretical autocorrelation coefficients ρ_j can be derived (derivations are given in Nelson, 1977, and Box and Jenkins, 1970). For the first-order autoregressive model $Y_t = \phi_0 + \phi_1 Y_{t-1} + \epsilon_t$, it can be proved that these theoretical autocorrelation coefficients are given by the geometric series

$$\rho_j = \phi_1^j, \qquad j = 1, 2, \ldots$$

Other Box-Jenkins models yield different theoretical autocorrelations.

EXAMPLE 16.12   Calculate the theoretical autocorrelations, for lags up to 10, for an AR(1) model with $\phi_1 = .80$. Do these autocorrelations resemble those we found in Example 16.11?

Solution   The theoretical autocorrelations are just successive powers of .80:

lag j:	1	2	3	4	5	6	7	8	9	10
ρ_j:	.8000	.6400	.5120	.4096	.3277	.2621	.2097	.1678	.1342	.1074

These values of ρ_j are plotted in Figure 16.10 (page 770). Note how the theoretical autocorrelations for an AR(1) model with $\phi_1 > 0$ gradually decay toward zero. Although we never know the actual value of ϕ_1 (or equivalently the ρ_j's), the sample autocorrelations for an AR(1) model should possess a pattern similar to that for the ρ_j's. The autocorrelations in Example 16.11 do not possess such a pattern, so the AR(1) model is not reasonable.   ■

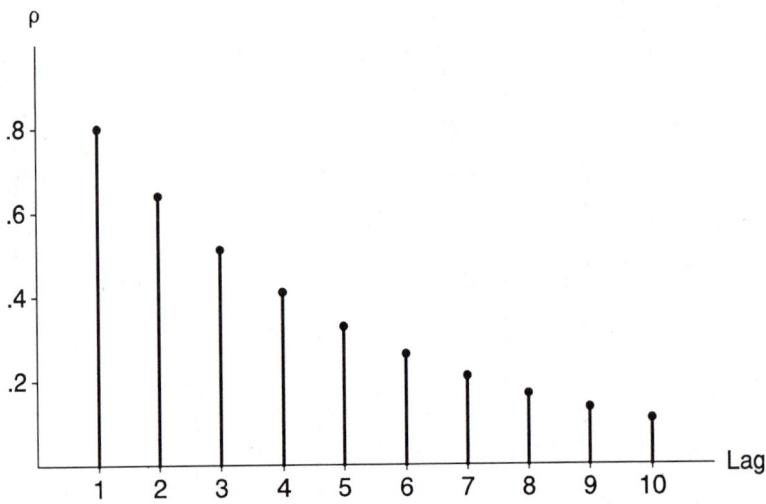

FIGURE 16.10   Correlogram of the Theoretical Autocorrelations for an AR(1) Model with $\phi_1 = .80$; Example 16.12

The theoretical autocorrelations for an AR(1) model with $\phi_1 < 0$ also decay toward zero, but the sign of ρ_j alternates from positive to negative (see Figure 16.11).

higher-order autoregressive models

There are many other Box-Jenkins models. The autoregressive idea can be extended to higher-order (longer lags) models. The pth-order autoregressive model AR(p) is

$$Y_t = \phi_0 + \phi_1 Y_{t-1} + \cdots + \phi_p Y_{t-p} + \epsilon_t$$

where the errors ϵ_t are assumed to satisfy the "white noise" assumptions.

moving-average model

There is also a different type of model, called a **moving-average model**.* The first-order moving-average model MA(1) is

$$Y_t = \theta_0 + \epsilon_t - \theta_1 \epsilon_{t-1}$$

where the ϵ's are assumed to be white noise.[†]

We can see the difference between autoregressive and moving-average models when we consider the effect of past ϵ values on current y values. Think of the ϵ values as random "shocks" input to an economic system, and y values as the output of the system. By appropriate substitutions (for Y_{t-1}, then Y_{t-2}, etc.) in a first-order autoregressive model, the weight given the lag j shock is seen to be ϕ_1^j. Assuming that $|\phi_j| < 1$, it follows that the weights of long-ago shocks decline steadily. In contrast, the first-order moving-average model gives a weight of $-\theta_1$

---

* The phrase *moving average* is used in a different sense in Box-Jenkins models than in smoothing models.

† The minus sign on θ_1 is conventional, allowing for a convenient "backshift" notation in Box and Jenkins (1970).

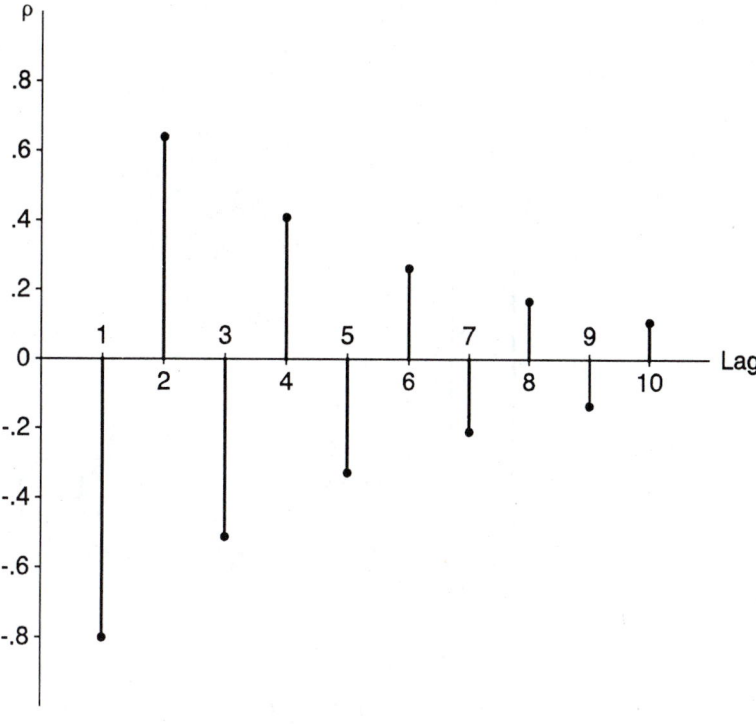

FIGURE 16.11   Correlogram of the Theoretical Autocorrelations for an AR(1) Model with $\phi_1 = -.80$

to ϵ_{t-1} and no weight at all to shocks with longer lags. In a pure moving-average model, the effect of a shock persists for a specified number of time periods, then disappears suddenly. In a pure autoregressive mode, the effect of a shock declines gradually. A moving-average model may be appropriate for a machine shop where ϵ_t represents a sudden burst of new orders and Y_t represents production. If all orders are filled in either the current month or the next month, the effect of two-month-old orders on production is zero. An autoregressive model may be appropriate for a model of sales of a certain kind of front-wheel-drive car. A positive ϵ shock may represent an upsurge in interest in such cars. We may reasonably assume such a shock to signal a longer-term increase in sales, but the effect should gradually decline because of such factors as new competitors and new technology.

The theoretical correlogram of a moving-average model reflects the difference between moving-average and autoregressive models. The general qth-order moving-average model, MA(q), is

$$Y_t = \theta_0 + \epsilon_t - \theta_1\epsilon_{t-1} - \cdots - \theta_{t-q}\epsilon_q$$

We assume the effect of a shock ϵ to persist up to lag q, then suddenly drop to zero. The theoretical autocorrelation reflects the drop-to-zero pattern. For the first-order moving-average model, $y_t = \theta_0 + \epsilon_t - \theta_1\epsilon_{t-1}$, the theoretical

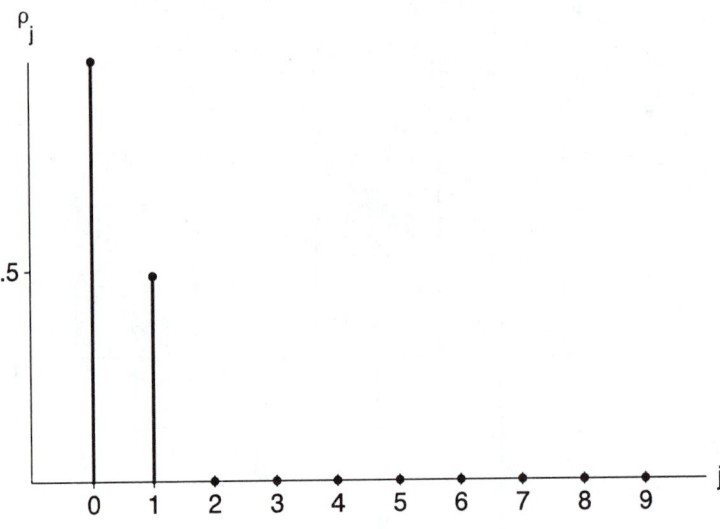

$$\begin{array}{ll}\text{FIGURE 16.12}\end{array}$$ Correlogram for a MA(1) Model with $\theta_1 = -.80$

autocorrelations are

$$\rho_j = \begin{cases} 1 & \text{for } j = 0 \\ \dfrac{-\theta_1}{1 + \theta_1^2}, & \text{for } j = 1 \\ 0, & \text{for } j \geq 2 \end{cases}$$

Thus the correlogram for a MA(1) model has a single spike; all autocorrelations beyond $j = 1$ are zero, as shown in Figure 16.12. Note the difference between the correlograms for AR(1) and MA(1) models. The theoretical correlogram for a pure moving-average process MA(q) tapers off gradually for $j < q$, then suddenly drops to zero for $j > q$. The sample correlogram of a pure moving-average process behaves similarly, but with a degree of random error. For any sample autocorrelations, $1/\sqrt{T}$ provides a rough approximation for the standard error of the sample autocorrelation (assuming the true autocorrelation is zero), where T is the number of observations. A sample correlogram that suddenly drops to within $\pm 1/\sqrt{T}$ of zero is a good candidate for a pure moving-average model.

EXAMPLE 16.13   The following data represent weekly sales of prime-grade steak (in hundreds of pounds) from a butcher shop. The shop does not run special sales. It often receives orders to be filled the next week, but it rarely defers orders for two or more weeks.

1	6994.35	16	6791.99	31	7083.95	46	6875.10
2	6819.14	17	6638.27	32	6905.47	47	6672.32
3	6627.76	18	6582.60	33	6795.83	48	6795.10
4	6903.73	19	6632.22	34	7343.88	49	6789.81
5	6803.14	20	7052.64	35	7038.02	50	6702.24

(*continued*)

6	6824.55	21	7150.16	36	7209.44	51	7009.77
7	6673.45	22	6505.49	37	7077.90	52	6986.91
8	7016.25	23	6771.53	38	7180.69	53	6765.67
9	7102.40	24	6952.84	39	7102.36	54	6916.01
10	6703.55	25	6791.50	40	6895.34	55	7028.07
11	7006.72	26	6549.27	41	6792.30	56	6678.84
12	7212.95	27	6895.45	42	6848.69	57	6898.03
13	7162.09	28	7655.78	43	6797.44	58	6999.30
14	7023.16	29	7201.25	44	6485.33	59	6850.31
15	6553.88	30	7028.80	45	6514.20	60	6675.30

The theoretical autocorrelations (based on an estimated $\theta_1 = .600$) are

ORDER

1,

2 and higher

AUTOCORR

4412

000

a. Plot theoretical (T) and sample (S) correlograms on the same plot.
b. Does the "sudden-zero" property of moving-average models show up in the data?

Solution a. The sample correlations are plotted in Figure 16.13. The first-order theoretical autocorrelation of .4412 is slightly larger than the sample value of .353, while all other theoretical autocorrelations are zero.

b. The second-order sample autocorrelation is very near zero. The higher-order autocorrelations wander around with no obvious pattern. ∎

EXAMPLE 16.14 Refer to the correlogram of Example 16.11 shown in Figure 16.9. Identify an appropriate candidate for a Box-Jenkins model.

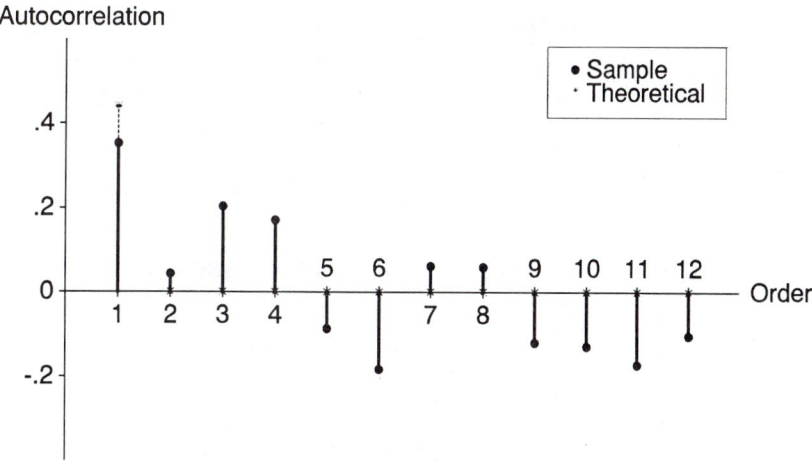

Autocorrelation

FIGURE 16.13   Sample Autocorrelations for Data of Example 16.13

Solution   For $T = 24$, $1/\sqrt{24} = .20$ represents an approximate standard error for any autocorrelation coefficient r_j. Because all autocorrelations are within $2(.20) = .40$ of zero except $r_1 = .455$ and only the long lag (9 and 10) autocorrelations are greater than .20, an MA(1) is a likely candidate for a Box-Jenkins model.   ■

general model

Autoregressive and moving-average models may be combined. The general autoregressive–moving-average model ARMA (p, q) is written

$$Y_t = \phi_0 + \phi_1 Y_{t-1} + \phi_2 Y_{t-2} + \cdots + \phi_p Y_{t-p} + \epsilon_t - \theta_1 \epsilon_{t-1} - \theta_2 \epsilon_{t-2} - \cdots - \theta_q \epsilon_{t-q}$$

If the lags p and q are large, very complex models can result. The usual strategy is to try to find a simple model (with very small p and q lags) that fits the data adequately and approximates the autocorrelations of the series. There are several strategies for identifying such models. One is based on an examination of the estimated correlogram. As we have seen, the theoretical correlogram for a pure autoregressive process tapers gradually to zero as the lag increases, while the theoretical correlogram of a pure moving-average process drops suddenly to zero. A combination autoregressive and moving-average process exhibits a combination of these phenomena in its correlogram: The correlogram tapers off, then drops sharply, then tapers off again. The lag just before the drop-off is a good candidate for the maximum lag q of the moving-average part. The maximum lag for the autoregressive component is harder to identify in the correlogram. Other Box-Jenkins methods, such as partial autocorrelation, are needed for precise identification of reasonable Box-Jenkins models. Box and Jenkins (1970) and Nelson (1977) contain good tips on the difficult task of model identification.

Once the maximum lags for an ARMA model have been specified, the next task is to estimate the ϕ or θ model parameters. The basic idea is to search for the

least-squares fit

least-squares fit. The process of finding the least-squares estimates is complex, especially if there is a moving-average component in the model. Any of the standard Box-Jenkins computer programs estimates the model parameters.

EXAMPLE 16.15   A time series contains the following data for a 40-month period:

134.59	97.60	74.03	55.75	84.24	126.61	141.67	128.72	146.22	157.66
158.57	157.85	154.02	113.37	109.29	160.06	177.27	161.21	123.35	124.43
170.74	175.41	201.49	227.60	233.43	239.80	184.09	133.22	119.65	123.52
139.92	175.82	166.81	163.33	122.41	111.96	151.67	160.21	180.46	188.86

The following autocorrelations are obtained:

Lag:	1	2	3	4	5	6	7	8	9	10
Correlation:	.767	.382	.093	$-.040$	$-.014$	.022	.035	.035	$-.019$	$-.050$

Plot the correlogram. What ARMA models are indicated?

Solution   See Figure 16.14. Only the first two (possibly three) autocorrelations differ from zero by any substantial amount. Given the steep drop to zero, you might try a moving average of two or three terms. Perhaps you can try a first-order (or at

Autocorrelations

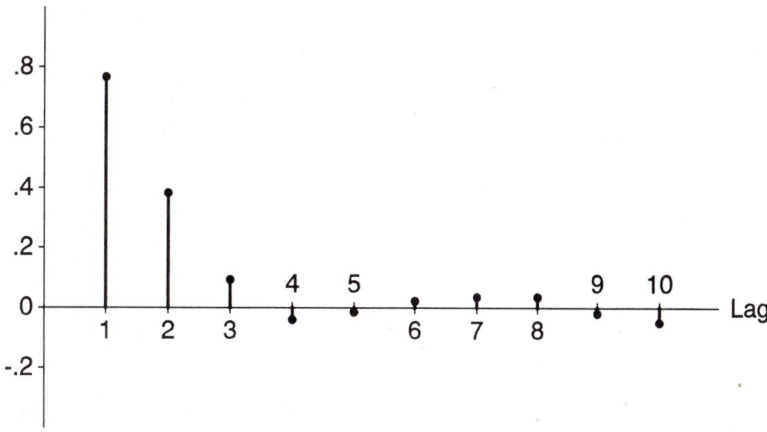

FIGURE 16.14   Correlogram for Example 16.15

most a second-order) autoregressive term, given that there is some suggestion of a decay toward zero in the correlogram.   ∎

EXAMPLE 16.16   ARMA models with $q = 1$ were estimated for $p = 1$ and 2 for the data of Example 16.15. The respective average squared errors were 432.95 and 424.65. Does the more complex model with $p = 2$ do much better?

Solution   The average squared error for the more complicated model is only very slightly (about 2%) smaller, which hardly seems to be very useful.   ∎

Box-Jenkins seasonal models   In our discussion of Box-Jenkins models, we have indicated how trends can be removed by differencing (of logs, if necessary) and how such models can capture apparent cyclic effects. We haven't said anything about seasonal effects; Box-Jenkins models can be extended to capture seasonal effects, too. In fact, one of the most popular deseasonalizing methods used by U.S. government agencies, the X-11 procedure of the census bureau, is closely related to Box-Jenkins methods (see Pierce, 1980). We do not go into detail here, except to note that the basic idea is to include autoregressive and moving-average terms with lag 4 for quarterly data, lag 12 for monthly data, and so on. The Nelson (1977) and Box and Jenkins (1970) texts contain full discussions.

Box-Jenkins forecasting   Once a model has been adopted and the coefficients estimated, a Box-Jenkins model can be used for forecasting. For the first-order autoregressive model, the one-period-ahead forecast is $\hat{y}_{t+1} = \hat{\phi}_0 + \hat{\phi}_1 y_t$; the two-period-ahead forecast is

$$\hat{y}_{t+2} = \hat{\phi}_0 + \hat{\phi}_1 y_{t+1}$$

but y_{t+1} is not yet known and must be replaced by $\hat{y}_{t+1}$ (at the cost of additional random error). This process can be continued for forecasts of any period ahead; the obvious extension works for any higher-order autoregressive model. Moving-average models are trickier to use for forecasting. In the first-order moving-average model,

$$y_{t+1} = \hat{\theta}_0 - \hat{\theta}_1 \epsilon_t$$

but ϵ_t is the unknown true error at time t and must itself be estimated. Estimation of error terms in moving-average (or general ARMA) models is done by a rather elaborate computerized method involving (among other things) backward forecasting. Any good Box-Jenkins program can handle the technical problems. One good approach to checking Box-Jenkins models uses the concept of validation of Chapter 15: Fit the model based on, say, the first 80% of the data, then generate forecasts of the remaining data. While there are more sophisticated model-selection methods available, this approach should detect any gross deviations from a model.

EXAMPLE 16.17   An ARMA model with $p = 1$ and $q = 1$ is fit to the first 32 periods of the data of Example 16.15, as is an ARMA model with $p = 1$ and $q = 2$. Forecasts are generated for periods 33–40, with the following results:

Actual	ARMA(1, 1)	Error	ARMA(1, 2)	Error
166.81	188.55	−21.74	191.71	−24.90
163.33	175.40	−12.07	180.67	−17.34
122.41	166.94	−44.53	165.43	−43.02
111.96	161.51	−49.55	154.83	−42.87
151.67	158.02	−6.35	149.84	1.83
160.21	155.78	4.43	148.59	11.62
180.46	154.33	26.13	149.00	31.46
188.86	153.41	35.45	149.79	39.07
Mean		−8.53		−5.52
Standard deviation		30.41		31.67

Is there compelling evidence in favor of the more complicated ARMA(1, 2) model?

Solution   Neither model seems to grossly over- or underestimate the data in the validation sample. Both commit some rather large errors. While the average error for the ARMA(1, 2) model is slightly better than that for the ARMA(1, 1) model, the standard deviation is higher. We don't feel compelled to use the more complicated model.   ■

The Box-Jenkins approach to time-series data is in many ways attractive. The general ARMA structure is rich and allows for a wide variety of auto-correlation patterns. Many kinds of cyclic and seasonal patterns can be captured by Box-Jenkins models. Yet it is important for a manager to realize that these models aren't magic. A typical Box-Jenkins model used in forecasting a time series is based entirely on the past history of the series itself, and it doesn't allow for any predictive value of other variables. The virtue of such an approach is that it requires only readily available data—only the past history of the series. The weakness of the approach is that it doesn't take advantage of the predictive value of other, related series. The Box-Jenkins approach is a useful technique, and it can be applied within a regression context. But it is not a cure-all.

SECTION 16.4 EXERCISES

16.23 Examination of the sales records of a firm for 60 months yields the following data on monthly sales of a standard product:

90.8	94.8	100.1	104.8	112.2	121.9	124.6	137.5	156.0	165.3	173.7	182.4
178.7	174.0	175.4	173.3	175.7	176.0	179.7	178.2	186.4	195.7	204.9	214.3
222.5	227.3	222.6	219.8	220.5	220.4	228.3	227.2	228.3	235.7	241.2	248.8
257.3	267.4	276.9	288.8	299.6	315.8	322.8	332.2	347.0	357.7	363.2	366.7
371.9	373.7	371.8	371.4	359.7	355.4	348.4	342.6	337.7	329.8	327.7	324.5

a. Plot the data against time. Is there an evident trend?
b. The month-to-month changes in sales are

3.9	5.3	4.7	7.4	9.7	2.7	12.9	18.5	9.3	8.4	8.7	−3.7
−4.7	1.4	−2.1	2.4	.3	3.7	−1.5	8.2	9.2	9.1	9.4	8.2
4.8	−4.7	−2.8	.7	.1	7.9	−1.1	1.1	7.4	5.5	7.6	8.5
10.1	9.5	11.9	10.8	16.2	7.0	9.4	14.8	10.7	5.5	3.5	5.2
1.8	−1.9	−.4	−11.7	−4.3	−7.0	−5.8	−4.9	−7.9	−2.1	−3.2	

Plot change against time. Is there an evident linear trend in the changes? Does there appear to be some cyclic behavior?

16.24 Autocorrelations are calculated for the change data of Exercise 16.23. The results are

Lag:	1	2	3	4	5	6
Correlation:	.693	.581	.490	.285	.154	.049
Lag:	7	8	9	10	11	12
Correlation:	−.042	−.208	−.232	−.250	−.284	−.231

a. Verify the calculation of the lag 1 correlation.
b. Plot the correlations against lag numbers. Is there any lag at which the lag correlations drop off suddenly?

16.25 A first-order autoregressive model is fit to the change data of Exercise 16.23. The estimated autoregressive model is

$$\hat{y}_t = 1.093 + .709\, y_{t-1}$$

The predicted values are

3.8	3.9	4.9	4.4	6.3	7.9	3.1	10.2	14.2	7.7	7.0	7.3
−1.6	−2.2	2.1	−.4	2.8	1.3	3.7	.0	6.9	7.7	7.6	7.8
6.9	4.5	−2.2	−.9	1.6	1.1	6.6	.3	1.9	6.3	5.0	6.5
7.1	8.2	7.9	9.5	8.8	12.6	6.0	7.7	11.6	8.7	5.0	3.6
4.8	2.4	−.3	.8	−7.2	−1.9	−3.9	−3.0	−2.4	−4.5	−.4	

with a mean squared error of 21.67. Plot predicted and actual change values over time. Does it appear that the model yields useful forecasts of changes in sales?

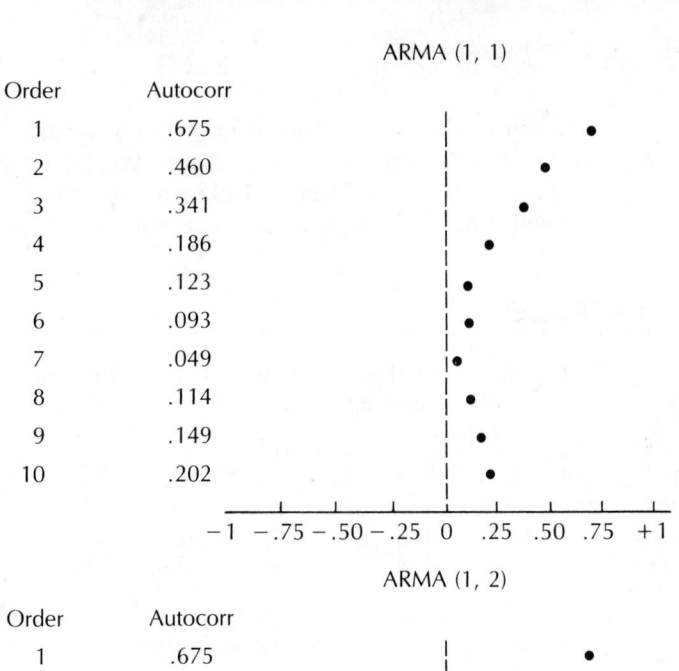

ARMA (1, 1)

Order	Autocorr
1	.675
2	.460
3	.341
4	.186
5	.123
6	.093
7	.049
8	.114
9	.149
10	.202

−1 −.75 −.50 −.25 0 .25 .50 .75 +1

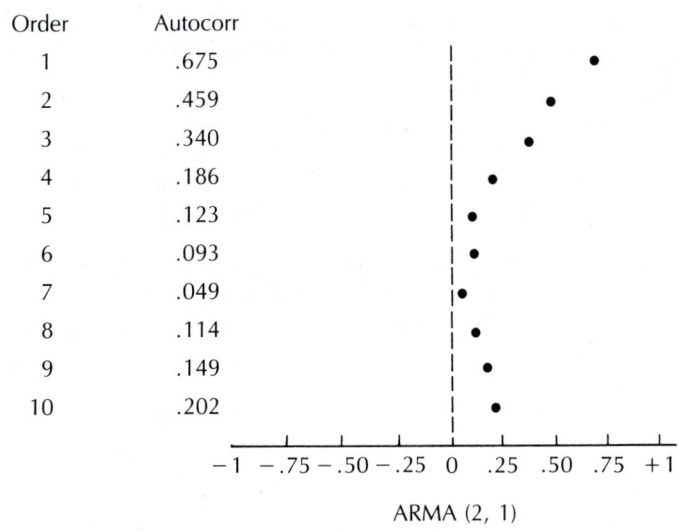

ARMA (1, 2)

Order	Autocorr
1	.675
2	.459
3	.340
4	.186
5	.123
6	.093
7	.049
8	.114
9	.149
10	.202

−1 −.75 −.50 −.25 0 .25 .50 .75 +1

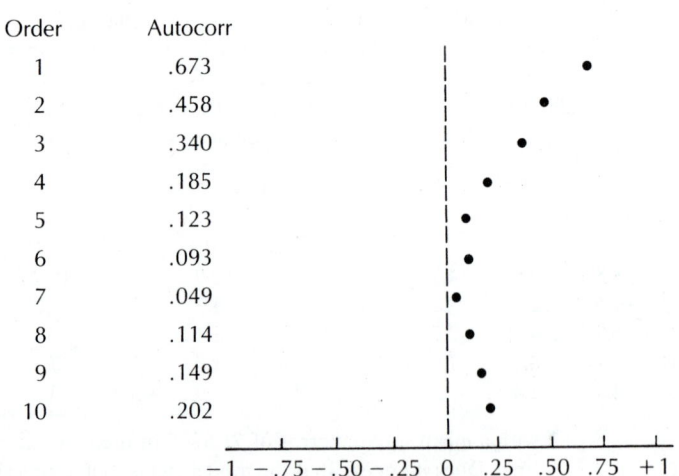

ARMA (2, 1)

Order	Autocorr
1	.673
2	.458
3	.340
4	.185
5	.123
6	.093
7	.049
8	.114
9	.149
10	.202

−1 −.75 −.50 −.25 0 .25 .50 .75 +1

FIGURE 16.15   Box-Jenkins Models; Exercise 16.28

16.26 The estimated lag correlations for the model of Exercise 16.25 are

Lag:	1	2	3	4	5	6
Correlation:	.690	.556	.472	.260	.121	.023
Lag:	7	8	9	10	11	12
Correlation:	−.094	−.229	−.258	−.265	−.289	−.240

How do the estimated lag correlations based on the model compare to the computed lag correlations of Exercise 16.24?

16.27 A manufacturer of novelty items produces (among other items) pennants for sports teams. Weekly production figures include both long-term runs, which are items that sell fairly steadily with slow fluctuation, and short-term runs, which are items that sell in sudden one- or two-week bursts. Data are collected on weekly production for the preceding 156 weeks. There is virtually no trend in the data. Lag correlations are as follows:

Lag:	1	2	3	4	5	6	7	8	9	10
Correlation:	.826	.556	.397	.258	.166	.117	.094	.131	.183	.222

a. Plot these correlations against lag number. Is there any lag at which correlations drop off suddenly?

b. What autoregressive and moving-average terms would you suggest for inclusion in a Box-Jenkins model for these data?

16.28 The data of Exercise 16.27 are fitted to three possible Box-Jenkins models: ARMA(1, 1), ARMA(1, 2), and ARMA(2, 1) (see Figure 16.15). Do the more complicated models—ARMA(1, 2) and ARMA(2, 1)—yield obviously better correlograms than the ARMA(1, 1) model?

16.29 The sum of squared errors for the three models of Exercise 16.28 are as follows:

Model:	ARMA(1, 1)	ARMA(1, 2)	ARMA(2, 1)
SSE:	15,279.47	15,279.64	15,279.41

Is there any evidence to indicate that the more complicated models fit much better?

Summary

This chapter deals with time-series data: Data collected on one or more variables over time. We begin our consideration of such data with a discussion of index numbers; these numbers are the result of attempts to summarize complicated patterns of price or quantity movement.

The special price-level problem of economic time series can be partially remedied by the use of price indices. The construction of price indices involves a choice of quantity weights. Because such choices are not logically inevitable, they are another source of variability and uncertainty in time-series analysis.

The analysis of time-series data requires sophisticated approaches, and a number of methods have been proposed. The classical trend-cycle-season-irregularity approach is useful in isolating trends and correcting for seasonal factors, but it is less successful in dealing with cyclic behaviors. Various smoothing techniques, including moving-average, running-median, and exponential-smoothing methods, are useful in generating forecasts once the time series has been purged of trend and seasonal factors.

The Box-Jenkins approach is an alternative forecasting scheme that involves explicit models for the evolution of a time series. This style of time-series analysis raises an interesting question about cycles. Though no explicit cycle feature appears in any Box-Jenkins model, data that apparently follow a cyclic pattern can fit such models very well.

KEY FORMULAS: Time-Series Analysis

1. Simple aggregate price index in year k, with base year 0

$$I_k = \frac{\sum p_{ki}}{\sum p_{0i}} \times 100$$

2. Weighted aggregate price index

$$I_k = \frac{\sum p_{ki} q_i}{\sum p_{0i} q_i} \times 100$$

3. Multiplicative model involving trend, cyclic, seasonal, and irregular components

$$y_t = T_t C_t S_t I_t$$

4. Additive model

$$y_t = T_t + C_t + S_t + I_t$$

5. Exponential smoothing

$$\hat{y}_{t+1} = \alpha y_t + \alpha(1 - \alpha)y_{t-1} + \alpha(1 - \alpha)^2 y_{t-2} + \cdots$$
$$= \alpha y_t + (1 - \alpha)\hat{y}_t$$

6. First-order autoregressive model, AR(1)

$$Y_t = \phi_0 + \phi_1 Y_{t-1} + \epsilon_t$$

7. jth-order sample autocorrelation coefficient

$$r_j = \frac{\sum\limits_{t=j+1}^{T} (y_t - \bar{y})(y_{t-j} - \bar{y})}{\sum\limits_{t=1}^{T} (y_t - \bar{y})^2}$$

8. Theoretical autocorrelation coefficients for an AR(1) model

$$\rho_j = \phi_1^j, \qquad j = 0, 1, 2, \ldots$$

9. pth-order autoregressive model, AR(p)

$$Y_t = \phi_0 + \phi_1 Y_{t-1} + \cdots + \phi_p Y_{t-p} + \epsilon_t$$

10. First-order moving-average model, MA(1)

$$Y_t = \theta_0 + \epsilon_t - \theta_1 \epsilon_{t-1}$$

11. Theoretical autocorrelation coefficients for a MA(1)

$$\rho_j = \begin{cases} 1, & \text{for } j = 0 \\ \dfrac{-\theta_1}{1 + \theta_1^2}, & \text{for } j = 1 \\ 0, & \text{for } j \geq 2 \end{cases}$$

12. qth-order moving-average model, MA(q)

$$Y_t = \theta_0 + \epsilon_t - \theta_1 \epsilon_{t-1} - \cdots - \theta_q \epsilon_{t-q}$$

13. Mixed autoregressive, moving-average model, ARMA(p, q)

$$Y_t = \phi_0 + \phi_1 Y_{t-1} + \cdots + \phi_p Y_{t-p} + \epsilon_t - \theta_1 \epsilon_{t-1} - \cdots - \theta_q \epsilon_{t-q}$$

14. Forecasting using Box-Jenkins models

AR(1): $\hat{y}_{t+1} = \hat{\phi}_0 + \hat{\phi}_1 y_t, \hat{y}_{t+2} = \hat{\phi}_0 + \hat{\phi}_1 \hat{y}_{t+1}, \ldots$

MA(1): $\hat{\theta}_0 - \hat{\theta}_1 \hat{\epsilon}_t$, where $\hat{\epsilon}_t$ is estimated using backward forecasting

CHAPTER 16 EXERCISES

16.30 A manufacturer of snack foods compiles dollar-sales volume monthly for four years. Because prices have changed substantially, the firm uses a price index to deflate the dollar figures. The results are shown below (sales in thousands of dollars per month):

Year 1	J	F	M	A	M	J	J	A	S	O	N	D
Sales	421.9	447.0	439.3	479.3	478.5	481.2	506.8	477.5	480.5	502.5	527.9	521.8
Deflated sales	413.7	440.4	429.1	465.4	454.9	466.3	486.9	457.9	455.1	477.3	498.1	487.7
Index	102.0	101.5	102.4	103.0	105.2	103.2	104.1	104.3	105.6	105.3	106.0	107.0

Year 2												
Sales	526.3	527.7	543.3	519.5	579.3	570.1	570.7	603.1	609.8	600.7	637.1	655.8
Deflated sales	492.4	491.8	503.6	481.1	525.7	520.2	515.6	538.5	545.0	530.7	555.5	568.3
Index	106.9	107.3	107.9	108.0	110.2	109.6	110.7	112.0	111.9	113.2	114.7	115.4

Year 3												
Sales	632.6	631.5	661.8	670.5	677.2	701.4	711.1	700.3	712.2	750.9	729.7	764.2
Deflated sales	548.7	544.4	560.9	563.5	565.8	583.6	592.1	582.2	586.7	609.5	588.0	608.0
Index	115.3	116.0	118.0	119.0	119.7	120.2	120.1	120.3	121.4	123.2	124.1	125.7

Year 4											
Sales	738.8	784.8	780.8	795.9	832.9	828.4	845.0	874.8	885.6	884.5	884.5	895.4
Deflated sales	586.4	620.4	615.3	612.3	634.9	630.5	637.8	658.3	662.9	660.6	653.3	652.2
Index	126.0	126.5	126.9	130.0	131.2	131.4	132.5	132.9	133.6	133.9	135.4	137.3

a. Plot the dollar-volume sales figures over time (months 1–48). What sort of trend equation seems appropriate?

b. Plot the deflated sales figures over time. What sort of trend equation seems appropriate for these deflated values?

c. Can you explain the discrepancy in the trends of parts (a) and (b)?

16.31 a. Calculate a linear trend equation for the deflated sales values of Exercise 16.30. The following summary figures have been obtained:

$$\sum y_t = 26{,}359.5, \qquad \sum ty_t = 690{,}868.6, \qquad \sum t = 1176$$
$$\sum t^2 = 38{,}024, \qquad n = 48$$

b. Plot the trend line on the same plot as the deflated sales values. Does there appear to be any seasonal or cyclic fluctuation around the trend?

16.32 The deflated sales figures of Exercise 16.30 are divided by the trend values obtained in Exercise 16.31 to obtain the following detrended values:

Year 1:	.95	1.00	.97	1.04	1.00	1.02	1.05	.98	.96	1.00	1.03	1.00
Year 2:	1.00	.99	1.00	.95	1.03	1.01	.99	1.02	1.02	.99	1.03	1.04
Year 3:	.99	.98	1.00	1.00	.99	1.01	1.02	.99	.99	1.02	.98	1.00
Year 4:	.96	1.01	.99	.98	1.01	.99	1.00	1.02	1.02	1.01	.99	.98

a. Calculate a seasonal index by averaging the values for each month separately.

b. Calculate detrended, deseasonalized values for the last six months of year 4.

16.33 An intercity transportation company maintains quarterly records on the number of riders on its "milk run" (short distance, many stops) bus routes. The data (in thousands of riders per quarter) are

	Quarter			
Year	1	2	3	4
1	3.83	4.61	5.68	3.90
2	4.17	4.92	6.29	4.18
3	4.63	5.45	6.79	4.55
4	4.95	5.92	7.32	4.98
5	5.41	6.55	7.94	5.41
6	6.16	6.98	8.71	6.06
7	6.45	7.63	9.55	6.43
8	6.75	8.38	10.67	7.04

a. Plot the data (ridership vs. quarters 1–32).

b. What sort of trend equation seems appropriate?

16.34 Fit an exponential trend curve to the data of Exercise 16.33. The following summary figures have been calculated:

$$\sum \log y_t = 57.313, \qquad \sum t = 528, \qquad n = 32$$
$$\sum t \log y_t = 1004.30, \qquad \sum t^2 = 11,440$$

16.35 The following detrended values are calculated by dividing the data of Exercise 16.33 by trend values (from the equation obtained in Exercise 16.34).

	Quarter			
Year	1	2	3	4
1	.891	1.050	1.266	.851
2	.891	1.028	1.287	.837
3	.907	1.045	1.275	.836
4	.890	1.042	1.261	.840
5	.893	1.058	1.255	.837
6	.933	1.034	1.263	.860
7	.896	1.038	1.271	.838
8	.861	1.044	1.303	.840

    a. Does there appear to be a strong seasonal component in the data?

    b. Calculate seasonal indices for each quarter by simple averaging.

16.36 a. Calculate exponentially smoothed forecasts of the detrended values of Exercise 16.35. Use $\alpha = .5$.

    b. Do these forecasts work well for quarter 3 in various years? Can you think of an explanation?

16.37 a. Calculate 5-quarter moving averages for the data of Exercise 16.35.

    b. Calculate 5-quarter running medians for these data.

    c. Would these figures, used as forecasts, do well for quarter 3?

    d. What further step would you suggest for improving moving-average or running-median forecasting for this situation?

16.38 A food-service company provides vending machines for a growing number of companies in a metropolitan area. Data have been collected for the past seven years on the quarterly prices of the major lines of business—sandwiches, hot meals, beverages, and desserts. In addition, total dollar-sales data are available. The data on prices are as follows:

	Quarter			
Year 1	1	2	3	4
Sandwiches	.62	.62	.65	.66
Hot meals	.80	.83	.86	.88
Beverages	.20	.20	.20	.20
Desserts	.35	.35	.36	.38
Year 2				
Sandwiches	.65	.68	.69	.71
Hot meals	.88	.91	.93	.99

(*continued*)

Year 2	Quarter			
	1	2	3	4
Beverages	.20	.20	.21	.23
Desserts	.38	.38	.39	.41
Year 3				
Sandwiches	.73	.75	.78	.80
Hot meals	1.01	1.04	1.07	1.11
Beverages	.23	.25	.25	.26
Desserts	.41	.42	.45	.45
Year 4				
Sandwiches	.82	.85	.85	.87
Hot meals	1.14	1.19	1.20	1.22
Beverages	.30	.30	.30	.32
Desserts	.45	.47	.48	.50
Year 5				
Sandwiches	.90	.94	.97	1.00
Hot meals	1.26	1.32	1.35	1.40
Beverages	.32	.35	.35	.37
Desserts	.50	.51	.53	.56
Year 6				
Sandwiches	1.02	1.05	1.08	1.10
Hot meals	1.43	1.47	1.53	1.55
Beverages	.37	.38	.39	.39
Desserts	.57	.58	.61	.63
Year 7				
Sandwiches	1.12	1.15	1.20	1.23
Hot meals	1.56	1.61	1.70	1.74
Beverages	.40	.40	.41	.41
Desserts	.65	.66	.69	.71

The data on total sales (in thousands of dollars per quarter) are

Year	Quarter			
	1	2	3	4
1	138.93	143.60	150.47	155.77
2	158.00	164.89	171.77	184.48
3	189.45	198.38	209.69	220.37
4	231.40	244.36	249.67	260.99
5	271.25	289.20	300.49	316.63
6	327.25	340.49	357.53	367.32
7	376.85	389.49	411.34	422.54

a. Assume that the relative quantity weights are sandwiches, .30; hot meals, .28; beverages, .26; and desserts, .16. Calculate price indices for the fourth quarter in years 1 to 7.

b. Recalculate the price indices using the relative quantity weights sandwiches, .25; hot meals, .35; beverages, .28; and desserts, .12.

c. How much difference does it make which set of weights is used? Why?

16.39 The total-sales data of Exercise 16.38 are deflated by a price index based on the quantity weights shown in part (a). The deflated values are

Year	Quarter			
	1	2	3	4
1	138.93	141.48	143.17	144.76
2	147.52	149.63	152.41	155.42
3	156.82	158.96	162.05	165.69
4	168.29	171.36	173.98	176.94
5	179.40	182.70	185.03	187.46
6	190.38	192.91	195.27	197.38
7	199.29	201.08	202.73	203.63

a. Plot the values. What form of trend equation seems appropriate?

b. Calculate a linear trend equation.

16.40 Differences of successive quarterly values for the data of Exercise 16.39 are calculated. The following lag correlations are computed for these differences:

Lag:	0	1	2	3	4	5	6
Correlation:	1.000	.318	.152	.170	.127	.050	.148

Lag:	7	8	9	10	11	12
Correlation:	−.058	−.198	−.160	−.140	−.123	−.307

a. Plot the correlations against lag number.

b. Is there any visually obvious place where the lag correlations fall off sharply?

c. What Box-Jenkins model would you fit to the difference data?

16.41 Autoregressive models of order $p = 1$ and $p = 2$ are fit to the data of Exercise 16.40. The following results are obtained:

	AR(1) Model	
Parameter	Estimate	Standard Error
Autoregressive lag 1	.409	.211
Constant	1.401	—
Residual standard deviation	.602	(25 d.f.)
Sum of squared residuals	9.076	

(continued)

	AR(2) Model	
Parameter	Estimate	Standard Error
Autoregressive lag 1	.378	.222
Autoregressive lag 2	.108	.228
Constant	1.205	—
Residual standard deviation	.612	(24 d.f.)
Sum of squared residuals	9.000	

    a. Write the respective models.

    b. Does the more complicated AR(2) model have a dramatically smaller average squared error?

    c. Which of the two models would you use?

16.42 A motel along a major highway just outside a small city caters to vacation travellers and business customers. It's been established for many years, as have its major competitors. The motel has data on the average number of daily room rentals each week, out of a capacity of 241 rooms. The occupancy data for three years (156 weeks) is in the 'CH16C1.DAT' file on the data disk, with occupancy in column 1 and week number in column 2.

    a. Would you expect to see a strong trend in this situation? Plot occupancy against week number; by eye, is there an evident trend?

    b. Use a regression program to calculate a trend equation. Assume a linear, rather than an exponential trend. Does the magnitude of the slope indicate that there is a substantial trend?

    c. Have the computer program calculate predicted values based on the trend equation and subtract these from actual values to obtain residuals. (Many computer packages calculate "studentized" residuals when asked directly for residuals; the two-step procedure of calculating predicted values, then differences, ensures that we get "unstudentized" residuals, as desired.)

    d. The last week of each year (weeks 52, 104, and 156) attracts holiday travelers, but few business travelers. Find the average value of these three residuals. What does this average indicate about the seasonal pattern for the end of the year?

16.43 a. Use a computer package to calculate autocorrelation coefficients for lags of 1, 2, 3, up to about 10 weeks based on the residuals from Exercise 16.42. Obtain a plot of the correlations against lag number.

    b. In your judgment, is there a lag number at which the autocorrelations drop off suddenly to near 0? What does your answer indicate about the kind of ARMA model that should be fit?

16.44 a. Use a Box-Jenkins (ARMA) computer program to fit a first-order autoregressive model to the residuals from Exercise 16.42. Locate the average squared error of the model.

    b. Do the same for a first-order moving average model.

    c. Which of the two models appears to fit the data better? Is there a clear choice between the two?

16.45 Local television channels rely heavily on their early-evening news broadcasts for advertising revenue. The ratings for these broadcasts are critical in determining the advertising rates they can charge. The 'CH16C2.DAT' file contains ratings (in column 1) of one such broadcast, as well as week number (in column 2), from week 1 to week 104.

a. Plot ratings against week number. Is there evidence of a trend?

b. Use a regression program to fit a linear trend of ratings against week number. What does the sign of the trend equation indicate about how well the broadcast is doing?

c. What does the magnitude of the slope indicate about the extent of the trend? Note that multiplying the slope by 52 gives the predicted change in ratings over a one-year period.

16.46 Obtain predicted values for the trend equation in Exercise 16.45. Subtract these from the actual values to obtain residuals. You might expect the "dog days" of summer (roughly weeks 30 through 34 and 82 through 87) to give lower ratings if many people are on vacation. Alternatively, people might have more time and actually watch the news more. Average the residuals for these weeks. What does the average value indicate about a seasonal effect of these weeks?

16.47 a. Calculate autocorrelation coefficients for lags 1, 2, 3, up to 10 or so weeks. Obtain a plot of autocorrelations against lag numbers.

b. In your opinion, is there a lag at which the autocorrelations drop suddenly to 0?

c. Fit autoregressive models of orders 1, 2, and 3. Do the more complex AR models fit the data conspicuously better than the first-order AR model?

16.48 Electrical utilities must gear their capacity planning to peak demand periods. Data on peak demands each week for 260 weeks for one such utility are stored in column 1 of the 'CH16C3.DAT' file on the data disk; week number is in column 2.

a. Plot the demands against week number. Is there evidence of a trend?

b. Fit a linear trend to the demand data, using a regression program. Obtain predicted values and residual (actual − predicted) values. If there is a general pattern that the residuals at both ends of the data have one sign, and the residuals in the middle have the opposite sign, there is reason to think that a curved trend equation would work better. In your opinion, is this pattern in fact the case?

c. Have a computer program calculate the logarithms of the peak demands. Fit a linear trend corresponding to an exponential trend in the original data to the logarithms. Obtain residuals from this trend equation. Is there a pattern of "same signs at the ends, opposite sign in the middle" evident in these residuals?

16.49 a. Would you expect to see seasonal patterns in peak demand for electricity? From what you know generally, at what times would you expect to see the highest demands?

b. The week numbers in the data begin with week 1 at the beginning of January. Define the week numbers that you would expect to have the highest demands. Find the average of the residuals (from the logarithmic model of Exercise 16.48, part (c)). Does this average confirm your opinion about the demands in these weeks?

16.50 Use the residuals from the logarithmic model of Exercise 16.48, part (c). If a program is available to you that fits Box-Jenkins models with a seasonal component, obtain models with a first-order autoregressive term only, and with a first-order moving average term only (plus seasonal components). Which model seems to fit better?

C A S E　　Time Series

A production manager for a packaged cereal manufacturer has asked you for help in scheduling production of one of its established cereals. The product is a mature one with reasonably consistent sales from year to year. As a mature product, it is usually promoted through local stores' coupons and point-of-sale displays; the national advertising budget is negligible.

Production is scheduled based on periods of five working days each. Holidays aren't counted in the periods. The product isn't produced on weekends because the overtime cost would be excessive. Actual production of the cereal is done, whenever possible, in a single run per five-day period. Multiple runs are undesirable, because the production line is used for several products and must be thoroughly cleaned each time a product change occurs. The manager tries to keep a low level of inventory, both to save inventory cost and to make sure that fresh product is shipped. The manager's basic problem is to determine the amount to produce per period in order to match outgoing shipments.

The manager has written the following to you:

> We'd like to use our shipment data as the basis for forecasting outgoing shipments for the next period; the next two periods would be even better. We've tried to use information about promos and coupons to guess the demand, but there's so many deals and you never can tell how well they'll work, so that hasn't worked at all.
>
> It seems like there's surges and slow spells in our shipments. We ought to be able to use the pattern to get decent forecasts. I'm sending you two year's worth of shipment data, which is basically all we have since they gave us some new shipping territory. It's all measured in equivalent cases shipped; an equivalent case is like twelve 16-ounce boxes with 192 ounces of cereal in one box or another. I don't have any problem with the different box sizes; I can change sizes on the packing line in three minutes flat. Can you give me some way to predict the overall demand for the next period or two?

The data are shown below for 100 periods. See what forecasting you can do using the data; you'll probably want to use a computer program. Any of the standard smoothing or modelling methods could be used. The production manager has computer facilities available. Write a report to the manager with your recommendations. Remember that the production manager is a production manager, not a statistician; explain any technical ideas clearly in English.

12412	10695	10784	12702	12025	12469	13365	13416	13978	12264
13178	10078	9312	9980	11072	11149	9634	11156	9561	9045
12018	11334	10298	10384	11426	10138	9613	11430	10587	12001
10938	10964	8943	10858	11879	10647	11491	10585	12146	13114
11145	13016	12839	12726	14868	13192	12752	14178	14484	14657
12641	14914	14410	13737	15278	14062	11844	10167	8904	10023
9924	11389	12680	12139	11392	11715	12223	10110	9249	13526
15046	12976	10988	11032	11163	10869	9224	9094	10927	10363
11098	10893	14124	15378	15142	16080	12376	13017	11398	12839
14637	12689	12364	11969	12689	15353	12292	11075	8948	9919

17

DECISIONS, UNCERTAINTY, AND INFORMATION

Now we can integrate statistical ideas and economic concepts. Statistics provide an important framework for economic decisions. The economic decisions a manager makes are made in the face of uncertainty. Statistical thinking and language is geared to uncertainty. In this chapter, we introduce the basic notions of statistical decision theory.

The key definitions are in Section 17.1; here we consider actions to take, uncertain outcomes that will occur, the economic payoffs that result from combinations of actions and outcomes, and specified probabilities for the outcomes. Then in Section 17.2 we discuss expected value as a basic decision criterion. We first present the important idea of sensitivity analysis in this section, and we will continue to use it in the rest of the chapter. Uncertainty introduces risk in decision making. The amount of risk may be measured in terms of variance; this is a particularly useful idea in the context of a portfolio of many investments. Alternatively, we can use statistical utility functions to deal with uncertainty. The subject of Section 17.3 is the treatment of risk.

We can reduce uncertainty with information, but information is costly in money and time. In Section 17.4, we consider how we can evaluate information in a decision framework. Bayes' Theorem is a key idea in this section and was first considered in Chapter 3; it might be useful to review that theorem. A very useful visual device for understanding how probability, information, and payoffs all fit into decision theory is a decision tree, which we explain in Section 17.5. We explore some important special results for information about means and proportions in Section 17.6. Finally, in Section 17.7, we contrast the ways in which decision theory and hypothesis testing treat information.

The management decisions presented in this chapter are scaled down in size and complexity from those most managers face. These simplified situations allow us to consider the essential ideas without the distraction of lots of detail. Once we understand the basic ideas, we can apply them in complex situations.

17.1   THE ELEMENTS OF DECISION THEORY   ∎

Managers must routinely make decisions. Almost always, these decisions have to be made without as much information as a manager would like to have. The decision may involve a recurring, day-to-day problem like deciding how many loaves of bread to stock tomorrow in a supermarket. Or it may involve a major strategic issue that will have long-term effects on a company, such as choosing a particular architecture for the next microcomputer. The uncertainty involved may be as simple as the demand for bread tomorrow, or as complex as what industry-wide standards will be adopted for the operating system of microcomputers. In this section, we'll present some formal structures that can help managers think systematically about making decisions in the face of uncertainty.

We will consider four fundamental issues involved in any decision under uncertainty:

1. What possible **actions** may be chosen?
2. What are the possible, uncertain **outcomes** to be considered?
3. What is the consequence, the **payoff**, for each combination of action and outcome?
4. What **probabilities** should be assigned to each outcome?

When managers use statistical decision theory they are forced to consider these fundamental questions explicitly and systematically.

The first essential ingredient of decision theory is the decision to be made. To use decision theory, it is necessary to specify the possible actions (decisions) that may be taken. The set of possible actions is called the **action space** A; individual actions are labeled a_1, a_2, and so on.

action space

$$A = \{a_1, a_2, \ldots, a_n\}$$

We assume that the actions are defined in such a way that exactly one action will be chosen.

EXAMPLE 17.1   A grocery manager must decide how much bread to stock each day. Available space accommodates up to 84 loaves. Define an action space.

Solution   Because the manager must select the number of loaves to stock, the possible actions are the integers between 0 and 84, inclusive.

$$A = \{0, 1, 2, \ldots, 83, 84\}$$ ∎

EXAMPLE 17.2   A product manager has two new frozen dinner products that might be marketed. For each product, the manager can take one of the following actions: Introduce it, scrap it, or send it back to the laboratory kitchens for further development. Define an action space that encompasses the two new products.

Solution   The requirement that one and only one action is taken makes it convenient to combine the various possible decisions for each frozen dinner product into overall actions. Because there are three possible decisions for each product, there are nine possible actions. These are listed in the action space.

$$A = \{(\text{introduce } 1, \text{introduce } 2), (\text{introduce } 1, \text{scrap } 2),$$
$$(\text{introduce } 1, \text{redevelop } 2), (\text{scrap } 1, \text{introduce } 2), (\text{scrap } 1, \text{scrap } 2),$$
$$(\text{scrap } 1, \text{redevelop } 2), (\text{redevelop } 1, \text{introduce } 2),$$
$$(\text{redevelop } 1, \text{scrap } 2), (\text{redevelop } 1, \text{redevelop } 2)\} \qquad \blacksquare$$

Decision theory has to do with decisions made under uncertainty. To use it, there must be uncertainty about something. The something may be relatively concrete, such as tomorrow's demand for bread, or relatively amorphous, such as next year's consumer confidence level. The idea is that the eventual degree of success of any selected action depends on which one of several future outcomes* actually occurs.

outcomes

  The second essential element of decision theory is the list of possible outcomes. This set is essentially the sample space we introduced in Chapter 3. It is customary to denote the possible **outcomes** as $\theta_1, \theta_2, \dots$. The set of possible outcomes is $\Theta = \{\theta_1, \theta_2, \dots\}$.

EXAMPLE 17.3

In Example 17.1, the store's profit from stocking a certain number of loaves of bread depends on the actual demand of customers for bread. Define an appropriate sample space.

Solution

One good way to define the set of possible outcomes is to specify the possible numbers of loaves demanded.

$$\Theta = \{0, 1, 2, \dots, 83, 84 \text{ or more}\} \qquad \blacksquare$$

EXAMPLE 17.4

In Example 17.2, the success of the possible actions depends on consumer preference for the new products compared to current competitors. It also depends on consumer preferences for potential redeveloped products (but for simplicity we ignore that). Assume that preference can adequately be specified as very high, high, medium, low, or very low for each of the two products. Define an appropriate set of possible outcomes.

Solution

Again, we want to define the set so that exactly one outcome occurs. One possibility is that both products receive very high preference; call this outcome $(\text{VH}_1, \text{VH}_2)$. Using this code, we can write the possible outcomes as

$$\Theta = \{(\text{VH}_1, \text{VH}_2), (\text{VH}_1, \text{H}_2), (\text{VH}_1, \text{M}_2), (\text{VH}_1, \text{L}_2), (\text{VH}_1, \text{VL}_2),$$
$$(\text{H}_1, \text{VH}_2), (\text{H}_1, \text{H}_2), \dots, (\text{VL}_1, \text{L}_2), (\text{VL}_1, \text{VL}_2)\}$$

The set comprises 25 different outcomes. $\blacksquare$

  One of the virtues of decision theory is that it forces a manager to be explicit about the possible actions that may be taken. It is worthwhile to take some time

---

* These outcomes are sometimes called *states of nature*, but there is no requirement for them to refer to natural phenomena.

to consider whether the action space A really includes all the possible actions that may plausibly be taken. Having specified the possible actions, a manager must consider outcomes associated with these actions. Fortunately, it is usually not crucial to list all the possible outcomes; even a considerable simplification of the outcome set won't seriously distort the relative desirability of the various actions. In Example 17.4 we could have defined 50 acceptance levels for each product rather than five. It is unlikely that the increased complexity would lead to any substantial change in the relative merits of the actions.

payoff function   **The third component of statistical decision theory is the payoff function.** For each possible action and each resulting outcome, one must specify a numerical value

$$v(a_i, \theta_j)$$

that represents the profit (or desirability) of action a_i given that outcome θ_j actually occurs. Often the payoffs are arranged in a matrix and sometimes they are specified by a mathematical function.

EXAMPLE 17.5   Suppose that the store in the bread inventory problem of Examples 17.1 and 17.3 earns a profit of 7 cents per loaf sold and loses 3 cents per loaf of unsold bread (which must be discounted on the day-old shelf). For simplicity, limit the action space for loaves ordered to $A = \{0, 1, 2\}$ and the outcome space for loaves demanded to $\Theta = \{0, 1, 2\}$. Compute the values for the payoff function $v(a_i, \theta_j)$.

Solution   If $a_i = 0$, no bread is ordered and there is no profit (or loss) no matter what the outcome. Hence

$$v(0, \theta_j) = 0, \quad \text{for all } \theta_j$$

If $a_i = 1$ and $\theta_j = 0$, the one loaf ordered is not sold, and

$$v(1, 0) = -3$$

If $a_i = 1$ and $\theta_j = 1$, the one loaf ordered is sold, so

$$v(1, 1) = 7$$

In general, the profit depends on whether the demand is greater than or less than the number of loaves ordered. If $\theta_j \geq a_i$, all a_i loaves are sold, for a total profit of $7a_i$. If $\theta_j < a_i$, only θ_j loaves are sold and $a_i - \theta_j$ are left unsold, for a profit of $7\theta_j - 3(a_i - \theta_j)$. It follows that

$$v(a_i, \theta_j) = \begin{cases} 7a_i, & \text{if } \theta_j \geq a_i \\ 7\theta_j - 3(a_i - \theta_i), & \text{if } \theta_j < a_i \end{cases}$$

A portion of the payoff matrix for Examples 17.1 and 17.3 is shown below.

			Outcome θ_j			
Action a_i	0	1	2	3	4	...
0	0	0	0	0	0	
1	-3	7	7	7	7	

Action a_i	Outcome θ_j					
	0	1	2	3	4	...
2	-6	4	14	14	14	...
3	-9	1	11	21	21	
4	-12	-2	8	18	28	
$\vdots$						

numerical payoffs

The requirement of a **numerical payoff** function is a limitation on the applicability of statistical decision theory. Most managers have a very hard time assigning numerical, quantitative values (the v's) to intangible, qualitative results. While an insurer can quantify the value of the loss of a worker's life as the stated policy coverage, we could hope that the managers of the worker's plant have a more complicated, less numerical loss. There are two extreme positions that can be (and are) taken concerning the applicability of decision theory in light of the requirement of a numerical payoff function.

1. Decision theory should restrict itself to the readily quantified aspects of a decision. The manager can weigh these results against the qualitative aspects of the problem.
2. Decisions involving intangibles are made every day. These decisions implicitly put a quantitative value $v(a_i, \theta_j)$ on each qualitative, intangible result. If decision theorists are clever enough, they can obtain these values and incorporate them in a numerical analysis.

We suspect that most decision theorists hold something like the second position; it leads to a wide scope of application and to many interesting research activities. But a skeptical manager might do well to stick with something like the first position, even while testing out methods for evaluating intangible results. It may not be wise to make hard decisions based on soft numbers.

sensitivity analysis

We believe there is a third position. It usually is not necessary to specify each value $v(a_i, \theta_j)$ to the nearest penny. By a **sensitivity analysis**, which we discuss in the next section, it is often possible to find an action that looks good over a fairly wide range of possible values of $v(a_i, \theta_j)$ assigned to the intangible results (a_i, θ_j). Such analyses are particularly useful when payoffs can be specified only within limits.

The fourth component of statistical decision theory is the probability to be assigned to each possible, uncertain outcome. For repetitive decisions such as the number of loaves of bread to be stocked, past data can be very helpful in assigning probabilities. A histogram of past bread sales gives a pretty good idea of the distribution of demand, though a supermarket manager should recognize that sales may fall short of demand if "stockouts" have occurred. Even in such routine decisions, historical data may not give relevant probabilities for the particular problem (in many places, a forecast of heavy snow for the day after tomorrow can increase the demand for bread enormously).

Some decision problems are found in a "one-shot" context, where historical data is of limited (though not zero) value. A computer designer faced with a choice of architecture may be uncertain of the standards that will be adopted by an industry group for the next generation operating system. There haven't been many computer standards groups in the past, and what groups there have been have not operated in exactly the same environment. Therefore, a computer designer would have to use personal judgment to decide on reasonable **subjective** probabilities.

Subjective probabilities can be tricky because there is no provably "right" subjective probability for an outcome. At the least, subjective probability considerations should be logically consistent; for example, probabilities should never be negative, they should add to 1 over all outcomes, and if events are thought to be independent, the probabilistic definition of independence should hold. One way to specify subjective probabilities is simply to list the possible outcomes and to state a probability for each one directly. For example, the computer designer might consider three possible outcomes by the standards group: Adopt the dominant manufacturer's standard, adopt the standard of a consortium of competitors, or adopt a compromise. Believing that the committee is weighted toward the consortium and that the dominant manufacturer's standard is technically inferior, the designer might assign $P(\text{consortium}) = .60$ and $P(\text{compromise}) = .30$; necessarily, it would follow that $P(\text{dominant}) = .10$. There's no point and no need to assign probabilities to several decimal places; nobody is that accurate, and decisions don't normally hinge on extremely small differences in probabilities.

For purposes of "sensitivity analysis," to be discussed in a later section, it's a good idea to specify a range of probabilities, from "seems a little low" to "seems a little high," for each outcome. For example, the designer might feel that $P(\text{consortium})$ is between .50 and .70 and $P(\text{compromise})$ is between .20 and .40. Of course, it's impossible to have both $P(\text{consortium}) = .70$ and $P(\text{compromise}) = .40$; usually we would combine a "seems low" probability for one outcome with a "seems high" probability for another.

A useful device for assessing subjective probabilities is the **probability wheel** described in the article by Spetzler and Stael von Holstein (1975). This is a two-color wheel where the proportions of (say) blue and yellow can be adjusted. A probability assessor can ask, "Which bet would you prefer—that the event in question will happen or that a random pointer will land in the blue part?" By varying the proportions of the two colors, it's fairly easy to get a good indication of probability beliefs. This method—and virtually all others—won't work well in assessing extremely small probabilities. It is quite difficult for us to assess whether we think that a probability is one in a hundred, one in a thousand, or one in ten thousand. Sensitivity analysis is critical in such situations.

With development of the basic elements of decision theory (action space, outcome space, payoff function, and probability) we can illustrate how to use these elements in making decisions.

SECTION 17.1   EXERCISES

17.1   An independent automobile rental firm must decide how many cars to purchase three months in advance of a new model year. The company currently uses 80 cars, which all must be replaced. A maximum of 100 cars can be stored and serviced, and a minimum of 40 cars must be on hand to provide competitive service. The desired number of cars depends heavily on the level of business travel when the cars become available. The level of travel may be very light, light, moderate, heavy, or very heavy.

a. Identify an action space.

b. Identify the set of possible outcomes (states of nature).

17.2   The car rental firm of Exercise 17.1 analyzes the possible results for ordering 50, 60, 70, 80, 90, and 100 cars. The following approximate payoff matrix (in thousands of dollars profit per month) is obtained:

	Outcome, Travel Level				
Action, Cars Ordered	VL	L	M	H	VH
50	30	40	40	40	40
60	35	50	55	55	55
70	20	40	60	70	70
80	25	30	55	80	85
90	−10	20	50	80	110
100	−25	10	45	80	105

a. Show that ordering 50 cars is an unreasonable action. (Hint: Compare the payoffs to 50 and 60 cars for each possible travel level.) In the language of decision theory, ordering 50 cars is an inadmissible action.

b. Are there any other actions that are clearly unreasonable?

17.3   The concession holder at a major league baseball stadium must decide how many refreshment stands to open for each game. One stand is adequate for about 1000 fans. Every stand that is open, with enough fans in attendance, yields a profit of $800. Each excess stand results in a net loss of $200. So, if there are 10 stands open but only 9000 fans, 9 stands make a total of $7200 in profits but the tenth stand loses $200, for a net profit of $7000. Assume that the maximum possible crowd is 30,000, that there are 30 stands that can be opened, and that the number of fans is an exact multiple of 1000.

a. Specify an action set.

b. Specify a set of possible outcomes.

c. Construct the payoff matrix.

17.4   Are there any obviously unreasonable actions in the action set of Exercise 17.3; that is, can any action be ruled out as always being inferior to another one for all possible outcomes?

17.5   An investor has the opportunity to buy all or part of an apartment complex that can possibly be converted into condominiums; the investor can buy a 100%, 75%, 50%, 25%, or 0% share. The return on investment depends on two factors—whether or not a condominium-conversion law is passed in the city and whether rental levels rise or stay the same. If the law is not passed, the complex will be converted, and the profit for a 100% share will be $100,000 (present value). If the law is passed and the rental level rises, the profit for a 100% share will be $40,000. If the law is passed and the rental level stays the same, there will be a loss of $20,000 for a 100% share. Profits or losses for partial shares are proportional to the size of a share; thus, for instance, the profit to a 75% share of a converted complex is $75,000.

a. Specify the action space.

b. Specify the set of possible outcomes.

c. Construct the payoff matrix.

17.6   A firm is facing a lawsuit charging discrimination against older employees. Attorneys for the firm believe that an out-of-court settlement can be reached at a cost of $80,000. Alternatively, the firm can contest the suit. If it is found not guilty, legal fees will cost $20,000. If the suit is tried by Judge A and the firm is found guilty, the cost is expected to be $150,000. If it is tried by Judge B and the firm is found guilty, the cost is expected to be $180,000.

    a. Describe an action space and a set of possible outcomes.

    b. Construct a payoff matrix. Express costs as negative profits.

17.2   DECISION MAKING USING EXPECTED VALUES   ■

In this section we combine the elements defined in Section 17.1 to assess the merits of various possible actions. The basic selection criterion we use is the **expected payoff** action a_i that results in the largest **expected payoff**. This criterion combines the payoff and probability aspects of a decision problem to give a numerical measure of the expected return to each possible action.

    Recall from Chapter 4 that the expected value of any (discrete) random variable Y with probability distribution $P_Y(y)$ is

$$E(Y) = \sum y P_Y(y)$$

that is, $E(Y)$ is the probability-weighted average of the possible Y values. In decision theory, the random variable is the payoff $v(a_i, \theta_j)$ associated with a particular action a_i and outcome θ_j. The possible outcomes are assigned prob- **expected return** abilities $P(\theta_j)$. The expected payoff, or **expected return**, to action a_i is often denoted $R(a_i)$.

■

Expected Return to Action a_i

$$R(a_i) = \sum_j v(a_i, \theta_j) P(\theta_j)$$

where $v(a_i, \theta_j)$ is the payoff for action a_i if outcome θ_j occurs.

■

EXAMPLE 17.6   The manager of a clothing store must decide how many extra salespeople to schedule for the store's annual clearance sale. If the number of additional customers is small, the existing sales force can handle the load. If the crowds turn out to be heavier, additional salespeople are needed to avoid the loss of sales and goodwill. The manager's estimated payoffs (in thousands of dollars per day) are listed in the following table for the action space $A = \{0, 1, 2, 3\}$ and outcome space $\Theta = \{\text{small, moderate, large}\}$. The manager's estimates for the outcome probabilities $P(\theta_j)$ are also listed.

Actions, Additional	Outcome, Additional Customers		
Salespeople	Small	Moderate	Large
0	1	1	1
1	−1	2	3
2	−3	3	6
3	−5	3	10
$P(\theta_j)$	.2	.6	.2

Compute the expected return for each action and determine the action with the highest expected return.

Solution   Taking the actions, payoffs, and outcome probabilities, we obtain the following expected payoffs:

Action, Additional Salespeople	Expected Payoff $R(a_i)$
0	$1(.2) + 1(.6) + 1(.2) = 1.0$
1	$-1(.2) + 2(.6) + 3(.2) = 1.6$
2	$-3(.2) + 3(.6) + 6(.2) = 2.4$
3	$-5(.2) + 3(.6) + 10(.2) = 2.8$

The action with the highest expected payoff is to schedule three extra salespeople. The selection of the action with the highest expected return can also be done **expected-value tree**   using an **expected-value tree**. For these same data, the expected-value tree would be as shown here:

Action a_i	Outcome θ_j	Payoff $v(a_i, \theta_j)$	Probabilities $P(\theta_j)$	Expected return $R(a_i)$
	small	1	.2	
Add 0	moderate	1	.6	1.0
	large	1	.2	
	small	-1	.2	
Add 1	moderate	2	.6	1.6
	large	3	.2	
	small	-3	.2	
Add 2	moderate	3	.6	2.4
	large	6	.2	
	small	-5	.2	
Add 3	moderate	3	.6	2.8
	large	10	.2	

■

As we noted previously, the expected-value criterion is to select the action that has the highest expected return. This criterion is appealing in several respects. The required calculations are very easy. More important, this criterion is desirable in the long run. A manager who takes action based on the expected-value criterion will have higher average payoffs in the long run than one who takes action on some other basis. This argument has particular force for decisions that must be made repeatedly under identical (or at least similar) conditions. In such cases, the long-run average return per action approximates the expected return, so of course selecting the highest expected return gives the best long-run result.

risk   The hitch in this argument is that applying a strategy that maximizes the expected payoff ignores short-run **risk**. A long-run argument isn't much consolation to the owners of a small firm that goes bankrupt taking a short-run loss. We discuss the assessment of risk in the next section.

We have seen that the expected return to a particular action is determined by the payoffs to various actions given various outcomes and by the probabilities of those outcomes. These quantities can be estimated in many situations, but it is rare that they are known exactly. Instead, these quantities are more or less rough estimates. The potential effect of misestimation on the supposedly optimal action **sensitivity analysis**   (and its near-optimal competitors) can be found by **sensitivity analysis**.

The idea of sensitivity analysis is to vary the basic quantities of the analysis to see if the best action remains optimal, or nearly so. The underlying quantity estimates can be varied one at a time or in combination. (A spreadsheet computer program is very helpful here.) There are usually many ways to vary the estimates. Ideally, the best action remains optimal (or nearly optimal) when the estimates are altered in ways that are unfavorable to that action. In such a case a manager can be confident that the selected action is a good one.

EXAMPLE 17.7   In Example 17.6, the highest expected return was obtained by scheduling three additional salespeople. Suppose that the store manager is uncertain about the payoffs when there is a large number of additional customers, and also about the respective probabilities of small, moderate, and large numbers of additional customers. The payoffs (in hundreds of dollars per day) for the action space $A = \{$schedule 0, 1, 2, or 3 additional salespeople$\}$ and the outcome (large) can be as low as 1, 2.5, 6, and 9 or as high as 1, 4, 8, and 12. The probabilities $P(\theta_j)$ for small, moderate, and large numbers can be as pessimistic as .3, .6, and .1 or as optimistic as .1, .5, and .4. Conduct a sensitivity analysis by computing the expected payoffs under these extreme situations when there are large numbers of additional customers.

Solution   There are four combinations of changes in payoffs and outcome probabilities that can be made:

Payoffs, $v(a_i, \text{large})$		Outcome Probabilities, $P(\theta_j)$
(1, 2.5, 6, 9)	with	(.3, .6, .1)
(1, 2.5, 6, 9)	with	(.1, .5, .4)
(1, 4, 8, 12)	with	(.3, .6, .1)
(1, 4, 8, 12)	with	(.1, .5, .4)

We can (and you should) calculate the expected returns for each combination to see if a_4 (schedule 3 additional salespeople) remains optimal. In this example, the critical combination is clear. The reason that a_4 was originally declared optimal is that there was a high payoff for a large number of additional customers, and P(large) was fairly high. We should calculate expected returns assuming the lower $(1, 2.5, 6, 9)$ payoffs and the pessimistic $(.3, .6, .1)$ probabilities, as indicated in the following revised payoff table:

| Action, Additional | *Outcome, Additional Customers* | | |
Salespeople	Small	Moderate	Large
0	1	1	1
1	−1	2	2.5
2	−3	3	9
3	−5	3	9
$P(\theta_j)$	.3	.6	.1

The expected payoffs using this revised table are shown below:

Action, Additional Salespeople	Expected Payoff $R(a_i)$
0	$1(.3) + 1(.6) + 1(.1) = 1.0$
1	$-1(.3) + 2(.6) + 2.5(.1) = 1.15$
2	$-3(.3) + 3(.6) + 6(.1) = 1.5$
3	$-5(.3) + 3(.6) + 9(.1) = 1.2$

By changing payoffs and probabilities in an unfavorable direction, we observe that the action a_4 (schedule 3 additional salespeople) becomes the second-best decision to a_3 (schedule 2 additional salespeople). The difference in payoffs between a_3 and a_4 is $300 per day. Because the advantage of a_3 over a_4 is small even when we loaded the deck in its favor, however, we would conclude that a_4 is a near-optimal solution that is reasonably insensitive to changes in the underlying payoffs and probabilities. ∎

SECTION 17.2 EXERCISES

17.7 A drug manufacturer has applied to the Food and Drug Administration for approval of a new prescription drug. A ruling to be made in 18 months will either allow the firm to market the drug immediately, require additional information, or completely reject the drug. The firm can choose to begin full production now, so that on approval the drug can be marketed immediately, go into limited production, or await the final decision. Payoffs to the various actions are as follows (in hundreds of thousands of dollars):

	Approved	Additional Information	Disapproved
Full production	9.7	−2.9	−3.9
Limited production	3.6	−0.7	−1.7
Await decision	0	0	0

The probability of approval is assessed at .7, of additional information at .2, and of disapproval at .1. Based on the expected-value criterion, which is the best action?

17.8 Refer to Exercise 17.7. An executive of the firm claims that the payoffs to full production are closer to 6.0 (approved), −3.5 (additional information), and −4.5 (disapproved). Another executive asserts that the respective probabilities are .5, .2, and .3.

    a. Which is the best action (in expected value), assuming the revised payoffs and the original probabilities?

    b. Which is the best action (in expected value), assuming the original payoffs and the revised probabilities?

    c. Which is the best action (in expected value), assuming the revised payoffs and the revised probabilities?

    d. Summarize the results of this sensitivty analysis.

17.9 A firm is considering three price levels for a new product. The payoffs depend on the time required for another company to market its competitive product. The relevant assumed values are

	Profits *(Millions of Dollars, Present Value)*		
Price	at 1 Year	at 1.5 Years	at 2 Years
Low	3.2	3.4	3.5
Moderate	2.9	4.5	4.8
High	2.0	4.0	5.5
Probabilities	.25	.50	.25

What price level yields the highest expected profit?

17.10 Refer to Exercise 17.9. The firm's marketing staff believes that the profits for moderate prices are close to correct but that the profits for low and high prices could be in error by as much as half a million dollars in either direction for each amount of time required.

    a. In which direction should the profits for low and high prices be changed to perform a sensitivity analysis?

    b. Does the originally optimal action remain so with the modified profit figures?

17.11 Refer to Exercises 17.9 and 17.10.

    a. What action has the highest expected payoff if the probabilities for 1 year, 1.5 years, and 2 years are .4, .3, and .3, respectively, and if the payoffs of Exercise 7.9 are correct?

    b. Which action has the highest expected payoff if these modified probabilities hold and if the profit figures for low and high prices are each raised by half a million dollars?

c. Summarize the results of this sensitivity analysis.

17.12 In Exercise 17.6, a firm facing a discrimination suit had to decide whether to settle or to contest the suit. The relevant outcomes were whether the case would be assigned to Judge A or Judge B and whether the firm is found guilty or not. Regardless of outcome, the cost (negative profit) of settling is $80,000. If the firm contests the suit, the costs depend on the outcome. If (Judge A, guilty), the cost is $150,000; if (Judge B, guilty), the cost is $180,000; if (either judge, not guilty), the cost is $20,000. Assume that the case will be assigned to Judge A with probability .7 and to Judge B with probability .3. Whichever judge handles the case, the probability that the firm will be found guilty is .4. Which action has the lower expected cost (less negative profit)?

17.13 Refer to Exercise 17.12. Does the optimal action change if the probability that the firm will be found guilty is increased to .6? decreased to .3?

17.3   THE ELEMENT OF RISK

In the last section we suggested that expected return is a good, basic, long-run criterion for selecting a desirable action. The difficulty with expected return as a criterion is that it ignores the element of risk. According to the expected-payoff criterion, an investment strategy with an action that has payoffs of $500 or $1500 with equal probabilities $(1/2)$ is no more or less desirable than an action that has a $50,000 loss or $52,000 gain with equal probabilities. Both have an expected payoff of $1000. However, when one considers the severe risk associated with the win $52,000 – lose $50,000 situation, it is not difficult to select the less risky investment. In this section we discuss one way to evaluate risk. In the next section we discuss some methods that have been proposed for combining the aspects of expected return and risk.

There are two standard approaches to dealing with risk; we'll consider them both in this section. First, we can use variance (or standard deviation) as a measure of riskiness. Alternatively, we will consider statistical utility theory as a way of combining analyses of expected payoff and risk.

variance and risk
Generally speaking, for a given expected return, risk increases as the probabilities of both extremely good and extremely bad payoffs increase; the more spread out the payoff probabilities, the riskier the decision. Beginning in Chapter 2, we have used variance (or standard deviation) as a measure of the spread in sample data. In the same spirit, variance can be considered as a measure of risk; the greater the variance (variability) for a given action, the larger the risk associated with that action.

The variance for a particular action a_i is defined below in the notation of decision theory:

Variance of an Action Var(a_i)

$$\text{Var}(a_i) = \sum_j [v(a_i, \theta_j) - R(a_i)]^2 P(\theta_j)$$

A shortcut formula is

$$\text{Var}(a_i) = \sum_j [v(a_i, \theta_j)]^2 P(\theta_j) - [R(a_i)]^2$$

Standard deviation $(a_i) = \sqrt{\text{Var}(a_i)}$ ∎

EXAMPLE 17.8   Calculate $\text{Var}(a_i)$ for each of the actions a_i for the scheduling problem we discussed in Example 17.6.

Solution   The payoffs, outcome probabilities, and expected payoffs for the action space $A = \{$schedule 0, 1, 2, or 3 additional salespeople$\}$ are summarized here:

Action, Additional Salespeople	Outcome, Additional Customers			Expected Payoff $R(a_i)$
	Small	Moderate	Large	
0	1	1	1	1.0
1	−1	2	2	1.6
2	−3	3	6	2.4
3	−5	3	10	2.8
$P(\theta_j)$	.2	.6	.2	

Using the shortcut formula for $\text{Var}(a_i)$, we can compute the risk for each action as follows:

Action, Additional Salespeople	Risk; $\text{Var}(a_i)$
0	$1(.2) + 1(.6) + 1(.2) - (1)^2 = 0$
1	$1(.2) + 4(.6) + 9(.2) - (1.6)^2 = 1.84$
2	$9(.2) + 9(.6) + 36(.2) - (2.4)^2 = 8.64$
3	$25(.2) + 9(.6) + 100(.2) - (2.8)^2 = 22.56$

Although action a_4 (schedule 3 additional salespeople) has the highest expected payoff, it also has the highest risk. You, as a manager, may be willing to take an action with a lower expected payoff and correspondingly lower risk.   ∎

Variance is a particularly useful measure for assessing the combined risk of a portfolio. In this context we need the concept of covariance we introduced in Chapter 4. Recall that the covariance of two random variables X and Y, $\text{Cov}(X, Y)$, is a measure of the strength of the (linear) relation between them. In the Appendix of Chapter 4 we proved that, for any random variables X and Y,

$$\text{Var}(X + Y) = \text{Var}(X) + \text{Var}(Y) + 2\,\text{Cov}(X, Y)$$

Thus, if the returns to two investments tend to be either both large or both small, the covariance is positive, which inflates the variance of the total return. But if one of the investments tends to give a large return when the other gives a small return, the covariance is negative, and the variance of the total return is smaller.

We need some definitions. Suppose that a manager has d dollars or other forms of capital that can be distributed among k different investments. Let

Y_i = return per dollar assigned to investment i $(i = 1, 2, \ldots, k)$, a random variable with mean μ_i and variance σ_i^2

σ_{ij} = covariance between the return on investments Y_i and Y_j

d_i = dollar amount assigned to investment i $(i = 1, 2, \ldots, k)$

$d = \sum_i d_i$

The payoff (return to the portfolio) for any given action $(d_1, d_2, \ldots, d_k)$ and outcome $(Y_1, Y_2, \ldots, Y_k)$ is

$$d_1 Y_1 + d_2 Y_2 + \cdots + d_k Y_k = \sum d_i Y_i$$

where k is the number of distinct investments.

EXAMPLE 17.9   Suppose an investor has $50,000 to invest and would like to invest in some combination of stock A (1), stock B (2), bond (3), and treasury bill (4). Assume that the expected dollar returns for these investments over a one-year period are

Investment:	Stock A (1)	Stock B (2)	Bond (3)	Bill (4)
Expected return/dollar, μ_i:	1.130	1.120	1.095	1.088

Also assume that the variances and covariances for the returns per dollar invested are as shown below:

	Investment			
	1	2	3	4
Investment				
1	.0597	.0369	.0051	.0000
2		.0421	.0013	.0000
3			.0049	.0000
4				.0000

Identify μ_1, μ_3, σ_2^2, σ_4^2, σ_{13}, and σ_{23}.

Solution   The expected returns per dollar invested are given in the first table above: $\mu_1 = 1.130$ and $\mu_3 = 1.095$. Variances and covariances are presented in the second table. Note that variances appear along the diagonal and covariances off the diagonal.

$$\sigma_2^2 = .0421, \qquad \sigma_4^2 = .0000$$

and

$$\sigma_{13} = .0051, \qquad \sigma_{23} = .0013 \qquad\blacksquare$$

According to the basic properties of expected value we developed in Chapter 4, the expected return to the portfolio is just the sum of dollars invested times expected earnings per dollar:

$$E\left(\sum_i d_i Y_i\right) = \sum_i d_i E(Y_i) = \sum d_i \mu_i$$

Variance (or risk) computations are more complicated, because both variances and covariances are involved. For a portfolio with $k = 2$ investments, it can be shown that the variance (risk) of the portfolio is

portfolio risk

$$\text{Var}(d_1 Y_1 + d_2 Y_2) = d_1^2 \text{Var}(Y_1) + d_2^2 \text{Var}(Y_2) + 2d_1 d_2 \text{Cov}(Y_1, Y_2)$$
$$= d_1^2 \sigma_1^2 + d_2^2 \sigma_2^2 + 2d_1 d_2 \sigma_{12}$$

In general, the variance of the portfolio payoff is

$$\text{Var}\left(\sum_i d_i Y_i\right) = \sum_i d_i^2 \text{Var}(Y_i) + 2 \sum_{i<j} d_i d_j \text{Cov}(Y_i, Y_j)$$

$$= \sum_i d_i^2 \sigma_i^2 + 2 \sum_{i<j} d_i d_j \sigma_{ij}$$

where the notation $\sum_{i<j}$ means sum over all possible pairs where i is less than j.

EXAMPLE 17.10

Refer to the investment problem of Example 17.9. Suppose that the manager of the account wants to place $20,000 in stock A (1), $10,000 in stock B (2), $15,000 in bond (3), and $5000 in treasury bill (4).
  a. Identify d.
  b. Identify the particular action (d_1, d_2, d_3, d_4).
  c. Compute the expected return for this investment action.
  d. Compute the variance (and standard deviation) of the investment return for this action.

Solution

a. The total number of dollars available for investment is $d = \$50,000$.
  b. The investment action chosen by the manager is $(d_1 = \$20,000, d_2 = \$10,000, d_3 = \$15,000, d_4 = \$5000)$.
  c. The expected return for this action is

$$E\left(\sum_i d_i Y_i\right) = \sum d_i \mu_i$$

Substituting for the d_i and μ_i, we obtain

$$E\left(\sum d_i Y_i\right) = 20,000(1.130) + 10,000(1.120) + 15,000(1.095)$$
$$+ 5000(1.088) = \$55,665$$

d. We can use the expression for $\text{Var}(\sum d_i Y_i)$ to compute the variance for the investment return associated with the action ($d_1 = \$20,000$, $d_2 = \$10,000$, $d_3 = \$15,000$, $d_4 = \$5000$).

$$\text{Var}\left(\sum d_i Y_i\right) = \sum d_i^2 \text{Var}(Y_i) + 2 \sum_{i<j} d_i d_j \text{Cov}(Y_i, Y_j)$$

The first term in this formula is

$$\sum d_i^2 \text{Var}(Y_i) = (20,000)^2(.0597) + (10,000)^2(.0421)$$
$$+ (15,000)^2(.0049) + (5000)^2(.0000)$$
$$= 29,192,500$$

The second term is

$$2 \sum_{i<j} d_i d_j \text{Cov}(Y_i, Y_j) = 2\,[20,000(10,000)(.0369) + 20,000(15,000)(.0051)$$
$$+ 20,000(5000)(.0000) + 10,000(15,000)(.0013)$$
$$+ 10,000(5000)(.0000) + (15,000)(5000)(.0000)]$$
$$= 18,210,000$$

Hence $\text{Var}(\sum d_i Y_i) = 29,192,500 + 18,210,000 = 47,402,500$ and the standard deviation of investment return is $\sqrt{47,402,500} = \$6884.95$. ∎

risk and return   There is typically a positive relation between risk (variance) and expected return; individual investments with high returns also carry high risks, and low-risk investments yield low returns. But by judicious combination of investments, it may be possible to obtain a fairly high expected return with a fairly low variance.

EXAMPLE 17.11   Refer to Examples 17.9 and 17.10. Compute the expected return, variance, and standard deviation for an investment action that places all $50,000 in treasury bills (4).

Solution   The particular action chosen is ($d_1 = 0$, $d_2 = 0$, $d_3 = 0$, $d_4 = \$50,000$). The expected payoff and variance for this action are easy to compute, because $d_1 = d_2 = d_3 = 0$.

$$E\left(\sum d_i Y_i\right) = \sum d_i \mu_i = \$50,000(1.088) = \$54,400$$

$$\text{Var}\left(\sum d_i Y_i\right) = d_4^2 \text{Var}(Y_4) = (50,000)^2(.0000) = .0000$$

Compared to the action ($d_1 = \$20,000$, $d_2 = \$10,000$, $d_3 = \$15,000$, $d_4 = \$5000$), the action ($d_1 = d_2 = d_3 = 0$, $d_4 = \$50,000$) has a lower expected return, but the net gain of $4400 (versus $5665) is without risk. ∎

Variance (or standard deviation) has been widely used as the basic measure of risk in financial portfolio analysis. As a risk measure, it is fairly easy to

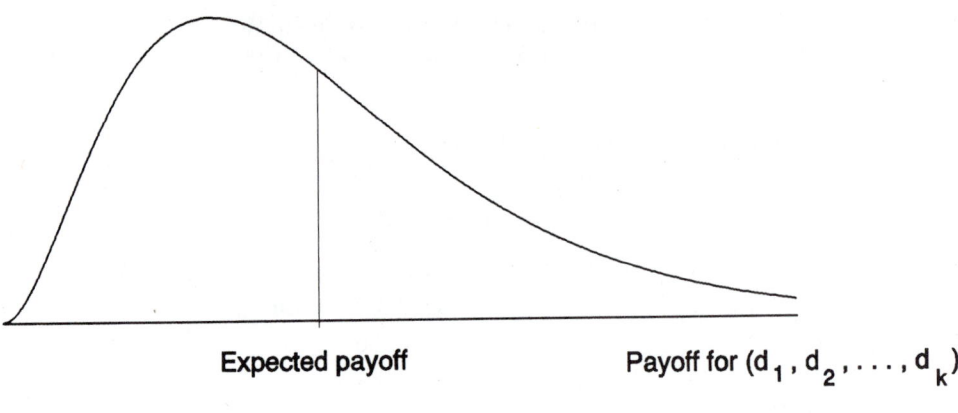

Expected payoff   Payoff for $(d_1, d_2, \ldots, d_k)$

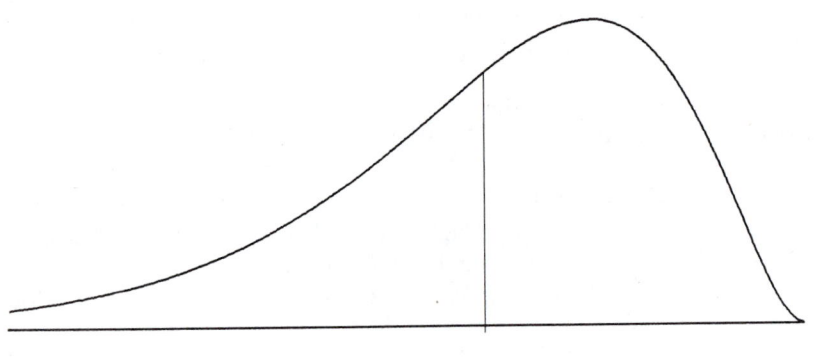

Expected payoff   Payoff for $(d'_1, d'_2, \ldots, d'_k)$

FIGURE 17.1   Possible Payoff Distributions

calculate. One very convenient property is that the portfolio variance is calculated simply from individual variances and from covariances of pairs of investment outcomes Y_i, Y_j. A limitation of variance as a risk measure is that it treats above-expected and below-expected returns symmetrically. For example, suppose the payoff $\sum d_i Y_i$ for a particular action $(d_1, d_2, \ldots, d_k)$ has a probability distribution as indicated in Figure 17.1a. The expected payoff and variance for the investment action are $\sum d_i \mu_i$ and $\mathrm{Var}(\sum d_i Y_i)$, respectively. Consider a second investment action $(d_1, d_2, \ldots, d_k)$, which has the same expected payoff and variance but a "flipped over" probability distribution (Figure 17.1b). Should we consider the two investment actions to be equally risky? The second investment action clearly has a higher "down-side risk" than the first investment action, even though the risks (as measured by the variances) are identical. When the **skewness problem**   probability distribution of payoffs is highly skewed, variance may be a somewhat deceptive measure of risk. Fortunately, the return of a portfolio of many investments is likely to have a roughly symmetric, normal distribution, thanks to the Central Limit Theorem. For these symmetric distributions, it seems eminently reasonable to equate higher variance with higher risk. Thus, for portfolio analysis in particular, variance appears to be a very suitable and convenient risk measure.

An alternative approach to making decisions under uncertainty uses **expected utility**. Rather than finding separate return and risk measures—expected value and variance—and asking a manager to make a tradeoff, with the utility approach the manager lists risk preferences and tolerances. The utility approach then uses the manager's preferences to find a single **utility function**. The relative desirability of various uncertain results is then established simply by computing the expected value of this function. This approach originated with von Neumann and Morganstern (1967).

utility function

EXAMPLE 17.12   Suppose that a manager of a multinational firm has accounts receivable (six months from now) of several million French francs. Three possible "hedging" actions can be taken against the possibility of changes in currency exchange rates, by purchasing futures contracts: The entire balance due can be hedged, or half can be, or none. The payoffs (including commission charges) to each action and the relevant outcome probabilities can be summarized as follows:

	Outcome θ_j		
	Franc Loses		Franc Gains
Action a_i	Value	No Change	Value
Full hedge	-20	-20	-20
Half hedge	-50	-10	30
No hedge	-80	0	80
$P(\theta_j)$	.30	.40	.30

Assume that the following utility function applies:

Payoff:	-80	-50	-20	-10	0	30	80
Utility:	0	40	65	74	80	90	100

    a. Find the expected payoff for each action. Which action has the highest expected payoff?

    b. Find the expected utility for each action. Which action is preferable?

Solution   a.

Action	Expected Payoff
Full hedge	$-20(.3) - 20(.4) - 20(.3) = -20$
Half hedge	$-50(.3) - 10(.4) + 30(.3) = -10$
No hedge	$-80(.3) + 0(.4) + 80(.3) = 0$ (highest)

The expected-payoff criterion selects the no-hedge action.

b. Replace each payoff by its utility and again, compute the expected values.

Action	Expected Utility
Full hedge	$65(.3) + 65(.4) + 65(.3) = 65.0$
Half hedge	$40(.3) + 74(.4) + 90(.3) = 68.6$ (highest)
No hedge	$0(.3) + 80(.4) + 100(.3) = 62.0$

The half-hedge action is preferable according to the expected-utility criterion, apparently as a balancing of small expected loss and modest risk. ∎

A utility function reflects, rather than determines, a manager's willingness to accept risks in pursuit of profits. The idea is not that a manager should possess this utility function as opposed to that one. Rather, the idea is that a utility function corresponds to a manager's specified risk willingness. The technical details of utility-function construction are presented in the Appendix to this chapter.

risk and utility

The utility functions of Figure 17.2 curve downward, substantially for U_1, slightly for U_2. Technically, they are called concave functions. It's not hard to show that use of a linear utility function (which has no curvature) is equivalent to use of the expected-payoff criterion. In this situation, the element of risk is ignored. A concave utility function does take risk into account.

EXAMPLE 17.13

For the problem of Example 17.12, the following three utility functions are considered:

Payoff $v(a_i, \theta_j)$	−80	−50	−20	−10	0	30	80
Utility function U_1	0	40	65	74	80	90	100
Utility function U_2	0	30	55	65	70	83	100
Utility function U_3	0	18.75	37.50	43.75	50	68.75	100

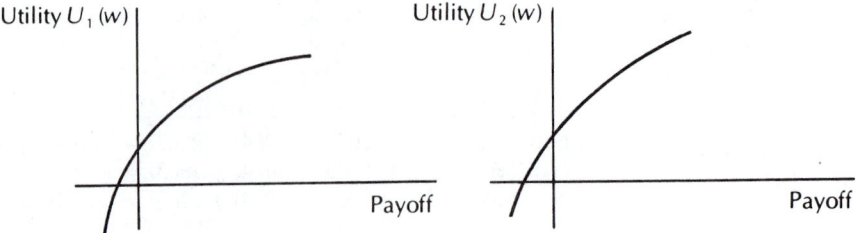

Utility $U_1(w)$ Payoff   Utility $U_2(w)$ Payoff

FIGURE 17.2   Typical Utility Functions

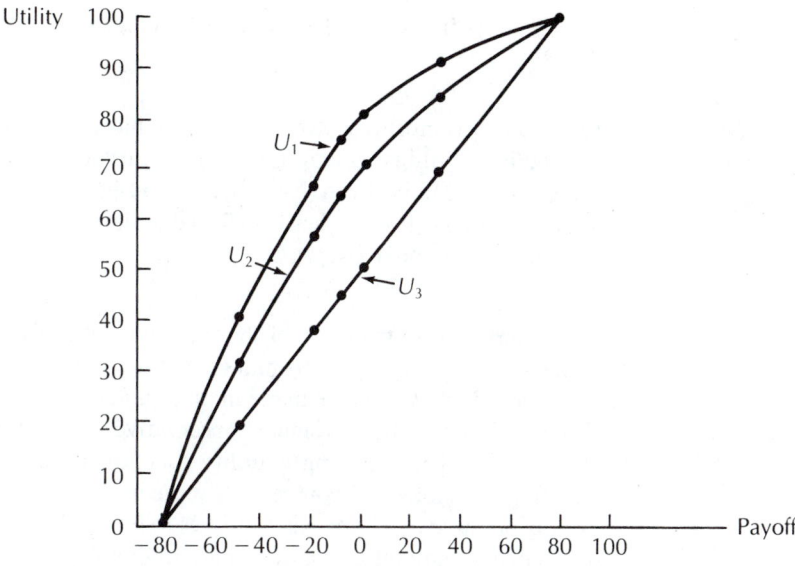

FIGURE 17.3   Utility Functions for Example 17.13

a. Draw smooth curves representing each utility function. Compare the degrees of curvature.

b. Compute expected utilities for each action under each utility function.

Solution   a. The utility functions are shown in Figure 17.3. Clearly U_1 has the most severe curvature, U_2 less severe curvature, and U_3 none at all.

b. Expected utilities for U_1 were computed in Example 17.12. Similar computations give the following table of expected utilities:

Action	U_1	U_2	U_3
Full hedge	65.0	55.0	37.50
Half hedge	68.6	59.9	43.75
No hedge	62.0	58.0	50.00

risk aversion   The degree of curvature of the utility function reflects the decision maker's attitude toward risk. A downward curving (concave) utility function implies **risk aversion**. A risk-averse manager having a choice between two actions with equal expected payoffs prefers the action with less variability. A severely curved utility function indicates a strongly risk-averse decision maker; a linear function indicates no risk aversion at all.*

* It is possible to have an upward-curving (convex) utility function—for a manager who actually prefers risk.

EXAMPLE 17.14   Which utility function in Example 17.13 indicates strongest risk aversion? which least?

Solution   Function U_1 is most risk-averse because it has the strongest curvature. Function U_3, the linear utility function, shows no curvature and no risk aversion at all. Function U_2 is in between. Note that the no-hedge action has the highest return and highest risk. It is the least preferred action under U_1, second under U_2, and most preferred under U_3.   ■

The main contribution of the expected-utility approach to decision making is that it forces managers to make consistent, explicit, quantitative judgments about risk. If decisions are made in an organization on an ad hoc basis, some of them are likely to be extremely conservative while others are wildly risky. The effort involved in selecting a utility function is repaid by the consistency of resulting decisions. Of course utility theory is not a magical cure-all. It's not usually possible to assign exact utilities to all possible payoffs, particularly when intangible, nonquantitative outcomes are involved. Utility calculations must be regarded as approximations and must be used thoughtfully.

SECTION 17.3   EXERCISES

17.14 A fuel oil dealer must decide how much oil to purchase at the beginning of the heating season. The basic options are full capacity (enough oil to fill all storage tanks), 90% capacity, 80% capacity, or 70% capacity. The crucial unpredictable variable is the weather during the heating season. In a severe winter, the dealer can sell the full-capacity amount at a good profit, but with a warm winter, excess oil must be carried over to the following summer at a serious interest penalty. Also, if too little oil is ordered initially, a refill of more expensive oil must be purchased. The dealer classifies the possible outcomes as severe, cold, normal, mild, or warm winter. The payoff matrix (profits in thousands of dollars) and assessed probabilities of the possible outcomes are

| | | Winter | | |
Order	Severe	Cold	Normal	Mild	Warm
Full	120	90	60	30	0
90%	80	90	80	70	60
80%	50	70	75	70	65
70%	30	40	50	60	70
Probabilities	.10	.20	.40	.20	.10

a. Which order quantity yields the highest expected profit?
b. Which order quantity yields the lowest standard deviation (risk)?

c. Is there any conflict between the goals of maximizing expected return and minimizing risk?

17.15 Refer to Exercise 17.14. Suppose that, because of forecasts of a relatively cold winter, the assessed outcome probabilities are revised to .20, .30, .30, .15, and .05 for severe, cold, normal, mild, and warm winter, respectively.

a. Recalculate expected profits and standard deviations for the various actions.

b. Is there any reason to modify the choice of optimal action found in Exercise 17.14?

17.16 A revised forecast of interest rates and replacement fuel oil prices leads to the following payoff matrix for Exercise 17.14:

			Winter		
Order	Severe	Cold	Normal	Mild	Warm
Full	120	80	40	0	−40
90%	75	90	75	60	45
80%	40	65	75	65	55
70%	15	30	45	60	70

Use the probabilities shown in Exercise 17.14.

a. Which order quantity yields the highest expected return?

b. Which quantity has the lowest risk (standard deviation)?

c. Is the preferred action sensitive to this modification of the payoff matrix?

17.17 The random variables Y_1 and Y_2 represent one-year net returns to $1000 investments in project 1 and project 2. The probability distribution $P_{Y_1 Y_2}(y_1, y_2)$ is as follows:

					y_2				
		70	80	90	100	110	120	130	$P_{Y_1}(y_1)$
	80	.01	.01	.03	.09	.06	.07	.03	.30
y_1	100	.01	.02	.11	.12	.11	.02	.01	.40
	120	.03	.07	.06	.09	.03	.01	.01	.30
	$P_{Y_2}(y_2)$	.05	.10	.20	.30	.20	.10	.05	

a. Calculate the covariance of Y_1 and Y_2.

b. Calculate the correlation of Y_1 and Y_2.

17.18 a. Refer to Exercise 17.17. Calculate the expected return of a portfolio consisting of $3000 invested in project 1 and $2000 invested in project 2.

b. Calculate the variance of this portfolio.

c. Compare the return and risk of this portfolio to that of an investment of $2000 in project 1 and $3000 in project 2.

17.19 The treasurer of a certain firm has a short-term surplus of $1 million in cash to invest. The money will be needed in one year, but not before. Three possible investments for the cash have been suggested. The expected returns per dollar, variances, and covariances are shown below:

	Investment		
	A	B	C
Expected return per dollar, μ_i	1.088	1.091	1.095
Var(A) = .00	Cov(A, B) = .00 Var(B) = .022		Cov(A, C) = .00 Cov(B, C) = .020 Var(C) = .068

a. Find the expected return and variance for a portfolio with equal amounts in each investment.

b. Compute the expected return and risk for (1) .5 million dollars invested in each of A and C; (2) 1 million dollars invested in B. Compare your results.

17.20 An investor has a choice of three stocks to purchase. Expected returns, variances, and covariances (per dollar invested) are

Stock:	1	2	3
Expected return:	1.090	1.088	1.091

Variance-Covariance Matrix

	1	2	3
1	.095	.020	.080
2	.020	.104	.030
3	.080	.030	.095

Thus, for example, the variance per dollar invested in stock 2 is .104 and the covariance for stocks 1 and 2 is .020.

a. What is the expected return to a portfolio with $1000 invested in each of the three stocks?

b. What is the variance of this portfolio?

17.21 In Exercise 17.20, stock 2 has both the lowest expected return and the highest variance. Even so, show that an investor who desires low risk might prefer the portfolio of Exercise 17.20 to a portfolio with $1500 invested in each of stocks 1 and 3.

17.22 A company with a current net worth of $2 million is considering an expansion program. The success of this program depends largely on future demand for the company's product line. The payoff matrix and assessment of outcome probabilities are given next, where payoffs are expressed as net worth in millions of dollars after three years.

	Demand		
Action	Steady	Small Increase	Large Increase
Expansion	1.50	2.40	3.80
No expansion	2.10	2.40	2.70
Probabilities	.40	.30	.30

Assume that the firm's utility function can be taken as $U(x) = 1 - e^{-.05x}$, where x is net worth after three years.

a. Show that expansion has a higher expected payoff but also a higher standard deviation.

b. Which action has higher expected utility?

17.23 Refer to Exercise 17.22. Are the conclusions of that exercise affected if the demand probabilities are changed to .50, .30, and .20 for steady, small increase, and large increase, respectively?

17.24 Refer to Exercise 17.22. Are the conclusions of that exercise affected if the utility function is changed to $U(x) = 1 - e^{-.06x}$?

17.25 An investor has a current wealth of $400,000 and is considering five possible investment strategies. The wealth position after one year depends on the chosen strategy and on the change in the economic climate over the year, as follows (in thousands of dollars):

	Economic Climate Change			
Strategy	Decline	Constant	Small Increase	Strong Increase
1	270	370	470	570
2	310	385	460	535
3	350	400	450	500
4	390	415	440	465
5	430	430	430	430

The assumed prior probabilities of decline, constant, small increase, and strong increase in economic climate are .10, .20, .40, and .30, respectively.

a. Show that the expected return is highest for strategy 1 and then declines to lowest for strategy 5.

b. Show that the variance is also highest for strategy 1 and declines to lowest for strategy 5.

17.26 Refer to Exercise 17.25. If the investor's utility as a function of wealth position is expressed as $U(x) = \log_{10} x$, which investment strategy is preferable?

17.4   BUYING AND USING INFORMATION ∎

The discussion of decision theory thus far ignores one important managerial option: A manager can often buy more information. Information can be used to improve forecasts of future outcomes. Because these outcomes determine the relative success or failure of the actions, better information should lead to better decisions. The value of information may be measured by how much influence it has on decision making.

Information is expensive. Gathering and using data almost always cost money. Just as important, the information process takes time. It's easy to forget that while time goes by, profits and gains are being lost and costs are piling up. The relevant question for a manager is, will this information have enough value in decision making to justify the money and time expense to gather it? In this section we introduce some decision-theory ideas about how information can be used to

money and time costs

modify decisions and about how to weigh the benefits of information against the money and time costs of gathering it.

Suppose that an oil company has the option of purchasing the rights to all natural gas and oil that may be found under a certain tract of land in southern Wyoming. The company has identified three possible actions: Purchase all rights and bear all expenses, purchase a half share of all rights and bear half the expenses, or purchase none of the rights. The payoff to these actions obviously depends on the extent of underground oil and gas deposits actually present. Suppose that the company breaks down the possible outcomes as follows: No gas or oil, gas only, small oil deposit only, large oil deposit only, both oil and gas. Further, suppose that the net payoffs (in millions of dollars) and (prior) probabilities are as follows:

Action a_i	Outcome θ_j				
	No Gas or Oil	Gas Only	Small Oil	Large Oil	Both
Full rights	−10	8	18	40	58
Half rights	−5	4	9	20	29
No rights	0	0	0	0	0
$P(\theta_j)$	.70	.10	.10	.05	.05

We assume that the issue of risk can be neglected, so the expected-value criterion applies. The respective expected returns for the three possible actions are

E(return | full rights):

$$(-10)(.70) + 8(.10) + 18(.10) + 40(.05) + 58(.05) = .5$$

E(return | half rights):

$$(-5)(.70) + 4(.10) + 9(.10) + 20(.05) + 29(.05) = .25$$

E(return | no rights):

$$(0)(.70) + 0(.10) + 0(.10) + 0(.05) + 0(.05) = 0$$

The highest expected value corresponds to the full-rights action.

Before embarking on this action, however, it may be desirable for the company to seek additional information. If a "dry hole" (no gas or oil) could be ruled out, the expected profit to a full share would rise dramatically. On the other hand, if it could be known in advance that there was no gas or oil, a considerable loss could be spared. In practice, the company would't be able to know the outcome with certainty unless it bought the rights and drilled. But it's a useful **perfect information** fiction to imagine a source of **perfect information**—a magical worm that can report unerringly about "what's down there." How much would such a beast be worth?

According to the prior probabilities, there is a .7 chance that the perfect-information service reports no oil or gas; if so, the proper action is to claim no rights. If the source reports gas only, small oil, large oil, or both gas and oil, the proper action is to buy full rights. Such reports occur with respective probabilities .10, .10, .05, and .05. We can compute the expected return given perfect information using the abbreviated table below.

| | Outcome θ_j | | | | |
Action a_i	No Gas or Oil	Gas Only	Small Oil	Large Oil	Both
Full rights	—	8	18	40	58
Half rights	—	—	—	—	—
No rights	0	—	—	—	—
$P(\theta_j)$	.70	.10	.10	.05	.05

The expected return for perfect information is

(Payoff to no rights given no oil or gas) P(no oil or gas)
+ (payoff to full rights given gas only) P(gas only)
+ (payoff to full rights given small oil) P(small oil)
+ (payoff to full rights given large oil) P(large oil)
+ (payoff to full rights given both gas and oil) P(both gas and oil)
$$= 0(.70) + 8(.10) + 18(.10) + 40(.05) + 58(.05)$$
$$= 7.5$$

■

Expected Value of Perfect Information (EVPI)

The **expected value of perfect information** is the difference between the expected return under perfect information and the maximum expected return based on prior probabilities only.

The expected return under perfect information is

$$\sum_i (\text{maximum payoff given outcome } \theta_j) \, P(\theta_j)$$

■

In our illustration, EVPI $= 7.5 - 0.5 = 7.0$.

EXAMPLE 17.15   A manufacturing firm develops a security system for the door locks of hotel and motel rooms. The (present value of) future returns on sales of this system depend heavily on whether the system can be patented. An inventor has developed a somewhat similar system and holds a patent on it. The firm's possible actions are to buy patent rights from the inventor, to apply for its own patent, or to sell the rights to its system to a competitor. The payoffs, in millions of dollars (present value), are estimated as follows:

| | Outcome θ_j | |
Action a_i	System Patentable	System Not Patentable
Buy rights	18.6	16.4
Apply	20.8	8.2
Sell	15.4	15.4
$P(\theta_j)$	.80	.20

The firm's patent attorney estimates that there is a .80 probability that the firm's system is patentable, and therefore a .20 probability that it is not.

    a. Under current information conditions, what is the best action to take?

    b. What is the EVPI?

Solution   a. The respective expected returns on the possible actions are

E(return on buy): $18.6(.8) + 16.4(.2) = 18.16$
E(return on apply): $20.8(.8) + 8.2(.2) = 18.28$
E(return on sell): $15.4(.8) + 15.4(.2) = 15.4$

The highest expected return is for Apply. Neglecting risk, it is the best action.

    b. If it were known that the system was patentable, the firm would apply and earn 20.8. If it were known that the system was not patentable, the firm would buy rights and earn 16.4. The expected return under perfect information is $20.8(.8) + 16.4(.2) = 19.92$. Hence EVPI $= 19.92 - 18.28 = 1.64$.   ■

The EVPI puts an upper limit on the value of information. If the cost of gathering information, whether perfect or imperfect, exceeds the EVPI, there's no point in paying for information. In the oil and gas example, if the cost of a seismic study of the tract is $7.7 million, it would be foolish to do the study. Even perfect information is worth only $7.0 million.

EXAMPLE 17.16   Refer to Example 17.15. Suppose that an opinion from a patent specialist can be obtained for a total cost of $.4 million. Is the cost justified?

Solution   Possibly. The EVPI is $1.64 million; if the specialist's opinion is reliable enough, it could be worth the $.4 million cost.   ■

In practice, information is not perfect. Forecasts are subject to error. Therefore imperfect information is worth less than the EVPI. To assess the value and effect of sample (imperfect) information, we must consider how such information can affect decisions.

    The idea is fairly simple: Given any particular result from sample information, revise the probabilities $P(\theta_j)$ of all outcomes according to Bayes' Theorem

(Chapter 3). Use these revised (posterior) probabilities $P(\theta_j | \text{sample result } I)$ to select the best decision according to the expected-value criterion. To carry out this idea, we must specify the likelihoods of various sample results conditional on the eventual outcomes.

For instance, in the oil and gas illustration, suppose that a seismic test can be conducted that yields three possible outcomes: Poor promise of success, modest promise of success, or good promise of success. Assuming that the test has been used in other explorations, it is possible to assess its reliability by computing the chance (or likelihood) of each test result given a possible outcome. Such an assessment of previous success yields the likelihoods shown next.

	Likelihood (Sample Result $I | \theta_j$)				
	Outcome θ_j				
Sample Result I	No Oil or Gas	Gas Only	Small Oil	Large Oil	Both
Poor	.80	.50	.40	.20	.10
Modest	.15	.30	.40	.30	.30
Good	.05	.20	.20	.50	.60

Bayes' Theorem can be used to calculate the (posterior) probabilities of each outcome given any particular test result. For example,

$$P(\text{no oil or gas} | \text{poor}) = \frac{P(\text{poor} | \text{no oil or gas})P(\text{no oil or gas})}{P(\text{poor})}$$

where

$$P(\text{poor}) = P(\text{poor} | \text{no oil or gas})P(\text{no oil or gas}) + P(\text{poor} | \text{gas})P(\text{gas})$$
$$+ \cdots + P(\text{poor} | \text{both})P(\text{both})$$

$P(\text{no oil or gas} | \text{poor})$

$$= \frac{(.80)(.70)}{(.80)(.70) + (.50)(.10) + (.40)(.10) + (.20)(.05) + (.10)(.05)}$$

$$= \frac{.5600}{.6650} = .8421$$

Similar calculations or a probability tree can be made to yield each entry in the following table:

	P(Outcome θ_j	Sample Result I)	
	Sample Result I		
Outcome θ_j	Poor	Modest	Good
No oil or gas	.8421	.5122	.2692
Gas only	.0752	.1463	.1538
Small oil	.0602	.1951	.1538

$P(Outcome\ \theta_j\,|\,Sample\ Result\ I)$			
		Sample Result I	
Outcome θ_j	Poor	Modest	Good
Large oil	.0150	.0732	.1923
Both	.0075	.0732	.2308
P(Sample result I)	.6650	.2050	.1300

These probabilities are used in the standard expected-value calculations to assess the best action given a particular test result. For example, if the full-rights action is taken in the face of a poor test result, the expected return (using payoffs from page 814) is

$$-10(.8421) + 8(.0752) + 18(.0602) + 40(.0150) + 58(.0075) = -5.70$$

The remaining expected returns are computed in a similar way.

$E(return\ on\ a_i\,|\,Sample\ Result\ I)$			
		Sample Result I	
Action a_i	Poor	Modest	Good
Full rights	-5.70	6.73	22.39
Half rights	-2.85	3.37	11.19
No rights	.00	.00	.00

Based on the expected-return criterion, the best action is to choose no rights given a poor test result and full rights given either a modest or a good test result.

EXAMPLE 17.17   The manufacturing firm of Example 17.15 has the option of consulting a patent specialist, who will state that the patentability is likely, uncertain, or unlikely. The specialist is something less than infallible. From past history, it appears that the likelihoods of the specialist's opinion, given the eventual outcome, are

$Likelihood\ (Sample\ Result\ I\,|\,\theta_j)$		
	Outcome θ_j	
Sample Result I	Patentable	Not Patentable
Likely	.50	.25
Uncertain	.30	.30
Unlikely	.20	.45

a. Calculate the posterior probabilities $P(\theta_j\,|\,\text{opinion})$.
b. Given each possible opinion of the specialist, compute the expected return for each action based on the posterior probabilities of part (a).

a. For example, the posterior probability

$$P(\text{patentable}\,|\,\text{likely}) = \frac{P(\text{likely}\,|\,\text{patentable})P(\text{patentable})}{P(\text{likely})}$$

where

$$P(\text{likely}) = P(\text{likely}\,|\,\text{patentable})P(\text{patentable})$$
$$+ P(\text{likely}\,|\,\text{not patentable})P(\text{not patentable})$$
$$= .50(.80) + .25(.20) = .45$$

Hence

$$P(\text{patentable}\,|\,\text{likely}) = \frac{.50(.80)}{.45} = .889$$

Similar calculations yield the table of the posterior probabilities shown here:

$P(\text{Outcome } \theta_j\,|\,\text{Sample result } I)$			
	Sample Result I		
Outcome θ_j	Likely	Uncertain	Unlikely
Patentable	.889	.800	.640
Not patentable	.111	.200	.360
$P(\text{Sample result } I)$	.45	.30	.25

b. If the opinion is likely and the payoffs are as indicated on page 816, the expected return to the buy-rights action is

$$E(\text{return on buy}\,|\,\text{likely}) = 18.6(.889) + 16.4(.111) = 18.36$$

Similar calculations give the following table:

$Expected\ (Return\ on\ a_i\,|\,Sample\ Result\ I)$			
	Sample Result I		
Action a_i	Likely	Uncertain	Unlikely
Buy rights	18.36	18.16	17.81
Apply	19.40	18.28	16.26
Sell	15.40	15.40	15.40
$P(\text{Sample result } I)$	.45	.30	.25

■

We define the expected value of sample information (EVSI) similarly to the expected value of perfect information (EVPI).

Expected Value of Sample Information (EVSI)

1. Calculate the posterior outcome probabilities $P(\text{outcome } \theta_j | \text{sample result } I)$ given each sample (information) result, and also the probabilities of each sample result.
2. Calculate the expected return to each action $E(\text{action } a_i | \text{sample result } I)$ using each set of posterior probabilities.
3. EVSI = the maximum expected return using sample information less the maximum expected return using no sample information.
   $= \sum (\text{maximum expected return} | \text{sample result}) P(\text{sample result})$
   $-$ maximum expected return using no sample information. ∎

In the oil and gas illustration, we can use the middle table, page 818. The best action given a poor result is the choice of no rights, expected return 0. The best action given a modest result is the choice of full rights (expected return 6.73), and the best result given a good result is the choice of full rights (expected return 22.39). The probabilities of poor, modest, and good results were calculated as .6650, .2050, and .1300, respectively. The maximum expected return using no information was calculated as .50 (see page 814). Therefore

$$\text{EVSI} = (0)(.6650) + (6.73)(.2050) + (22.39)(.1300) - .50 = 3.790$$

If the test costs \$4.0 million, it is not worth the cost; if it costs \$3.0 million, it is worth the cost.

EXAMPLE 17.18   Refer to Examples 17.15 and 17.17. Suppose the patent specialist's fee is \$.40 million. Is the information worth the cost?

Solution   Calculate the EVSI. The best action for each opinion, the expected return for the best action, and the probability of a given opinion are displayed here. These were obtained from the solution to Example 17.17, part (b).

Opinion	Best Action | Opinion	Expected Return	P(Opinion)
Likely	Apply	19.40	.45
Uncertain	Apply	18.28	.30
Unlikely	Buy	17.81	.25

The maximum expected return with no additional information was computed to be 18.28 in Example 17.15. Hence

$$\text{EVSI} = 19.40(.45) + 18.28(.30) + 17.81(.25) - 18.28 = .387$$

Because the EVSI is less than the cost of the information, the information is not worth the cost. ∎

SECTION 17.4 EXERCISES

17.27 An entrepreneur is considering building a system of fish farms near major cities to supply freshwater fish (primarily walleyed pike and sauger) to the hotel and restaurant trade. The profitable scale of such an operation depends on the yield of edible fish after a 4-year growth period. Anticipated net profits are as follows (in millions of dollars per year):

	Yield		
Scale	Good	Fair	Poor
Large	10.5	2.2	−5.8
Medium	6.1	2.4	−1.2
Small	3.2	1.9	−0.6
None	.0	.0	.0

After discussion with several specialists, the entrepreneur assesses the probabilities of good, fair, and poor yields as .2, .5, and .3, respectively.

a. What scale of operations has the highest expected return?

b. Imagine that a pilot project could, at the cost of $1.0 million, identify yield exactly. Would such a project be desirable?

17.28 Refer to Exercise 17.27. It is possible to establish a pilot project that will give a fairly accurate indication of yield. The likelihoods (conditional probabilities) of various pilot project results given yields are assumed to be as follows:

	Yield		
Results	Good	Fair	Poor
Favorable	.9	.2	.1
Mediocre	.1	.7	.2
Unfavorable	.0	.1	.7

a. Find the revised (posterior) probabilities of good, fair, and poor yields given a favorable pilot project result.

b. Find the scale that has the greatest expected profit, given a favorable result.

c. What is the probability of a favorable result?

d. Answer parts (a), (b), and (c) for a mediocre result, and then for a poor result.

17.29 The pilot project of Exercise 17.28 costs $.6 million. Is the information provided worth the cost?

17.30 A supermarket chain must decide how much shelf space and what form of display to use for generic food products. These products are offered by some of the chain's major competitors. The crucial unknown factor is the degree to which generic products "cannibalize" sales of national and house brands. A staff report indicates the following display options, three-month profit figures (in hundreds of thousands of dollars), and probabilities:

| | Degree of Cannibalization | | | |
Display	25%	50%	75%	100%
30 ft., consolidated	2.4	1.2	.0	−1.2
30 ft., scattered	3.6	2.0	−1.1	−1.8
15 ft., consolidated	1.5	.8	−.4	−.8
15 ft., scattered	2.0	1.2	−.6	−1.0
None	−.3	−.5	−.7	−.9
Probabilities	.50	.25	.20	.05

a. Is any display option always worse than some other option?
b. Which option has the highest expected profit?
c. Suppose an extremely extensive survey costing $240,000 can indicate the degree of cannibalization perfectly. Is such a survey worth its cost?

17.31 Refer to Exercise 17.30. Suppose a limited survey of shoppers at the chain can be undertaken at a cost of $40,000. Because the survey is based on a modest sample and tends to indicate higher substitution of generic products than actually occurs, the following conditional probabilities apply:

| Survey Result (How Much Substitution?) | Degree of Cannibalization | | | |
	25%	50%	75%	100%
Little	.1	.1	.0	.0
Some	.3	.2	.1	.0
Half	.3	.3	.1	.0
Most	.2	.3	.5	.1
All	.1	.1	.3	.9

a. What is the probability that the survey result is little?
b. If the result is little, what are the posterior probabilities of each possible degree of cannibalization?
c. If the result is little, what is the optimal display option?
d. Answer questions (a), (b), and (c) for each of the other possible survey results.

17.32 Is the survey of Exercise 17.31 worth its cost?

17.5   DECISION TREES

The calculations involved in assessing the value of information are not terribly hard, but there are many of them. Any device for keeping the calculations straight is useful. In this section we introduce such a device—decision trees. The concept of a decision tree is very similar to that of a probability tree (Chapter 3) and to that of an expected-value tree (Section 17.2).

The simplest decision trees involve a single decision and a single chance outcome. For example, the dispatchers for a bulk chemical carrier must decide how many trucks to reserve each day for their contract customers. By carrier policy, there must be at least one reserved truck, but the dispatchers are allowed to reserve two (out of the total of three available bulk trucks). The carrier's profit for the day depends on the number of calls received that day for contract (C) and freelance (F) delivery, according to the following table (profits in hundreds of dollars).

C:	0				1				2			
F:	0	1	2	3	0	1	2	3	0	1	2	3
Reserve 1:	−8.0	−2.0	4.0	9.5	−2.0	4.5	10.5	10.2	10.0	16.5	10.5	6.5
Reserve 2:	−8.0	−2.0	3.0	2.0	−2.0	4.5	9.5	9.2	10.0	16.5	15.5	15.0

Demand records indicate that the probabilities that $C = 0, 1$, or 2 are .20, .60, and .20, respectively; that the probabilities for $F = 0, 1, 2$, or 3 are .10, .20, .50, and .20, respectively; and that the C and F demands are statistically independent. We can construct a decision tree to find which number of reserved trucks has the higher expected value. The first step is a decision branch, indicated by a rectangle; here the decision is to reserve 1 truck or 2. Next, a simple decision tree has a single chance branch, indicated by an ellipse or circle. We can combine the C and F calls as outcomes, and use independence to calculate probabilities; for example, $P(C = 0 \text{ and } F = 0) = P(C = 0)P(F = 0) = (.20)(.10) = .02$. We enter probabilities (conditional on any events to the left, just like probability trees) under each chance branch. We indicate payoffs at the end of each path. A partial decision tree is shown in Figure 17.4 (page 824); you should be able to figure out what the remaining paths are.

To complete the tree, work from right to left. Calculate expected values for each chance branch and insert the result in the ellipse for use in further calculations to the left. For each decision branch, find the best choice (the highest expected value, if we're maximizing profit) and put that value in the rectangle. Continue working right to left until the optimal initial decision is determined. In the bulk carrier problem there are only two chance branches (ellipses); the expected values are:

Reserve 1: $\quad -8.0(.02) + (-2.0)(.04) + 4.0(.10) + \cdots + 10.5(.10) + 6.5(.04) = 7.504$
Reserve 2: $\quad -8.0(.02) + (-2.0)(.04) + 3.0(.10) + \cdots + 15.5(.10) + 15.0(.04) = 7.524$

The higher expected profit is 7.524, corresponding to reserving two trucks; this value is inserted at the initial decision branch, which indicates the optimal decision.

Decision trees are especially helpful, though rather large, when there is a whole sequence of decision and chance steps. For example, a law firm dealing with growing business is considering how large a lease to sign for new space. The firm can either rent two floors for three years or three floors for three years. If it rents three floors, it can sublet the third floor after a year. The profitability of the firm depends seriously on the decision. If the firm rents two floors and meets its target growth, the firm's accumulated earnings will be 2.0 million dollars after three years; if it rents two floors but has low growth, the earnings will be

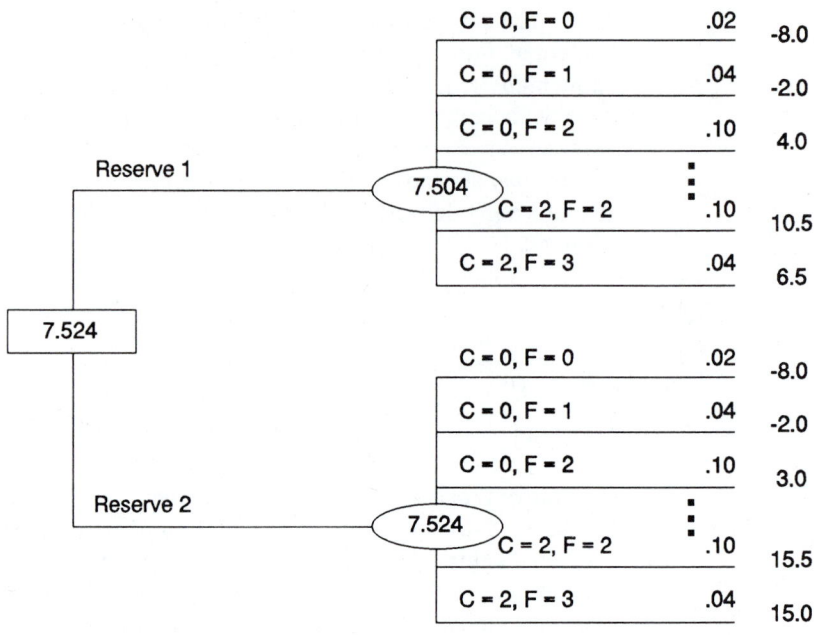

C = 0, F = 0	.02	-8.0
C = 0, F = 1	.04	-2.0
C = 0, F = 2	.10	4.0
7.504	⋮	
C = 2, F = 2	.10	10.5
C = 2, F = 3	.04	6.5

Reserve 1

7.524

Reserve 2

C = 0, F = 0	.02	-8.0
C = 0, F = 1	.04	-2.0
C = 0, F = 2	.10	3.0
7.524	⋮	
C = 2, F = 2	.10	15.5
C = 2, F = 3	.04	15.0

FIGURE 17.4   Partial Decision Tree for Bulk Carrier Problem

1.2 million. If the firm rents three floors, the situation is more complicated: An on-target performance the first year, no sublet, and another on-target performance in subsequent years yields a 2.4 (million dollar) profit, but if the first-year performance is on-target, the firm doesn't sublet, and the subsequent performance is low, the profit is only 1.4. Various other combinations of performance and subletting the third floor are evaluated as follows:

(On-target first, sublet, on-target later): 2.0 million
(On-target first, sublet, low later): 1.8 million
(Low first, non-subletting, on-target later): 1.8 million
(Low first, non-subletting, low later): 0.8 million
(Low first, subletting, on-target later): 1.4 million
(Low first, subletting, low later): 1.2 million

The firm's managing partner thinks that the probability of being on-target the first year is .5 if the firm leases two floors, .6 for three floors. Assuming that the firm leases three floors, the probability of being on-target later given an on-target first-year performance is .6, regardless of sublet decisions; similarly, the probability of on-target performance later, given low first-year performance, is .30. What should the firm do?

A decision tree for the problem is shown in Figure 17.5. The tree is filled in from right to left; for example, given that the firm rents three floors, is on-target the first year, and doesn't sublet, the expected profit is 2.4(.60) + 1.4(.40) = 2.00. Working backward, the best decision about subletting is "no" if the first-year

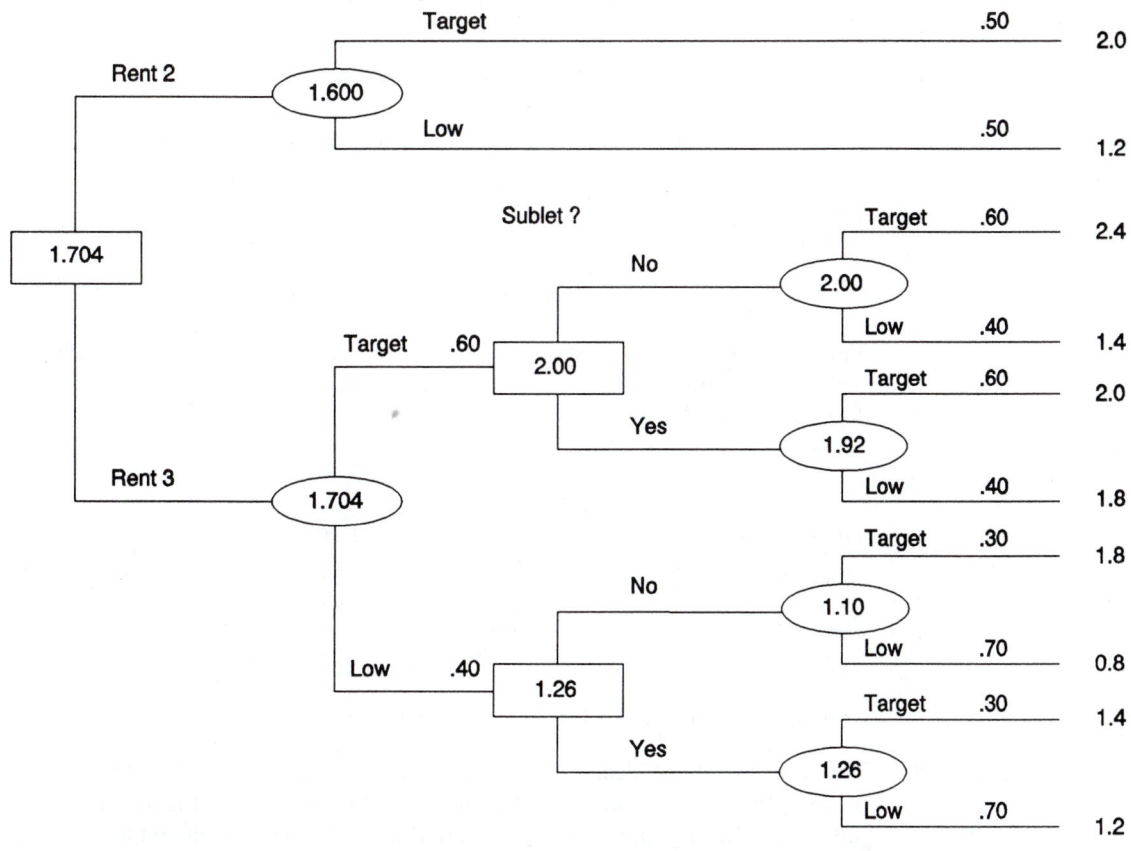

FIGURE 17.5   Decision Tree for Law Firm Leasing Problem

performance is on-target, "yes" otherwise. Working backward some more, the expected value for the "rent 3" decision is 1.704, substantially better than the 1.600 expected value of the "rent 2" decision. Before you examine the details of the tree, you might try to work out the optimal decision by hand, unaided. We wish you great good luck. The optimal decision turns out to be: Rent 3 floors originally, sublet if and only if the first-year performance is low.

One example of multistage decision trees is the problem of buying information. If there is an option to obtain (somewhat reliable) information before making a decision, a tree can help to clarify the costs and benefits. The only new feature is that conditional probabilities may have to be calculated using Bayes' Theorem for insertion in the tree.

EXAMPLE 17.19   A publisher of newspapers serving various suburban communities is considering adding a paper (either a fully separate paper or a spinoff edition of an existing one) to serve a growing area. The success of such a paper depends heavily on the future growth of businesses in the area. The publisher's payoffs and prior probabilities are shown below:

	Outcome θ_j		
Action a_i	Rapid	Moderate	Little
Full paper	5.2	−1.2	−3.6
Spin-off	2.6	1.2	−.4
No paper	.0	.0	.0
$P(\theta_j)$	.50	.30	.20

The publisher can hire a specialist to survey the suburb at a cost of $100,000 (i.e., $.10 million). The specialist will give a positive or negative recommendation. The likelihoods are assumed to be

	Outcome θ_j		
Sample Result I	Rapid	Moderate	Little
Positive	.70	.50	.20
Negative	.30	.50	.80
$P(\theta_j)$	.50	.30	.20

Construct a decision tree for the publisher's problem.

Solution   The publisher must decide whether to hire the specialist, receive the opinion (if any), then choose the desired action, and finally observe the actual growth outcome. The tree paths occur in that order. The net payoffs depend on the growth outcome and the specialist's fee. The relevant probabilities are those for the specialist's opinion and for outcomes given the opinion. Given no opinion, the prior probabilities .50, .30, and .20 apply. A probability tree for the specialist's opinions and prior probabilities is shown in Figure 17.6. From the probability tree it follows that

$$P(\text{positive}) = .35 + .15 + .04 = .54$$
$$P(\text{negative}) = .15 + .15 + .16 = .46$$

Posterior probabilities $P(\theta_j \mid \text{sample result } I)$ are then

	Sample Result I	
Outcome θ_j	Positive	Negative
Rapid	$\dfrac{.35}{.54} = .648$	$\dfrac{.15}{.46} = .326$
Moderate	$\dfrac{.15}{.54} = .278$	$\dfrac{.15}{.46} = .326$
Little	$\dfrac{.04}{.54} = .074$	$\dfrac{.16}{.14} = .348$

The resulting decision tree is shown in Figure 17.7 (page 828).

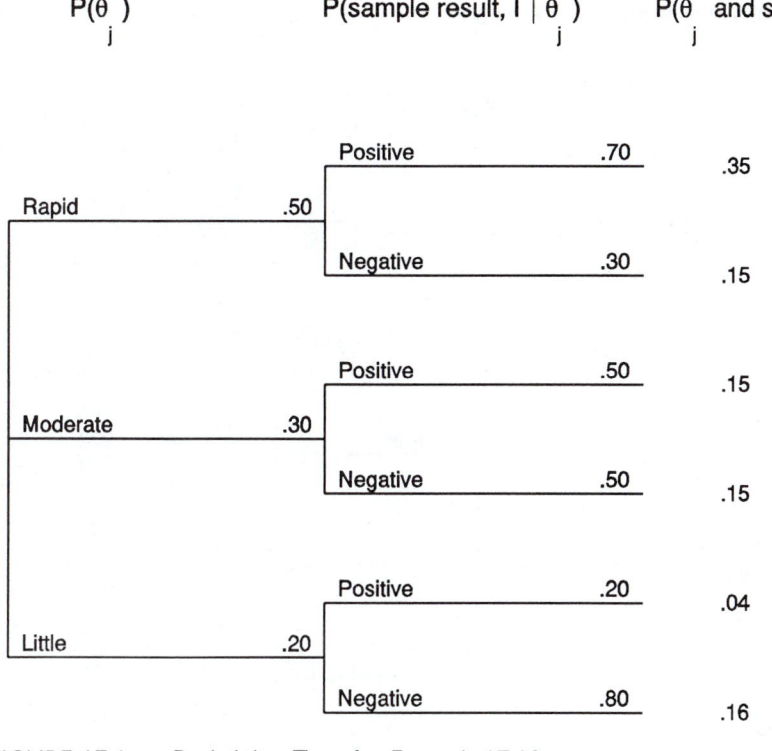

$$P(\theta_j) \qquad\qquad P(\text{sample result, I} \mid \theta_j) \qquad P(\theta_j \text{ and sample result, I})$$

		Positive	.70	.35
Rapid	.50			
		Negative	.30	.15
		Positive	.50	.15
Moderate	.30			
		Negative	.50	.15
		Positive	.20	.04
Little	.20			
		Negative	.80	.16

FIGURE 17.6   Probability Tree for Example 17.19

The optimal action sequence is to buy the opinion—if it is positive, to bring out the full paper, and if it is negative, to use the spin-off edition. ■

The virtue of a decision tree is that it forces step-by-step logic on the part of a manager facing a complex decision. Of course, trees can become very large when there are many stages, decisions, and outcomes. It is precisely in these conditions that the step-by-step logic of decision theory is most useful.

Constructing a Decision Tree

1. Identify the series of decision and chance stages. Usually this series proceeds in a natural chronological order.
2. Construct all branches, with rectangles indicating decisions and ellipses indicating chance stages.
3. On the far right, indicate the net payoff for each branch.
4. At each chance stage, insert the appropriate result probabilities. Bayes' Theorem calculations or a separate probability tree may be needed.
5. Fill in ellipses and rectangles from right to left. Each ellipse is filled by an expected-value calculation, each rectangle by a choice of the maximum expected value. Nonoptimal decisions are ignored.

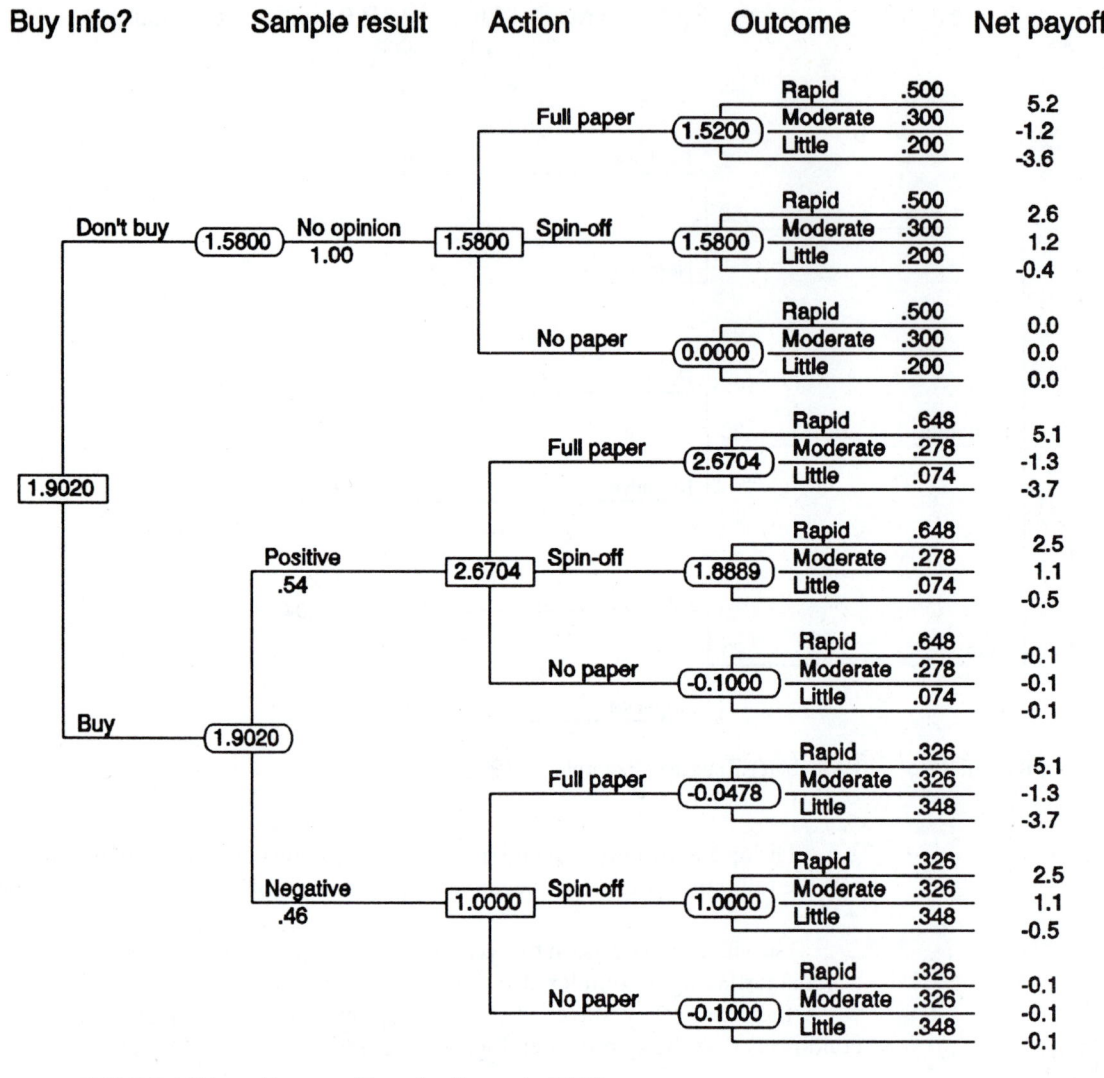

FIGURE 17.7   Decision Tree for Example 17.19

SECTION 17.5   EXERCISES

17.33 In Exercises 17.30 through 17.32 a supermarket management was considering displaying generic food products. The profitability of various actions depends on the degree of "cannibalization" of national and house brands, with the following payoffs (in hundreds of thousands of dollars) and probabilities.

	Degree of Cannibalization			
Display	25%	50%	75%	100%
30 ft., consolidated	2.4	1.2	.0	−1.2
30 ft., scattered	3.6	2.0	−1.1	−1.8
15 ft., consolidated	1.5	.8	−.4	−.8
15 ft., scattered	2.0	1.2	−.6	−1.0
Probabilities	.50	.25	.20	.05

A small survey can be run at a cost of $40,000, with the following probabilities of various survey results, given the actual degree of substitution:

	Degree of Cannibalization			
Survey Result	25%	50%	75%	100%
Little	.1	.1	.0	.0
Some	.3	.2	.1	.0
Half	.3	.3	.1	.0
Most	.2	.3	.5	.1
All	.1	.1	.3	.9

Construct a decision tree to determine whether or not to run the survey and, if it is run, what is the optimal response to each possible survey result.

17.34 Suppose that the prior probabilities given in Exercise 17.30 are changed to .40, .30, .20, and .10 for 25%, 50%, 75%, and 100%, respectively. Construct a probability tree to recalculate the probabilities for the decision tree of Exercise 17.33. Using the recalculated probabilities, find new optimal decisions. Are there any changes in optimal decisions?

17.35 A home center store that sells hardware, paint, lumber, tools, and the like must decide each week on how extensively to advertise special prices for the upcoming weekend. The store managers can prepare small, medium, or large advertising circulars. After the managers commit to the circular, they learn whether their chief competitor is advertising a major sale; at that point (Friday), they can decide whether or not to schedule extra sales staff. The net profit for the weekend depends on their decisions, the competitor's decision, and the weather (poor, fair, or good) during the weekend. The weekend profits, in thousands of dollars, are shown in the following table:

		Competitor Sale, Weather					
		(Y, P)	(Y, F)	(Y, G)	(N, P)	(N, F)	(N, G)
	(S, Y)	−5.0	−0.2	5.8	2.0	12.0	20.0
	(S, N)	2.2	2.4	5.6	5.4	13.0	16.0
Circular,	(M, Y)	−5.0	0.0	10.8	3.0	13.2	24.0
extra staff?	(M, N)	1.0	0.6	9.4	6.6	13.2	19.6
	(L, Y)	−4.6	2.2	15.8	3.6	13.8	26.6
	(L, N)	−1.2	3.0	13.0	8.8	13.6	20.4

That is, if the managers decide (S,Y), a small circular and yes to extra staff, and if the competitor decides yes to a sale and the weather is poor, the store loses $5,000 for the weekend. Other entries in the table are interpreted similarly. The competitor advertises a major sale on about 10% of all weekends. The weather forecast for the upcoming weekend has a 10% chance of poor weather, 30% chance of fair weather, and 60% chance of good weather.

a. Construct a decision tree for the manager's problem by specifying the sequence of decision and chance steps, the payoff to each path, and the probabilities associated with each chance branch.

b. At the rightmost chance step, calculate the expected profit. Enter it in the tree.

c. Working back from the right, select the optimal decisions in the rightmost decision step.

d. Continuing to work back from the right, calculate the next expected value and select the next optimal decision.

e. Summarize the optimal decisions.

17.36 The superiors of the managers in Exercise 17.35 demand that an extra 0.5 thousand dollars be added to the payoff whenever a medium-sized circular is ordered, and an extra 1.0 thousand dollars whenever a large-sized circular is ordered, to account for the general value of advertising.

a. Recalculate the decision tree.

b. How do the optimal decisions change, if at all?

17.37 The managers in Exercises 17.35 and 17.36 learn from sales representatives of suppliers that the competitor has placed several unusually large orders. They decide to increase the probability to .30 that the competitor will have a major sale.

a. Recalculate the decision tree, as modified in Exercise 17.36.

b. How do the optimal decisions change, if at all?

17.38 Refer to the security system problem of Examples (not Exercises) 17.15, 17.17, and 17.18 (pages 815, 818, and 820).

a. Construct a decision tree by entering the decision whether to buy information, the result of the sample, the action taken, and the resulting chance outcome. Enter appropriate payoffs and probabilities.

b. Working from right to left, fill in the chance-step expected values and the decision-step optimal choices. What are the optimal decisions?

17.39 Suppose the probabilities of likely, uncertain, and unlikely given that the system is not patentable are changed to .30, .40, and .30, respectively, in Exercise 17.38.

a. What parts of the decision tree can possibly change?

b. Does any optimal decision change?

17.40 Construct a decision tree to answer Exercises 17.28 and 17.29.

17.41 Suppose that the returns to a large-scale operation, shown in Exercise 17.27, are modified to be 9.9, 2.0, and -6.2 under good, fair, and poor yields, respectively. Modify the decision tree of Exercise 17.40 appropriately. Are any optimal decisions affected?

17.6   DECISIONS BASED ON A MEAN OR A PROPORTION ($\int$) ∎

In the examples of the first two sections of this chapter, the number of actions and outcomes has been quite small. In some managerial situations, the actions and outcomes may cover an entire numerical interval. The market share of a new product can range anywhere between 0 and 100%. The mean useful lifetime of commercial washing machines can be anywhere from nearly zero to some very long time. The introductory advertising expense for a new product can be almost anything. The possible replacement times for office copiers can range widely. In this section we introduce decision theory for cases in which either the action space or the outcome space covers a continuous range of possibilities.

When the decision problem involves a continuous random variable (outcome), one strategy is to model the variable directly (for example, to specify a mean and standard deviation for a roughly normal distribution). That strategy is the basic aim of this section. However, a good alternative approach is to approximate the distribution by specifying a few discrete quantities. One could define the possible results as "near the middle" (the mode or median is one of the judgments), "on the low side" (where a low percentile like the 10th is to be specified), or "on the high side" (where a high percentile like the 90th is to be specified). Keefer and Bodily (1983) discuss this approach. Given that the relevant probabilities of the decision problem are subjective estimates, we wouldn't want to claim that there is an absolute, logical preference for one approach or the other.

The basic elements of continuous-variable decision theory are the same as always; we must consider actions, outcomes, payoffs, and (when we evaluate information) likelihoods. Either the action set A or the outcome set (sample space) Θ may be continuous. The custom is to talk about losses rather than payoffs. We define the **loss** (sometimes called the **regret**) of a given action under an outcome as the difference between the maximum payoff under an outcome and the payoff to the specified action under the outcome.

loss

EXAMPLE 17.20   Suppose that the following payoff $v(a_i, \theta_j)$ table applies:

	Outcome θ_j						Expected
Action a_i	1	2	3	4	5	6	Payoff
A	12	16	12	8	4	0	10.0
B	10	15	20	15	10	5	14.5
C	4	12	18	24	18	12	16.0
D	0	7	14	21	28	21	14.7
Prior probability $P(\theta_j)$	.1	.2	.3	.2	.1	.1	

a. Calculate a loss table.
b. Show that action C minimizes expected loss.

Solution   a. The maximum payoffs for each outcome are

Outcome: 1   2   3   4   5   6
Best payoff: 12   16   20   24   28   21

The loss function is found by subtracting all payoffs in a column from the maximum payoff in that column.

	Outcome θ_j					
Action a_i	1	2	3	4	5	6
A	0	0	8	16	24	21
B	2	1	0	9	18	16
C	8	4	2	0	10	9
D	12	9	6	3	0	0
Prior probability $P(\theta_j)$	.1	.2	.3	.2	.1	.1

b. The expected losses are A, 10.1; B, 5.6; C, 4.1; D, 5.4. Therefore C is the best action. It minimizes the expected loss, or correspondingly, it maximizes the expected payoff. In fact, the difference in expected losses for different actions equals the difference in expected payoffs. Action C is 6.0 units better than action A, 1.5 better than action B, and 1.3 better than action D.   ■

It can be proved that the same action that maximizes the expected payoff also minimizes the expected loss, so it really doesn't matter whether we speak of payoffs or of losses.

loss functions   In principle, any loss table or function may be specified by a manager. In keeping with standard decision-theory notation, we label actions as a, outcomes as θ, and loss functions as $L(a, \theta)$. To keep the mathematics relatively simple, we limit our consideration to three types of loss functions for continuous outcomes and action spaces. These loss functions are

Squared error: $L(a, \theta) = c(a - \theta)^2$

Absolute error: $L(a, \theta) = c|a - \theta|$

Angle-shaped error: $L(a, \theta) = \begin{cases} c_1(a - \theta), & \text{if } a \geq \theta \\ c_2(\theta - a), & \text{if } a < \theta \end{cases}$

These loss functions are shown in Figure 17.8. Here the c's represent appropriate constants. The manager should choose an action a to minimize expected value of the selected loss function $L(a, \theta)$.

If an action can be selected anywhere in a numerical range, the optimal action is specified by some useful theorems. We assume that the outcome θ ranges

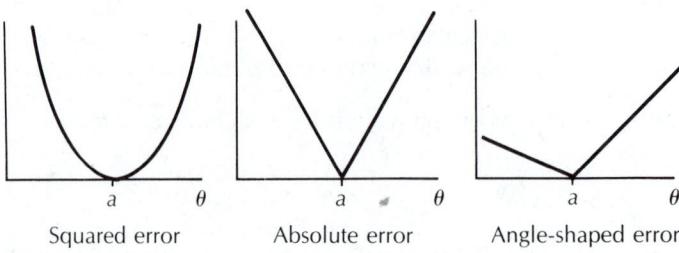

Squared error   Absolute error   Angle-shaped error

FIGURE 17.8   Three Possible Loss Functions

over a continuous interval and has a prior probability density $f(\theta)$. Then the optimal action $a*$ for each of the three types of loss functions is given below.

Squared error loss: $a* = E(\theta) = \displaystyle\int_{-\infty}^{\infty} \theta f(\theta) \, d\theta$

Absolute error loss: $a* = $ median of $f(\theta)$

Angle-shaped loss: $a* = \left(\dfrac{c_2}{c_1 + c_2} \times 100\right)$th percentile of $f(\theta)$

EXAMPLE 17.21   Suppose that the daily demand θ for beef for a large supermarket chain is assumed to have a normal density with expected value 2000 pounds and standard deviation 150 pounds. Note that we can consider both the action space and the outcome space to be continuous. The action a is the amount of beef supplied. Find the optimal action under each of the following loss functions.

   a. $L_1(a, \theta) = .005(a - \theta)^2$
   b. $L_2(a, \theta) = .5|a - \theta|$
   c. $L_3(a, \theta) = \begin{cases} 2(a - \theta), & \text{if } a \geq \theta \\ 8(\theta - a), & \text{if } a < \theta \end{cases}$

Solution   a. For loss function 1, $a* = E(\theta) = 2000$.
       b. For loss function 2, $a* = $ the median of $f(\theta)$. For a normal density the median equals the expected value, 2000.
       c. For loss function 3, $c_1 = 2$ and $c_2 = 8$, so we want the $8/(2 + 8) \times 100 = 80$th percentile of the θ distribution. According to the table of normal probabilities, the 80th percentile is at $z = .84$ standard deviation above the mean, so $a* = 2000 + .84(150) = 2126$.   ■

If θ is continuous but there are only a finite number of possible actions, we must compute the expected loss for each value of a and select the action with the smallest expected loss, $EL(a, \theta) = \int_{\text{all } \theta} L(a, \theta) f(\theta) \, d\theta$.

$\int$EXAMPLE 17.22   A computer firm develops a new high-speed printer for use with very small minicomputers. The decision whether or not to market the product depends heavily on its potential market share θ. The break-even point is $\theta = .25$. For each .01 below .25, the loss by taking action a_1 (market the product) is \$20,000. For each .01 above .25, the loss by taking action a_2 (don't market the product) is \$80,000. Thus

$$L(a_1, \theta) = \begin{cases} 20,000(.25 - \theta)100, & \text{if } \theta < .25 \\ 0, & \text{if } \theta \geq .25 \end{cases}$$

$$L(a_2, \theta) = \begin{cases} 80,000(\theta - .25)100, & \text{if } \theta > .25 \\ 0, & \text{if } \theta \leq .25 \end{cases}$$

The assumed prior probabilities for the market share θ are summarized in the continuous density function $f(\theta) = 12\theta - 24\theta^2 + 12\theta^3, 0 < \theta < 1$. Which action has the lower expected loss?

Solution

$$EL(a_1, \theta) = \int_0^1 L(a_1, \theta) f(\theta) \, d\theta$$

$$= \int_0^{.25} 20{,}000(.25 - \theta)100(12\theta - 24\theta^2 + 12\theta^3) \, d\theta$$

$$+ \int_{.25}^1 0(12\theta - 24\theta^2 + 12\theta^3) \, d\theta$$

$$= 48{,}047$$

$$EL(a_2, \theta) = \int_0^1 L(a_2, \theta) f(\theta) \, d\theta$$

$$= \int_{.25}^1 80{,}000(\theta - .25)100(12\theta - 24\theta^2 + 12\theta^3) \, d\theta$$

$$+ \int_0^{.25} 0(12\theta - 24\theta^2 + 12\theta^3) \, d\theta$$

$$= 1{,}392{,}187.5$$

Action a_1 (market the product) has a much smaller expected loss.   ■

In this section, the selection of an action has been based entirely on prior probabilities using an expected-value criterion. We have said nothing about the potential value of information or about how to use it. One concept of value of information, the expected value of perfect information (EVPI), translates very conveniently into terms of loss.

A decision maker who can forecast the final outcome perfectly will pick the action that gives the minimum loss. The minimum loss for any given outcome is zero, by definition of the loss function. Therefore the expected loss under perfect information must be zero. Under current information (using only prior probabilities), the optimal expected loss is $EL(a^*, \theta)$. Therefore

$$EVPI = EL(a^*, \theta) - 0 = EL(a^*, \theta)$$

The value and use of sample, error-prone information isn't easy. In principle, the basic idea isn't hard: Use sample information to calculate posterior probabilities using Bayes' Theorem, then select the optimal action using these posterior probabilities. Unfortunately, the mathematics required is rather extensive. We state only two useful special cases. A general treatment is given in DeGroot (1970).

normal prior distribution

One important special case occurs when the outcome θ is a population mean and is assumed to have **normal prior distribution**. Assume that the information consists of a random sample of n observations $Y_1, \ldots, Y_n$, which have expected value θ and known variance* σ^2. Then it can be proven that the posterior density of θ, given the sample information, is also normal with the

---

* The more realistic case of unknown variance gives generally similar results, but the math isn't easy. See DeGroot (1970).

expected value

$$\frac{\dfrac{\mu_0}{\sigma_0^2} + \bar{y}\left(\dfrac{n}{\sigma^2}\right)}{\dfrac{1}{\sigma_0^2} + \dfrac{n}{\sigma^2}}$$

and variance

$$\frac{1}{\dfrac{1}{\sigma_0^2} + \dfrac{n}{\sigma^2}}$$

where

μ_0 = prior expected value
σ_0^2 = prior variance
$\bar{y}$ = sample mean
σ^2 = variance of each observation (population variance)

The posterior mean (which for a normal distribution is also the median) is a weighted average of the prior mean and the sample mean. The weights depend on the sample size n, the prior variance σ_0^2, and the population variance σ^2.

EXAMPLE 17.23   A new type of bit for digging wells has been developed. The crucial property for such bits is the average useful life—the number of hours the bit can be used before it wears out. Based on general engineering principles, the manufacturer's best guess is that the mean life is 120 hours. Until a field test is conducted, there is uncertainty about the actual mean life. A normal prior distribution for μ with expected value 120 hours and standard deviation 20 hours fairly represents the uncertainty (and a great deal of uncertainty it is; there is a subjective probability of about .05 that the mean is less than 80 hours or greater than 160 hours). A set of 15 bits is tested and the life of each bit is normally distributed with the unknown mean and an assumed standard deviation of 10 hours.

    a. Assume that the sample mean lifetime is 135 hours. Find the posterior distribution of the true mean lifetime.

    b. An analysis of the potential losses and profits indicates that the bit should be marketed only if the probability that the mean life exceeds 125 hours is at least .9. Should the bit be marketed?

Solution   a. The following parameters are specified: The prior mean, $\mu_0 = 120$; the prior standard deviation, $\sigma_0 = 20$; the sample size, $n = 15$; and the population standard deviation, $\sigma = 10$. The posterior distribution of μ is normal, with expected value

$$\frac{\dfrac{\mu_0}{\sigma_0^2} + \bar{y}\left(\dfrac{n}{\sigma^2}\right)}{\dfrac{1}{\sigma_0^2} + \dfrac{n}{\sigma^2}} = \frac{\dfrac{120}{(20)^2} + 135\left[\dfrac{15}{(10)^2}\right]}{\dfrac{1}{(20)^2} + \dfrac{15}{(10)^2}}$$

$$= 134.75$$

and variance

$$\frac{1}{\frac{1}{\sigma_0^2} + \frac{n}{\sigma^2}} = 6.557$$

Note that the posterior expected value is heavily weighted toward the sample mean, because the prior uncertainty about the mean is very high.

b. By standard normal calculations

$$P(\theta > 125) = P\left(Z > \frac{125 - 134.75}{\sqrt{6.557}}\right)$$

$$= P(Z > -3.81) \approx 1.00$$

Therefore the company should market the bit.   ∎

Another special case occurs when θ is a population proportion of individuals having some property with assumed prior density

$$f(\theta) = \frac{(\alpha + \beta - 1)!}{(\alpha - 1)!(\beta - 1)!} \theta^{\alpha - 1}(1 - \theta)^{\beta - 1}, \qquad 0 \le \theta \le 1$$

beta prior density   This prior density is called a **beta density.*** A wide variety of shapes for $f(\theta)$ may be generated by taking various values for α and β (see Figure 17.9).

In this situation, assume that the sample information is Y, the number of individuals that have the specified property. Variable Y is assumed to have a binomial distribution. Then it can be shown that the posterior density of θ is also a beta density with parameters α' and β', where

$$\alpha' = \alpha + y$$
$$\beta' = \beta + n - y$$

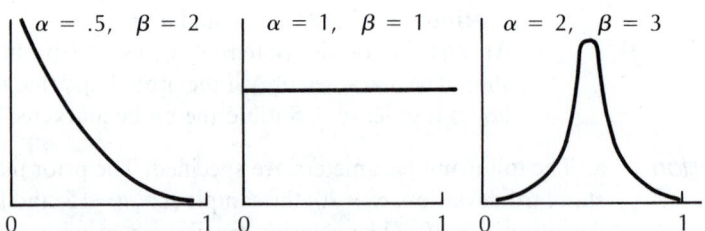

FIGURE 17.9   Beta Densities

---

* α and β may take on noninteger values. In such a case, the factorials must be interpreted by the gamma function.

The expected value of this density is $\alpha'/(\alpha' + \beta')$. For large values of α' and β' (say, both α' and β' at least 10), the density is approximately normal with variance $\alpha'\beta'/[(\alpha' + \beta')^2(\alpha' + \beta' + 1)]$.

EXAMPLE 17.24   Refer to Example 17.22. Suppose that the computer firm test-markets the printer to a random sample of 40 potential buyers, and that 8 actually buy the printer while the other 32 choose competitive products.

     a. Show that the prior density for θ, the true proportion of buyers, given by

$$f(\theta) = 12\theta - 24\theta^2 + 12\theta^3, \qquad 0 \le \theta \le 1$$

     is a beta density.

     b. Find the posterior distribution of θ.

     c. What is the approximate probability that $\theta > .25$, the break-even value?

Solution   a. $f(\theta)$ can be rewritten as

$$f(\theta) = 12\theta^{2-1}(1 - \theta)^{3-1}$$

a beta density with $\alpha = 2$ and $\beta = 3$. The expected value for this prior distribution is $\alpha/(\alpha + \beta) = .4$.

     b. We have $y = 8$ and $n - y = 32$. The posterior density is again a beta density with

$$\alpha' = 2 + 8 = 10 \qquad \text{and} \qquad \beta' = 3 + 32 = 35$$

The posterior expected value of the true proportion is $\alpha'/(\alpha' + \beta') = .222$. This is somewhat above the sample proportion .200 but well below the prior expected value $2/(2 + 3) = .400$.

     c. For these values of α' and β', a normal approximation is decent. The variance is $\alpha'\beta'/[(\alpha' + \beta')^2(\alpha' + \beta' + 1)] = .00376$, so the standard deviation is $\sqrt{.00376} = .0613$.

$$P(\theta > .25) = P\left(Z > \frac{.25 - .222}{.0613}\right)$$

$$= P(Z > .46) = .32 \qquad \blacksquare$$

These cases assume some very special probability distributions. It can be proved that these assumptions are not crucial. If the relevant sample size is reasonably large, the posterior distribution is approximately normal. The same

Central Limit Theorem   general guidelines as those for application of the **Central Limit Theorem** should apply here. Almost always, the posterior expected value falls between the prior expected value and the sample mean. The relative weights given to the prior mean and the sample mean depend on the prior uncertainty and the standard error of the sample mean. As the sample size gets larger, it often occurs that the posterior expected value approximates the sample mean (or more generally, the maximum likelihood estimate of θ). The value of incorporating prior information about θ is greatest when the sample size is small or when there is accurate information about θ.

SECTION 17.6   EXERCISES

17.42 In Exercise 17.14, a fuel oil dealer had to decide how much oil to stock at the beginning of the heating season. The payoffs depend on the severity of winter weather, as shown in the following table, with prior probabilities.

			Winter		
Order	Severe	Cold	Normal	Mild	Warm
Full	120	90	60	30	0
90%	80	90	80	70	60
80%	50	70	75	70	65
70%	30	40	50	60	70
Probabilities	.10	.20	.40	.20	.10

    a. Construct a loss table that corresponds to the payoff matrix.

    b. Verify that the order quantity that minimizes expected loss is the same quantity that maximizes expected payoff.

17.43 The benefits department of a large corporation is considering modifying the health insurance coverage for its employees. The critical unknown factor in the decision is the proportion of employees who will actually select option A. The corporation must estimate this proportion when selecting the health insurance policy. If the actual proportion turns out to be less than or equal to the estimate, the cost per year to the corporation is $100,000 times the estimated proportion. If the actual proportion exceeds the estimate, the cost per year is $200,000 times the actual proportion minus $100,000 times the estimate.

    a. Construct a payoff matrix for actual proportions $\theta = .10, .20, \ldots, .90$ and estimates $a = .10, .20, \ldots, .90$. (Note: payoff = negative of cost.)

    b. Calculate a table of losses (opportunity costs) based on this payoff matrix.

    c. Show that the loss function equals the absolute error loss with $c = 100,000$.

17.44 Refer to Exercise 17.43. The personnel department is quite uncertain about the actual proportion θ of employees who will select option A. The assumed prior density of θ is

$$f(\theta) = 6(\theta - \theta^2), \qquad \text{for } 0 \le \theta \le 1$$

    a. Show that this density is a beta density.

    b. What are the mean and median for this density?

    c. What is the optimal estimate for the corporation?

17.45 Refer to Exercises 17.43 and 17.44. Suppose that a random sample of 100 employees shows that 40 will select option A. For practical purposes, the sampling distribution may be assumed to be binomial.

    a. Calculate the posterior density of θ.

    b. Find the mean and median of this density, using a normal approximation.

    c. What is the new optimal estimate?

    d. Explain why the estimate is above .40 but only slightly so.

17.46 A chain of hardware stores is planning a "do-it-yourself" sale based on heavy local advertising. The crucial decision is how much initial inventory to stock in each store. If demand per store is greater than or equal to stock, the chain's profit per store is

$1.00 for each dollar stocked plus $.70 for each dollar of excess demand. If demand is less than stock, the profit is $1.00 for each dollar of demand less $.10 for each dollar of excess stock.

    a. Construct a payoff matrix depending on stock a and demand θ. Both stock and demand should range from 5 to 50 (in thousands of dollars per store).

    b. Calculate a loss table from this payoff matrix.

    c. Show that the loss function is angle-shaped with $c_1 = .1$ and $c_2 = .3$.

17.47 Assume that the prior distribution of demand θ in Exercise 17.46 is normal with mean 30 and standard deviation 8 (in units of thousands of dollars per store). What is the optimal amount to stock?

17.48 Refer to Exercises 17.46 and 17.47. The chain tests the sales campaign in a random sample of 12 stores. The mean demand per store in the sample is $34,000. Assume that the true standard deviation of sales is $12,000.

    a. What is the posterior distribution of θ, the demand per store for all stores in the chain?

    b. What is the optimal value of a, the amount stocked per store?

17.49 A steel producer is considering installing heat-recovery equipment to reduce energy costs. A critical unknown parameter in the decision is the amount of recoverable energy per ton of steel. This parameter determines the desired size of the equipment. Careful analysis of cost factors indicates that the loss (opportunity cost) function is

$$L(a, \theta) = 1000(a - \theta)^2 \text{ dollars}$$

where a is size and θ is recoverable energy per ton. Engineering estimates suggest that the recoverable energy is normally distributed with mean 2000 units per ton. There is considerable uncertainty in this estimate, however, as indicated by a standard deviation of 150 units per ton.

    a. Based on the engineering estimates, what is the optimal size of the equipment?

    b. What is the expected loss? [Hint: $E(\theta - a)^2 = \text{Var}(\theta) + (E(\theta) - a)^2$.]

17.50 Refer to Exercise 17.49. Ten lots of steel are produced. The mean recoverable energy per ton in the sample is 1890 units and the standard deviation (assumed to be the true one) is 120 units.

    a. Find the posterior distribution of the heat loss per ton.

    b. What is the optimal size of the equipment?

    c. What is the expected loss?

17.51 Suppose that the standard deviation in Exercise 17.50 had been 140. How would the answers to that exercise change?

17.7   BAYESIAN DECISION THEORY AND HYPOTHESIS TESTING

Many managerial problems involving statistical information can be stated in terms of either decision theory or hypothesis testing. A natural question is, Which way is better? The question has been debated for a long time to no final conclusion. In this section we make a few suggestions.

    The first thing to point out is that often it doesn't matter which approach is used. In many cases, probably the majority, the two approaches yield very similar answers. If the statistical evidence favoring one action over another is strong, either approach so indicates.

**advantage of
decision theory**

Classical significance-testing procedures were not really developed for decision problems. Rather, they were developed for inference, to answer the question, Can this apparent effect be attributable merely to random variation? Some care is needed to adapt hypothesis-testing procedures to a decision situation. As we indicated in Chapter 9, in such situations both the costs of the two kinds of error and the prior probabilities of the hypothesis should be considered in selecting α and β probabilities. Decision theory has the advantage that it incorporates these factors explicitly.

**disadvantage of
decision theory**

One disadvantage of decision-theory methods is that they require more judgment and more computation. In classical methods, once the sample size, test statistic, and α level are specified, the procedure is routine and can be computerized. To use decision theory, a manager must specify prior probabilities, likelihoods, and payoffs or losses. It isn't always easy to make these specifications in any precise, numerical form. While sensitivity analysis can be used to test the effect of changes in specification, the requirements for the use of Bayesian methods are definitely more demanding than those for the use of hypothesis testing. This is particularly true for more complex problems, such as those of multiple regression.

At a minimum, the ideas of decision theory can be used in a rough, approximate way to illuminate hypothesis-testing methods. If the cost of falsely rejecting a null hypothesis is high and the prior probability of that null hypothesis being true is substantial, a prudent manager should demand extremely strong evidence (a very small p-value) before rejecting it. If the cost of a Type II error or the prior plausibility of a research hypothesis is high, a manager might well act as if the research hypothesis is true even if the hypothesis test yields very weak evidence favoring it. It may be difficult to put precise numerical values on these high versus low judgments, but ignoring them altogether is not the answer.

Finally, all these methods are intended to help people think clearly in conditions of uncertainty. A manager who understands what the methods are (and are not) intended for, what factors are (and aren't) being considered, and what assumptions are being made should profit from their use.

Summary

This chapter has introduced some fundamental concepts and methods of statistical decision theory. The essential definitions are the action space, the outcome space, and the payoff function. Probabilities are applied to outcomes, not actions. The basic criterion for a good action, which we describe in Section 17.2, is the expected payoff to each action. The element of risk may be treated either by using variances (especially handy in portfolio analysis) or by using utility functions.

To understand how information enters decision theory, we can use Bayes' Theorem to revise probabilities in light of new information, and we can select what actions will be optimal if and when each possible piece of information occurs. We can assess the value of either hypothetically perfect information or obtainable sample information by finding the difference between the optimal payoffs with information and the optimal payoff without it. A decision tree is a useful visual way to understand the evaluation. The results for sample means and proportions in Section 17.6 may be viewed as useful shortcuts for two common situations.

KEY FORMULAS: Some Basic Ideas of Decision Theory

1. Expected return to action a_i, $R(a_i)$

$$R(a_i) = \sum_j v(a_i, \theta_j)P(\theta_j)$$

2. Variance of action a_i

$$\text{Var}(a_i) = \sum_j [v(a_i, \theta_j)]^2 P(\theta_j) - [R(a_i)]^2$$

3. $\text{Cov}(X, Y) = \sum_{x,y} (x - \mu_x)(y - \mu_y)P_{XY}(x, y) = \left(\sum_{x,y} xy P_{XY}(x, y)\right) - \mu_X \mu_Y$

4. Portfolio analysis
   a. Expected return for action $(d_1, d_2, \ldots, d_k)$

$$E\left(\sum_i d_i Y_i\right) = \sum_i d_i \mu_i$$

   b. Variance of action $(d_1, d_2, \ldots, d_k)$

$$\text{Var}\left(\sum_i d_i Y_i\right) = \sum_i d_i^2 \text{Var}(Y_i) + 2 \sum_{i<j} d_i d_j \text{Cov}(Y_i, Y_j)$$

5. Expected value of perfect information (EVPI)

$$\text{EVPI} = \sum_j (\text{maximum payoff given outcome } \theta_j)P(\theta_j)$$

$$- \text{ maximum expected return when no additional information is available}$$

6. Summary table: Likelihood (sample result I | outcome θ_j)

	Outcome θ_j		
Sample Result I	θ_1	θ_2	$\cdots$
1			
2		Likelihood (sample result I | θ_j)	
$\vdots$			

7. Posterior probability, $P(\text{outcome } \theta_j \mid \text{sample result } I)$

$$P(\theta_j \mid \text{sample result } I) = \frac{P(\text{sample result } I \mid \theta_j)P(\theta_j)}{\sum_j P(\text{sample result } I \mid \theta_j)P(\theta_j)}$$

		Sample Result I		
Outcome θ_j	1	2	3	$\cdots$
θ_1				
θ_2		$P(\theta_j \mid \text{Sample result } I)$		
$\vdots$				
$P(\text{Sample result } I)$				

8. Expected return on action a_i given sample result I

$$E(\text{return on } a_i \mid \text{sample result } I)$$
$$= \sum_j v(a_i, \theta_j) P(\text{outcome } \theta_j \mid \text{sample result } I)$$

		Sample Result I		
Action a_i	1	2	3	$\cdots$
a_1				
a_2		$E(\text{return on } a_i \mid \text{sample result } I)$		
$\vdots$				

9. Expected value of sample information (EVSI)

$$\sum_I (\text{maximum expected return} \mid \text{sample result I}) P(\text{sample result } I)$$
$$- \text{Maximum expected return using no sample information}$$

10. Loss functions
   a. Square error: $L(a, \theta) = c(a - \theta)^2$
   b. Absolute error: $L(a, \theta) = c|a - \theta|$
   c. Angle-shaped error: $L(a, \theta) = \begin{cases} c_1(a - \theta), & \text{if } a \geq \theta \\ c_2(\theta - a), & \text{if } a < \theta \end{cases}$

CHAPTER 17   EXERCISES

17.52 A consumer-products manufacturer is considering two possible promotion campaigns for its line of skin care products. The aim of each campaign is to increase
market share. Success depends heavily on whether the company's two main
competitors also have campaigns; both, either one, or neither competitor may do so.
a. Specify an action space.
b. Specify a set of states of nature (outcomes).

17.53 The market research staff of the company of Exercise 17.52 estimates the following
market share payoffs:

	Competing Promotions			
	Both	A only	B only	Neither
Promotion 1	28	35	37	44
Promotion 2	34	37	36	40

The company's executives believe that there is a 60% chance that either competitor will have a promotional campaign, independently of the other competitor (and of their own company's decision). The costs of the two promotions are virtually equal.
a. Calculate the expected market share for each of the two promotion campaigns.
b. Calculate the standard deviation of market share for each campaign. Which campaign has lower risk?

17.54 Refer to Exercise 17.53. Assume a utility function for market share x of the form

$$U(x) = x - .002x^2$$

a. Sketch $U(x)$. Does this function reflect risk aversion?
b. Which promotion has a higher expected utility?
c. Does the preferred promotion have higher expected payoff? lower risk? both?

17.55 Refer to Exercises 17.53 and 17.54. Do any of the conclusions change if the probability that either competing firm stages a campaign is decreased to .5 or increased to .7?

17.56 A soft-drink bottler is considering the possibility of either replacing or upgrading its facilities for making nonreturnable bottles. A key element in the decision is whether the state passes a bottle bill requiring returnable, deposit soft-drink bottles. Both 5-cent deposit and 10-cent deposit bills have been proposed. The following payoffs have been estimated:

	Bottle Bill		
Action	None	5-Cent	10-Cent
No change	25	20	15
Replace	50	10	-30
Upgrade	35	20	5

The firm believes that there is a 60% chance of no bottle bill being passed, a 30% chance of a 5-cent bill, and a 10% chance of a 10-cent bill.
a. Which action has the highest expected payoff?
b. Which action has the lowest variance?

17.57 Refer to Exercise 17.56. Assume that the bottler's utility, as a function of payoff x, is

$$U(x) = \log_{10}(x + 200)$$

Which action has the highest expected utility?

17.58 Refer to Exercises 17.56 and 17.57. The payoffs for the upgrade action may all be in error by as much as ± 5 units. The probabilities of no bill and the 5-cent bill may be .7 and .2 in one direction or .5 and .4 in the other. Conduct a sensitivity analysis of the bottler's decision problem. Four extreme combinations of payoffs and probabilities may be obtained by varying the upgrade payoffs and the probabilities in both directions.

17.59 The joint probability distribution $P_{XY}(x, y)$ of $x =$ return of $1 invested in stock A and $y =$ return to $1 invested in stock B is as follows:

		\multicolumn{5}{c}{y}
		.08	.09	.10	.11	.12
	.08	.00	.00	.02	.04	.09
	.09	.00	.01	.09	.09	.01
x	.10	.00	.06	.18	.06	.00
	.11	.01	.09	.09	.01	.00
	.12	.09	.04	.02	.00	.00

a. Calculate $\text{Cov}(X, Y)$ and $P_{XY}(x, y)$.
b. Explain why the covariance is negative.

17.60 Refer to the joint distribution of Exercise 17.59.
a. Calculate the expected return and risk for a portfolio with $500 invested in each of the two stocks.
b. Calculate the expected return and risk for an investment of $1000 in stock A.
c. Why is the risk for the portfolio in part (a) so much lower than the risk for the investment in part (b)?

17.61 A growing company plans to issue additional stock in two months, and it must decide whether to offer all common, all preferred, or half of each. The company's treasurer predicts the yields of each choice, depending on the state of the stock market at the time of issue, as follows (all figures in millions of dollars):

	\multicolumn{5}{c}{State of Market}
Offer	Down 8%	Down 4%	Steady	Up 4%	Up 8%
Common	92.0	96.0	100.0	104.0	108.0
Preferred	97.0	98.0	99.0	100.0	101.0
Half/half	94.5	97.0	99.5	102.0	104.5

The treasurer assesses the probabilities of the five market states (from lowest to highest) as .25, .30, .20, .15, and .10.
a. Which action has the highest expected yield?
b. Which action has the lowest variance?

17.62 The president of the company of Exercise 17.61 assesses the market probabilities as .10, .30, .40, .15, and .05. Do the answers to that exercise change if these revised probabilities are used?

17.63 Refer to Exercises 17.61 and 17.62. Assume the utility function $U(x) = 1 - e^{-.01x}$, where $x =$ yield in millions of dollars.
a. Which action has the highest expected utility based on the treasurer's probabilities of Exercise 17.61?

b. Which action has the highest expected utility based on the president's probabilities of Exercise 17.62?

17.64 A trust officer for a bank assesses the expected returns, variances, and covariances for four investment opportunities. The results (expressed as return per dollar) are

Investment:	1	2	3	4
Expected return, μ_i:	1.089	1.090	1.091	1.086

	Variance-Covariance Matrix			
	1	2	3	4
1	.048	.049	.050	−.038
2	.049	.052	.052	−.041
3	.050	.052	.058	−.043
4	−.038	−.041	−.043	.060

(Variances are along the diagonal of this matrix; all other entries are covariances.)

a. Calculate the expected return and standard deviation for a portfolio consisting of $4000 invested in each of investments 1, 2, and 3.

b. Calculate the expected return and standard deviation for a portfolio consisting of $3000 invested in each of investments 1, 2, 3, and 4.

c. Is either portfolio clearly preferred to the other (assuming a somewhat risk-averse investor)?

17.65 Assume that the investor's expected utility function in Exercise 17.64 is equal to

expected return − .001 variance

Which portfolio has the higher expected utility?

17.66 The admissions staff at a selective university must decide each year on an admissions policy—tight, normal, or relaxed. The desirability of each policy, as measured on a 60-point scale, depends on the "yield," the percentage of accepted applicants who actually enroll. For a tight admissions policy the desirability of high, normal, and low yields are 50, 40, and 30, with respective probabilities .2, .4, and .4. For a normal policy, the corresponding desirability numbers are 46, 42, and 36 and the probabilities are .3, .4, and .3, respectively. For a relaxed policy, the desirability numbers are 44, 40, and 37, with probabilities .4, .4, and .2.

a. Construct a decision tree for the staff's problem.

b. What is the optimum policy, assuming that high expected desirability numbers are preferable?

17.67 The decision problem for the admissions staff of Exercise 17.66 is complicated by the possibility of establishing a wait list. If the original yield to normal or relaxed policies is low, the staff will consider a partial dip into the wait list. If the policy is normal, a partial dip will yield high, medium, or low success with probabilities .1, .4, and .5 and desirabilities 44, 39, and 35. If the policy is relaxed, a partial dip will yield high, medium, or low success with probabilities .2, .4, and .4 and desirabilities 42, 40, and 36. If the original yield to a tight policy is normal, the staff can consider a partial dip (probabilities .2, .5, .3, desirabilities 46, 42, 38 for the three success categories). If the original yield for a tight policy is low, the staff can consider a partial dip (probabilities .2, .4, .4, desirabilities 42, 34, 28) or a full dip (probabilities .1, .3, .6, desirabilities 42, 38, 30). In all other cases, no recourse to the wait list is considered, and the desirability numbers of Exercise 17.66 still hold. If the staff chooses not to dip into the wait list, the desirability numbers also hold.

a. Create a multistage decision tree for this problem.

b. In each case where a wait list decision is contemplated, what is the optimal action?

c. What is the optimal initial admissions policy?

17.68 One member of the admissions staff of Exercises 17.66 and 17.67 thinks that the claimed yield and weight list probabilities are too optimistic. Instead, this staffer believes that the original high, normal, and low yield probabilities should be .1, .4, and .5, regardless of the admission policy, and that the wait list probabilities for high, medium, and low success should be .1, .5, and .4, uniformly for all decisions. If these probabilities are used, how (if at all) do the optimal decisions change?

17.69 The production engineering staff of a manufacturing company has developed two possible redesigns of its production process. Method 1 requires substantial additional training of workers and a relatively modest investment. Method 2 requires less training than even the current method but a heavy investment in automated equipment. The net profit attributable to each method depends on the rate of turnover of workers as shown in the following payoff matrix (in thousands of dollars):

Process	Turnover Rate		
	Down 10%	No Change	Up 10%
Method 1	+80	+40	−100
Method 2	−40	+20	+50
Current	30	0	−40

The labor relations manager believes that there is a 30% chance that, over the relevant time period, the turnover rate will go down by 10%, a 60% chance of no change, and a 10% chance that it will go up by 10%.

a. Which process has the highest expected return?

b. How valuable would perfect information about turnover rate be?

17.70 The company of Exercise 17.69 can hire a consultant to survey a sample of workers and provide an opinion about likely future turnover. The following likelihoods are assumed for the consultant's opinion:

Consultant's Opinion	Actual Turnover Rate		
	Down 10%	No Change	Up 10%
Down sharply	.30	.05	.00
Down slightly	.40	.20	.10
Constant	.20	.50	.20
Up slightly	.10	.20	.40
Up sharply	.00	.05	.30

a. Calculate the probabilities of each possible opinion and the posterior probabilities of actual rates given each opinion. You may want to use a probability tree.

b. Calculate the action that has the highest expected value given each opinion. You may want to use a decision tree.

c. The consultant's fee is $4000. Should the company hire the consultant?

17.71 The likelihoods assumed in Exercise 17.70 are not known with complete accuracy. As part of a sensitivity analysis, the following alternative likelihoods are assumed:

Consultant's Opinion	Actual Turnover Rate		
	Down 10%	No Change	Up 10%
Down sharply	.40	.00	.00
Down slightly	.50	.15	.00
Constant	.10	.70	.10
Up slightly	.00	.15	.50
Up sharply	.00	.00	.40

a. Do these alternative likelihoods indicate greater or lesser value to the consultant's opinion as compared to the likelihoods of Exercise 17.70?

b. Rework Exercise 17.70 assuming the alternative likelihoods. Which decisions, if any, should be changed?

17.72 The director of media selection for an advertising agency must decide on placement for an ad campaign promoting a "full-flavor" beer. The basic choice is between television commercials on broadcasts of professional football only and commercials on both baseball and football telecasts. If the football audience also constitutes the baseball audience, there is little gain to advertising in both places. After analysis, it is determined that the both-place strategy is preferable only if the proportion θ of baseball watchers who are also football watchers is less than .60. Complete accurate data on this proportion is unavailable. A reasonable prior density for θ is

$$f(\theta) = 20(\theta^3 - \theta^4), \quad \text{for } 0 \le \theta \le 1$$

a. Verify that this density is a beta density.

b. Sketch the density.

c. What is the prior probability that the proportion θ is less than .6?

17.73 Refer to Exercise 17.72. A random sample of television viewers shows that, of 128 baseball watchers, 70 are also football watchers.

a. Find the posterior distribution of the proportion θ.

b. What is the expected value of θ?

c. Use a normal approximation to calculate the probability that the proportion is less than .60.

17.74 Refer to Exercise 17.73. Do the hypothesis-testing methods of Chapter 9 lead to the rejection of $H_0: \theta \ge .60$ and support of $H_a: \theta < .60$ with an α of .05? Compare the conclusion of such a test to the answer to Exercise 17.73, part (c).

17.75 A trucking firm regularly sends loads from Chicago to Baltimore. The standard route for these loads passes over many toll roads, so the toll cost is substantial. An alternate route has become feasible with the opening of a new interstate highway. The new route will be cheaper if the mean additional travel time is less than 2 hours. Calculation of relative mileage and terrain leads to a normal prior distribution of this mean. The prior expected value is 1.40 hours with a prior standard deviation of .40 hours. Find the prior probability that the true mean is less than 2 hours.

17.76 The trucking firm of Exercise 17.75 tests the new route by sending nine loads. The times required may be regarded as the results of a random sample. The sample mean additional time is 1.33 hours and the standard deviation (which may be assumed to be the true one) is 1.80 hours.

a. What is the posterior distribution of the true mean additional time?

b. What is the probability that the true mean is less than 2 hours?

17.77 a. Use the hypothesis-testing methods of Chapter 9 on the random sample in Exercise 17.76. Show that $H_a: \mu < 2$ is not supported at $\alpha = .05$ $\alpha = .10$.

b. The answer to part (b) of Exercise 17.76 gave a high probability that the mean is less than 2. Why do the two approaches yield apparently conflicting answers?

17.78 A chain of auto supply stores is preparing a promotion for its line of car radios and cassette decks. A debate arises over whether to aim the promotion primarily at new car buyers or at current owners. The profitability of the two actions depends on new car sales for the last three months of the year. The payoff matrix in thousands of dollars is estimated to be

	Sales				
Aim	Down 10%	Down 5%	Steady	Up 5%	Up 10%
New car buyers	25	75	125	175	225
Current owners	100	80	60	40	20

As of May, when the planning stage for the promotion is in process, the prior probabilities for last-quarter sales are .10, .20, .30, .30, and .10 for down 10%, down 5%, steady, up 5%, and up 10%, respectively.

a. Which action maximizes the expected payoff?

b. Calculate a loss table. Which action minimizes the expected loss?

17.79 Refer to Exercise 17.78. Rather than making an immediate decision, the company can defer its choice until new-car sales data are available for the summer months (June, July, and August). These data may lead to changes in the probabilities for last-quarter sales. Historical data on the relation between summer sales and last-quarter sales yield the following likelihoods:

Summer Sales	Last-Quarter Sales				
	Down 10%	Down 5%	Steady	Up 5%	Up 10%
Down 10%	.30	.20	.10	.15	.05
Down 5%	.30	.25	.20	.20	.15
Steady	.20	.20	.40	.20	.20
Up 5%	.15	.20	.20	.25	.30
Up 10%	.05	.15	.10	.20	.30

a. Calculate posterior probability distributions for last-quarter sales, given each possible value of summer sales.

b. What is the optimal action given each possible value of summer sales?

17.80 The cost to the company in Exercise 17.79 of delaying its choice is $4000, primarily in the cost of preparing duplicate materials. Should the company wait?

17.81 A chain of appliance dealers must place an order for two new models of dishwashers. The total order size is fixed; the manufacturer will supply only 10,000 units. The chain can order any proportion of deluxe and standard units. An analysis of the profitability of sales of the units produces the following table of profits (in thousands of dollars):

Proportion of Deluxe Units Ordered, a	Proportion of Deluxe Units Demanded, θ					
	.05	.10	.15	.20	.25	.30
.05	110	110	110	110	110	110
.10	95	120	120	120	120	120
.15	80	105	130	130	130	130
.20	65	90	115	140	140	140
.25	50	75	100	125	150	150
.30	35	60	85	110	135	160

This table can be extended to other proportions.
a. Calculate a loss table.
b. Show that the loss function is angle shaped, with $c_1 = 300$ and $c_2 = 200$.
c. What is the optimal value of a for a specified prior density $f(\theta)$?

17.82 A commercial real estate agency is planning to adopt a local area network system to enable its agents to share information about conditions of various properties and about potential clients. A decision must be made whether to set up an in-house training program or to contract the training out. The payoff to the network depends heavily on the turnover rate of agents. The president of the agency estimated the payoffs in thousands of dollars over a two-year period according to the following table.

Training	Turnover		
	Low	Normal	High
In-house	75	65	55
Contract	85	60	35

The president noted that many of the current agents were in personal situations that would make it easy for them to move. Therefore, it seemed reasonable to assess the probability of low turnover as about .1, of normal turnover as about .5, and of high turnover as about .4.
a. Which action has the higher expected payoff?
b. Which action has the higher variance?
c. How much of a problem does the agency president have in trading off risk for return?
d. Do your answers to the previous three questions change if the probabilities of low, normal, and high turnover are changed to .2, .6, and .2, respectively?

17.83 The president of the agency in Exercise 17.82 could defer a decision until next spring, when demand for office space becomes known, at a substantial cost in lost efficiency and sales. Demand has some relation to agent turnover; higher demand creates more opportunities for agents to move. Demand is by no means an infallible indicator, however. Based on experience, the president estimates the following likelihoods of demands given turnover rates.

| | | Turnover | |
Demand	Low	Normal	High
Poor	.5	.2	.1
Fair	.3	.6	.4
Good	.2	.2	.5

Assume that the original probabilities (.1, .5, .4) of low, normal, and high turnover apply.

a. Calculate revised probabilities of turnover rates given each of the three possible demands.

b. Show that the optimal (highest expected payoff) training decision is to use in-house training, regardless of the demand level.

c. How much would the information about spring demand be worth to the agency president? (This question may not require any calculation. If information can't change the decision, then what is its value?)

17.84 Construct a decision tree for Exercise 17.83, assuming that the cost of waiting for demand information is $20,000. What is the difference in payoffs between "wait" and "don't wait" decisions? Why?

17.85 An airline has the option to expand its operations at an airport where it is a strong competitor. It can buy rights to use 0, 1, or 2 extra gates now; when a new terminal is completed in a year, it can buy rights to an additional 0, 1, or 2 extra gates. The value of extra gates depends on the growth of the regional economy in the next year, and on whether takeoff and landing rights at peak times must be restricted when the new terminal opens. The airline's economists estimate that the probabilitiy of a regional growth rate 1% higher than forecast is .20, the probability of regional growth right at forecast is .50, and the probability of regional growth 1% lower than forecast is .30. The local operations manager believes that the probability of takeoff/landing restrictions is .60 if growth is higher than forecast, .40 if it's right at forecast, and .20 if growth is lower than forecast. After accounting for operating profits and the value of gate rights, accountants for the airline have come up with the following table for various combinations of gate rights, growth, and restrictions.

| | | Growth, Restriction | | | | | |
		$(+1, Y)$	$(+1, N)$	$(0, Y)$	$(0, N)$	$(-1, Y)$	$(-1, N)$
	(0, 0)	13.8	15.7	5.1	5.8	6.2	8.0
	(0, 1)	13.0	17.8	3.9	6.5	3.6	9.0
	(0, 2)	12.0	19.9	2.5	7.2	0.6	10.0
Gates now,	(1, 0)	16.0	18.8	7.3	7.8	2.4	5.5
gates next	(1, 1)	14.7	21.0	5.8	9.1	0.2	6.8
year	(1, 2)	13.2	23.0	4.0	10.3	-2.8	8.1
	(2, 0)	18.0	21.6	5.6	6.3	-8.0	3.3
	(2, 1)	15.5	23.0	3.6	7.4	-11.4	4.3
	(2, 2)	12.0	25.4	1.4	8.5	-16.8	5.2

Is any choice of gates clearly unreasonable because that choice is inferior to another regardless of growth and restriction? (Note: A choice can't be unreasonable if it's best for a particular combination of growth and restriction.)

17.86 a. Construct a decision tree for Exercise 17.85. Specify decision and chance steps. Note that the airline must decide now whether to buy additional gate rights in the old terminal, but it can wait until after observing growth to decide on gate rights in the new terminal.

b. Calculate expected values and optimal decisions, using the tree. What is the optimal number of gates to buy now?

17.87 The airline's accounting staff discovers an error in computing the profit for the $(0, 0)$, $(+1, Y)$ entry in the table of Exercise 17.85. It should be 11.0, not 13.8. Modify the decision tree in Exercise 17.86. How, if at all, do optimal decisions change?

CASE Decisions, Uncertainty, and Information

One of the recurring tasks of the treasurer of a small company is to invest short-term cash surpluses. Typically, the company accumulates a surplus of about $200,000 in September, which can be invested until major payments come due in March. The company has a long-standing banking relationship, so that the treasurer feels compelled to use the bank's investment vehicles.

There are basically three possibilities for the company's short-term investments: A certificate of deposit (CD) that yields 4.1% for six months, a bond, and a mutual fund. The return to the bond and the mutual fund depend on the interest rate at the end of the period. The bond also will yield 4.1% (net after commissions) if there is no change in interest rate. For every percentage point of increase in the interest rate in March, the yield decreases by 0.8%. The mutual fund yields 4.0% (after commissions); the effect of an interest rate change is less clear than for a bond, but a reasonable guess is that a one-point increase in interest decreases yield by 0.6%. The interest rate effect works in the other direction, too; each percentage point of decrease in interest rate increases the bond yield by 0.8% and the mutual fund yield by 0.6%.

Obviously, the key issue is the possible change in interest rates. The treasurer believes that there is just about a 50-50 chance that the interest rate will stay the same over the relevant period. If it does change, it is somewhat more likely to go up than to go down. In any case, the change (up or down) shouldn't be more than a full percentage point; more likely, any change will be half a percentage point.

The treasurer has an additional option, to subscribe to a rate forecasting service at a cost of $300. The treasurer isn't very impressed with the forecasts. In the past, when interest rates stayed where they were, the forecast said so half the time; the other half, the forecast divided equally between increase and decrease. When there was a full point increase, the forecast called for an increase only about half the time, said no change a quarter of the time, and actually predicted a decrease the other quarter of the time. When there was a full point decrease, it was more or less the reverse, the forecast calling for a lower rate half the time, unchanged a quarter of the time, and increase the other quarter of the time. Presumably, when the actual change was half a point or so, the forecast accuracy would be in between the results for change and the results for no change.

The treasurer has asked you to prepare a report on the question of which investment to choose and whether to subscribe to the forecasting service. Because these questions come up every year, the treasurer would like to have a standard procedure to analyze the problem under various possible future economic conditions. The company owns several computers with spreadsheet programs that can do the arithmetic quickly. The procedure will have to be approved by the president of the company, who has a severe allergy to mathematical formulas but is quite good at dealing with words, graphs, and numbers.

Appendix: More on Expected-Utility Theory

In any decision-theory problem we begin with a set of mutually exclusive actions A, a set of possible outcomes Θ, payoffs $v(a_i, \theta_j)$ associated with each action a_i and outcome θ_j, and outcome probabilities $P(\Theta_j)$. It is then possible to compute the expected payoff and variance for each action. Utility theory is used to bridge the gap between a decision rule using expected payoffs (which ignores risk) and one that uses a risk criterion, the variance of payoffs, but ignores the expected payoff. Utility theory offers a compromise between these two outcomes by incorporating risk into a payoff decision rule. This is done by converting the expected payoff for a given action into an expected utility.

gambles

Utility theory is based on **gambles**. A gamble is an action defined by a set of possible payoffs and a set of probabilities associated with the payoffs. The payoffs in this book are numerical results (e.g., dollars). In principle, the payoffs need not be numerical, but is appears to be somewhat difficult to evaluate nonnumerical gambles in terms of numerical utilities.

utility

The **utility** of a gamble to a particular manager can be inferred from the manager's preference for a gamble relative to another action that has a fixed, certain payoff. For example, suppose as an investment manager you are faced with the problem of choosing between the following two actions with corresponding payoffs:

a_1:   Receive $10 for certain
a_2:   Receive $120 with probability .5 or lose $80 with probability .5

The expected payoffs for the two actions are

$$R(a_1) = \$10 \quad \text{and} \quad R(a_2) = 120(.5) - 80(.5) = \$20$$

Since a_2 has the higher expected payoff, you may well choose action a_2 if you can sustain an $80 loss. For this situation, action a_2 has a higher utility for you than action a_1.

Now suppose that you are faced with a choice between two similar types of actions—but with stakes (payoffs and risks) that are quite a bit higher:

a_1:   Receive a certain, fixed payoff of $100,000
a_2:   Receive a payoff of $1,000,000 with probability .5 or a loss of $600,000 with probability .5

For this situation, the expected payoffs are

$$R(a_1) = \$100{,}000$$

and

$$R(a_2) = \$1{,}000{,}000(.5) - \$600{,}000(.5) = \$200{,}000$$

Even though the expected payoff for action a_2 is \$100,000 more than the expected payoff for action a_1, you may consider action a_1 to be more desirable since your firm may not be able to sustain a loss of \$600,000. Under these circumstances, action a_1 has a higher utility for you even though it has a lower expected payoff.

The selection of an action in the last two examples depends on the evaluation of risk relative to the payoff. That's what utility theory is all about. By forcing a manager to make choices between various gambles and other actions with certain payoffs, we can examine how a manager evaluates risk in light of the expected payoffs for various actions.

We can illustrate the assignment of numerical utilities to actions with an example. Suppose that we want to find a manager's utilities for possible payoffs for five different actions. These result in possible changes in the firm's net worth after one year ranging from -2 to $+3$ (millions of dollars). We can assign arbitrary utility values to any two selected payoffs. For example, the outcome -2 (a decrease of 2 million dollars net worth) is least desirable, and the outcome $+3$ is most desirable. A utility value of 0 for outcome -2, $U(-2) = 0$, and a utility value of 1 for outcome $+3$, $U(3) = 1$, may be assigned arbitrarily.* Based on these two utilities and on the manager's preference, we can define certain gambles and determine the utilities for other actions. A gamble that has .5 probabilities for -2 and 3 has expected utility $.5U(-2) + .5U(3) = .5$. Suppose that a manager feels that this gamble is no better and no worse than an action that guarantees 0 change. Because the manager is indifferent about a guaranteed 0 change and the 50-50 gamble between -2 and $+3$, the utility of a guaranteed 0 payoff is $U(0) = .5U(-2) + .5U(3) = .5$.

Now suppose that the manager is indifferent to a 50-50 gamble between 0 and 3 and a guaranteed payoff of 1.2; then the utility of the 1.2 payoff is $U(1.2) = .5U(0) + .5U(3) = .5(.5) + .5(1) = .75$. So far, we have

Payoff:	-2	0	1.2	3
U(outcome):	.00	.50	.75	1.00

By obtaining the manager's preferences among many such gambles, we can eventually obtain a whole curve of utilities, which might look something like the curve in Figure 17.10.

EXAMPLE 17.25   Suppose that a manager can equate the following 50–50 gambles to actions that would result in the corresponding fixed, certain payoffs.

---

* This is true because neither adding a constant to all utilities nor multiplying them by a positive constant changes the relative ranking of expected utilities.

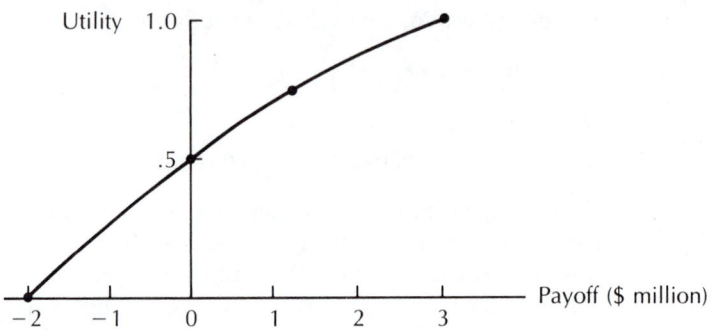

FIGURE 17.10   Hypothetical Utility Curve

Payoffs for 50–50 Gambles	Guaranteed Payoff Equivalent
Gamble 1: loss −10, gain 30	0
Gamble 2: lose 0, gain 30	10
Gamble 3: gain 10, gain 30	18
Gamble 4: loss −10, gain 0	−6

Using these specified gambles and the alternate actions with fixed, guaranteed payoffs, develop appropriate utilities and sketch a utility function.

Solution   We may arbitrarily set the utility for the lowest payoff $U(-10) = 0$ and the utility for the largest payoff $U(30) = 1$. For the first gamble, $U(0) = .5U(-10) + .5U(30) = .5$. From the second gamble, $U(10) = .5U(0) + .5U(30) = .75$. From the third gamble, $U(18) = .5U(10) + .5U(30) = .875$. Finally, $U(-6) = .5U(-10) + .5U(0) = .25$. The utility function might appear as shown in Figure 17.11.

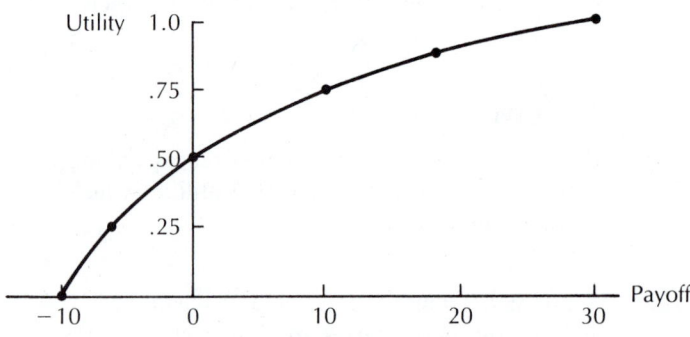

FIGURE 17.11   Approximate Utility Function for Example 17.25   ∎

CHAPTER
18

SOME ALTERNATIVE SAMPLING METHODS

sample random sample

We discussed the basic idea of random sampling in Chapter 6. There we defined a **simple random sample**: A set of n observations chosen from a population of size N in such a way that all possible samples of size n have an equal chance of being selected. The formulas (particularly those for standard errors) of later chapters were based on an assumption of simple random sampling. There are other ways of choosing random samples, and in this chapter we discuss a few of them. The chapter serves as an introduction to a broad area of statistical theory called **sample survey design**.

sample survey design

Why should a manager bother with fancy sample survey designs? The purpose of selecting a sample is to obtain the most accurate information possible for a given expenditure (of both time and money). Accuracy is measured by amount of bias, which ideally is zero, and by probable sampling variability as summarized by a standard error. In some situations it may be possible to break the population down into subpopulations, called **strata**, that have relatively small within-strata variability. Then **stratified sampling** can yield better accuracy for a given sample size. Stratified sampling is the subject of Section 18.2. There are other situations in which simple random sampling is too expensive; for example, if we tried to interview a simple random sample of 1000 adult Americans, the travel costs for interviewers would be horrendous. An alternative sampling procedure is to select 50 ZIP code areas randomly and then interview 20 randomly selected individuals in each area. This procedure is an example of two-stage **cluster sampling**; we discuss cluster sampling in Sections 18.3 and 18.4. The advantage of cluster sampling is that the cost per observation can be much lower than the cost of simple random sampling. These sampling methods (and some other slightly more complex ones we discuss in Section 18.5) can be useful in getting good information economically.

stratified sampling

cluster sampling

One obvious area of application of sample survey design is in market research. Another rapidly growing area of application is in accounting, particularly auditing. We can expect the use of these methods to grow even more in the future.

18.1   TAKING A SIMPLE RANDOM SAMPLE ∎

Selecting a good simple random sample takes planning and effort. A sloppy sample can reflect several potential biases. Because most good approaches to sampling involve simple random sampling (from the whole population, or from strata, or of clusters), it is worthwhile to consider some pitfalls to avoid in sampling.

One kind of potential bias arises in selecting the entities (people, accounts, or whatever) to be sampled. Survey statisticians distinguish the **target population** (the set of entities that ideally should be sampled) from the **sampling frame** (the set of entities that actually can be sampled). In a study of consumer satisfaction with the service departments of new-car dealers, the target population may be all private purchasers of new cars within the past two years. The sampling frame may well be the set of all purchasers for whom dealers have current addresses. Purchasers who have moved (without forwarding addresses) are part of the target population, but because they cannot be sampled, they are not part of the sampling frame. Naturally, the best possible situation is that the target population and sampling frame be identical. This is often possible in auditing situations, but it is very difficult to achieve in sampling human populations. When the target population and sampling frame differ, a manager must usually assume that those entities that cannot be sampled have the same characteristics as those that can. If the assumption is false, one kind of **selection bias** occurs.

target population

sampling frame

selection bias

EXAMPLE 18.1   A chain of paint and wallpaper stores in a mid-size city is considering strategies for pricing its house brand of interior paints. A critical element of this strategy is consumer perception of the quality of its paints. A survey is planned of current homeowners in the city. A list of those who paid real-estate taxes the previous year is used to select a sample of 200 homeowners. Identify the target population and the sampling frame. Are there any major selection biases?

Solution   The target population presumably is all current homeowners in the city, but ideally it is the persons in each home who decide on paint purchases. The sampling frame is all homeowners who paid real-estate taxes the previous year. A minor selection bias is the omission of homeowners who paid no taxes, because it seems plausible that their homes would be neglected and poor candidates for painting. A more serious bias is the omission of those who purchased homes in the current year. These people are likely to be major paint purchasers and quite possibly less familiar with local (as opposed to national) paint brands. ∎

A subtle form of selection bias can occur if members of the sampling frame have unequal probabilities of being sampled. We would not be very impressed by a study of consumer satisfaction with new-car dealers' service departments that proceeded by taking a random sample of service orders and interviewing the car owners. People who were happy with the service would bring their cars back several times and therefore would have a high probability of being sampled. Conversely, people who didn't like the service would have a low selection

size bias
: probability. This kind of bias is called a **size bias** because it often reflects the size or number of transactions of an individual in the sampling frame.

EXAMPLE 18.2

A brokerage firm anticipates an increase in the margin requirements for purchasers of common stock and wishes to estimate what fraction of its customers would have been affected by such an increase during the past year. A clerk randomly samples 1000 purchases of common stocks during the year and determines the fraction of these purchases that would have been affected. Identify a size bias.

Solution

The target population is customers, not purchases. The sampling procedure is biased toward those customers who purchased stock frequently during the past year.   ∎

There is a different kind of bias that can arise even though no selection biases are present. Once selected, individuals in a sample may not give accurate responses. At the extreme, many individuals may not respond at all. As many as

nonresponse bias
: 80% or even more of individuals contacted by mail surveys do not respond; a 30% nonresponse rate in telephone surveys is considered better than average. In any competent survey, a follow-up mechanism is provided to give some indication as to whether (first-round) nonrespondents differ from respondents, but this device has only limited value. The problem of nonresponse is perhaps the most serious limitation of the usefulness of surveys of human populations. A great deal of ingenuity has been expended to minimize nonresponse rates, because this is a crucial part of any survey design.

sensitive-question bias
: In addition, those who do respond may not respond accurately. Questions can be ambiguous or "loaded" to favor a certain answer. In some situations, certain answers may be more socially acceptable or polite than others. Pretesting usually reveals any serious defects in questions. You can use the randomized-response technique we will discuss in Section 18.5 to deal with sensitive questions.

This litany of potential problems doesn't mean that surveys are impossible, but it does mean that they must be done carefully.

Assuming that a survey design has removed potential biases, the remaining source of error is "luck of the draw": Pure random variability. Here is where the standard-error formulas of statistical theory are useful. In the next several sections we set out standard errors for various types of survey design. The aim of a survey typically is estimation (rather than hypothesis testing). The desired population parameter may be the population mean μ, the population proportion π, or the total value in the population, which we denote by τ. Because the population mean is the total divided by the population size N (that is, $\mu = \tau/N$), it follows that $\tau = N\mu$. If the sample mean $\bar{y}$ is used to estimate μ, a natural estimate of the population total τ is $N\bar{y}$.

We developed confidence-interval methods for a mean in Chapter 8. We found that t tables should be used for small samples. In most sample surveys, sample sizes are large enough that normal tables may be used. Remember that the normal table "magic number" for 95% confidence intervals is 1.96.

Estimation of μ and τ Using Simple Random Sampling

Point estimate

of μ: $\bar{y}$
of τ: $N\bar{y}$

95% confidence interval

for μ: $\bar{y} \pm 1.96\hat{\sigma}_{\bar{Y}}$
for τ: $N\bar{y} \pm 1.96N\hat{\sigma}_{\bar{Y}}$

where

$$\hat{\sigma}_{\bar{Y}} = \sqrt{\frac{s^2}{n}\left(\frac{N-n}{N-1}\right)}$$

The quantity $(N - n)/(N - 1)$, called a **finite population correction factor**, accounts for the fact that there is slightly more information in a sample of 50 from a population of 100 than in a sample of 50 from a population of 10,000. Recall that the absolute sample size primarily determines sample accuracy.

EXAMPLE 18.3   An industrial firm is concerned about the time per week spent by employees on certain trivial tasks. The time-log sheets of a simple random sample of 50 employees in one week show that the average amount of time spent on these tasks is 10.31 hours with a sample variance of 2.25. If the corporation employs 750 people, estimate the total number of hours lost per week on these trivial tasks. Give a 95% confidence interval for τ.

Solution   We are told that the population consists of $N = 750$ employees, from which a random sample of $n = 50$ time-log sheets is obtained. The mean amount of work lost for the sampled employees is 10.31. An estimate of the total amount of time lost per week is

$$N\bar{y} = 750(10.31) = 7732.5 \text{ hours}$$

The 95% confidence interval for τ is

$$N\bar{y} \pm 1.96N\hat{\sigma}_{\bar{Y}}$$

where

$$\hat{\sigma}_{\bar{Y}} = \sqrt{\frac{s^2}{n}\left(\frac{N-n}{N-1}\right)}$$

Substituting into the formula for $\hat{\sigma}_{\bar{Y}}$, we obtain

$$\hat{\sigma}_{\bar{Y}} = \sqrt{\frac{2.25}{50}\left(\frac{750-50}{750-1}\right)} = .205$$

The corresponding 95% confidence interval for τ, the total number of hours lost per week on these trivial tasks for the 750 employees, is

$$7732.5 \pm 1.96(750)(.205)$$

or

$$7732.5 \pm 301.4$$

Thus we are 95% confident that the time lost per week is between 7431.1 and 8033.9 hours. This is a staggering amount—approximately 26% of the scheduled work hours. ∎

Rather than estimating a population mean or total, sample surveys are frequently conducted to estimate the proportion of experimental units in a population that possess a specified characteristic. For example, suppose we are interested in determining a television program's rating by estimating the proportion of families in a given district who watch the program during a given week. Let $y_i = 0$ if the ith family in a simple random sample of n does not possess the characteristic of interest (did not watch the show) and $y_i = 1$ if the ith family does possess the characteristic of interest. Then the proportion of elements in the sample possessing the specified characteristic also represents the sample mean of the y_i's. With this convention, $\hat{\pi}$ is actually $\bar{y}$, and π can be thought of as the mean for the entire population of 0's and 1's. Thus formulas developed for estimating μ can also be used for estimating π. Fortunately, these formulas simplify considerably, as shown below:

Estimation of π Using Simple Random Sampling

Point estimate of π: $\qquad\qquad \hat{\pi} = \dfrac{y}{n}$

95% confidence interval for π: $\qquad \hat{\pi} \pm z_{\alpha/2}\hat{\sigma}_{\hat{\pi}}$

where

$$\hat{\sigma}_{\hat{\pi}} = \sqrt{\frac{\hat{\pi}(1 - \hat{\pi})}{n}\left(\frac{N - n}{N - 1}\right)}$$

EXAMPLE 18.4   A business manager in charge of a large-volume product is concerned about the proportion of customers with delinquent accounts and the proportion of customers with a balance due exceeding $500. An internal audit is made of a random sample of 120 accounts from a total of 2280 accounts. From this sample, 17 are found to be delinquent and 64 have balances due in excess of $500. Use these data to give a 95% confidence interval for

    a. the proportion of delinquent accounts;
    b. the proportion of accounts with balances in excess of $500.

Solution   a. The point estimate of the proportion of customers with delinquent accounts is

$17/120 = .14$. The 95% confidence interval for π is

$$.14 \pm 1.96 \sqrt{\frac{.14(.86)}{120}\left(\frac{2280 - 120}{2280 - 1}\right)}$$

or

$$.14 \pm .060$$

We are 95% confident that the actual proportion of delinquent accounts is between .080 and .200.

b. In a similar way, the point estimate of the proportion of accounts with balances in excess of $500 is $64/120 = .53$. The corresponding approximate 95% confidence interval for π is

$$.53 \pm 1.96 \sqrt{\frac{.53(.47)}{120}\left(\frac{2280 - 120}{2280 - 1}\right)}$$

or

$$.53 \pm .087$$

We are 95% confident that the actual proportion of accounts with balances in excess of $500 is between .443 and .617.   ∎

The ideas in this section are essentially a review of ideas from Chapters 6–8. The procedures of the next sections extend these ideas to more complicated sample survey designs. While the formulas become more complicated, the essential idea of estimate plus or minus 1.96 standard errors for 95% confidence still holds.

SECTION 18.1   EXERCISES

18.1   Refer to Example 18.1. Suppose that the paint store chain conducts a telephone survey based on random selection of telephone numbers. (Business phones can be excluded.) Identify the sampling frame and any major selection biases.

18.2   A state commission investigates problems of wheelchair-bound people in obtaining access to public transit and to state offices. A survey is planned in which 150 wheelchair-bound people each keep a diary recording all instances of inaccessibility. The 150 people are selected from the membership list of a statewide association for handicapped persons. Identify the target population, the sampling frame, and possible selection bias.

18.3   Assume that the survey of the previous exercise can be regarded as a simple random sample. Suppose that 66 of the 150 persons report encountering an inaccessible public building. Give a 95% confidence interval for the population proportion.

18.4   An organization that specializes in arranging rentals and trades of vacation homes wishes to survey the condominium apartments on a certain large island off the Florida coast. Interviewers are instructed to call on randomly chosen apartments during the month of March between 10 A.M. and noon. Follow-up calls are made between 3 P.M. and 5 P.M. the next day, and then again between 7 P.M. and 9 P.M. the following day. Apartment owners are interviewed to determine their interest in renting out their apartments during specified times. What biases could be present in this study?

18.5 Assume that the survey conducted in Exercise 18.4 can be regarded as a simple random sample. Suppose that, of 221 apartment owners who respond, 83 are willing to rent their apartments. The mean availability of the 83 apartments is 4.2 weeks and the standard deviation is 2.8 weeks.

   a. Find a 95% confidence interval for the population proportion of rentable apartments.

   b. Find a 95% confidence interval for the true mean availability of rentable apartments.

18.6 In an audit of sales for a certain store, an accounting clerk is told to keep a running total of sales accounts. Every sale that takes the total into the next $10,000 interval is selected for examination. For example, a sale that took the total from $29,972 to $30,041 would be selected. The sales are assumed to be in random order, for all practical purposes. Does this procedure yield a practically unbiased simple random sample of all sales?

18.7 Suppose that the sample of Exercise 18.6 yields 267 sales with a mean amount of $112.24 and a standard deviation of $91.49. Calculate a 95% confidence interval for the true mean sale amount, assuming that the sample constitutes a simple random sample.

18.8 Did you identify any bias in Exercise 18.6? What effect do you think it has on the confidence interval of Exercise 18.7?

18.2   STRATIFIED RANDOM SAMPLING

Stratification offers an alternative to simple random sampling and in many instances increases the accuracy of information available for estimating μ or τ.

Stratified Random Sample

A stratified random sample is a sample obtained by dividing the population of experimental units into nonoverlapping groups, called *strata*. A simple random sample is selected from each stratum.

The first step in selecting a stratified random sample is to clearly specify the strata, making certain that each experimental unit can be classified into only one stratum. For example, in a local election survey we may wish to stratify registered voters according to one of five voting precincts. If precinct boundary lines are clearly defined and the voter registration lists are up to date, there should be no problem in placing registered voters into the appropriate precincts (strata).

After the experimental units are divided into strata, we select a simple random sample of unit from each stratum.

Before presenting the formulas for the estimates of μ (or π) and τ, we need the following notation:

I: Number of strata
N_i: Number of elements in stratum i ($i = 1, 2, \ldots, I$)
n_i: Sample size in stratum i
N: Total population size; $N = \sum_i N_i$
n: Total sample size; $n = \sum_i n_i$

$\bar{y}_i$:   Sample mean in stratum i
s_i^2:   Sample variance in stratum i

The point estimation procedures for μ and τ are given next.

Estimation of μ and τ Using Stratified Random Sampling

Point estimate

of μ: $\bar{y}_{ST} = \dfrac{\sum_i N_i \bar{y}_i}{N}$

of τ: $N\bar{y}_{ST}$

95% confidence interval

for μ: $\bar{y}_{ST} \pm z_{\alpha/2}\hat{\sigma}_{\bar{Y}_{ST}}$
for τ: $N\bar{y}_{ST} \pm z_{\alpha/2}N\hat{\sigma}_{\bar{Y}_{ST}}$

where

$$\hat{\sigma}_{\bar{Y}_{ST}} = \frac{1}{N}\sqrt{\sum N_i^2\left(\frac{N_i - n_i}{N_i - 1}\right)\frac{s_i^2}{n_i}}$$

EXAMPLE 18.5   A wholesale food distributor in a large metropolitan area would like to know if demand is great enough to justify adding a new product to the stock. To aid in making the decision, the wholesaler plans to add this product to a sample of the stores serviced to estimate average monthly sales. Because only four large chains are serviced in the metropolitan area, it is administratively convenient to stratify the stores, with each chain serving as a stratum. There are 24 stores in stratum 1, 36 in stratum 2, 30 in stratum 3, and 30 in stratum 4. The wholesaler decides that there is enough money to obtain data in a total of 20 retail stores. If we allocate the total sample size among the strata with each sample size proportional to the stratum size, we obtain sample sizes of 4, 6, 5, and 5 for the four chains, respectively. Thus the product is introduced into 4 stores chosen at random from chain 1, 6 stores from chain 2, and 5 stores each from chains 3 and 4. The sales (in hundreds of dollars, after a one-month trial period) are tabulated below. Estimate the average sales for the month and give a 95% confidence interval for μ.

	Stratum (Chain)			
	1	2	3	4
	89	91	108	102
	80	99	96	120
	92	93	100	104
	100	105	93	101
		111	93	123
		101		
Sample mean	89	100	98	110
Sample variance	78.67	55.60	39.50	112.50

Solution   The point estimate of μ, the average monthly sales for all stores across the four chains, is

$$\bar{y}_{ST} = \frac{\sum_i N_i \bar{y}_i}{N} = \frac{24(89) + 36(100) + 30(98) + 30(110)}{120} = 99.8$$

The 95% confidence interval for μ is

$$\bar{y}_{ST} \pm 1.96 \hat{\sigma}_{\bar{y}_{ST}}$$

where

$$\hat{\sigma}_{\bar{y}_{ST}} = \frac{1}{N} \sqrt{\sum_i N_i^2 \left(\frac{N_i - n_i}{N_i - 1}\right)\left(\frac{s_i^2}{n_i}\right)}$$

$$= \frac{1}{120}\left[(24)^2 \left(\frac{24 - 4}{24 - 1}\right)\frac{78.67}{4} + (36)^2 \left(\frac{36 - 6}{36 - 1}\right)\frac{55.60}{6} \right.$$

$$\left. + (30)^2 \left(\frac{30 - 5}{30 - 1}\right)\frac{39.50}{5} + (30)^2 \left(\frac{30 - 5}{30 - 1}\right)\frac{112.5}{5} \right]^{1/2}$$

$$= \frac{1}{120}\sqrt{43731.0} = 1.74$$

The corresponding confidence interval is

$$99.8 \pm 1.96(1.74), \qquad \text{or} \qquad 99.8 \pm 3.41$$

We are 95% confident that the average monthly sales for these 120 stores are in the interval 96.39 to 103.21 (thousand dollars). ∎

The standard error of $\bar{y}_{ST}$ depends on the estimated variances s_i^2 in the various strata, while the standard error of $\bar{y}$ based on simple random sampling depends on s^2, which estimates the overall population variance. If there is relatively little variability in each strata as compared to the overall population variability, stratification yields a smaller standard error, and hence more accurate estimation, than does simple random sampling. In the language of Chapter 12, **variability within and between strata**   it is desirable to have relatively low **variability within strata** as compared to the **variability between strata**. In other words, it is desirable to divide the population into relatively homogeneous (low-variability) strata.

EXAMPLE 18.6   Refer to Example 18.5 and assume that the tabulated data were obtained from a simple random sample of stores. Compute a 95% confidence interval for μ and compare it to the one obtained in Example 18.5 using stratified random sampling.

Solution   One can easily verify that the sample mean and variance for the $n = 20$ observations are $\bar{y} = 99.8$ and $s^2 = 111.85$ with $N = 120$. The 95% confidence interval for μ is

$$99.8 \pm 1.96 \hat{\sigma}_{\bar{y}}$$

where

$$\hat{\sigma}_{\bar{y}} = \sqrt{\frac{s^2}{n}\left(\frac{N - n}{N - 1}\right)} = \sqrt{\frac{111.85}{20}\left(\frac{120 - 20}{119}\right)} = 2.17$$

so the 95% confidence interval for μ using simple random sampling is

$$99.8 \pm 1.96(2.17), \quad \text{or} \quad 99.8 \pm 4.25$$

Note that this interval is wider than that for stratified random sampling. This will not always be so; but when stratification produces smaller, homogeneous groups, stratified random sampling is an improvement over simple random sampling. ■

The mathematics behind the formulas for stratified random sampling follows from the formulas for linear combinations of independent random variables (see Appendix 4A). The point estimate $\bar{y}_{ST}$ is a weighted average of the strata means $\bar{y}_i$; the weights are the strata sizes N_i. Thus

$$\sigma_{\bar{Y}_{ST}}^2 = \text{Var}\left(\sum_i \frac{N_i}{N} \bar{y}_i\right) = \sum_i \frac{N_i^2}{N^2} \sigma_{\bar{Y}_i}^2$$

Because a simple random sample is taken within each stratum,

$$\sigma_{\bar{Y}_i}^2 = \frac{\sigma_i^2}{n_i}\left(\frac{N_i - n_i}{N_i - 1}\right)$$

The standard-error formula for $\bar{y}_{ST}$ follows by estimating each true stratum variance σ_i^2 by the sample variance s_i^2.

Stratified sampling can also be used to estimate a population proportion π. For example, suppose that the personnel department of a large corporation is interested in estimating the proportion of all vested employees who participate in a company-run stock savings program. If the divisions of the corporation represent strata and a simple random sample of n_i employee records is obtained from stratum i ($i = 1, \ldots, I$), then a point estimate and approximate confidence interval can be obtained using the following formulas:

Estimation of π Using Stratified Random Sampling

Point estimate: $\hat{\pi}_{ST} = \dfrac{1}{N} \sum N_i \hat{\pi}_i$

95% confidence interval: $\hat{\pi}_{ST} \pm z_{\alpha/2} \hat{\sigma}_{\hat{\pi}_{ST}}$

where

$$\hat{\sigma}_{\hat{\pi}_{ST}} = \frac{1}{N} \sqrt{\sum_i N_i^2 \left(\frac{N_i - n_i}{N_i - 1}\right) \frac{\hat{\pi}_i(1 - \hat{\pi}_i)}{n_i}}$$

EXAMPLE 18.7   The sample data for the survey of vested employees is shown for each of the three divisions of the corporation. Use these data to estimate π, the proportion of all vested employees who participate in the company-run stock program.

Stratum (Division)	Number N_i of Vested Employees	Sample Size n_i	Number Who Participate
1	450	45	12
2	300	30	15
3	760	76	30

Solution The point estimate of π is

$$\hat{\pi}_{ST} = \frac{1}{N} \sum_i N_i \hat{\pi}_i = \frac{1}{1510} [450(.27) + 300(.50) + 760(.39)] = .38$$

The 95% confidence interval for π can be found after we compute $\hat{\sigma}_{\hat{\pi}_{ST}}$.

$$\hat{\sigma}_{\hat{\pi}_{ST}} = \frac{1}{N} \sqrt{\sum_i N_i^2 \left(\frac{N_i - n_i}{N_i - 1}\right) \frac{\hat{\pi}_i(1 - \hat{\pi}_i)}{n_i}}$$

$$= \frac{1}{1510} \left[(450)^2 \left(\frac{450 - 45}{450 - 1}\right) \frac{(.27)(.73)}{45} + (300)^2 \left(\frac{300 - 30}{300 - 1}\right) \frac{(.5)(.5)}{30} \right.$$

$$\left. + (760)^2 \left(\frac{760 - 76}{760 - 1}\right) \frac{(.39)(.61)}{76} \right]^{1/2}$$

$$= \frac{1}{1510} \sqrt{3106.67} = .037$$

The corresponding 95% confidence interval for π is

$$.38 \pm 1.96(.037), \quad \text{or} \quad .38 \pm .073$$

The actual proportion of vested employees in the corporation who participate in the stock program is estimated to be in the interval .307–.453. ∎

advantages of stratified random sampling   There are several reasons that stratified random sampling often results in an increase in information for a given cost. First, the data often are more homogeneous within each stratum than in the population as a whole. Taking advantage of the reduced variability within each stratum, we obtain estimates that have smaller confidence intervals than comparable estimates from a simple random sample of the same size. Second, the cost of conducting a stratified random sample tends to be less than that for a simple random sample. The elements in each stratum are usually located within a smaller geographic area, and separate teams of interviewers can be sent to the strata for collection of the sample data. Third, separate estimates of population parameters for each stratum can be obtained without additional sampling.

SECTION 18.2   EXERCISES

18.9 A group of college students conducts a survey to determine the average number of college hours (credits) an undergraduate student must earn for various majors to obtain a bachelor's degree from a large university. To do this, the departments of the university are stratified by colleges. Use the sample data shown below to estimate μ, the average number of credit hours required for a bachelor's degree. Construct a 95% confidence interval.

College	Number of Departments	Sample Data
Architecture and fine arts	7	192, 199, 188, 191
Arts and sciences	40	186, 195, 186, 189,
		186, 192, 193, 195,
		200, 183, 187, 192
Business administration	6	193, 186, 180, 182
Education	8	197, 198, 188, 196
Engineering	20	202, 203, 213, 202,
		204, 206, 210, 206

18.10 Refer to Example 18.5. Use the sales data from all 20 stores as a single random sample. Estimate the mean sales with a 95% confidence interval. Compare your results to those of Example 18.5. Does it appear that stratification has helped?

18.11 A study of television-viewing habits stratifies people in a metropolitan area by gender and age. Random samples chosen within strata, and the sampled individuals record one week's prime-time viewing in diaries. The results are as follows:

Gender	Age	Number in Population (Thousands)	Number in Sample	Mean	Standard Deviation
F	18–34	312	127	10.4	4.2
M	18–34	317	129	11.2	3.8
F	35–49	285	116	9.8	3.9
M	35–49	279	114	10.3	4.1
F	50–64	248	101	10.6	4.5
M	50–64	221	90	11.0	4.8
F	65+	189	77	10.1	4.4
M	65+	114	46	10.9	3.9
		1965	800		

a. Calculate a 95% confidence interval for the overall mean viewing time.
b. Calculate a 95% confidence interval for the mean viewing times of all people age 65 and over. Note that only the last two strata are relevant.

18.12 Recalculate a 95% confidence interval for the overall mean viewing time in Exercise 18.11, assuming that the eight strata represent equal proportions of the population. Is there a substantial shift in the interval? Explain why.

18.13 In a study of the 2000 largest nonfinancial corporations, a sample of 250 firms is chosen and the number of firms that value inventory on the LIFO principle is determined. The sample is stratified into five major industries. The results are as follows:

Industry Type	Number of Firms	Number Sampled	Number Using LIFO
A	425	66	16
B	489	61	10
C	443	55	9
D	379	47	11
E	165	21	4

Calculate a 95% confidence interval for the overall proportion of firms using LIFO.

18.14 Refer to the data of Exercise 18.13. Calculate a 95% confidence interval assuming (incorrectly) that the data resulted from a simple random sample. Do the point estimate and confidence interval differ substantially from those found in Exercise 18.13? Can you explain why?

18.3   CLUSTER SAMPLING ∎

When units to be sampled are grouped together, possibly geographically, a third type of sampling, cluster sampling, can often give more information for a given cost than simple or stratified random sampling. In cluster sampling, just as in stratified sampling, we think of the individual units as being divided in groups. One difference is that stratification is based on a characteristic of interest such as gender, age, or educational level, whereas clusters are based on physical nearness in space or time. Another difference is that we sample units in all strata, but only in some clusters.

one-stage cluster sample   A **one-stage cluster sample** is obtained by taking a simple random sample of clusters and then observing all the units in the sampled clusters. For example, a suburban town council considering a major house reassessment project might divide the town into blocks, choose a random sample of blocks, and send an assessor to value each house on the sampled blocks. In this way, the assessor can spend more time assessing and less time running around town, which wouldn't be the case for a simple random sample of individual houses scattered throughout the town.

advantage of cluster sampling   In general, the advantage of cluster sampling increases as units become more separated, and the cost of proceeding from one unit to another increases. The limitation of cluster sampling is that one tends to get less information per unit sampled because the units within a cluster tend to be similar. For example, in our assessment example, houses in a block tend to be similarly valued. Once an assessor finds, for example, that one house in a block is valued at 180% of the old assessment, it's very likely that all the other houses will have similar values, so the extra information from the other houses won't tell us much. In contrast to stratified sampling, we would like to have little variability among clusters and high variability within clusters; unfortunately, clusters tend to be rather homogeneous in practice.

If a cluster sample is taken, the point estimates of a mean or a proportion are, in effect, the sample mean or sample proportion. The standard error for cluster sampling is somewhat more complicated than for simple random sampling. It must reflect the possible relation among units in a single cluster. The notation is as follows:

N: Number of clusters

n: Number of clusters selected in a simple random sample

m_i: Number of elements in cluster i ($i = 1, 2, \ldots, N$)

$\bar{m}$:   Average cluster size for the sampled clusters; $\bar{m} = \sum_i m_i / n$

M: Number of elements in the population; $M = \sum_i m_i$

$\bar{M}$:   Average cluster size for the population; $\bar{M} = M/N$; if $\bar{M}$ is unknown, it may be estimated by $\bar{m}$

T_i: Total for all observations in the ith cluster

The estimation procedures for μ and τ are presented next.

Estimation of μ and τ Using Cluster Sampling

Point estimate

of μ: $\bar{y}_c = \dfrac{\sum T_i}{\sum m_i}$

of τ: $M\bar{y}_c$

95% confidence interval

for μ: $\bar{y}_c \pm z_{\alpha/2}\hat{\sigma}_{\bar{y}_c}$

for τ: $M\bar{y}_c \pm z_{\alpha/2}M\hat{\sigma}_{\bar{y}_c}$

where

$$\hat{\sigma}_{\bar{y}_c} = \sqrt{\left(\frac{N-n}{nN\bar{M}^2}\right)\frac{\sum_i (T_i - \bar{y}_c m_i)^2}{n-1}}$$

EXAMPLE 18.8   Interviews are conducted in each of 25 blocks sampled from a set of 415 blocks in a city. The data on income for adult males are presented below. Use the data to estimate the average income per adult male in the city using a 95% confidence interval.

Cluster i	Number of Adult Males m_i	Total Income per Cluster T_i	Cluster i	Number of Adult Males m_i	Total Income per Cluster T_i
1	8	$96,000	4	5	$65,000
2	12	121,000	5	6	52,000
3	4	42,000	6	6	40,000

Cluster i	Number of Adult Males m_i	Total Income per Cluster T_i	Cluster i	Number of Adult Males m_i	Total Income per Cluster T_i
7	7	75,000	17	6	32,000
8	5	65,000	18	5	22,000
9	8	45,000	19	5	45,000
10	3	50,000	20	4	37,000
11	2	85,000	21	6	51,000
12	6	43,000	22	8	30,000
13	5	54,000	23	7	39,000
14	10	49,000	24	3	47,000
15	9	53,000	25	8	41,000
16	3	50,000			
	$\sum_i m_i = 151$	$\sum_i T_i = \$1,329,000$			

Solution   The best estimate of the population mean μ is

$$\bar{y}_c = \frac{\sum_i T_i}{\sum_i m_i} = \frac{\$1,329,000}{151} = \$8801$$

To calculate the confidence interval, we must compute

$$\sum_i (T_i - \bar{y}_c m_i)^2 = \sum_i T_i^2 - 2\bar{y}_c \sum_i T_i m_i + \bar{y}_c^2 \sum_i m_i^2$$

Thus we have

$$\sum_i T_i^2 = T_1^2 + T_2^2 + \cdots + T_{25}^2$$

$$= (96,000)^2 + (121,000)^2 + \cdots + (41,000)^2 = 82,039,000,000$$

$$\sum_i m_i^2 = m_1^2 + m_2^2 + \cdots + m_{25}^2 = (8)^2 + (12)^2 + \cdots + (8)^2 = 1047$$

$$\sum_i T_i m_i = T_1 m_1 + T_2 m_2 + \cdots + T_{25} m_{25}$$

$$= (96,000)(8) + (121,000)(12) + \cdots + (41,000)(8)$$

$$= 8,403,000$$

and hence

$$\sum_i (T_i - \bar{y}_c m_i)^2 = 82,039,000,000 - 2(8801)(8,403,000) + (8801)^2(1047)$$

$$= 15,227,502,247$$

Because M is not known, the $\bar{M}$ appearing in the formula for standard error must be estimated by $\bar{m}$, where

$$\bar{m} = \frac{\sum_i m_i}{n} = \frac{151}{25} = 6.04$$

Then

$$\left(\frac{N-n}{Nn\bar{M}^2}\right)\left(\frac{\sum_i(T_i - \bar{y}_c m_i)^2}{n-1}\right) = \left(\frac{415-25}{(415)(25)(6.04)^2}\right)\left(\frac{15,227,502,247}{24}\right)$$

$$= 653,785$$

and the approximate 95% confidence interval is

$$8801 \pm 1.96\sqrt{653,785}, \quad \text{or} \quad 8801 \pm 1584.8$$

We are 95% confident that the mean income for adult males in the city lies between $7216.20 and $10,385.80. Although the width of this confidence interval is rather large, it can be reduced by sampling more clusters, thereby increasing the sample size. ∎

A population proportion can also be estimated using cluster sampling. For example, in a survey of rank-and-file workers, the leaders of a labor union may be interested in the proportion of members who favor a proposed new benefits package. If the locals of the labor union represent the clusters and a simple random sample of clusters is selected, we can estimate the population proportion π in the following way. Let a_i denote the number of laborers in cluster i who favor the new benefits package ($i = 1, 2, \ldots, n$) and let m_i denote the number of members of the local in the ith cluster. Then an estimate of π is given by

$$\hat{\pi}_c = \frac{\sum_i a_i}{\sum_i m_i}$$

The details are given below:

Estimation of π Using Cluster Sampling

Point estimate:
$$\hat{\pi}_c = \frac{\sum_i a_i}{\sum_i m_i}$$

95% confidence interval:
$$\hat{\pi}_c \pm z_{\alpha/2}\hat{\sigma}_{\hat{\pi}_c}$$

where

$$\hat{\sigma}_{\hat{\pi}_c} = \sqrt{\left(\frac{N-n}{nN\bar{M}^2}\right)\frac{\sum(a_i - \hat{\pi}_c m_i)^2}{n-1}}$$

Note: n should be 20 or more unless all the cluster sizes are approximately the same. ∎

EXAMPLE 18.9 Suppose that a random sample of 25 local unions is selected from the total of 520 possible clusters. The sample data from the 25 clusters are shown in the following table. Use these data to construct an approximate 95% confidence interval for π.

Cluster	Number of Members m_i	Number Favoring a_i	Cluster	Number of Members m_i	Number Favoring a_i
1	65	30	14	115	60
2	78	35	15	150	92
3	80	49	16	43	31
4	40	16	17	67	17
5	50	32	18	39	24
6	100	51	19	26	14
7	120	75	20	98	56
8	75	40	21	106	52
9	80	39	22	112	76
10	85	52	23	59	33
11	90	55	24	71	47
12	73	19	25	82	55
13	61	34			

Solution   For these data, you should verify that

$$\sum m_i = 1965, \qquad \sum m_i^2 = 174{,}499, \qquad \bar{m} = 78.60$$
$$\sum a_i = 1084, \qquad \sum a_i^2 = 56{,}424, \qquad \sum a_i m_i = 97{,}669$$

The estimate of π, the proportion of all union members favoring the new benefits package, is

$$\hat{\pi}_c = \frac{\sum a_i}{\sum m_i} = \frac{1084}{1965} = .55$$

To calculate $\hat{\sigma}_{\hat{\pi}_c}$ we need

$$\sum (a_i - \hat{\pi}_c m_i)^2 = \sum a_i^2 - 2\hat{\pi}_c \sum a_i m_i + \hat{\pi}_c^2 \sum m_i^2$$
$$= 56{,}424 - 2(.55)(97{,}669) + (.55)^2(174{,}499)$$
$$= 1774.05$$

Because we do not know the exact number of union members M, we can use $\bar{m}$ for $\bar{M}$ in the formula for $\hat{\sigma}_{\hat{\pi}_c}$:

$$\hat{\sigma}_{\hat{\pi}_c} = \sqrt{\left(\frac{N-n}{nN\bar{M}^2}\right)\frac{\sum_i (a_i - \hat{\pi}_c m_i)^2}{n-1}}$$
$$= \sqrt{\left(\frac{520-25}{25(520)(78.60)^2}\right)\frac{1774.05}{24}} = .21$$

Hence the approximate 95% confidence interval for π is

$$.55 \pm 1.96(.021), \qquad \text{or} \qquad .55 \pm .041$$

We are 95% confident that the actual proportion of union members favoring the new benefits package is between .509 and .591. It appears that a majority favor the package.   ∎

SECTION 18.3   EXERCISES

18.15 A utility that supplies natural gas to a suburban area needs to estimate the average R value of insulation in the attic area of homes in its service area. A random sample of 18 out of 19,790 blocks is selected from the area, and the R value is found for each house in the selected blocks. The data are as follows:

Block:	1	2	3	4	5	6	7	8	9
Mean:	10.1	12.5	14.0	13.5	9.3	8.0	7.0	9.0	11.2
Number of houses:	20	16	10	8	14	16	22	15	12

Block:	10	11	12	13	14	15	16	17	18
Mean:	12.0	15.0	10.2	16.0	12.0	8.2	10.0	14.2	9.0
Number of houses:	10	7	14	6	12	22	16	10	21

Relevant summary figures are

$$\sum T_i = 2610.8, \quad \sum m_i = 251, \quad \sum T_i m_i = 38{,}556.6$$
$$\sum T_i^2 = 395{,}206.4, \quad \sum m_i^2 = 3931$$

a. Calculate a 95% confidence interval for the true mean R level.
b. Why might this form of sampling be adopted in preference to a simple random sample of houses?

18.16 Suppose that the data of Exercise 18.15 are wrongly assumed to have arisen from a simple random sample.

a. Calculate a 95% confidence interval for the population mean. The sample mean and variance of the R values for the 251 houses included are 10.40 and 29.97, respectively.
b. How does the width of this interval compare to that of the interval in Exercise 18.15?

18.17 A lumber company must precisely estimate the number of board-feet of lumber available in harvest-age trees. The company owns 1200 ten-acre stands of trees, from which 60 stands are selected at random. Inspectors assess the usable board-feet per tree in each stand. Summary figures are shown below.

$$\sum T_i = 4{,}735{,}000, \quad \sum m_i = 47{,}200, \quad \sum T_i m_i = 3{,}806{,}930{,}000$$
$$\sum T_i^2 = 380{,}989{,}000{,}000, \quad \sum m_i^2 = 38{,}074{,}000$$

a. Calculate $\bar{y}_c$.
b. Calculate a 95% confidence interval for the mean number of board-feet per tree.

18.18 A chain of retail stores is considering discontinuing advertising mailings to its inactive accounts (those with less than $25 purchased in the past six months). There are 97 stores in the chain with an average of 1827 accounts per store. It is not possible to process the records of all stores, so a random sample of 20 stores is chosen. Analysis of the records of these stores yields the following data:

	Store									
	1	2	3	4	5	6	7	8	9	10
Number of accounts	2020	1659	1854	1371	2530	1614	1901	2301	1745	1299
Total purchases ($000)	186	153	162	114	259	158	224	261	189	117
Number of inactive accounts	429	371	403	327	580	312	365	417	357	226

	Store									
	11	12	13	14	15	16	17	18	19	20
Number of accounts	1884	1901	1624	1346	1403	2119	1946	1784	1974	1838
Total purchases ($000)	219	198	146	132	265	243	216	168	199	174
Number of inactive accounts	394	373	327	301	415	401	373	361	411	340

a. Calculate $\bar{y}_c$ for purchase amounts.

b. Calculate a 95% confidence interval for the true mean sales per account in the past six months.

c. Calculate a 95% confidence interval for the proportion of inactive accounts.

18.4   SELECTING THE SAMPLE SIZE   ∎

So far, we have assumed that the sample size of a survey is known. Of course the selection of a sample size is one of the most important parts of a sample survey design. We discussed the issue of sample-size determination for simple random sampling in Section 8.3. Now we extend the discussion to cover stratified and cluster sampling.

The width of a 95% confidence interval is a useful measure of the probable accuracy of a sample estimator. Because sample information is costly, the aim is to find the smallest sample size that yields a 95% (or whatever level is desired) confidence interval of a specified width, using a particular sample survey design.* In general, the width of a confidence interval depends not only on the design and sample size but also on one or more unknown variances. These variances may be estimated either in a preliminary study or by a manager's "horseback guess." Then we can find the desired sample size by trial and error or by formula.

half-width   Formulas for the sample size are usually stated in terms of the desired **half-width** E of a confidence interval. An interval of the form point estimate $\pm E$ has width $2E$ and therefore half-width E. Sample sizes needed to yield a desired half-width are shown below. In the case of stratified sampling, it is assumed that the overall sample size is allocated among strata in proportion to strata sizes, so that n_i, the sample size for stratum i, equals nN_i/N. If some other allocation is chosen, the formula is a first approximation. Trial and error can be used to find a more exact value of n.

∎

Sample Sizes for Estimating μ

Simple random sampling:

$$n = \frac{Ns^2}{(N-1)\dfrac{E^2}{z_{\alpha/2}^2} + s^2}$$

where s^2 is an estimate of the overall population variance.

* If several designs are available, with possibly differing costs per observation, you can compute the costs and the required sample sizes and select the least expensive design.

Stratified random sampling:

$$n = \frac{\sum_i N_i s_i^2}{(N-1)\frac{E^2}{z_{\alpha/2}^2} + \frac{1}{N}\sum_i N_i s_i^2}$$

where s_i^2 is an estimate of the variance in stratum i.

Cluster sampling:

$$n = \frac{N s_c^2}{(N-1)\frac{E^2 \bar{M}^2}{z_{\alpha/2}^2} + s_c^2}$$

where s_c^2 is an estimate of the variance of cluster totals. If the estimate is based on a preliminary sample of n' clusters,

$$s_c^2 = \frac{\sum(T_i - \bar{y}_c m_i)^2}{n' - 1}$$

EXAMPLE 18.10

Use the data of Example 18.8 as preliminary information in a pilot study to calculate the sample size required to obtain a 95% confidence interval of width $500 with cluster sampling.

Solution

From Example 18.8 we have $\sum(T_i - \bar{y}_c m_i)^2 = 15{,}227{,}502{,}247$; $N = 415$ and $\bar{m} = 6.04$. Therefore

$$s_c^2 = \frac{\sum(T_i - \bar{y}_c m_i)^2}{n' - 1} = \frac{15{,}227{,}502{,}247}{24} = 634{,}479{,}260.3$$

If the desired width is 500, $E = 250$. Substituting into the formula for n with $\bar{M}$ approximated by $\bar{m}$, we obtain

$$n = \frac{415(634{,}479{,}260.3)}{414(250)^2(6.04)^2}{(1.96)^2} + 634{,}479{,}260.3} = 302$$

A cluster sample of size 302 is needed to obtain a 95% confidence interval for μ with width $500 (i.e., $\pm\$250$).

In the same way, we can calculate approximate sample sizes for estimating either τ or π for each of the three sample survey designs, as shown in the following:

Approximate Sample Size for Estimating τ

Simple random sampling:

$$n = \frac{N s^2}{\frac{(N-1)E^2}{4N^2} + s^2}$$

Stratified random sampling:

$$n = \frac{\sum_i N_i s_i^2}{\dfrac{(N-1)E^2}{4N^2} + \dfrac{1}{N}\sum N_i s_i^2}$$

Cluster sampling:

$$n = \frac{N s_c^2}{\dfrac{(N-1)E^2}{4N^2} + s_c^2}$$

where $s_c^2 = [\sum_i(y_i - \bar{y}_c m_i)^2]/(n'-1)$ from a preliminary sample of n' clusters.

Approximate Sample Size for Estimating π

Simple random sampling:

$$n = \frac{N\hat{\pi}(1-\hat{\pi})}{\dfrac{(N-1)E^2}{z_{\alpha/2}^2} + \hat{\pi}(1-\hat{\pi})}$$

where $\hat{\pi}$ is the estimated proportion from a preliminary sample or is a guessed value.

Stratified random sampling:

$$n = \frac{\sum_i N_i\hat{\pi}_i(1-\hat{\pi}_i)}{\dfrac{(N-1)E^2}{z_{\alpha/2}^2} + \dfrac{1}{N}\sum_i N_i\hat{\pi}_i(1-\hat{\pi}_i)}$$

where $\hat{\pi}_i$ is the estimated proportion obtained from a preliminary sample from the ith stratum.

Cluster sampling:

$$n = \frac{N s_c^2}{\dfrac{(N-1)E^2\bar{M}^2}{z_{\alpha/2}^2} + s_c^2}$$

where $s_c^2 = [\sum_i(a_i - \hat{\pi}_c m_i)^2]/(n'-1)$ is from a preliminary sample of n' clusters.

Note: If no preliminary information is available and it is difficult to guess π_i, substitute $\hat{\pi}_i = .5$ to obtain a conservative sample size (one that is likely to be larger than needed).

EXAMPLE 18.11   The manager for a chain of department stores wants to conduct an in-house survey to estimate the proportion of accounts that have been delinquent by one month or more at least once in the previous calendar year. The chain consists of five stores. To reduce the cost of sampling, it is decided to use a stratified random sample with the stores serving as strata. Use the information shown here to determine the sample size (and allocation) necessary to achieve a 95% confidence interval for π with a width of .02.

Stratum	Stratum Size N_i	Estimate of π_i from Previous Year
1	1000	.22
2	2500	.35
3	3200	.24
4	1700	.30
5	4100	.15

Solution The formula for n is

$$n = \frac{\sum_i N_i \hat{\pi}_i (1 - \hat{\pi}_i)}{\dfrac{(N-1)E^2}{z_{\alpha/2}^2} + \dfrac{1}{N} \sum_i N_i \hat{\pi}_i (1 - \hat{\pi}_i)}$$

We'll use the previous year's estimates for the $\hat{\pi}_i$'s in the formula and set the interval half-width $E = .01$. Then

$$\sum_i N_i \hat{\pi}_i (1 - \hat{\pi}_i) = 1000(.22)(.78) + 2500(.35)(.65) + \cdots + 4100(.15)(.85)$$

$$= 2203.78$$

The required sample size is

$$n = \frac{2203.78}{12,499 \dfrac{(.01)^2}{(1.96)^2} + \dfrac{2203.78}{12,500}} = \frac{2203.78}{.4888} \approx 4509$$

The required total sample size is approximately 4509. The allocation of this sample size to the strata utilizes the formula $n_i = n(N_i/N)$. Thus

$$n_1 = 4509\left(\frac{1000}{12,500}\right) \approx 361$$

$$n_2 = 4509\left(\frac{2500}{12,500}\right) \approx 902$$

$$n_3 = 4509\left(\frac{3200}{12,500}\right) \approx 1154$$

$$n_4 = 4509\left(\frac{1700}{12,500}\right) \approx 613$$

$$n_5 = 4509\left(\frac{4100}{12,500}\right) = 1479$$

■

SECTION 18.4   EXERCISES

18.19 In planning a stratified sample, a manager guesses that all strata variances equal approximately 40. Each of the 10 strata is made up of 1000 individuals, and equal sample sizes are to be taken in all strata. How large a sample is required to estimate the population mean to within $\pm.5$ unit with 95% confidence?

18.20 The variance for the overall population of Exercise 18.19 is guessed as approximately 80.

    a. If a simple random sample is taken, how large a sample is required to estimate the mean to within $\pm.5$ unit with 95% confidence?

    b. Is there any major advantage to stratification in this situation? Why?

18.21 A population is divided into 3000 clusters, with an average cluster size of 40. The variance of total cluster scores s_c^2 is estimated to be roughly 20,000. How many clusters must be sampled to yield a 95% confidence interval for the population mean with a half-width of 4?

18.22 Refer to Exercise 18.15. How many blocks have to be sampled to yield a 90% confidence interval with a half-width of 2.0?

18.23 The utility company of Exercise 18.15 also wants to estimate the proportion of homes with insulation that meet minimum government standards. A (very) preliminary sample of five blocks is taken. If the number of houses per block is 20, 15, 16, 18, and 22 and the number of houses per block with at least the minimum insulation is 3, 6, 4, 3, and 5, respectively, how many additional blocks must be sampled to estimate this proportion to within $\pm.2$ with 95% confidence?

18.5   OTHER SAMPLING TECHNIQUES   ∎

The sample survey designs that we have discussed in this chapter are among the most widely used designs in business surveys. There are, however, many extensions to these designs and other sampling techniques. We discuss a few of these briefly.

systematic sampling   **Systematic sampling** provides a useful alternative to simple random sampling that is easier to use and hence less subject to interviewer errors. To select a systematic sample, we imagine the elements of the population numbered from 1 to N. A random selection of one element is made from the first k elements of the population. Every kth element of the population is selected thereafter. This is called a 1-in-k systematic sample. For example, suppose a manager wants to sample $n = 200$ of a total of $N = 1000$ invoices to determine the proportion of invoices with one or more errors. A 1-in-5 systematic sample gives the desired sample size and is easy to obtain. Imagine that the invoices are numbered from 1 to 1000, as shown in Figure 18.1 (page 878).

To obtain a 1-in-5 systematic sample, we make a random selection of one invoice from the first five. Suppose number 2 is selected. Then we take every fifth invoice from there on. The 200 invoices to be included in the sample are invoices numbered 2, 7, 12, 17, ..., 997. The formulas for point estimates of μ, τ, and π and the corresponding 95% confidence intervals are the same as those for simple random sampling.

If systematic sampling is easier to use and the formulas are the same as for simple random sampling, why would we ever use simple random sampling?

Invoice #	Invoice sampled
1	
2	2
3	
4	
5	
6	
7	7
8	
9	
10	
⋮	⋮
996	
997	997
998	
999	
1000	

FIGURE 18.1   A 1-in-5 Systematic Sample

Sometimes the elements of the population, when ordered, have inherent cycles. For example, sales volumes for grocery stores tend to have weekly cycles with greater sales volumes toward the end of the week. Similarly, retail sales of over-the-counter cough syrups and other cold preparations have cyclic sales patterns over the year, as do prices on agricultural commodities. If a systematic sample is used and the sampling pattern corresponds to the inherent cycle (see Figure 18.2), a bias is introduced; the population parameter of interest is either consistently overestimated or underestimated. Systematic sampling should also be avoided if the manager has no information about the population size N, because it is then impossible to determine the sampling rate (value of k) to achieve the desired sample size. For further details, see Scheaffer, Mendenhall, and Ott (1986).

You will recall that, with cluster sampling, the elements of the population are arranged in naturally occurring groups (clusters) and a simple random sample of clusters is selected. Each element in the selected clusters is surveyed.

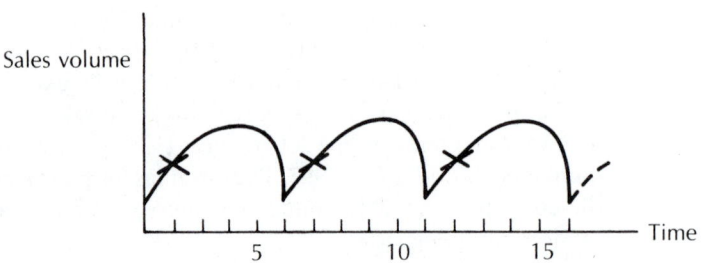

FIGURE 18.2   Cyclic Pattern in Sales: Systematic Sample Marked in X

two-stage cluster sampling

Sometimes, however, the cluster sizes are too large to make it feasible to sample all elements in the selected clusters. In these situations, we employ **two-stage cluster sampling**. First we obtain a simple random sample of clusters, then we select a simple random sample of elements from the selected clusters. Pollsters in national surveys often use two-stage cluster sampling. For example, a national public opinion survey on the mood of the nation could be done using geographic areas (such as states or counties) as clusters and then taking a simple random sample of elements within the sampled clusters.

There are obvious extensions to two-stage clustering. In the previous example, we could use multistage cluster sampling by first obtaining a simple random sample of states, then a simple random sample of counties within the sampled states, then a simple random sample of voting districts within the selected counties, and finally a simple random sample of people within the selected voting districts. By subdividing the population a number of times, it is possible to use well-defined sampling units at each stage, and the final stage (e.g., voting district) has a readily available list of elements (frame) from which to draw the simple random sample of opinions. For further details on multistage cluster sampling, see Cochran (1977), Kish (1965), and Scheaffer, Mendenhall, and Ott (1986).

randomized-response methods

The **randomized-response technique** was developed by Warner (1965) to improve the response rate of individuals surveyed about sensitive or embarrassing questions. Direct questions about involvement with such activities as shoplifting, abortion, tax evasion, drug usage, and sexual harassment, for example, are often difficult to respond to truthfully.

We illustrate the randomized-response technique for the situation in which a "yes" or "no" answer is required. Extensions to this original work are discussed in Greenberg et al. (1971). The randomized-response technique involves pairing the sensitive question with an innocuous question. For example, in a survey of factory supervisors, those surveyed could be asked to answer "yes" or "no" to one of the two questions:

(sensitive) A: Have you been involved in sexual harassment of employees of the opposite sex?

(nonsensitive) B: Is your birthday in January, February, or March?

The particular question given to an interviewee is unknown to the interviewer. Typically, a box containing a certain number of red and white balls is presented to the interviewee. The interviewee selects one of the balls without revealing the color to the interviewer. If the ball selected is red, the interviewee answers "yes" or "no" to the A question. Otherwise the interviewee answers "yes" or "no" to the B question.

The interesting result is that, without knowing which question individuals answer but knowing the proportion of red balls in the box and the proportion of "yes" responses (to either question) in the sample, it is possible to estimate π, the proportion of persons who have been involved with sexual harassment. The randomized response technique is described in greater detail in Warner (1965) and Greenberg et al. (1971).

18.6   CHOOSING A SAMPLING METHOD ∎

In this chapter we have presented several sampling approaches: Simple random sampling, stratified sampling, one-stage and two-stage cluster sampling, and systematic sampling. What are the considerations when deciding which sampling method to use?

What methods are feasible? There must be a method to ensure (nearly) unbiased sampling. Haphazard, unplanned sampling is almost worthless. A good sampling frame of individual units or of clusters is highly desirable. With a table of random numbers (or computer-generated random numbers) one can guarantee legitimate random sampling. If an explicit sampling frame can't be constructed, there should be a method that clearly guarantees randomness and avoids bias. One-in-k systematic sampling is such a method, *provided* that one can safely assume that there are no cycles in the units that might match the cycle of sampling. Random sampling can be done at random times; there are watches available that "beep" at random times. An important question about any sampling method is, Are there particular types of units that systematically, predictably will be overrepresented or underrepresented? If there are, the method is biased and undesirable.

When there are several feasible methods, the decision can be based on efficiency. If the units can be grouped according to a basis of interest such as age or educational level, stratified sampling of the groups should be considered. This method will be particularly advantageous if the groups (strata) are relatively homogeneous, with little variability within strata. If the units can be divided into subsets that are easily sampled together—whether because they are geographically close together, in the same computer subfile, or for some other reason—then cluster sampling may allow for a larger sample at lower cost. If measuring every unit in a cluster is not desirable because the clusters are too big or because the units in a cluster are so similar as to be uninformative, two-stage cluster sampling might well be useful. It can be tempting to define a very elaborate, multistage sampling scheme involving layers of stratification and clusterings; the old acronym K.I.S.S.—Keep It Simple, Stupid—applies to sampling methods, too.

Before the measurements are actually made on the sampled units, it's crucial to make sure of what is being measured. If a questionnaire is being used, it should be pretested for clarity and lack of ambiguity. If there are sensitive questions involved, the randomized response technique may be helpful. If financial data from many companies are being collected, it's important that the accounting ground rules be the same for all companies. A little anticipation can save a great deal of grief.

However the sample is finally conducted, as long as it's conducted thoughtfully, the important payoff is that sampling allows managers to get useful information, at a reasonable cost, that otherwise would be prohibitively difficult to obtain.

Summary

The first and simplest type of sampling procedure we discussed was simple random sampling. We obtain a simple random sample of n elements if each sample of size n from the N elements in the population has the same probability of being selected. For estimating a population mean μ or total τ, we use the sample mean $\bar{y}$ or sample total $N\bar{y}$, respectively. The procedure for estimating a population proportion can be thought of as a variation on estimating a population mean. By assigning a 1 to each element possessing the characteristic of interest and a 0 to all others, the population and sample proportions π and $\hat{\pi}$ are also the population and sample mean μ and $\bar{y}$, respectively.

The second sampling procedure we presented was stratified random sampling. We obtain a stratified random sample by separating the population of elements into groups (strata) such that each element belongs to one and only one stratum. A simple random sample is then selected from each of the strata. Stratified random sampling has three major advantages over simple random sampling. First, the variance of estimation procedures for μ and τ are usually reduced because the variance of observations within each stratum is usually smaller than the overall population variance. Second, the cost of collecting observations is often reduced when the population of elements is separated into smaller groups. And finally, separate estimates of parameters in each stratum can also be computed from the same sample data.

The next sampling procedure we presented was cluster sampling. In this procedure the elements of the population are separated into groups called *clusters*, and the experimenter selects a simple random sample of clusters. An observation is obtained from each element in the sampled clusters. Cluster sampling may provide more information per unit cost than simple random sampling or stratified random sampling either when a list of the elements in the population is not available or when the cost of obtaining observations increases as the distance between elements increases.

We discussed sample-size considerations for estimating μ, τ, and π under simple random sampling, stratified random sampling, and cluster sampling in Section 18.4. For each design, we presented a formula for computing the sample size necessary to achieve a 95% confidence interval of a specified width. These formulas require information from a preliminary sample or guessed values for sample variances.

Finally two extensions to the three sample survey designs and one other sampling technique were presented.

KEY FORMULAS: Some Alternative Sampling Methods

1. Estimation of μ or τ under simple random sampling

   Point estimate

   of μ: $\bar{y}$

   of τ: $N\bar{y}$

95% confidence interval

for μ: $\bar{y} \pm z_{\alpha/2}\hat{\sigma}_{\bar{Y}}$
for τ: $N\bar{y} \pm z_{\alpha/2}N\hat{\sigma}_{\bar{Y}}$

where

$$\hat{\sigma}_{\bar{Y}} = \sqrt{\frac{s^2}{n}\left(\frac{N-n}{N-1}\right)}$$

2. Estimation of π using simple random sampling

Point estimate $\hat{\pi} = \dfrac{y}{n}$

95% confidence interval $\hat{\pi} \pm z_{\alpha/2}\hat{\sigma}_{\hat{\pi}}$

where

$$\hat{\sigma}_{\hat{\pi}} = \sqrt{\frac{\hat{\pi}(1-\hat{\pi})}{n}\left(\frac{N-n}{N-1}\right)}$$

3. Estimation of μ and τ using stratified random sampling

Point estimate

of μ: $\bar{y}_{ST} = \dfrac{\sum_i N_i\bar{y}_i}{N}$

of τ: $N\bar{y}_{ST}$

95% confidence interval

for μ: $\bar{y}_{ST} \pm z_{\alpha/2}\hat{\sigma}_{\bar{y}_{ST}}$
for τ: $N\bar{y}_{ST} \pm z_{\alpha/2}N\hat{\sigma}_{\bar{y}_{ST}}$

where

$$\hat{\sigma}_{\bar{y}_{ST}} = \frac{1}{N}\sqrt{\sum_i N_i^2\left(\frac{N_i-n_i}{N_i-1}\right)\frac{s_i^2}{n_i}}$$

4. Estimation of π using stratified random sampling

Point estimate $\hat{\pi}_{ST} = \dfrac{1}{N}\sum_i N_i\hat{\pi}_i$

95% confidence interval $\hat{\pi}_{ST} \pm z_{\alpha/2}\hat{\sigma}_{\hat{\pi}_{ST}}$

where

$$\hat{\sigma}_{\hat{\pi}_{ST}} = \frac{1}{N}\sqrt{\sum_i N_i^2\left(\frac{N_i-n_i}{N_i-1}\right)\frac{\hat{\pi}_i(1-\hat{\pi}_i)}{n_i}}$$

5. Estimation of μ and τ using cluster sampling

Point estimate

of μ:

$$\bar{y}_c = \frac{\sum_i T_i}{\sum_i m_i}$$

of π: $M\bar{y}_c$

95% confidence interval

for μ: $\bar{y}_c \pm z_{\alpha/2}\hat{\sigma}_{\bar{Y}_c}$

for τ: $M\bar{y}_c \pm z_{\alpha/2}M\hat{\sigma}_{\bar{Y}_c}$

where

$$\hat{\sigma}_{\bar{Y}_c} = \sqrt{\left(\frac{N-n}{nN\bar{M}^2}\right)\frac{\sum_i(T_i - \bar{y}_c m_i)^2}{n-1}}$$

6. Estimation of π using cluster sampling

Point estimate $\hat{\pi}_c = \dfrac{\sum_i a_i}{\sum_i m_i}$

95% confidence interval $\hat{\pi}_c \pm z_{\alpha/2}\hat{\sigma}_{\hat{\pi}_c}$

where

$$\hat{\sigma}_{\hat{\pi}_c} = \sqrt{\left(\frac{N-n}{nN\bar{M}^2}\right)\frac{\sum_i(a_i - \hat{\pi}_c m_i)^2}{n-1}}$$

7. Sample sizes for estimating μ

Sample random sampling:

$$n = \frac{Ns^2}{(N-1)\dfrac{E^2}{z_{\alpha/2}^2} + s^2}$$

Stratified random sampling:

$$n = \frac{\sum_i N_i s_i^2}{(N-1)\dfrac{E^2}{z_{\alpha/2}^2} + \dfrac{1}{N}\sum_i N_i s_i^2}$$

Cluster sampling:

$$n = \frac{Ns_c^2}{(N-1)\dfrac{E^2\bar{M}^2}{z_{\alpha/2}^2} + s_c^2}$$

8. Sample sizes for estimating τ

Simple random sampling:

$$n = \frac{Ns^2}{\dfrac{(N-1)E^2}{z_{\alpha/2}^2 N^2} + s^2}$$

Stratified random sampling:

$$n = \frac{\sum_i N_i s_i^2}{\dfrac{(N-1)E^2}{z_{\alpha/2}^2 N^2} + \dfrac{1}{N}\sum_i N_i s_i^2}$$

Cluster sampling:

$$n = \frac{Ns_c^2}{\dfrac{(N-1)E^2}{z_{\alpha/2}^2 N^2} + s_c^2}$$

9. Sample sizes for estimating π

Simple random sampling:

$$n = \frac{N\hat{\pi}(1-\hat{\pi})}{\dfrac{(N-1)E^2}{z_{\alpha/2}^2} + \hat{\pi}(1-\hat{\pi})}$$

Stratified random sampling:

$$n = \frac{\sum_i N_i \hat{\pi}_i(1-\hat{\pi}_i)}{\dfrac{(N-1)E^2}{z_{\alpha/2}^2} + \dfrac{1}{N}\sum_i N_i \hat{\pi}_i(1-\hat{\pi}_i)}$$

Cluster sampling:

$$n = \frac{Ns_c^2}{\dfrac{(N-1)E^2\bar{M}^2}{z_{\alpha/2}^2} + s_c^2}$$

CHAPTER 18 EXERCISES

18.24 A publisher of college dictionaries surveys bookstores in the neighborhoods of various colleges and universities to determine the average number of dictionaries displayed on shelves. To do this, the publisher selects 12 colleges and universities at random from a list of all accredited institutions of higher education. Every bookstore on or near these 12 campuses is visited and the number of dictionaries on display is counted.

a. Identify the sample survey method used.

b. Why might this method be preferred to a simple random sample of bookstores?

18.25 The survey of Exercise 18.24 yields the following data:

School	Number of Stores	Number of Dictionaries
1	2	4, 6
2	6	8, 3, 4, 5, 2, 5
3	3	5, 7, 2
4	1	6
5	2	4, 8
6	4	3, 2, 5, 2
7	3	4, 7, 3
8	1	5
9	2	6, 3
10	4	4, 4, 2, 6
11	3	3, 2, 3
12	2	5, 5

a. Calculate a 95% confidence interval for the true mean number of displayed dictionaries.

b. What is the 95% confidence interval if the data are assumed (incorrectly) to be the result of a simple random sample?

c. How large a sample of universities is required to estimate the mean within $\pm.1$ with 95% confidence?

18.26 An auto parts firm wants to estimate the average time required to fill its orders. The orders are classified into four types:

A: single item, off the shelf

B: single item, production required

C: multiple item, off the shelf

D: multiple item, production required

Random samples of 30 orders of each of the four types are selected, and times are determined.

a. Identify the type of sample survey design.

b. Why might this kind of design be preferable to a simple random sample of 120 orders?

18.27 Suppose that the orders of the previous exercise are numbered (without regard to type) from 0001 to 8260, and suppose that you have a table of 4-digit random numbers. How would you go about actually drawing the sample? You can expect to get some numbers larger than 8260 and some repetitions. It is very unlikely that the first 120 orders selected would contain exactly 30 of each type.

18.28 Suppose that the survey of Exercise 18.26 yields the following results (times in days):

Type	Mean	Standard Deviation
A	3.21	.82
B	7.39	2.14
C	4.65	1.05
D	9.27	3.65

Assume that the four types of orders are equally represented in the population of all orders. Calculate a 95% confidence interval for the true mean time.

18.29 Assume that the population of orders in Exercise 18.28 consists of 2216 A's, 2715 B's, 1874 C's, and 1455 D's.
   a. Recalculate the 95% confidence interval.
   b. How sensitive is the interval to assumptions about the number of each type of order?

18.30 Assume that the population of orders is as given in Exercise 18.29. How large a sample is needed to estimate the mean time within $\pm.3$ day with 95% confidence? How should the sample be allocated among the four types?

18.31 An economic survey is designed to estimate the average amount spent on utilities for households in a city. Because no list of households is available, cluster sampling is used with divisions (wards) forming the clusters. A simple random sample of 20 wards is selected from the 60 wards of the city. Interviewers then obtain the cost of utilities from each household within the sampled wards. The total costs are tabulated below:

Ward	Number of Households	Total Amount Spent	Ward	Number of Households	Total Amount Spent
1	55	$2210	11	73	$2930
2	60	2390	12	64	2470
3	63	2430	13	69	2830
4	58	2380	14	58	2370
5	71	2760	15	63	2390
6	78	3110	16	75	2870
7	69	2780	17	78	3210
8	58	2370	18	51	2430
9	52	1990	19	67	2730
10	71	2810	20	70	2880

Estimate the average amount a household in the city spends on utilities and calculate a 95% confidence interval.

18.32 Refer to Exercise 18.31. Use the sample data to estimate τ, the total amount spent on utilities. Calculate a 95% confidence interval. The total number of households in the city is 3950.

18.33 The parts warehouse of a foreign-car importer contains 81,513 items. A complete inventory of all these items would obviously be very expensive; therefore sampling is employed. The parts are listed in nine categories. Random samples are taken of items in each category, and the dollar value of "shrinkage" in each sampled item is determined. Identify the sample survey design.

18.34 One inventory check for the importer of Exercise 18.33 yields the following data:

Category	Items Sampled	Items Included	Mean Shrinkage/Item	Variance
1	125	12,461	1.310	.125
2	84	8,402	.272	.092
3	10	6,977	.149	.011
4	92	9,206	.117	.021
5	118	11,817	1.970	.214
6	100	10,048	.132	.032
7	94	9,372	.098	.062
8	80	7,965	.216	.042
9	53	5,265	.020	.017

Calculate a 90% confidence interval for the total inventory shrinkage.

18.35 What total sample size is needed to make the confidence interval of Exercise 18.34 have a half-width of $300? If the sample size is allocated to categories in proportion to the number of items in the categories, how many items should be sampled in each category?

18.36 A large hospital surveys its accounts for the past year to see what proportion of accounts were not settled within 60 days. The accounts are stratified by size, and random samples are taken of all accounts. The following data are obtained:

Stratum	Account Size	Total Number of Accounts	Number of Accounts Sampled	Number of Accounts Not Settled in 60 Days
A	Under $100	8251	41	5
B	100–499	2917	29	6
C	500–999	843	42	8
D	1000–2499	487	49	15
E	2500 or over	202	40	23

Calculate a 95% confidence interval for the true proportion of accounts not settled in 60 days.

18.37 The formula for required stratified sample size given in Section 18.4 is based on the assumption that the sample size is allocated among strata in proportion to the relative sizes of the strata. This assumption does not hold for Exercise 18.36.

a. Use the formula to calculate the sample size required to give the half-width that was actually obtained in Exercise 18.36.

b. How much difference in required sample size is caused by the difference in allocation?

18.38 A campus survey is conducted to determine the average occupancy per car for staff and faculty members entering the university during the 7:30–9:00 A.M. rush-hour period for a representative mid-week day. There are four legal entrances to the university and it is assumed that data are collected from these checkpoints. The day chosen for study is a Wednesday in the middle of the semester. One person is stationed at each checkpoint and instructed to sample every second car. For each car included in the sample, the person first checks the sticker on the front of the car to verify that it is a faculty or staff member's car. Then the number of occupants (including the driver) is recorded. Assuming that the four checkpoints represent four strata and that the method of sampling simulates simple random sampling of each stratum, use the data in the following table to estimate the average occupancy per car. Give a 95% confidence interval.

Stratum (Entrance)	N_i	n_i	$\sum_i y_i$	s_i^2
North	294	147	185	.24
South	150	75	89	.26
East	230	115	144	.26
West	322	161	203	.18

18.39 Is simple random sampling an alternative to stratified random sampling for estimating μ in Exercise 18.38? Explain.

18.40 Refer to Exercise 18.38. Estimate τ, the total number of occupants entering the campus during the 7:30–9:00 A.M. period. Find a 95% confidence interval.

C A S E   Sampling Methods

A motel chain recently introduced a special club for high-usage customers, mostly those who use the chain frequently on business trips. The club offers various "perks" for its members; the chain hopes to make up the cost by increased usage and by expenditures of club members in motel restaurants and lounges. Club members make reservations through a centralized system, so the chain can determine usage directly. However, restaurant and lounge expenditures aren't available centrally and the totals they report aren't really useful because they combine club members and nonmembers.

To get an indication of the average restaurant/lounge expenditure per club member and the proportion of club members who used the restaurant or lounge at all, the chain picked 30 of its 612 motels. Each motel determined how many club members stayed at the motel during a specified week, how many used the motel's restaurant and lounge facilities, and the total dollar restaurant/lounge expenditure of club members at the motel during that week. The chain's records showed that there had been 61,518 club members staying at some motel in the chain during that week, an average of 100.52 per motel.

The data have been provided to you with a request that you give the chain's director of promotions estimates of the chain-wide proportion of users and average expenditure per user. The director vaguely remembers what a confidence interval is, but will need clear explanations of any technical terms in your report.

In addition, the director is considering a longer-range study. The chain divides its motels into urban, small-city, and roadside units. The director has speculated that restaurant use by club members would vary greatly among the three types of motels. You have been invited to make suggestions about how to obtain data to check this speculation.

motel	totalnum	numused	total$
541	82	65	1789.66
603	136	103	2992.73
118	90	70	2115.65
285	77	48	1629.12
378	121	98	4477.40
116	88	68	2387.59
233	144	115	2638.08
322	111	96	1872.58
528	92	80	2520.17
245	94	71	1764.60
384	79	62	1922.76
383	108	81	3211.59
69	93	77	2231.67
181	85	66	2007.10
508	152	122	4651.71
78	108	80	2110.06
184	91	74	2437.86
202	88	62	1910.82
244	94	77	2474.85
144	113	90	4593.19
502	88	66	1158.76
172	84	62	2449.39
342	121	95	2198.28
547	106	88	2358.49
320	97	71	2830.13
40	79	55	970.76
610	133	111	2967.30
536	87	70	2409.40
391	94	71	1380.08
70	90	60	2318.05

DATA MANAGEMENT AND REPORT PREPARATION

In the past 18 chapters we've discussed particular statistical methods, how those methods are applied to specific data sets, and how findings from statistical analyses in the form of computer output are interpreted. We have not concentrated on the processing steps that one follows between the time the data are received and the time the data are available in computer-readable form for analysis, nor have we discussed the form and content of the report that summarizes the results of a statistical analysis. In this chapter we consider the data-processing steps and statistical report writing. This chapter is not a complete manual with all the tools required; rather, it is an overview—what a manager should know about these steps. As an example, the chapter reflects standard procedures in the pharmaceutical industry, which is highly regulated. Procedures differ somewhat in other industries.

19.1 PREPARING DATA FOR STATISTICAL ANALYSIS ■

We begin with a discussion of the steps involved in processing data from a study. In practice, these steps may consume 75% of the total effort from the receipt of the raw data to the presentation of results from the analysis. What are these steps, why are they so important, and why are they so time-consuming?

To answer these questions, let's list the major data-processing steps in the cycle, which begin with receipt of the data and end when the statistical analysis begins. Then we'll discuss each step separately.

Steps in Preparing Data for Analysis

1. Receiving the raw data source
2. Creating the data base from the raw data source
3. Editing the data base

4. Correcting and clarifying the raw data source
5. Finalizing the data base
6. Creating data files from the data base

■

raw data source

1. Receiving the raw data source. For each study that is to be summarized and analyzed, the data arrive in some form, which we'll refer to as the **raw data source**. For a clinical trial, the raw data source is usually case report forms, sheets of $8\frac{1}{2}'' \times 11''$ paper, that have been used to record study data for each patient entered into the study. For other types of studies, the raw data source may be sheets of paper from a laboratory notebook, a magnetic tape (or any other form of machine-readable data), hand-tabulations, and so on.

data trail

It is important to retain the raw data source because it is the beginning of the **data trail**, which leads from the raw data to the conclusions drawn from a study. Many consulting operations involved with the analysis and summarization of many different studies keep a log that contains vital information related to the study and raw data source. General information contained in a study log is shown below:

■

Log for Study Data

1. Data received, and from whom
2. Study investigator
3. Statistician (and others) assigned
4. Brief description of study
5. Treatments (compounds, preparations, etc.) studied
6. Raw data source
7. Response(s) measured
8. Reference number for study
9. Estimated (actual) completion date
10. Other pertinent information

■

Later, when the study has been analyzed and results have been communicated, additional information can be added to the log on how the study results were communicated, where these results are recorded, what data files have been saved, and where these files are stored.

2. Creating the data base from the raw data source. For most studies that are scheduled for a statistical analysis, a machine-readable data base is created. The steps taken to create the data base and the eventual form of the data base vary from one operation to another, depending on the software systems to be used in the statistical analysis. However, we can give a few guidelines based on the form of the entry system.

When the data are to be *key-entered* at a terminal, the raw data are first checked for legibility. Any illegible numbers or letters or other problems should be brought to the attention of the study coordinator. Then a coding guide that assigns column numbers and variable names to the data is filled out. Certain codes for missing values (e.g., not available) are also defined here. Also, it is helpful to give a brief description of each variable. The data file keyed in at the terminal is referred to as the **machine-readable data base**. A listing of the data base should be obtained and checked carefully against the raw data source. Any errors should be corrected at the terminal and verified against an updated listing.

machine-readable data base

Sometimes data are received in machine-readable form. For these situations the magnetic tape or disk file is considered to be the data base. You must, however, have a coding guide to "read" the data base. Using the coding guide, obtain a listing of the data base and check it *carefully* to see that all numbers and characters look reasonable and that proper formats were used to create the file. Any problems that arise must be resolved before proceeding further.

Some data sets are so small that it is not necessary to create a machine-readable data file from the raw data source. Instead, calculations are performed by hand or the data are entered into an electronic calculator. For these situations check any calculations to see that they make sense. Don't believe everything you see; redoing the calculations is not a bad idea.

3. Editing the data base. The types of edits done and the completeness of the editing process really depend on the type of study and how concerned you are about the accuracy and completeness of the data prior to the analysis. For example, in using SAS files it is wise to examine the minimum, maximum, and frequency distribution for each variable to make certain nothing looks unreasonable.

Certain other checks should be made. Plot the data and look for problems. Also, certain **logic checks** should be done depending on the structure of the data. If, for example, data are recorded for patients at several different visits, then the data recorded for visit 2 can't be earlier than the data for visit 1; similarly, if a patient is lost to follow-up after visit 2, we can't have any data for that patient at later visits.

logic checks

For small data sets we can do these data edits by hand, but for large data sets the job may be too time-consuming and tedious. If machine editing is required, look for a software system that allows the user to specify certain data edits. Even so, for more complicated edits and logic checks it may be necessary to have a customized edit program written in order to machine edit the data. This programming chore can be a time-consuming step; plan for this well in advance of the receipt of the data.

4. Correcting and clarifying the raw data source. Questions frequently arise concerning the legibility or accuracy of the raw data during any one of the steps from the receipt of the raw data to the communication of the results from the statistical analysis. We have found it helpful to keep a list of these problems or discrepancies in order to define the data trail for a study. If a correction (or clarification) is required to the raw data source, this should be indicated on the form and the appropriate change made to the raw data source. If no correction is required, this should be indicated on the form as well. Keep in mind that the machine-readable data base should be changed to reflect any changes made to the raw data source.

5. Finalizing the data base. You may have been led to believe that all data for a study arrive at one time. This, of course, is not always the case. For example, with a marketing survey, different geographic locations may be surveyed at different times and hence those responsible for data processing do not receive all the data at one time. All these subsets of data, however, must be processed through the cycles required to create, edit, and correct the data base. Eventually the study is declared complete and the data is processed into the data base. At this time the data base should be reviewed again and final corrections made before beginning the analysis. The reason for this is that, for large data sets, the analysis and summarization chores take considerable manpower and computer time. It's better to agree on a final data base analysis than to have to repeat all analyses on a changed data base at a later date.

    6. Creating data files from the data base. Generally there are one or two sets of data files created from the machine-readable data base. The first set, referred to as **original files**, reflects the basic structure of the data base. A listing of the files is checked against the data base listing to verify that the variables have been read with correct formats and missing value codes have been retained. For some studies the original files are actually used for editing the data base.

original files

work files

    A second set of data files, called **work files**, may be created from the original files. Work files are designed to facilitate the analysis. They may require restructuring of the original files, a selection of important variables, or the creation or addition of new variables by insertion, computation, or transformation. A listing of the work files is checked against that of the original files to ensure proper restructuring and variable selection. Computed and transformed variables are checked by hand calculations to verify the program code.

    If original and work files are SAS data sets, you should utilize the documentation features provided by SAS. At the time an SAS data set is created, a descriptive label for the data set, of up to 40 characters, should be assigned. The label can be stored with the data set imprinted wherever the contents procedure is used to print the data set's contents. All variables can be given descriptive names, up to 8 characters in length, which are meaningful to those involved in the project. In addition, variable labels up to 40 characters in length can be used to provide additional information. Title statements can be included in the SAS code to identify the project and describe each job. For each file, a listing (proc print) and a dictionary (proc contents) can be retained.

    For files created from the data base using other software packages, you should utilize the labeling and documentation features available in the computer program.

    Even if appropriate statistical methods are applied to data, the conclusions drawn from the study are only as good as the data on which they are based. So you be the judge. The amount of time spent on these data-processing chores before analysis really depends on the nature of the study, the quality of the raw data source, and how confident you want to be about the completeness and accuracy of the data.

19.2   GUIDELINES FOR A STATISTICAL ANALYSIS AND REPORT

In this section we briefly discuss a few guidelines for a statistical analysis and some important elements of a statistical report for communicating results. The statistical analysis of a large study can usually be broken down into three types of analyses: (1) preliminary analyses, (2) primary analyses, and (3) backup analyses.

preliminary analyses

The **preliminary analyses**, which are often descriptive or graphic, familiarize the statistician with the data and provide a foundation for all subsequent analyses. These analyses may include frequency distributions, histograms, descriptive statistics, an examination of comparability of the treatment groups, correlations, or univariate and bivariate plots.

primary analyses
backup analyses

Primary analyses are those used to address the objectives of the study and the analyses on which conclusions are drawn. **Backup analyses** include alternate methods for examining the data that confirm the results of the primary analyses; they may also include new statistical methods that are not as readily accepted as the more standard methods. Several guidelines for analyses are presented below:

Preliminary, Primary, and Backup Analyses

1. Analyses should be performed with software that has been extensively tested.
2. Computer output should be labeled to reflect which study is analyzed, what subjects (animals, patients, etc.) are used in the analysis, and a brief description of the analysis preferred. For example, TITLE statements in SAS are very helpful.
3. Variable labels and value labels (e.g., $0 =$ none, $1 =$ mild) should appear on the output.
4. A list of the data used in each analysis should be provided.
5. The output for all analyses should be checked *carefully*. Did the job run successfully? Are the sample sizes, means, and degrees of freedom correct? Other checks may be necessary as well.
6. All preliminary, primary, and backup analyses that provide the informational base from which study conclusions are drawn should be saved.

After the statistical analysis is completed, conclusions must be drawn and the results communicated to the intended audience. Sometimes it is necessary to communicate these results as a formal written statistical report. A general outline for a statistical report that we have found useful and informative is listed below:

General Outline for a Statistical Report

1. Summary
2. Introduction
3. Experimental design and study procedures
4. Descriptive statistics
5. Statistical methodology
6. Results and conclusions

7. Discussion
8. Data listings

19.3   DOCUMENTATION AND STORAGE OF RESULTS

The final part of this cycle of data processing, analysis, and summarization concerns the documentation and storage of results. For formal statistical analyses that are subject to careful scrutiny by others, it is important to provide detailed documentation for all data processing and the statistical analyses so that the data trail is clear and the data base or work files are readily accessible. Then the reviewer can follow what has been done, redo it, or extend the analyses. The elements of a documentation and storage file depend on the particular setting in which you work. The contents for a general documentation storage file are shown below:

Study Documentation and Storage File

1. Statistical report
2. Study description
3. Random code (used to assign subjects to treatment groups)
4. Important correspondence
5. File creation information
6. Preliminary, primary, and backup analyses
7. Raw data source
8. A data management sheet, which includes the log as well as information on the storage of the data files

Summary

We hope the information presented in this chapter has opened your eyes and broadened your perspective on data processing and statistical analysis. Most textbooks assume that the data are ready for analysis when received or displayed. In practice, however, much work is required to prepare the data for analysis and to write a report. The material presented here gives the flavor of what is being done in the pharmaceutical industry. Because many other businesses or experimental settings are less highly regulated, it may be possible to relax some of the steps that have been outlined here. The important point is that you should actively consider whether these steps are required for a study; don't just ignore them.

Besides discussing the steps required to prepare data for analysis, we have presented a few guidelines for a statistical analysis, a general outline for a statistical report, and the contents of a documentation and storage system. Remember, these are only examples of what can be done. Other variations are certainly reasonable and appropriate.

APPENDIX

Table 1
Binomial probabilities (n between 2 and 6)

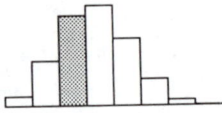

n = 2

y↓	.05	.10	.15	.20	.25	.30	.35	.40	.45	.50	
0	.9025	.8100	.7225	.6400	.5625	.4900	.4225	.3600	.3025	.2500	2
1	.0950	.1800	.2550	.3200	.3750	.4200	.4550	.4800	.4950	.5000	1
2	.0025	.0100	.0225	.0400	.0625	.0900	.1225	.1600	.2025	.2500	0
	.95	.90	.85	.80	.75	.70	.65	.60	.55	.50	y↑

n = 3

y↓	.05	.10	.15	.20	.25	.30	.35	.40	.45	.50	
0	.8574	.7290	.6141	.5120	.4219	.3430	.2746	.2160	.1664	.1250	3
1	.1354	.2430	.3251	.3840	.4219	.4410	.4436	.4320	.4084	.3750	2
2	.0071	.0270	.0574	.0960	.1406	.1890	.2389	.2880	.3341	.3750	1
3	.0001	.0010	.0034	.0080	.0156	.0270	.0429	.0640	.0911	.1250	0
	.95	.90	.85	.80	.75	.70	.65	.60	.55	.50	y↑

n = 4

y↓	.05	.10	.15	.20	.25	.30	.35	.40	.45	.50	
0	.8145	.6561	.5220	.4096	.3164	.2401	.1785	.1296	.0915	.0625	4
1	.1715	.2916	.3685	.4096	.4219	.4116	.3845	.3456	.2995	.2500	3
2	.0135	.0486	.0975	.1536	.2109	.2646	.3105	.3456	.3675	.3750	2
3	.0005	.0036	.0115	.0256	.0469	.0756	.1115	.1536	.2005	.2500	1
4	.0000	.0001	.0005	.0016	.0039	.0081	.0150	.0256	.0410	.0625	0
	.95	.90	.85	.80	.75	.70	.65	.60	.55	.50	y↑

n = 5

y↓	.05	.10	.15	.20	.25	.30	.35	.40	.45	.50	
0	.7738	.5905	.4437	.3277	.2373	.1681	.1160	.0778	.0503	.0313	5
1	.2036	.3281	.3915	.4096	.3955	.3602	.3124	.2592	.2059	.1563	4
2	.0214	.0729	.1382	.2048	.2637	.3087	.3364	.3456	.3369	.3125	3
3	.0011	.0081	.0244	.0512	.0879	.1323	.1811	.2304	.2757	.3125	2
4	.0000	.0005	.0022	.0064	.0146	.0284	.0488	.0768	.1128	.1563	1
5	.0000	.0000	.0001	.0003	.0010	.0024	.0053	.0102	.0185	.0313	0
	.95	.90	.85	.80	.75	.70	.65	.60	.55	.50	y↑

n = 6

y↓	.05	.10	.15	.20	.25	.30	.35	.40	.45	.50	
0	.7351	.5314	.3771	.2621	.1780	.1176	.0754	.0467	.0277	.0156	6
1	.2321	.3543	.3993	.3932	.3560	.3025	.2437	.1866	.1359	.0938	5
2	.0305	.0984	.1762	.2458	.2966	.3241	.3280	.3110	.2780	.2344	4
3	.0021	.0146	.0415	.0819	.1318	.1852	.2355	.2765	.3032	.3125	3
4	.0001	.0012	.0055	.0154	.0330	.0595	.0951	.1382	.1861	.2344	2
5	.0000	.0001	.0004	.0015	.0044	.0102	.0205	.0369	.0609	.0938	1
6	.0000	.0000	.0000	.0001	.0002	.0007	.0018	.0041	.0083	.0156	0
	.95	.90	.85	.80	.75	.70	.65	.60	.55	.50	y↑

Table 1 (continued)
Binomial probabilities (n between 7 and 10)

n = 7 π

y↓	.05	.10	.15	.20	.25	.30	.35	.40	.45	.50	
0	.6983	.4783	.3206	.2097	.1335	.0824	.0490	.0280	.0152	.0078	7
1	.2573	.3720	.3960	.3670	.3115	.2471	.1848	.1306	.0872	.0547	6
2	.0406	.1240	.2097	.2753	.3115	.3177	.2985	.2613	.2140	.1641	5
3	.0036	.0230	.0617	.1147	.1730	.2269	.2679	.2903	.2918	.2734	4
4	.0002	.0026	.0109	.0287	.0577	.0972	.1442	.1935	.2388	.2734	3
5	.0000	.0002	.0012	.0043	.0115	.0250	.0466	.0774	.1172	.1641	2
6	.0000	.0000	.0001	.0004	.0013	.0036	.0084	.0172	.0320	.0547	1
7	.0000	.0000	.0000	.0000	.0001	.0002	.0006	.0016	.0037	.0078	0
	.95	.90	.85	.80	.75	.70	.65	.60	.55	.50	y↑

n = 8 π

y↓	.05	.10	.15	.20	.25	.30	.35	.40	.45	.50	
0	.6634	.4305	.2725	.1678	.1001	.0576	.0319	.0168	.0084	.0039	8
1	.2793	.3826	.3847	.3355	.2670	.1977	.1373	.0896	.0548	.0313	7
2	.0515	.1488	.2376	.2936	.3115	.2965	.2587	.2090	.1569	.1094	6
3	.0054	.0331	.0839	.1468	.2076	.2541	.2786	.2787	.2568	.2188	5
4	.0004	.0046	.0185	.0459	.0865	.1361	.1875	.2322	.2627	.2734	4
5	.0000	.0004	.0026	.0092	.0231	.0467	.0808	.1239	.1719	.2188	3
6	.0000	.0000	.0002	.0011	.0038	.0100	.0217	.0413	.0703	.1094	2
7	.0000	.0000	.0000	.0001	.0004	.0012	.0033	.0079	.0164	.0313	1
8	.0000	.0000	.0000	.0000	.0000	.0001	.0002	.0007	.0017	.0039	0
	.95	.90	.85	.80	.75	.70	.65	.60	.55	.50	y↑

n = 9 π

y↓	.05	.10	.15	.20	.25	.30	.35	.40	.45	.50	
0	.6302	.3874	.2316	.1342	.0751	.0404	.0207	.0101	.0046	.0020	9
1	.2985	.3874	.3679	.3020	.2253	.1556	.1004	.0605	.0339	.0176	8
2	.0629	.1722	.2597	.3020	.3003	.2668	.2162	.1612	.1110	.0703	7
3	.0077	.0446	.1069	.1762	.2336	.2668	.2716	.2508	.2119	.1641	6
4	.0006	.0074	.0283	.0661	.1168	.1715	.2194	.2508	.2600	.2461	5
5	.0000	.0008	.0050	.0165	.0389	.0735	.1181	.1672	.2128	.2461	4
6	.0000	.0001	.0006	.0028	.0087	.0210	.0424	.0743	.1160	.1641	3
7	.0000	.0000	.0000	.0003	.0012	.0039	.0098	.0212	.0407	.0703	2
8	.0000	.0000	.0000	.0000	.0001	.0004	.0013	.0035	.0083	.0176	1
9	.0000	.0000	.0000	.0000	.0000	.0000	.0001	.0003	.0008	.0020	0
	.95	.90	.85	.80	.75	.70	.65	.60	.55	.50	y↑

n = 10 π

y↓	.05	.10	.15	.20	.25	.30	.35	.40	.45	.50	
0	.5987	.3487	.1969	.1074	.0563	.0282	.0135	.0060	.0025	.0010	10
1	.3151	.3874	.3474	.2684	.1877	.1211	.0725	.0403	.0207	.0098	9
2	.0746	.1937	.2759	.3020	.2816	.2335	.1757	.1209	.0763	.0439	8
3	.0105	.0574	.1298	.2013	.2503	.2668	.2522	.2150	.1665	.1172	7
4	.0010	.0112	.0401	.0881	.1460	.2001	.2377	.2508	.2384	.2051	6
5	.0001	.0015	.0085	.0264	.0584	.1029	.1536	.2007	.2340	.2461	5
6	.0000	.0001	.0012	.0055	.0162	.0368	.0689	.1115	.1596	.2051	4
7	.0000	.0000	.0001	.0008	.0031	.0090	.0212	.0425	.0746	.1172	3
8	.0000	.0000	.0000	.0001	.0004	.0014	.0043	.0106	.0229	.0439	2
9	.0000	.0000	.0000	.0000	.0000	.0001	.0005	.0016	.0042	.0098	1
10	.0000	.0000	.0000	.0000	.0000	.0000	.0000	.0001	.0003	.0010	0
	.95	.90	.85	.80	.75	.70	.65	.60	.55	.50	y↑

Table 1 (continued)
Binomial probabilities (n between 12 and 16)

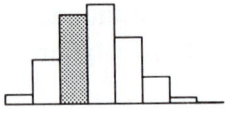

n = 12 π

y↓	.05	.10	.15	.20	.25	.30	.35	.40	.45	.50	
0	.5404	.2824	.1422	.0687	.0317	.0138	.0057	.0022	.0008	.0002	12
1	.3413	.3766	.3012	.2062	.1267	.0712	.0368	.0174	.0075	.0029	11
2	.0988	.2301	.2924	.2835	.2323	.1678	.1088	.0639	.0339	.0161	10
3	.0173	.0852	.1720	.2362	.2581	.2397	.1954	.1419	.0923	.0537	9
4	.0021	.0213	.0683	.1329	.1936	.2311	.2367	.2128	.1700	.1208	8
5	.0002	.0038	.0193	.0532	.1032	.1585	.2039	.2270	.2225	.1934	7
6	.0000	.0005	.0040	.0155	.0401	.0792	.1281	.1766	.2124	.2256	6
7	.0000	.0000	.0006	.0033	.0115	.0291	.0591	.1009	.1489	.1934	5
8	.0000	.0000	.0001	.0005	.0024	.0078	.0199	.0420	.0762	.1208	4
9	.0000	.0000	.0000	.0001	.0004	.0015	.0048	.0125	.0277	.0537	3
10	.0000	.0000	.0000	.0000	.0000	.0002	.0008	.0025	.0068	.0161	2
11	.0000	.0000	.0000	.0000	.0000	.0000	.0001	.0003	.0010	.0029	1
12	.0000	.0000	.0000	.0000	.0000	.0000	.0000	.0000	.0001	.0002	0
	.95	.90	.85	.80	.75	.70	.65	.60	.55	.50	y↑

n = 14 π

y↓	.05	.10	.15	.20	.25	.30	.35	.40	.45	.50	
0	.4877	.2288	.1028	.0440	.0178	.0068	.0024	.0008	.0002	.0001	14
1	.3593	.3559	.2539	.1539	.0832	.0407	.0181	.0073	.0027	.0009	13
2	.1229	.2570	.2912	.2501	.1802	.1134	.0634	.0317	.0141	.0056	12
3	.0259	.1142	.2056	.2501	.2402	.1943	.1366	.0845	.0462	.0222	11
4	.0037	.0349	.0998	.1720	.2202	.2290	.2022	.1549	.1040	.0611	10
5	.0004	.0078	.0352	.0860	.1468	.1963	.2178	.2066	.1701	.1222	9
6	.0000	.0013	.0093	.0322	.0734	.1262	.1759	.2066	.2088	.1833	8
7	.0000	.0002	.0019	.0092	.0280	.0618	.1082	.1574	.1952	.2095	7
8	.0000	.0000	.0003	.0020	.0082	.0232	.0510	.0918	.1398	.1833	6
9	.0000	.0000	.0000	.0003	.0018	.0066	.0183	.0408	.0762	.1222	5
10	.0000	.0000	.0000	.0000	.0003	.0014	.0049	.0136	.0312	.0611	4
11	.0000	.0000	.0000	.0000	.0000	.0002	.0010	.0033	.0093	.0222	3
12	.0000	.0000	.0000	.0000	.0000	.0000	.0001	.0005	.0019	.0056	2
13	.0000	.0000	.0000	.0000	.0000	.0000	.0000	.0001	.0002	.0009	1
14	.0000	.0000	.0000	.0000	.0000	.0000	.0000	.0000	.0000	.0001	0
	.95	.90	.85	.80	.75	.70	.65	.60	.55	.50	y↑

n = 16 π

y↓	.05	.10	.15	.20	.25	.30	.35	.40	.45	.50	
0	.4401	.1853	.0743	.0281	.0100	.0033	.0010	.0003	.0001	.0000	16
1	.3706	.3294	.2097	.1126	.0535	.0228	.0087	.0030	.0009	.0002	15
2	.1463	.2745	.2775	.2111	.1336	.0732	.0353	.0150	.0056	.0018	14
3	.0359	.1423	.2285	.2463	.2079	.1465	.0888	.0468	.0215	.0085	13
4	.0061	.0514	.1311	.2001	.2252	.2040	.1553	.1014	.0572	.0278	12
5	.0008	.0137	.0555	.1201	.1802	.2099	.2008	.1623	.1123	.0667	11
6	.0001	.0028	.0180	.0550	.1101	.1649	.1982	.1983	.1684	.1222	10
7	.0000	.0004	.0045	.0197	.0524	.1010	.1524	.1889	.1969	.1746	9
8	.0000	.0001	.0009	.0055	.0197	.0487	.0923	.1417	.1812	.1964	8
9	.0000	.0000	.0001	.0012	.0058	.0185	.0442	.0840	.1318	.1746	7
10	.0000	.0000	.0000	.0002	.0014	.0056	.0167	.0392	.0755	.1222	6
11	.0000	.0000	.0000	.0000	.0002	.0013	.0049	.0142	.0337	.0667	5
	.95	.90	.85	.80	.75	.70	.65	.60	.55	.50	y↑

n = 16 continued on next page

Table 1 (continued)
Binomial probabilities (n between 16 and 20)

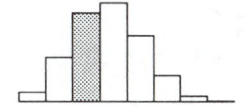

n = 16 (continued from previous page) π

y↓	.05	.10	.15	.20	.25	.30	.35	.40	.45	.50	
12	.0000	.0000	.0000	.0000	.0000	.0002	.0011	.0040	.0115	.0278	4
13	.0000	.0000	.0000	.0000	.0000	.0000	.0002	.0008	.0029	.0085	3
14	.0000	.0000	.0000	.0000	.0000	.0000	.0000	.0001	.0005	.0018	2
15	.0000	.0000	.0000	.0000	.0000	.0000	.0000	.0000	.0001	.0002	1
	.95	.90	.85	.80	.75	.70	.65	.60	.55	.50	y↑

n = 18 π

y↓	.05	.10	.15	.20	.25	.30	.35	.40	.45	.50	
0	.3972	.1501	.0536	.0180	.0056	.0016	.0004	.0001	.0000	.0000	18
1	.3763	.3002	.1704	.0811	.0338	.0126	.0042	.0012	.0003	.0001	17
2	.1683	.2835	.2556	.1723	.0958	.0458	.0190	.0069	.0022	.0006	16
3	.0473	.1680	.2406	.2297	.1704	.1046	.0547	.0246	.0095	.0031	15
4	.0093	.0700	.1592	.2153	.2130	.1681	.1104	.0614	.0291	.0117	14
5	.0014	.0218	.0787	.1507	.1988	.2017	.1664	.1146	.0666	.0327	13
6	.0002	.0052	.0301	.0816	.1436	.1873	.1941	.1655	.1181	.0708	12
7	.0000	.0010	.0091	.0350	.0820	.1376	.1792	.1892	.1657	.1214	11
8	.0000	.0002	.0022	.0120	.0376	.0811	.1327	.1734	.1864	.1669	10
9	.0000	.0000	.0004	.0033	.0139	.0386	.0794	.1284	.1694	.1855	9
10	.0000	.0000	.0001	.0008	.0042	.0149	.0385	.0771	.1248	.1669	8
11	.0000	.0000	.0000	.0001	.0010	.0046	.0151	.0374	.0742	.1214	7
12	.0000	.0000	.0000	.0000	.0002	.0012	.0047	.0145	.0354	.0708	6
13	.0000	.0000	.0000	.0000	.0000	.0002	.0012	.0045	.0134	.0327	5
14	.0000	.0000	.0000	.0000	.0000	.0000	.0002	.0011	.0039	.0117	4
15	.0000	.0000	.0000	.0000	.0000	.0000	.0000	.0002	.0009	.0031	3
16	.0000	.0000	.0000	.0000	.0000	.0000	.0000	.0000	.0001	.0006	2
17	.0000	.0000	.0000	.0000	.0000	.0000	.0000	.0000	.0000	.0001	1
	.95	.90	.85	.80	.75	.70	.65	.60	.55	.50	y↑

n = 20 π

y↓	.05	.10	.15	.20	.25	.30	.35	.40	.45	.50	
0	.3585	.1216	.0388	.0115	.0032	.0008	.0002	.0000	.0000	.0000	20
1	.3774	.2702	.1368	.0576	.0211	.0068	.0020	.0005	.0001	.0000	19
2	.1887	.2852	.2293	.1369	.0669	.0278	.0100	.0031	.0008	.0002	18
3	.0596	.1901	.2428	.2054	.1339	.0716	.0323	.0123	.0040	.0011	17
4	.0133	.0898	.1821	.2182	.1897	.1304	.0738	.0350	.0139	.0046	16
5	.0022	.0319	.1028	.1746	.2023	.1789	.1272	.0746	.0365	.0148	15
6	.0003	.0089	.0454	.1091	.1686	.1916	.1712	.1244	.0746	.0370	14
7	.0000	.0020	.0160	.0545	.1124	.1643	.1844	.1659	.1221	.0739	13
8	.0000	.0004	.0046	.0222	.0609	.1144	.1614	.1797	.1623	.1201	12
9	.0000	.0001	.0011	.0074	.0271	.0654	.1158	.1597	.1771	.1602	11
10	.0000	.0000	.0002	.0020	.0099	.0308	.0686	.1171	.1593	.1762	10
11	.0000	.0000	.0000	.0005	.0030	.0120	.0336	.0710	.1185	.1602	9
12	.0000	.0000	.0000	.0001	.0008	.0039	.0136	.0355	.0727	.1201	8
13	.0000	.0000	.0000	.0000	.0002	.0010	.0045	.0146	.0366	.0739	7
14	.0000	.0000	.0000	.0000	.0000	.0002	.0012	.0049	.0150	.0370	6
15	.0000	.0000	.0000	.0000	.0000	.0000	.0003	.0013	.0049	.0148	5
16	.0000	.0000	.0000	.0000	.0000	.0000	.0000	.0003	.0013	.0046	4
17	.0000	.0000	.0000	.0000	.0000	.0000	.0000	.0000	.0002	.0011	3
18	.0000	.0000	.0000	.0000	.0000	.0000	.0000	.0000	.0000	.0002	2
	.95	.90	.85	.80	.75	.70	.65	.60	.55	.50	y↑

Table 1 (continued)
Binomial probabilities (n = 50 and 100)

n = 50   π

y↓	.05	.10	.15	.20	.25	.30	.35	.40	.45	.50	
0	.0769	.0052	.0003	.0000	.0000	.0000	.0000	.0000	.0000	.0000	50
1	.2025	.0286	.0026	.0002	.0000	.0000	.0000	.0000	.0000	.0000	49
2	.2611	.0779	.0113	.0011	.0001	.0000	.0000	.0000	.0000	.0000	48
3	.2199	.1386	.0319	.0044	.0004	.0000	.0000	.0000	.0000	.0000	47
4	.1360	.1809	.0661	.0128	.0016	.0001	.0000	.0000	.0000	.0000	46
5	.0658	.1849	.1072	.0295	.0049	.0006	.0000	.0000	.0000	.0000	45
6	.0260	.1541	.1419	.0554	.0123	.0018	.0002	.0000	.0000	.0000	44
7	.0086	.1076	.1575	.0870	.0259	.0048	.0006	.0000	.0000	.0000	43
8	.0024	.0643	.1493	.1169	.0463	.0110	.0017	.0002	.0000	.0000	42
9	.0006	.0333	.1230	.1364	.0721	.0220	.0042	.0005	.0000	.0000	41
10	.0001	.0152	.0890	.1398	.0985	.0386	.0093	.0014	.0001	.0000	40
11	.0000	.0061	.0571	.1271	.1194	.0602	.0182	.0035	.0004	.0000	39
12	.0000	.0022	.0328	.1033	.1294	.0838	.0319	.0076	.0011	.0001	38
13	.0000	.0007	.0169	.0755	.1261	.1050	.0502	.0147	.0027	.0003	37
14	.0000	.0002	.0079	.0499	.1110	.1189	.0714	.0260	.0059	.0008	36
15	.0000	.0001	.0033	.0299	.0888	.1223	.0923	.0415	.0116	.0020	35
16	.0000	.0000	.0013	.0164	.0648	.1147	.1088	.0606	.0207	.0044	34
17	.0000	.0000	.0005	.0082	.0432	.0983	.1171	.0808	.0339	.0087	33
18	.0000	.0000	.0001	.0037	.0264	.0772	.1156	.0987	.0508	.0160	32
19	.0000	.0000	.0000	.0016	.0148	.0558	.1048	.1109	.0700	.0270	31
20	.0000	.0000	.0000	.0006	.0077	.0370	.0875	.1146	.0888	.0419	30
21	.0000	.0000	.0000	.0002	.0036	.0227	.0673	.1091	.1038	.0598	29
22	.0000	.0000	.0000	.0001	.0016	.0128	.0478	.0959	.1119	.0788	28
23	.0000	.0000	.0000	.0000	.0006	.0067	.0313	.0778	.1115	.0960	27
24	.0000	.0000	.0000	.0000	.0002	.0032	.0190	.0584	.1026	.1080	26
25	.0000	.0000	.0000	.0000	.0001	.0014	.0106	.0405	.0873	.1123	25
26	.0000	.0000	.0000	.0000	.0000	.0006	.0055	.0259	.0687	.1080	24
27	.0000	.0000	.0000	.0000	.0000	.0002	.0026	.0154	.0500	.0960	23
28	.0000	.0000	.0000	.0000	.0000	.0001	.0012	.0084	.0336	.0788	22
29	.0000	.0000	.0000	.0000	.0000	.0000	.0005	.0043	.0208	.0598	21
30	.0000	.0000	.0000	.0000	.0000	.0000	.0002	.0020	.0119	.0419	20
31	.0000	.0000	.0000	.0000	.0000	.0000	.0001	.0009	.0063	.0270	19
32	.0000	.0000	.0000	.0000	.0000	.0000	.0000	.0003	.0031	.0160	18
33	.0000	.0000	.0000	.0000	.0000	.0000	.0000	.0001	.0014	.0087	17
34	.0000	.0000	.0000	.0000	.0000	.0000	.0000	.0000	.0006	.0044	16
35	.0000	.0000	.0000	.0000	.0000	.0000	.0000	.0000	.0002	.0020	15
36	.0000	.0000	.0000	.0000	.0000	.0000	.0000	.0000	.0001	.0008	14
37	.0000	.0000	.0000	.0000	.0000	.0000	.0000	.0000	.0000	.0003	13
38	.0000	.0000	.0000	.0000	.0000	.0000	.0000	.0000	.0000	.0001	12
	.95	.90	.85	.80	.75	.70	.65	.60	.55	.50	y↑

n = 100   π

y↓	.05	.10	.15	.20	.25	.30	.35	.40	.45	.50	
0	.0059	.0000	.0000	.0000	.0000	.0000	.0000	.0000	.0000	.0000	100
1	.0312	.0003	.0000	.0000	.0000	.0000	.0000	.0000	.0000	.0000	99
2	.0812	.0016	.0000	.0000	.0000	.0000	.0000	.0000	.0000	.0000	98
3	.1396	.0059	.0001	.0000	.0000	.0000	.0000	.0000	.0000	.0000	97
4	.1781	.0159	.0003	.0000	.0000	.0000	.0000	.0000	.0000	.0000	96
5	.1800	.0339	.0011	.0000	.0000	.0000	.0000	.0000	.0000	.0000	95
6	.1500	.0596	.0031	.0001	.0000	.0000	.0000	.0000	.0000	.0000	94
7	.1060	.0889	.0075	.0002	.0000	.0000	.0000	.0000	.0000	.0000	93
8	.0649	.1148	.0153	.0006	.0000	.0000	.0000	.0000	.0000	.0000	92
9	.0349	.1304	.0276	.0015	.0000	.0000	.0000	.0000	.0000	.0000	91
10	.0167	.1319	.0444	.0034	.0001	.0000	.0000	.0000	.0000	.0000	90
11	.0072	.1199	.0640	.0069	.0003	.0000	.0000	.0000	.0000	.0000	89
	.95	.90	.85	.80	.75	.70	.65	.60	.55	.50	y↑

n = 100 continued on next page

Table 1 (continued)
Binomial probabilities (n = 100)

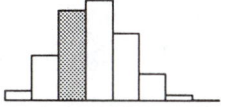

n = 100 (continued from previous page)   π

y↓	.05	.10	.15	.20	.25	.30	.35	.40	.45	.50	
12	.0028	.0988	.0838	.0128	.0006	.0000	.0000	.0000	.0000	.0000	88
13	.0010	.0743	.1001	.0216	.0014	.0000	.0000	.0000	.0000	.0000	87
14	.0003	.0513	.1098	.0335	.0030	.0001	.0000	.0000	.0000	.0000	86
15	.0001	.0327	.1111	.0481	.0057	.0002	.0000	.0000	.0000	.0000	85
16	.0000	.0193	.1041	.0638	.0100	.0006	.0000	.0000	.0000	.0000	84
17	.0000	.0106	.0908	.0789	.0165	.0012	.0000	.0000	.0000	.0000	83
18	.0000	.0054	.0739	.0909	.0254	.0024	.0001	.0000	.0000	.0000	82
19	.0000	.0026	.0563	.0981	.0365	.0044	.0002	.0000	.0000	.0000	81
20	.0000	.0012	.0402	.0993	.0493	.0076	.0004	.0000	.0000	.0000	80
21	.0000	.0005	.0270	.0946	.0626	.0124	.0009	.0000	.0000	.0000	79
22	.0000	.0002	.0171	.0849	.0749	.0190	.0017	.0001	.0000	.0000	78
23	.0000	.0001	.0103	.0720	.0847	.0277	.0032	.0001	.0000	.0000	77
24	.0000	.0000	.0058	.0577	.0906	.0380	.0055	.0003	.0000	.0000	76
25	.0000	.0000	.0031	.0439	.0918	.0496	.0090	.0006	.0000	.0000	75
26	.0000	.0000	.0016	.0316	.0883	.0613	.0140	.0012	.0000	.0000	74
27	.0000	.0000	.0008	.0217	.0806	.0720	.0207	.0022	.0001	.0000	73
28	.0000	.0000	.0004	.0141	.0701	.0804	.0290	.0038	.0002	.0000	72
29	.0000	.0000	.0002	.0088	.0580	.0856	.0388	.0063	.0004	.0000	71
30	.0000	.0000	.0001	.0052	.0458	.0868	.0494	.0100	.0008	.0000	70
31	.0000	.0000	.0000	.0029	.0344	.0840	.0601	.0151	.0014	.0001	69
32	.0000	.0000	.0000	.0016	.0248	.0776	.0698	.0217	.0025	.0001	68
33	.0000	.0000	.0000	.0008	.0170	.0685	.0774	.0297	.0043	.0002	67
34	.0000	.0000	.0000	.0004	.0112	.0579	.0821	.0391	.0069	.0005	66
35	.0000	.0000	.0000	.0002	.0070	.0468	.0834	.0491	.0106	.0009	65
36	.0000	.0000	.0000	.0001	.0042	.0362	.0811	.0591	.0157	.0016	64
37	.0000	.0000	.0000	.0000	.0024	.0268	.0755	.0682	.0222	.0027	63
38	.0000	.0000	.0000	.0000	.0013	.0191	.0674	.0754	.0301	.0045	62
39	.0000	.0000	.0000	.0000	.0007	.0130	.0577	.0799	.0391	.0071	61
40	.0000	.0000	.0000	.0000	.0004	.0085	.0474	.0812	.0488	.0108	60
41	.0000	.0000	.0000	.0000	.0002	.0053	.0373	.0792	.0584	.0159	59
42	.0000	.0000	.0000	.0000	.0001	.0032	.0282	.0742	.0672	.0223	58
43	.0000	.0000	.0000	.0000	.0000	.0019	.0205	.0667	.0741	.0301	57
44	.0000	.0000	.0000	.0000	.0000	.0010	.0143	.0576	.0786	.0390	56
45	.0000	.0000	.0000	.0000	.0000	.0005	.0096	.0478	.0800	.0485	55
46	.0000	.0000	.0000	.0000	.0000	.0003	.0062	.0381	.0782	.0580	54
47	.0000	.0000	.0000	.0000	.0000	.0001	.0038	.0292	.0736	.0666	53
48	.0000	.0000	.0000	.0000	.0000	.0001	.0023	.0215	.0665	.0735	52
49	.0000	.0000	.0000	.0000	.0000	.0000	.0013	.0152	.0577	.0780	51
50	.0000	.0000	.0000	.0000	.0000	.0000	.0007	.0103	.0482	.0796	50
51	.0000	.0000	.0000	.0000	.0000	.0000	.0004	.0068	.0386	.0780	49
52	.0000	.0000	.0000	.0000	.0000	.0000	.0002	.0042	.0298	.0735	48
53	.0000	.0000	.0000	.0000	.0000	.0000	.0001	.0026	.0221	.0666	47
54	.0000	.0000	.0000	.0000	.0000	.0000	.0000	.0015	.0157	.0580	46
55	.0000	.0000	.0000	.0000	.0000	.0000	.0000	.0008	.0108	.0485	45
56	.0000	.0000	.0000	.0000	.0000	.0000	.0000	.0004	.0071	.0390	44
57	.0000	.0000	.0000	.0000	.0000	.0000	.0000	.0002	.0045	.0301	43
58	.0000	.0000	.0000	.0000	.0000	.0000	.0000	.0001	.0027	.0223	42
59	.0000	.0000	.0000	.0000	.0000	.0000	.0000	.0001	.0016	.0159	41
60	.0000	.0000	.0000	.0000	.0000	.0000	.0000	.0000	.0009	.0108	40
61	.0000	.0000	.0000	.0000	.0000	.0000	.0000	.0000	.0005	.0071	39
62	.0000	.0000	.0000	.0000	.0000	.0000	.0000	.0000	.0002	.0045	38
63	.0000	.0000	.0000	.0000	.0000	.0000	.0000	.0000	.0001	.0027	37
64	.0000	.0000	.0000	.0000	.0000	.0000	.0000	.0000	.0001	.0016	36
65	.0000	.0000	.0000	.0000	.0000	.0000	.0000	.0000	.0000	.0009	35
66	.0000	.0000	.0000	.0000	.0000	.0000	.0000	.0000	.0000	.0005	34
67	.0000	.0000	.0000	.0000	.0000	.0000	.0000	.0000	.0000	.0002	33
68	.0000	.0000	.0000	.0000	.0000	.0000	.0000	.0000	.0000	.0001	32
69	.0000	.0000	.0000	.0000	.0000	.0000	.0000	.0000	.0000	.0001	31
	.95	.90	.85	.80	.75	.70	.65	.60	.55	.50	y↑

Source: Computed by D. K. Hildebrand

Table 2
Poisson Probabilities (μ between .1 and 5.0)

y	.1	.2	.3	.4	.5	.6	.7	.8	.9	1.0
0	.9048	.8187	.7408	.6703	.6065	.5488	.4966	.4493	.4066	.3679
1	.0905	.1637	.2222	.2681	.3033	.3293	.3476	.3595	.3659	.3679
2	.0045	.0164	.0333	.0536	.0758	.0988	.1217	.1438	.1647	.1839
3	.0002	.0011	.0033	.0072	.0126	.0198	.0284	.0383	.0494	.0613
4	.0000	.0001	.0003	.0007	.0016	.0030	.0050	.0077	.0111	.0153
5	.0000	.0000	.0000	.0001	.0002	.0004	.0007	.0012	.0020	.0031
6	.0000	.0000	.0000	.0000	.0000	.0000	.0001	.0002	.0003	.0005

y	1.1	1.2	1.3	1.4	1.5	1.6	1.7	1.8	1.9	2.0
0	.3329	.3012	.2725	.2466	.2231	.2019	.1827	.1653	.1496	.1353
1	.3662	.3614	.3543	.3452	.3347	.3230	.3106	.2975	.2842	.2707
2	.2014	.2169	.2303	.2417	.2510	.2584	.2640	.2678	.2700	.2707
3	.0738	.0867	.0998	.1128	.1255	.1378	.1496	.1607	.1710	.1804
4	.0203	.0260	.0324	.0395	.0471	.0551	.0636	.0723	.0812	.0902
5	.0045	.0062	.0084	.0111	.0141	.0176	.0216	.0260	.0309	.0361
6	.0008	.0012	.0018	.0026	.0035	.0047	.0061	.0078	.0098	.0120
7	.0001	.0002	.0003	.0005	.0008	.0011	.0015	.0020	.0027	.0034
8	.0000	.0000	.0001	.0001	.0001	.0002	.0003	.0005	.0006	.0009

y	2.1	2.2	2.3	2.4	2.5	2.6	2.7	2.8	2.9	3.0
0	.1225	.1108	.1003	.0907	.0821	.0743	.0672	.0608	.0550	.0498
1	.2572	.2438	.2306	.2177	.2052	.1931	.1815	.1703	.1596	.1494
2	.2700	.2681	.2652	.2613	.2565	.2510	.2450	.2384	.2314	.2240
3	.1890	.1966	.2033	.2090	.2138	.2176	.2205	.2225	.2237	.2240
4	.0992	.1082	.1169	.1254	.1336	.1414	.1488	.1557	.1622	.1680
5	.0417	.0476	.0538	.0602	.0668	.0735	.0804	.0872	.0940	.1008
6	.0146	.0174	.0206	.0241	.0278	.0319	.0362	.0407	.0455	.0504
7	.0044	.0055	.0068	.0083	.0099	.0118	.0139	.0163	.0188	.0216
8	.0011	.0015	.0019	.0025	.0031	.0038	.0047	.0057	.0068	.0081
9	.0003	.0004	.0005	.0007	.0009	.0011	.0014	.0018	.0022	.0027
10	.0001	.0001	.0001	.0002	.0002	.0003	.0004	.0005	.0006	.0008
11	.0000	.0000	.0000	.0000	.0000	.0001	.0001	.0001	.0002	.0002

y	3.1	3.2	3.3	3.4	3.5	3.6	3.7	3.8	3.9	4.0
0	.0450	.0408	.0369	.0334	.0302	.0273	.0247	.0224	.0202	.0183
1	.1397	.1304	.1217	.1135	.1057	.0984	.0915	.0850	.0789	.0733
2	.2165	.2087	.2008	.1929	.1850	.1771	.1692	.1615	.1539	.1465
3	.2237	.2226	.2209	.2186	.2158	.2125	.2087	.2046	.2001	.1954
4	.1733	.1781	.1823	.1858	.1888	.1912	.1931	.1944	.1951	.1954
5	.1075	.1140	.1203	.1264	.1322	.1377	.1429	.1477	.1522	.1563
6	.0555	.0608	.0662	.0716	.0771	.0826	.0881	.0936	.0989	.1042
7	.0246	.0278	.0312	.0348	.0385	.0425	.0466	.0508	.0551	.0595
8	.0095	.0111	.0129	.0148	.0169	.0191	.0215	.0241	.0269	.0298
9	.0033	.0040	.0047	.0056	.0066	.0076	.0089	.0102	.0116	.0132
10	.0010	.0013	.0016	.0019	.0023	.0028	.0033	.0039	.0045	.0053
11	.0003	.0004	.0005	.0006	.0007	.0009	.0011	.0013	.0016	.0019
12	.0001	.0001	.0001	.0002	.0002	.0003	.0003	.0004	.0005	.0006
13	.0000	.0000	.0000	.0000	.0001	.0001	.0001	.0001	.0002	.0002

y	4.1	4.2	4.3	4.4	4.5	4.6	4.7	4.8	4.9	5.0
0	.0166	.0150	.0136	.0123	.0111	.0101	.0091	.0082	.0074	.0067
1	.0679	.0630	.0583	.0540	.0500	.0462	.0427	.0395	.0365	.0337
2	.1393	.1323	.1254	.1188	.1125	.1063	.1005	.0948	.0894	.0842
3	.1904	.1852	.1798	.1743	.1687	.1631	.1574	.1517	.1460	.1404
4	.1951	.1944	.1933	.1917	.1898	.1875	.1849	.1820	.1789	.1755
5	.1600	.1633	.1662	.1687	.1708	.1725	.1738	.1747	.1753	.1755
6	.1093	.1143	.1191	.1237	.1281	.1323	.1362	.1398	.1432	.1462
7	.0640	.0686	.0732	.0778	.0824	.0869	.0914	.0959	.1002	.1044
8	.0328	.0360	.0393	.0428	.0463	.0500	.0537	.0575	.0614	.0653
9	.0150	.0168	.0188	.0209	.0232	.0255	.0281	.0307	.0334	.0363
10	.0061	.0071	.0081	.0092	.0104	.0118	.0132	.0147	.0164	.0181
11	.0023	.0027	.0032	.0037	.0043	.0049	.0056	.0064	.0073	.0082
12	.0008	.0009	.0011	.0013	.0016	.0019	.0022	.0026	.0030	.0034
13	.0002	.0003	.0004	.0005	.0006	.0007	.0008	.0009	.0011	.0013
14	.0001	.0001	.0001	.0001	.0002	.0002	.0003	.0003	.0004	.0005
15	.0000	.0000	.0000	.0000	.0001	.0001	.0001	.0001	.0001	.0002

Table 2 (continued)
Poisson Probabilities (μ between 5.5 and 20.0)

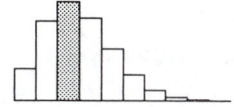

y	5.5	6.0	6.5	7.0	7.5	8.0	8.5	9.0	9.5	10.0
0	.0041	.0025	.0015	.0009	.0006	.0003	.0002	.0001	.0001	.0000
1	.0225	.0149	.0098	.0064	.0041	.0027	.0017	.0011	.0007	.0005
2	.0618	.0446	.0318	.0223	.0156	.0107	.0074	.0050	.0034	.0023
3	.1133	.0892	.0688	.0521	.0389	.0286	.0208	.0150	.0107	.0076
4	.1558	.1339	.1118	.0912	.0729	.0573	.0443	.0337	.0254	.0189
5	.1714	.1606	.1454	.1277	.1094	.0916	.0752	.0607	.0483	.0378
6	.1571	.1606	.1575	.1490	.1367	.1221	.1066	.0911	.0764	.0631
7	.1234	.1377	.1462	.1490	.1465	.1396	.1294	.1171	.1037	.0901
8	.0849	.1033	.1188	.1304	.1373	.1396	.1375	.1318	.1232	.1126
9	.0519	.0688	.0858	.1014	.1144	.1241	.1299	.1318	.1300	.1251
10	.0285	.0413	.0558	.0710	.0858	.0993	.1104	.1186	.1235	.1251
11	.0143	.0225	.0330	.0452	.0585	.0722	.0853	.0970	.1067	.1137
12	.0065	.0113	.0179	.0263	.0366	.0481	.0604	.0728	.0844	.0948
13	.0028	.0052	.0089	.0142	.0211	.0296	.0395	.0504	.0617	.0729
14	.0011	.0022	.0041	.0071	.0113	.0169	.0240	.0324	.0419	.0521
15	.0004	.0009	.0018	.0033	.0057	.0090	.0136	.0194	.0265	.0347
16	.0001	.0003	.0007	.0014	.0026	.0045	.0072	.0109	.0157	.0217
17	.0000	.0001	.0003	.0006	.0012	.0021	.0036	.0058	.0088	.0128
18	.0000	.0000	.0001	.0002	.0005	.0009	.0017	.0029	.0046	.0071
19	.0000	.0000	.0000	.0001	.0002	.0004	.0008	.0014	.0023	.0037
20	.0000	.0000	.0000	.0000	.0001	.0002	.0003	.0006	.0011	.0019
21	.0000	.0000	.0000	.0000	.0000	.0001	.0001	.0003	.0005	.0009
22	.0000	.0000	.0000	.0000	.0000	.0000	.0001	.0001	.0002	.0004
23	.0000	.0000	.0000	.0000	.0000	.0000	.0000	.0000	.0001	.0002

y	11.0	12.0	13.0	14.0	15.0	16.0	17.0	18.0	19.0	20.0
0	.0000	.0000	.0000	.0000	.0000	.0000	.0000	.0000	.0000	.0000
1	.0002	.0001	.0000	.0000	.0000	.0000	.0000	.0000	.0000	.0000
2	.0010	.0004	.0002	.0001	.0000	.0000	.0000	.0000	.0000	.0000
3	.0037	.0018	.0008	.0004	.0002	.0001	.0000	.0000	.0000	.0000
4	.0102	.0053	.0027	.0013	.0006	.0003	.0001	.0001	.0000	.0000
5	.0224	.0127	.0070	.0037	.0019	.0010	.0005	.0002	.0001	.0001
6	.0411	.0255	.0152	.0087	.0048	.0026	.0014	.0007	.0004	.0002
7	.0646	.0437	.0281	.0174	.0104	.0060	.0034	.0019	.0010	.0005
8	.0888	.0655	.0457	.0304	.0194	.0120	.0072	.0042	.0024	.0013
9	.1085	.0874	.0661	.0473	.0324	.0213	.0135	.0083	.0050	.0029
10	.1194	.1048	.0859	.0663	.0486	.0341	.0230	.0150	.0095	.0058
11	.1194	.1144	.1015	.0844	.0663	.0496	.0355	.0245	.0164	.0106
12	.1094	.1144	.1099	.0984	.0829	.0661	.0504	.0368	.0259	.0176
13	.0926	.1056	.1099	.1060	.0956	.0814	.0658	.0509	.0378	.0271
14	.0728	.0905	.1021	.1060	.1024	.0930	.0800	.0655	.0514	.0387
15	.0534	.0724	.0885	.0989	.1024	.0992	.0906	.0786	.0650	.0516
16	.0367	.0543	.0719	.0866	.0960	.0992	.0963	.0884	.0772	.0646
17	.0237	.0383	.0550	.0713	.0847	.0934	.0963	.0936	.0863	.0760
18	.0145	.0255	.0397	.0554	.0706	.0830	.0909	.0936	.0911	.0844
19	.0084	.0161	.0272	.0409	.0557	.0699	.0814	.0887	.0911	.0888
20	.0046	.0097	.0177	.0286	.0418	.0559	.0692	.0798	.0866	.0888
21	.0024	.0055	.0109	.0191	.0299	.0426	.0560	.0684	.0783	.0846
22	.0012	.0030	.0065	.0121	.0204	.0310	.0433	.0560	.0676	.0769
23	.0006	.0016	.0037	.0074	.0133	.0216	.0320	.0438	.0559	.0669
24	.0003	.0008	.0020	.0043	.0083	.0144	.0226	.0328	.0442	.0557
25	.0001	.0004	.0010	.0024	.0050	.0092	.0154	.0237	.0336	.0446
26	.0000	.0002	.0005	.0013	.0029	.0057	.0101	.0164	.0246	.0343
27	.0000	.0001	.0002	.0007	.0016	.0034	.0063	.0109	.0173	.0254
28	.0000	.0000	.0001	.0003	.0009	.0019	.0038	.0070	.0117	.0181
29	.0000	.0000	.0001	.0002	.0004	.0011	.0023	.0044	.0077	.0125
30	.0000	.0000	.0000	.0001	.0002	.0006	.0013	.0026	.0049	.0083
31	.0000	.0000	.0000	.0000	.0001	.0003	.0007	.0015	.0030	.0054
32	.0000	.0000	.0000	.0000	.0001	.0001	.0004	.0009	.0018	.0034
33	.0000	.0000	.0000	.0000	.0001	.0001	.0002	.0005	.0010	.0020

Source: Computed by D. K. Hildebrand.

Table 3
Normal curve areas

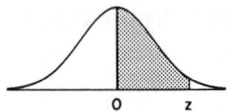

z	.00	.01	.02	.03	.04	.05	.06	.07	.08	.09
0.00	.0000	.0040	.0080	.0120	.0160	.0199	.0239	.0279	.0319	.0359
0.10	.0398	.0438	.0478	.0517	.0557	.0596	.0636	.0675	.0714	.0753
0.20	.0793	.0832	.0871	.0910	.0948	.0987	.1026	.1064	.1103	.1141
0.30	.1179	.1217	.1255	.1293	.1331	.1368	.1406	.1443	.1480	.1517
0.40	.1554	.1591	.1628	.1664	.1700	.1736	.1772	.1808	.1844	.1879
0.50	.1915	.1950	.1985	.2019	.2054	.2088	.2123	.2157	.2190	.2224
0.60	.2257	.2291	.2324	.2357	.2389	.2422	.2454	.2486	.2517	.2549
0.70	.2580	.2611	.2642	.2673	.2704	.2734	.2764	.2794	.2823	.2852
0.80	.2881	.2910	.2939	.2967	.2995	.3023	.3051	.3078	.3106	.3133
0.90	.3159	.3186	.3212	.3238	.3264	.3289	.3315	.3340	.3365	.3389
1.00	.3413	.3438	.3461	.3485	.3508	.3531	.3554	.3577	.3599	.3621
1.10	.3643	.3665	.3686	.3708	.3729	.3749	.3770	.3790	.3810	.3830
1.20	.3849	.3869	.3888	.3907	.3925	.3944	.3962	.3980	.3997	.4015
1.30	.4032	.4049	.4066	.4082	.4099	.4115	.4131	.4147	.4162	.4177
1.40	.4192	.4207	.4222	.4236	.4251	.4265	.4279	.4292	.4306	.4319
1.50	.4332	.4345	.4357	.4370	.4382	.4394	.4406	.4418	.4429	.4441
1.60	.4452	.4463	.4474	.4484	.4495	.4505	.4515	.4525	.4535	.4545
1.70	.4554	.4564	.4573	.4582	.4591	.4599	.4608	.4616	.4625	.4633
1.80	.4641	.4649	.4656	.4664	.4671	.4678	.4686	.4693	.4699	.4706
1.90	.4713	.4719	.4726	.4732	.4738	.4744	.4750	.4756	.4761	.4767
2.00	.4772	.4778	.4783	.4788	.4793	.4798	.4803	.4808	.4812	.4817
2.10	.4821	.4826	.4830	.4834	.4838	.4842	.4846	.4850	.4854	.4857
2.20	.4861	.4864	.4868	.4871	.4875	.4878	.4881	.4884	.4887	.4890
2.30	.4893	.4896	.4898	.4901	.4904	.4906	.4909	.4911	.4913	.4916
2.40	.4918	.4920	.4922	.4925	.4927	.4929	.4931	.4932	.4934	.4936
2.50	.4938	.4940	.4941	.4943	.4945	.4946	.4948	.4949	.4951	.4952
2.60	.4953	.4955	.4956	.4957	.4959	.4960	.4961	.4962	.4963	.4964
2.70	.4965	.4966	.4967	.4968	.4969	.4970	.4971	.4972	.4973	.4974
2.80	.4974	.4975	.4976	.4977	.4977	.4978	.4979	.4979	.4980	.4981
2.90	.4981	.4982	.4982	.4983	.4984	.4984	.4985	.4985	.4986	.4986
3.00	.4987	.4987	.4987	.4988	.4988	.4989	.4989	.4989	.4990	.4990

z	area
3.50	.49976737
4.00	.49996833
4.50	.49999660
5.00	.49999971

Source: Computed by P. J. Hildebrand.

Table 4
Percentage points of the *t* distribution

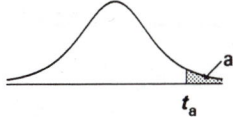

df	a = .1	a = .05	a = .025	a = .01	a = .005	a = .001
1	3.078	6.314	12.706	31.821	63.657	318.309
2	1.886	2.920	4.303	6.965	9.925	22.327
3	1.638	2.353	3.182	4.541	5.841	10.215
4	1.533	2.132	2.776	3.747	4.604	7.173
5	1.476	2.015	2.571	3.365	4.032	5.893
6	1.440	1.943	2.447	3.143	3.707	5.208
7	1.415	1.895	2.365	2.998	3.499	4.785
8	1.397	1.860	2.306	2.896	3.355	4.501
9	1.383	1.833	2.262	2.821	3.250	4.297
10	1.372	1.812	2.228	2.764	3.169	4.144
11	1.363	1.796	2.201	2.718	3.106	4.025
12	1.356	1.782	2.179	2.681	3.055	3.930
13	1.350	1.771	2.160	2.650	3.012	3.852
14	1.345	1.761	2.145	2.624	2.977	3.787
15	1.341	1.753	2.131	2.602	2.947	3.733
16	1.337	1.746	2.120	2.583	2.921	3.686
17	1.333	1.740	2.110	2.567	2.898	3.646
18	1.330	1.734	2.101	2.552	2.878	3.610
19	1.328	1.729	2.093	2.539	2.861	3.579
20	1.325	1.725	2.086	2.528	2.845	3.552
21	1.323	1.721	2.080	2.518	2.831	3.527
22	1.321	1.717	2.074	2.508	2.819	3.505
23	1.319	1.714	2.069	2.500	2.807	3.485
24	1.318	1.711	2.064	2.492	2.797	3.467
25	1.316	1.708	2.060	2.485	2.787	3.450
26	1.315	1.706	2.056	2.479	2.779	3.435
27	1.314	1.703	2.052	2.473	2.771	3.421
28	1.313	1.701	2.048	2.467	2.763	3.408
29	1.311	1.699	2.045	2.462	2.756	3.396
30	1.310	1.697	2.042	2.457	2.750	3.385
40	1.303	1.684	2.021	2.423	2.704	3.307
60	1.296	1.671	2.000	2.390	2.660	3.232
120	1.289	1.658	1.980	2.358	2.617	3.160
240	1.285	1.651	1.970	2.342	2.596	3.125
∞	1.282	1.645	1.960	2.326	2.576	3.090

Source: Computed by P. J. Hildebrand.

Table 5
Percentage points of the χ^2 distribution (a > .5)

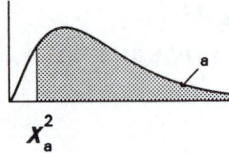

χ^2_a

df	a = .999	a = .995	a = .99	a = .975	a = .95	a = .9
1	.000002	.000039	.000157	.000982	.003932	.01579
2	.002001	.01003	.02010	.05064	.1026	.2107
3	.02430	.07172	.1148	.2158	.3518	.5844
4	.09080	.2070	.2971	.4844	.7107	1.064
5	.2102	.4117	.5543	.8312	1.145	1.610
6	.3811	.6757	.8721	1.237	1.635	2.204
7	.5985	.9893	1.239	1.690	2.167	2.833
8	.8571	1.344	1.646	2.180	2.733	3.490
9	1.152	1.735	2.088	2.700	3.325	4.168
10	1.479	2.156	2.558	3.247	3.940	4.865
11	1.834	2.603	3.053	3.816	4.575	5.578
12	2.214	3.074	3.571	4.404	5.226	6.304
13	2.617	3.565	4.107	5.009	5.892	7.042
14	3.041	4.075	4.660	5.629	6.571	7.790
15	3.483	4.601	5.229	6.262	7.261	8.547
16	3.942	5.142	5.812	6.908	7.962	9.312
17	4.416	5.697	6.408	7.564	8.672	10.09
18	4.905	6.265	7.015	8.231	9.390	10.86
19	5.407	6.844	7.633	8.907	10.12	11.65
20	5.921	7.434	8.260	9.591	10.85	12.44
21	6.447	8.034	8.897	10.28	11.59	13.24
22	6.983	8.643	9.542	10.98	12.34	14.04
23	7.529	9.260	10.20	11.69	13.09	14.85
24	8.085	9.886	10.86	12.40	13.85	15.66
25	8.649	10.52	11.52	13.12	14.61	16.47
26	9.222	11.16	12.20	13.84	15.38	17.29
27	9.803	11.81	12.88	14.57	16.15	18.11
28	10.39	12.46	13.56	15.31	16.93	18.94
29	10.99	13.12	14.26	16.05	17.71	19.77
30	11.59	13.79	14.95	16.79	18.49	20.60
40	17.92	20.71	22.16	24.43	26.51	29.05
50	24.67	27.99	29.71	32.36	34.76	37.69
60	31.74	35.53	37.48	40.48	43.19	46.46
70	39.04	43.28	45.44	48.76	51.74	55.33
80	46.52	51.17	53.54	57.15	60.39	64.28
90	54.16	59.20	61.75	65.65	69.13	73.29
100	61.92	67.33	70.06	74.22	77.93	82.36
120	77.76	83.85	86.92	91.57	95.70	100.62
240	177.95	187.32	191.99	198.98	205.14	212.39

Table 5 (continued)
Percentage points of the χ^2 distribution (a < .5)

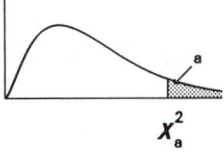

a = .1	a = .05	a = .025	a = .01	a = .005	a = .001	df
2.706	3.841	5.024	6.635	7.879	10.83	1
4.605	5.991	7.378	9.210	10.60	13.82	2
6.251	7.815	9.348	11.34	12.84	16.27	3
7.779	9.488	11.14	13.28	14.86	18.47	4
9.236	11.07	12.83	15.09	16.75	20.52	5
10.64	12.59	14.45	16.81	18.55	22.46	6
12.02	14.07	16.01	18.48	20.28	24.32	7
13.36	15.51	17.53	20.09	21.95	26.12	8
14.68	16.92	19.02	21.67	23.59	27.88	9
15.99	18.31	20.48	23.21	25.19	29.59	10
17.28	19.68	21.92	24.72	26.76	31.27	11
18.55	21.03	23.34	26.22	28.30	32.91	12
19.81	22.36	24.74	27.69	29.82	34.53	13
21.06	23.68	26.12	29.14	31.32	36.12	14
22.31	25.00	27.49	30.58	32.80	37.70	15
23.54	26.30	28.85	32.00	34.27	39.25	16
24.77	27.59	30.19	33.41	35.72	40.79	17
25.99	28.87	31.53	34.81	37.16	42.31	18
27.20	30.14	32.85	36.19	38.58	43.82	19
28.41	31.41	34.17	37.57	40.00	45.31	20
29.62	32.67	35.48	38.93	41.40	46.80	21
30.81	33.92	36.78	40.29	42.80	48.27	22
32.01	35.17	38.08	41.64	44.18	49.73	23
33.20	36.42	39.36	42.98	45.56	51.18	24
34.38	37.65	40.65	44.31	46.93	52.62	25
35.56	38.89	41.92	45.64	48.29	54.05	26
36.74	40.11	43.19	46.96	49.65	55.48	27
37.92	41.34	44.46	48.28	50.99	56.89	28
39.09	42.56	45.72	49.59	52.34	58.30	29
40.26	43.77	46.98	50.89	53.67	59.70	30
51.81	55.76	59.34	63.69	66.77	73.40	40
63.17	67.50	71.42	76.15	79.49	86.66	50
74.40	79.08	83.30	88.38	91.95	99.61	60
85.53	90.53	95.02	100.43	104.21	112.32	70
96.58	101.88	106.63	112.33	116.32	124.84	80
107.57	113.15	118.14	124.12	128.30	137.21	90
118.50	124.34	129.56	135.81	140.17	149.45	100
140.23	146.57	152.21	158.95	163.65	173.62	120
268.47	277.14	284.80	293.89	300.18	313.44	240

Source: Computed by P. J. Hildebrand

Table 6

Percentage points of the F distribution (df_2 between 1 and 6)

df_2	a	df_1 1	2	3	4	5	6	7	8	9	10
1	.25	5.83	7.50	8.20	8.58	8.82	8.98	9.10	9.19	9.26	9.32
	.10	39.86	49.50	53.59	55.83	57.24	58.20	58.91	59.44	59.86	60.19
	.05	161.4	199.5	215.7	224.6	230.2	234.0	236.8	238.9	240.5	241.9
	.025	647.8	799.5	864.2	899.6	921.8	937.1	948.2	956.7	963.3	968.6
	.01	4052	5000	5403	5625	5764	5859	5928	5981	6022	6056
2	.25	2.57	3.00	3.15	3.23	3.28	3.31	3.34	3.35	3.37	3.38
	.10	8.53	9.00	9.16	9.24	9.29	9.33	9.35	9.37	9.38	9.39
	.05	18.51	19.00	19.16	19.25	19.30	19.33	19.35	19.37	19.38	19.40
	.025	38.51	39.00	39.17	39.25	39.30	39.33	39.36	39.37	39.39	39.40
	.01	98.50	99.00	99.17	99.25	99.30	99.33	99.36	99.37	99.39	99.40
	.005	198.5	199.0	199.2	199.2	199.3	199.3	199.4	199.4	199.4	199.4
	.001	998.5	999.0	999.2	999.2	999.3	999.3	999.4	999.4	999.4	999.4
3	.25	2.02	2.28	2.36	2.39	2.41	2.42	2.43	2.44	2.44	2.44
	.10	5.54	5.46	5.39	5.34	5.31	5.28	5.27	5.25	5.24	5.23
	.05	10.13	9.55	9.28	9.12	9.01	8.94	8.89	8.85	8.81	8.79
	.025	17.44	16.04	15.44	15.10	14.88	14.73	14.62	14.54	14.47	14.42
	.01	34.12	30.82	29.46	28.71	28.24	27.91	27.67	27.49	27.35	27.23
	.005	55.55	49.80	47.47	46.19	45.39	44.84	44.43	44.13	43.88	43.69
	.001	167.0	148.5	141.1	137.1	134.6	132.8	131.6	130.6	129.9	129.2
4	.25	1.81	2.00	2.05	2.06	2.07	2.08	2.08	2.08	2.08	2.08
	.10	4.54	4.32	4.19	4.11	4.05	4.01	3.98	3.95	3.94	3.92
	.05	7.71	6.94	6.59	6.39	6.26	6.16	6.09	6.04	6.00	5.96
	.025	12.22	10.65	9.98	9.60	9.36	9.20	9.07	8.98	8.90	8.84
	.01	21.20	18.00	16.69	15.98	15.52	15.21	14.98	14.80	14.66	14.55
	.005	31.33	26.28	24.26	23.15	22.46	21.97	21.62	21.35	21.14	20.97
	.001	74.14	61.25	56.18	53.44	51.71	50.53	49.66	49.00	48.47	48.05
5	.25	1.69	1.85	1.88	1.89	1.89	1.89	1.89	1.89	1.89	1.89
	.10	4.06	3.78	3.62	3.52	3.45	3.40	3.37	3.34	3.32	3.30
	.05	6.61	5.79	5.41	5.19	5.05	4.95	4.88	4.82	4.77	4.74
	.025	10.01	8.43	7.76	7.39	7.15	6.98	6.85	6.76	6.68	6.62
	.01	16.26	13.27	12.06	11.39	10.97	10.67	10.46	10.29	10.16	10.05
	.005	22.78	18.31	16.53	15.56	14.94	14.51	14.20	13.96	13.77	13.62
	.001	47.18	37.12	33.20	31.09	29.75	28.83	28.16	27.65	27.24	26.92
6	.25	1.62	1.76	1.78	1.79	1.79	1.78	1.78	1.78	1.77	1.77
	.10	3.78	3.46	3.29	3.18	3.11	3.05	3.01	2.98	2.96	2.94
	.05	5.99	5.14	4.76	4.53	4.39	4.28	4.21	4.15	4.10	4.06
	.025	8.81	7.26	6.60	6.23	5.99	5.82	5.70	5.60	5.52	5.46
	.01	13.75	10.92	9.78	9.15	8.75	8.47	8.26	8.10	7.98	7.87
	.005	18.63	14.54	12.92	12.03	11.46	11.07	10.79	10.57	10.39	10.25
	.001	35.51	27.00	23.70	21.92	20.80	20.03	19.46	19.03	18.69	18.41

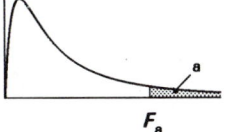

F_a

				df$_1$								
12	**15**	**20**	**24**	**30**	**40**	**60**	**120**	**240**	**∞**	**a**	**df$_2$**
9.41	9.49	9.58	9.63	9.67	9.71	9.76	9.80	9.83	9.85	.25	1
60.71	61.22	61.74	62.00	62.26	62.53	62.79	63.06	63.19	63.33	.10	
243.9	245.9	248.0	249.1	250.1	251.1	252.2	253.3	253.8	254.3	.05	
976.7	984.9	993.1	997.2	1001	1006	1010	1014	1016	1018	.025	
6106	6157	6209	6235	6261	6287	6313	6339	6353	6366	.01	
3.39	3.41	3.43	3.43	3.44	3.45	3.46	3.47	3.47	3.48	.25	2
9.41	9.42	9.44	9.45	9.46	9.47	9.47	9.48	9.49	9.49	.10	
19.41	19.43	19.45	19.45	19.46	19.47	19.48	19.49	19.49	19.50	.05	
39.41	39.43	39.45	39.46	39.46	39.47	39.48	39.49	39.49	39.50	.025	
99.42	99.43	99.45	99.46	99.47	99.47	99.48	99.49	99.49	99.50	.01	
199.4	199.4	199.4	199.5	199.5	199.5	199.5	199.5	199.5	199.5	.005	
999.4	999.4	999.4	999.5	999.5	999.5	999.5	999.5	999.5	999.5	.001	
2.45	2.46	2.46	2.46	2.47	2.47	2.47	2.47	2.47	2.47	.25	3
5.22	5.20	5.18	5.18	5.17	5.16	5.15	5.14	5.14	5.13	.10	
8.74	8.70	8.66	8.64	8.62	8.59	8.57	8.55	8.54	8.53	.05	
14.34	14.25	14.17	14.12	14.08	14.04	13.99	13.95	13.92	13.90	.025	
27.05	26.87	26.69	26.60	26.50	26.41	26.32	26.22	26.17	26.13	.01	
43.39	43.08	42.78	42.62	42.47	42.31	42.15	41.99	41.91	41.83	.005	
128.3	127.4	126.4	125.9	125.4	125.0	124.5	124.0	123.7	123.5	.001	
2.08	2.08	2.08	2.08	2.08	2.08	2.08	2.08	2.08	2.08	.25	4
3.90	3.87	3.84	3.83	3.82	3.80	3.79	3.78	3.77	3.76	.10	
5.91	5.86	5.80	5.77	5.75	5.72	5.69	5.66	5.64	5.63	.05	
8.75	8.66	8.56	8.51	8.46	8.41	8.36	8.31	8.28	8.26	.025	
14.37	14.20	14.02	13.93	13.84	13.75	13.65	13.56	13.51	13.46	.01	
20.70	20.44	20.17	20.03	19.89	19.75	19.61	19.47	19.40	19.32	.005	
47.41	46.76	46.10	45.77	45.43	45.09	44.75	44.40	44.23	44.05	.001	
1.89	1.89	1.88	1.88	1.88	1.88	1.87	1.87	1.87	1.87	.25	5
3.27	3.24	3.21	3.19	3.17	3.16	3.14	3.12	3.11	3.10	.10	
4.68	4.62	4.56	4.53	4.50	4.46	4.43	4.40	4.38	4.36	.05	
6.52	6.43	6.33	6.28	6.23	6.18	6.12	6.07	6.04	6.02	.025	
9.89	9.72	9.55	9.47	9.38	9.29	9.20	9.11	9.07	9.02	.01	
13.38	13.15	12.90	12.78	12.66	12.53	12.40	12.27	12.21	12.14	.005	
26.42	25.91	25.39	25.13	24.87	24.60	24.33	24.06	23.92	23.79	.001	
1.77	1.76	1.76	1.75	1.75	1.75	1.74	1.74	1.74	1.74	.25	6
2.90	2.87	2.84	2.82	2.80	2.78	2.76	2.74	2.73	2.72	.10	
4.00	3.94	3.87	3.84	3.81	3.77	3.74	3.70	3.69	3.67	.05	
5.37	5.27	5.17	5.12	5.07	5.01	4.96	4.90	4.88	4.85	.025	
7.72	7.56	7.40	7.31	7.23	7.14	7.06	6.97	6.92	6.88	.01	
10.03	9.81	9.59	9.47	9.36	9.24	9.12	9.00	8.94	8.88	.005	
17.99	17.56	17.12	16.90	16.67	16.44	16.21	15.98	15.86	15.75	.001	

Table 6 (continued)
Percentage points of the F distribution (df_2 between 7 and 12)

						df_1					
df_2	a	1	2	3	4	5	6	7	8	9	10
7	.25	1.57	1.70	1.72	1.72	1.71	1.71	1.70	1.70	1.69	1.69
	.10	3.59	3.26	3.07	2.96	2.88	2.83	2.78	2.75	2.72	2.70
	.05	5.59	4.74	4.35	4.12	3.97	3.87	3.79	3.73	3.68	3.64
	.025	8.07	6.54	5.89	5.52	5.29	5.12	4.99	4.90	4.82	4.76
	.01	12.25	9.55	8.45	7.85	7.46	7.19	6.99	6.84	6.72	6.62
	.005	16.24	12.40	10.88	10.05	9.52	9.16	8.89	8.68	8.51	8.38
	.001	29.25	21.69	18.77	17.20	16.21	15.52	15.02	14.63	14.33	14.08
8	.25	1.54	1.66	1.67	1.66	1.66	1.65	1.64	1.64	1.63	1.63
	.10	3.46	3.11	2.92	2.81	2.73	2.67	2.62	2.59	2.56	2.54
	.05	5.32	4.46	4.07	3.84	3.69	3.58	3.50	3.44	3.39	3.35
	.025	7.57	6.06	5.42	5.05	4.82	4.65	4.53	4.43	4.36	4.30
	.01	11.26	8.65	7.59	7.01	6.63	6.37	6.18	6.03	5.91	5.81
	.005	14.69	11.04	9.60	8.81	8.30	7.95	7.69	7.50	7.34	7.21
	.001	25.41	18.49	15.83	14.39	13.48	12.86	12.40	12.05	11.77	11.54
9	.25	1.51	1.62	1.63	1.63	1.62	1.61	1.60	1.60	1.59	1.59
	.10	3.36	3.01	2.81	2.69	2.61	2.55	2.51	2.47	2.44	2.42
	.05	5.12	4.26	3.86	3.63	3.48	3.37	3.29	3.23	3.18	3.14
	.025	7.21	5.71	5.08	4.72	4.48	4.32	4.20	4.10	4.03	3.96
	.01	10.56	8.02	6.99	6.42	6.06	5.80	5.61	5.47	5.35	5.26
	.005	13.61	10.11	8.72	7.96	7.47	7.13	6.88	6.69	6.54	6.42
	.001	22.86	16.39	13.90	12.56	11.71	11.13	10.70	10.37	10.11	9.89
10	.25	1.49	1.60	1.60	1.59	1.59	1.58	1.57	1.56	1.56	1.55
	.10	3.29	2.92	2.73	2.61	2.52	2.46	2.41	2.38	2.35	2.32
	.05	4.96	4.10	3.71	3.48	3.33	3.22	3.14	3.07	3.02	2.98
	.025	6.94	5.46	4.83	4.47	4.24	4.07	3.95	3.85	3.78	3.72
	.01	10.04	7.56	6.55	5.99	5.64	5.39	5.20	5.06	4.94	4.85
	.005	12.83	9.43	8.08	7.34	6.87	6.54	6.30	6.12	5.97	5.85
	.001	21.04	14.91	12.55	11.28	10.48	9.93	9.52	9.20	8.96	8.75
11	.25	1.47	1.58	1.58	1.57	1.56	1.55	1.54	1.53	1.53	1.52
	.10	3.23	2.86	2.66	2.54	2.45	2.39	2.34	2.30	2.27	2.25
	.05	4.84	3.98	3.59	3.36	3.20	3.09	3.01	2.95	2.90	2.85
	.025	6.72	5.26	4.63	4.28	4.04	3.88	3.76	3.66	3.59	3.53
	.01	9.65	7.21	6.22	5.67	5.32	5.07	4.89	4.74	4.63	4.54
	.005	12.23	8.91	7.60	6.88	6.42	6.10	5.86	5.68	5.54	5.42
	.001	19.69	13.81	11.56	10.35	9.58	9.05	8.66	8.35	8.12	7.92
12	.25	1.46	1.56	1.56	1.55	1.54	1.53	1.52	1.51	1.51	1.50
	.10	3.18	2.81	2.61	2.48	2.39	2.33	2.28	2.24	2.21	2.19
	.05	4.75	3.89	3.49	3.26	3.11	3.00	2.91	2.85	2.80	2.75
	.025	6.55	5.10	4.47	4.12	3.89	3.73	3.61	3.51	3.44	3.37
	.01	9.33	6.93	5.95	5.41	5.06	4.82	4.64	4.50	4.39	4.30
	.005	11.75	8.51	7.23	6.52	6.07	5.76	5.52	5.35	5.20	5.09
	.001	18.64	12.97	10.80	9.63	8.89	8.38	8.00	7.71	7.48	7.29

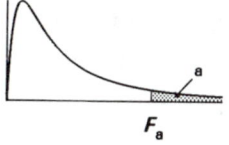

					df$_1$						
12	**15**	**20**	**24**	**30**	**40**	**60**	**120**	**240**	**∞**	**a**	**df$_2$**
1.68	1.68	1.67	1.67	1.66	1.66	1.65	1.65	1.65	1.65	.25	7
2.67	2.63	2.59	2.58	2.56	2.54	2.51	2.49	2.48	2.47	.10	
3.57	3.51	3.44	3.41	3.38	3.34	3.30	3.27	3.25	3.23	.05	
4.67	4.57	4.47	4.41	4.36	4.31	4.25	4.20	4.17	4.14	.025	
6.47	6.31	6.16	6.07	5.99	5.91	5.82	5.74	5.69	5.65	.01	
8.18	7.97	7.75	7.64	7.53	7.42	7.31	7.19	7.13	7.08	.005	
13.71	13.32	12.93	12.73	12.53	12.33	12.12	11.91	11.80	11.70	.001	
1.62	1.62	1.61	1.60	1.60	1.59	1.59	1.58	1.58	1.58	.25	8
2.50	2.46	2.42	2.40	2.38	2.36	2.34	2.32	2.30	2.29	.10	
3.28	3.22	3.15	3.12	3.08	3.04	3.01	2.97	2.95	2.93	.05	
4.20	4.10	4.00	3.95	3.89	3.84	3.78	3.73	3.70	3.67	.025	
5.67	5.52	5.36	5.28	5.20	5.12	5.03	4.95	4.90	4.86	.01	
7.01	6.81	6.61	6.50	6.40	6.29	6.18	6.06	6.01	5.95	.005	
11.19	10.84	10.48	10.30	10.11	9.92	9.73	9.53	9.43	9.33	.001	
1.58	1.57	1.56	1.56	1.55	1.54	1.54	1.53	1.53	1.53	.25	9
2.38	2.34	2.30	2.28	2.25	2.23	2.21	2.18	2.17	2.16	.10	
3.07	3.01	2.94	2.90	2.86	2.83	2.79	2.75	2.73	2.71	.05	
3.87	3.77	3.67	3.61	3.56	3.51	3.45	3.39	3.36	3.33	.025	
5.11	4.96	4.81	4.73	4.65	4.57	4.48	4.40	4.35	4.31	.01	
6.23	6.03	5.83	5.73	5.62	5.52	5.41	5.30	5.24	5.19	.005	
9.57	9.24	8.90	8.72	8.55	8.37	8.19	8.00	7.91	7.81	.001	
1.54	1.53	1.52	1.52	1.51	1.51	1.50	1.49	1.49	1.48	.25	10
2.28	2.24	2.20	2.18	2.16	2.13	2.11	2.08	2.07	2.06	.10	
2.91	2.85	2.77	2.74	2.70	2.66	2.62	2.58	2.56	2.54	.05	
3.62	3.52	3.42	3.37	3.31	3.26	3.20	3.14	3.11	3.08	.025	
4.71	4.56	4.41	4.33	4.25	4.17	4.08	4.00	3.95	3.91	.01	
5.66	5.47	5.27	5.17	5.07	4.97	4.86	4.75	4.69	4.64	.005	
8.45	8.13	7.80	7.64	7.47	7.30	7.12	6.94	6.85	6.76	.001	
1.51	1.50	1.49	1.49	1.48	1.47	1.47	1.46	1.45	1.45	.25	11
2.21	2.17	2.12	2.10	2.08	2.05	2.03	2.00	1.99	1.97	.10	
2.79	2.72	2.65	2.61	2.57	2.53	2.49	2.45	2.43	2.40	.05	
3.43	3.33	3.23	3.17	3.12	3.06	3.00	2.94	2.91	2.88	.025	
4.40	4.25	4.10	4.02	3.94	3.86	3.78	3.69	3.65	3.60	.01	
5.24	5.05	4.86	4.76	4.65	4.55	4.45	4.34	4.28	4.23	.005	
7.63	7.32	7.01	6.85	6.68	6.52	6.35	6.18	6.09	6.00	.001	
1.49	1.48	1.47	1.46	1.45	1.45	1.44	1.43	1.43	1.42	.25	12
2.15	2.10	2.06	2.04	2.01	1.99	1.96	1.93	1.92	1.90	.10	
2.69	2.62	2.54	2.51	2.47	2.43	2.38	2.34	2.32	2.30	.05	
3.28	3.18	3.07	3.02	2.96	2.91	2.85	2.79	2.76	2.72	.025	
4.16	4.01	3.86	3.78	3.70	3.62	3.54	3.45	3.41	3.36	.01	
4.91	4.72	4.53	4.43	4.33	4.23	4.12	4.01	3.96	3.90	.005	
7.00	6.71	6.40	6.25	6.09	5.93	5.76	5.59	5.51	5.42	.001	

Table 6 (continued)
Percentage points of the *F* distribution (df$_2$ between 13 and 18)

df$_2$	a	1	2	3	4	5	6	7	8	9	10
							df$_1$				
13	.25	1.45	1.55	1.55	1.53	1.52	1.51	1.50	1.49	1.49	1.48
	.10	3.14	2.76	2.56	2.43	2.35	2.28	2.23	2.20	2.16	2.14
	.05	4.67	3.81	3.41	3.18	3.03	2.92	2.83	2.77	2.71	2.67
	.025	6.41	4.97	4.35	4.00	3.77	3.60	3.48	3.39	3.31	3.25
	.01	9.07	6.70	5.74	5.21	4.86	4.62	4.44	4.30	4.19	4.10
	.005	11.37	8.19	6.93	6.23	5.79	5.48	5.25	5.08	4.94	4.82
	.001	17.82	12.31	10.21	9.07	8.35	7.86	7.49	7.21	6.98	6.80
14	.25	1.44	1.53	1.53	1.52	1.51	1.50	1.49	1.48	1.47	1.46
	.10	3.10	2.73	2.52	2.39	2.31	2.24	2.19	2.15	2.12	2.10
	.05	4.60	3.74	3.34	3.11	2.96	2.85	2.76	2.70	2.65	2.60
	.025	6.30	4.86	4.24	3.89	3.66	3.50	3.38	3.29	3.21	3.15
	.01	8.86	6.51	5.56	5.04	4.69	4.46	4.28	4.14	4.03	3.94
	.005	11.06	7.92	6.68	6.00	5.56	5.26	5.03	4.86	4.72	4.60
	.001	17.14	11.78	9.73	8.62	7.92	7.44	7.08	6.80	6.58	6.40
15	.25	1.43	1.52	1.52	1.51	1.49	1.48	1.47	1.46	1.46	1.45
	.10	3.07	2.70	2.49	2.36	2.27	2.21	2.16	2.12	2.09	2.06
	.05	4.54	3.68	3.29	3.06	2.90	2.79	2.71	2.64	2.59	2.54
	.025	6.20	4.77	4.15	3.80	3.58	3.41	3.29	3.20	3.12	3.06
	.01	8.68	6.36	5.42	4.89	4.56	4.32	4.14	4.00	3.89	3.80
	.005	10.80	7.70	6.48	5.80	5.37	5.07	4.85	4.67	4.54	4.42
	.001	16.59	11.34	9.34	8.25	7.57	7.09	6.74	6.47	6.26	6.08
16	.25	1.42	1.51	1.51	1.50	1.48	1.47	1.46	1.45	1.44	1.44
	.10	3.05	2.67	2.46	2.33	2.24	2.18	2.13	2.09	2.06	2.03
	.05	4.49	3.63	3.24	3.01	2.85	2.74	2.66	2.59	2.54	2.49
	.025	6.12	4.69	4.08	3.73	3.50	3.34	3.22	3.12	3.05	2.99
	.01	8.53	6.23	5.29	4.77	4.44	4.20	4.03	3.89	3.78	3.69
	.005	10.58	7.51	6.30	5.64	5.21	4.91	4.69	4.52	4.38	4.27
	.001	16.12	10.97	9.01	7.94	7.27	6.80	6.46	6.19	5.98	5.81
17	.25	1.42	1.51	1.50	1.49	1.47	1.46	1.45	1.44	1.43	1.43
	.10	3.03	2.64	2.44	2.31	2.22	2.15	2.10	2.06	2.03	2.00
	.05	4.45	3.59	3.20	2.96	2.81	2.70	2.61	2.55	2.49	2.45
	.025	6.04	4.62	4.01	3.66	3.44	3.28	3.16	3.06	2.98	2.92
	.01	8.40	6.11	5.18	4.67	4.34	4.10	3.93	3.79	3.68	3.59
	.005	10.38	7.35	6.16	5.50	5.07	4.78	4.56	4.39	4.25	4.14
	.001	15.72	10.66	8.73	7.68	7.02	6.56	6.22	5.96	5.75	5.58
18	.25	1.41	1.50	1.49	1.48	1.46	1.45	1.44	1.43	1.42	1.42
	.10	3.01	2.62	2.42	2.29	2.20	2.13	2.08	2.04	2.00	1.98
	.05	4.41	3.55	3.16	2.93	2.77	2.66	2.58	2.51	2.46	2.41
	.025	5.98	4.56	3.95	3.61	3.38	3.22	3.10	3.01	2.93	2.87
	.01	8.29	6.01	5.09	4.58	4.25	4.01	3.84	3.71	3.60	3.51
	.005	10.22	7.21	6.03	5.37	4.96	4.66	4.44	4.28	4.14	4.03
	.001	15.38	10.39	8.49	7.46	6.81	6.35	6.02	5.76	5.56	5.39

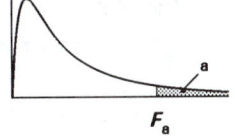

F_a

					df_1						
12	**15**	**20**	**24**	**30**	**40**	**60**	**120**	**240**	**∞**	**a**	**df_2**
1.47	1.46	1.45	1.44	1.43	1.42	1.42	1.41	1.40	1.40	.25	13
2.10	2.05	2.01	1.98	1.96	1.93	1.90	1.88	1.86	1.85	.10	
2.60	2.53	2.46	2.42	2.38	2.34	2.30	2.25	2.23	2.21	.05	
3.15	3.05	2.95	2.89	2.84	2.78	2.72	2.66	2.63	2.60	.025	
3.96	3.82	3.66	3.59	3.51	3.43	3.34	3.25	3.21	3.17	.01	
4.64	4.46	4.27	4.17	4.07	3.97	3.87	3.76	3.70	3.65	.005	
6.52	6.23	5.93	5.78	5.63	5.47	5.30	5.14	5.05	4.97	.001	
1.45	1.44	1.43	1.42	1.41	1.41	1.40	1.39	1.38	1.38	.25	14
2.05	2.01	1.96	1.94	1.91	1.89	1.86	1.83	1.81	1.80	.10	
2.53	2.46	2.39	2.35	2.31	2.27	2.22	2.18	2.15	2.13	.05	
3.05	2.95	2.84	2.79	2.73	2.67	2.61	2.55	2.52	2.49	.025	
3.80	3.66	3.51	3.43	3.35	3.27	3.18	3.09	3.05	3.00	.01	
4.43	4.25	4.06	3.96	3.86	3.76	3.66	3.55	3.49	3.44	.005	
6.13	5.85	5.56	5.41	5.25	5.10	4.94	4.77	4.69	4.60	.001	
1.44	1.43	1.41	1.41	1.40	1.39	1.38	1.37	1.36	1.36	.25	15
2.02	1.97	1.92	1.90	1.87	1.85	1.82	1.79	1.77	1.76	.10	
2.48	2.40	2.33	2.29	2.25	2.20	2.16	2.11	2.09	2.07	.05	
2.96	2.86	2.76	2.70	2.64	2.59	2.52	2.46	2.43	2.40	.025	
3.67	3.52	3.37	3.29	3.21	3.13	3.05	2.96	2.91	2.87	.01	
4.25	4.07	3.88	3.79	3.69	3.58	3.48	3.37	3.32	3.26	.005	
5.81	5.54	5.25	5.10	4.95	4.80	4.64	4.47	4.39	4.31	.001	
1.43	1.41	1.40	1.39	1.38	1.37	1.36	1.35	1.35	1.34	.25	16
1.99	1.94	1.89	1.87	1.84	1.81	1.78	1.75	1.73	1.72	.10	
2.42	2.35	2.28	2.24	2.19	2.15	2.11	2.06	2.03	2.01	.05	
2.89	2.79	2.68	2.63	2.57	2.51	2.45	2.38	2.35	2.32	.025	
3.55	3.41	3.26	3.18	3.10	3.02	2.93	2.84	2.80	2.75	.01	
4.10	3.92	3.73	3.64	3.54	3.44	3.33	3.22	3.17	3.11	.005	
5.55	5.27	4.99	4.85	4.70	4.54	4.39	4.23	4.14	4.06	.001	
1.41	1.40	1.39	1.38	1.37	1.36	1.35	1.34	1.33	1.33	.25	17
1.96	1.91	1.86	1.84	1.81	1.78	1.75	1.72	1.70	1.69	.10	
2.38	2.31	2.23	2.19	2.15	2.10	2.06	2.01	1.99	1.96	.05	
2.82	2.72	2.62	2.56	2.50	2.44	2.38	2.32	2.28	2.25	.025	
3.46	3.31	3.16	3.08	3.00	2.92	2.83	2.75	2.70	2.65	.01	
3.97	3.79	3.61	3.51	3.41	3.31	3.21	3.10	3.04	2.98	.005	
5.32	5.05	4.78	4.63	4.48	4.33	4.18	4.02	3.93	3.85	.001	
1.40	1.39	1.38	1.37	1.36	1.35	1.34	1.33	1.32	1.32	.25	18
1.93	1.89	1.84	1.81	1.78	1.75	1.72	1.69	1.67	1.66	.10	
2.34	2.27	2.19	2.15	2.11	2.06	2.02	1.97	1.94	1.92	.05	
2.77	2.67	2.56	2.50	2.44	2.38	2.32	2.26	2.22	2.19	.025	
3.37	3.23	3.08	3.00	2.92	2.84	2.75	2.66	2.61	2.57	.01	
3.86	3.68	3.50	3.40	3.30	3.20	3.10	2.99	2.93	2.87	.005	
5.13	4.87	4.59	4.45	4.30	4.15	4.00	3.84	3.75	3.67	.001	

Table 6 (continued)
Percentage points of the F distribution (df_2 between 19 and 24)

		df_1									
df_2	a	1	2	3	4	5	6	7	8	9	10
19	.25	1.41	1.49	1.49	1.47	1.46	1.44	1.43	1.42	1.41	1.41
	.10	2.99	2.61	2.40	2.27	2.18	2.11	2.06	2.02	1.98	1.96
	.05	4.38	3.52	3.13	2.90	2.74	2.63	2.54	2.48	2.42	2.38
	.025	5.92	4.51	3.90	3.56	3.33	3.17	3.05	2.96	2.88	2.82
	.01	8.18	5.93	5.01	4.50	4.17	3.94	3.77	3.63	3.52	3.43
	.005	10.07	7.09	5.92	5.27	4.85	4.56	4.34	4.18	4.04	3.93
	.001	15.08	10.16	8.28	7.27	6.62	6.18	5.85	5.59	5.39	5.22
20	.25	1.40	1.49	1.48	1.47	1.45	1.44	1.43	1.42	1.41	1.40
	.10	2.97	2.59	2.38	2.25	2.16	2.09	2.04	2.00	1.96	1.94
	.05	4.35	3.49	3.10	2.87	2.71	2.60	2.51	2.45	2.39	2.35
	.025	5.87	4.46	3.86	3.51	3.29	3.13	3.01	2.91	2.84	2.77
	.01	8.10	5.85	4.94	4.43	4.10	3.87	3.70	3.56	3.46	3.37
	.005	9.94	6.99	5.82	5.17	4.76	4.47	4.26	4.09	3.96	3.85
	.001	14.82	9.95	8.10	7.10	6.46	6.02	5.69	5.44	5.24	5.08
21	.25	1.40	1.48	1.48	1.46	1.44	1.43	1.42	1.41	1.40	1.39
	.10	2.96	2.57	2.36	2.23	2.14	2.08	2.02	1.98	1.95	1.92
	.05	4.32	3.47	3.07	2.84	2.68	2.57	2.49	2.42	2.37	2.32
	.025	5.83	4.42	3.82	3.48	3.25	3.09	2.97	2.87	2.80	2.73
	.01	8.02	5.78	4.87	4.37	4.04	3.81	3.64	3.51	3.40	3.31
	.005	9.83	6.89	5.73	5.09	4.68	4.39	4.18	4.01	3.88	3.77
	.001	14.59	9.77	7.94	6.95	6.32	5.88	5.56	5.31	5.11	4.95
22	.25	1.40	1.48	1.47	1.45	1.44	1.42	1.41	1.40	1.39	1.39
	.10	2.95	2.56	2.35	2.22	2.13	2.06	2.01	1.97	1.93	1.90
	.05	4.30	3.44	3.05	2.82	2.66	2.55	2.46	2.40	2.34	2.30
	.025	5.79	4.38	3.78	3.44	3.22	3.05	2.93	2.84	2.76	2.70
	.01	7.95	5.72	4.82	4.31	3.99	3.76	3.59	3.45	3.35	3.26
	.005	9.73	6.81	5.65	5.02	4.61	4.32	4.11	3.94	3.81	3.70
	.001	14.38	9.61	7.80	6.81	6.19	5.76	5.44	5.19	4.99	4.83
23	.25	1.39	1.47	1.47	1.45	1.43	1.42	1.41	1.40	1.39	1.38
	.10	2.94	2.55	2.34	2.21	2.11	2.05	1.99	1.95	1.92	1.89
	.05	4.28	3.42	3.03	2.80	2.64	2.53	2.44	2.37	2.32	2.27
	.025	5.75	4.35	3.75	3.41	3.18	3.02	2.90	2.81	2.73	2.67
	.01	7.88	5.66	4.76	4.26	3.94	3.71	3.54	3.41	3.30	3.21
	.005	9.63	6.73	5.58	4.95	4.54	4.26	4.05	3.88	3.75	3.64
	.001	14.20	9.47	7.67	6.70	6.08	5.65	5.33	5.09	4.89	4.73
24	.25	1.39	1.47	1.46	1.44	1.43	1.41	1.40	1.39	1.38	1.38
	.10	2.93	2.54	2.33	2.19	2.10	2.04	1.98	1.94	1.91	1.88
	.05	4.26	3.40	3.01	2.78	2.62	2.51	2.42	2.36	2.30	2.25
	.025	5.72	4.32	3.72	3.38	3.15	2.99	2.87	2.78	2.70	2.64
	.01	7.82	5.61	4.72	4.22	3.90	3.67	3.50	3.36	3.26	3.17
	.005	9.55	6.66	5.52	4.89	4.49	4.20	3.99	3.83	3.69	3.59
	.001	14.03	9.34	7.55	6.59	5.98	5.55	5.23	4.99	4.80	4.64

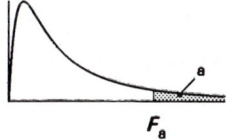

F_a

			df$_1$									
12	**15**	**20**	**24**	**30**	**40**	**60**	**120**	**240**	**∞**	**a**	**df$_2$**
1.40	1.38	1.37	1.36	1.35	1.34	1.33	1.32	1.31	1.30	.25	19
1.91	1.86	1.81	1.79	1.76	1.73	1.70	1.67	1.65	1.63	.10	
2.31	2.23	2.16	2.11	2.07	2.03	1.98	1.93	1.90	1.88	.05	
2.72	2.62	2.51	2.45	2.39	2.33	2.27	2.20	2.17	2.13	.025	
3.30	3.15	3.00	2.92	2.84	2.76	2.67	2.58	2.54	2.49	.01	
3.76	3.59	3.40	3.31	3.21	3.11	3.00	2.89	2.83	2.78	.005	
4.97	4.70	4.43	4.29	4.14	3.99	3.84	3.68	3.60	3.51	.001	
1.39	1.37	1.36	1.35	1.34	1.33	1.32	1.31	1.30	1.29	.25	20
1.89	1.84	1.79	1.77	1.74	1.71	1.68	1.64	1.63	1.61	.10	
2.28	2.20	2.12	2.08	2.04	1.99	1.95	1.90	1.87	1.84	.05	
2.68	2.57	2.46	2.41	2.35	2.29	2.22	2.16	2.12	2.09	.025	
3.23	3.09	2.94	2.86	2.78	2.69	2.61	2.52	2.47	2.42	.01	
3.68	3.50	3.32	3.22	3.12	3.02	2.92	2.81	2.75	2.69	.005	
4.82	4.56	4.29	4.15	4.00	3.86	3.70	3.54	3.46	3.38	.001	
1.38	1.37	1.35	1.34	1.33	1.32	1.31	1.30	1.29	1.28	.25	21
1.87	1.83	1.78	1.75	1.72	1.69	1.66	1.62	1.60	1.59	.10	
2.25	2.18	2.10	2.05	2.01	1.96	1.92	1.87	1.84	1.81	.05	
2.64	2.53	2.42	2.37	2.31	2.25	2.18	2.11	2.08	2.04	.025	
3.17	3.03	2.88	2.80	2.72	2.64	2.55	2.46	2.41	2.36	.01	
3.60	3.43	3.24	3.15	3.05	2.95	2.84	2.73	2.67	2.61	.005	
4.70	4.44	4.17	4.03	3.88	3.74	3.58	3.42	3.34	3.26	.001	
1.37	1.36	1.34	1.33	1.32	1.31	1.30	1.29	1.28	1.28	.25	22
1.86	1.81	1.76	1.73	1.70	1.67	1.64	1.60	1.59	1.57	.10	
2.23	2.15	2.07	2.03	1.98	1.94	1.89	1.84	1.81	1.78	.05	
2.60	2.50	2.39	2.33	2.27	2.21	2.14	2.08	2.04	2.00	.025	
3.12	2.98	2.83	2.75	2.67	2.58	2.50	2.40	2.35	2.31	.01	
3.54	3.36	3.18	3.08	2.98	2.88	2.77	2.66	2.60	2.55	.005	
4.58	4.33	4.06	3.92	3.78	3.63	3.48	3.32	3.23	3.15	.001	
1.37	1.35	1.34	1.33	1.32	1.31	1.30	1.28	1.28	1.27	.25	23
1.84	1.80	1.74	1.72	1.69	1.66	1.62	1.59	1.57	1.55	.10	
2.20	2.13	2.05	2.01	1.96	1.91	1.86	1.81	1.79	1.76	.05	
2.57	2.47	2.36	2.30	2.24	2.18	2.11	2.04	2.01	1.97	.025	
3.07	2.93	2.78	2.70	2.62	2.54	2.45	2.35	2.31	2.26	.01	
3.47	3.30	3.12	3.02	2.92	2.82	2.71	2.60	2.54	2.48	.005	
4.48	4.23	3.96	3.82	3.68	3.53	3.38	3.22	3.14	3.05	.001	
1.36	1.35	1.33	1.32	1.31	1.30	1.29	1.28	1.27	1.26	.25	24
1.83	1.78	1.73	1.70	1.67	1.64	1.61	1.57	1.55	1.53	.10	
2.18	2.11	2.03	1.98	1.94	1.89	1.84	1.79	1.76	1.73	.05	
2.54	2.44	2.33	2.27	2.21	2.15	2.08	2.01	1.97	1.94	.025	
3.03	2.89	2.74	2.66	2.58	2.49	2.40	2.31	2.26	2.21	.01	
3.42	3.25	3.06	2.97	2.87	2.77	2.66	2.55	2.49	2.43	.005	
4.39	4.14	3.87	3.74	3.59	3.45	3.29	3.14	3.05	2.97	.001	

Table 6 (continued)
Percentage points of the F distribution (df_2 between 25 and 30)

df_2	a	1	2	3	4	5	6	7	8	9	10
25	.25	1.39	1.47	1.46	1.44	1.42	1.41	1.40	1.39	1.38	1.37
	.10	2.92	2.53	2.32	2.18	2.09	2.02	1.97	1.93	1.89	1.87
	.05	4.24	3.39	2.99	2.76	2.60	2.49	2.40	2.34	2.28	2.24
	.025	5.69	4.29	3.69	3.35	3.13	2.97	2.85	2.75	2.68	2.61
	.01	7.77	5.57	4.68	4.18	3.85	3.63	3.46	3.32	3.22	3.13
	.005	9.48	6.60	5.46	4.84	4.43	4.15	3.94	3.78	3.64	3.54
	.001	13.88	9.22	7.45	6.49	5.89	5.46	5.15	4.91	4.71	4.56
26	.25	1.38	1.46	1.45	1.44	1.42	1.41	1.39	1.38	1.37	1.37
	.10	2.91	2.52	2.31	2.17	2.08	2.01	1.96	1.92	1.88	1.86
	.05	4.23	3.37	2.98	2.74	2.59	2.47	2.39	2.32	2.27	2.22
	.025	5.66	4.27	3.67	3.33	3.10	2.94	2.82	2.73	2.65	2.59
	.01	7.72	5.53	4.64	4.14	3.82	3.59	3.42	3.29	3.18	3.09
	.005	9.41	6.54	5.41	4.79	4.38	4.10	3.89	3.73	3.60	3.49
	.001	13.74	9.12	7.36	6.41	5.80	5.38	5.07	4.83	4.64	4.48
27	.25	1.38	1.46	1.45	1.43	1.42	1.40	1.39	1.38	1.37	1.36
	.10	2.90	2.51	2.30	2.17	2.07	2.00	1.95	1.91	1.87	1.85
	.05	4.21	3.35	2.96	2.73	2.57	2.46	2.37	2.31	2.25	2.20
	.025	5.63	4.24	3.65	3.31	3.08	2.92	2.80	2.71	2.63	2.57
	.01	7.68	5.49	4.60	4.11	3.78	3.56	3.39	3.26	3.15	3.06
	.005	9.34	6.49	5.36	4.74	4.34	4.06	3.85	3.69	3.56	3.45
	.001	13.61	9.02	7.27	6.33	5.73	5.31	5.00	4.76	4.57	4.41
28	.25	1.38	1.46	1.45	1.43	1.41	1.40	1.39	1.38	1.37	1.36
	.10	2.89	2.50	2.29	2.16	2.06	2.00	1.94	1.90	1.87	1.84
	.05	4.20	3.34	2.95	2.71	2.56	2.45	2.36	2.29	2.24	2.19
	.025	5.61	4.22	3.63	3.29	3.06	2.90	2.78	2.69	2.61	2.55
	.01	7.64	5.45	4.57	4.07	3.75	3.53	3.36	3.23	3.12	3.03
	.005	9.28	6.44	5.32	4.70	4.30	4.02	3.81	3.65	3.52	3.41
	.001	13.50	8.93	7.19	6.25	5.66	5.24	4.93	4.69	4.50	4.35
29	.25	1.38	1.45	1.45	1.43	1.41	1.40	1.38	1.37	1.36	1.35
	.10	2.89	2.50	2.28	2.15	2.06	1.99	1.93	1.89	1.86	1.83
	.05	4.18	3.33	2.93	2.70	2.55	2.43	2.35	2.28	2.22	2.18
	.025	5.59	4.20	3.61	3.27	3.04	2.88	2.76	2.67	2.59	2.53
	.01	7.60	5.42	4.54	4.04	3.73	3.50	3.33	3.20	3.09	3.00
	.005	9.23	6.40	5.28	4.66	4.26	3.98	3.77	3.61	3.48	3.38
	.001	13.39	8.85	7.12	6.19	5.59	5.18	4.87	4.64	4.45	4.29
30	.25	1.38	1.45	1.44	1.42	1.41	1.39	1.38	1.37	1.36	1.35
	.10	2.88	2.49	2.28	2.14	2.05	1.98	1.93	1.88	1.85	1.82
	.05	4.17	3.32	2.92	2.69	2.53	2.42	2.33	2.27	2.21	2.16
	.025	5.57	4.18	3.59	3.25	3.03	2.87	2.75	2.65	2.57	2.51
	.01	7.56	5.39	4.51	4.02	3.70	3.47	3.30	3.17	3.07	2.98
	.005	9.18	6.35	5.24	4.62	4.23	3.95	3.74	3.58	3.45	3.34
	.001	13.29	8.77	7.05	6.12	5.53	5.12	4.82	4.58	4.39	4.24

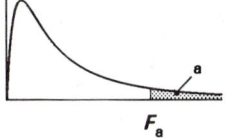

F_a

					df$_1$							
12	**15**	**20**	**24**	**30**	**40**	**60**	**120**	**240**	**∞**	**a**	**df$_2$**
1.36	1.34	1.33	1.32	1.31	1.29	1.28	1.27	1.26	1.25	.25	25
1.82	1.77	1.72	1.69	1.66	1.63	1.59	1.56	1.54	1.52	.10	
2.16	2.09	2.01	1.96	1.92	1.87	1.82	1.77	1.74	1.71	.05	
2.51	2.41	2.30	2.24	2.18	2.12	2.05	1.98	1.94	1.91	.025	
2.99	2.85	2.70	2.62	2.54	2.45	2.36	2.27	2.22	2.17	.01	
3.37	3.20	3.01	2.92	2.82	2.72	2.61	2.50	2.44	2.38	.005	
4.31	4.06	3.79	3.66	3.52	3.37	3.22	3.06	2.98	2.89	.001	
1.35	1.34	1.32	1.31	1.30	1.29	1.28	1.26	1.26	1.25	.25	26
1.81	1.76	1.71	1.68	1.65	1.61	1.58	1.54	1.52	1.50	.10	
2.15	2.07	1.99	1.95	1.90	1.85	1.80	1.75	1.72	1.69	.05	
2.49	2.39	2.28	2.22	2.16	2.09	2.03	1.95	1.92	1.88	.025	
2.96	2.81	2.66	2.58	2.50	2.42	2.33	2.23	2.18	2.13	.01	
3.33	3.15	2.97	2.87	2.77	2.67	2.56	2.45	2.39	2.33	.005	
4.24	3.99	3.72	3.59	3.44	3.30	3.15	2.99	2.90	2.82	.001	
1.35	1.33	1.32	1.31	1.30	1.28	1.27	1.26	1.25	1.24	.25	27
1.80	1.75	1.70	1.67	1.64	1.60	1.57	1.53	1.51	1.49	.10	
2.13	2.06	1.97	1.93	1.88	1.84	1.79	1.73	1.70	1.67	.05	
2.47	2.36	2.25	2.19	2.13	2.07	2.00	1.93	1.89	1.85	.025	
2.93	2.78	2.63	2.55	2.47	2.38	2.29	2.20	2.15	2.10	.01	
3.28	3.11	2.93	2.83	2.73	2.63	2.52	2.41	2.35	2.29	.005	
4.17	3.92	3.66	3.52	3.38	3.23	3.08	2.92	2.84	2.75	.001	
1.34	1.33	1.31	1.30	1.29	1.28	1.27	1.25	1.24	1.24	.25	28
1.79	1.74	1.69	1.66	1.63	1.59	1.56	1.52	1.50	1.48	.10	
2.12	2.04	1.96	1.91	1.87	1.82	1.77	1.71	1.68	1.65	.05	
2.45	2.34	2.23	2.17	2.11	2.05	1.98	1.91	1.87	1.83	.025	
2.90	2.75	2.60	2.52	2.44	2.35	2.26	2.17	2.12	2.06	.01	
3.25	3.07	2.89	2.79	2.69	2.59	2.48	2.37	2.31	2.25	.005	
4.11	3.86	3.60	3.46	3.32	3.18	3.02	2.86	2.78	2.69	.001	
1.34	1.32	1.31	1.30	1.29	1.27	1.26	1.25	1.24	1.23	.25	29
1.78	1.73	1.68	1.65	1.62	1.58	1.55	1.51	1.49	1.47	.10	
2.10	2.03	1.94	1.90	1.85	1.81	1.75	1.70	1.67	1.64	.05	
2.43	2.32	2.21	2.15	2.09	2.03	1.96	1.89	1.85	1.81	.025	
2.87	2.73	2.57	2.49	2.41	2.33	2.23	2.14	2.09	2.03	.01	
3.21	3.04	2.86	2.76	2.66	2.56	2.45	2.33	2.27	2.21	.005	
4.05	3.80	3.54	3.41	3.27	3.12	2.97	2.81	2.73	2.64	.001	
1.34	1.32	1.30	1.29	1.28	1.27	1.26	1.24	1.23	1.23	.25	30
1.77	1.72	1.67	1.64	1.61	1.57	1.54	1.50	1.48	1.46	.10	
2.09	2.01	1.93	1.89	1.84	1.79	1.74	1.68	1.65	1.62	.05	
2.41	2.31	2.20	2.14	2.07	2.01	1.94	1.87	1.83	1.79	.025	
2.84	2.70	2.55	2.47	2.39	2.30	2.21	2.11	2.06	2.01	.01	
3.18	3.01	2.82	2.73	2.63	2.52	2.42	2.30	2.24	2.18	.005	
4.00	3.75	3.49	3.36	3.22	3.07	2.92	2.76	2.68	2.59	.001	

Table 6 (continued)
Percentage points of the F distribution (df_2 at least 40)

		df_1									
df_2	a	1	2	3	4	5	6	7	8	9	10
40	.25	1.36	1.44	1.42	1.40	1.39	1.37	1.36	1.35	1.34	1.33
	.10	2.84	2.44	2.23	2.09	2.00	1.93	1.87	1.83	1.79	1.76
	.05	4.08	3.23	2.84	2.61	2.45	2.34	2.25	2.18	2.12	2.08
	.025	5.42	4.05	3.46	3.13	2.90	2.74	2.62	2.53	2.45	2.39
	.01	7.31	5.18	4.31	3.83	3.51	3.29	3.12	2.99	2.89	2.80
	.005	8.83	6.07	4.98	4.37	3.99	3.71	3.51	3.35	3.22	3.12
	.001	12.61	8.25	6.59	5.70	5.13	4.73	4.44	4.21	4.02	3.87
60	.25	1.35	1.42	1.41	1.38	1.37	1.35	1.33	1.32	1.31	1.30
	.10	2.79	2.39	2.18	2.04	1.95	1.87	1.82	1.77	1.74	1.71
	.05	4.00	3.15	2.76	2.53	2.37	2.25	2.17	2.10	2.04	1.99
	.025	5.29	3.93	3.34	3.01	2.79	2.63	2.51	2.41	2.33	2.27
	.01	7.08	4.98	4.13	3.65	3.34	3.12	2.95	2.82	2.72	2.63
	.005	8.49	5.79	4.73	4.14	3.76	3.49	3.29	3.13	3.01	2.90
	.001	11.97	7.77	6.17	5.31	4.76	4.37	4.09	3.86	3.69	3.54
90	.25	1.34	1.41	1.39	1.37	1.35	1.33	1.32	1.31	1.30	1.29
	.10	2.76	2.36	2.15	2.01	1.91	1.84	1.78	1.74	1.70	1.67
	.05	3.95	3.10	2.71	2.47	2.32	2.20	2.11	2.04	1.99	1.94
	.025	5.20	3.84	3.26	2.93	2.71	2.55	2.43	2.34	2.26	2.19
	.01	6.93	4.85	4.01	3.53	3.23	3.01	2.84	2.72	2.61	2.52
	.005	8.28	5.62	4.57	3.99	3.62	3.35	3.15	3.00	2.87	2.77
	.001	11.57	7.47	5.91	5.06	4.53	4.15	3.87	3.65	3.48	3.34
120	.25	1.34	1.40	1.39	1.37	1.35	1.33	1.31	1.30	1.29	1.28
	.10	2.75	2.35	2.13	1.99	1.90	1.82	1.77	1.72	1.68	1.65
	.05	3.92	3.07	2.68	2.45	2.29	2.18	2.09	2.02	1.96	1.91
	.025	5.15	3.80	3.23	2.89	2.67	2.52	2.39	2.30	2.22	2.16
	.01	6.85	4.79	3.95	3.48	3.17	2.96	2.79	2.66	2.56	2.47
	.005	8.18	5.54	4.50	3.92	3.55	3.28	3.09	2.93	2.81	2.71
	.001	11.38	7.32	5.78	4.95	4.42	4.04	3.77	3.55	3.38	3.24
240	.25	1.33	1.39	1.38	1.36	1.34	1.32	1.30	1.29	1.27	1.27
	.10	2.73	2.32	2.10	1.97	1.87	1.80	1.74	1.70	1.65	1.63
	.05	3.88	3.03	2.64	2.41	2.25	2.14	2.04	1.98	1.92	1.87
	.025	5.09	3.75	3.17	2.84	2.62	2.46	2.34	2.25	2.17	2.10
	.01	6.74	4.69	3.86	3.40	3.09	2.88	2.71	2.59	2.48	2.40
	.005	8.03	5.42	4.38	3.82	3.45	3.19	2.99	2.84	2.71	2.61
	.001	11.10	7.11	5.60	4.78	4.25	3.89	3.62	3.41	3.24	3.09
∞	.25	1.32	1.39	1.37	1.35	1.33	1.31	1.29	1.28	1.27	1.25
	.10	2.71	2.30	2.08	1.94	1.85	1.77	1.72	1.67	1.63	1.60
	.05	3.84	3.00	2.60	2.37	2.21	2.10	2.01	1.94	1.88	1.83
	.025	5.02	3.69	3.12	2.79	2.57	2.41	2.29	2.19	2.11	2.05
	.01	6.63	4.61	3.78	3.32	3.02	2.80	2.64	2.51	2.41	2.32
	.005	7.88	5.30	4.28	3.72	3.35	3.09	2.90	2.74	2.62	2.52
	.001	10.83	6.91	5.42	4.62	4.10	3.74	3.47	3.27	3.10	2.96

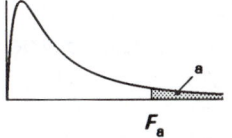

F_a

					df_1						
12	**15**	**20**	**24**	**30**	**40**	**60**	**120**	**240**	**∞**	**a**	**df₂**
1.31	1.30	1.28	1.26	1.25	1.24	1.22	1.21	1.20	1.19	.25	40
1.71	1.66	1.61	1.57	1.54	1.51	1.47	1.42	1.40	1.38	.10	
2.00	1.92	1.84	1.79	1.74	1.69	1.64	1.58	1.54	1.51	.05	
2.29	2.18	2.07	2.01	1.94	1.88	1.80	1.72	1.68	1.64	.025	
2.66	2.52	2.37	2.29	2.20	2.11	2.02	1.92	1.86	1.80	.01	
2.95	2.78	2.60	2.50	2.40	2.30	2.18	2.06	2.00	1.93	.005	
3.64	3.40	3.14	3.01	2.87	2.73	2.57	2.41	2.32	2.23	.001	
1.29	1.27	1.25	1.24	1.22	1.21	1.19	1.17	1.16	1.15	.25	60
1.66	1.60	1.54	1.51	1.48	1.44	1.40	1.35	1.32	1.29	.10	
1.92	1.84	1.75	1.70	1.65	1.59	1.53	1.47	1.43	1.39	.05	
2.17	2.06	1.94	1.88	1.82	1.74	1.67	1.58	1.53	1.48	.025	
2.50	2.35	2.20	2.12	2.03	1.94	1.84	1.73	1.67	1.60	.01	
2.74	2.57	2.39	2.29	2.19	2.08	1.96	1.83	1.76	1.69	.005	
3.32	3.08	2.83	2.69	2.55	2.41	2.25	2.08	1.99	1.89	.001	
1.27	1.25	1.23	1.22	1.20	1.19	1.17	1.15	1.13	1.12	.25	90
1.62	1.56	1.50	1.47	1.43	1.39	1.35	1.29	1.26	1.23	.10	
1.86	1.78	1.69	1.64	1.59	1.53	1.46	1.39	1.35	1.30	.05	
2.09	1.98	1.86	1.80	1.73	1.66	1.58	1.48	1.43	1.37	.025	
2.39	2.24	2.09	2.00	1.92	1.82	1.72	1.60	1.53	1.46	.01	
2.61	2.44	2.25	2.15	2.05	1.94	1.82	1.68	1.61	1.52	.005	
3.11	2.88	2.63	2.50	2.36	2.21	2.05	1.87	1.77	1.66	.001	
1,26	1.24	1.22	1.21	1.19	1.18	1.16	1.13	1.12	1.10	.25	120
1.60	1.55	1.48	1.45	1.41	1.37	1.32	1.26	1.23	1.19	.10	
1.83	1.75	1.66	1.61	1.55	1.50	1.43	1.35	1.31	1.25	.05	
2.05	1.94	1.82	1.76	1.69	1.61	1.53	1.43	1.38	1.31	.025	
2.34	2.19	2.03	1.95	1.86	1.76	1.66	1.53	1.46	1.38	.01	
2.54	2.37	2.19	2.09	1.98	1.87	1.75	1.61	1.52	1.43	.005	
3.02	2.78	2.53	2.40	2.26	2.11	1.95	1.77	1.66	1.54	.001	
1.25	1.23	1.21	1.19	1.18	1.16	1.14	1.11	1.09	1.07	.25	240
1.57	1.52	1.45	1.42	1.38	1.33	1.28	1.22	1.18	1.13	.10	
1.79	1.71	1.61	1.56	1.51	1.44	1.37	1.29	1.24	1.17	.05	
2.00	1.89	1.77	1.70	1.63	1.55	1.46	1.35	1.29	1.21	.025	
2.26	2.11	1.96	1.87	1.78	1.68	1.57	1.43	1.35	1.25	.01	
2.45	2.28	2.09	1.99	1.89	1.77	1.64	1.49	1.40	1.28	.005	
2.88	2.65	2.40	2.26	2.12	1.97	1.80	1.61	1.49	1.35	.001	
1.24	1.22	1.19	1.18	1.16	1.14	1.12	1.08	1.06	1.00	.25	∞
1.55	1.49	1.42	1.38	1.34	1.30	1.24	1.17	1.12	1.00	.10	
1.75	1.67	1.57	1.52	1.46	1.39	1.32	1.22	1.15	1.00	.05	
1.94	1.83	1.71	1.64	1.57	1.48	1.39	1.27	1.19	1.00	.025	
2.18	2.04	1.88	1.79	1.70	1.59	1.47	1.32	1.22	1.00	.01	
2.36	2.19	2.00	1.90	1.79	1.67	1.53	1.36	1.25	1.00	.005	
2.74	2.51	2.27	2.13	1.99	1.84	1.66	1.45	1.31	1.00	.001	

Source: Computed by P. J. Hildebrand.

Table 7

Critical values for the Wilcoxon signed-rank test (n = 5(1)54)

One-sided	Two-sided	n = 5	n = 6	n = 7	n = 8	n = 9	n = 10	n = 11	n = 12	n = 13	n = 14
p = .1	p = .2	2	3	5	8	10	14	17	21	26	31
p = .05	p = .1	0	2	3	5	8	10	13	17	21	25
p = .025	p = .05		0	2	3	5	8	10	13	17	21
p = .01	p = .02			0	1	3	5	7	9	12	15
p = 005	p = .01				0	1	3	5	7	9	12
p = .0025	p = .005					0	1	3	5	7	9
p = .001	p = .002						0	1	2	4	6

One-sided	Two-sided	n = 15	n = 16	n = 17	n = 18	n = 19	n = 20	n = 21	n = 22	n = 23	n = 24
p = .1	p = .2	36	42	48	55	62	69	77	86	94	104
p = .05	p = .1	30	35	41	47	53	60	67	75	83	91
p = .025	p = .05	25	29	34	40	46	52	58	65	73	81
p = .01	p = .02	19	23	27	32	37	43	49	55	62	69
p = 005	p = .01	15	19	23	27	32	37	42	48	54	61
p = .0025	p = .005	12	15	19	23	27	32	37	42	48	54
p = .001	p = .002	8	11	14	18	21	26	30	35	40	45

One-sided	Two-sided	n = 25	n = 26	n = 27	n = 28	n = 29	n = 30	n = 31	n = 32	n = 33	n = 34
p = .1	p = .2	113	124	134	145	157	169	181	194	207	221
p = .05	p = .1	100	110	119	130	140	151	163	175	187	200
p = .025	p = .05	89	98	107	116	126	137	147	159	170	182
p = .01	p = .02	76	84	92	101	110	120	130	140	151	162
p = 005	p = .01	68	75	83	91	100	109	118	128	138	148
p = .0025	p = .005	60	67	74	82	90	98	107	116	126	136
p = .001	p = .002	51	58	64	71	79	86	94	103	112	121

One-sided	Two-sided	n = 35	n = 36	n = 37	n = 38	n = 39	n = 40	n = 41	n = 42	n = 43	n = 44
p = .1	p = .2	235	250	265	281	297	313	330	348	365	384
p = .05	p = .1	213	227	241	256	271	286	302	319	336	353
p = .025	p = .05	195	208	221	235	249	264	279	294	310	327
p = .01	p = .02	173	185	198	211	224	238	252	266	281	296
p = 005	p = .01	159	171	182	194	207	220	233	247	261	276
p = .0025	p = .005	146	157	168	180	192	204	217	230	244	258
p = .001	p = .002	131	141	151	162	173	185	197	209	222	235

One-sided	Two-sided	n = 45	n = 46	n = 47	n = 48	n = 49	n = 50	n = 51	n = 52	n = 53	n = 54
p = .1	p = .2	402	422	441	462	482	503	525	547	569	592
p = .05	p = .1	371	389	407	426	446	466	486	507	529	550
p = .025	p = .05	343	361	378	396	415	434	453	473	494	514
p = .01	p = .02	312	328	345	362	379	397	416	434	454	473
p = 005	p = .01	291	307	322	339	355	373	390	408	427	445
p = .0025	p = .005	272	287	302	318	334	350	367	384	402	420
p = .001	p = .002	249	263	277	292	307	323	339	355	372	389

Source: Computed by P. J. Hildebrand.

TABLE 8 Percentage Points of the Studentized Range

Error d.f.	α	t = number of treatment means									
		2	3	4	5	6	7	8	9	10	11
5	.05	3.64	4.60	5.22	5.67	6.03	6.33	6.58	6.80	6.99	7.17
	.01	5.70	6.98	7.80	8.42	8.91	9.32	9.67	9.97	10.24	10.48
6	.05	3.46	4.34	4.90	5.30	5.63	5.90	6.12	6.32	6.49	6.65
	.01	5.24	6.33	7.03	7.56	7.97	8.32	8.61	8.87	9.10	9.30
7	.05	3.34	4.16	4.68	5.06	5.36	5.61	5.82	6.00	6.16	6.30
	.01	4.95	5.92	6.54	7.01	7.37	7.68	7.94	8.17	8.37	8.55
8	.05	3.26	4.04	4.53	4.89	5.17	5.40	5.60	5.77	5.92	6.05
	.01	4.75	5.64	6.20	6.62	6.96	7.24	7.47	7.68	7.86	8.03
9	.05	3.20	3.95	4.41	4.76	5.02	5.24	5.43	5.59	5.74	5.87
	.01	4.60	5.43	5.96	6.35	6.66	6.91	7.13	7.33	7.49	7.65
10	.05	3.15	3.88	4.33	4.65	4.91	5.12	5.30	5.46	5.60	5.72
	.01	4.48	5.27	5.77	6.14	6.43	6.67	6.87	7.05	7.21	7.36
11	.05	3.11	3.82	4.26	4.57	4.82	5.03	5.30	5.35	5.49	5.61
	.01	4.39	5.15	5.62	5.97	6.25	6.48	6.67	6.84	6.99	7.13
12	.05	3.08	3.77	4.20	4.52	4.75	4.95	5.12	5.27	5.39	5.51
	.01	4.32	5.05	5.50	5.84	6.10	6.32	6.51	6.67	6.81	6.94
13	.05	3.06	3.73	4.15	4.45	4.69	4.88	5.05	5.19	5.32	5.43
	.01	4.26	4.96	5.40	5.73	5.98	6.19	6.37	6.53	6.67	6.79
14	.05	3.03	3.70	4.11	4.41	4.64	4.83	4.99	5.13	5.25	5.36
	.01	4.21	4.89	5.32	5.63	5.88	6.08	6.26	6.41	6.54	6.66
15	.05	3.01	3.67	4.08	4.37	4.59	4.78	4.94	5.08	5.20	5.31
	.01	4.17	4.84	5.25	5.56	5.80	5.99	6.16	6.31	6.44	6.55
16	.05	3.00	3.65	4.05	4.33	4.56	4.74	4.90	5.03	5.15	5.26
	.01	4.13	4.79	5.19	5.49	5.72	5.92	6.08	6.22	6.35	6.46
17	.05	2.98	3.63	4.02	4.30	4.52	4.70	4.86	4.99	5.11	5.21
	.01	4.10	4.74	5.14	5.43	5.66	5.85	6.01	6.15	6.27	6.38
18	.05	2.97	3.61	4.00	4.28	4.49	4.67	4.82	4.96	5.07	5.17
	.01	4.07	4.70	5.09	5.38	5.60	5.79	5.94	6.08	6.20	6.31
19	.05	2.96	3.59	3.98	4.25	4.47	4.65	4.79	4.92	5.04	5.14
	.01	4.05	4.67	5.05	5.33	5.55	5.73	5.89	6.02	6.14	6.25
20	.05	2.95	3.58	3.96	4.23	4.45	4.62	4.77	4.90	5.01	5.11
	.01	4.02	4.64	5.02	5.29	5.51	5.69	5.84	5.97	6.09	6.19
24	.05	2.92	3.53	3.90	4.17	4.37	4.54	4.68	4.81	3.92	5.01
	.01	3.96	4.55	4.91	5.17	5.37	5.54	5.69	5.81	5.92	6.02
30	.05	2.89	3.49	3.85	4.10	4.30	4.46	4.60	4.72	4.82	4.92
	.01	3.89	4.45	4.80	5.05	5.24	5.40	5.54	5.65	5.76	5.85
40	.05	2.86	3.44	3.79	4.04	4.23	4.39	4.52	4.63	4.73	4.82
	.01	3.82	4.37	4.70	4.93	5.11	5.26	5.39	5.50	5.60	5.69
60	.05	2.83	3.40	3.74	3.98	4.16	4.31	4.44	4.55	4.65	4.73
	.01	3.76	4.28	4.59	4.82	4.99	5.13	5.25	5.36	5.45	5.53
120	.05	2.80	3.36	3.68	3.92	4.10	4.24	4.36	4.47	4.56	4.64
	.01	3.70	4.20	4.50	4.71	4.87	5.01	5.12	5.21	5.30	5.37
∞	.05	2.77	3.31	3.63	3.86	4.03	4.17	4.29	4.39	4.47	4.55
	.01	3.64	4.12	4.40	4.60	4.76	4.88	4.99	5.08	5.16	5.23

TABLE 8 (*continued*)

12	13	14	15	16	17	18	19	20	α	Error d.f.
				t = number of treatment means						
7.32	7.47	7.60	7.72	7.83	7.93	8.03	8.12	8.21	.05	5
10.70	10.89	11.08	11.24	11.40	11.55	11.68	11.81	11.93	.01	
6.79	6.92	7.03	7.14	7.24	7.34	7.43	7.51	7.59	.05	6
9.48	9.65	9.81	9.95	10.08	10.21	10.32	10.43	10.54	.01	
6.43	6.55	6.66	6.76	6.85	6.94	7.02	7.10	7.17	.05	7
8.71	8.86	9.00	9.12	9.24	9.35	9.46	9.55	9.65	.01	
6.18	6.29	6.39	6.48	6.57	6.65	6.73	6.80	6.87	.05	8
8.18	8.31	8.44	8.55	8.66	8.76	8.85	8.94	9.03	.01	
5.98	6.09	6.19	6.28	6.36	6.44	6.51	6.58	6.64	.05	9
7.78	7.91	8.03	8.13	8.23	8.33	8.41	8.49	8.57	.01	
5.83	5.93	6.03	6.11	6.19	6.27	6.34	6.40	6.47	.05	10
7.49	7.60	7.71	7.81	7.91	7.99	8.08	8.15	8.23	.01	
5.71	5.81	5.90	5.98	6.06	6.13	6.20	6.27	6.33	.05	11
7.25	7.36	7.46	7.56	7.65	7.73	7.81	7.88	7.95	.01	
5.61	5.71	5.80	5.88	5.95	6.02	6.09	6.15	6.21	.05	12
7.06	7.17	7.26	7.36	7.44	7.52	7.59	7.66	7.73	.01	
5.53	5.63	5.71	5.79	5.86	5.93	5.99	6.05	6.11	.05	13
6.90	7.01	7.10	7.19	7.27	7.35	7.42	7.48	7.55	.01	
5.46	5.55	5.64	5.71	5.79	5.85	5.91	5.97	6.03	.05	14
6.77	6.87	6.96	7.05	7.13	7.20	7.27	7.33	7.39	.01	
5.40	5.49	5.57	5.65	5.72	5.78	5.85	5.90	5.96	.05	15
6.66	6.76	6.84	6.93	7.00	7.07	7.14	7.20	7.26	.01	
5.35	5.44	5.52	5.59	5.66	5.73.	5.79	5.84	5.90	.05	16
6.56	6.66	6.74	6.82	6.90	6.97	7.03	7.09	7.15	.01	
5.31	5.39	5.47	5.54	5.61	5.67	5.73	5.79	5.84	.05	17
6.48	6.57	6.66	6.73	6.81	6.87	6.94	7.00	7.05	.01	
5.27	5.35	5.43	5.50	5.57	5.63	5.69	5.74	5.79	.05	18
6.41	6.50	6.58	6.65	6.73	6.79	6.85	6.91	6.97	.01	
5.23	5.31	5.39	5.46	5.53	5.59	5.65	5.70	5.75	.05	19
6.34	6.43	6.51	6.58	6.65	6.72	6.78	6.84	6.89	.01	
5.20	5.28	5.36	5.43	5.49	5.55	5.61	5.66	5.71	.05	20
6.28	6.37	6.45	6.52	6.59	6.65	6.71	6.77	6.82	.01	
5.10	5.18	5.25	5.32	5.38	5.44	5.49	5.55	5.59	.05	24
6.11	6.19	6.26	6.33	6.39	6.45	6.51	6.56	6.61	.01	
5.00	5.08	5.15	5.21	5.27	5.33	5.38	5.43	5.47	.05	30
5.93	6.01	6.08	6.14	6.20	6.26	6.31	6.36	6.41	.01	
4.90	4.98	5.04	5.11	5.16	5.22	5.27	5.31	5.36	.05	40
5.76	5.83	5.90	5.96	6.02	6.07	6.12	6.16	6.21	.01	
4.81	4.88	4.94	5.00	5.06	5.11	5.15	5.20	5.24	.05	60
5.60	5.67	5.73	5.78	5.84	5.89	5.93	5.97	6.01	.01	
4.71	4.78	4.84	4.90	4.95	5.00	5.04	5.09	5.13	.05	120
5.44	5.50	5.56	5.61	5.66	5.71	5.75	5.79	5.83	.01	
4.62	4.68	4.74	4.80	4.85	4.89	4.93	4.97	5.01	.05	∞
5.29	5.35	5.40	5.45	5.49	5.54	5.57	5.61	5.65	.01	

TABLE 9   Random Numbers

Line/Col.	(1)	(2)	(3)	(4)	(5)	(6)	(7)	(8)	(9)	(10)	(11)	(12)	(13)	(14)
1	10480	15011	01536	02011	81647	91646	69179	14194	62590	36207	20969	99570	91291	90700
2	22368	46573	25595	85393	30995	89198	27982	53402	93965	34095	52666	19174	39615	99505
3	24130	48360	22527	97265	76393	64809	15179	24830	49340	32081	30680	19655	63348	58629
4	42167	93093	06243	61680	07856	16376	39440	53537	71341	57004	00849	74917	97758	16379
5	37570	39975	81837	16656	06121	91782	60468	81305	49684	60672	14110	06927	01263	54613
6	77921	06907	11008	42751	27756	53498	18602	70659	90655	15053	21916	81825	44394	42880
7	99562	72905	56420	69994	98872	31016	71194	18738	44013	48840	63213	21069	10634	12952
8	96301	91977	05463	07972	18876	20922	94595	56869	69014	60045	18425	84903	42508	32307
9	89579	14342	63661	10281	17453	18103	57740	84378	25331	12566	58678	44947	05585	56941
10	85475	36857	53342	53988	53060	59533	38867	62300	08158	17983	16439	11458	18593	64952
11	28918	69578	88231	33276	70997	79936	56865	05859	90106	31595	01547	85590	91610	78188
12	63553	40961	48235	03427	49626	69445	18663	72695	52180	20847	12234	90511	33703	90322
13	09429	93969	52636	92737	88974	33488	36320	17617	30015	08272	84115	27156	30613	74952
14	10365	61129	87529	85689	48237	52267	67689	93394	01511	26358	85104	20285	29975	89868
15	07119	97336	71048	08178	77233	13916	47564	81056	97735	85977	29372	74461	28551	90707
16	51085	12765	51821	51259	77452	16308	60756	92144	49442	53900	70960	63990	75601	40719
17	02368	21382	52404	60268	89368	19885	55322	44819	01188	65255	64835	44919	05944	55157
18	01011	54092	33362	94904	31273	04146	18594	29852	71585	85030	51132	01915	92747	64951
19	52162	53916	46369	58586	23216	14513	83149	98736	23495	64350	94738	17752	35156	35749
20	07056	97628	33787	09998	42698	06691	76988	13602	51851	46104	88916	19509	25625	58104
21	48663	91245	85828	14346	09172	30168	90229	04734	59193	22178	30421	61666	99904	32812
22	54164	58492	22421	74103	47070	25306	76468	26384	58151	06646	21524	15227	96909	44592
23	32639	32363	05597	24200	13363	38005	94342	28728	35806	06912	17012	64161	18296	22851
24	29334	27001	87637	87308	58731	00256	45834	15398	46557	41135	10367	07684	36188	18510
25	02488	33062	28834	07351	19731	92420	60952	61280	50001	67658	32586	86679	50720	94953

REFERENCES

BOOKS AND ARTICLES

Belsley, D. A., Kuh, E., and Welsch, R. E. (1980). *Regression Diagnostics: Identifying Influential Data and Sources of Collinearity.* New York: Wiley.

Box, G. E. P., Hunter, W. G., and Hunter, J. S. (1978). *Statistics for Experimenters: An Introduction to Design, Data Analysis and Model Building.* New York: Wiley.

Box, G. E. P., and Jenkins, G. (1970) *Time Series Analysis: Forecasting and Control.* San Francisco: Holden-Day.

Buckley, J. J. (1988). "A Mathematical Programming Approach to Sensitivity Analysis in Single-Stage Decision Making." *Decision Sciences 19*: 211–232.

Cochran, W. G. (1977). *Sampling Techniques.* New York: Wiley.

Cochran, W. G., and Cox, G. M. (1957). *Experimental Designs,* 2nd ed. New York: Wiley.

Cook, R. D., and Weisberg, S. (1982). *Residuals and Influence in Regression.* New York: Chapman and Hall.

DeGroot, M. H. (1970). *Optimal Statistical Decisions.* New York: McGraw-Hill.

Deming, W. E. (1986). *Out of the Crisis.* Cambridge, MA: MIT Center for Advanced Engineering Study.

Draper, N. R., and Smith, H. (1981). *Applied Regression Analysis,* 2nd ed. New York: Wiley.

Greenberg, B. G., Kuebler, R. R., Abernathy, J. R., and Horvitz, D. G. (1971). "Application of Randomized Response Technique in Obtaining Quantitative Data." *Journal of the American Statistical Association 66*: 245–250.

Hildebrand, D. K., Laing, J. D., and Rosenthal, H. (1977). *Prediction Analysis of Cross Classifications.* New York: Wiley.

Hollander, M., and Wolfe, D. (1973). *Nonparametric Statistical Methods.* New York: Wiley.

Holloway, C. A. (1979). *Decision Making Under Uncertainty: Models and Choices.* Englewood Cliffs, NJ: Prentice-Hall, 1979.

Johnston, J. (1977). *Econometric Methods,* 2nd ed. New York: McGraw-Hill.

Keefer, D. L., and Bodily, S. E. (1983). "Three-Point Approximations for Continuous Random Variables." *Management Science 29*: 595–609.

Kish, L. (1965). *Survey Sampling.* New York: Wiley.

Larsen, R. J., and Marx, M. L. (1986). *An Introduction to Mathematical Statistics and Its Applications*. Englewood Cliffs, NJ: Prentice-Hall.

Mallows, C. L. (1973). "Some Comments on C_p." *Technometrics 15*: 661–675.

Mendenhall, W. (1968). *Introduction to Linear Models and the Design and Analysis of Experiments*. Belmont, CA: Wadsworth.

Mood, A. M., Graybill, F. A., and Boes, D. C. (1974). *Introduction to the Theory of Statistics*, 3rd ed. New York: McGraw-Hill.

Nelson, C. R. (1977). *Applied Time Series Analysis for Managerial Forecasting*. San Francisco: Holden-Day.

Ott, L. (1989). *An Introduction to Statistical Methods and Data Analysis*, 3rd ed. Boston: PWS-KENT.

Ott, L., Larson, R. F., and Mendenhall, W. (1987). *Statistics: A Tool for the Social Sciences*, 4th ed. Boston: PWS-KENT.

Phadke, M. S. (1986). "Design Optimization Case Studies." *AT&T Technical Journal 65*(2): 39–50.

Pierce, D. A. (1980). "A Survey of Recent Developments in Seasonal Adjustment." *The American Statistician 34*: 125–134.

Pignatiello, J. J., and Ramberg, J. S. (1985). "Discussion." *Journal of Quality Technology 17*: 198–206.

Schaeffer, R. L., Mendenhall, W., and Ott, L. (1986). *Elementary Survey Sampling*, 3rd ed. Boston: PWS-KENT.

Shoemaker, A. C., and Kacker, R. N. (1988). "A Methodology for Planning Experiments in Robust Product and Process Design." *Quality and Reliability Engineering International 4*: 95–103.

Spetzler, C. S., and Stael von Holstein, C.A. (1975). "Probability Encoding in Decision Analysis." *Management Science 22*: 340–358.

Taguchi, G. (1980). *Introduction to Off-Line Quality Control*. Tokyo: Japanese Standards Association.

Tukey, J. W. (1977). *Exploratory Data Analysis*. Reading, MA: Addison-Wesley.

von Neumann, J., and Morganstern, O. (1967). *Theory of Games and Economic Behavior*, 3rd ed. New York: Wiley.

Walton, M. (1986). *The Deming Management Method*. New York: Dodd, Mead.

Warner, S. L. (1965). "Randomized Response: A Survey Technique for Eliminating Evasive Answer Bias." *Journal of the American Statistical Association 60*: 63–69.

Welch, B. L. (1938). "The Significance of the Differences Between Two Means When the Population Variances Are Unequal." *Biometrika 29*: 350–362.

STATISTICAL PROGRAM PACKAGES

(BMDP)

Dixon, W. J., chief editor, Brown, M. B., Engelman, L., and Jennrich, R. I., assistant editors (1990). *BMDP Statistical Software Manual, 1990 Revision*. Berkeley, CA: University of California Press.

(Execustat)

Strategy Plus, Inc. (1990). *EXECUSTAT*. Boston: PWS-KENT, 1990.

(IDA)

Ling, R. F., and Roberts, H. V. (1980). *User's Manual for IDA*. Palo Alto, CA: Scientific Press.

(Minitab)

Schaefer, R. L., and Anderson, R. B. (1989). *The Student Edition of Minitab*. Reading, MA: Addison-Wesley.

(SAS)

SAS Institute (1985). *SAS User's Guide: Basics, Version 5 Edition*. Cary, NC: SAS Institute, Inc.

(SPSS-X)

SPSS, Inc. (1988). *SPSS-X User's Guide, 3rd ed.* Chicago: SPSS, Inc.

(Statgraphics)

STSC, Inc. (1986). *Statgraphics Users Guide*. Rockville, MD: STSC, Inc.

(Systat)

Wilkinson, L. (1987). *SYSTAT: The System for Statistics*. Evanston, IL: SYSTAT, Inc.

ANSWERS TO EXERCISES

CHAPTER 2   Section 2.1, pg. 15

2.1 a.

Class	Midpoint	Frequency
320–329	325	1
330–339	335	1
340–349	345	0
350–359	355	1
360–369	365	6
370–379	375	7
380–389	385	11
390–399	395	1

Note that this is just *one* of many possible frequency tables.

b.

32	4									
33	9									
34										
35	9									
36	6	0	6	3	7	4				
37	5	5	9	4	7	1	9			
38	5	0	4	3	6	7	4	6	5	1	5
39	0									

2.2 a.

Class	Midpoint	Frequency
810–819	815	1
820–829	825	1
830–839	835	4
840–849	845	7
850–859	855	2
860–869	865	1
870–879	875	1

b.

81	2						
82	4						
83	8	8	6	9			
84	7	9	1	6	9	6	3
85	2	0					
86	4						
87	1						

2.3 a.

Class	Midpoint	Frequency
11.80–11.89	11.85	1
11.90–11.99	11.95	2
12.00–12.09	12.05	6
12.10–12.19	12.15	4
12.20–12.29	12.25	6
12.30–12.39	12.35	1

MANUFACTURER E

b.

Class	Midpoint	Frequency
11.80–11.89	11.85	1
11.90–11.99	11.95	2
12.00–12.09	12.05	5
12.10–12.19	12.15	1
12.20–12.29	12.25	1
12.30–12.39	12.35	0

MANUFACTURER S

Class	Midpoint	Frequency
11.80–11.89	11.85	0
11.90–11.99	11.95	0
12.00–12.09	12.05	1
12.10–12.19	12.15	3
12.20–12.29	12.25	5
12.30–12.39	12.35	1

c. The combined histogram shows 2 modal classes. The separate histograms show that each has one different modal class.

2.4 a. One possible summary, using a class width of 5:

Interval	Midpoint	Frequency
7.5–12.4	10	7
12.5–17.4	15	5
17.5–22.4	20	4
22.5–27.4	25	1
27.5–32.4	30	2
32.5–37.4	35	3
37.5–42.4	40	1
42.5–47.4	45	1

Total 24

Divide by 24 to obtain relative frequencies.

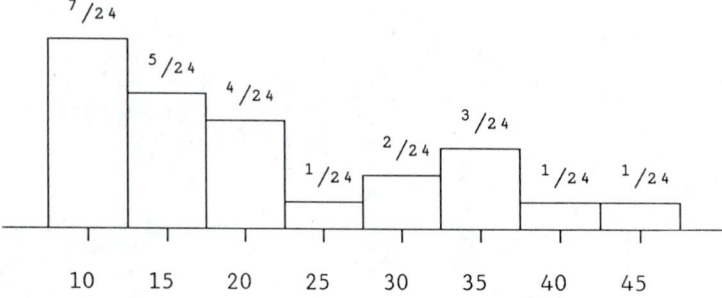

b. We could record the third digit as follows.

0	7.7	8.5	9.6	9.7			
1	0.3	3.6	4.5	0.1	1.4	4.2	3.7
1	9.5	7.8	5.9				
2	0.7	2.1					
2	5.9	9.1					
3	2.6	2.4					
3	6.7	5.9					
4	0.1						
4	5.9						

The stem-and-leaf diagram shows the data.

2.5 a. Histogram with first rectangle Nonsmoking (height 18), second rectangle Wrong Bed (height 13), and so on.

b. No. The three major reasons are all related to check-in, not maintenance.

Section 2.2, pg. 23

2.6 mean = 15.1875, median = 14.5, mode = 18

2.7 a. One possibility is to use a class width of 300.

Class	Midpoint	Frequency
150–449	300	3
450–749	600	3
750–1049	900	6
1050–1349	1200	3
1350–1649	1500	6
1650–1949	1800	0
1950–2249	2100	2

Total 23

b. $\bar{y}$ is roughly 1200.

c. median = 1039, mean = 1091.96

d. mean slightly larger; slight right-skewness.

2.8 a. Not for quantitative data.

b. median = 688

c. mean = 679.4

d. left-skewness

2.9

54	7						
⋮							
62	5						
63	0						
64							
65	6						
66	4	7	7				
67	7	9					
68	8	8	8	8	8		
69	1	4	7	9			
70	0	1	2	3	3	3	8
71	1						

Yes, data are left-skewed.

2.10 a.

Number of members	mean	median
1	93.750	78.5

b. right-skewed

c. right-skewed

2.11 a. Yes;
$$108.723 = [20(93.75) + \cdots + 10(131.90)]/83$$
b. No; the weighted average of medians is 98.98, but the overall median is 104.

2.12 a. No; there is considerable variability within levels.
b. Yes, they overlap.
c. No, somewhat right-skewed.

Section 2.3, pg. 35

2.13 a. Sample 1: range $= 10$
Sample 2: range $= 12$
b. Sample 1: $\bar{y} = 20$; $s^2 = 17.33$; $s = 4.16$
Sample 2: $\bar{y} = 20$; $s^2 = 8.50$; $s = 2.92$
c. Sample 1 has more variability.

2.14 a. $\bar{y} = 679.4$, $s = 34.8$
b. 23/26, or 88.5%, of the data fall in this range. The Empirical Rule works poorly for these data.

2.15 a. median $= 688$, IQR $= 34$
b. Inner: 616 and 752
Outer: 565 and 803
The 547 value is a severe outlier.
c. The box goes from 667 to 701 with a line at 688. The whiskers go down to 625 and up to 711. The severe outlier, 547, is indicated by a o symbol.

2.16 Operator skill differs, as does complexity of requests. You may think of others.

2.17 a. 759.98 to 828.48
b. 51/60 is 85%, not 68%. The data aren't mound shaped; a huge outlier at 601, inflating s.

2.18 There are several outliers; they increase s greatly.

2.19 a. Increase the mean, decrease the standard deviation.
b. Mean increased slightly, standard deviation decreased greatly.

2.20 a. Only about 1.6% late.
b. Weather, reasonableness of schedule, air traffic control delays, late passengers, etc.
c. 88.62 to 114.54

2.21 a. Yes, except for two "outside values."
b. 36/38 $= 94.7\%$

2.22 Apparent decreasing trend.

2.23 a. There may be fewer sources of variation.
b. Flight 483 only.

2.24 a. No up or down trend; two high scores in the middle.
b. 82.75 to 117.25; 118 is barely out of control.

2.25 a. mean $= [600(1) + \cdots + 840(4)]/60 = 794.00$
variance
$$= [(600 - 794)^2(1) + \cdots + (840 - 794)^2(4)]/59$$
$$= 1210.85$$
standard deviation $= \sqrt{1210.85} = 34.80$
b. Very close to 794.23 and 34.25.

2.26 a. Decrease mean by 0.5, standard deviation unchanged.
b. mean $= 793.50$, standard deviation $= 34.80$

2.27 a. Mean trends downward.
b. No problem.

2.28 Bad lot would mean a jump, drift would mean a trend. Heating is the problem.

Section 2.4, pg. 44

2.29 a. "SKEWNESS" $= 1.766$;
"KURTOSIS" $= 4.372$
b. The histogram shows slight right-skewness. Skewness $= 1.67$. Slight difference.

2.30 a. KURTOSIS $= 3.88$
b. Slightly more heavy-tailness than the normal distribution.

2.31 a. right-skewness
b. slight left-skewness
c. symmetric

2.32 a. Year 1: $\bar{y} = 2.083$, $s = 2.158$
Year 2: $\bar{y} = 2.308$, $s = 2.293$

b.

Year	$(\bar{y} - \text{median})/s$	Third-Power Skewness
1	.525	1.048
2	.309	1.435

Strong right-skewness is indicated.

2.33 a. $\bar{y} = 2.196$, the average of the yearly means
b. $s = 2.181$, not an average

2.34 a. left-skewness
b. measure $= -.247$

2.35 a. Nothing extreme.
b. measure $= .104$, moderate right-skewness

2.36 Kurtosis $= 2.467$. Data are slightly light-tailed.

Chapter 2 Exercises, pg. 49

2.37 a. $\bar{y} = 4$; $s^2 = 52.85$; $s = 7.27$
b. $\bar{y} \pm 1s$: -3.27 to 11.27
Actual: 90%
Empirical Rule: 68%
The discrepancy is due to right-skewness.
c. Skewness $= +.344$, indicating right-skewness.

2.39 a.

Class	Midpoint	Frequency
8–12	10	10
13–17	15	0
18–22	20	5
23–27	25	0
28–32	30	10

The data are symmetric (no skewness) and tri-modal.
b. The mean and median are exactly the same, 20.
c. $s = 9.18$
The skewness coefficient must equal 0.
d. $\bar{y} \pm 1s$: 10.82 to 29.18
Actual: 36%
Empirical Rule: 68%
Discrepancy is due to the trimodal distribution of the data.
e. $\bar{y} \pm 2s$: 1.64 to 38.36
Actual: 100%
Chebyshev's: at least 75%

2.40 a. $\bar{y} = 0$; $s^2 = 117.43$; $s = 10.84$
b. skewness $= -.092$ using $(\bar{y} - \text{median})/s$
skewness $= -2.49$ using alternative formula
c. Skewed right but with a left outlier.
d. The outlier at -36.

2.41 No obvious increasing or decreasing trend.

2.42 No clear trend.

2.43 a. 0.86 and 3.14; no means out of control
b. No, unless production slowed to do so.

2.44 Possible right-skewness.

2.45 Last five numbers are higher.

2.46 On four of the last five days.

2.47 a. 0.60 and 2.40 minutes
b. days 22, 30, 32, 54, 55, 57, and 58

2.48 Yes, high variability at the end of the period.

2.49 a. Quality of representatives, local economic conditions, differences in competition, etc.
b. No evident skewness, several candidate outliers.
c. skew = 0.0055, practically no skewness

2.50 May be slight downward trend.

2.51 Nonsense; half the values will always be below the median.

2.52 a. smaller
b. smaller
c. Server 2 has smallest mean, server 1, smallest standard deviation.

2.53 Server 2 has smallest MEAN, server 1, smallest STDEV.

2.54 Nothing at all; the data are qualitative.

2.55 a. codes 6, 9, and 7
b. All pay-related.

2.56 Pay clearly contains most of the data.

2.57 a. Without sorting the "leaves"

1	6 8 7 6 9 6 9 2 8 0 6 2 9 5 4 8 7 4 0 4 3 2 1 9 1 2 3 9 5 7
2	9 6 7 2 5 7 5 4 5 5 5 0 0 1 9 0 8 1 0 7 8
3	7 5
4	7 9 0 5 6 1 0
5	3 7 6

b.

1	2 0 2 4 4 0 4 3 2 1 1 2 3
1	6 8 7 6 9 6 9 8 6 9 5 8 7 9 9 5 7
2	2 4 0 0 1 0 1 0
2	9 6 7 5 7 5 5 5 5 9 8 7 8
3	
3	7 5
4	0 1 0
4	7 9 5 6
5	3
5	7 6

c. Right-skewed, possibly bimodal, in either display.

2.58 a. Histogram is also right-skewed.
b. Uses different intervals.

2.59 The right "whisker" is longer than the left one; there are also outliers on the right.

2.60 The mean is one-third of a standard deviation above the median.

2.61 a. No.
b. Some jumps.

2.62 a. No; too big.
b. Variability.

2.63 a. Maybe 57 or 60.
b. Roughly 1.

2.64 a. Perhaps the BIDPERHR mean is a bit above 1.
b. No; MINPRBID is much more severely skewed.

2.65 a. 62.462 and 1.432. No; 60/62.462 is not close to 1.432.
b. MINPRBID is much more skewed.

2.66 b. right-skewed

2.67 a. No; right-skewed.
b. Not obvious.

2.68 a. right-skewness and outliers
b. right-skewness

2.69 Right skew and several outliers on the right.

2.70 a. Histogram ordered by frequency.

2.71 For qualitative data, only the mode is a sensible "average."

2.72 b. Slight right skew.
c. About 65 or 66.
d. About 2 or 3.
e. mean 66.024, standard deviation 2.115

2.73 a. Slight right skew.
b. Mean 13.946, median 13.840, standard deviation 0.771
c. (mean − median)/st.dev. = .137

2.74 b. One mild outlier, low side.
c. mean = 0.826; ratio of means = 0.826 in this case

2.75 a. Symmetric, two outliers.
b. Observations 5 (high) and 25 (low)
c. mean 1985.5, st. dev. 200.8
d. mean 1992.3, st. dev. (greater change) 146.9

2.76 b. No trend.
c. No obvious cycle.

2.77 b. Some left skew, outlier at 42.
c. Yes; many 5's and 0's in the leaves.

2.78 a. mean 79.42, st.dev. 6.97.
b. st.dev. of means = 4.647
d. Day 50 has a mean below 66.06.

b. Apart from code 11, codes 01 and 02 are most important, and relate to the manuals and operators' ability to use them.

CHAPTER 3   Section 3, pg. 78

3.1 a. If the editor calls on past experience, the long-run relative frequency interpretation. If the textbook is one of a kind, the subjective interpretation.
b. Long-run relative frequency interpretation.
c. Classical interpretation: A random sample (all probabilities equal) of 100 employees.
d. If one is willing to assume that economic conditions in Germany are going to be the same next year as in previous years, the long-run interpretation. If one is not willing to assume the same economic conditions for the next year, the subjective interpretation.
e. Long-run relative frequency interpretation.

3.2 No "correct" answers.

3.3 a. $P(C) = 541/723 = .748$
b. $P(serious) = 453/723 = .627$
c. $P(not\ reimbursed) = 22/723 = .030$

3.4 a. $P(engine \mid C) = 106/541 = .196$

b.

		Engine	Transmission	Exhaust	Fit/Finish	Other	Total
Brand	C	.196	.390	.124	.246	.044	1.000
	G	.115	.632	.088	.132	.033	1.000

The probabilities are quite different.

3.5 a. $P(>1$ problem$) = 92/609 = .151$
b. $P(>1$ problem$|C) = 71/453 = .157$

3.6

		Number of Problems			
		1	2	3	Total
Brand	C	.843	.119	.038	1.000
	G	.865	.103	.032	1.000

The probabilities are nearly identical.

3.7 No; also depends on the number sold of each brand.

3.8 a. $P(gas) = 186/1236 = .150$
b. $P(food) = 734/1236 = .594$

3.9 $P(dairy|food) = 207/734 = .282$

3.10 a. $P(recalled) = .580$
b. $P(recalled) = 1 - .420 = .580$

3.11 $P(man$ or favorable$) = 157/250 = .628$
$= P(man) + P(favorable)$
$- P(both)$

3.12 a. $P(incorr|m) = .42, P(favor|m) = .38,$
$P(unfavor|m) = .20$
$P(incorr|w) = .42, P(favor|w) = .38,$
$P(unfavor|w) = .20$
b. The responses are identical by gender.

Section 3.2, pg. 83

3.13 The sample space, S, consists of 45 outcomes: (A12), (A13), ..., (C56).

3.14 $P(same$ division$) = 3/45 = .067$
$P(different$ divisions$) = 12/45 = .267$

3.15 An outcome would be a string of 100 numbers, each number being a 0 or a 1. The outcomes aren't equally likely.

3.16 $P(A) = .80; P(B) = .50; P(A$ and B both occur$) = .35; P(either$ A or B, or both$) = .95$

3.17 $P(A$ or B$) = .95 \neq P(A) + P(B) = 1.30.$ A and B aren't mutually exclusive.

3.18 a. If model number is an outcome
$S = \{1, 2, 3, 4, 5, 6, 7, 8, 9\}.$
b. $P(standard) = .84$
c. $P(standard$ or both drives$) = 1.000$

3.19 "Probability" greater than 1.0; the events aren't mutually exclusive.

Section 3.3, pg. 91

3.20 $\bar{A}$ is the event that generator 1 fails. $(A \cup B)$ is the event that generator 1 works properly or generator 2 works properly or both generator 1 and 2 work properly.
$(A \cap B)$ is the event that both generator 1 and 2 work properly.
$(\bar{A} \cap \bar{B})$ is the event that both generator 1 and 2 fail.
The complement of $A \cup B$ is $\bar{A} \cap \bar{B}$.

3.21 $P(A \cap \bar{B}) = .03; P(\bar{A} \cap B) = .01; P(\bar{A} \cap \bar{B}) = .03$

3.22 $P(B|A) = .969.$ Given that generator 1 works properly, the probability that 2 also works is .969.
$P(\bar{B}|A) = .031.$
$P(B|\bar{A}) = .25.$ Given that generator 1 fails, the probability that 2 works properly is .25.
$P(\bar{B}|\bar{A}) = .75.$
$P(B|A) + P(\bar{B}|A) = 1$ but $P(B|A) + P(B|\bar{A}) \neq 1$

3.23 $P(A \cap B) \neq 0;$ therefore, A and B are not mutually exclusive.
$P(A \cup B) = .97$

3.24 Not mutually exclusive pairs. $(A \cap B \cap C)$ is the event that the grant was ineligible and it was incomplete and received past the deadline.

3.25

3.26 $P(\bar{A} \cap \bar{B} \cap \bar{C}) = .769$; $P(A \cup B \cup C) = .231$;
$P(\bar{A} \cap \bar{B}) = .817$
$\bar{A} \cap \bar{B} \cap \bar{C}$ is "none of the events occur";
$A \cup B \cup C$ is "at least one occurs"; $\bar{A} \cap \bar{B}$ is "neither A nor B occurs."

3.27 a. P(defective and detected) $= .09$
b. P(defective and not detected) $= .01$

3.28 a. P(defective and not detected) $= .002$
b. P(defective and not detected) is lower when the original probability of defective drilling is lower.

3.29 P(defective and never detected) $= .002$

Section 3.4, pg. 95

3.30 a. $P(A) = .40$, $P(A \cap B) = .12$, $P(B \mid A) = .30$
b. $P(B \mid A) = P(B) = .30$. Therefore A and B are statistically independent.
c. Not at all useful.

3.31 a. $P(A \cap \bar{B}) = .28$, $P(\bar{B} \mid A) = .70$
b. $P(\bar{B} \mid A) = P(\bar{B}) = .70$. Therefore A and $\bar{B}$ are statistically independent.

3.32 A is the event "worker comes from Plant 1." B is the event "response is poor."
a. $P(A) = .436$; $P(B) = .291$; $P(A \cap B) = .109$
b. $P(A \cap B) \neq P(A)P(B)$; therefore A and B are not independent.
c. $P(B \mid A) = .25 \neq P(B \mid \bar{A}) = .323$

3.33 Because $P(B \mid A) = P(B)$ and $P(B \mid \bar{A}) = P(B)$ by independence, $P(B \mid A) = P(B \mid \bar{A})$.

3.34 P(no substitute needed at any school) $= .18$

3.35 Not a realistic; take the case of a flu epidemic.

3.36 a. P(both drives | standard) $= .24/.84 = .286$
b. P(standard | both drives) $= .24/.40 = .600$
c. No; P(both drives | standard) is not equal to P(both drives).

3.37 Yes, the probabilities work out to be independent.

3.38 No, these events should not be independent.

3.39 Yes, these events might well be independent.

Section 3.5, pg. 104

3.40 a. Joint probability table:

		Retest			
		Major	Minor	None	
First Test	Major	.18	.30	.12	.60
	Minor	.03	.09	.18	.30
	None	.00	.02	.08	.10
		.21	.41	.38	1.00

b. P(Major at retest) $= .21$
c. P(Minor at retest) $= .41$;
P(none at retest) $= .38$

3.41 P(Major at retest) $= .21$; P(Minor at retest) $= .41$; P(None at retest) $= .38$

3.42 b. P(program will show major bugs at all three tests) $= .018$
c. P(program will show major bugs at third test) $= .021$
d. P(program shows no bugs at second and third tests) $= .896$

3.43 a. P(first time bidder $\cap$ satisfactory service) $= .06$
b. P(satisfactory service) $= .84$
c. P(first time bidder | satisfactory service) $= .071$

3.44 a. P(failure and poor) $= .30$
b.

	Poor	Fair	Good
Failure	.30	.18	.12
Moderate	.06	.12	.12
Major	.01	.03	.06

c. P(failure | good) $= .40$

3.45 P(major | poor) $= .01/.37 = .027$

3.46 a. The tree should have four levels of branches for the four calls. Each branch is either C (Contract) with probability .4, or O (Occasional) with probability .6.
b. P(decline) $= P$(at least 3 C's) $= .1792$

3.47 P(4 C's | decline) $= .0256/.1792 = .143$

Section 3.6, pg. 110

3.48 a. $P(\text{defaulted} \mid \text{poor}) = .029$

b. $P(\text{defaulted} \mid \text{poor}) = .029$

3.49 $P(\text{defaulted} \mid \text{fair}) = P(\text{defaulted}) = .01$, independent

3.50 $P(A \mid \text{defective}) = .5$, higher than the prior probability, $1/3$.

3.51 $P(\text{type 1} \mid \text{fire}) = .40$

3.52 $P(\text{unsuccess} \mid \text{good}) = .714 > P(\text{unsuccess}) = .40$

3.53 $P(A_2 \mid B_1) = .443$; $P(A_2 \mid B_2) = .226$; $P(A_2 \mid B_3) = .513$; $P(A_2 \mid B_4) = .276$

3.54 a. The prior probabilities are for weak, normal, and strong markets. The likelihoods are for poor, fair, and good sales.

b. The probability of a weak year should decrease.

c. $P(\text{weak} \mid \text{good}) = .08/(.08 + .10 + .06) = .333$

3.55 a. $P(\text{weak} \mid \text{good}) = .08/.24 = .333$
$P(\text{normal} \mid \text{good}) = .10/.24 = .417$
$P(\text{strong} \mid \text{good}) = .06/.24 = .250$

b. No, it is still the least probable, because of the low prior probability.

3.56 a. The probability of a strike should increase.

b. $P(\text{strike} \mid \text{full catch-up}) = .14/.46 = .304$

c. $P(\text{strike} \mid \text{full catch-up}) = .14/.46$

3.57 No change; "stay even" is independent of "strike."

Chapter 3 Exercises, pg. 113

3.58 A typical outcome of this experiment would be one with (say) 18 B's, 22 C's, and 20 D's. All outcomes should not be equally likely.

3.59 Let A be "MBA degree," and B be "undergraduate business degree."

a. Venn diagram

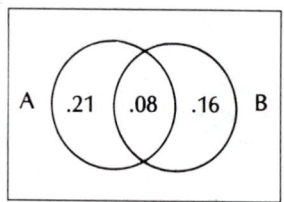

b. $P(A \cup B) = .45$

c. $P(\bar{A} \cap \bar{B}) = .55$

3.60 $P(\text{exactly one of A or B}) = .37$

3.61 Let A be "air-conditioning," and B be "power steering."

a. Venn diagram

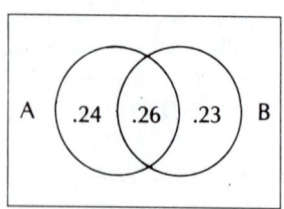

b. $P(A \cap \bar{B}) = .24$

c. $P(\bar{A} \cap \bar{B}) = .27$

3.62 Let C be the event "automatic transmission."

a. Venn diagram

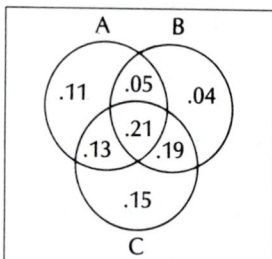

b. $P(A \cup B \cup C) = .88$

c. $P(\text{exactly 1 option ordered}) = .30$

3.63 A and C are independent.

3.64 a. $P(\text{all 8 stocks beat the market}) = .5^8 = .00390625$

b. Independence among stocks and even chance of the stock doing better or worse than the market.

3.65 a. $P(\text{no analyst gets 8 "winners"}) = [1 - (.5)^8]^{100} = .676$

b. $P(\text{at least one analyst gets 8 "winners"}) = .324$

3.66 a. Joint probability table

		Sales level for week 1				
		10	20	30	40	
	10	.16	.12	.08	.04	.40
Sales level for	20	.12	.09	.06	.03	.30
week 2	30	.08	.06	.04	.02	.20
	40	.04	.03	.02	.01	.10
		.40	.30	.20	.10	1.00

b. P(average sales level per week $= 25) = .20$

3.67 If a recently released book makes the best seller list one week, sales the following week could be greatly affected.

3.68 a. P(received on time $\cap$ specifications met) $= .60$

b. Joint probability table

	Received on time	Received late	
Specifications met	.60	.15	.75
Specifications not met	.15	.10	.25
	.75	.25	1.00

c. P(specifications met) $= .75$

3.69 a. P(all 4 orders meet specifications) $= .316$

b. The orders are independent of each other.

3.70 a. P(both pay) $= .25$

b. P(pay in full twice) $= .25$

c. Independence; unreasonable in b.

3.71 a. P(pay in full twice) $= .45$

b. P(pay in full neither month) $= .45$

c. P(exactly one month) $= .10$

3.72 $P(\text{first} | \text{second}) = .90$

3.73 a. P(no alteration) $= .52$

b. P(exactly one alteration) $= .26$

3.74 not independent

3.75 a. P(both jackets need alteration) $= .16$

b. Same P(alteration) and independence. Independence is dubious.

3.76 a. P(not perfect) $= 1 - .8847 = .1153$

b. $P(\text{not usable} | \text{not perfect}) = .0025/.1153 = .0217$

Review Exercises, Chapters 2–3, pg. 117

R1 a.

Supplier	Mean	Std. Dev.	Median	Skew = (mean − median)/St. Dev.
A	26.71	9.21	23.25	.38
B	31.33	8.49	28.2	.37
C	22.77	9.02	19.8	.33
D	28.05	11.95	24.0	.34

b. No, the data are severely right-skewed.

R2 $\bar{y} = 27.215$ is the average of supplier means. $s^2 = 97.56$ is not an average.

R3 $P(\text{decrease} | \text{not correct}) = .160$

R4 a. The qualitative variable "type of bank" is excluded.

Variable	Deposits	Capital	Reserves	Bad Debts
$\bar{y}$	8.683	2.617	2.475	1.794
s	9.112	3.229	2.647	1.333

b.

Variable	Deposits	Capital	Reserves	Bad Debts
25th %ile	3.67	.85	.92	.97
75th %ile	11.64	4.03	3.28	2.00
IQR	7.97	3.18	2.36	1.03
Lower inner fence	negative	negative	negative	negative
Upper inner fence	23.595	8.80	6.82	3.545
Lower outer fence	negative	negative	negative	negative
Upper outer fence	35.55	13.57	10.36	5.09
Outliers	31.62(*)	10.63(*)	9.22(*)	3.97(*)
				4.31(*)

(* = mild, o = severe)

R5 $P(\text{unacceptable} \mid \text{test shows excess}) = .0092/.0488$
$$= .19$$

R6 $P(\text{borderline} \mid \text{acceptable})$
   $= P(\text{borderline} \mid \text{not acceptable})$
   $= .05$

R7   a. $\bar{y} = 2.31, s = 1.38$
   b. Meaningless; X_3 is qualitative.

R8

Variable	X_4	X_5	Y
Mean	32,938	40,977	8,038
St. dev.	21,561	26,433	6,256
Median	21,200	36,000	5,000

The mean of Y is (except for roundoff) equal to $\bar{x}_5 - \bar{x}_4$.
There is no such relation for medians or standard deviations.

R9 $(\bar{y} - \text{median})/s = .486$, more right-skewness than is suggested by a histogram.

R10   a. $P(\text{cancelled}) = .587$
   b. $P(\text{bottom third} \mid \text{cancelled}) = .425/.587 = .724$

R11   No; $P(\text{bottom third} \mid \text{cancelled}) \neq P(\text{bottom third}) = .50$. Independence would mean that highly ranked shows were just as likely to be cancelled as poorly ranked ones. Not so!

R12   a. $P(\text{excellent} \cap \text{definite}) = .0432$
   b. Independence, an unreasonable assumption. The calculated probability should be too low.

R13   a. $\bar{y} = 2.477$
   b. $s = 1.834$. As a population, $\sigma = 1.833$.
   c. The range contains 1134/1533, or 74.0%, of the data, fairly close to 68%.

R14   a. $P(\text{at least 1}) = .869$
   b. $P(\text{at most 3} \mid \text{at least 1}) = .738$

R15   a. The two should be nearly equal. Median = 35.55; $\bar{y} = 35.41$.
   b. Range for men = 11.3, range for women = 22.2; there are outliers in the data for women.

R16   For men, the box goes from 33.8 to 36.7 with a line at 35.55, whiskers down to 31.6 and up to 40.2, and a moderate outlier at 28.9. For women, the box goes from 30.5 to 33.6 with a line at 32.15, whiskers down to 29.8 and up to 38.1, a moderate outlier at 22.5, and a severe outlier at 44.7.

R17 $\bar{y} = 34.08$, a weighted average; median = 34.0, not related to the group medians.

R18   a. $P(\text{engine} \cap \text{not interior} \cap \text{not exterior}) = .32$
   b. $P(\text{exactly one}) = .63$
   c. No;
   $P(\text{engine} \cap \text{interior}) = .23$
   $\neq P(\text{engine})P(\text{interior})$.

R19   a. Each plot is somewhat right-skewed.
   b.

	Base	Corn	Oats	Wheat
Mean		11.25	12.97	32.14
Median		10.75	12.25	31.0
n		20	18	29

In each case the mean is larger than the median, indicating right-skewness.

R20 $\bar{y} = 20.75$, median = 15. Neither is typical.

CHAPTER 4   Sections 4.1 and 4.2, pg. 128

4.1   a. Let A through C represent the women recruiters, and D through H the men recruiters. The sample space consists of 56 outcomes: (AB), (AC), ..., (HG).

   b. The number of women selected for each outcome in the sample space is given in the order in which the outcomes are listed above: 2, 2, ..., 0.

4.2

y	0	1	2
$P_Y(y)$	.357	.536	.107

4.3

y	0	1	2
$F_Y(y)$	.357	.893	1.00

4.4 b. $P(Y \le 2) = .50$
c. $P(Y \ge 7) = .13$
d. $P(1 \le Y \le 5) = .71$

4.5

y	0	1	2	3	4	5	6	7	8	9	10
$F_Y(y)$	.10	.25	.50	.64	.73	.81	.87	.92	.96	.985	1.00

$P(Y \le 2) = .50$ $P(Y \ge 7) = .13$
$P(1 \le Y \le 5) = .71$

4.6 a. $P(X \ge 3) = .64$
b. $P(2 \le X \le 6) = .60$
c. $P(X \ge 9) = .07$

4.7 a.

x	0	1	2	3	4	5	6	7	8	9	10
$F_X(x)$	.06	.20	.36	.50	.62	.72	.80	.87	.93	.97	1.00

b. $1 - F_X(2) = .64$, $F_X(6) - F_X(1) = .60$,
$1 - F_X(8) = .07$

Section 4.3, pg. 135

4.8 a. Table of $F_Y(y)$ values

y	$F_Y(y) = 5y^4 - 4y^5$
0	0
.1	.00046
.2	.00672
.3	.03078
.4	.08704
.5	.18750
.6	.33696
.7	.52822
.8	.73728
.9	.91854
1.0	1.00000

b. $P(Y \le .8) = .73728$; $P(Y \ge .6) = .66304$;
$P(.5 \le Y \le .9) = .73104$

4.9 a. Table of $F_Y(y)$ values

y	$F_Y(y) = 1 - e^{-.5y}$
0	0
1	.3935
2	.6321
3	.7769
4	.8647
5	.9179
6	.9502
7	.9698
8	.9817

b. $P(Y \le .75) = .3127$; $P(Y \ge 4) = .1353$;
$P(2 \le Y \le 3.5) = .1941$

4.10 a. $f_Y(y) = 5(4)y^3 - 4(5)y^4$ $0 \le y \le 1$
b. Integrate $f_Y(y)$; $P(.2 \le Y \le .7) = .5215$;
$P(Y \le .6) = .33696$; $P(Y \ge .5) = .8125$
c. $P(.2 \le Y \le .7) = .5215$; $P(Y \le .6) = .33696$;
$P(Y \ge .5) = .8125$

4.11 a. Table of $f_Y(y)$ values

y	$f_Y(y) = (4/27)(9y - 6y^2 + y^3)$
0	0
.25	.2801
.50	.4629
.75	.5625
1.00	.5926
1.50	.5000
2.00	.2963
2.50	.0926
3.00	0

b. $P(Y \le 1.5) = .6875$; $P(Y \ge 2.0) = .1111$;
$P(1 \le Y \le 2.5) = .5764$

c. Table of $F_Y(y)$ values

y	$F_Y(y) = \dfrac{4}{27}\left(\dfrac{9y^2}{2} - \dfrac{6y^3}{3} + \dfrac{y^4}{4}\right)$
0	0
.5	.1319
1.0	.4074
1.5	.6875
2.0	.8889
2.5	.9838
3.0	1.0000

Sections 4.4 and 4.5, pg. 142

4.16 b. $E(Y) = 4.32$
c. $E(Y)$ is pulled to the right, because of the right-skewness of the data.

4.17 a. $\sigma_Y = 2.2798$
b. $\sigma_Y = \sqrt{23.86 - (4.32)^2} = 2.2798$

4.18 Actual probability: $P(2.0402 \leq Y \leq 6.5998) = .63$
Empirical Rule: $P(2.0402 \leq Y \leq 6.5998) = .68$
The right-skewness of the population distribution.

4.19 a. Apartment #1: $E(Y) = 100$
Apartment #2: $E(Z) = 105$
b. Apartment #1: $\text{Var}(Y) = 2500$; $\sigma_Y = 50$
Apartment #2: $\text{Var}(Z) = 8475$; $\sigma_Z = 92.06$

4.20 a. Apartment #2 has higher return, but also higher risk.
b. For many people, the less risky apartment #1 would be preferred.

4.21 a. $\mu_X = 3.97$
b. $\sigma_X^2 = 7.0891$
c. $\sigma_X^2 = 22.85 - (3.97)^2 = 7.0891$

4.22 $P(-1.35 < X < 9.29) = .97$, close to .95 (Empirical Rule) and well above .75 (Chebyshev's Inequality).

4.23 a. $\mu_Y = 1.5$, the long-run average Y value
b. $\sigma_Y = .866$

4.24 a. The density is very right-skewed.
b. No; right-skewness.
$P(.634 < Y < 2.366) = P(1 < Y < 2.366) = .924$, not close to .68.

4.25 a. $\mu_Y = 10$ by symmetry
b. $\sigma_Y = .039$

4.12 $P(Y > 115) = .0430$

4.13 $F_Y(y) = .0009375$
$\times [-10,400/3 + 40y - .1(y - 100)^3/3]$,
$80 < y < 120$

4.14 a. $P(2 < Y < 4) = .1094$, regardless of the inclusion of 2.00000... and 4.00000...
b. $P(0.5 < Y < 1.5) = P(1 < Y < 1.5) = .7037$

4.15 a. $F_Y(y) = 1 - 1/y^3$, for $y > 1$
b. $1 - 1/y^3 = .99$ if $y = 4.642$

4.26 a. The possibilities are $y = 0$, 1, or 2.
b. $P_Y(0) = .84$, $P_Y(1) = .12$, $P_Y(2) = .04$

4.27 a. $\mu_Y = 0.20$; in the long run, a controller averages 0.20 rework cycles.
b. $\sigma_Y^2 = 0.24$, $\sigma_Y = 0.4899$

4.28 a. $P_Y(0) = .920$, $P_Y(1) = .048$, $P_Y(2) = .032$
b. $P(\text{scrapped})$ originally was .004, now is .0064.
c. μ_Y should decrease. In fact, μ_Y becomes 0.112.

4.29 a.

y	0	1	2	3
$P_Y(y)$	.343	.441	.189	.027

b. Same probability of each bid's being accepted and independence of results. Both seem reasonable.

4.30 $\mu_Y = 0.90$, $\sigma_Y^2 = 0.63$

4.31 The mean should be unchanged, but the variance should increase.

4.32 a. $P(X < 0) = 1 - 6.625e^{-2.5} = .4562$
b. $P(X > 0.176) = 8.2618e^{-2.94} = .4368$, not extremely high

4.33 a. $E(X) = 0.20$; in the long run, the two-year net return for such projects will be 20 cents per dollar.
b. $\text{Var}(X) = \text{Var}(Y) = 0.48$
c. W has higher expected return and lower variability (uncertainty), and usually would be preferred.

Section 4.6, pg. 149

4.34 a. $P(X = 1, Y = 2) = .055$
b. $P(X \le 2, Y \le 2) = .21$
c.

x	1	2	3	4
$P_X(x)$	.23	.27	.27	.23

y	1	2	3	4
$P_Y(y)$	.23	.27	.27	.23

d. $P_{XY}(1, 1) = .03 \neq P_X(1)P_Y(1) = .0529$. Not statistically independent.

4.35 Plug in x and y values.

4.36 a. Joint probability table

		0	1	y 2	3	4	5
	0	.01	.03	.025	.02	.01	.005
	1	.04	.12	.10	.08	.04	.02
x	2	.025	.075	.0625	.05	.025	.0125
	3	.02	.06	.05	.04	.02	.01
	4	.005	.015	.0125	.01	.005	.0025

b.

x	0	1	2	3	4	
$P_X(x)$	.10	.40	.25	.20	.05	

y	0	1	2	3	4	5
$P_Y(y)$	.10	.30	.25	.20	.10	.05

4.37 The assumption of independence is doubtful.

4.38 a. $P_{XY}(2, 2) = .100$
b. $P(X = 2 \cap Y \le 2) = .175$
c. $P(X \le 2 \cap Y \le 2) = .325$

4.39 a.

x	0	1	2	3	4
$P_X(x)$	.180	.195	.250	.195	.180

y	0	1	2	3	4
$P_Y(y)$	.150	.225	.250	.225	.150

No: For example,
$$P_{XY}(0, 0) = .010 \neq P_X(0)P_Y(0)$$
$$= (.180)(.150) = .027$$

4.40 $P_{Y|X}(y \mid x)$

				y		
		0	1	2	3	4
	0	.0556	.0833	.1667	.4167	.2778
	1	.1026	.1538	.2308	.3077	.2051
x	2	.1200	.1800	.4000	.1800	.1200
	3	.2051	.3077	.2308	.1538	.1026
	4	.2778	.4167	.1667	.0833	.0556

Not independent; the conditional probabilities change as x changes.

Sections 4.7 and 4.8, pg. 158

4.41 a. $\mu_X = \mu_Y = 2$, by symmetry
b. $\sigma_X = 1.353$, $\sigma_Y = 1.285$

4.42 a. $\text{Cov}(X, Y) = -.70$
b. $\text{Corr}(X, Y) = -.403$. As X increases, Y tends to decrease; the two are dependent.

4.43

x	0	1	2	3	4
$\mu_{Y|X=x}$	2.778	2.359	2.000	1.641	1.222

The conditional expectation decreases as x increases.

4.44 a.

t	0	1	2	3	4	5	6	7	8
$P_T(t)$	.010	.035	.090	.205	.320	.205	.090	.035	.010

b. $\mu_T = 4$, $\sigma_T^2 = 2.08$
c. $\mu_T = 2 + 2$, $\sigma_T^2 = 1.83 + 1.65 + 2(-.70)$

4.45 a.

x	0	1	2
$P_X(x)$	.81	.18	.01

b. $\mu_X = .20$, $\sigma_X^2 = .18$
c. Independence; unreasonable if blocks were sampled one after another.

4.46 $P_{XY}(x, y)$

		0	y 1	2	
	0	.8100	0	0	.81
x	1	.0180	.1620	0	.18
	2	.0001	.0018	.0081	.01
		.8281	.1638	.0081	

4.47 a. $\mu_Y = .1800$, $\sigma_Y = .4047$
b. $\text{Corr}(X, Y) = .943$
c. The more defectives, the more detected.

4.48 a.

y	0	1	2	3
$P_Y(y)$	.080	.314	.414	.192

b. $P(Y \ge 2) = .606$

c.

y	0	1	2	3
$F_Y(y)$	.080	.394	.808	1.000

$P(Y \geq 2) = 1 - .394$

4.49 $\mu_Y = 1.718$, $\sigma_Y = .8640$

4.50 a.

x	0	100	150	200	250	300	350	400
$P_X(x)$	.080	.020	.070	.224	.030	.096	.288	.192

b. $\mu_X = 280.8$, $\sigma_X = 128.69$

4.51 a. $\mu_T = 5054.4$
$\sigma_T^2 = 298,104.48$
b. Independence is reasonable.

4.52 a. Density is left-skewed.
b. $P(.7 < Y < .9) = .4655$
c. $P(Y > .8) = .3446$

4.53 $\mu_Y = 0.7143$, $\sigma_Y = 0.1597$

4.54 a. $F_X(x) = (6/125)(2.5x^2 - x^3/3)$, for $0 < x < 5$
b. $P(X \geq 3) = 1 - F_X(3) = .352$
c. $\mu_X = 2.5$, $\sigma_X = 1.118$

4.55 $\text{Corr}(X, Y) = 0$ if X and Y are independent.

4.56 a. $f_Y(y) = .0625e^{-.5y}y^2$, for $y > 0$
b. $f_{X|Y=y}(x \mid y) = xe^{-x/y}/y^2$, for $x > 0$
c. Not independent; complex calls make both X and Y large. Note that $f_{X|Y}(x \mid y)$ depends on y, so X and Y are not independent.

4.57 $\mu_{X|Y=y} = 2y$

4.58 $\text{Cov}(X, Y) = 96 - (6)(12) = 24$

Chapter 4 Exercises, pg. 162

4.59 Let 1 through 3 represent the field engineers over 40
4 represent the field engineer under 40
5 and 6 represent the sales reps over 40
7 through 10 represent the sales reps under 40
a. The sample space consists of 60 possible outcomes for the three people chosen.
b. $y =$ the number of persons over 40

y	0	1	2	3
$P_Y(y)$	.100	.433	.417	.050
$F_Y(y)$	.100	.533	.950	1.00

4.60 $E(Y) = 1.417$; $\text{Var}(Y) = .543$ $\sigma_Y = .737$

4.61 a. Table of $F_Y(y)$ values:

y	$F_Y(y)$
0	.02
1	.15
2	.35
3	.65
4	.84
5	.99
6	1.00

b. $E(Y) = 3$; $\sigma_Y = 1.33$
c. Actual probability: $P(1.67 \leq Y \leq 4.33) = .69$
Empirical Rule: $P(1.67 \leq Y \leq 4.33) = .68$

4.62 a. $E(Y) = .6666$; $\sigma_Y = .1785$
b. Actual probability:
$P(.3096 \leq Y \leq 1.0236) = .9654$

4.63 a. Table of $F_Y(y)$ values

y	$F_Y(y) = 10y^3 - 15y^4 + 6y^5$
0	0
.25	.10352
.50	.5000
.75	.9058
1.00	1.000

b. $P(Y \leq .5) = .5$;
$P(.4 \leq Y \leq .6) = .36512$;
$P(Y \geq .7) = .16308$

4.64 a. $f_y(y) = 30y^2 - 60y^3 + 30y^4$
b. Table of $f_Y(y)$ values

y	$f_y(y) = 30y^2 - 60y^3 + 30y^4$
0	0
.25	1.054
.50	1.875
.75	1.054
1.00	0

c. $E(Y) = .5$;
$\text{Var}(Y) = .0357$;
$\sigma_Y = .1889$
d. $\mu_Y \pm \sigma_Y$ gives the interval $(.3111, .6889)$.
$P(.3111 \leq Y \leq .6889) = .6438$; Empirical Rule probability is .68.

4.65 a. Table of $F_Y(y)$ values

y	$F_Y(y)$
0	.21
1	.59
2	.79
3	.90
4	.96
5	.99
6	1.00

b. $E(Y) = 1.56$
$\sigma_Y = 1.34$

4.66 a. Joint probability table

		y_2						
		0	1	2	3	4	5	6
	0	.0441	.0798	.0420	.0231	.0126	.0063	.0021
	1	.0798	.1444	.0760	.0418	.0228	.0114	.0038
	2	.0420	.0760	.0400	.0220	.0120	.0060	.0020
y_1	3	.0231	.0418	.0220	.0121	.0066	.0033	.0011
	4	.0126	.0228	.0120	.0066	.0036	.0018	.0006
	5	.0063	.0114	.0060	.0033	.0018	.0009	.0003
	6	.0021	.0038	.0020	.0011	.0006	.0003	.0001

b. Table of $P_S(s)$ values

s	$P_S(s)$	s	$P_S(s)$
0	.0441	7	.0328
1	.1596	8	.0142
2	.2284	9	.0058
3	.1982	10	.0021
4	.1488	11	.0006
5	.1022	12	.0001
6	.0631		

c. $E(S) = 3.12$;
$\sigma_S = 1.9007$

4.67 a. $P(0 < X < .5 \cap 0 < Y < .5) = .0371$
b. $P(Y > 1) = .7688$

4.68 a. $f_X(x) = (3/320)(128/3 + 32x - 16x^2)$
b. $f_{Y|X}(y|x) = (48 - 12x^2 - 3y^2 + 12xy)/$
$(128 + 96x - 48x^2)$

4.69 No; longer programs should have longer times. The conditional density of Y varies with x, so there is dependence.

4.70 a. $P(X > .5 \cap Y > .5) = .0586$
b. $P(.1 < Y < .3) = .3903$

4.71 a. $f_X(x) = 12x(1 - x)^2$, $f_Y(y) = 20y(1 - y)^3$
b. $\text{Cov}(X, Y) = 0$, by independence

4.72 a.

y	.70	.75	.80	.85	.90	.95
$f_Y(y)$	0.5848	1.4059	2.8751	4.8161	5.9888	3.9622

Density is left-skewed, with its peak near $y = .90$.

b. $y = .90$ is the mode.
c. $P(Y \geq .90) = .3516$; $P(Y \leq .85) = .3705$

4.73 a. $\mu_Y = 0.8636$
b. $\sigma_Y = .0716$
c. $P(Y \leq 0.649) = .0084$

4.74 a. X should not be large, unless most people are betting on a decline in the market. For example, $f_X(0) = 0$, $f_X(.1) = 5.6002$, $f_X(.2) = 1.9140$, $f_X(.3) = 0.3874$, and $f_X(.4) = 0.0512$; highest values of the density are near $x = .10$.
b. $P(X < .10) = .5182$

4.75 a. $\mu_X = 0.1111$
b. It is the long-run (over many trading periods) average proportion of short sales, not the most likely (mode) value.
c. $\text{Var}(X) = 0.005198$, $\sigma_X = .0721$; if we take "reasonable range" to mean two standard deviations below and above the mean, that range is -0.0331 (really 0) to 0.2553.

4.76 a. No. The conditional density of Y given x changes as x changes.
b. Not independent. If independent, the conditional expected value wouldn't depend on x. It does indicate that high individual purchases go together with high short sales.

4.77 a. $P(Y > 8) = .0625$
b. $P(8 < Y < 9) = .0502$

4.78 a. $f_Y(y) = 4(y - 6)^{-5}$, for $y > 7$
   b. $P(7.0 < Y < 7.5) = .8025$

4.79 a. $P(X \geq .8) = .3446$
   b. $P(X < .5) = .1094$

4.80 $P(X < .9 \mid X \geq .8) = .6685$

4.81 a. $P(2 < Y < 4) = .0886$
   b. $P(Y > 10) = .00000004$

4.82 a. $f_Y(y) = 4ye^{-2y}$, $y > 0$
   b. mode $= 0.5$

4.83 a.

y	7.0	7.5	8.0	8.5
$f_Y(y)$	4.0000	0.5267	0.1250	0.0410

   Definitely right-skewed
   b. Perhaps 7.2 or 7.3.
   c. $\mu_Y = 7.3333$, $\sigma_Y = 0.4714$
   d. No, because of skewness.
   $P(6.8619 \leq Y \leq 7.8047)$
   $= P(7 \leq Y \leq 7.8047) = .9057$, not close to .68

4.84 a. $E(X) = .7143$ is the long-run average proportion of promptly answered calls.
   b. $\text{Var}(X) = 0.02551$, $\sigma_X = 0.1597$

4.85 $\mu + 2\sigma = 0.7143 + 2(0.1597) = 1.0337$, but X must be less than 1.0. The distribution cannot be bell-shaped.

4.86 a. $P(0 < X < 0.5, 0.5 < Y < 1) = .1406$
   b. $f_X(x) = 3x - 1.5x^2$, $0 < x < 1$;
   $f_Y(y) = 1.5 - y$, $0 < y < 1$
   c. $P(0 < X < 0.5) = .3125$;
   $P(0.5 < Y < 1) = .3750$
   d. No. For example, the probability in part (a) is not the product of the probabilities in part (c).

4.87 a. Should have negative sign
   b. $\text{Cov}(X, Y) = -1/96$ and has a negative sign.
   c. $\sigma_X = .2437$, $\sigma_Y = .2764$, $\rho_{X,Y} = -0.1547$, a weak correlation

4.88 a. $f_X(x) = 12x^2(1 - x)$, $0 < x < 1$;
   $P(0.5 < X < 1) = .6875$
   b. $f_{Y|X}(y \mid x) = (1/x)e^{-y/x}$, $y > 0$.
   $P(Y > 1 \mid X = .5) = e^{-2} = 0.1353$

4.89 a. $E(Y \mid x) = x$, which says that the average time between orders is the average time between orders!
   b. Increases as x increases, so positive covariance and correlation

4.90 $\text{Cov}(X, Y) = 0.04$ is, indeed, positive.

CHAPTER 5   Section 5.1, pg. 177

5.1 $\binom{7}{3} = 35$ panels

5.2 $\binom{5}{2}\binom{2}{1} = 20$ panels with exactly 2
$\binom{5}{2}\binom{2}{1} + \binom{5}{3}\binom{2}{0} = 30$ panels with at least 2

5.3 $\binom{8}{4} = 70$ choices

5.4 $\binom{4}{3}\binom{4}{1} = 16$ choices

Section 5.2, pg. 183

5.5 a. $\binom{10}{3}(.2)^3(.8)^7 = .2013$

   b. $\binom{4}{2}(.4)^2(.6)^2 = .3456$

   c. $\binom{16}{12}(.7)^{12}(.3)^4 = .2040$

5.6 a.

y	1	2	3
$P_Y(y)$	.35596	.29663	.13184
Table 1	.3560	.2966	.1318

   b. The histogram is right-skewed.
   c. $\mu_1 = 1.50$, $\sigma_Y = 1.0607$.

5.7 $P(Y \geq 4) = .9840$
   b. $P(Y > 4) = .9490$
   c. $P(Y \leq 10) = .8723$
   d. $P(Y \geq 16) = .0000$

5.8 $P(Y \leq 16) = .9840$ and $P(Y < 16) = .9490$
   The events are logically identical, with renaming of success/failure.

5.9 a. Yes; each customer is a trial, the success probability shouldn't change, and the results should be independent.
b. $P(Y = 5) = .1789$
c. $P(Y \le 5) = .4163$
d. mode = 6

5.10 $\mu_Y = 6, \sigma_Y = 2.05$

5.11 $P(3.95 \le Y \le 8.05) = .7796$, not overly close to .68

5.12 a. Independence may not hold, because successes may depend on storms, etc.
b. $P(Y \ge 85) = .9601$

5.13 $\mu_Y = 90, \sigma_Y = 3$

5.14 a. Taking $\pi = .10$, $P(Y = 0) = .4305$
b. $P(Y \ge 2) = .1869$
c. $\mu_Y = .80$

5.15 Histogram is very right-skewed.

Section 5.3, pg. 186

5.16 a.

y	0	1	2	3
$P_Y(y)$	4/35	18/35	12/35	1/35

b. The distribution is slightly right-skewed.

5.17 $\mu_Y = 1.2857, \sigma_Y = 0.6999$

5.18 a. $P_Y(2) = .3$
b. $P_Y(2) = .4286$
c. $P_Y(2) = .5$

5.19 a. $P_Y(0) = .0776$
b. $P_Y(0) = 0$

5.20 a. $P_Y(4) = 1/70 = .014$

b.

y	0	1	2	3	4
$P_Y(y)$	1/70	16/70	36/70	16/70	1/70

5.21 $P(\text{at least } 1) = 1 - \binom{2375}{50} \bigg/ \binom{2500}{50}$

5.22 $\mu_Y = 2.5, \sigma_Y^2 = 2.328$

5.23 $P(Y \ge 1) = .923$ with $n = 50$ and $\pi = .05$
$\mu_Y = 2.5, \sigma_Y^2 = 2.375$, close to the correct values.

Section 5.5, pg. 193

5.24 a. From Table 2, $P_Y(1) = .2681$, .3476, and .0395, respectively.
b. $P(Y \le 3) = .9211$ and .0817, respectively.
c. $P(Y \le 10) = 1.0000$ and .5831, respectively.

5.25 The distribution is highly right-skewed.

5.26 a. $P(Y \le 10) = .7060$
b. $P(Y \ge 7) = .7932$
c. $P(7 \le Y \le 11) = .5962$

5.27 $E(Y) = 9; \sigma_Y = 3$

5.28 If a fire burns several neighboring houses and two or more of them were insured by this firm, then the assumption that events happen one at a time doesn't hold.

5.29 a. $P(Y = 0) = .6703$
b. $P(Y \ge 2) = .0616$

5.30 $E(Y) = .4; \sigma_Y = .632$

5.31 a. $P(Y = 0) = .0003$
b. $P(Y \ge 5) = .900$

Section 5.6, pg. 195

5.32 $P(60 < Y < 85) = 25/110$

5.33 $\mu_Y = 65, \sigma_Y = 31.75$

5.34 a. $P(10 < Y < 50) = 40/200 = .2$
b. $P(Y > 50) = 150/200 = .75$
c. $P(Y \le 120) = 120/200 = .60$

5.35 a. $P(300 \le Y \le 1300) = 1000/10,000 = .1$
b. $\sigma_Y^2 = (10,000)^2/12 = 8,333,333.3$

5.36 a. $P(Y \ge 8) = (20 - 8)/20 = .60$
b. $\sigma_Y = \sqrt{(20)^2/12} = 5.774$

Section 5.7, pg. 197

5.37 For $f_Y(y) = 0.4e^{-y/2.5}$ we have

y	0	.5	1.0	1.5	2.0
$f_Y(y)$	.4000	.3275	.2681	.2195	.1797

The density is highly right-skewed.

5.38 a. $P(Y > 2) = e^{-2/2} = .3679$
b. $P(Y > 1) = e^{-1/2} = .6065$
c. $P(1 < Y < 2) = e^{-1/2} - e^{-2/2} = .2386$
d. $P(1 \leq Y \leq 2) = P(1 < Y < 2)$ for a continuous random variable.

5.39 With $\mu = 1.25$, $P(Y > 1) = e^{-1/1.25} = .4493$ and $P(Y \geq 2) = e^{-2/1.25} = .2019$

5.40 a. $P_Y(0) = e^{-.8} = .4493$
b. $P_Y(0) = e^{-.8(2)} = .2019$
c. Same probabilities because same events.

5.41 a. $P(Y < 2.5) = 1 - e^{-2.5/5} = .3935$
b. $P(Y > 10) = e^{-10/5} = .1353$

5.42 a. $\mu = 1/5 = 0.2$
b. Poisson with $\mu = (0.2)(2.5) = 0.5$
$P(Y \geq 1) = 1 - P_Y(0) = .3935$
c. with $\mu = (0.2)(10) = 2.0$, $P(Y = 0) = .1353$

5.43 a. $P(20 < Y < 60) = .3834$
b. $\sigma_Y = 40$

5.44 The expected rate may not be constant.

5.45 a. $P(Y > 5) = .0163$
b. $P(\text{arrival time} < 3) = .4512$

5.46 With $\mu_Y = 12(1/4) = 3$, $P(Y \geq 6) = .0838$

5.47 a. $P(W > 7) = .2466$
b. $P(W > 14) = .0608$

5.48 With $\mu = 7(0.2) = 1.4$, $P(Y \geq 4) = .0538$

Section 5.8, pg. 203

5.49 a. $P(0 \leq Z \leq 1.00) = .3413$
b. $P(0 \leq Z \leq 1.65) = .4505$
c. $P(-1.00 \leq Z \leq 0) = .3413$
d. $P(-1.28 \leq Z \leq 0) = .3997$
e. $P(-1.65 \leq Z \leq 1.65) = .9010$
f. $P(-1.28 \leq Z \leq 1.28) = .7994$
g. $P(-1.07 \leq Z \leq 2.33) = .8478$
h. $P(Z \geq 2.65) = .0040$
i. $P(Z \leq -2.42) = .0078$
j. $P(Z \geq 1.39 \text{ or } Z \leq -1.39) = .1646$

5.50 a. $k = 2.33$
b. $k = 2.33$
c. $k = 2.33$
d. $k = 1.00$
e. $k = 2.00$
f. $k = -1.645$

5.51 From Exercise 6.25 d and e:
$P(-1 \leq Z \leq 1) = .6826$ and
$P(-2 \leq Z \leq 2) = .9544$
From the Empirical Rule:
$P(-1 \leq Z \leq 1) \cong .68$ and
$P(-2 \leq Z \leq 2) \cong .95$

5.52 a. $P(Y \leq 130) = P(Z \leq 2)$
b. $P(Y \geq 82.5) = P(Z \geq -1.167)$
c. $P(Y \leq 130) = .9772$; $P(Y \geq 82.5) = .8790$
d. $P(Y > 106) = .3446$; $P(Y < 94) = .3446$;
$P(94 < y < 106) = .3108$
e. $P(Y \leq 70) = .0228$; $P(Y \geq 130) = .0228$;
$P(70 < Y < 130) = .9544$

5.53 a. $k = 24.75$
b. $k = 24.75$
c. $k = 112.6$
d. $k = 92.2$
e. $k = 112.6$
f. $k = 92.2$

5.54 a. $P(Y \geq 1000) = .3085$
b. $P(Y \leq 940) = .1587$
c. $P(960 \leq Y \leq 1060) = .6687$

5.55 a. $k = 928.8$
b. $k = 970$

5.56 a. $P(Y > 5.40) = .2266$
b. $P(4.70 < Y < 5.50) = .6826$
c. $P(Y > 3.90) = .9987$

Section 5.9, pg. 207

5.57 a. $P(40 \leq Y \leq 60) = .965$
b. $P(40 \leq Y \leq 60) = .9544$
The normal approximation to the binomial is quite good.

5.58 Using a continuity-corrected normal approximation: $P(39.5 \leq Y \leq 60.5) = .9642$, very close to the correct value.

5.59 A reasonable approximation if the input errors occurred independently of each other during a given time period.

5.60 a. $E(Y) = 8$; $\sigma_Y = 2.828$
b. $P(5 \leq Y \leq 11) = .7884$

5.61 $P(4.5 \leq Y \leq 11.5) = .785$

Chapter 5 Exercises, pg. 211

5.62 a. Yes, the binomial assumptions are met.
b. $P(Y \geq 24) = .012$
c. Assuming the claim is true, then $P(Y \geq 24) = .012$. We would doubt the manufacturer's claim.

5.63 a. $E(Y) = 15$; $\sigma_y^2 = 12.75$
b. $P(Y \geq 24) = .0059$; $P(Y \geq 23.5) = .0087$; fairly close.

5.64 a. $P(Y \leq 1) = .2794$
b. $P(Y \geq 4) = .2396$

5.65 a. $P(Y \leq 1) = .2873$
b. $P(Y \geq 4) = .2424$
A fairly good approximation

5.66 a. $\binom{30000}{100}$
b. $\binom{29700}{100}$
c. $\binom{29700}{100} / \binom{30000}{100}$
d. $\sum_{k=0}^{2} \binom{300}{k}\binom{29700}{100-k} / \binom{30000}{100}$

5.67 a. $P(Y = 0) = \binom{100}{0}(.01)^0(.99)^{100}$;
$P(Y \leq 2) = \sum_{Y=0}^{2} \binom{100}{Y}(.01)^Y(.99)^{100-Y}$
b. $P(Y = 0) = .3678$; $P(Y \leq 2) = .9197$

5.68 a. $\binom{30}{14} = 145,422,675$
b. $\binom{6}{5}\binom{24}{9} = 7,845,024$
c. .059

5.69 a. $P(Y = 1) = .3614$; $P(Y \leq 1) = .6626$
b. $E(Y) = 1.2$; $\sigma_Y = 1.095$

5.70 Not accurate because $\mu < 5$.

5.71 a. $P(Y \leq 72.8) = .6915$;
$P(71.2 \leq Y \leq 72.8) = .3830$
b. $P(Y \geq 74) = .1056$
c. $k = 75.73$

5.72 a. $P(Y > 73) = .2659$
b. $P(Y = 3) = .055$

5.73 a. $P(Y > 5) = .0668$
b. $P(Y \leq 6) \approx 1$

5.74 a. $P(Y \geq 8) \approx 0$
b. Conclusively indicates that the cutter was inefficient.

5.75 a. $P(Y < 8) = .8666$
b. It is likely that the occurrence of errors in transmission are dependent during a given time period.

5.76 $P(Y < 8) = .2203$

5.77 a. Binomial with $n = 1000$ and $\pi = .50$ under reasonable assumptions
b. $\mu_Y = 500$, $\sigma_Y = 15.811$

5.78 $P(Y \leq 460) \approx .0057$; accurate because $n\pi = n(1 - \pi) = 500$

5.79 a. $P(Y \leq 5) = \sum_{y=0}^{5} \binom{250}{y}(.01)^y(.99)^{250-y}$
b. Independence and constant probability seem to be reasonable.

5.80 a. $P(Y \leq 5) = .9441$
b. $P(Y \leq 5) = .9580$
c. Poisson, because $\mu_Y < 5$

5.81 a. $\mu_Y = 100$; $\sigma_Y = 99.499$
b. $P_Y(1) = .01 > P_Y(100) = .00370$

5.82 a. $P(Y \geq 400)$
$$= \sum_{y=400}^{\infty} \frac{(y-1)!}{(4-1)!(y-4)!}(.01)^4(.99)^{y-4}$$
b. $\sigma_Y^2 = 39,600$

5.83 a. 120 choices
b. $P(Y \geq 2) = 110/455$

5.84 $\mu_Y = 1.0$, $\sigma_Y^2 = .4762$

5.85 a. $P(Y > 7) = .2466$
b. $P(Y > 14) = .0608$

5.86 $\mu_Y = 5$, $\sigma_Y = 5$

5.87   Nonclumping of crashes and independence of time periods. Independence would be violated.

5.88   a. $P(Y \leq 57.5) \approx P(Z < -2.81) = .0025$
b. Yes; $n\pi = 80$ and $n(1 - \pi) = 320$
c. Not plausible

5.89   a. $P(Y \leq 56) = \sum_{y=0}^{56} \binom{400}{y}(.2)^y(.8)^{400-y}$
b. $P(Y \leq 56) = .0013$ or $P(Y \leq 56.5) = .0016$
c. No; result is unlikely assuming $\pi = .20$.

5.90   Poisson ($\mu = 0.5$) probability $= .3935$

5.91 $P(\text{win}) = 1/3,838,380 = .0000002605$

5.92   a. $P(\text{exactly 4}) = .002192$
b. $P(\text{at least 4}) = .002246$

5.93   a. $P(\text{win})$ should decrease a bit.
b. $P(\text{win}) = .0000001906$
c. Decreased quite substantially

5.94   a. Binomial with $n = 1,000,000$ and $\pi = 1/3,838,380$
b. $P_Y(0) = \binom{1,000,000}{0}(1/3,838,380)^0$
$\times (1 - 1/3,838,380)^{1,000,000}$
c. $P(Y \geq 2)$
$= 1 - \sum_{y=0}^{1} \binom{1,000,000}{y}\pi^y(1 - \pi)^{1,000,000-y}$
where $\pi = 1/3,838,380$

5.95   a. $\mu_Y = 0.2605$, $\sigma_Y^2 = 0.2605$

5.95 (cont.) b. $P(Y = 0) = e^{-0.2605} = .7707$
$P(Y \geq 2)$
$= 1 - e^{-0.2605} - e^{-0.2605}\frac{(.2605)^1}{1!} = .0286$
Should be close; n is large and $n\pi < 1$.
c. $P(Y = 0) = .771$
$P(Y \geq 2) = .028$

5.96   No; $n\pi = 0.2605 < 5$

5.97   a. Geometric with $\pi = 1 - .771 = .229$
b. $\mu_X = 4.37$, $\sigma_X = 3.834$
c. $P_X(3) = (.771)^2(.229)$

5.98   The probability of success would increase (depending on the previous results).

5.99   a. $\mu = 3.5$
b. Poisson $P(Y \geq 4) = .4634$
c. Nonclumping and independence. Basically the assumptions seem sensible.

5.100 $P(W > 3) = .2231$, $\mu_W = 2$

5.101   a. $\mu_Y = 12$, $\sigma_Y = 3.464$
b. $P(Y > 8) = .8450$

5.102 $P(W \geq 2) = .0498$

5.103   a. No. Constant rate is irrelevant for Poisson probabilities.
b. No. Constant rate is irrelvant for Poisson probabilities.

CHAPTER 6   Section 6.1, pg. 221

6.1   Select 375, 779 (ignore 995, 963, 895, and 854), 289, 635, 094, 103, 071, 510, 023, and 010.

6.2   Selection bias favoring those at home at those times.

6.3   a. Not all combinations of books have the same probability.

b. Select books from an inventory list, using random numbers.

6.4   Use random numbers between 0001 and 4256.

6.5   Size bias favoring holders of many seats.

6.6   First strategy probably would check only the work of a few employees.

Section 6.2, pg. 225

6.7   Biased toward those machines that are in poorest condition.

6.8   One possible approach: Obtain records for the population of all machines in the chain of laundromats, randomly choose 100 records.

6.9   We would make sure not to "tinker" with any transactions with serial numbers ending in 00.

6.10   Collect all transaction numbers for each day and select 1% of them via random number generator.

6.11   a. Both are symmetric; there is less variability for $n = 3$.
b. $P(\bar{Y}$ will be no more than $.50 away from the mean) $= .60$

6.12 Sampling distribution, $n = 2$: $E(\bar{Y}) = 4$; $\sigma_{\bar{Y}}^2 = .75$
Sampling distribution, $n = 3$: $E(\bar{Y}) = 4$;
$\sigma_{\bar{Y}}^2 = .3334$
The sample size does not affect the expected values. As the sample size increases, the variance decreases.

6.13 b. $\mu = E(Y) = 7$
c. $E(\bar{Y}) = 7$; $\sigma_{\bar{Y}}^2 = 1.575$
d. Probability $= .8401$

6.14 a. The histogram of the sampling distribution of $\bar{Y}$ shows smaller variance.
b. The histogram of the sampling distribution of $\bar{Y}$ shows less skewness.

6.15 b. The histogram looks very much like the theoretical probability histogram. The Monte Carlo simulation appears to be a good approximation to the sampling distribution of $\bar{Y}$.

Section 6.3, pg. 230

6.16 $E(\bar{Y}) = \mu = 7$; $\sigma_{\bar{Y}}^2 = 1.575$. The values agree.

6.17 a. $E(T) = 46{,}350$; $\sigma_T = 6158.9$
b. $E(\bar{Y}) = 927$; $\sigma_{\bar{Y}} = 123.2$

6.18 a. $E(\bar{Y}) = 28.2$; $\sigma_{\bar{Y}} = .218$
b. $E(\bar{Y}) = 28.2$; $\sigma_{\bar{Y}} = .109$

Section 6.4, pg. 236

6.19 a. $E(T) = 3270$; $\sigma_T = 107.52$
b. $P(3150 \leq T \leq 3390) = .7372$
c. $\mu_{\bar{Y}} = 327$; $\sigma_{\bar{Y}} = 10.76$;
$P(314 \leq \bar{Y} \leq 339) = .7555$

6.20 Range: $327 - 21$ to $327 + 21$ or 306 to 348

6.21 a. The population distribution is skewed right.

b.

Sample Size	$P(\mu - 2\sigma_{\bar{Y}} < \bar{Y} < \mu + 2\sigma_{\bar{Y}})$	Normal Approximation
2	.9664	.95
4	.9479	.95
8	.9681	.95
16	.9532	.95
32	.9533	.95

c.

Sample Size	$P(\mu - \sigma_{\bar{Y}} < \bar{Y} < \mu + \sigma_{\bar{Y}})$	Normal Approximation
2	.7840	.68
4	.6739	.68
8	.6946	.68
16	.6638	.68
32	.6984	.68

6.22 a. Sampling distribution of $\bar{Y}$ is approximately normal with $\mu_{\bar{Y}} = 927$ and $\sigma_{\bar{Y}} = 123.2$.
b. $P(\bar{Y} > 1100) = .0808$

6.23 The population might well be very skewed, so $n = 50$ may not be enough.

6.24 $P(\bar{Y} > 1100) = .0808$. One might conclude that the repair claims this year will be a bit higher than in the past.

$P(\bar{Y} > 1000) = .2776$. We might conclude that the repair claims this year will be similar to those in the past.

6.25 a. $P(Y > 170) = P(Z > 1.05) = .1469$
b. $P(135 < \bar{Y} < 155) = P(-2.14 < Z < 1.15)$
$= .8587$

6.26 a. Left-skewed distribution.
b. The Central Limit Theorem effect will "deskew" the distribution of means, but not the distribution of individual values.

6.27 a. $P(0.997 < Y < 1.003) =$
$P(-0.50 < Z < 0.50) = .3830$
b. $P(0.997 < \bar{Y} < 1.003) =$
$P(-2.24 < Z < 2.24) = .9750$
c. Should decrease the probability of a good quality pin. $P(0.997 < Y < 1.003) =$
$P(-0.15 < Z < 0.15) = .1192$, lower than the answer to part (a).
d. $P(0.997 < \bar{Y} < 1.003) =$
$P(-0.67 < Z < 0.67) = .4972$

6.28 No. The Central Limit Theorem works effectively for outlier-prone distributions with $n = 20$.

6.29 a. $P(Y > 80) = .2743$
b. $P(\bar{Y} > 80) = .0287$

6.30 No; $n = 10$ is too small to "deskew" the distribution, especially for a one-tail probability without compensating errors.

Section 6.6, pg. 248

6.31 a. Expected value and standard error of $\bar{Y}$
b. Close to $\mu_{\bar{Y}} = 50$ and $\sigma_{\bar{Y}} = 5$

6.32 Expected value is close to 0 and standard error is close to .2.

6.33 Both histogram and normal plot indicate normal distribution, possibly with a very few mild outliers.

6.34 a. $\mu = 3, \sigma = 1.265$

b. $n = 10$: $\mu_{\bar{Y}} = 3, \sigma_{\bar{Y}} = .400$
$n = 30$: $\mu_{\bar{Y}} = 3, \sigma_{\bar{Y}} = .231$
c. Means very close, standard deviations a bit smaller.

6.35 a. $\mu_{\bar{Y}} = 0, \sigma_{\bar{Y}} = .4472$
b. Both the average and the standard deviation are very close.

6.36 The plot indicates a normal distribution.

Chapter 6 Exercises, pg. 252

6.37 a. Plausibly, $\mu = 50(.2) = 10$
b. The paddle obtains an unbiased sample.

6.38 Paddle sampling appears to be slightly biased.

6.39 a. Testing would wear the mechanisms so they couldn't be sold.
b. Supplier could add five good mechanisms to a bad lot.

6.40 Sample *size* is the important factor, not the fraction. Also, suppliers of unknown quality should be tested more rigorously.

6.41 a. $E(\bar{Y}) = 4200$
b. $\sigma_{\bar{Y}} = \dfrac{3400}{\sqrt{20}} \sqrt{\dfrac{4980}{4999}} = 758.82$; if $N = 10,000$,
$\sigma_{\bar{Y}} = 759.54$ instead.
c. Not normal, but right skewed.
d. Not really; $n = 20$ is not large enough if the process data are seriously skewed.

6.42 No, because of $\sqrt{n}$ appearing in the standard error.

6.43 a. $E(T) = 213K$
b. $\sigma_T = 8.3K$

6.44 Amount of bad sectors is independent from disk to disk. If not, the standard deviation will be wrong.

6.45 Normal; the Central Limit Theorem effect will work well for $n = 100$.

6.46 a. We could simply sample from a list to obtain a sample of 200.
b. If the distribution of percentage income tax payments in the population is skewed, so will be the distribution of percentage income tax in the sample.

6.47 a. The weekly demand is the sum of many individual demands. Therefore, by CLT, the weekly demand can be expected to be roughly normally distributed.
b. One way to select a random sample of size $n = 15$ would be to visit the store on a randomly selected day of the week at a randomly selected time of the day and observe the number of sacks of flour bought by the first 15 customers to go through the checkout lines.

6.48 a. $P(\bar{Y} > 73.0) = .0078$
b. 95% range for $\bar{Y}$: 71.1905 to 72.8095

6.49 a. We can obtain a listing of all of the 2571 sales categories and sample every 25th sales category or have a lottery with sales category codes.
b. It's possible that there will not be equal representation from the various departments in the department store.
Group the 2571 into various departments and randomly choose an equal number from within each department to make up the sample.

6.50 a. $E(\bar{Y}) = 2.2$; $\sigma_{\bar{Y}} = .16$
b. $E(\bar{Y}) = 2.2$; $\sigma_{\bar{Y}} = .1568$; very little difference
c. $P(Y > 2.4) = .1056$

6.51 We would expect the normal approximation to be fairly good barring severe skewness.

6.52 a. $\mu = 100$; $\sigma = 21.07$
b. The distribution is perfectly symmetric. These are two extreme (symmetric) outlier values.

6.53

a.

Sample Size	$P(\mu - \sigma_{\bar{Y}} < \bar{Y} < \mu + \sigma_{\bar{Y}})$	Normal Approximation
2	.8224	.6828
4	.8202	.6828
8	.7088	.6828

b. Approximation is good for $n = 8$.

c.

Sample Size	$P(\mu - 2\sigma_{\bar{Y}} < \bar{Y} < \mu + 2\sigma_{\bar{Y}})$	Normal Approximation
2	.9224	.95
4	.9024	.95
8	.9334	.95

Again, for $n = 8$, approximation is decent.

6.54 a. No; right-skewed.

b. Mean 3.62, st. dev. 2.904 (dividing by $\sqrt{533}$ would give 2.901).

d. Shape nearly normal; Central Limit Theorem.

6.55 a. Our samples yielded st. dev. = 0.574; yours will differ somewhat. This approximates the standard error of the mean, 0.581.

6.56 b. Not uniform, but normal, by Central Limit Theorem.

c. Theoretical st. dev. = .0833. We got .0805; yours will differ slightly.

d. Theoretical mean = 0.5000; we got 0.489.

Review Exercises, Chapters 4–6, pg. 256

R21 a. $P(Y > 210) = .4013$
b. $P(\bar{Y} > 210) = .1056$

R22 Part a poorer; part b is influenced by Central Limit Theorem.

R23 a. $P(Y \le 3) = \sum_{y=0}^{3} \binom{50}{y}(.05)^y(.95)^{50-y}$
b. $P(Y \le 3) = .7604$
c. Binomial assumptions; assumptions seem fairly sensible.

R24 a. $\mu_X = 6.66667$, $\sigma_X = 2.687$
b. $P(X \ge 3) = .909$

R25 a. $\mu_T = 26.66668$, $\sigma_T^2 = 28.444$
b. Independence, only in variance calculation.

R26 $P(\bar{X} > 7) = .0401$; good approximation with $n = 200$.

R27 a. For a continuous random variable, probability is an area, not a sum.
b. $P(5 \le Y \le 8) = .5067$
c. $\mu_Y = 6$, $\sigma_Y = 2$

R28 $P(Y < 8 \mid Y > 5) = .7370$

R29 Poisson; $P_Y(0) = .3012$

R30 Nonclumping and independence of impurities

R31 Not independent

		0	1	2	3	4	5	$P_X(x)$
	0	.0000	.2400	.1200	.0200	.0120	.0080	.40
	1	.0300	.1200	.0750	.0450	.0150	.0150	.30
x	2	.0075	.0450	.0600	.0150	.0120	.0105	.15
	3	.0030	.0150	.0220	.0300	.0200	.0100	.10
	4	.0005	.0020	.0075	.0150	.0200	.0050	.05
$P_Y(y)$		.0410	.4220	.2845	.1250	.0790	.0485	

R32 $\mu_Y = 1.9245$, $\sigma_Y = 1.2074$

R33 a. $P(Y \ge 2) = .2641$
b. Binomial assumptions

R34 No; not sampling a fixed number, and order is relevant.

R35 $\mu_Y = 2.07$, $\sigma_Y^2 = .2851$

R36 a. $P(0 < X < .3 \cap 0 < Y < .5) = .44625$
b. $f_X(x) = 2(1 - x)$, for $0 < x < 1$
c. Yes; $f_{XY}(x, y) = f_X(x)f_Y(y)$

R37 $\mu_Y = .25$, $\sigma_Y = .194$

R38 $\mu_W = 18.33$, $\sigma_W^2 = 103.90$

R39 $P(\bar{Y} > 265) = .0089$

R40 Used Central Limit Theorem; poor approximation if individual values are highly skewed.

R41 $P(Y \le 3) = .0281$

R42 Binomial assumptions seem plausible.

R43 a. $P_{Y|X}(y \mid x) = (xy + 1)/(5 + 10x)$
b. No; as x gets larger, y (reasonably) tends to get larger.

R44 $\mu_Y = 2.743$, $\sigma_Y^2 = 1.448$

R45 Poisson; $P(Y \ge 10) = .2833$

R46 Nonclumping and independence appear plausible.

R47 $P(200 < X < 300 \cap 30 < Y < 50) = .0496$

R48 $f_{Y|X}(y \mid x) = .000006y(100 - y)$, for $0 < y < 100$
Independent

R49 $\mu_X = 170$, $\sigma_X^2 = 2500$
$\mu_Y = 50$, $\sigma_Y^2 = 500$
$\mu_T = 220$, $\sigma_T^2 = 3000$

R50 $\mu_{X'} = .170$, $\sigma_{X'}^2 = .002500$
$\mu_{Y'} = .050$, $\sigma_{Y'}^2 = .000500$
$\mu_{T'} = .220$, $\sigma_{T'}^2 = .003000$

R51 a. $P(\bar{X}' > .180) \approx .001$
b. Yes; $n = 250$ is large and the Central Limit Theorem applies.

CHAPTER 7   Section 7.1, pg. 266

7.1 a. $\bar{y} = 23.985$, median $= 23.8$
b. $\bar{y}_t = 23.8438$

7.2 a. Frequency distribution table is shown below:

Class	Midpoint	Frequency	Relative Frequency
15.9–18.9	17.4	3	.15
19.0–22.0	20.5	2	.10
22.1–25.1	23.6	8	.40
25.2–28.2	26.7	5	.25
28.3–31.3	29.8	1	.05
31.4–34.4	32.9	1	.05

b. Data are fairly close to normally distributed.
c. The sample mean is most efficient for normal populations.

7.3 a. All estimators appear unbiased. (The averages are all very close to 100.)
b. The mean appears most efficient; it has the smallest variance.

7.4 a. $\bar{y} = 236.4$, median $= 234.5$
b. $\bar{y}_t = 233.875$

7.5 a. The most conspicuous aspect of the display is the value 379, an obvious outlier.
b. No. Mean has been thrown off by the outlier.

7.6 a. Yes; $E(\hat{\mu}_1) = E(\hat{\mu}_2) = \mu$.
b. $\text{Var}(\hat{\mu}_1) = .25\sigma^2 < \text{Var}(\hat{\mu}_2) = .26\sigma^2$

7.7 a. Yes; boxplots center at 0.
b. Median has narrowest boxplot.

7.8 Averages are essentially 0; median has smallest standard deviation.

7.9 a. All should be unbiased, by symmetry.
b. Mean has smallest standard deviation.

7.10 Yes, unbiased and mean boxplot narrowest.

7.11 a. No evidence of *systematic* tendency to over- or underestimate (bias)
b. May be inefficient due to outliers

7.12 a. Mean may be inefficient due to outliers.

Section 7.2, pg. 271

7.13 No. Sample fraction isn't relevant; sample size is.

7.14 a. Without; no reason to measure twice
b. Standard error of the mean if $N = 2200$ is 0.3356; if $N = 1760$ it's 0.3347, a minor difference.

7.15 A sample *size* of 10 will give poor accuracy.

7.16 a. Sample without replacement.
b. Assuming sampling with replacement,
$\sigma_{\bar{y}} = .0422$
c. Assuming sampling without replacement,
$\sigma_{\bar{y}} = .0392$
d. The standard error sampling without replacement is smaller by 3/1000.

7.17 Projections are based on absolute sample size, not percentages. For example, all projections may be based on samples of 50,000, which may be 1% of N.Y. but 20% of Wyoming.

Section 7.3, pg. 276

7.18 a, b. Below is a table of likelihoods for specified values of θ.

θ	Likelihood $= \theta^4 e^{-8\theta}$
.1	.000045
.2	.000323
.3	.000735
.4	.001044
.5	.001145
.6	.001067
.7	.000888
.8	.000681
.9	.000490
1.0	.000335

c. MLE of θ is .5

7.19 Take derivative, set to zero, and solve.

7.20 a. Direct computation.
b. According to the table in part a, the MLE of θ is 1.5.

7.21 Take derivative, set to zero, and solve.

7.22 a. $\bar{y} = 5.4$, median $= 5.0$
b. $L(5.4) = .000007027$
$L(5.0) = .00001910$
c. At $\bar{y} = 5.4$, the likelihood is not as large as at 5.0; $\bar{Y}$ is not the maximum likelihood estimator.

Chapter 7 Exercises, pg. 278

7.23 a. Yes; averages are near 300, the population mean.
b. Trimmed mean has smallest variance.

7.24 a. No; for a skewed distribution, mean, median, and trimmed mean should differ.
b. Yes; the averages differ.

7.25 a. Yes; the box plots are symmetric around 0.
b. No! The box plot for the mean is much wider.

7.26 Yes. The averages are nearly 0; the standard deviation for the mean is much larger.

7.27 For outlier-prone data or (possibly) for highly skewed data.

7.28 No; proportion sampled is not critical for accuracy.

7.29 All are unbiased.

7.30 $\hat{\theta}_3$ has smallest variance; it gives most weight to Y_1, which has smaller variance.

7.31 a. $k = 3$.
b.

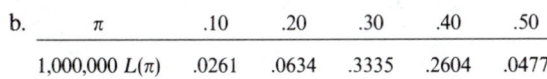

π	.10	.20	.30	.40	.50
1,000,000 $L(\pi)$	.0261	.0634	.3335	.2604	.0477

c. The maximum will occur at about $\pi = .30$.

7.32 $\hat{\pi} = .3333$

7.33 a. $L(\theta) = \theta^3 (25.36443)^{-(\theta+1)}$
b.

θ	1	2	3
$L(\theta)$	.00155	.00049	.000065

$\theta = 1$ is closest

7.34 $\hat{\theta} = 0.928 = n/\log_e[(1 + y_1)\cdots(1 + y_n)]$

7.35 a. MEAN 100.71   MEDIAN 100.10
b. Median; data indicate outliers.

7.36 a. **S**-shape indicates outliers.
b. Yes; the histogram showed outliers.

7.37 No; data appear to be roughly normal.

7.38 Plot is roughly a straight line, indicating near-normal data.

7.39 a. Second method, if population really is normal.
b. First method.
c. Skewness; first method.

7.40 Check if averages are close to correct value; then check for smallest standard deviation.

7.41 a. With replacement, $\sigma_y = 0.600$; without, $\sigma_{\bar{y}} = 0.593$.
b. Without; minor effect.
c. No; if sample is random, sample *size* is key.

7.42 a.

θ	25	24	23	22	21
Likelihood	.00000256	.00000301	.00000357	.00000427	.00000514

The likelihood for $\theta = 20$ is 0.
b. MLE = 21.

7.43 a. MLE = largest serial number.
b. Biased to underestimate.

7.44 a. Both averages near 0.500; seem unbiased.
b. Standard deviation for mean is smaller; mean more efficient.

CHAPTER 8   Section 8.1, pg. 290

8.1 a. 95%: $22.2 \le \mu \le 25.7$
b. 99%: $21.68 \le \mu \le 26.29$

8.2 We would expect that 95% of all confidence intervals calculated in this manner would include the parameter μ.

8.3 It seems reasonable to assume near-normality.

8.4 $2.631 \le \mu \le 2.769$

8.5 $4.4\% \le \mu \le 7.2\%$

8.6 For $n = 36$ and possibly severe skewness, the normal approximation may not be good.

8.7 a. $12.424 \le \mu \le 13.784$. Long run, 95% of such intervals will include the true mean service time.
b. No; 12.5 is within the reasonable range for μ.

8.8 Yes; 12.500 is not included in the interval. Lower confidence, narrower interval.

8.9 a. right skew
b. Not badly, by Central Limit Theorem.

Section 8.2, pg. 293

8.10 95% confidence interval for π: $.414 \le \pi \le .502$

8.11 We are 95% confident that the true long-run proportion of new product placements is in the interval (.414, .502).

8.12 90% confidence interval for π: $.60 \le \pi \le .74$

8.13 Yes. $n\hat{\pi} = 84$ and $n(1 - \hat{\pi}) = 41$ are both greater than 5, so that the normal approximation to the binomial is accurate.

8.14 $.096 \le \pi \le .304$

Section 8.3, pg. 296

8.15 a. For width .50: $n \cong 693$.
For width .25: $n \cong 2771$.
For width .125: $n \cong 11,084$.
b. Quadruple the sample size to cut the width in half.

8.16 For width of $.3\sigma$: $n \cong 171$.
For width of $.4\sigma$: $n \cong 96$.

8.17 For width of $50: n \cong 983$.

8.18 a. If $\sigma = 300$, $n \cong 553$. If $\sigma = 450$, $n \cong 1245$.

b. If $n = 1245$ and σ is 300, interval width is only about 33, smaller than the desired width of 50.

8.19 Yes. The sample size ($n = 983$) is much larger than needed in assuming normality of $\bar{Y}$.

8.20 a. Using $\hat{\pi} = .5$: $n \cong 9604$
b. Using $\hat{\pi} = .005$: $n \cong 191$
Using $\hat{\pi} = .08$: $n \cong 2827$.
The sample size need only be 2827 for a width no larger than .02, if $.005 \le \pi \le .08$.

Section 8.4, pg. 301

8.21 a. $P(t > 1.638) = .1$
b. $P(t > 5.841) = .005$
c. $P(t < -2.353) = .05$
d. $P(-2.353 < t < 2.353) = .9$
e. $P(|t| > 3.182) = .05$
f. $P(|t| > 4.541) = .02$

8.22 $P(t > 1.638) = .10; P(z > 1.638) = .0507$
$P(|t| > 1.638) = .20; P(|z| > 1.638) = .1014$
The mistaken assumption causes understatement of the probabilities.

8.23 a. Table of simulated and theoretical relative frequencies:

Range	Actual Frequencies	Relative Frequencies	Theoretical Relative Frequencies
$t < -2.353$	44	.04	.05
$-2.353 < t < -1.638$	59	.0536	.05
$-1.638 < t < 1.638$	896	.8145	.80
$1.638 < t < 2.353$	47	.0427	.05
$2.353 < t$	54	.0491	.05
	1100	1.000	1.00

b. There is no evidence of a systematic departure.

8.24 $t_{.10,72} = 1.2946 \qquad t_{.05,72} = 1.6684$
$t_{.01,72} = 2.3836$

Section 8.5, pg. 304

8.25 a. $\bar{y} = 56.87; s = 28.97$
b. $40 \le \mu \le 74$

8.26 $n \cong 252$

8.27 $\bar{y} = 328.64; s = 15.49$
$319.7 \le \mu \le 337.6$

8.28 a. Using t with 19 d.f., $46.6 \le \mu \le 63.2$.
b. Data are outlier-prone; mean is inefficient.

8.29 a. $1.071 \le \mu \le 1.189$
b. $1.074 \le \mu \le 1.186$
c. z interval is (artificial and) narrower.

8.30 The 95% claim is slightly suspect for $n = 31$.

Sections 8.6 and 8.7, pg. 311

8.31 a. Stem-and-leaf display of the data:

```
29 | 8
30 | 7
31 | 9  6
32 | 6  0  9
33 | 1  5  5
34 | 1  7  6
35 | 1
```

b. No blatant skewness or extreme outliers, no reason to doubt the approximate correctness of the 95% confidence level.

8.32 $316 \le$ median ≤ 346

8.33 a. $12.060 \le \mu \le 13.184$
b. $11.8 \le$ median ≤ 13.3

8.34 a. The data appear nearly normal.
b. The more efficient mean has the narrower interval.

8.35 The normal plot is close to a straight line. There is no obvious nonnormality.

Section 8.8, pg. 317

8.36 a. $P(Y > 46.96) = .01$
b. $P(Y > 18.11) = .90$
c. $P(Y < 12.88) = .01$
d. $P(12.88 < Y < 46.96) = .98$

8.37 a. $\chi^2_{.025} = 21.92$
b. $\chi^2_{.975} = 3.816$

8.38 a. $\chi^2_{.025} \approx 324.51, \chi^2_{.975} \approx 232.33$

8.39 a. $0.0162 \le \sigma \le 0.0209$
b. No; 0.030 (and larger) is well outside the interval.

8.40 a. Concerned only about too large a σ.
b. $\sigma \le 0.0204$; 0.030 (and larger) not included, not plausible.

8.41 a. $0.000226221 \le \sigma^2 \le 0.000393669$, or $0.0150 \le \sigma \le 0.0198$
b. Very similar interval.

8.42 a. By chi-square, $0.0243 \le \sigma \le 0.0314$; by jack-knife, $0.0229 \le \sigma \le 0.0303$, very similar.
b. The interval for supplier B is completely above the one for A; B has more variability.

Chapter 8 Exercises, pg. 321

8.43 $3.99 \le \mu \le 6.41$

8.44 a. No; right-skewed.
b. May be poor approximation with $n = 22$.

8.45 $n = 1537$

8.46 No. With $n = 1537$, the CLT certainly applies.

8.47 $.295 \le \pi \le .393$

8.48 a. $n = 1527$
b. $n = 1692$

8.49 $.498 \le \pi \le .622$
$.438 \le \pi \le .562$
$.398 \le \pi \le .522$

8.50 Nonsense, assuming a random sample.

8.51 $97.6 \le \mu \le 102.4$

8.52 a. No; the fraction isn't relevant to accuracy.
b. Yes; sample wasn't random. The machine may have cyclic behavior.

8.53 $.0168 \le \mu \le .0252$

8.54 Correction factor is .9989 and has no real effect.

8.55 Data severely right-skewed and $n = $ only 22. Confidence level may be wrong.

8.56 a. Data are roughly normal, perhaps with slight outliers.
b. The mean interval should be narrower, barring outliers; $59.903 \le \mu \le 63.017$
c. $60 \le$ median ≤ 64
Actually, the median interval is a trifle wider.

8.57 Basically a line, indicating normal data.

8.58 a. $16.48 \le \mu \le 20.15$

b. $16.32 \le \mu \le 20.30$
c. $s = 6.29$ is larger than the assumed $\sigma = 6.00$; $t_{.05} = 1.701$ is larger than $z_{.05} = 1.645$.

8.59 Severely right-skewed.

8.60 a. $9.43 \le \mu \le 9.93$, assuming 0.95983 is the *sample* standard deviation.
b. Yes; the interval excludes 10.00 ounces.

8.61 Nearly normal. Even if it hadn't been normal, $n = 61$ would make the confidence level close to correct.

8.62 No clear trend, not obvious.

8.63 a. $0.815 \le \sigma \le 1.169$
b. σ definitely larger than 0.75.

8.64 a. $1.890 \le \mu \le 3.944$
b. $\mu = 2.50$ is included, so plausible.

8.65 Underestimate; too low.

8.66 a. Negative values aren't possible; data likely are right-skewed.
b. Slight skew, not severe.

8.67 a. $1.449 \le \sigma \le 2.375$
b. Claimed 95% confidence would not be correct.

8.68 a. $6.10 \le \mu \le 12.88$
b. No; interval is for population *mean*, not individual values.

8.69 a. $4.690 \le$ median ≤ 8.000
b. Data are right-skewed, so mean and median differ.

8.70 No obvious trend or cycle, but apparent outlier.

8.71 a. $0.99371 \le \mu \le 1.00597$
b. No; interval is for the mean, not individual values.

8.72 a. $0.991 \le$ median ≤ 1.004
b. Quite similar; data basically symmetric without serious outliers.

8.73 a. $0.0302 \le \sigma \le 0.0390$
b. About 68% of actual prices will be within ± 0.039 (3.9 percent) of estimated. (This assumes $\mu = 1.000$.)

8.74 No evident pattern.

8.75 a. $104.55 \le \mu \le 130.79$
b. No; 105.20 is still plausible, but so is 130.79, a large increase.

8.76 a. $108 \le$ median ≤ 131, 96.16% confidence
b. Slightly narrower; outlier made mean inefficient.

8.77 $15.44 \le \sigma \le 32.02$, but outlier-prone population makes claimed chi-square probability incorrect.

8.78 a. $0.071 \le \pi \le 0.179$
b. No; $\pi = 0.20$ is excluded, not plausible.

8.79 a. $n = 1537$, assuming $\pi = 0.20$
b. Not unless the yard has a terrible supplier.

8.80 a. Supplier could ship a bad lot with a good right rear pallet load.
b. True random sampling would be expensive, but any method shouldn't be predictable.

8.81 a. $n = 1692$
b. $n = 863$, assuming $\pi = .15$
c. Almost a 50% reduction.

8.82 $.030 \le \pi_{\text{by passed}} \le .057$
$.037 \le \pi_{\text{failure}} \le .066$
$.076 \le \pi_{\text{nonworking}} \le .114$

8.83 Not all combinations of meters have the same probability of being sampled.

8.84 a. We are 95% sure that the true mean is between 4.42 and 5.94 (thousand dollars). For 186 d.f., the difference between t and z is negligible.
b. $4.80 \le \sigma \le 5.88$

8.85 Central Limit Theorem effect makes confidence for mean a good approximation, but not the confidence level for the standard deviation.

8.86 a. $\pm .0253$
b. $\pm .0248$, very similar.
c. To allow a small margin for bias.

8.87 $\pm .0071$

8.88 a. $n = 271$, assuming $= .50$
b. No, only to .0707.

8.89 a. That only half are satisfied, not a testimonial to the dealer.
b. $n = 174$, assuming $\pi = .80$

8.90 Extreme right-skewness makes the population mean and median very different.

8.91 a. mean 5.524, st.dev. 2.598
b. $5.17 \le \mu \le 5.87$
c. 95% of such intervals will include the population mean.

8.92 a. Severely right-skewed.
b. No; for $n = 215$, Central Limit Theorem applies.

8.93 a. mean 227.3, st.dev. 79.7
b. $210.3 \le \mu \le 244.4$

8.94 a. Yes, nearly normal.
b. Apparent cycles; nonindependent data.

8.95 b. $0.544 \le \mu \le 4.356$
c. B has lower average.

8.96 a. No.
b. No.

8.97 $3.10 \le \sigma \le 5.95$

CHAPTER 9   Section 9.1, pg. 341

9.1 a. $\pi =$ long-run proportion of bids resulting in takeovers
b. $H_0: \pi = .35$
c. $H_a: \pi < .35$
d. From Appendix Table 1 with $n = 20$, $P(Y \le 3 | \pi = .35) = .0445$.

9.2 Yes. $y = 2$ is in the rejection region.

9.3 a. The proportion, π, of houses with swimming pools that must be purchased by the realtor.
b. $H_a: \pi > .05$ (one-sided)
c. $H_0: \pi \le .05$
d. R.R.: If $y \ge 6$, reject H_0

9.4 Because $y = 7$, reject H_0 at $\alpha = .05$ level.

9.5
  a. The population parameter, π, is the proportion of applications prepared by the new manager that are accepted for funding.

  b. $\pi = .50$

  c. $H_a: \pi \neq .5$, because a change in either direction would be relevant.

  d. R.R.: If $y \leq 4$ or $y \geq 14$, reject H_0

9.6   Because $y = 7$, do not reject H_0 at $\alpha = .05$ level.

9.7   For example, if the decision to accept an application from the city is based on the number of applications already accepted, trials are not independent and probabilities are not constant.

9.8
  a. $\pi = .40$

  b. The selection method might decrease the rate of desirability of products, as well as increase it.

  c. The intent is to improve desirability of products; $H_a: \pi > .40$

9.9
  a. $\mu = 20(.40) = 8.0$

  b. Reject H_0 if $y \leq 3$ or if $y \geq 13$
$$P(Y \leq 3 \cup Y \geq 13 \,|\, \pi = .40) = .0370$$

9.10   Independence is violated.

Section 9.2, pg. 344

9.11
  a. $\beta = P(Y \geq 4 \,|\, \pi = .25) = .7749$

  b. power $= P(Y \leq 3 \,|\, \pi = .25) = .2251$

9.12   As the population parameter gets farther from the H_0 value, β should decrease.

9.13 $\beta = P(Y \leq 5 \,|\, \pi = .10) = .6161$

9.14   False positive (Type I) error

9.15
  a. All else equal, β decreases as n increases.

  b. $\beta = P(Y \leq 9 \,|\, \pi = .10) = .4513$, which is indeed smaller than $\beta = .6161$ in Exercise 9.13.

9.16   Type I (false positive): Claim a different marketing rate, when in fact the rate is the same.

Type II (false negative): Claim the same marketing rate, when in fact the rate is different.

9.17 $\beta = P(H_0 \text{ not rejected}) = P(4 \leq Y \leq 12)$ with $n = 20$.

π	.45	.50	.55	.65	.75	.80
β	.9370	.8671	.7477	.3990	.9019	.0322

The β curve decreases in an **S**-shape.

9.18
  a. power$(\pi = .50) = 1 - \beta_{.50} = .1329$

  b. As n increases, power increases.

Sections 9.3 and 9.4, pg. 357

9.19
  a. The mean waiting time of nonemergency patients.

  b. $H_0: \mu \leq 30$
     $H_a: \mu > 30$

  c. T.S. $z = \dfrac{\bar{y} - \mu_0}{\sigma/\sqrt{n}} = \dfrac{\bar{y} - 30}{10/\sqrt{22}}$
    R.R. at $\alpha = .05$, reject H_0 if $z > 1.645$

9.20   T.S. $z = 3.7992$
Conclusion: Reject H_0 at $\alpha = .05$ level

9.21 $\beta = P(z < -.2311) = .4086$ for $\mu_a = 34$
Table of β probabilities:

μ_a	$\beta = P(H_0 \text{ not rejected} \,|\, H_a \text{ true})$
32	.7602
34	.4086
36	.1212
38	.0175
40	.0012

9.22   Independence would be a bad assumption.

9.23 $H_0: \mu = 1.5$
$H_a: \mu \neq 1.5$
T.S.: $z = -.5887$
RR: At $\alpha = .05$, reject H_0 if $z \geq 1.96$ or $z < -1.96$
Conclusion: Do not reject H_0.

9.24   Table of β probabilities:

μ_a	β
1.0	.7365
1.2	.8750
1.4	.9419
1.6	.9419
1.8	.8750
2.0	.7365

9.25 Plot of the data:

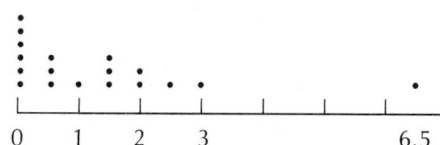

Because n is small (18) and the data are clearly skewed, the assumption of normality is not appropriate.

Section 9.5, pg. 361

9.26 p-value $= P(z \geq 3.7992) \approx .0001$

9.27 p-value $= P(Y \leq 4 \mid \pi = .15) = .1122$

9.28 p-value $= P(z \leq -1.19) = .1174$

9.29
a. $z = 1.14$
b. "P VALUE": p-value $= .26$
c. A two-tailed p-value is appropriate. The company is concerned with *any* deviation from the goal of 40%.

9.30
a. The p-value of .26 > usual α values. The sales manager is correct.
b. The term "proved" is much too strong.

9.31
a. $H_0: \mu \geq 20{,}000$
   $H_a: \mu < 20{,}000$
b. T.S. $z = -2.9524$
   p-value $= P(z < -2.95) = .0016$

9.32 The result is statistically significant at the usual α values. The result, however, is not what would be termed "practically significant."

Section 9.6, pg. 366

9.33 $H_0: \mu \leq 1600$
$H_a: \mu > 1600$
T.S.: $t = 3.64$
RR: at $\alpha = .10$, reject H_0 if $t > 1.333$
Conclusion: Reject H_0.

9.34 p-value $< .005$, and H_a is strongly supported.

9.35
a. $H_0: \mu = 0$
   $H_a: \mu > 0$
b. T.S.: $t = .3509$
   R.R.: At $\alpha = .05$, reject H_0 if $t > 1.943$
   Conclusion: Do not reject H_0.

9.36 $-2.3 \leq \mu_0 \leq 3.3$. Because $\mu = 0$ is contained in this interval, we cannot reject $H_0: \mu = 0$ at $\alpha = .10$.

9.37 Because the confidence interval is quite wide, the β risk for alternative μ values may be large, and it is unwise to conclude "no change."

9.38
a. $\bar{d} = 1.8$; $s_d = 1.9889$
b. $H_0: \mu_d = 0$
   $H_a: \mu_d > 0$
   T.S.: $t = 2.8619$
   R.R.: At $\alpha = .01$, reject H_0 if $t > 2.821$
   Conclusion: Reject H_0.

Section 9.8, pg. 369

9.39
a. The histogram or stem-and-leaf display shows no obvious nonnormality.
b. No; the data appear normal.

9.40
a. $H_0: \mu = 315$
   $H_a: \mu \neq 315$

T.S.: $t = 3.2955$
R.R.: At $\alpha = .05$, reject H_0 if $t > 2.16$ or $t < -2.16$
Conclusion: Reject H_0.
p-value $< .01$

b. H_0: median $= 315$
H_a: median $\neq 315$
T.S.: $y = 12$
R.R.: at $\alpha = .05$, reject H_0 if $y \geq 12$ or $y \leq 2$
Conclusion: Reject H_0.
p-value $= .0130$
c. No, no serious difference in the conclusions of parts a and b

9.41 $316 \leq$ population median ≤ 346

9.42 a. H_0: $\mu \leq 45$
H_a: $\mu > 45$
T.S.: $t = 1.965$
R.R.: At $\alpha = .05$, reject H_0 if $t > 1.717$
Conclusion: Reject H_0.
b. Because the data are clearly skewed, the test based on the assumption of symmetry in part a is not appropriate.

9.43 a. H_0: median ≤ 45
H_a: median > 45
T.S.: $y = 11$, $z = 0$
R.R.: At $\alpha = .05$, reject H_0 if $z > 1.645$
Conclusion: Do not reject H_0.
b. Yes. In 9.44(a), a one-sided test was performed on skewed data. The test for the population median is designed to deal with this problem.

9.44 a. $\mu = 55$ but H_0: $\mu = 50$. The simulation is evaluating $P(\text{reject } H_0 \mid H_a \text{ true}) = \text{power}$.
b. The power is higher for the t test, for any α.

Section 9.10, pg. 374

9.45 a. Yes; $\mu = 4.62$ is well within the 95% confidence interval.
b. No; interval includes a wide range of plausible values besides 4.62.

9.46 No, by the Central Limit Theorem with $n = 187$.

9.47 a. $0.539 \leq \mu \leq 2.017$
b. $\mu = 1.50$ is within the 95% confidence interval.

9.48 a. $43.55 \leq \mu \leq 51.65$
b. $\mu = 44.0$ is included in the interval.
c. $\mu = 44.0$ is close to the end of the interval.

9.49 a. $19,428 \leq \mu \leq 19,962$
b. $\mu = 20,000$ is not included in the 99% confidence interval.

c. No; the mean is detectably lower by a small amount.

9.50 a. $10,888.9 \leq \mu \leq 12,871.9$
b. $\mu = 11,260$ is included in the 95% interval

9.51 No; the interval is very wide.

9.52 Generally upward trend

9.53 a. $9.01\% \leq \mu \leq 9.21\%$
b. 9.26% is not included in the 99% confidence interval.

9.54 No; modest, detectable improvement.

9.55 No, by the Central Limit Theorem.

Section 9.11, pg. 377

9.56 a. .975   b. .95   c. .99

9.57 H_0: $\sigma^2 = .15^2 = .0225$
H_a: $\sigma^2 < .0225$
T.S.: $\chi^2 = 46.464$
R.R.: Reject H_0 if $\chi^2 < 43.19$
Conclusion: Do not reject H_0.

9.58 H_0: $\sigma^2 = .0225$
H_a: $\sigma^2 > .0225$
T.S.: $\chi^2 = 46.464$
R.R.: Reject H_0 if $\chi^2 > 79.08$

Conclusion: Retain H_0.
This choice of H_a is more generous.

9.59 a. $\bar{y} = 3.999$; $s = .0159$
b. H_0: $\sigma^2 = .011^2 = .000121$
H_a: $\sigma^2 > .000121$
T.S.: $\chi^2 = 52.23$
R.R.: Reject H_0 if $\chi^2 > 37.65$
Conclusion: Reject H_0.

9.60 90% confidence interval: $.0002 < \sigma^2 < .0004$; $.0130 < \sigma < .0208$

9.61 The distribution may be heavy-tailed. Although the probabilities may not be accurate, the conclusion seems appropriate.

9.62 $H_0: \sigma^2 = 4$ T.S.: $\chi^2 = 64.8$
$H_a: \sigma^2 < 4$ R.R.: Reject H_0 if $\chi^2 < 60.39$
Conclusion: Do not reject H_0.

9.63 p-value $\simeq .1$

Section 9.12, pg. 379

9.64 a. $H_0: \pi \geq .135$
$H_a: \pi < .135$
b. Rejection of H_0 implies that the miller does not pay the full price of the grain to the seller. Not rejecting H_0 implies that the full price is paid.
c. If α is very small, it is more difficult to reject H_0. This would be disadvantageous to the miller if H_0 is false.

9.65 i. Implies that the cost of a Type I error is very high and as such α should be very small.

ii. Implies that the cost of a Type II error is not great and so the β value can be allowed to be fairly large.
iii. Makes the miller skeptical of any sample that indicates rejection of H_0, indicating that α should be small.

9.66 The cost of a Type I error is much higher than the cost of a Type II error. For these reasons, the α value is set very low.

Chapter 9 Exercises, pg. 382

9.67 $H_0: \pi \leq .1$
$H_a: \pi > .1$
T.S.: $y = 9$
R.R.: At $\alpha = .05$, reject H_0 if $y \geq 10$
Conclusion: Do not reject H_0.

9.68 p-value $= P(Y \geq 9 \,|\, \pi = .1) = .0579$

9.69 One-sided alternative: We should only be concerned if the mpg is overestimated and the consumer is misled by misadvertising.
Two-sided alternative: for technological reasons, a two-sided alternative may be desirable.

9.70 $H_0: \mu = 28.2$
$H_a: \mu \neq 28.2$
T.S.: $z = -2.0203$
R.R.: At $\alpha = .01$, reject H_0 if $z < -2.576$
Conclusion: Do not reject H_0.

9.71 p-value $= 2P(z \geq 2.0203) = .0434$

9.72 One would seriously question the acceptance of 28.2 mpg as "truth."

9.73 99% confidence interval for μ: $24.8 \leq \mu \leq 28.6$. Reliably assume that the true mean is between 24.8 and 28.6 mpg.

9.74 a. 95% confidence interval for μ:
$3.03 \leq \mu \leq 3.07$

b. Because 3 does not lie in the 95% confidence interval for μ, H_0 can be rejected at $\alpha = .05$.

9.75 a. Yes, the results were statistically significant.
b. The deviation from "average" is so small that people would most probably ignore it.

9.76 p-value $= 2(z \geq 3.9648) \approx .00006$

9.77 a. $H_a: \mu < 20$, $H_0: \mu = 20$
b. $z = \dfrac{\bar{Y} - 20}{6.0/\sqrt{29}}$
c. R.R.: $z < -1.645$; Conclusion: $z = -1.52$, so retain H_0.

9.78 $P(z < -1.52) = .064$

9.79 Right-skewed; with small n, claimed probabilities are incorrect.

9.80 $t = -1.45 > -1.701$; retain H_0.

9.81 a. $H_a: \mu$ not equal to 10.0, $H_0: \mu = 10.0$
b. $z = \dfrac{\bar{Y} - 10.0}{1.0/\sqrt{61}}$
c. $|z| = |-2.50| > z_{.05} = 1.645$. Reject H_0.

9.82 p-value $= P(|z| > 2.50) = .0124$, two-tailed

9.83 $|t| = |-2.60|$; reject H_0 at $\alpha = .10$ (or at $\alpha = .05$).

9.84 $.01 < p < .02$

9.85 $\chi^2 = 55.28 > \chi^2_{.95} = 43.19$, and $\chi^2 < \chi^2_{.05} = 79.08$; retain H_0.

9.86   a. $t = 1.14$; retain H_0.
b. No; deviation *might* be the result of randomness.

9.87 $p > .10$

9.88 $1.89 \leq \mu \leq 3.84$ includes 2.50. Wide interval, so low power.

9.89   a. $H_a: \mu > 7.5 \, K$
b. $t = 1.19$; not significant

9.90 $p > .10$

9.91   Yes; severe skew, modest n

9.92   a. Outlier-prone.
b. No; heavy-tailed.

9.93   No; S-shape of outlier-prone data.

9.94   Yes; 30.4 not included.
b. No; outliers make interval wide but correct.

9.95   Yes, confidence incorrect; more serious for variance.

9.96   a. Yes; "so reject H_0."
b. Yes.
c. $p = .0126 < \alpha = .10$; reject H_0.

9.97   a. $t > -1.65$; p-value $> .05$
b. No; *may* have been no decrease.

9.98   a. right skew
b. Not with $n = 144$.

9.99   a. $2.22 \leq \sigma \leq 2.80$
b. No; Central Limit Theorem doesn't apply.

9.100   From the ongoing process.

9.101   a. mean $= 2067.2$, st. dev. $= 251.0$
b. one-tailed p-value $= .0000$
c. Thoroughly.

9.102   a. No problem.
b. Definite cyclic pattern.

9.103   a. mean 2.804, st. dev. 0.633
b. Yes; p-value .0001.

9.104   a. Two outliers, one of them major.
b. Slight **S**-shape, indicating outliers.

9.105   a. Mean 5.04, median 4.00, st. dev. 4.02 suggests right-skewness.
b. Definite right-skewness.

9.106   a. $t = -1.16$
b. One-sided p-value about .13.

Review Exercises, Chapters 7–9, pg. 389

R52   a. $240.40 \leq \mu \leq 266.24$
b. The sample mean should be reasonably efficient.

R53   Reject H_0; 230.2 is not in the interval.

R54 $H_0: \mu = 230.2$
$H_a: \mu \neq 230.2$
T.S. $z = \dfrac{\bar{y}. - \mu_0}{\sigma/\sqrt{n}}$
R.R.: $|z| > 2.58$
Conclusion: $z = 4.62$; reject H_0.

R55 p-value $= 2p(z > 4.62) \approx 2P(z > 4.50) = .0000068$ (two-sided)

R56   Using $t_{.005, 49 \, d.f.} \approx 2.684$ by interpolation, $239.62 \leq \mu \leq 267.02$; reject $H_0: \mu = 230.2$
Formal test T.S.: $t = 4.53 > 2.684$, reject H_0, p-value $< 2(.001)$
Same conclusions.

R57 $233 \leq \text{median} \leq 275$; reject H_0

R58   The median interval is wider; $\bar{y}$ is more efficient here.

R59   R.R.: Reject H_0 if $y \leq 36$;
$P(Y \leq 36 | \pi = .45) = .0429$

R60   R.R.: Reject H_0 if $y \leq 33$;
$P(Y \leq 33 | \pi = .45) = .0097$

R61   Yes; $y = 32 \leq 36$, so reject H_0.

R62   Yes; $y = 32 \leq 33$, so reject H_0 with p-value $< .01$.

R63   a. $H_0: \mu = 272.6$; $H_a: \mu > 272.6$ because higher yield is desired.
b. $H_0: \mu = 272.6$
$H_a: \mu > 272.6$
T.S.: $z = \dfrac{\bar{y} - 272.6}{67.3/\sqrt{25}}$
R.R.: Reject H_0 if $z > 1.645$

R64 $\beta = P(Z > .76) = .2236$

R65   The β probability is larger with μ_a closer to μ_0.

R66 $z = 3.09$; reject H_0

R67 p-value $= .001$

R68 Data are modestly left-skewed with possible outliers. A fences calculation shows that 135 and 185 are (oh, deer!) outliers. The mean may not be efficient.

R69

π	.2	.3	.4	.5
$1{,}000{,}000\ L(\pi)$	.0792	.0164	.0009	.00001

$\hat{\pi} = .2$ or less

R70 a. $\hat{\pi} = 1/6 = .1667$
b. $\hat{\pi} = 1/(1 + \bar{x})$

R71 $\hat{\pi}$ is a (slightly) biased estimator.

R72 $.102 \le \pi \le .229$

R73 a. $n = 589.3$, rounded up to 590
b. $n = 1068$

R74 Yes; $n\hat{\pi} = 22$ and $n(1 - \hat{\pi}) = 111$ are much greater than 5.

R75 Biased in favor of large accounts.

R76 a. Using $t_{.025,\,240\,d.f.} = 1.970$, $5093 \le \mu \le 5669$
b. Skewness is a minor problem. The major problem is the biased sampling.

R77 $78.91 \le \mu \le 81.83$

R78 Using a z approximation, $k = 8$; so $80.3 \le \text{median} \le 82.5$.

R79 The median interval is shorter, indicating that the sample median is more efficient. A plot shows left-skewness with outliers.

R80 $|t| = |-1.90|$, $.05 < p\text{-value} < .10$

R81 power $= 1 - P(Z > 2.49) = .9936$

R82 The given means were hypothetical population means: The p-value refers to a particular sample.

R83 $\hat{\theta} = 1.833$

R84 $\hat{\theta} = \left[\sum_{i=1}^{n} \log_e(1 + y_i) \right] \Big/ n$

R85 It is unbiased and most efficient.

CHAPTER 10 Section 10.1, pg. 398

10.1 a. $-2.6791 \le \mu_1 - \mu_2 \le 15.8791$
b. $H_0: \mu_1 - \mu_2 = 0$
$H_a: \mu_1 - \mu_2 \ne 0$
T.S.: $z = 1.3941$
R.R.: Reject H_0 if $|z| > 1.96$
Conclusion: Do not reject H_0.
Note also that 0 is included in the confidence interval.

10.2 p-value $= .165$

10.3 a. $-.4782 \le \mu_1 - \mu_2 \le -.0218$
b. $H_0: \mu_1 - \mu_2 = 0$
$H_a: \mu_2 - \mu_2 \ne 0$
T.S.: $z = -1.8025$
R.R.: Reject H_0 if $|z| > 1.645$
Conclusion: Reject H_0.

10.4 p-value $= .0718$

10.5 We can be confident in the z probabilities (especially because n_1 and n_2 are large).

10.6 a. $\mu_{\bar{K} - \bar{R}} = 78.28 - 75.79 = 2.49$
b. $\sigma_{\bar{K} - \bar{R}} = \sqrt{\dfrac{(9.63)^2}{8} + \dfrac{(11.25)^2}{12}} = 4.705$

10.7 μ would not change; $\sigma_{\bar{K} - \bar{R}} = 4.853$

10.8 a. $\mu_{\bar{Y}_1 - \bar{Y}_2} = -4.21$
b. $\sigma^2_{\bar{Y}_1 - \bar{Y}_2} = 2.31172$

10.9 The dependent sampling makes the variance wrong.

Section 10.2, pg. 407

10.10 a. $s_p^2 = 1.1601$; $s_p = 1.077$
b. $-1.2619 \le \mu_1 - \mu_2 \le .5619$
c. $H_0: \mu_1 - \mu_2 = 0$
$H_a: \mu_1 - \mu_2 \ne 0$
T.S.: $t = -.7959$
R.R.: Reject H_0 if $|t| > 2.074$
Conclusion: Retain H_0.

10.11 $p > .2$

10.12 a. With unequal n's and variances, t' should give closer α probabilities.
b. Yes; the t' probabilities are very close to the nominal α probabilities, but the pooled variance t probabilities are not.

10.13 The assumption of normality is mildly suspect. Both sets of data appear slightly bimodal. The conclusion of no difference in means seems appropriate given the mild problem.

10.14 a. $\bar{y}_1 = 10.37$; $\bar{y}_2 = 9.83$; $s_1 = .3234$; $s_2 = .2406$
b. $t = 4.2368$
c. $t' = 4.2368$
d. $t = t'$ because $n_1 = n_2$

10.15

a.

Sample 1		Sample 2	
9.8–.9	×	9.4–.5	×
10.0–.1	×	9.6–.7	× × ×
10.2–.3	× × ×	9.8–.9	× × ×
10.4–.5	×	10.0–.1	× ×
10.6–.7	× × ×	10.2–.3	×
10.8–.9	×		

b. The assumption of normal populations does not appear seriously violated. Because $n_1 = n_2$, the assumption of equal variances is not inappropriate.

10.16 a. $p = .0005$, two-tailed
b. The data give strong support to H_a that there is a decrease in mean potency.

10.17 a. $s_p^2 = \dfrac{9(10.46)^2 + 15(8.67)^2}{24} = 88.010$
b. With 24 d.f., $t_{.005} = 2.797$.
$2.92 \le \mu_A - \mu_B \le 24.08$
c. Yes; $\mu_A - \mu_B = 0.00$ is not included in the interval.

10.18 $1.95 \le \mu_A - \mu_B \le 25.05$
By either method, 0.00 isn't included. The more believable t' confidence interval is somewhat wider.

10.19 a.

Sample	$\bar{y}$	s
I	13.43	5.738
II	15.21	6.174

b. $t = -.668$
c. $t' = -.668$
d. $t = t'$ whenever $n_1 = n_2$

10.20 a. No; $|t| < 2.101$.
b. 2-tailed p-value $> .2$
c. d.f. ≈ 17
d. Same conclusion.

Section 10.3, pg. 414

10.21 a. Sample 1 rank sum $= 146$; Sample 2 rank sum $= 64$
b. $z = 3.0743$
c. H_0: Populations are identical.
H_a: Population 1 is shifted to the right of population 2.
d. R.R.: Reject H_0 if $z > 2.326$.
Conclusion: Reject H_0. The research hypothesis is supported at $\alpha = .01$ level.

10.22 a. A one-tailed p-value should be reported: $p = .001$.
b. The conclusions are the same.

10.23 a.

A: 39 41 42 44 49 53 56 57 63 71
Rank: 11 13 14 16 18 21 23 24 25 26

B: 27 28 29 30 31 33 35 36 37 38 40 43 45 50 52 54
Rank: 1 2 3 4 5 6 7 8 9 10 12 15 17 19 20 22

b. $T_1 = 191$, $T_2 = 160$
c. $z = 2.95 > 2.58$; yes, significant.

10.24 There is no clear preference; both methods yield the same conclusion.

10.25 a. $|z| = |-1.66| < 1.96$; retain H_0.
b. p-value $= .097$

10.26 Both samples are highly right-skewed. The rank sum test is preferred.

10.27 a. The means are unequal, so H_a is true; power $= P(\text{reject } H_0 \mid H_0 \text{ true})$.
b. The rank sum test.

Sections 10.4 and 10.5, pg. 423

10.28 a. $H_0: \mu_d = 0$
$H_a: \mu_d \neq 0$
T.S.: $t = 4.0602$
R.R.: Reject H_0 if $|t| > 1.761$.
Conclusion: Reject H_0.
b. 90% confidence interval: $1.965 \leq \mu_d \leq 4.975$

10.29 a. H_0: The distribution of differences is symmetric around 0.
H_a: The differences tend to be larger than 0 or smaller than 0.
T.S.: $T = 7$
R.R.: Reject H_0 if $T \leq 25$
Conclusion: Reject H_0.
b. Display A has a better effect on sales than Display B.

10.30 Paired-sample t test: p-value $< .002$
Wilcoxon signed-rank test: p-value $< .005$

10.31 a. $H_0: \mu_1 - \mu_2 = 0$
$H_a: \mu_1 - \mu_2 \neq 0$
T.S.: $t = .7600$
R.R.: Reject H_0 if $|t| > 1.701$
Conclusion: Retain H_0.
b. The pairing process effectively eliminates store-to-store variation.

10.32 H_0: The median difference is zero.
H_a: The median difference is not zero.
T.S.: $y = 12$
R.R.: Reject H_0 if $y \leq 3$ or $y \geq 11$
Discard the 0 difference; take $n = 14$.
Conclusion: Reject H_0.

10.33 The signed-rank test has better power.

10.34 a. $t = 2.86$
b. $T = 6$

c.

t Test

$H_0: \mu_d = 0$
$H_a: \mu_d \neq 0$
T.S.: $t = 2.86$
R.R.: Reject H_0 if $|t| > 2.262$
Conclusion: Reject H_0.

Wilcoxon Signed-Rank Test

H_0: Differences are symmetric about 0.
H_a: Differences are greater or less than 0.
T.S.: $T = 6$
R.R.: Reject H_0 if $T \leq 8$
Conclusion: Reject H_0.

10.35 t test: p-value $= .0187$
Wilcoxon: p-value $= .0310$
Reject H_0.

10.36 Paired sampling is more effective because of the great variability in delivery times among the different destinations. To select destinations, choose as wide a variety as possible.

10.37 a. The same ZIP codes are used for both samples.
b. For A-B differences, $\bar{d} = -.375$, $s_d = .920$.
c. $t = -1.41 > -1.796$; retain H_0.
d. $.05 < p$-value $< .10$, one-tailed

10.38 a. $T = T_+ = 23 > 17$; retain H_0.
b. p-value $> .1$
c. Yes, at $\alpha = .05$.

10.39 No; H_0 is retained but not proved.

10.40 a. The data are paired by task (finding the same combinations).
b. $-48.1 \leq \mu_d \leq 5.5$, where $d = $ Program 1 $-$ Program 2
c. Retain H_0 at $\alpha = .05$; 0.0 is included.

10.41 $T = |T_+| = 9 > 3$; retain H_0.

10.42 The same conclusion is found.

10.43 a. $-89.8 \leq \mu_1 - \mu_2 \leq 47.2$
b. Pairing was quite helpful in reducing variability.

10.44 Outlier-prone data.

10.45 **S**-shape; outlier-prone.

10.46 $t = 1.806, .05 < p < .10$

10.47 a. Yes; $p = .003$.
b. Yes; $p = .007$.
c. Sign, signed rank tests are more conclusive for outlier-prone data.

Section 10.6, pg. 431

10.48 90% confidence interval: $.0076 \leq \pi_1 - \pi_2 \leq .0304$

10.49
a. $H_0: \pi_1 - \pi_2 = 0$
   $H_a: \pi_1 - \pi_2 \neq 0$
   T.S.: $z = 2.7536$
   R.R.: Reject H_0 if $|z| > 1.645$
   Conclusion: Reject H_0.
b. Modified standard error $= \sigma_{\hat{\pi}} = .0075$
   Modified z T.S.: $z = 2.5333$
   Conclusion: Reject H_0.
   The modification does not affect the conclusion.

10.50 z statistic: p-value $= .006$
Modified z statistic: p-value $= .0114$

10.51
a. 95% confidence interval for true difference:
   $.0785 \leq \pi_1 - \pi_2 \leq .1467$
b. $H_0: \pi_1 - \pi_2 = 0$
   $H_a: \pi_1 - \pi_2 > 0$
   T.S.: $z = 6.4713$
   R.R.: Reject H_0 if $|z| > 1.645$
   Conclusion: Reject H_0.

10.52 p-value $= P(Z > 6.4713) \approx 0$. Strongly support the research hypothesis.

10.53 Modified standard error: $\sigma_{\hat{\pi}} = .0180$
Modified z T.S.: $z = 6.2556$
p-value $= P(z > 6.2556) \approx 0$
Use of the modified standard error does not affect the conclusion.

10.54
a. $z = 2.31 > 1.645$; reject H_0
b. p-value $= .0208$, two-tailed

10.55 $z = 2.29$; essentially the same result

10.56
a. $.038 \leq \pi_1 - \pi_2 \leq .166$
b. Yes, more than adequate.
c. Yes; .000 is not included.

10.57 $z = 3.13$ (or $z = 3.11$ with the pooled proportion); reject H_0.

10.58
a. $z = 1.64$
   (or $z = 1.61$ using $\bar{\pi}$) < 1.96; retain H_0.
b. No; H_0 is retained, not proved.

10.59 $-.039 \leq \pi_1 - \pi_2 \leq .439$
Supplier 1 may produce anywhere from 3.9% fewer reliable motors to 43.9% more reliable motors than supplier 2! The interval is uninformatively wide.

Section 10.7, pg. 437

10.60
a. The times to onset of relief may be skewed.
b. $H_0: \sigma_1^2 = \sigma_2^2$
   $H_a: \sigma_1^2 \neq \sigma_2^2$
   T.S.: $F = 1.5376$
   R.R.: Reject H_0 if $F > 2.53$ or $F < .395$
   Conclusion: Do not reject H_0.

10.61 $.607 \leq \sigma_1^2/\sigma_2^2 \leq 2.53$

10.62 Yes; the nominal α is much too small.

10.63
a. $0.310 \leq \dfrac{\sigma_A^2}{\sigma_B^2} \leq 0.634$
b. A standard deviation is lower.

10.64
a. $0.292 \leq \dfrac{\sigma_A^2}{\sigma_B^2} \leq 0.638$
b. A standard deviation is lower.
c. Similar results.

Chapter 10 Exercises, pg. 441

10.65
a. $-.0241 \leq \pi_1 - \pi_2 \leq .0547$
b. $H_0: \pi_1 - \pi_2 = 0$
   $H_a: \pi_1 - \pi_2 \neq 0$
   T.S.: $z = .7612$
   R.R.: Reject H_0 if $|z| > 1.96$
   Conclusion: Retain H_0.

10.66 p-value $= .4472$

10.67
a. $\$9.39 \leq \mu_1 - \mu_2 \leq \$28.83$
b. We are 90% confident that the mean error of those accounts in error at Bank B is at least \$9.39 larger than the mean error of those accounts in error at Bank A and at most \$28.83.

c. $H_0: \mu_1 - \mu_2 = 0$
$H_a: \mu_1 - \mu_2 > 0$
T.S.: $z = 3.2333$
R.R.: Reject H_0 if $t > 1.96$.
Conclusion: Reject H_0.

10.68 p-value $< .002$

10.69 a. $H_0: \mu_1 - \mu_2 = 0$
$H_a: \mu_1 - \mu_2 \neq 0$
T.S.: $t = 3.2707$
R.R.: Reject H_0 if $|t| > 1.994$ (interpolated).
Conclusion: Reject H_0.
b. $H_0: \mu_1 - \mu_2 = 0$
$H_a: \mu_1 - \mu_2 \neq 0$
T.S.: $t' = 3.2333$
R.R.: Reject H_0 if $|t'| > 2.03$.
Conclusion: Reject H_0.
Note that the t' statistic equals the large sample z statistic.

10.70 a. $H_0: \mu_1 - \mu_2 = 0$
$H_a: \mu_1 - \mu_2 \neq 0$
T.S.: $t = .7999$
R.R.: Reject H_0 if $|t| > 1.321$.
Conclusion: Retain H_0.
b. H_0: The two populations are identical.
H_a: Population 1 is shifted to the right of Population 2.
T.S.: $z = .6928$
R.R.: Reject H_0 if $z > 1.282$.
Conclusion: Retain H_0.

10.71 The t test is more powerful. Choosing the more appropriate test is not critical.

10.72 t test: $.10 < p$-value
Wilcoxon rank sum test: p-value $\approx .25$

10.73 a. $H_0: \mu_d = 0$
$H_a: \mu_d > 0$
T.S.: $t = 3.1542$
R.R.: Reject H_0 if $t > 1.363$
Conclusion: Reject H_0.
b. H_0: The distribution of differences is symmetric around 0.
H_a: The differences tend to be larger than 0.
T.S.: $T = 8$
R.R.: Reject H_0 if $T \leq 17$.
Conclusion: Reject H_0.

10.74 In the case of heavy tails, the signed rank test is more powerful. The conclusions of both tests are the same.

10.75 t test: $.001 < p$-value $< .005$
Wilcoxon: $.005 < p$-value $< .01$

10.76 A paired sample experiment eliminates the effect of variability on the two varieties of trees. In selecting plots, choose a wide range.

10.77 a. $t = 5.9126$
b. $t' = 4.4491$
c. $H_0: \mu_1 - \mu_2 = 0$
$H_a: \mu_1 - \mu_2 \neq 0$
T.S.: $t = 5.9126$
R.R.: Reject H_0 if $|t| > 2.66$.
Conclusion: Reject H_0.
p-value $= .0001$
$H_0: \mu_1 - \mu_2 = 0$
$H_a: \mu_1 - \mu_2 \neq 0$
T.S.: $t' = 4.4491$
R.R.: Reject H_0 if $|t'| > 2.831$.
Conclusion: Reject H_0.
p-value $= .0002$
H_a is strongly supported in both tests.

10.78 The t' statistic seems to be more reliable for this experiment. The conclusions are the same.

10.79 a. $T = $ sum of ranks for sample $R = 345$
b. $z = -4.2963$; p-value $= .0000$
c. H_0: the two populations are identical.
H_a: Population 1 is shifted to the right of Population 2.
T.S.: $z = -4.2963$
R.R.: Reject H_0 if $|z| > 2.58$.
Conclusion: Reject H_0.

10.80 a. Avoid biases; conceal labels, etc.
b. Avoid time effects; flip coins, etc.

10.81 a. Paired by panelist.
b. Reject H_0 at $\alpha = .05$.
c. Using 60 d.f., $-0.091 \leq \mu_d \leq 0.789$; retain H_0 at $\alpha = .01$.

10.82 $.01 < p < .05$

10.83 a. Paired data.
b. Retain H_0.
c. Much wider; pairing helped.

10.84 Slightly less conclusive.

10.85 Only slight skew, no outliers.

10.86 a. No; $p = .060 > \alpha$.
b. No! Difference is large and close to significant.

10.87 Right-skewed or outliers.

10.88 a. No; skew.
b. Outliers.

10.89 a. Yes; less sensitive to outliers.
b. Yes; $p = .032$ compared to $p = .060$.

10.90 a. No; $p = .926$.
b. May be differences other than means.

10.91 a. F (as source 2/source 1) = 3.937, $p < .002$
b. Source 2 is clearly more variable, poorer quality.

10.92 a. Very similar.
b. Source 2 more variable.
c. Close to normal.

10.93 a. (Equal Vars.)
b. Yes, at $\alpha = .01$.
c. Yes; $p = .0008$.
d. No; (Unequal Vars.) is similar.

10.94 Yes, $\alpha = .05$.

10.95 a. Nearly normal.
b. No problem.

10.96 a. Yes; $p = .0050$.
b. Similar conclusions.

10.97 a. Code 1: mean 23.95, st.dev. 12.55, n 21. Code 2: mean 27.24, st.dev. 3.54, n 59.
b. Both plots show some right-skewness.
c. Rank sum for skewness, or possibly t' because skew not too bad. Given unbalanced data, don't use pooled-variance t.
d. Using rank sum, p-value = .0079; using t', p-value = .25.

10.98 a. Using rank sum, from -11.00 to 0.00; 0 is right on the edge of the interval. Using t', -11.2 to 4.58; 0 is included.
b. Rank sum is borderline reject/retain at $\alpha = .01$; t' retains hypothesis of 0 difference because 0 is included.

10.99 $F = 12.57$, p-value much less than .001; yes, they differ.

10.100 a. Paired samples.
b. Maybe slight skew, but plot is basically straight.
c. $t = 2.85$, two-tailed p-value = .0064.
d. No overwhelmingly obvious reason to do a one-sided test.

10.101 a. p-value .018, less conclusive than t test.
b. p-value .25, much less conclusive.

10.102 a. p-value .14
b. Matching was very useful in reducing variability.

10.103 a. Both somewhat right-skewed.
b. -11.3 to -0.6 for pooled variance; -11.4 to -0.6 for t'; in both cases, reject null hypothesis of 0.
c. Virtually identical.

10.104 a. p-value .031 for both tests.
b. p-value .024.
c. Rank sum is slightly more conclusive and can be believed.

CHAPTER 11   Section 11.1, pg. 456

11.1 a and b

Number of Arrivals per Minute	Theoretical Proportions π_i	Expected Frequencies $E_i = n\pi_i$
0	.0224	44.8
1	.0850	179
2	.1615	323
3	.2046	409.2
4	.1944	388.8
5	.1477	295.4
6	.0936	187.2
7	.0508	101.6
8	.0241	48.2
9 or more	.0159	31.8

c. $H_0: \pi_i = \pi_{i,0}$
$H_a: H_0$ is not true
T.S.: $\chi^2 = 77.2595$
R.R.: Reject H_0 if $\chi^2 > 21.67$
Conclusion: Reject H_0.

11.2 It appears that in the last four cells, the Poisson model systematically overestimates the number.

11.3 a. The expected frequencies are 7.5, 11.25, and 6.25.
b. $H_0: \pi_i = \pi_{i,0}$
$H_a: H_0$ is not true
T.S.: $\chi^2 = 4.4933$
R.R.: Reject H_0 if $\chi^2 > 5.991$
Conclusion: Retain H_0.

11.4 a. $H_0: \pi_i = \pi_{i,0}$
$H_a: H_0$ is not true
T.S.: $\chi^2 = 44.933$
R.R.: Reject H_0 if $\chi^2 > 5.991$
Conclusion: Reject H_0.

b. The probability of a Type II error is small compared to the previous situation, where it was very likely that H_0 would not be rejected when it is false.

Section 11.2, pg. 462

11.5 a. $\chi^2 = 15.96704$
b. p-value $= .0139$
c. The presence of some relationship is indicated.
d. Yes. Not all the expected cell values are greater than or equal to five.

b. d.f. $= 3$
c. H_0: Age and promotion are independent
H_a: Age and promotion are dependent
T.S.: $\chi^2 = 13.0252$
R.R.: Reject H_0 at $\alpha = .05$ if $\chi^2 > 7.815$.
Conclusion: Reject H_0.

11.6

	Outstanding	Average	Poor
Most desirable	43.75%	52.08%	4.17%
Good	30.30	54.55	15.15
Adequate	16.00	56.00	28.00
Undesirable	17.65	47.06	35.29

The percentage of Poor ratings increases as the desirability of the school decreases.

11.8 $.001 < p$-value $< .005$

11.9 a. Expected numbers under independence

	-39	$40+$	Total
Promoted	38.4	41.6	80
Not promoted	81.6	88.4	170
Total	120	130	250

11.7 a. Expected numbers under independence

	Under 30	30–39	40–49	Over 50	Total
Promoted	16	22.4	25.6	16	80
Not promoted	34	47.6	54.4	34	170
Total	50	70	80	50	250

b. H_0: Age and promotion are independent
H_a: Age and promotion are dependent
T.S.: $\chi^2 = .0118$
R.R.: Reject H_0 at $\alpha = .05$ if $\chi^2 > 3.841$
Conclusion: Retain H_0.
c. In part (a), combining age group had the effect of completely masking a relationship that was present.

Chapter 11 Exercises, pg. 469

11.10 a. The relevant data are the column totals (i.e., 210, 240, and 150, respectively).
b. H_0: The proportions .25, .40, and .35 describe union preference among industrial laborers.
H_a: The proportions are something else.
T.S.: $\chi^2 = 41.1429$
R.S.: Reject H_0 at $\alpha = .01$ if $\chi^2 > 9.21$.
Conclusion: Reject H_0 overwhelmingly.

11.11 p-value $< .001$

11.12 H_0: Union preference is independent of membersip status.
H_a: Membership status and union preference are related.
T.S.: $\chi^2 = 162.795$
R.R.: Reject H_0 at $\alpha = .05$ if $\chi^2 > 5.99$.
Conclusion: Reject H_0.

11.13

	Favor	Indifferent	Opposed
Members	70.0%	21.0%	9.0%
Nonmembers	17.5%	49.5%	33.0%

Far more members than nonmembers are in favor; far more nonmembers than members are opposed.

11.14 $\lambda = .272$, indicating a strong relation; recall that $\lambda > .3$ is rare.

11.15 a. Expected numbers under independence

		Opinion					
		1	2	3	4	5	
	A	42	107	78	34	39	300
Commercial	B	42	107	78	34	39	300
	C	42	107	78	34	39	300
		126	321	234	102	117	900

b. d.f. $= 8$

c. H_0: Opinion distribution is the same for each of three commercials.

  H_a: Opinion distribution and commercial viewed are somehow related.

  T.S.: $\chi^2 = 72.5208$

  R.R.: Reject H_0 at $\alpha = .01$ if $\chi^2 > 20.09$.

  Conclusion: Reject H_0.

11.16 p-value $< .001$

11.17   For predicting opinion given commercial: $\lambda = .0069$.

  For predicting commercial given opinion: $\lambda = .1567$.

  A weak relationship between commercial and opinion exists.

11.18   a. Same probability of an order, for all forms.

  b. No; p shown as .000.

11.19 $\lambda = .0000$, misses predictive value.

11.20   a. Yes; ROW PERCENTS differ. No relation would mean same ROW PERCENTS.

  b. Yes; p shown as .000.

11.21   Knowing SOPHIST reduces error predicting PREFER by 20.13%; moderate predictability.

11.22   a. $18.51 \leq$ PERCENT ≤ 30.27

  b. Systat is more conservative.

11.23   a. 11, 30, 88, and 87, respectively.

  b. $\chi^2 = 86.48$; reject at all reasonable α.

11.24   a. χ^2 is 61.04, p-value very small. Reject H_0 emphatically.

  b. The result is so conclusive that even a poor approximation is usable.

11.25   As frequency increases, opinion of adequacy decreases.

11.26   a. Opinion is mostly lower (favoring HMO) for younger ages, higher (favoring traditional) for older ages.

  b. $\chi^2 = 37.82 > 26.30$; yes, reject.

11.27   a. Yes; $\chi^2 = 62.3$.

  b. Yes; $\chi^2 = 82.4$.

  c. No; neither χ^2 is even close to significant.

CHAPTER 12   Sections 12.1 and 12.2, pg. 484

12.1   a. $\bar{y} = 1118.525$

  b. SS(Between) $= 105,529.85$

  c. SS(Within) $= 38,244.08$

  d. SSB d.f. $= 4$; SSW d.f. $= 35$

12.2   See 12.1 b and c

12.3 $H_0: \mu_1 = \mu_2 = \mu_3 = \mu_4 = \mu_5$

  H_a: Not all μ_i equal $(i = 1, \ldots, 5)$.

  T.S.: $F = 24.145$

  R.R.: At $\alpha = .05$, reject H_0 if $F > 2.64$ (interpolated).

  Conclusion: Reject H_0.

  p-value $< .001$

12.4   The assumption of equal variances for the 5 distributions is the problem here. Equal sample sizes take care of this problem, and the result is very conclusive.

12.5 H_0: The distributions are identical.

  H_a: The distributions differ in location.

  T.S.: $H = 115.9976$

  R.R.: At $\alpha = .05$, reject H_0 if $H > 9.49$.

  Conclusion: Reject H_0.

  $p < .001$

12.6   The conclusions of the F test and the Kruskal-Wallis test agree; therefore, the choice is not crucial.

12.7   a. SS(Between) $= 3478.17505669$; SS(Within) $= 7782.06984127$

  b. $F = 4.92$

  c. $H_0: \mu_1 = \mu_2 = \mu_3 = \mu_4 = \mu_5$

  H_a: Not all means are equal.

  T.S.: $F = 4.92$

  R.R.: At $\alpha = .01$, reject H_0 if $F > 3.78$ (interpolated).

  Conclusion: Reject H_0.

12.8   The assumptions appear reasonable for the data.

12.9   a. $H = 16.10$

  b. H_0: The distributions are identical.

  H_a: The distributions differ in location.

  T.S.: $H = 16.10$

  R.R.: At $\alpha = .05$, reject H_0 if $H > 9.49$.

  Conclusion: Reject H_0.

  c. Choice is not crucial.

12.10 a.

Policy	1	2	3
$\bar{y}$	7.94375	2.76000	7.55000
s	3.48750	2.18795	5.29449
n	16	10	10

Grand mean $= 6.39444$

b. SS(Between) $= 183.851$,
SS(Within) $= 477.808$

c. Between: d.f. $= 2$, MS $= 91.93$; Within:
d.f. $= 33$, MS $= 14.479$

12.11 a. $F = 6.349$
b. Yes; $F > F_{.01} = 5.3$, roughly.
c. $.001 < p < .005$

12.12 a. Right-skewed displays.
b. No; skewed to long times.
c. No; Central Limit Theorem applies.

12.13 a. No evident pattern.
b. Independence.

12.14 a. Yes; $p < .001$.
b. Not at all.
c. Very similar.

12.15 a. Yes; $F > F_{.05} = 2.9$, roughly.
b. Very conclusive.

12.16 Nothing terrible.

12.17 Yes; $H > \chi^2_{.01} = 11.34$.

12.18 $.001 < p < .005$; slightly higher p-value.

12.19 a. No; F is small.
b. None at all.

12.20 a. right-skewed.
b. Normal distribution.

12.21 Still not conclusive.

Section 12.3, pg. 491

12.22 a. Tukey method confidence intervals (95%):

$$-105.81 \le \mu_A - \mu_B \le -10.67$$
$$-2.19 \le \mu_A - \mu_C \le 92.95$$
$$-17.07 \le \mu_A - \mu_D \le 78.07$$
$$-135.94 \le \mu_A - \mu_E \le -40.80$$
$$56.05 \le \mu_B - \mu_C \le 151.19$$
$$41.17 \le \mu_B - \mu_D \le 136.31$$
$$-77.70 \le \mu_B - \mu_E \le 17.44$$
$$-62.45 \le \mu_C - \mu_D \le 32.69$$
$$-181.32 \le \mu_C - \mu_E \le -86.18$$
$$-166.44 \le \mu_D - \mu_E \le -71.30$$

b. The differences are significant at $\alpha = .05$:

$$\mu_A - \mu_B, \mu_B - \mu_D, \mu_A - \mu_E, \mu_C - \mu_E,$$
$$\mu_B - \mu_C, \mu_D - \mu_E$$

12.23 a. 99.5% confidence intervals:

$$-118.2746 \le \mu_A - \mu_B \le 1.7946$$
$$-14.8469 \le \mu_A - \mu_C \le 105.6069$$
$$-25.1842 \le \mu_A - \mu_D \le 86.1842$$
$$-141.4834 \le \mu_A - \mu_E \le -35.2566$$
$$53.6438 \le \mu_B - \mu_C \le 153.5962$$
$$44.3431 \le \mu_B - \mu_D \le 133.1369$$
$$-71.2564 \le \mu_B - \mu_E \le 10.9964$$
$$-59.5365 \le \mu_C - \mu_D \le 29.7765$$

$$-175.1565 \le \mu_C - \mu_E \le -92.3435$$
$$-153.3367 \le \mu_D - \mu_E \le -84.4033$$

b. The overall probability of error will be no
more than $10(.005) = .05$. However, if all
the assumptions for use of the t statistic are
not met, the .005 probabilities of error may
not be accurate.

12.24 Five of the 99.5% confidence intervals calculated using a t statistic are smaller in width than
the 95% confidence intervals calculated using
Tukey's Method.

12.25 According to the 99% CI limits, none of the
pairs of means can be declared significantly
different at $\alpha = .01$.

12.26 a. With $n = 11.43$ and using 30 d.f. for 33 d.f.,
$$1.25 \le \mu_1 - \mu_2 \le 9.12$$
$$-3.54 \le \mu_1 - \mu_3 \le 4.33$$
$$-8.72 \le \mu_2 - \mu_3 \le -0.86$$
b. 1 from 2; 2 from 3

12.27 Using random numbers.

12.28 Using 30 d.f. in table,
$$-8.56 \le \mu_1 - \mu_2 \le 18.36$$
$$0.59 \le \mu_1 - \mu_3 \le 27.46$$
etc.
1 is significantly different from 3 and 4.

Section 12.4, pg. 505

12.29   a. $\bar{y}_{...} = 67$ is the overall average value, equally weighted over regions and products.

b.

Region	Region Effect	Product	Product Effect
1	8	A	−5
2	−8	B	5
3	0	C	0
4	4		
5	−4		

c. On the average, consumers rated Product A five points lower and Product B five points higher than the average rating of all three products over all 5 regions.

12.30   Table of interactions:

Product Region	Product A	B	C
1	−2	0	2
2	1	0	−1
3	0	0	0
4	1	0	−1
5	0	0	0

12.31   The profile plot consists of five lines, each with an elbow. The lines all increase, then decrease, but they are not exactly parallel.

12.32   a. Yes, interaction is present because graph by regions is not parallel.

b. Yes, Product B is the favored product in every region.

12.33   a. $\bar{y}_{...} = 1.4$

b.

Row (Plan)	Row Effect	Column (Areas)	Column Effect
A	.3	1	.2
B	.4	2	0
C	−.7	3	−.2
		4	0

c. SS(Plan) $= 80[(.3)^2 + (.4)^2 + (−.7)^2]$
$= 59.20$

12.34   ANOVA Table:

Source	SS	d.f.	MS	F	p-value	Conclusion
Plan	59.2	2	29.6	24.67	$p < .001$	Reject H_0
Area	4.8	3	1.6	1.33	$p > .25$	Retain H_0
Interaction	2.4	6	.4	.33	$p > .25$	Retain H_0
Error	273.6	228	1.2			
Total	340.0	239				

12.35   b. A profile plot of the data suggests the possibility that some interaction is present.

c. Although the plot indicates some interaction, it is not enough for statistical significance.

12.36   Tukey 95% confidence intervals:
$-.51 \le \mu_1 - \mu_2 \le .31$
$.59 \le \mu_1 - \mu_3 \le 1.41$ significantly different
$.69 \le \mu_2 - \mu_3 \le 1.51$ significantly different

12.37   a. SS(Tank type) = 3259.375;
SS(Location) = 29,976.875

b. $F_{\text{Tank type}} = 13.138$; $F_{\text{Location}} = 51.785$

c. H_0: No significant differences among tank types.

H_a: H_0 is false.
T.S.: $F = 13.138$
R.R.: At $\alpha = .01$, reject H_0 if $F > 4.87$.
Conclusion: Reject H_0.

12.38   p-value ≈ 0

12.39   SS(Location) would become part of SS(Residual).
Conclusion: Do not reject H_0.
Here the differences among tank types are masked when location is not considered as a factor in ANOVA.

12.40   a. Mean yields by tank type:
$\bar{y}_1. = 136.375$; $\bar{y}_2. = 128.625$;
$\bar{y}_3. = 112.125$; $\bar{y}_4. = 114.125$.

b. The following pairs of means are significantly different as determined by the Tukey 99% confidence interval method: μ_1 and μ_3, μ_2 and μ_3, and μ_1 and μ_4.

12.41 a. No; major interaction.
b. Profiles cross, showing interaction.

12.42 a. p-value = .0001
b. Optimal mixture depends on altitude.
c. Not very.

12.43 a. method 1
b. Yes; fresher is always better.
c. Yes; little interaction.

12.44 a. No; $p = 0.608$.
b. Conclusively, it matters.
c. Yes; $p = 0.006$.

12.45 Using 40 error d.f., not 45, and $\alpha = .05$, only 1 vs. 3 is significant.

Section 12.5, pg. 513

12.46 a.
System:	I	II	III	IV
Mean:	189.833	173.833	211.000	164.333

Task:	1	2	3	4	5	6
Mean:	54.00	326.75	195.25	86.75	38.25	407.50

Grand mean = 184.75
b. SS(System = 7505.5,
SS(Tank) = 472,214.5,
SS(Total) = 481,758.5,
SS(Error) = 2038.5
c. $F = 18.41$; p-value < .001

12.47 For treatments (systems) $A_I = 1139$, $A_{II} = 1043$, $A_{III} = 1266$, $A_{IV} = 986$. $T = 4434$. SS(System) = 7505.5; similar calculations yield other SS.

12.48 Systems: All differences are significant except I vs. II and II vs. IV
Tasks: All differences are significant except 1 vs. 5.

12.49 a. Treatments are mixtures, blocks are investigators.
b. To control for possible variation among investigators.

12.50 a. MIXT is significant (p-value = .0001 < .05) but INVEST is not (p-value = .2273 > .05).

b. Mixture 2 has mean 2653.2; by the Tukey method, it is different from each of the others.

12.51 No; F for INVEST isn't significant. If it had been, we would have evidence of variation among the investigators in their average measurements.

12.52 a. $F = 5.51$, $.01 < p$-value < .025
b. $F = 6.91$, $p < .001$; significant at $\alpha = .01$
Clearly, different people assign different average scores.

12.53 a. Tukey: $2.17 \leq \mu_1 - \mu_2 \leq 19.33$, $-.16 \leq \mu_1 - \mu_3 \leq 17.00$, $-10.91 \leq \mu_2 - \mu_3 \leq 6.25$
b. Only 1 vs. 2 is detectable (significant).

12.54 SS(FORM) = $12[(57.667 - 51.278)^2 + (46.917 - 51.278)^2 + (49.250 - 51.278)^2]$ = 767.41

Section 12.6, pg. 522

12.55

a.
Source	F value
INSUQUAL	33.34
LAYOUT	24.72
INSUQUAL * LAYOUT	0.03
FAMTYPE	44.29
INSUQUAL * FAMTYPE	0.01
LAYOUT * FAMTYPE	24.21
INSUQUAL * LAYOUT * FAMTYPE	0.03

b. All the main factors are significant at $\alpha = .01$. The LAYOUT/FAMILY TYPE interaction is the only significant interaction.

12.56 b. The profile plots agree with the conclusion of the corresponding F tests.

12.57 a. The Tukey 95% confidence interval is $-8.12 \leq \mu_1 - \mu_2 \leq -3.88$. This confidence interval agrees with the F test that there is a significant difference in mean electricity usage for the two insulation qualities.

b. No; interaction for the two factors.

c. All *but* the following pairs of means are significant as determined by the Tukey method: μ_3 and μ_6, μ_4 and μ_5, μ_4 and μ_6, and μ_5 and μ_6.

12.58
a. Each pair—for example (B1, C1), (B1, C2), (B2, C1), (B2, C2)—is represented in 4 rows (12 observations).

b. Each row with $O = 1$ is duplicated with $O = 2$.

c. Respectively, columns 4, 2, 1, and 7.

12.59
a. B, C, E, and O

b. $B * O, C * O$

12.60
a. $B = 2, C = 1, E = 2, O = 1$

b. $C = 1, O = 1$

12.61
a. No ERROR d.f., no ERROR MS

b. $B, D * O, B * C * O$

12.62 Better (lower) variance if $B = 1$.

12.63 $B = 1$ for variance; $C = 1, E = 2, O = 1$ for means; don't care about D.

12.64
a. The first 16 rows (and the second 16) in the A, B, C columns are the same as OA_{16}.

b. 1, 1 becomes $D = 1$; 1, 2 is $D = 3$; 31 is $D = 3$; 32 is $D = 4$.

12.65
a. D, G, I, and $I * G$

b. B, F

c. A, C, E, H, $I * B, I * C, G * B$

12.66
a. equal

b. level 4

12.67 2 vs. 4 and 3 vs. 4

12.68
a. The $I = 2, G = 1$ mean is much higher.

b. $I = 2$, and $G = 1$, both on average and in combination.

Chapter 12 Exercises, pg. 532

12.69
a. Design A: $\bar{y}_1 = 492.2, s_1^2 = 12351.29$
Design B: $\bar{y}_2 = 476.5, s_2^2 = 8360.06$
Design C: $\bar{y}_3 = 573.5, s_3^2 = 6258.94$

b., c. SS(Between) = 54,217.2667 and SS(Within) = 242,732.61

12.70 $H_0: \mu_1 = \mu_2 = \mu_3$
$H_a: H_0$ is false.

T.S.: $F = \dfrac{27,108.634}{8990.096} = 3.015$

R.R.: At $\alpha = .05$, reject H_0 if $F > 3.35$.
Conclusion: Do not reject H_0.
$.05 < p\text{-value} < .10$

12.71 H_0: The distributions are identical.
H_a: The distributions differ in location.
T.S.: $H = 6.3277$
R.R.: At $\alpha = .05$, reject H_0 if $H > 5.99$.
Conclusion: Reject H_0.
$.025 < p\text{-value} < .05$

12.72 Because the sample sizes are small, the Central Limit Theorem may not have its effect and the Kruskal-Wallis conclusion may be preferred.

12.73 None of the pairwise confidence intervals indicates significant differences among means.

12.74
a. $F = 23.10$

b. $H_0: \mu_1 = \mu_2 = \mu_3$
H_a: All means are not equal.
T.S.: $F = 23.10$
R.R.: At $\alpha = .01$, reject H_0 if $F > 5.42$.
Conclusion: Reject H_0.

c. $p\text{-value} = .0001$

12.75 H_0: The distributions are identical.
H_a: The distributions have different locations.
T.S.: $H = 18.87$
R.R.: At $\alpha = .01$, reject H_0 if $H > 9.21$.
Conclusion: Reject H_0.

12.76
b. There appear to be slight violations of the ANOVA assumptions.

c. Choice of the more appropriate test is not necessary here.

12.77 The Tukey 99% confidence intervals are

$$-24.77 \le \mu_1 - \mu_2 \le -2.73$$
$$-35.44 \le \mu_1 - \mu_3 \le -13.40$$
$$-21.69 \le \mu_2 - \mu_3 \le 0.35$$

μ_1, and μ_2; μ_1 and μ_3 are significantly different.

12.78 a. The null hypothesis of equality of house prices is totally irrelevant here. The F test concurs; $F = 122.58$ has a p-value of 0.0001.
b. $F = 10.66$
c. The null hypothesis is rejected at all typical α levels; the p-value is .0001.

12.79 The Tukey 95% confidence intervals are

$$0.85 \leq \mu_1 - \mu_2 \leq \; 8.49$$
significantly different

$$-5.65 \leq \mu_1 - \mu_3 \leq \; 1.99$$

$$-6.40 \leq \mu_1 - \mu_4 \leq \; 1.24$$

$$-10.32 \leq \mu_2 - \mu_3 \leq -2.68$$
significantly different

$$-11.07 \leq \mu_2 - \mu_4 \leq -3.43$$
significantly different

$$-4.57 \leq \mu_3 - \mu_4 \leq \; 3.07$$

12.80 a. $F = .34$; retain H_0.
b. The variation in houses completely masks the variation in appraisers that we are attempting to study.

12.81 b. H_0: No interaction between design and depth.
H_a: H_0 is false.
T.S.: $F = .93$
R.R.: At $\alpha = .05$, reject H_0 if $F > 3.89$.
Conclusion: Do not reject H_0.
c. A profile plot of the data indicates no substantial interaction.

12.82 a. H_0: no design effect
H_a: H_0 is false.
T.S.: $F = 6.35$
R.R.: At $\alpha = .05$, reject H_0 if $F > 3.89$.
Conclusion: There are significant effects of design.
p-value = .0131
b. $F = 178.68$; there are significant depth effects.

12.83 $$22.882 \leq \mu_A - \mu_B \leq 159.118$$
significantly different

$$-19.118 \leq \mu_A - \mu_C \leq 117.118$$

$$-110.118 \leq \mu_B - \mu_C \leq \; 26.118$$

12.84 a. $F = .44$; retain H_0.
b. The graphs are not seriously nonparallel, the interaction may not be substantial; it is not statistically significant.

12.85 Summary of F tests; all conclusions are based on $\alpha = .05$.

Null Hypothesis	F statistic	p-value	Conclusion
No three-factor interaction	.44	.6459	Retain H_0
No sweetness-acidity interaction	8.89	.0004	Reject H_0
No sweetness-color interaction	3.70	.0307	Reject H_0
No acidity-color interaction	2.92	.0927	Retain H_0
No sweetness effect	75.51	.0000	Reject H_0
No acidity effect	22.72	.0000	Reject H_0
No color effect	116.46	.0000	Reject H_0

12.86 a. 95% confidence interval:
$3.42 \leq \mu_1 - \mu_2 \leq 8.36$. The difference in average ratings is significant at $\alpha = .05$.
b. All differences that are larger in absolute value) than 10.29 are significant.

12.87 a. SS(Between) = 678.21,
SS(Within) = 902.46
b.

Source	SS	df	MS
Between	678.2	5	135.6
Within	902.5	30	30.1

c. $F = 4.51 > 2.53$; detectable.
$.001 < p < .005$

12.88 1 vs. 2, 1 vs. 5, 4 vs. 5

12.89 To avoid any order-related biases.

12.90 Two factor (bases, coloring agents).

12.91 a. No; F is small.
b. $F_{color} = 1.71 < F_{.10}$
$F_{base} = 10.19 > F_{.001}$

12.92 a. $$-15.61 \leq \mu_1 - \mu_2 \leq -4.55$$
$$-11.20 \leq \mu_1 - \mu_3 \leq -0.14$$
$$-1.12 \leq \mu_2 - \mu_3 \leq \; 9.94$$
b. 1 vs. 2 and 1 vs. 3

12.93 Yes; $p < .05$.

12.94 Yes; $H > 7.815$; same conclusion.

12.95 Design 3 is highest; significantly better than all others.

12.96 a. Yes, the means for typetv = 1 and 2 are larger.
b. Differences between mean for 3 and the other means are significant.

12.97   a. $p = .0000$
b. No, but a very conclusive difference.

12.98   Yes; 3 is in a different group.

12.99   a. Not evident.
b. The first level is a bit more variable.

12.100   The p-value is also very small.

12.101   a. None, for any reasonable α.
b. fabric

12.102   How light was it outside?!

12.103   a. none
b. fabric and liner
c. Yes, properly analyzed.

12.104   "Daynumber" is clearly important.

12.105   b. Modest interaction.

12.106   a. No; SS = 972 is small relative to others or to total.
b. Type, yes; color, no.

12.107   No; residuals fairly close to normally distributed.

12.108   a. No; several severe outliers on the high side; often right-skewed.
b. p-value .085, significant at .10, not at .05

12.109   a. $H = 15.08$, significant at .05, not at .025
b. Kruskal-Wallis is somewhat more conclusive because of the outlier-proneness of the data.

12.110   b. $F = 3.33$, p-value about .02
c. Randomized block study assumes no interaction.

12.111 $W = 0.389$; service 1 is significantly lower than 4, but not quite significantly lower than service 2 and 3.

12.112   b. Yes; MS(Error) = 5.33, not 0.559. Blocking was highly useful in controlling for variability.

12.113   a. No; variability gets much bigger as predicted value increases.
b. $F = 5.09$, $p < .005$
c. Still have a nonconstant variance problem.

Review Exercises, Chapters 10–12, pg. 546

R86   a. $-11.70 \le \mu_{old} - \mu_{new} \le 2.90$
b. Retain H_0; 0.00 is included in the interval.
c. Paired samples (same testers)

R87   a. $2.14 \le \mu_d \le 6.66$
b. Yes; 0.00 is not included.
c. Differences appear nearly normal.

R88   Signed-rank test; discard the 0 difference, so $n = 39$. $T = |T_-| = 151.5 \le 249$. Reject H_0; same conclusion.

R89 $t = 3.95$, p-value $< .002$; signed-rank p-value $< .002$ also.

R90   The paired-sample interval is much narrower; pairing was highly desirable.

R91   a. $F = 4.25 > F_{.01, 3, 60} = 4.13$; reject H_0. We have good evidence that at least one (sub)population mean differs from the others.
b. $.005 < p$-value $< .01$
c. Conclusion is still valid, but a rank test might be more effective.

R92   a. Using the Tukey method,
$-17.06 \le \mu_1 - \mu_2 \le 2.70$,
$-17.63 \le \mu_1 - \mu_3 \le 2.13$,
$-20.25 \le \mu_1 - \mu_4 \le -0.49$,
$-10.45 \le \mu_2 - \mu_3 \le 9.31$,
$-13.07 \le \mu_2 - \mu_4 \le 6.69$, and
$-12.50 \le \mu_3 - \mu_4 \le 7.26$.
b. Only the difference between means 1 and 4 is significant (either at $\alpha = .05$ or at $\alpha = .01$).

R93   a. Yes; $H > \chi^2_{.01, 3 d.f.} = 11.34$.
b. p-value $< .001$
c. The p-value for the Kruskal-Wallis test is (even) more conclusive, presumably because of the outliers in the data.

R94   a. $\chi^2 = 5.675 < 9.488$; not detectable (significant).
b. p-value $> .10$
c. Mildly. The expected values are small; 3 of the 9 are less than 5.

R95   Using degree of control to predict rating, $\lambda = .107$, indicating a modest relation.

R96   No. H_0 is retained, not proved, especially when n is small.

R97   Using $t_{.025, 45 d.f.} = 2.016$ by interpolation, $-115.5 \le \mu_1 - \mu_2 \le -51.5$. Reject H_0 at $\alpha = .05$ because 0 is not included.

R98 The sample sizes and sample variances are unequal (in the dangerous way—the larger n with the smaller s^2). The data are clearly left-skewed.

R99 Using t' with 19 d.f., $-122.8 \leq \mu_1 - \mu_2 \leq -44.2$. Again, reject H_0 at $\alpha = .05$.

R100 $z = -3.70$, $p < 2(.00024) = .00048$

R101 a. $F = 2.61$, $.01 < p\text{-value} < .025$ (assuming $F_{14, 31} \approx F_{14, 30}$). Retain H_0 at $\alpha = .01$.
b. Yes; the data are skewed to the left, and this F test is sensitive to nonnormality.

R102 a.

Program	A	B	C	(Grand Mean)
Mean	38.55	35.00	37.30	36.95

$$SS(\text{Program}) = 20[(38.55 - 36.95)^2$$
$$+ (35 - 36.95)^2$$
$$+ (37.30 - 36.95)^2]$$
$$= 129.7$$
$$SS(\text{Error}) = 9[(5.190)^2 + (3.342)^2$$
$$+ \cdots + (4.971)^2]$$
$$= 1393.55$$

b. $F = 2.51 < F_{.05, 2, 54} \approx 3.2$, not significant

R103 No program means differ by 3.87, so none of them is significant at $\alpha = .05$.

R104 The program means aren't a good indicator.

R105 Yes, the standard deviations for the inexperienced preparers are consistently quite a bit lower.

R106 $\chi^2 = 8.441 < 9.488$; retain H_0. The frequencies are (barely) consistent with the theory.

R107 No; all *expected* frequencies are greater than 5.

R108 $t = t' = 4.027$, $p\text{-value} < .001$

R109 $T_1 = 254.5$, $z = -4.21$, $p\text{-value} < .0001$

R110 The rank test is preferred because of the outlier at 4.7. The conclusion is the same.

R111 $F = 4.598 > F_{.01, 19, 19} \approx 3.03$. Support H_a.

R112 Normality is crucial; the outlier makes the assumptions shaky.

R113 a. $-.256 \leq \pi_1 - \pi_2 \leq .016$
b. Retain H_0: $\pi_1 - \pi_2 = 0$.

R114 Retain H_0; $|z| = |-1.73| < 1.96$.

R115 Trials are not independent.

R116 $\chi^2 = 9.289$ with 3 d.f., $.025 < p\text{-value} < .05$

R117 None obvious; in particular, all $\hat{E}_{ij} > 5$.

R118 a. Paired-sample
$t = 3.777 > t_{.025, 19 \text{ d.f.}} = 2.093$; reject H_0.
b. $p < .002$ (two-tailed); printer A clearly is slower.

R119 Signed-rank test; $T = |T_-| = 24 \leq 26$, so $p\text{-value} < .002$ as for the t test.

R120 s_d is much smaller than $\sqrt{s_A^2 + s_B^2} = 12.17$, indicating that a paired-sample method is much more effective.

R121 a. $SS(\text{Between}) = 12(21.17 - 22.718)^2 + 9(15.44 - 22.718)^2 + 18(27.39 - 22.718)^2 = 898.4$, as shown except for roundoff.
$SS(\text{Within}) = 11(8.26)^2 + 8(7.32)^2 + 17(8.15)^2 = 2308.3$, again as shown except for roundoff.
b. $F = 7.00 > F_{.05, 2, 36} = 3.28$ (by rough interpolation); significant.

R122 Kruskal-Wallis $H = 10.12 > 5.991$, significant at $\alpha = .05$; $.005 < p\text{-value} < .01$.

R123 The F test assumes normality, so the Kruskal-Wallis is more appropriate.

R124 $\chi^2 = 16.61 > 9.488$; reject H_0.

R125 The χ^2 statistic is so far beyond the table value that the conclusion seems safe.

CHAPTER 13 Sections 13.1 and 13.2, pg. 568

13.1 c. The plot of y vs. x' appears more nearly linear.

13.2 a. $\hat{y} = 14.29167 + 1.47500x$
b. $s_\epsilon = 1.35$

13.3 a. $\hat{y} = 14.876 + 10.522x'$
b. $s_\epsilon = 1.13$

13.4 The residual standard deviation in Exercise 13.3 is smaller. Concurs with Exercise 13.1.

13.5 a. A plot of the data indicates that a linear equation is plausible.
b. $\hat{y} = 1.76685 + .001110x$
c. $s_\epsilon = .558$

13.6 Nothing blatant.

13.7 a. Downward curving relation
b. $X = 100$, $Y = 3.2$ is a low-influence outlier.

13.8 a. intercept $= 6.030$, slope $= -0.01700$
b. Lifetime decreases as speed increases.
c. $s_\epsilon = 0.632368$; about 68% of Y values should be within ± 0.63 of predicted.

13.9 a. 5.01, 4.67, 4.33, 3.99, 3.65
b. Larger for $x = 80$, 100, 120; smaller for $x = 60$, 140. Curved relation.

13.10 a. Linear, increasing.
b. $x = 65.0$, $Y = 110.0$ is a high-influence outlier.

13.11 a. Predicted $Y = 47.15048348 + 1.80264021x$
b. Two purchasers differing in income by 1.0 will differ in sale price by 1.80. Intercept isn't meaningful.
c. $s = 14.45$

13.12 Predicted $Y = 24.35754491 + 2.46196748x$; slope increased substantially when outlier was deleted.

Section 13.3, pg. 574

13.13 a. $.00934 \leq \beta \leq .01266$
b. The number of independent businesses (x) in sample zip-code areas has no effect in predicting the number of bank branches in these areas.
c. $H_a: \beta_1 > 0$
d. $H_0: \beta_1 = 0$
$H_a: \beta_1 > 0$
T.S.: $t = 13.14$
R.R.: At $\alpha = .05$, reject H_0 if $t > 1.812$.
Conclusion: Reject H_0.

13.14 p-value $< .001$

13.15 $.390 \leq \sigma_\epsilon \leq .979$

13.16 a. Linear equation relating y to x seems

plausible. There is one very extreme point (runsize $= 20.0$, total cost $= 1146$).
b. $\hat{y} = 99.77704 + 51.91785x$;
$s_\epsilon = 12.2068$
c. $50.717 \leq \beta_1 \leq 53.118$; the slope, β_1, could be interpreted as the variable cost per sticker, while the intercept, β_0, could be interpreted as the fixed cost.

13.17 a. $t = 88.527$
b. p-value $= 0.0000$ (two-tailed)

13.18 a. $F = 7836.946$; p-value $= 0.0000$
b. The conclusions of the F test and the t test are identical.

13.19 $10.05 \leq \sigma_\epsilon \leq 15.70$

Section 13.4, pg. 580

13.20 a. $E(Y_{n+1}) = \hat{y}_{n+1} = 203.6$
b. $198.9 \leq E(Y_{n+1}) \leq 208.3$

13.21 Because $x_{x+1} = 2.0$ is close to $\bar{x} = 2.967$, we would not expect major extrapolation.

13.22 a. $\hat{y}_{n+1} = 203.6$ $178.2 \leq Y_{n+1} \leq 229.0$
b. Yes; $250 does not fall in the 95% prediction interval.

13.23 a. $\hat{y}_{n+1} = 15.837$; $14.055 \leq Y_{n+1} \leq 17.619$
b. The prediction is a considerable extrapolation from the data.

13.24 a. $\hat{y}_{n+1} = 43.79$
b. $\hat{y}_{n+1} = 28.57$
c. The s_ϵ of predicting y with x' is 1.13; this is smaller than the s_ϵ of predicting y with x, which is 1.36. Therefore, it seems that prediction with x' is more reasonable.

13.25 $25.383 \leq Y_{n+1} \leq 31.751$

Sections 13.5 and 13.6, pg. 589

13.26 $r_{yx} = .972$

13.27 a. $H_0: \rho_{yx} = 0$
$H_a: \rho_{yx} > 0$
T.S.: $t = 13.14$
R.R.: At $\alpha = .05$, reject H_0 if $t > 1.812$.
Conclusion: Reject H_0.
b. The t's are equal except for rounding.

13.28 a. $r_{yx}^2 = .9964$
b. Because $\hat{\beta}_1$ is positive, it follows that r_{yx} is positive.

13.29 With a smaller x (RUNSIZE) range, the correlation would probably be lower.

13.30 a. $r_{yx} = .9561$
b. $r_s = .9879$
c. A plot of the data indicates a nonlinear increasing relation between y and x.

13.31 a. Perhaps some noticeable trend.
b. Case 11 (SALARY $= 37.9$, EXPER $= 14.0$)

13.32 Definitely increasing with one outlier.

13.33 a. Predicted $Y = 40.507 + 1.470X$
1.470 is predicted SALARY difference for one year's EXPER difference. 40.507 is predicted SALARY with no EXPER; it is not absurd and is (barely) within the data.
b. $s_\epsilon = 5.40$; about 68% of prediction errors are within ± 5.40 (thousand dollars).
c. Yes; p-value of t (or F) $= 0.000$.
d. $r^2 = .494$

13.34 a. Should and did increase slope.
b. Decreased by almost 25%.
c. Increased from .703 to .842.

Chapter 13 Exercises, pg. 594

13.35 b. $\hat{y} = 2.025 + 2.350x$
c. $\hat{y} = 51.37$

13.36 a. $s_\epsilon = 1.958$
b. $-3.916 < (y - \hat{y}) < 3.916$; all of the residuals for these data lie within this interval.

13.37 b. $\hat{y} = 5.859 + .015x$
c. $H_0: \beta_1 = 0$
$H_a: \beta_1 > 0$
T.S.: $t = 5.812$
R.R.: At $\alpha = .05$, reject H_0 if $t > 2.015$.
Conclusion: Reject H_0.
p-value $< .001$

13.38 b. $\hat{y} = 1.008 + 5.312x'$
c. $H_0: \beta_1 = 0$
$H_a: \beta_1 > 0$
T.S.: $t = 7.019$
R.R.: At $\alpha = .05$, reject H_0 if $t > 2.015$.
Conclusion: Reject H_0.
p-value $< .001$

13.39 The regression line in Exercise 13.38 appears to be the better fit.

13.40 a. $1.988 \le \beta_1 \le 2.712$
b. $1.494 \le \sigma_\epsilon^2 \le 23.063$

13.41 a. $\hat{y} = 2.3548 + 42.3246\sqrt{x}$
b. $t = 15.1 \qquad p \ll .002$

13.42 $.377 \le Y_{n+1} \le 13.635$ (may contain roundoff error)

13.43 a. $\hat{y} = 149.056 + 50.118x$
b. $r_{yx}^2 = .8231$

13.44 a. SS(Residual) $= 875,124$; $s_\epsilon = 94.525$
b. $45.45 < \beta_1 < 54.79$
c. There is no point in testing $H_0: \beta_1 = 0$. Obviously, longer flights take more fuel; $\beta_1 > 0$.

13.45 a. $629.233 \le E(Y_{n+1}) \le 671.239$
b. $460.962 \le Y_{n+1} \le 839.510$; $Y_{n+1} = 570$ is contained in this interval.

13.46 β_1 is the fuel used for each hundred miles of air mileage. β_0 might be interpreted as the fuel needed to take off.

13.47 a. $r_{yx} = .864$
b. $t = 5.417$, p-value $< .001$

13.48 a. 1. The advertising expense accounts for $r_{yx}^2 = .746$ of the variability of sales.
2. From Exercise 13.47b the correlation between advertising expense and sales is statistically significant.
b. Marketing strategy, competition, etc. These factors are represented in the regression model via the random error term.

c. The data have been collected over time, and therefore represent a time series.

13.49 $69.22 \le Y_{n+1} \le 137.93$

13.50 b. $y = 556.13 - 26.13x$
$H_0: \beta_1 = 0$
$H_a: \beta_1 \neq 0$
T.S.: $t = -2.823$
R.R.: At $\alpha = .05$, reject H_0 if $|t| > 2.228$.
Conclusion: Reject H_0.
c. $210.87 \le Y_{n+1} \le 326.51$

13.51 a. $r_s = -.678$
b. $t = -2.917$
Conclusion: Reject H_0.
c. From part (b), we have significant evidence to conclude that the number of housing starts decreases with interest rates.

13.52 SS(Total) $= S_{yy} = 2508.62$, of which 2356.13, or 93.9%, is accounted for by SS(Between).

13.53 a. $\hat{y} = 68 + 5.75x_2$
b. $H_0: \beta_2 = 0$
$H_a: \beta_2 \neq 0$
T.S.: $t = .897$
R.R.: At $\alpha = .05$, reject H_0 if $|t| > 2.228$.
Conclusion: Do not reject H_0.
p-value: $.20 < p\text{-value} < .50$

13.54 a. $\hat{y} = 55.73 + 2.311x$
b. $s_\epsilon = 4.4445$

13.55 When $x_{n+1} = 21$, $\hat{y}_{n+1} = 104.268$; when $x_{n+1} = 40$, $\hat{y}_{n+1} = 148.183$. The $\pm$ term when $x_{n+1} = 21$ is 10.296; the $\pm$ term when $x_{n+1} = 40$ is 14.341. The plus-or-minus increases as one forecasts farther into the future.

13.56 $1.949 \le \beta_1 \le 2.673$; the value of β_1 is the monthly growth rate in sales.

13.57 a. $\hat{y} = 9.771 + .0501$ MILEAGE; $s_\epsilon = 2.202$
b. $.0486 \le \beta_1 \le .0516$

13.58 A linear equation relating y to x seems plausible. It appears that the variability of y increases with x.

13.59 $22.32 \le y_{n+1} \le 31.30$; the extrapolation problem is not extremely serious.

13.60 a. negative
b. No; slight positive slope.

13.61 Yes; high-influence outlier.

13.62 a. Very large outlier with high influence.
b. Yes; negative slope.

13.63 From possibly positive to clearly negative.

13.64 From positive to negative.

13.65 a. From small positive to clearly negative.
b. High influence of the one outlier town.

13.66 a. Yes; strong linear relation.
b. Observation 27 (size = 2.00, price = 19.10); not high leverage.
c. Predicted price = 51.08 + 59.15 size
d. Predicted price = 53.99 + 59.04 size; little change in slope, by low leverage.
e. 29.14 vs. 20.96; outlier inflates standard deviation badly.

13.67 a. Predicted price of a 0 square foot house is $53,990; no house has that size!
b. That price didn't change at all as the house got bigger; rejected with p-value less than .001.
c. $49.35 \le \beta_1 \le 68.73$, using 40 d.f.

13.68 a. $297.98 \le$ price ≤ 400.39; gross extrapolation.
b. Variability seems to increase with size.
c. Interval isn't wide enough.

13.69 a. Correlation $= -0.771$; lower sales at higher densities.
b. sales $= 141.5 - 12.89$ density. Predicted sales with no houses per acre(!) $= 141.5$; predicted sales decrease by 12.89 per unit increase in density.
c. Standard deviation $= 21.74$; prediction $\pm$ (95% confidence) is about 43.5.

13.70 a. $t = -6.63$; strongly conclusive.
b. $-16.87 \le \beta_1 \le -8.92$

13.71 No; definitely curved.

13.72 a. Measure of lot size; e.g., 0.50 acres per house in that ZIP code area.
b. Much closer to straight line.
c. Correlation $= 0.952$; much stronger because closer to straight line fit.

13.73 a. Predicted durability $= 47.02 + 0.308$ concentration; if concentration is one unit higher, durability is predicted to be 0.308 units higher.
b. $r^2 = .116$; little predictive value.

13.74 Yes, barely; p-value $= .008$.

13.75 a. *Not* a straight line in plot.
b. Underestimates the predictability.

CHAPTER 14   Sections 14.1 and 14.2, pg. 618

14.1   a. $\hat{y} = 326.39 + 136.10\text{PROMO}$
$- 61.18\text{DEVEL} - 43.70\text{RESEARCH}$
b. $s_\epsilon = 25.63$
c. $\text{SS(Residual)} = 13{,}136.23$

14.2 $\hat{\beta}_1$ is the expected change in y(sales), per unit change in x (promotion expenses), provided that all other x's (direct development expenditures and research effort) stay constant.

14.3   b. The plot of x vs. w indicates zero correlation.
c. $\hat{y} = 14.5 + 7x$
d. $s_\epsilon = 3.782$
e. $r^2_{yx} = .733$

14.4   a. $\hat{y} = 10 + 5x + 2w + 1v$; $s_\epsilon = 2.646$
b. $R^2_{y \cdot xwv} = .895 > .733$ and $2.646 < 3.782$

14.5   a. $y = 50.0195 + 6.64357143 \text{ CAT1}$
$+ 7.3145 \text{ CAT2} - 1.23142857 \text{ CAT1SQ}$
$- .7724 \text{ CAT1CAT2} - 1.1755 \text{ CAT2SQ}$
b. $\text{SS(Residual)} = 71.48900671$;
$s_\epsilon = 2.25972512$

14.6 $r^2_{y \cdot x_1 x_2 x_3 x_4 x_5} = .862$

Section 14.3, pg. 624

14.7   a. $F = 22.28$
b. $H_0: \beta_1 = \beta_2 = \beta_3 = 0$
H_a: At least one $\beta_j \neq 0$
T.S.: $F = 22.28$
R.R.: At $\alpha = .01$, reject H_0 if $F > 4.94$.
Conclusion: Reject H_0.
c. $t = 4.84$
d. $H_0: \beta_1 = 0$
$H_a: \beta_1 \neq 0$
T.S.: $t = 4.84$
R.R.: At $\alpha = .05$, reject H_0 if $|t| > 2.086$.
Conclusion: Reject H_0.
e. Promotion has additional predictive value.

14.8 p-value $= .0001$, a two-tailed value.

14.9   DEVEL and RESEARCH each may have no additional predictive value in predicting y, as the "last predictor in." PROMO has additional predictive value in predicting y.

14.10   a. $\text{MS(Regression)} = 159.67$;
$\text{MS(Residual)} = 7.00$
b. $F = 22.81$
c. p-value $< .001$
d. $H_0: \beta_2 = \beta_3 = \beta_4 = 0$

14.11   a. $\hat{y} = 7.204 + 1.363\text{METAL} + .306\text{TEMP}$
$+ .0102\text{WATTS} - .00278\text{MET}$
$\times \text{TEMP}$
b. Only WATTS has some proven additional predictive value.

Section 14.4, pg. 630

14.12   a. $R^2 = .769693$
b. $F = 22.28$
c. The F value on the output is the same as the value in part (b).

14.13   a. $R^2 = .352298$
b. $F = 18.12$
c. $H_0: \beta_2 = \beta_3 = 0$
d. $H_0: \beta_2 = \beta_3 = 0$
$H_a: H_0$ is not true.
T.S.: $F = 18.12$
R.R.: At $\alpha = .01$, reject H_0 if $F > 5.85$.
Conclusion: Reject H_0.

14.14   a. $R^2 = .7444$
b. $R^2 = .7567$

c. $\beta_3 = \beta_4 = 0$; that is, BUSIN and COMPET have no predictive value once INCOME is included as predictor.
d. $H_0: \beta_3 = \beta_4 = 0$ T.S.: $F = .430$
$H_a: H_0$ is not true.
T.S.: $F = .430$
R.R.: At $\alpha = .05$, reject H_0 if $F > 6.11$.
Conclusion: Retain H_0.

14.15   a. $\hat{y} = 50.0195 + 6.64357143\text{CAT1}$
$+ 7.3145\text{CAT2} - 1.23142857\text{CAT1SQ}$
$- .7724\text{CAT1CAT2} - 1.1755\text{CAT2SQ}$
b. $\hat{y} = 70.31 - 2.676\text{CAT1} - .8802\text{CAT2}$
c. Complete model $R^2 = .862437$;
reduced model $R^2 = .588452$

d. $H_0: \beta_3 = \beta_4 = \beta_5 = 0$
   $H_a: H_0$ is not true.
   T.S.: $F = 9.29$
   R.R.: At $\alpha = .05$, reject H_0 if $F > 3.34$.

Conclusion: Reject H_0; yes, the addition of the second-order terms has improved the predictive value of the model.

Section 14.5, pg. 633

14.16 a. For observation 21,
   $54.7081 \le Y_{n+1} \le 65.1438$.
   For observation 22,
   $57.0829 \le Y_{n+1} \le 67.6528$.
   b. For observation 21,
   $50.0281 \le Y_{n+1} \le 65.6985$.

For observation 22,
   $51.0525 \le Y_{n+1} \le 66.4345$.
c. Yes, the confidence limits for the model of part (a) are tighter.

Section 14.6, pg. 640

14.17 c. $\hat{\beta} = \begin{bmatrix} 50.733 \\ 1.667 \\ 1.060 \end{bmatrix}$

14.18 a. $\mathbf{Y'Y} = 39,341$
   b. SS(Residual) $= 118.7$
   c. $s_\epsilon = 3.145$

14.19 a. $F = 31.048$
   b. $H_0: \beta_1 = \beta_2 = 0$
   $H_a: H_0$ is not true.
   T.S.: $F = 31.048$
   R.R.: At $\alpha = .01$, reject H_0 if $F > 6.93$.
   Conclusion: Reject H_0.

14.20 $H_0: \beta_1 = 0$
   $H_a: \beta_1 \ne 0$
   T.S.: $t = 5.926$
   R.R.: At $\alpha = .05$, reject H_0 if $|t| > 2.178$.
   Conclusion: Reject H_0.

   $H_0: \beta_2 = 0$
   $H_a: \beta_2 \ne 0$
   T.S.: $t = 5.329$
   R.R.: At $\alpha = .05$, reject H_0 if $|t| > 2.178$.
   Conclusion: Reject H_0.

14.21 b. $\hat{\beta} = \begin{bmatrix} 20.00000 \\ 1.20833 \\ .66667 \end{bmatrix}$
   c. $s_\epsilon = 3.321$

14.22 a. $s_{\hat{\beta}_1} = 2.8493$; $s_{\hat{\beta}_2} = 1.7503$
   b. $-3.84 \le \beta_1 \le 6.25$; $-2.45 \le \beta_2 \le 3.77$
   c. $H_0: \beta_1 = 0$
   $H_a: \beta_1 > 0$
   T.S.: $t = .424$
   R.R.: At $\alpha = .05$, reject H_0 if $t > 1.771$.
   Conclusion: Retain H_0.

14.23 a. SS(Residual) $= 143.375$; SS(Regression) $= 208.625$; SS(Total) $= 352$
   b. $R^2_{y \cdot x_2 x_2} = .593$
   c. $H_0: \beta_1 = \beta_2 = 0$
   $H_a: H_0$ is not true.
   T.S.: $F = 9.46$
   R.R.: At $\alpha = .01$, reject H_0 if $F > 6.70$.
   Conclusion: Reject H_0.

14.24 a. $\hat{y}_{n+1} = 24.417$
   b. $18.045 \le Y_{n+1} \le 30.788$
   c. $\hat{y}_{n+1} = 20.417$
   d. $0.179 \le Y_{n+1} \le 40.655$

Chapter 14 Exercises, pg. 643

14.25 a. $\hat{y} = -1.31949 + 5.54983 \text{ EDUC} + .88514 \text{ INCOME} + 1.92483 \text{ POP} - 11.38928 \text{ FAMSIZE}$
   $\quad\quad\quad\quad\quad$ (2.70228) $\quad\quad$ (1.30846) $\quad\quad\quad$ (1.37081) $\quad\quad\quad$ (6.66931)
   b. $R^2 = .9625$, $s_\epsilon = 2.6863$

14.26 Collectively, the independent variables have at least some value. There is little evidence as to which predictors have "last in" value.

14.27 a. $R^2 = .9423$
b. $F = 1.885 < 4.74$; retain H_0.

14.28 a. $\hat{y} = -16.81979712 + 1.47018752x1 + .99477822x2 - .02400705x1x2 - .01031004x2SQ + .00024957x1x2SQ$; $s_\epsilon = 3.39011256$
b. The variable x_3 represents the interaction effect.
c. $H_0: \beta_3 = 0$
$H_a: \beta_3 \neq 0$
T.S.: $t = -1.01$
R.R.: At $\alpha = .05$, reject H_0 if $|t| > 2.087$.
Conclusion: Retain H_0.

14.29 a. $\hat{y} = -16.81979712 + 1.47018752x1 + .99477822x2 - .02400705x1x2 - .01031004x2SQ + .00024957x1x2SQ$
(Complete Model);
$\hat{y} = .84008527 + 1.01583472x1 + .05582624x2$ (Reduced Model)
b. $H_0: \beta_3 = \beta_4 = \beta_5 = 0$
T.S.: $F = .867$
Conclusion: Retain H_0.
p-value $> .25$

14.30 a. $\hat{y} = .87272 + 2.54794SIZE +$
(1.20083)
$+ .22028PARKING$
$(.15539)$
$+ .58932INCOME$
$(.17806)$
b. The intercept, .873, is predicted SALES with 0 floor space, 0 parking, and 0 income—a less-than-promising parlay. The coefficient of SIZE is the predicted increase in SALES from an additional 1000 square feet of floor space holding PARKING and INCOME constant. Similar interpretations hold for the other coefficients.
c. $R^2 = .7912$, $s_\epsilon = .7724$

14.31 $F = 15.158$ indicates that there's predictive value there somewhere. The t tests show that INCOME definitely has incremental predictive value and that SIZE may have incremental value. There is no evidence that PARKING adds anything.

14.32 a. $\hat{y} = 102.7083 - .83333PROTEIN - 1.375SUPPLEM - 4.0ANTIBIO$

b. $s_\epsilon = 1.7096$
c. $R^2 = .9007$

14.33 a. $\hat{y}_{n+1} = 77.333$
b. No extrapolation.
c. $76.469 \leq E(Y_{n+1}) \leq 78.197$

14.34 a. $\hat{y} = 89.83334 - .83333PROTEIN$
b. $R^2 = .5057$
c. $H_0: \beta_{ANTIBIO} = \beta_{SUPPLEM} = 0$
$H_a: H_0$ is not true.
T.S.: $F = 27.84$
R.R.: At $\alpha = .05$, reject H_0 if $F > 3.74$.
Conclusion: Reject H_0.

14.35 a. $\hat{y} = 18.678 + .5420SENIOR + 1.2074SEX + 8.7779RANKD1 + 4.4211RANKKD2 + 2.7165RANKD3 + .9225DOCT$
b. Given RANK, SENIOR, and DOCT, a male professor is predicted to have a salary 1.2074 thousand dollars higher than a comparable woman professor.
c. A full professor (of specified seniority, sex, and doctorate holding) is predicted to have a salary 8.7779 thousand dollars higher than a similar lecturer/instructor.

14.36 a. $t = 1.134 < 1.714$; retain H_0.
b. Not proved; may be true, may be false.

14.37 a. $F = 64.646$
b. That none of the (obviously relevant) variables predicts salaries.
c. Yes; the p-value $= .0001$. A silly H_0 is rejected.

14.38 a. $R^2 = .9403$
b. $F < 1$; no evidence of incremental predictive value.

14.39 a. Predicted salary $= 25.54 + 0.00389$ numempl $+ 0.0957$ profit $+ 0.216$ IPcost; two companies differing by one employee, having the same profit and IPcost, are predicted to differ by 0.00389 on salary. Similar interpretations hold for other slopes.
b. Yes; $F = 13.10$, $p < .001$.
c. All of them.

14.40 a. $R^2 = 0.384$
b. $r^2 = 0.0358$
c. $F = 17.8$ with 2, 65 d.f.; reject H_0 and conclude that the other predictors do add value.

14.41 Only large correlation is 0.531 (profit, IPcost); collinearity isn't too serious here.

14.42 a. No; largest correlation among X's is only 0.342.

b. At extreme right of plot against number of employees and well off apparent line (or curve).

c. Predicted overhead = 78.35 + 0.00264 employees + 1.576 size − 0.245 personnel

d. Predicted overhead = 75.05 + 0.00516 employees + 1.363 size − 0.205 personnel; slope of "employees" almost doubles.

14.43 a. $F = 16.35$; reject H_0 that none of the variables have any predictive value.

b. $t = 4.63, 2.05, -2.62$, respectively. All three variables seem to add at least some predictive value.

14.44 $58.18 \leq$ overhead ≤ 81.35; 88.90 appears to be high.

14.45 a. All positive.

b. Predicted sales = $-10.09 + 0.449$ titles + 0.308 footage + 0.0696 IBM − 0.0126 Apple. Apple coefficient is (slightly) negative.

c. $-0.063 \leq \beta_{\text{titles}} \leq 0.961$, interpolating in table; 0 is included.

14.46 a. Yes, indeed! $F = 116.7$.

b. None of them.

14.47 Horrendous collinearity; all correlations exceed 0.9.

14.48 $R^2 = .9085$ for all variables; $r^2 = .9007$ for titles alone. $F = 1.336$ with 3, 47 d.f.; cannot reject H_0.

CHAPTER 15   Sections 15.1–15.3, pg. 659

15.1 a. $r_{y_t x_t} = .635$

b. $r_{y_t x_{t-1}} = .974$

c. The "lag one" correlation is stronger. There is a delay.

15.2 a. $y_t = 2.82 + 1.73 x_{t-1}$

b. $s_e = .2157$

c. $13.91 \leq y_{13} \leq 14.93$

15.3 With only two points, the correlation is either 1 or -1.

15.4 a. The dummy variables are DIV2 and DIV3. If both DIV2 = 0 and DIV3 = 0, it follows by elimination that division = 1.

b. β_2 is the difference in expected ACTUAL sales between division 1 and division 2 for a fixed forecast. Similarly, β_3 is the difference in expected ACTUAL sales between division 1 and division 3 for a fixed forecast.

c. $H_0: \beta(\text{DIV2}) = 0$ T.S.: $t = -5.67$
Conclusion: Reject H_0 because p-value = .0001.

$H_0: \beta(\text{DIV3}) = 0$ T.S.: $t = 1.25$
Conclusion: Retain H_0 because p-value = .2205.

15.5 We would have to run a simple regression model (using FORECAST as the only predictor variable).

15.6 a. $H_0: \beta_1 = \beta_2 = \beta_3 = 0$, which says that none of the variables in the multiple regression has any predictive value at all.

b. $F = 109.47$; at $\alpha = .01$, $F_{.01} = 4.60$, therefore reject H_0; p-value = .0001

15.7 a. $\hat{y} = \text{FORECAST}$; the coefficient would be 1.000.

b. $1.184 \leq \beta_1 \leq 1.524$; the confidence interval doesn't include the value 1.

Section 15.4, pg. 668

15.8 a. Pre-tax and post-tax income are highly correlated. Number of employees and gross sales are not necessarily highly correlated.

b. Collinearity; it's likely that profitability in total dollars would be strongly correlated with size of firm. Some sort of ratio to size is needed.

15.9 a. Defining the "industry-type" variable as indicated would not be a good idea because a one-unit increase in INDUSTRY could mean either a change from the chemicals industry to the data-processing industry or a change from the data-processing industry to the electronics industry.

b. Define three dummy variables.

c. Dummy variable: 1 if matches, 0 if not.

15.10 a. A regression analysis based on CONTRIB, INCOME, and MATCHING would be bedeviled by collinearity and nonconstant variance. It's likely that INCOME and SIZE are highly correlated.

b. CONTRIB/INCOME represents the proportion of pre-tax income contributed by the corporation.

15.11 Modify the regression model by introducing cross-product terms, involving SIZE and industry dummies.

15.12 a. $(EDLEVEL)^2$ incorporated into the model.

b. Residuals from a first-order regression model

vs. EDLEVEL would show a parabolic pattern.

15.13 a. No collinearity present in the data.

b. Zero correlation between MELT and CHILL as well as MELT and REPEL.

15.14 There is no obvious evidence of nonlinearity.

15.15 a. The difference in R^2 values is $.913828 - .903581 = .010247$

b. $H_0: \beta_{\text{MELTSQ}} = \beta_{\text{CHILLSQ}} = 0$
T.S.: $F = 1.427$
R.R.: At $\alpha = .05$, reject H_0 if $F > 3.40$.
Conclusion: Retain H_0.

c. Neither MELTSQ or KNIFESQ is a statistically significant predictor as "last predictor in."

Section 15.5, pg. 677

15.16 a. REPEL, KNIFE, CHILL, MELT, SPEED (not entered)

b. REPEL, KNIFE, CHILL, MELT, SPEED

c. The ordering of the variables is the same.

15.17 $H_0: \beta_4 = \beta_5 = 0$
T.S.: $F = 3.11$
R.R.: At $\alpha = .05$, reject H_0 if $F > 3.35$.
Conclusion: Retain H_0, in a close call.

15.18 a. $H_0: \beta_1 = \cdots = \beta_7 = 0$
T.S.: $F = 1.019$
Conclusion: The p-value $> .25$, retain H_0.

b. None of them.

15.19 a. The increment to R^2 is $.192 - .060 = .132$

b. $H_0: \beta_1 = \beta_2 = \beta_5 = 0$
T.S.: $F = 1.805$
R.R.: At $\alpha = .05$, reject H_0 if $F > 2.92$.
Conclusion: Retain H_0.

c. Neither is good.

Sections 15.6 and 15.7, pg. 696

15.20 a. There doesn't seem to be any nonlinearity.

b. There doesn't seem to be a nonconstant variance problem.

15.21 a. $\hat{y} = 5759.7 + 230.79(\text{MILAGE})$
$- 8.4934(\text{GASPRI})$
$- 14.538(\text{PREGAS})$
$- 251.70(\text{INTRAT})$
$- 56.437(\text{CARPRI})$

b. 47.543

15.22 a. A (positive) autocorrelation problem;
$d = .7999$.

b. There is a rather strong pattern in the sequence plot of residuals.

15.23 a. $\hat{y} = -.66169 - 89.662\text{CPRIMI}$
$- 221.95\text{CLAGPR}$
$- 109.50\text{CINTRA}$
$+ 5.8950\text{CCARPR}$

b. $s_\epsilon = 37.339$

c. Not this time.

Section 15.8, pg. 701

15.24 a. No; average error is -2.0016, and standard deviation of errors is 58.224.

b. It is 58.224, as compared to 37.339.

15.25 a. In the full model, a negative bias. There isn't a similar pattern for the simpler model.

b. In the simpler model, the standard deviation is actually smaller, at .0079447.

c. No; both bias and standard deviation results indicate that the model should be kept.

Chapter 15 Exercises, pg. 703

15.26 a. Nonconstant variance.

b. We might well expect the problem of nonconstant variance to disappear.

15.27 a. The X correlations are 0.

b. We would not expect to find a problem of autocorrelation.

c. "Heteroscedascity" is a possibility. A plot of residuals vs. predicted would be useful.

15.28 a. Nonconstant variance; outliers.

b. No evidence of the problem of nonconstant variance exists. The point in the upper left corner is an outlier.

15.29 a. Number of installations in previous months and number of installations in four preceding months.

b. No severe interaction could be expected.

c. Possible need for nonlinear terms in the model.

15.30 a. Two possible outliers.

b. Autocorrelation problem.

15.31 There may be a slight nonconstant variance problem.

15.32 a. BCURRSQ, ACURRSQ, BPREV, APREV, BPREC4, BCURR, ACURR, APREC4—a rather strange sequence!

b. Increment to $R^2 = $
.0228 + .0095 + .0030 + .0030 = .0383

15.33 a. Yes; there is a cyclic pattern in the plot of residuals and time.

b. Yes; in Figure 15.21(a), "the plot thickens."

15.34 The sequence is very different.

15.35 a. No; there's no cyclic pattern.

b. Not really; the plot in Figure 15.22(a) shows no pattern.

15.36 a. $\hat{y} = .520634 + 1.334738$DACURR
$+ 1.063336$DAPREV

$+ 2.025487$DBCURR
$+ .396343$DBPREV
$- .020037$DBCURRSQ
$+ .119333$DAPREC4
$+ .009662$DACURRSQ
$+ .058331$DBPREC4

b. Yes; $F = 40.08$ with p-value .0000.

c. DACURR, DAPREV, DBCURR, DBPREV

d. $R^2 = .941$; variation in all eight predictors accounts for 94.1% of the variation in Y.

e. $s_\epsilon = 3.356$

15.37 a. Residuals -3.78, -2.03, 2.01, 4.94, 1.71, -1.78; $s = 3.25$

b. It's essentially the same.

c. Yes; ± 2 standard deviations is less than 7 units.

15.38 a. The SPECIALS variable is a dummy or indicator variable. SPECIALS should not be coded as 0, 1, and 2.

b. β_8 is the difference in expected time between "no special packing" and "special packing at A" orders for a fixed NUMFREQ, NUMMOD, NUMRARE, NUMLOOSE, AVSZCAR, AVSZLB, and SKIDS. Similarly, β_9 is the difference in expected time for "no special packing" and "special packing at B" orders for a fixed NUMFREQ, NUMMOD, NUMRARE, NUMLOOSE, AVSZCAR, AVZZLB, and SKIDS.

c. The supervisor expected travel time not to be directly proportional to the number of items.

d. Interaction terms might be useful because the supervisor expected assembly-station time to depend on NUM and AVSZ.

15.39 a. There is one very obvious outlier.

b. Nonconstant variance does not appear to be a problem.

c. We would not expect to find autocorrelation.

15.40 Square roots is the more effective transformation.

15.41
a. Increased $R^2 = .0124$
b. $H_0: \beta_4 = \beta_5 = 0$
T.S.: $F = 20.39$
R.R.: At $\alpha = .05$, reject H_0 if $F \geq 3.23$.
Conclusion: Reject H_0.

15.42
a. $\hat{y} = .02436 + 1.80133$ (SQTNFPER)
$\quad + 1.63110$ (SQTNMPER)
$\quad + 2.73480$ (SQTNRPER)
$\quad + 1.14912$ (NUMLPER)
$\quad + .36002$ (ASZCRPER)
$\quad + .21039$ (ASZLPER)
$\quad + 1.87525$ (SPECAPER)
$\quad + 2.92493$ (SPECBPER)
$\quad + 1.28820$ (SKIDSPER)
Residual standard deviation $= .0492$
b. All the residual plots indicate no violation of assumptions.

15.43
a. Standard deviation of the regression prediction errors $= .08848$. Standard deviation of the superintendent's prediction errors $= .15273$.
b. The standard deviation in Exercise 15.42 was .0492. The regression standard deviation has increased to .08848.
c. Yes; the error should be cut in half, roughly.

15.44
a. No reason to assume linear relation in departure time; day really isn't a quantitative variable.
b. Predicted demand $= -4.042 + 17.74$ peak-dummy $+ 0.5233$ share $+ 4.180$ income
c. Predicted demand $= 1.305 - 20.03$ peakdummy $+ 0.5141$ share $+ 3.760$ income $+ 0.04982$ peak*share $+ 3.044$ peak*income
d. $F = 7.43$ with 2, 318 d.f.; reject H_0. There is clear evidence of interaction.

15.45
b. No real evidence of nonlinearity.
c. Nothing to see.

15.46
a. No evident cycles.
b. Durbin-Watson $= 2.10$, no problem.

15.47
a. used-car sales
b. Predicted sales $= 933.3 - 5.682$ lowtemp $+ 0.4843$ advertising $- 0.001095$ used-car $+ 2.429$ month
c. $s = 37.69$ vs. $s = 69.56$ in the original model.

15.48
a. Not too serious; largest magnitude is -0.670 (used-car and lagged advertising).
b. $F = 160.3$, $p < .001$
c. $p < .001$ for lowtemp, month, lagged advertising; $p = .317$ for used-car.

15.49
a. No evidence of increasing variance.
b. No evidence of nonlinearity.
c. Obvious autocorrelation against month.
d. Durbin-Watson $= 1.1$; no serious problem.

15.50 Lag advertising by 1 month; drop used-car as a predictor. The Durbin-Watson statistic is low, so calculate differences. Omit differences of month number (all of which are 1). The model has acceptable Durbin-Watson and smaller standard deviation than the original.

15.51
a. Serious collinearity; all X correlations exceed 0.8.
b. No dummy or lagged variables needed.
c. $R^2 = 0.838$

15.52
a. Some possible "fan," not glaring.
b. One possible outlier at the right on the "helpers" plot; perhaps a curved relation.
c. Not time-series data.

15.53
a. In terms of natural (base e) logarithms, predicted logsqft $= 3.013 + 0.390$ logskilled $+ 0.206$ loghelpers $+ 0.252$ logvehicles.
b. No serious curvature.
c. Predicted sqft $= e^{3.013}$ (skilled)$^{.390}$ (helpers)$^{.206}$ (vehicles)$^{.252}$

Review Exercises, Chapters 13–15, pg. 726

R126
a. $S_{xy} = 35,178,250$ and $S_{xx} = 1.010.887.8$
$\hat{y} = 1013.1027 + 34.79936x$
b. Predicted increase in direct cost per additional direct labor hour
c. fixed cost
d. $s = 3396.71$

R127 $r_{xy} = .9031$; variation in direct labor hours accounts for $(.9031)^2 = .8156$, or 81.56%, of total direct cost.

R128
a. $s_{\hat{\beta}_1} = 3.3784$
b. $27.82 \leq \beta_1 \leq 41.77$

R129 No; direct cost certainly should increase as direct labor hours increase. $t = 10.30$ is conclusive evidence to reject H_0.

R130 a. $\hat{y} = 31,985$; $25,481 \le Y_{n+1} \le 38,489$
b. $10,262 \le Y_{n+1} \le 22,108$
c. The interval in part (a) is wider (extrapolation penalty).

R131 a. The constant-variance assumption appears to be wrong.
b. The prediction intervals in R130 are most questionable.

R132 a. PURCH $= -.744 + .0329$ AGE
$+ .00900$ INCOME
$+ .115$ OWNER
$+ .00818$ EDUCN
b. For given income, ownership, and education, each one-year increase in age predicts a .0329 unit increase in purchases. The other slopes have similar interpretation.
c. Meaningless; there are extremely few 0-year-old, income-less, education-less cardholders.

R133 a. That all predictors were worthless.
b. $F > 600$
c. AGE definitely adds predictive value, OWNER and EDUCN most likely add value, and INCOME may add value.

R134 Yes; in particular, AGE and INCOME are rather highly correlated.

R135 a. To test whether the effects of AGE, INCOME, and EDUCN on PURCH depend on OWNER.
b. $F = 1.52 < F_{.10,3,152} \approx 2.12$; retain H_0

R136 The variance is not constant.

R137 There is an evident outlier at the lower left of the plot.

R138 a. Yes; R^2 is slightly higher and s is lower.
b. Yes. Everything else is the same.
c. The t for LOGINC is larger.

R139 Yes; LEADING, RATE, and MONTH all are very highly correlated.

R140 a. $F = 321.310$ with p-value .0001
b. Yes for SUPPLY and RATE, no for LEADING.

R141 ROOT MSE $= .0359 = \sqrt{\text{MS(ERROR)}}$
This standard deviation is considerably lower than the standard deviation of SPREAD, a good predictive value.

R142 a. Definite cyclic pattern indicates autocorrelation.
b. $d = 0.807$
c. The claimed standard deviation and standard errors are too low, and R^2 is too high.

R143 a. They are quite similar.
b. No change; we would believe the results for the difference data.
c. Yes; $d = 2.003$.

R144 No particular pattern; there shouldn't be a cyclic pattern with $d = 2.003$.

R145 The correlations among independent variables are much lower.

R146 a. $\hat{y} = -3.333 + .0794\text{GAS} + 7.861\text{TRAFFIC} - .132$ AVGINC
b. No; Gas $= 0$, TRAFFIC $= 0$, and AVGINC $= 0$ are all impossible.

R147 a. SS(Regression) $= 480.17195$
b. GAS accounts for 457.428, AVGINC adds an additional 0.919, and TRAFFIC adds 21.825.
c. AVGINC seems to be of little value.
d. Delete AVGINC and TRAFFIC.

R148 a. Not extreme; highest correlation of independent variables is .566.
b. The data aren't a time series.

R149 One outlier (upper right); no other pattern evident.

R150 a. The coefficient of TRAFFIC has decreased considerably.
b. $s = 3.26$ compared to previous $s = 4.34$
c. $R^2 = .513$ compared to previous $R^2 = .600$

R151 $F = 0.54$, not close to significant.

R152 a. The plot is perfectly rectangular.
b. $r_{\text{TEMP,PRES}} = 0$
c. no collinearity

R153 a. YIELD $= -2.41 + .0262\text{TEMP} + 5.33\text{PRES}$
b. $\pm.962$

R154 $F = 82.14$, t's $= 9.09$ and 9.04; TEMP and PRES definitely have predictive value.

R155 There's a clear curve in the plot.

R156 a. Not at all.
b. Only modestly; s decreases slightly and R^2 increases slightly. The t statistic is not highly significant.

R157   a. Yes; $t = 8.33$.
      b. $R^2 = .759$

R158   Autocorrelation is shown by Durbin-Watson statistic $= 0.43$. R^2 is too high; s and the standard errors are too low.

R159   a. Yes; $t = 18.16$.
      b. $R^2 = .940$
      c. Surprisingly, both values are larger.

R160   Not entirely; $d = 1.43$.

R161   a. That pressure difference didn't affect YIELD.
      b. $F = 414.234$, $t = 20.353$

R162 $s = \text{ROOT MSE} = 2.435 = \sqrt{\text{MS(Error)}}$
Most (95%) prediction errors will be within $\pm 2(2.435) = \pm 4.870$.

R163   a. Yes, there's a clear curve in the plot.
      b. No obvious outliers.

R164 $R^2 = .9437$ is larger than the previous R^2 of $.9367$.

CHAPTER 16   Section 16.1, pg. 748

16.1   a. $I_2 = 109.8$; $I_3 = 120.8$
      b. $I_2 = 109.2$; $I_3 = 120.2$

16.2   a. $I_2 = 109.2$; $I_3 = 118.5$; $I_3 = 128.6$
      b. $I_2 = 105.7$; $I_3 = 112.8$; $I_4 = 119.0$
      c. $I_2 = 107.9$; $I_3 = 112.3$; $I_4 = 112.7$

16.3   a. The weighted index value is consistently lower.
      b. Change in relative weights.

16.4   a. $I_2 = 102.9$; $I_3 = 113.2$; $I_4 = 129.1$; $I_5 = 133.3$
      b. $I_2 = 107.5$; $I_3 = 115.8$; $I_4 = 128.9$; $I_5 = 139.2$
      c. Any differences can be attributed to the relatively large steel weights.

Section 16.2, pg. 757

16.5   Obvious upward trend. Seasonal pattern; the sales peak in September.

16.6 $\hat{y}_t = 100.513 + .5963t$

16.7   The sales peak occurs in September.

16.8   a.

Month	J	F	M	A	M	J
Value	.985	.983	.981	.987	.988	.983

Month	J	A	S	O	N	D
Value	.988	.989	.987	.987	.989	.987

      b.

t	61	62	63	64	65	66
forecast	137.1611	124.1477	124.6861	125.2246	139.4118	125.8819

t	67	68	69	70	71	72
forecast	140.4651	154.8854	169.8476	156.0526	142.4217	143.0163

16.9   No obvious pattern.

16.10   b. Linear trend should be adequate.
      c. There doesn't seem to be any cyclical or seasonal pattern.

16.11 $\log \hat{y}_t = 4.56295 + .0197t$

16.12   b. There don't seem to be any seasonal or cyclical effects.

16.13

t	33	34	35	36
forecast	183.6533	187.3072	191.0337	194.8344

Section 16.3, pg. 764

16.14 a.

Month	3-Month	5-Month
1	*	*
2	*	*
3	95.7	*
4	122.0	*
5	129.7	115.0
6	131.7	118.6
7	109.0	119.2
8	101.0	118.2
9	95.0	102.4
10	94.0	97.8
11	109.7	105.0
12	115.0	106.0
13	114.7	106.0
14	95.0	105.0
15	91.0	104.2
16	95.7	97.6
17	109.3	101.6
18	115.0	104.4
19	109.3	106.2
20	99.3	106.6
21	92.3	102.4
22	92.3	96.0
23	95.7	95.0
24	102.7	98.4

c. Average squared-error for 3-month moving average = 627.613; for 5-month moving average = 337.6589

16.15 a.

Month	3-Month	5-Month
1	*	*
2	*	*
3	97	*
4	101	*
5	120	101
6	120	107
7	107	107
8	100	107
9	96	100
10	96	97
11	97	97
12	105	97
13	105	97
14	96	97
15	93	96
16	93	96
17	110	96
18	110	110
19	110	110
20	95	110
21	93	95
22	93	93
23	93	93
24	105	95

c. Average squared-error for 3-month running median = 557.8571; for 5-month running median = 291.0526

16.16 a.

Month	Forecast	Month	Forecast
1	89.00	13	110.71
2	89.00	14	98.94
3	95.40	15	86.99
4	99.88	16	91.80
5	154.38	17	106.36
6	126.88	18	121.27
7	110.98	19	112.25
8	102.20	20	96.85
9	97.24	21	95.37
10	90.65	22	90.27
11	95.73	23	92.45
12	133.55	24	102.49

b. Average squared error = 502.0

16.17 The 5-month running median is best.

16.18 b. The 3-week moving average.

16.19 b. The 3-week running median.

16.20 Yes. The 3-week running median method is best on both criteria.

16.21 c. Perhaps $\alpha = .8$ is overresponding.

16.22 $\alpha = .8$

Section 16.4, pg. 777

16.23 a. There is a long-term upward trend.
b. There does not seem to be any evidence of a linear trend.

16.24 a. $r_1 = .693$, by calculation.
b. The lag correlations taper off, rather than dropping to 0.

16.25 It appears that the model yields useful forecasts of changes in sales.

16.26 The estimated lag correlations for the data of Exercise 16.24 are close to but higher than the estimated lag correlations for the model of Exercise 16.25.

16.27 a. There is a suggestion of a sharp drop between lags 1 and 2.

b. An autoregressive parameter is needed as suggested by the gradual tapering of auto-correlations. The suggestion of a drop at lag 2 indicates that at least one moving average term could be used.

16.28 No

16.29 No

Chapter 16 Exercises, pg. 781

16.31 a. $\hat{y}_t = 429.30 + 4.892t$

16.32 a.

Month	J	F	M	A	M	J
Index	.975	.995	.990	.9925	1.0075	1.0075

Month	J	A	S	O	N	D
Index	1.015	1.0025	.9975	1.005	1.0075	1.005

b.

Month	J	A	S	O	N	D
Index	.985	1.017	1.023	1.005	.983	.975

16.33 There is some curvature; try an exponential trend.

16.34 $\log \hat{y}_t = 1.4363 + .0215t$

16.35 a. There appears to be a seasonal component in the data. The data values peak in the 3rd quarter.

b.

Quarter	1	2	3	4
Index	.89525	1.042375	1.272625	.842375

	Quarter			
Year	1	2	3	4
1	.891	.445	.856	.853
2	.872	.950	1.119	1.042
3	.975	1.010	1.142	.989
4	.939	.991	1.126	.983
5	.938	.998	1.126	.982
6	.957	.996	1.129	.995
7	.945	.992	1.131	.985
8	.923	.983	1.143	.992

16.36 b. Quarter 3 is consistently underestimated.

16.37 a.

Quarter	5-Quarter Moving Average	Quarter	5-Quarter Moving Average
1	***	17	.9852
2	***	18	1.0188
3	***	19	1.0614
4	***	20	.9766
5	.9898	21	.9952
6	1.0172	22	1.0234
7	1.0646	23	1.0644
8	.9788	24	.9854
9	.9900	25	.9972
10	1.0208	26	1.0182
11	1.0702	27	1.0656
12	.98	28	.9806
13	.9906	29	.9808
14	1.0176	30	1.0104
15	1.0608	31	1.0634
16	.9738	32	.9772

b.

Quarter	5-Quarter Running Median	Quarter	5-Quarter Running Median
1	***	17	.893
2	***	18	1.042
3	***	19	1.058
4	***	20	.893
5	.891	21	.933
6	1.028	22	1.034
7	1.028	23	1.034
8	.891	24	.933
9	.907	25	.933
10	1.028	26	1.034
11	1.045	27	1.038
12	.907	28	.896
13	.907	29	.896
14	1.042	30	1.038
15	1.042	31	1.044
16	.890	32	.861

c. No. The figures are clearly not good predictors.

d. Work with a seasonal adjustment.

16.38   a. $I_1 = 107.6$; $I_2 = 118.8$; $I_3 = 133.3$; $I_4 = 147.8$; $I_5 = 169.5$; $I_6 = 186.5$; $I_7 = 207.9$

b. $I_1 = 107.8$; $I_2 = 119.6$; $I_3 = 134.2$; $I_4 = 148.9$; $I_5 = 170.9$; $I_6 = 188.0$; $I_7 = 209.5$

c. The difference is very small.

16.39   a. A positive linear trend equation seems appropriate.

b. $\hat{y}_t = 135.204 + 2.559t$

16.40   b. The lag correlations decrease smoothly.

c. AR[1], AR[2]

16.41   a. $\hat{y}_t = 1.401 + 409y_{t-1}$
$\hat{y}_t = 1.205 + .378y_{t-1} + .108y_{t-2}$

b. no

c. The AR(1) model seems adequate.

16.42   a. No suggestion of trend.

b. Slope $= -0.04544$ indicates a decrease of about $(.045)(52)$ or about 2 per year; not a strong trend.

d. Mean $= -30.88$; the last week of the year averages about 30 fewer daily room rentals than typical.

16.43   b. Drops near 0 after lag 1; try a one-period MA model.

16.44   c. MA model seems slightly better.

16.45   a. Perhaps slightly decreasing.

b. Slope $= -0.00813$ per week; losing ratings over time.

c. Losing about $(.008)(52)$, or roughly .4 ratings point per year.

16.46   Mean $= 0.6837$; slightly *higher* summer ratings.

16.47   b. No; there's a gradual decline.

c. No; mean square error similar for all three.

16.48   a. Definite increasing trend.

b. Not an evident pattern.

c. Still no evident pattern.

16.49   a. Highest demand in summer.

b. For example, weeks 21–36, 73–88, 125–140, etc., average is $+0.2077$, indicating higher than trend demand.

16.50   AR model better.

CHAPTER 17   Section 17.1, pg. 794

17.1   a. $A = \{40, 41, \ldots, 100\}$

b. $\Theta = \{$very light, light, moderate, heavy, very heavy$\}$

17.2   a. Ordering 50 cars is worse than 60.

b. Ordering 100 cars is also clearly unreasonable, compared to 90.

17.3   a. $A = \{1, 2, \ldots, 30\}$

b. $\Theta = \{1000, 2000, \ldots, 30,000\}$

17.4   There are no inadmissable actions.

17.5   a. $A = \{100\%, 75\%, 50\%, 25\%, 0\%\}$

b. $\Theta = \{$(law not passed), (law passed and rental level rises), (law passed and rental level stays the same)$\}$

c. payoff matrix

	θ_1	θ_2	θ_3
A_1	100,000	40,000	$-20,000$
A_2	75,000	30,000	$-15,000$
A_3	50,000	20,000	$-10,000$
A_4	25,000	10,000	$-5,000$
A_5	0	0	0

17.6   a. $A = \{\text{settle, contest}\}$;
          $\Theta = \{(\text{found not guilty})$,
                  $(\text{found guilty by Judge A})$,
                  $(\text{found guilty by Judge B})\}$

b. payoff matrix

	θ_1	θ_2	θ_3
A_1	$-80{,}000$	$-80{,}000$	$-80{,}000$
A_2	$-20{,}000$	$-150{,}000$	$-180{,}000$

Section 17.2, pg. 799

17.7   "Full production" has the highest payoff.

17.8   a. "Full production" has the highest payoff.
     b. "Full production" has the highest payoff.
     c. "Limited production" has the highest payoff.
     d. The action "full production" remains optimal if the payoffs and probabilities are varied one at a time. But if we vary both the payoffs and probabilities, the action "full production" becomes second best to "limited production."

17.9   "Moderate" has the highest payoff.

17.10   a. Add .5 million to the profits for "low" and "high" prices.
      b. "High" has the highest payoff.

17.11   a. "Moderate" has the highest payoff.
      b. "High" has the highest payoff.
      c. The action "moderate" remains optimal if the probabilities are varied. But if we vary the payoffs, either alone or in combination with varied probabilities, the action "moderate" becomes a second best decision to "high."

17.12   "Go to trial" has the lower expected cost.

17.13   "Settlement" has the lower expected cost if the probability is increased to .6. "Go to trial" has the lower expected cost if the probability is decreased to .3.

Section 17.3, pg. 810

17.14   a. "90%" has the highest expected profit.
      b. "80%" has the lowest standard deviation.
      c. Yes, there is a conflict.

17.15   a. "90%" has the highest expected profit.
      b. If our goal was to maximize expected return, optimal action is found in Exercise 17.14. However, if our goal was to minimize risk, we would change our initial choice "80%" to "90%."

17.16   a. "90%" has the highest expected return.
      b. "80%" has the lowest risk.
      c. No, the optimal actions do not change.

17.17   a. Cov. $(Y_1 Y_2) = -84$
      b. $\rho_{Y_1 Y_2} = -.374$

17.18   a. Expected return $= 500$
      b. Variance $= 1992$
      c. Expected return $= 500$; variance $= 1842$

17.19   a. Expected return $= 1{,}091{,}333.332$;
         variance $= 14{,}444{,}444{,}000$
      b. Expected return $= 1{,}091{,}500$;
         variance $= 17{,}000{,}000{,}000$
         Expected return $= 1{,}091{,}000$;
         variance $= 22{,}000{,}000{,}000$

17.20   a. Expected return $= 3269$
      b. Variance $= 554{,}000$

17.21   Expected return $= 3271.50$; variance $= 787{,}500$. If an investor desires low risk, he would prefer the portfolio of Exercise 17.20.

17.22   a. "Expansion" has a higher expected payoff but also a higher standard deviation.
      b. "Expansion" has a higher expected utility.

17.23   The optimal choice changes from "expansion" to "no expansion."

17.24   "Expansion" has the higher expected utility.

17.25   a. Expected return table

		$R(a_i)$
	1	$270(.10) + 370(.20) + 470(.40) + 570(.30) = 460$
	2	$310(.10) + 385(.20) + 460(.40) + 535(.30) = 452.5$
Strategy	3	$350(.10) + 400(.20) + 450(.40) + 500(.30) = 445$
	4	$390(.10) + 415(.20) + 440(.40) + 465(.30) = 437.5$
	5	$430(.10) + 430(.20) + 430(.40) + 430(.30) = 430$

The expected return is highest for "strategy 1" and declines to lowest for "strategy 5."

b. Variance table

Var(a_i)

1	$[(270)^2(.10) + (370)^2(.20) + (470)^2(.40) + (570)^2(.30) - (460)^2] = 8900$
2	$[(310)^2(.10) + (385)^2(.20) + (460)^2(.40) + (535)^2(.30) - (452.5)^2] = 5006.25$
Strategy 3	$[(350)^2(.10) + (400)^2(.20) + (450)^2(.40) + (500)^2(.30) - (445)^2] = 2225$
4	$[(390)^2(.10) + (415)^2(.20) + (440)^2(.40) + (465)^2(.30) - (437.5)^2] = 556.25$
5	$[(430)^2(.10) + (430)^2(.20) + (430)^2(.40) + (430)^2(.30) - (430)^2] = 0$

The variance is highest for "strategy 1" and declines to lowest for "strategy 5."

17.26   Investment "strategy 1" has the highest expected utility.

Section 17.4, pg. 821

17.27   a. "Medium" has the highest expected return.
b. EVPI = 1.24. The pilot project would be desirable.

17.28   a. P(good yield | favorable) = .581;
P(fair yield | favorable) = .322;
P(poor yield | favorable) = .097
b. "Large" has the best expected value.
c. P(favorable) = .31
d. P(good yield | mediocre) = .047;
P(fair yield | mediocre) = .814;
P(poor yield | mediocre) = .139; "medium" has the best expected value; P(mediocre) = .43. P(good yield | unfavorable) = 0;
P(fair yield | unfavorable) = .192;
P(poor yield | unfavorable) = .808;
"No scale" has the best expected value;
P(unfavorable) = .26

17.29   EVSI = .768; the pilot project would be desirable.

17.30   a. The "no display" option is always worse than the "15 ft., consolidated" option.
b. "30 ft., scattered" has the highest expected profit.
c. EVPI = .27, the survey is not worth its cost, 2.4.

17.31   a. P(little) = .075
b. P(25% | little) = .667; P(50% | little) = .333;
P(75% | little) = 0; P(100% | little) = 0
c. "30 ft., scattered" has the highest expected profit, given a "little" result.
d. P(some) = .22; P(25% | some) = .682;
P(50% | some) = .227; P(75% | some) = .091;
P(100% | some) = 0; "30 ft., scattered" has the highest expected profit, given a "some" result. P(half) = .245; P(25% | half) = .612;
P(50% | half) = .306; P(75% | half) = .082;
P(100% | half) = 0; "30 ft., scattered" has the highest expected profit, given a "half" result.
P(most) = .28; P(100% | most) = .018;
"30 ft., scattered" has the highest expected profit, given a "most" result. P(all) = .18;
P(25% | all) = .278; P(50% | all) = .139;
P(75% | all) = .333; P(100% | all) = .250;
"30 ft. consolidated" has the highest expected profit, given an "all" result.

17.32   EVSI = .014; the survey is not worthwhile, at a cost of .4.

Section 17.5, pg. 828

17.33   Do not run survey. Choose 30 ft., scattered display, with expected payoff 1.990.

17.34   No changes.

17.35   e. Prepare a large circular. Whether or not the competitor has a sale, schedule extra sales staff. The expected profit is 19.382.

17.36   b. Same optimal decisions; the change favors the previously optimal decision.

17.37   b. No changes in optimal decisions.

17.38   Don't consult the specialist. Apply for a patent.

17.39 a. Probabilities change. Payoffs don't change.

b. No change in optimal decisions, because the revised probabilities make the specialist's opinion even less valuable.

17.40 Buy.

17.41 Buy.

Section 17.6, pg. 838

17.42 a. Loss table

		Severe	Cold	Normal	Mild	Warm
				Outcome θ_j		
	Full	0	0	20	40	70
Order	90%	40	0	0	0	10
a_i	80%	70	20	5	0	5
	70%	90	50	30	10	0
Probability		.10	.20	.40	.20	.10

b. The quantity that minimizes expected loss is "90%"; this is the same optimal quantity found in Exercise 17.14.

17.43 a. Payoff table

		.10	.20	.30	.40	.50	.60	.70	.80	.90
					Actual Proportions, θ					
	.10	.10	.30	.50	.70	.90	1.10	1.30	1.50	1.70
	.20	.20	.20	.40	.60	.80	1.00	1.20	1.40	1.60
	.30	.30	.30	.30	.50	.70	.90	1.10	1.30	1.50
Estimates	.40	.40	.40	.40	.40	.60	.80	1.00	1.20	1.40
a	.50	.50	.50	.50	.50	.50	.70	.90	1.10	1.30
	.60	.60	.60	.60	.60	.60	.60	.80	1.00	1.20
	.70	.70	.70	.70	.70	.70	.70	.70	.90	1.10
	.80	.80	.80	.80	.80	.80	.80	.80	.80	1.00
	.90	.90	.90	.90	.90	.90	.90	.90	.90	.90

b. Loss table

		.10	.20	.30	.40	.50	.60	.70	.80	.90
	.10	.00	.10	.20	.30	.40	.50	.60	.70	.80
	.20	.10	.00	.10	.20	.30	.40	.50	.60	.70
	.30	.20	.10	.00	.10	.20	.30	.40	.50	.60
Estimates	.40	.30	.20	.10	.00	.10	.20	.30	.40	.50
a_i	.50	.40	.30	.20	.10	.00	.10	.20	.30	.40
	.60	.50	.40	.30	.20	.10	.00	.10	.20	.30
	.70	.60	.50	.40	.30	.20	.10	.00	.10	.20
	.80	.70	.60	.50	.40	.30	.20	.10	.00	.10
	.90	.80	.70	.60	.50	.40	.30	.20	.10	.00

c. The loss function is an absolute error loss function with $c = 100,000$ (or $c = 1$ (100,000)). For example, $L(.20, .10) = 1|.20 - .10| = .10$.

17.44 a. The given prior density is a beta density with $\alpha = 2$ and $\beta = 2$.

b. The mean = median = .5.

c. $a^* = .5$

17.45 a. The posterior density of θ is a beta density with $\alpha' = 42$ and $\beta' = 62$.

b. For large values of α' and β', the density is approximately normal with mean, .4038, and variance, .0023; the median = .4038.

c. $a^* = .4038$

d. Because of the large sample size ($n = 100$), the sample result $p = 40/100$ carries more weight than the prior density estimate of $p = .50$.

17.46 a.

				Demand θ				
	5	6	7	8	9	10	...	50
5	5	5.70	6.40	7.10	7.80	8.50	...	
6	4.90	6	6.70	7.40	8.10	8.80	...	
7	4.80	5.90	7	7.70	8.40	9.10	...	
Stock 8	4.70	5.80	6.90	8	8.70	9.40	...	
a 9	4.60	5.70	6.80	8.90	9	9.70	...	
10	4.50	5.60	6.70	8.80	8.90	10.00		
50	:	:	:	:	:	:	:	50

b. Loss table

				Demand θ				
	5	6	7	8	9	10	...	50
5	0	.30	.60	.90	1.2	1.5	...	
6	.10	0	.30	.60	.90	1.2	...	
7	.20	.10	0	.30	.60	.90	...	
Stock 8	.30	.20	.10	0	.30	.60	...	
a 9	.40	.30	.20	.10	0	.30	...	
10	.50	.40	.30	.20	.10	0	...	
50	:	:	:	:	:	:		0

c. The loss function is an angle-shaped loss function with $c_1 = .1$ and $c_2 = .3$. For example,

$L(5, 7) = .3(7 - 5) = .60$

$L(7, 5) = .1(7 - 5) = .20$

17.47 $a^* = 35.36$ (thousands)

17.48 a. The posterior distribution of θ is normal with mean 33.37 and standard deviation 3.179 (thousands).

b. $a^* = 35.499$ (thousands)

17.49 a. $a^* = 2000$

b. $E[L(a, \theta)] = 22,500,000$

17.50 a. The posterior distribution of μ is normal with mean 1898.78 and variance 1355.01.

b. $a^* = 1898.78$

c. $E[L(a, \theta)] = 1,355,010$

17.51 The posterior distribution of μ is normal with mean 1900.88 and variance 1805.05; $a^* = 1900.88$; $E(L(a, \theta)) = 1,805,050$.

Chapter 17 Exercises, pg. 842

17.52 a. $A = \{$(promotion 1), (promotion 2)$\}$

b. $\Theta = \{$(both competitors, A and B),
(competitor A only),
(competitor B only),
(neither A nor B)$\}$

17.53 a. "Promotion 2" has the higher expected payoff.

b. "Promotion 2" has the lower risk.

17.54 a. A plot of the utility function indicates risk aversion.

b. "Promotion 2" has the higher expected utility.

c. The preferred promotion, "Promotion 1," has also lower risk but not higher expected payoff.

17.55 "Promotion 2" has the higher expected payoff and "Promotion 1" has the lower risk if the probability is decreased to .5. "Promotion 2" has the higher expected payoff and "Promotion 1" has the lower risk if the probability is increased to .7. The conclusions of Exercise 17.54 do not change.

17.56 a. "Replace" has the highest expected payoff.

b. "No change" has the lowest variance.

17.57 "Replace" has the highest expected utility.

17.58 Revision 1—"replace" and "upgrade" have the highest expected payoff.
Revision 2—"upgrade"
Revision 3—"replace"
Revision 4—"replace"

17.59 a. $Cov(X, Y) = -.000108$; $\rho_{xy} = -.783$
b. The covariance is negative because there is a tendency for Project 2 net returns to decrease as Project 1 net returns increase.

17.60 a. Expected return $= 100$; variance $= 10$
b. Expected return $= 100$; variance $= 160$
c. The risk is lower because of cancelling variations (due to the negative covariance).

17.61 a. "Preferred" has the highest expected payoff.
b. "Preferred" has the lowest variance.

17.62 "Common" has the highest expected payoff; "preferred" has the lowest variance. The revised probabilities have affected the decision about the action with the highest expected payoff.

17.63 a. "Preferred" has the highest expected utility.
b. "Common" has the highest expected utility.

17.64 a. Expected return $= 13,080$;
variance $= 7,360,000$;
standard deviation $= 2712.93$

b. Expected return $= 13,068$;
variance $= 2,484,000$;
standard deviation $= 1576.07$
c. Assuming a somewhat risk-averse investor, the portfolio consisting of $3000 invested in each of the four investments is preferred.

17.65 The portfolio consisting of $3000 invested in each of the four investments has the higher expected utility.

17.66 b. Normal policy, with expected desirability 41.4.

17.67 b. For (tight, low), choose full dip into wait list. For all other cases in which the wait list is considered, choose partial.
c. Normal policy, with expected desirability 41.85.

17.68 No change in any optimal decisions.

17.69 a. "Method 1" has the highest expected return.
b. Perfect information is worth $15,000.

17.70 a. $P(\text{down sharply}) = .12$; $P(\text{down slightly}) = .25$; $P(\text{constant}) = .38$; $P(\text{up slightly}) = .19$; $P(\text{up sharply}) = .06$
Posterior probabilities

	θ_j		
	Down	No Change	Up 10%
Down sharply	.750	.250	0
Down slightly	.480	.480	.040
Constant	.158	.789	.053
Up slightly	.158	.632	.210
Up sharply	0	.500	.500

b.

Opinion:	Down sharply	Down slightly	Constant	Up slightly	Up sharply
Optimal Method:	1	1	1	1	2

c. EVSI $= 3.8968$; the company should not hire the consultant.

17.71 a. The alternative likelihoods indicate greater value to the consultant's opinion.
b. Posterior probabilities

	Outcome θ_j		
	Down	No Change	Up 10%
Down sharply	1	0	0
Down slightly	.625	.375	0
Constant	.065	.913	.022
Up slightly	0	.643	.357
Up sharply	0	0	1

$P(\text{down sharply}) = .12$; $P(\text{down slightly}) = .24$; $P(\text{constant}) = .46$; $P(\text{up slightly}) = .14$; $P(\text{up sharply}) = .05$
The action that has the highest expected value given each of the opinions DOWN SHARPLY, DOWN SLIGHTLY, and CONSTANT is "Method 1." The action that has the highest expected value given the opinions UP SLIGHTLY and UP SHARPLY is "Method 2."
The overall decision changes from Exercise 17.70. The decision in this exercise is to hire the consultant.

17.72 a. Beta density with $\alpha = 4$ and $\beta = 2$.

b.

θ	0	.2	.4	.6	.8	1.0
$f(\theta)$	0	.128	.768	1.728	2.048	0

c. $P(\theta < .6) = .33696$

17.73 a. The posterior density of θ is a beta density with $\alpha' = 74$ and $\beta' = 60$.

b. For large α' and β', the density is approximately normal with mean .552 and variance .00183; $P(\theta < .6) = .8686$.

17.74 $H_0: \theta \geq .60$
$H_a: \theta < .60$
T.S.: $z = -1.227$
R.R.: At $\alpha = .05$, reject if $z < -1.645$.
Conclusion: Retain H_0.
From Exercise 17.73, we see that there is a fairly high probability of obtaining a proportion value less than .60. Yet, the preceding test leads us not to conclude $\theta < .60$.

17.75 $P(\mu < 2) = .9332$

17.76 a. Normal with mean 1.378 and variance .111.
b. $P(\mu < 2) = 0.97$

17.77 a. $H_0: \mu = 2$
$H_a: \mu < 2$
T.S.: $z = -1.117$
R.R.: At $\alpha = .05$, reject H_0 if $z < -1.645$; at $\alpha = .10$, reject H_0 if $z < -1.28$.
Conclusion: Retain H_0.

b. The variance in the decision theory approach is smaller using the prior distribution approach rather than the single random sampling hypothesis.

17.78 a. "New car buyers" has the highest expected payoff.
b. "New car buyers" has the lowest expected loss.

17.79 $P(\text{down } 10\%) = .15$; $P(\text{down } 5\%) = .215$; $P(\text{steady}) = .26$; $P(\text{up } 5\%) = .22$; $P(\text{up } 10\%) = .155$.

a. Posterior probabilities

	Down 10%	Down 5%	Steady	Up 5%	Up 10%
Down 10%	.200	.267	.200	.300	.033
Down 5%	.139	.233	.279	.279	.070
Steady	.077	.154	.462	.230	.077
Up 5%	.068	.182	.273	.341	.136
Up 10%	.032	.194	.194	.387	.194

b. The optimal aim for each possible value of summer sales is "new car."

17.80 The company should not defer its choice at a cost of $4000.

17.81 a. Loss table

		θ_j (Proportion Demanded)					
		.05	.10	.15	.20	.25	.30
	.05	0	10	20	30	40	50
	.10	15	0	10	20	30	40
a_j	.15	30	15	0	10	20	30
Proportion	.20	45	30	15	0	10	20
Ordered	.25	60	45	30	15	0	10
	.30	75	60	45	30	15	0

b. The loss function is angle shaped with $c_1 = 300$ and $c_2 = 200$. For example,
$L(.05, .10) = 200(.10 - .05) = 10$
$L(.10, .05) = 300(.10 - .05) = 15$
c. $a^* = $ 40th percentile of $f(\theta)$

17.82 a. in-house
b. contract
c. none
d. no change

17.83 a.

	Turnover		
Given Demand	Low	Normal	High
Poor	5/19	10/19	4/19
Fair	3/49	30/49	16/49
Good	2/32	10/32	20/32

b.

Expected payoff given	Decision	
	In-house	Contract
Poor	65.53	61.32
Fair	62.35	53.37
Good	59.38	45.94

In-house has higher expected payoff in each case.

c. Nothing. The decision is the same, regardless of the information.

17.84 20, because waiting has cost but no value.

17.85 None of them.

17.86 a. First branch (decision) is "gates now," next branch (chance) is "growth," third branch (decision) is "gates next year," and last branch (chance) is "restriction."

b. Buy one gate now.

17.87 Not at all; the change makes a nonoptimal decision even poorer.

CHAPTER 18   Section 18.1, pg. 860

18.1 A serious bias would be the omission of those who have nonpublished phone numbers.

18.2 A possible selection bias would be the omission of those wheelchair-bound people who are not members of the statewide association.

18.3 $.36 \leq \pi \leq .52$

18.4 Omission of those owners not available for contact during the month of March.

18.5 a. $.312 \leq \pi \leq .439$
b. $3.83 \leq \mu \leq 4.57$

18.6 Large sales have a tendency to push the running totals over a \$10,000 interval, and thereby would be more likely to be in the sample.

18.7 $\$101.27 \leq \mu \leq \$123.21$

18.8 The bias to larger sales will probably give an inflated estimate of the mean and variance.

Section 18.2, pg. 865

18.9 $192.998 \leq \mu \leq 195.782$

18.10 $95.93 \leq \mu \leq 104.17$ (in thousands of dollars); stratification has helped.

18.11 a. $10.235 \leq \mu \leq 10.18$
b. $9.66 \leq \mu \leq 11.14$

18.12 $10.23 \leq \mu \leq 10.85$; there is no substantial shift in the confidence interval.

18.13 $.1535 \leq \pi \leq .2461$

18.14 $.153 \leq \pi \leq .247$; the individual strata proportions are very much alike, so that the stratified calculation is very close to the simple random sampling calculation.

Section 18.3, pg. 872

18.15 a. $9.31 \leq \mu \leq 11.49$
b. A simple random sample would have the survey team riding all over town searching for individual houses. Cluster sampling merely requires the identification for city blocks.

18.16 a. $9.772 \leq \mu \leq 11.078$
b. The width of the interval assuming a simple random sample is smaller.

18.17 a. $\bar{y}_c = 100.32$
b. $99.56 \leq \mu \leq 101.08$

18.18 a. $\bar{y}_c = .1048$
b. $.0977 \leq \mu \leq .1119$ (in thousands)
c. $.1982 \leq \pi \leq .2162$

Section 18.4, pg. 877

18.19 $n = 602; n_i = 61 \ (i = 1, \ldots, 10)$

18.20 a. $n = 1135$
b. Yes. The within-stratum variance is lower.

18.21 $n = 4$

18.22 $n = 4$

18.23 Additional 70

Chapter 18 Exercises, pg. 885

18.24 a. cluster sampling
b. Cluster sampling is preferred, as in this case, when the elements of the population are located over a large area.

18.25 a. $-3.79 \leq \mu \leq 4.87$
b. $3.728 \leq \mu \leq 4.932$
c. $n \approx 366$

18.26 a. stratified random sampling
b. Confidence intervals should be smaller than those constructed assuming simple random sample.

18.27 The simplest procedure would be to continue drawing random numbers until there are 30 samples of each type.

18.28 $5.736 \leq \mu \leq 6.524$

18.29 a. $5.623 \leq \mu \leq 6.337$
b. Assuming equal representation:
$5.736 \leq \mu \leq 6.524$
Assuming unequal representation:
$5.623 \leq \mu \leq 6.337$, not drastically different.

18.30 $n = 187; n_1 = 50; n_2 = 62; n_3 = 42; n_4 = 33$

18.31 $\$39.54 \leq \mu \leq \$40.80$

18.32 $\$156{,}192.51 \leq \mu \leq \$161{,}150.49$

18.33 Stratified sampling

18.34 $46{,}735.48 \leq \mu \leq 49{,}417.26$

18.35 $n = 13{,}252; n_1 = 2026; n_2 = 1366; n_3 = 1134;$
$n_4 = 1921; n_5 = 1921; n_6 = 1633; n_7 = 1524;$
$n_8 = 1295; n_9 = 856$

18.36 $.086 \leq \pi \leq .234$

18.37 a. $n = 94$
b. The effect of using proportional allocation is to more than halve the sampling size.

18.38 $1.401 \leq \mu \leq 1.459$

18.39 Simple random sampling is not advisable. If two (or more) riders in the same carpool were sampled, a car's total occupancy would be counted more than once.

18.40 $1395 \leq \tau \leq 1454$

INDEX